THE **52ND** ANNUAL OF ADVERTISING,
EDITORIAL AND TELEVISION ART & DESIGN WITH
THE **13TH** ANNUAL COPY AWARDS

THE 52ND ANNUAL OF ADVERTISING, EDITORIAL AND TELEVISION ART & DESIGN WITH THE 13TH ANNUAL COPY AWARDS

THE ONE SHOW

The 52nd Annual of Advertising,
Editorial & Television Art & Design
with the 13th Annual Copy Awards

Published by Watson-Guptill Publications
a division of Billboard Publications, Inc.
One Astor Plaza, New York, N.Y. 10036
Library of Congress catalog number 22-5058
ISBN 0-8230-1905-5

Art Director/Designer: Dave Epstein
Editor: Jo Yanow
Editorial Coordinator: Jennifer Place
Editorial Advisor: Susan E. Meyer
Writer/Art Directors Hall of Fame: Jerome Snyder
Writer/Copywriters Hall of Fame: Steve Lance
Assistant Editor: Jack Anson Finke
Editorial Assistants: Glenda Spencer, Jackie Weir, Wendy Smith
Production Coordinator: Frank DeLuca
Assistant Production Coordinator: Hector Campbell
Page Design/Show Section: James Craig, Robert Fillie
Mechanicals: Michael Jimenez
Photo/Gold Award: Carl Fischer
Photo/Empire State Bldg.: © 1964 Dexter Press, Inc.,
(West Nyack, N.Y., all rights reserved)
Photos/Hall of Fame Awards: Carl Fischer, Pete Turner
Cover Color Print: Peterson Color Laboratories, Inc.
Cover Color Retouching: Forway Studios, Inc.
Typographer: Atlantic Linotype Co.
Headlines: Sans-Serif No. 1 Condensed
Body Face: Helvetica Light and Demibold
Printing: Economy Graphics, Inc.
Binding: Economy Bookbinding Corporation
Color Separations: Pioneer-Moss
Cover Paper: Permalin
Text Paper: Finch Filmtext
4/C Illustration Paper: Oxford Starflex Dull
Cover Illustration Printer: Algen Press

It was my pleasure to be at the inaugural One Show Awards Presentation Dinner to welcome some of the foremost creative talents in the city and the country.

Professional communicators make an important contribution to our society. The quality of their work in The One Show speaks for itself, so I recommend that you enjoy it as I have.

The City of New York congratulates The Art Directors Club, Inc. and The Copy Club of New York.

John V. Lindsay
Mayor, The City of New York

The One Show

This book, the 52nd in a series of annual reviews of the best our business has to offer, is more significant than all of its predecessors, save two.

The first Art Directors Annual must go down in the history of our business as one of its most important documents. Likewise, the 29th, in which we see, for the first time, a section devoted to television commercials.

This year's Annual deserves a place beside them because of the creation of The One Show.

Art directors and copywriters have been working in teams since the early days of Doyle Dane Bernbach. A new rapport has been developing between editorial art directors and the writers and editors with whom they work. And graphic designers have developed a new sensitivity to the content of the words they deal with.

The One Show is a symbol and focal point for this growing link between the visual and verbal aspects of our crafts.

Representatives from The Art Directors Club, The Copy Club of New York, and renegades from last year's Andy Board spent countless hours hammering out a workable set of criteria and rules for judging this new show. As a result, the 150 people who dedicated thousands of hours to its supervision and judging helped create a show that was not only one of the most honest and carefully judged, but also one of the most historically significant.

If The One Show exhibits any trend, it is a renewed interest in information. While entertainment and persuasive logic are still among our favorite tools, an increasingly vocal consumerist trend and more attention to our work from the FTC and FDA has resulted in a somewhat more literate, informative brand of advertising.

The One Show is an exciting measure of the vitality of our business, a tribute to the origination of its concept (Shep Kurnit, George Lois, and Ed McCabe) and a credit to The Art Directors Club and The Copy Club.

Joint Directors:
Shep Kurnit
George Lois
Ed McCabe
Co-Chairmen:
Peter Nord
Charles Rosner
Joint Study Committee:
Dave Altschiller
Ed Butler
Bill Cadge
Jerry Della Femina
Lou Dorfsman
Dick Jackson
George Krikorian
Bob Levenson
Helen Nolan
Stuart Pittman
Pat Del Vecchio
Special Editorial Study Committee:
Herb Bleiweiss
Bill Cadge
Bob Ciano
Lou Silverstein

Co-Chairmen:
Dan Bingham
R. O. Blechman
Neil Calet
Bob Ciano
Thierry DaRold
Pat Del Vecchio
Larry Dunst
Mel Freedman
Adam Hanft
Harvey Herman
Tony Isidore
Steve Kambanis
Dick Luden
Leon Meadow
Michael Pateman
Bob Reed
Mel Rustom
Don Slater
Dick Tarlow
Bob White
Francine Wilvers

Judges:
Peter Adler
Walter Allner
Ted Andresakes
Ruth Ansel
Tom Atkinson
Ed Bianchi
Barry Biederman
Peter Bradford
Paula Brown
Bruno Brugnatelli
Aaron Burns
C. P. Burtin
Sandi Butchkiss
Tony Cappiello
Josh Carlisle
Kathy Carlisle
Sue Citron
Harvey Cohen
Rita Conner
Verdun Cook
David Deutsch
Rosalind Dunn
Jim Durfee
Guy Durham
Dave Epstein
Bob Fearon
Gene Federico
Marcella Free
Len Fury
Flora Goldenson
George Gomes
Barry Greenspan
Joe Gregorace
Mike Gross
Al Grossman
Ed Hanft
Peter Hirsch
Linda Howard
Marvin Jacobson
Walter Kaprielian
Kay Kavanaugh
Jess Korman
George Krikorian
Bob Kuperman
Ann Marie Light
Dick Lopez
Dee Maskaleris
Dennis Mazzella
Holden McAlister
Bill McCaffery
Al Meadow
Tom Messner
Jeff Metzner
Bob Meury
Bert Neufeld
Frank Nicolo
Bernie Owett
Lore Parker
Alan Peckolick
Phil Peppis
Paul Posnick
Orville Roberts
Arnold Roston
Mort Rubenstein
Vince Salmieri
Hank Seiden
Lew Sherwood
Mark Shoenfield
Mel Stabin
Ira Sturtevant
Jerry Sussman
Milt Sutton
Jim Symon
Bill Taubin
Alex Tsao
George Tscherny
Ned Viseltear
Dick Wasserman
Kurt Weihs
Bob Wilvers
Joe Wojtala
Henry Wolf
Tom Yobbagy

CONTENTS

The Art Directors Club Hall of Fame Award

PHOTO BY PETE TURNER

The relatively recent invention of the Art Director, his coming-of-age, and the Hall of Fame.

In the beginning it was all very simple:
The artist worked for kings and their courts (and Holbein painted Henry VIII, Velazquez, the Infantas, and Leonardo designed fortifications for the Duke of Sforza). Or they worked for the Church and illustrated religious belief (producing the Sistine ceiling and hundreds of Madonnas and Resurrections). They also designed the castles which housed their patrons. Later, the merchant princes joined the ranks of the employers, and Rembrandt and Rubens painted their allegorical and often flattering portraits. Even later, Renoir glorified fin-de siecle family life for the wealthy bourgeoisie. At about that same time, along came yet another client: Industry.

With industry, motivations were not as simple, or relationships as one-to-one, as they used to be. industry replaced the Medicis, but the form of expression became more complex. Designers were needed to give shape to industry's products, and advertising became the new way to let people know about those products. In its infancy, industry commissioned the artist much as its leaders did in private. (Toulouse-Lautrec did many posters.)

As things got more complex, a go-between was needed to interpret the goals of the client to the artist and make the often gruff captains-of-industry aware of the contribution "Art" could make. This necessity invented the "Art Director."

Even though the invention is recent—not much more than a half-century old—the contribution has been enormous. Never before has imagery been disseminated so rapidly or so profusely. An art director's single piece of work is seen by more people in one week than Leonardo's total output was in his entire lifetime.

The art director is largely responsible for the visual images that confront us everywhere, and therefore responsible for the visual education of everyone. All this frantic activity has produced a large body of work, a mythology of its own, and some very real heroes. It became apparent that this phenomenon had to be chronicled, its history preserved, and its giants honored for their far-reaching contributions. The Art Directors Hall of Fame was created for this purpose.

We have a short but crowded past to catch up with before all the nominations can become current. Last year eight men were honored. All had a hand in shaping the new disciplines and giving it some masterpieces. This year, we are honoring three more for their imagination, their understanding of our craft, and their success in translating their visions into separate realities.

We have, as Art Directors and within only fifty years, regained the old one-to-one status with the patrons which is indispensable for the creation of valid work. The talent will take care of itself.

Henry Wolf

THE ART DIRECTORS HALL OF FAME

1972	M. F. Agha
	Lester Beall
	Alexey Brodovitch
	A. M. Cassandre
	René Clarke
	Robert Gage
	William Golden
	Paul Rand
1973	Charles Coiner
	Paul Smith
	Jack Tinker

Marcus: artist Everett Henry
Ford: artist James Williamson
Lincoln: artist Leslie Saalburg

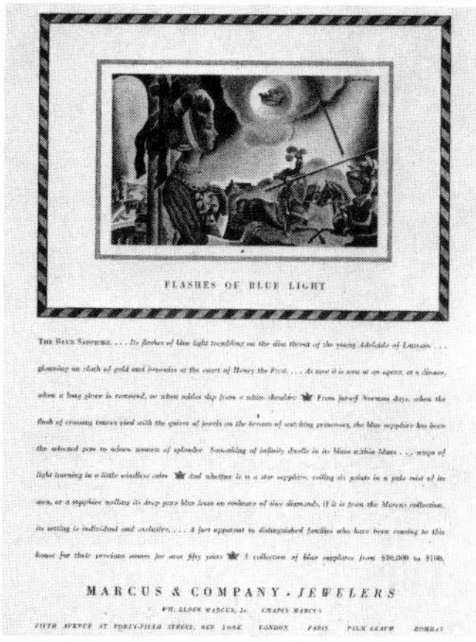

"Watch The Fords Go By"
THE FORD V·8

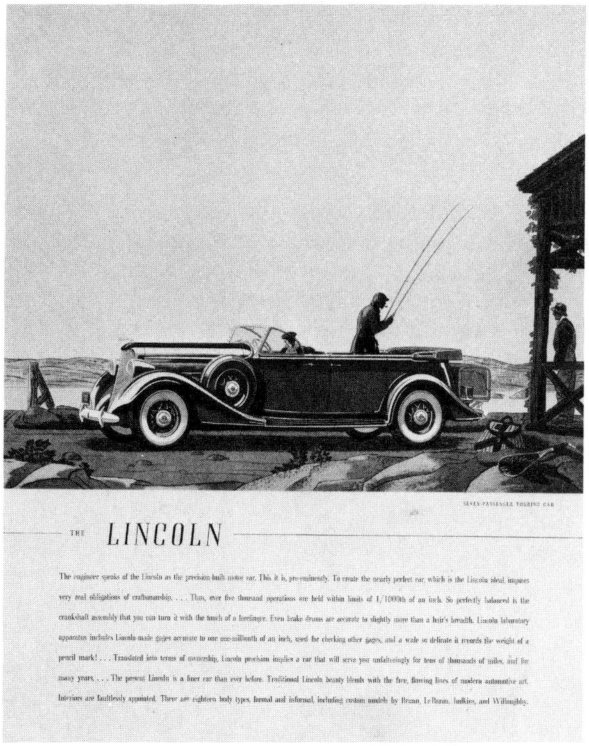

Charles Coiner

Many have used art and artists well but, perhaps, none with the versatility, elegance, and thoroughness found in the continuous body of Charles Coiner's work. Coiner holds a special copyright when it comes to the merger of the fine and applied arts in advertising.

He spent his 40 year career art directing at N. W. Ayer & Son. As a staunch advocate of art as a vital element in modern communications, the most glittering talents of the day—Dufy, Georgia O'Keefe, Norman Rockwell, and a hundred more all worked for him and with him on the agency's ads. They were artists whose works were filling museums and the pages of *Collier's, The Saturday Evening Post, Vanity Fair,* and the other magazines. Often they worked with Coiner when they were not accessible to others in the 'advertising world.'

Appropriately, Coiner's peers in 1949 honored him as the first American to receive the National Society of Art Directors Annual Award for distinction in the practice of his profession. The N. S. A. D. citation aptly presented his credo: "From the very start of his long career, he has stood for the principle that regardless of the type of product or type of people who used it, better art would make better advertising. He has not succumbed to trick fads but has stood consistently in the vanguard of those whose work combines the sound foundation of the traditional with freshness of today and tomorrow."

Coiner's art advocacy was without cant or artifice. Simply—the best advertising demanded the best in art. What is unique to the artist's vision can impart a rare excellence to the visual language of advertising.

A native of California, he studied painting at the Chicago Academy of Fine Arts and then set out on his own course of education spending a long period in Europe in the '20s. Propitiously, he absorbed the spirit of the classic tradition of Western art while finding himself at the center of the burgeoning modern art movement there.

COVARRUBIAS
To all Americas, U. S. foods go in paper packages.
CONTAINER CORPORATION OF AMERICA

Brighten the corner where you are
Cannon

Container Corporation: artist Covarrubias
Cannon: photographer Edward Steichen

Upon his return to America, he found in Ayer a special empathic understanding that narrowed the distinction between the two cultures. The era was a turning point in communications. Much of modern art so long influenced by technology and contemporary graphic communication could be joined naturally with another channel of contemporary communication —advertising.

By 1936, Coiner assumed complete charge of Ayer's vast art department. His warmth and perception and intelligence inevitably identified with the Ayer working atmosphere which became known as a professional environment where the young found confidence and guidance and the older, more experienced could function in an unfettered creative collaboration. Solely because of Coiner, many of the best talents of the time were drawn there. Leo Lionni, Robert Bach, Leon Karp, William Free, Jack Tinker, Neil Fujita, Ken Stuart, and Arthur Blomquist, to name a few.

Coiner's cavalcade of campaigns were innovative, intrinsically appropriate, and, in the style of the true master, seemingly effortless. Coiner cast great artists in fresh roles for unconventional graphic ambience. For instance: the soaring imaginations of Georgia O'Keefe, A. M. Cassandre, and Migel Covarrubias brought a personal poetic dimension to Dole Pineapple ads. A Coiner-Edward Steichen collaboration for Cannon Towels was the first known use of a nude photograph—then a feat. Coiner's imagery was rich—from Norman Rockwell's pin-pointed documentary naturalism in solutions for Bell Telephone to lyrical soft-sell De Beers diamond ads by brilliant artists. Or another first: a wartime series for Caterpillar Tractors built on the themes "Ever watch a forest die" and "Watch the farms go by" touching on environmental questions years ahead of their time. Copy in Coiner ads was well-honed and rich in ideas. Consider the famed *Ladies Home Journal* ads headlined "Never underestimate the power of a woman" (now a part of our vocabulary). But perhaps none were more significant than the Container Corporation "Great Ideas" series which 'advertised' its corporate sponsor, but also elevated intellectually and artistically.

CONCENTRATION
RESEARCH, EXPERIENCE AND TALENT FOCUSSED ON ADVANCED PAPERBOARD PACKAGING
CONTAINER CORPORATION OF AMERICA
A.M.CASSANDRE

τ'αέρα
To Grecian islands—U. S. supplies in paper packages. CONTAINER CORPORATION OF AMERICA

In the Dark of the Hour
CAPEHART - PANAMUSE - FARNSWORTH

●Hawaiian Pineapple Company, Ltd., invited the world-famed American artist, Georgia O'Keeffe, to visit Hawaii and paint her impressions of the color and brilliance of the Islands. She chose the magnificent Haliconia flower, called by some the "Mock Bird of Paradise."
PAINTED IN HAWAII, HOME OF DOLE PINEAPPLE JUICE, BY GEORGIA O'KEEFFE
Hospitable Hawaii cannot send you its abundance of flowers or its sunshine. But it sends you something reminiscent of both—golden, fragrant Dole Pineapple Juice. As you drink this pure, unsweetened juice of luscious, sun-ripened pineapples, you will know that only Nature could give Dole Pineapple Juice its marvelous flavor. For breakfast . . . when you are tired or thirsty between meals . . . whenever you, your children or guests crave refreshment, serve tall glasses of DOLE PINEAPPLE JUICE FROM HAWAII

Container Corporation: A.M. Cassandre
Dole Pineapple: Georgia O'Keefe
Container Corporation: artist Baplaz
Capehart-Panamuse: artist Raymond Breinin
supervisor Walter Reinsit

Nothing else in the world
... not all the armies
... is so powerful as an idea
whose time has come.
Great Ideas of Western Man ...
one of a series
Victor Hugo, 1802-1885, The Future of Man
Container Corporation of America
Artist: Robert Vickrey

Container Corporation: artist Robert Vickrey

Thus, Coiner, a graphic architect, helped hold creative links together. He was not revolutionary in the light of the changing trends or modes, but he helped make a silent 'taste' revolution.

The man Charles Coiner was also engaged in a wide variety of activities. While an active art director, he was concerned with the education of young designers and was a trustee and advisor for the Philadelphia Museum and its College of Art and served on the Boards of other art schools.

Other achievements: design of the NRA "Blue Eagle" emblem, creation of all the Civilian Defense designs during World War II, creation of the Red Feather insignia of the Community Fund, designer of the War Fund insignia.

Coiner retired from Ayer in 1964. A vigorous, healthy, handsome man, he turned his resourcefulness to painting and to the outdoors surrounding his Bucks County Pennsylvania home. Ever a painter, Coiner's work hangs in New York's Whitney Museum and the Philadelphia Museum and is still exhibited and runs in leading magazines. His entry into the Art Directors Hall of Fame is really a kind of a manifest destiny. Coiner stands for the best of artistic traditions, for esteemed creativity, and the highest standards of performance and integrity.

Caterpillar
Ever watch a forest die?
No? Well, I have. It started two days ago. Seems like two years. "Big fire over the ridge," they told me. "Everybody's needed."
So I've been fighting it for forty-eight hours. Sweating and choking in the smoke till my eyes and lungs feel burnt out. Didn't have enough to eat in that time. Don't know as I'm hungry right now, though. I'm just plain beat.
The paper'll talk about a million-dollar loss. But when you read it you won't see the red hell that turned big trees into living torches. You won't hear the roar of it or know the black discouragement of falling back, defeated, time after time.
What am I thinking about, besides my aches and pains? Well, I remember a lucky deer that raced past . . . a bear and her two cubs that got away. And the scorched young trees that would have been forest some day. Then I think of the boys on the big yellow bulldozers, ramming through brush and trees and blinding smoke to cut the firebreak along the ridge. That's what finally licked it.
Last of all I think of you. Was it you who dropped the match? You, who tossed the cigarette out the car window, or left the campfire smoldering? If it was, I wish you'd been here with me to see this forest die.
Caterpillar Tractor Co., Peoria, Illinois, U. S. A.
CATERPILLAR
DIESEL ENGINES • TRACTORS • MOTOR GRADERS • EARTHMOVING EQUIPMENT
WHEN YOU THINK OF
FORESTS, THINK OF THE BIG
YELLOW MACHINES THAT HELP GUARD THEM

"Merry Christmas, Grandma . . . we came in our new PLYMOUTH!"

Plymouth: artist Norman Rockwell

Paul Smith

"I awoke one morning and found myself famous," Byron said. How did I get to be famous the famous ask—seldom sure of what it all is. There often is an elegant insouciance that comes with greatness.

Paul Smith is cast out of that classic mold. He was a Renaissance agency man long before the concept came into vogue. His qualities—enormous versatility, probing intellectuality, and voracious interest in the spectrum of human endeavor. Some accomplishments—art director, artist, writer, executive, industry leader, engineer, inventor, teacher of celestial navigation! Yet, all that Smith will say is that he is a "professional dilettante. I'm one by choice since I don't believe in spectator sports."

As unorthodox in his academic background as he is in person, Smith managed to attend both college and high school without graduating from either. He became a scientist—an electrical engineer, a technical designer, inventor of electronic devices, and an accomplished amateur astronomer out of sheer grit and intellectual curiosity.

TO A HAIR'S BREADTH

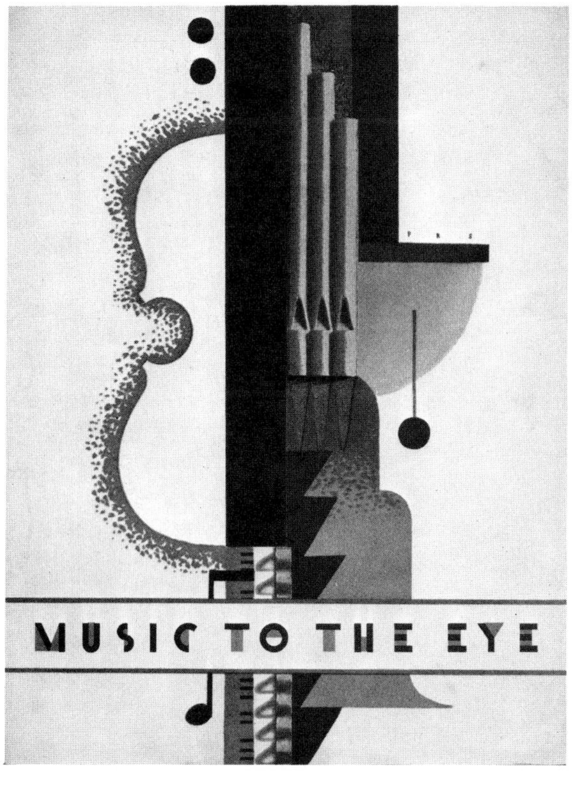
MUSIC TO THE EYE

IT MAKES THE GENIUS

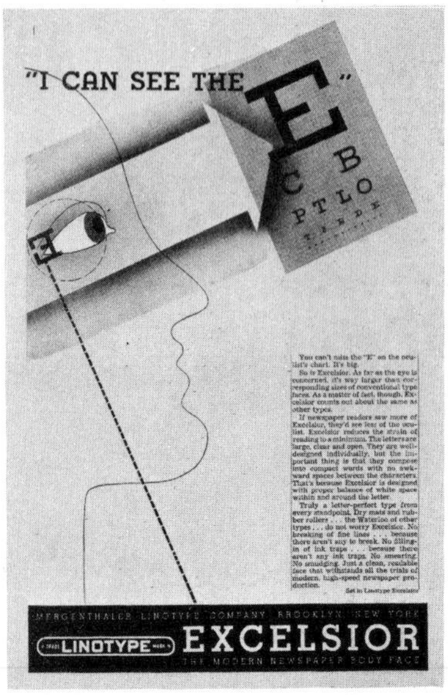

In the same resolute manner that has exemplified his style in everything, artist Smith rejected the 'confining' classification of artist, thinking himself perhaps more of a scientist than artist. His scientific expertise helped him to make his special contribution to our industry. For instance, some 14 years after Smith was a well-accepted art director with work appearing in every Art Directors Club annual exhibition, he wrote and illustrated a technical manual for the United States Navy. Today, that manual is still required material, carried by every plane in the Navy and Air Force.

From the start of his varied career—as a young man in 1925—the combative artist and scientist facets of his personality never allowed him to be content with peer esteem. He felt a deep theoretical responsibility to his profession. In outlining his contributions, it is good to start here. In 1958, Smith organized the landmark ADC's third communications conference. Its preemptive theme—Creativity. Smith then stated prophetically: "Providing a favorable climate for the creative personality in our culture is one of the most urgent problems in America today. The better we understand the vital process of creative power, the better equipped we will be to realize our potentials as individuals, as corporations, as a nation." Creativity became *the* issue soon after. Later Smith edited a successful book reprinting the Conference proceedings—read worldwide. It's still read.

Smith was one of the many to have come out of the midwest to enrich New York's environs. Originally a writer, he was drawn to avant garde art, which had a body of sturdy advocates in Chicago around 1928. The self-taught (a watercolor-a-day) Smith turned to art directing the following year. His acceptance in the Chicago Art Director Shows and the winning of four awards was proof that the young man was right on target. By 1932, he had transferred his fortunes and talents to New York, joining the fledgling Kenyon & Eckhardt agency. After 10 years, he moved to D'Arcy, where he brought his own aura of enlightenment to the wartime Coca-Cola campaign. (His "Yes" Poster broke with the past's stifling patterns and became a classic.) His closeness to contemporary painting enabled him to add a breadth of illustrative concept to a campaign that, in lesser hands, would have been mired in banality.

In this period—his reputation well solidified—Smith was elected to the presidency of the New York Art Directors Club. He held the post for two years. Just before the end of the forties, he formed his own agency enlarged with a hop-scotch of mergers into what became the longest title of the time—Calkins and Holden, Carlock, McClinton and Smith. They did some of the boldest advertising of the day.

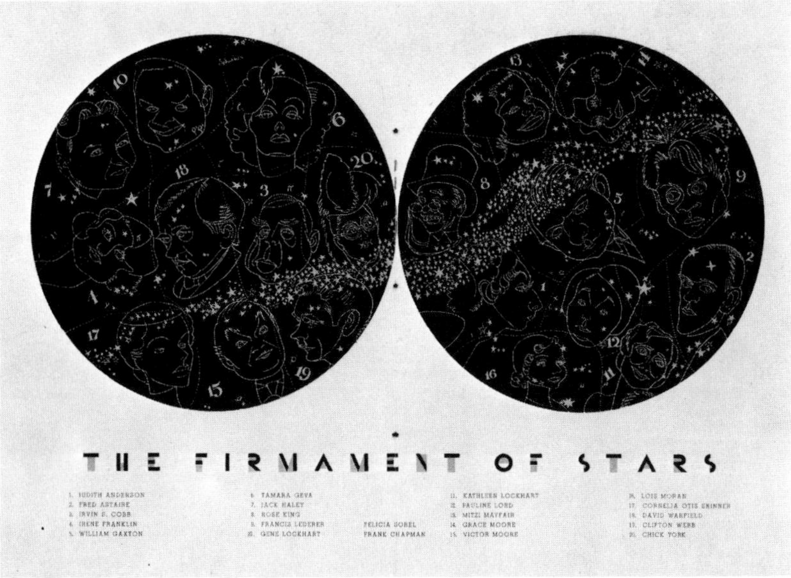
THE FIRMAMENT OF STARS
1. JUDITH ANDERSON
2. FRED ASTAIRE
3. IRVIN S. COBB
4. IRENE FRANKLIN
5. WILLIAM GAXTON
6. TAMARA GEVA
7. JACK HALEY
8. ROSE KING
9. FRANCIS LEDERER
10. GENE LOCKHART
FELICIA SOREL
FRANK CHAPMAN
11. KATHLEEN LOCKHART
12. PAULINE LORD
13. MITZI MAYFAIR
14. GRACE MOORE
15. VICTOR MOORE
16. LOIS MORAN
17. CORNELIA OTIS SKINNER
18. DAVID WARFIELD
19. CLIFTON WEBB
20. CHICK YORK

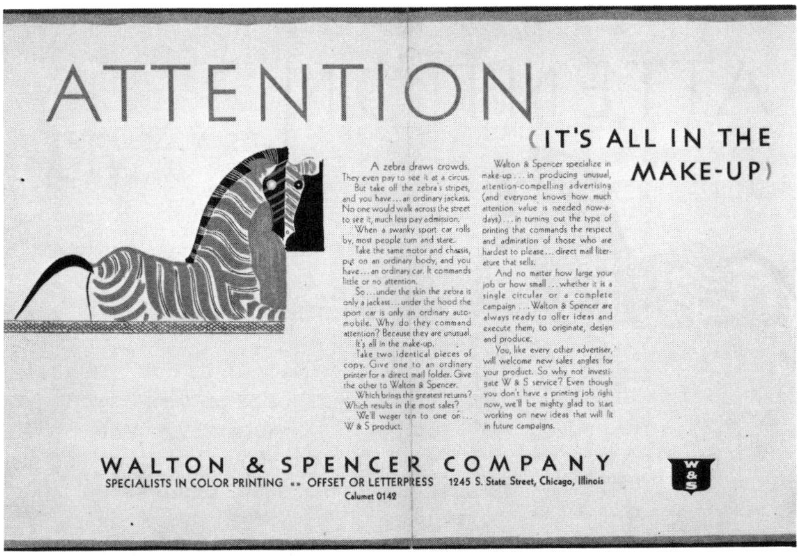
ATTENTION
(IT'S ALL IN THE MAKE-UP)
A zebra draws crowds. They even pay to see it at a circus.
But take off the zebra's stripes, and you have... an ordinary jackass. No one would walk across the street to see it, much less pay admission.
When a swanky sport car rolls by, most people turn and stare.
Take the same motor and chassis, put on an ordinary body, and you have... an ordinary car. It commands little or no attention.
So... under the skin the zebra is only a jackass... under the hood the sport car is only an ordinary automobile. Why do they command attention? Because they are unusual.
It's all in the make-up.
Take two identical pieces of copy. Give one to an ordinary printer for a direct mail folder. Give the other to Walton & Spencer.
Which brings the greatest returns? Which results in the most sales?
We'll wager ten to one on... W & S product.
Walton & Spencer specialize in make-up... in producing unusual, attention-compelling advertising (and everyone knows how much attention value is needed now-a-days)... in turning out the type of printing that commands the respect and admiration of those who are hardest to please... direct mail literature that sells.
And no matter how large your job or how small... whether it is a single circular or a complete campaign.... Walton & Spencer are always ready to offer ideas and execute them, to originate, design and produce.
You, like every other advertiser, will welcome new sales angles for your product. So why not investigate W & S service? Even though you don't have a printing job right now, we'll be mighty glad to start working on new ideas that will fit in future campaigns.
WALTON & SPENCER COMPANY
SPECIALISTS IN COLOR PRINTING • • OFFSET OR LETTERPRESS
1245 S. State Street, Chicago, Illinois
Calumet 0142
W & S

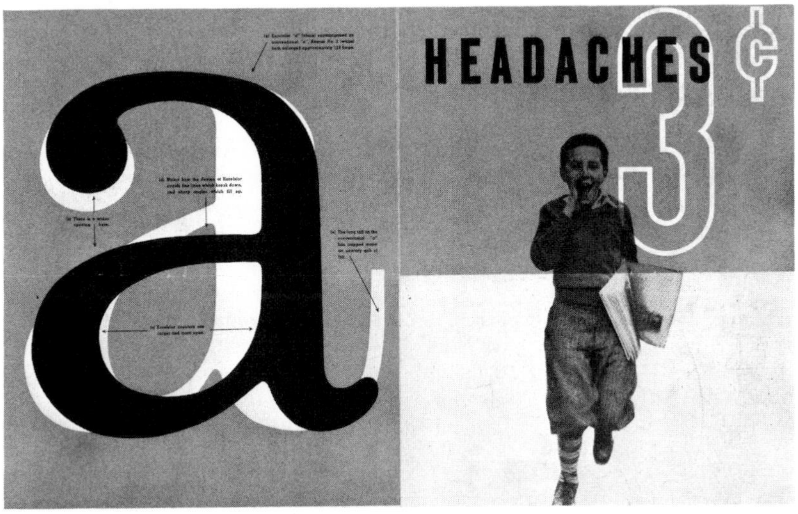
HEADACHES 3¢
a

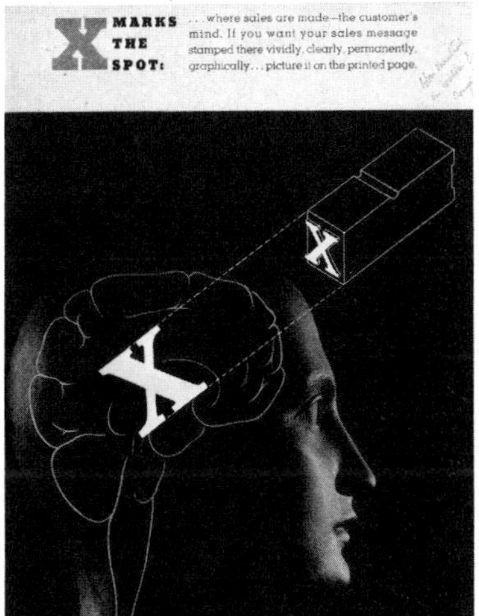
X MARKS THE SPOT:
...where sales are made—the customer's mind. If you want your sales message stamped there vividly, clearly, permanently, graphically... picture it on the printed page.
WALKER ENGRAVING CORPORATION • 141 East 25th Street, New York, N. Y.

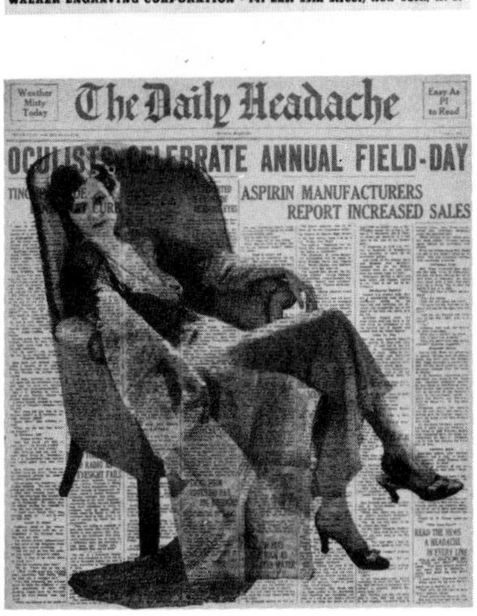
The Daily Headache
OCULISTS CELEBRATE ANNUAL FIELD-DAY
ASPIRIN MANUFACTURERS REPORT INCREASED SALES

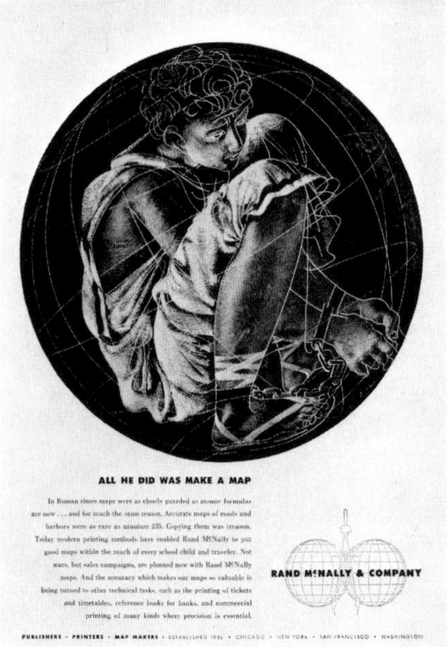
ALL HE DID WAS MAKE A MAP
In Roman times maps were as closely guarded as atomic formulas are now . . . and for much the same reason. Accurate maps of roads and harbors were as rare as uranium 235. Copying them was treason. Today modern printing methods have enabled Rand McNally to put good maps within the reach of every school child and traveler. Not wars, but sales campaigns, are planned now with Rand McNally maps. And the accuracy which makes our maps so valuable is being turned to other technical tasks, such as the printing of tickets and timetables, reference books for banks, and commercial printing of many kinds where precision is essential.
RAND McNALLY & COMPANY
PUBLISHERS · PRINTERS · MAP MAKERS

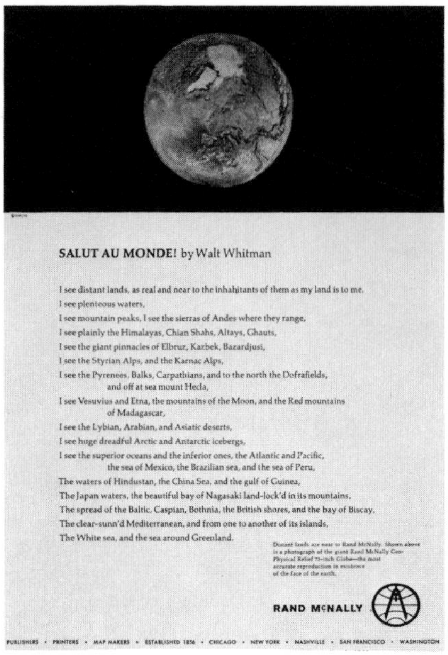
SALUT AU MONDE! by Walt Whitman
I see distant lands, as real and near to the inhabitants of them as my land is to me.
I see plenteous waters,
I see mountain peaks, I see the sierras of Andes where they range,
I see plainly the Himalayas, Chian Shahs, Altays, Ghauts,
I see the giant pinnacles of Elbruz, Kazbek, Bazardjusi,
I see the Styrian Alps, and the Karnac Alps,
I see the Pyrenees, Balks, Carpathians, and to the north the Dofrafields,
and off at sea mount Hecla,
I see Vesuvius and Etna, the mountains of the Moon, and the Red mountains
of Madagascar,
I see the Lybian, Arabian, and Asiatic deserts,
I see huge dreadful Arctic and Antarctic icebergs,
I see the superior oceans and the inferior ones, the Atlantic and Pacific,
the sea of Mexico, the Brazilian sea, and the sea of Peru,
The waters of Hindustan, the China Sea, and the gulf of Guinea,
The Japan waters, the beautiful bay of Nagasaki land-lock'd in its mountains,
The spread of the Baltic, Caspian, Bothnia, the British shores, and the bay of Biscay,
The clear-sunn'd Mediterranean, and from one to another of its islands,
The White sea, and the sea around Greenland.
RAND McNALLY
PUBLISHERS · PRINTERS · MAP MAKERS · ESTABLISHED 1856 · CHICAGO · NEW YORK · NASHVILLE · SAN FRANCISCO · WASHINGTON

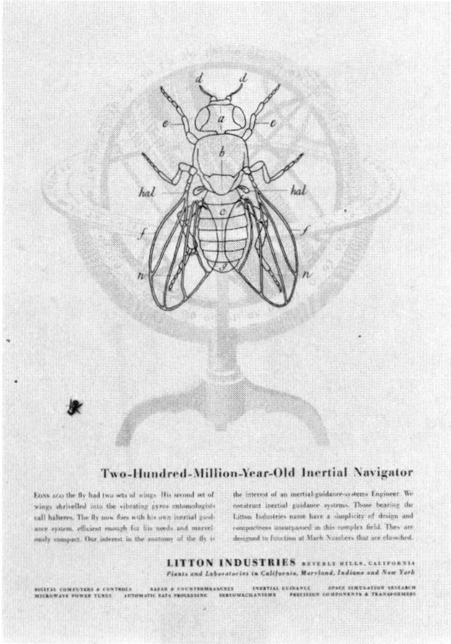
Two-Hundred-Million-Year-Old Inertial Navigator
LITTON INDUSTRIES
Plants and Laboratories in California, Maryland, Indiana and New York

Fly-by-Night Bachelors of Science
LITTON INDUSTRIES
Plants and Laboratories in California, Maryland, Indiana and New York

As an independent and as part of an archipelago of names—Smith produced a memorable body of work. Probably most dramatic and seminal were a series of posters he directed with George Krikorian for *The New York Times* that marvelously combated its stuffy image. The ultra-modern series was shown at the Museum of Modern Art (the year, 1952). Smith's campaigns continued with preemptive ideas—for Boeing (one sold the positiveness of the jet age), for Celanese (a campaign hit financial analysts), for Prudential, The New York Stock Exchange, Rand McNally. Each with its specific ideological, marketing or industrial problem, demonstrated his skill in selling ideas, often abstract ones. Smith enjoyed the job of interpreting corporations to each other and to the "various publics they wanted to reach." The duality of his intellect was in perfect consonance with problems broader than selling—broader than the ordinary commodity to consumer line. It was a high time in the development of corporate advertising.

In his last years before retiring, Smith wrote and art directed a long campaign for Celanese—the last of which was illustrated by René Magritte.

Smith has lived in Bermuda with his family since 1970. Retirement seems inappropriate to Paul Smith—who, we have said, does not like spectator sports. Smith currently is involved—making astronomical telescopes, playing the classical guitar, sailing, painting.

In our era of intense specialization, someone of the dimension and breadth of a Paul Smith is, indeed, a "rara avis." His contribution has been a fusion of independent vision and intellect which has enhanced the role and prestige of the art director.

Yes
Coca-Cola

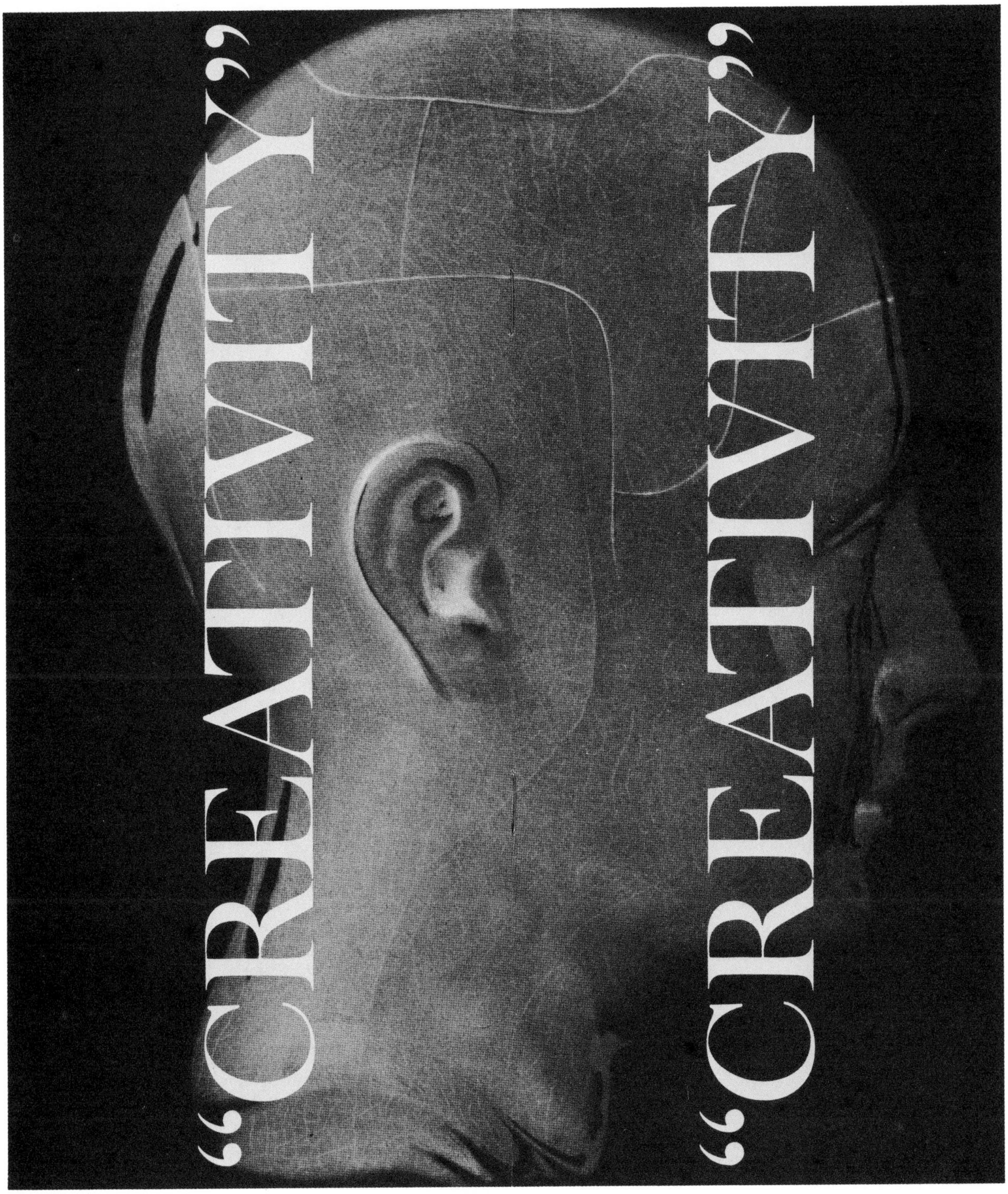
“CREATIVITY”
“CREATIVITY”

Jack Tinker

Jack Tinker is best known—particularly to younger people—for his creative think-tank that helped spawn many of the trends of the 'creative revolution' of the sixties. But for 30 years before that, he had been a bright light—an art director of protean skills. And Tinker has been an important presence in the industry.

The word "communicator" applied to the art director, writer, or creative director is relatively new to our lexicon. Tinker—who has been in advertising all his adult life as a creator and executive—always considered himself a communicator first.

His advertising story began in 1927—a time in American life still suffused with the optimism of the American Dream. A crisp 21, two years out of the warm embrace of Philadelphia's venerable Pennsylvania Academy of Fine Arts, Jack Tinker was for all the surrounding optimism, just one more impecunious artist casting about for a place in commerce's chilly environment. Interestingly, as he looks back at that time, he recalls there being no surging youthful ambition pushing him toward advertising. "I guess I was old enough and wise enough to know that an agency used whatever talents I might have, moreover they paid for them." Tinker's story throughout reveals how eventful events, never even perceived by lesser talents can, in gifted hands, be turned into successes.

to a man
at that
dangerous
age!
When life goes stale and you feel you're building up to an explosion, this is the time to let yourself go in a sleek new Riviera.
If your common sense tells you that you don't really need a luxurious, powerful new sports coupe, tell your common sense to be quiet. "Look," you can say to yourself, "you work hard enough . . . you deserve a little fun."
After you've agreed with this undeniable truth, daydream a little. You're behind the wheel of this tailored beauty with 325 horses at your command (more than you find on Wagon Train). You ride in airy elegance, pleasantly conscious of admiring looks. The bucket seats, the rich appointments add to your big time feeling . . . you're quite a guy . . . successful, and if you aren't exactly handsome, the car can do a lot for almost any face. Another argument (if you need one) . . . an imported car of this caliber would cost twice Riviera's price.
So if you're at that dangerous age, pamper yourself with a Riviera. It's an astonishing combination of classic elegance and spectacular sports car performance.
See your Buick dealer for a demonstration.
THE RIVIERA
BY BUICK

THE HOUSE THAT BIT!
By Mr. Friendly
Imagine, living day and night
Inside a house that's apt to bite!
With leaping rugs that try to down you,
Tubs that gaily try to drown you,
Switches, that I'm loath to say
Treat you in a *shocking* way!
No wonder Lee turned white with fright
And ran out shrieking in the night!
Then Mr. Friendly reached the scene
And handed Lee *"Watch" magazine!**
"This new American Mutual guide to
home safety," he said, lapsing into prose,
"shows you more than 50 ways to tame
the most dangerous house!"
Thanks to American Mutual, Lee
Lives in a house that is accident-free!
In fact it's so safe, so quiet, so still
Lee hammers his head now,
just for a thrill!
*IMPORTANT NEW OFFER THAT CAN SAFEGUARD YOUR HOME!
For only 15¢ (to cover mailing costs) you get a fully-illustrated 50¢ magazine full of new information about home safety. With dramatic illustrations and clear, easy-to-follow instructions, this new issue of "Watch" is the latest guide to safer living! Send 15¢ today to Institute For Safer Living of American Mutual Liability Insurance Company, Dept. A-132, 142 Berkeley Street, Boston 16, Massachusetts.
AMERICAN MUTUAL
A M
Service from salaried representatives in 77 offices!
Savings from regular substantial dividends!
©1952, AMERICAN MUTUAL LIABILITY INSURANCE COMPANY

Advertising in Philadelphia in the late twenties meant N. W. Ayer & Son, a distinguished agency with a somewhat unorthodox attitude about employing the non-commercial artist. In what became a tradition, many of its art directors achieved a measure of distinction in the fine arts in addition to their achievements in advertising. In two years the inexperienced but ingenuous painter had emerged as one of the key creative people on Ayer's directorial staff, a position of increasing luminance he held for seven years while working on Yardley and other important accounts. It is a point of nostalgic pride to him that it was his ads that introduced the unforgettable Model A Ford to the American public.

Alka-Seltzer®

On The Rocks

You haven't tried it yet?
Oh boy.
Alka-Seltzer On The Rocks works just like Alka-Seltzer Off The Rocks . . . only it's good enough to drink. Maybe even delicious? And even today, in 1966, nothing relieves an upset stomach and summer headache faster . . . or better than good old Alka-Seltzer.
Try it at a picnic.
Try it at the beach.
Plop two Alka-Seltzers in water. Let it bubble away a few seconds. Add ice. A slice of lime. Cheers.

With a solid record of achievement he was next beckoned to New York and the J. M. Mathes Agency, where for five years he lent his skill, wit and creativity to a range of campaigns that encompassed innumerable industrial enterprises as well as household products (Canada Dry, Lux Toilet Soap, American Viscose being only some of them). But it was the McCann-Erickson base from 1939-1960 (minus a short period with J. Walter Thompson) where he assumed various executive posts to eventually become its creative director and senior vice president. Ads—in their entirety or components bearing the Tinker stamp—were regularly selected for the Art Directors Annual Exhibitions and frequently took awards. In 1952, he received the coveted National Society of Art Directors "Art Director of the Year" Award. (An issue of *Advertising Age* called him "One of the greatest art directors of all time.")

Tinker wrote, designed, created, supervised, drew the famous "Mr. Friendly" series for American Mutual Insurance. Louis Dorfsman, also a much-honored art director at CBS, vividly recalls one of those vignettes that demonstrated Tinker's low-keyed manner and penetrating creative insights. It was during a discussion of a CBS Radio campaign. The meeting room was filled with smoke and banalities. Tinker cut through the enveloping murk with a succinct description of an ad: It was simply a lone automobile making its dusty way along a desert highway. It said "The driver of this car is being sold a refrigerator." That was 17 years ago. The ad's freshness, pertinence, and sprightly sense of communication remain unfaded by time.

The smile of Business - NO 5
Birth of a smile... "Gulp type!" Usually follows a change of plans by the brass!
Jack Tinker

In 1960, the Interpublic Group, under the aegis of Marion Harper, established a company whose sole function was creative exploration and development. This company, of course, became the famous Jack Tinker and Partners where, for a full decade, Tinker provided the spiritual wherewithal, creative resources, and rare leadership that united a diverse and gifted group. They began with four: Tinker; Dan Calhoun, art director; Myron McDonald, marketing generalist; Herta Hertzog, research. Ineluctably, the unique concept had to give way to carrying out the functions of an ad agency. After acquiring the Alka-Seltzer account they became a full-service agency to respond to its clients' needs. However miraculous, they kept their specialness—and the graduate members of the team reads like an Advertising "Who's Who": Mary Wells, Bob Wilvers, Henry Wolf, Stewart Greene are but a few who labored in this unusual and fruitful vineyard. A few of its memorable achievements: the first of the new Alka-Seltzer campaigns that helped to make captivating advertising a part of the contemporary language, Braniff Airlines, Buick Riviera, Accutron Watch. The free-flowing group had far-flung influence beyond expectations.

What was the agency like? Said Mary Wells: "Some people run agencies like banks or religious organizations or like Bellevue Hospital. Jack ran his like a Scott Fitzgerald novel. He created a witty, glamorous atmosphere that was intensely personal and tremendously productive."

Bob Wilvers: "Jack was the genius catalyst who created and held together an environment in which sensitive, well-intentioned, creative people could work. There can't be a warmer, kinder, more generous man or a man with more style."

To Tinker, advertising is not a medium for sales, but is a way of reaching people in effective salutary, humane form. He feels advertising is the province of the young—a medium of the immediate now. "It is not the forte of the ancient."

Prolific as a book illustrator, totally versatile as a magazine and advertising writer—there was and is an unquenchable vivacity to Jack Tinker. Although a serious illness forced him to withdraw from the active agency front in 1971, he recovered with typical buoyancy and is now pursuing the fullness of life as an artist, writer, and keen observer of the advertising he knew and helped build and lives in Upper New York and Florida with his wife, Martha.

Tinker very properly belongs in the Hall of Fame. He gave dedicated effort to the idea that art direction was an important segment of the world of communication. He helped shape a profession in which the creative mind and hand could flourish.

The Stereophonic Smile or Client-Bellow!... Means "By God
A.B. that's funny as hell!" "How about one more all around?

the Smile of Business NO 5
The Flash Smile:
means, "what did I say that was so funny?"

The Smile of Business — NO. 2
the smile of the Fox ... The chickens are usually gone when you see this ... you have only the feathers!

The Smile of Business — NO. 1
The warm executive smile -

The Copy Club Hall of Fame Award

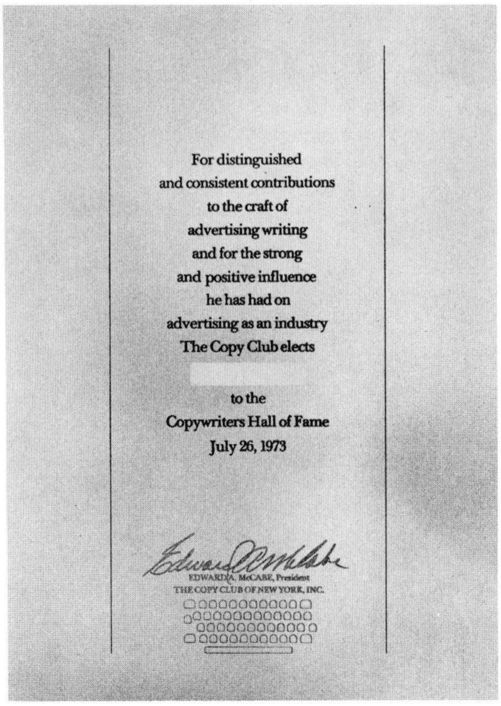
For distinguished
and consistent contributions
to the craft of
advertising writing
and for the strong
and positive influence
he has had on
advertising as an industry
The Copy Club elects
to the
Copywriters Hall of Fame
July 26, 1973
EDWARD A. McCABE, President
THE COPY CLUB OF NEW YORK, INC.

PHOTO BY CARL FISCHER

The Great "Ghosts"

They worked with ideas. They used words that excited people. Words that sold automobiles, and life insurance and soft drinks. And yet they were anonymous to the world. They signed their work with the name of their clients.

But other copywriters knew who was writing the great advertising successes. Who was making things happen with words. And we envied and applauded their skill. So 12 years ago we began to honor our own. To pay tribute not to just a given print ad or commercial but to a whole body of work, we invented the Copy Hall of Fame. The men and women we have so honored have indeed been giants in the profession. They have written brilliant, successful advertisements. In most cases, they have set whole new directions. They won their fame and our respect and deserve both.

Bob Fearon

THE COPYWRITERS HALL OF FAME

1961	Leo Burnett
1962	George H. Gribbin
1963	David Ogilvy
1964	William Bernbach
1965	Rosser Reeves
1966	Julian Koenig
1967	Bernice Fitz-Gibbon
	Claude Hopkins
1968	Phyllis Robinson
1969	Mary Wells Lawrence
1970	Howard Gossage
1971	Ron Rosenfeld
1972	Robert Levenson
1973	John Caples
	James Webb Young

John Caples

With a certain degree of selfishness, stemming, perhaps, from a need for self-aggrandizement, we need to believe that the creative process in advertising improves with time. In reality, what changes is style, and the universal constant of good writing remains throughout the years. Those who are good, cease being so only when their style cannot change with the years. Those who are great, adapt.

For 43 years, John Caples has stood as axiomatic proof of this theory. The father of direct response advertising, he continues to create some of the most successful ads of their kind as vice president and creative director of BBD&O's direct response division.

There lies, in direct response advertising, a satisfaction often unavailable in other areas of copywriting: Tangible evidence of results. Coupons can be counted. And the variations in appeal and direction can be measured in returns received—not just in the subjective minds of agency and client.

For John Caples, this special nature of direct response has always appealed to his duality, in its appeasement of his creative abilities and its challenge in the proof of results. Over the years, Caples has responded to this challenge by pioneering techniques and tests which stand as monuments to his genius as writer and researcher.

A New Yorker all his life, Caples came into advertising shortly after his graduation from Annapolis. Going to work for Ev Grady at Ruthrauff & Ryan, it was as a copy cub that he wrote "They Laughed When I Sat Down At the Piano . . ." opening a new technique in mail order and still standing today as one of the greatest ads ever written.

For two years, Caples studied under Grady. In 1927, influenced by Bill Orchard's advertising course, he joined BBD&O as writer and account executive. Given the Phoenix Mutual account, this first assignment earned him his second entry into *The 100 Greatest Ads* with his appeal "To Men Who Want to Quit Work Some Day" (the forerunner of "How I Retired in 15 years at $100 a Month").

For the next fifteen years, Caples' interest in testing dominated his activities. As director of readership research and copy testing at BBD&O, he implemented testing methods for advertising, developing new ones where direct mail standards didn't apply. This work—still used in copy testing—served as the basis for the three advertising books he wrote during that period.

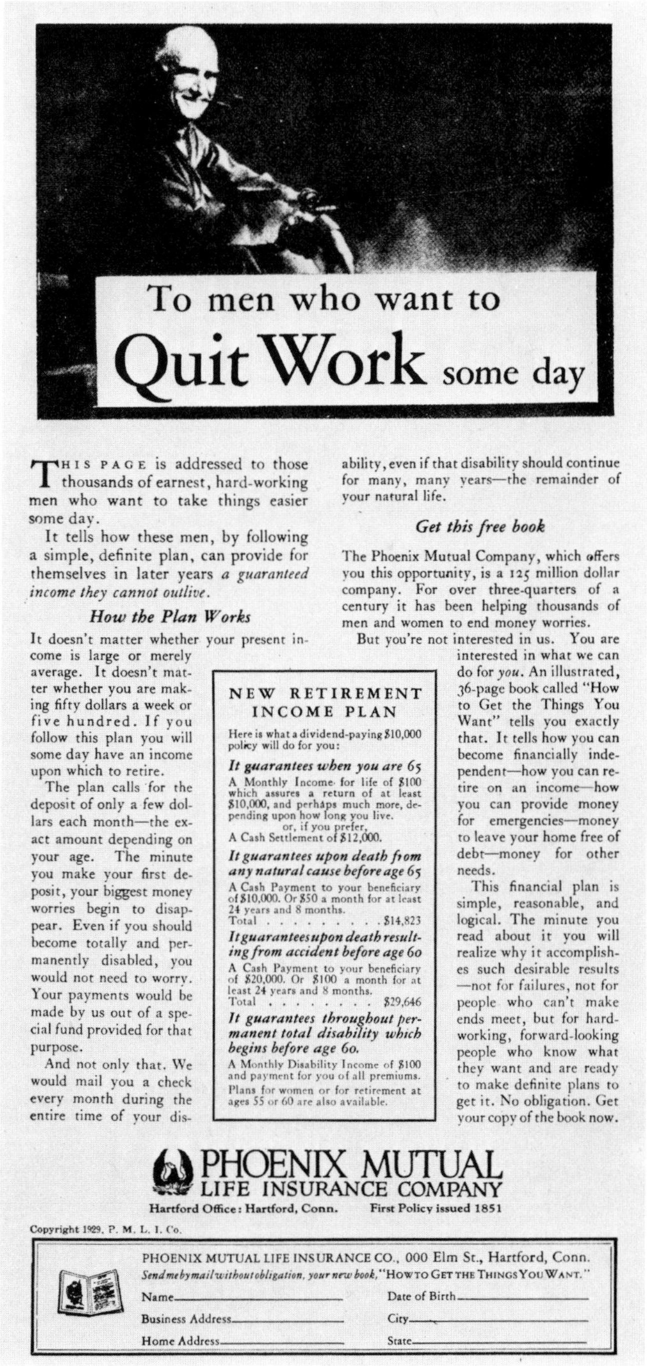

To men who want to
Quit Work some day
THIS PAGE is addressed to those thousands of earnest, hard-working men who want to take things easier some day.
It tells how these men, by following a simple, definite plan, can provide for themselves in later years a guaranteed income they cannot outlive.
How the Plan Works
It doesn't matter whether your present income is large or merely average. It doesn't matter whether you are making fifty dollars a week or five hundred. If you follow this plan you will some day have an income upon which to retire.
The plan calls for the deposit of only a few dollars each month—the exact amount depending on your age. The minute you make your first deposit, your biggest money worries begin to disappear. Even if you should become totally and permanently disabled, you would not need to worry. Your payments would be made by us out of a special fund provided for that purpose.
And not only that. We would mail you a check every month during the entire time of your disability, even if that disability should continue for many, many years—the remainder of your natural life.
NEW RETIREMENT INCOME PLAN
Here is what a dividend-paying $10,000 policy will do for you:
It guarantees when you are 65
A Monthly Income for life of $100 which assures a return of at least $10,000, and perhaps much more, depending upon how long you live.
or, if you prefer,
A Cash Settlement of $12,000.
It guarantees upon death from any natural cause before age 65
A Cash Payment to your beneficiary of $10,000. Or $50 a month for at least 24 years and 8 months.
Total $14,823
It guarantees upon death resulting from accident before age 60
A Cash Payment to your beneficiary of $20,000. Or $100 a month for at least 24 years and 8 months.
Total $29,646
It guarantees throughout permanent total disability which begins before age 60.
A Monthly Disability Income of $100 and payment for you of all premiums.
Plans for women or for retirement at ages 55 or 60 are also available.
Get this free book
The Phoenix Mutual Company, which offers you this opportunity, is a 125 million dollar company. For over three-quarters of a century it has been helping thousands of men and women to end money worries.
But you're not interested in us. You are interested in what we can do for you. An illustrated, 36-page book called "How to Get the Things You Want" tells you exactly that. It tells how you can become financially independent—how you can retire on an income—how you can provide money for emergencies—money to leave your home free of debt—money for other needs.
This financial plan is simple, reasonable, and logical. The minute you read about it you will realize why it accomplishes such desirable results—not for failures, not for people who can't make ends meet, but for hard-working, forward-looking people who know what they want and are ready to make definite plans to get it. No obligation. Get your copy of the book now.
PHOENIX MUTUAL
LIFE INSURANCE COMPANY
Hartford Office: Hartford, Conn.
First Policy issued 1851
Copyright 1929, P. M. L. I. Co.
PHOENIX MUTUAL LIFE INSURANCE CO., 000 Elm St., Hartford, Conn.
Send me by mail without obligation, your new book, "HOW TO GET THE THINGS YOU WANT."
Name
Date of Birth
Business Address
City
Home Address
State

"Can he really play?" a girl whispered. "Heavens no!" Arthur exclaimed. "He never played a note in his life."

They Laughed When I Sat Down At the Piano But When I Started to Play!—

ARTHUR had just played "The Rosary." The room rang with applause. I decided that this would be a dramatic moment for me to make my debut. To the amazement of all my friends, I strode confidently over to the piano and sat down.

"Jack is up to his old tricks," somebody chuckled. The crowd laughed. They were all certain that I couldn't play a single note.

"Can he really play?" I heard a girl whisper to Arthur.

"Heavens, no!" Arthur exclaimed. "He never played a note in all his life. . . But just you watch him. This is going to be good."

I decided to make the most of the situation. With mock dignity I drew out a silk handkerchief and lightly dusted off the piano keys. Then I rose and gave the revolving piano stool a quarter of a turn, just as I had seen an imitator of Paderewski do in a vaudeville sketch.

"What do you think of his execution?" called a voice from the rear.

"We're in favor of it!" came back the answer, and the crowd rocked with laughter.

Then I Started to Play

Instantly a tense silence fell on the guests. The laughter died on their lips as if by magic. I played through the first few bars of Beethoven's immortal Moonlight Sonata. I heard gasps of amazement. My friends sat breathless — spellbound!

I played on and as I played I forgot the people around me. I forgot the hour, the place, the breathless listeners. The little world I lived in seemed to fade — seemed to grow dim—unreal. Only the music was real. Only the music and visions it brought me. Visions as beautiful and as changing as the wind blown clouds and drifting moonlight that long ago inspired the master composer. It seemed as if the master musician himself were speaking to me—speaking through the medium of music—not in words but in chords. Not in sentences but in exquisite melodies!

A Complete Triumph!

As the last notes of the Moonlight Sonata died away, the room resounded with a sudden roar of applause. I found myself surrounded by excited faces. How my friends carried on! Men shook my hand — wildly congratulated me — pounded me on the back in their enthusiasm! Everybody was exclaiming with delight—plying me with rapid questions. . . . "Jack! Why didn't you tell us you could play like that?" . . . "Where *did* you learn?"—"How long have you studied?"—"Who *was* your teacher?"

"I have never even *seen* my teacher," I replied. "And just a short while ago I couldn't play a note."

"Quit your kidding," laughed Arthur, himself an accomplished pianist. "You've been studying for years. I can tell."

"I have been studying only a short while," I insisted. "I decided to keep it a secret so that I could surprise all you folks."

Then I told them the whole story.

"Have you ever heard of the U. S. School of Music?" I asked.

A few of my friends nodded. "That's a correspondence school, isn't it?" they exclaimed.

"Exactly," I replied. "They have a new simplified method that can teach you to play any instrument by mail in just a few months."

How I Learned to Play Without a Teacher

And then I explained how for years I had longed to play the piano.

"A few months ago," I continued, "I saw an interesting ad for the U. S. School of Music—a new method of learning to play which only cost a few cents a day! The ad told how a woman had mastered the piano in her spare time at home—and *without a teacher!* Best of all, the wonderful new method she used, required no laborious scales — no heartless exercises — no tiresome practising. It sounded so convincing that I filled out the coupon requesting the Free Demonstration Lesson.

"The free book arrived promptly and I started in that very night to study the Demonstration Lesson. I was amazed to see how easy it was to play this new way. Then I sent for the course.

"When the course arrived I found it was just as the ad said — as easy as A.B.C.! And, as the lessons continued they got easier and easier. Before I knew it I was playing all the pieces I liked best. Nothing stopped me. I could play ballads or classical numbers or jazz, all with equal ease! And I never did have any special talent for music!"

• • • •

Pick Your Instrument

Piano	'Cello
Organ	Harmony and Composition
Violin	Sight Singing
Drums and Traps	Ukulele
Banjo	Guitar
Tenor Banjo	Hawaiian Steel Guitar
Mandolin	Harp
Clarinet	Cornet
Flute	Piccolo
Saxophone	Trombone

Voice and Speech Culture
Automatic Finger Control
Piano Accordion

Play Any Instrument

You too, can now *teach yourself* to be an accomplished musician—right at home—in half the usual time. You can't go wrong with this simple new method which has already shown 350,000 people how to play their favorite instruments. Forget that old-fashioned idea that you need special "talent." Just read the list of instruments in the panel, decide which one you want to play and the U. S. School will do the rest. And bear in mind no matter which instrument you choose, the cost in each case will be the same—just a few cents a day. No matter whether you are a mere beginner or already a good performer, you will be interested in learning about this new and wonderful method.

Send for Our Free Booklet and Demonstration Lesson

Thousands of successful students never dreamed they possessed musical ability until it was revealed to them by a remarkable "Musical Ability Test" which we send entirely without cost with our interesting free booklet.

If you are in earnest about wanting to play your favorite instrument—if you really want to gain happiness and increase your popularity—send at once for the free booklet and Demonstration Lesson. No cost — no obligation. Right now we are making a Special offer for a limited number of new students. Sign and send the convenient coupon now — before it's too late to gain the benefits of this offer. Instruments supplied when needed, cash or credit. **U. S. School of Music, 1031 Brunswick Bldg., New York City.**

U. S. School of Music,
1031 Brunswick Bldg., New York City.

Please send me your free book, "Music Lessons in Your Own Home", with introduction by Dr. Frank Crane, Demonstration Lesson and particulars of your Special Offer. I am interested in the following course:

. . . .

Have you above instrument? . . . .

Name . . . .
(Please write plainly)

Address . . . .

City . . . . **State** . . . .

At the outbreak of World War II, Caples returned to the Navy in charge of the Officer Candidate Program for the Third Naval District—processing 35,000 candidates in two years. In 1944, a Commander, he went to the Bureau of Naval Personnel in Washington to take charge of their Field Research Program surveying personnel needs and opinions.

In 1945, with a letter of commendation from the Secretary of the Navy, he returned full time to BBD&O and immediately proved he hadn't lost his touch; writing *The Wall Street Journal's* "How to Get Ahead in Business" campaign.

Throughout the fifties and sixties, Caples continued refining and developing testing methods for advertising. As a lecturer at Columbia University and the New York Advertising Club, he continued to teach others the way to make advertising work. His fourth book, *Making Ads Pay,* stands as a summation to his understanding of the essence of direct response advertising. Still active in testing and development at BBD&O, he is, as always, the only John Caples listed in the New York phone book.

There is, after all, only one John Caples.

I Was Going Broke on $9,000 a Year

So I sent $7 to The Wall Street Journal

High prices and taxes were getting me down. I had to have more money or reduce my standard of living. Like Alice in Wonderland, I had to run faster to stay in the same place.

So I sent $7 for a Trial Subscription to The Wall Street Journal. I heeded its warnings. I cashed in on the ideas it gave me for increasing my income and cutting expenses. I got the money I needed. Now I'm slowly forging ahead. Believe me, reading The Journal every day is a wonderful get-ahead plan.

This experience is typical. The Journal is a wonderful aid to salaried men making $7,500 to $30,000 a year. It is valuable to the owner of a small business. It can be of priceless benefit to young men who want to win advancement.

The Wall Street Journal is the complete business DAILY. Has largest staff of writers on business and finance. The only business paper served by all three big press associations. It costs $24 a year, but you can get a Trial Subscription for three months for $7. Just tear out this ad and attach check for $7 and mail. Or tell us to bill you. **NYT 0-00**

Address: The Wall Street Journal, 44 Broad St., New York 4, N.Y.

James Webb Young

"Knowledge," Jim Young once wrote, "is the power to predict. What an area of ignorance that leaves in advertising!"

In a career as copywriter and educator that bridged two centuries, James Webb Young would do much to dispel that ignorance. Though never formally educated, he engaged in a process of self-education that lasted a lifetime. With a wry, down-home humor masking an instinctive business genius, Young let the world give him an education. In return, it taught him how to sell.

In his mid-teens, as an office boy with the Western Methodist Book Concern, he tried his hand at direct mail letters for the firm. When his results drew a 1000 percent increase in response, James Young had found his calling and his philosophy. As he later remarked—he ". . . always thought the only difference between ad men and preachers was a sense of direction."

There isn't a girl who can't have the irresistible, appealing loveliness of perfect daintiness

Within the Curve of a Woman's Arm

A frank discussion of a subject too often avoided

A woman's arm! Poets have sung of its grace; artists have painted its beauty.

It should be the daintiest, sweetest thing in the world. And yet, unfortunately, it isn't, always.

There's an old offender in this quest for perfect daintiness—an offender of which we ourselves may be ever so unconscious, but which is just as truly present.

Shall we discuss it frankly?

Many a woman who says, "No, I am never annoyed by perspiration," does not know the facts—does not realize how much sweeter and daintier she would be if she were *entirely* free from it.

Of course, we aren't to blame because nature has so made us that the perspiration glands under the arms are more active than anywhere else. Nor are we to blame because the perspiration which occurs under the arm does not evaporate as readily as from other parts of the body. The curve of the arm and the constant wearing of clothing have made normal evaporation there impossible.

Would you be absolutely sure of your daintiness?

It is the chemicals of the body, not uncleanliness, that cause odor. And even though there is no active perspiration—no apparent moisture—there may be under the arms an odor unnoticed by ourselves, but distinctly noticeable to others. For it is a physiological fact that persons troubled with perspiration odor seldom can detect it themselves.

Fastidious women who want to be absolutely sure of their daintiness have found that they could not trust to their own consciousness; they have felt the need of a toilet water which would insure them against any of this kind of underarm unpleasantness, either moisture or odor.

To meet this need, a physician formulated Odorono—a perfectly harmless and delightful toilet water. With particular women Odorono has become a toilet necessity which they use regularly two or three times a week.

So simple, so easy, so sure

No matter how much the perspiration glands may be excited by exertion, nervousness, or weather conditions, Odorono will keep your underarms always sweet and naturally dry. You then can dismiss all anxiety as to your freshness, your perfect daintiness.

The right time to use Odorono is at night before retiring. Pat it on the underarms with a bit of absorbent cotton, only two or three times a week. Then a little talcum dusted on and you can forget all about that worst of all embarrassments—perspiration odor or moisture. Daily baths do not lessen the effect of Odorono at all.

Does excessive perspiration ruin your prettiest dresses?

Are you one of the many women who are troubled with excessive perspiration, which ruins all your prettiest blouses and dresses? To endure this condition is so unnecessary! Why, you need ***never*** spoil a dress with perspiration! For this severer trouble Odorono is just as effective as it is for the more subtle form of perspiration annoyance. Try it tonight and notice how exquisitely fresh and sweet you will feel.

If you are troubled in any unusual way or have had any difficulty in finding relief, let us help you solve your problem. We shall be so glad to do so. Address Ruth Miller, The Odorono Co., 719 Blair Avenue, Cincinnati, Ohio.

At all toilet counters in the United States and Canada, 60c and $1.00. Trial size, 30c. By mail postpaid if your dealer hasn't it.

Dr. Lewis B. Allyn, head of the famous Westfield Laboratories, Westfield, Massachusetts, says:

"Experimental and practical tests show that Odorono is harmless, economical and effective when employed as directed, and will injure neither the skin nor the health."

Address mail orders or requests as follows:

For Canada to The Arthur Sales Co., 61 Adelaide St., East, Toronto, Ont. For France to The Agence Américaine, 38 Avenue de l'Opéra, Paris. For Switzerland to The Agence Américaine, 17 Boulevard Helvetique, Geneve. For England to The American Drug Supply Co., 6 Northumberland Ave., London, W. C. 2. For Mexico to H. E. Gerber & Cia, 2a Gante, 19, Mexico City. For U. S. A. to The Odorono Co., 719 Blair Avenue, Cincinnati, Ohio.

By 1919, Young was joint manager of J. Walter Thompson's Western Operations—less than six years after joining the firm in Cincinnati. An association with them—as copywriter, client, and consultant—continued throughout his career. His talents as organizer made him one of the key architects of Thompson's international expansion during the twenties . . . at the same time his talents as writer made his reputation within the industry. In these, his most productive years, he wrote "Within the Curve of a Woman's Arm" . . . the first of his three ads included in *The 100 Greatest Advertisements.* It has been called the ad that introduced sex into advertising. Though over 200 readers cancelled their subscriptions, Young kept his perspective as copywriter when he remarked: "Several

Ad Council

women who learned I had written this advertisement said they would never speak to me again—that it was 'disgusting' and 'an insult to women'. But the deodorant's sales increased 112 percent that year."

For the next ten years, Young withdrew from the agency side of advertising, dividing his time between farming and education. In addition to three textbooks on advertising, he lectured on Business and Advertising at the University of Chicago and completed a study of the agency compensation system for the industry.

In 1939, the war drew Young out of retirement. Sensing America's impending involvement, he accepted a job with the Commerce Department developing a series of ads to counteract the effects of Nazi propaganda in South America. As the war neared, he rejoined Thompson and set out to create the War Advertising Council.

Less than two months before Pearl Harbor, Young addressed the first joint meeting of the AAAA and ANA with his proposal for a vast public service operation. Recognizing the need to make advertising an integral part of the war effort, the idea eventually raised millions on behalf of War Bonds, the Red Cross, USO, Victory Gardens and War Plant Punctuality. At war's end, recognizing the council's benefits, he converted it to peacetime use—becoming founder and first chairman of the Advertising Council.

Although in his sixties, James Webb Young became even more productive in the postwar years. Awarded an honorary law degree, he continued to make advertising responsive to the needs of a growing America, serving as consultant to information for the Marshall Plan. While supervising the first nationally run and quoted cosmetic success, "She's lovely. She's engaged. She uses Ponds," Young wrote a fourth advertising textbook and a novel each year over a ten year span.

In 1964, he retired a second time from Thompson to return again to his farm in New Mexico. Continuing his role as advisor and educator, he became deeply involved in the problems and culture of the Southwest Indians playing an active part there until his death in Santa Fe in the Spring of 1973.

James Webb Young was many things to many people. He lived his life with the same fullness he gave to advertising: "Written with passion, as good copy ought to be."

THE GOLD AWARDS

11
Art Director: Jim Handloser
Copywriter: Frank DiGiacomo
Designer: Jim Handloser
Photographer: WABC-TV News
Agency: Della Femina, Travisano & Partners, Inc.
Client: WABC-TV

13
Art Director: Stan Block
Copywriter: Adam Hanft
Photographer: Bruce Buchenholz
Agency: Rosenfeld, Sirowitz & Lawson
Client: WABC-TV

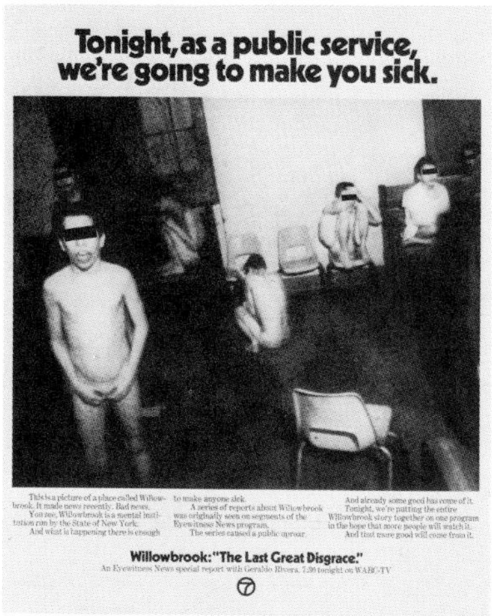

THIS JUNKIE HAS A FIFTY DOLLAR A DAY HABIT.
He won't be born for 6 months. He weighs one thirteenth of an ounce and is less than an inch long.
And he's as much of a junkie as someone who's 35 years old and shoots into the vein of his leg.
Tonight, Geraldo Rivera will take a close hard look at the junkie population of New York that hasn't even been born yet. Last year alone, 1,500 mothers with a monkey on their back gave birth to babies with a monkey on theirs.
Sometimes, if the mother goes through withdrawal while she's pregnant, the baby never gets born. He goes through cold turkey, too. And in the process will simply kick himself to death.
The program is an Eyewitness News Special called "The Littlest Junkie." And it not only explores the problem with agonizing honesty.
But it sets forth what's being done, what should be done before it's too late. And what a pregnant mother can do if she's not only eating for two, but shooting for two.
So watch tonight and see what the 70's have done to the miracle of childbirth.
TONIGHT 7:30
THE LITTLEST JUNKIE
With Eyewitness News Correspondent, Geraldo Rivera.

First the agency people told me I could say anything I wanted to about scotch. Then they censored me.

BY TOMMY SMOTHERS

I'VE BEEN CENSORED one way or another practically all my life.

It all started when my mother used to stick a pacifier into my mouth anytime I opened it.

When Dick and I were kids, once Mother got him a dog and me a muzzle.

Even my dreams have snips cut out of them. Always the good parts, too. [redacted].

That's the way it's always been.

So I wasn't surprised when one of the major networks joined the fun. It was annoying, I'll admit, but when it was all over all I could say was "et tu, CBS."

But all that is censorship under the bridge.

And speaking of censorship, it's certainly changed a lot since its beginning. Today, you can say anything as long as no one hears you. So probably the only way to steer clear of censors is to steer yourself into a closet and talk only to yourself.

Anyway, when the Teacher's advertising people heard I drink their scotch, they asked me to talk about it.

They gave me carte blanche, a yellow pad and a No. 2 pencil. Of course, the pencil had no point, but I got around that. [redacted].

Well, first I wrote about how happy I was that everybody and his brother doesn't drink Teacher's. Which, in my case, is a definite plus.

No problems so far.

Then I started reminiscing about my experiences with scotch, pre-Teachers.

The first time I tasted scotch I tried to belt it down like they always do in the movies when the hero has just lost his girl.

Ecccch. [redacted].

If this was what scotch tasted like, I vowed never to lose my girl or be a hero in a movie.

My stomach was the first casualty. Then my eyes started to water. And finally my tongue made itself heard. It gave me a severe tongue lashing.

However, I wasn't going to let myself be licked by a mere tongue, a pair of eyes and a stomach.

So I came back for less.

This time, I started with a Presbyterian. 2 parts this, 3 parts that, 4 parts something else and, if there's any room left over, scotch. [redacted].

The trouble with that was I got tired of walking up to bars and ordering one Presbyterian only to have the bartender tell me I was in the wrong place and down the street at the church I could find all the Presbyterians I wanted.

Next I moved to scotch and soda. Or more accurately, scotch and soda, soda, soda and soda.

After that, it was the big time. Scotch on the rocks. Straight. But I did such a terrific job of nursing my drink the Red Cross would have been proud of me.

All of which brings me to Teacher's. The first time I ever tasted it was the first time I ever finished my scotch on the rocks before it turned to water.

Teacher's, my tongue thanks you, my eyes thank you, my stomach thanks you. Even my sex life thanks you.

Once there was this girl and [redacted] back seat of this old DeSoto [redacted].

Boy, those Teacher's people let you say anything.

So anyway, [redacted]

86 PROOF SCOTCH WHISKY BLENDED AND BOTTLED IN SCOTLAND BY WM. TEACHER & SONS, LTD. © SCHIEFFELIN & CO., N.Y., IMPORTERS

28

Art Directors: Nick Gisonde
Bob Kuperman
Copywriters: Neil Drossman
Jerry Della Femina
Designers: Nick Gisonde
Bob Kuperman
Photographers: Arnold Beckerman
Anthony Edgeworth
Agency: Della Femina, Travisano & Partners, Inc.
Client: Teacher's Scotch

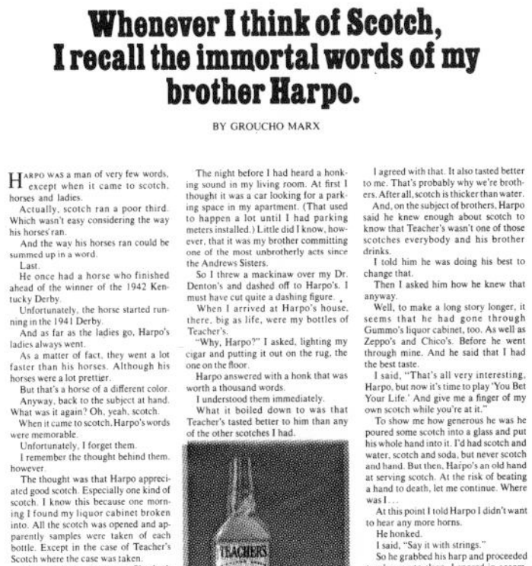
Whenever I think of Scotch, I recall the immortal words of my brother Harpo.
BY GROUCHO MARX

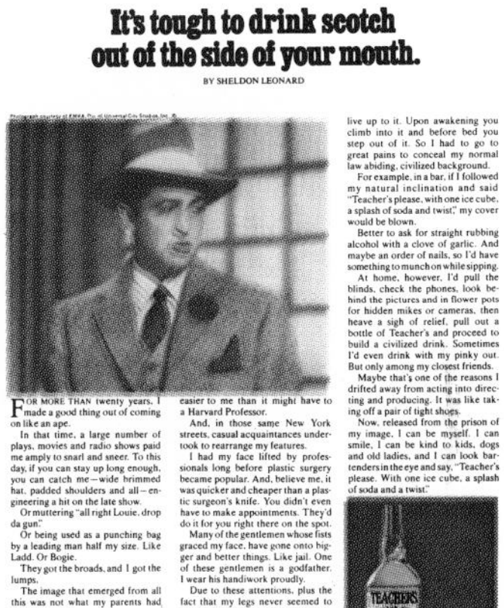
It's tough to drink scotch out of the side of your mouth.
BY SHELDON LEONARD

52
Art Director: Roy Grace
Copywriter: Marcia Bell Grace
Designer: Roy Grace
Photographer: Dick Stone
Agency: Doyle Dane Bernbach Inc.
Client: American Tourister Luggage

3,000 LB. CAR LOWERED ONTO SUITCASE TO SIMULATE ACTUAL INCIDENT.

"Dear American Tourister: You make a fabulous jack."

This unsolicited testimonial comes from The J. C. Quinly family of Walnut Creek, California.

Who jacked up their car to change a tire and left their American Tourister standing near.

All of a sudden, the car slid backward, fell off the jack, and landed square on their suitcase.

Where it remained until the Quinlys finished changing their tire.

Of course, the suitcase got dented. (Mr. Quinly had to fix it with a hammer.) And of course, you realize we don't build American Touristers to go through extraordinary things like supporting a car. We build American Touristers for the ordinary perils of ordinary travel.

So we build our case with 16 different strong materials.

We give it a tough stainless steel frame.

We reinforce American Touristers with fiberglass. Not just on the corners, but through and through.

Most important of all, we put in nonspring locks designed not to spring open on impact.

Remember, the beautiful thing about traveling with an American Tourister isn't that it holds up a car.

But simply that it holds up.

American Tourister

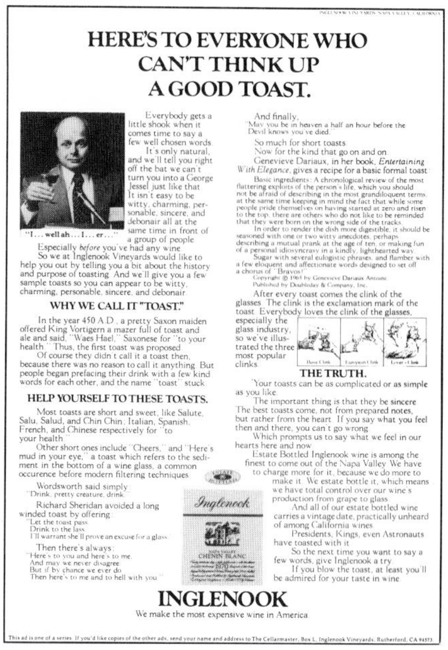
HERE'S TO EVERYONE WHO CAN'T THINK UP A GOOD TOAST.
"I... well ah... I... er..."
Everybody gets a little shook when it comes time to say a few well chosen words.
It's only natural, and we'll tell you right off the bat we can't turn you into a George Jessel just like that. It isn't easy to be witty, charming, personable, sincere, and debonair all at the same time in front of a group of people.
Especially before you've had any wine.
So we at Inglenook Vineyards would like to help you out by telling you a bit about the history and purpose of toasting. And we'll give you a few sample toasts so you can appear to be witty, charming, personable, sincere, and debonair.
WHY WE CALL IT "TOAST."
In the year 450 A.D., a pretty Saxon maiden offered King Vortigern a mazer full of toast and ale and said, "Waes Hael," Saxonese for "to your health." Thus, the first toast was proposed.
Of course they didn't call it a toast then, because there was no reason to call it anything. But people began prefacing their drink with a few kind words for each other, and the name "toast" stuck.
HELP YOURSELF TO THESE TOASTS.
Most toasts are short and sweet, like Salute, Salu, Salud, and Chin Chin: Italian, Spanish, French, and Chinese respectively for "to your health."
Other short ones include "Cheers," and "Here's mud in your eye," a toast which refers to the sediment in the bottom of a wine glass, a common occurence before modern filtering techniques.
Wordsworth said simply:
"Drink, pretty creature, drink."
Richard Sheridan avoided a long winded toast by offering:
"Let the toast pass.
Drink to the lass.
I'll warrant she'll prove an excuse for a glass."
Then there's always:
"Here's to you and here's to me.
And may we never disagree.
But if by chance we ever do
Then here's to me and to hell with you."
And finally,
"May you be in heaven a half an hour before the Devil knows you've died."
So much for short toasts.
Now for the kind that go on and on.
Genevieve Dariaux, in her book, Entertaining With Elegance, gives a recipe for a basic formal toast:
Basic ingredients: A chronological review of the most flattering exploits of the person's life, which you should not be afraid of describing in the most grandiloquent terms, at the same time keeping in mind the fact that while some people pride themselves on having started at zero and risen to the top, there are others who do not like to be reminded that they were born on the wrong side of the tracks.
In order to render the dish more digestible, it should be seasoned with one or two witty anecdotes, perhaps describing a mutual prank at the age of ten, or making fun of a personal idiosyncrasy in a kindly, lighthearted way.
Sugar with several eulogistic phrases, and flamber with a few eloquent and affectionate words designed to set off a chorus of "Bravos!"
Copyright © 1965 by Genevieve Dariaux Antoine
Published by Doubleday & Company, Inc.
After every toast comes the clink of the glasses. The clink is the exclamation mark of the toast. Everybody loves the clink of the glasses, especially the glass industry, so we've illustrated the three most popular clinks.
THE TRUTH.
Your toasts can be as complicated or as simple as you like.
The important thing is that they be sincere. The best toasts come, not from prepared notes, but rather from the heart. If you say what you feel then and there, you can't go wrong.
Which prompts us to say what we feel in our hearts here and now.
Estate Bottled Inglenook wine is among the finest to come out of the Napa Valley. We have to charge more for it, because we do more to make it. We estate bottle it, which means we have total control over our wine's production from grape to glass.
And all of our estate bottled wine carries a vintage date, practically unheard of among California wines.
Presidents, Kings, even Astronauts have toasted with it.
So the next time you want to say a few words, give Inglenook a try.
If you blow the toast, at least you'll be admired for your taste in wine.
Inglenook
CHENIN BLANC
INGLENOOK
We make the most expensive wine in America.
This ad is one of a series. If you'd like copies of the other ads, send your name and address to The Cellarmaster, Box L, Inglenook Vineyards, Rutherford, CA 94573.

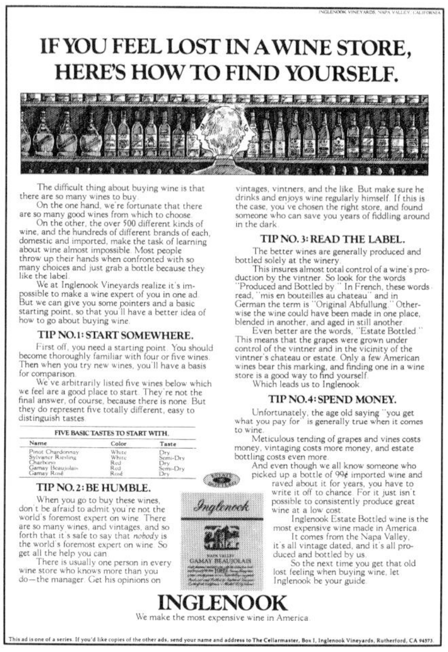
INGLENOOK VINEYARDS, NAPA VALLEY, CALIFORNIA
IF YOU FEEL LOST IN A WINE STORE, HERE'S HOW TO FIND YOURSELF.
The difficult thing about buying wine is that there are so many wines to buy.
On the one hand, we're fortunate that there are so many good wines from which to choose.
On the other, the over 500 different kinds of wine, and the hundreds of different brands of each, domestic and imported, make the task of learning about wine almost impossible. Most people throw up their hands when confronted with so many choices and just grab a bottle because they like the label.
We at Inglenook Vineyards realize it's impossible to make a wine expert of you in one ad. But we can give you some pointers and a basic starting point, so that you'll have a better idea of how to go about buying wine.
TIP NO.1: START SOMEWHERE.
First off, you need a starting point. You should become thoroughly familiar with four or five wines. Then when you try new wines, you'll have a basis for comparison.
We've arbitrarily listed five wines below which we feel are a good place to start. They're not the final answer, of course, because there is none. But they do represent five totally different, easy to distinguish tastes.
FIVE BASIC TASTES TO START WITH.
Name / Color / Taste
Pinot Chardonnay / White / Dry
Sylvaner Riesling / White / Semi-Dry
Charbono / Red / Dry
Gamay Beaujolais / Red / Semi-Dry
Gamay Rosé / Rosé / Dry
TIP NO.2: BE HUMBLE.
When you go to buy these wines, don't be afraid to admit you're not the world's foremost expert on wine. There are so many wines, and vintages, and so forth that it's safe to say that nobody is the world's foremost expert on wine. So get all the help you can.
There is usually one person in every wine store who knows more than you do—the manager. Get his opinions on vintages, vintners, and the like. But make sure he drinks and enjoys wine regularly himself. If this is the case, you've chosen the right store, and found someone who can save you years of fiddling around in the dark.
TIP NO.3: READ THE LABEL.
The better wines are generally produced and bottled solely at the winery.
This insures almost total control of a wine's production by the vintner. So look for the words "Produced and Bottled by." In French, these words read, "mis en bouteilles au chateau" and in German the term is "Original Abfullung." Otherwise the wine could have been made in one place, blended in another, and aged in still another.
Even better are the words, "Estate Bottled." This means that the grapes were grown under control of the vintner and in the vicinity of the vintner's chateau or estate. Only a few American wines bear this marking, and finding one in a wine store is a good way to find yourself.
Which leads us to Inglenook.
TIP NO.4: SPEND MONEY.
Unfortunately, the age old saying "you get what you pay for" is generally true when it comes to wine.
Meticulous tending of grapes and vines costs money, vintaging costs more money, and estate bottling costs even more.
And even though we all know someone who picked up a bottle of 99¢ imported wine and raved about it for years, you have to write it off to chance. For it just isn't possible to consistently produce great wine at a low cost.
Inglenook Estate Bottled wine is the most expensive wine made in America.
It comes from the Napa Valley, it's all vintage dated, and it's all produced and bottled by us.
So the next time you get that old lost feeling when buying wine, let Inglenook be your guide.
Inglenook
GAMAY BEAUJOLAIS
INGLENOOK
We make the most expensive wine in America.
This ad is one of a series. If you'd like copies of the other ads, send your name and address to The Cellarmaster, Box I, Inglenook Vineyards, Rutherford, CA 94573.

IN ORDER TO TALK ABOUT WINE, YOU HAVE TO LEARN THE LANGUAGE.
Wine has its own language, not in order to be uppity or anything like that.
Rather, wine words are used in an effort to describe taste sensations—an impossible task from the start since taste can't really be put into words, and everyone has a different sense of it.
Be that as it may, here is a glossary of wine terms brought to you by Inglenook, the most expensive wine made in America.
We've divided our vocabulary into two sections in order to cover those words which describe taste sensations observed in the mouth and those observed in the nose.
WORDS OF MOUTH.
ACIDITY: The essential natural sourness which gives bite on the tongue. It is an important keeping quality and contributes to bouquet.
BALANCED: The best combination of physical components—fruit, alcohol, tannin, acid, and the less tangible grace elements of "breed," "character," and "finesse."
BIG: A wine strong of flavor and high in alcohol and acidity.
BODY: The feeling of weight in the mouth, a tactile sense of substance that depends on the solids in solution and which distinguishes heavy from light wines.
CHARACTER: Complexity in a wine that shows unmistakable and distinctive features, possibly defying precise description.
DELICATE: A light and agreeable balance of flavor and quality.
DEPTH: Subtle richness giving a feeling of many flavor-layers.
DRY: Complete absence of sweetness.
EARTHY: A mineral or organic taste of the soil or terrain.
FINE: Superior overall quality and complexity.
FINISH: The "aftertaste," or the firm and distinctive flavor remaining after swallowing a well-balanced wine.
FOXY: Describing the distinctive spicy tang of native American grapes.
FULL-BODIED: Thick in the tactile sense.
LIGHT: Slender of body.
LUSCIOUS: All the balance qualities of softness, sweetness, fruitiness and ripeness.
MELLOW: Soft, ripe and well-matured.
NOBLE: Wine of consistent and continuing great quality and elegance.
NUTTY: A crisp, almost salty taste used to describe some heavy, dry white wines and Sherry.
RICH: A full, but not necessarily sweet, combination of fruit, flavor and body.
RIPE: Wine in its full bloom of maturity and mellowness.
ROBUST: Tough, full-bodied wine with much tannin that makes it appear immature, though it may develop in time.
VELVETY: An expression of soft, silky smoothness, implying complexity and quality.
VIGOROUS: A lively, healthy, winey sense of taste descriptive of developing young wines.
Foxy wine.
WORDS OF NOSE.
ACIDITY: Present and natural in all grapes and wines. Proper acidity in a young wine gives it liveliness and a pleasant mouthwatering quality.
AROMA: The perfume of the grape, in contrast to "bouquet" which is the smell of the wine itself.
BOUQUET: The smell of wine, being characteristic odors developed by oxidation of fruit acids and alcohol.
CLEAN: The absence of foreign or unpleasant smells.
DEEP: A bouquet of full, rich and lasting quality.
FLINTY: The smell of struck flint, typical of certain austere dry wines from high mineral soil.
FRAGRANT: Attractively and naturally scented.
FRUITY: A pleasantly ripe but not necessarily grapy smell.
GRAPY: A rich, sweet aroma produced by certain grape varieties.
NOSE: The combined bouquet and aroma of a wine.
PERFUME: A quality of bouquet developed in the maturing process, as opposed to aroma.
SPICY: Rich and herb-like.
STALKY: A descriptive smell of damp twigs.
WOODY: A particular smell derived from aging in oak casks.
Bouquet.
The nose of wine.
WINE LANGUAGE, SELF TAUGHT.
Of course, the best way to learn the language of wine is not from a book or a list of words like this, but rather from the wine you drink.
And if you buy the best wine you can afford, expressions like "such body," "such balance," and "such bouquet" will spring to mind.
Such is the case with Inglenook.
When tasted against the finest French wines at the National Auction of Rare European and American wines, Inglenook Estate Bottled wine evoked an outpouring of superlatives which included most of the above and some no one had ever heard of.
Try Inglenook yourself.
It's guaranteed to improve your vocabulary with only one glass.
Inglenook
WHITE PINOT
INGLENOOK
We make the most expensive wine in America.
This ad is one of a series. If you'd like copies of the other ads, send your name and address to The Cellarmaster, Box L, Inglenook Vineyards, Rutherford, CA 94573.

78
Art Director: Thomas O. Tieche
Copywriter: Patrick Kelly
Designer: Gloria Baker
Artist: Chås. B. Slackman
Photographer: Ron Quilici
Agency: McCann-Erickson, Inc.
Client: United Vintners, Inc.

Are you overlooking an enormous market?

For approximately four million American men, your large assortment of underwear probably isn't large enough: men 6'2" and taller and men 220 pounds and heavier.

To cover this market, Jockey makes two special lines of underwear, Big Man And Tall Man, in a variety of styles: T-shirt, V-neck T-shirt and athletic shirt; Brief, boxer and Midway:

Each line has a greater profit margin than regular sizes.

So you can make big money by putting big men into our underwear.

Jockey Tall Man and Big Man Underwear

Jockey International Inc., Kenosha, Wisconsin 53140 U.S.A.

108
Art Director: Lou Colletti
Copywriter: Larry Spector
Designer: Lou Colletti
Photographer: Tony Petrucelli
Agency: Levine, Huntley, Schmidt
Client: Jockey International, Inc.

131
Art Director: Sam Scali
Copywriter: Ed McCabe
Designer: Sam Scali
Photographers: Alan Dolgins
　　　　　　　Phil Mazzurco
Agency: Scali, McCabe, Sloves, Inc.
Client: Perdue Farms Inc.

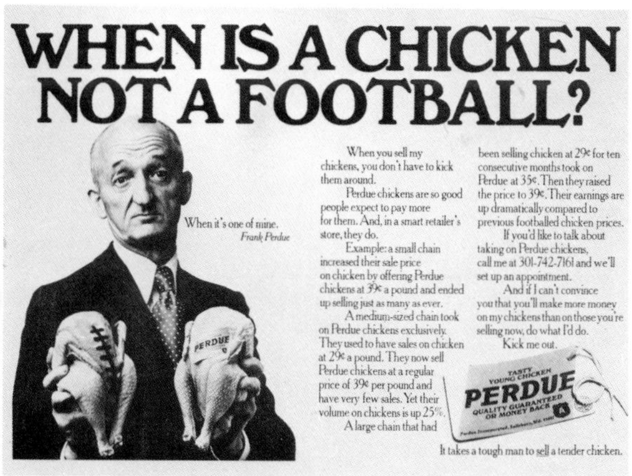

157
Art Director: Joe Cappadona
Copywriter: Ed Butler
Designer: Joe Cappadona
Photographer: Menken/Seltzer
Agency: Doyle Dane Bernbach Inc.
Client: Volkswagen of America

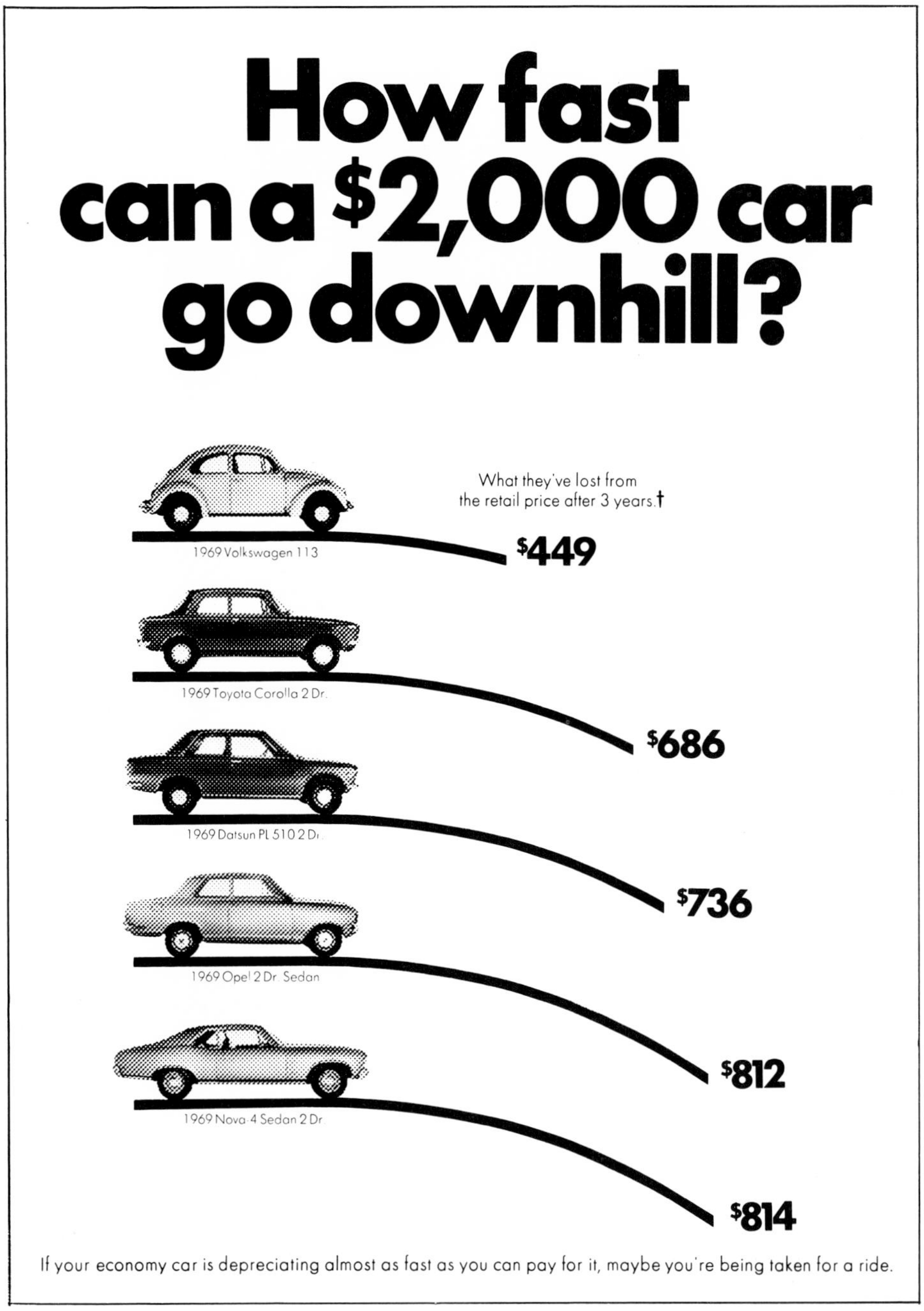

How fast can a $2,000 car go downhill?
What they've lost from the retail price after 3 years.†
1969 Volkswagen 113
$449
1969 Toyota Corolla 2 Dr.
$686
1969 Datsun PL 510 2 D
$736
1969 Opel 2 Dr. Sedan
$812
1969 Nova 4 Sedan 2 Dr.
$814
If your economy car is depreciating almost as fast as you can pay for it, maybe you're being taken for a ride.

IS YOUR CAR PASSING INSPECTION BUT FLUNKING LIFE?
The true test of a car's condition is not that it passes state inspection but rather how many annual inspections it's around to take. In Sweden, where the yearly government inspection covers about 200 points, Volvos have a life expectancy of 14 years.
So if you think your car is just scraping by, get a Volvo from us. It's built to be more than just passable.
DEALER NAME
©VOLVO, INC., 1972

WHERE VOLVOS COME FROM, A CAR MUST EAT UP THE ROAD. NOT VICE VERSA.
Swedish winters are car killers. With slush and raw salt on the road half the year, a car can be eaten away in short order. Unless it's protected as well as a Volvo. Every Volvo in our showroom has *two* undercoats protecting its underside. Vulnerable body parts are made of anti-corrosive galvanized steel. And instead of shiny chrome trim, which rusts, Volvo has shiny, stainless steel and aluminum, which don't.
So come buy a Volvo from us. Even if the winters aren't kind to it, the years should be.
DEALER NAME

171
Art Directors: Joe Schindelman
Bill Berenter
Copywriters: Ray Myers
Tom Nathan
Designer: Joe Schindelman
Photographers: Joel Meyerowitz
Malcolm Kirk
Agency: Scali, McCabe, Sloves, Inc.
Client: Volvo, Inc.

When was the last time you had your period?
If you're two weeks overdue, don't wait. Consult your doctor. And if you *are* pregnant and you want an abortion, consult us.
We can help you get a legal, safe, inexpensive abortion. By an M.D. in a clinic or hospital.
If you have the abortion during the first 10 weeks of pregnancy, it will cost only about $150. And no matter when you have it, there's no charge for our service.
Even if you got your period yesterday, we're a good number to remember: (212) 489-7794 Monday through Friday, between 10 a.m. and 5 p.m. New York time.
Free Abortion Referral Service from ZPG-New York

173
Art Director: Don Slater
Copywriter: Jim Parry
Agency: Parry Associates
Client: Zero Population Growth

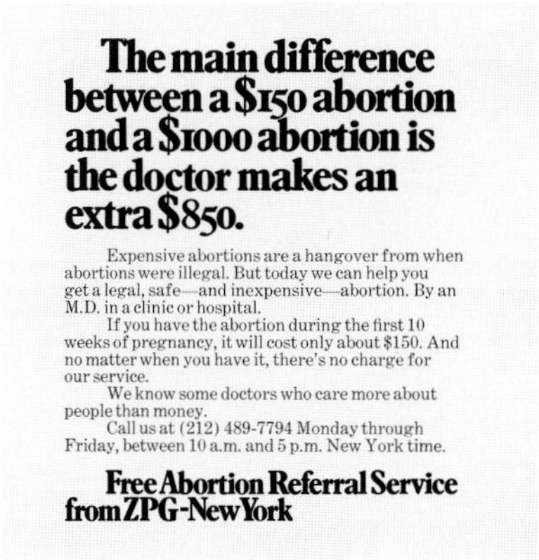
The main difference between a $150 abortion and a $1000 abortion is the doctor makes an extra $850.
Expensive abortions are a hangover from when abortions were illegal. But today we can help you get a legal, safe—and inexpensive—abortion. By an M.D. in a clinic or hospital.
If you have the abortion during the first 10 weeks of pregnancy, it will cost only about $150. And no matter when you have it, there's no charge for our service.
We know some doctors who care more about people than money.
Call us at (212) 489-7794 Monday through Friday, between 10 a.m. and 5 p.m. New York time.
Free Abortion Referral Service from ZPG-New York

The alternative to a wire coat hanger is (212) 489-7794.
There is such a thing as a legal, safe, inexpensive abortion. By an M.D. in a clinic or hospital. And we can help you get it.
If you have the abortion during the first 10 weeks of pregnancy, it will cost only about $150. And no matter when you have it, there's no charge for our service.
In the long run, a do-it-yourself abortion can be a lot costlier.
Call us at (212) 489-7794 Monday through Friday, between 10 a.m. and 5 p.m. New York time.
Free Abortion Referral Service from ZPG-New York

Shake and bake.

American Airlines to Hawaii

176
Art Director: Stan Jones
Copywriter: David Butler
Photographer: Carl Furuta
Agency: Doyle Dane Bernbach Inc.
Client: American Airlines

194
Art Director: Joe Gregorace
Copywriter: Peter Nord
Designer: Joe Gregorace
Photographer: David Spindell
Agency: Solow-Wexton, Inc.
Client: ILGWU

Made in Japan.

Every year, Americans salute more and more American flags that weren't made in America. Flags that bear the stars and stripes and little tags reading Made in Japan or Taiwan or Hong Kong.

Those flags aren't the only things with such labels. As low-wage, foreign goods flood the market, American industries shut down. As industries shut down, people lose jobs.

When people lose their jobs, they can't buy the things you make. Chances are if Betsy Ross (the Philadelphia seamstress who made the first American flag for George Washington) were alive today, she'd be standing in line for her unemployment check.

So help yourself and help us by looking for the union label in everything you buy. You can find our label in women's and children's garments.

This label stands for the creativity of American design, the skill of American workmanship, the importance of American jobs.

Ladies Garment Workers Union ILGWU Union Made AFL-CIO
Made in U.S.A.

490

Union Label Department, International Ladies' Garment Workers' Union, 22 W. 38th Street, New York, N.Y. 10018

POSITION AVAILABLE

Requires the patience of Job, the wisdom of Solomon, the strength of Hercules, the compassion of Florence Nightingale, the understanding of Martin Luther King, and pays $145. a month. That's about all there is to being a foster parent. For particulars, call or write The Children's Aid Society, 150 E. 45 St. (682-9040 Ext. 329)

231
Art Director: Rene Vidmer
Copywriter: Lew Petterson
Designer: Rene Vidmer
Agency, Hecht, Vidmer, Inc.
Client: Children's Aid Society

230
Art Director: Bob Kwait
Copywriter: Aaron Buchman
Designer: Bob Kwait
Photographer: Anonymous
Agency: Aaron Buchman
Client: United Jewish Appeal

מדינת היהודים
JEWISH STATE
HAGANA SHIP—JEWISH STATE
NOBODY BOUGHT A ROUND TRIP TICKET.
All they left behind was fear and grief and despair. Nothing worth even a backward glance.
They'd rather be refugees. And reach for a very old dream.
Israel.
There's only one catch. Israel doesn't have enough money to provide for them.
She has to keep spending more than she can bear until she finally wins her fight to be left alone.
Until then, there won't be enough money for a thousand things a thousand immigrants a week dearly need.
Unless you help the United Jewish Appeal come up with it.
You must.
Because for two and a half million Jews and more coming, there's no alternative to Israel.
Keep the promise.
The United Jewish Appeal.

SOME PEOPLE COME TO ISRAEL TO DIE.
Keep the promise.

SO FAR, THEY'VE ONLY BEEN SCARED TO DEATH.
Keep the promise.

McGraphic.

NIXON REVEALED!

250
Art Directors: Seymour Chwast
Herb Lubalin
Editor: Bill Maloney
Designers: Herb Lubalin
Seymour Chwast
Artist: Ellen Shapiro
Agency: Lubalin, Smith, Carnase, Inc.
Push Pin Studio
Client: Citizens Committee for
McGovern/Shriver

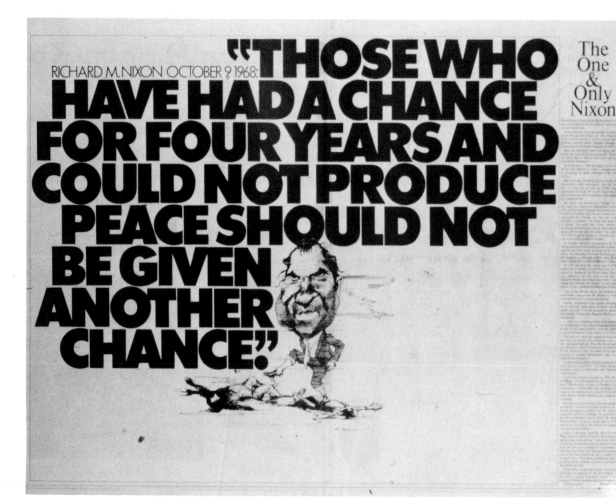

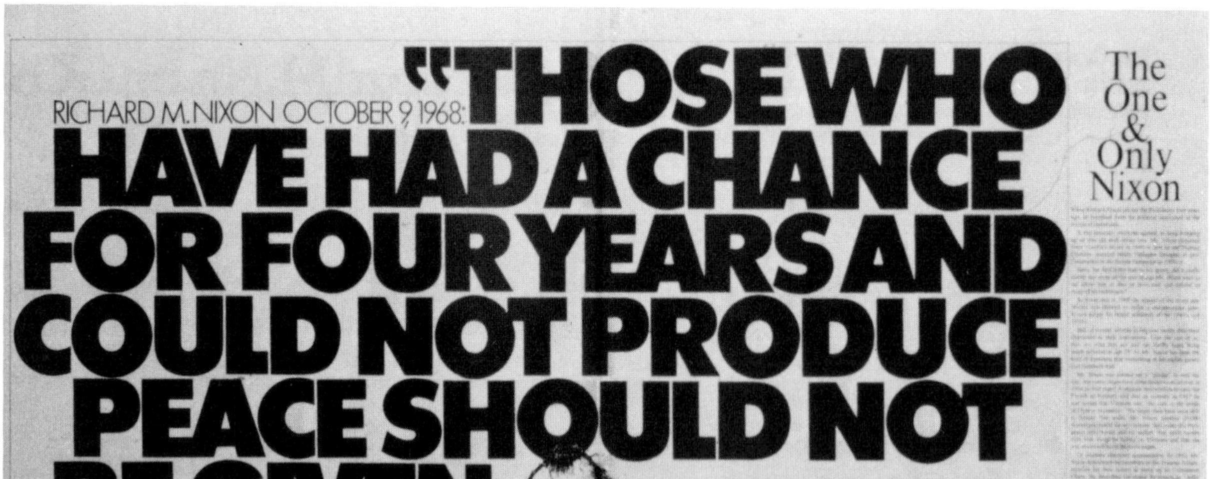

RICHARD M. NIXON OCTOBER 9, 1968: "THOSE WHO HAVE HAD A CHANCE FOR FOUR YEARS AND COULD NOT PRODUCE PEACE SHOULD NOT BE GIVEN ANOTHER CHANCE."

The One & Only Nixon

256
Copywriter: Ed McCabe
Producer: Ed McCabe
Production Company: The Mix Place
Agency: Scali, McCabe, Sloves, Inc.
Client: Perdue Farms, Inc.

Giblets
60-second

ANNCR.: Ladies and gentlemen, the President of Perdue Farms, Mr. Frank Perdue. . .

FRANK PERDUE: Some women have told me that when they get a chicken home, they find they've been gypped on the giblets. They bought a chicken without an interior. I wouldn't stand for that. I think when you pay for a chicken, you should get a whole chicken. Not an empty shell. I pack my tender, young Perdue chickens with all the things a chicken should be packed with. Liver, gizzard, heart, neck, and recipe. The recipe is there so that you'll know what to do with the giblets once you've got them. Instead of wasting them all on your cat.

If you're willing to settle for less in a chicken, that's your business. But I can't see it. Next thing you know someone will be trying to make the wings optional.

ANNCR.: When it comes to chicken, Frank Perdue is even tougher than you are. He *has* to be. Because every one of his chickens comes with a money-back quality guarantee.

It takes a tough man to make a tender chicken.

Perdue.

271
Composers: William Backer
Billy Davis
Roger Cook
Roger Greenaway
Billy Ed Wheeler
Producer: Billy Davis
Production Company: A.I.R. London
Sherman, Kahan
Agency: McCann-Erickson, Inc.
Client: Coca-Cola, U.S.A.

Getting This World Together
60-second

(WORDS AND MUSIC)

SONG: Together—together—together
—together . . .

Getting this world together
Getting this world together
Putting our dreams together
Putting our dreams together
Pull up a friendly chair
Show someone that you care . . .

(Hey) talk about what you feel now
Talk about what you feel now
Talk about what is real now
Talk about what is real now
Let's have some Coca-Cola
And talk it over now . . .

Getting this world together . . . (getting this world together)
Putting our dreams together . . . (sharing our dreams)
More people talk it over
Having a Coca-Cola
For sitting and talking it over
It's the real thing . . . (Coca-Cola) . . .

Let's have some Coke together
It's the real thing . . . (Coke is) . . . (Coca-Cola)
Coca-Cola . . . (getting this world together)
It's the real thing
Coca-Cola
Let's have some Coke together
It's the real thing
Coke is . . .

Life Is
60-second

Have a Good Day
60-second

291
Art Director: Roy Grace
Copywriter: Marcia Bell Grace
Designer: Roy Grace
TV Directors: Roy Grace
Bob Gaffney
TV Producer: Susan Calhoun
Production Company: Associates & Lofaro
Agency: Doyle Dane Bernbach Inc.
Client: American Luggage Works

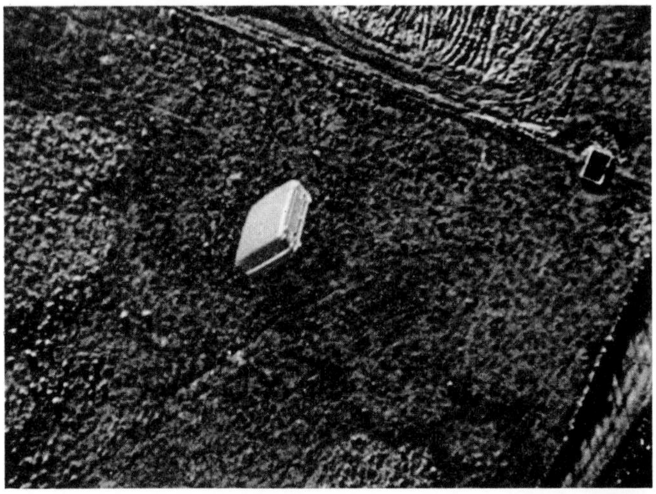

Flying
30-second

OPEN ON SUITCASE FALLING OUT OF UNSEEN HELICOPTER

SUPER: SLOW MOTION PHOTOGRAPHY

(SFX THROUGHOUT: WIND WHIRLING)

SLOW MOTION SHOTS (FROM GROUND) OF SUITCASE TUMBLING THROUGH THE SKY

MAN: What would you call a suitcase . . .

SUITCASE STILL FALLING

that could fall five hundred and fifty feet . . .

and survive twenty-two out of twenty-six times?

SUITCASE LANDS ON THE GRASS
(SFX: CRASH AS LANDS)
SUITCASE BOUNCES, THEN SETTLES

WOMAN: Fantastic!

MAN: No. American Tourister.

SUPER: AMERICAN TOURISTER FROM $20

311
Art Director: Sam Scali
Copywriter: Ed McCabe
TV Director: Franta Herman
TV Producers: Sam Scali
Ed McCabe
Production Company: Televideo Productions
Agency: Scali, McCabe, Sloves, Inc.
Client: Perdue Farms, Inc.

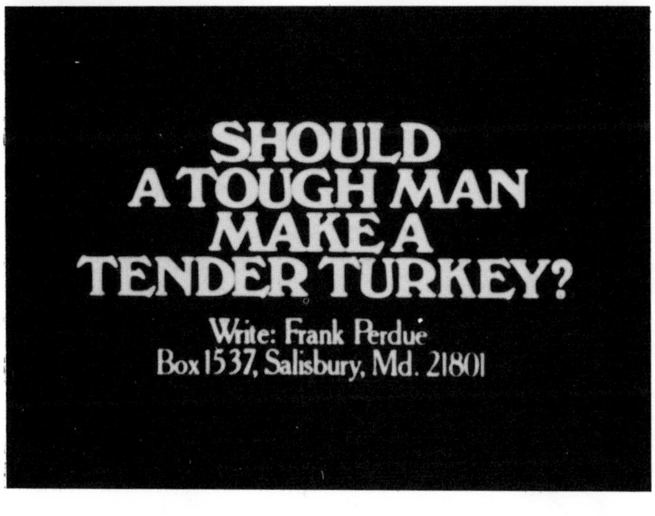

Turkey
30-second

FRANK PERDUE ALONE IN HIS DEN READING A BOOK ON "CARE AND FEEDING OF TURKEYS"

(SILENT)

PERDUE (FACE FRONT): Recently, a lady told me she had a great Perdue turkey. That's odd. I never raised a turkey.

I'm strictly a chicken man . . . But it's not a bad idea.

PERDUE SERIOUS (FORWARD)

A turkey as good as a Perdue chicken. It would require a lot of work. And I'm not going to waste my time if you're happy with the turkeys you're getting now.

Let me know what you think.

(PERDUE GOES BACK TO READING "THE CARE AND FEEDING OF TURKEYS")

SUPER: SHOULD A TOUGH MAN MAKE A TENDER TURKEY? Write: Frank Perdue

Parts Inspection
30-second

Parts
30-second

324
Art Director: Jeff Cohen
Copywriter: Lester Colodny
TV Producers: Syd Rangell
Allen Kay
Lois Korey
Production Company: Richards & Myers Films
Agency: Needham, Harper & Steers
Client: Xerox Corporation

Football
90-second

THE DAY OF THE "BIG GAME"
LESS THAN TWO MINUTES TO GO:

COACH (EXCITEDLY): Allright now. Pressure's on. Two minutes to go. No. No. No. Kramer, you idiot. Whatever happened to the game play we talked about? Come on. Come on. Never mind the tarp. Make that block stick. No. No. No.

COACH LOOKS FOR A SUB.

Colodny . . . Colodny . . . Colodny. Quick, Colodny, this is critical. All right. This is R 78, power reverse. I've got to get this into the ballgame as soon as I can.

SKETCHES A PLAY

This is . . . Colodny, pay attention. This is as important as anything you're going to do for this club. Way to go, Colodny. . . .

COLODNY DASHES UP TO XEROX IN LOCKER ROOM,

ANNCR. (VO): Xerox is . . . applying its technology to all phases of communication, whether it be . . . in business, government, education. . . .
. . . medicine, . . . or even landing men on the moon . . .
. . . at Xerox, we're working to find new ways of getting information . . .
. . . to people who need it.

COACH: Here it is. Everyone gets one. Okay, here we go.

ANNCR. (VO): And most important . . . When they need it.

QUARTERBACK FLIPS TOWEL ON CENTER'S BACKSIDE, TUCKS XEROX IN PLAYERS PEER AT PLAYS ON GROUND, IN HAND, OFF TO THE SIDE, ETC.

QUARTERBACK: . . . 385, . . . 384 . . .

BALL SNAPS BACK TO QUARTERBACK . . . WHO HANDS IT TO BACK CARRYING HIS COPY, HANDS BALL TO END

PAST GOAL LINE, END READS PLAY. MEANWHILE, OPPONENTS TACKLE WRONG PLAYERS. LONG PASS THROWN TO END, LOOKS UP FROM PLAY JUST IN TIME TO CATCH GAME WINNING PASS

SUPER: XEROX

333
Art Director: John Danza
Copywriter: Ed McCabe
TV Director: Bo Widerberg
TV Producers: John Danza
Ed McCabe
Production Company: James Garrett & Partners
Agency: Scali, McCabe, Sloves, Inc.
Client: Volvo, Inc.

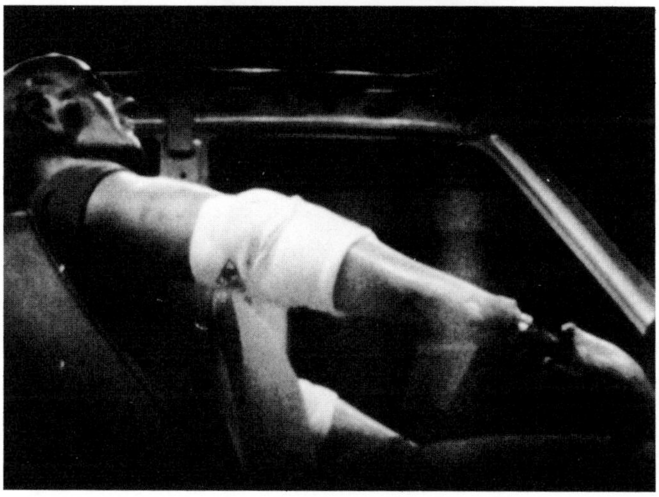

Engineering
60-second

SCENE TAKES PLACE IN A VOLVO FACTORY IN SWEDEN.

OPEN ON CU OF PRECISION WORK BEING DONE BEFORE BLUEPRINT AND DIALS

MAN (VO): In Sweden precision is a national preoccupation.

CAMERA MOVES TO CORRIDOR WHERE ENGINEERS ARE ALL AT WORK

Ours is a nation of engineers. Engineering is the largest industry, employing nearly 40 percent of the total labor force.

CAMERA ROAMS FACTORY WITH VIEWS OF ENGINEERS AT THEIR WORK

MOVE TO CAR ON LIFT

(SFX: UNDER)

Thirty-five engineers to every styling. Which shows where we put the emphasis.

We have to. Since Volvo is the largest selling car in Sweden a lot of our customers are engineers too.

CU MAN WORKING ON CAR

LONG VIEW OF CAR ON RACK

MAN AT CONTROL PANEL

VIEW OF VOLVO

VIEW INSIDE OF MECHANICAL MAN GIVING CAR A WORKOUT

(SFX)

Volvo. We build them the way we build them because we have to.

SUPER: VOLVO over tracks.

Sauna
60-second

Swedish Winter
60-second

344/360
Art Directors: Bob McDonald
Manny Perez
Copywriter: Helen Nolan
Cameraman: Steve Horn
TV Director: Steve Horn
TV Producer: Manny Perez
Production Company: Horn/Griner Productions
Agency: Young & Rubicam International, Inc.
Client: New York City Drug Addiction Agency

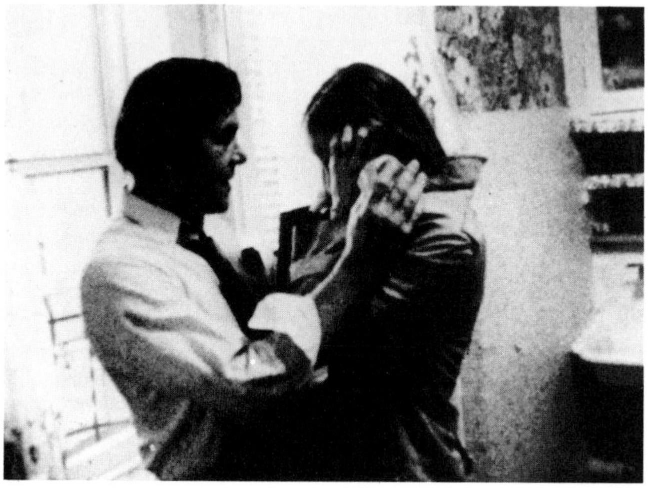

Karen
60-second

FATHER: Karen, are you going to have something to eat?

KAREN (AGITATED): I can't. I'm going out. Daddy, I need $20.00.

FATHER: What for? Hey, hey, what's the matter?

KAREN: Daddy, I'm sick . . . I did it again.

FATHER: You mean, you're back on drugs? Are you back on drugs, Karen?

KAREN: Yes, yes, yes, yes.

FATHER: But you promised. . . .

KAREN: I'm sorry. I'm sorry, it's the last time, Daddy. I promise, it's the last time. I'll go to the hospital, I'll get help, it's the last time, Daddy. Daddy, you've got to give me $20.00.

FATHER: No.

KAREN: I need the money, I need it now, Daddy, please, help me, help me .

FATHER: All right, baby. All right. Here, here, that's all I've got.

ANNCR. (VO): The only thing worse than what drug addicts do to the people they love, is what they do to themselves.

The Animal
60-second

JOEY: Hey man, what's happenin'? I'm sick. I need a bag.

PUSHER: Ten dollars, Joey.

JOEY: I only got five.

PUSHER: Ten dollars.

JOEY: Hey come on, you know I'm good for it.

PUSHER: Joey, the stuff is dynamite. Ten dollars or nothing.

JOEY: Please, please man . . .

PUSHER: Joey, get the money.

ANNCR. (VO): This is a drug addict. Unlike a man, he has no sense of right and wrong. No use for reason. He only feels. And what he feels most of the time is fear. He runs away from reality, because reality is what scares him most of all. He lives off human beings . . . because he's afraid to live like a human being. He's alive . . . but you couldn't call this really living.

Peer Group
60-second

Karen
60-second

HERO
WORSHIP
An international gallery of supersandwiches to serve the whole family during the hot days to come—and just the thing for the summer-bachelor days of your very own hero

393
Art Director: Alvin Grossman
Writer: Alvin Grossman
Designer: Alvin Grossman
Artist: William Steig
Photographer: Irwin Horowitz
Publisher: McCall Publishing Company
McCall's Magazine

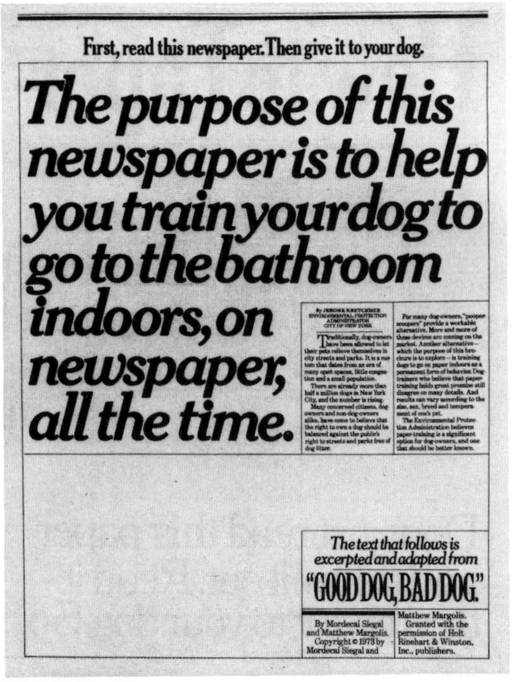
First, read this newspaper. Then give it to your dog.
The purpose of this newspaper is to help you train your dog to go to the bathroom indoors, on newspaper, all the time.
The text that follows is excerpted and adapted from
"GOOD DOG, BAD DOG."
By Mordecai Siegal and Matthew Margolis. Copyright © 1973 by Mordecai Siegal and Matthew Margolis. Granted with the permission of Holt, Rinehart & Winston, Inc., publishers.

374
Art Director: Lawrence Miller
Writers: Modecai Siegal
Matthew Margolis
Lawrence Miller
Designers: Lawrence Miller
Vance Jonson
Artist: Reynold Ruffins
Publisher: N.Y.C. Environmental Protection Administration
Agency: Marketing Design Alliance
Client: N.Y.C. Environmental Protection Administration

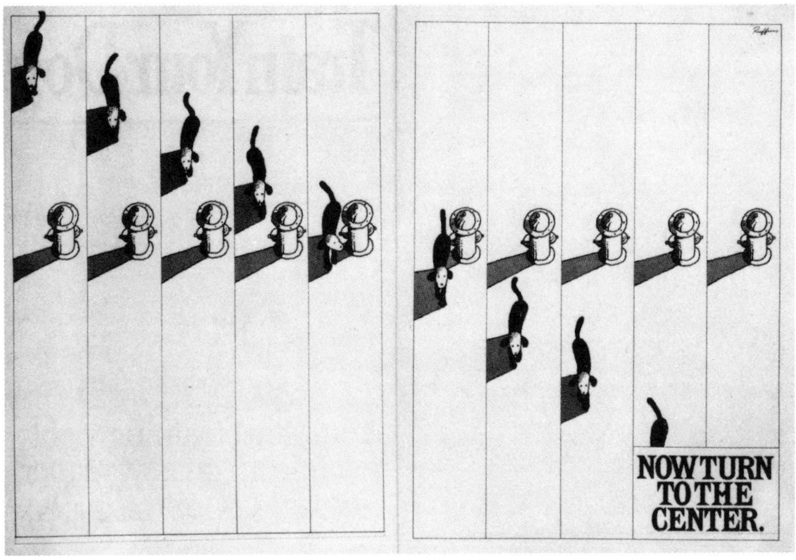
NOW TURN TO THE CENTER.

AFTER FIVE DAYS, NARROW DOWN THE SPACE THE PAPERS COVER.
THE KEY TO ENJOYING SUCCESS WITH THIS TECHNIQUE IS CONSISTENCY.
Once your dog has been paper-trained, he/she is always- and only-to use the newspapers.
THE DOG SHOULD NOT BE GIVEN FOOD OR WATER-EXCEPT AT THE SAME SCHEDULED TIMES EACH DAY.
Once the dog has accomplished his/her task, it is to be praised, then removed from papers.
Remember: Your dog is to be fed, watered, and papered. In that order.
FOUR STEP PROCEDURE AND TECHNIQUE.
Step One: Proper diet & scheduling.
Step Two: Confining your dog.
Step Three: Using an odor-neutralizer.
Step Four: Proper correction.
SCHEDULE FOR WORKING PEOPLE

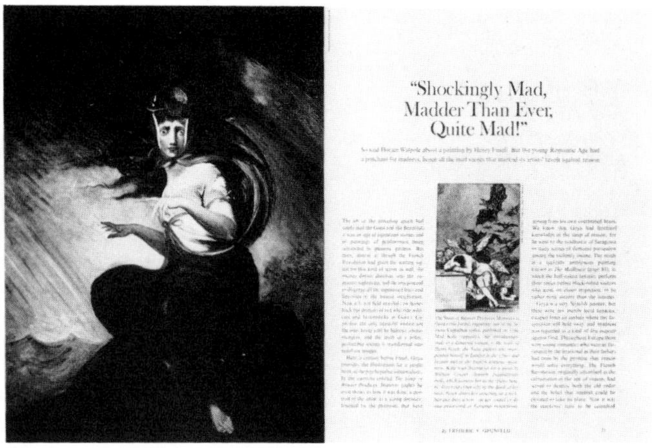
"Shockingly Mad,
Madder Than Ever,
Quite Mad!"

419
Art Director: Kenneth Munowitz
Editor: Charles L. Mee, Jr.
Designer: Kenneth Munowitz
Publisher: American Heritage Publishing
Horizon

424
Art Director: Joseph R. Morgan
Editor: Leonard Reed
Designers: Judith Mays
David Moore
Joseph Morgan
Robert Banks
Thurman French
Picture Editor: Lee Battaglia
Publisher: U.S. Information Agency
America Illustrated

447
Art Directors: Milton Charles
Alan Peckolick
Designer: Alan Peckolick
Photographer: Frank Moscati
Publisher: World Publishing
Agency: Alan Peckolick Graphic Design

452
Art Director: Acy Lehman
Designer: Acy Lehman
Photographer: Nick Sangiamo
Client: RCA Records

476
Art Director: Lawrence Miller
Writers: Mordecai Siegal
Matthew Margolis
Lawrence Miller
Designers: Lawrence Miller
Vance Jonson
Artist: Reynold Ruffins
Publisher: N.Y.C. Environmental
Protection Administration
Agency: Marketing Design Alliance
Client: N.Y.C. Environmental
Protection Administration

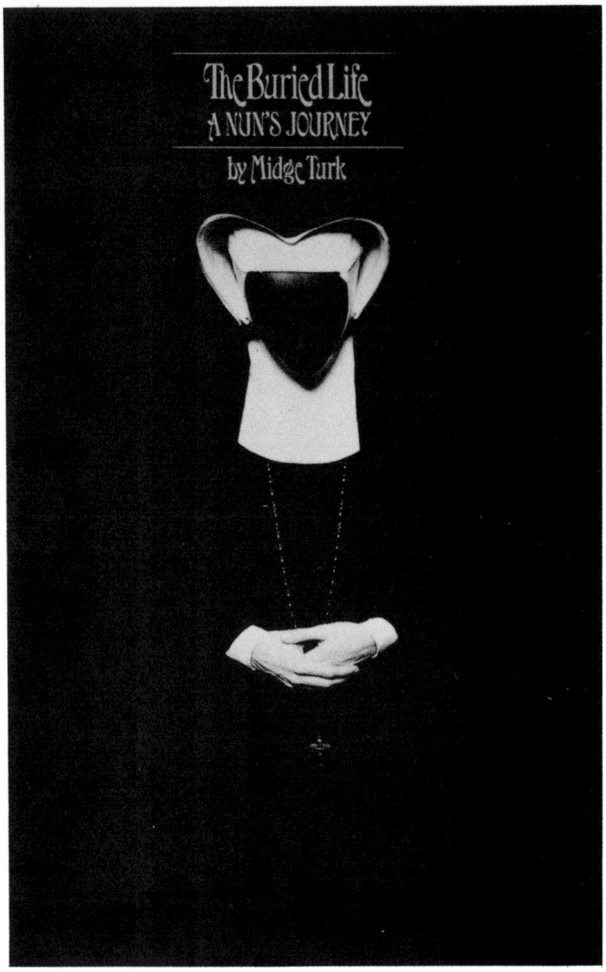
The Buried Life
A NUN'S JOURNEY
by Midge Turk

birth day
the new birth
RCA

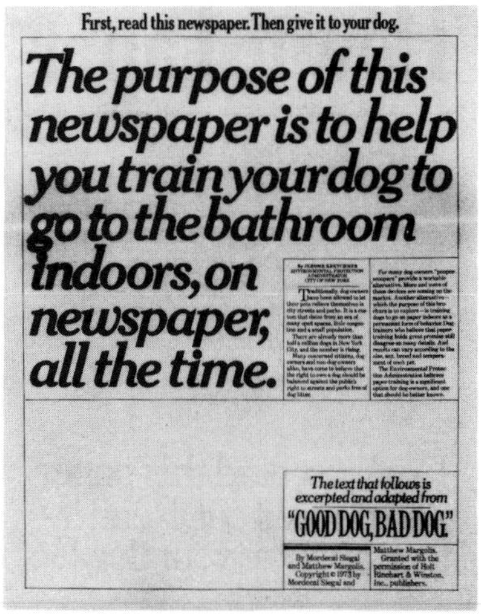
First, read this newspaper. Then give it to your dog.
The purpose of this newspaper is to help you train your dog to go to the bathroom indoors, on newspaper, all the time.
The text that follows is excerpted and adapted from
"GOOD DOG, BAD DOG"

514
Art Director: Meg Crane
Designers: Ira Sturtevant
Meg Crane
Photographer: Ivor Parry
Copywriter: Ira Sturtevant
Agency: Ponzi & Weill
Client: The Flavorbank Company, Inc.

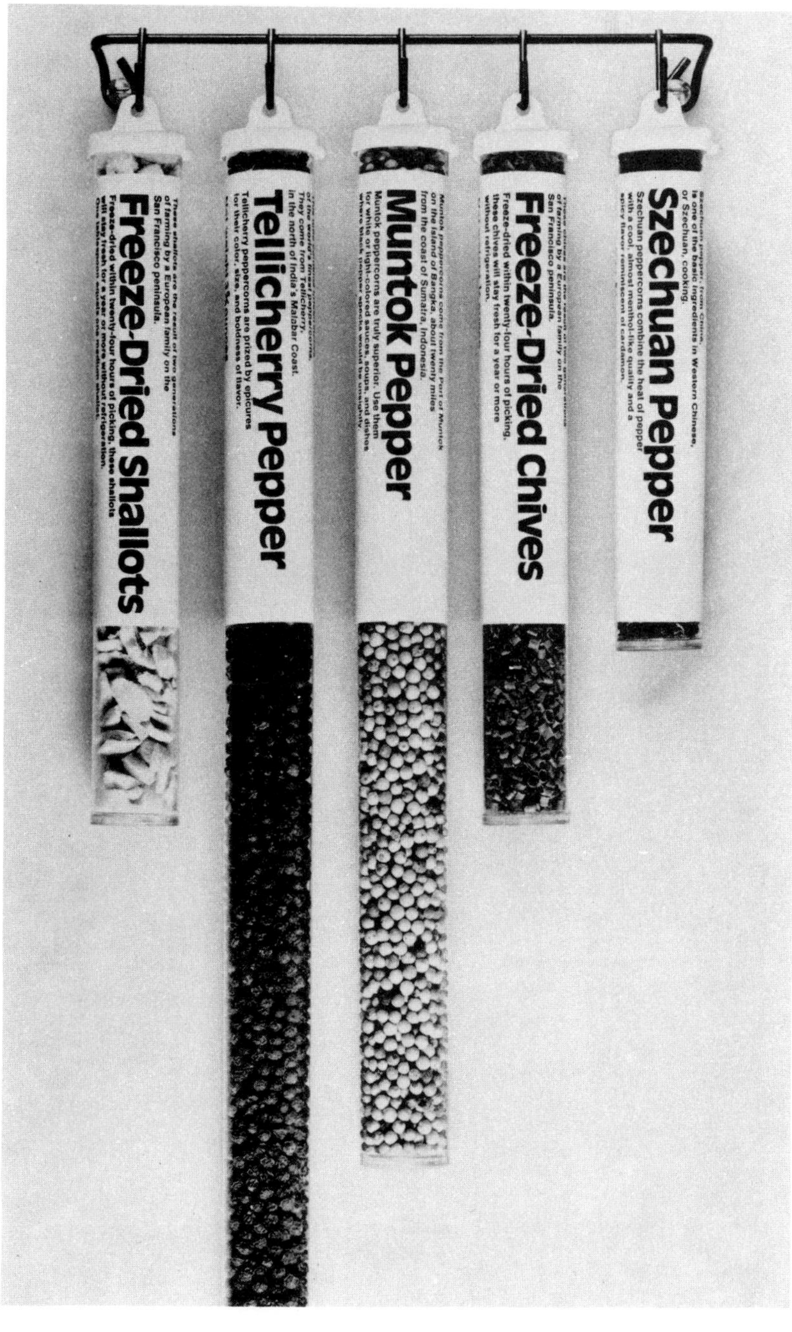

541
Art Director: Bill Berenter
Copywriter: Tom Nathan
Designer: Bill Berenter
Agency: Scali, McCabe, Sloves, Inc.
Client: Volvo, Inc.

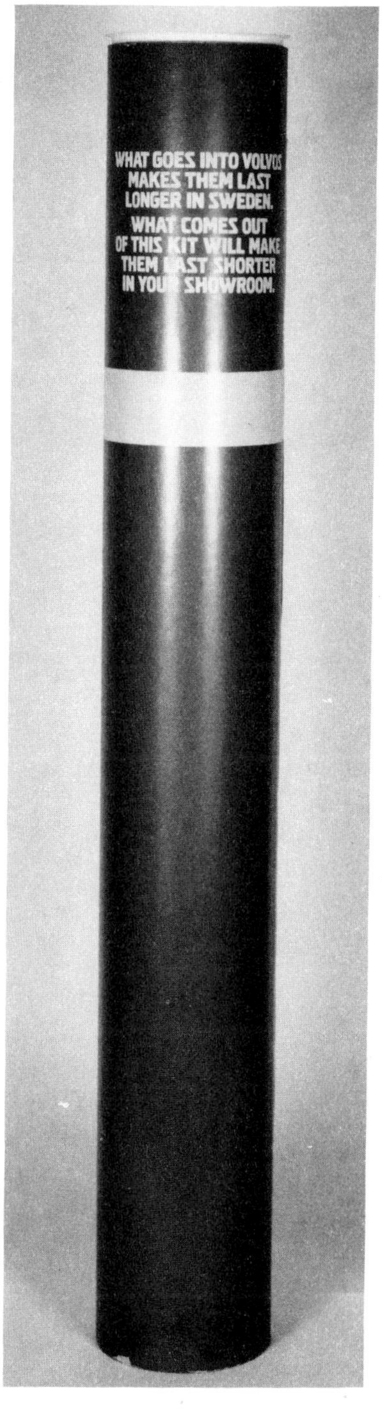

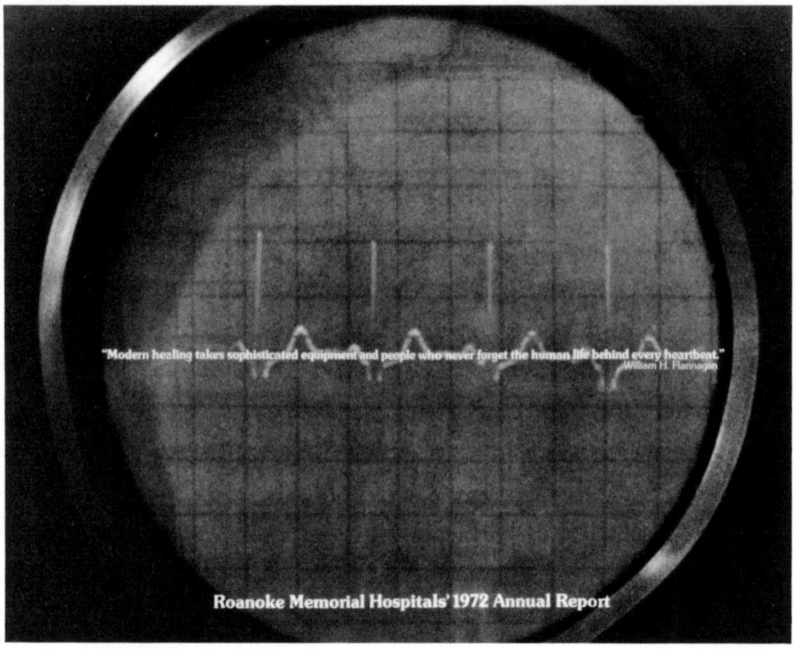

560
Art Directors: John Chepelsky
Kent Puckett
Copywriter: Doris Sanders
Designer: John Chepelsky
Photographer: The Workshop, Inc.
Agency: Brand Edmonds Packett
Client: Roanoke Memorial Hospitals

582
Designer: Bill Bonnell III
Agency: Container Corporation of America
Client: Container Corporation of America

Sippin' the sauce was a whole lot simpler in the old cowboy days. All the bartender had to know was how to pour without spilling. Most bars had bourbon, rye and beer and champagne for those special occasions like waking up alive in the morning.
First Union National
CUT OUT AND FOLD HERE
RED EYE

Quality Real Estate Investments
650 South Grand Avenue, Suite 900, Los Angeles, California 90017 Telephone 213 627-6580

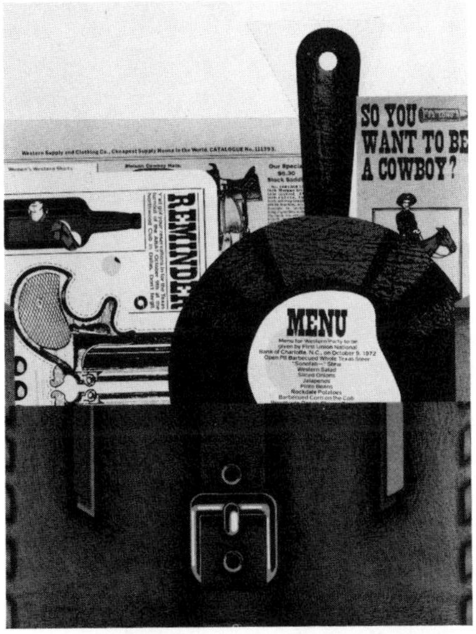
SO YOU WANT TO BE A COWBOY?
REMINDER
MENU

593

Art Director: Frank Rogers
Copywriter: Jack O'Brien
Designer: Mabey Trousdell
Artist: Mabey Trousdell
Agency: Kincaid Advertising
Client: First National City Bank

620
Art Directors: Dennis Juett
Don Weller
Designers: Dennis Juett
Don Weller
Jack Hermsen
Artist: Bob Maile
Photographer: Don Weller
Agency: Weller & Juett Inc.
Client: Quality Real Estate Investments

657
Art Director: Michael Reid
Designer: Michael Reid
Artist: Halina Logay
Agency: Michael Reid Design
Client: Rush-Presbyterian-St. Luke's
Medical Center

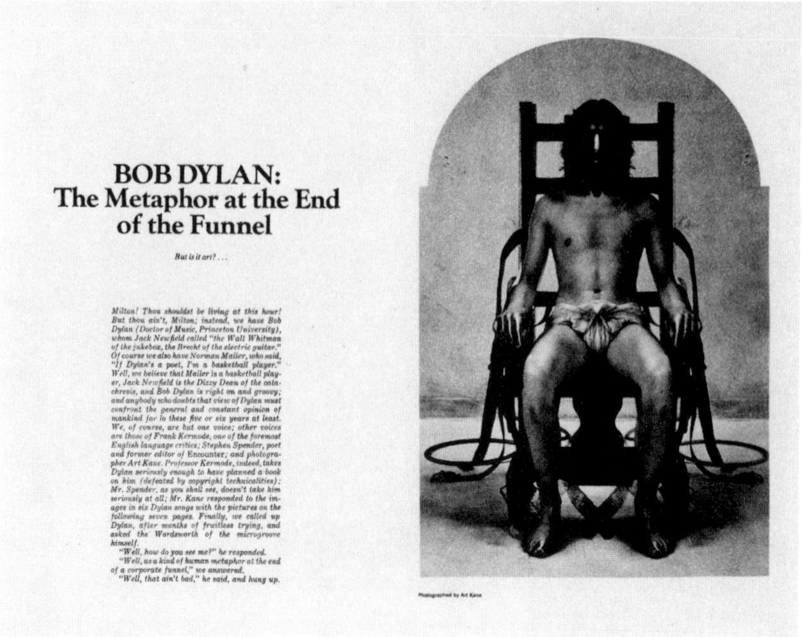

BOB DYLAN: The Metaphor at the End of the Funnel

But is it art? . . .

Milton! Thou shouldst be living at this hour! But thou ain't, Milton; instead, we have Bob Dylan (Doctor of Music, Princeton University), whom Jack Newfield called "the Walt Whitman of the jukebox, the Brecht of the electric guitar." Of course we also have Norman Mailer, who said, "If Dylan's a poet, I'm a basketball player." Well, we believe that Mailer is a basketball player, Jack Newfield is the Dizzy Dean of the catachresis, and Bob Dylan is right on and groovy; and anybody who doubts that view of Dylan must confront the general and constant opinion of mankind for lo these five or six years at least. We, of course, are but one voice; other voices are those of Frank Kermode, one of the foremost English language critics; Stephen Spender, poet and former editor of Encounter*; and photographer Art Kane. Professor Kermode, indeed, takes Dylan seriously enough to have planned a book on him (defeated by copyright technicalities); Mr. Spender, as you shall see, doesn't take him seriously at all; Mr. Kane responded to the images in six Dylan songs with the pictures on the following seven pages. Finally, we called up Dylan, after months of fruitless trying, and asked the Wordsworth of the microgroove himself.*

"Well, how do you see me?" he responded.

"Well, as a kind of human metaphor at the end of a corporate funnel," we answered.

"Well, that ain't bad," he said, and hung up.

Photographed by Art Kane

682
Art Director: Richard Weigand
Photographer: Art Kane
Writer: Bob Dylan
Publication: Esquire Magazine

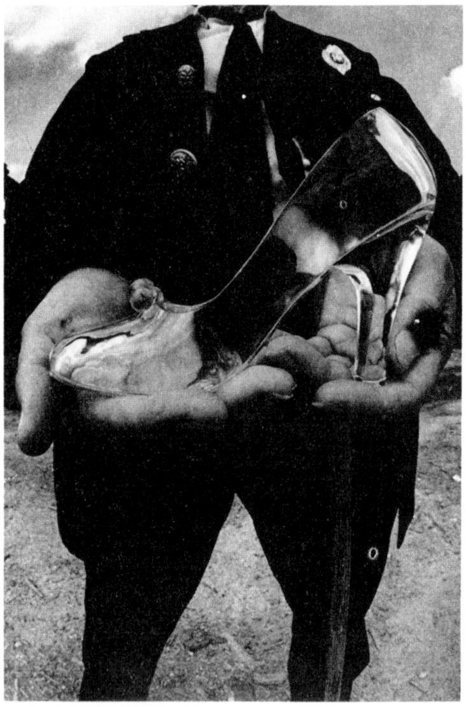

706
Art Director: Stan Jones
Photographer: Dick Richards
Copywriter: John Annarino
Agency: Twentieth Century Fox
Client: Twentieth Century Fox

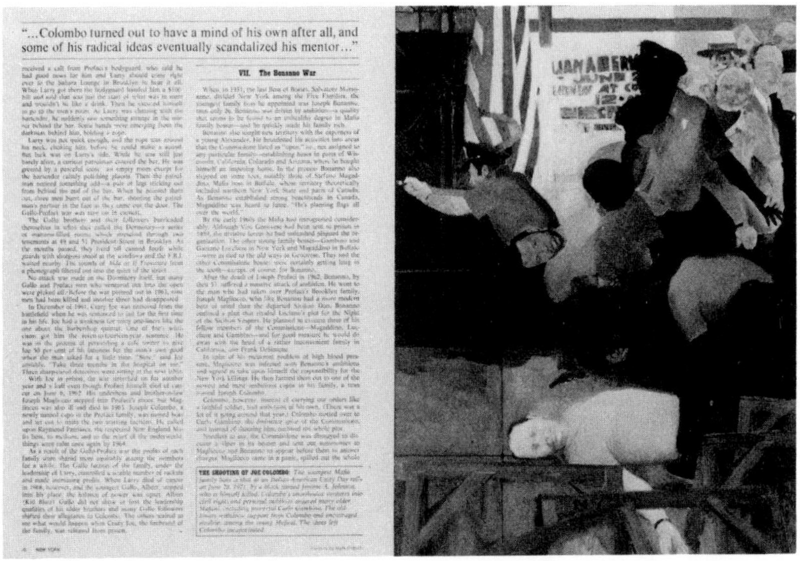
"...Colombo turned out to have a mind of his own after all, and some of his radical ideas eventually scandalized his mentor..."
VII. The Bonanno War
THE SHOOTING OF JOE COLOMBO:

740
Art Directors: Milton Glaser
Walter Bernard
Designers: Walter Bernard
Rochelle Udell
Artists: Paul Davis
Mark English
Burt Silverman
Publisher: New York Magazine

THE SHOOTING OF FRANK COSTELLO: The successor to Lucky Luciano was walking through the lobby of his apartment building on May 2, 1957, when he heard someone say, "This is for you, Frank." The speaker was a henchman of Vito Genovese, who wanted Costello's job as Mafia boss. Costello was only wounded, but he got the message and took an early retirement.
NEW YORK

THE KILLING OF JOEY GALLO: Blamed for planning the shooting of Joe Colombo, Gallo is shot to death and his bodyguard wounded at 5:30 a.m. on April 7, 1972, in Umberto's Clam House in Little Italy. Gallo was celebrating his 43rd birthday with people close to him, including his bride and her young daughter. A Colombo associate named Joseph Luparelli later turned himself in to the F.B.I., saying that he waited outside in a getaway car while four Colombo men took part in the Gallo killing.
NEW YORK

788
Art Directors: Howard C. Grant
Richard P. Ritter
Designers: Howard C. Grant
Richard P. Ritter
Photographer: Ryszard Horowitz
Copywriter: Diamond Information Center
Agency: N. W. Ayer & Son, Inc.
Ayer Design
Client: De Beers Consolidated Mines, Ltd.

794
Art Director: Barry Vetere
Copywriter: Jan Zechman
TV Director: Joe Sedelmaier
TV Producers: Jan Zechman
Barry Vetere
Production Company: Sedelmaier Film Productions, Inc.
Agency: Zechman Lyke Vetere, Inc.
Client: KMOX-TV

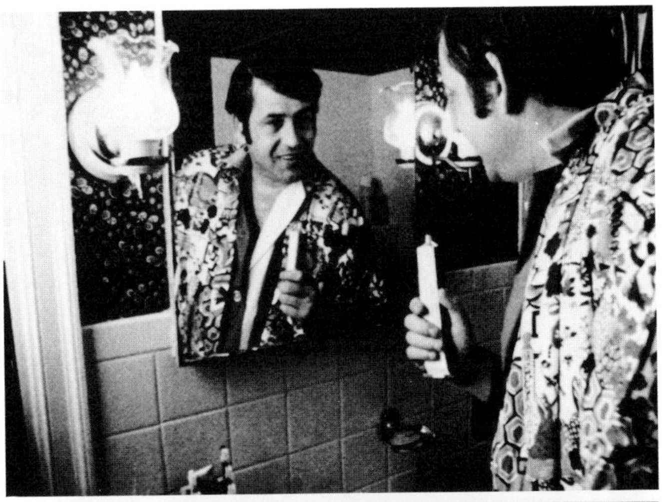

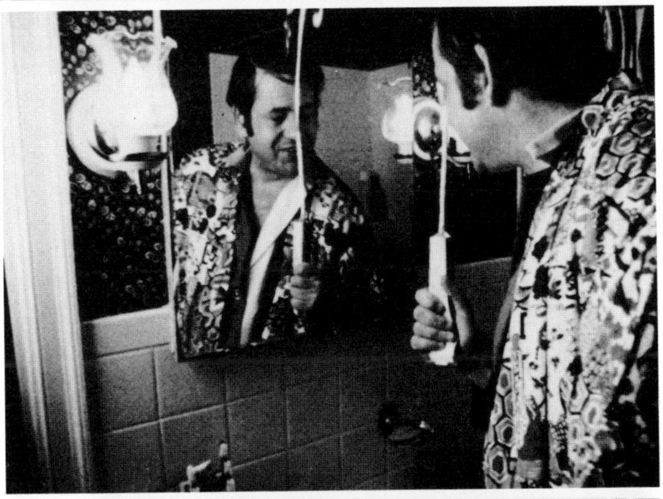

Bob Buck
10-second

OPEN ON BATHROOM. BOB BUCK ENTERS. WALKS JAUNTILY TO SINK, UP TO MIRROR

ANNCR. (VO): We've always insisted on 24 hour-a-day sportscasters.

BUCK PICKS UP TOOTHPASTE TUBE AND HOLDS IT LIKE HAND MIKE

BUCK: (A LITTLE LIKE HOWARD COSELL) Hello sports fans!

IN HIS ENTHUSIASM, BUCK SQUEEZES THE TOOTHPASTE ALL OVER HIS HAND AND PAJAMA TOP

ANNCR. (VO): What have we done?

SUPER: NEWS SERVICE
6 & 10 P.M.

Jim Bolen
10-second

Max Roby
10-second

Tom Jones
10-second

THE SHOW

ADVERTISING

Print
Radio Commercials
Television Commercials

This program is so beautiful, it has to die.

That was, as you will see, the strange verdict pronounced by many television critics about a new series, "The Waltons."

The audience reaction has been unusual, too. Little children get all smiley and weepy about it, the way they do for things like My Friend Flicka, Little Women, and the Cookie Monster stubbing his toe.

But from there on up in age and sophistication, overt emotions disappear. To be replaced by little smiles of recognition. An occasional gulp. Red eyes.

And in grown men, funny little sounds and fumblings in the dark, designed to hide the fact that a man is doing something as "unmanly" as being moved by a tender, sentimental story.

We at CBS would like to tell you what "The Waltons" is all about, but it won't be easy. Because everything we tell you can turn you off, if you relate it to similar programs with similar themes.

"The Waltons" is different. Not because it isn't "with it" and it isn't cutesy. Which it isn't. Not because it isn't exciting. Which it is. But because it's an honest attempt to portray a particular kind of American family during a particular time in history.

The Waltons are a large family. Seven children, the eldest eighteen, the youngest six. A mother and father. A grandmother and grandfather. Even a dog. Not a heroic Lassie dog. Not a funny, mangy dog. A dog dog.

And it's about the 1930's. Depression days. In the Blue Ridge Mountains of Virginia. The family is poor. One of the kids plays the harmonica. And it's all about how they all face life.

And that's what makes the Waltons special. *The kind of life they face.*

It has the feel of truth. The look, the texture. You can believe that there were people like this who led lives like this during times like these.

You can believe that maybe this was really how it was to grow up in tough country during tough times. How it really was to be part of a big, loving family.

It's about people who love each other, and love others. About people who care for their aged as well as their young.

And it's funny, too, because it's about a sprawling family of bright, vital individualists.

But it isn't puppy-cute. It isn't pat. And each program doesn't tightly package a moral, like a fortune cookie.

Though there is a moral, overall. Life can be tough. It can also be beautiful. Not easy. Beautiful.

"The Waltons" is on Thursdays. Opposite that funny man, Flip Wilson. And the exciting action show, "The Mod Squad."

It will remain alive until the end of this season, because some people here at CBS believe that there are enough of us around – even in this super-sophisticated day and age – who can still respond to some old-fashioned notions like respect, and dignity, and love. Who aren't embarrassed by an honest lump in the throat.

If there are enough of us, "The Waltons" may even fool the critics and live next year.

Watch "The Waltons" tonight, for a change. It may bring out the best in you.

It did in us.

"Please, folks, don't let this one die."
THE PITTSBURGH PRESS

"What will happen is that The Waltons will receive rave reviews, be embraced by a small, but enthusiastic audience, collect a number of awards —and vanish from the air with hardly a ripple."
DALLAS TIMES HERALD

"...the only entirely honest and rewarding hour I have spent on television this season."
SAN FRANCISCO CHRONICLE

"When these kids run down the dirt road in their bare feet, you can feel the dirt between your own toes."
THE PITTSBURGH PRESS

"Totally unique, exciting TV experience."
THE ATLANTA CONSTITUTION

"The show is so natural, so totally out of the TV mode, you have to worry about its survival."
CHICAGO TODAY

"Best family series on air."
THE INDIANAPOLIS STAR

"...a family in which people, real people, talk to one another... There's respect here, and affection openly displayed, and both young and old have their own dignity."
THE NEW YORK TIMES

"It's easy to get wrapped up with The Waltons. They happen to be real."
NEW YORK POST

"Breaks all the rules. Except one: It's entertaining."
CHICAGO TRIBUNE

"Quite wonderful in every respect... beautiful in its conjuring up of a more innocent day, poignant in its relationships, a perfect gem of a tale."
THE BOSTON EVENING GLOBE

"Probably will compare with the few great ones of television history."
THE DETROIT NEWS

"Might be the best show commercial television has produced in years."
DAYTON DAILY NEWS

Save "The Waltons"

See them tonight at 8:00 on Channel 2.

Newspaper/Single

1
Art Director: Lou Dorfsman
Copywriters: Lou Dorfsman
Peter Nord
Designers: Lou Dorfsman
Ted Andresakes
Photographer: CBS Photo
Agency: CBS/Broadcast Group
Client: CBS Television Network

2 Silver Award
Art Director: Charles Piccirillo
Copywriter: Tom Yobbagy
Photographer: Daily News Photo
Agency: Doyle Dane Bernbach Inc.
Client: Volkswagen of America

4
Art Director: Sam Scali
Copywriter: Ed McCabe
Designer: Sam Scali
Photographer: Phil Mazzurco
Agency: Scali, McCabe, Sloves, Inc.
Client: Perdue Farms, Inc.

©WORLD-WIDE VOLKSWAGEN CORP.
NEW YORK DAILY NEWS photo
Water Bug.
When the weather looks its worst, a Volkswagen looks its best.
And this was the picture, last Monday morning, as reported the next day in the New York Daily News:
Rush hour. On the Saw Mill River Parkway.
While thousands were stuck at home or on the road, the man in the VW was sailing along. And was one of the few who made it to work.
What made it possible?
Quite possibly the way we make the Volkswagen.
We seal the bottom of our car to the top of our car. To help protect everything inside against most things outside. Including dampness.
We put our engine in the rear. Above the drive wheels. For extra traction.
We cover our car with 13 pounds of paint—outside and inside. Even in places you can't see, but which corrosion can find.
In fact, the VW is so well put-together, it's practically airtight. And some of the stories you may have heard about VWs in water, aren't just stories.
But even more amazing than what a VW will go through, is what a VW goes for:
$1999.*
What other car gives you this kind of quality at this kind of price?
$1999.*

2

4

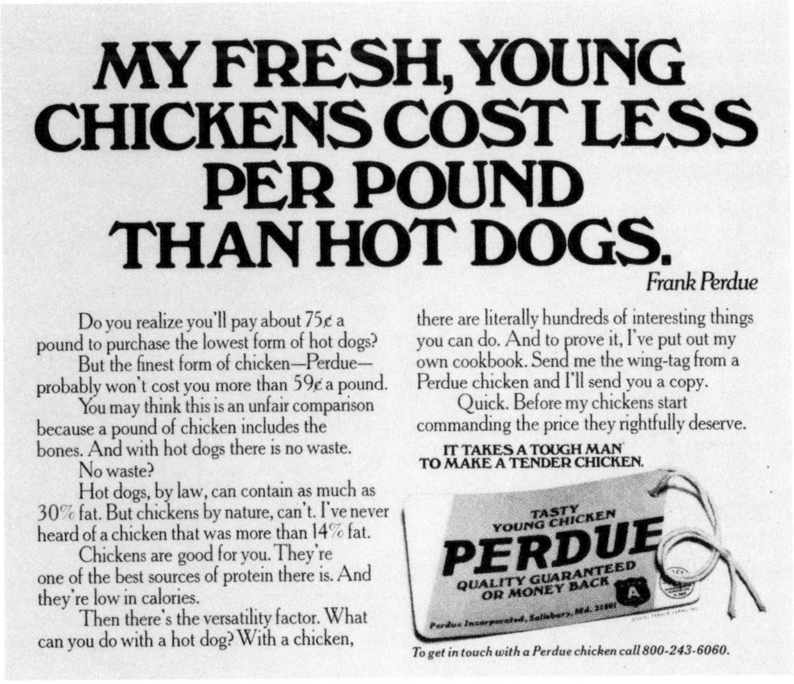
MY FRESH, YOUNG CHICKENS COST LESS PER POUND THAN HOT DOGS.
Frank Perdue
Do you realize you'll pay about 75¢ a pound to purchase the lowest form of hot dogs?
But the finest form of chicken—Perdue—probably won't cost you more than 59¢ a pound.
You may think this is an unfair comparison because a pound of chicken includes the bones. And with hot dogs there is no waste.
No waste?
Hot dogs, by law, can contain as much as 30% fat. But chickens by nature, can't. I've never heard of a chicken that was more than 14% fat.
Chickens are good for you. They're one of the best sources of protein there is. And they're low in calories.
Then there's the versatility factor. What can you do with a hot dog? With a chicken, there are literally hundreds of interesting things you can do. And to prove it, I've put out my own cookbook. Send me the wing-tag from a Perdue chicken and I'll send you a copy.
Quick. Before my chickens start commanding the price they rightfully deserve.
IT TAKES A TOUGH MAN TO MAKE A TENDER CHICKEN.
TASTY YOUNG CHICKEN
PERDUE
QUALITY GUARANTEED OR MONEY BACK
Perdue Incorporated, Salisbury, Md. 21801
To get in touch with a Perdue chicken call 800-243-6060.

5

In a 45 mph crash, the average head hits the average windshield with a force of over a ton.
Does that make a lasting impact on your brain?
It could.
When your car hits a stationary object at 45 mph, your brain can smash against the inside of your windshield the way a bug splatters against the outside.
And if you survive somehow, you might rather be dead than live with what's left of your face.
We're talking about passengers now, of course.
Drivers' heads don't get to the windshield so often. The driver can depend on the steering wheel to hold him back. And to tear his insides out in the process.
Now most passengers and drivers know these gruesome facts. So you'd think they'd protect themselves from windshields and steering wheels by wearing seat belts. But fewer than 40% do. You'd think they'd use shoulder belts. But fewer than 10% do.
Those are facts. Here's another:
Some 6500 men, women and children would be alive this year if they'd been wearing seat belts at one unpredictable moment last year.
Does that make a lasting impact on your brain?
Buckle up. Everybody. Every time. Please.
We want you to live. Mobil

5
Art Director: Lee Epstein
Copywriter: Hal Silverman
Designer: Lee Epstein
Photographer: Carl Fischer
Agency: Doyle Dane Bernbach Inc.
Client: Mobil Oil Corporation

6
Art Director: Joseph H. Phair
Copywriter: Arthur X. Tuohy
Designer: Katsuji Asada
Artist: J. Barry O'Rourke
Agency: Ketchum, MacLeod & Grove, Inc.
Client: American Insurance Association

7
Art Director: Ted Shaine
Copywriter: Diane Rothschild Hyatt
Designer: Mike Uris
Photographer: Anonymous
Agency: Doyle Dane Bernbach Inc.
Client: El Al Israel Airlines

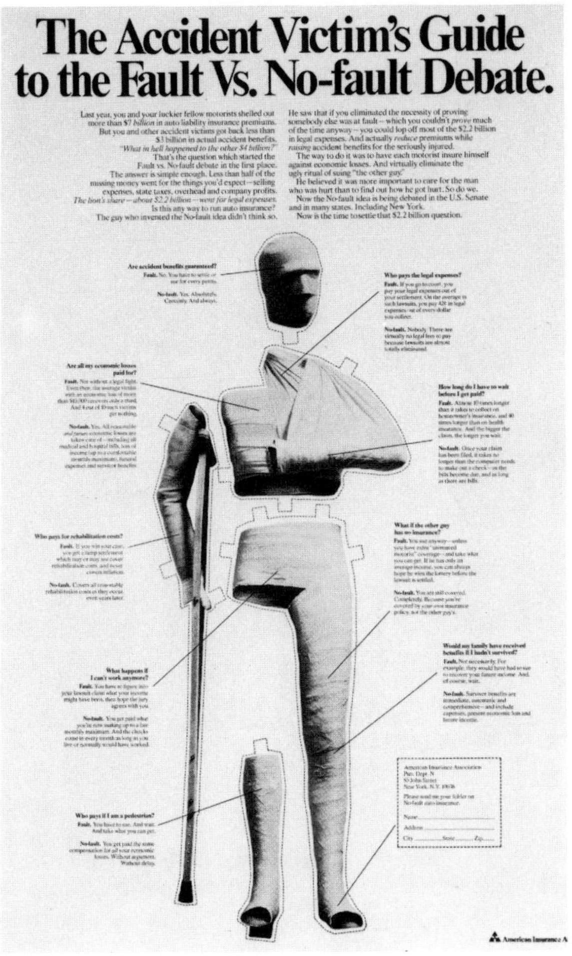
The Accident Victim's Guide to the Fault Vs. No-fault Debate.
Last year, you and your luckier fellow motorists shelled out more than $7 billion in auto liability insurance premiums.
But you and other accident victims got back less than $3 billion in actual accident benefits.
"What in hell happened to the other $4 billion?"
That's the question which started the Fault vs. No-fault debate in the first place.
The answer is simple enough. Less than half of the missing money went for the things you'd expect—selling expenses, state taxes, overhead and company profits.
The lion's share—about $2.2 billion—went for legal expenses.
Is this any way to run auto insurance?
The guy who invented the No-fault idea didn't think so.
He saw that if you eliminated the necessity of proving somebody else was at fault—which you couldn't prove much of the time anyway—you could lop off most of the $2.2 billion in legal expenses. And actually reduce premiums while raising accident benefits for the seriously injured.
The way to do it was to have each motorist insure himself against economic losses. And virtually eliminate the ugly ritual of suing "the other guy."
He believed it was more important to care for the man who was hurt than to find out how he got hurt. So do we.
Now the No-fault idea is being debated in the U.S. Senate and in many states. Including New York.
Now is the time to settle that $2.2 billion question.
Are accident benefits guaranteed?
Who pays the legal expenses?

6

"At last, Israel and Africa on the same tour."
El Al Israel Airlines

7

How far do you think you can get for $94 on your summer vacation?
If you want to go someplace interesting and different for your vacation this summer but you don't have a lot of money to spend, we have a few good suggestions.
The Bahamas, Puerto Rico or Jamaica.
Our prices are lower because it's the off-season.
And the only thing that's really off is the price.
Because our price includes your round trip air fare, first class hotel with private bath and some other nice things. Like perfect weather. Beautiful beaches. And fewer people around.
You can get a whole week in the Bahamas for $94, including air fare, hotel and some other nice things.
A week in Nassau is a great way to get away from it all.
There are white beaches for you to lie on. Plenty of warm sunshine for you to soak up. And lots of things for you to do.
And we can take you to all this for only $94.
When you arrive, we'll meet you at the airport.
We'll put you up in a first class hotel for 8 days and 7 nights.
We'll take you on a sightseeing tour of Paradise Island.
We'll take you to a night club show, and buy you a drink.
We'll pay your greens fees for a round of golf.
We'll give you a scuba diving lesson and a sailing lesson, if you want them.
And when your week is up and you're ready (or as ready as you'll ever be) to go back home, we'll drive you back to the airport.
The cost of all this, including your round trip air fare and double-occupancy hotel room, is only $94.
And we have a similar one-week vacation, for the same price, to Freeport.
Or you can get a whole week in Jamaica for $119, including air fare, hotel and some other nice things.
Nobody has to tell you what a beautiful place Jamaica is for a vacation.
And at this price, it's even more beautiful.
We put you up in a first class hotel in Montego Bay for 8 days and 7 nights.
We buy you a drink to welcome you.
We take you on a glass-bottom boat tour.
And, if you want, we even introduce you to some people who live in Jamaica, so you'll feel at home, right away.
The cost for the week in Montego Bay, including round trip air fare and double-occupancy hotel room, is only $119 if you travel in mid-week or $129 if you travel on a weekend.
And we have another vacation, in Ocho Rios.
You get 8 days and 7 nights in a first class hotel.
You get a car for the whole time you're there (you pay only for the gas and mileage).
And the cost, including your round trip air fare and double-occupancy hotel room, is only $138 if you travel in mid-week or $148 if you travel on a weekend.
Or you can get a whole week in Puerto Rico for $179, including air fare, hotel and some other nice things.
We put you up in a first class hotel in San Juan for 8 days and 7 nights.
We buy you a drink at two top night spots.
We give you a clubhouse pass to El Comandante Race Track. (And wish you luck.)
We give you a book of Discount Certificates good for special savings at many San Juan stores.
And after we give you all of this, we give you something else.
A day in St. Thomas.
Because as great as San Juan is, St. Thomas has something it doesn't have.
A free port.
Which means you can buy cameras, liquor, jewelry, watches and just about anything else you can think of at prices lower than just about any place else you can think of.
And not only are the prices low. Your flight to St. Thomas is included.
When you arrive in St. Thomas, we meet you and take you to town.
We give you a free sightseeing tour of the city.
And when you've finished shopping and sightseeing, we take you back to the airport and back to San Juan.
To sum it all up, you get the best of San Juan and the best of St. Thomas.
All for the price of San Juan alone.
And the cost, including your round trip air fare and double-occupancy hotel room, is only $179.
These are just some of the islands we can take you to at our off-season prices this summer. In fact we have more bargain vacations to more islands in the Caribbean than any other airline.
And in addition to our one-week vacations, we also have weekend and mid-week vacations.
If you would like to know more about how you can have a lot of vacation this summer, without spending a lot of money, just call a Pan Am travel agent or Pan Am office.
Or send in our coupon.
Pan American World Airways
100 South Biscayne Blvd.
Miami, Florida 33131
Yes, I'd like more information on how to have a great summer vacation without spending a lot of money.
Please send me your brochure.
Name
Street
City
State Zip
My Pan Am Travel Agent is:
Pan Am
The world's most experienced airline.

8

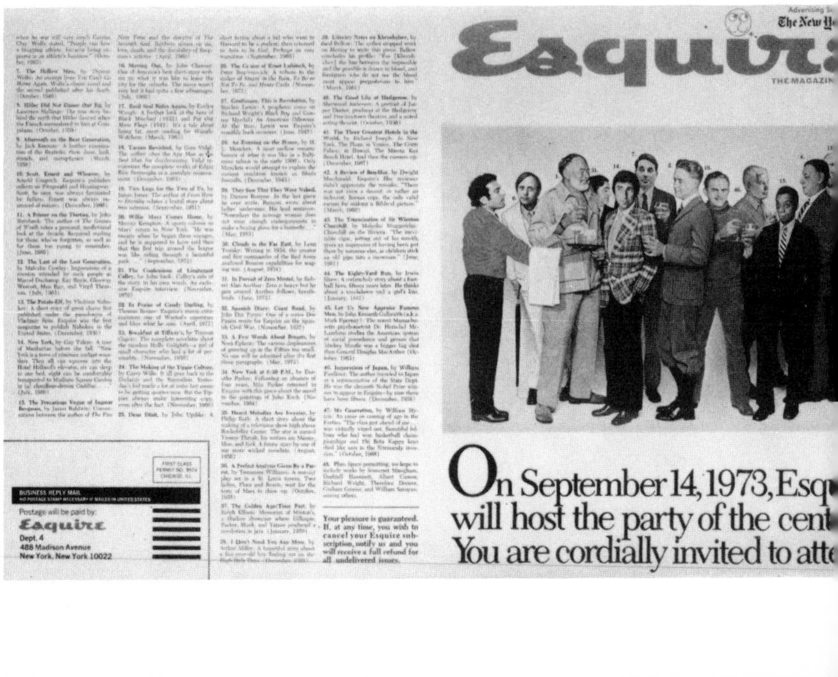

Esquire
BUSINESS REPLY MAIL
Postage will be paid by
Esquire
Dept. 4
488 Madison Avenue
New York, New York 10022
Your pleasure is guaranteed. If, at any time, you wish to cancel your Esquire subscription, notify us and you will receive a full refund for all undelivered issues.

8
Art Director: Mike Tesch
Copywriter: Dick Fitzhugh
Designer: Mike Tesch
Photographers: Harold Krieger
Robert Freson
Denny Tillman
Agency: Carl Ally Inc.
Client: Pan American Airways

10
Art Director: Bert Greene
Copywriter: Lee Eisenberg
Designer: Tom Houtz
Photographer: Jean-Paul Goude
Agency: Esquire
Client: Esquire

11 Gold Award
Art Director: Jim Handloser
Copywriter: Frank DiGiacomo
Designer: Jim Handloser
Photographer: WABC-TV News
Agency: Della Femina, Travisano & Partners, Inc.
Client: WABC-TV

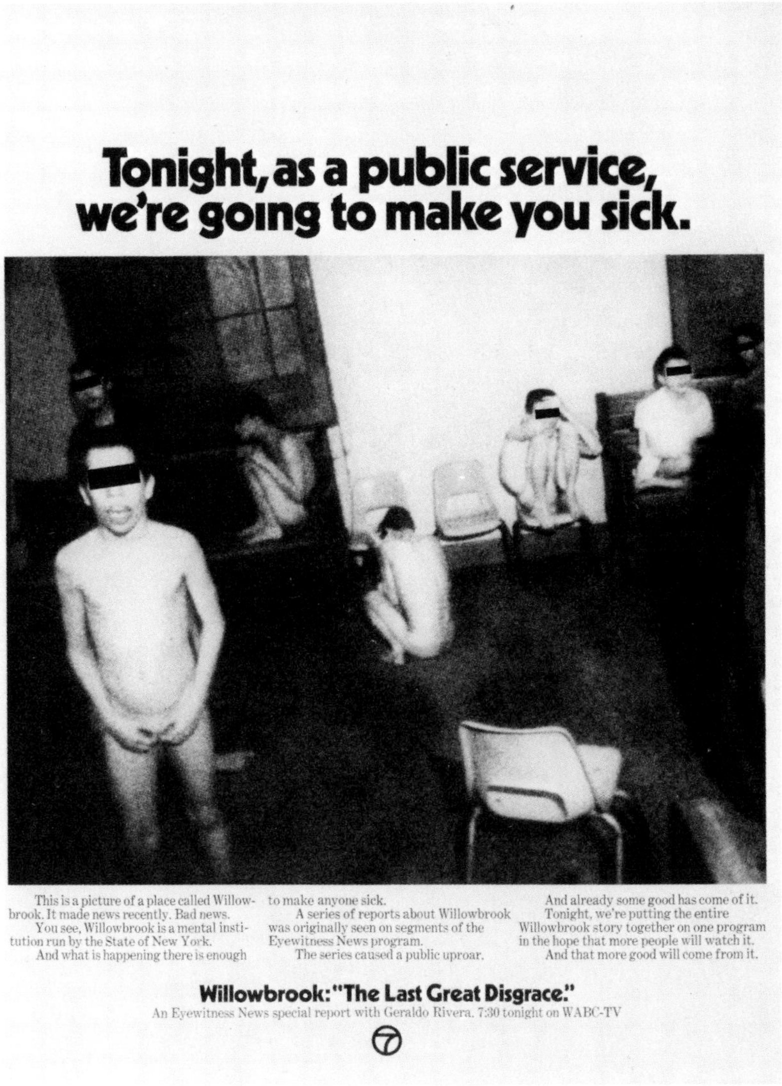
Tonight, as a public service, we're going to make you sick.
This is a picture of a place called Willowbrook. It made news recently. Bad news.
You see, Willowbrook is a mental institution run by the State of New York.
And what is happening there is enough to make anyone sick.
A series of reports about Willowbrook was originally seen on segments of the Eyewitness News program.
The series caused a public uproar.
And already some good has come of it.
Tonight, we're putting the entire Willowbrook story together on one program in the hope that more people will watch it.
And that more good will come from it.
Willowbrook: "The Last Great Disgrace."
An Eyewitness News special report with Geraldo Rivera. 7:30 tonight on WABC-TV

11

10

Newspaper/Single

12
Art Directors: Sam Scali
Ray Alban
Copywriters: Ed McCabe
Hy Abady
Designers: Sam Scali
Ray Alban
Photographer: James Moore
Agency: Scali, McCabe, Sloves, Inc.
Client: Barney's

13 Gold Award
Art Director: Stan Block
Copywriter: Adam Hanft
Photographer: Bruce Buchenholz
Agency: Rosenfeld, Sirowitz & Lawson
Client: WABC-TV

12

Calling all women to Barney's.

13

THIS JUNKIE HAS A FIFTY DOLLAR A DAY HABIT.
He won't be born for 6 months. He weighs one thirteenth of an ounce and is less than an inch long.
And he's as much of a junkie as someone who's 35 years old and shoots into the vein of his leg.
Tonight, Geraldo Rivera will take a close hard look at the junkie population of New York that hasn't even been born yet. Last year alone, 1,500 mothers with a monkey on their back gave birth to babies with a monkey on theirs.
Sometimes, if the mother goes through withdrawal while she's pregnant, the baby never gets born. He goes through cold turkey, too. And in the process will simply kick himself to death.
The program is an Eyewitness News Special called "The Littlest Junkie." And it not only explores the problem with agonizing honesty.
But it sets forth what's being done, what should be done before it's too late. And what a pregnant mother can do if she's not only eating for two, but shooting for two.
So watch tonight and see what the 70's have done to the miracle of childbirth.
7 TONIGHT 7:30
THE LITTLEST JUNKIE
With Eyewitness News Correspondent, Geraldo Rivera

14
Art Director: Bill Hogan
Copywriter: Bob Fearon
Designer: Bob Fearon
Photographer: Jeremy Blodgett
Agency: Doremus & Company
Client: Doremus & Company

16
Art Director: Reinhold Schwenk
Copywriter: Diane Rothschild Hyatt
Designer: Reinhold Schwenk
Photographer: Steve Nichols
Agency: Doyle Dane Bernbach Inc.
Client: Sony Corporation

14

DOREMUS
LIVES
Our problem is monumental. We turn out fresh, original advertising and yet we're often thought of as a solid, conservative agency specializing in what's commonly called "tombstone" advertising.
Sure, it's true that Doremus places more financial notice advertising than any other agency in the world.
And we like being best in this exacting, highly specialized area of advertising.
But light the neon: we're also a lively, growing general advertising agency. "One of the most under-appreciated," said an impressed prospect after seeing a presentation of our broad and varied work.
Commercials and print ads that sell the products and services of some of America's most prestigious companies to some of America's most thoughtful, discriminating people. Quality advertising. Intelligent. Lean. To the point. Advertising that works. Because Doremus understands what turns business on. And what turns people on.
If yours is a quality product and you want to reach a quality audience, we can help you get through to them. Persuasively. Convincingly.
Doremus & Company, 120 Broadway, New York, N.Y. 10005 (212) 964-0700.

16

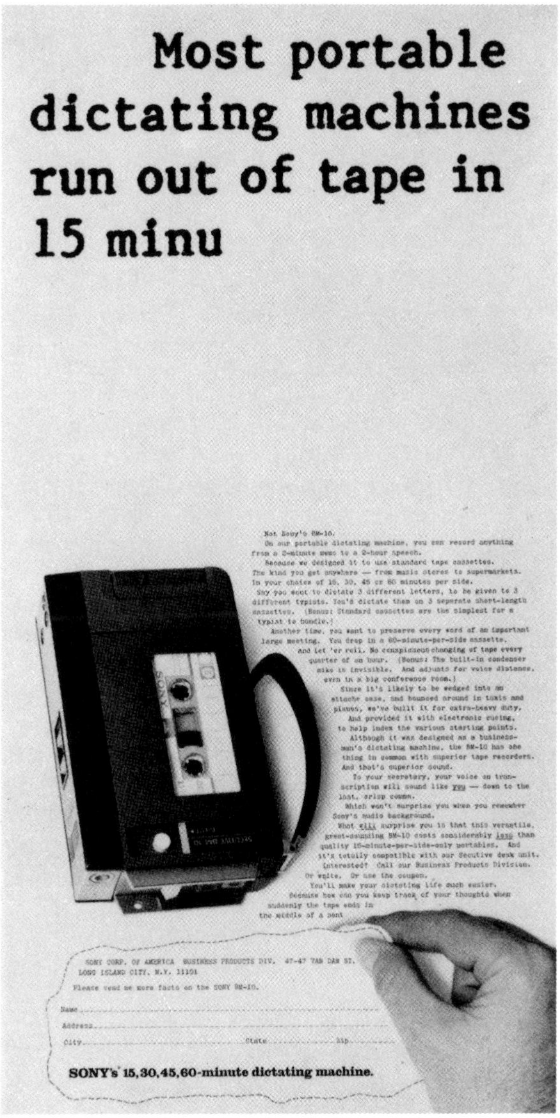

17
Art Director: Jon Guliner
Copywriter: Steve Smith
Artist: Chas. B. Slackman
Photographers: Henry Sandbank
Charles Santore
Joe Toto
Agency: Benton & Bowles, Inc.
Client: Crum & Forster

18
Art Director: Pete Coutroulis
Copywriter: Howard Krakow
Designer: Pete Coutroulis
Photographer: Victor Skrebneski
Agency: Jim Weller & Partners
Client: Florence Eiseman

HOW WE MANAGED TO ACHIEVE ANONYMITY IN JUST 75 YEARS.
And other amazing true stories about Crum & Forster and its insurance companies.
Average reading time: 4 minutes.
Crum & Forster is not exactly a household phrase. That's because Crum & Forster is an insurance holding company. And the insurance we sell is sold by the insurance companies that make up our holdings. So you're more likely to be familiar with their names than with ours.
Our companies include: United States Fire, Industrial Indemnity, The North River, Westchester Fire, International Insurance, American Eagle Life, International Surplus Lines, and Constitution Reinsurance—a company that specializes in reinsuring other insurance companies.
And while we may be "Crum and Who?" to the general public, we have made quite a name for ourselves in insurance circles.
Our companies sell enough insurance to make us the 16th largest property and casualty insurance group in the U.S.
When we opened our door on November 2, 1896, Frederick H. Crum and John A. Forster were general insurance agents selling other companies' insurance. We ended up buying those companies and selling our insurance through independent agents.
We depend on independent agents. You should, too.
We've gotten where we are, in large part, because of the efforts of one of the most unique sales forces in any business.
Crum & Forster companies sell their insurance through independent insurance agents and brokers. And while there are over 400,000 independent agents and brokers in the U.S., only 8,000 have been appointed to sell our insurance.
Their qualifications alone make them unique. But what makes them even more unique as a sales force is the fact that because they are independent, they not only represent Crum & Forster companies, they also represent competitors as well.
And for exactly that reason it is our firm belief that the independent agent and broker can best represent our interests and yours.
He provides you with personal service and an expert, objective opinion, because he isn't forced to rely on the services of one company. Rather he can look at your needs from your point of view and pick the right companies with the right coverages and services.
He provides us with the continuing motivation to offer a wide variety of coverages and services. And to continually improve them.
For example: A New Orleans agent who had the opportunity to write the property coverage for the $150.6 million Louisiana Superdome, now in construction, came to Crum & Forster. We had the capacity to provide the coverage and the necessary safety engineering.
The Crum & Forster companies were among the leaders in providing commercial package insurance for many industries.
As a result of the needs of an independent agent in Iowa, C&F developed a Nursing Home Program package. Rates were high for this type of package. We were able to develop a total property and casualty program at a better price. And this program included safety procedure recommendations to be used in nursing homes for the well-being of the residents.
Our claims to fame.
While others pioneered more efficient ways of collecting premiums, our companies have pioneered more efficient ways of paying claims.
We developed a telephone adjusting plan where we contact people the same day they report claims to determine the type and extent of loss or injury. This speeds up payments by speeding the information about the loss.
We pioneered advance payment claim handling. Which means that we pay the part of the claim that everyone has agreed on even if the total claim is still being worked out. Before that, you waited for the complete settlement. And in the case of a small business, the advance payment could mean the difference between staying open or closing down until the total claim is settled.
Further, we have a standby catastrophe task force that operates in addition to our regular claims people, in the event of a major disaster. This speeds up claims service when people need it most. We believe we are unique in having such a large group of property claims specialists operating exclusively in the handling of catastrophe claims.
We not only support no-fault auto insurance, we helped design it.
No-fault auto insurance was a popular topic of discussion at Crum & Forster back in 1967, long before it became a popular topic of conversation.
And that discussion led us to help design a basic no-fault program as part of our work with the American Insurance Association.
Since then, we've worked to encourage the states to adopt meaningful no-fault auto insurance laws.
We're still working.
Some of our other assets.
Since 1966, premiums have increased at a better-than-industry-average rate of 13.9% to $605.8 million in 1971. During the same period, net income rose from $17.7 million to $36 million.
And in the first 9 months of 1972, premiums increased 10.8% over the first 9 months of 1971. Net income increased 29.6%.
For a copy of our most recent annual report, write to B. P. Russell, Chairman of the Board, Crum & Forster, 110 William Street, New York, New York 10038.
And now that we've become better acquainted, let's keep in touch.
CRUM & FORSTER INSURANCE COMPANIES
THE POLICY MAKERS.

17

For the child who hasn't a thing to wear.
Florence Eiseman clothes.

18

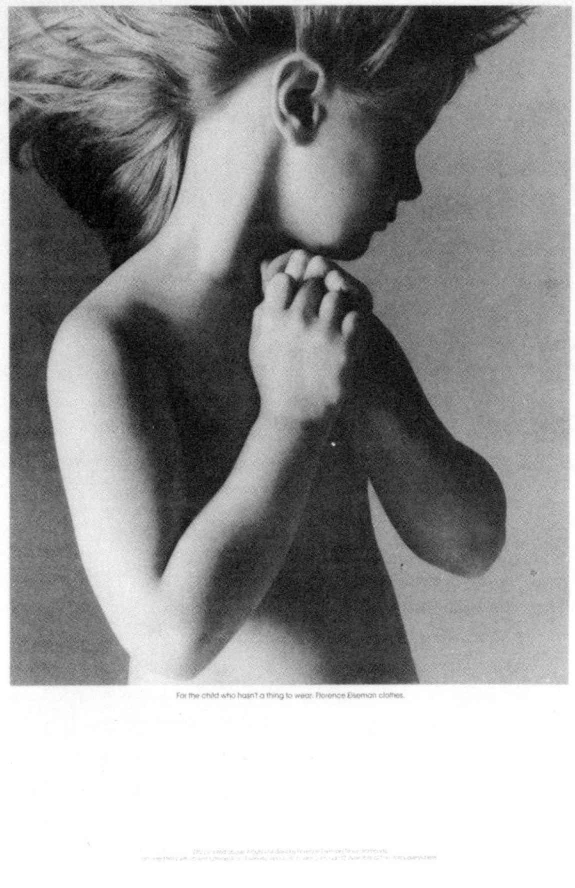
For the child who hasn't a thing to wear. Florence Eiseman clothes.

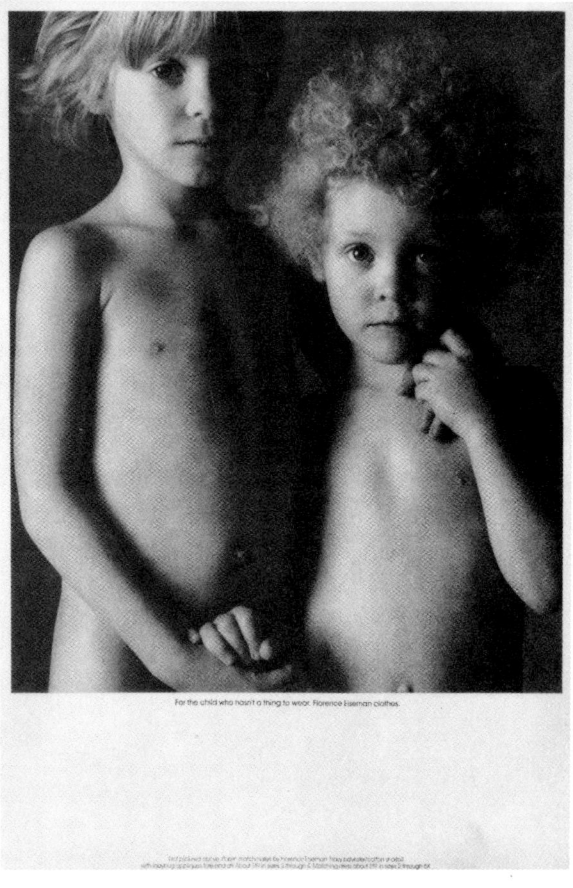
For the child who hasn't a thing to wear. Florence Eiseman clothes.

19

How to play
The Auto Insurance Shell Game.
The game, also known as *The Fault Vs. No-fault Debate*, is being played all over the country these days. The stakes are high.
More than $2,000,000,000 in auto liability insurance premiums. That's two *billion* dollars.
And you, the motorist, are the pawn. Like it or not.
On one side of the game, the idea is to convince state legislators and the public that the present fault system of auto liability insurance – under which you must prove "the other guy" caused the accident before your claim is paid – should be sanctified rather than scrapped.
Or, failing that, to dress up the fault system in a phony no-fault wrapper and pass it off as the real thing.
In either case, the objective is to prevent tampering with the $2.2 billion in legal expenses that are paid out of auto insurance premiums each year.
On the other side of the game is true no-fault auto insurance which, by eliminating or curtailing lawsuits, would also virtually eliminate the legal expenses. Then that $2.2 billion would go instead to pay for your medical bills and reduce your premiums.
The "fault" players as well as the "phony no-fault" players are all touting your "right to sue" as some sort of sacred standard.
On our side, the "true no-fault" players see this right more as a sacred cow. In fact, no-fault came about because the fault system – "right to sue" and all – simply isn't working.
In the first place, almost no one actually exercises this "right" in a courtroom. And for good reason. It's too chancy.
Secondly, "right" or no "right," the fault system allots responsibility with considerably less than the wisdom of a Solomon. In most states, if the other driver is 90% at fault but you are 10% at fault, you don't get a cent.
Finally, despite this "right," the average seriously injured victim recovers only a third of his economic losses, and many get nothing at all.
Those of us on the true no-fault side of the game – the major consumer organizations, most newspapers and magazines as well as some insurance companies – believe the motorist loses under *any* system which takes 1 premium dollar out of every 3 for legal expenses.
That, then, is what the game is really all about. Whether that 1 premium dollar in every 3 – or $2.2 billion in all each year – shouldn't go instead to pay your medical bills and economic losses – and reduce your premiums.
We don't think the game needs to be played at all. But, if it must, it deserves to be played with everyone's eyes open.
And the facts straight.
Fault.
The settle-or-sue circus.
Phony No-fault.
True No-fault.
American Insurance Association

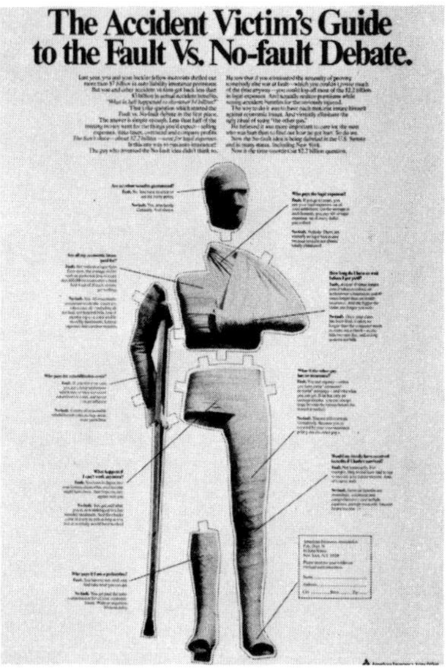
The Accident Victim's Guide to the Fault Vs. No-fault Debate.

19
Art Director: Joseph H. Phair
Copywriter: Arthur X. Tuohy
Designer: Katsuji Asada
Photographers: J. Barry O'Rourke
Jeff Nikki
Agency: Ketchum, MacLeod & Grove, Inc.
Client: American Insurance Association

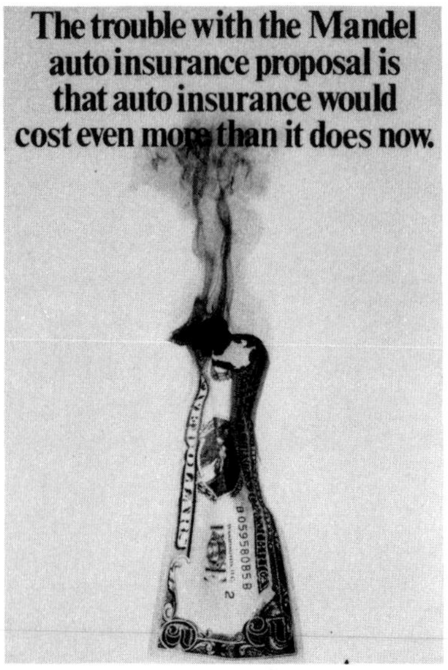
The trouble with the Mandel auto insurance proposal is that auto insurance would cost even more than it does now.

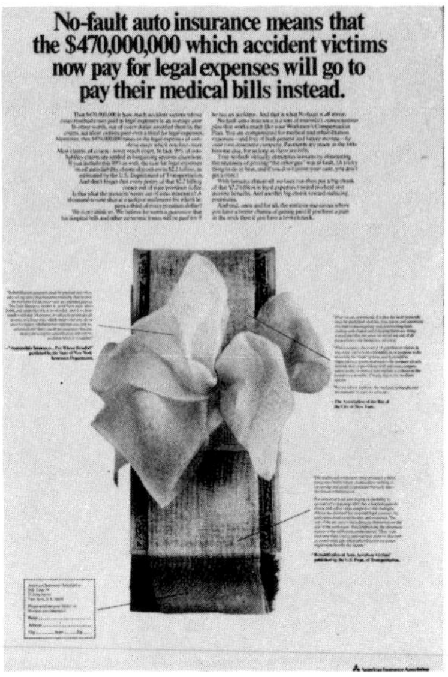
No-fault auto insurance means that the $470,000,000 which accident victims now pay for legal expenses will go to pay their medical bills instead.

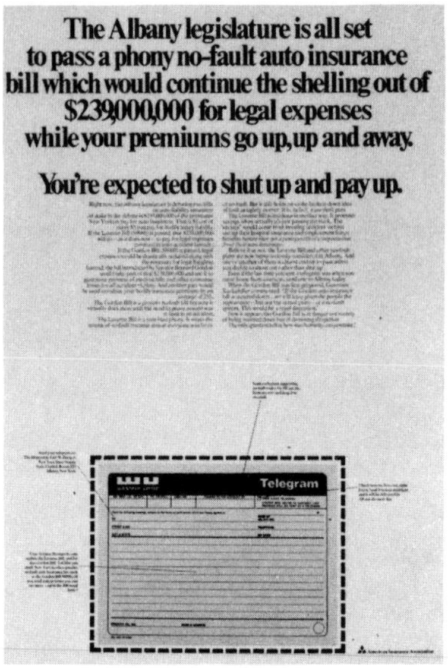
The Albany legislature is all set to pass a phony no-fault auto insurance bill which would continue the shelling out of $239,000,000 for legal expenses while your premiums go up, up and away.
You're expected to shut up and pay up.
Telegram

20
Art Directors: Elliott Manketo
Ed DiBenedetto
Copywriters: Jerry Pfiffner
Dean Crebbin
Tad Dillon
Photographers: George Haling
Tony Pappas
Michael O'Neill
Agency: N.W. Ayer & Son, Inc., New York
Client: Union Dime Savings Bank

20

Union Dime. 40th&Avenue of the Americas, right in the neighborhood.

Union Dime. 50th&Park, right in the neighborhood.

Union Dime. 39th&Madison, right in the neighborhood.

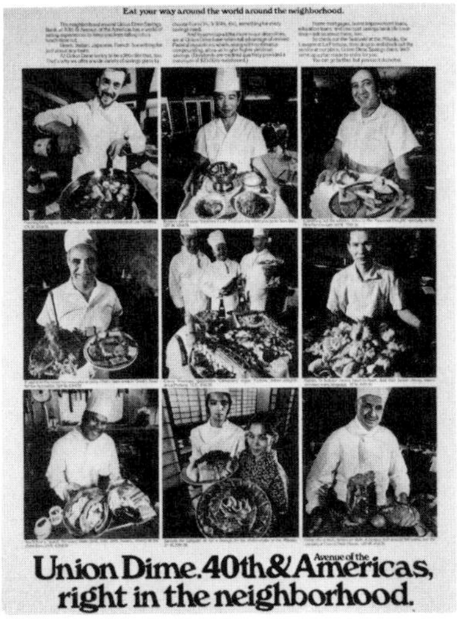
Union Dime. 40th&Avenue of the Americas, right in the neighborhood.

INTRODUCING THE CLIPPER.
A CONDOMINIUM SO UNBEATABLE,
WE PREDICT ITS 149 APARTMENTS
WILL BE COMPLETELY SOLD
BY MARCH 25, 1973.
STUDIO
1 BEDROOM
2 BEDROOM/2 BATH
THE CLIPPER. A HIGH-RISE CONDOMINIUM ON BISCAYNE BAY AT NORTHEAST 69TH STREET. IMMEDIATE OCCUPANCY. 754-5411.

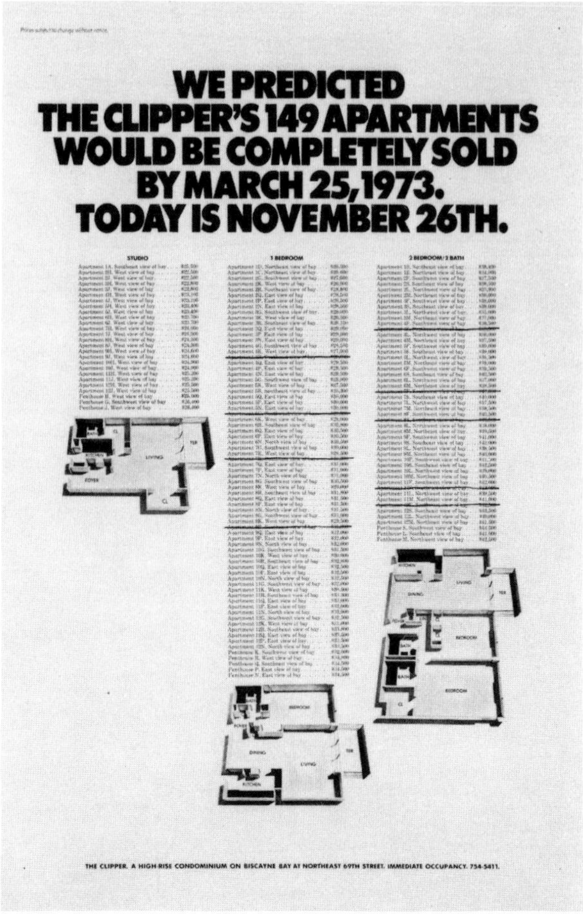
WE PREDICTED
THE CLIPPER'S 149 APARTMENTS
WOULD BE COMPLETELY SOLD
BY MARCH 25, 1973.
TODAY IS NOVEMBER 26TH.
STUDIO
1 BEDROOM
2 BEDROOM/2 BATH
THE CLIPPER. A HIGH-RISE CONDOMINIUM ON BISCAYNE BAY AT NORTHEAST 69TH STREET. IMMEDIATE OCCUPANCY. 754-5411.

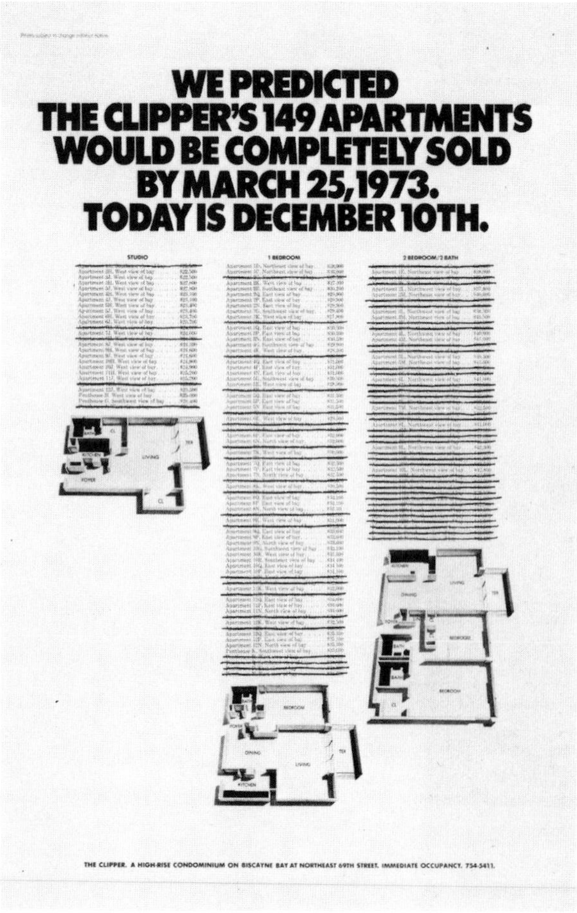
WE PREDICTED
THE CLIPPER'S 149 APARTMENTS
WOULD BE COMPLETELY SOLD
BY MARCH 25, 1973.
TODAY IS DECEMBER 10TH.
STUDIO
1 BEDROOM
2 BEDROOM/2 BATH
THE CLIPPER. A HIGH-RISE CONDOMINIUM ON BISCAYNE BAY AT NORTHEAST 69TH STREET. IMMEDIATE OCCUPANCY. 754-5411.

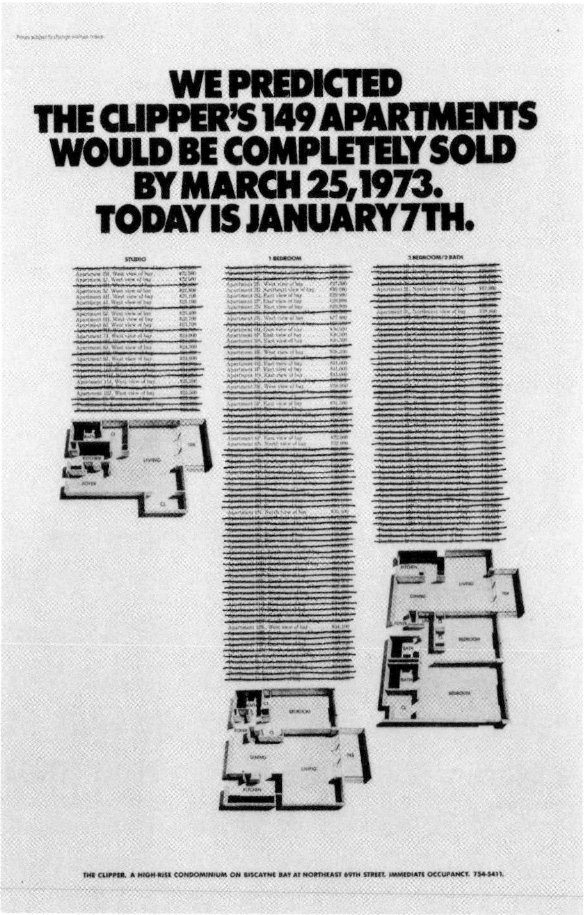
WE PREDICTED
THE CLIPPER'S 149 APARTMENTS
WOULD BE COMPLETELY SOLD
BY MARCH 25, 1973.
TODAY IS JANUARY 7TH.
STUDIO
1 BEDROOM
2 BEDROOM/2 BATH
THE CLIPPER. A HIGH-RISE CONDOMINIUM ON BISCAYNE BAY AT NORTHEAST 69TH STREET. IMMEDIATE OCCUPANCY. 754-5411.

22

House of ill repute?
The Houses of Congress are in ill repute these days—and they don't deserve it.
The general view holds that they're full of small, pliant men...outdated and inefficient...unresponsive to the popular will...subservient to the President.
Unfair and untrue, says the January Fortune. The quality of individual Senators and Representatives is higher today than at any time in our history. But with American life getting more complex and diverse, we need a much stronger "people's branch" of government.
So Fortune Magazine, in the first of two major stories on Congress, puts forward a set of hard, specific proposals for making it what it should be. This program is going to stir heated debate in Washington and everyplace else where decisions are made.
Helping decision-makers is what Fortune is all about. Take the 18-month economic forecast in this month's issue. We see real G.N.P. growing at least as fast in 1973 as in 1972—*without increased inflation.* (Pay attention, because Fortune's forecasts are consistently the most accurate in business publishing.)
Take a story like *"Du Pont 'Gave Away' Billions—and Prospered."* While consumer prices were going up 41 percent, Du Pont's prices were coming down 24 percent. It's a classic example of how to serve the public best by doing your own job well.
"How A & P Got Creamed." Here are the how and why and when-will-it-ever-end in the bloodiest price war in food store history.
"The Underwriters Have to Offer Even More" tells all about the new competition in underwriting and why investment bankers are going to have to run even faster to stay in place.
And so it goes as the New Fortune enters the New Year. There's controversy here. And strong stands on vital issues. And a view of the future you'll find nowhere else.
As reader or advertiser, you're going to profit from Fortune in 1973. Because a lot of the forward-thinking starts right here...
ONLY IN FORTUNE

21
Art Director: Lou Masciovecchio
Copywriter: Burt Klein
Designer: Lou Masciovecchio
Artist: Bob Gelberg
Agency: Bogorad, Klein, Schulwolf, Masciovecchio, Inc.
Client: Transcontinental Realty Corporation

22
Art Director: Bob Czernysz
Copywriter: Richard Olmstead
Designer: Bob Czernysz
Photographers: Cailor/Resnick
Peter Papadopolous
Black Star
DeWayne Dalrymple
Louis Kraar
Agency: Young & Rubicam International, Inc.
Client: Fortune

New York, where they milk the horses.
ONLY IN FORTUNE

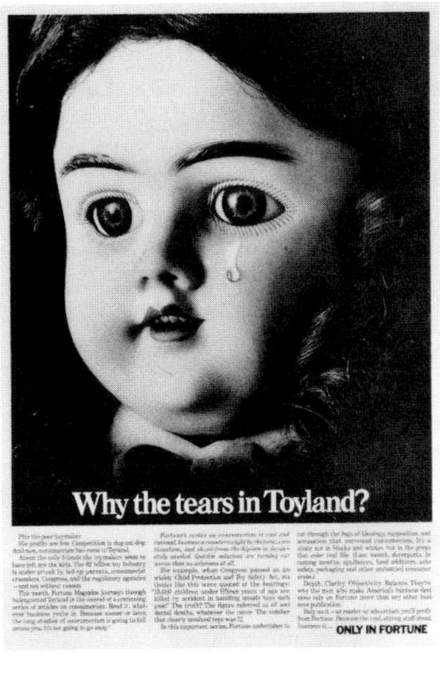
Why the tears in Toyland?
ONLY IN FORTUNE

Newspaper/Campaign

23

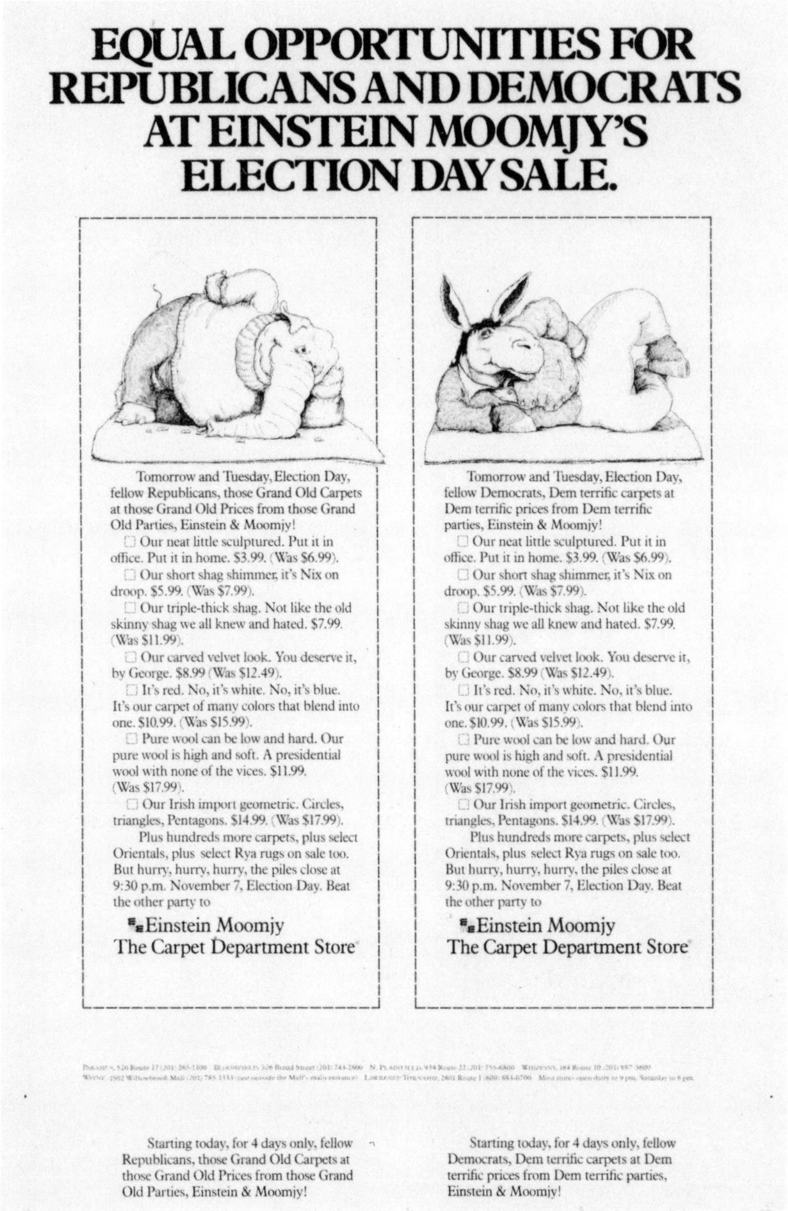

EQUAL OPPORTUNITIES FOR REPUBLICANS AND DEMOCRATS AT EINSTEIN MOOMJY'S ELECTION DAY SALE.
Tomorrow and Tuesday, Election Day, fellow Republicans, those Grand Old Carpets at those Grand Old Prices from those Grand Old Parties, Einstein & Moomjy!
☐ Our neat little sculptured. Put it in office. Put it in home. $3.99. (Was $6.99).
☐ Our short shag shimmer, it's Nix on droop. $5.99. (Was $7.99).
☐ Our triple-thick shag. Not like the old skinny shag we all knew and hated. $7.99. (Was $11.99).
☐ Our carved velvet look. You deserve it, by George. $8.99 (Was $12.49).
☐ It's red. No, it's white. No, it's blue. It's our carpet of many colors that blend into one. $10.99. (Was $15.99).
☐ Pure wool can be low and hard. Our pure wool is high and soft. A presidential wool with none of the vices. $11.99. (Was $17.99).
☐ Our Irish import geometric. Circles, triangles, Pentagons. $14.99. (Was $17.99).
Plus hundreds more carpets, plus select Orientals, plus select Rya rugs on sale too. But hurry, hurry, hurry, the piles close at 9:30 p.m. November 7, Election Day. Beat the other party to
Einstein Moomjy
The Carpet Department Store
Tomorrow and Tuesday, Election Day, fellow Democrats, Dem terrific carpets at Dem terrific prices from Dem terrific parties, Einstein & Moomjy!
☐ Our neat little sculptured. Put it in office. Put it in home. $3.99. (Was $6.99).
☐ Our short shag shimmer, it's Nix on droop. $5.99. (Was $7.99).
☐ Our triple-thick shag. Not like the old skinny shag we all knew and hated. $7.99. (Was $11.99).
☐ Our carved velvet look. You deserve it, by George. $8.99 (Was $12.49).
☐ It's red. No, it's white. No, it's blue. It's our carpet of many colors that blend into one. $10.99. (Was $15.99).
☐ Pure wool can be low and hard. Our pure wool is high and soft. A presidential wool with none of the vices. $11.99. (Was $17.99).
☐ Our Irish import geometric. Circles, triangles, Pentagons. $14.99. (Was $17.99).
Plus hundreds more carpets, plus select Orientals, plus select Rya rugs on sale too. But hurry, hurry, hurry, the piles close at 9:30 p.m. November 7, Election Day. Beat the other party to
Einstein Moomjy
The Carpet Department Store
Starting today, for 4 days only, fellow Republicans, those Grand Old Carpets at those Grand Old Prices from those Grand Old Parties, Einstein & Moomjy!
Starting today, for 4 days only, fellow Democrats, Dem terrific carpets at Dem terrific prices from Dem terrific parties, Einstein & Moomjy!

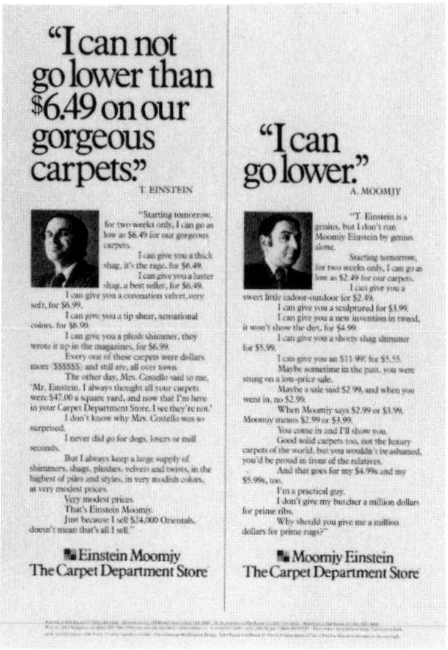

"I can not go lower than $6.49 on our gorgeous carpets."
T. EINSTEIN
"Starting tomorrow, for two weeks only, I can go as low as $6.49 for our gorgeous carpets.
I can give you a thick shag, it's the rage, for $6.49.
I can give you a luster shag, a best seller, for $6.49.
I can give you a coronation velvet, very soft, for $6.99.
I can give you a tip shear, sensational colors, for $6.99.
I can give you a plush shimmer, they wrote it up in the magazines, for $6.99.
Every one of these carpets were dollars more ($$$$$$) and still are, all over town.
The other day, Mrs. Costello said to me, 'Mr. Einstein, I always thought all your carpets were $47.00 a square yard, and now that I'm here in your Carpet Department Store, I see they're not.'
I don't know why Mrs. Costello was so surprised.
I never did go for dogs, losers or mill seconds.
But I always keep a large supply of shimmers, shags, plushes, velvets and twists, in the highest of piles and styles, in very modish colors, at very modest prices.
Very modest prices.
That's Einstein Moomjy.
Just because I sell $24,000 Orientals, doesn't mean that's all I sell."
Einstein Moomjy
The Carpet Department Store
"I can go lower."
A. MOOMJY
"T. Einstein is a genius, but I don't run Moomjy Einstein by genius alone.
Starting tomorrow, for two weeks only, I can go as low as $2.49 for our carpets.
I can give you a sweet little indoor-outdoor for $2.49.
I can give you a sculptured for $3.99.
I can give you a new invention in tweed, it won't show the dirt, for $4.99.
I can give you a shorty shag shimmer for $5.99.
I can give you an $11.99! for $5.55.
Maybe sometime in the past, you were stung on a low-price sale.
Maybe a sale said $2.99, and when you went in, no $2.99.
When Moomjy says $2.99 or $3.99, Moomjy means $2.99 or $3.99.
You come in and I'll show you.
Good solid carpets too, not the luxury carpets of the world, but you wouldn't be ashamed, you'd be proud in front of the relatives.
And that goes for my $4.99s and my $5.99s, too.
I'm a practical guy.
I don't give my butcher a million dollars for prime ribs.
Why should you give me a million dollars for prime rugs?"
Moomjy Einstein
The Carpet Department Store

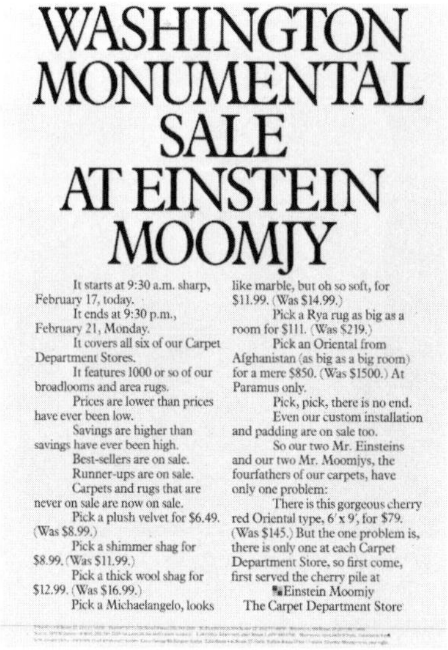

WASHINGTON MONUMENTAL SALE AT EINSTEIN MOOMJY
It starts at 9:30 a.m. sharp, February 17, today.
It ends at 9:30 p.m., February 21, Monday.
It covers all six of our Carpet Department Stores.
It features 1000 or so of our broadlooms and area rugs.
Prices are lower than prices have ever been low.
Savings are higher than savings have ever been high.
Best-sellers are on sale.
Runner-ups are on sale.
Carpets and rugs that are never on sale are now on sale.
Pick a plush velvet for $6.49. (Was $8.99.)
Pick a shimmer shag for $8.99. (Was $11.99.)
Pick a thick wool shag for $12.99. (Was $16.99.)
Pick a Michaelangelo, looks like marble, but oh so soft, for $11.99. (Was $14.99.)
Pick a Rya rug as big as a room for $111. (Was $219.)
Pick an Oriental from Afghanistan (as big as a big room) for a mere $850. (Was $1500.) At Paramus only.
Pick, pick, there is no end.
Even our custom installation and padding are on sale too.
So our two Mr. Einsteins and our two Mr. Moomjys, the fourfathers of our carpets, have only one problem:
There is this gorgeous cherry red Oriental type, 6' x 9', for $79. (Was $145.) But the one problem is, there is only one at each Carpet Department Store, so first come, first served the cherry pile at
Einstein Moomjy
The Carpet Department Store

23
Art Director: Harvey Baron
Copywriter: Carole Anne Fine
Agency: Rosenfeld, Sirowitz & Lawson
Client: Einstein Moomjy

24

"When I started turning gray, I turned white."
New Great Day Concentrate

More and more men with gray hair are combing the streets.
A/C EMPLOYMENT AGENCIES
PERMANENT
TEMPORARY
New Great Day Concentrate

24 Silver Award
Art Director: Paul Guliner
Copywriter: Hy Abady
Designer: Paul Guliner
Photographers: Joe Toto
Ken Duskin
Agency: Doyle Dane Bernbach Inc.
Client: Clairol Great Day Concentrate

What to do if your Prince Charming is snow white.
After all the time you spend trying to look younger than you are, your gray-haired husband is unintentionally telling people your age.
Causing all that vanity to be in vain.
Well, Clairol can once again help you look younger, and it isn't with a new lipstick, or a new conditioner, or a new eyeliner.
It's with a new hair coloring. For men. (Obviously, if your husband looks younger, you'll look younger.)
Great Day Concentrate penetrates inside the gray hair shaft and turns it dark again. Without changing colors (the way other men's hair coloring does) and looking just as natural as his hair was before he turned gray.
Wouldn't it be nice for you to look 5 or 10 years younger without even doing a thing to yourself? And wouldn't it be even nicer for your husband to look 5 or 10 years younger at the office?
By shampooing Great Day Concentrate in, he (and you) can control how much younger you (and he) would like to look.
He can get rid of just a little gray, half of the gray, leave a little gray at the temples, or go completely dark again by shampooing it in regularly once a week.
And then, someday, your prince will come back.
SPECIAL OFFER:
For a $2.50 tube of New Great Day Concentrate, send 50¢ to Great Day, Box 1015E, Yonkers, New York 10701
Name
Address
City
State Zip
New Great Day Concentrate

To the 56,000,000 people who smoke cigarettes.
A lot of people have been telling you not to smoke, especially cigarettes with high 'tar' and nicotine. But smoking provides you with a pleasure you don't want to give up.
Naturally, we're prejudiced. We're in the business of selling cigarettes.
But there is one overriding fact that transcends whether you should or shouldn't smoke and that fact is that you do smoke.
And what are they going to do about that?
They can continue to exhort you not to smoke. Or they might look reality in the face and recommend that, if you smoke and want low 'tar' and nicotine in a cigarette, you smoke a cigarette like Vantage.
And we'll go along with that, because there is no other cigarette like Vantage. Except Vantage.
Vantage has a unique filter that allows rich flavor to come through it and yet substantially cuts down on 'tar' and nicotine. It has only 12 milligrams 'tar' and 0.8 milligrams nicotine.
It is not a heavy drag cigarette. You don't have to work so hard pulling the smoke through it that all the joy of smoking is lost.
Not that Vantage is the lowest 'tar' and nicotine cigarette. (But you probably wouldn't like the lowest 'tar' and nicotine cigarette anyway.)
The plain truth is that smoke has to come through a filter if taste is to come through a filter. And where there is taste there has to be some 'tar.'
But Vantage is the only cigarette that gives you so much flavor with so little 'tar' and nicotine.
So much flavor that you'll never miss your high 'tar' cigarette.
VANTAGE
VANTAGE
VANTAGE

If you smoke.
We're not telling you anything you don't know when we acknowledge that a controversy about smoking exists.
And since we're in the business of selling cigarettes, you obviously know where we stand.
So if you don't smoke, we're not about to persuade you to start.
But if you do, we'd like to persuade you to try a cigarette you may wish to smoke more than the one you're smoking now.
We mean Vantage, of course.
Vantage gives you flavor like a full-flavor cigarette. Without anywhere near the 'tar' and nicotine.
That's a simple statement of truth.
We don't want you to misunderstand us. Vantage is not the lowest 'tar' and nicotine cigarette you can buy.
It's simply the lowest 'tar' and nicotine cigarette you'll enjoy smoking.
We just don't see the point in putting out a low 'tar' and nicotine cigarette you have to work so hard getting some taste out of, you won't smoke it.
If you agree with us, we think you'll enjoy Vantage.
VANTAGE MENTHOL
VANTAGE MENTHOL
MENTHOL 11 mg. 'tar' 0.8 mg. nicotine
VANTAGE
VANTAGE
FILTER 12 mg. 'tar' 0.9 mg. nicotine
Warning: The Surgeon General Has Determined That Cigarette Smoking Is Dangerous to Your Health.
Filter: 12 mg. "tar", 0.9 mg. nicotine, Menthol: 11 mg. "tar", 0.8 mg. nicotine—av. per cigarette, FTC Report Apr. '77.

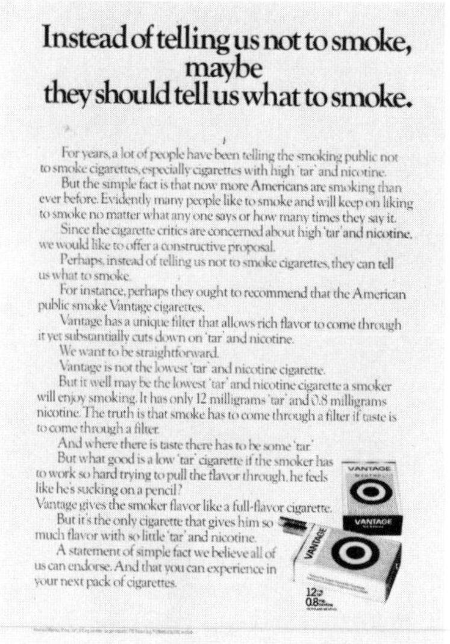
Instead of telling us not to smoke, maybe they should tell us what to smoke.
For years, a lot of people have been telling the smoking public not to smoke cigarettes, especially cigarettes with high 'tar' and nicotine.
But the simple fact is that now more Americans are smoking than ever before. Evidently many people like to smoke and will keep on liking to smoke no matter what any one says or how many times they say it.
Since the cigarette critics are concerned about high 'tar' and nicotine, we would like to offer a constructive proposal.
Perhaps, instead of telling us not to smoke cigarettes, they can tell us what to smoke.
For instance, perhaps they ought to recommend that the American public smoke Vantage cigarettes.
Vantage has a unique filter that allows rich flavor to come through it yet substantially cuts down on 'tar' and nicotine.
We want to be straightforward.
Vantage is not the lowest 'tar' and nicotine cigarette.
But it well may be the lowest 'tar' and nicotine cigarette a smoker will enjoy smoking. It has only 12 milligrams 'tar' and 0.8 milligrams nicotine. The truth is that smoke has to come through a filter if taste is to come through a filter.
And where there is taste there has to be some 'tar.'
But what good is a low 'tar' cigarette if the smoker has to work so hard trying to pull the flavor through, he feels like he's sucking on a pencil?
Vantage gives the smoker flavor like a full-flavor cigarette.
But it's the only cigarette that gives him so much flavor with so little 'tar' and nicotine.
A statement of simple fact we believe all of us can endorse. And that you can experience in your next pack of cigarettes.
VANTAGE
VANTAGE
VANTAGE

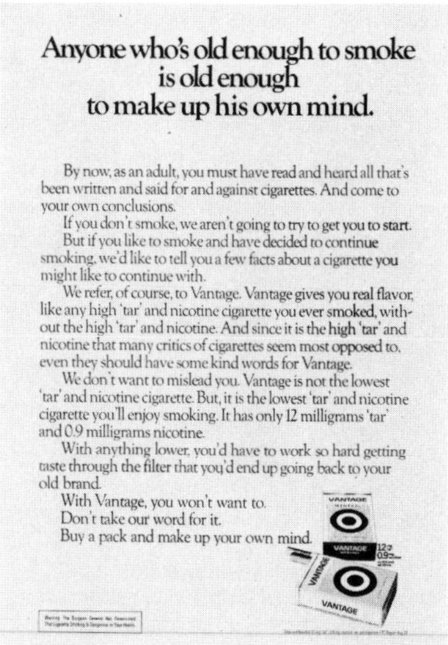
Anyone who's old enough to smoke is old enough to make up his own mind.
By now, as an adult, you must have read and heard all that's been written and said for and against cigarettes. And come to your own conclusions.
If you don't smoke, we aren't going to try to get you to start.
But if you like to smoke and have decided to continue smoking, we'd like to tell you a few facts about a cigarette you might like to continue with.
We refer, of course, to Vantage. Vantage gives you real flavor, like any high 'tar' and nicotine cigarette you ever smoked, without the high 'tar' and nicotine. And since it is the high 'tar' and nicotine that many critics of cigarettes seem most opposed to, even they should have some kind words for Vantage.
We don't want to mislead you. Vantage is not the lowest 'tar' and nicotine cigarette. But, it is the lowest 'tar' and nicotine cigarette you'll enjoy smoking. It has only 12 milligrams 'tar' and 0.9 milligrams nicotine.
With anything lower, you'd have to work so hard getting taste through the filter that you'd end up going back to your old brand.
With Vantage, you won't want to.
Don't take our word for it.
Buy a pack and make up your own mind.
VANTAGE
VANTAGE
VANTAGE

26
Art Director: Joseph Cipolla
Copywriter: George Adels
Concept: George Adels
Joseph Cipolla
Bob Wilvers
Jack Silverman
Designer: Joseph Cipolla
Agency: Leber Katz Partners
Client: R. J. Reynolds

27
Art Director: Don Ozyp
Copywriter: Denny Oakerbloom
Designer: Mabey Trousdell
Artist: Mabey Trousdell
Agency: The Marschalk Company
Client: The Illuminating Company

OVEN CLEANER!
Look what you're missing with a flameless electric self-cleaning oven.
The ILLUMINATING Company

GeeWillikers
Most people save about $30 when they buy a flameless electric dryer.

27

How clean it is with a flameless electric range.

28

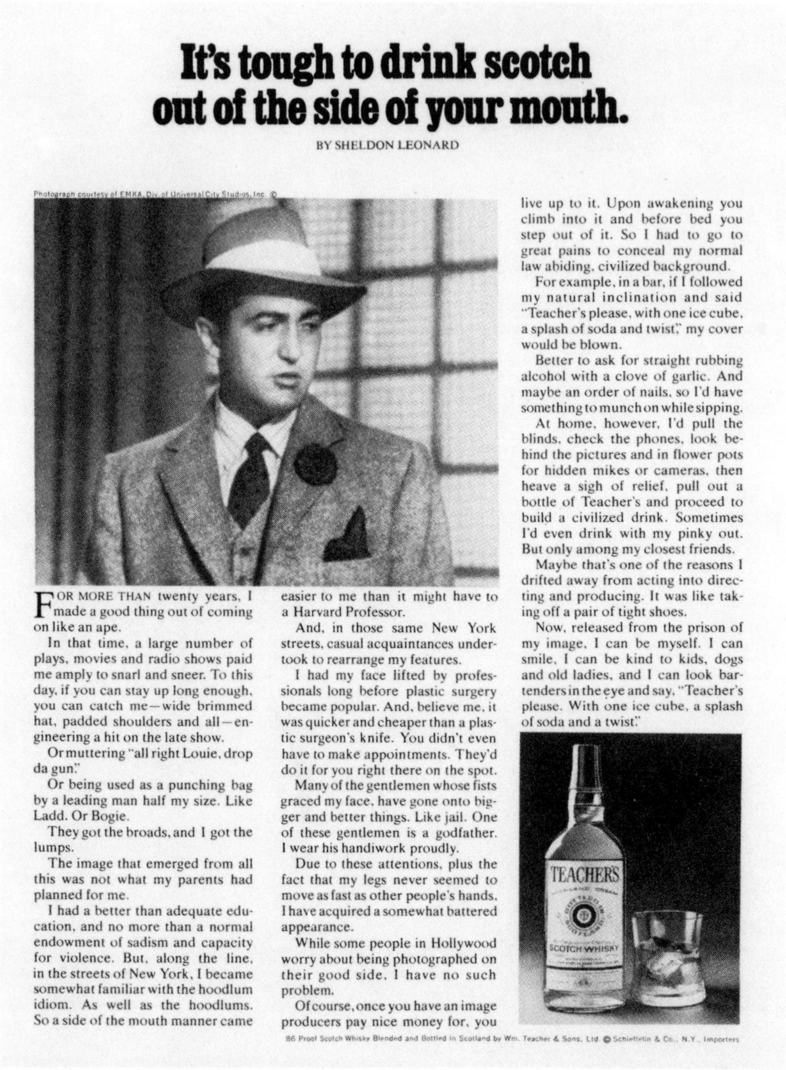

It's tough to drink scotch out of the side of your mouth.
BY SHELDON LEONARD
Photograph courtesy of EMKA, Div. of Universal City Studios, Inc. ©
FOR MORE THAN twenty years, I made a good thing out of coming on like an ape.
In that time, a large number of plays, movies and radio shows paid me amply to snarl and sneer. To this day, if you can stay up long enough, you can catch me—wide brimmed hat, padded shoulders and all—engineering a hit on the late show.
Or muttering "all right Louie, drop da gun."
Or being used as a punching bag by a leading man half my size. Like Ladd. Or Bogie.
They got the broads, and I got the lumps.
The image that emerged from all this was not what my parents had planned for me.
I had a better than adequate education, and no more than a normal endowment of sadism and capacity for violence. But, along the line, in the streets of New York, I became somewhat familiar with the hoodlum idiom. As well as the hoodlums. So a side of the mouth manner came easier to me than it might have to a Harvard Professor.
And, in those same New York streets, casual acquaintances undertook to rearrange my features.
I had my face lifted by professionals long before plastic surgery became popular. And, believe me, it was quicker and cheaper than a plastic surgeon's knife. You didn't even have to make appointments. They'd do it for you right there on the spot.
Many of the gentlemen whose fists graced my face, have gone onto bigger and better things. Like jail. One of these gentlemen is a godfather. I wear his handiwork proudly.
Due to these attentions, plus the fact that my legs never seemed to move as fast as other people's hands, I have acquired a somewhat battered appearance.
While some people in Hollywood worry about being photographed on their good side, I have no such problem.
Of course, once you have an image producers pay nice money for, you live up to it. Upon awakening you climb into it and before bed you step out of it. So I had to go to great pains to conceal my normal law abiding, civilized background.
For example, in a bar, if I followed my natural inclination and said "Teacher's please, with one ice cube, a splash of soda and twist," my cover would be blown.
Better to ask for straight rubbing alcohol with a clove of garlic. And maybe an order of nails, so I'd have something to munch on while sipping.
At home, however, I'd pull the blinds, check the phones, look behind the pictures and in flower pots for hidden mikes or cameras, then heave a sigh of relief, pull out a bottle of Teacher's and proceed to build a civilized drink. Sometimes I'd even drink with my pinky out. But only among my closest friends.
Maybe that's one of the reasons I drifted away from acting into directing and producing. It was like taking off a pair of tight shoes.
Now, released from the prison of my image, I can be myself. I can smile, I can be kind to kids, dogs and old ladies, and I can look bartenders in the eye and say, "Teacher's please. With one ice cube, a splash of soda and a twist."
TEACHER'S
SCOTCH WHISKY
86 Proof Scotch Whisky Blended and Bottled in Scotland by Wm. Teacher & Sons, Ltd. © Schieffelin & Co., N.Y., Importers

28 Gold Award
Art Directors: Nick Gisonde
Bob Kuperman
Copywriters: Neil Drossman
Jerry Della Femina
Designers: Nick Gisonde
Bob Kuperman
Photographers: Arnold Beckerman
Anthony Edgeworth
Agency: Della Femina, Travisano & Partners, Inc.
Client: Teacher's Scotch

29
Art Director: George Lois
Copywriter: Rudy Fiala
Designers: Dennis Mazzella
Tom Courtos
Photographer: Carl Fischer
Agency: Lois Holland Callaway Inc.
Client: Olivetti Corporation of America

I told the scotch people I don't drink any more. Then again, I don't drink any less, either.
BY REDD FOXX

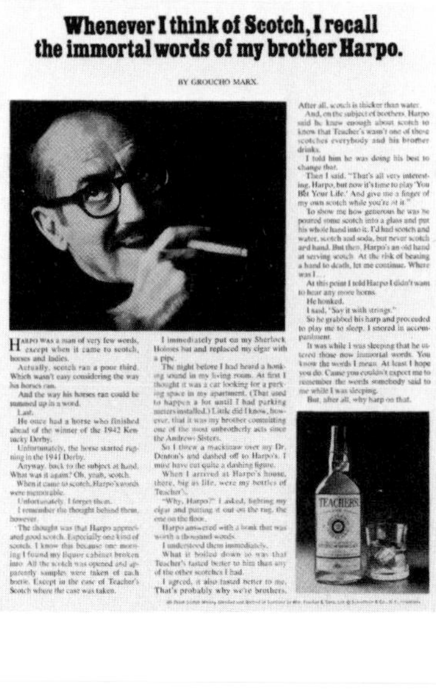

Whenever I think of Scotch, I recall the immortal words of my brother Harpo.
BY GROUCHO MARX

First the agency people told me I could say anything I wanted to about scotch. Then they censored me.
BY TOMMY SMOTHERS

Join the Olivetti girls.
Hey!
If you work
in an office
and type on an
electric typewriter,
join us.
Be an Olivetti girl!
To qualify, all you have to do is
talk your boss into getting you an
Olivetti typewriter.
That's asking a lot, we know.
But whatever you have to go through to make the
change will be worth it. Because this is the typewriter
with the brain inside that makes the four most common
typing mistakes absolutely impossible. No flying caps!
No improper spacing! No shading or ghosting! No crowding or piling!
It takes the "oooops" out of typing. So you can type faster, neater, sharper.
And have more fun. Let's face it, you just can't beat those Olivetti girls!
So why not join 'em?
olivetti
The Beautiful Dream Machines

Who is the Olivetti girl?
And why are people saying
such terribly nice things
about her.
The Olivetti girl is a secretary/typist who's been attracting
lots of attention lately for her amazing performance on the typewriter.
Because no matter how fast she types she rarely makes a mistake!
Now, she may be prettier than other typists,
but she's not necessarily any brainier.
Then what makes an Olivetti girl such a phenomenal typist?
Her brainy Olivetti Electric Typewriter, of course!
This typewriter can actually think for itself. Because it has a brain inside
that makes the four most common typing mistakes absolutely
impossible. No flying caps!
No improper spacing!
No shading or ghosting!
No crowding or piling!
That's why an Olivetti girl can really belt it out.
And is sharper, looser, never uptight.
That's why an Olivetti girl has more fun.
And that is why people are saying such terribly
nice things about her.
olivetti
The American Dream Machines

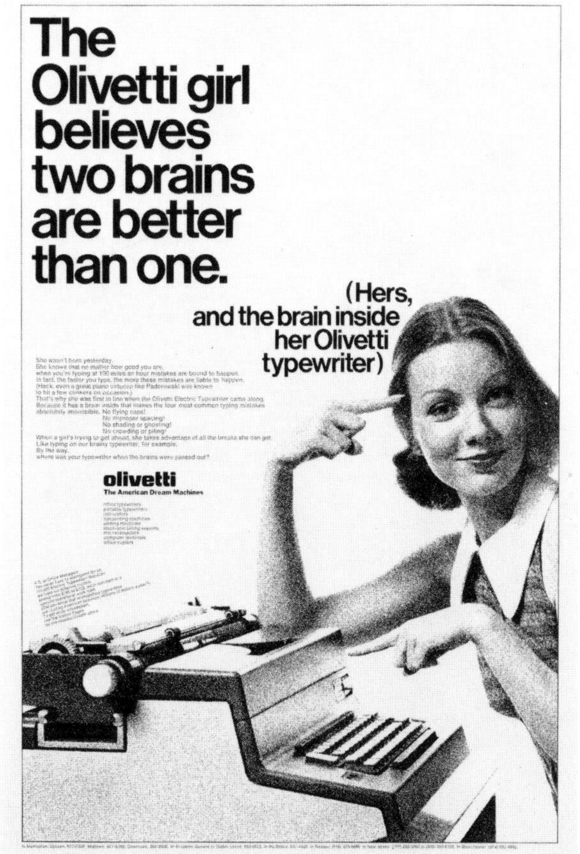

The
Olivetti girl
believes
two brains
are better
than one.
(Hers,
and the brain inside
her Olivetti
typewriter)
olivetti
The American Dream Machines

"It's more important,"
said our fastidious Mabel Wheeler,
"that our pie filling have more blueberry
than more blueberries."
Comstock Blueberry Pie Filling has more fruit per ounce than the next two leading brands. 5% more than Brand II. And 24% more than Brand III.*
That's because years ago Mabel asked us if we wanted to make a pie filling with more blueberries or more blueberry.
At first, we thought she was playing games with us. But she wasn't.
"Let me tell you all about blueberries. There are two kinds the lowbush and the highbush."
And then Mabel told us that the lowbush blueberry was puny and full of seeds. And that if we used them in our pie filling we would have to use more.
But she went on to say that the highbush berry was bigger, juicier with smaller seeds. And that they would give our pie filling more blueberry.
Well, ever since that day, we've been making our blueberry pie filling only with the highbush blueberry.
So please try our pie filling, we think you'll like it.
Try it in Mabel's recipe for blueberry pie on our label. It's the very same recipe that stopped Mr. Wheeler from beating around the bush and to settling down.
Or in any of the other ways, Mabel has used over the years to keep the bloom in Mr. W's eye:
1. Stir into pancake batter, add a little orange juice and make blueberry pancakes.
2. Bake with cottage cheese and noodles to make a noodle pudding.
3. Mix with cranberry sauce and lemon rind and serve with duck or goose.
4. Spoon into omelets, roll up and sprinkle with confectionery sugar.
5. Mix with sour cream and a little brown sugar to make blue pudding.
6. Serve with melon balls, nectarine slices and cottage cheese for a summery salad.
7. Roll in dough like a jelly roll, cut in slices, sprinkle with nuts and bake.
Now this is where we need your help. The only way we can get Mabel to share her recipes is by promising her some of yours. So please send your favorite recipe for blueberry pie filling to Comstock, Box 267, Newark, New York 14513.
A long time ago, Mabel convinced us that success isn't always a question of quantity, but quality.
It's still true today.
10¢ Off
Any can of Comstock's Pie Filling.
10¢ Off
Comstock
blueberry
PIE FILLING
BORDEN
Comstock. The pie filling made by persnickety old ladies.

Harriet Foster said they never get bruised if you pit them with a new hairpin.
It took us a long time to convince her there are other ways.
Harriet Foster is our cherry lady here at Comstock. We're not exactly sure how old she is. But we know she's over 21 because she grew up pitting cherries with a new hairpin. And when we tried to move in our cherry-pitting machine, she said until we could prove to her it was as gentle as a hairpin, it would be over her dead body.
We tried five machines until we found one that passed inspection.
Harriet, you see, really knows her cherries. She knows that even one single bruised cherry will make a less than perfect pie. She knows that the Montmorency variety is the best pie-cherry because they're tart and thin-skinned. That they peak between July 15 and August 15. And that they're perfectly ripe when they're plump, shiny, firm and juicy.
Of course, nobody would believe us if we said Comstock was run by a bunch of little old ladies. But the truth is, they know more about pie fillings than anybody else. So out front, we have a lot of serious types in expensive suits shuffling papers. And out back where the real work is done, are Harriet and her cronies packing plenty of cherries into every can. (Nothing's worse in her eyes than a cherry pie with more goo than cherries.)
Harriet's recipe for plain old-fashioned cherry pie is on the label. And here are a few more of her secrets for what to do with our pie fillings:
1. Pour it over an angel food cake filled with vanilla pudding.
2. Mix it with sliced apples and stuff a chicken.
3. Add hot brandy and serve flaming over vanilla ice cream.
4. Make an upside-down cake.
5. Baste a duck with it. Or pork chops. Or a ham.
6. Serve over pancakes and waffles.
7. Thin it with sour cream and a little sherry; chill and serve as a cold soup.
The only way we could weasel these ideas out of Harriet was to promise her some new ones in exchange. So please clip this coupon and try our cherry pie filling. See if you can come up with some ideas of your own. Then to keep Harriet happy, mail your recipe for cherry pie filling to Comstock Cherry Pie Filling, Box 267, Newark, N.Y. We'll gather them all together in a recipe booklet (giving credit where it's due) and send you a copy.
Now if you're getting a little weary of all this cherry pie talk, we also make other pie fillings including blueberry, peach and apple. They're not in Harriet's department, but they each have their own persnickety old lady running the show. And by the way, these ladies sell more pie fillings than anybody else.
We're very grateful to them. Particularly to Harriet. Who still keeps a new hairpin in her apron pocket. Just in case the cherry-pitting machine breaks down.
10¢
10¢ off any can of Comstock Pie Filling
cherry
PIE FILLING
10¢
10¢
BORDEN
Comstock. The pie filling made by persnickety old ladies.

30

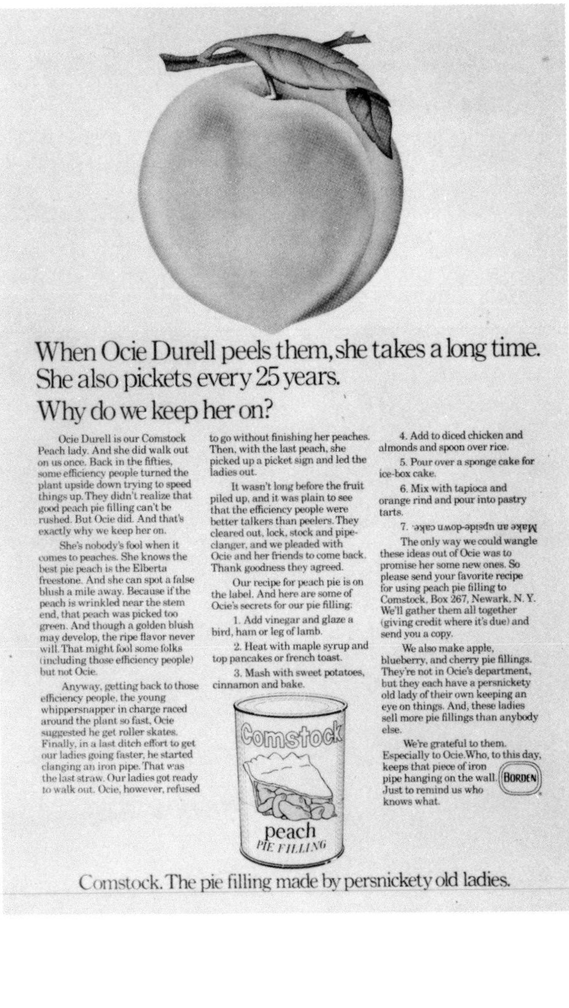
When Ocie Durell peels them, she takes a long time.
She also pickets every 25 years.
Why do we keep her on?
Ocie Durell is our Comstock Peach lady. And she did walk out on us once. Back in the fifties, some efficiency people turned the plant upside down trying to speed things up. They didn't realize that good peach pie filling can't be rushed. But Ocie did. And that's exactly why we keep her on.
She's nobody's fool when it comes to peaches. She knows the best pie peach is the Elberta freestone. And she can spot a false blush a mile away. Because if the peach is wrinkled near the stem end, that peach was picked too green. And though a golden blush may develop, the ripe flavor never will. That might fool some folks (including those efficiency people) but not Ocie.
Anyway, getting back to those efficiency people, the young whippersnapper in charge raced around the plant so fast, Ocie suggested he get roller skates. Finally, in a last ditch effort to get our ladies going faster, he started clanging an iron pipe. That was the last straw. Our ladies got ready to walk out. Ocie, however, refused to go without finishing her peaches. Then, with the last peach, she picked up a picket sign and led the ladies out.
It wasn't long before the fruit piled up, and it was plain to see that the efficiency people were better talkers than peelers. They cleared out, lock, stock and pipe-clanger, and we pleaded with Ocie and her friends to come back. Thank goodness they agreed.
Our recipe for peach pie is on the label. And here are some of Ocie's secrets for our pie filling:
1. Add vinegar and glaze a bird, ham or leg of lamb.
2. Heat with maple syrup and top pancakes or french toast.
3. Mash with sweet potatoes, cinnamon and bake.
4. Add to diced chicken and almonds and spoon over rice.
5. Pour over a sponge cake for ice-box cake.
6. Mix with tapioca and orange rind and pour into pastry tarts.
7. Make an upside-down cake.
The only way we could wangle these ideas out of Ocie was to promise her some new ones. So please send your favorite recipe for using peach pie filling to Comstock, Box 267, Newark, N.Y. We'll gather them all together (giving credit where it's due) and send you a copy.
We also make apple, blueberry, and cherry pie fillings. They're not in Ocie's department, but they each have a persnickety old lady of their own keeping an eye on things. And, these ladies sell more pie fillings than anybody else.
We're grateful to them. Especially to Ocie. Who, to this day, keeps that piece of iron pipe hanging on the wall. Just to remind us who knows what.
BORDEN
Comstock
peach
PIE FILLING
Comstock. The pie filling made by persnickety old ladies.

A good landlord is hard to find.
Except when the rent is due.
It's time for a change
The key financial advantages
What you get for what you pay
Make your move
East Bluff Condominium
located at Northport Dr. & Sherman
Ave., just across from Warner Park
and Lake Mendota 244-4522

Newspaper/Campaign

30
Art Director: Gayle Gleckler
Copywriters: Patti Mullen
Geraldine Newman
Designer: Gayle Gleckler
Artist: Sagebrush Studio
Agency: Tinker, Dodge & Delano
Client: Borden Inc.

31
Art Directors: Pete Coutroulis
Tom Conrad
Copywriter: Howard Krakow
Designers: Pete Coutroulis
Tom Conrad
Artists: Charles White III
Robert Grossman
Janie Case
Christie Sheets
Agency: Jim Weller & Partners
Client: East Bluff Northridge Lakes

31

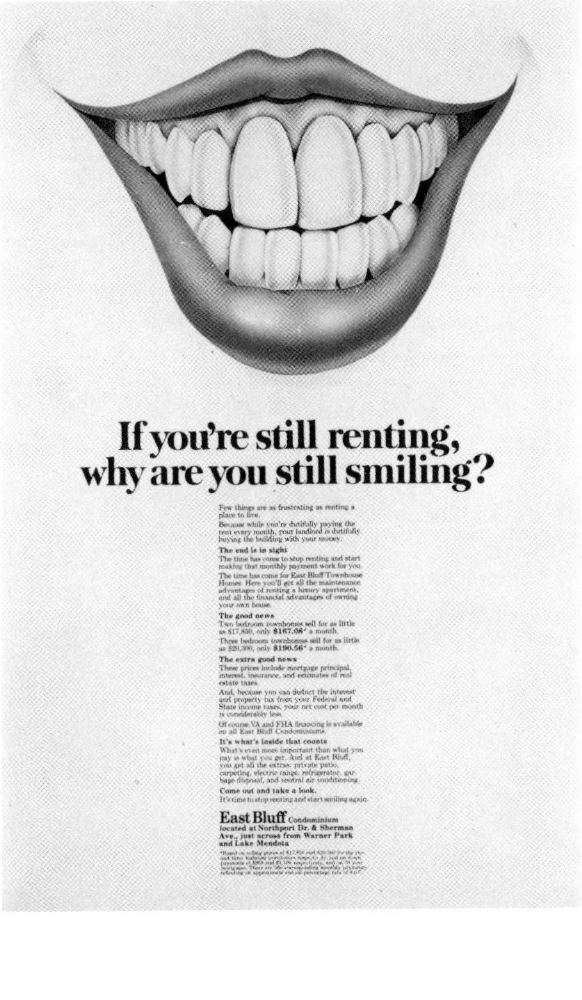
If you're still renting,
why are you still smiling?
Few things are as frustrating as renting a place to live.
Because while you're dutifully paying the rent every month, your landlord is dutifully buying the building with your money.
The end is in sight
The time has come to stop renting and start making that monthly payment work for you.
The time has come for East Bluff Townhouse Homes. Here you'll get all the maintenance advantages of renting a luxury apartment, and all the financial advantages of owning your own house.
The good news
Two bedroom townhomes sell for as little as $17,850, only $167.08* a month.
Three bedroom townhomes sell for as little as $20,300, only $190.56* a month.
The extra good news
These prices include mortgage principal, interest, insurance, and estimates of real estate taxes.
And, because you can deduct the interest and property tax from your Federal and State income taxes, your net cost per month is considerably less.
Of course, VA and FHA financing is available on all East Bluff Condominiums.
It's what's inside that counts
What's even more important than what you pay is what you get. And at East Bluff, you get all the extras: private patio, carpeting, electric range, refrigerator, garbage disposal, and central air conditioning.
Come out and take a look.
It's time to stop renting and start smiling again.
East Bluff Condominium
located at Northport Dr. & Sherman
Ave., just across from Warner Park
and Lake Mendota

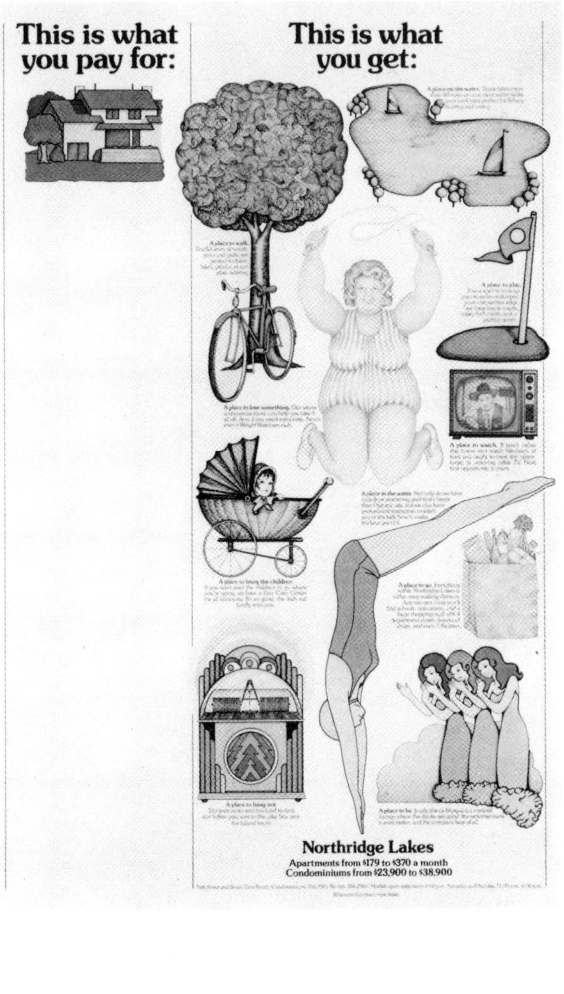
This is what
you pay for:
This is what
you get:
Northridge Lakes
Apartments from $179 to $370 a month
Condominiums from $23,900 to $38,900

Consumer Magazine/Single

32
Art Director: John Danza
Copywriter: Ed McCabe
Designer: John Danza
Photographer: Malcolm Kirk
Agency: Scali, McCabe, Sloves, Inc.
Client: Volvo, Inc.

33
Art Directors: David Deutsch
Rocco E. Campanelli
Copywriter: Bruce T. Barton
Designers: David Deutsch
Rocco E. Campanelli
Photographer: Ben Somoroff Studios
Agency: David Deutsch Associates, Inc.
Client: Oneida Ltd. Silversmiths

IN SWEDEN, YOU DRIVE A GOOD CAR. OR ELSE.
Cars in Sweden are subject to spot inspections at any time. It's part of a continuing campaign to rid the road of defective cars. Any car that fails is taken off the road.
Cars over one year old have to go through the annual automobile inspections as well. And it isn't easy. 200 components are thoroughly examined. If your car fails, you're either served with a summons ordering you to have it fixed. Fast. Or you're forbidden to drive it at all. It has to be towed away.
So when Swedes buy a new car, how well it will do in the inspections is one of their biggest concerns. And they can get a good idea of just how well that will be. Published reports give the results on all cars sold in Sweden.
Obviously, these reports can really hurt an automobile manufacturer if they're bad. Or really help him if they're good.
The largest selling car in Sweden is Volvo.
You see, when we build a Volvo, how well it will do in the inspections is one of our biggest concerns too.
Volvo.
We build them the way we build them because we have to.
VOLVO
W63803

32

33

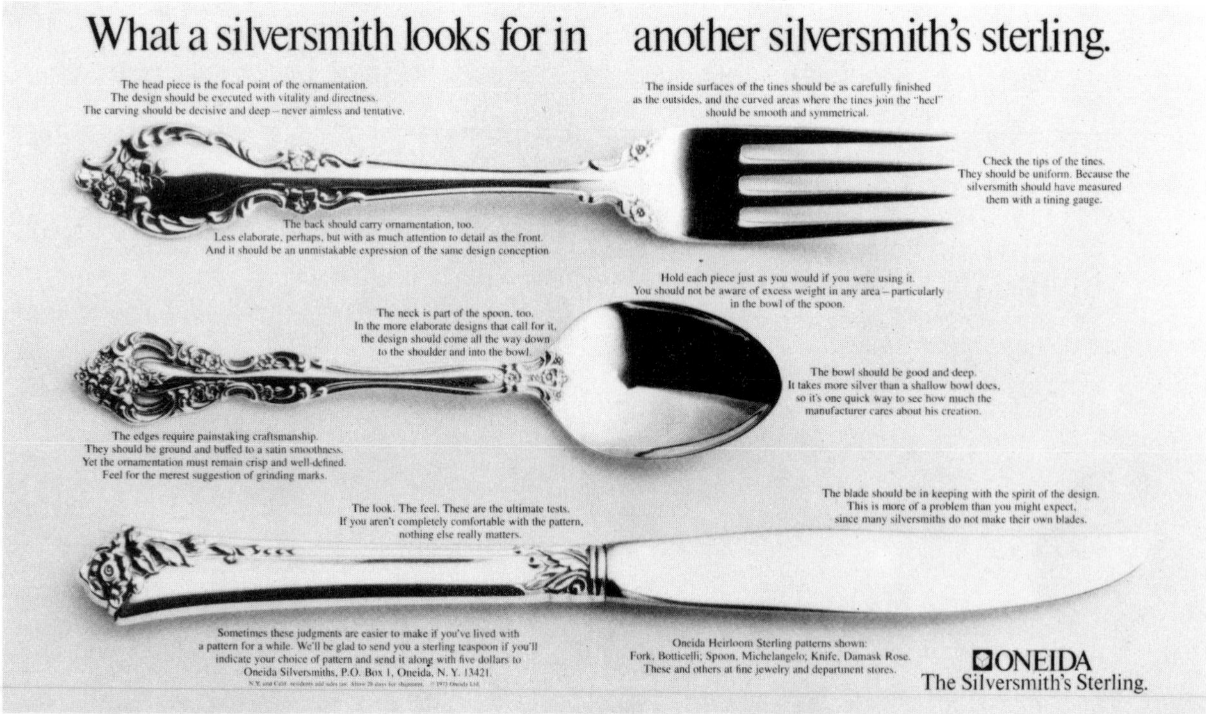
What a silversmith looks for in another silversmith's sterling.
The head piece is the focal point of the ornamentation. The design should be executed with vitality and directness. The carving should be decisive and deep—never aimless and tentative.
The inside surfaces of the tines should be as carefully finished as the outsides, and the curved areas where the tines join the "heel" should be smooth and symmetrical.
Check the tips of the tines. They should be uniform. Because the silversmith should have measured them with a tining gauge.
The back should carry ornamentation, too. Less elaborate, perhaps, but with as much attention to detail as the front. And it should be an unmistakable expression of the same design conception.
Hold each piece just as you would if you were using it. You should not be aware of excess weight in any area—particularly in the bowl of the spoon.
The neck is part of the spoon, too. In the more elaborate designs that call for it, the design should come all the way down to the shoulder and into the bowl.
The bowl should be good and deep. It takes more silver than a shallow bowl does, so it's one quick way to see how much the manufacturer cares about his creation.
The edges require painstaking craftsmanship. They should be ground and buffed to a satin smoothness. Yet the ornamentation must remain crisp and well-defined. Feel for the merest suggestion of grinding marks.
The look. The feel. These are the ultimate tests. If you aren't completely comfortable with the pattern, nothing else really matters.
The blade should be in keeping with the spirit of the design. This is more of a problem than you might expect, since many silversmiths do not make their own blades.
Sometimes these judgments are easier to make if you've lived with a pattern for a while. We'll be glad to send you a sterling teaspoon if you'll indicate your choice of pattern and send it along with five dollars to Oneida Silversmiths, P.O. Box 1, Oneida, N. Y. 13421.
Oneida Heirloom Sterling patterns shown: Fork, Botticelli; Spoon, Michelangelo; Knife, Damask Rose. These and others at fine jewelry and department stores.
ONEIDA
The Silversmith's Sterling.

IN EUROPE, WHERE THEY'VE BEEN BUYING SMALL CARS FOR THREE GENERATIONS, THEY BUY MORE FIATS THAN ANYTHING ELSE.
For every Volkswagen sold in Italy, 6 Fiats are sold in Germany.
For every Renault sold in Italy, 2 Fiats are sold in France.
For every Volvo sold in Italy, 9 Fiats are sold in Sweden.
All this becomes even more meaningful when you consider that, over there, they have fifty different kinds of cars to choose from.
And that their choice is based on sixty years of driving these various cars under conditions that run all the way from the sub-zero winters of Sweden to the Alpine roads of northern Italy to the traffic jams of Paris to the no speed limit driving of the German autobahn.
Now, if you've been trying to decide between the dozen or so small cars sold here in the States, the above facts should make your decision easier.
After all, when it comes to small cars, you can't fool a European.
FIAT
The biggest selling car in Europe.

34

35

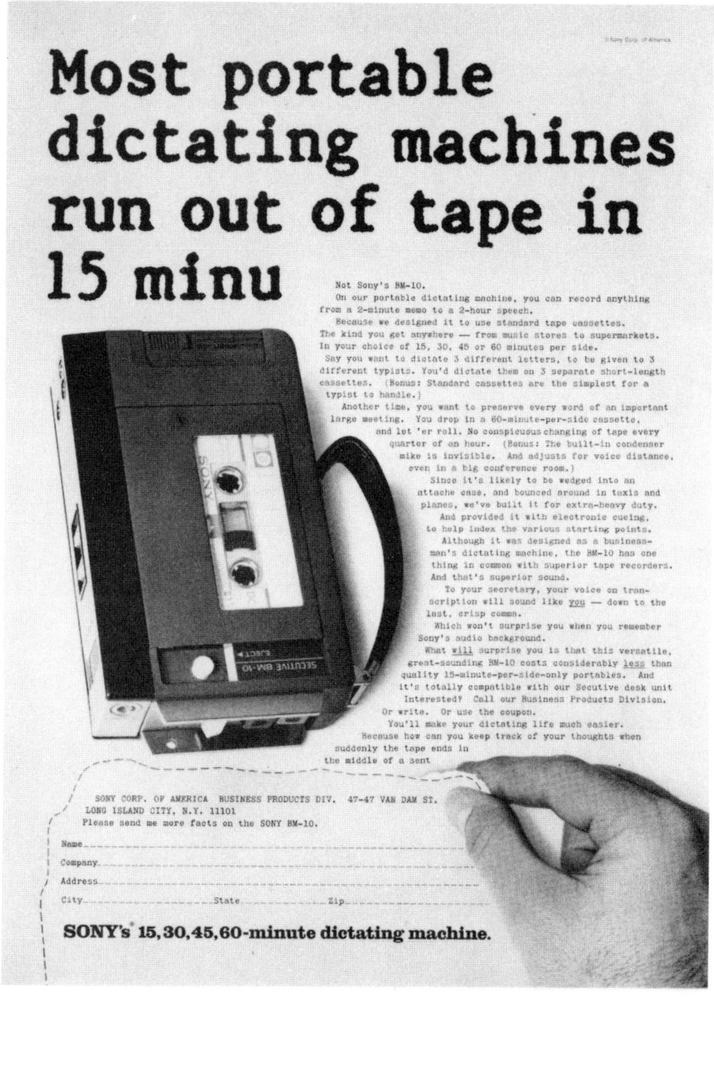
Most portable dictating machines run out of tape in 15 minu
Not Sony's BM-10.
On our portable dictating machine, you can record anything from a 2-minute memo to a 2-hour speech.
Because we designed it to use standard tape cassettes. The kind you get anywhere — from music stores to supermarkets. In your choice of 15, 30, 45 or 60 minutes per side.
Say you want to dictate 3 different letters, to be given to 3 different typists. You'd dictate them on 3 separate short-length cassettes. (Bonus: Standard cassettes are the simplest for a typist to handle.)
Another time, you want to preserve every word of an important large meeting. You drop in a 60-minute-per-side cassette, and let 'er roll. No conspicuous changing of tape every quarter of an hour. (Bonus: The built-in condenser mike is invisible. And adjusts for voice distance, even in a big conference room.)
Since it's likely to be wedged into an attache case, and bounced around in taxis and planes, we've built it for extra-heavy duty.
And provided it with electronic cueing, to help index the various starting points.
Although it was designed as a businessman's dictating machine, the BM-10 has one thing in common with superior tape recorders. And that's superior sound.
To your secretary, your voice on transcription will sound like you — down to the last, crisp comma.
Which won't surprise you when you remember Sony's audio background.
What will surprise you is that this versatile, great-sounding BM-10 costs considerably less than quality 15-minute-per-side-only portables. And it's totally compatible with our Secutive desk unit
Interested? Call our Business Products Division. Or write. Or use the coupon.
You'll make your dictating life much easier.
Because how can you keep track of your thoughts when suddenly the tape ends in the middle of a sent
SONY CORP. OF AMERICA BUSINESS PRODUCTS DIV. 47-47 VAN DAM ST. LONG ISLAND CITY, N.Y. 11101
Please send me more facts on the SONY BM-10.
Name
Company
Address
City State Zip
SONY's 15, 30, 45, 60-minute dictating machine.

34
Art Director: Ralph Ammirati
Copywriter: Marty Puris
Designer: Ralph Ammirati
Photographer: George Gomes
Agency: Carl Ally Inc.
Client: Fiat

35
Art Director: Reinhold Schwenk
Copywriter: Diane Rothschild Hyatt
Designer: Reinhold Schwenk
Photographer: Steve Nichols
Agency: Doyle Dane Bernbach Inc.
Client: Sony Corporation

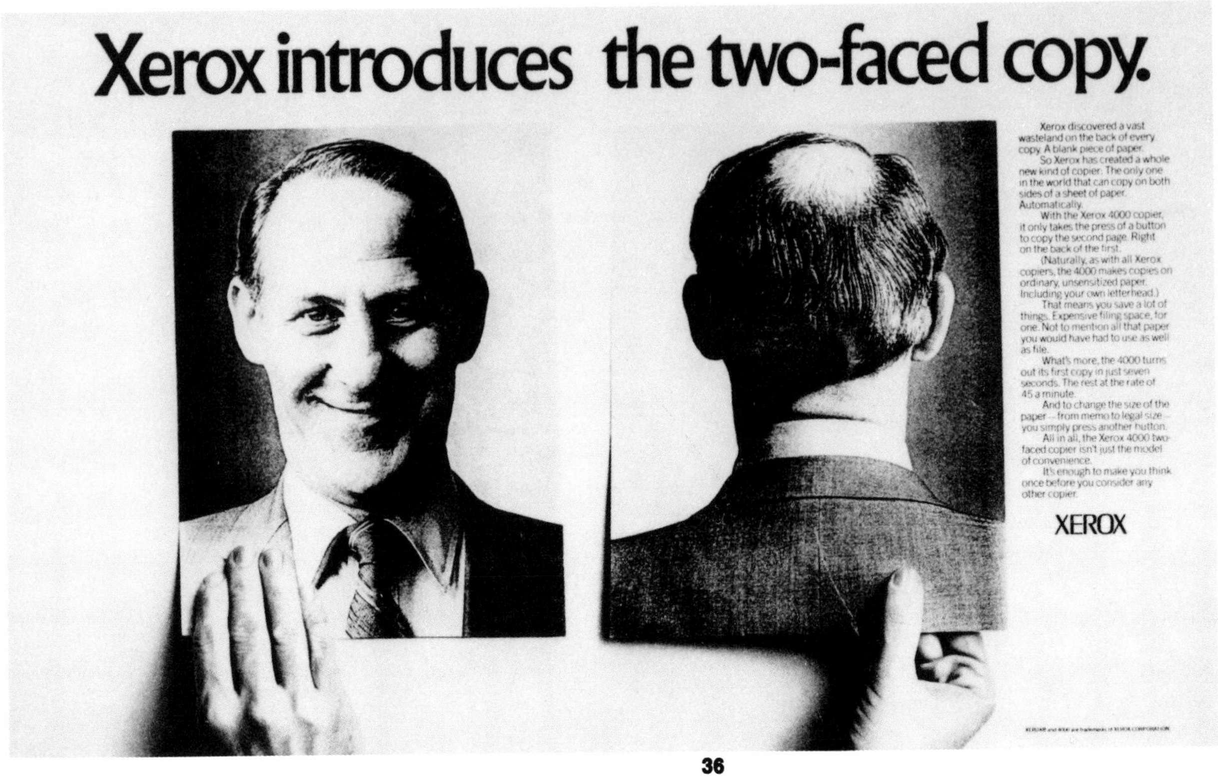
Xerox introduces the two-faced copy.
Xerox discovered a vast wasteland on the back of every copy. A blank piece of paper.
So Xerox has created a whole new kind of copier. The only one in the world that can copy on both sides of a sheet of paper. Automatically.
With the Xerox 4000 copier, it only takes the press of a button to copy the second page. Right on the back of the first.
(Naturally, as with all Xerox copiers, the 4000 makes copies on ordinary, unsensitized paper. Including your own letterhead.)
That means you save a lot of things. Expensive filing space, for one. Not to mention all that paper you would have had to use as well as file.
What's more, the 4000 turns out its first copy in just seven seconds. The rest at the rate of 45 a minute.
And to change the size of the paper – from memo to legal size – you simply press another button.
All in all, the Xerox 4000 two-faced copier isn't just the model of convenience.
It's enough to make you think once before you consider any other copier.
XEROX

36

37

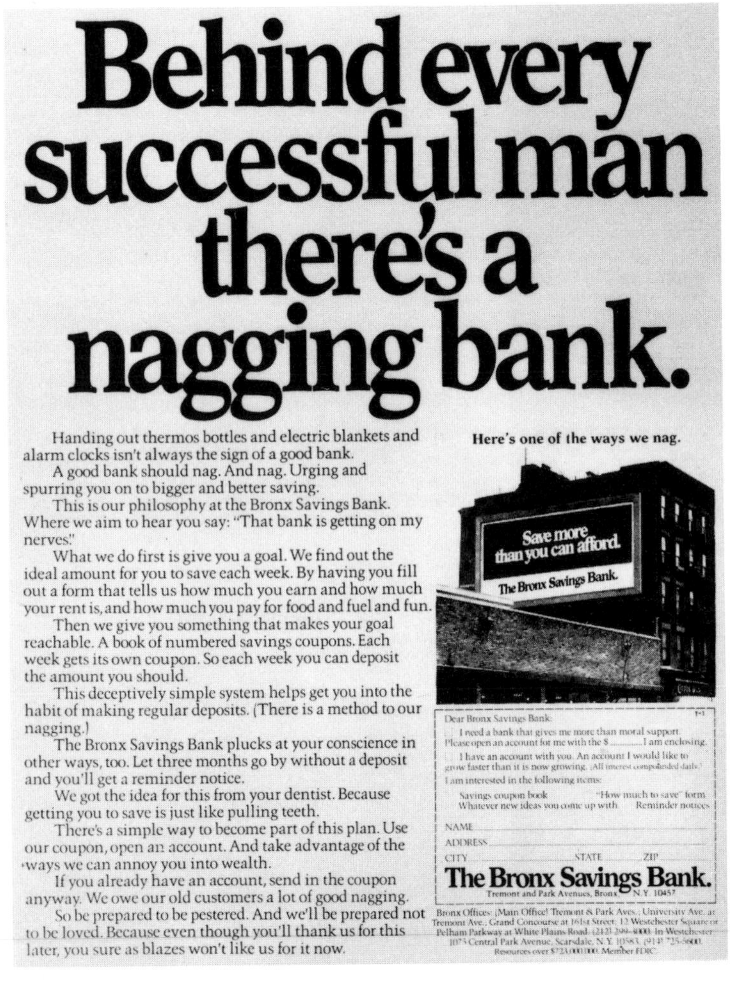
Behind every successful man there's a nagging bank.
Handing out thermos bottles and electric blankets and alarm clocks isn't always the sign of a good bank.
A good bank should nag. And nag. Urging and spurring you on to bigger and better saving.
This is our philosophy at the Bronx Savings Bank. Where we aim to hear you say: "That bank is getting on my nerves."
What we do first is give you a goal. We find out the ideal amount for you to save each week. By having you fill out a form that tells us how much you earn and how much your rent is, and how much you pay for food and fuel and fun.
Then we give you something that makes your goal reachable. A book of numbered savings coupons. Each week gets its own coupon. So each week you can deposit the amount you should.
This deceptively simple system helps get you into the habit of making regular deposits. (There is a method to our nagging.)
The Bronx Savings Bank plucks at your conscience in other ways, too. Let three months go by without a deposit and you'll get a reminder notice.
We got the idea for this from your dentist. Because getting you to save is just like pulling teeth.
There's a simple way to become part of this plan. Use our coupon, open an account. And take advantage of the ways we can annoy you into wealth.
If you already have an account, send in the coupon anyway. We owe our old customers a lot of good nagging.
So be prepared to be pestered. And we'll be prepared not to be loved. Because even though you'll thank us for this later, you sure as blazes won't like us for it now.
Here's one of the ways we nag.
Save more than you can afford.
The Bronx Savings Bank.
Dear Bronx Savings Bank:
I need a bank that gives me more than moral support. Please open an account for me with the $ .... I am enclosing.
I have an account with you. An account I would like to grow faster than it is now growing. (All interest compounded daily.)
I am interested in the following items:
Savings coupon book
"How much to save" form
Whatever new ideas you come up with
Reminder notices
NAME
ADDRESS
CITY
STATE
ZIP
The Bronx Savings Bank.
Tremont and Park Avenues, Bronx, N.Y. 10457
Bronx Offices: (Main Office) Tremont & Park Aves.; University Ave. at Tremont Ave.; Grand Concourse at 161st Street; 12 Westchester Square or Pelham Parkway at White Plains Road. In Westchester
Central Park Avenue, Scarsdale, N.Y.
Member FDIC.

36
Art Director: Allen Kay
Copywriters: Lois Korey
Roger Levinsohn
Photographer: Stephen Steigman
Agency: Needham, Harper & Steers
Client: Xerox

37
Art Director: Don Slater
Copywriter: Adam Hanft
Photographer: Arnold Beckerman
Agency: Smith/Greenland Company Inc.
Client: The Bronx Savings Bank

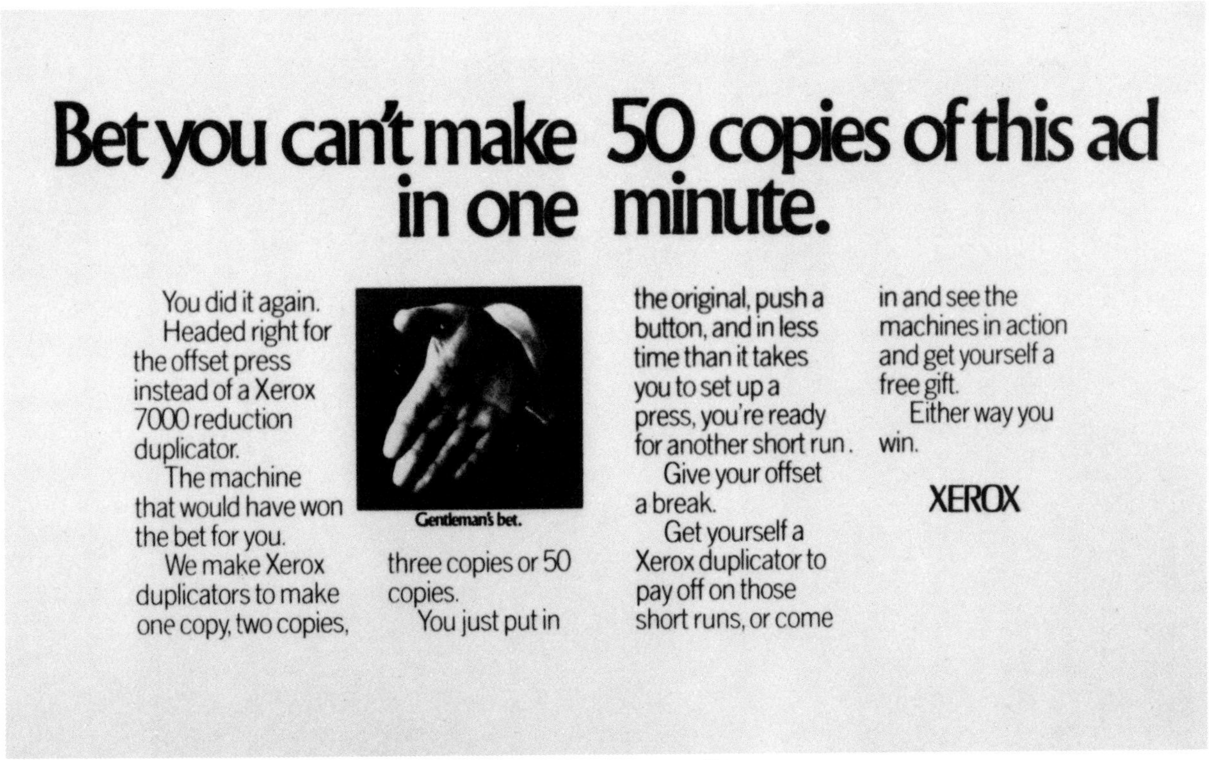
Bet you can't make 50 copies of this ad in one minute.
You did it again.
Headed right for the offset press instead of a Xerox 7000 reduction duplicator.
The machine that would have won the bet for you.
We make Xerox duplicators to make one copy, two copies, three copies or 50 copies.
You just put in the original, push a button, and in less time than it takes you to set up a press, you're ready for another short run.
Give your offset a break.
Get yourself a Xerox duplicator to pay off on those short runs, or come in and see the machines in action and get yourself a free gift.
Either way you win.
XEROX
Gentleman's bet.

38

39

IN SWEDEN, VOLVOS AND PEOPLE LAST LONGER.
The life expectancy of a Swede is 77 years. The longest on earth.
Swedes have a passion for fitness.
Thinking, perhaps, the more they can endure, the longer they will last.
The Swedes are big on saunas. They'll work up a sweat in the sauna's 200° heat and run outside for an invigorating plunge into ice water.
The man in the picture has been doing it twice a week since he was six. He's now 75 years old.
The greatest number of entrants for any competitive event in the world turn out each year in Sweden the day of the "Vasa Lopp." About 8000 people compete in this grueling 52-mile cross country ski race.
In a country where people demand so much of themselves, the car most in demand is a Volvo. It would be inconsistent for it to be anything else.
In Sweden Volvos have a life expectancy of 14 years—longer than any other make.
Volvo.
We build them the way we build them because we have to.
VOLVO

38
Art Director: Allen Kay
Copywriter: Lois Korey
Photographer: Bill Stettner
Agency: Needham, Harper & Steers
Client: Xerox

39
Art Director: John Danza
Copywriter: Ed McCabe
Designer: John Danza
Photographer: Malcolm Kirk
Agency, Scali, McCabe, Sloves, Inc.
Client: Volvo, Inc.

Consumer Magazine/Single

40
Art Director: Rocco E. Campanelli
Copywriter: Lou Centlivre
Designer: Rocco E. Campanelli
Artist: Al Bensusen
Agency: David Deutsch Associates, Inc.
Client: Hild Sails

40

Herb Hild Introduces An Automatic Shift For Sailboats.

You know what a drifter is. It's a baggy sail that you use to catch the wind when there isn't much wind to catch. Darn few sailors own one because it's so limited. When the wind increases, a big puddin' bag of a sail isn't of much use.

The drifter of yesteryear was limited.

Not so with the new Hildamatic Drifter. It has drawstrings on the foot and leach that let you adjust to shifts in wind velocity. You can flatten the sail when the wind comes up. Or you can give the sail a draft when the wind is light.

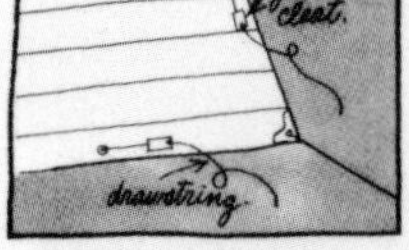

Loosen the drawstrings for a flat sail.

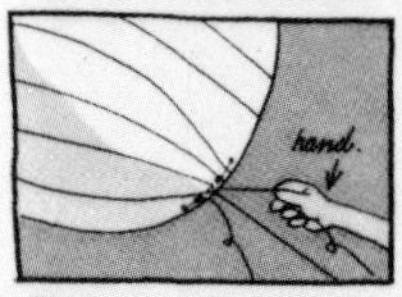

Tighten the drawstrings for a full sail.

The Hildamatic Drifter is as simple to operate as an automatic

The Hildamatic Drifter automatically adjusts from a flat sail to a full sail with a thousand in-between positions.

shift. All you do is loosen or tighten the drawstrings. And there's a jam cleat built onto the sail. Jam the strings into the cleat (think of it as the gear shift) and the sail keeps the shape you set it for. There are literally thousands of adjustments you can make for pinpoint sailing.

This is a great sail to have when you're racing. You can get greater speed out of your boat in light wind. And you can save precious seconds because there is no need to change the sail once the wind increases.

No Need To Race

But even if you don't enter a lot of races, you should still invest a few dollars in a Hildamatic. First, you have two sails in one bag. (For about the price of one.) But, more important, the Hildamatic Drifter will give you more fun than any sail you've ever used before.

This has got to be one of the most versatile and economical sails you'll ever buy. You don't have to spend money on a lot of additional equipment. No spinnaker pole is needed. No guys, no halyard; just a great little sail that does twice the work of other sails in light to medium air.

Herb's Philosophy

You won't find a sail like this anywhere else. Which is our way of letting you know Herb Hild is different from other sailmakers. His philosophy is, it isn't difficult to help champion sailors win additional trophies. The challenge is helping someone win their first championship. Making extraordinary sailors out of ordinary sailors is Herb Hild's goal.

Two sails in one sail bag.

If you'd like to have an automatic shift for your boat, we have a suggestion. Get it in gear. Send Herb a letter or visit him this week. Off-season discounts are in effect now.

Herb Hild Sails, Inc.
225 Fordham St., City Island, N.Y.

THE BIGGEST SELLING SMALL CAR IN EUROPE
VS. THE BIGGEST SELLING SMALL CAR IN AMERICA.
This year, millions of Americans will go out to buy their very first small car.
Many will find themselves confused as to which small car is best.
Which is why we think it might be helpful for you to know that in Europe, where they've been comparing small cars for three generations, they buy more Fiats than anything else.
Volkswagens included.
One of the big reasons for this is the Fiat 128, which we're bringing to America for the first time this year.
And to give you an idea of how good it is, here's how it stacks up, point by point, against America's favorite, the Volkswagen.
And not just the regular Volkswagen. But the Super Beetle.
OUR PERFORMANCE VERSUS THEIR PERFORMANCE.
The most obvious difference between the Fiat 128 and the Volkswagen Super Beetle is the engine.
Ours is in front—theirs is in back. We have front wheel drive—they have rear wheel drive.
Front wheel drive gives you better handling because the wheels that are moving the car are also the wheels that are turning the car. And also because pulling is a much more efficient way to move something than pushing.
Front wheel drive also gives you better traction on ice and snow. (As proof, last year, the Fiat 128 won the Canadian Winter Rally, which is run over ice and snow the likes of which we hardly ever see in the States.)
You'll also notice, if you glance at the chart on the right, that under passing conditions the Fiat accelerates faster than the Volkswagen. (If you've ever passed a giant truck on a highway, you know how important that is.)
Now, since engines alone do not determine how well a car performs, there are a few other subjects we'd like to cover.
For instance, the Fiat 128—which has self-adjusting front disc brakes—can bring you to a complete stop in a shorter distance than the Volkswagen, which does not have disc brakes.
Secondly, the Fiat 128 has rack and pinion steering, which is a more positive kind of steering system generally found on such cars as Ferraris, Porsches, and Jaguars. The Volkswagen doesn't.
And lastly, the Fiat comes with radial tires; the Volkswagen doesn't.
OUR ROOM VERSUS THEIR ROOM.
The trouble with most of the small cars around is that while they help solve the serious problem of space on the road, they create a serious problem of space inside the car.
And while the Volkswagen is far from the worst offender in this area, it still doesn't give you anywhere near the amount of space you get in the Fiat 128.
As you can see on the measurement chart, the Fiat 128 is a full 10 inches shorter on the outside than the Volkswagen. Yet it has more room on the inside than an Oldsmobile Cutlass, let alone the Volkswagen.
Compared to the Super Beetle, it's wider in front, wider in back, and 5 inches wider between the front and back seat. Which should be good news for your knees.
And in the trunk of the Fiat 128, where lack of room is taken for granted in small cars, you'll find 13 cubic feet of room. In the Volkswagen you'll find 9.2.
OUR COST VERSUS THEIR COST.
Aside from the fact that the Fiat 128 costs $167 less than the Super Beetle, there's another cost advantage we're rather proud of. According to tests run by the North American Testing Company, the Fiat 128 gets better gas mileage than the Super Beetle.
Now we don't for one minute expect that, even in the face of all the aforementioned evidence, you will rush out and buy a Fiat. All we suggest is that you take the time to look at a Fiat.
Recently, the president of Volkswagen of America was quoted as saying that 42% of all the people who buy Volkswagens have never even looked at another kind of car.
And we think that people who don't look before they buy never know what they've missed.
FIAT
ACCELERATION
FIAT 20-50 mph ... 9.405 secs.
VW 20-50 mph ... 11.635 secs.
FIAT 40-70 mph ... 17.86 secs.
VW 40-70 mph ... 20.09 secs.
BRAKING
FIAT 20-0 mph ... 13.2 ft.
VW 20-0 mph ... 14.6 ft.
FIAT 60-0 mph ... 139.7 ft.
VW 60-0 mph ... 155.2 ft.
BUMPER TO BUMPER
FIAT ... 151.81 in.
VW ... 160.24 in.
FRONT SEAT–SIDE TO SIDE
FIAT ... 53.50 in.
VW ... 46.0 in.
REAR SEAT–SIDE TO SIDE
FIAT ... 49.875 in.
VW ... 47.125 in.
BACK SEAT–KNEE ROOM
FIAT ... 31.00 in.
VW ... 25.75 in.
COST
FIAT ... $1,992*
VW ... $2,159*

42

43

A CAR WITH ONLY THREE COATS COULD FREEZE TO DEATH IN SWEDEN.
So before a Volvo sedan leaves the factory, it's dressed accordingly.
The outside has seven coats of protection. The inside has six. A Volvo also has underwear—two undercoats.
Where some cars have chrome, Volvos have stainless steel. There isn't a piece of non-functional chrome trim on the entire Volvo body.
Volvo comes with a heater designed for use above the arctic circle. A sizeable piece of Sweden lies within it. There are *nine* hot air outlets.
An electrically heated rear window defroster, powerful enough to melt a sheet of ice, is standard equipment.
You see, when you build a car in a country where the temperature can be below freezing six months of the year, where they use raw salt on the roads, and where automobile inspections are so stiff that badly rusted cars are ordered off the road, you build to suit.
Volvo.
We build them the way we build them because we have to.
WA 8405
VOLVO

42
Art Director: Ralph Ammirati
Copywriter: Marty Puris
Designer: Ralph Ammirati
Photographer: Carl Fischer
Agency: Carl Ally Inc.
Client: Fiat

43
Art Director: John Danza
Copywriter: Ed McCabe
Designer: John Danza
Photographer: Malcolm Kirk
Agency: Scali, McCabe, Sloves, Inc.
Client: Volvo, Inc.

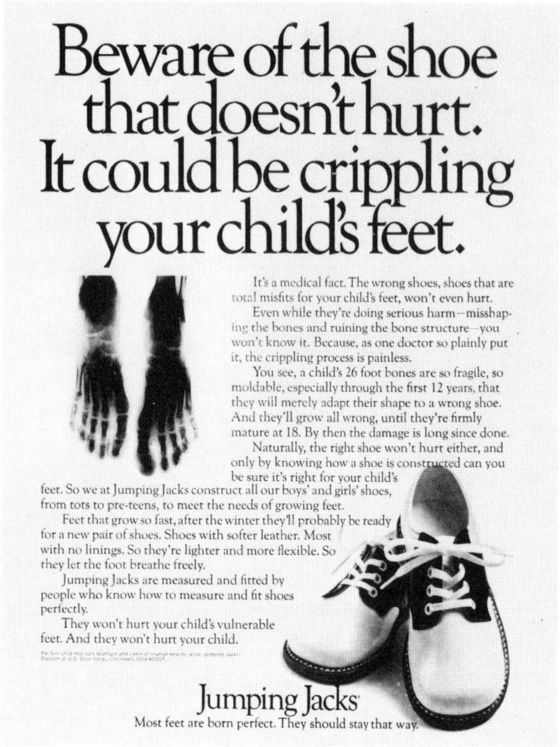
Beware of the shoe that doesn't hurt. It could be crippling your child's feet.
It's a medical fact. The wrong shoes, shoes that are total misfits for your child's feet, won't even hurt.
Even while they're doing serious harm—misshaping the bones and ruining the bone structure—you won't know it. Because, as one doctor so plainly put it, the crippling process is painless.
You see, a child's 26 foot bones are so fragile, so moldable, especially through the first 12 years, that they will merely adapt their shape to a wrong shoe. And they'll grow all wrong, until they're firmly mature at 18. By then the damage is long since done.
Naturally, the right shoe won't hurt either, and only by knowing how a shoe is constructed can you be sure it's right for your child's feet. So we at Jumping Jacks construct all our boys' and girls' shoes, from tots to pre-teens, to meet the needs of growing feet.
Feet that grow so fast, after the winter they'll probably be ready for a new pair of shoes. Shoes with softer leather. Most with no linings. So they're lighter and more flexible. So they let the foot breathe freely.
Jumping Jacks are measured and fitted by people who know how to measure and fit shoes perfectly.
They won't hurt your child's vulnerable feet. And they won't hurt your child.
Jumping Jacks
Most feet are born perfect. They should stay that way.

44

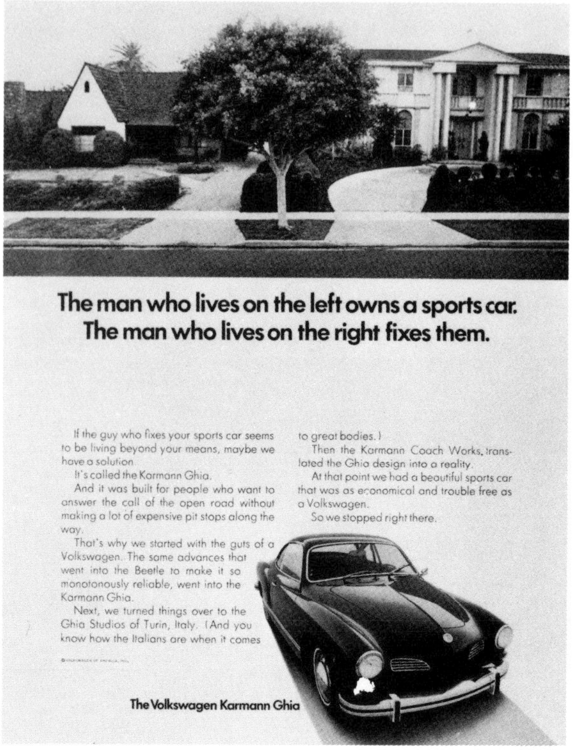
The man who lives on the left owns a sports car.
The man who lives on the right fixes them.
If the guy who fixes your sports car seems to be living beyond your means, maybe we have a solution.
It's called the Karmann Ghia.
And it was built for people who want to answer the call of the open road without making a lot of expensive pit stops along the way.
That's why we started with the guts of a Volkswagen. The same advances that went into the Beetle to make it so monotonously reliable, went into the Karmann Ghia.
Next, we turned things over to the Ghia Studios of Turin, Italy. (And you know how the Italians are when it comes to great bodies.)
Then the Karmann Coach Works, translated the Ghia design into a reality.
At that point we had a beautiful sports car that was as economical and trouble free as a Volkswagen.
So we stopped right there.
The Volkswagen Karmann Ghia

45

44
Art Director: Stanley Schofield
Copywriters: Martin Cohen
Jack Silverman
Designer: Stanley Schofield
Photographers: Joe Toto
Luis Pacheco
Agency: Leber Katz Partners
Client: U.S. Shoe Corporation

45
Art Director: Mike Lawlor
Copywriter: Ed Butler
Designer: Mike Lawlor
Photographer: Tony Petrucelli
Agency: Doyle Dane Bernbach Inc.
Client: Volkswagen of America

I got stuck in a church pew before I lost 70 pounds.

By Joyce Caldwell—as told to Ruth L. McCarthy

I belong to the New Hope Baptist Church in Pelzer, South Carolina and when our pastor told everyone in the congregation to bow down on their knees and pray, I'll tell you I needed new hope to pull myself up.

I sing with the choir, so I was right up front where everybody could see me. And at 212 pounds, it took every bit of angling I could do to get myself on my feet. I'd like to have died.

That wasn't the only embarrassing incident that happened in church, either. Another time, when I was singing, my panty hose slipped with every breath I took. Why, I was afraid to let out a high note for fear they'd drop right down.

You'd have thought with all that I'd have done something about my weight long ago, especially since I'm a Licensed Practical Nurse. Working in the hospital, I knew from the doctors that I ought to get those pounds off. But somehow my own homemade chocolate pound cake and pies were my weakness and my temptation. It wasn't that I ate so much at meals. It was that I ate so often. There were never any scraps around our house. Why, I had the "poorest" dog in town.

Once I tried some reducing pills, but I got so nervous, my husband could barely live with me. So I finally gave them up, even though I knew deep down he wanted me to lose. He never said so, but when we'd go to some social at the news office where he works, I'd accuse him of not introducing me to his friends. Guess it was my own conscience, making me feel inferior.

No matter whether I was photographed up close or at a distance, I still looked fat. Since I weighed 212 pounds, it's no wonder my son called me "Big Mama."

I never could have worn this bulky sweater and jacket if I hadn't lost 70 pounds. But buying clothes for vacation time is a pleasure, now that I'm down to 142 pounds.

Actually, it took a trip to Washington, D.C. and the discovery that I needed slacks with a 36 waist to open my eyes. Not only that—when I returned home and looked in the mirror, I suddenly saw myself in years to come—a big, big woman. I knew then that it was time to do something.

I talked to one of my neighbors about my problem and it was a good day that I did. You see, she knew about those reducing-plan candies, Ayds*, which incidentally contain vitamins and minerals, but no drugs. The Ayds plan worked just fine for her, so she gave me a handful of the candies to try. Soon after, I bought a box of the chocolate fudge kind at the drugstore and started on the plan myself.

I'd take two before breakfast like the directions say – with a hot drink (for me, coffee). Then I'd have an egg and toast. At noon, maybe I'd have soup or a hamburger and, of course, Ayds the same way. And in the evening I'd have pretty much the same meal as I'd cook for my family—meat and a vegetable or a salad, sometimes banana pudding or a little piece of cheese cake. But thanks to taking Ayds, I'd eat much smaller portions than I used to, because the Ayds plan really helped me cut back.

Well, I started losing one or two pounds a week. Doing it that way kept my skin firm, too. And, believe me, I had the kind of fat that's difficult to lose. Not fluffy like, but real hard. Why, you could hardly pinch me.

One thing I'd like to say. Occasionally, when I was losing, I'd get a hunger spell. It was psychological, I know. Like a terrible urge to eat. So I'd let myself breakover and have what I wanted. To my way of thinking, you just have to get that feeling out of your system. Then I'd go back on the Ayds plan. And you can see from my pictures, it worked. I took off 70 pounds, enough to make people where I'm now employed say: "Didn't you have a sister working here some time ago?"

I'll tell you this. When you hear something like that, you know that there's always new hope. I found mine, quite simply, in a box of Ayds.

BEFORE AND AFTER MEASUREMENTS

	Before	After
Height	5'4"	5'4"
Weight	212 lbs.	142 lbs.
Bust	44"	38"
Waist	36"	28½"
Hips	*	37½"
Dress	18½	12-14

**Joyce has no record of her hip measurements, but she thinks it was about 44 inches.*

46

46
Art Director: Charles Aromando
Copywriter: Ruth L. McCarthy
Designer: Charles Aromando
Photographer: Jerry Cohen
Agency: Wilson, Haight & Welch, Inc.
Client: Campana Corporation

47
Art Director: Joe Gregorace
Copywriter: Edward Smith
Designer: Joe Gregorace
Photographer: Tony Petrucelli
Agency: Doyle Dane Bernbach Inc.
Client: Volkswagen of America

47

© VOLKSWAGEN OF AMERICA, INC.

Which man would you vote for?

Ah yes, what could be more dazzling than watching the candidates parading about, kissing babies and flashing winning smiles.

Consider the man in the picture on the left.

He promises to spend your tax dollars wisely.

But see how he spends his campaign dollars.

On a very fancy convertible.

Resplendent with genuine leather seats. A big 425-horsepower engine.

And a price tag that makes it one of the most expensive convertibles you can buy.

Now consider his opponent.

He promises to spend your tax dollars wisely.

But see how he spends his campaign dollars.

On a Volkswagen Convertible.

Resplendent with a hand-fitted vinyl top.

A warranty and four free diagnostic check-ups that cover you for 24 months or 24,000 miles.*

And a price tag that makes it the least expensive four-passenger convertible you can buy.

So maybe this year you'll find a politician who'll do what few politicians ever do:

Keep his promises before he's elected.

*If an owner maintains and services his vehicle in accordance with the Volkswagen maintenance schedule any factory part found to be defective in material or workmanship within 24 months or 24,000 miles, whichever comes first (except normal wear and tear and service items), will be repaired or replaced by any U.S. or Canadian Volkswagen Dealer. And this will be done free of charge. See your Volkswagen dealer for details.

How to tell your parents you want to join the Army.

You're graduating from high school and not going to college. And you're not really prepared for a job. You're not even certain you know what you want to do. Or can do.

Tell your parents you can find out in the Women's Army Corps. Find out which of the many fields you might do well in. Like personnel management, data processing, stock control, administrative procedures, communications, medical or dental.

And tell them we'll train you for a career in that field. And pay you while you learn. At a starting salary of $288 a month. And since so many things in the Army are free—meals, housing, medical and dental care—you may save most of your salary.

Or spend it on the 30 days paid vacation we'll give you every year. Go just about anywhere in the world. Europe, Hawaii, Panama, the Far East, or any of those great places you've always wanted to see in the States. All at a very low cost.

Tell them that you can continue your education, too. Take special courses. Even go for your college degree. And that we'll pay for most of it.

Tell them that in today's Army you may discover abilities you never knew you had. And get to use them in a rewarding, responsible job. You'll find new friends. Meet people. Mature.

And if you need more good reasons, see your local Army Representative.

Today's Army wants to join you.

48
Art Director: Pam Dawson
Copywriter: Boris Todrin
Photographer: Tony Petrucelli
Agency: N. W. Ayer & Son, Inc., Phila.
Client: United States Army Recruiting Command

49

49
Art Director: Mark Shap
Copywriter: Brian Olesky
Designer: Mark Shap
Artists: Tim Lewis
Sandra Shap
Photographer: Mel Sokolsky
Agency: Wells, Rich, Greene, Inc.
Client: Trans World Airlines

50
Art Director: Jim Brown
Copywriter: Norman Muchnic
Designer: Jim Brown
Photographer: Bob Gomel
Agency: Doyle Dane Bernbach Inc.
Client: General Telephone & Electronics

50

Which one is the night game?
The only way to know for sure is to be there in person.
Because both these pictures were taken at Cincinnati's new Riverfront Stadium, where the field is lit by 1648 thousand-watt Metalarc lamps from our GTE Sylvania company.
And the light is so even and natural that color TV cameras can operate at night as though they were under a sunny sky.
It's so uniform there are almost no shadows or hot spots on the field.
At this point, you could say, "Well, that's fine for the Cincinnati Reds, but what does Metalarc lighting do for me?"
Well, consider what it did for the people of Wichita, Kansas, and the kids of Hammonton, New Jersey.
When Metalarc lamps replaced the old lamps in downtown Wichita, they not only lowered the accident rate, but saved the local taxpayers some money.
(Most Sylvania Metalarc lighting costs about a fifth as much to operate as equivalent incandescent illumination. And Metalarc lamps last about 7½ times as long.)
The people of Hammonton, New Jersey chose Metalarc lamps to replace the incandescents in their kids' Little League stadium. And they don't even televise. They just want everyone involved to have a better look at what's going on.
Now, back to our question. The night game is the one on the right. (Don't take a closer look. It won't help.)
The Metalarc lamp was developed at our lighting research center in Massachusetts. It's just one of literally thousands of types of lighting with the GTE Sylvania name on them.
Here at General Telephone & Electronics, we believe there's no excuse for anybody ever to be left in the dark.
GTE
GENERAL TELEPHONE & ELECTRONICS

Consumer Magazine/Single

51
Art Director: Ed Rotondi
Copywriter: Art Naiman
Designer: Ed Rotondi
Artist: David Wilcox
Agency: Young & Rubicam International, Inc.
Client: Dr. Pepper

52 Gold Award
Art Director: Roy Grace
Copywriter: Marcia Bell Grace
Designer: Roy Grace
Photographer: Dick Stone
Agency: Doyle Dane Bernbach Inc.
Client: American Tourister Luggage

51

We lived in shame for 57 years.
by Chester Trachtenberg
IT ALL BEGAN IN 1914. Velma and I were sashaying home from a school dance when we stopped off for a bit of liquid refreshment. I reached into the soft drink cooler for a bottle of Koala Cola, our favorite.
Imagine my amazement when I found a bottle of Dr Pepper in my hand instead! "What is it?" asked Velma, fully as startled as I.
"I don't know," I said. "Looks like some kind of medicine." Acting brave to impress her, I suggested we try some.
"Gee, Chester, I'm not sure," she said. "Maybe this stuff is like cornsilk. Or even stronger!"
Well, our first taste of Dr Pepper erased all our doubts. We discovered it was a uniquely delicious soft drink blended from 23 different flavors, and we've been drinking it ever since.
Now, we're peaceable folks, and we don't like to cause a fuss. So it wasn't until you started talking about Dr Pepper all over the place—right out in the open!—that Velma and I took our Dr Pepper out of the paper bags and let the world know what we had been enjoying in private all these years. The veil of secrecy had lifted from our lives.
Like any pioneers against misunderstanding, Velma and I have suffered. But the refreshing taste of Dr Pepper has always amply rewarded us.
Dr Pepper.
America's most misunderstood soft drink.
WILCOX

52

"Dear American Tourister: You make a fabulous jack."
This unsolicited testimonial comes from The J. C Quinly family of Walnut Creek, California.
Who jacked up their car to change a tire and left their American Tourister standing near. All of a sudden, the car slid backward, fell off the jack, and landed square on their suitcase.
Where it remained until the Quinlys finished changing their tire.
Of course, the suitcase got dented. (Mr. Quinly had to fix it with a hammer.)
And of course, you realize we don't build American Touristers to go through extraordinary things like supporting a car. We build American Touristers for the ordinary perils of ordinary travel.
So we build our case with 16 different strong materials, and give it a tough stainless steel frame.
We reinforce American Touristers with fiberglass. Not just on the corners, but through and through.
Most important of all, we put in nonspring locks designed not to spring open on impact.
Remember, the beautiful thing about traveling with an American Tourister isn't that it holds up a car.
But simply that it holds up.
American Tourister

53
Art Director: Bob Needleman
Copywriter: Judy Merrill
Designer: Bob Needleman
Photographer: Steve Horn
Agency: Smith/Greenland Company Inc.
Client: Somerset Importers, Ltd.

54
Art Director: Joe Gregorace
Copywriter: Peter Nord
Designer: Joe Gregorace
Artist: Mabey Trousdell
Agency: Solow-Wexton, Inc.
Client: No-Cal Soda Corporation

53

He knows if you've been bad or good or exceedingly successful.
Johnnie Walker
Black Label Scotch
YEARS 12 OLD

54

EAT YOUR HEART OUT, HERSHEY'S.
NEW FLAVOR
SUGAR FREE
NO SUGAR
NO-CAL
CHOCOLATE
16 FL.OZ.
There are people who think that eating a chunk of chocolate is the second greatest thing in the whole world.
Eating two chunks is the first greatest.
They are the chocoholics. And they would sell their souls for a bar of, a hunk of, a chunk of, a square of, a nibble of, a lick of, a whiff of, a sip of, a drink of, a swallow of, some rich, sweet, velvety, creamy, excruciatingly delicious chocolate.
No-Cal has come out with a Chocolate Soda just for them. It's everything a chocolate fanatic has ever lusted for in a rich, sweet, velvety, creamy, excruciatingly delicious chocolate soda.
Except.
It's got no sugar. No sugar at all.
And what that means is this: now for the first time in the history of the entire world, you, the chocolate fanatic, can have chocolate after chocolate after chocolate and have nothing... but nothing... to show for it.
OUR NEW SUGAR-FREE NO-CAL CHOCOLATE SODA.

In our Feb. 8 mail there were two complaints. Find them.
We reprint here every single comment about the performance of Sony color TV that we received on Tuesday, Feb. 8. Two unhappy comments and 154 happy-to-ecstatic ones.
All were written on the warranty cards returned to us by recent purchasers. 400 additional cards with no comments presumably came from happy owners. Grand total: 554 yes's, 2 no's. It was a typical day.
We're pleased, of course. But not surprised. Because our all-solid-state Trinitron system is so radically different, it gives you a radically different color picture.
And the chance that you'll love it is excellent. About 554 to 2.
TRINITRON
SONY COLOR TV

55

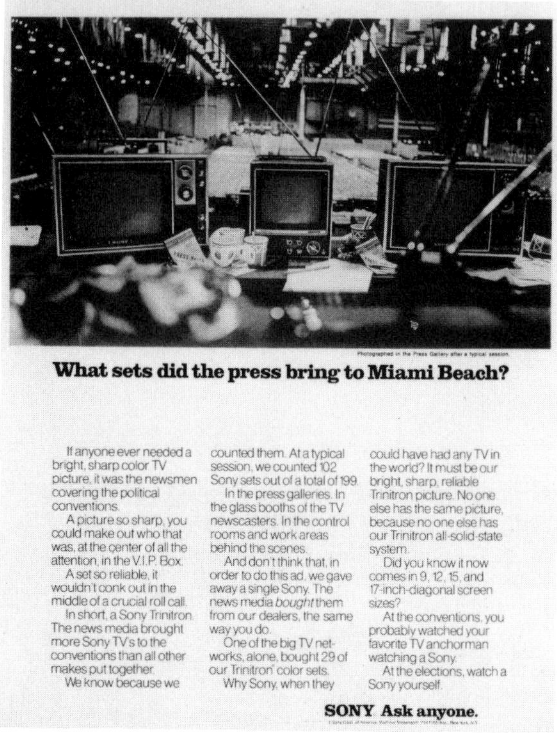
What sets did the press bring to Miami Beach?
If anyone ever needed a bright, sharp color TV picture, it was the newsmen covering the political conventions.
A picture so sharp, you could make out who that was, at the center of all the attention, in the V.I.P. Box.
A set so reliable, it wouldn't conk out in the middle of a crucial roll call.
In short, a Sony Trinitron. The news media brought more Sony TV's to the conventions than all other makes put together.
We know because we counted them. At a typical session, we counted 102 Sony sets out of a total of 199.
In the press galleries. In the glass booths of the TV newscasters. In the control rooms and work areas behind the scenes.
And don't think that, in order to do this ad, we gave away a single Sony. The news media bought them from our dealers, the same way you do.
One of the big TV networks, alone, bought 29 of our Trinitron color sets.
Why Sony, when they could have had any TV in the world? It must be our bright, sharp, reliable Trinitron picture. No one else has the same picture, because no one else has our Trinitron all-solid-state system.
Did you know it now comes in 9, 12, 15, and 17-inch-diagonal screen sizes?
At the conventions, you probably watched your favorite TV anchorman watching a Sony.
At the elections, watch a Sony yourself.
SONY Ask anyone.

56

57

His mother needed a steam shovel.
All you need is Birds Eye Combinations.
"Boy, do I love vegetables!"
"Open wide, Mike, here comes another load.
"That's a good boy..."
Oh, the things mother had to go through to get your man to eat his vegetables when he was a boy.
They should have given her time and a half.
At Birds Eye, we never forget the little boy who lives inside every man.
That's why we've come up with Birds Eye Combinations: 18 interesting vegetable combinations a man can love.
Our peas aren't just peas. We've added potatoes, with a little something extra: a cream sauce. We've combined lima beans and corn and peas and carrots. In a mild onion sauce.
Tonight, serve him Birds Eye Combinations.
And watch him dig in.
Because your vegetables will be as irresistible as his mother's stories.
Mixed Vegetables with Onion Sauce
Green Peas and Potatoes with Cream Sauce
The vegetables mother never had.

58

First the agency people told me I could say anything I wanted to about scotch. Then they censored me.
BY TOMMY SMOTHERS
I'VE BEEN CENSORED one way or another practically all my life.
It all started when my mother used to stick a pacifier into my mouth anytime I opened it.
When Dick and I were kids, once Mother got him a dog and me a muzzle.
Even my dreams have snips cut out of them. Always the good parts, too. [redacted].
That's the way it's always been.
So I wasn't surprised when one of the major networks joined the fun. It was annoying, I'll admit, but when it was all over all I could say was "et tu, CBS."
But all that is censorship under the bridge.
And speaking of censorship, it's certainly changed a lot since its beginning. Today, you can say anything as long as no one hears you. So probably the only way to steer clear of censors is to steer yourself into a closet and talk only to yourself.
Anyway, when the Teacher's advertising people heard I drink their scotch, they asked me to talk about it.
They gave me carte blanche, a yellow pad and a No. 2 pencil. Of course, the pencil had no point, but I got around that. [redacted].
Well, first I wrote about how happy I was that everybody and his brother doesn't drink Teacher's. Which, in my case, is a definite plus.
No problems so far.
Then I started reminiscing about my experiences with scotch, pre-Teachers.
The first time I tasted scotch I tried to belt it down like they always do in the movies when the hero has just lost his girl.
Eeecch. [redacted].
If this was what scotch tasted like, I vowed never to lose my girl or be a hero in a movie.
My stomach was the first casualty. Then my eyes started to water. And finally my tongue made itself heard. It gave me a severe tongue lashing.
However, I wasn't going to let myself be licked by a mere tongue, a pair of eyes and a stomach.
So I came back for less.
This time, I started with a Presbyterian. 2 parts this, 3 parts that, 4 parts something-else and, if there's any room left over, scotch. [redacted].
The trouble with that was I got tired of walking up to bars and ordering one Presbyterian only to have the bartender tell me I was in the wrong place and down the street at the church I could find all the Presbyterians I wanted.
Next I moved to scotch and soda. Or more accurately, scotch and soda, soda, soda and soda.
After that, it was the big time. Scotch on the rocks. Straight. But I did such a terrific job of nursing my drink the Red Cross would have been proud of me.
All of which brings me to Teacher's. The first time I ever tasted it was the first time I ever finished my scotch on the rocks before it turned to water.
Teacher's, my tongue thanks you, my eyes thank you, my stomach thanks you. Even my sex life thanks you.
Once there was this girl and [redacted] back seat of this old DeSoto [redacted].
Boy, those Teacher's people let you say anything.
So anyway, [redacted].
TEACHER'S
SCOTCH WHISKY

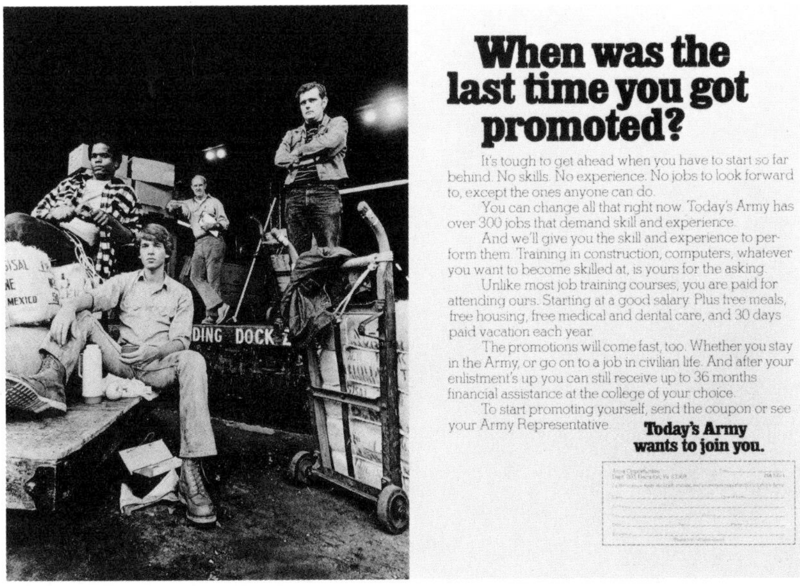

DING DOCK
When was the last time you got promoted?
It's tough to get ahead when you have to start so far behind. No skills. No experience. No jobs to look forward to, except the ones anyone can do.
You can change all that right now. Today's Army has over 300 jobs that demand skill and experience.
And we'll give you the skill and experience to perform them. Training in construction, computers, whatever you want to become skilled at, is yours for the asking.
Unlike most job training courses, you are paid for attending ours. Starting at a good salary. Plus free meals, free housing, free medical and dental care, and 30 days paid vacation each year.
The promotions will come fast, too. Whether you stay in the Army, or go on to a job in civilian life. And after your enlistment's up you can still receive up to 36 months financial assistance at the college of your choice.
To start promoting yourself, send the coupon or see your Army Representative.
Today's Army wants to join you.

59

60

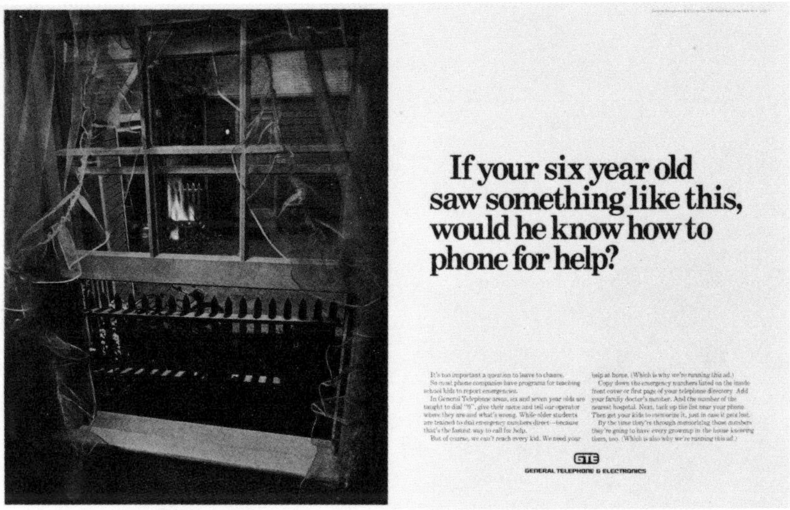

If your six year old saw something like this, would he know how to phone for help?
GTE
GENERAL TELEPHONE & ELECTRONICS

55
Art Director: Mike Lawlor
Copywriter: Lore Parker
Designer: Mike Lawlor
Photographer: Carl Fischer
Agency: Doyle Dane Bernbach Inc.
Client: Sony Corporation

56
Art Director: Mike Lawlor
Copywriter: Lore Parker
Designer: Mike Lawlor
Photographer: Tibor Hirsch
Agency: Doyle Dane Bernbach Inc.
Client: Sony Corporation

57
Art Director: Woody Litwhiler
Copywriter: Don Marowski
Designer: Woody Litwhiler
Artist: Charles White
Photographer: Joe Toto
Agency: Young & Rubicam International, Inc.
Client: General Foods

58 Silver Award
Art Director: Nicholas Gisonde
Copywriter: Neil Drossman
Designer: Nicholas Gisonde
Photographer: Arnold Beckerman
Agency: Della Femina, Travisano, & Partners, Inc.
Client: Teacher's Scotch

59
Art Director: Joseph Caserta
Copywriters: Ted Regan
Pat Cunningham
Photographer: Cailor/Resnick
Agency: N. W. Ayer & Son, Inc., Phila.
Client: United States Army Recruiting Command

60
Art Director: Jim Brown
Copywriter: Richard Vitaliano
Designer: Jim Brown
Photographer: Carl Fischer
Agency: Doyle Dane Bernbach Inc.
Client: General Telephone & Electronics

61

Your baby's crying
for Wa-Wa & Woo-Woo.
The most adorable playmates ever created for baby are really nursers that hold eight full ounces and loads of happy gurgles.
One's a raccoon. The other's a bear.
We call them Wa-Wa and Woo-Woo, because we think babies should be able to pronounce their playmates' names.
Both come with Evenflo's famous No Work, No Worry Nipple.
And in case you hadn't noticed, they're 3-dimensional—so easy for baby to hold.
Wa-Wa and Woo-Woo want to play. Don't keep your baby waiting.
evenflo
Roger Hane

61
Art Director: Tony Apilado
Copywriter: John Paul Itta
Artist: Roger Hane
Agency: John Paul Itta, Inc.
Client: Evenflo Baby Products

62
Art Director: Lou Principato
Copywriter: Adrienne Cohen
Designer: Lou Principato
Photographer: Joe Toto
Agency: Young & Rubicam International, Inc.
Client: Eastern Airlines

63
Art Director: Georgia Shankle
Copywriter: Evelyn Lewis
Designer: Georgia Shankle
Photographer: Otto Storch
Agency: Young & Rubicam International, Inc.
Client: General Foods

Don't take someone else's honeymoon.
Honeymoons are not made in heaven. There's nothing heavenly about a flashy 31-story hotel with an over-anxious social directress if you're longing for solitude.
Or a cottage on a lonely island when you like plenty of night life. Or a steady diet of fresh-caught fish when your taste runs to hamburgers.
No, honeymoons have their disappointments just like anything else – if you choose the wrong one.
And that's an easy thing to do. Just read the travel brochures – did you ever see one that didn't look good? Or let a few friends or relatives tell you where they went, and you'll end up taking their honeymoon. Not yours.
We think your honeymoon should be what you are. Not what somebody thinks you are.
And nobody knows you better than you – what you like and don't like, what's important to you and what isn't. So we've developed a way for you to tell us, so we can help you plan the honeymoon that was meant for you.
Our questionnaire below probes your interests, attitudes, values, even your subconscious desires. You can fill it out alone, but it's better if you fill it out together. Then send it to us.
We'll send a personal letter back telling you which destination and accommodations fulfill your wants. After that, call us. We want your honeymoon to be everything you want it to be, and we'll do everything we can to see that it is
12 questions to make sure the honeymoon you take is the one you want.
With the exception of questions 6 and 7, please circle just one answer.
1. What kind of a couple do you see yourselves as?
a. Outgoing b. Whimsical c. Old-fashioned d. Serious e. Confident f. Sophisticated g. Lighthearted
2. Associate yourselves with one of these words:
a. Fireside b. Unicorn c. Stadium d. Escargot e. Bach f. Safari g. Bubble bath
3. Associate your honeymoon with one of these words:
a. Serenade b. Raft c. Schooner d. Ivy e. Plaza f. Flamingo g. Daiquiri h. Windmill i. Casino j. Lime k. Coq au vin l. Marquee
4. Where would you be happy?
a. In the mountains b. At the seashore c. In a big cultural city d. Cruising on the water
5. Where would you be happiest?
a. On a small island away from it all
b. In a place with a stimulating foreign flavor
c. At a smart resort where the international set gathers
d. In a lively resort city on the beach
e. In a bustling metropolis
f. On the high seas heading for the tropics
6. As a participant, what do you enjoy? (pick three)
a. Golfing b. Swimming c. Sailing d. Sightseeing e. Playing tennis f. Dancing g. Skin diving h. Water skiing i. Fishing j. Biking k. Horseback riding l. Duty-free shopping m. Gambling
7. As a spectator, what do you enjoy? (pick three)
a. Floor shows b. People c. Horse races d. Concerts e. Dog races f. Jai alai g. Bull fights h. Ballet i. Theatre j. Opera k. Native dancing l. Museums m. Nature
8. Which environment do you feel most comfortable in?
a. Solitary b. Primitive c. Pampered d. Old World e. Social f. Eventful g. Vigorous
9. Which word best describes the place you'd like to stay?
a. Posh b. Adventurous c. Casual d. Independent e. Festive f. Convivial
10. Which honeymoon most definitely belongs to someone else?
a. A villa on a lonely island with little night life
b. A plush hotel on an island with gambling casinos
c. A luxurious hotel in the heart of a big city
d. A hillside cottage with private beach
e. A spacious apartment overlooking the sea
f. A villa with a private pool and a full staff of servants
g. An Old World chateau
h. A floating hotel with five meals a day
11. How long can you spend on your honeymoon?
a. A long weekend b. 7 days c. 14 days d. 21 days e. A month
12. What kind of accommodations can you afford?
a. Moderate b. In-between c. Deluxe
Eastern Airlines The Honeymoon You Want
P.O. Box 399 Radio City Station
New York, N.Y. 10019
Name
Address
City & State
Zip Phone #
Date of Wedding
Please enclose a quarter for postage and handling.
EASTERN The Wings of Man.

62

63

Log Cabin and the Sweet Soul Picnic. July 4th. Memphis, Tennessee.
Sweet soul food. An American tradition that's a fabulous blend of Southern, West Indian, French Creole, and African foods.
Sweet because of the syrup that swirls through the black-eyed peas. That glazes the candied yams. That even goes into the sweet potato pie. The Log Cabin brand that has been around this country since 1887. And great Black cooks, creative as they are, no doubt have discovered how the special taste of Log Cabin fits right into their way of cooking.
Soul because of the love. The care. The long hours of preparation. The wisdom of knowing how to please. The ingenuity of knowing how to make superb dishes out of whatever was on hand, which is the secret of great cooking traditions everywhere.
If you want to know what goes into the cookery of a sweet soul picnic, here's an idea. It all begins the night before. Talk about preparation! The family would get together in Grandma Ella Jackson's big kitchen. There'd be lots of greens to wash. Lots of yams to be peeled. Lots of chicken to cut. And lots of black-eyed peas to soak. Grandma's kitchen was a ceaseless hive of activity in preparation for the day ahead. The great sweet soul picnic. A classical Southern feast.
Here are some great soul food recipes from the Log Cabin kitchens, beginning with the most classic of all, Southern Fried Chicken.
Log Cabin and the Southern Fried Chicken
Dip 3-lb. frying chicken pieces in ½ cup Log Cabin Syrup; coat with 1 cup seasoned all-purpose flour; then sprinkle with remaining flour and set aside 15 minutes. Fry chicken, a few pieces at a time, in ½ inch of hot shortening (half butter and half vegetable shortening) in large skillet, until golden brown. Place in shallow baking pan; bake at 350° for 30 minutes, or until tender. Garnish. Makes 4 to 6 servings.
Note: Recipe may be doubled.
Throughout Black homes in this country, black-eyed peas are traditionally served on New Year's Day as an assurance of good luck for the coming year. It's called Hoppin' John. Of course, it's not only served on New Year's Day. Black-eyed peas are a staple in soul food cooking and are served throughout the year. No matter what the occasion. Like for the soul food picnic. The black-eyed peas are baked with pork and sweetened with Log Cabin.
Log Cabin and the Baked Black-Eyed Peas
Soak 1 lb. dried black-eyed peas in water overnight; drain. In large saucepan combine ½ lb. salt pork and enough water to cover. Bring to boil; simmer 1½ hours. Drain, measuring broth; add water to make 4 cups liquid. Combine peas and measured liquid in saucepan; top with pork. Bring to boil; simmer 30 minutes. Stir in 1 cup catsup, ⅔ cup Log Cabin Syrup, 2 tbsp. vinegar, 2 tsp. salt, and ¾ tsp. dry mustard. Pour into 3-qt. casserole. Bake at 350° for 2 hours. Makes about 10 cups or 10 servings.
The only way to end a really great picnic is to serve a really great dessert. And what dessert could have more soul than sweet potato pie?
Log Cabin and the Sweet Potato Pie
Combine 2½ cups mashed cooked sweet potatoes (about 4 medium), ¼ cup sugar, and ¼ cup softened butter; gradually beat in ⅔ cup Log Cabin Syrup. Add 3 eggs, one at a time, beating well after each addition. Blend in ¾ cup milk, then ½ tsp. salt, ¼ tsp. each nutmeg, allspice, and cinnamon, and 1 tsp. vanilla. Pour into 1 unbaked 9-inch fluted pie shell. Bake at 425° for 10 minutes; then at 325° for 1 hour. Cool.
Soul food was born in the homes of Black cooks. And because recipes were seldom written down, a young girl learned from experience by watching her mother and grandmother. As she grew older she instinctively added her own little touches. Thus making soul food what it is today.
Log Cabin has been refined and fussed with over the years, too. To satisfy America's changing tastes.
Log Cabin and the sweet soul picnic. Two of America's No. 1 favorites. Make them a part of your 4th of July celebration.
The Log Cabin Brand. America grew up on it.

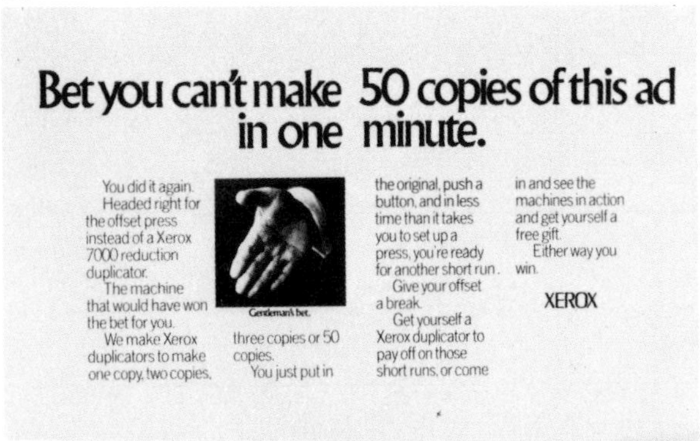
Bet you can't make 50 copies of this ad in one minute.
Gentleman's bet.
You did it again.
Headed right for the offset press instead of a Xerox 7000 reduction duplicator.
The machine that would have won the bet for you.
We make Xerox duplicators to make one copy, two copies, three copies or 50 copies.
You just put in the original, push a button, and in less time than it takes you to set up a press, you're ready for another short run.
Give your offset a break.
Get yourself a Xerox duplicator to pay off on those short runs, or come in and see the machines in action and get yourself a free gift.
Either way you win.
XEROX

NEVER FOLD WHAT YOU CAN SHRINK
XEROX

Xerox makes copiers for fathers and sons.
JOHN MILLER
PUBLIC ACCOUNT
It was my son, the president, who said to me one day:
"Dad, why don't you get yourself a Xerox copier?"
"Sure," I said. "I'll just move my desk into the hall."
"No, Dad. You don't understand. I mean a little copier you can put anywhere in the office."
"What do I need one for? I'm not the big businessman my son is."
"Well, for one thing, you could keep better track of client records that come in and out every day. And wouldn't it be nice to keep your files in better order? And you could send out flyers and mailers and maybe drum up some new business."
"Sounds great. I'll sell the house and buy one."
"Dad, it's not expensive. There's not even a monthly minimum copy charge on the 660. Besides a small use fee, you only pay for the copies you make.
"And it copies on almost any paper. You can even use the beige letterhead Mom gave you.
"What more could you ask for, Pa?"
"A son that calls once in a while."
J. MILLER INC.
XEROX®, 660 and 720 are trademarks of XEROX CORPORATION.
Besides the Millers' 660 and 720, Xerox makes all kinds of copiers for all kinds of families.
XEROX

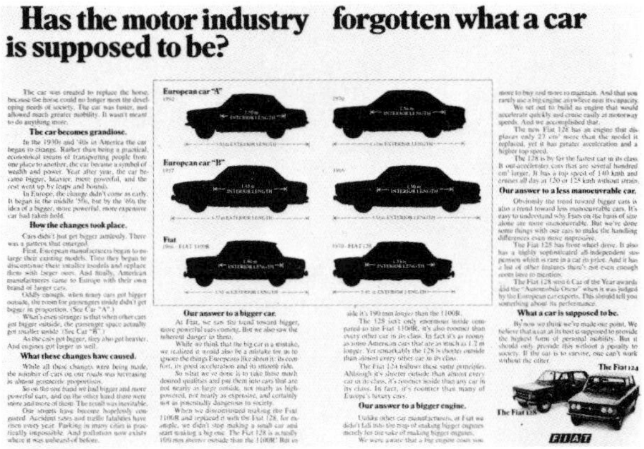
Has the motor industry forgotten what a car is supposed to be?
The Fiat 124
The Fiat 128
FIAT

64
Art Directors: Allen Kay
Jeff Cohen
Mel Gottlieb
Copywriters: Lois Korey
Roger Levinsohn
Peter Dichter
Alan Fraser
Photographers: Stephen Steigman
Michael O'Neill
Tony Petrucelli
Agency: Needham, Harper & Steers
Client: Xerox

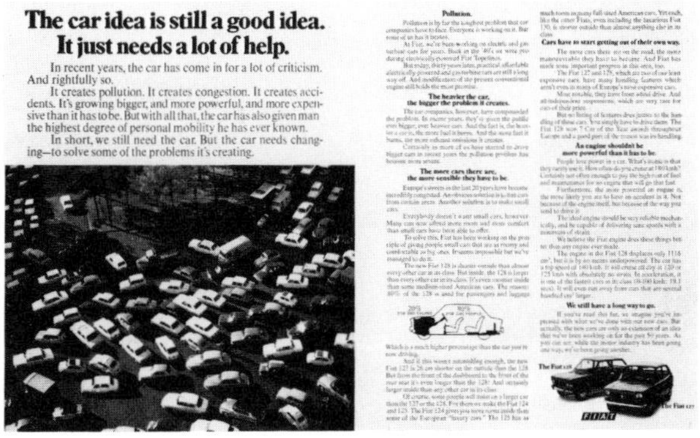

65

65
Art Director: Ron Barrett
Copywriter: David Altschiller
Designer: Ron Barrett
Photographer: Hans Hansen
Agency: Carl Ally Inc.
Client: Fiat

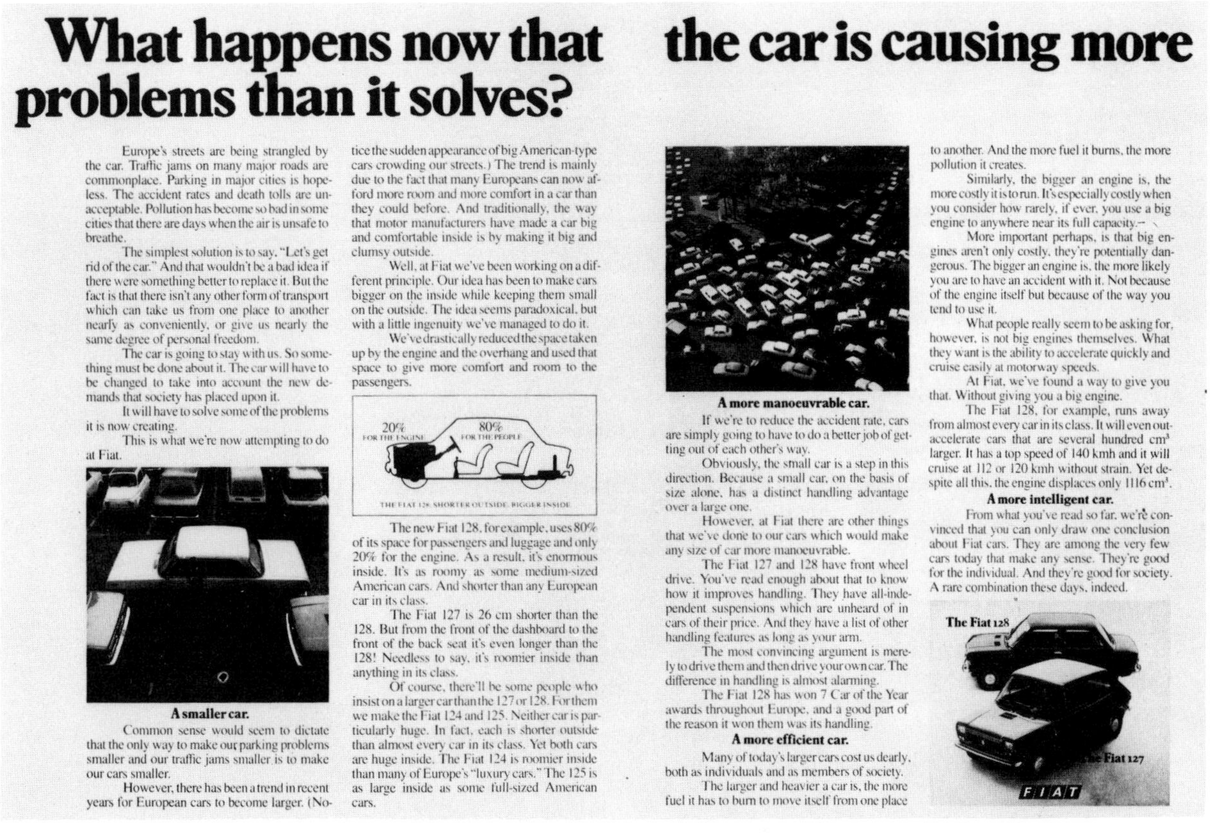
What happens now that the car is causing more problems than it solves?
Europe's streets are being strangled by the car. Traffic jams on many major roads are commonplace. Parking in major cities is hopeless. The accident rates and death tolls are unacceptable. Pollution has become so bad in some cities that there are days when the air is unsafe to breathe.
The simplest solution is to say, "Let's get rid of the car." And that wouldn't be a bad idea if there were something better to replace it. But the fact is that there isn't any other form of transport which can take us from one place to another nearly as conveniently, or give us nearly the same degree of personal freedom.
The car is going to stay with us. So something must be done about it. The car will have to be changed to take into account the new demands that society has placed upon it.
It will have to solve some of the problems it is now creating.
This is what we're now attempting to do at Fiat.
A smaller car.
Common sense would seem to dictate that the only way to make our parking problems smaller and our traffic jams smaller is to make our cars smaller.
However, there has been a trend in recent years for European cars to become larger. (Notice the sudden appearance of big American-type cars crowding our streets.) The trend is mainly due to the fact that many Europeans can now afford more room and more comfort in a car than they could before. And traditionally, the way that motor manufacturers have made a car big and comfortable inside is by making it big and clumsy outside.
Well, at Fiat we've been working on a different principle. Our idea has been to make cars bigger on the inside while keeping them small on the outside. The idea seems paradoxical, but with a little ingenuity we've managed to do it.
We've drastically reduced the space taken up by the engine and the overhang and used that space to give more comfort and room to the passengers.
20% FOR THE ENGINE
80% FOR THE PEOPLE
THE FIAT 128: SHORTER OUTSIDE, BIGGER INSIDE
The new Fiat 128, for example, uses 80% of its space for passengers and luggage and only 20% for the engine. As a result, it's enormous inside. It's as roomy as some medium-sized American cars. And shorter than any European car in its class.
The Fiat 127 is 26 cm shorter than the 128. But from the front of the dashboard to the front of the back seat it's even longer than the 128! Needless to say, it's roomier inside than anything in its class.
Of course, there'll be some people who insist on a larger car than the 127 or 128. For them we make the Fiat 124 and 125. Neither car is particularly huge. In fact, each is shorter outside than almost every car in its class. Yet both cars are huge inside. The Fiat 124 is roomier inside than many of Europe's "luxury cars." The 125 is as large inside as some full-sized American cars.
A more manoeuvrable car.
If we're to reduce the accident rate, cars are simply going to have to do a better job of getting out of each other's way.
Obviously, the small car is a step in this direction. Because a small car, on the basis of size alone, has a distinct handling advantage over a large one.
However, at Fiat there are other things that we've done to our cars which would make any size of car more manoeuvrable.
The Fiat 127 and 128 have front wheel drive. You've read enough about that to know how it improves handling. They have all-independent suspensions which are unheard of in cars of their price. And they have a list of other handling features as long as your arm.
The most convincing argument is merely to drive them and then drive your own car. The difference in handling is almost alarming.
The Fiat 128 has won 7 Car of the Year awards throughout Europe, and a good part of the reason it won them was its handling.
A more efficient car.
Many of today's larger cars cost us dearly, both as individuals and as members of society.
The larger and heavier a car is, the more fuel it has to burn to move itself from one place to another. And the more fuel it burns, the more pollution it creates.
Similarly, the bigger an engine is, the more costly it is to run. It's especially costly when you consider how rarely, if ever, you use a big engine to anywhere near its full capacity.
More important perhaps, is that big engines aren't only costly, they're potentially dangerous. The bigger an engine is, the more likely you are to have an accident with it. Not because of the engine itself but because of the way you tend to use it.
What people really seem to be asking for, however, is not big engines themselves. What they want is the ability to accelerate quickly and cruise easily at motorway speeds.
At Fiat, we've found a way to give you that. Without giving you a big engine.
The Fiat 128, for example, runs away from almost every car in its class. It will even outaccelerate cars that are several hundred cm³ larger. It has a top speed of 140 kmh and it will cruise at 112 or 120 kmh without strain. Yet despite all this, the engine displaces only 1116 cm³.
A more intelligent car.
From what you've read so far, we're convinced that you can only draw one conclusion about Fiat cars. They are among the very few cars today that make any sense. They're good for the individual. And they're good for society. A rare combination these days, indeed.
The Fiat 128
The Fiat 127
FIAT

66

WHY VOLVO CAN'T BUILD A SMALL CAR.
Swedes tend to be tall. And Volvos are intended to accommodate them.
The average height of Swedish men is 5'10". The man in the picture is taller than average. But a Volvo still has room for him. There is leg and headroom for drivers up to 6'6½".
And Volvos aren't big in the front at the expense of people in the back. As you've no doubt heard, Sweden is a country of tall, blonde, statuesque passengers.
Volvos also have extra-wide opening doors. And a trunk befitting the most mobile people in Europe.
The fact is, you just don't get to be the biggest-selling car in Sweden by building a little car.
If we did, our people wouldn't be able to fit into it.
VOLVO

IN A NATION OF ENGINEERS, BAD CARS DON'T SELL.
TEKNISK AB
VOLVO

IN MOST COUNTRIES THE BEST SELLING CAR IS ALSO CHEAP. NOT IN SWEDEN.
VOLVO

66
Art Director: John Danza
Copywriter: Ed McCabe
Designer: John Danza
Photographer: Malcolm Kirk
Agency: Scali, McCabe, Sloves, Inc.
Client: Volvo, Inc.

67
Art Director: Stanley Schofield
Copywriter: Jack Silverman
Designer: Stanley Schofield
Photographers: Dennis Chalkin
Bill Dolce
Bob Golden
Agency: Leber Katz Partners
Client: Utica Mutual Insurance

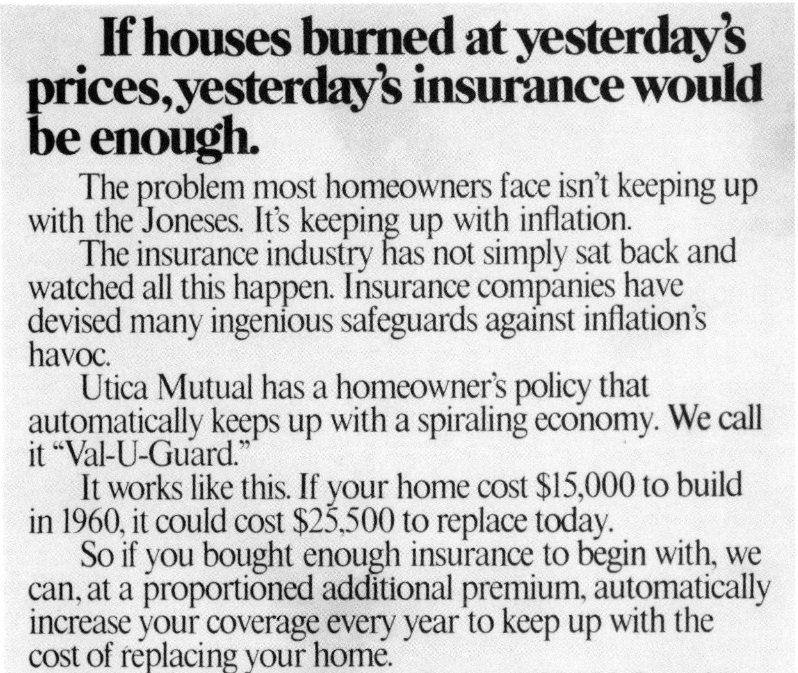
If houses burned at yesterday's prices, yesterday's insurance would be enough.
The problem most homeowners face isn't keeping up with the Joneses. It's keeping up with inflation.
The insurance industry has not simply sat back and watched all this happen. Insurance companies have devised many ingenious safeguards against inflation's havoc.
Utica Mutual has a homeowner's policy that automatically keeps up with a spiraling economy. We call it "Val-U-Guard."
It works like this. If your home cost $15,000 to build in 1960, it could cost $25,500 to replace today.
So if you bought enough insurance to begin with, we can, at a proportioned additional premium, automatically increase your coverage every year to keep up with the cost of replacing your home.
Your Utica Agent knows all about "Val-U-Guard." Call him, he's in the Yellow Pages or write us c/o P.O. Box 530, Utica, N.Y.
Because no matter how up-to-date your house is, the most modern thing you can have in it is the insurance you have on it.
UTICA
MUTUAL
A MEMBER OF UTICA NATIONAL
INSURANCE GROUP
INSURANCE THAT STARTS WITH YOU

The song of the open road. Tra-la.
You can hardly count on getting from here to there these days without something going wrong.
Even if you do everything right.
Because the roads you're driving on probably aren't being repaired right. And you can expect other drivers to do nothing right.
So the insurance industry has been devising new ways to make life on the road a lot less worrisome.
Our Utica Mutual Carefree Driving Club is one really unusual antidote.
With a Utica Mutual Auto Insurance Policy, you can join the Club for $12 a year ($6 for each additional car) and you'll never get stranded. If you're in an accident, we'll get you up to $25 a day for hotels, meals, telephone or transportation.
And a phone call will get you a bail bond for up to $5,000.
Your Utica Agent knows about these and all the other benefits you get when you join our "Carefree Driving Club". Call him, he's in the Yellow Pages. Or write us c/o P.O. Box 530, Utica, N.Y. for more information.
After all, why should your plans break down just because your car has?
UTICA
MUTUAL
A MEMBER OF UTICA NATIONAL
INSURANCE GROUP

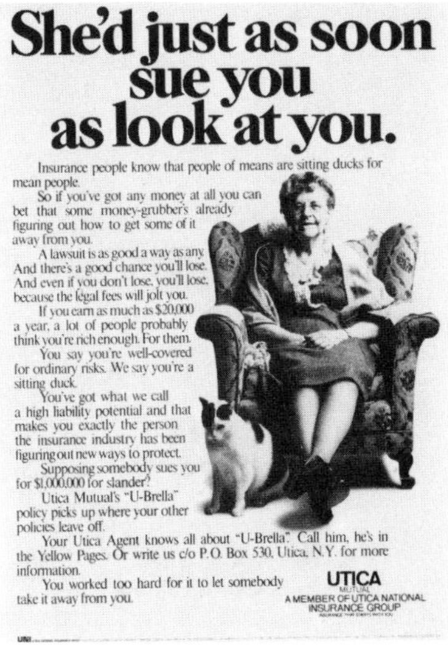
She'd just as soon sue you as look at you.
Insurance people know that people of means are sitting ducks for mean people.
So if you've got any money at all you can bet that some money-grubber's already figuring out how to get some of it away from you.
A lawsuit is as good a way as any. And there's a good chance you'll lose. And even if you don't lose, you'll lose, because the legal fees will jolt you.
If you earn as much as $20,000 a year, a lot of people probably think you're rich enough. For them.
You say you're well-covered for ordinary risks. We say you're a sitting duck.
You've got what we call a high liability potential and that makes you exactly the person the insurance industry has been figuring out new ways to protect.
Supposing somebody sues you for $1,000,000 for slander?
Utica Mutual's "U-Brella" policy picks up where your other policies leave off.
Your Utica Agent knows all about "U-Brella". Call him, he's in the Yellow Pages. Or write us c/o P.O. Box 530, Utica, N.Y. for more information.
You worked too hard for it to let somebody take it away from you.
UTICA
MUTUAL
A MEMBER OF UTICA NATIONAL
INSURANCE GROUP

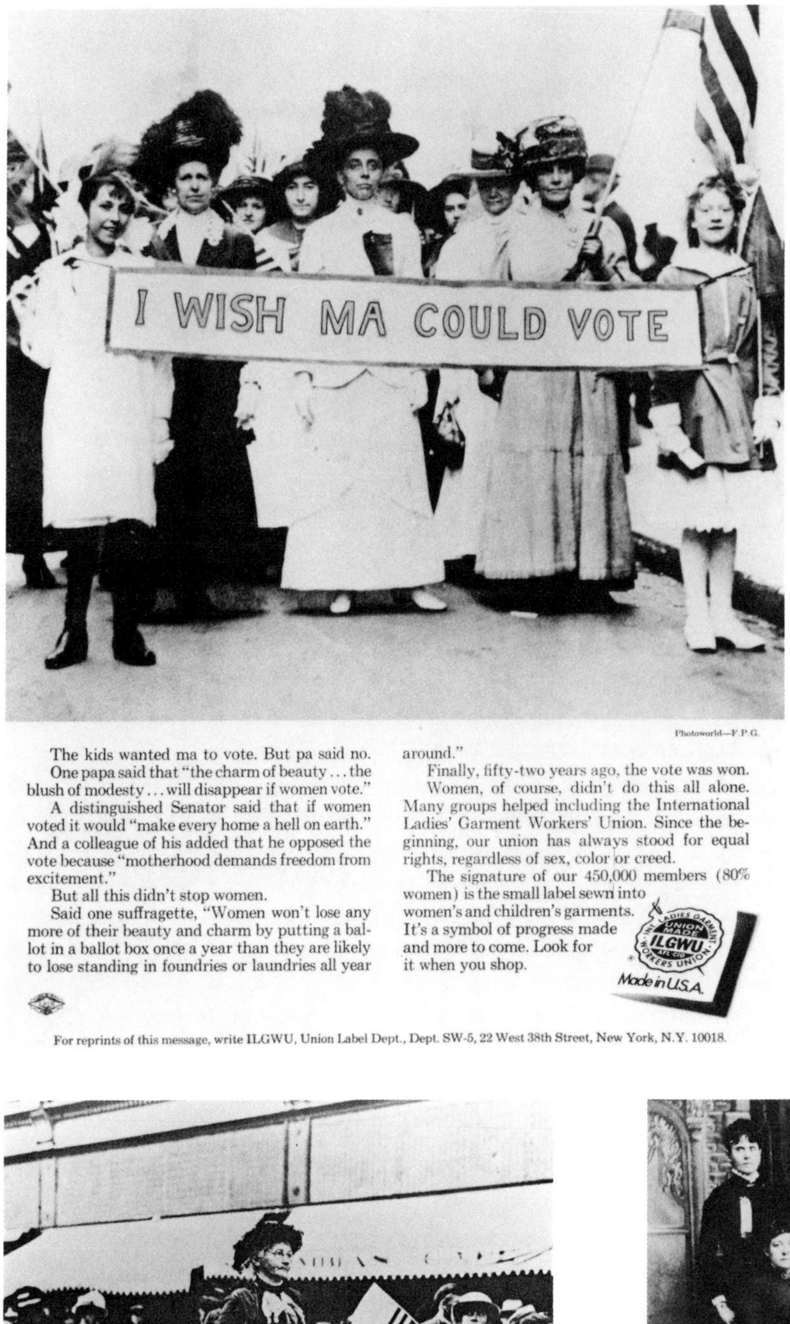
I WISH MA COULD VOTE
Photoworld—F.P.G.
The kids wanted ma to vote. But pa said no.
One papa said that "the charm of beauty... the blush of modesty... will disappear if women vote."
A distinguished Senator said that if women voted it would "make every home a hell on earth." And a colleague of his added that he opposed the vote because "motherhood demands freedom from excitement."
But all this didn't stop women.
Said one suffragette, "Women won't lose any more of their beauty and charm by putting a ballot in a ballot box once a year than they are likely to lose standing in foundries or laundries all year around."
Finally, fifty-two years ago, the vote was won.
Women, of course, didn't do this all alone. Many groups helped including the International Ladies' Garment Workers' Union. Since the beginning, our union has always stood for equal rights, regardless of sex, color or creed.
The signature of our 450,000 members (80% women) is the small label sewn into women's and children's garments. It's a symbol of progress made and more to come. Look for it when you shop.
INT. LADIES GARMENT WORKERS UNION
UNION MADE
ILGWU
AFL-CIO
Made in U.S.A.
For reprints of this message, write ILGWU, Union Label Dept., Dept. SW-5, 22 West 38th Street, New York, N.Y. 10018.

68
Art Director: Joe Gregorace
Copywriter: Martin Solow
Designer: Joe Gregorace
Photographer: Photo World Stock
Agency: Solow-Wexton, Inc.
Client: ILGWU

69
Art Director: Charles Aromando
Copywriter: Ruth McCarthy
Designer: Charles Aromando
Photographer: Jerry Cohen
Agency: Wilson, Haight & Welch, Inc.
Client: Campana Corporation

68

"I reside wherever there is a good fight against wrong."
She was called the "Joan of Arc" of the coal fields.
One newspaper described Mother Jones as "the most dangerous woman in the country." Another said, "There is no more patriotic person in America."
"Her personal non-resistance," said Clarence Darrow, "was far more powerful than any appeal to force."
We, in the International Ladies' Garment Workers' Union, honor the memory of Mother Jones, a labor organizer and a fighter for human rights, on this, the 45th anniversary of her death.
Once, she was asked where she lived, and replied: "I reside wherever there is a good fight against wrong."
ILGWU
Made in U.S.A.
The union label stands for the creativity of American design. The skill of American workmanship. The importance of American jobs.
For 64-page publication containing historic photographs, send 50¢ to ILGWU, Union Label Dept., 22 West 38th Street, New York, N. Y. 10018, Dept. SW-1

"My husband always believed that women should do anything they liked that was good..."
So she joined the union.
Mother of twelve children, Mrs. George Rodgers brought her youngest with her to the union convention.
Together with other delegates, she posed for a photograph.
It was to let everyone know that women were members of the Noble and Holy Order of the Knights of Labor—the federation of unions of a century ago.
Today there are many women union members. For instance, eighty per cent of the International Ladies' Garment Workers' Union—founded over 70 years ago—are women.
Over seven decades, ILGWU members have not only worked to provide a better living for their families, but have helped improve conditions of all working people. Without regard for race, religion, origin or sex.
You can help in this long crusade. When you buy women's or children's apparel, look for the union label.
It is a symbol of progress made.
And more to come.
ILGWU
Made in U.S.A.
For 64-page publication containing historic photographs, send 50¢ to Union Label Dept., ILGWU, 22 W. 38th Street, New York, N.Y. 10018, Dept. SW-3

As seen in Ms. Magazine September 1972.

I lost 66¼ inches and 75 pounds. Isn't that beautiful?

By Joanne Irell—as told to Ruth L. McCarthy

I was some fat pineapple — nearly 205 ugly pounds —when this photograph was taken in Hawaii.

Shoulders 8"
Bust 9½"
Arms 6¼"
Abdomen 14¾"
Waist 6"
Hips 9½"
Thighs 7½"
Knees 1¾"
Calves 2"
Ankles 1"

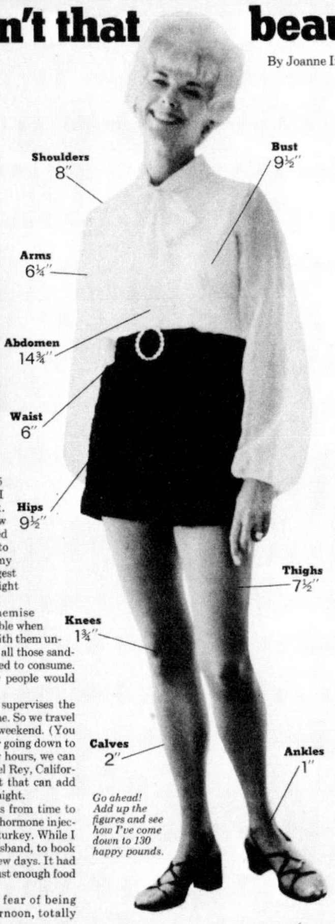

Go ahead! Add up the figures and see how I've come down to 130 happy pounds.

The day I discovered I was 205 pounds, it was such a shock, I went to bed for one solid week. Even my husband didn't know what was wrong with me. I refused to tell him, just as I had refused to get on a scale for a good part of my adult life. That's one of the biggest mistakes any person with a weight problem can make.

In the beginning, I wore chemise dresses. They'd become fashionable when I started to gain. I simply grew with them until I looked like a balloon. It was all those sandwiches, chili dogs and cakes I used to consume. I'd eat them as easily as other people would light up cigarettes.

On top of that, my husband supervises the catering division of a major airline. So we travel a lot—like flying to Alaska for a weekend. (You get three meals on the plane.) Or going down to Mexico City for dinner. In a few hours, we can make it from our home, Playa Del Rey, California, to a fantastic *festin*, a feast that can add two pounds to your weight overnight.

Of course, I'd go on wild diets from time to time. For instance, the one with hormone injections, hard boiled eggs and cold turkey. While I was on that, I got Harry, my husband, to book a hotel suite in San Diego for a few days. It had a refrigerator so we could keep just enough food to make us both miserable.

We didn't go out much for fear of being tempted by food, but one afternoon, totally bored, we went to a movie. It was disastrous. A man, sitting in front of us, was munching popcorn. I'll tell you, I nearly grabbed the bag out of his hands. Instead, I jumped up and ran out with Harry after me.

That was the end of the diet. Soon after, I went on an eating spree that would have made most people ill. Not me. Instead, I wound up weighing 205 pounds. At the same time, my sister announced she could no longer sew for me. That, I think, was the most shattering blow of all. But it was also the moment of truth for me. I knew I could no longer go on like this. So I prepared myself, mentally, to reduce. I took all of my measurements; then I looked for something to help me slim down.

I had read those stories of people who had lost weight with the help of the reducing-plan candy, Ayds®. I also had talked to people about them. When I learned they contained vitamins and minerals, but no drugs, I bought a box of the plain chocolate fudge kind at the drugstore. Then I started on the plan.

Before breakfast, I took a couple of Ayds with a hot drink like the directions say. Then I had grapefruit juice and a soft boiled egg. At noon, I'd have Ayds again—this time with bouillon—and maybe cheese. And for dinner, Ayds and coffee, followed by meat or fish, vegetables, tomatoes or sometimes celery and carrot sticks. I found that Ayds really helped curb my appetite, and I was satisfied with less food. In three months, I had lost 35 pounds on the Ayds plan.

But I still had at least that much more to lose. I knew this for sure after a trip to Acapulco, where I was taken for pregnant! I was wearing hot pants and an overblouse, while watching someone para-gliding behind a speed boat. Suddenly I said to Harry: "I wouldn't mind taking a turn at that!" Immediately, a man beside me said: "Go ahead. I'll even pay for it. To see the 'both' of you being pulled would be worth it." And he didn't mean Harry. I was humiliated.

Well, it took me several more months to get down to 130 pounds. But I did it! I can hardly believe it even now and neither can my son. Especially after we added up all the inches I've lost — around my shoulders, arms, thighs, and stomach. Fact is, thanks to the Ayds plan, I've lost over 1½ yards of fat. Just as important, I've also gained a much better disposition.

BEFORE AND AFTER MEASUREMENTS		
	Before	After
Height	5'6"	5'6"
Weight	205 lbs.	130 lbs.
Bust	47½"	38"
Waist	35"	29"
Hips	45½"	36"
Dress	20	12-14

I got stuck in a church pew before I lost 70 pounds.

By Joyce Caldwell—as told to Ruth L. McCarthy

This picture made me lose 58 pounds. See!

By Sandy Vargo—as told to Ruth L. McCarthy

I didn't want to lose him, so I lost 59 pounds.

By Shirley Gallagher—as told to Ruth L. McCarthy

Watch me lose 125 pounds —a picture at a time.

By Betty O'Neal—as told to Ruth L. McCarthy

270 pounds

255 pounds

232 pounds

215 pounds

195 pounds

145 pounds

When I was fat, I had to "act" happy. But at 128 pounds, I can be myself.

By Lorraine Marks—as told to Ruth L. McCarthy

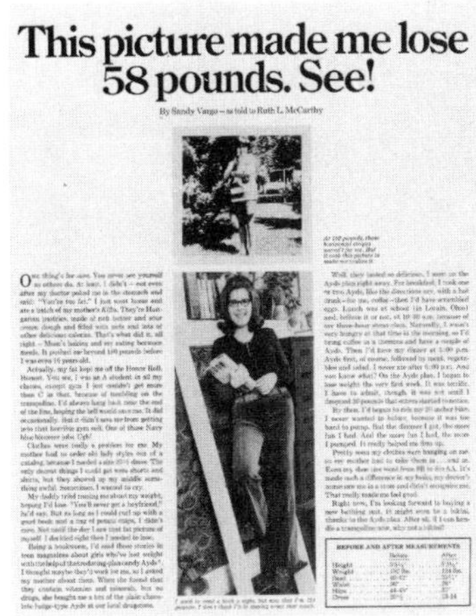

70

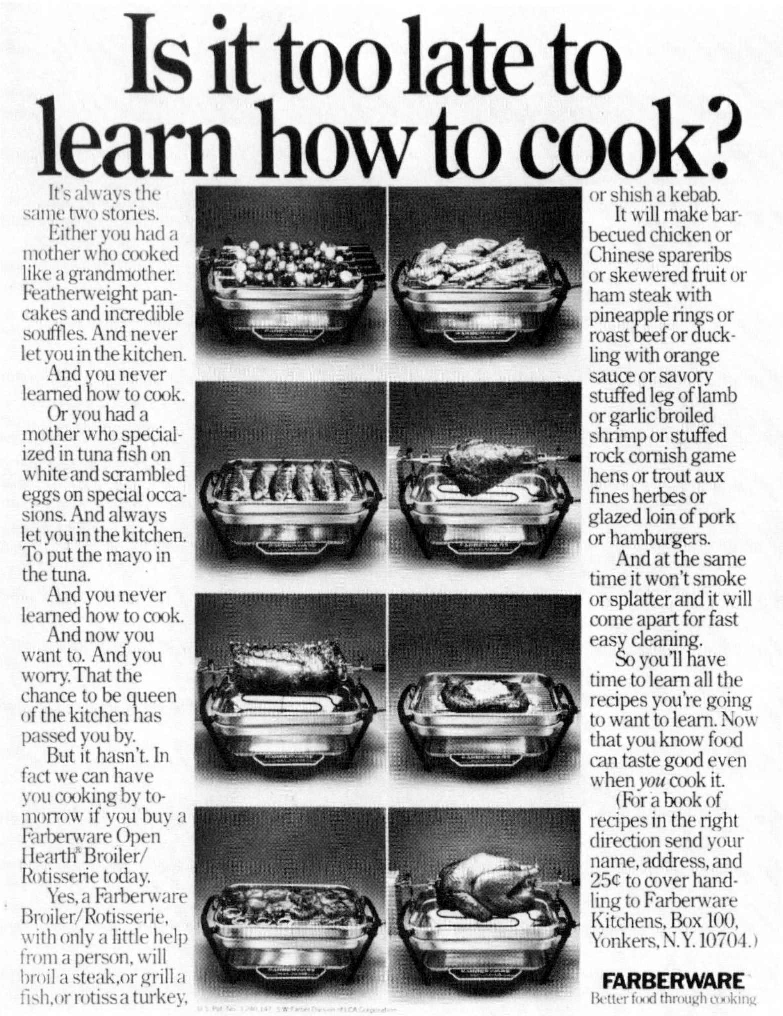
Is it too late to learn how to cook?
It's always the same two stories.
Either you had a mother who cooked like a grandmother. Featherweight pancakes and incredible souffles. And never let you in the kitchen.
And you never learned how to cook.
Or you had a mother who specialized in tuna fish on white and scrambled eggs on special occasions. And always let you in the kitchen. To put the mayo in the tuna.
And you never learned how to cook.
And now you want to. And you worry. That the chance to be queen of the kitchen has passed you by.
But it hasn't. In fact we can have you cooking by tomorrow if you buy a Farberware Open Hearth® Broiler/Rotisserie today.
Yes, a Farberware Broiler/Rotisserie, with only a little help from a person, will broil a steak, or grill a fish, or rotiss a turkey, or shish a kebab.
It will make barbecued chicken or Chinese spareribs or skewered fruit or ham steak with pineapple rings or roast beef or duckling with orange sauce or savory stuffed leg of lamb or garlic broiled shrimp or stuffed rock cornish game hens or trout aux fines herbes or glazed loin of pork or hamburgers.
And at the same time it won't smoke or splatter and it will come apart for fast easy cleaning.
So you'll have time to learn all the recipes you're going to want to learn. Now that you know food can taste good even when *you* cook it.
(For a book of recipes in the right direction send your name, address, and 25¢ to cover handling to Farberware Kitchens, Box 100, Yonkers, N.Y. 10704.)
FARBERWARE
Better food through cooking

70
Art Director: Don Slater
Copywriter: Elon Specht
Photographer: Charles Gold
Agency: Smith/Greenland Company Inc.
Client: Farberware

71
Art Director: Joseph Cipolla
Copywriters: George Adels
Concept: George Adels
Joseph Cipolla
Bob Wilvers
Jack Silverman
Designer: Joseph Cipolla
Agency: Leber Katz Partners
Client: R. J. Reynolds

Anything they can cook you can cook better.
FARBERWARE

Now that we've taught you how to cook we refuse to let you ruin it with a rotten cup of coffee.
How to use a pot.
FARBERWARE

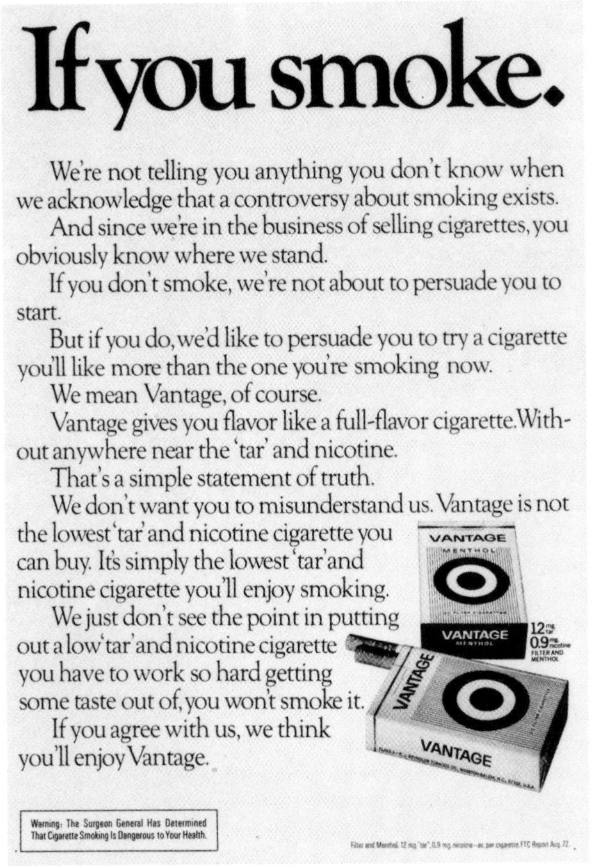
If you smoke.
We're not telling you anything you don't know when we acknowledge that a controversy about smoking exists.
And since we're in the business of selling cigarettes, you obviously know where we stand.
If you don't smoke, we're not about to persuade you to start.
But if you do, we'd like to persuade you to try a cigarette you'll like more than the one you're smoking now.
We mean Vantage, of course.
Vantage gives you flavor like a full-flavor cigarette. Without anywhere near the 'tar' and nicotine.
That's a simple statement of truth.
We don't want you to misunderstand us. Vantage is not the lowest 'tar' and nicotine cigarette you can buy. It's simply the lowest 'tar' and nicotine cigarette you'll enjoy smoking.
We just don't see the point in putting out a low 'tar' and nicotine cigarette you have to work so hard getting some taste out of, you won't smoke it.
If you agree with us, we think you'll enjoy Vantage.
VANTAGE
MENTHOL
VANTAGE
MENTHOL
12 mg. tar
0.9 mg. nicotine
FILTER AND MENTHOL
VANTAGE
VANTAGE
Warning: The Surgeon General Has Determined That Cigarette Smoking Is Dangerous to Your Health.
Filter and Menthol: 12 mg. "tar", 0.9 mg. nicotine—av. per cigarette, FTC Report Aug. '72.

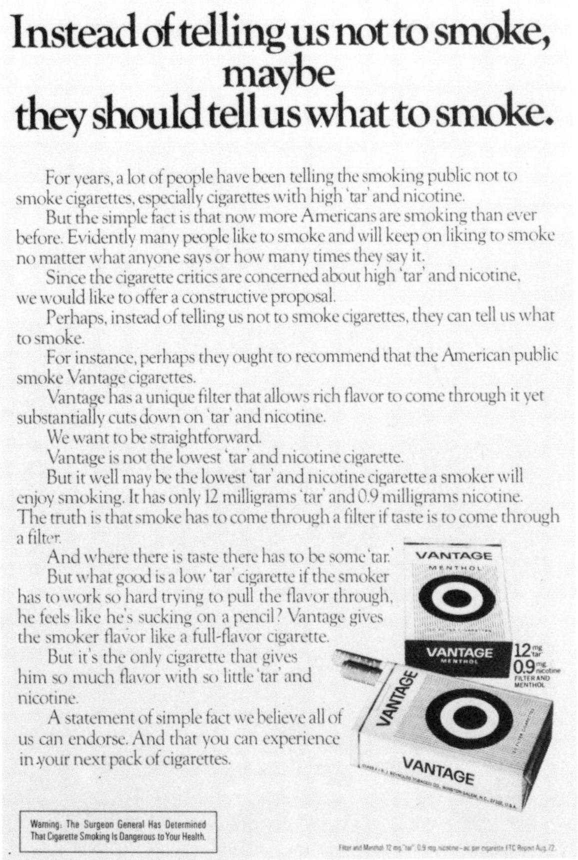
Instead of telling us not to smoke, maybe they should tell us what to smoke.
For years, a lot of people have been telling the smoking public not to smoke cigarettes, especially cigarettes with high 'tar' and nicotine.
But the simple fact is that now more Americans are smoking than ever before. Evidently many people like to smoke and will keep on liking to smoke no matter what anyone says or how many times they say it.
Since the cigarette critics are concerned about high 'tar' and nicotine, we would like to offer a constructive proposal.
Perhaps, instead of telling us not to smoke cigarettes, they can tell us what to smoke.
For instance, perhaps they ought to recommend that the American public smoke Vantage cigarettes.
Vantage has a unique filter that allows rich flavor to come through it yet substantially cuts down on 'tar' and nicotine.
We want to be straightforward.
Vantage is not the lowest 'tar' and nicotine cigarette.
But it well may be the lowest 'tar' and nicotine cigarette a smoker will enjoy smoking. It has only 12 milligrams 'tar' and 0.9 milligrams nicotine.
The truth is that smoke has to come through a filter if taste is to come through a filter.
And where there is taste there has to be some 'tar.'
But what good is a low 'tar' cigarette if the smoker has to work so hard trying to pull the flavor through, he feels like he's sucking on a pencil? Vantage gives the smoker flavor like a full-flavor cigarette.
But it's the only cigarette that gives him so much flavor with so little 'tar' and nicotine.
A statement of simple fact we believe all of us can endorse. And that you can experience in your next pack of cigarettes.
VANTAGE
MENTHOL
VANTAGE
MENTHOL
12 mg. tar
0.9 mg. nicotine
FILTER AND MENTHOL
VANTAGE
VANTAGE
Warning: The Surgeon General Has Determined That Cigarette Smoking Is Dangerous to Your Health.

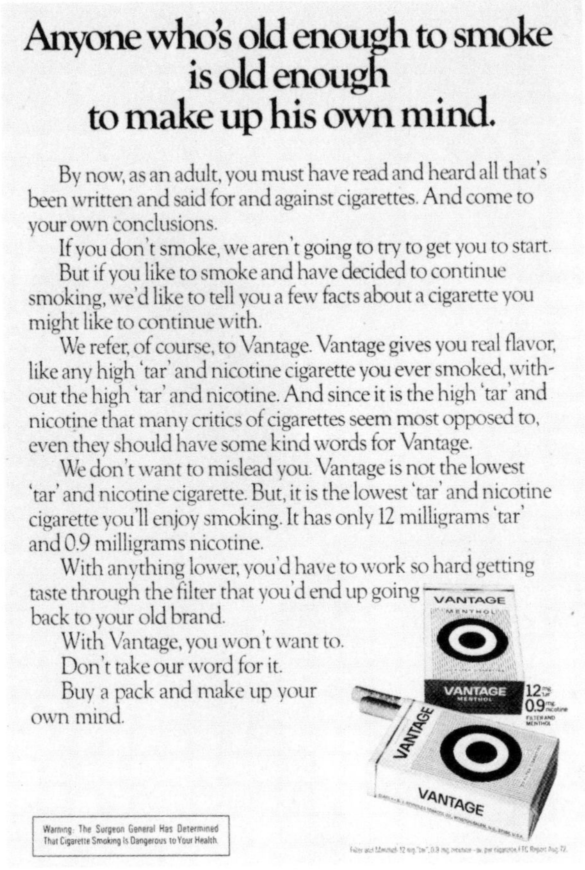
Anyone who's old enough to smoke is old enough to make up his own mind.
By now, as an adult, you must have read and heard all that's been written and said for and against cigarettes. And come to your own conclusions.
If you don't smoke, we aren't going to try to get you to start.
But if you like to smoke and have decided to continue smoking, we'd like to tell you a few facts about a cigarette you might like to continue with.
We refer, of course, to Vantage. Vantage gives you real flavor, like any high 'tar' and nicotine cigarette you ever smoked, without the high 'tar' and nicotine. And since it is the high 'tar' and nicotine that many critics of cigarettes seem most opposed to, even they should have some kind words for Vantage.
We don't want to mislead you. Vantage is not the lowest 'tar' and nicotine cigarette. But, it is the lowest 'tar' and nicotine cigarette you'll enjoy smoking. It has only 12 milligrams 'tar' and 0.9 milligrams nicotine.
With anything lower, you'd have to work so hard getting taste through the filter that you'd end up going back to your old brand.
With Vantage, you won't want to.
Don't take our word for it.
Buy a pack and make up your own mind.
VANTAGE
MENTHOL
VANTAGE
MENTHOL
12 mg. tar
0.9 mg. nicotine
FILTER AND MENTHOL
VANTAGE
VANTAGE
Warning: The Surgeon General Has Determined That Cigarette Smoking Is Dangerous to Your Health.

To the 56,000,000 people who smoke cigarettes.
A lot of people have been telling you not to smoke, especially cigarettes with high 'tar' and nicotine. But smoking provides you with a pleasure you don't want to give up.
Naturally, we're prejudiced. We're in the business of selling cigarettes.
But there is one overriding fact that transcends whether you should or shouldn't smoke and that fact is that you do smoke.
And what are they going to do about that?
They can continue to exhort you not to smoke. Or they might look reality in the face and recommend that, if you smoke and want low 'tar' and nicotine in a cigarette, you smoke a cigarette like Vantage.
And we'll go along with that, because there is no other cigarette like Vantage. Except Vantage.
Vantage has a unique filter that allows rich flavor to come through it and yet substantially cuts down on 'tar' and nicotine.
Not that Vantage is the lowest 'tar' and nicotine cigarette.
(But you probably wouldn't like the lowest 'tar' and nicotine cigarette anyway.)
The plain truth is that smoke has to come through a filter if taste is to come through a filter. And where there is taste there has to be some 'tar.'
But Vantage is the only cigarette that gives you so much flavor with so little 'tar' and nicotine.
So much flavor that you'll never miss your high 'tar' cigarette.
VANTAGE
MENTHOL
VANTAGE
MENTHOL
12 mg. tar
0.9 mg. nicotine
FILTER AND MENTHOL
VANTAGE
VANTAGE
Warning: The Surgeon General Has Determined That Cigarette Smoking Is Dangerous to Your Health.

72

What parents do to their children's feet on Sunday is a sin.
Maybe they just don't know about those angelic little dress-up shoes that try to get by on looks alone.
But some bright color and a cute strap are far from enough to suit a child's growing foot.
A foot with 26 delicate bones that take a full 18 years to mature and are at their most fragile through the first 12 years.
So we at Jumping Jacks insist on making a lot more than a pretty shoe.
We make a shoe with leather almost as tender as a child's foot. Most with no linings inside. So the shoe is that much lighter and softer, more free and flexible.
It lets the foot breathe easy and doesn't distort a child's normal way of walking.
And the man who fits Jumping Jacks shoes knows how to fit. Exactly.
Baby feet aren't baby teeth. A child gets only one pair. One time. That's why abusing them leads 8 out of 10 people into lifelong foot problems.
That's why you should look over our children's shoes from tots to pre-teens, for both boys and girls.
And look them over inside and out.
Then you can dress up your child beautifully on Sunday—without worrying about it every Monday.
Jumping Jacks
Most feet are born perfect. They should stay that way.

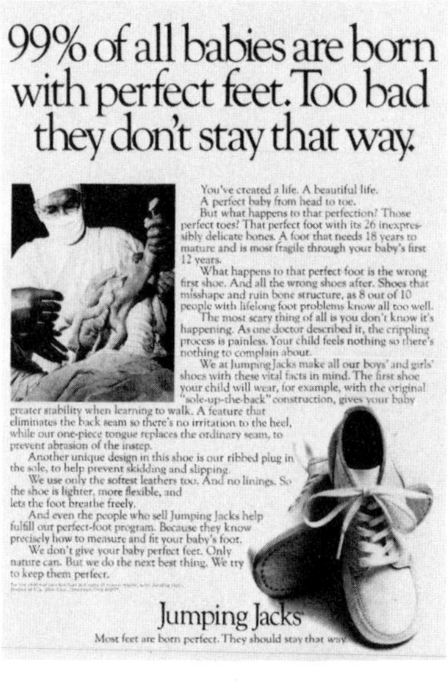

99% of all babies are born with perfect feet. Too bad they don't stay that way.

72
Art Director: Stanley Schofield
Copywriters: Martin Cohen
Jack Silverman
Designer: Stanley Schofield
Photographers: Joe Toto
Luis Pacheco
Agency: Leber Katz Partners
Client: U.S. Shoe Corporation

73
Art Director: Dick Gage
Copywriters: Bill Hamilton
Mark Meyers
Designer: Dick Gage
Photographer: Bill Bruin
Agency: Humphrey, Browning, MacDougall
Client: Acushnet Golf Equipment

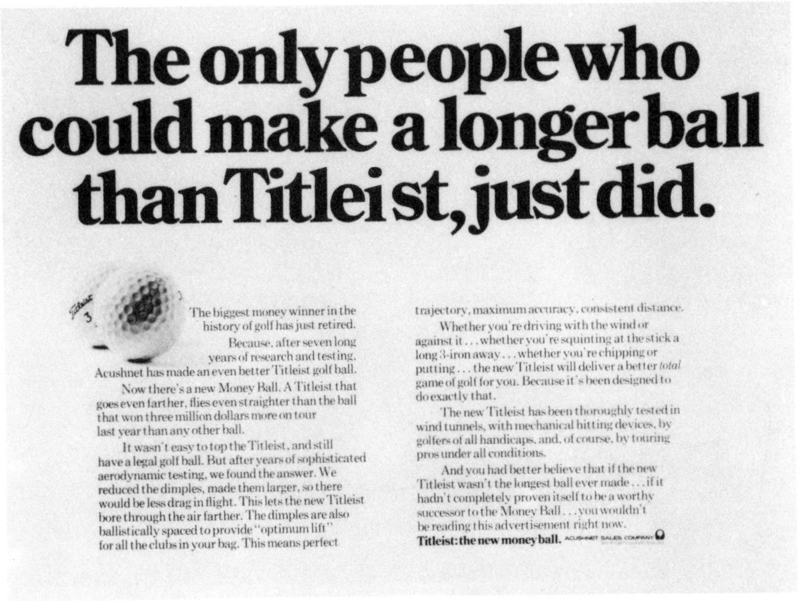
The only people who could make a longer ball than Titleist, just did.
Titleist 3
The biggest money winner in the history of golf has just retired.
Because, after seven long years of research and testing, Acushnet has made an even better Titleist golf ball.
Now there's a new Money Ball. A Titleist that goes even farther, flies even straighter than the ball that won three million dollars more on tour last year than any other ball.
It wasn't easy to top the Titleist, and still have a legal golf ball. But after years of sophisticated aerodynamic testing, we found the answer. We reduced the dimples, made them larger, so there would be less drag in flight. This lets the new Titleist bore through the air farther. The dimples are also ballistically spaced to provide "optimum lift" for all the clubs in your bag. This means perfect trajectory, maximum accuracy, consistent distance.
Whether you're driving with the wind or against it . . . whether you're squinting at the stick a long 3-iron away . . . whether you're chipping or putting . . . the new Titleist will deliver a better total game of golf for you. Because it's been designed to do exactly that.
The new Titleist has been thoroughly tested in wind tunnels, with mechanical hitting devices, by golfers of all handicaps, and, of course, by touring pros under all conditions.
And you had better believe that if the new Titleist wasn't the longest ball ever made . . . if it hadn't completely proven itself to be a worthy successor to the Money Ball . . . you wouldn't be reading this advertisement right now.
Titleist: the new money ball.
ACUSHNET SALES COMPANY

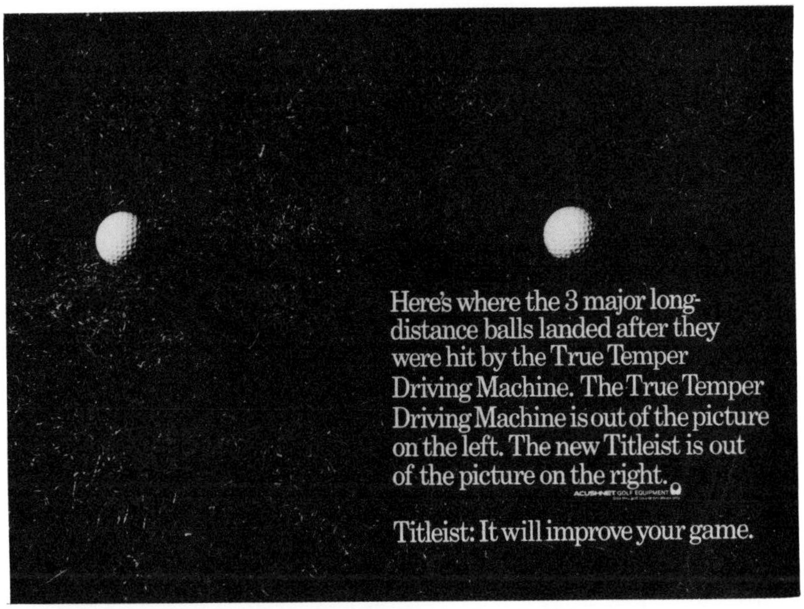
Here's where the 3 major long-distance balls landed after they were hit by the True Temper Driving Machine. The True Temper Driving Machine is out of the picture on the left. The new Titleist is out of the picture on the right.
ACUSHNET GOLF EQUIPMENT
Titleist: It will improve your game.

Titleist golfers of America:
You are about to hit the longest drive of your life.
The first time you start getting back into the groove this year, it's going to happen. You're going to put some wood behind that ball. And you're going to hit it farther than you've ever hit a golf ball before.
It won't be your winter isometrics that did it. It won't be your new golf book that did it, either. It'll be us that did it. After 7 years of research, we came out with a new Titleist golf ball – a ball that has extra yards built into it.
You'll notice some changes right away when you hold a new Titleist golf ball in your hand. The dimples are larger and shallower. This lets the new Titleist bore through the air farther to give you extra yards.
You've read some ads about long distance balls. We want to prove to you that the new Titleist is the longest ball made today – right on your own course.
If you're used to hitting to a particular tree, you're going to be hitting beyond that tree this year.
Is there a fairway trap somewhere on your course that's been driving you nuts? You're going to clear it more often this year.
There may be a dogleg you've always been tempted to try and cut. Try and cut it this year.
Many Titleist golfers will find that, instead of playing a safe shot short of a brook, they can now easily carry over the brook to the green.
You will find that some wood shots have now become iron shots. That some big water hazards have gotten smaller. And that some impossible par 4's have become possible par 4's.
The new Titleist is going to make a noticeable difference in the way you get around your course. It's going to improve your game this year.
You've got some very satisfying weekends coming up, Titleist golfer. Because you're about to play the best golf of your life.
ACUSHNET
Titleist 3
Titleist: It will improve your game.

One world. One piano.
No one is quite sure when it happened.
But sometime between the orbital journeys of Philias Phogg and Yuri Gagarin, the Steinway piano, too, circled the earth.
It didn't happen in 80 days or 108 minutes. And it created no stir to speak of. But one after another, as surely and predictably as the tides, the immortals of the music world chose the Steinway.®
Today, in international music competitions everywhere, Steinway is the one piano most often played.
From the Bolshoi Theatre to Carnegie Hall, it is the piano on which concert artists most often perform. In Aukland and Ottawa, in Jerusalem and Chicago, wherever music is loved and played, the Steinway continues to be the world standard of how a piano should sound.
And you can own one.
For more information please write to John H. Steinway, 109 West 57th Street, New York 10019.
Steinway & Sons

A Steinway is a Steinway is a Steinway.
There are different sizes. And different prices.
But large or small, when a piano bears the Steinway name you may be certain that it was built to the standard set by Henry E. Steinway 425,000 pianos ago: "Build the finest piano possible and sell it at the lowest price consistent with quality."
From smallest vertical to concert grand, all Steinway pianos are built by the same hands. Regardless of size, they share patented and exclusive features (like Steinway's Diaphragmatic® Sound Board). Features which endow the instrument with the Steinway sound.
We make no "cheaper" piano. We make no second-line piano sold under another name. We make only the Steinway.®
And no one else has ever managed to build anything quite like it.
For more information please write to John H. Steinway, 109 West 57th Street, New York 10019.
Steinway & Sons

Our simplest part.
We don't even make it ourselves.
It's so simple that we can entrust it to someone else.
This isn't anything unusual, especially when you consider the fact that there are over 12,000 parts in a single Steinway grand. Many of them standard enough that we can have them made for us, and still expect them to measure up.
But there are some things that no one but a Steinway craftsman can touch. Things like our intricate and patented Accelerated Action. Or the soundboard. Or just about anything that we consider critical to sound and tone.
Because when all is said and done, it's our name that goes on each piano.
For more information, please write John H. Steinway, 109 West 57th Street, New York, N.Y. 10019.
Steinway & Sons

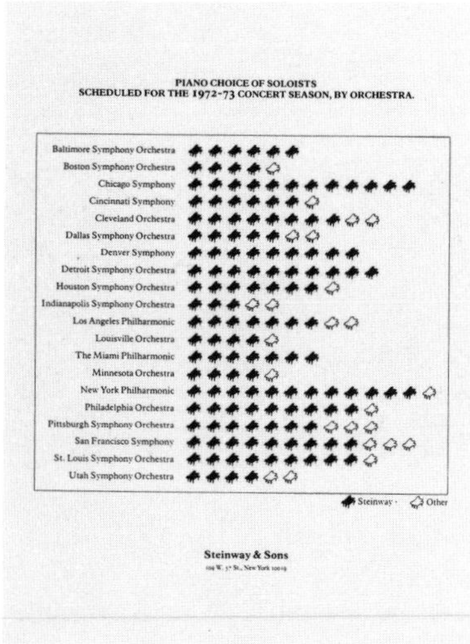
PIANO CHOICE OF SOLOISTS
SCHEDULED FOR THE 1972-73 CONCERT SEASON, BY ORCHESTRA.
Baltimore Symphony Orchestra
Boston Symphony Orchestra
Chicago Symphony
Cincinnati Symphony
Cleveland Orchestra
Dallas Symphony Orchestra
Denver Symphony
Detroit Symphony Orchestra
Houston Symphony Orchestra
Indianapolis Symphony Orchestra
Los Angeles Philharmonic
Louisville Orchestra
The Miami Philharmonic
Minnesota Orchestra
New York Philharmonic
Philadelphia Orchestra
Pittsburgh Symphony Orchestra
San Francisco Symphony
St. Louis Symphony Orchestra
Utah Symphony Orchestra
Steinway
Other
Steinway & Sons

& Sons
Theodore.
John.
Henry.
Today's Steinways.
Their father built pianos. And their grand-father. And their great-grandfather.
Today they work together to build the kind of instrument decreed by Henry E. Steinway some 420,000 pianos ago; "build the finest piano possible; sell it for the lowest price consistent with quality."
This *was* the Steinway standard.
This *is* the Steinway standard.
It means a piano which has features found in no other piano.
It means an "action" patented by one Steinway in 1966, mounted on an "action rail" patented by his great-uncle in 1868. It means a lot of time spent to build a few instruments.
It means a piano that is more expensive.
It means a piano that is more piano.
For more information please write to the one in the middle, John H. Steinway, 109 West 57th Street, New York, N.Y. 10019.
Steinway & Sons

If Pirelli snow tires can climb our hills, they can climb yours.
Maybe you've heard of our hills, the Alps, the Apennines.
For a snow tire to be able to get around in that kind of crowd, it has to have just a bit more than the ordinary snow tire.
It has to have gripping power so fierce it can dig in and pull you out of spots conventional snow tires couldn't even get you into.
Not just in deep snow, but also on hard packed snow and ice, and even mud.
And not only must it be able to outclimb and outpull conventional snow tires, it has to be able to outstop them, out-turn them, and just outhandle them in general.
We make a snow tire that can do all that.
The Pirelli Cinturato Etna.
It has a special radial ply construction that flattens out and grips the road much like the treads of a tank.
Which might explain why, in a country like Italy which has some of the toughest hills in the world, Pirelli Cinturato Etnas are the number one selling snow tire.
And, by the way, we realize that most roads aren't paved with ice and snow all winter long, so you'll be happy to know that the Etna rides cool and quiet on dry roads.
And it comes with another nice feature we haven't mentioned so far. An affordable price. (It can also be equipped with ice spikes, where legal, if you're the kind of guy who can't be too careful.)
The Pirelli Cinturato Etna.
If it can get around in our neighborhood, it can get around in yours.
PIRELLI
Radial Snow Tires

74
Art Directors: Thierry DaRold
Dick Thomas
Cathie Campbell
Copywriters: Arthur Einstein
Thierry DaRold
Hank Prowitt
Dick Thomas
Cynthia Johnson
Designers: Thierry DaRold
Dick Thomas
Cathie Campbell
Photographers: Irving Penn
Carl Fischer
Cathie Campbell
NASA
Agency: Lord, Geller, Federico, Peterson, Inc.
Client: Steinway & Sons

75
Art Directors: Larry Osborne
Ron Becker
Copywriters: Joe Tantillo
Neil Drossman
Steve Penchina
Designers: Larry Osborne
Ron Becker
Photographers: Hal Davis
Mike Raab
Harold Krieger
Agency: DKG Inc.
Client: Pirelli Tires

75

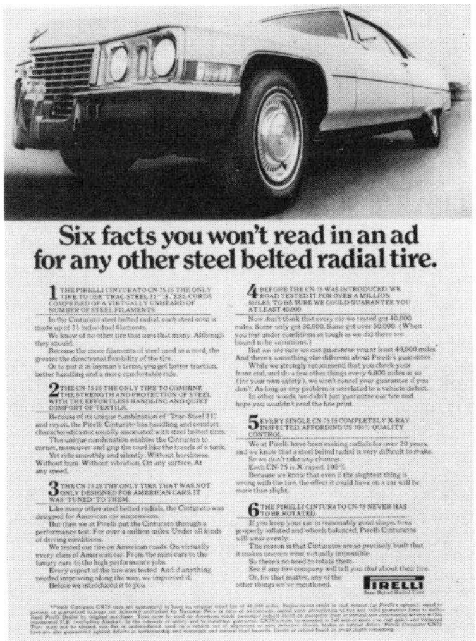

76

JOHNNIE WALKER® BLACK LABEL 12 YEAR OLD BLENDED SCOTCH WHISKY, 86.8 PROOF. BOTTLED IN SCOTLAND. IMPORTED BY SOMERSET IMPORTERS, LTD., N.Y., N.Y.
Johnnie Walker
Black Label
BOTTLED IN SCOTLAND
YEARS 12 OLD
JOHN WALKER & SONS

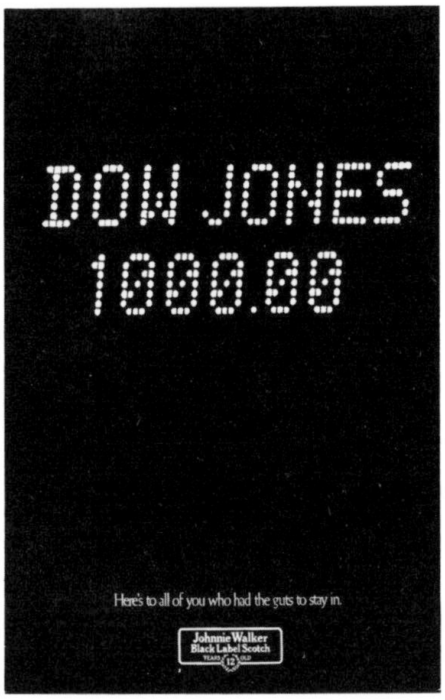
DOW JONES
1000.00
Here's to all of you who had the guts to stay in.
Johnnie Walker
Black Label Scotch
YEARS 12 OLD

To Dad,
This little bottle's here to say
you've made me what I am today.
Your stories of bankers, your stories
of kings, your stories of conglomerates,
they taught me things.
So today I'm rich, today I'm wiser.
But as this gift shows, Dad,
I'm not a miser.
Johnnie Walker
Black Label Scotch
YEARS 12 OLD

Johnnie Walker
Black Label Scotch
Refills available. About $60.
Johnnie Walker Black Label Six Pack, about $60. Sold separately, about $10 a fifth.

76
Art Director: Steve Singer
Copywriter: Jennifer Berne
Photographers: Dave Willardson
Cailor/Resnick
Agency: Smith/Greenland Company Inc.
Client: Somerset Importers, Ltd.

77
Art Director: George Fithian
Copywriters: Jo Anne Findley
Ed Curran
Designer: Ed Curran
Photographer: Bill Holland
Agency: Aitkin-Kynett & Co.
Client: F. J. Cooper, Inc.

This diamond is called "The Sultan of Morocco," says Douglas Cooper, but for $250,000 I will name it after you. It's that easy.

Mr. Cooper, the Philadelphia jeweler, has a flair for the never-before. This time it's the world's largest known blue-gray (steel-blue?) diamond. To wit: 35.27 carats.

The history of the Sultan, or the .... Diamond (why not fill in your name now and see how it sounds?) is somewhat fragmentary, to say the least. The gem was unearthed in India in the 18th century or earlier. Its uniqueness and unusual cut suggest that it once occupied a place of honor in the coffers of Catherine The Great. (Possibly she was wearing it on the occasion of her untimely demise.)

At any rate, from there it vanished. And the following account was laced together from bits of rumors, legends, folderol and some actual facts: an exiled monk, in payment for her silence, gave the gem to a favored Circassian slave. She was later to become the mother of Sultan Abd ul-Aziz IV, who was famous for collecting taxes at the point of a sword. The Sultan fell prey to an unscrupulous vizier who, pandering to his worst traits, squandered the Sultan's treasure. Unreliable sources report that the diamond somehow then came into the possession of a Dutch libertine who narrowly escaped death by firing squad in Casablanca in 1908, along with 5 other deserters from the Foreign Legion.

Two World Wars and a shroud of mystery account for another half-century during which the stone never surfaced. Though the diamond was rumored to be in the western part of the United States, Mr. Cooper's man recently trailed a Riffian tribesman from a bazaar in Ksar-es-Souk to the grandnephew of the former legionnaire and the fabled Sultan of Morocco.

Mr. Cooper has since set the Sultan as a ring, with diamonds in platinum. (See it below actual size.) It should be noted that any museum would give its eye-teeth to add this incredible gem to its collection. Ask Mr. Cooper or your accountant for the interesting specifics tax-wise. At your leisure, Mr. Cooper will fly the Sultan to you for your approval.

Speaking of flying, in all the excitement we forgot to tell you about Señor Toucan (rhamphastidae), who just flew in from Paraguay (the long way around), crossing the Andes at altitudes of up to 10,000 feet (which isn't easy with a diamond in your beak). Shown actual size in 18 karat gold with ruby eyes. $220.

Mail address: 1406 Chestnut St., Philadelphia, Pa. 19110. Add 6% for Penna. delivery. (Our magnificent Christmas catalog is ready. You may now write for it.)

F·J·COOPER INC
jewelers by birth . . . since 1883
1416 Chestnut Street, Philadelphia, Pa.
2 Orange St. at Union, Montego Bay, Jamaica
F. R. Cooper, Colchester, England

"Only great alexandrites pass this test," says Mr. Cooper. "And few can hold a candle to this one." (Forgive the pun. We couldn't resist it.)

Isn't it ironic that with all the scientific equipment at his disposal, Douglas Cooper, the Philadelphia jeweler, still tests his chrysoberyl alexandrites the way Alexander II of Russia did? The tsar was indeed partial to alexandrites. They were discovered in the Urals in 1833 on the day the young tsarevitch celebrated his majority and they were named after him, don't you see.

The extraordinary thing, of course, was that the alexandrite, a shimmering sea green by day, turned Titian red by night (or candlelight). The redder the better.

As time went on, the tsar and the gem were to share more than just their name. Alexander was noted for his subtlety and discretion. The same qualities were to endear his namesake to gem connoisseurs the world over.

Mr. Cooper's rare chrysoberyl alexandrite ring is shown above actual size. It was red when we photographed it and wreathed in 18 karat gold acanthus leaves with diamonds. $39,500. Mr. Cooper will gladly hold a candle to it for you, if you should like a closer look.

What do you do as an encore to a gem that changes its color? How about the ring below that changes its clothes? The bunches of diamonds you see actual size are one convertible ring: first in an 18 karat gold daytime jacket, then in 18 karat white gold for evening. With almost 4 carats of diamonds, a great stocking stuffer, don't you think, at $2,880?

The duck at the end of this paragraph has been quacking incessantly since the beginning of this ad. "Tell them about me, tell them about me." Okay, okay. For the record, he's lapis-lazuli and 18 karat gold as a brooch. $100. Mail address: 1406 Chestnut Street, Philadelphia, Pennsylvania 19110. Add 6% for Pennsylvania delivery. Did you know our new catalog was ready? Write for it soon.

F·J·COOPER INC
jewelers by birth . . . since 1883
1416 Chestnut Street, Philadelphia, Pa.
2 Orange St. at Union, Montego Bay, Jamaica
F. R. Cooper, Colchester, England

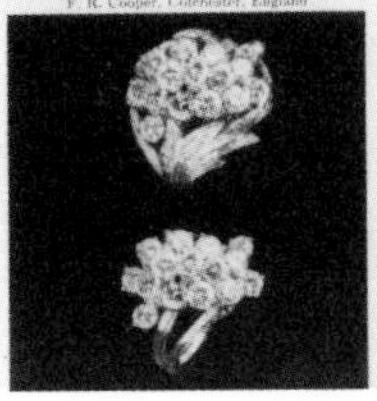

"The emerald that is not sold will be mine for my birthday," says Mrs. Cooper. Mr. Cooper says nothing.

Years of scouring the Far East for treasures like the seated Lohan (Ming Dynasty temple priest) have taught Douglas Cooper something about oriental inscrutability.

And years as the wife of the Philadelphia jeweler have taught Diene Cooper something about detachment. Mrs. Cooper is usually not this covetous. But emeralds are usually not this special.

Few can boast the clarity and the color of Mr. Cooper's (Mrs. Cooper's?). Not to mention their credentials: for centuries they shared a place of honor in *the* magnificent collection belonging to the Imperial House of Russia.

They are both shown below actual size set as rings. The one on the top, with diamonds in 18 karat gold and platinum, $125,000. And just below, the other ensconced in diamonds and platinum, $225,000. Since even our excellent photographer can not do justice to these remarkable gems, Mr. Cooper will be glad to fly them to you for your amazement.

The erudite owl has been taking all of this in but, taking his example from Mr. Cooper and the Lohan, says nothing. When absolutely pressed for information, he doesn't give a hoot. As a brooch in 14 karat gold with peridot eyes, $75. Mail address: 1406 Chestnut Street, Philadelphia, Pennsylvania 19110. Add 6% for Pennsylvania delivery.

F·J·COOPER INC
jewelers by birth . . . since 1883
1416 Chestnut Street, Philadelphia, Pa.
2 Orange St. at Union, Montego Bay, Jamaica
F. R. Cooper, Colchester, England

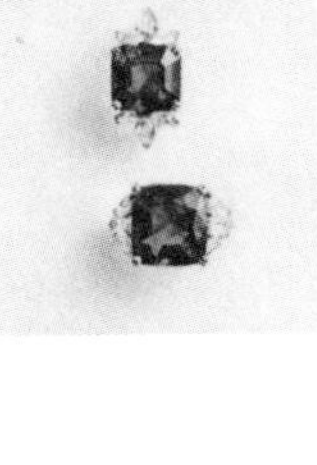

"Jamaica is a land where frogs live in trees and birds ride on cows," says Mr. Cooper. "What better setting for my storybook ruby?"

Ho-hum rubies are not at home in the Isle of Springs, the land of the Arawak and the sanctuary of the buccaneer. Douglas Cooper's latest contribution to the island's color and excitement is the fabulous gem ruby shown below actual size.

A personal audience with the Cooper ruby would expose the rare, exquisite pigeon's-blood vibrancy that makes connoisseurs go crazy with lust.

Mr. Cooper will tell you that this is among the finest rubies he has ever seen (and he has seen a few).

If you would like to inspect it, come to the Georgian Corner (shown in our photograph) and ask for Mr. Cooper's, mon. Or call Mr. Cooper in Montego Bay 952-5705. The ruby, awash with diamonds as a ring, in 18 karat yellow gold and platinum is $88,000.

The Jamaican Doctor Bird over there to the right has never hitched a ride on a cow like his friend, the cattle egret. But he has a specialty of his own—flying backwards at 3600 WPM's (Wingbeats Per Minute). As a brooch, in 18 karat gold and enamel with a ruby eye (so everyone can have a ruby). $165.

And unlike Annie Palmer, the Lucrezia Borgia of Montego Bay, the little spider starting things off is nonpoisonous. This fellow is making a repeat appearance with us, back by popular demand. His body is a black star sapphire. As a brooch in 14 karat gold with a spiral back, $24.

Come see us at No. 2 Orange Street at Union, or write to 1406 Chestnut Street, Philadelphia, Pa. 19110. Add 6% for Pennsylvania delivery.

F·J·COOPER INC
jewelers by birth . . . since 1883
1416 Chestnut Street, Philadelphia, Pa.
2 Orange St. at Union, Montego Bay, Jamaica
F. R. Cooper, Colchester, England

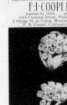

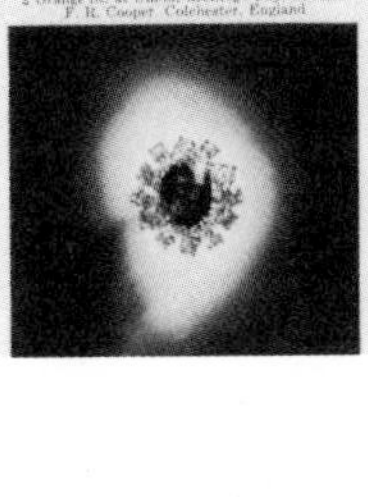

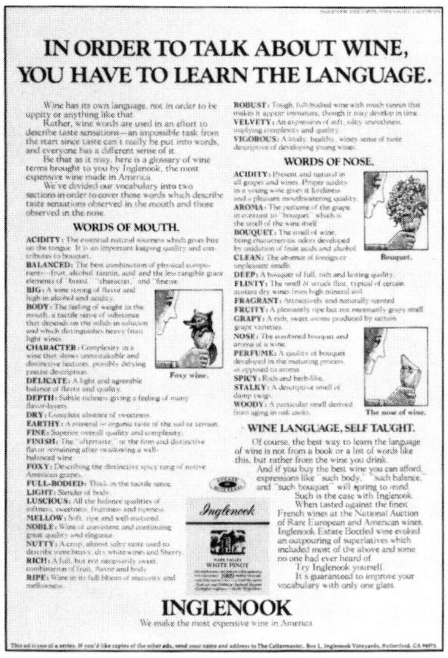
IN ORDER TO TALK ABOUT WINE, YOU HAVE TO LEARN THE LANGUAGE.
WORDS OF MOUTH.
WORDS OF NOSE.
WINE LANGUAGE, SELF TAUGHT.
INGLENOOK
We make the most expensive wine in America.

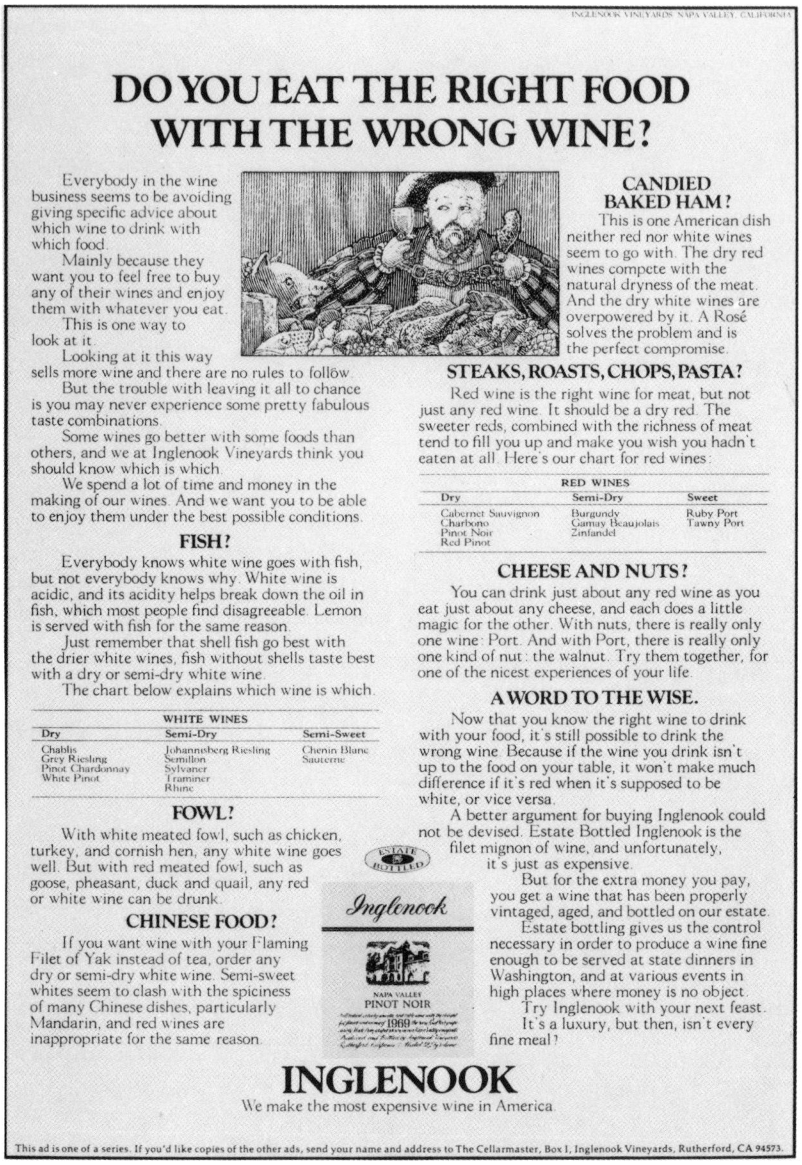
INGLENOOK VINEYARDS, NAPA VALLEY, CALIFORNIA
DO YOU EAT THE RIGHT FOOD WITH THE WRONG WINE?
Everybody in the wine business seems to be avoiding giving specific advice about which wine to drink with which food.
Mainly because they want you to feel free to buy any of their wines and enjoy them with whatever you eat.
This is one way to look at it.
Looking at it this way sells more wine and there are no rules to follow.
But the trouble with leaving it all to chance is you may never experience some pretty fabulous taste combinations.
Some wines go better with some foods than others, and we at Inglenook Vineyards think you should know which is which.
We spend a lot of time and money in the making of our wines. And we want you to be able to enjoy them under the best possible conditions.
FISH?
Everybody knows white wine goes with fish, but not everybody knows why. White wine is acidic, and its acidity helps break down the oil in fish, which most people find disagreeable. Lemon is served with fish for the same reason.
Just remember that shell fish go best with the drier white wines, fish without shells taste best with a dry or semi-dry white wine.
The chart below explains which wine is which.
WHITE WINES
Dry: Chablis, Grey Riesling, Pinot Chardonnay, White Pinot
Semi-Dry: Johannisberg Riesling, Semillon, Sylvaner, Traminer, Rhine
Semi-Sweet: Chenin Blanc, Sauterne
FOWL?
With white meated fowl, such as chicken, turkey, and cornish hen, any white wine goes well. But with red meated fowl, such as goose, pheasant, duck and quail, any red or white wine can be drunk.
CHINESE FOOD?
If you want wine with your Flaming Filet of Yak instead of tea, order any dry or semi-dry white wine. Semi-sweet whites seem to clash with the spiciness of many Chinese dishes, particularly Mandarin, and red wines are inappropriate for the same reason.
CANDIED BAKED HAM?
This is one American dish neither red nor white wines seem to go with. The dry red wines compete with the natural dryness of the meat. And the dry white wines are overpowered by it. A Rosé solves the problem and is the perfect compromise.
STEAKS, ROASTS, CHOPS, PASTA?
Red wine is the right wine for meat, but not just any red wine. It should be a dry red. The sweeter reds, combined with the richness of meat tend to fill you up and make you wish you hadn't eaten at all. Here's our chart for red wines:
RED WINES
Dry: Cabernet Sauvignon, Charbono, Pinot Noir, Red Pinot
Semi-Dry: Burgundy, Gamay Beaujolais, Zinfandel
Sweet: Ruby Port, Tawny Port
CHEESE AND NUTS?
You can drink just about any red wine as you eat just about any cheese, and each does a little magic for the other. With nuts, there is really only one wine: Port. And with Port, there is really only one kind of nut: the walnut. Try them together, for one of the nicest experiences of your life.
A WORD TO THE WISE.
Now that you know the right wine to drink with your food, it's still possible to drink the wrong wine. Because if the wine you drink isn't up to the food on your table, it won't make much difference if it's red when it's supposed to be white, or vice versa.
A better argument for buying Inglenook could not be devised. Estate Bottled Inglenook is the filet mignon of wine, and unfortunately, it's just as expensive.
But for the extra money you pay, you get a wine that has been properly vintaged, aged, and bottled on our estate.
Estate bottling gives us the control necessary in order to produce a wine fine enough to be served at state dinners in Washington, and at various events in high places where money is no object.
Try Inglenook with your next feast.
It's a luxury, but then, isn't every fine meal?
ESTATE BOTTLED
Inglenook
NAPA VALLEY
PINOT NOIR
1969
INGLENOOK
We make the most expensive wine in America.
This ad is one of a series. If you'd like copies of the other ads, send your name and address to The Cellarmaster, Box I, Inglenook Vineyards, Rutherford, CA 94573.

78

HERE'S TO EVERYONE WHO CAN'T THINK UP A GOOD TOAST.
WHY WE CALL IT "TOAST."
HELP YOURSELF TO THESE TOASTS.
THE TRUTH.
INGLENOOK
We make the most expensive wine in America.

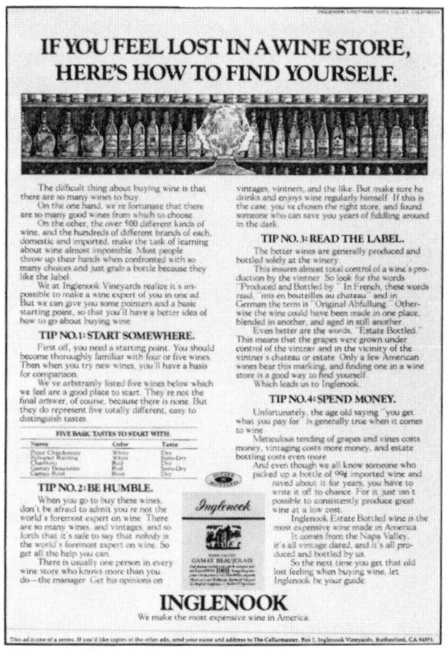
IF YOU FEEL LOST IN A WINE STORE, HERE'S HOW TO FIND YOURSELF.
TIP NO. 1: START SOMEWHERE.
TIP NO. 2: BE HUMBLE.
TIP NO. 3: READ THE LABEL.
TIP NO. 4: SPEND MONEY.
INGLENOOK
We make the most expensive wine in America.

You were born with fluoride in your teeth.
So why use Crest?
Crest
Fighting cavities is the whole idea behind Crest.

How to introduce a little person to a big dentist.
Fighting cavities is the whole idea behind Crest.

78 Gold Award
Art Director: Thomas O. Tieche
Copywriter: Patrick Kelly
Designer: Gloria Baker
Artist: Chas. B. Slackman
Photographer: Ron Quilici
Agency: McCann-Erickson, Inc.
Client: United Vintners, Inc.

79 Silver Award
Art Directors: Jim Burton
Burt Blum
Copywriters: Marv Jacobson
Bob Collins
Ellen Massoth
Artist: Kim Whitesides
Photographers: Joe Toto
John Amos Miller
Agency: Benton & Bowles, Inc.
Client: Procter & Gamble

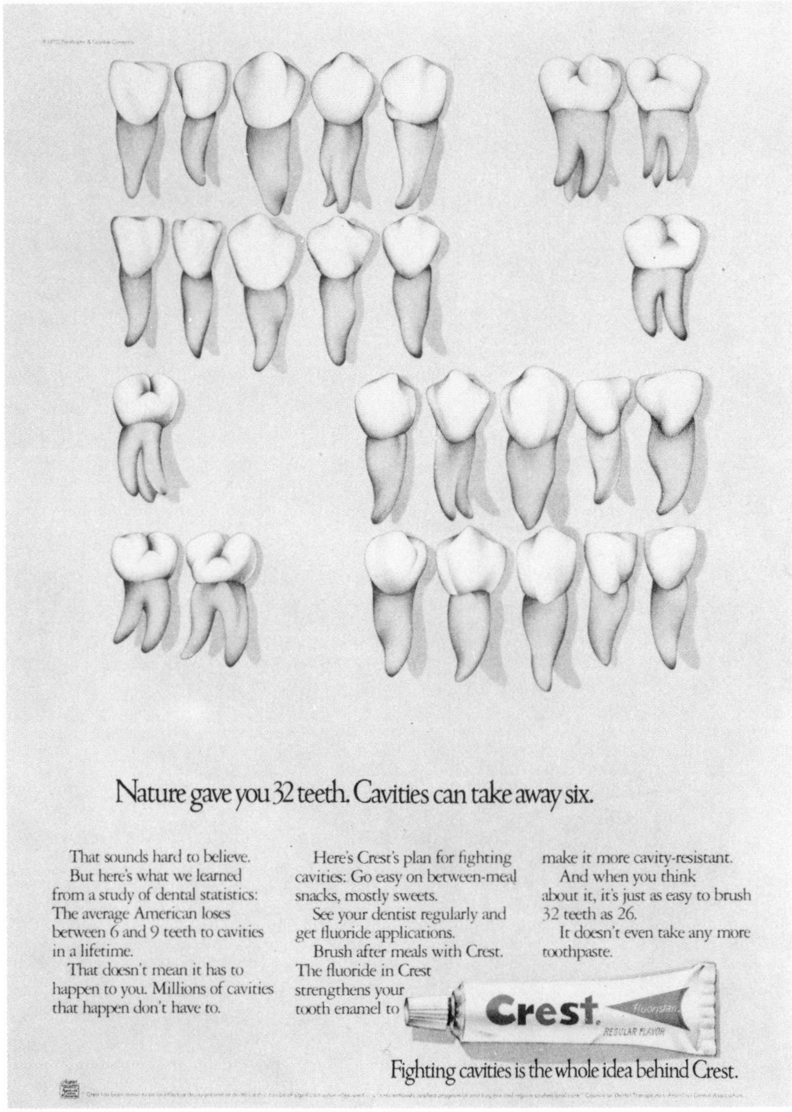
Nature gave you 32 teeth. Cavities can take away six.
That sounds hard to believe. But here's what we learned from a study of dental statistics: The average American loses between 6 and 9 teeth to cavities in a lifetime.
That doesn't mean it has to happen to you. Millions of cavities that happen don't have to.
Here's Crest's plan for fighting cavities: Go easy on between-meal snacks, mostly sweets.
See your dentist regularly and get fluoride applications.
Brush after meals with Crest. The fluoride in Crest strengthens your tooth enamel to make it more cavity-resistant.
And when you think about it, it's just as easy to brush 32 teeth as 26.
It doesn't even take any more toothpaste.
Crest
REGULAR FLAVOR
Fighting cavities is the whole idea behind Crest.

80

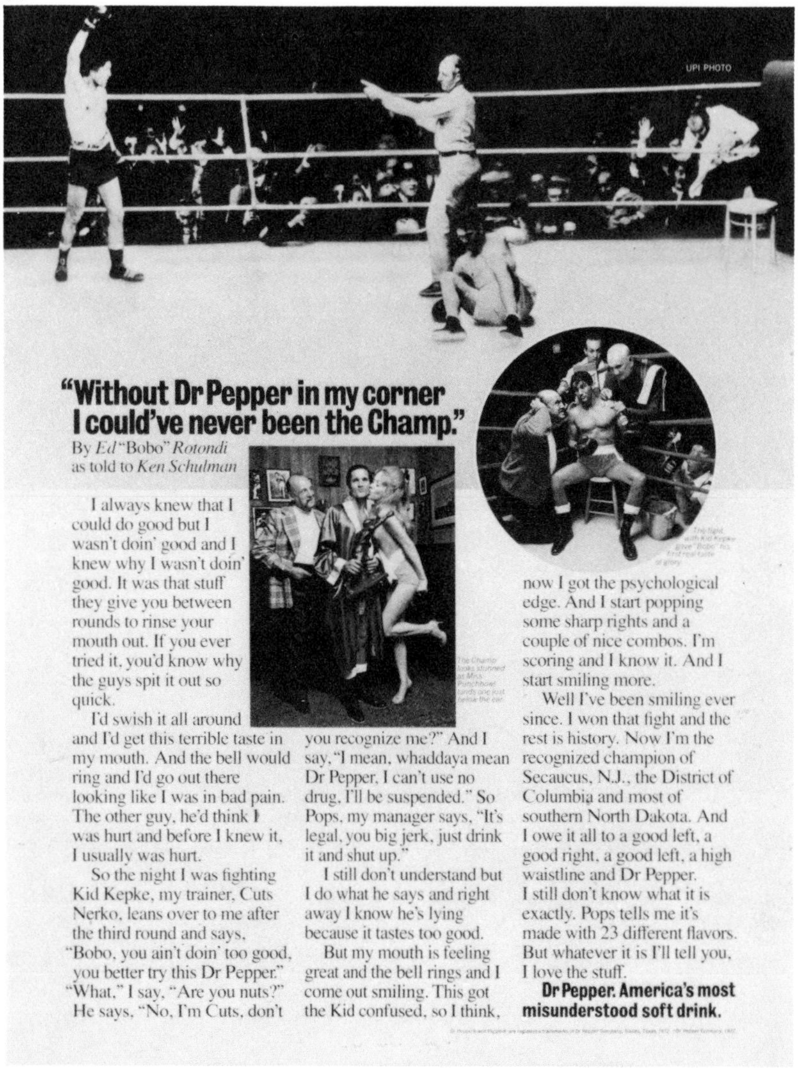
UPI PHOTO
"Without Dr Pepper in my corner I could've never been the Champ."
By *Ed* "Bobo" *Rotondi* as told to *Ken Schulman*
I always knew that I could do good but I wasn't doin' good and I knew why I wasn't doin' good. It was that stuff they give you between rounds to rinse your mouth out. If you ever tried it, you'd know why the guys spit it out so quick.
I'd swish it all around and I'd get this terrible taste in my mouth. And the bell would ring and I'd go out there looking like I was in bad pain. The other guy, he'd think I was hurt and before I knew it, I usually was hurt.
So the night I was fighting Kid Kepke, my trainer, Cuts Nerko, leans over to me after the third round and says, "Bobo, you ain't doin' too good, you better try this Dr Pepper." "What," I say, "Are you nuts?" He says, "No, I'm Cuts, don't you recognize me?" And I say, "I mean, whaddaya mean Dr Pepper, I can't use no drug, I'll be suspended." So Pops, my manager says, "It's legal, you big jerk, just drink it and shut up."
I still don't understand but I do what he says and right away I know he's lying because it tastes too good.
But my mouth is feeling great and the bell rings and I come out smiling. This got the Kid confused, so I think, now I got the psychological edge. And I start popping some sharp rights and a couple of nice combos. I'm scoring and I know it. And I start smiling more.
Well I've been smiling ever since. I won that fight and the rest is history. Now I'm the recognized champion of Secaucus, N.J., the District of Columbia and most of southern North Dakota. And I owe it all to a good left, a good right, a good left, a high waistline and Dr Pepper.
I still don't know what it is exactly. Pops tells me it's made with 23 different flavors. But whatever it is I'll tell you, I love the stuff.
Dr Pepper. America's most misunderstood soft drink.

We lived in shame for 57 years.

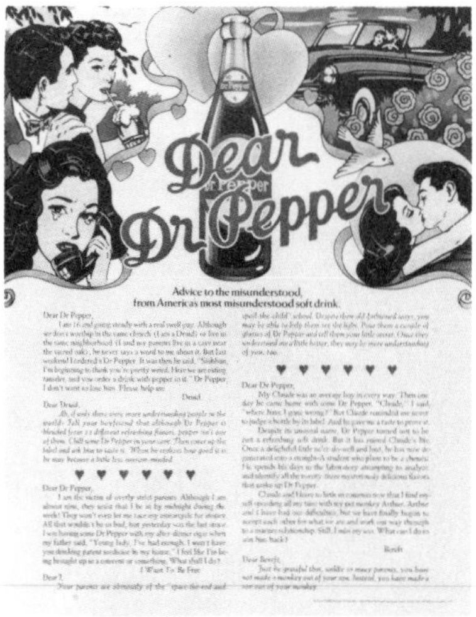
Dear Dr Pepper
Advice to the misunderstood, from America's most misunderstood soft drink.

80
Art Director: Ed Rotondi
Copywriters: Ken Schulman
Art Naiman
Designer: Ed Rotondi
Artists: David Wilcox
David Willardson
Photographer: Joe Toto
Agency: Young & Rubicam International, Inc.
Client: Dr. Pepper

81
Art Director: Roy Grace
Copywriter: Marcia Bell Grace
Designer: Roy Grace
Photographer: Dick Stone
Agency: Doyle Dane Bernbach Inc.
Client: American Tourister Luggage

"Dear American Tourister: You saved my life."
On October 20, 1969, Charles Pendley and his American Tourister were hit by a car going 40 miles an hour.
Luckily for Mr. Pendley, the American Tourister absorbed the force of the blow. If it hadn't, the doctor later told him, he probably wouldn't be alive.
Mr. Pendley suffered a broken wrist. The American Tourister suffered some too. But the locks, which weren't even locked, stayed shut. Nothing inside (including a bottle of after-shave lotion and a camera) got hurt.
Now, while we don't build an American Tourister to withstand things like speeding cars and onrushing trains, we do build an American Tourister well.
We mold every piece out of sixteen different strong materials, and wrap it all up with a tough stainless steel frame. Instead of putting reinforcement at the corners, we reinforce it with fiberglass all over. We give each bag nonspring locks, designed not to spring open on impact.
Maybe American Tourister can't promise to save your life. But think what we do to save your underwear.
American Tourister

"Dear American Tourister: Your suitcase took an unexpected trip."
We could tell you ourselves how we build American Touristers out of 16 different strong materials. And give them tough stainless steel frames. But James Edelstein of West Allis, Wis. says it better: "At 70 mph it flew off the luggage rack. Not a single bottle inside got broken."
We could go on about the fiberglass reinforcement we put all through every case. But why not let Mrs. W. W. Hairston of Florence, Ala. do the talking: "My suitcase fell off the luggage rack and skidded down the highway for 1500 feet. There was one small dent in it."
We could mention how our nonspring locks are designed not to spring open on impact. But who knows more about impact than Robert Ammon of Bloomfield Hills, Mich.: "After hitting the pavement at 80 mph and plunging down a 40-foot embankment, the bag stayed closed."
Naturally we can't promise that flying off a car won't scratch or dent or split an American Tourister. We don't build them to go on trips like these. But trips like these were exactly what happened to Robert Funk of Sioux City, Iowa, Mrs. Frank O'Brien of Birmingham, Ala., Robert Geroy of Winston-Salem, N.C., Mrs. Houston Hodges of Austin, Tex., Brother Richard Belles of Selma, Ala., Mrs. Robert Rapp of San Leandro, Calif. And dozens more.
Ask any of them, when the unexpected happens, what you can expect from a suitcase made by American Tourister.
American Tourister

"Dear American Tourister: You make a fabulous jack."
This unsolicited testimonial comes from The J. C. Quinly family of Walnut Creek, California.
Who jacked up their car to change a tire and left their American Tourister standing near. All of a sudden, the car slid backward, fell off the jack, and landed square on their suitcase.
Where it remained until the Quinlys finished changing their tire.
Of course, the suitcase got dented. (Mr. Quinly had to fix it with a hammer.)
And of course, you realize we don't build American Touristers to go through extraordinary things like supporting a car. We build American Touristers for the ordinary perils of ordinary travel.
So we build our case with 16 different strong materials, and give it a tough stainless steel frame.
We reinforce American Touristers with fiberglass. Not just on the corners, but through and through.
Most important of all, we put in nonspring locks designed not to spring open on impact.
Remember, the beautiful thing about traveling with an American Tourister isn't that it holds up a car.
But simply that it holds up.
American Tourister

"Dear American Tourister: I dropped my suitcase."
"1500 feet.
From a helicopter.
Onto ground frozen hard at 40 below."
Ah well, accidents happen. And while we don't promise to survive the unusual, we do build American Touristers unusually well.
We mold 16 different strong materials into every piece we build.
We reinforce American Touristers with fiberglass. All over, not just on the corners.
We wrap every American Tourister with a tough stainless steel frame. And put in nonspring locks, the kind designed not to spring open on impact.
So when D. H. Bennyhoff of Alaska dropped his American Tourister 1500 feet from a helicopter, everything inside stayed inside. And nothing inside got hurt.
"We think a suitcase should stand up to the everyday perils of everyday travel," says American Tourister.
"I think it's amazing," says Mr. Bennyhoff.
American Tourister

82

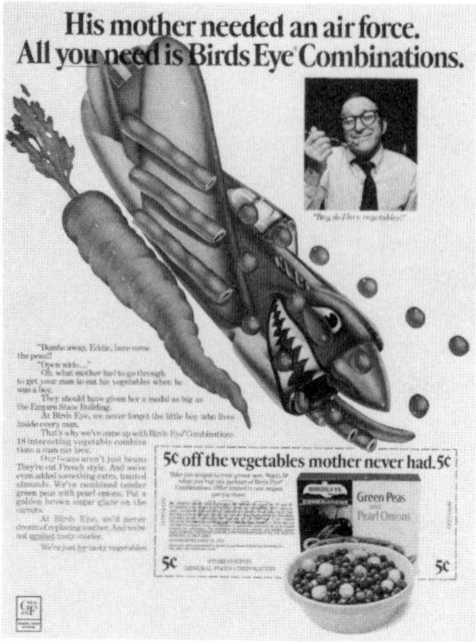
His mother needed an air force.
All you need is Birds Eye Combinations.
5¢ off the vegetables mother never had. 5¢
Green Peas
5¢
5¢

His mother needed a railroad.
All you need is Birds Eye® Combinations.
"Boy, do I love vegetables!"
"Open wide, Joey, here comes the caboose!!
"ChooChooChooChoo ChooChooChooChoo."
Oh, the things mother had to go through to get your man to eat his vegetables when he was a boy.
They should have made her a saint. At least.
At Birds Eye,® we never forget the little boy who lives inside every man.
That's why we've come up with Birds Eye® Combinations: 20 interesting vegetable combinations a man can love.
Our peas aren't just peas. We've combined them with tender cauliflower. And we've even added a smooth cream sauce. Our baby lima beans come with a mild seasoned sauce, Southern style.
Next time, serve him Birds Eye® Combinations.
And when he asks for seconds, be proud.
Because your vegetables will be as unforgettable as his mother's stories.
Two new vegetables mother never had.
BIRDS EYE
COMBINATIONS
Green Peas and Cauliflower with Cream Sauce
NEW!
Baby Lima Beans with Seasoned Sauce, Southern Style
NEW!
GF
GENERAL FOODS KITCHENS

82
Art Director: Woody Litwhiler
Copywriter: Don Marowski
Designer: Woody Litwhiler
Artist: Charles White
Photographer: Joe Toto
Agency: Young & Rubicam International, Inc.
Client: General Foods

83

Chances are you choose an airline exactly wrong.
"Fly with us and get the world's biggest sandwich."
"Fly with us and get the world's smilingest stewardesses."
"Fly with us and get the world's longest movies."
"Fly with us and get the world's liveliest color coordinations."
Pan Am

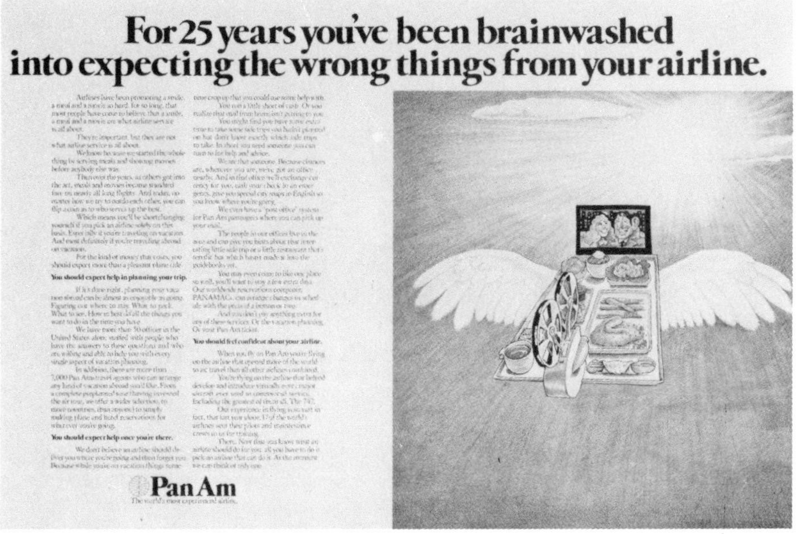

For 25 years you've been brainwashed into expecting the wrong things from your airline.
Pan Am

Picking an airline for its food is like picking a restaurant for its flying ability.
RALPH'S
Pan Am

83
Art Director: Amil Gargano
Copywriters: Jim Durfee
Bob Kaplan
Artist: Rick Meyrowitz
Agency: Carl Ally Inc.
Client: Pan American Airways

Consumer Magazine/Campaign

84
Art Directors: Nicholas Gisonde
Bob Kuperman
Copywriters: Neil Drossman
Jerry Della Femina
Designers: Nicholas Gisonde
Bob Kuperman
Photographer: Arnold Beckerman
Agency: Della Femina, Travisano & Partners, Inc.
Client: Teacher's Scotch

85
Art Directors: Joe LaRosa
Rafael Morales
Copywriter: Judy Blumenthal
Photographer: David Langley
Agency: Waring & LaRosa, Inc.
Client: Fisher-Price Toys

84

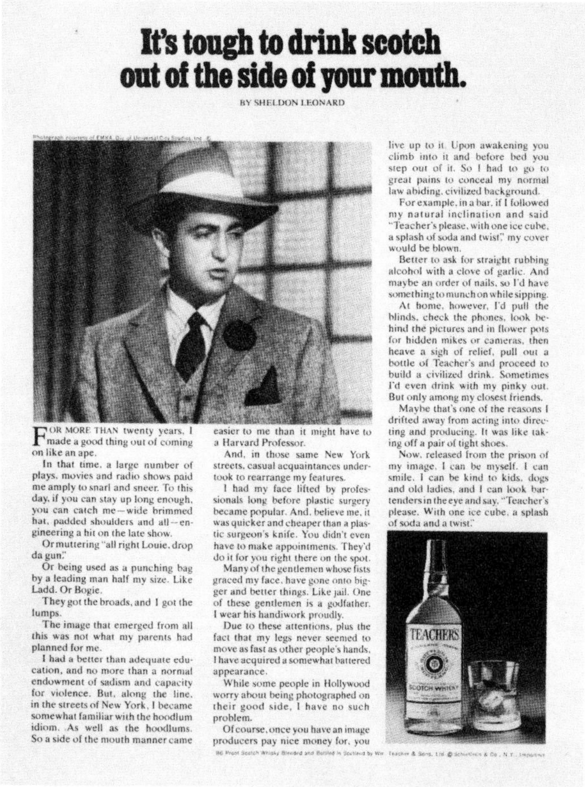
It's tough to drink scotch out of the side of your mouth.
BY SHELDON LEONARD
FOR MORE THAN twenty years, I made a good thing out of coming on like an ape.
In that time, a large number of plays, movies and radio shows paid me amply to snarl and sneer. To this day, if you can stay up long enough, you can catch me—wide brimmed hat, padded shoulders and all—engineering a hit on the late show.
Or muttering "all right Louie, drop da gun."
Or being used as a punching bag by a leading man half my size. Like Ladd. Or Bogie.
They got the broads, and I got the lumps.
The image that emerged from all this was not what my parents had planned for me.
I had a better than adequate education, and no more than a normal endowment of sadism and capacity for violence. But, along the line, in the streets of New York, I became somewhat familiar with the hoodlum idiom. As well as the hoodlums. So a side of the mouth manner came easier to me than it might have to a Harvard Professor.
And, in those same New York streets, casual acquaintances undertook to rearrange my features.
I had my face lifted by professionals long before plastic surgery became popular. And, believe me, it was quicker and cheaper than a plastic surgeon's knife. You didn't even have to make appointments. They'd do it for you right there on the spot.
Many of the gentlemen whose fists graced my face, have gone onto bigger and better things. Like jail. One of these gentlemen is a godfather. I wear his handiwork proudly.
Due to these attentions, plus the fact that my legs never seemed to move as fast as other people's hands, I have acquired a somewhat battered appearance.
While some people in Hollywood worry about being photographed on their good side, I have no such problem.
Of course, once you have an image producers pay nice money for, you live up to it. Upon awakening you climb into it and before bed you step out of it. So I had to go to great pains to conceal my normal law abiding, civilized background.
For example, in a bar, if I followed my natural inclination and said "Teacher's please, with one ice cube, a splash of soda and twist," my cover would be blown.
Better to ask for straight rubbing alcohol with a clove of garlic. And maybe an order of nails, so I'd have something to munch on while sipping.
At home, however, I'd pull the blinds, check the phones, look behind the pictures and in flower pots for hidden mikes or cameras, then heave a sigh of relief, pull out a bottle of Teacher's and proceed to build a civilized drink. Sometimes I'd even drink with my pinky out. But only among my closest friends.
Maybe that's one of the reasons I drifted away from acting into directing and producing. It was like taking off a pair of tight shoes.
Now, released from the prison of my image, I can be myself. I can smile. I can be kind to kids, dogs and old ladies, and I can look bartenders in the eye and say, "Teacher's please. With one ice cube, a splash of soda and a twist."
TEACHERS
SCOTCH WHISKY

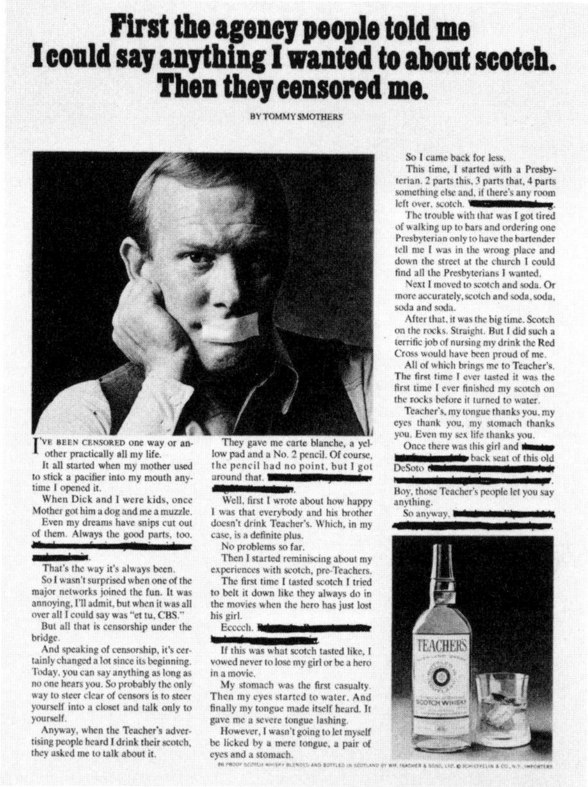
First the agency people told me I could say anything I wanted to about scotch. Then they censored me.
BY TOMMY SMOTHERS
I'VE BEEN CENSORED one way or another practically all my life.
It all started when my mother used to stick a pacifier into my mouth anytime I opened it.
When Dick and I were kids, once Mother got him a dog and me a muzzle.
Even my dreams have snips cut out of them. Always the good parts, too. [redacted].
That's the way it's always been.
So I wasn't surprised when one of the major networks joined the fun. It was annoying, I'll admit, but when it was all over all I could say was "et tu, CBS."
But all that is censorship under the bridge.
And speaking of censorship, it's certainly changed a lot since its beginning. Today, you can say anything as long as no one hears you. So probably the only way to steer clear of censors is to steer yourself into a closet and talk only to yourself.
Anyway, when the Teacher's advertising people heard I drink their scotch, they asked me to talk about it.
They gave me carte blanche, a yellow pad and a No. 2 pencil. Of course, the pencil had no point, but I got around that. [redacted].
Well, first I wrote about how happy I was that everybody and his brother doesn't drink Teacher's. Which, in my case, is a definite plus.
No problems so far.
Then I started reminiscing about my experiences with scotch, pre-Teachers.
The first time I tasted scotch I tried to belt it down like they always do in the movies when the hero has just lost his girl.
Ecccch. [redacted].
If this was what scotch tasted like, I vowed never to lose my girl or be a hero in a movie.
My stomach was the first casualty. Then my eyes started to water. And finally my tongue made itself heard. It gave me a severe tongue lashing.
However, I wasn't going to let myself be licked by a mere tongue, a pair of eyes and a stomach.
So I came back for less.
This time, I started with a Presbyterian. 2 parts this, 3 parts that, 4 parts something else and, if there's any room left over, scotch. [redacted].
The trouble with that was I got tired of walking up to bars and ordering one Presbyterian only to have the bartender tell me I was in the wrong place and down the street at the church I could find all the Presbyterians I wanted.
Next I moved to scotch and soda. Or more accurately, scotch and soda, soda, soda and soda.
After that, it was the big time. Scotch on the rocks. Straight. But I did such a terrific job of nursing my drink the Red Cross would have been proud of me.
All of which brings me to Teacher's. The first time I ever tasted it was the first time I ever finished my scotch on the rocks before it turned to water.
Teacher's, my tongue thanks you, my eyes thank you, my stomach thanks you. Even my sex life thanks you.
Once there was this girl and [redacted] back seat of this old DeSoto [redacted].
Boy, those Teacher's people let you say anything.
So anyway, [redacted].
TEACHERS
SCOTCH WHISKY

I told the scotch people I don't drink any more. Then again, I don't drink any less, either.

Whenever I think of Scotch, I recall the immortal words of my brother Harpo.

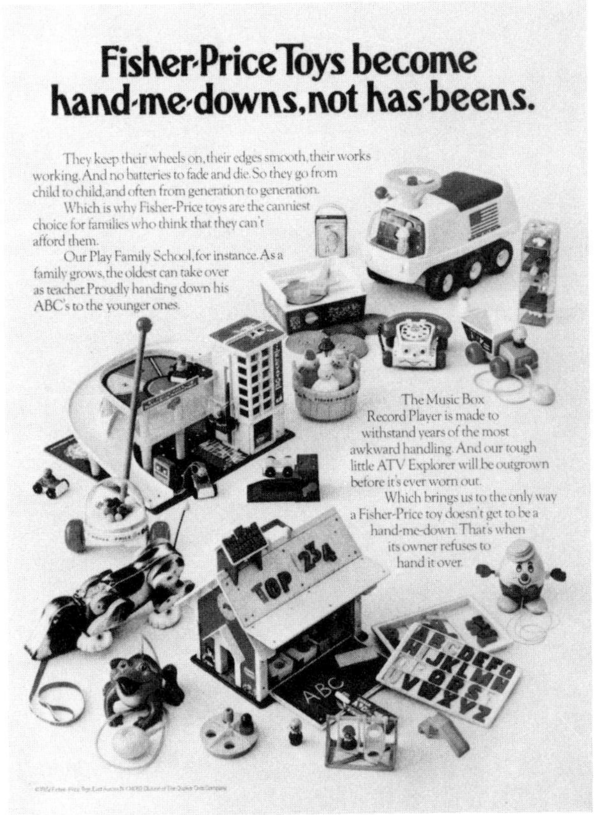
Fisher-Price Toys become hand-me-downs, not has-beens.
They keep their wheels on, their edges smooth, their works working. And no batteries to fade and die. So they go from child to child, and often from generation to generation.
Which is why Fisher-Price toys are the canniest choice for families who think that they can't afford them.
Our Play Family School, for instance. As a family grows, the oldest can take over as teacher. Proudly handing down his ABC's to the younger ones.
The Music Box Record Player is made to withstand years of the most awkward handling. And our tough little ATV Explorer will be outgrown before it's ever worn out.
Which brings us to the only way a Fisher-Price toy doesn't get to be a hand-me-down. That's when its owner refuses to hand it over.

Fisher-Price Toys come without instructions.
Even our Play Family School, newest addition to the Play Family world. (That bright, durable world where things run smoothly and imagination takes over.) No one ever had to show a child how to play school.
Then there's our new Music Box Record Player. Leave a child on his own with it. He'll figure out how it works. No needles, no batteries or electric cord. And discs made especially for small hands.
Not only do we omit directions for children, there are none for adults to struggle through either. Forget blueprints, nuts and bolts, last-minute frenzies. Because every Fisher-Price toy comes out of its box all put together.
The rest is child's play.

Fisher-Price Toys run on child power.
Because when a toy is fueled by imagination it travels farther than anything.
The Jet that takes off from Play Family Airport lands on cloud cities.
And there's a musical Merry-Go-Round where no one ever asks for your ticket.
Our new Play Family Houseboat makes the bathtub a sea. With knees for islands.
And since child-power is half imagination, half pure energy, Fisher-Price puts in dozens of realistic details. Details that do things.
Look at our new Airport. With its own passenger jet, helicopter and a fleet of trucks and cars. The nozzle on the jet fueler fits every vehicle. The baggage rack can revolve. And the copter goes, "Whomp whomp." Children can appreciate that kind of thing.
So there they go. Into the air. Over the waves. Round and round in circles. That's child power.

Fisher-Price Toys don't need batteries.
They run the old-fashioned way. On child power. The strength of young imaginations. The endless energy of small bodies.
The push and pull of a child's curiosity on the way to learning something new.
Because Fisher-Price believes there's too much push-button entertainment today. And once you've pressed a button, what else is there to do, Mommy?
Even our new Music Box Record Player is a toy of involvement. Not only doesn't it need batteries (it winds up), it doesn't even need a Mommy to supervise.
Our Play Family Toys, including a brand new Schoolhouse, give children the chance to run things their own way, on their own steam.
That's another great thing about child power. When it's exhausted, it goes to bed for the night. And wakes up—recharged.

Consumer Magazine/Campaign

86
Art Director: Jim Brown
Copywriter: Norman Muchnic
Designer: Jim Brown
Photographer: Henry Sandbank
Agency: Doyle Dane Bernbach Inc.
Client: General Telephone & Electronics

86

If your six year old saw something like this, would he know how to phone for help?
It's too important a question to leave to chance.
So most phone companies have programs for teaching school kids to report emergencies.
In General Telephone areas, six and seven year olds are taught to dial "0", give their name and tell our operator where they are and what's wrong. While older students are trained to dial emergency numbers direct—because that's the fastest way to call for help.
But of course, we can't reach every kid. We need your help at home. (Which is why we're running this ad.)
Copy down the emergency numbers listed on the inside front cover or first page of your telephone directory. Add your family doctor's number. And the number of the nearest hospital. Next, tack up the list near your phone. Then get your kids to memorize it, just in case it gets lost.
By the time they're through memorizing those numbers they're going to have every grownup in the house knowing them, too. (Which is also why we're running this ad.)
GTE
GENERAL TELEPHONE & ELECTRONICS

Before it flashes at your daughter's wedding, it has to do a lot more in our lab.
That's why we have a lab in the first place.
Because when your daughter gets married, we want you to have as much confidence in our flashcubes as we do.
And since we invented the flashcube, it's only right we give ours the toughest tests in the business before sending it out in the world.
But what is there for a flashcube to do besides flash?
Well, for your once-in-a-lifetime indoor shots to come out right, it has to flash at the right time and for the right length of time, to begin with.
At the same time, it has to flash with the right intensity.
And there's no better time to start finding out if it will than before each individual bulb is put into the cube.
We do that much on a device we call a photometer.
The next test comes two weeks later, when we check each flashcube, bulb by bulb, to see if the blue dot has turned pink.
If it has, we know that air has gotten in and the bulb won't fire at all.
These we don't even bother to test. We simply throw the whole cube out.
But don't get the idea that all flashcubes that pass make it out of the plant.
We store some of each day's output under warehouse conditions right on the premises for periods of 30 days. 60 days. 6 months. A year.
And then we test them all over again.
For that matter, even after a Blue Dot flashcube has made it out of the plant, it still hasn't seen the last of us. We recall a few cases a year from every single GTE Sylvania warehouse in the world for re-testing.
For timing. For brightness. For that nasty pink dot.
Our 40 full-time testers work very hard at what they do to minimize the chance of failure.
Because we know that what really matters is not that we invented the flashcube, but that we make the best one.
And keep on making it.
GTE
GENERAL TELEPHONE & ELECTRONICS

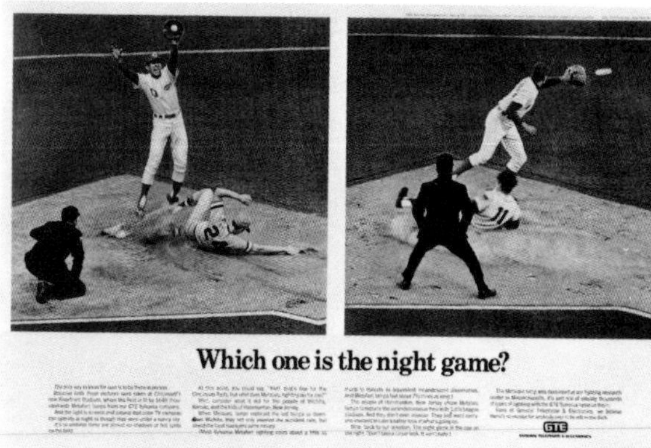
Which one is the night game?
GTE

87
Art Director: Fred Kittel
Copywriters: Granger Tripp
Bill Lane
Designers: Fred Kittel
Bob Moscarello
Photographers: Tom McCarthy
Tony Petrucelli
Bill Binzen
Agency: J. Walter Thompson Company
Client: Eastman Kodak Company

87

Would you risk
this moment
on anything
less than
Kodak film?

Would you risk this moment
on anything less than Kodak film?

Would you risk
this moment
on anything
less than
Kodak film?

Would you risk this moment
on anything less than Kodak film?
Kodak makes your pictures count.

Would you risk this moment
on anything less than Kodak film?
Kodak makes your pictures count.

Consumer Magazine / Campaign

88
Art Directors: Allan Beaver
Lou Colletti
Copywriters: Larry Plapler
Larry Spector
Designers: Allan Beaver
Lou Colletti
Photographer: Richard Noble
Agency: Levine, Huntley, Schmidt
Client: Jockey International, Inc.

Somehow the Fifties look a lot better in the Seventies.
Jockey Golden Oldies Group
DACRON

88

Our vacation prints. While a guy takes in the scenic beauty he gives a little back.
Jockey Sportswear.

DACRON
Jockey does something terrific for guys.
Jockey does something terrific for guys.
Jockey Sportswear.

89

Art Directors: Harry Webber
Julio Dilorio
Copywriter: Gene Case
Photographer: Manny Gonzalez
Agency: Case & McGrath Inc.
Client: Gravymaster Co., Inc.

89

"When my husband says the grace, I'm afraid I know why he's praying."
He's so sweet, he'd never say something I cooked was bad. He'd just say it's "not one of his favorites."
But there's one thing he loves that I make as good as anybody:
Gravy. I make great gravy. I follow the pictures on the Gravy Master bottle.
The gravy comes out dark and rich and smooth, with a little taste of parsley and things.
I've never messed it up yet.
Knock on wood.
Looking for some new recipes?
Write Gravy Master, Dept. AY, Long Island City, N. Y. 11101.

"My gravy is fine. It's what's underneath that makes me cry."
My husband loves my gravy. He uses it to hide the lumps in my mashed potatoes.
But friends who make the fluffiest potatoes tell me it's gravy that gives them fits.
So I say: Follow the pictures on the Gravy Master bottle. Gravy Master gravy has a little taste of parsley and things, and it comes out rich and smooth.
And if The Lump Queen here can make gravy rich and smooth, anybody can.
Memo to you good cooks: For some interesting recipes, write Gravy Master, Dept. KX, Long Island City, N. Y. 11101.

"Everyone gives thanks for my gravy but not for my turkey."
Mrs. D. G., White Plains, N.Y.
My turkey's always so dry! The white meat's like some new kind of building material.
Oh well, I'll just make lots of gravy. And Boy do I make good gravy!
I follow the pictures on the Gravy Master bottle. Sesame Street couldn't make it any plainer.
The gravy comes out smooth and brown, with a little taste of celery and parsley and things.
Gravy Master costs about 3¢ a meal. A bottle lasts 10 meals.
That's about how long my turkey lasts.

"My gravy's so good, it gives guests a false sense of security."
Mrs. P.M., Greenburgh, N.Y.
Gravy is on all my friends' Disaster List. So when they come to dinner and taste my gravy, they probably think I'm one of those born cooks you read about.
Wrong! I'm a nervous wreck in the kitchen before a big meal.
So what I do with gravy is, I just follow the pictures on the Gravy Master bottle.
It's like having a piece of a cookbook glued right there on the bottle.
The gravy comes out smooth and brown, with a little taste of celery and parsley and things.
And Gravy Master costs only 3¢ a meal.

"I'm a bum cook. But I make great gravy."
Some of my rice.
My rice is a pot of glue.
My hamburgers are like grey rocks.
My fried eggs have plastic placemats for bottoms.
But weird as it sounds, I have no trouble with gravy.
I follow the pictures on the Gravy Master bottle.
Sesame Street couldn't make it any plainer.
The gravy comes out smooth and brown, with a little taste of celery and parsley and things.
Gravy Master costs about 3¢ a meal. A bottle lasts 10 meals.
I can hide a lot of mistakes under that much good gravy.

Log Cabin® and the Sweet Soul Picnic. July 4th. Memphis, Tennessee.

Sweet soul food. An American tradition that's a fabulous blend of Southern, West Indian, French Creole, and African foods.

Sweet because of the syrup that swirls through the black-eyed peas. That glazes the candied yams. That even goes into the sweet potato pie. The Log Cabin® brand that has been around this country since 1887. And great Black cooks, creative as they are, no doubt have discovered how the special taste of Log Cabin fits right into their way of cooking.

Soul because of the love. The care. The long hours of preparation. The wisdom of knowing how to please. The ingenuity of knowing how to make superb dishes out of whatever was on hand, which is the secret of great cooking traditions everywhere.

If you want to know what goes into the cookery of a sweet soul picnic, here's an idea. It all begins the night before. Talk about preparation! The family would get together in Grandma Ella Jackson's big kitchen. There'd be lots of greens to wash. Lots of yams to be peeled. Lots of chicken to cut. And lots of black-eyed peas to soak. Grandma's kitchen was a ceaseless hive of activity in preparation for the day ahead. The great sweet soul picnic. A classical Southern feast.

Here are some great soul food recipes from the Log Cabin kitchens, beginning with the most classic of all, Southern Fried Chicken.

Log Cabin and the Southern Fried Chicken

Dip 3-lb. frying chicken pieces in ½ cup Log Cabin Syrup; coat with 1 cup seasoned all-purpose flour; then sprinkle with remaining flour and set aside 15 minutes. Fry chicken, a few pieces at a time, in ½ inch of hot shortening (half butter and half vegetable shortening) in large skillet, until golden brown. Place in shallow baking pan; bake at 350° for 30 minutes, or until tender. Garnish. Makes 4 to 6 servings. *Note:* Recipe may be doubled.

Throughout Black homes in this country, black-eyed peas are traditionally served on New Year's Day as an assurance of good luck for the coming year. It's called Hoppin' John. Of course, it's not only served on New Year's Day. Black-eyed peas are a staple in soul food cooking and are served throughout the year. No matter what the occasion. Like for the soul food picnic. The black-eyed peas are baked with pork and sweetened with Log Cabin.

Log Cabin and the Baked Black-Eyed Peas

Soak 1 lb. dried black-eyed peas in water overnight; drain. In large saucepan combine ½ lb. salt pork and enough water to cover. Bring to boil; simmer 1½ hours. Drain, measuring broth; add water to make 4 cups liquid. Combine peas and measured liquid in saucepan; top with pork. Bring to boil; simmer 30 minutes. Stir in 1 cup catsup, ⅔ cup Log Cabin Syrup, 2 tbsp. vinegar, 2 tsp. salt, and ¾ tsp. dry mustard. Pour into 3-qt. casserole. Bake at 350° for 2 hours. Makes about 10 cups or 10 servings.

The only way to end a really great picnic is to serve a really great dessert. And what dessert could have more soul than sweet potato pie?

Log Cabin and the Sweet Potato Pie

Combine 2½ cups mashed cooked sweet potatoes (about 4 medium), ¼ cup sugar, and ¼ cup softened butter; gradually beat in ⅔ cup Log Cabin Syrup. Add 3 eggs, one at a time, beating well after each addition. Blend in ¾ cup milk, then ½ tsp. salt, ¼ tsp. *each* nutmeg, allspice, *and* cinnamon, and 1 tsp. vanilla. Pour into 1 unbaked 9-inch fluted pie shell. Bake at 425° for 10 minutes; then at 325° for 1 hour. Cool.

Soul food was born in the homes of Black cooks. And because recipes were seldom written down, a young girl learned from experience by watching her mother and grandmother. As she grew older she instinctively added her own little touches. Thus making soul food what it is today.

Log Cabin has been refined and fussed with over the years, too. To satisfy America's changing tastes.

Log Cabin and the sweet soul picnic. Two of America's No. 1 favorites. Make them a part of your 4th of July celebration.

The Log Cabin Brand. America grew up on it.

Log Cabin® and a pie Johnny Appleseed would have been proud of.

Homemade apple pie, fresh-out-of-the-oven, cooling on the back porch of an old country farmhouse in Lisbon, Ohio. Golden, flaky crust hiding the delights that lie beneath. The tender, juicy apples mingled with a touch of lemon, a bit of cinnamon, some butter, sugar and a little Log Cabin Syrup to make the apples even more luscious.

Every good American cook has her own special favorite secrets, and this one's the mapley touch of Log Cabin Syrup.

Log Cabin and Johnny Appleseed Pie.

Combine 1/4 cup Log Cabin Syrup, 1/2 cup sugar, 2 tablespoons Minute® Tapioca, 1 tablespoon lemon juice, 1 teaspoon cinnamon, 1/2 teaspoon

nutmeg, and 1/4 teaspoon salt; gently stir in 6 cups peeled, sliced apples (about 6 apples) and let stand 15 minutes. Line a 9-inch pie pan with pastry. Pack apple mixture tightly into bottom crust and dot with 2 tablespoons butter. Cut design or slits in top crust, put on pie, press edges together and crimp. Open cuts to let steam escape. Bake at 450° for about 1 hour, or until filling bubbles and pastry is golden. For glazed crust, brush top crust with 2 tablespoons Log Cabin Syrup after 40 minutes of baking; then continue baking. Cool before cutting.

Apple pie is one of the greatest of all American cooking traditions, no doubt because the apple is such a hearty fruit. It became a very important part of the pioneers' way of life. Apples were used in every imaginable way. But of all the wonderful apple treats pioneer women made, a warm apple pie was something the men looked forward to when they came home from a hard day in the fields.

Perhaps we owe the fact that apple trees are still growing in abundance around us to a man named John Chapman, known in American legend as Johnny Appleseed. A man who traveled through the wilderness of the Ohio River Valley, stopping and clearing a patch of land, and then planting that land with apple seeds.

The Log Cabin brand has been around about as long as the legend. Since 1887, to be exact. It was just about the first blended syrup ever, refined and fussed with over the years, of course, just like the original apple pie recipe. But always a favorite with America's cooks.

Here's a recipe from the Log Cabin kitchens for an apple pie Johnny Appleseed himself would have been proud of.

Apple orchards. Beautiful in springtime when pink and white blossoms crowd the branches of the trees and scent the air with nature's own perfume. Stately in summer with leaves of apple green. And generous in autumn with boughs presenting their gifts of fruit glistening in the sun. Fruits for wonderful apple pies. That was Johnny Appleseed's legacy to America.

Our legacy to the American cooking heritage is Log Cabin's delicious blend of syrups.

The Log Cabin Brand. America grew up on it.

A Log Cabin® breakfast around berry picking time. Salem, Oregon.

Sweet berries and Log Cabin® Syrup over scrumptious sourdough pancakes. That's what breakfast in Salem, Oregon, is all about. Especially this time of year when the berries are just ripe to be picked.

This breakfast became a tradition years ago when pioneers were settling the hillsides and valleys of the American Northwest.

They brought with them their sourdough starter

of flour, water and yeast. Salt, sugar, baking soda and eggs were later added to make wonderful breads, biscuits and pancakes.

What a blessing this sight must have been to those good cooks; fresh wild berries of every imaginable kind growing in fertile abundance in the Oregon soil.

Here are some recipes from the Log Cabin kitchens including special tips on how to make the "starter" for the sourdough pancakes.

How to make Sourdough Pancakes.

First make the starter. Sprinkle 1 package active dry yeast into 2-1/2 cups *warm,* not hot, water in large glass mixing bowl. Gradually stir in 3 cups unsifted all-purpose flour; then beat until very smooth. Cover with towel and place in warm, draft-free place for 24 hours to ripen. (Mixture should then be bubbly; if not, discard and begin again.) Store in tightly covered glass container in refrigerator. Mixture will keep several weeks.

To make batter, blend 2 cups *warm,* not hot, water and 2 cups unsifted all-purpose flour into starter; then beat until smooth. Cover with towel; place in warm, draft-free place overnight. Measure 4 cups, refrigerate remainder in covered glass container to use at another time—keeps several weeks.

To make pancakes, add 1 egg, slightly beaten, 1/4 cup evaporated milk, and 2 tablespoons salad oil to the 4 cups batter; beat until smooth. Combine 2 tablespoons sugar, 1 teaspoon baking soda, and 1/2 teaspoon salt; add to batter and mix just to blend. Let stand 15 minutes. Bake on hot griddle, turning to brown on both sides. Serve with syrup made from Log Cabin and berries. Makes about 24 to 30 (4-inch) pancakes.

When a woman spends the time and effort to give her family a special breakfast of sourdough pancakes, it seems natural that she'd want to make her berry syrups with a traditional syrup like Log Cabin. After all, the Log Cabin brand has been around this country since 1887. The tartness of fresh berries mingled with the sweet, mellow, rich taste of Log Cabin does justice to even the sourdough pancake.

Log Cabin and Berry Syrup

Combine 1/2 cup Log Cabin Syrup and 2/3 to 3/4 cup fresh blueberries, strawberries, blackberries, or boysenberries. Serve on pancakes. Makes about 1 cup.

Over the years Americans have discovered how Log Cabin fits right into their own style of cooking. It's been refined and fussed with just to suit America's changing tastes.

Why not try sourdough pancakes for a change topped with a berry syrup made from Log Cabin, one of America's all-time favorites.

The Log Cabin Brand. America grew up on it.

It may be a hamburger to you, but it's chopped beef to us.
There's a world of difference in the world of hamburgers. We call our hamburger chopped beef because it's a lot more than just an ordinary hamburger, it's 100% government-inspected pure beef chopped fine, broiled to your order, and served on a warmed sesame seed roll. Whatever you choose to call our hamburger, you get it (along with a generous portion of French fries) at Ponderosa for a ridiculously low 59 cents.*
Ponderosa® You don't know how good it is until you eat someplace else.

90
Art Director: Georgia Shankle
Copywriter: Evelyn Lewis
Designer: Georgia Shankle
Photographer: Otto Storch
Agency: Young & Rubicam International, Inc.
Client: General Foods

91
Art Director: William Taubin
Copywriter: Larry Levenson
Photographer: George Ratkai
Agency: Doyle Dane Bernbach Inc.
Client: Ponderosa Steak House

91

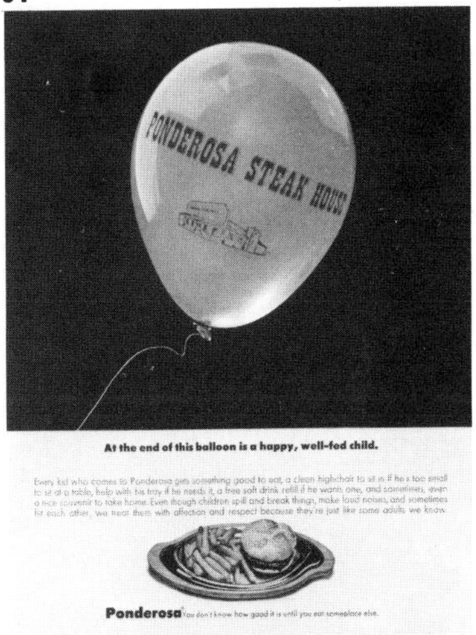
PONDEROSA STEAK HOUSE
At the end of this balloon is a happy, well-fed child.
Ponderosa® You don't know how good it is until you eat someplace else.

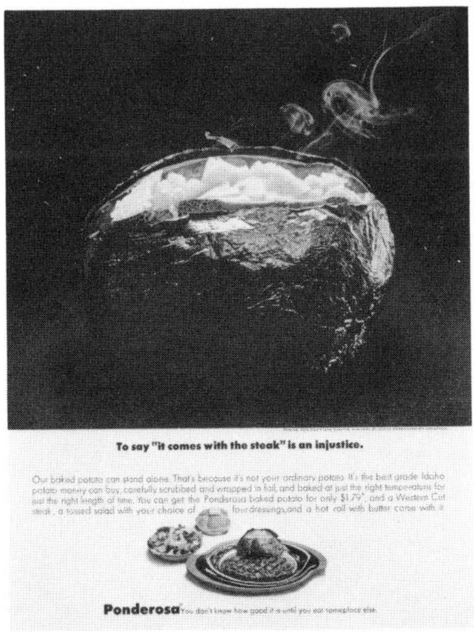
To say "it comes with the steak" is an injustice.
Ponderosa® You don't know how good it is until you eat someplace else.

How many fresh vegetables do you put in a salad?
Ponderosa® You don't know how good it is until you eat someplace else.

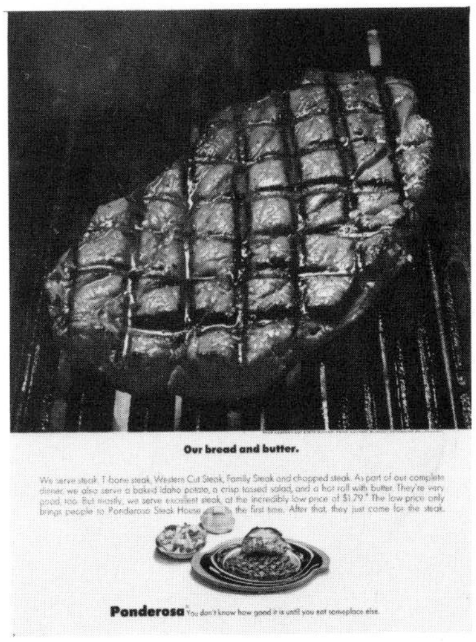
Our bread and butter.
Ponderosa® You don't know how good it is until you eat someplace else.

To tell you the truth, I've lost the urge.
Lack of exercise, insufficient fluid intake, diet deficient in bulk, and certain medications can all contribute to constipation in the aging. Gradually the normal defecation "urge" is lost. And help is needed to restore the normal bowel function.
FLEET ENEMA works quickly – usually within 2 to 5 minutes. Unlike oral laxatives, which can take up to 24 hours. And oral laxatives may actually irritate the intestinal tract or retard digestion and further inhibit regularity.
FLEET ENEMA is gentle, too. Works without the burning often experienced with suppositories. Without the discomfort of soapsuds enemas.
FLEET ENEMA induces a physiological pattern of evacuation in the left colon and the rectum. Where it's needed. Helpful especially for the geriatric patient with poor intestinal tone.
And FLEET ENEMA is easy. Ready to use. Completely disposable. A timesaving plus in nursing home care – or at home.
FLEET ENEMA. For geriatric patients. Helps restore the urge.
Warning: Frequent or prolonged use of enemas may result in dependence. Take only when needed or when prescribed by a physician. Do not use when nausea, vomiting, or abdominal pain is present. Caution: Do not administer to children under two years of age unless directed by a physician.
FREE BOOKLET. The Professional Treatment of Constipation. Specifically prepared to assist you in providing your older patients with more detailed information about constipation and its treatment. For copies simply write to C.B.FLEET CO.,INC., P.O. Box 1100, Lynchburg, Va. 24505.
Fleet® Enema
The professional aid to constipation relief
Fleet
pharmaceuticals
C. B. FLEET CO., INC.
Lynchburg, Va. 24505

Trade Magazine/Single

93

94

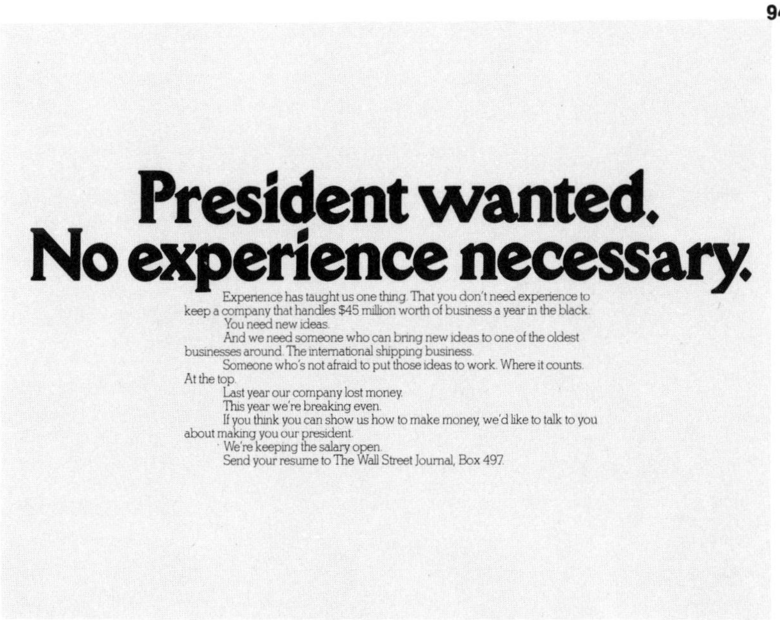

President wanted.
No experience necessary.
Experience has taught us one thing. That you don't need experience to keep a company that handles $45 million worth of business a year in the black.
You need new ideas.
And we need someone who can bring new ideas to one of the oldest businesses around. The international shipping business.
Someone who's not afraid to put those ideas to work. Where it counts. At the top.
Last year our company lost money.
This year we're breaking even.
If you think you can show us how to make money, we'd like to talk to you about making you our president.
We're keeping the salary open.
Send your resume to The Wall Street Journal, Box 497.

92
Art Directors: Lester Barnett
George Toubin
Copywriter: Karen Blunt
Photographer: Steve Steigman
Agency: Klemtner Advertising Agency
Client: C. B. Fleet Co.

93
Art Director: Irwin Rothman
Photographer: Irv Bahrt
Client: Pioneer-Moss Engraving

94
Art Director: Ken Berris
Copywriter: John Russo
Designer: Ken Berris
Agency: Della Femina, Travisano & Partners, Inc.
Client: Emery Air Freight

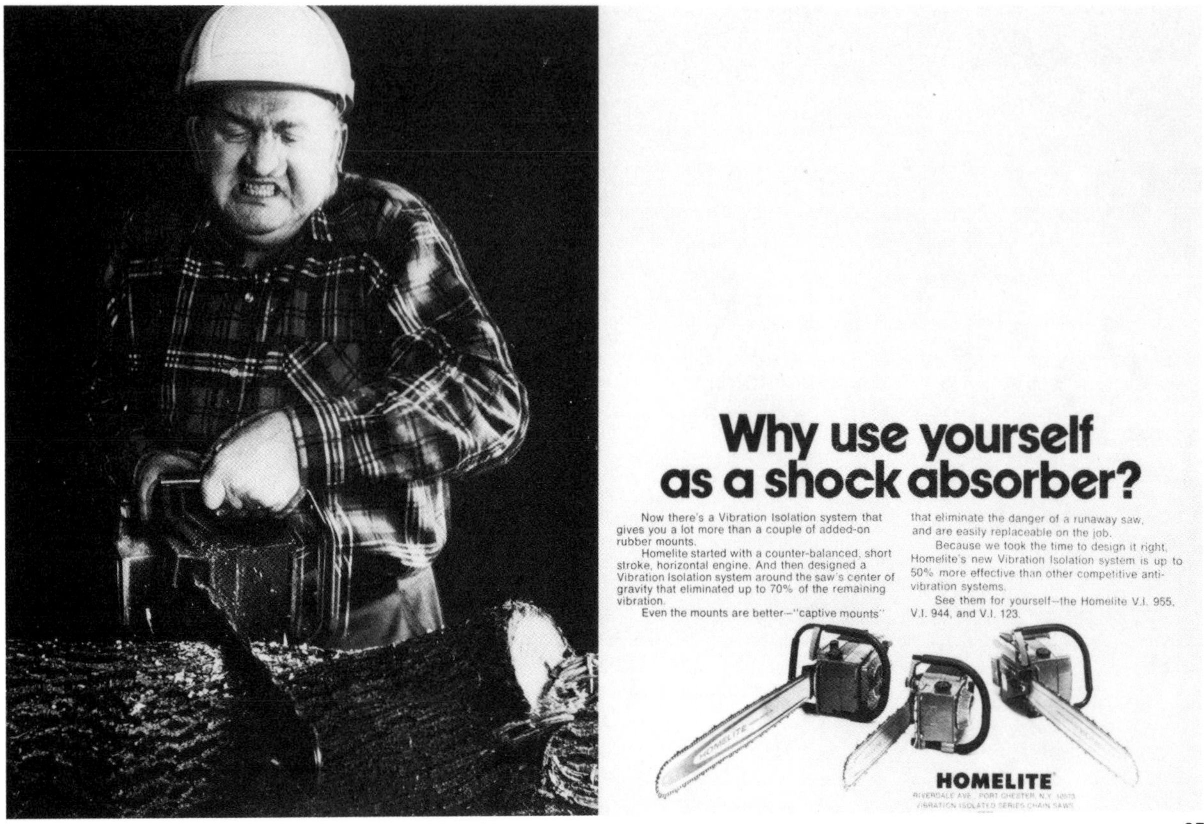
Why use yourself as a shock absorber?
Now there's a Vibration Isolation system that gives you a lot more than a couple of added-on rubber mounts.
Homelite started with a counter-balanced, short stroke, horizontal engine. And then designed a Vibration Isolation system around the saw's center of gravity that eliminated up to 70% of the remaining vibration.
Even the mounts are better—"captive mounts" that eliminate the danger of a runaway saw, and are easily replaceable on the job.
Because we took the time to design it right, Homelite's new Vibration Isolation system is up to 50% more effective than other competitive anti-vibration systems.
See them for yourself—the Homelite V.I. 955, V.I. 944, and V.I. 123.
HOMELITE
RIVERDALE AVE., PORT CHESTER, N.Y.
VIBRATION ISOLATED SERIES CHAIN SAWS

95

96

PEOPLE BROWSE IN OTHER DECORATING MAGAZINES. THEY BUY IN OURS.
1,001 DECORATING IDEAS
Colonial...
to mix or match!
The other decorating magazines feature priceless things like an original oil painting or a two hundred year old bed. That's the stuff that fills dreams.
But when people actually want to fill a home, they open a copy of 1,001 Decorating Ideas.
Everything in it is affordable and currently on the market.
That's because our philosophy of decorating is that everything we show should not only be beautiful, but also practical.
As one example, we're running a series of articles showing how to decorate one house four different ways. To prove that no matter what style the exterior, the interior of a house can be any style people choose.
Our concept of decorating accounts for why approximately a million people buy each issue of our magazine, why two million people read each issue and why 58.4%* of the people who buy our magazine keep it around the house for at least three years.
But more important for you is the fact that people not only read our magazine, they buy what's in it.
That's the basic difference between 1,001 and other decorating magazines.
While they fill the heads of their readers with dreams, we fill the homes of our readers with products.
1,001 DECORATING IDEAS
1,001 Decorating Ideas, 149 Fifth Avenue, New York, New York 10010, (212)-677-0870
A Consolidated Foods Company • Responsive to consumer needs. *Source: A study of 1,001 Decorating Ideas—Compiled by A.C. Neilsen, 1971.

This page is missing from your telephone book.

These are the brand-new toll-free numbers to call when you want to send a passenger or cargo on TAP to Portugal and points beyond.
In some states you must dial '1' before using the '800' WATS numbers.
And to use the Enterprise (E) numbers, simply dial the operator and have her place the call.
Tear out this page and keep it. You'll probably have a call for it.

TAP
THE INTERCONTINENTAL AIRLINE OF PORTUGAL
We're as big as an airline should be.
In New York City: 421-8500

Alabama	800 221-2085	New York	
Arizona	800 221-7260	Albany	E 6176
Arkansas	800 221-2085	Buffalo	E 6019
California	800 221-7260	Hempstead	E 6019
Colorado	800 221-7260	Hicksville	E 6019
Connecticut	800 221-2001	Huntington	E 6214
Delaware	800 221-2001	Levittown	E 6019
Dist. of Columbia	800 221-2035	Mount Vernon	E 6019
Florida	800 221-2085	Nassau County	E 6019
Georgia	800 221-2061	New Rochelle	E 6019
Idaho	800 221-7260	Northport	E 6214
Illinois	800 221-2061	Rochester	E 6019
Indiana	800 221-2061	Schenectady	E 6176
Iowa	800 221-2085	Syracuse	E 6019
Kansas	800 221-2085	Troy	E 6176
Kentucky	800 221-2061	Valley Stream	E 6019
Louisiana	800 221-2085	White Plains	E 6019
Maine	800 221-2035	Yonkers	E 6019
Maryland	800 221-2035	North Carolina	800 221-2061
Massachusetts	800 221-2001	North Dakota	800 221-7260
Michigan	800 221-2061	Ohio	800 221-2035
Minnesota	800 221-2085	Oklahoma	800 221-7260
Mississippi	800 221-2085	Oregon	800 221-7260
Missouri	800 221-2085	Pennsylvania	800 221-2035
Montana	800 221-7260	Rhode Island	800 221-2001
Nebraska	800 221-2085	South Carolina	800 221-2061
Nevada	800 221-7260	South Dakota	800 221-2085
New Hampshire	800 221-2001	Tennessee	800 221-2061
New Jersey	800 221-2001	Texas	800 221-7260
New Mexico	800 221-7260	Utah	800 221-7260
		Vermont	800 221-2001
		Virginia	800 221-2035
		Washington State	800 221-7260
		West Virginia	800 221-2035
		Wisconsin	800 221-2061
		Wyoming	800 221-7260

97

Trade Magazine/Single

95
Art Director: Richard Brown
Copywriter: Jim Coufal
Photographer: Joe Morello
Agency: Needham, Harper & Steers
Client: Homelite

96
Art Director: Lou Colletti
Copywriter: Larry Spector
Designer: Lou Colletti
Photographer: Joe DiBartolo
Agency: Levine, Huntley, Schmidt
Client: Conso Publishing Co.

97
Art Director: Lou Coletti
Copywriter: Lew Sherwood
Agency: Herbert Arthur Morris Advertising
Client: TAP Airline of Portugal

98
Art Director: Dick Calderhead
Copywriter: Dick Jackson
Designer: Barbara Schubeck
Art Source: The Bettmann Archive
Agency: Calderhead, Jackson Inc.
Client: Calderhead, Jackson, Inc.

98

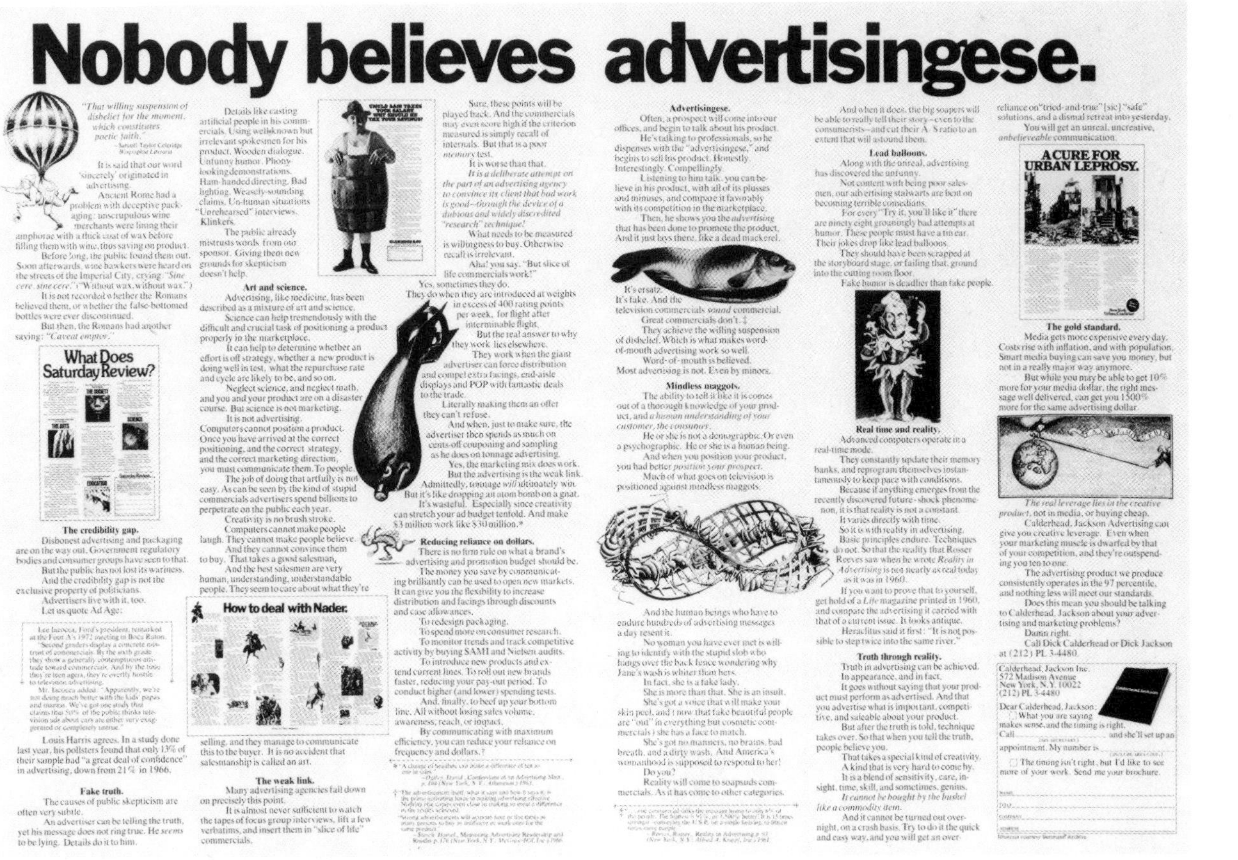

Nobody believes advertisingese.
What Does Saturday Review?
How to deal with Nader.
A CURE FOR URBAN LEPROSY.

Trade Magazine/Single

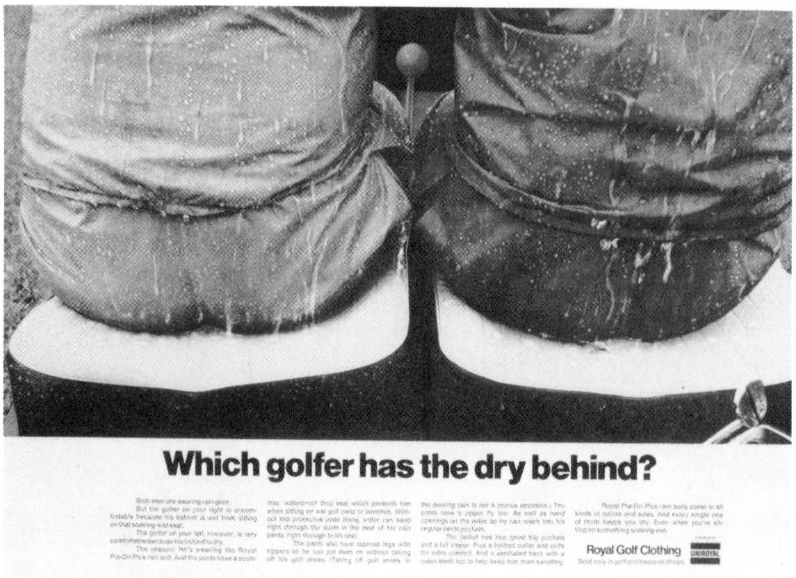
Which golfer has the dry behind?
Royal Golf Clothing

99

100

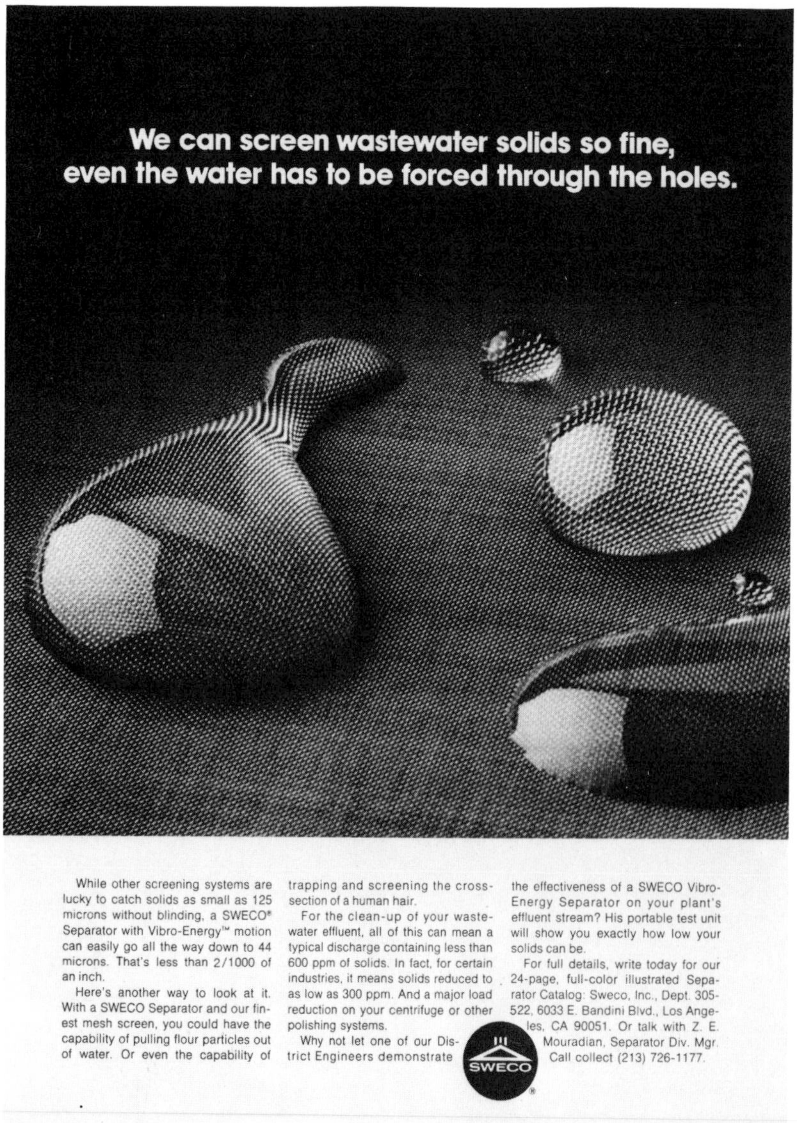
We can screen wastewater solids so fine, even the water has to be forced through the holes.
While other screening systems are lucky to catch solids as small as 125 microns without blinding, a SWECO® Separator with Vibro-Energy™ motion can easily go all the way down to 44 microns. That's less than 2/1000 of an inch.
Here's another way to look at it. With a SWECO Separator and our finest mesh screen, you could have the capability of pulling flour particles out of water. Or even the capability of trapping and screening the cross-section of a human hair.
For the clean-up of your wastewater effluent, all of this can mean a typical discharge containing less than 600 ppm of solids. In fact, for certain industries, it means solids reduced to as low as 300 ppm. And a major load reduction on your centrifuge or other polishing systems.
Why not let one of our District Engineers demonstrate the effectiveness of a SWECO Vibro-Energy Separator on your plant's effluent stream? His portable test unit will show you exactly how low your solids can be.
For full details, write today for our 24-page, full-color illustrated Separator Catalog: Sweco, Inc., Dept. 305-522, 6033 E. Bandini Blvd., Los Angeles, CA 90051. Or talk with Z. E. Mouradian, Separator Div. Mgr. Call collect (213) 726-1177.
SWECO

99
Art Director: Teddy Hwang
Copywriter: Peter Murphy
Designer: Teddy Hwang
Photographer: Matthew Klein
Agency: Doyle Dane Bernbach Inc.
Client: Uniroyal

100
Art Director: Ralph Lenac
Copywriter: David Warford
Designer: Ralph Lenac
Photographer: Tachibana-N-Tropp
Agency: Cochrane Chase & Co.
Client: Sweco, Inc.

101
Art Director: Allan Beaver
Copywriter: Larry Plapler
Designer: Allan Beaver
Agency: Levine, Huntley, Schmidt
Client: E. F. Timme & Son

102
Art Director: Lou Colletti
Copywriter: Neil Drossman
Designer: Lou Colletti
Photographer: Joe DiBartolo
Agency: Levine, Huntley, Schmidt
Client: Conso Publishing Co.

OUR WARP KNITS ARE SIX MONTHS AHEAD OF THE TIMES.

OUR DELIVERIES AREN'T SIX MONTHS BEHIND THE TIMES.

We have a genius group of designers. Guys who consistently come up with the ideas the rest of the industry consistently copies.

And we have a 140,000 square foot, science-fiction type plant that enables us to make fabrics others can't.

This marriage of brain power and machine power produces the most originally conceived and perfectly made warp knits available for men's and women's wear.

What's more our new plant, complete with it's own dyeing and finishing facilities, enables us to do something else very unusual in warp knits; maintain a respectable delivery schedule.

Timme warp knits: We do our darndest to design ahead of our time. And deliver on time.

TIMME

E.F. Timme & Son, Inc. 200 Madison Avenue, N.Y.C. Makers of fake fur and fabric for just about everything else.

101

102

OUR DECORATING MAGAZINE IS AROUND HOMES SO LONG IT BECOMES A PIECE OF FURNITURE.

According to studies, 58.4% of the people who lay their hands on our magazine hold on to it for at least three years.

So when you run an advertisement in 1,001 Decorating Ideas, it will usually be decorating a home for a long time.

Which means your ad will be read while other ads are being forgotten.

And now that we've told you how long people keep our magazine, we'll tell you why a million or so buy each issue in the first place.

Unlike some other decorating publications, we don't offer pie in the sky. Virtually everything we show is affordable and currently on the market. In short, our magazine appeals to doers, not dreamers.

What's more, in addition to newsstands and supermarkets, the majority of our magazines are sold where your products are sold: In department stores and specialty shops.

1,001 Decorating Ideas: Like a good piece of furniture, it's made to last.

1,001 DECORATING IDEAS

1,001 Decorating Ideas, 149 Fifth Avenue, New York, New York 10010, (212)-677-0870

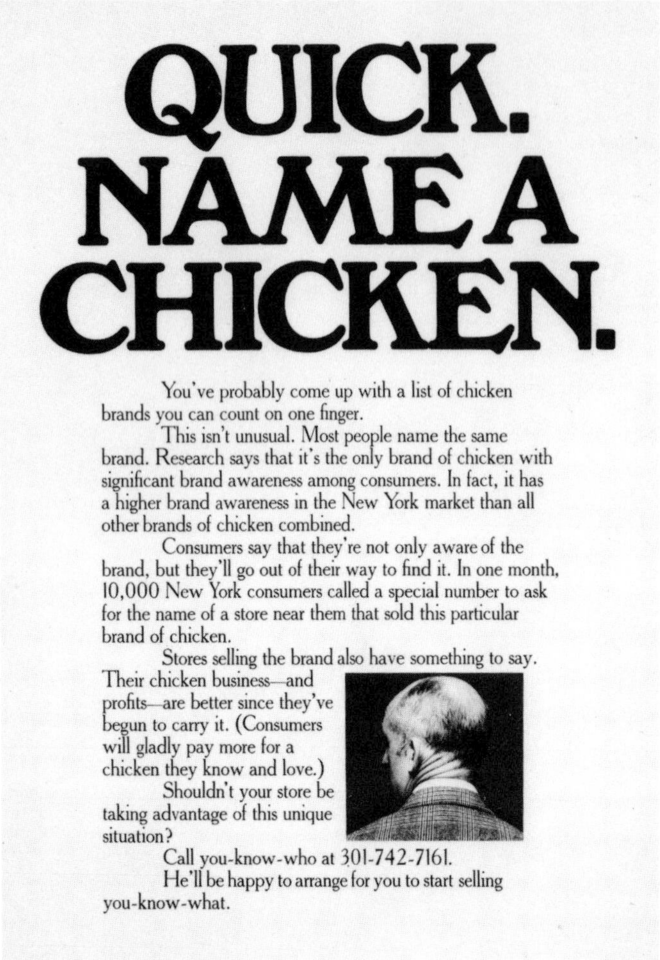
QUICK.
NAME A
CHICKEN.
You've probably come up with a list of chicken brands you can count on one finger.
This isn't unusual. Most people name the same brand. Research says that it's the only brand of chicken with significant brand awareness among consumers. In fact, it has a higher brand awareness in the New York market than all other brands of chicken combined.
Consumers say that they're not only aware of the brand, but they'll go out of their way to find it. In one month, 10,000 New York consumers called a special number to ask for the name of a store near them that sold this particular brand of chicken.
Stores selling the brand also have something to say. Their chicken business—and profits—are better since they've begun to carry it. (Consumers will gladly pay more for a chicken they know and love.)
Shouldn't your store be taking advantage of this unique situation?
Call you-know-who at 301-742-7161.
He'll be happy to arrange for you to start selling you-know-what.

103

103 Silver Award
Art Director: Sam Scali
Copywriter: Ed McCabe
Designer: Sam Scali
Photographer: Phil Mazzurco
Agency: Scali, McCabe, Sloves, Inc.
Client: Perdue Farms Inc.

104
Art Director: John Assante
Copywriter: Floyd Stone
Designer: John Assante
Photographer: Robert Swanson
Agency: Doyle Dane Bernbach Inc.
Client: Polaroid Corporation

104

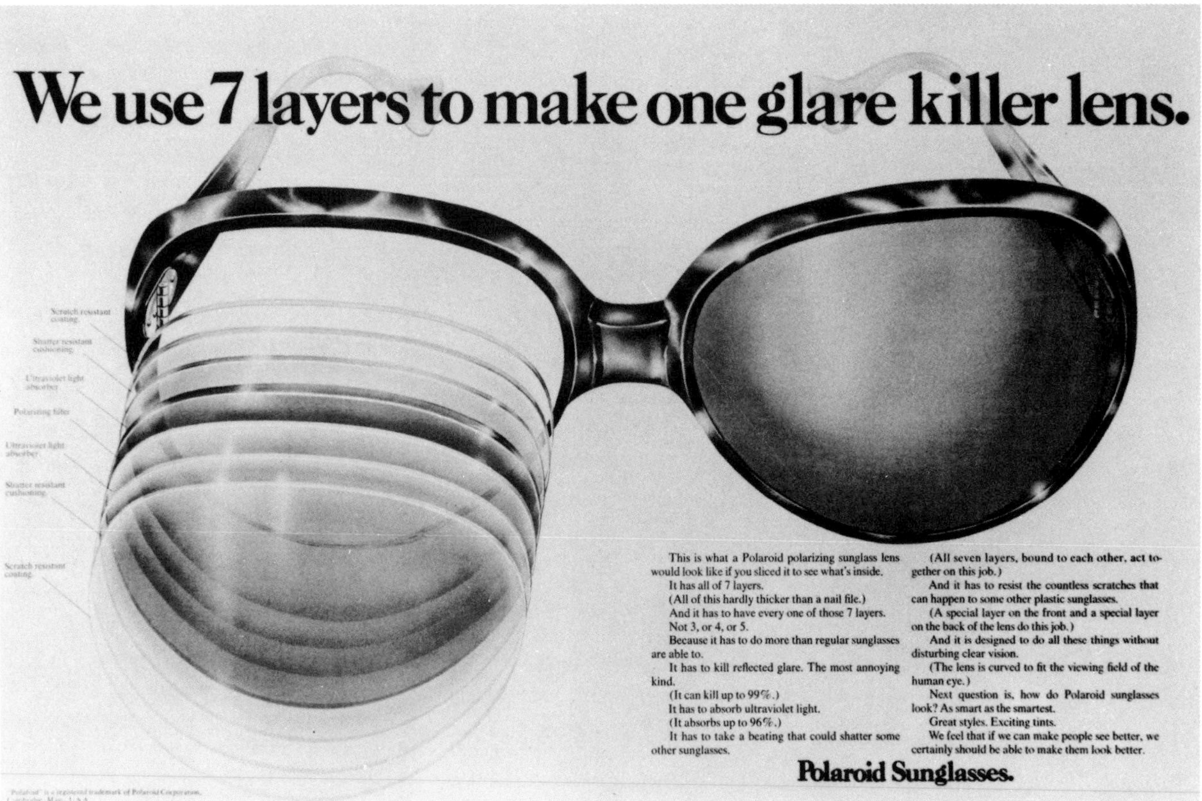
We use 7 layers to make one glare killer lens.
This is what a Polaroid polarizing sunglass lens would look like if you sliced it to see what's inside.
It has all of 7 layers.
(All of this hardly thicker than a nail file.)
And it has to have every one of those 7 layers.
Not 3, or 4, or 5.
Because it has to do more than regular sunglasses are able to.
It has to kill reflected glare. The most annoying kind.
(It can kill up to 99%.)
It has to absorb ultraviolet light.
(It absorbs up to 96%.)
It has to take a beating that could shatter some other sunglasses.
(All seven layers, bound to each other, act together on this job.)
And it has to resist the countless scratches that can happen to some other plastic sunglasses.
(A special layer on the front and a special layer on the back of the lens do this job.)
And it is designed to do all these things without disturbing clear vision.
(The lens is curved to fit the viewing field of the human eye.)
Next question is, how do Polaroid sunglasses look? As smart as the smartest.
Great styles. Exciting tints.
We feel that if we can make people see better, we certainly should be able to make them look better.
Polaroid Sunglasses.

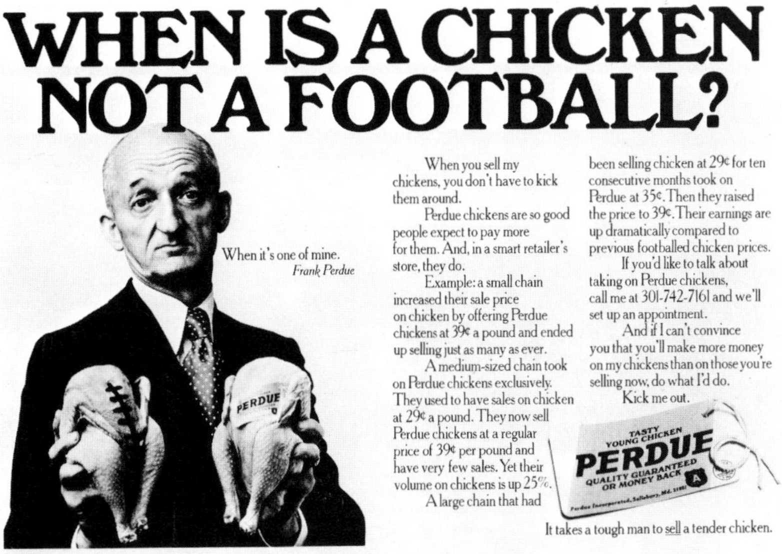
WHEN IS A CHICKEN NOT A FOOTBALL?
When it's one of mine.
Frank Perdue
When you sell my chickens, you don't have to kick them around.
Perdue chickens are so good people expect to pay more for them. And, in a smart retailer's store, they do.
Example: a small chain increased their sale price on chicken by offering Perdue chickens at 39¢ a pound and ended up selling just as many as ever.
A medium-sized chain took on Perdue chickens exclusively. They used to have sales on chicken at 29¢ a pound. They now sell Perdue chickens at a regular price of 39¢ per pound and have very few sales. Yet their volume on chickens is up 25%.
A large chain that had been selling chicken at 29¢ for ten consecutive months took on Perdue at 35¢. Then they raised the price to 39¢. Their earnings are up dramatically compared to previous footballed chicken prices.
If you'd like to talk about taking on Perdue chickens, call me at 301-742-7161 and we'll set up an appointment.
And if I can't convince you that you'll make more money on my chickens than on those you're selling now, do what I'd do.
Kick me out.
TASTY YOUNG CHICKEN
PERDUE
QUALITY GUARANTEED OR MONEY BACK
It takes a tough man to sell a tender chicken.

105

105
Art Director: Sam Scali
Copywriter: Ed McCabe
Designer: Sam Scali
Photographer: Alan Dolgins
Agency: Scali, McCabe, Sloves, Inc.
Client: Perdue Farms Inc.

106
Art Director: Dick Calderhead
Copywriter: Dick Jackson
Designer: Barbara Schubeck
Art Source: The Bettmann Archive
Agency: Calderhead, Jackson Inc.
Client: Calderhead, Jackson Inc.

107
Art Director: Jim Handloser
Copywriter: Frank DiGiacomo
Designer: Jim Handloser
Photographer: WABC-TV News
Agency: Della Femina, Travisono & Partners, Inc.
Client: WABC-TV

106

How to deal with Nader.

107

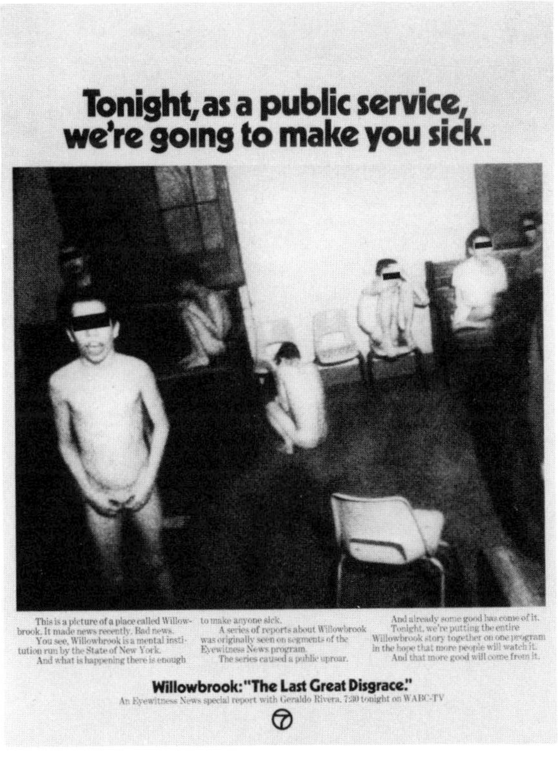
Tonight, as a public service, we're going to make you sick.
This is a picture of a place called Willowbrook. It made news recently. Bad news.
You see, Willowbrook is a mental institution run by the State of New York.
And what is happening there is enough to make anyone sick.
A series of reports about Willowbrook was originally seen on segments of the Eyewitness News program.
The series caused a public uproar.
And already some good has come of it.
Tonight, we're putting the entire Willowbrook story together on one program in the hope that more people will watch it.
And that more good will come from it.
Willowbrook: "The Last Great Disgrace."
An Eyewitness News special report with Geraldo Rivera. 7:30 tonight on WABC-TV

Are you overlooking an enormous market?
For approximately four million American men, your large assortment of underwear probably isn't large enough: men 6'2" and taller and men 220 pounds and heavier.
To cover this market, Jockey makes two special lines of underwear, Big Man And Tall Man, in a variety of styles: T-shirt, V-neck T-shirt and athletic shirt; Brief, boxer and Midway.
Each line has a greater profit margin than regular sizes.
So you can make big money by putting big men into our underwear.
Jockey Tall Man and Big Man Underwear

108

109

A face only a mother and 5½ million readers could love.
These days, the hockey goalie makes Frankenstein look like a movie star. But every month, Sport Magazine's audience idolizes this monster, along with a whole tribe of 7 foot giants and 300 pound brutes.
In fact, Sport Magazine's action closeups and penetrating editorials don't just report the mayhem these athletes are creating. They surround our readers with it. Make them part of the fury on the ice. The violence on the turf. The desperation on the courts.
Then Sport takes them past the roar of the arena. Into the noise of the locker room. Into the pride and fears a player takes home with him.
And while Sport surrounds fans with more and more action, advertisers are surrounding them with more and more products.
Last year we scored an unbelievable 75% increase in ad pages over the year before. And our winning streak is now extended to 23 consecutive months of growth.
Advertisers are simply learning Sport's golden rule: that when our audience grabs all the excitement on our editorial pages, they don't let go when they come to our ad pages.
Sport delivers an audience concentration that's 94% male, with over half between the prime ages of 18 to 34. And 70% living in the prime A and B counties.
All delivered with unbeatable efficiency, at an unbeatable $10,041 four color page price. So if you want to reach men, reach them in Sport. It's filled with the faces that launched a thousand sales.
SPORT
If you got any closer to the action, you might get hurt.

110

Until we got into the vitamin business, one in every pot was just a promise.
Roche, the nutrition experts.

Trade Magazine / Single

108 Gold Award
Art Director: Lou Colletti
Copywriter: Larry Spector
Designer: Lou Colletti
Photographer: Tony Petrucelli
Agency: Levine, Huntley, Schmidt
Client: Jockey International, Inc.

109
Art Director: Alfonso Marino
Copywriter: Martin Friedman
Photographer: Stock
Agency: Herbert Arthur Morris Advertising
Client: Bartell Media Corp.
Sport Magazine

110
Art Director: Harold Gropper
Copywriter: William Zeitung
Designer: Harold Gropper
Photographer: Carl Fischer
Agency: Marsteller Inc.
Client: Hoffmann-La Roche

111
Designer: Bernie Zlotnick
Copywriter: Irwin Rothman
Artist: Hiroshige
Client: Pioneer-Moss Reproductions

112
Art Director: Frank Biancalana
Copywriter: Ethan Revsin
Designer: Frank Biancalana
Artist: Charles White III
Agency: Lee King & Partners
Client: GATX

many impressions from worn blocks. Very often poor quality duplicate blocks were produced that bore little relationship to the original blocks.
Since the prints were used as illustrations for books in many cases they inevitably assumed a political character. Important officials of the day were represented in various and unflattering ways. In 1789 the prints became subject to censorship. In 1842 the censor's personal seal appeared on all prints. In 1847 the censors worked in pairs with two seals appearing on the prints and in 1852 a combination date and censor's seal appeared. These seals did more to help collectors date the prints than restrict the subject matter, since artists and publishers found many ways to circumvent the censorship.
Prior to the works of Hokusai and Hiroshige most prints dealt with heroic subjects, the theatre and beautiful women. Hokusai perfected the color print as a medium for landscapes and Hiroshige within a few years rivaled Hokusai in this field only with less seriousness and with somewhat of a self-taught western influence and perspective. In 1849 the great Hokusai died, leaving Hiroshige the undisputed master in the landscape field. Hiroshige traveled extensively in search of material and turned out a large number of print series including the famous work on the To-kaido (eastern seaboard highway extending from Edo to Kyoto). He died in 1858 at the age of 62 during a cholera epidemic that raged through Japan and killed 28,000 in Edo alone. His farewell poem reads: "Leaving my brush on the Azuma (To-kaido) road, I depart to enjoy the wondrous sights of paradise."
In 1861, Kuniyoshi died, followed by Kunisada in 1864. This left Kyosai and Yoshitoshi (pupils of Kuniyoshi) as the only first rate artists among the mediocre artists of the Imperial Restoration period that began in 1868. This era marked the end of the ukiyo-e period. Chemical colors, over-refined engraving and printing methods and European drawing techniques eliminated the simple beauty of the ukiyo-e print. Among the impressions left on western painters by the Japanese print were Whistler's "Nocturnes" and the terrible copies in oil by Van Gogh of Hiroshige's "Ohashi Bridge" and "Plum-blossom Garden". In 1861 Captain Sherard Osborn, an English naval officer published a book reproducing Hiroshige prints. In describing one of his prints he writes "... our embryo Turner has striven hard to reproduce the combined effects of water, mountain, cloud, and spray touched by the bright beams of a rising sun". Turner of course was acclaimed by the following generation of western art lovers as one of the greatest landscape artists of all time. Hiroshige undoubtedly belongs in this category as well.

The enclosed reproduction of an original Ukiyo-e 19th century Japanese print is presented to you by Pioneer-Moss, as part of its program of showing the role graphic arts innovations and inventions have had in developing cultural and educational as well as communication advances. The marriage of artistic techniques and abilities to those of graphic arts advances helped not only to speed the use of illustrations in daily newspapers, magazines and books but helped create a brand new art form which is as popular today as it was when it was first developed. In addition to its popularity, printmaking has gained recognition as an art form by art critics, museums and collectors.
Pioneer-Moss is proud of John Calvin Moss's contribution to the use of illustrations in communications. One hundred years ago he invented photoengravings which he called "a superior substitute for wood engravings". Pioneer-Moss today produces engravings and color separations for any printing process, using the latest machinery and techniques combined with the master craftsmanship needed to satisfy the stringent demands of our customers. We hope that these print reproductions provide a measure of enjoyment and satisfaction to everyone who sees them. The Curtis paper used for the Japanese prints was chosen because of its high quality and its similarity to the original paper used for these prints.
If you would like additional copies of these inserts, please write to Print Reproductions Editor, Pioneer-Moss Reproductions Corp., 460 West 34 St., New York, N.Y. 10001 or Curtis Paper Company, Newark, Del. 19711.

Hiroshige 1797-1858. Mt. Fuji viewed from Mt. Rokuso-Zan across the lake. No. 35 of "The 36 Views of Mt. Fuji" 8⅞ x 13¼ signed Hiroshige Ga. Published by Tsuta-ya 1858

The Japanese Print—One of a series
Color separations and reproduction by Pioneer-Moss Reproductions Corp.
Lithographed on Curtis Rag 70 lb. offset

浮
世
絵

Ukiyo-e was originally a Buddhist expression translated as "The every day world of sorrows and troubles" emphasizing the transitory nature of human life as opposed to blissful eternal life. As time passed the meaning of the expression changed and its religious and solemn overtones were replaced with a new emphasis on the pursuit of a pleasurable and lighthearted life and an interest in "now." The word ukiyo-e contains three characters, "uki" which means "floating" or transitory" —"yo" signifying "world" and "e" meaning pictures". Translated, ukiyo-e becomes "pictures of the floating world." Today this term is generally applied to the prints and paintings of the latter part of the 17th century through the 19th century that were produced in the area of Edo (today called Tokyo). In its period ukiyo-e also applied to the other popular and stylish fads of the day, and was used as a prefix for activities devoted to daily amusements, whims and pleasures without any concern for tomorrow.
The ukiyo-e artist was the illustrator of his day. He chose his subjects from the theatre, the "pleasure districts" and other everyday scenes. Moronobu (1618-1695) was the first artist to make use of woodcuts as an inexpensive means of reproducing drawings of the contemporary life of the people. The production of color prints flourished in the late 18th century after full range color printing was developed about 1765 and it was no longer necessary to hand color black and white block prints.
The beautiful results obtained by the outstanding ukiyo-e artists such as Harunobu, Shunsho, Kiyonaga, Sharaku, Utamaro, Hokusai, Toyokuni, Hiroshige, Eisen, Kuniyoshi, Kunisada and the last of their era, Kyosai and Yoshitoshi, are all the more wonderous when the methods of producing these prints are known. The artist's drawing was made with India ink and brushed on very thin rice paper. This was laid face down on a cherrywood block by the engraver. He then proceeded to cut the reversed design in relief on the block. Proofs were pulled from this block and the artist would specify the colors and positions on the proof. The engraver then cut a block for each color required. In order to register the blocks, the engraver cut a small line at the lower right hand side, and a corner cut in the top left hand side in the same position of each block. When the blocks were completed to the artist's satisfaction they were turned over to the printer. He inked each block with the proper color and pressed a sheet of paper that had been dampened slightly to the block, using a bamboo fiber mat as his press. He used the corner lines on the block as a guide, feeding the edges of the paper to these two register marks. The prints were produced and printed under the direction of the publisher. To a great extent the taste of the publisher and his marketing ability determined both the quality and commercial success of the final print. A combination of talents by the artist, engraver and printer was required to obtain a worthwhile print. Both the artist and publisher were extremely zealous in choosing engravers and printers who would interpret and produce the print to their satisfaction. Many poor prints were made by inferior craftsmen and also by running too

111

112

What was good for your grandmother isn't necessarily good for you.

When grandma went to put up some peaches, she simply trotted down to the cellar and tapped her private supply of jars.
At maybe five cents apiece, she could afford to keep enough jars on hand to cover herself, whether it was a bumper year for peaches or not.
You, on the other hand, don't have that luxury.
Besides the capital you tie up in building your own storage facilities, you still have to worry about supply fluctuations. (Maybe the only thing worse than an expensive terminal is an idle one.)
So instead of building, we suggest you lease from us. We'll lease you just the space you need in principal North American ports, plus Europe and Asia.
Complete attendant services are available as well, from mixing to blending to drumming.
Our charter tanker fleet and lease tank cars are also at your disposal. (Flexibility in transfer and storage becomes even more important during the current energy crisis.)
The nice thing is, you can do all these things with us without investing so much as a nickel.
Now admit it, even your grandmother couldn't do that.

GATX

General American Transportation Corp., Chicago, IL 60680

What's a nice girl like her doing in a place like this?

If someone told John Calvin Moss 100 years ago that a woman would represent his company, it's difficult to say how he would react. After all he did invent photoengraving as "a superior substitute for wood engraving" which revolutionized the use of photos in the print media.

With his advanced ideas he might very well accept a woman representative. Especially when she has an eye for color that is second to none. And the training in color that only a Japanese woodcut artist receives.

Today at Pioneer-Moss we try to emulate our founder's pioneer spirit of 100 years ago. We constantly look for better ways to do things including having Sanae as our representative.

We admit that sometimes our clients are surprised when Sanae responds to a call to review a color ad. But the surprise soon gives way to respect and appreciation for her color knowledge.

Call Sanae at LO 4-2640. You don't have to be a Ms. to call Sanae. A Mr., Mrs., or Miss will also appreciate her talents. And those of our other representatives George, Richard, Jerry, Jeff, Bill, Sheldon, Stanley and Irwin as well.

113

You run Airports. We run Restaurants. Let's get together.

Simple. We build great restaurants.

Airport Restaurants—from luxury units to snack bars—that leap across the entire spectrum of airport potential; the First Class passenger thru the mechanics and baggage handlers.

We started with the Newarker, at Newark Airport, in 1953. Then we took over food operations at LaGuardia, including LaGuardia Terrace. Next, at JFK we built great facilities at the Pan Am Terminal, TWA's Terminal, Air Canada and the International Arrival Building. During all this, we set up AGE Food Services, and won our first in-flight food operations from Milwaukee and Philadelphia Airports. (And operated in Friendship Airport in Baltimore.)

Anyway, we earned our way by doing what we always do. At Mamma Leone's, at the Four Seasons, even with Zum Zum, our chain of Wurst Snack Bars. (The latest one we put in the Orange Bowl.)

This same pursuit of excellence made our Treadway Inns successful, made Barricini Chocolates a national treat, and it makes our airport restaurants as different from the usual airport facilities as good food is from bad.

One of our best men, Fred Haverly, Director of Airport Marketing Services, will be at your conference. Say hello to him. (You'll like the way he talks.)

The Restaurant division of Restaurant Associates Industries.

RA INDUSTRIES

114

116

It's impossible to know everybody in a big company.

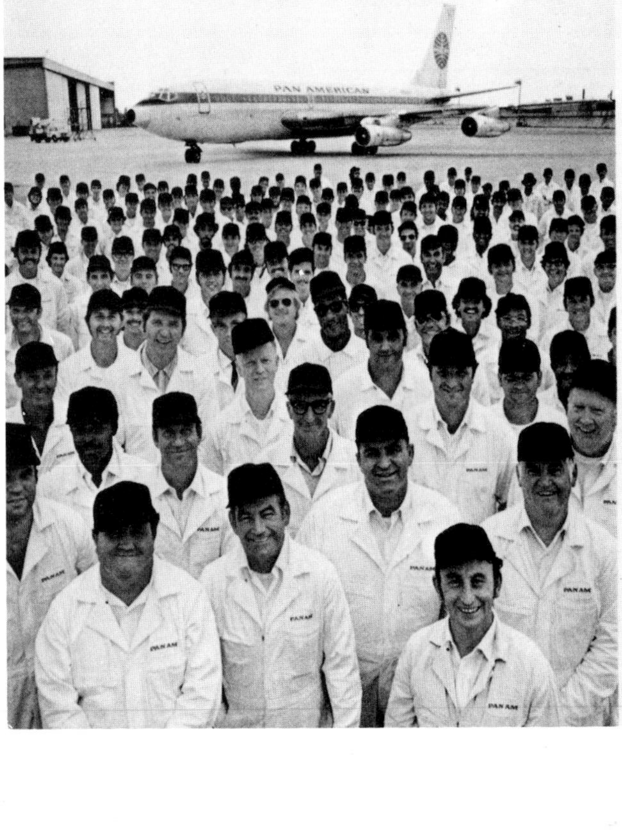

But it is possible to make sure they belong.

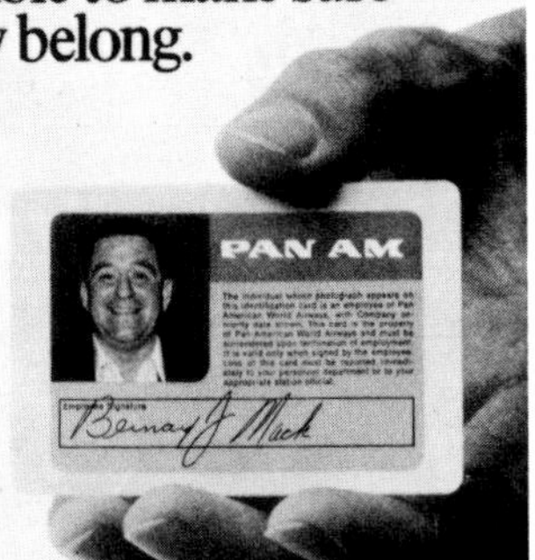

Just match the card with the face.

With a color portrait, there's no mistaking who the person is.

But the Polaroid Portrait ID card doesn't only give you a good picture. It's the most secure ID card you can issue. It's practically impossible to tamper with the card without detection.

And a firm can make its own cards easily with a Polaroid Land Identification System. It produces a full color, laminated ID card in two minutes or less.

This means you can issue permanent identification to a new employee in minutes, and he can go on the job right away. You don't have to fill out temporary identification papers every time you hire somebody.

In addition to showing his face and signature, it can show his function in the organization—for example, by the color of the background.

If the subject has blinked or doesn't like the way he looks, the picture can be retaken on the spot. (You don't have to wait for days to see how the picture came out and call him back for another try.)

Over 5000 organizations throughout the world are using Polaroid Portrait ID cards. They're used for identification in industry, universities, research centers, banks and government. They're also used as credit cards and drivers' licenses.

What's more, people like to carry them.

Because it's nice to have your own portrait in color.

And in today's complicated world, you never know when you'll need to prove you're you.

The Polaroid 2-Minute Identification Card

Some of the organizations that use our ID system:

Hong Kong International Airport—Hong Kong/**Volvo**—Sweden/**The New York Times**—U.S./**The Marconi Company Limited**—U.K./**Owens-Corning Fiberglas**—U.S./**Canadian Broadcasting Corporation**—Canada/**Porsche**—Germany/**Bacardi**—Puerto Rico/**Union Carbide**—U.S./**Singer Sewing Machine**—Philippines/**3M Company**—Australia, Canada, Italy, U.S./**The Coca-Cola Company**—U.S./**Empresas Electricas Asociadas**—Peru/**Rhodia Industrias Quimicas E Texteis**—Brazil/**American Motors**—U.S./**Esso Standard**—France/**Lanerossi S.p.A.**—Italy/**Uniroyal**—U.S./**Winthrop Laboratories**—U.K., U.S./**Banca Commerciale Italiana**—Italy/**Mexicana de Aviacion**—Mexico/**IBM**—Australia, Belgium, France, Germany, Holland, U.K., U.S./**Christiania Bank og Kreditkasse**—Norway/**Georgia Power**—U.S./**Burlington Industries**—U.S./**International Nickel**—Canada/**Union de Transports Aeriens (UTA)**—France/**Ansett Airlines**—Australia/**Volkswagen**—Germany/**Scott Paper**—U.S./**Time, Inc.**—U.S./**Aerospatiale**—France/**ICI Fibres**—U.K./**Stockholms Läns Allmänna Försäkringskassa**—Sweden/**Olympic Airways**—Greece/**Puerto Rican Cement**—Puerto Rico/**Ente Nazionale Idrocarburi (ENI)**—Italy/**General Electric**—U.S./**Renault**—France/**Schiphol Airport**—Holland/**Lord & Taylor**—U.S./**Australia and New Zealand Banking Group**—Australia/**S.E.A.—Societa Esercizi Aeroportuali—Linate and Malpensa Airports (Milan)**—Italy/**Thomson C.S.F.**—France/**Bankers Trust**—U.S./**Bell Laboratories**—U.S./**Avions Marcel Dassault**—France/**U.S. Steel**—U.S./**International Computers Limited**—U.K./**British European Airways**—U.K./**First National City Bank**—Panama/**A.E.G.**—Germany/**Ciba-Geigy**—Switzerland.

Polaroid®

Creative Glass.
First you buy it. Then you decide what to do with it.
When Corning set out to make Creative Glass, we had only one thing in mind. To make it beautiful.
The rest, we decided, would be up to your imagination.
So we designed 15 pieces of the most artful, intelligent glassware you've ever seen. Then we made them heat-resistant and cold-resistant. And we priced them as beautifully as we designed them. From $5.00 for a mysterious set of salt and pepper shakers you don't have to turn upside down to shake; to $10 for the Super-Server you see above filled with shrimp and ice.
Creative Glass. We were creative when we designed it. So you could be creative when you use it.
Creative Glass by Corning. A product of imagination... yours and ours.

117

118

Made in Japan.
Every year, Americans salute more and more American flags that weren't made in America. Flags that bear the stars and stripes and little tags reading Made in Japan or Taiwan or Hong Kong.
Those flags aren't the only things with such labels. As low-wage, foreign goods flood the market, American industries shut down. As industries shut down, people lose jobs.
When people lose their jobs, they can't buy the things you make. Chances are if Betsy Ross (the Philadelphia seamstress who made the first American flag for George Washington) were alive today, she'd be standing in line for her unemployment check.
So help yourself and help us by looking for the union label in everything you buy. You can find our label in women's and children's garments.
This label stands for the creativity of American design, the skill of American workmanship, the importance of American jobs.
ILGWU
Made in U.S.A.
Union Label Department, International Ladies' Garment Workers' Union, 22 W. 38th Street, New York, N.Y. 10018

Trade Magazine/Single

113
Art Director: Bernie Zlotnick
Copywriter: Irwin Rothman
Designer: Bernie Zlotnick
Photographer: Irwin Rothman
Client: Pioneer-Moss Reproductions

114
Art Director: Dennis Mazzella
Copywriter: Ron Holland
Designer: Dennis Mazzella
Agency: Lois Holland Callaway Inc.
Client: Restaurant Associates

116
Art Directors: Lee Epstein
Norman Schwartz
Copywriter: Andy Certner
Designers: Lee Epstein
Norman Schwartz
Photographer: Tony Petrucelli
Agency: Doyle Dane Bernbach Inc.
Client: Polaroid Corporation

117
Art Director: Paul Jervis
Copywriter: John LaRock
Designer: Paul Jervis
Photographer: Cailor/Resnick
Agency: DKG Inc.
Client: Corning Glass Works

118 Distinctive Merit Award
Art Director: Joe Gregorace
Copywriter: Peter Nord
Designer: Joe Gregorace
Photographer: Dave Spindell
Agency: Solow-Wexton, Inc.
Client: ILGWU

There are some things only glass can do right.
When it comes to hospital use, nothing quite beats glass.
Take glass I.V. bottles.
If you want to put additives into I.V. solutions in glass, you can. Fast, if you have to.
It's easy to connect glass bottles in series.
Graduations on glass are accurate and easy to read. And it's easy to add your own graduations for special situations.
The clarity of glass makes it easy to check the vital clarity of I.V. solutions.
And you don't need special racks to store glass I.V. bottles.
O-I Uni-Pak™ syringes also have special glass advantages.
They're chemically inert. Completely impervious to foreign materials and all but a very few chemicals.
They're easy to sterilize completely.
And the graduations, as always, are extra easy to read.
Then there are O-I Uni-Pak amber vials. Besides all the standard advantages of glass, they have the added protection of amber. Naturally, like all O-I amber products, they meet the U.S. Pharmacopeia and the National Formulary requirements for light resistance.
One more advantage of glass. It can always be recycled. So when it's through helping save a life, it helps save the environment.
Safe, dependable, versatile glass.
Anything else is something less.
Owens-Illinois

119

120

In the twenties, lettermen loaned these sweaters to their girlfriends.
Fifty years later, guys are ready to take them back.
Jockey Letterman Sweaters

119
Art Director: Paulette Kaplan
Copywriter: Joe McClinton
Photographer: Phil Marco
Agency: Meldrum & Fewsmith
Client: Owens-Illinois

120
Art Director: Lou Colletti
Copywriter: Larry Spector
Designer: Lou Colletti
Photographer: Richard Noble
Agency: Levine, Huntley, Schmidt
Client: Jockey International, Inc.

121
Art Director: Courtland Thomas White
Copywriter: Neil Drossman
Designer: Courtland Thomas White
Agency: Courtland Thomas White, Inc.
Client: Segmented Sampling, Inc.

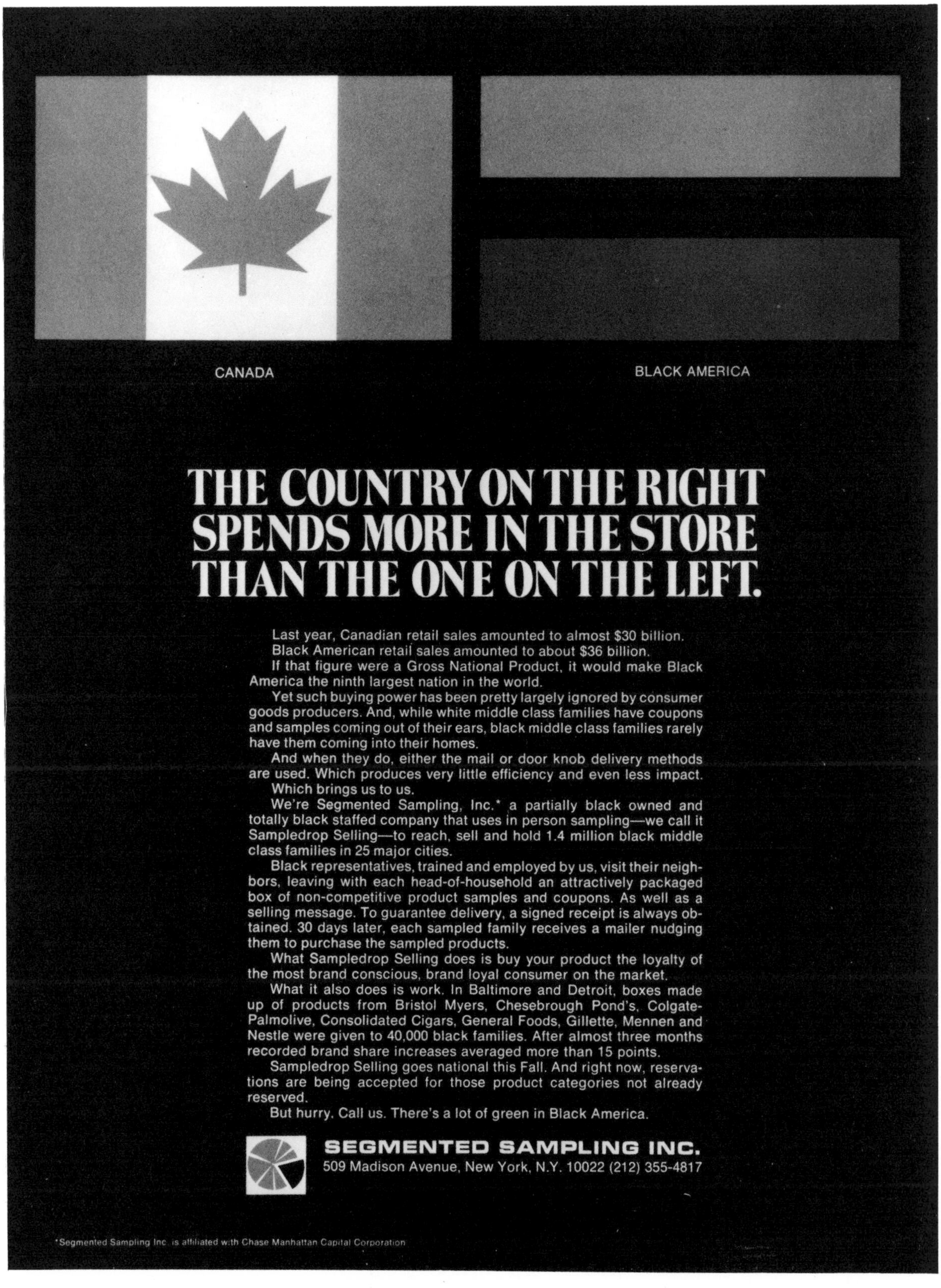
CANADA
BLACK AMERICA
THE COUNTRY ON THE RIGHT SPENDS MORE IN THE STORE THAN THE ONE ON THE LEFT.
Last year, Canadian retail sales amounted to almost $30 billion.
Black American retail sales amounted to about $36 billion.
If that figure were a Gross National Product, it would make Black America the ninth largest nation in the world.
Yet such buying power has been pretty largely ignored by consumer goods producers. And, while white middle class families have coupons and samples coming out of their ears, black middle class families rarely have them coming into their homes.
And when they do, either the mail or door knob delivery methods are used. Which produces very little efficiency and even less impact.
Which brings us to us.
We're Segmented Sampling, Inc.* a partially black owned and totally black staffed company that uses in person sampling—we call it Sampledrop Selling—to reach, sell and hold 1.4 million black middle class families in 25 major cities.
Black representatives, trained and employed by us, visit their neighbors, leaving with each head-of-household an attractively packaged box of non-competitive product samples and coupons. As well as a selling message. To guarantee delivery, a signed receipt is always obtained. 30 days later, each sampled family receives a mailer nudging them to purchase the sampled products.
What Sampledrop Selling does is buy your product the loyalty of the most brand conscious, brand loyal consumer on the market.
What it also does is work. In Baltimore and Detroit, boxes made up of products from Bristol Myers, Chesebrough Pond's, Colgate-Palmolive, Consolidated Cigars, General Foods, Gillette, Mennen and Nestle were given to 40,000 black families. After almost three months recorded brand share increases averaged more than 15 points.
Sampledrop Selling goes national this Fall. And right now, reservations are being accepted for those product categories not already reserved.
But hurry. Call us. There's a lot of green in Black America.
SEGMENTED SAMPLING INC.
509 Madison Avenue, New York, N.Y. 10022 (212) 355-4817
*Segmented Sampling Inc. is affiliated with Chase Manhattan Capital Corporation

Bob Versandi was spraying bicycles.
Then he unplugged the fan.
Explosion-proof equipment could have prevented the fire.
And Graybar has it.
The kind of electrical equipment you need in areas where you find hazardous vapors. Gases. Dusts. Or easily ignitible fibers and flyings.
That covers a lot of industrial and commercial areas. And a lot of equipment. Like junction boxes, buzzers, motors, controls, lights, receptacles, hand tools. To name just a few.
But Graybar has more.
Graybar has know-how.
Because we serve so many customers, we've been involved in almost every kind of hazardous situation.
So we can help you with yours.
We know the problems involved with OSHA rules. We keep up with current regulations. We're familiar with just about all the hundreds of recent changes in the National Electrical Code. (If we've missed one, we'll check it out for you.)
All those changes can be confusing.
You know, of course, that new electrical installations in hazardous areas require explosion-proof equipment.
But hazardous areas in existing buildings now require the same.
That brings up problems.
So if you're not sure about where you stand, check us.
We're right in your back yard. We're your local supplier... because we're in over 150 locations across the country.
We supply electrical equipment from over 1,000 top manufacturers. Fast. And by ordering from one source, you save time. Trouble. Paperwork.
Call Graybar now. We'll take care of your complex needs. And keep you from blowing your stack.
Graybar Electric Company, Inc., 420 Lexington Avenue, New York, N.Y. 10017.
Go to the source: Graybar.

122

123

Sport's Top Performer of the Year turned water into gold.
Winning seven gold medals wasn't the
only reason Sport awarded Mark
its coveted title. The fact is
Sport felt he outperformed
every other athlete in every
other category in 1972.
So to the 5½ million
readers of Sport Magazine
who have been
arguing all year
about who'd
wear the
crown, our
February
issue is
worth its
weight in gold.
Actually they feel that
way about all our issues.
Because every month, when our
audience dives into our pages, they come up with
more than just statistics. They get involved with the men
and women who make the records. And the drives
and desires and defeats that got them there.
It's just this kind of involvement that makes Sport
unique. And with our new editor Dick Schaap
leading the team, our articles are really making waves.
our editorial is making our
think, our ads are making
spend.
Our advertisers know that.
why we've more than
our total ad pages in
2 years. In the first
of 1973, we're already
over 30% ahead
last year!
Sport delivers an
audience concen-
tration that
means money
in the bank;
male. Over half
between the ages
and 34. With 70% from
counties.
with an efficiency that makes
advertisers' heads swim: just $10,041 for a four
color page.
So if you've got a product to sell, put it in Sport.
And watch your ads turn to gold.
SPORT
Where the writing is just as exciting as the action.

122
Art Director: Robert Versandi
Copywriter: Sam Exler
Designer: Robert Versandi
Photographer: Freelance Photography Guild
Agency: Gaynor & Ducas, Inc.
Client: Graybar Electric

123
Art Director: Alfonso Marino
Copywriter: Janet Manning
Photographer: Stock
Agency: Herbert Arthur Morris Advertising
Client: Bartell Media Corp.
Sport Magazine

Trade Magazine/Campaign

124
Art Director: Lou Colletti
Copywriters: Larry Spector
Neil Drossman
Designer: Lou Colletti
Photographer: Joe DiBartolo
Agency: Levine, Huntley, Schmidt
Client: Conso Publishing Co.

THE DECORATING MAGAZINE WELL-UPHOLSTERED FAMILIES READ.
WALL STREET JOU
Consum
1,001 DECORATING IDEAS
Money
FORTUNE
Our readers are not only interested in decorating their homes, they're experts at feathering their nests.
In fact, the 1,001 readers' median income is $14,255*. That's a substantially higher figure than other decorating magazines offer, including House Beautiful ($11,666*) and House & Garden ($11,680*).
What this means is that the readers of our magazine can afford to buy the products in it—in other words they're buyers, not browsers.
What's more, virtually everything we show editorially is affordable and currently on the market. So, what a family saves decorating one room, they can spend beautifying another.
Which is one more reason over a million people buy each issue of our magazine and why 58.4%* of them keep it around the house for at least three years.
And since our magazine decorates so many homes, your ads should be decorating our magazine.
1,001 DECORATING IDEAS

124

OUR DECORATING MAGAZINE IS AROUND HOMES SO LONG IT BECOMES A PIECE OF FURNITURE.
According to studies, 58.4% of the people who lay their hands on our magazine hold on to it for at least three years.
So when you run an advertisement in 1,001 Decorating Ideas, it will usually be decorating a home for a long time.
Which means your ad will be read while other ads are being forgotten.
And now that we've told you how long people keep our magazine, we'll tell you why a million or so buy each issue in the first place.
Unlike some other decorating publications, we don't offer pie in the sky. Virtually everything we show is affordable and currently on the market. In short, our magazine appeals to doers, not dreamers.
What's more, in addition to newsstands and supermarkets, the majority of our magazines are sold where your products are sold: In department stores and specialty shops.
1,001 Decorating Ideas: Like a good piece of furniture, it's made to last.
1,001 DECORATING IDEAS
FUNK & WAGNALLS
STANDARD COLLEGE DICTIONARY

BY HELPING WOMEN SAVE MONEY, OUR MAGAZINE GETS THEM TO SPEND IT.
EXPENSIVE ROOM
LESS EXPENSIVE ROOM
Unlike some other magazines, 1,001 Decorating Ideas isn't filled with the stuff dreams are made of. Instead, it's filled with the stuff real living rooms, bedrooms and kitchens are made of.
Virtually everything we show is affordable and currently on the market.
Which could be why about a million people buy each issue of our magazine and why 58.4%* of them keep it around the house for at least 3 years. And that brings us to why advertisers buy our magazine.
First of all, since our magazine becomes a permanent member of the household, so do the ads in it.
Even more important, however, women don't look through our magazine with an eye to looking, they look with an eye to buying.
So, they not only buy our magazine, they buy what's in it, too.
Which is nice to know if you have something to sell.
1,001 DECORATING IDEAS

125

We're putting our fake fur on television alongside our competition's.

The most convincing way to demonstrate the authenticity of a Timme fake fur is to show it next to the real thing. So that's exactly what we're doing.

In a startling 30 second TV commercial, a beautiful girl tells you of the advantages of the Timme fake fur she's wearing. While she's sitting next to a real live 400 pound tiger. Our tiger commercial and an equally exciting one minute TV spot will be launched on the

NBC National Geographic Special on September 9. A TV Special which Timme alone is sponsoring.

And from then on our television campaign will saturate the New York, Los Angeles and Southern markets.

We're going to back our tiger commercial with an elephant sized budget.

TIMME

E.F. Timme & Son, Inc., 200 Madison Avenue, New York, N.Y. 10016

It's time chairs and sofas were as well dressed as people.

Long before Timme made fabric for furniture, we made fabric for clothing.

As a result, we offer something desperately needed in upholstery fabrics: fashion.

Timme offers the most exciting patterns, styles, and colors in the business.

We also offer another unusual feature. Thanks to a computerized system and a huge plant in North Carolina, we make our delivery dates.

And speaking of dates, we'd like to make one with you. To tell you more about our operation. And show you that our line of terrific upholstery fabrics we've been bragging about.

TIMME

E.F. Timme & Son, Inc. 200 Madison Avenue New York, N.Y. 10016 (212) MU 3-2886

OUR WARP KNITS ARE SIX MONTHS AHEAD OF THE TIMES.

OUR DELIVERIES AREN'T SIX MONTHS BEHIND THE TIMES.

We have a genius group of designers. Guys who consistently come up with the ideas the rest of the industry consistently copies.

And we have a 140,000 square foot, science-fiction type plant that enables us to make fabrics others can't.

This marriage of brain power and machine power produces the most originally conceived and perfectly made warp knits available for men's and women's wear.

What's more our new plant, complete with it's own dyeing and finishing facilities, enables us to do something else very unusual in warp knits; maintain a respectable delivery schedule.

Timme warp knits: We do our darndest to design ahead of our time. And deliver on time.

TIMME

E.F. Timme & Son, Inc. 200 Madison Avenue, N.Y.C. Makers of fake fur and fabric for just about everything else.

Trade Magazine/Campaign

126
Art Director: Robert Martin
Copywriter: Robert Tulp
Agency: Muller Jordan Herrick Inc.
Client: FMC Corporation

"Leave the XP-4 out one time and they stomp all over you."
Can't blame the critters.
FMC's new XP-4 is the tastiest phosphorus mineral feed supplement they've ever tasted. That's because of its acid pH.
But XP-4 is a lot more than just palatable to livestock and poultry.
It's economical. It comes in convenient dry form. And with a P-factor of 26.0% in readily available form, you know XP-4 will stimulate fast, healthy growth.
Another thing. Formulated into pellets or blocks, FMC's XP-4 easily picks up moisture from molasses or added water to form an excellent hydrate binding agent.
The stampede is on to XP-4, from FMC.
For details, write FMC Chemicals, Inorganic Chemicals Division, 633 Third Avenue, New York, N.Y. 10017.
FMC Chemicals

126

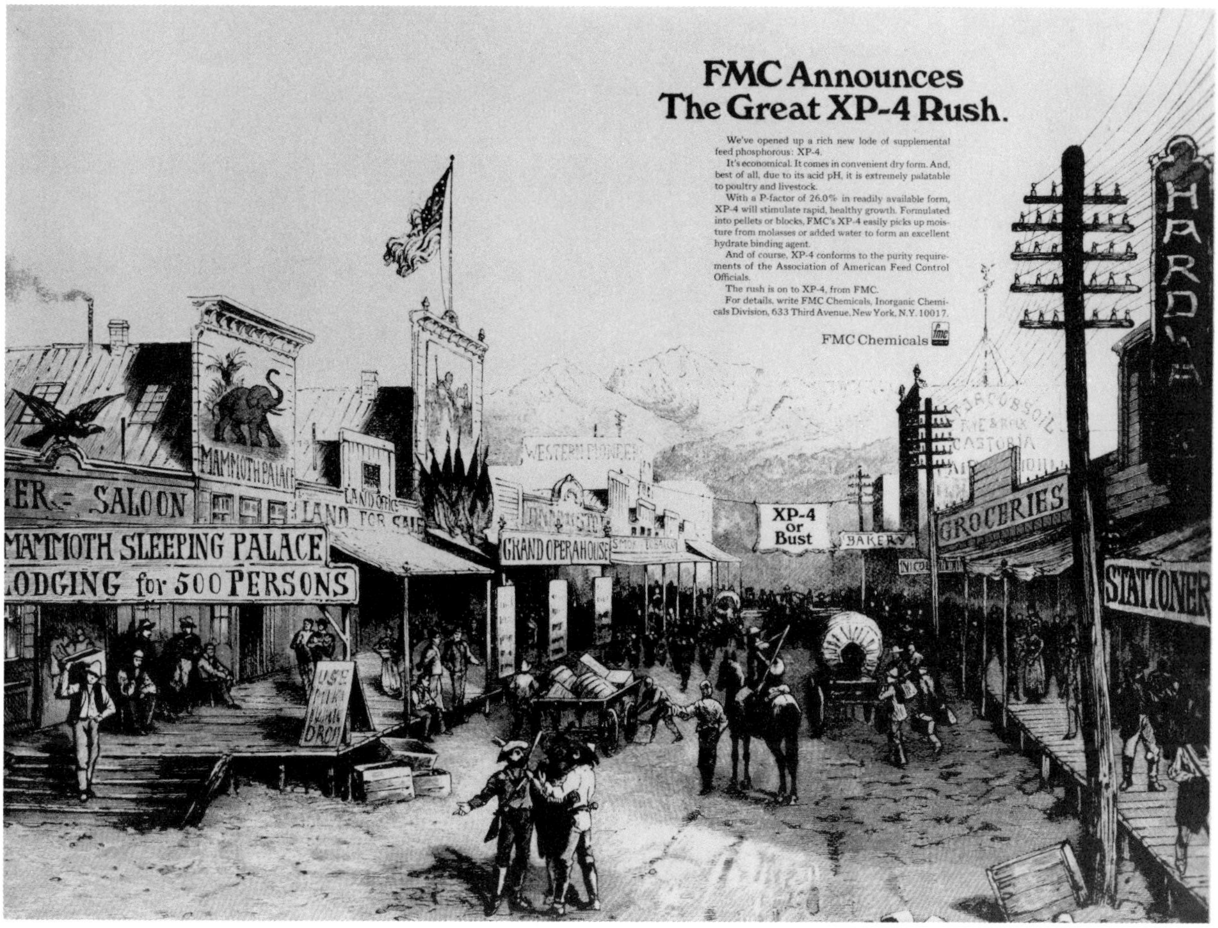
FMC Announces The Great XP-4 Rush.
We've opened up a rich new lode of supplemental feed phosphorous: XP-4.
It's economical. It comes in convenient dry form. And, best of all, due to its acid pH, it is extremely palatable to poultry and livestock.
With a P-factor of 26.0% in readily available form, XP-4 will stimulate rapid, healthy growth. Formulated into pellets or blocks, FMC's XP-4 easily picks up moisture from molasses or added water to form an excellent hydrate binding agent.
And of course, XP-4 conforms to the purity requirements of the Association of American Feed Control Officials.
The rush is on to XP-4, from FMC.
For details, write FMC Chemicals, Inorganic Chemicals Division, 633 Third Avenue, New York, N.Y. 10017.
FMC Chemicals
SALOON
MAMMOTH PALACE
MAMMOTH SLEEPING PALACE
LODGING for 500 PERSONS
GRAND OPERA HOUSE
XP-4 or Bust
BAKERY
GROCERIES

"We jes feed them critters XP-4 and let the chips fall where they may."
The evidence is piling up.
FMC's new XP-4 is the tastiest mineral feed supplement you can give livestock and poultry.
That's because of its acid pH.
And palatability is just the beginning of the advantages.
XP-4 is economical. It comes in convenient dry form.
And with a P-factor of 26.0% in readily available form, XP-4 stimulates fast, healthy growth.
Also, FMC's new XP-4 easily picks up moisture from molasses or added water to form an excellent hydrate binding agent for pellet or block formulation.
For details, write FMC Chemicals, Inorganic Chemicals Division, 633 Third Avenue, New York, N.Y. 10017.
FMC Chemicals

"Never mind the cash. Just stuff the XP-4 in a feed bag."
XP-4 is like money in the bank.
First of all, FMC's new phosphorus mineral feed supplement is palatable.
Its acid pH makes it the tastiest product your livestock and poultry have ever come across.
XP-4 is also economical. It comes in convenient dry form.
And a P-factor of 26.0% in readily available form assures you XP-4 will promote rapid, healthy growth.
Also, XP-4 easily picks up moisture from molasses, or added water, to form an excellent hydrate binding agent for pellet or block formulation.
Grab the XP-4 and run.
For details, write FMC Chemicals, Inorganic Chemicals Division, 633 Third Avenue, New York, N.Y. 10017.
FMC Chemicals

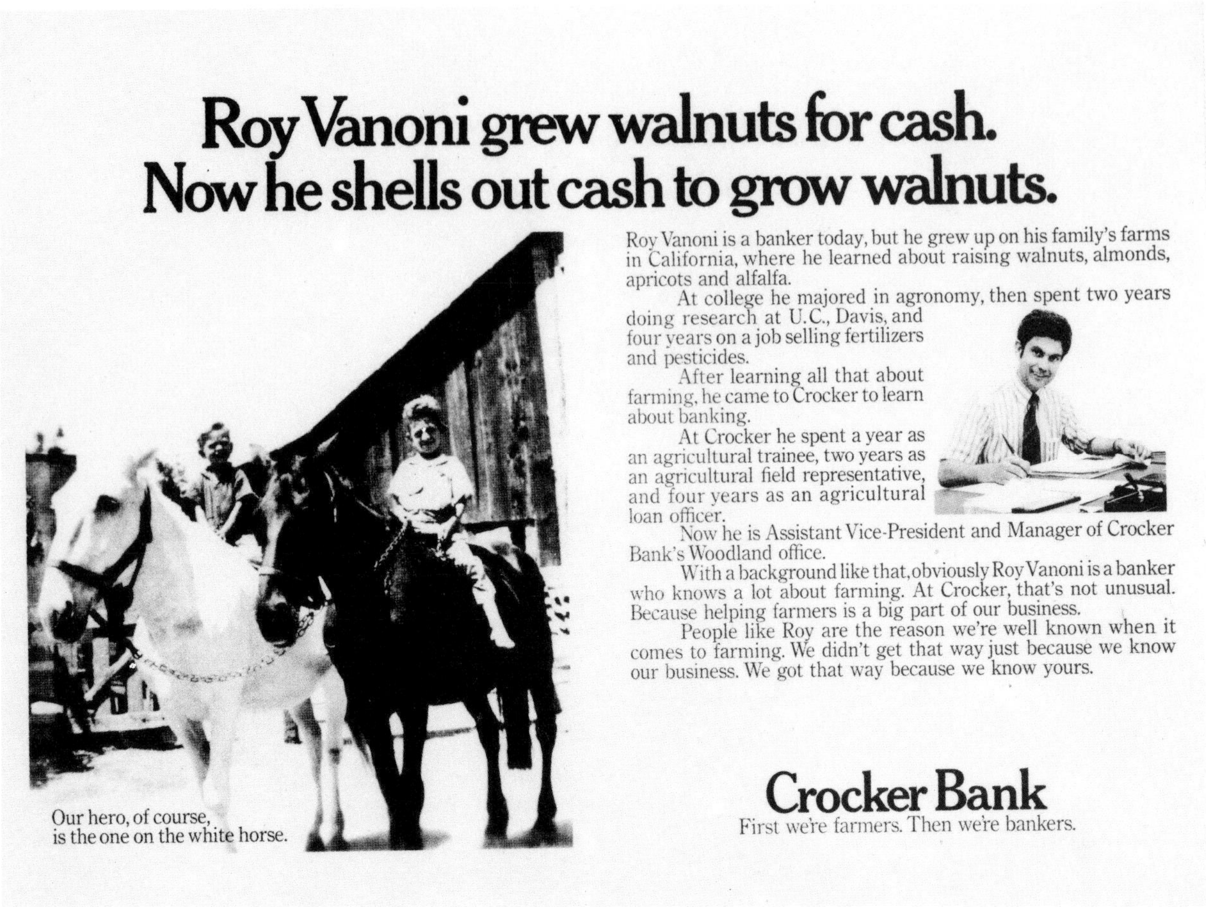

Roy Vanoni grew walnuts for cash.
Now he shells out cash to grow walnuts.
Roy Vanoni is a banker today, but he grew up on his family's farms in California, where he learned about raising walnuts, almonds, apricots and alfalfa.
At college he majored in agronomy, then spent two years doing research at U.C., Davis, and four years on a job selling fertilizers and pesticides.
After learning all that about farming, he came to Crocker to learn about banking.
At Crocker he spent a year as an agricultural trainee, two years as an agricultural field representative, and four years as an agricultural loan officer.
Now he is Assistant Vice-President and Manager of Crocker Bank's Woodland office.
With a background like that, obviously Roy Vanoni is a banker who knows a lot about farming. At Crocker, that's not unusual. Because helping farmers is a big part of our business.
People like Roy are the reason we're well known when it comes to farming. We didn't get that way just because we know our business. We got that way because we know yours.
Our hero, of course, is the one on the white horse.
Crocker Bank
First we're farmers. Then we're bankers.

Wayne Phelps knew about beans before he knew beans about banking.
Wayne Phelps is a banker today. But he grew up on a farm.
He learned about the land on a farm in Burino, New Mexico and in the San Joaquin Valley.
So Wayne has the kind of knowledge of farming that you don't get from books. And the kind that you do get from books. Because he spent four years at U.C. Davis, a good place to learn about agriculture.
When he got out of college, he went to work for the Farm Home Administration. Then, after several years with the Federal Land Bank and the Bureau of Reclamation, he came to work for Crocker, a good place to learn about banking.
He'd left the land. But we sent him back to it. Back to the farm to learn how a banker can best help a farmer.
He became an agricultural loan officer in Sacramento. Then he spent six years as a lending officer in Stockton, and seven years as an agricultural loan supervisor in Fresno. And now, he's an assistant vice president, agricultural loan officer in the Fresno main office.
Wayne Phelps is a banker who knows a lot about farming. But at Crocker, that's hardly unusual. It's because helping farmers has been a big part of our business for a long time.
Men like Wayne Phelps are the reason we're so well known when it comes to farming. We didn't get that way just because we know our business.
We got that way because we know yours.
Wayne Phelps being sheepish at age 12.
Crocker Bank
First we're farmers. Then we're bankers.

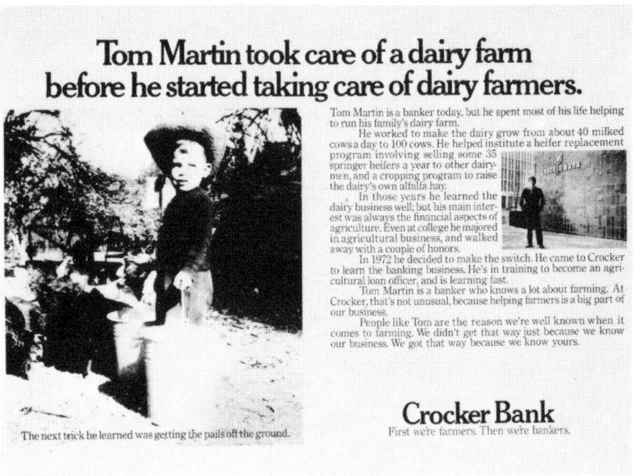

Tom Martin took care of a dairy farm before he started taking care of dairy farmers.
Tom Martin is a banker today, but he spent most of his life helping to run his family's dairy farm.
He worked to make the dairy grow from about 40 milked cows a day to 100 cows. He helped institute a heifer replacement program involving selling some 35 springer heifers a year to other dairymen, and a cropping program to raise the dairy's own alfalfa hay.
In those years he learned the dairy business well; but his main interest was always the financial aspects of agriculture. Even at college he majored in agricultural business, and walked away with a couple of honors.
In 1972 he decided to make the switch. He came to Crocker to learn the banking business. He's in training to become an agricultural loan officer, and is learning fast.
Tom Martin is a banker who knows a lot about farming. At Crocker, that's not unusual, because helping farmers is a big part of our business.
People like Tom are the reason we're well known when it comes to farming. We didn't get that way just because we know our business. We got that way because we know yours.
The next trick he learned was getting the pails off the ground.
Crocker Bank
First we're farmers. Then we're bankers.

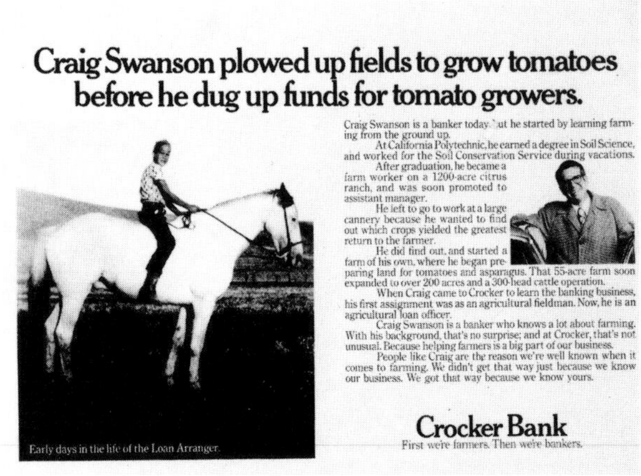

Craig Swanson plowed up fields to grow tomatoes before he dug up funds for tomato growers.
Craig Swanson is a banker today. But he started by learning farming from the ground up.
At California Polytechnic, he earned a degree in Soil Science, and worked for the Soil Conservation Service during vacations.
After graduation, he became a farm worker on a 1200-acre citrus ranch, and was soon promoted to assistant manager.
He left to go to work at a large cannery because he wanted to find out which crops yielded the greatest return to the farmer.
He did find out, and started a farm of his own, where he began preparing land for tomatoes and asparagus. That 55-acre farm soon expanded to over 200 acres and a 300-head cattle operation.
When Craig came to Crocker to learn the banking business, his first assignment was as an agricultural fieldman. Now, he is an agricultural loan officer.
Craig Swanson is a banker who knows a lot about farming. With his background, that's no surprise; and at Crocker, that's not unusual. Because helping farmers is a big part of our business.
People like Craig are the reason we're well known when it comes to farming. We didn't get that way just because we know our business. We got that way because we know yours.
Early days in the life of the Loan Arranger.
Crocker Bank
First we're farmers. Then we're bankers.

Fred Busch helped grow cotton before he helped cotton farmers grow.
Fred Busch wasn't always busy financing crops.
For a long time, he was busy raising them.
Fred's experience started early, on his family's ranch just southwest of Mendota. He went to Fresno State where he studied agriculture and graduated with a degree in business. Then he farmed on his own in Fresno and Madera counties.
When he came to work for Crocker, Fred started his education all over again. He graduated from our Administrative Training Program and Commercial and Agricultural Loan Workshops. He studied at the American Institute of Banking.
Then Fred graduated again—this time from the Pacific Coast School of Banking at the University of Washington.
Fred Busch is a banker who knows a lot about farming.
At Crocker, that's hardly unusual. It's because helping farmers has been a big part of our business for a long time.
Men like Fred Busch are why we're so well known in farming. We didn't get that way just because we know our business. We got that way because we know yours.
At age five, Fred couldn't decide between farming and flying.
Crocker Bank
First we're farmers. Then we're bankers.

We think you should get as much out of your Employee Benefits Program as your employees do.
It starts with appreciation.
When your employees appreciate all the benefits you're giving them, they're more willing to give of themselves. Their respect, their loyalty, their enthusiasm.
But if an employee doesn't realize exactly how much he's getting out of your company, he just may decide that your company is not for him.
Which means that motivating your employees depends as much on explaining their benefits as it does on providing them. That's where we can help you. We're Benefacts.
We can provide each one of your employees with a personalized annual statement that completely details every one of his benefits.
In plain dollars and cents English, not computerized gobbledygook.
At the same time, the statement itself will impress him. A lot. Benefacts statements are custom-designed especially for your company, handsomely illustrated, and carefully printed on quality stock.
We were the first to offer this kind of service. Today, over 300 leading companies don't use anything else—in-house or otherwise. In fact, we put together more statements for more companies and employees than all our competitors combined.
Benefacts. It can help you get more out of the benefits you're giving your employees.
For complete details, write Benefacts Inc., Hampton Plaza, 300 East Joppa Rd., Baltimore, Maryland 21204.
Or call us at (301) 296-5500.
Benefacts
It helps people remember why they came to work for you in the first place.

127
Art Director: Bruce Campbell
Copywriters: Alex Cichy
Fred Udall
Bruce Campbell
Hal Riney
Designers: Hal Riney
Mort Cohn
Photographers: Jim Marshall
Bruce Campbell
Agency: BBDO, San Francisco
Client: Crocker Bank

128
Art Director: Thomas Ruriani
Copywriter: Philip Dusenberry
Designer: Thomas Ruriani
Artist: Alan Brooks
Agency: Dusenberry, Ruriani, Kornhauser Inc.
Client: Alexander & Alexander—Benefacts

At least once a year, your employees should know what a great company they work for.
They should know about the one thing most employees are in the dark about. Their company benefits.
We don't have to tell you how much of an incentive benefits can be. Except when your people don't know what they are. Or understand them. In which case, the benefits aren't doing either of you much good.
Which is why you should know about Benefacts.
It's a personalized annual statement that spells out each benefit to each of your people. Clearly and quickly.
We were the first to come up with this kind of service. We turned computer statistics into language people understand. Plain English.
We've made Benefacts so accurate, many companies use it in auditing their pension funds. And it's so complete a service that over 300 of the nation's leading corporations wouldn't dream of using anything else. In-house or otherwise.
In fact, we put together more statements for more companies and employees than all our competitors combined.
For complete details, write or phone Benefacts Inc., Hampton Plaza, 300 E. Joppa Rd., Baltimore, Md. 21204 (301) 296-5500
Benefacts
It helps people remember why they came to work for you in the first place.

128

The reason your employees don't appreciate their benefits is because they don't understand them.
You hand a new employee a medical plan, an insurance plan, a pension plan, a disability plan, a profit-sharing plan, and everything ends up in a drawer.
And he winds up in the dark.
So while his benefits are piling up, he doesn't know exactly how he's benefitting from them. Instead of being impressed, he's merely confused.
So we suggest giving each one of your employees something to go along with his benefits. Benefacts. A personalized annual statement that completely explains just what the benefits are.
Each Benefacts statement says in effect, "Harry, so far you've got $2000 in the pension-fund, $5000 in profit-sharing, $25,000 insurance..." Etc.
At the same time, the statements look as attractive as the benefits they describe. They're custom-designed especially for your company, handsomely illustrated, and carefully printed on quality stock. A nice way of showing your people you think they're pretty important.
We were the first to offer this kind of service. Today, over 300 leading companies don't use anything else, in-house or otherwise. In fact, we put together more statements for more companies and employees than all our competitors combined.
Benefacts. It helps your employees appreciate their company benefits. And think a lot more of your company.
For complete details, write Benefacts, Inc., Hampton Plaza, 300 E. Joppa Rd., Baltimore, Md. 21204. Or call us at (301) 296-5500.
Benefacts
It helps people remember why they came to work for you in the first place.

WE'RE TEACHING A LOT OF AMERICANS A SECOND LANGUAGE. ENGLISH.

Throughout America, people are trapped in their own communities, unable to talk their way out.

They're imprisoned behind an impenetrable barrier because they can't speak English.

And since existing language programs reach only a few people, many Americans spend a lifetime trying to pick up a language they should be able to learn in a year.

But in San Francisco, things are changing.

A committee of Chinese citizens sought the help of KPIX, Group W's television station. Working with the community, KPIX helped create a new Chinese language curriculum and handbook and then televised sixty-five half hour TV programs entitled "Sut Yung Ying Yee" (Practical English). The shows were so successful an appliance store in the area had a run on TV sets.

In Boston, a series for Spanish-speaking youngsters ("Que Pasa") was produced and televised by Group W's WBZ-TV in cooperation with the Massachusetts Executive Committee for Educational Television. The programs were later rerun in public schools by the Boston educational TV station.

Both language series have been aired by other Group W stations. And there's interest in other cities, as well as by the Federal government in similar programs elsewhere.

Putting words into action is something responsible broadcasters believe in strongly.

And Group W stations like KPIX and WBZ-TV prove it.

Broadcasting does more with problems than talk about them.

GROUP W
WESTINGHOUSE BROADCASTING COMPANY

WBZ · WBZ-TV BOSTON · WINS NEW YORK · KYW · KYW-TV PHILADELPHIA · KDKA · KDKA-TV PITTSBURGH
WJZ-TV BALTIMORE · WOWO FT. WAYNE · WIND CHICAGO · KPIX SAN FRANCISCO · KFWB LOS ANGELES

THEY'RE PREPARING FOR WAR IN THE FORESTS OF CALIFORNIA.

At this moment, Air Force planes are being tested for special assignment in the forests of the west coast.

When they go into action, it could signal the end of devastating forest fires and the floods and mudslides which follow in their path.

This could greatly reduce the loss of 4½ million acres of forest a year. At the cost of some $600 million. *Every year.*

The idea originated with Group W's Los Angeles radio station, KFWB.

There were thousands of surplus Air Force planes gathering dust. Why not convert some of them into tankers, loaded with a fire-retardant chemical? Then, when brush fires broke out, the planes could be there in a matter of minutes.

KFWB proposed the plan in a series of editorials. And the first wave of support began rolling in. Not just from the public but also from municipal governments, the California legislature, Congress and the Air Force.

A year after the first radio editorial, a National Guard plane made eight test runs over a fire in Santa Barbara. And the technique worked.

The Air Force has now promised enough planes for a national fire-fighting program. The chemicals they drop will not only extinguish fires but will, at the same time, fertilize the scorched earth.

Putting words into action is something responsible broadcasters believe in strongly.

And Group W stations like KFWB prove it.

Broadcasting does more with problems than talk about them.

GROUP W
WESTINGHOUSE BROADCASTING COMPANY

WBZ · WBZ-TV BOSTON · WINS NEW YORK · KYW · KYW-TV PHILADELPHIA · KDKA · KDKA-TV PITTSBURGH
WJZ-TV BALTIMORE · WOWO FT. WAYNE · WIND CHICAGO · KPIX SAN FRANCISCO · KFWB LOS ANGELES

129

IN SOME STATES YOU CAN SPEND YOUR WHOLE LIFE PAYING FOR A CRIME YOU NEVER COMMITTED.

Calvin Reeves, a Chicago postman, was arrested in 1967 for a strange "crime." While inquiring at a police station about a neighbor's son, he was charged with interfering with the duties of a police officer.

There were three court appearances to hear his case. But the arresting officer never showed and the case was closed. Except for one thing.

The postman's fingerprints stayed in the police files. Which means that he had an arrest record. For life.

He turned to Illinois State Senator Richard Newhouse for help, who in turn came to WIND, Group W's radio station in Chicago.

We arranged for a lie-detector test. Produced a program. Even tried to persuade the police to destroy the files.

Finally, we helped introduce legislation. Bills were passed in 1969 and 1971. And now anyone falsely arrested (without a previous record) or anyone cleared of an alleged crime will have the records, including fingerprints, destroyed.

Which means that thousands of innocent persons, often turned down for jobs because of an archaic system of records, won't have to face that demoralization again.

Putting words into action is something responsible broadcasters believe in strongly.

And Group W stations like WIND prove it.

Broadcasting does more with problems than talk about them.

GROUP W
WESTINGHOUSE BROADCASTING COMPANY

WBZ · WBZ-TV BOSTON · WINS NEW YORK · KYW · KYW-TV PHILADELPHIA · KDKA · KDKA-TV PITTSBURGH
WJZ-TV BALTIMORE · WOWO FT. WAYNE · WIND CHICAGO · KPIX SAN FRANCISCO · KFWB LOS ANGELES

MAYBE THE BUILDING YOU THOUGHT WAS FIREPROOF IS REALLY ESCAPEPROOF.

Chances are the forty-story building you work in was designed as though it were fireproof. But due to a whole new set of fire hazards spawned by modern technology, you may well be working in a steel-and-glass firetrap. Without sprinklers. Without adequate exits. And with sealed windows.

And your home is probably not much safer.

Worst of all, many fire departments are still fighting fires the way they did fifty years ago.

It's the job of Group W's Urban America Unit to zero in on problems like this. To ask the right questions. Look for the solutions. And most important, to provoke action. That was the reason for our hour-long television documentary "Firetrap."

It was meant to alarm people. And it did.

One Congressman used the film and an actual demonstration from it when he introduced nine new fire-prevention bills. Elsewhere, state legislators have been spurred to action.

Architects, insurance companies and fire departments use "Firetrap" in their training programs.

Putting words into action is something responsible broadcasters believe in strongly.

And television programs like Group W's "Firetrap" prove it.

Broadcasting does more with problems than talk about them.

GROUP W
WESTINGHOUSE BROADCASTING COMPANY

WBZ · WBZ-TV BOSTON · WINS NEW YORK · KYW · KYW-TV PHILADELPHIA · KDKA · KDKA-TV PITTSBURGH
WJZ-TV BALTIMORE · WOWO FT. WAYNE · WIND CHICAGO · KPIX SAN FRANCISCO · KFWB LOS ANGELES

MAYBE WE'D BE BETTER OFF KEEPING DRUG OFFENDERS ON THE STREET INSTEAD OF IN JAIL.

Not every drug offender is a hard-core junkie.

A 17-year-old caught experimenting with marijuana can often be rehabilitated before he gets into more trouble.

Unfortunately, the drug laws in this country don't always give him that chance.

But in Massachusetts the laws have changed.

It began when WBZ, Group W's radio station in Boston, launched a ten-month effort on the drug problem. The station involved its audience. Not just in the problem. But in the solutions as well.

Listeners made suggestions. Some were incorporated into a bill. The bill was passed by the state legislature. And today a first offender convicted of possession of marijuana is no longer sent to jail. Instead, he's put on probation for 6 months. Then his record is wiped clean.

Putting words into action is something responsible broadcasters believe in strongly.

And Group W stations like WBZ prove it.

Broadcasting does more with problems than talk about them.

GROUP W
WESTINGHOUSE BROADCASTING COMPANY

WBZ · WBZ-TV BOSTON · WINS NEW YORK · KYW · KYW-TV PHILADELPHIA · KDKA · KDKA-TV PITTSBURGH
WJZ-TV BALTIMORE · WOWO FT. WAYNE · WIND CHICAGO · KPIX SAN FRANCISCO · KFWB LOS ANGELES

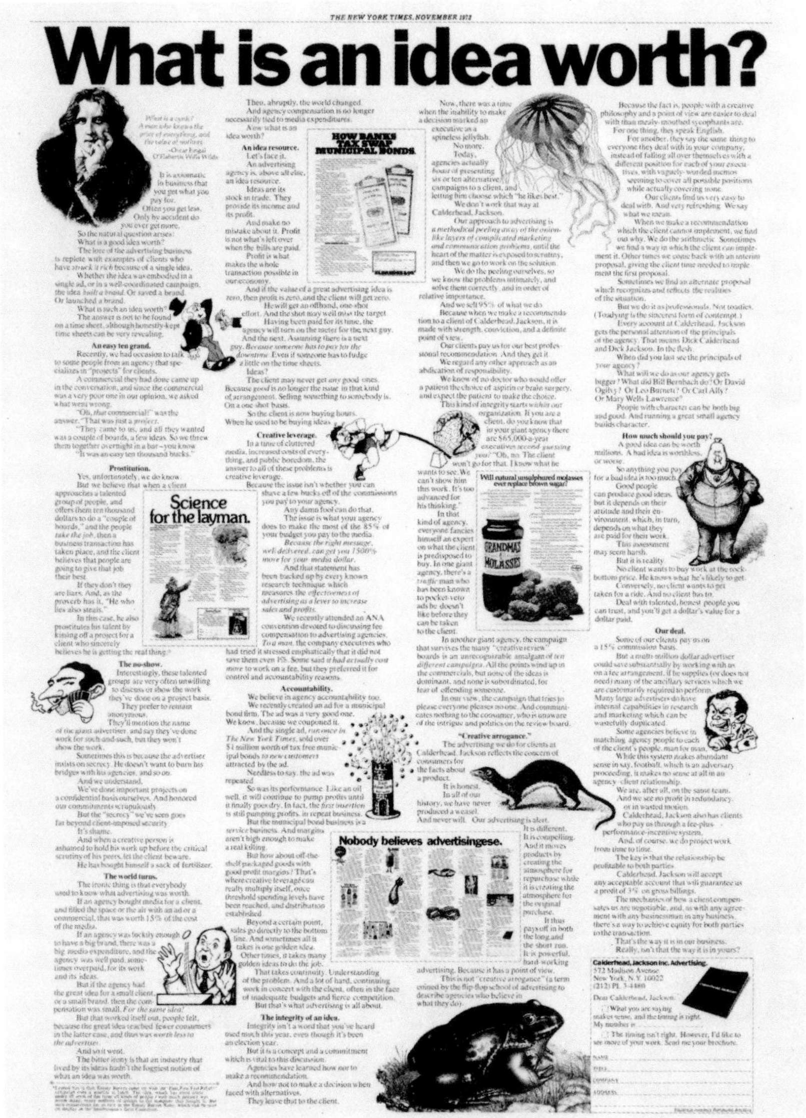
THE NEW YORK TIMES, NOVEMBER 1972
What is an idea worth?
Science for the layman.
Nobody believes advertisingese.
GRANDMA'S MOLASSES

129
Art Directors: Ron Becker
Larry Osborne
Copywriters: Larry Spector
Marshall Karp
Marc Shenfield
Designer: Ron Becker
Agency: DKG Inc.
Client: Westinghouse Broadcasting Company

130 Silver Award
Art Director: Dick Calderhead
Copywriter: Dick Jackson
Designer: Barbara Schubeck
Art Source: The Bettmann Archive
Agency: Calderhead, Jackson Inc.
Client: Calderhead, Jackson Inc.

130

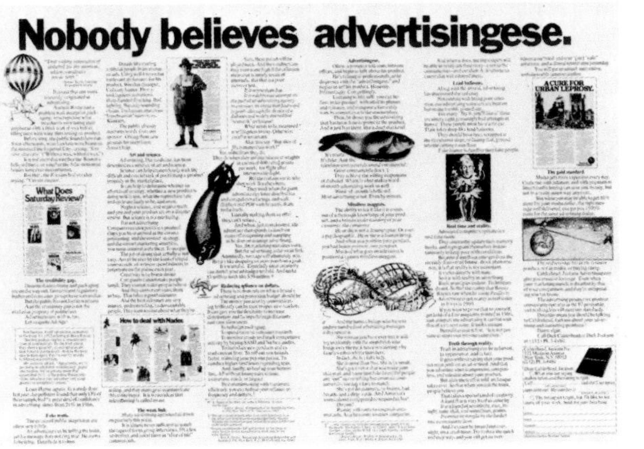
Nobody believes advertisingese.
What Does Saturday Review?
A CURE FOR URBAN LEPROSY.

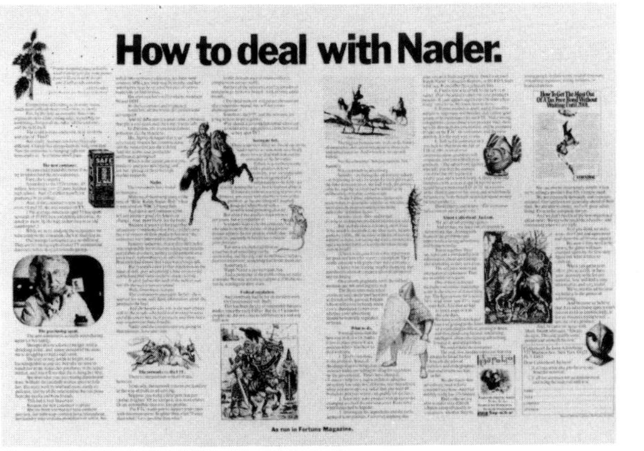
How to deal with Nader.
As run in Fortune Magazine.

WHEN IS A CHICKEN NOT A FOOTBALL?
When it's one of mine.
Frank Perdue
PERDUE
When you sell my chickens, you don't have to kick them around.
Perdue chickens are so good people expect to pay more for them. And, in a smart retailer's store, they do.
Example: a small chain increased their sale price on chicken by offering Perdue chickens at 39¢ a pound and ended up selling just as many as ever.
A medium-sized chain took on Perdue chickens exclusively. They used to have sales on chicken at 29¢ a pound. They now sell Perdue chickens at a regular price of 39¢ per pound and have very few sales. Yet their volume on chickens is up 25%.
A large chain that had been selling chicken at 29¢ for ten consecutive months took on Perdue at 35¢. Then they raised the price to 39¢. Their earnings are up dramatically compared to previous footballed chicken prices.
If you'd like to talk about taking on Perdue chickens, call me at 301-742-7161 and we'll set up an appointment.
And if I can't convince you that you'll make more money on my chickens than on those you're selling now, do what I'd do.
Kick me out.
TASTY YOUNG CHICKEN
PERDUE
QUALITY GUARANTEED OR MONEY BACK
Perdue Incorporated, Salisbury, Md. 21801
It takes a tough man to sell a tender chicken.

HOW I BECAME THE CHIQUITA OF THE CHICKEN BUSINESS.
By Frank Perdue
First I identified my fresh young Perdue chickens with special wing-tags to separate them from the competition.
Then I went on television, radio and down into the subways to tell people how good my chickens are. I told them about my rigid quality standards. And offered their money back if they weren't completely satisfied.
Then I supplied stores carrying Perdue chicken with posters promoting Perdue chickens.
You know what? People don't go into their stores and ask for chicken anymore. Now they ask for Perdue.
In fact, Perdue is far and away the largest-selling brand of chicken in New York. You might say I've become the top banana in the chicken business around here.
If you're still messing around with chicken why don't you start selling Perdue? Call our Sales Manager, Tom Robinson, at 212-245-8532 for more information. If the line is busy, please try again. A lot of guys are going out of the chicken business these days.
PERDUE
IT TAKES A TOUGH MAN TO SELL A TENDER CHICKEN.

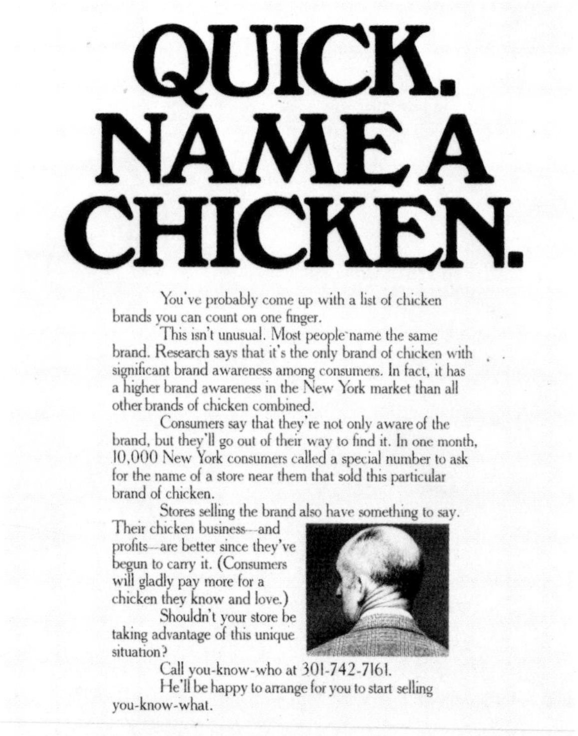
QUICK. NAME A CHICKEN.
You've probably come up with a list of chicken brands you can count on one finger.
This isn't unusual. Most people name the same brand. Research says that it's the only brand of chicken with significant brand awareness among consumers. In fact, it has a higher brand awareness in the New York market than all other brands of chicken combined.
Consumers say that they're not only aware of the brand, but they'll go out of their way to find it. In one month, 10,000 New York consumers called a special number to ask for the name of a store near them that sold this particular brand of chicken.
Stores selling the brand also have something to say. Their chicken business—and profits—are better since they've begun to carry it. (Consumers will gladly pay more for a chicken they know and love.)
Shouldn't your store be taking advantage of this unique situation?
Call you-know-who at 301-742-7161.
He'll be happy to arrange for you to start selling you-know-what.

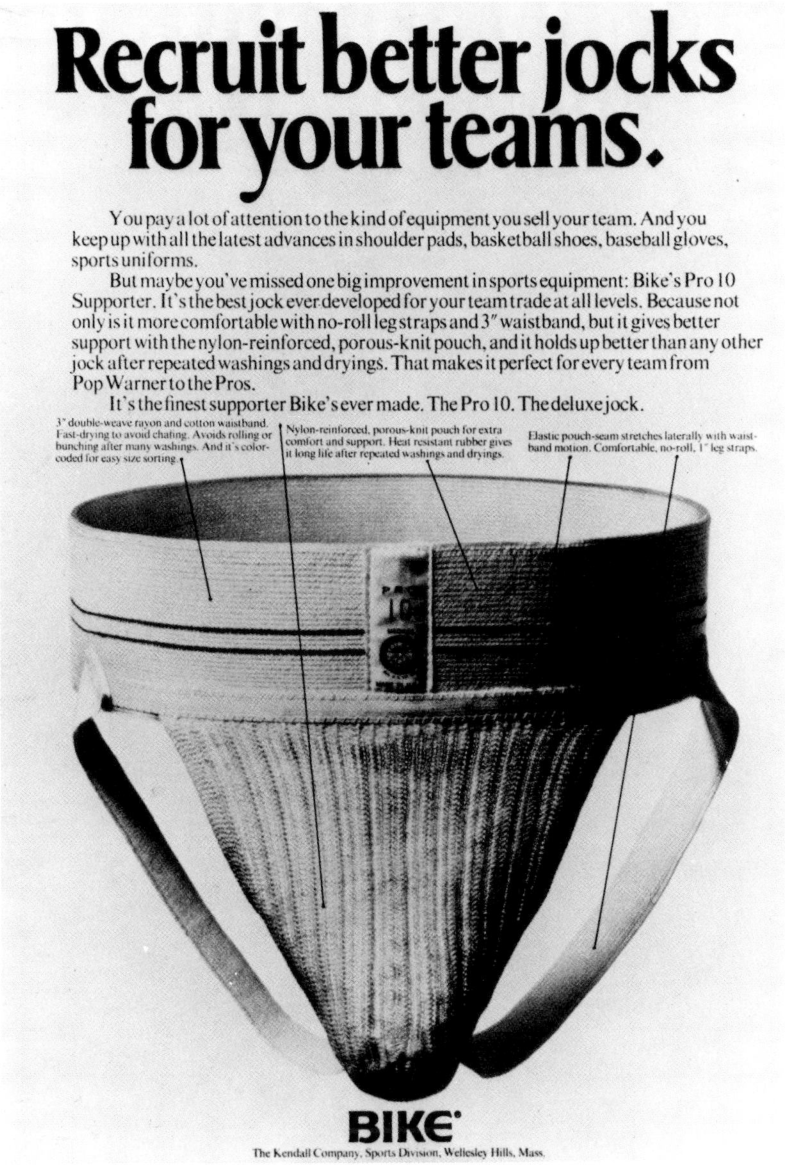

Recruit better jocks for your teams.
You pay a lot of attention to the kind of equipment you sell your team. And you keep up with all the latest advances in shoulder pads, basketball shoes, baseball gloves, sports uniforms.
But maybe you've missed one big improvement in sports equipment: Bike's Pro 10 Supporter. It's the best jock ever developed for your team trade at all levels. Because not only is it more comfortable with no-roll leg straps and 3" waistband, but it gives better support with the nylon-reinforced, porous-knit pouch, and it holds up better than any other jock after repeated washings and dryings. That makes it perfect for every team from Pop Warner to the Pros.
It's the finest supporter Bike's ever made. The Pro 10. The deluxe jock.
3" double-weave rayon and cotton waistband. Fast-drying to avoid chafing. Avoids rolling or bunching after many washings. And it's color-coded for easy size sorting.
Nylon-reinforced, porous-knit pouch for extra comfort and support. Heat resistant rubber gives it long life after repeated washings and dryings.
Elastic pouch-seam stretches laterally with waist-band motion. Comfortable, no-roll, 1" leg straps.
BIKE®
The Kendall Company, Sports Division, Wellesley Hills, Mass.

131 Gold Award
Art Director: Sam Scali
Copywriter: Ed McCabe
Designer: Sam Scali
Photographers: Alan Dolgins
Phil Mazzurco
Agency: Scali, McCabe, Sloves, Inc.
Client: Perdue Farms Inc.

132
Art Directors: Ralph Moxcey
Ken Amaral
Copywriter: Scott Miller
Designer: Ralph Moxcey
Photographer: Bill Bruin
Agency: Humphrey, Browning, MacDougall
Client: Kendall Company

132

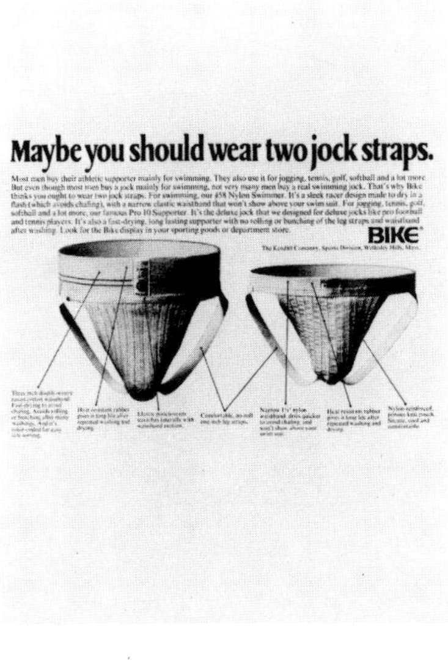

Maybe you should wear two jock straps.

Most men buy their athletic supporter mainly for swimming. They also use it for jogging, tennis, golf, softball and a lot more. But even though most men buy a jock mainly for swimming, not very many men buy a real swimming jock. That's why Bike thinks you ought to wear two jock straps. For swimming, our #58 Nylon Swimmer. It's a sleek racer design made to dry in a flash (which avoids chafing), with a narrow elastic waistband that won't show above your swim suit. For jogging, tennis, golf, softball and a lot more, our famous Pro 10 Supporter. It's the deluxe jock that we designed for deluxe jocks like pro football and tennis players. It's also a fast-drying, long lasting supporter with no rolling or bunching of the leg straps and waistband after washing. Look for the Bike display in your sporting goods or department store.

BIKE

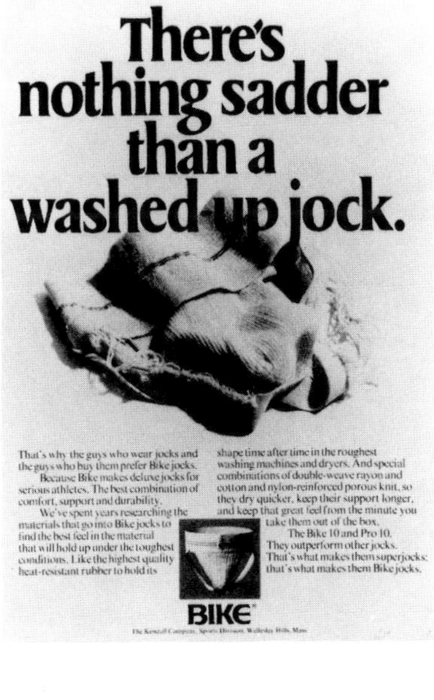

There's nothing sadder than a washed-up jock.
That's why the guys who wear jocks and the guys who buy them prefer Bike jocks.
Because Bike makes deluxe jocks for serious athletes. The best combination of comfort, support and durability.
We've spent years researching the materials that go into Bike jocks to find the best feel in the material that will hold up under the toughest conditions. Like the highest quality heat-resistant rubber to hold its shape time after time in the roughest washing machines and dryers. And special combinations of double-weave rayon and cotton and nylon-reinforced porous knit, so they dry quicker, keep their support longer, and keep that great feel from the minute you take them out of the box.
The Bike 10 and Pro 10. They outperform other jocks. That's what makes them superjocks: that's what makes them Bike jocks.
BIKE®

"Above everything else," George Jean Nathan declared, "a musical is first and last a girl show."
That was in the 20s and 30s. Before women's liberation and short money.
Newsweek Reporter Lorraine Kisly found that most magnificent of sex objects, the showgirl, was not only alive and kicking on Broadway but under all that flesh there was a woman.
Charlene Ryan ("A Funny Thing Happened on the Way to the Forum") not only has the kind of body that male chauvinist pigs dream of, she's gutsy, direct and "freaked out" by an Indian Guru. "I dig being a sex object," she says. "What else is it all about? I'm a damned good dancer and I know it. I have the potential to do a lot more, but I think that's pretty much true of everyone."
Suzanne Briggs ("Follies") is the ultimate in chic carnality. "I always aim for an elegance along with the sex thing I mix it with," she says. Men are inclined to send flowers or a bottle of champagne backstage ... It kind of gets in your blood. There's no way I could work in an office now."
Ursula Maschmeyer (also in "Follies") has a somewhat darker viewpoint. "There's no future in being a showgirl. Just beauty isn't that important any more."
"Ain't Supposed to Die a Natural Death" has a new kind of showgirl. She's black and beautiful Barbra Alston. "When we were kids my brother would say 'You're not going to do that dance in public are you?' But in the house we'd let it all out."
It was all let out in Newsweek (May 22). Senior Editor Jack Kroll wrote the story. "Girls! Girls! Girls!" was more than just an ordinary theater piece. It was a
The all-American sex object is alive and kicking.
window that let Newsweek's 15 million adult readers world-wide (10 million of them males) look into the lives of the girls most men dream of and not many (not even Newsweek readers) know.
Newsweek

133
Art Directors: Elliott Manketo
Jerry Pfiffner
George Tenne
Copywriters: Tad Dillon
Jerry Pfiffner
Peter Rodgers
Photographers: Frank Cowan
Joe Toto
Henry Wolf
Agency: N. W. Ayer & Son, Inc., New York
Client: Newsweek

134
Art Director: Ray Alban
Copywriters: Ed McCabe
Dan Bingham
Designer: Ray Alban
Photographer: Phil Mazzurco
Agency: Scali, McCabe, Sloves, Inc.
Client: Dictaphone

133

Bad News For IBM.
Dictaphone introduces the Thought Tank.
A new kind of continuous-flow thought processor that outdates conventional dictating equipment.
The Thought Tank is also bad news for Norelco, Edison, Gray, Stenorette, Stenocord or anyone else who makes conventional dictating equipment.
But it's beautiful news for you, because the Thought Tank can literally cut 38% off the time it used to take to get your correspondence out.
There are no belts or tapes to transfer. There are no separate dictating and transcribing procedures. There is nothing to load or unload.
A small unit that resembles a telephone sits on your desk, a small receiver with a signal light sits on your girl's desk. Somewhere in-between sits the Thought Tank.
The moment you start dictating, the Thought Tank lights the signal on your secretary's desk, and 12 seconds later, she starts typing—while you're still dictating.
So before you've finished dictating a second letter, the first letter is typed and on your desk ready to be signed.
It is the fastest, simplest method of dictating ever devised.
And it is a great deal more than that. You use the Thought Tank as a 24-hour, continuous-flow thought processor.
Any thought—a memo, a letter, a note to yourself, next week's lunch, theater tickets, a BLT with no mayo—any thought you think of, can be put into the Thought Tank.
And you can put your ideas into the Thought Tank from any outside telephone with a simple, inexpensive attachment.
Suppose you're relaxing at home when something occurs to you. You don't put the idea on a scrap of paper; you pick up your telephone and call your Thought Tank.
The Thought Tank lights the signal on your girl's unattended desk, and tells her there's something in the tank. She starts to work on it as soon as she gets to work.
Or say you're at an airport at 7:00 a.m. You have an important memo you want to get out, but your office isn't open.
With the Thought Tank, you simply call it in from a phone booth, and when your office opens in the morning, it's on your secretary's desk, ready to be done.
These are just two ways you can use the Thought Tank to speed up your ideas and get more work done.
You can take any six dictators in your office and each can be inexpensively hooked up to one Thought Tank. And on that basis alone, the Thought Tank could save your business thousands of dollars.
Which brings us to the question of dollars.
The basic Thought Tank costs less than a pair of most conventional dictating and transcribing machines.
Or, if you choose, you can lease a Thought Tank for as little as a dollar a day.
Think of it: a Thought Tank for a dollar a day.
This has to be great news for business.
Unless you're in the business of making conventional dictating machines.
Call this toll-free number for a free in-office demonstration of the Thought Tank. 800-243-6000. From Connecticut, call 1-800-882-6500 or see the Yellow Pages.
Dictaphone

How Dictaphone's Thought Tank Can Help You Get More Out Of IBM's Typewriter.
If you're important enough to require a secretary with one of the best electric typewriters IBM makes, you're also important enough to require the fastest dictating system anybody makes.
Dictaphone's Thought Tank.
It can literally cut 38% off the time it used to take to get your paperwork out. And it can get more work out of a typewriter than anyone ever dreamed of.
A small unit that resembles a telephone sits on your desk. A small unit with a signal light sits on your secretary's desk. The Thought Tank sits anywhere in-between.
For day-to-day dictating, you simply pick up the phone and start talking. A signal lights the unit on your secretary's desk and twelve seconds later she begins typing. While you're still dictating.
So before you've even finished dictating a second letter, your secretary can have the first letter back on your desk ready to be signed.
It is the fastest method of dictating ever invented, and it's a great deal more than that.
The Thought Tank is a 24-hour, continuous-flow thought processor.
You can put your ideas into the Thought Tank at any hour of the day or night from any telephone in the world with an inexpensive attachment, plus a monthly telephone charge.
Let's suppose a business trip takes you to a remote location. You've been through a day of wall-to-wall meetings and there are 10 million things on your mind that have to get done. But your office is closed and half-way across the country.
You don't scribble notes to yourself on a piece of paper.
You pick up the telephone in your hotel room, call your Thought Tank, tell it what you want done, and when your secretary arrives at work the next morning, she is greeted by a signal light and your voice telling her what needs to be done.
And it gets done.
Surprisingly, one Thought Tank costs less than many conventional dictating and transcribing systems, including our own.
Or, you can lease a Thought Tank for as little as one dollar a day.
Think about it: a Thought Tank for a dollar a day.
In an age where many companies are introducing the 4-day work week, the Thought Tank ushers in the 24-hour day.
Dictaphone

If Dictaphone Corporation Doesn't Use Dictating Machines, Why Should You?
After making great dictating machines for fifty years, last year we began to get rid of them.
Like most American businesses, we found ourselves overwhelmed by the amount of correspondence we had to get out each day.
And no dictating equipment made—not even our own—was able to keep up with it.
So, although we still make dictating machines, you won't find many left around our offices.
We've found something better.
The Thought Tank.
The Dictating Machine Traps Words. The Thought Tank Puts Them To Work.
When you dictate into a dictating machine, something very bad happens.
Nothing.
Your words just sit on the belt, tape or cassette. Languishing. Until they're finally removed and transcribed.
The Thought Tank, on the other hand, instantly puts your words where they belong.
On your secretary's desk.
E. L. Tabat, Dictaphone's President, practices what he preaches.
A small unit that resembles a telephone sits on your desk. A small unit with a signal light sits on your secretary's desk. Somewhere in-between sits the Thought Tank.
The moment you start dictating, the Thought Tank lights the signal on your secretary's desk.
12 seconds later, she can start typing—while you're still dictating.
That's all there is to it.
Nothing to load or unload.
No separate dictating and transcribing procedures.
And most important, not a moment's delay in getting your thoughts onto paper and out of the office.
Any Thought Worth Having Is Worth Putting Into The Thought Tank.
Because the Thought Tank is so simple to use (believe it or not, there are those who actually consider it fun), you'll find yourself using it for thoughts you wouldn't think of putting into a dictating machine.
Short letters, memos, next week's dental appointment, even brainstorms that you might ordinarily lose forever—put them into the Thought Tank and before you know it your secretary is putting them back on your desk.
The Thought Tank Works 24 Hours A Day.
As you probably know all too well, your mind doesn't stop working when you stop working.
Well, neither does the Thought Tank.
Any thought you have, whether you have it at home or Hong Kong, can—with an inexpensive attachment and small monthly telephone charge—be telephoned into the Thought Tank any time of the day or night.
When the President is out of town, he still gets work out of the office.
Or, if you choose, you can lease a Thought Tank for as little as a dollar a day.
The Thought Tank Costs Less Than You Think.
With all its amazing capabilities, the basic Thought Tank costs less than a pair of most conventional dictating and transcribing machines.
All things considered, it's no wonder that thousands of companies throughout the country have been switching from dictating machines to Thought Tanks.
Including the company that made dictating machines famous.
For more information on how the Thought Tank can help your business, call 914-967-7405, collect. Or mail the coupon below.
Please send your booklet on the Thought Tank "60 Ways to Improve Executive Communications."
Please arrange for a free demonstration of the Thought Tank, executive communications system, in my office.
The Thought Tank by Dictaphone
120 Old Post Road, Rye, New York 10580

You can sell Dickies for the same price as cheap pants.
PANTS $7
DICKIES $7
If you're a self-service mass merchandiser, you don't need us to tell you that the most important thing you can offer is a good, low price.
Instead we'll just remind you that the second most important thing is a good, reliable, well-known product.
And that it's still possible to offer both at the same time.
Dickies

A Dickies salesman may try to high-pressure you into a smaller order.
Dickies Order Form
Doz. Lot# 16-242R
100
Anybody will sell you what you want, and there are a few who'll try for more than that.
At Dickies, we'd rather sell you what you need. And after 50 years of selling pants and work wear, we have a pretty good idea of what that is.
This way we sometimes make a little less in the short run.
But we're one of the largest-selling clothing manufacturers in the country. We can afford to be interested in the long run.
Dickies
You can sell them for the same price as cheap pants.

Dickies can help keep your business from running you.
We have a solution for all the paperwork, inventories, and other forms of madness that make you work too hard.
A Dickies salesman.
Our salesman will help you do your inventories, provide instant service for fill-ins, help you plan your merchandise flow, help with displays, promotions and advertising, and probably buy you lunch now and then.
So if your business is running you, it doesn't surprise us.
After all, you're doing two jobs. Your own, and the one we're paying our salesmen to do for you.
Dickies
You can sell them for the same price as cheap pants.

Why stake your good name on pants that don't have any?
Dickies
You can sell them for the same price as cheap pants.

Only Dickies work clothes come in these popular sizes.
10"
12"
17"
21"
DICKIES
If you're interested in selling obscure work clothes, you have over 250 unheard-of names to choose from.
But if you're interested in selling work clothes advertised to over 150 million people on NFL football telecasts, then Dickies isn't just a logical choice.
It's the only possible one.
Dickies
You can sell them for the same price as cheap clothes.

We've put some of our most successful customers out of business.
Dickies provides a unique service to its retailers. We mind your business.
We provide you with a gigantic service organization on which you can dump all manner of time-consuming detail. Such as inventories, forecasting, instant fill-in servicing, and promotion.
So to get out on the golf course or tennis courts more often, sell Dickies. And join the growing number of successful retailers enjoying the fruits of our labors.
Dickies
You can sell them for the same price as cheap pants.

If you're still doing your own inventories, maybe you should change your pants.
Sell Dickies and two things will happen:
(1) Your pants won't stay around long enough for you to have trouble keeping track of them. (We produce 5 to 7 turnovers a year.)
(2) We'll keep track of your pants for you. We'll send you a monthly computer printout showing sales performance in each of your stores.
These labor-saving services are available now from Dickies—the people who believe your way of making a living shouldn't have to become your whole life.
Dickies
You can sell them for the same price as cheap pants.

A Dickies salesman actually shows up when you need him!
What do you do when there's a run on a certain style, and you're caught with your supply of pants down?
If you sell Dickies, you merely call a Dickies salesman.
He can get there faster because there are more of him to go around. (We have one of the largest sales/services organizations in the business.)
And he'll leave as quickly as he came.
A Dickies salesman actually goes away when you don't need him!
Dickies
You can sell them for the same price as cheap pants.

Now millions of people can pick up your pants at home.
Dickies
If you sell Dickies this year, your pants will appear on N.F.L. football, pro golf and tennis, pro basketball, and many other sports.
Each of our commercials will be seen by over 30 million people.
We don't guarantee they'll all run into your store.
But once people do get there, you'll be able to greet them with famous pants, instead of unheard-of ones.
Dickies
You can sell them for the same price as cheap pants.

136

Instant Non-food.
You're looking at the new Number 1 in non-foods, in chain after chain.
We've always had the reputation for being a fast developer.
In supermarkets we're even faster.
In just three years, Polaroid Colorpack Land film has become the number one dollar volume non-food item in hundreds of stores in major chains across the country.
(One midwestern chain of 105 stores recently sold about 7500 packs of film, in 13 days. That's about $30,000 worth at their prices!)
It's easy to see why.
Women buy 62% of all film sold.
And 7 out of 10 buy on impulse.
So when our colorful and convenient film prepacks (50 packs to a prepack) are displayed in the kind of a store where women buy more on impulse than anyplace else, what do you expect?
We'll tell you.
It sells so fast many store owners can pay for their film out of current sales.
And to make matters even nicer, we'll be playing radio commercials all across the country from now through July.
We want to stir up our instant non-food for the Holidays.
Polaroid Colorpack Film
The next best thing to food.
POLAROID COLORPACK FILM

60-second pictures. The next best thing to food.
You're looking at the new Number 1 in non-foods, in chain after chain.
In just 3 years, Polaroid Colorpack film has become the number one dollar volume non-food item in hundreds of stores in major chains across the country.
It came as no surprise to us.
We've known for a long time that 62% of all film is bought by women. And that 7 out of 10 buy it on impulse.
So what better place than food stores to sell Polaroid Land film, where women buy more on impulse than any place else.
With our convenient racks and prepacks, Polaroid film is easy to stock and attractive to display. It sells so fast, many store owners can pay for it out of current sales.
One of the most spectacular successes was a Southwestern chain of 150 stores which sold almost 160 prepack displays of film in one weekend. That's about 8000 packs of film!
Think of it this way.
There are millions of Polaroid Land camera owners out there.
And they all have to buy food sooner or later.
Polaroid Colorpack Film
POLAROID COLORPACK FILM
POLACOLOR LAND FILM TYPE 108
EIGHT 3¼ X 4¼ INCH PRINTS
POLAROID
108

Think of it as 20 cans of soup.
You're looking at the new Number 1 in non-foods, in chain after chain.
One pack of Polaroid Type 108 Colorpack film can put as much cash in the cash register as about twenty 10½ oz. cans of everybody's favorite soup (at typical prices).
And it does it in a hurry. In just three years, Polaroid Land film has become the number one dollar volume non-food item in hundreds of stores in major chains throughout the country.
(An Eastern chain of 100 stores recently sold over 17,000 packs of film in just 20 days!)
The reason is simple.
Most food shoppers are women.
Most film is bought by women. (62% to be exact.)
And 7 out of 10 times they buy on impulse.
With our rainbow colored boxes and convenient prepack displays it's almost impossible not to get impulsive.
It's selling so fast, in fact, many store owners can afford to pay for their film out of current sales.
Which is a nice way to run a business.
Polaroid Colorpack Film.
The next best thing to food.
POLAROID
108

135
Art Director: Art Shardin
Copywriter: Tom Thomas
Artist: Joe Genova
Agency: Kurtz & Symon, Inc.
Client: Williamson-Dickie Mfg. Co.

136
Art Director: John Assante
Copywriter: Brian Hennessy
Designer: John Assante
Photographer: Steve Eisenberg
Agency: Doyle Dane Bernbach Inc.
Client: Polaroid Corporation

WPRO has a very unusual kind of children's program. It's only for kids who've run away from home.
It's not for kids sitting snug in their rooms. It's for kids who thought they had enough of their rooms. *Run-Away* is a one-of-a-kind program developed by WPRO with the cooperation of the Missing Persons Bureaus of Rhode Island's local police. Its purpose: to broadcast descriptions of runaway children. And give parents a chance to say "Come home. We care." *Run-Away* is working. Reuniting a lot of scared kids with a lot of scared parents.
And helping them find out that a little running away is maybe what they really needed to put them back together.
WPRO
PROVIDENCE
One of the stations of Capital Cities Broadcasting. We talk to people.

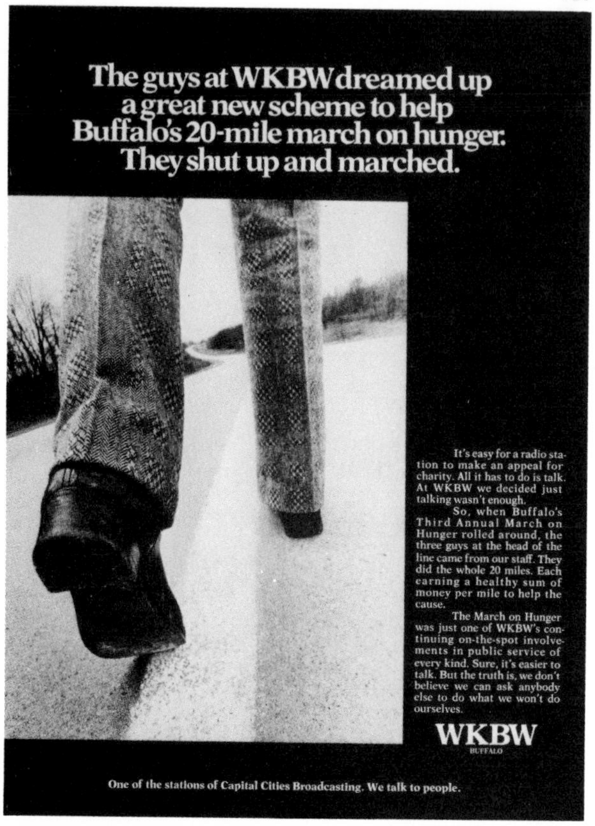
The guys at WKBW dreamed up a great new scheme to help Buffalo's 20-mile march on hunger. They shut up and marched.
It's easy for a radio station to make an appeal for charity. All it has to do is talk. At WKBW we decided just talking wasn't enough.
So, when Buffalo's Third Annual March on Hunger rolled around, the three guys at the head of the line came from our staff. They did the whole 20 miles. Each earning a healthy sum of money per mile to help the cause.
The March on Hunger was just one of WKBW's continuing on-the-spot involvements in public service of every kind. Sure, it's easier to talk. But the truth is, we don't believe we can ask anybody else to do what we won't do ourselves.
WKBW
BUFFALO
One of the stations of Capital Cities Broadcasting. We talk to people.

For one unforgettable week last May, every radio and TV station in Philly were on the same wave length.
Drugs. It's a dirty word. And last year WPVI decided to clean it up. With a powerful all-out, one-week broadcast attack.
Working with the Television and Radio Advertising Club, we marshalled every TV and radio station in the area. We assembled, taped and made available all of the known TV spots on drug abuse, besides producing a few of our own. And we even helped put together a few radio spots as well.
So that in Philly, that week of May 24th, all public announcements on all stations were turned over to a single subject—drugs. It was a million bucks of media time. And worth every cent. And this year we're going to do it again.
So if you're in Philadelphia during drug week this spring, listen in or look in. And see what happens when a lot of guys on a lot of stations get mad enough to work on the same wave length.
WPVI-TV
PHILADELPHIA
One of the stations of Capital Cities Broadcasting. We talk to people.

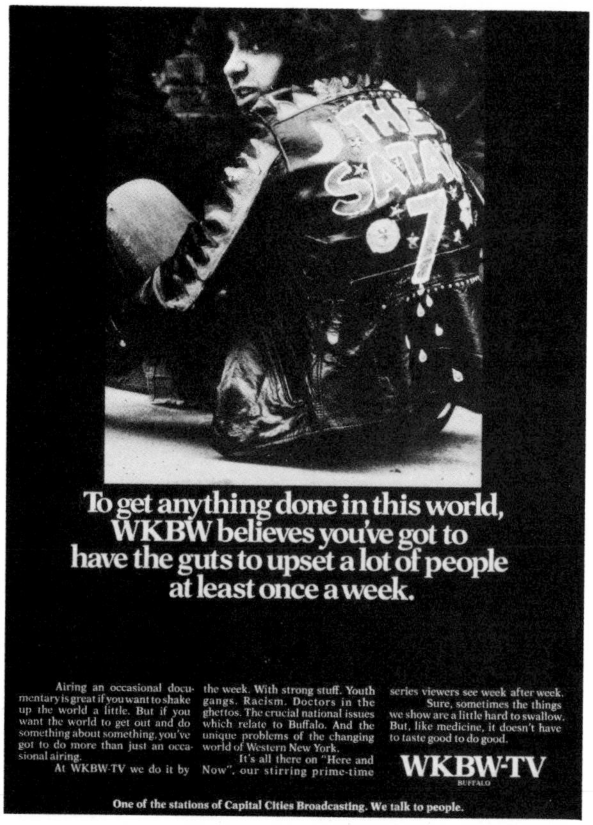
To get anything done in this world, WKBW believes you've got to have the guts to upset a lot of people at least once a week.
Airing an occasional documentary is great if you want to shake up the world a little. But if you want the world to get out and do something about something, you've got to do more than just an occasional airing.
At WKBW-TV we do it by the week. With strong stuff. Youth gangs. Racism. Doctors in the ghettos. The crucial national issues which relate to Buffalo. And the unique problems of the changing world of Western New York.
It's all there on "Here and Now", our stirring prime-time series viewers see week after week.
Sure, sometimes the things we show are a little hard to swallow. But, like medicine, it doesn't have to taste good to do good.
WKBW-TV
BUFFALO
One of the stations of Capital Cities Broadcasting. We talk to people.

Trade Magazine/Campaign

137
Art Director: Mike Withers
Copywriter: Joy Golden
Photographer: Michael Pateman
Agency: Zakin Selden Comerford Inc.
Client: Capital Cities Communications

138
Art Director: John Cenatiempo
Copywriter: Arnold Price
Designer: John Cenatiempo
Photographer: Bill Rosenbluth
Agency: Gaynor & Ducas, Inc.
Client: Storer Broadcasting Co.

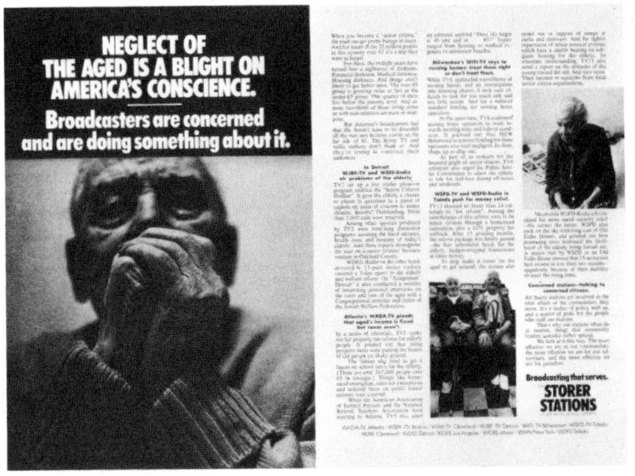
NEGLECT OF THE AGED IS A BLIGHT ON AMERICA'S CONSCIENCE.
Broadcasters are concerned and are doing something about it.
Broadcasting that serves.
STORER STATIONS

138

POVERTY IN A TRILLION-DOLLAR ECONOMY IS A CRYING SHAME.
Broadcasters are concerned and are doing something about it.
Broadcasting that serves.
STORER STATIONS

CARS AND THEIR DRIVERS KILL MORE CHILDREN EVERY YEAR THAN ALL ILLNESSES COMBINED.
Broadcasters are concerned and are doing something about it.
DEAD END
Broadcasting that serves.
STORER STATIONS

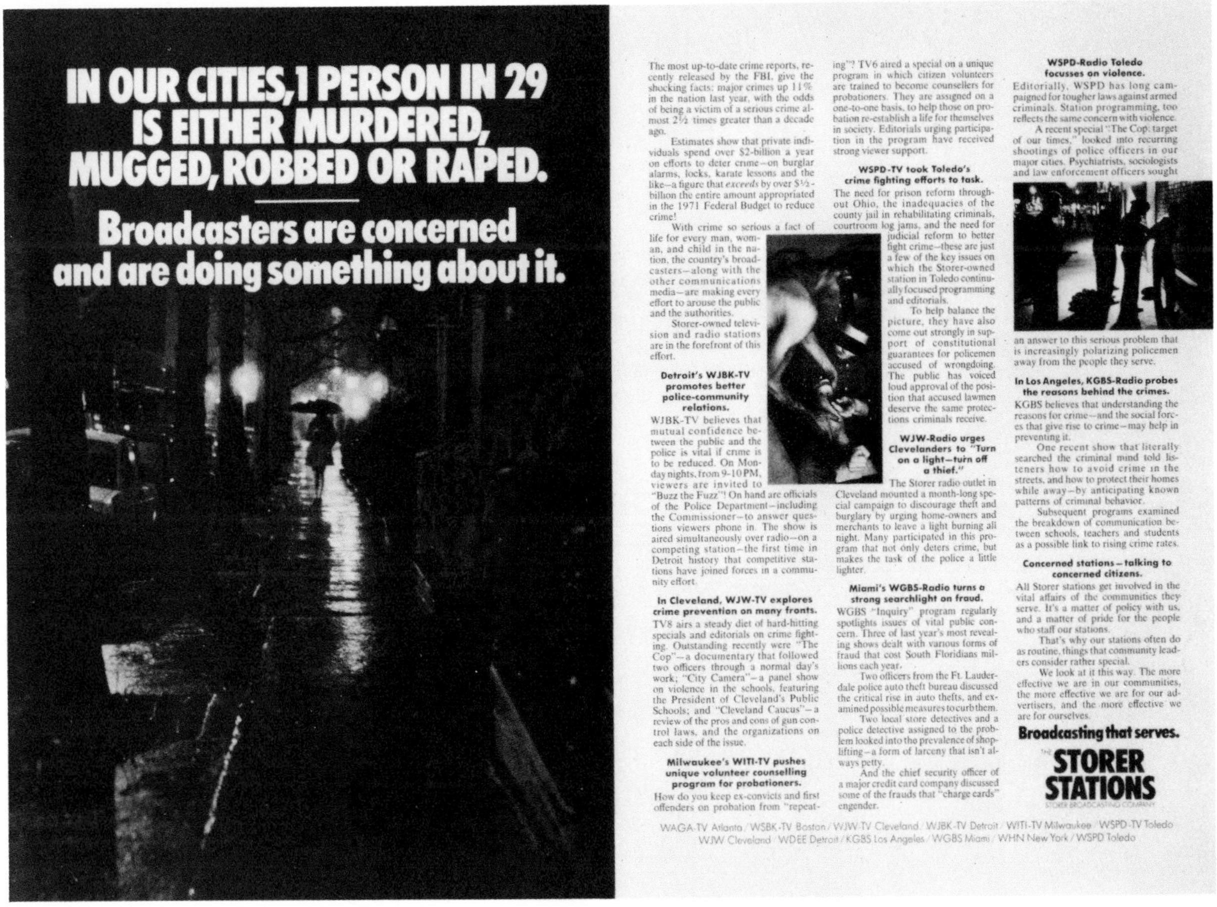

139

ABC Stations' news.
People watch us to learn what's going on in the world.
ABC Stations' movies.
People watch us to escape from what's going on in the world.

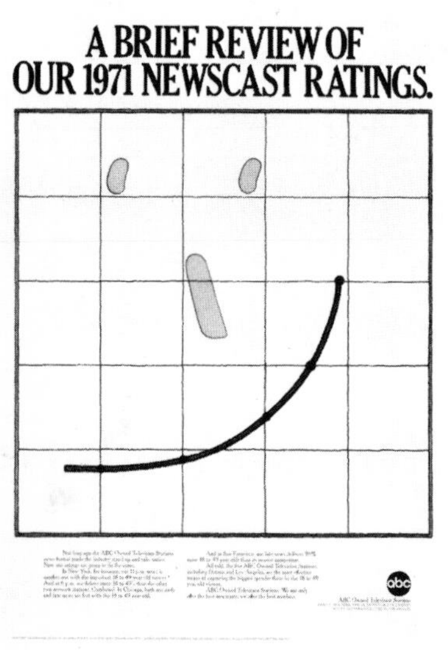
A BRIEF REVIEW OF OUR 1971 NEWSCAST RATINGS.

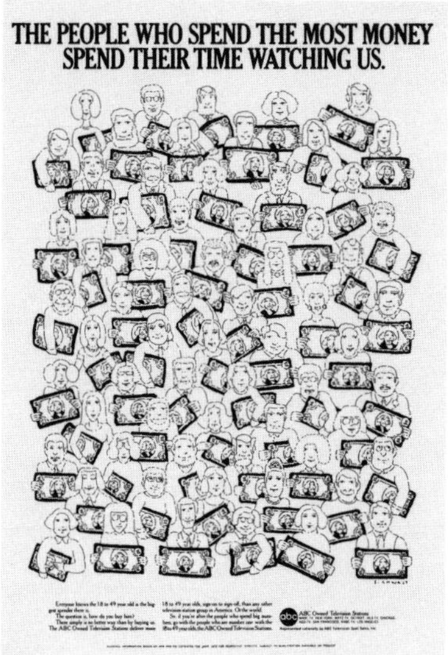
THE PEOPLE WHO SPEND THE MOST MONEY SPEND THEIR TIME WATCHING US.

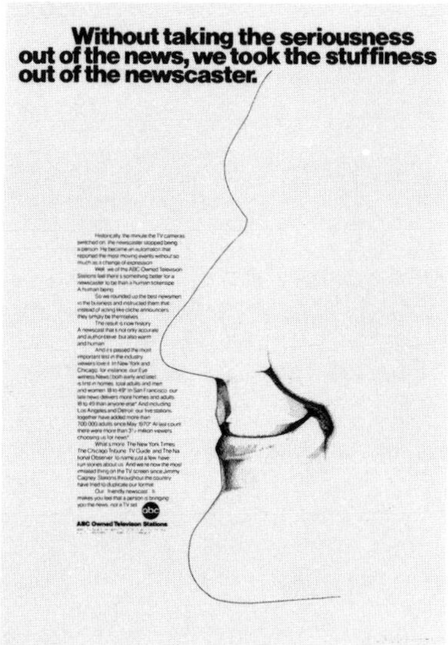
Without taking the seriousness out of the news, we took the stuffiness out of the newscaster.

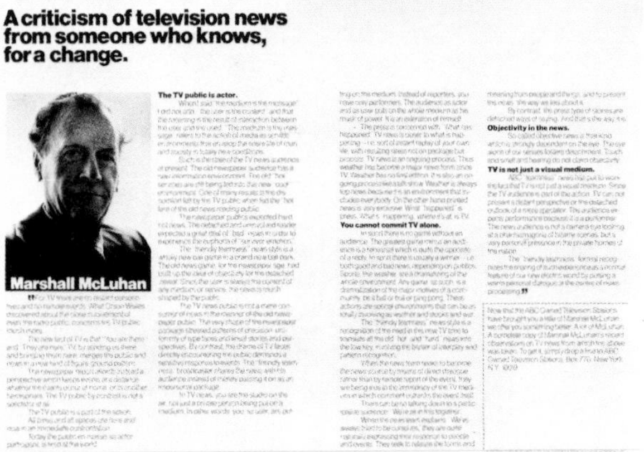

A criticism of television news from someone who knows, for a change.
Marshall McLuhan

Somehow we manage to tell people what's going on in the world, and still make a lot of friends.

139
Art Director: Allan Beaver
Copywriter: Larry Plapler
Designer: Allan Beaver
Photographers: U.P.I.
M.G.M.
Agency: H. E. Mahoney & Associates
Client: ABC Owned Television Stations

140
Art Director: Dave Perl
Copywriter: Hal Freedman
Designer: Dave Perl
Artist: Jerry Pinkney
Photographers: Carl Fischer
Pete Turner
John Paul Endress
Ursula G. Kreis
Robert Little
Cacchione/Sheehan
Agency: Warren, Muller, Dolobowsky
Client: Business Week

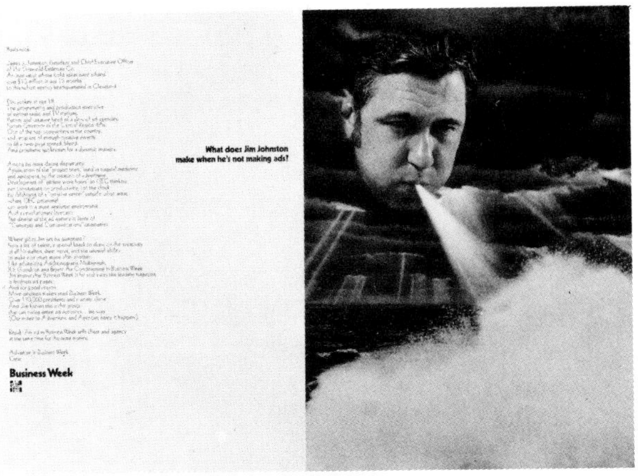

What does Jim Johnston make when he's not making ads?
Business Week

140

Look again.
Charles Moss, new President and Creative Director of Wells, Rich, Greene.
From copy trainee a mere ten years ago to kingpin of the $100-million plus ad agency that has taken the industry by storm.
What manner of performer is this?
The very best.
An accomplished actor at age 12 in "The Little Fugitive."
Cum laude graduate in English from Ithaca College.
A creative standout at ad agencies brimming with creative standouts (DDB and Tinker).
Author of national campaigns for Benson & Hedges, Braniff, TWA, American Motors, Safeguard, Royal Crown, et al.
Co-author of WRG/Dragoti's first feature film soon to be released.
A professional who has become so sensitive to marketing problems that his campaigns set records for sales as well as awards.
And a 33 year old, to boot.
What's behind this stellar rise?
Incisive research funneled to the creative staff.
Fostering a feeling of involvement up and down the line.
And the instinct for a sound business idea like advertising TWA in Business Week.
Charlie knows that in the race for business ads it's Business Week in a walk.
He knows that he and his client will be noticed by more decision makers per dollar than in any other business book.
More than 130,000 presidents and owners alone.
And he also knows that this audience has the clout to move entire ad accounts...his way.
(That's where our Index to Advertisers and Agencies comes in.)
Windup:
An ad in Business Week sells client and agency at the same time for the same money.
Advertise in Business Week.
Streak a little.
Business Week
What took Charlie Moss so long?

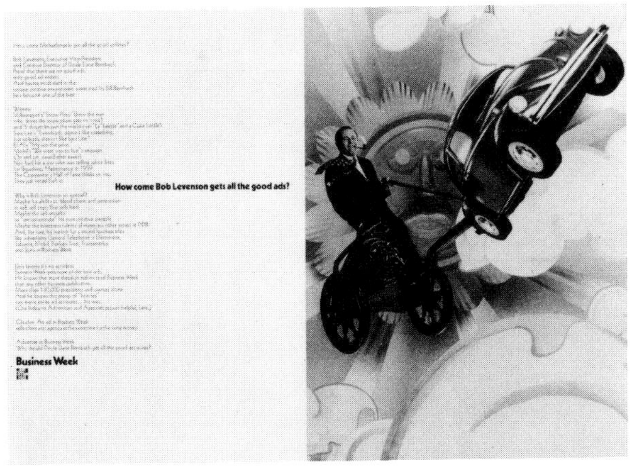

How come Bob Levenson gets all the good ads?
Business Week

Where did Bob Marker get his majesty?
Business Week

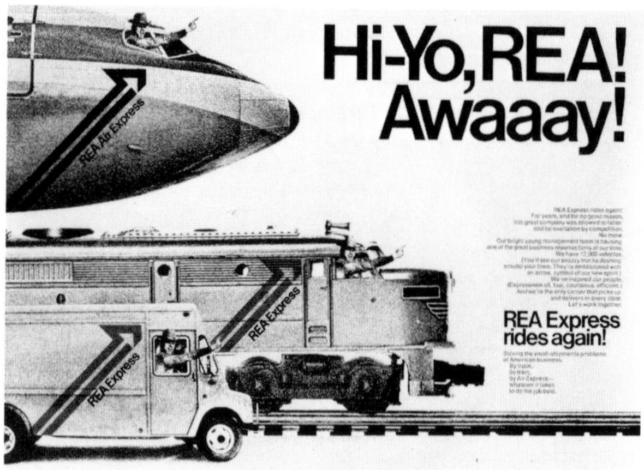
Hi-Yo, REA!
Awaaay!
REA Air Express
REA Express
REA Express rides again!

Hi-Yo, REA! Awaaay!
REA Air Express
REA Express
REA Express rides again!

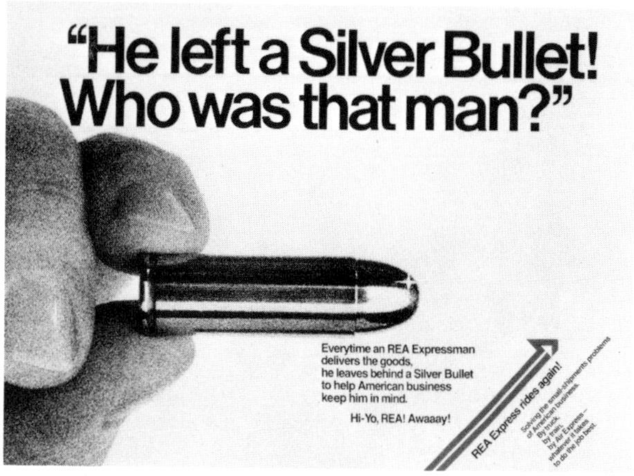
"He left a Silver Bullet!
Who was that man?"
Everytime an REA Expressman
delivers the goods,
he leaves behind a Silver Bullet
to help American business
keep him in mind.
Hi-Yo, REA! Awaaay!
REA Express rides again!
Solving the small-shipments problems
of American business.
By truck,
by train,
by Air Express—
whatever it takes
to do the job best.

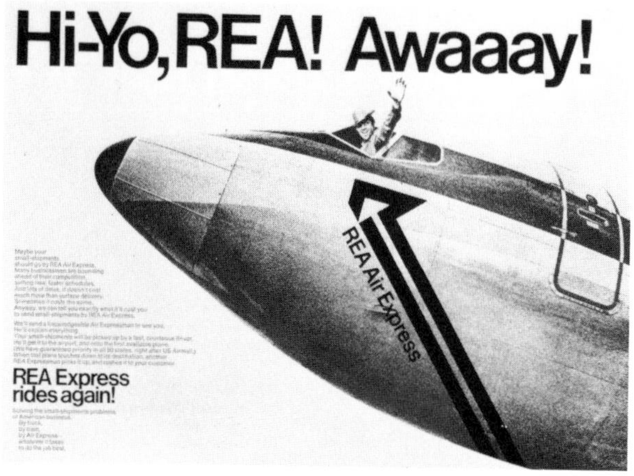
Hi-Yo, REA! Awaaay!
REA Air Express
REA Express
rides again!

"REA
Air Express
rides again!"
The only Air Express
is REA Air Express,
(because only REA is
in partnership
with all 33 airlines,
reaches 522 airports, and
serves 22,000 communities).
Read this list of how
we can help you
beat your competitors:
1. Only REA Air Express has priority air service.
Our priority isn't everything, but it helps. No freight
(except Airmail) can go on a plane until REA is aboard.
And we never hold Air Express for consolidation.
We route shipments to go on the first available plane.
2. 95% of all REA Air Express shipments are delivered
to major cities within 48 hours. 70% within 24 hours.
(12% are delivered the same day!)
3. Across the board, REA Air Express is now the lowest
priced air service. You'll love the door-to-door pickup
and delivery, at no extra cost, to a wide area around
all our airport markets.
4. When one company picks up your shipment,
and another one delivers it, it's a mess.
Pickup and delivery is always in our hands.
5. Carton, carton, who's got the carton?
You'll never ask. We manifest everything. And our
Destination Tracing System tells us where
your shipment is every mile of the way.
Air is the future.
Every year the gap between
surface prices and
Air Express prices narrows.
We proved 10,000,000 times last
year that REA Air Express
is the biggest, fastest carrier of
small-shipments known
to mankind
(at near the speed of sound)!
Hi-Yo, REA! Awaaay!
REA Air Express

How Kingfish Isaacs sold coaches on giving their players Southern Comfort™ before every game.
Kingfish Isaacs has been drunk for twenty-five years.
Drunk with an idea. Saturated with a concept. Intoxicated by one goal. Through the days as a player, as a coach, as a sports retailer, right up to the day he walked into Southern Athletic.
What obsessed Kingfish was the idea that nobody, but nobody in sports equipment manufacturing was really player-oriented.
And the best example of that problem was uniforms.
Jerseys used to drive players to drinking. Kingfish played football twenty-five years ago at Wake Forest. And, in many ways, the football equipment of those days seems pretty crude these days.
But, even then, the uniforms looked great from the stands. Those jetblack jerseys with the shiny gold pants looked pretty up-and-running good to the fan in row Z.
For the players, it was another story. Because the jerseys were wool or maybe heavy cotton. The pants were combat nylon. And the players were about to drop in their tracks. They would have driven as hard for six drops of water as for six points.
The problem was, sports uniforms were always designed by some guy up in row Z, not by a player or a coach.
How Southern Comfort solves a ball player's problems. That was all before Southern Comfort, Fred Isaacs' miracle fabric. Here was a fabric for both jerseys and pants that would look better, feel better, and wear better than anything before it.
The reason it does all that is a process called transverse-triangular knitting. That's what made double-knit and interlock obsolete.
That's what makes Southern Comfort the fabric that absolutely won't run. The best breathing fabric yet. The fabric that won't let dirt in. The fabric that fits closer, looks better, and gives less tackling surface. The fabric that won't absorb moisture. The fabric that gives maximum perspiration evaporation. The fabric that is stronger, and has the maximum recovery of shape. The fabric with the best heat dissipation. The most brilliant colors.
That's what makes Southern Comfort fabric semi-amazing. Just like a lot of other things at Southern Athletic.
And that's why, if you're not giving your players Southern Comfort uniforms, we'd love to talk to you.
If you still haven't written Kingfish, Knoxville, read this. Kingfish wants to tell you about his miraculous Southern Comfort uniforms almost as much as he wants to tell you about his greatest victories as a coach.
Write Southern Athletic, Box 666, Knoxville, Tennessee 37901.
SOUTHERN ATHLETIC
A subsidiary of the Kendall Company, Sports Division, Wellesley Hills, Mass.

141
Art Director: George Lois
Copywriter: Ron Holland
Designer: Dennis Mazzella
Tom Courtos
Photographer: Tasso Vendikos
Agency: Lois Holland Callaway Inc.
Client: REA Express

142
Art Director: Ralph Moxcey
Copywriter: Scott Miller
Designer: Ralph Moxcey
Photographer: Bill Bruin
Agency: Humphrey, Browning, MacDougall
Client: Kendall Company

142

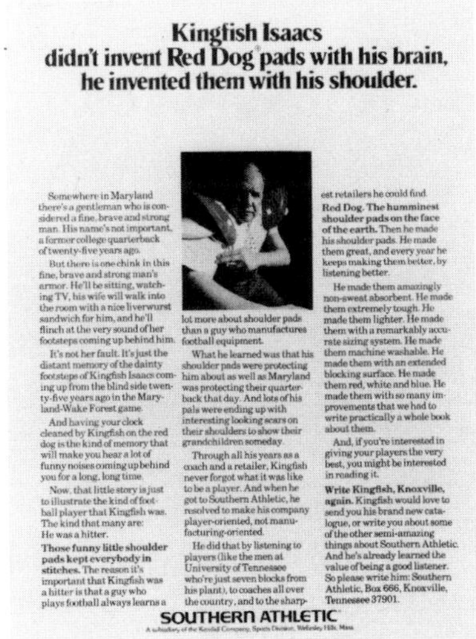

Kingfish Isaacs invented a whole new kind of uniform, but he wasn't satisfied until he invented a whole new way to sell it, too.

Kingfish Isaacs didn't invent Red Dog® pads with his brain, he invented them with his shoulder.

143

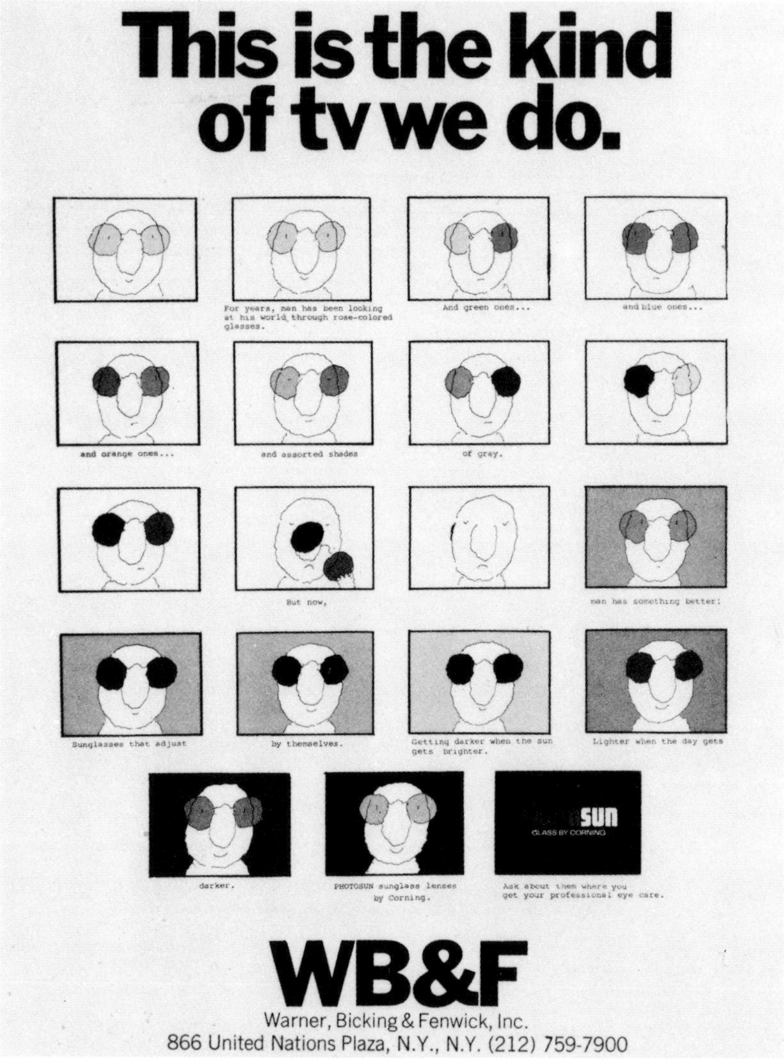
This is the kind of tv we do.
For years, man has been looking at his world through rose-colored glasses.
And green ones...
and blue ones...
and orange ones...
and assorted shades
of grey.
But now,
man has something better!
Sunglasses that adjust
by themselves.
Getting darker when the sun gets brighter.
Lighter when the day gets
darker.
PHOTOSUN sunglass lenses by Corning.
SUN
GLASS BY CORNING
Ask about them where you get your professional eye care.
WB&F
Warner, Bicking & Fenwick, Inc.
866 United Nations Plaza, N.Y., N.Y. (212) 759-7900

This is the kind of print we do.
Now one pair of sunglasses for all kinds of days.
PHOTOSUN
WB&F
Warner, Bicking & Fenwick, Inc.
866 United Nations Plaza, N.Y., N.Y. (212) 759-7900

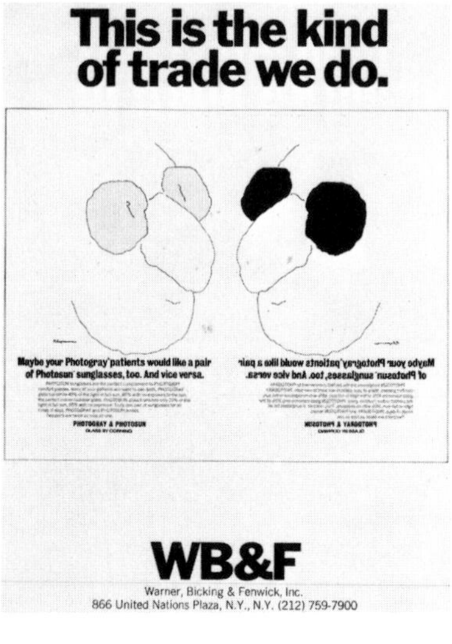
This is the kind of trade we do.
Maybe your Photogray patients would like a pair of Photosun sunglasses, too. And vice versa.
WB&F
Warner, Bicking & Fenwick, Inc.
866 United Nations Plaza, N.Y., N.Y. (212) 759-7900

143
Art Director: Rod Capawana
Copywriters: Charles Sawyer
Tyler Kaus
Photographers: Charles Wiesehahn
Bob Blechman
Rod Capawana
Agency: Warner, Bicking & Fenwick, Inc.
Client: Warner, Bicking & Fenwick, Inc.

144
Art Director: Ben Wong
Copywriter: Bob Lackovic
Designers: Ben Wong
Dave Willardson
Artist: Dave Willardson
Agency: Wenger-Michael, Inc.
Client: Fender Musical Instruments

The world's favorite road machine
"Making it" in music means getting on the road. With a Fender Precision Bass, it means travelling with the first electric bass. Professionals choose a Fender bass more often than any other. Together with a Fender Bass amp, you'll have companions who'll never let you down. Make your travels easier; go with Fender.
Fender
CBS Musical Instruments, A Division of CBS, Inc.
For a full-color 64 page Fender catalog, plus a full-color 22" x 25" poster version of this ad, send $1.00 for postage and handling to: Fender, Dept. K-1, Box 3410, Fullerton, California 92634.

The world's favorite space machine
Fender
Space, like music, is an endless frontier. To conquer either requires creative talent, dedication and the finest equipment. Our Research and Development team is dedicated to creating the finest guitars and amplifiers designed for each other. Your Fender® dealer has all the equipment you'll ever need. The rest is up to you.

The world's favorite love machine
Love makes the world go round. Music sets the mood, heightens the emotion and provides the beat. Love takes two. Fender® guitars and amps are compatible—made for each other. If you really want to make it, in love or music, try a little Fenderness.

The world's favorite recording machine
Listening to records is real pleasure. Making records is all business. Everything rides on the sound, and more professionals choose the "Fender Sound" . . . controlled distortion or pure clean projection. Listen to your favorite record. Chances are it was cut using Fender.® Fender amps are the number one selling amps in the world. For business and pleasure, turn on to Fender . . . guitars and amps that are made for each other.
Fender

Fender
The world's favorite blending machine
Good music, like good food, needs just the proper combination of ingredients. Mixed together in exact proportions. Until the sound produced is smooth and balanced. Carefully controlled and blended all the way. New Fender® PA Systems provide a mix that is matchless. See your Fender dealer . . . he'll gladly turn one on for you.

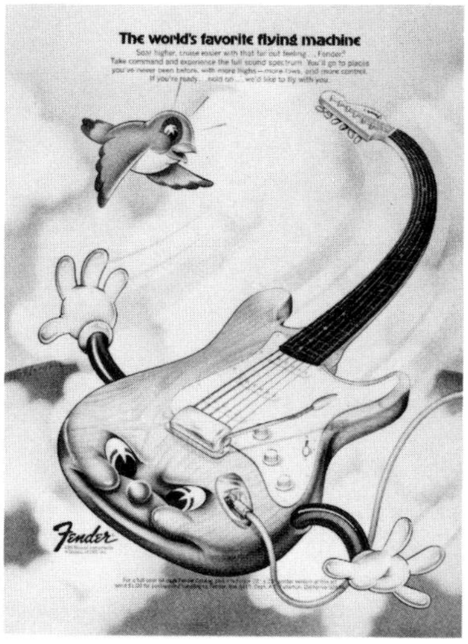
The world's favorite flying machine
Soar higher, cruise easier with that far out feeling . . . Fender®
Take command and experience the full sound spectrum. You'll go to places you've never been before, with more highs—more lows, and more control.
If you're ready . . . hold on . . . we'd like to fly with you.
Fender

145

American Electric Power puts on the fifth of the world's largest double reheat boilers.

It's the Appalachian Power Company's Unit No. 2 at the John E. Amos plant, West Virginia.

This makes five Foster Wheeler coal-fired, 800 MW once-through boilers AEP has put in service since 1969.

They're the five largest units of their kind. And a lot more.

Each of the boilers was delivered and started up on time, and has achieved some remarkable availability records.

For example, Unit No. 1 at the Amos plant (the most recent to complete a year of service) has racked up a boiler operating availability record of over 96% in its first year of operation.

This kind of success is largely the result of Foster Wheeler's design approach.

Like the way we design our multiple series passes to limit super-critical fluid enthalpy inbalance.

It's done by frequent mixing between passes. Which results in furnace circuits that are extremely stable and insensitive to heat absorption upsets.

Small wonder that on initial start-up, AEP's Amos #1 ramped up to full load without delay.

And after coming down only for turbine strainer removal, it immediately went back on line and operated for 120 consecutive days at full power.

Quite a break-in record. And even then, it took a bolt of lightning to shut it down.

Makes us proud to be an American Electric Power supplier.

Foster Wheeler Corporation, 666 Fifth Avenue, New York, N.Y. 10019

FOSTER WHEELER

If they're giving you trouble, we'll pulverize them.

FOSTER WHEELER

We've developed a certain sensitivity to NOx emissions.

FOSTER WHEELER

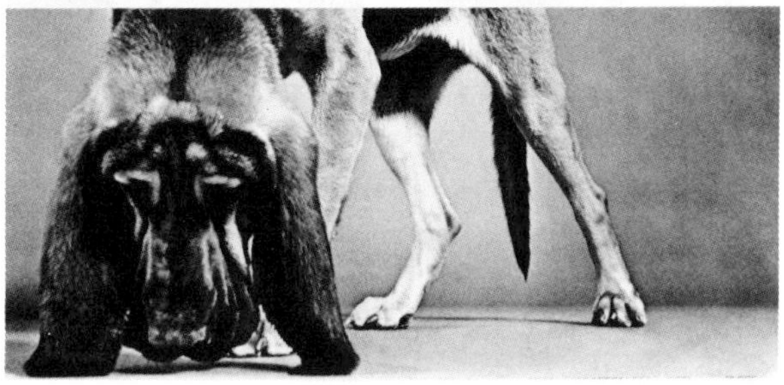

Our steam generator design began with an ideal.

FOSTER WHEELER

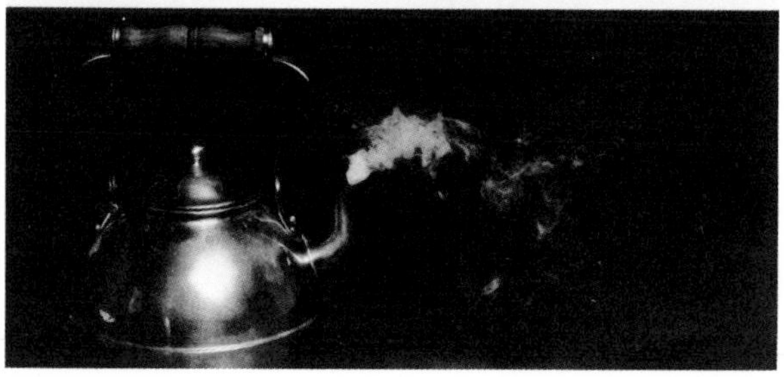

Under the octane gun.

The first step, and beyond. How we can help.

FOSTER WHEELER

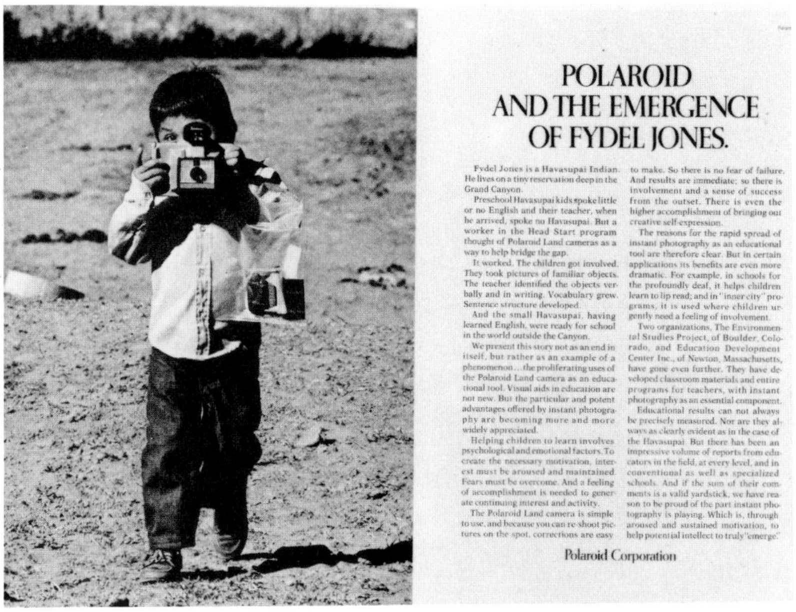
The instant image
and tumor detection.
POLAROID
AND THE EMERGENCE
OF FYDEL JONES.
Fydel Jones is a Havasupai Indian. He lives on a tiny reservation deep in the Grand Canyon.
Preschool Havasupai kids spoke little or no English and their teacher, when he arrived, spoke no Havasupai. But a worker in the Head Start program thought of Polaroid Land cameras as a way to help bridge the gap.
It worked. The children got involved. They took pictures of familiar objects. The teacher identified the objects verbally and in writing. Vocabulary grew. Sentence structure developed.
And the small Havasupai, having learned English, were ready for school in the world outside the Canyon.
We present this story not as an end in itself, but rather as an example of a phenomenon... the proliferating uses of the Polaroid Land camera as an educational tool. Visual aids in education are not new. But the particular and potent advantages offered by instant photography are becoming more and more widely appreciated.
Helping children to learn involves psychological and emotional factors. To create the necessary motivation, interest must be aroused and maintained. Fears must be overcome. And a feeling of accomplishment is needed to generate continuing interest and activity.
The Polaroid Land camera is simple to use, and because you can re-shoot pictures on the spot, corrections are easy to make. So there is no fear of failure. And results are immediate; so there is involvement and a sense of success from the outset. There is even the higher accomplishment of bringing out creative self-expression.
The reasons for the rapid spread of instant photography as an educational tool are therefore clear. But in certain applications its benefits are even more dramatic. For example, in schools for the profoundly deaf, it helps children learn to lip read; and in "inner city" programs, it is used where children urgently need a feeling of involvement.
Two organizations, The Environmental Studies Project, of Boulder, Colorado, and Education Development Center Inc., of Newton, Massachusetts, have gone even further. They have developed classroom materials and entire programs for teachers, with instant photography as an essential component.
Educational results can not always be precisely measured. Nor are they always as clearly evident as in the case of the Havasupai. But there has been an impressive volume of reports from educators in the field, at every level, and in conventional as well as specialized schools. And if the sum of their comments is a valid yardstick, we have reason to be proud of the part instant photography is playing. Which is, through aroused and sustained motivation, to help potential intellect to truly "emerge."
Polaroid Corporation

145
Art Director: Raymond Fedynak
Copywriter: Robert Tulp
Photographers: Joel Baldwin
Leon Kuzmanoff
Ken Ambrose
Agency: Muller Jordan Herrick Inc.
Client: Foster Wheeler Corporation

146
Art Director: Lee Epstein
Copywriter: Fred Udall
Designer: Lee Epstein
Photographers: Terry Eiler
Henry Sandbank
Agency: Doyle Dane Bernbach Inc.
Client: Polaroid Corporation

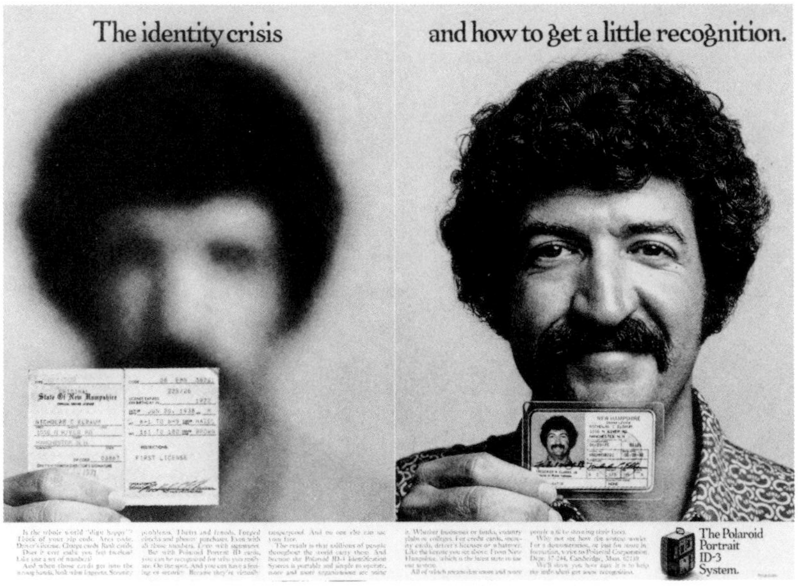
The identity crisis
and how to get a little recognition.
The Polaroid Portrait ID-3 System.

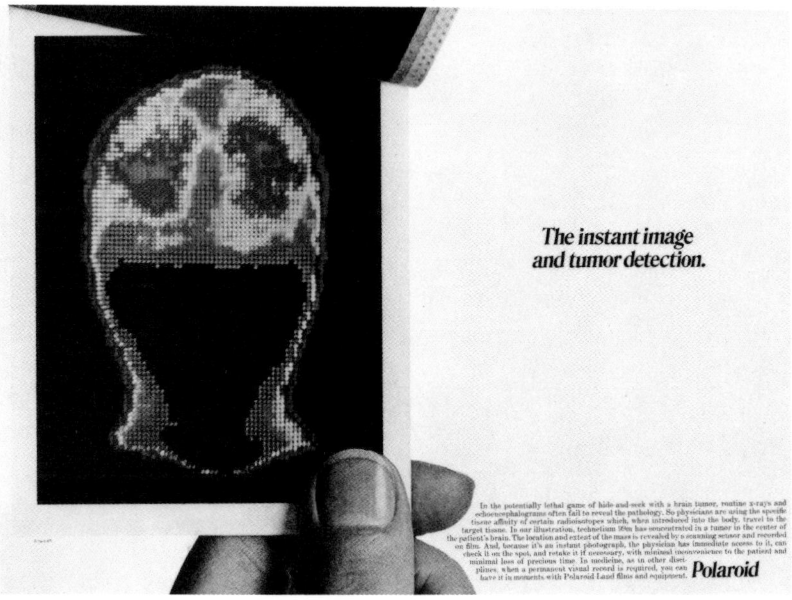

146

147

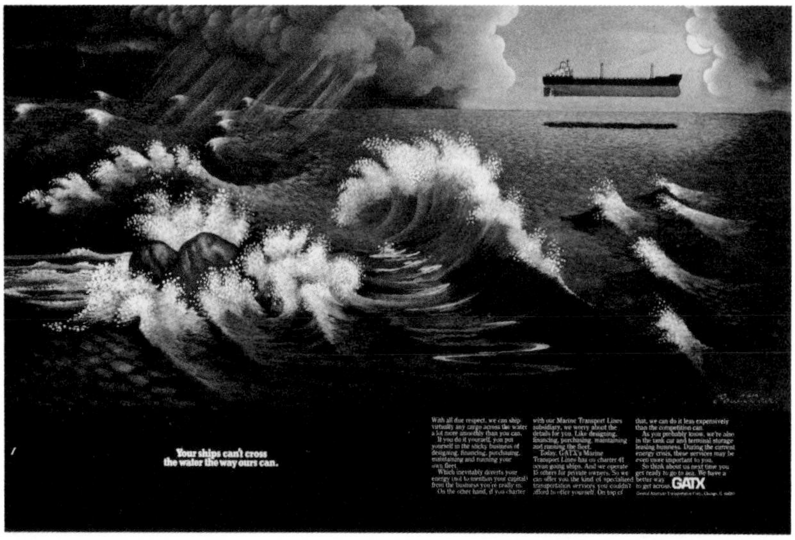
Your ships can't cross
the water the way ours can.
With all due respect, we can ship virtually any cargo across the water a lot more smoothly than you can.
If you do it yourself, you put yourself in the sticky business of designing, financing, purchasing, maintaining and running your own fleet.
Which inevitably diverts your energy (not to mention your capital) from the business you're really in.
On the other hand, if you charter with our Marine Transport Lines subsidiary, we worry about the details for you. Like designing, financing, purchasing, maintaining and running the fleet.
Today, GATX's Marine Transport Lines has on charter 41 ocean going ships. And we operate 15 others for private owners. So we can offer you the kind of specialized transportation services you couldn't afford to offer yourself. On top of that, we can do it less expensively than the competition can.
As you probably know, we're also in the tank car and terminal storage leasing business. During the current energy crisis, these services may be even more important to you.
So think about us next time you get ready to go to sea. We have a better way to get across.
GATX

Old tank cars don't die,
they just slowly depreciate.
When you own your own fleet of tank cars, you make certain people happy.
Like your tax man. Even though you may tie up millions, he can make the depreciation look very lucrative over a period of, say, ten years.
Like your maintenance staff. As long as you own your own cars they can repair them and keep them looking nice.
Like the folks in accounting. One of the joys of owning your own is keeping on top of the paper work.
Like top management. A thrill for them is the challenge of keeping the tank cars filled.
If this is for you, fine, we'll gladly sell you tank cars.
On the other hand, you can lease all your tank cars from us. (Not to mention ships and terminal storage facilities. Important leasing services to have available during the current energy crisis.)
Leasing from us saves you the investment, frees you from maintenance, traffic and accounting headaches, and gives you the flexibility to use only the tank cars you need.
Thus, owning no tank cars at all should make everyone happy. Except for the man behind the ledgers.
But whoever heard of a happy tax man anyhow?
GATX

What was good for your grandmother
isn't necessarily good for you.
When grandma went to put up some peaches, she simply trotted down to the cellar and tapped her private supply of jars.
At maybe five cents apiece, she could afford to keep enough jars on hand to cover herself, whether it was a bumper year for peaches or not.
You, on the other hand, don't have that luxury.
Besides the capital you tie up in building your own storage facilities, you still have to worry about supply fluctuations. (Maybe the only thing worse than an expensive terminal is an idle one.)
So instead of building, we suggest you lease from us. We'll lease you just the space you need in principal North American ports, plus Europe and Asia.
Complete attendant services are available as well, from mixing to blending to drumming.
Our charter tanker fleet and lease tank cars are also at your disposal. (Flexibility in transfer and storage becomes even more important during the current energy crisis.)
The nice thing is, you can do all these things with us without investing so much as a nickel.
Now admit it, even your grandmother couldn't do that.
GATX

147
Art Director: Frank Biancalana
Copywriter: Ethan Revsin
Designer: Frank Biancalana
Artists: Charles White III
David Wilcox
Paul Davis
Agency: Lee King & Partners
Client: GATX

148
Art Director: Clyde Davis
Copywriter: Fred Mann
Designer: George Toubin
Photographer: Henry Sandbank
Agency: Klemtner Advertising Agency
Client: Pfizer Inc.

Typical appearance of the throat in acute exudative pharyngitis with pharyngeal mucosa red and swollen; tonsils may be enlarged, red and spotted with a yellowish-white purulent exudate oozing from the crypts. (Large photo below offers a unique view of the same area from the inside looking out. Done with true-to-life, plastic model of tonsils and pharynx.)

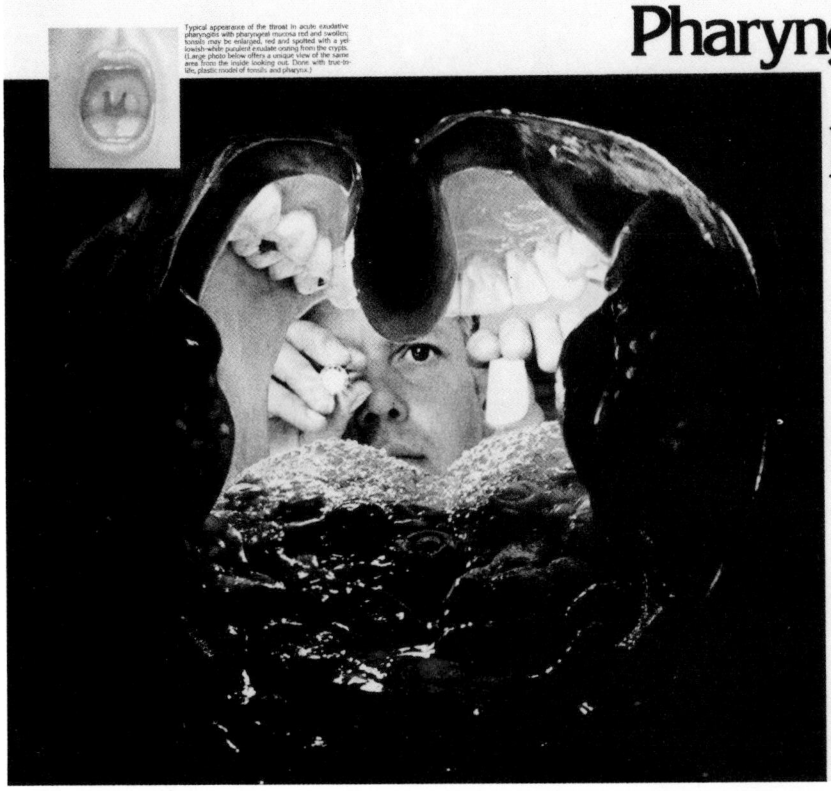

Pharyngitis/tonsillitis from the pathogen's point of view

Vibramycin (doxycycline) penetrates tonsil tissue to reach susceptible pathogens

Therapeutic tissue concentrations contribute to the clinical effectiveness of Vibramycin in bacterial throat infections. Vibramycin is active against a wide range of susceptible bacteria including strains of such causative organisms* as Streptococcus pyogenes† and Haemophilus influenzae.

Vibramycin is valuable in the treatment of tonsillitis due to susceptible pathogens because it reaches high concentrations in tonsil tissue (see table below).

Vibramycin tissue levels in tonsils of patients given 200 mg. the first day of therapy and 100 mg. daily for two additional days.[1]

1 hour after last Vibramycin dose			24 hours after last Vibramycin dose		
	Tissue Levels (µg./Gm.)			Tissue Levels (µg./Gm.)	
Patient	Right Tonsil	Left Tonsil	Patient	Right Tonsil	Left Tonsil
(A)	2.80	3.00	(D)	2.04	2.00
(B)	5.60	5.60	(E)	4.30	3.60
(C)	3.20	3.96	(F)	1.84	1.56
(D)	4.20	5.00	(G)	2.52	2.56
(E)	2.50	3.20	(H)	2.16	2.26

1. Adapted from Berrettini, B.: Chemotherapy 13:362, 1968

*Because not all strains of pathogens are susceptible, it is recommended that routine culture and susceptibility studies be performed.
†When using Vibramycin in infections caused by Group A beta-hemolytic streptococcus, therapy should be continued for 10 days. For upper respiratory infections due to this organism, penicillin is the drug of choice.

Vibramycin® (doxycycline hyclate)

See Brief Summary on following page for information on side effects and contraindications.

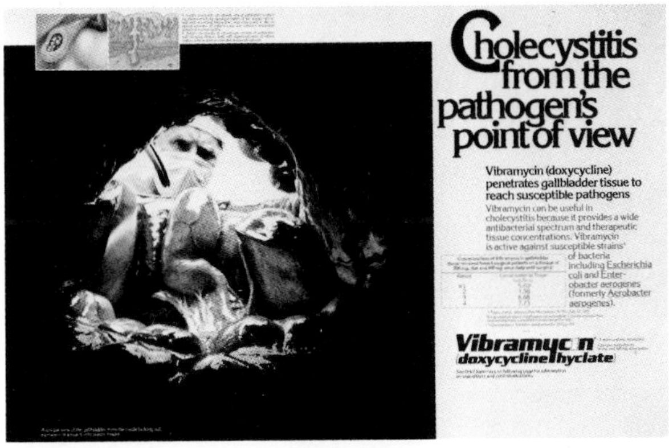
Cholecystitis from the pathogen's point of view
Vibramycin (doxycycline) penetrates gallbladder tissue to reach susceptible pathogens
Vibramycin can be useful in cholecystitis because it provides a wide antibacterial spectrum and therapeutic tissue concentrations. Vibramycin is active against susceptible strains* of bacteria including Escherichia coli and Enterobacter aerogenes (formerly Aerobacter aerogenes).
Vibramycin (doxycycline hyclate)

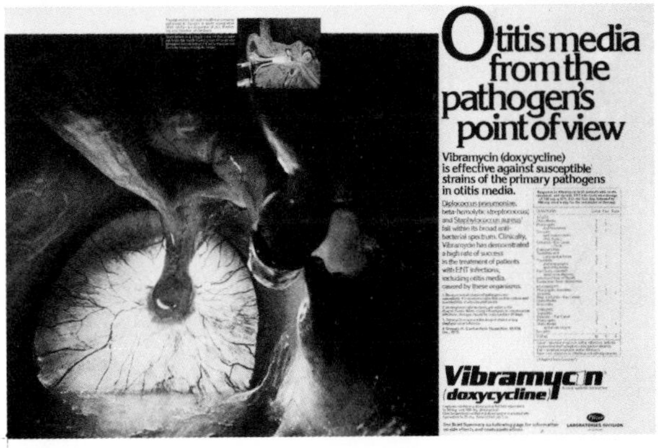
Otitis media from the pathogen's point of view
Vibramycin (doxycycline) is effective against susceptible strains of the primary pathogens in otitis media.
Vibramycin (doxycycline)
LABORATORIES DIVISION

Acute sinusitis from the pathogen's point of view
Vibramycin (doxycycline) penetrates sinus secretions to reach susceptible pathogens
Vibramycin (doxycycline)

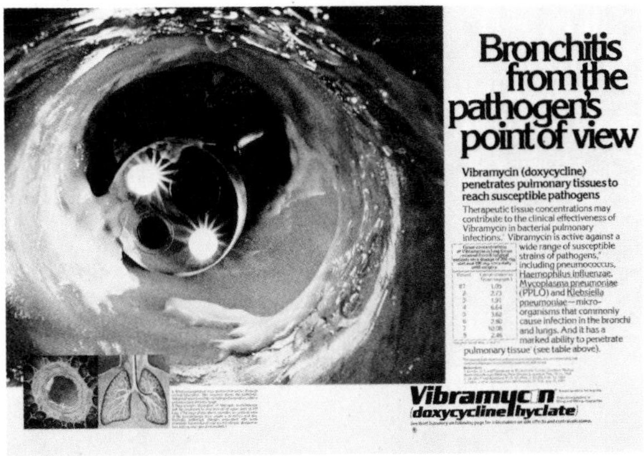
Bronchitis from the pathogen's point of view
Vibramycin (doxycycline) penetrates pulmonary tissues to reach susceptible pathogens
Therapeutic tissue concentrations may contribute to the clinical effectiveness of Vibramycin in bacterial pulmonary infections. Vibramycin is active against a wide range of susceptible strains of pathogens, including pneumococcus, Haemophilus influenzae, Mycoplasma pneumoniae (PPLO) and Klebsiella pneumoniae—microorganisms that commonly cause infection in the bronchi and lungs. And it has a marked ability to penetrate pulmonary tissue (see table above).
Vibramycin (doxycycline hyclate)

149

149
Art Director: A. Neal Siegel
Copywriter: Roger Ross
Designer: A. Neal Siegel
Photographer: Phil Marco
Agency: Smith Kline & French Laboratories
Client: Smith Kline & French Laboratories

150
Designer: Bernie Zlotnick
Copywriter: Irwin Rothman
Artist: Hiroshige
Client: Pioneer-Moss Reproductions

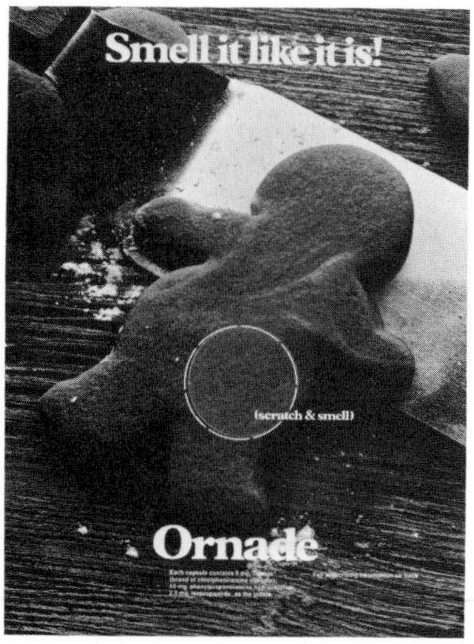

many impressions from worn blocks. Very often poor quality duplicate blocks were produced that bore little relationship to the original blocks.
Since the prints were used as illustrations for books in many cases, they inevitably assumed a political character. Important officials of the day were represented in various and unflattering ways. In 1790 the prints became subject to censorship. In 1842 the censor's personal seal appeared on all prints. In 1847 the censors worked in pairs with two seals appearing on the prints and in 1852 a combination date and censor's seal appeared. These seals did more to help collectors date the prints than restrict the subject matter, since artists and publishers found many ways to circumvent the censorship.
Prior to the works of Hokusai and Hiroshige most prints dealt with heroic subjects, the theatre and beautiful women. Hokusai perfected the color print as a medium for landscapes and Hiroshige within a few years rivaled Hokusai in this field only with less seriousness and with somewhat of a self-taught western influence and perspective. In 1849 the great Hokusai died, leaving Hiroshige the undisputed master in the landscape field. Hiroshige traveled extensively in search of material and turned out a large number of print series including the famous work on the To-kaido (eastern seaboard highway extending from Edo to Kyoto). He died in 1858 at the age of 62 during a cholera epidemic that raged through Japan and killed 28,000 in Edo alone. His farewell poem reads: "Leaving my brush on the Azuma (To-kaido) road, I depart to enjoy the wondrous sights of paradise."
In 1861, Kuniyoshi died, followed by Kunisada in 1864. This left Kyosai and Yoshitoshi (pupils of Kuniyoshi) as the only first rate artists among the mediocre artists of the Imperial Restoration period that began in 1868. This era marked the end of the ukiyo-e period. Chemical colors, over-refined engraving and printing methods and European drawing techniques eliminated the simple beauty of the ukiyo-e print. Among the impressions left on western painters by the Japanese print were Whistler's "Nocturnes" and the terrible copies in oil by Van Gogh of Hiroshige's "Ohashi Bridge" and "Plum-blossom Garden". In 1861 Captain Sherard Osborn, an English naval officer published a book reproducing Hiroshige prints. In describing one of his prints he wrote: "... our embryo Turner has striven hard to reproduce the combined effects of water, mountain, cloud, and spray enriched by the bright beams of a rising sun". Turner of course was acclaimed by the following generation of western art lovers as one of the greatest landscape artists of all time. Hiroshige undoubtedly belongs in this category as well.

The enclosed reproduction of an original Ukiyo-e 19th century Japanese print is presented to you by Pioneer-Moss, as part of its program of showing the role graphic arts innovations and inventions have had in developing cultural and educational as well as communication advances. The marriage of artistic techniques and abilities to those of graphic arts advances helped not only to speed the use of illustrations in daily newspapers, magazines and books but helped create a brand new art form which is as popular today as it was when it was first developed. In addition to its popularity, printmaking has gained recognition as an art form by art critics, museums and collectors.
Pioneer-Moss is proud of John Calvin Moss's contribution to the use of illustrations in communications. One hundred years ago he invented photoengravings which he called "a superior substitute for wood engravings".
Pioneer-Moss today produces engravings and color separations for any printing process, using the latest machinery and techniques combined with the master craftsmanship needed to satisfy the stringent demands of our customers. We hope that these print reproductions provide a measure of enjoyment and satisfaction to everyone who sees them. The Curtis paper used for the Japanese prints was chosen because of its high quality and its similarity to the original paper used for these prints.
If you would like additional copies of these inserts, please write to Print Reproductions Editor, Pioneer-Moss Reproductions Corp., 460 West 34 St., New York, N.Y. 10001 or Curtis Paper Company, Newark, Del. 19711.

Hiroshige 1797-1858. Azuma Bridge and Kinru-Zan Temple from the series One Hundred Famous Views of Edo. 8 13/16 x 13 5/8 signed Hiroshige Ga published by Uoyei 1857

The Japanese Print—One of a series
Color separations and reproduction by Pioneer-Moss Reproductions Corp.
Lithographed on Curtis Rag 70 lb. offset

浮世絵

Ukiyo-e was originally a Buddhist expression translated as "The every day world of sorrows and troubles" emphasizing the transitory nature of human life as opposed to blissful eternal life. As time passed the meaning of the expression changed and its religious and solemn overtones were replaced with a new emphasis on the pursuit of a pleasurable and lighthearted life and an interest in "now."
The word ukiyo-e contains three characters "uki" which means "floating" or transitory" —"yo" signifying "world" and "e" meaning pictures". Translated, ukiyo-e becomes "pictures of the floating world." Today this term is generally applied to the prints and paintings of the latter part of the 17th century through the 19th century that were produced in the area of Edo (today called Tokyo). In its period ukiyo-e also applied to the other popular and stylish fads of the day, and was used as a prefix for activities devoted to daily amusements, whims and pleasures without any concern for tomorrow.
The ukiyo-e artist was the illustrator of his day. He chose his subjects from the theatre, the "pleasure districts" and other everyday scenes. Moronobu (1618-1695) was the first artist to make use of woodcuts as an inexpensive means of reproducing drawings of the contemporary life of the people. The production of color prints flourished in the late 18th century after full range color printing was developed about 1765 and it was no longer necessary to hand color black and white block prints.
The beautiful results obtained by the outstanding ukiyo-e artists such as Harunobu, Shunsho, Kiyonaga, Sharaku, Utamaro, Hokusai, Toyokuni, Hiroshige, Eisen, Kuniyoshi, Kunisada and the last of their era, Kyosai and Yoshitoshi, are all the more wonderous when the methods of producing these prints are known. The artist's drawing was made with India ink and brushed on very thin rice paper. This was laid face down on a cherrywood block by the engraver. He then proceeded to cut the reversed design in relief on the block. Proofs were pulled from this block and the artist would specify the colors and positions on the proof. The engraver then cut a block for each color required. In order to register the blocks, the engraver cut a small line at the lower right hand side, and a corner cut in the top left hand side in the same position of each block. When the blocks were completed to the artist's satisfaction they were turned over to the printer. He inked each block with the proper color and pressed a sheet of paper that had been dampened slightly to the block, using a bamboo fiber mat as his press. He used the corner lines on the block as a guide, feeding the edges of the paper to these two register marks. The prints were produced and printed under the direction of the publisher. To a great extent the taste of the publisher and his marketing ability determined both the quality and commercial success of the final print. A combination of talents by the artist, engraver and printer was required to obtain a worthwhile print. Both the artist and publisher were extremely zealous in choosing engravers and printers who would interpret and produce the print to their satisfaction. Many poor prints were made by inferior craftsmen and also by running too

Trade Magazine/Campaign

151
Art Directors: Allan Beaver
Lou Colletti
Copywriters: Larry Plapler
Larry Spector
Designers: Allan Beaver
Lou Colletti
Artist: Gary Overacre
Photographer: Tony Petrucelli
Agency: Levine, Huntley, Schmidt
Client: Jockey International, Inc.

151

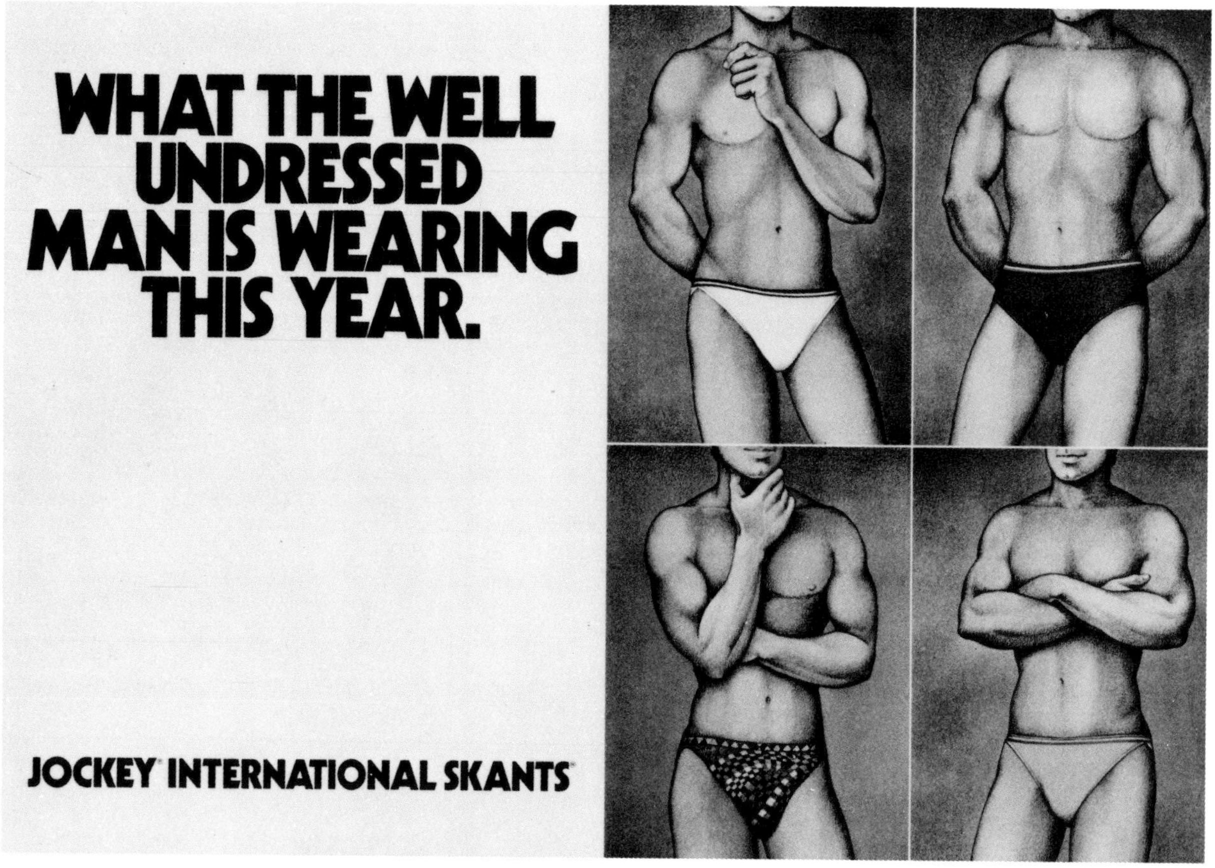
WHAT THE WELL UNDRESSED MAN IS WEARING THIS YEAR.
JOCKEY INTERNATIONAL SKANTS

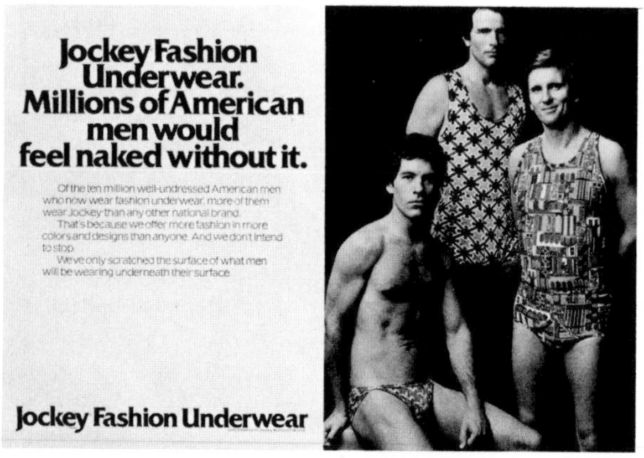
Jockey Fashion Underwear. Millions of American men would feel naked without it.
Of the ten million well-undressed American men who now wear fashion underwear, more of them wear Jockey than any other national brand.
That's because we offer more fashion in more colors and designs than anyone. And we don't intend to stop.
We've only scratched the surface of what men will be wearing underneath their surface.
Jockey Fashion Underwear

Are you overlooking an enormous market?
For approximately four million American men, your large assortment of underwear probably isn't large enough: men 6'2" and taller and men 220 pounds and heavier.
To cover this market, Jockey makes two special lines of underwear, Big Man And Tall Man, in a variety of styles: T-shirt, V-neck T-shirt and athletic shirt; Brief, boxer and Midway.
Each line has a greater profit margin than regular sizes.
So you can make big money by putting big men into our underwear.
Jockey Tall Man and Big Man Underwear

Small Space/Single

152
Art Director: Tom Stoerrle
Copywriter: Frank DiGiacomo
Designer: Tom Stoerrle
Agency: Della Femina, Travisano & Partners, Inc.
Client: Yonkers Raceway Corp.

153
Art Director: George Lois
Copywriter: Ron Holland
Designer: Dennis Mazzella
Agency: Lois Holland Callaway Inc.
Client: Restaurant Associates

152

Tomorrow night, anybody from Yonkers who shows, wins.
YONKERS AREA NIGHT ADMISSION COUPON
This coupon and 75¢ service charge admits one to Grandstand on Wednesday, Feb. 7, 1973 ONLY.
NIGHT HARNESS RACING AT THE NEW YONKERS RACEWAY
NON-TRANSFERABLE AND NOT FOR SALE
CLIP COUPON AND PRESENT AT GRANDSTAND GATE
That's right, anybody from Yonkers who shows up at Gate 5 tonight with this coupon gets into the grandstand for just a 75¢ service charge. Which means you'll come out $1.50 ahead before the first race.
Now how can you beat that?
THE NEW YONKERS RACEWAY

153

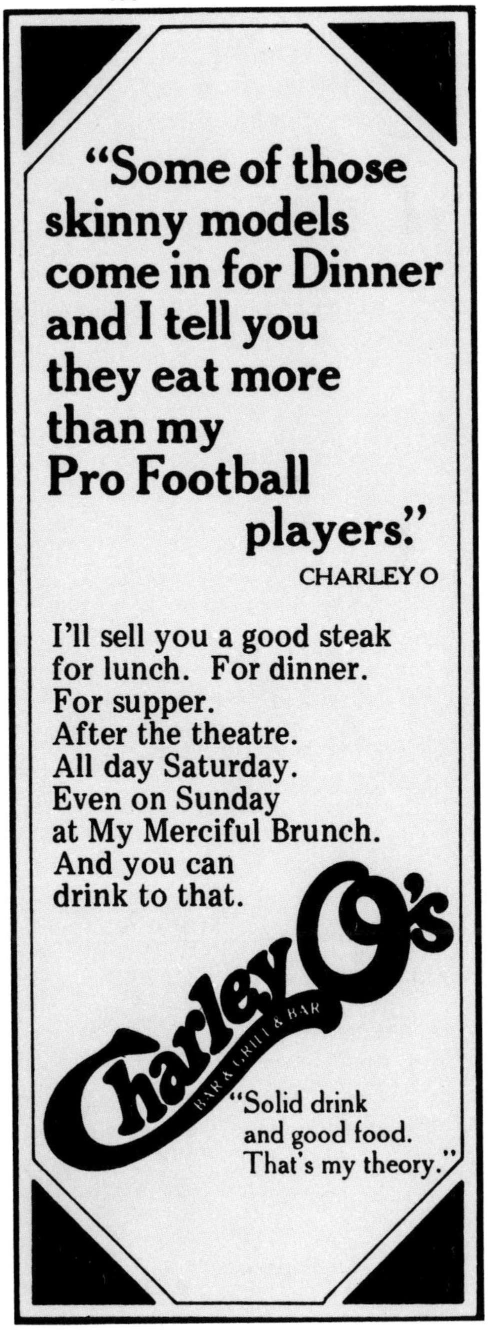

"Some of those skinny models come in for Dinner and I tell you they eat more than my Pro Football players."
CHARLEY O
I'll sell you a good steak for lunch. For dinner. For supper. After the theatre. All day Saturday. Even on Sunday at My Merciful Brunch. And you can drink to that.
Charley O's
BAR & GRILL & BAR
"Solid drink and good food. That's my theory."

TO GET IN TOUCH WITH A PERDUE CHICKEN, CALL 800-243-6000.

Tell the operator you want a tender, golden-yellow, juicy, succulent, young Perdue chicken.

Then tell her where you live.

She'll tell you where to go.

There is no charge for this call, this service is free.

In Conn. call: 1-800-882-6500.

154

"My gravy is fine.
It's what's underneath
that makes me cry."
My husband loves my gravy. He uses it to hide the lumps in my mashed potatoes.
But friends who make the fluffiest potatoes tell me it's gravy that gives them fits.
So I say: Follow the pictures on the Gravy Master bottle. Gravy Master gravy has a little taste of parsley and things, and it comes out rich and smooth.
And if The Lump Queen here can make gravy rich and smooth, anybody can.
Memo to you good cooks: For some interesting recipes, write Gravy Master, Dept. KX, Long Island City, N. Y. 11101.

155

156

The main difference between a $150 abortion and a $1000 abortion is the doctor makes an extra $850.

Expensive abortions are a hangover from when abortions were illegal. But today we can help you get a legal, safe—and inexpensive—abortion. By an M.D. in a clinic or hospital.

If you have the abortion during the first 10 weeks of pregnancy, it will cost only about $150. And no matter when you have it, there's no charge for our service.

We know some doctors who care more about people than money.

Call us at (212) 489-7794 Monday through Friday, between 10 a.m. and 5 p.m. New York time.

Free Abortion Referral Service from ZPG-New York

157

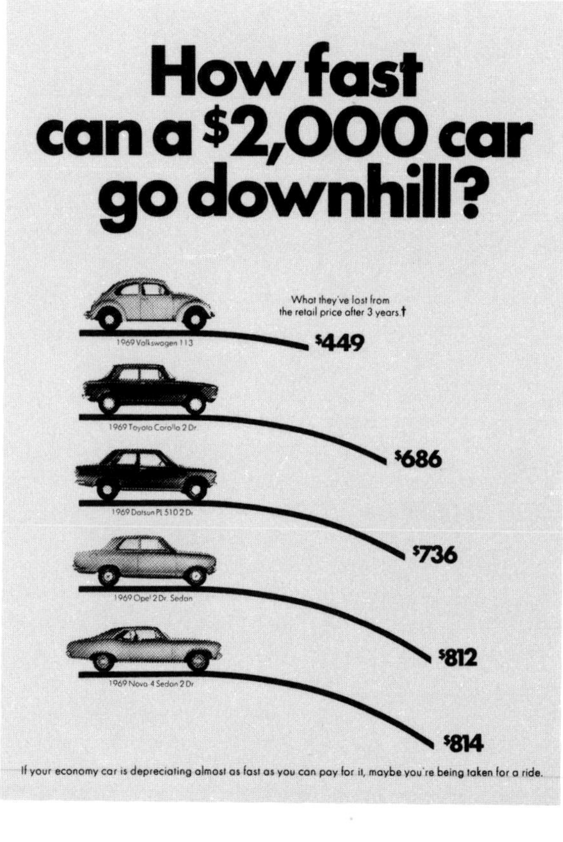
How fast can a $2,000 car go downhill?
What they've lost from the retail price after 3 years.†
1969 Volkswagen 113
$449
1969 Toyota Corolla 2 Dr
$686
1969 Datsun PL 510 2 Dr
$736
1969 Opel 2 Dr. Sedan
$812
1969 Nova 4 Sedan 2 Dr
$814
If your economy car is depreciating almost as fast as you can pay for it, maybe you're being taken for a ride.

WE'RE LOOKING FOR BROKERS WITH A PAST IN FUTURES.

If you know your way around hog runs, platinum lodes and soy bean fields, Hornblower would like to hear from you.

We need good people who can sell. And Hornblower will give you every opportunity to prove how good you are. We do it by limiting a major obstacle: competition.

At Hornblower, only commodities specialists deal in commodities.

To help you move fast, Hornblower runs telephone hot lines direct to the commodities exchanges. Push a button and you're talking to a Hornblower man right on the floor. You can place an order, change an order, change your mind and get confirmation while your customer's on "Hold."

Since research is crucial to you, we give our analysts incentives to be right. How much they earn is based on how accurately they analyze.

If you think your future in futures might be brighter at Hornblower, contact us. Send a resume of your educational and business background, along with specifics on your commodities experience to:

Mr. Robert Robens, National Commodity Sales Manager, Hornblower & Weeks-Hemphill, Noyes Incorporated, 72 West Adams Street, Chicago, Illinois 60603. Your inquiry will be held in strictest confidence, of course.

HORNBLOWER
HORNBLOWER & WEEKS-HEMPHILL, NOYES
Incorporated

72 West Adams Street
Chicago, Ill. 60603 Tel. 641-5000

158

159

"COME WIZ ME TO ZE BRASSERIE."

Nothing makes women more beautiful
than stepping 7 steps down to the Brasserie.
You'll see.
After theatre, you'll decide upon supper.
After theatre, wonderful people flock here.
After theatre, she'll forget curfew.
(The Brasserie never closes.)
Remember: The Brasserie is an informal
French restaurant that stays open
24 heures a day.

BRASSERIE
100 East 53rd Street
PLaza 1-4840

Another Restaurant Associates Great Place.

154
Art Director: Sam Scali
Copywriter: Ed McCabe
Designer: Sam Scali
Agency: Scali, McCabe, Sloves, Inc.
Client: Perdue Farms Inc.

155
Art Director: Harry Webber
Copywriter: Gene Case
Photographer: Manny Gonzalez
Agency: Case & McGrath Inc.
Client: Gravymaster Co., Inc.

156
Art Director: Don Slater
Copywriter: Jim Parry
Agency: Parry Associates
Client: Zero Population Growth

157 Gold Award
Art Director: Joe Cappadona
Copywriter: Ed Butler
Designer: Joe Cappadona
Photographer: Menken/Seltzer
Agency: Doyle Dane Bernbach Inc.
Client: Volkswagen of America

158
Art Director: Ray Alban
Copywriter: Tom Nathan
Designer: Ray Alban
Agency: Scali, McCabe, Sloves, Inc.
Client: Hornblower & Weeks-Hemphill, Noyes

159
Art Director: George Lois
Copywriter: Ron Holland
Designer: Dennis Mazzella
Agency: Lois Holland Callaway Inc.
Client: Restaurant Associates

The alternative to a wire coat hanger is (212) 489-7794.

There is such a thing as a legal, safe, inexpensive abortion. By an M.D. in a clinic or hospital. And we can help you get it.

If you have the abortion during the first 10 weeks of pregnancy, it will cost only about $150. And no matter when you have it, there's no charge for our service.

In the long run, a do-it-yourself abortion can be a lot costlier.

Call us at (212) 489-7794 Monday through Friday, between 10 a.m. and 5 p.m. New York time.

Free Abortion Referral Service from ZPG-New York

160

When was the last time you had your period?

If you're two weeks overdue, don't wait. Consult your doctor. And if you *are* pregnant and you want an abortion, consult us.

We can help you get a legal, safe, inexpensive abortion. By an M.D. in a clinic or hospital.

If you have the abortion during the first 10 weeks of pregnancy, it will cost only about $150. And no matter when you have it, there's no charge for our service.

Even if you got your period yesterday, we're a good number to remember: (212) 489-7794 Monday through Friday, between 10 a.m. and 5 p.m. New York time.

Free Abortion Referral Service from ZPG-New York

161

162

"When my husband says the grace, I'm afraid I know why he's praying."

He's so sweet, he'd never say something I cooked was bad. He'd just say it's "not one of his favorites."

But there's one thing he loves that I make as good as anybody:

Gravy. I make great gravy. I follow the pictures on the Gravy Master bottle.

The gravy comes out dark and rich and smooth, with a little taste of parsley and things. I've never messed it up yet.

Knock on wood.

Looking for some new recipes?
Write Gravy Master, Dept. AY, Long Island City, N. Y. 11101.

Small Space/Single

See everything from א to ת.
Israel is the ruins of a 20,000-seat race track the Romans built in 2 A.D. And Greek relics. And caves that Stone Age men lived in 120 centuries ago.
And 20 minutes later it's "Love Story" in a Haifa theatre.
Or Tel Aviv's version of the Beatles, singing "My beby does the Henky Penky" in a discotheque.
Israel is also a Mediterranean Miami Beach called Herzliya. Where you can check into a luxury hotel and lie in the sun all day. So you should go home with a tan.
It's an American film company shooting a television commercial in the Negev. And the Chagall windows in the Hadassah Medical Center.
It's falafel, latkes, kosher coq au vin, and pizza.
The Hatikvah before a soccer game.
And blocks of shops where you can buy anything from the world's softest leather trench coat, to a stack of Hebrew comic books.
If you bring your clubs, there's even golf in Israel.
And if you bring any feeling at all, there are moments that will stay with you forever.
The Wailing Wall on the Sabbath.
The silence at the tombs of Abraham, Isaac and Jacob.
The sight of a blue and white Magen David-Israeli flag flapping over a children's village in the Galilee.
Altogether, there is more in Israel that's exciting, fattening, and profoundly moving than you can begin to imagine.
And we'd like to show you every bit of it.
Just call us or your travel agent for more information.
In the words of that old Israeli expression, you're in for the time of your חיים.
The Airline of Israel

163

164

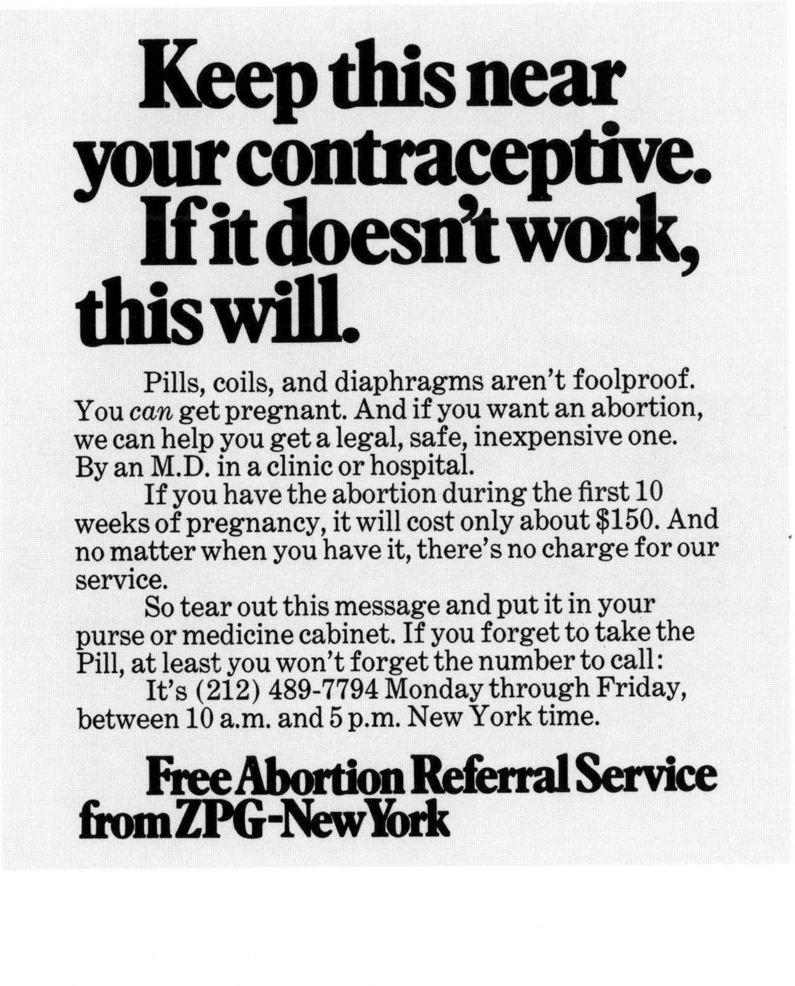

Keep this near your contraceptive. If it doesn't work, this will.
Pills, coils, and diaphragms aren't foolproof. You *can* get pregnant. And if you want an abortion, we can help you get a legal, safe, inexpensive one. By an M.D. in a clinic or hospital.
If you have the abortion during the first 10 weeks of pregnancy, it will cost only about $150. And no matter when you have it, there's no charge for our service.
So tear out this message and put it in your purse or medicine cabinet. If you forget to take the Pill, at least you won't forget the number to call:
It's (212) 489-7794 Monday through Friday, between 10 a.m. and 5 p.m. New York time.
Free Abortion Referral Service from ZPG-New York

160
Art Director: Don Slater
Copywriter: Jim Parry
Agency: Parry Associates
Client: Zero Population Growth

161
Art Director: Don Slater
Copywriter: Jim Parry
Agency: Parry Associates
Client: Zero Population Growth

162
Art Director: Harry Webber
Copywriter: Gene Case
Photographer: Manny Gonzalez
Agency: Case & McGrath Inc.
Client: Gravymaster Co., Inc.

163
Art Director: Stu Weisselberg
Copywriter: Diane Rothschild Hyatt
Designer: Stu Weisselberg
Agency: Doyle Dane Bernbach Inc.
Client: El Al Israel Airlines

164 Silver Award
Art Director: Don Slater
Copywriter: Jim Parry
Agency: Parry Associates
Client: Zero Population Growth

165
Art Director: Tom Ladyga
Copywriter: Mike Marino
Designer: Tom Ladyga
Agency: Griswold-Eshleman Co.
Client: Industry Week

166
Art Director: Frank Ginsberg
Copywriter: Lou Linder
Artist: Burt Blum
Agency: The Marschalk Company, Inc.
Client: Coca-Cola U.S.A.

165

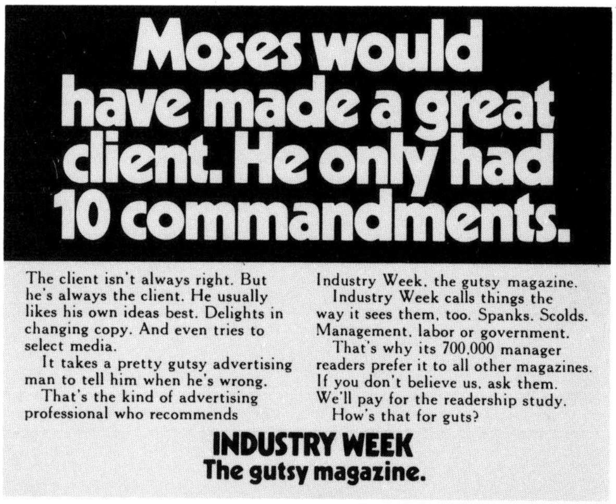
Moses would have made a great client. He only had 10 commandments.
The client isn't always right. But he's always the client. He usually likes his own ideas best. Delights in changing copy. And even tries to select media.
It takes a pretty gutsy advertising man to tell him when he's wrong.
That's the kind of advertising professional who recommends Industry Week, the gutsy magazine.
Industry Week calls things the way it sees them, too. Spanks. Scolds. Management, labor or government.
That's why its 700,000 manager readers prefer it to all other magazines. If you don't believe us, ask them. We'll pay for the readership study.
How's that for guts?
INDUSTRY WEEK
The gutsy magazine.

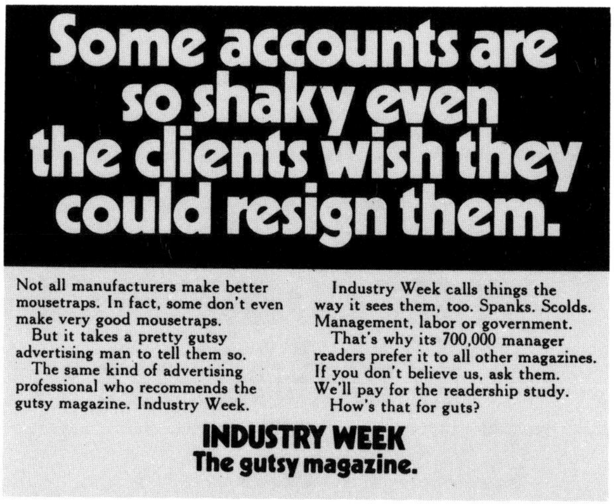
Some accounts are so shaky even the clients wish they could resign them.
Not all manufacturers make better mousetraps. In fact, some don't even make very good mousetraps.
But it takes a pretty gutsy advertising man to tell them so.
The same kind of advertising professional who recommends the gutsy magazine. Industry Week.
Industry Week calls things the way it sees them, too. Spanks. Scolds. Management, labor or government.
That's why its 700,000 manager readers prefer it to all other magazines. If you don't believe us, ask them. We'll pay for the readership study.
How's that for guts?
INDUSTRY WEEK
The gutsy magazine.

He was the world's greatest copywriter. Then they made him Creative Director.
Lost: a great copywriter.
Found: a lousy creative director.
Good copywriters don't always make good creative directors. But they sometimes make great media buyers.
They know good editorial content when they see it. And they've seen it in Industry Week. The gutsy magazine.
They like the way Industry Week calls things the way it sees them. The way it spanks. Scolds. Management, labor or government.
That's why its 700,000 manager readers prefer it to all other magazines. If you don't believe us, ask them. We'll pay for the readership study.
How's that for guts?
INDUSTRY WEEK
The gutsy magazine.

How do you hire a $40,000 a year media director for only $20,000?
You don't.
$40,000 media directors won't work for $20,000. And neither will any other $40,000 talent.
Good talent establishes its own value. Just like good magazines.
And one of the most valuable media buys these days is the gutsy magazine. Industry Week.
It's valuable because it's well read. And it's well read because it calls things the way it sees them. Spanks. Scolds. Management, labor or government.
That's why its 700,000 manager readers prefer it to all other magazines. If you don't believe us, ask them. We'll pay for the readership study.
How's that for guts?
INDUSTRY WEEK
The gutsy magazine.

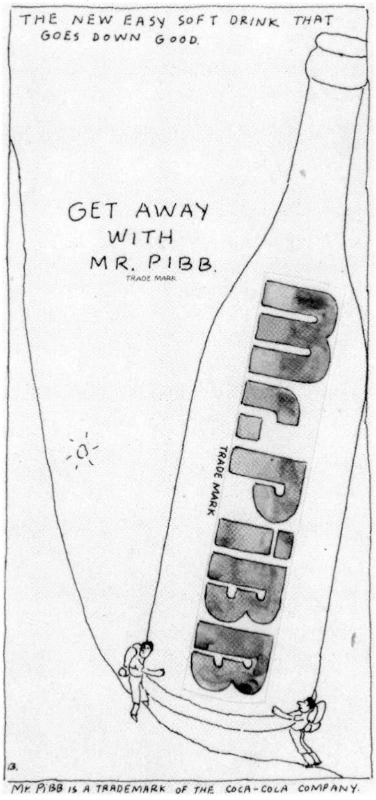
THE NEW EASY SOFT DRINK THAT GOES DOWN GOOD.
GET AWAY WITH MR. PIBB.
TRADE MARK
Mr. PiBB
TRADE MARK
B.
Mr. PiBB IS A TRADEMARK OF THE COCA-COLA COMPANY.

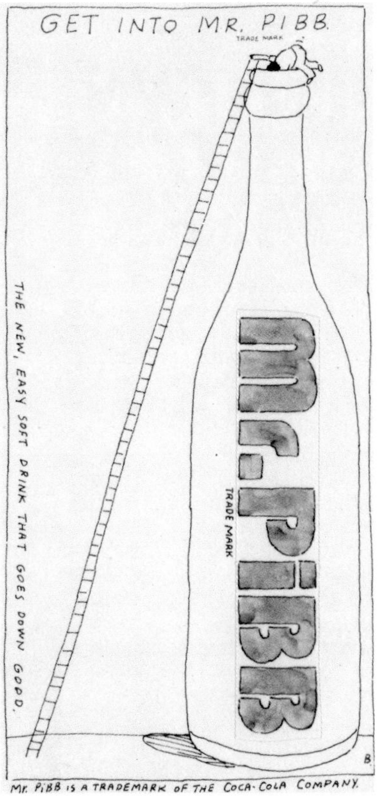
GET INTO MR. PIBB.
TRADE MARK
THE NEW, EASY SOFT DRINK THAT GOES DOWN GOOD.
Mr. PiBB
TRADE MARK
B.
Mr. PiBB IS A TRADEMARK OF THE COCA-COLA COMPANY.

B.
HAVE A BURGER WITH MR. PIBB.
TRADE MARK
Mr. PiBB
TRADE MARK
THE NEW, EASY SOFT DRINK THAT GOES DOWN GOOD.
Mr. PiBB IS A TRADEMARK OF THE COCA-COLA COMPANY.

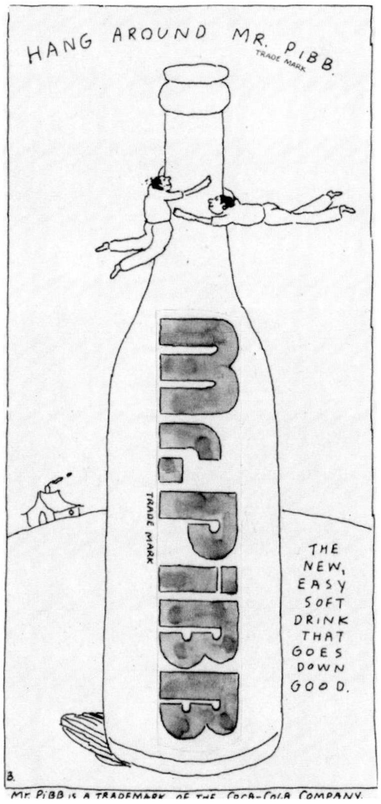
HANG AROUND MR. PIBB.
TRADE MARK
Mr. PiBB
TRADE MARK
THE NEW, EASY SOFT DRINK THAT GOES DOWN GOOD.
B.
Mr. PiBB IS A TRADEMARK OF THE COCA-COLA COMPANY.

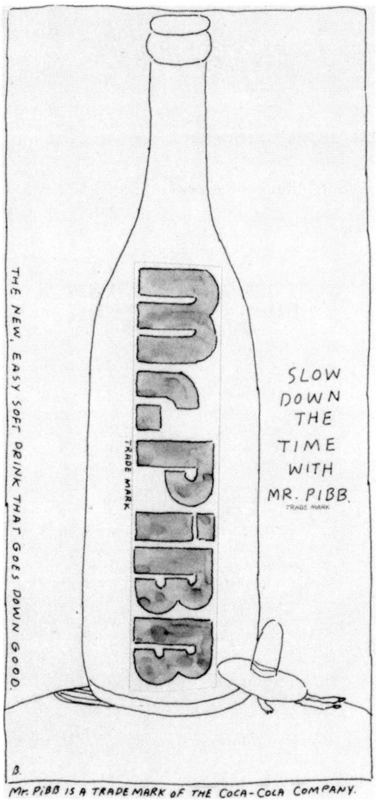
THE NEW, EASY SOFT DRINK THAT GOES DOWN GOOD.
Mr. PiBB
TRADE MARK
SLOW DOWN THE TIME WITH MR. PIBB.
TRADE MARK
B.
Mr. PiBB IS A TRADEMARK OF THE COCA-COLA COMPANY.

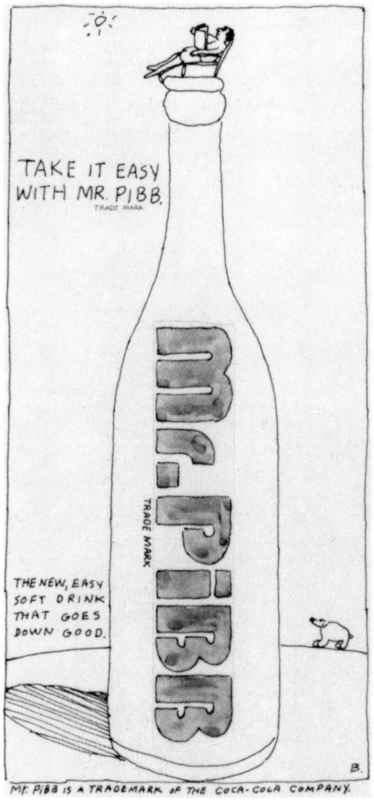
TAKE IT EASY WITH MR. PIBB.
TRADE MARK
Mr. PiBB
TRADE MARK
THE NEW, EASY SOFT DRINK THAT GOES DOWN GOOD.
B.
Mr. PiBB IS A TRADEMARK OF THE COCA-COLA COMPANY.

167

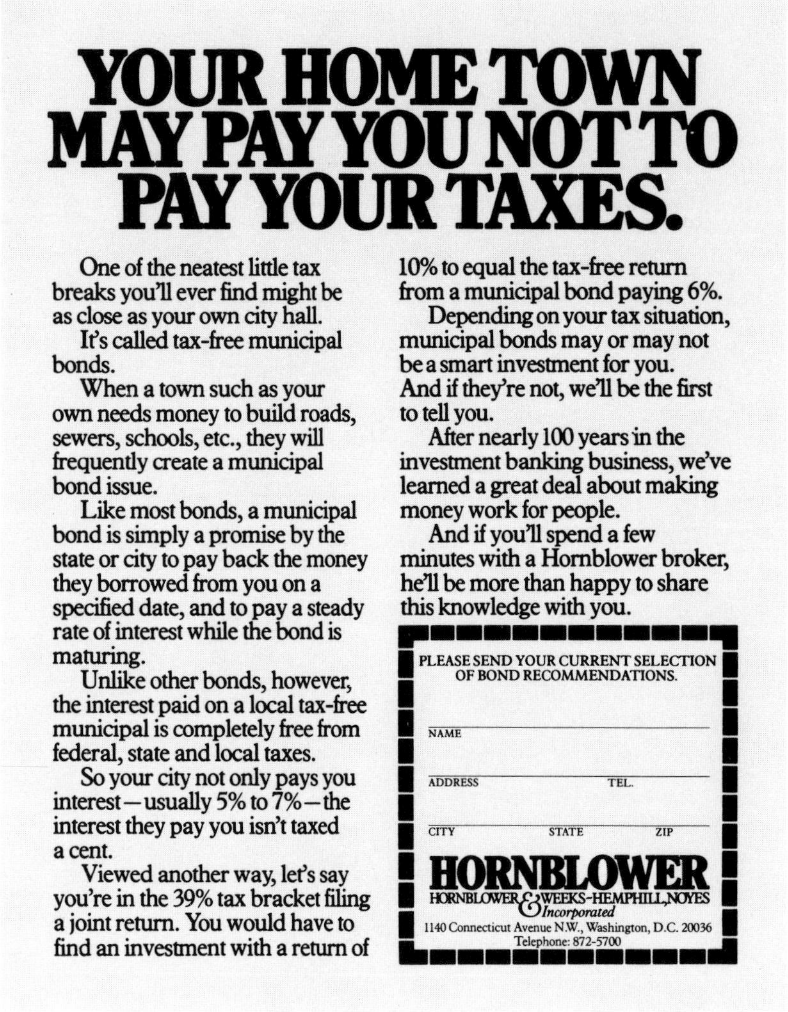
YOUR HOME TOWN MAY PAY YOU NOT TO PAY YOUR TAXES.
One of the neatest little tax breaks you'll ever find might be as close as your own city hall.
It's called tax-free municipal bonds.
When a town such as your own needs money to build roads, sewers, schools, etc., they will frequently create a municipal bond issue.
Like most bonds, a municipal bond is simply a promise by the state or city to pay back the money they borrowed from you on a specified date, and to pay a steady rate of interest while the bond is maturing.
Unlike other bonds, however, the interest paid on a local tax-free municipal is completely free from federal, state and local taxes.
So your city not only pays you interest—usually 5% to 7%—the interest they pay you isn't taxed a cent.
Viewed another way, let's say you're in the 39% tax bracket filing a joint return. You would have to find an investment with a return of 10% to equal the tax-free return from a municipal bond paying 6%.
Depending on your tax situation, municipal bonds may or may not be a smart investment for you. And if they're not, we'll be the first to tell you.
After nearly 100 years in the investment banking business, we've learned a great deal about making money work for people.
And if you'll spend a few minutes with a Hornblower broker, he'll be more than happy to share this knowledge with you.
PLEASE SEND YOUR CURRENT SELECTION OF BOND RECOMMENDATIONS.
NAME
ADDRESS
TEL.
CITY
STATE
ZIP
HORNBLOWER
HORNBLOWER & WEEKS-HEMPHILL, NOYES
Incorporated
1140 Connecticut Avenue N.W., Washington, D.C. 20036
Telephone: 872-5700

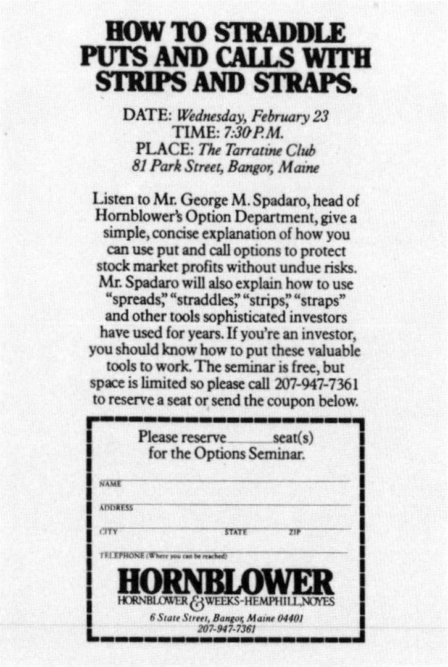
HOW TO STRADDLE PUTS AND CALLS WITH STRIPS AND STRAPS.
DATE: Wednesday, February 23
TIME: 7:30 P.M.
PLACE: The Tarratine Club
81 Park Street, Bangor, Maine
Listen to Mr. George M. Spadaro, head of Hornblower's Option Department, give a simple, concise explanation of how you can use put and call options to protect stock market profits without undue risks. Mr. Spadaro will also explain how to use "spreads," "straddles," "strips," "straps" and other tools sophisticated investors have used for years. If you're an investor, you should know how to put these valuable tools to work. The seminar is free, but space is limited so please call 207-947-7361 to reserve a seat or send the coupon below.
Please reserve ______ seat(s) for the Options Seminar.
NAME
ADDRESS
CITY
STATE
ZIP
TELEPHONE (Where you can be reached)
HORNBLOWER
HORNBLOWER & WEEKS-HEMPHILL, NOYES
6 State Street, Bangor, Maine 04401
207-947-7361

IF STOCKS AND BONDS DON'T INTEREST YOU, HOW ABOUT PORK BELLIES?
The Commodity Futures market (hogs, sugar, grain and the like) is one of the most exciting, volatile and riskiest areas of investing.
Weather, pestilence, crop failure—almost any factor can affect their prices. And it takes a specialist to know which factors these are.
Because of the highly-sensitive nature of Commodity trading, Hornblower has full-time Commodity specialists who, in our opinion, know more about crops and livestock than most farmers.
Their names are Mr. Donald Parker and Mr. Peter Caten and they would be more than happy to share their knowledge in this area with you.
At Hornblower, there's more to the stock market than just Bulls and Bears.
We also specialize in hogs and turkeys and cows.
HORNBLOWER
HORNBLOWER & WEEKS-HEMPHILL, NOYES
160 Franklin Street, Boston, Massachusetts
(617) 482-5545

167
Art Director: Ray Alban
Copywriter: Dan Bingham
Designer: Ray Alban
Agency: Scali, McCabe, Sloves, Inc.
Client: Hornblower & Weeks-Hemphill, Noyes

168
Art Director: Kurt Weihs
Copywriters: Barbara Brenner
Kurt Weihs
Dennis Mazzella
Designer: Dennis Mazzella
Photographer: Tom Weihs
Agency: Brenner, Mazzella, Weihs
Client: Myrtle Motors Corporation

What's the big deal?
Pontiac '73 is the great new car of '73. And that means a great deal.
Myrtle can afford to sell you the great Pontiac '73 at the lowest price. Because we are the biggest Pontiac dealer in New York. That's a big deal.
Myrtle will arrange financing, if you wish. Even with a low down payment. And that's a fair deal.
Myrtle will get your plates and title. That's a nice deal.
Myrtle always wants good, clean used cars. Therefore we will offer the best trade-in deal.
Now, what's a great dealer without a great service department? Myrtle enlarged to 22 super-trained mechanics. Fast. Efficient. Friendly! Call anytime during working hours for service. Isn't that a good deal?
That's the big deal!
Myrtle Motors Pontiac
Mm
Myrtle Motors Corp.
61-20 Fresh Pond Rd.
Maspeth, Queens
366-5050

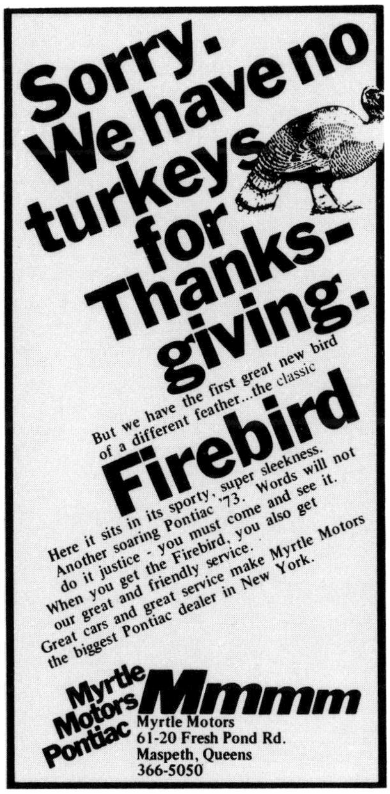
Sorry. We have no turkeys for Thanks-giving.
But we have the first great new bird of a different feather...the classic
Firebird
Here it sits in its sporty, super sleekness. Another soaring Pontiac '73. Words will not do it justice - you must come and see it. When you get the Firebird, you also get our great and friendly service.
Great cars and great service make Myrtle Motors the biggest Pontiac dealer in New York.
Myrtle Motors Pontiac
Mmmmm
Myrtle Motors
61-20 Fresh Pond Rd.
Maspeth, Queens
366-5050

These mechanics look after your car when you leave it with Myrtle Motors.
Angels with dirty faces.
Have you ever done time waiting for your car to be serviced? Never with us. A dealer is only as good as his product and service. And thanks to our great Pontiacs and our great servicemen, Myrtle Motors is the biggest Pontiac dealer in New York.
Myrtle Motors Pontiac
Mm
Myrtle Motors, Inc.
61-20 Fresh Pond Rd.
Maspeth, Queens
366-5050

"If I couldn't find my mamma in the kitchen, I knew she was having a baby."
MAMMA LEONE'S
"WHERE STRONG APPETITES ARE MET AND CONQUERED." OPEN DAILY FOR DINNER AND AFTER-THEATER SUPPER. WHAT A PLACE FOR PRIVATE PARTIES.
239 W. 48TH ST. JU 6-5151
"I love big tables. I can get more food on them."
MAMMA LEONE'S
"WHERE STRONG APPETITES ARE MET AND CONQUERED." OPEN DAILY FOR DINNER AND AFTER-THEATER SUPPER. WHAT A PLACE FOR PRIVATE PARTIES.
239 W. 48TH ST. JU 6-5151
"The devil must have tempted Eve with Fettucine. (Nobody'd cause all this trouble for an apple!)"
MAMMA LEONE'S
"WHERE STRONG APPETITES ARE MET AND CONQUERED." OPEN DAILY FOR DINNER AND AFTER-THEATER SUPPER. WHAT A PLACE FOR PRIVATE PARTIES.
239 W. 48TH ST. JU 6-5151
"As far as I'm concerned, the Superbowl is still my minestrone."
MAMMA LEONE'S
"WHERE STRONG APPETITES ARE MET AND CONQUERED." OPEN DAILY FOR DINNER AND AFTER-THEATER SUPPER. WHAT A PLACE FOR PRIVATE PARTIES.
239 W. 48TH ST. JU 6-5151
"Before you marry her, bring her to my place. See if she likes to eat."
MAMMA LEONE'S
"WHERE STRONG APPETITES ARE MET AND CONQUERED." OPEN DAILY FOR DINNER AND AFTER-THEATER SUPPER. WHAT A PLACE FOR PRIVATE PARTIES.
239 W. 48TH ST. JU 6-5151
"If he's giving you the cold shoulder, stop using frozen foods."
MAMMA LEONE'S
"WHERE STRONG APPETITES ARE MET AND CONQUERED." OPEN DAILY FOR DINNER AND AFTER-THEATER SUPPER. WHAT A PLACE FOR PRIVATE PARTIES.
239 W. 48TH ST. JU 6-5151
"Nobody ever filed for divorce on a full stomach."
MAMMA LEONE'S
"WHERE STRONG APPETITES ARE MET AND CONQUERED." OPEN DAILY FOR DINNER AND AFTER-THEATER SUPPER. WHAT A PLACE FOR PRIVATE PARTIES.
239 W. 48TH ST. JU 6-5151
"Be a career woman, but after you learn to cook."
MAMMA LEONE'S
"WHERE STRONG APPETITES ARE MET AND CONQUERED." OPEN DAILY FOR DINNER AND AFTER-THEATER SUPPER. WHAT A PLACE FOR PRIVATE PARTIES.
239 W. 48TH ST. JU 6-5151
"Nobody ever got in trouble hanging around their kitchen."
MAMMA LEONE'S
"WHERE STRONG APPETITES ARE MET AND CONQUERED." OPEN DAILY FOR DINNER AND AFTER-THEATER SUPPER. WHAT A PLACE FOR PRIVATE PARTIES.
239 W. 48TH ST. JU 6-5151

Small Space/Campaign

169
Art Director: Dennis Mazzella
Copywriter: Ron Holland
Designer: Dennis Mazzella
Agency: Lois Holland Callaway, Inc.
Client: Restaurant Associates

170
Art Director: Howard Benson
Copywriter: Pat Sutula
Artist: Larry Ross
Agency: Carl Ally Inc.
Client: Pan American Airways

Discover the virgin islands of the South Pacific.

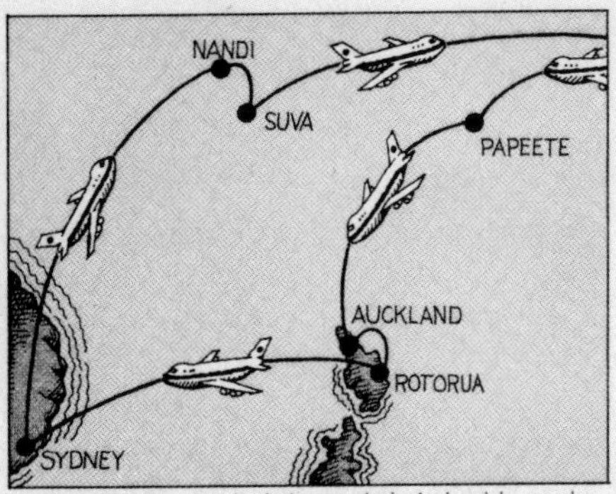

If you're looking for islands that everybody else hasn't been to, let Pan Am® fly you to the South Pacific. And the islands that were the historic landings of Captain Cook and HMS Bounty's Captain Bligh.

You'll tour Papeete in Tahiti, Nandi and Suva in Fiji and even a few cities in Australia and New Zealand.

We'll give you plenty of time to relax in the sun, shop for souvenirs or just lose yourself in the beauty of it all.

While it's still beautiful.

For more details on the Pan Am South Pacific Mini Holiday, call us.

(Travel agent name and tour price go here.)
This tour is valid April 1-November 30.

Our tour of Panama includes the discovery of an island 13 miles into the Pacific and 450 years into the past.

The tiny tropical island of Taboga, where nothing has changed much since the days of Francisco Pizarro.

A few days of relaxation here and you'll be ready for a few days of excitement in Panama City.

And you'll be on your own to explore mountain jungles, fish in the streams or the ocean, visit the racetrack, a nightclub or a casino, or just go shopping. You'll find bargains on everything from Peruvian silver to Chinese silk.

If you'd like to take the Pan Am® Panama Tour, call us.

(Travel agent name and tour price go here.)
This tour valid April 1—November 30.

16 days to become oriented to Tokyo, Bangkok and Hong Kong.

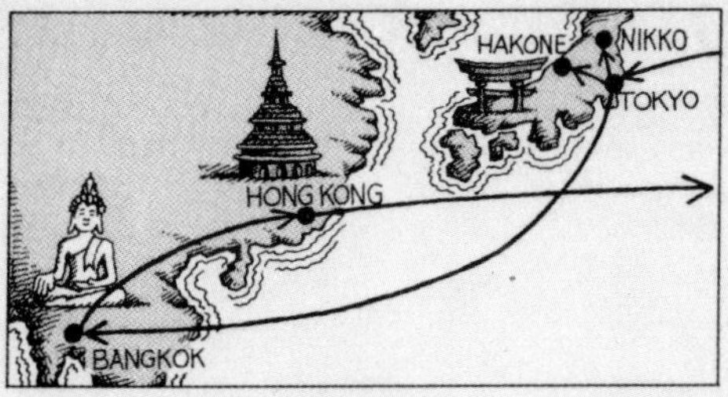

You'll be flown to these cities and back on Pan Am®.

In Tokyo, as well as Hong Kong and Bangkok, you'll stay in first class hotels with private bath. And get breakfast every morning.

And there'll be someone on hand to show you around or make sure you know how to get somewhere, when you want to get there on your own.

If you'd like to become oriented, call us and ask about the Pan Am Orient 16 Adventure.

(Travel agent name and tour price go here.)
This tour is valid April 1-November 30.

A tour that takes you from Lisbon to Madrid the long way. Through Morocco.

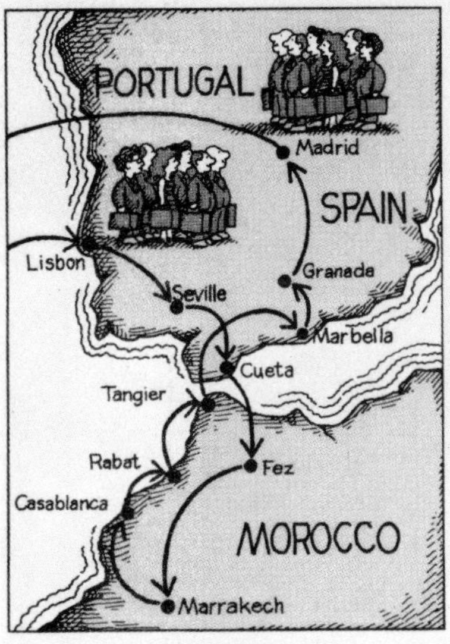

You'll be flown by Pan Am® to Lisbon. After a few days there, you'll be driven in a deluxe, air-conditioned motorcoach through the historic cities of Portugal and Spain. And the intriguing cities of Morocco. As well as the beautiful countryside in between.

In these cities you'll stay in first class hotels with most of your meals provided.

And the tour will end with a few days in Madrid before you're driven to the airport for your Pan Am flight back.

If you're interested in 22 days of history and intrigue, call us and ask about our Fantasia Tour.

(Travel agent name and tour price go here.)
This tour valid April 1-November 30.

VOLVOS ARE BUILT FOR PEOPLE WHO DEMAND MORE OF THEIR BODIES.

The Volvo factory is very conscientious about body building. Every Volvo is assembled from large steel sections instead of lots of smaller ones. 10,000 spot welds fuse these sections together in a single, solid unit.

Then six layers of primer and paint are applied to protect it from rust and corrosion. Which helps explain why Volvo is the car that sells best in Sweden. It's prepared for the worst.

If you'd like to have a body like that, come see us. And demand a Volvo.

DEALER NAME

WHERE VOLVOS COME FROM, A CAR MUST EAT UP THE ROAD. NOT VICE VERSA.

Swedish winters are car killers. With slush and raw salt on the road half the year, a car can be eaten away in short order. Unless it's protected as well as a Volvo. Every Volvo in our showroom has *two* undercoats protecting its underside. Vulnerable body parts are made of anti-corrosive galvanized steel. And instead of shiny chrome trim, which rusts, Volvo has shiny, stainless steel and aluminum, which don't.

So come buy a Volvo from us. Even if the winters aren't kind to it, the years should be.

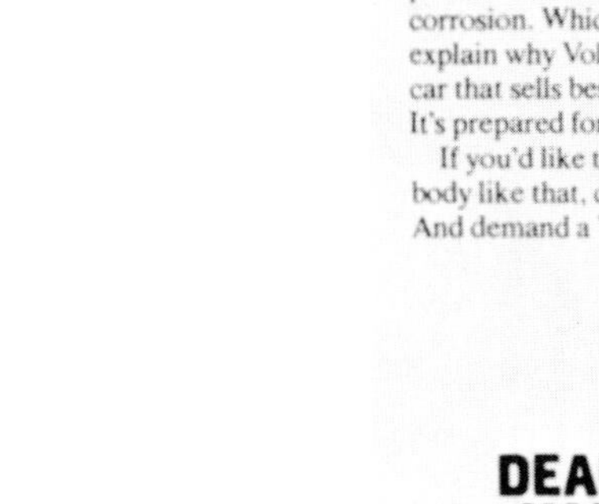

DEALER NAME

IS YOUR CAR PASSING INSPECTION BUT FLUNKING LIFE?

The true test of a car's condition is not that it passes state inspection but rather how many annual inspections it's around to take. In Sweden, where the yearly government inspection covers about 200 points, Volvos have a life expectancy of 14 years.

So if you think your car is just scraping by, get a Volvo from us. It's built to be more than just passable.

DEALER NAME

Small Space/Campaign

Tonight, if you're lucky, you won't have to work like a horse to put your kid through college.
Tonight at Yonkers, in addition to our nine exciting races, we've added another attraction. We're giving away a $2,000 college scholarship to one lucky Yonkers fan. You can use the scholarship for your child, donate it to your favorite organization, or even go back to school yourself.
So why not join us? We always like to see folks with a little horse sense.
COLLEGE SCHOLARSHIP NIGHT. POST TIME 8:00 P.M.
THE NEW YONKERS RACEWAY

Tonight at Yonkers your dark horse could turn out to be a free color TV.
That's right, because tonight we're giving away 3 color TVs after the 9th race. All you need to be eligible for these prizes is your admission ticket.
So come on out, because even if you don't win any green, you still might leave with a lot of color.
COLOR TV NIGHT. POST TIME 8:00 P.M.
THE NEW YONKERS RACEWAY

172

Tonight at Yonkers, even if you don't win any bread, you still get a shot at a toaster.
Or a color TV. Or a black and white TV. Or a stereo set. Or a digital clock radio. Or a rotisserie. Or an electric mixer.
You see, tonight is Appliance Give-Away Night at Yonkers. And we're giving away 9 great appliances to 9 lucky people.
So stick around after the 9th race. You might be in for a little shock.
APPLIANCE GIVE-AWAY NIGHT. POST TIME 8:00 P.M.
THE NEW YONKERS RACEWAY

171 Gold Award
Art Directors: Joe Schindelman
Bill Berenter
Copywriters: Ray Myers
Tom Nathan
Designer: Joe Schindelman
Photographers: Joel Meyerowitz
Malcolm Kirk
Agency: Scali, McCabe, Sloves, Inc.
Client: Volvo, Inc.

172
Art Directors: Bob Kuperman
Tom Stoerrle
Copywriters: Jerry Della Femina
Kathy Cole
Frank DiGiacomo
Designers: Bob Kuperman
Tom Stoerrle
Agency: Della Femina, Travisano & Partners, Inc.
Client: Yonkers Raceway

173 Gold Award
Art Director: Don Slater
Copywriter: Jim Parry
Agency: Parry Associates
Client: Zero Population Growth

174
Art Director: Charles Abrams
Copywriter: Brian Hennessy
Designer: Charles Abrams
Artist: David Palladini
Agency: Doyle Dane Bernbach Inc.
Client: Mobil Oil Corporation

The main difference between a $150 abortion and a $1000 abortion is the doctor makes an extra $850.

Expensive abortions are a hangover from when abortions were illegal. But today we can help you get a legal, safe—and inexpensive—abortion. By an M.D. in a clinic or hospital.

If you have the abortion during the first 10 weeks of pregnancy, it will cost only about $150. And no matter when you have it, there's no charge for our service.

We know some doctors who care more about people than money.

Call us at (212) 489-7794 Monday through Friday, between 10 a.m. and 5 p.m. New York time.

Free Abortion Referral Service from ZPG-New York

173

When was the last time you had your period?

If you're two weeks overdue, don't wait. Consult your doctor. And if you *are* pregnant and you want an abortion, consult us.

We can help you get a legal, safe, inexpensive abortion. By an M.D. in a clinic or hospital.

If you have the abortion during the first 10 weeks of pregnancy, it will cost only about $150. And no matter when you have it, there's no charge for our service.

Even if you got your period yesterday, we're a good number to remember: (212) 489-7794 Monday through Friday, between 10 a.m. and 5 p.m. New York time.

Free Abortion Referral Service from ZPG-New York

The alternative to a wire coat hanger is (212) 489-7794.

There is such a thing as a legal, safe, inexpensive abortion. By an M.D. in a clinic or hospital. And we can help you get it.

If you have the abortion during the first 10 weeks of pregnancy, it will cost only about $150. And no matter when you have it, there's no charge for our service.

In the long run, a do-it-yourself abortion can be a lot costlier.

Call us at (212) 489-7794 Monday through Friday, between 10 a.m. and 5 p.m. New York time.

Free Abortion Referral Service from ZPG-New York

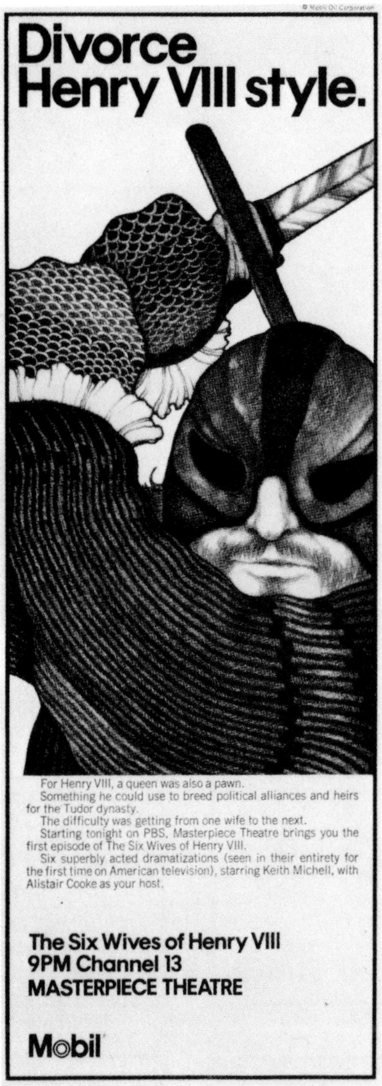
© Mobil Oil Corporation
Divorce Henry VIII style.
For Henry VIII, a queen was also a pawn.
Something he could use to breed political alliances and heirs for the Tudor dynasty.
The difficulty was getting from one wife to the next.
Starting tonight on PBS, Masterpiece Theatre brings you the first episode of The Six Wives of Henry VIII.
Six superbly acted dramatizations (seen in their entirety for the first time on American television), starring Keith Michell, with Alistair Cooke as your host.
The Six Wives of Henry VIII
9PM Channel 13
MASTERPIECE THEATRE
Mobil

© Mobil Oil Corporation
Anne Boleyn
you were undone.
Your mortal sin
you had no son.
Tonight. The second of
The Six Wives of Henry VIII
9PM Channel 13 (PBS)
MASTERPIECE THEATRE
Mobil

© Mobil Oil Corporation
Catherine of Aragon,
Eighteen years wed;
Banished from court,
And soon to be dead.
Tonight. The first of
The Six Wives of Henry VIII
9:30PM Channel 13 (PBS)
MASTERPIECE THEATRE
Mobil

Jane Seymour,
Reared like a nun,
Just has the strength
To bear him a son.
Tonight. The third of
The Six Wives of Henry VIII
9PM Channel 13 (PBS)
MASTERPIECE THEATRE
Mobil

Catherine Parr
must compromise.
But she's alive
when Henry dies.
Tonight. The sixth of
The Six Wives of Henry VIII
9PM Channel 13 PBS
MASTERPIECE THEATRE
Mobil

Anne of Cleves
avoids his bed.
A desperate plan
to save her head.
Tonight. The fourth of
The Six Wives of Henry VIII
9PM Channel 13 (PBS)
MASTERPIECE THEATRE
Mobil

Catherine Howard,
young deflowered,
Queen of England,
soon entowered.
Tonight. The fifth of
The Six Wives of Henry VIII
9PM Channel 13 PBS
MASTERPIECE THEATRE
Mobil

Small Space/Campaign

175 Silver Award
Art Directors: Sam Scali
Duane Plants
Copywriter: Tom Thomas
Designers: Sam Scali
Duane Plants
Agency: Scali, McCabe, Sloves, Inc.
Client: Village Voice

175

"I LOST MY JOB THROUGH THE VILLAGE VOICE."

Besides providing encouragement to leave your boring and irrelevant job, The Voice provides alternatives—film maker, travel agent, cab driver, etc.

New York's most interesting jobs are in The Voice.

THE VOICE.
IT KEEPS YOU AHEAD OF THE TIMES.

BUY PROPERTY WHERE IT'S STILL PRIVATE.

You can find country property in the secluded recesses of Vermont, Pennsylvania, Maine or even nearby New York in The Voice classifieds.

On sale at newsstands.

THE VOICE.
IT KEEPS YOU AHEAD OF THE TIMES.

FREE SUMMER HOUSES FOR RENT.

You'll find New York's most emancipated summer houses in The Voice.

On sale at newsstands.

THE VOICE.
IT KEEPS YOU AHEAD OF THE TIMES.

USE YOUR VOICE TO UNCLOG BATHROOM DRAINS.

You can find a plumber, a carpenter, a furniture mover or practically any other service you might need in The Voice classifieds.

On sale at newsstands.

THE VOICE.
IT KEEPS YOU AHEAD OF THE TIMES.

Outdoor/Single

176 Gold Award
Art Director: Stan Jones
Copywriter: David Butler
Photographer: Carl Furuta
Agency: Doyle Dane Bernbach Inc.
Client: American Airlines

177
Art Director: Si Lam
Copywriter: John Annarino
Photographer: Bernie Gardner
Agency: Doyle Dane Bernbach Inc.
Client: Volkswagen of America

176

177

Outdoor/Single

178
Art Director: John Brinkley
Copywriter: Robert Levenson
Photographer: Stan Caplan
Agency: Doyle Dane Bernbach Inc.
Client: Porsche Audi of America

179
Art Director: John Baeder
Copywriter: Stuart Pittman
Designers: John Baeder
Stuart Pittman
Agency: Smith/Greenland Company Inc.
Client: Somerset Importers, Ltd.

178

It's a lot of cars for the money.
The Audi.

180

Honor Thy Self.
Johnnie Walker
BLACK LABEL SCOTCH
12
YEARS OLD
12 Year Old Blended Scotch Whisky 86.8 Proof. Bottled in Scotland. Imported by Somerset Importers, Ltd., N.Y., N.Y.

180
Art Director: Si Lam
Copywriter: Janet Boden
Photographer: Robert Woodcock
Agency: Doyle Dale Bernbach Inc.
Client: Terminix-International Inc.

181
Art Director: Allan Beaver
Copywriter: Larry Plapler
Designer: Allan Beaver
Agency: Levine, Huntley, Schmidt, Inc.
Client: Bruce-Flournoy Ford

179

For free
termite inspection call
Terminix.

181

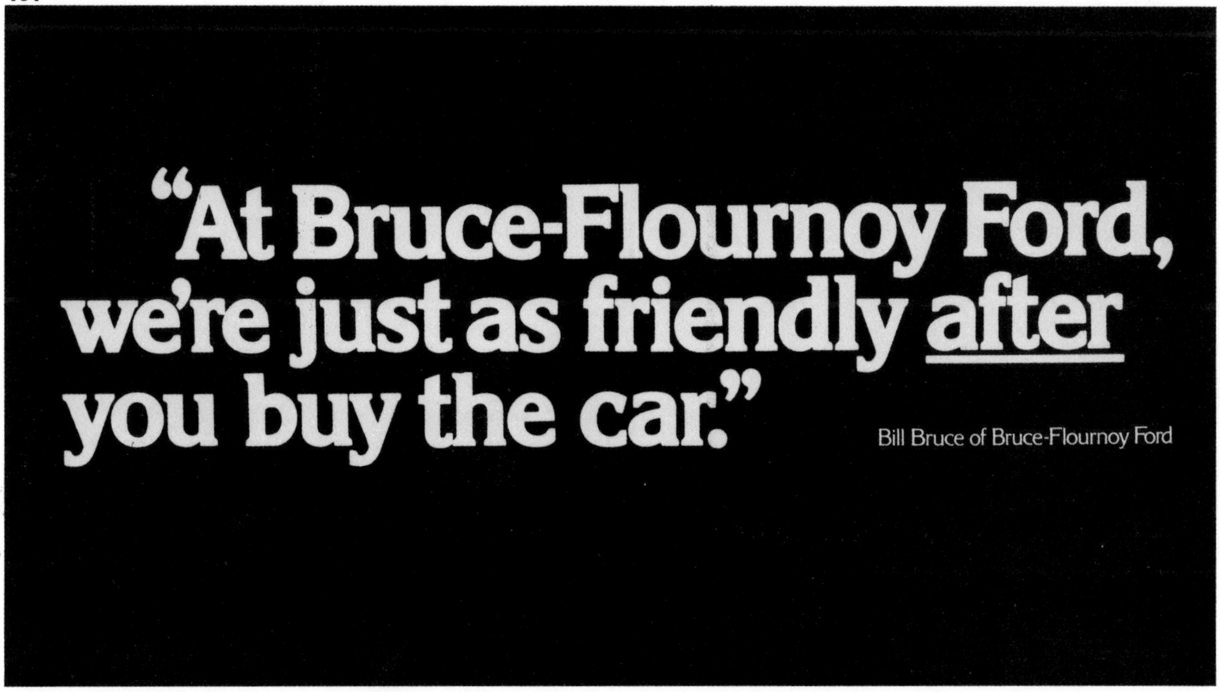
"At Bruce-Flournoy Ford,
we're just as friendly after
you buy the car."
Bill Bruce of Bruce-Flournoy Ford

Outdoor/Single

183
Art Director: Walter Kaprielian
Copywriter: Arthur X. Tuohy
Designers: Walter Kaprielian
Peter Welsch
Harold Florian
Katsuji Asada
Arton Associates, Inc.
Artist: J. McCaffery
Agency: Ketchum, MacLeod & Grove, Inc.
Client: Newark District Ford Dealers

184
Art Director: Paul Jervis
Copywriter: Sandy Berger
Designer: Paul Jervis
Photographer: Graphics Group
Agency: DKG Inc.
Client: Dollar Savings Bank

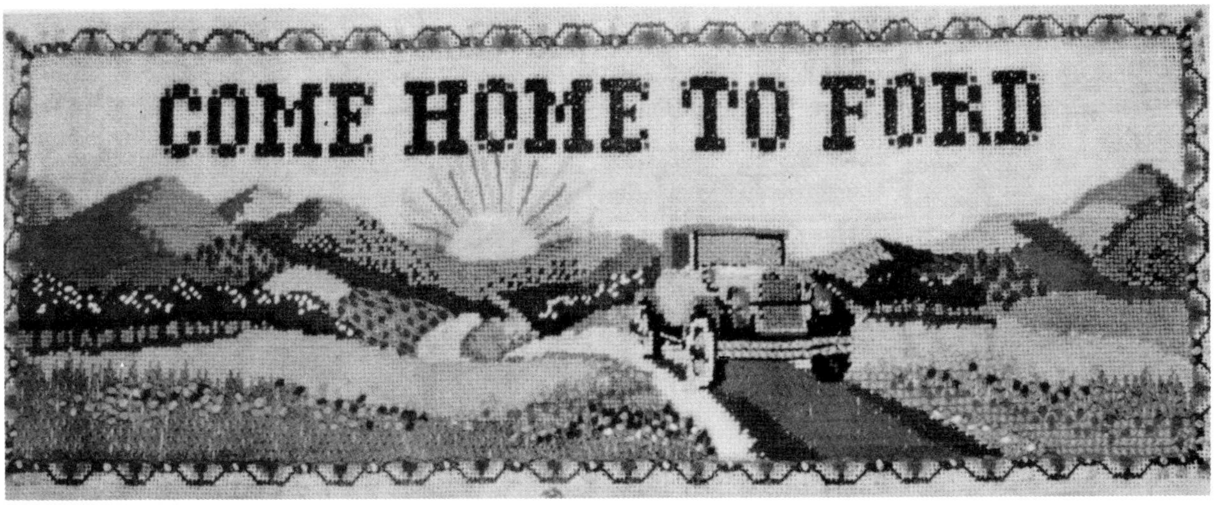

183

184

Barney wanted women
in the worst way.
And that's the way he got them.
Paramount Pictures presents A
Howard W. Koch Production of the
Neil Simon Play starring
Alan Arkin
as the
"Last of
the Red Hot
Lovers"
also starring, in order of appearance
Sally Kellerman
Paula Prentiss
Reneé Taylor
Screenplay by Neil Simon Produced by Howard W. Koch Directed by Gene Saks
Music Scored by Neal Hefti Color by MOVIELAB A Paramount Picture
PG

185

185
Art Director: Ed Brodkin
Copywriter: Hank Weintraub
Designer: Paul Crifo
Artist: Paul Crifo
Agency: Diener-Hauser-Greenthal
Client: Paramount Pictures

186

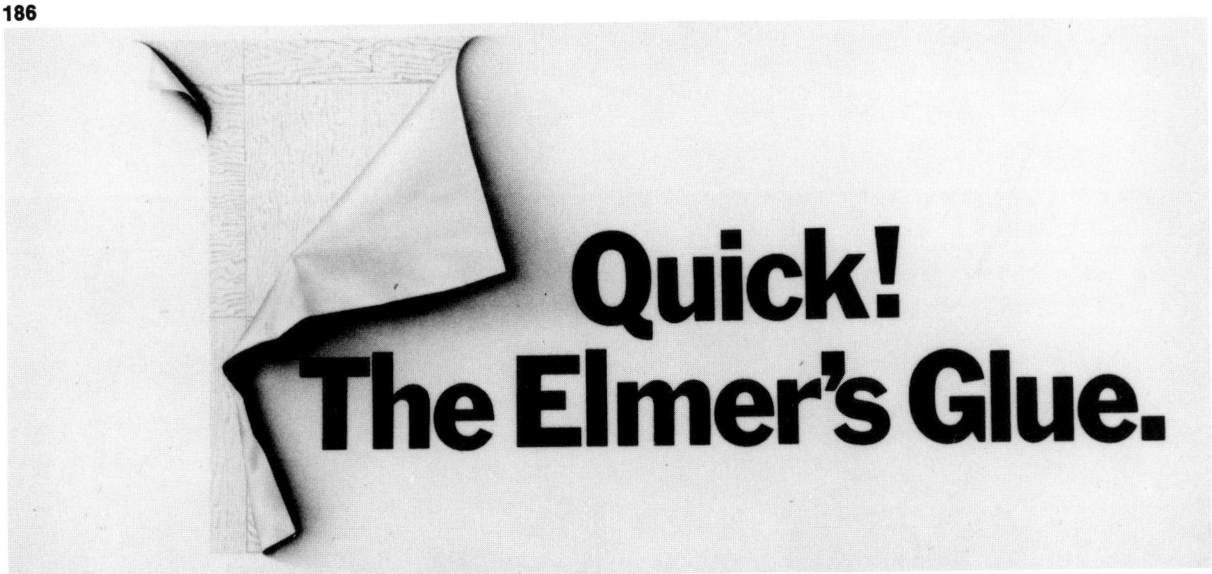
Quick!
The Elmer's Glue.

186 Silver Award
Art Director: Oscar Ross
Copywriter: Oscar Ross
Designer: Oscar Ross
Photographer: Bob Meecham
Agency: Goodis Goldberg Soren
Client: Borden Chemical Company

Dr Pepper may look the same but
it doesn't taste the same.

187

188

PEOPLE
WHO DRINK
NO-CAL.
HAVE NOTHING
TO SHOW FOR IT.
COLA
SUGAR FREE
NO-CAL
COLA

189

Continuous Performances at every table.
Benihana of Tokyo
Marina Del Rey: 14160 Panay Way
Beverly Hills: 38 N. La Cienega Blvd.
Encino: 16226 Ventura Blvd.
Las Vegas, San Francisco, Portland, Seattle, Hawaii

187
Art Director: Ed Rotondi
Copywriter: Neil Bearling
Photographer: George M. Cochran
Agency: Young & Rubicam International, Inc.
Client: Dr. Pepper

188
Art Director: Joe Gregorace
Copywriter: Martin Solow
Designers: Joe Gregorace
Pat Taranto
Photographer: Dean Nakahara
Agency: Solow-Wexton, Inc.
Client: No-Cal Soda Corporation

189
Art Directors: Bob Tore
Aaron Koster
Copywriter: Hans Kracauer
Designer: Bob Tore
Photographer: Alan Brooks
Agency: Kracauer & Marvin
Client: Benihana of Tokyo

189A
Art Director: William Herzog
Designer: William Herzog
Client: O'Mealia Outdoor Advertising Corporation

190
Art Director: George Lois
Copywriter: Ron Holland
Designer: Kurt Weihs
Photographer: Tasso Vendikos
Agency: Lois Holland Callaway, Inc.
Clients: Cutty Sark
Buckingham Corporation

FREE TICKETS
for speeders

189 A

190

If you still can't afford to move to Coral Gables...
CUTTY SARK
BLENDED
"Don't give up the ship!"
Sure your marina raised your dock rent again, but...
CUTTY SARK
BLENDED
"Don't give up the ship!"
Next time the stewardess says "Coffee, Tea or Milk" tell her...
CUTTY SARK
BLENDED
"Don't give up the ship!"
Whether you're a man or a Mouse...
CUTTY SARK
BLENDED
"Don't give up the ship!"
If every year first base seems farther away...
CUTTY SARK
BLENDED
"Don't give up the ship!"
Drink your Orange Juice every morning, but...
CUTTY SARK
BLENDED
"Don't give up the ship!"
Keep 'em flying, but...
CUTTY SARK
BLENDED
"Don't give up the ship!"
When your betting system is going to the dogs...
CUTTY SARK
BLENDED
"Don't give up the ship!"
If you just peel while others tan...
CUTTY SARK
BLENDED
"Don't give up the ship!"
If you're driving through Lion country and your windows won't close...
CUTTY SARK
BLENDED
"Don't give up the ship!"
Keep 'em flying, but...
CUTTY SARK
BLENDED
"Don't give up the ship!"
"I gave up all hopes of breaking 90, but...
CUTTY SARK
BLENDED
I won't give up the ship!"
If you're the first man on Mars, and you spy other footsteps...
CUTTY SARK
BLENDED
"Don't give up the ship!"
If you still can't afford to move to Palm Beach...
CUTTY SARK
BLENDED
"Don't give up the ship!"
When you realize the Doc gelded your fastest colt...
CUTTY SARK
BLENDED
"Don't give up the ship!"
Whether you're sneezy or sleepy or happy or grumpy...
CUTTY SARK
BLENDED
"Don't give up the ship!"
Go to jai alai or go to the dogs, but...
CUTTY SARK
BLENDED
"Don't give up the ship!"
Drink your Orange Juice every morning, but...
CUTTY SARK
BLENDED
"Don't give up the ship!"
Drink your Orange Juice every morning, but...
CUTTY SARK
BLENDED
"Don't give up the ship!"
Even when you're a thousand miles inland...
CUTTY SARK
BLENDED
"Don't give up the ship!"
Next time the stewardess says "Coffee, Tea or Milk" tell her...
CUTTY SARK
BLENDED
"Don't give up the ship!"
To every school clamoring to play in our Gator Bowl...
CUTTY SARK
BLENDED
"Don't give up the ship!"
Drink your Orange Juice every morning, but...
CUTTY SARK
BLENDED
"Don't give up the ship!"
Drink your Orange Juice every morning, but...
CUTTY SARK
BLENDED
"Don't give up the ship!"

191

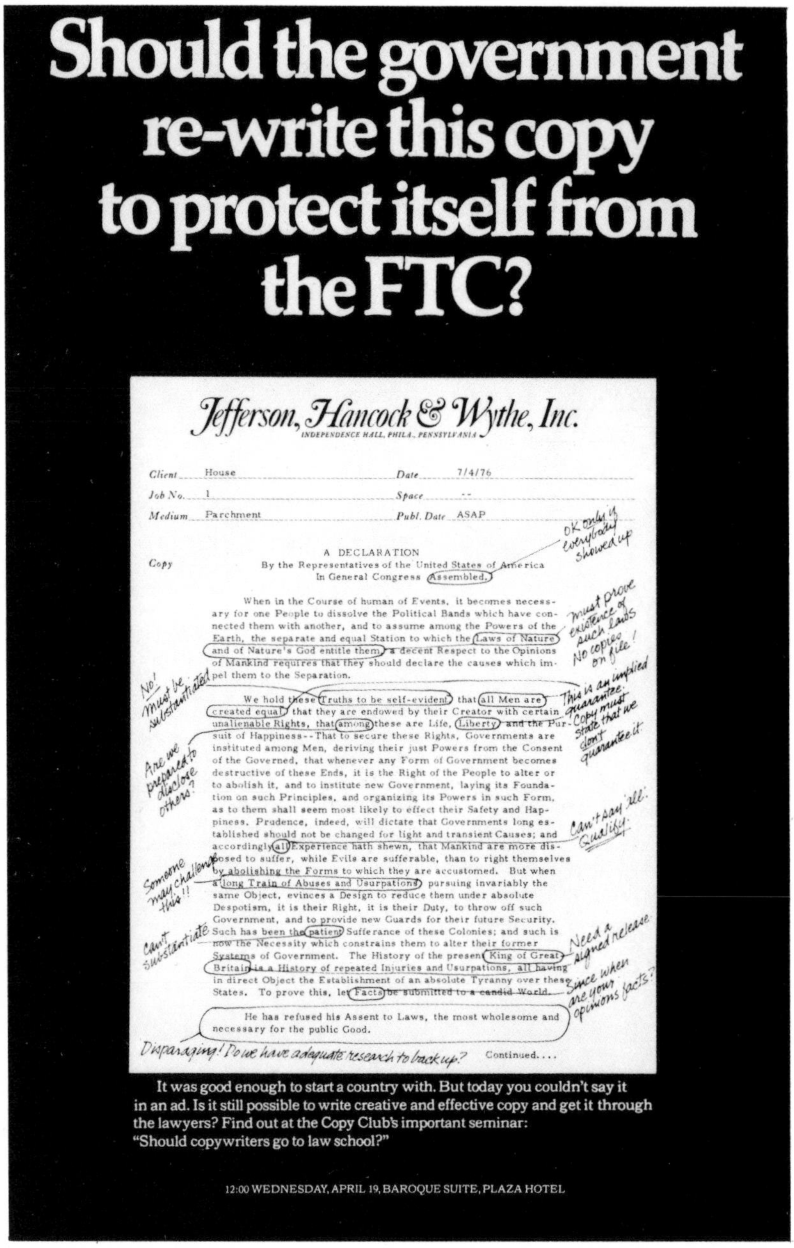
Should the government re-write this copy to protect itself from the FTC?
Jefferson, Hancock & Wythe, Inc.
INDEPENDENCE HALL, PHILA., PENNSYLVANIA
Client House
Date 7/4/76
Job No. 1
Space --
Medium Parchment
Publ. Date ASAP
Copy
A DECLARATION
By the Representatives of the United States of America
In General Congress Assembled.
When in the Course of human of Events, it becomes necessary for one People to dissolve the Political Bands which have connected them with another, and to assume among the Powers of the Earth, the separate and equal Station to which the Laws of Nature and of Nature's God entitle them, a decent Respect to the Opinions of Mankind requires that they should declare the causes which impel them to the Separation.
We hold these Truths to be self-evident, that all Men are created equal, that they are endowed by their Creator with certain unalienable Rights, that among these are Life, Liberty and the Pursuit of Happiness--That to secure these Rights, Governments are instituted among Men, deriving their just Powers from the Consent of the Governed, that whenever any Form of Government becomes destructive of these Ends, it is the Right of the People to alter or to abolish it, and to institute new Government, laying its Foundation on such Principles, and organizing its Powers in such Form, as to them shall seem most likely to effect their Safety and Happiness. Prudence, indeed, will dictate that Governments long established should not be changed for light and transient Causes; and accordingly all Experience hath shewn, that Mankind are more disposed to suffer, while Evils are sufferable, than to right themselves by abolishing the Forms to which they are accustomed. But when a long Train of Abuses and Usurpations, pursuing invariably the same Object, evinces a Design to reduce them under absolute Despotism, it is their Right, it is their Duty, to throw off such Government, and to provide new Guards for their future Security. Such has been the patient Sufferance of these Colonies; and such is now the Necessity which constrains them to alter their former Systems of Government. The History of the present King of Great Britain is a History of repeated Injuries and Usurpations, all having in direct Object the Establishment of an absolute Tyranny over these States. To prove this, let Facts be submitted to a candid World.
He has refused his Assent to Laws, the most wholesome and necessary for the public Good.
Continued....
OK only if everybody showed up
must prove existence of such laws No copies on file!
No! must be substantiated
This is an implied guarantee. Copy must state that we don't guarantee it.
Are we prepared to disclose others?
Can't say 'all'. Qualify.
Someone may challenge this!!
Can't substantiate
Need a signed release
Since when are your opinions facts?
Disparaging! Do we have adequate research to back up?
It was good enough to start a country with. But today you couldn't say it in an ad. Is it still possible to write creative and effective copy and get it through the lawyers? Find out at the Copy Club's important seminar: "Should copywriters go to law school?"
12:00 WEDNESDAY, APRIL 19, BAROQUE SUITE, PLAZA HOTEL

191 Silver Award
Art Director: Joe Schindelman
Copywriter: Ed McCabe
Designer: Joe Schindelman
Agency: Scali, McCabe, Sloves, Inc.
Client: The Copy Club of New York

192
Art Director: Bill Berenter
Copywriter: Tom Nathan
Designer: Bill Berenter
Artist: Milton Glaser
Agency: Scali, McCabe, Sloves, Inc.
Client: Volvo, Inc.

193
Art Director: Bill Berenter
Copywriter: Tom Nathan
Designer: Bill Berenter
Agency: Scali, McCabe, Sloves, Inc.
Client: Volvo, Inc.

194 Gold Award
Art Director: Joe Gregorace
Copywriter: Peter Nord
Designer: Joe Gregorace
Photographer: David Spindell
Agency: Solow-Wexton, Inc.
Client: ILGWU

192

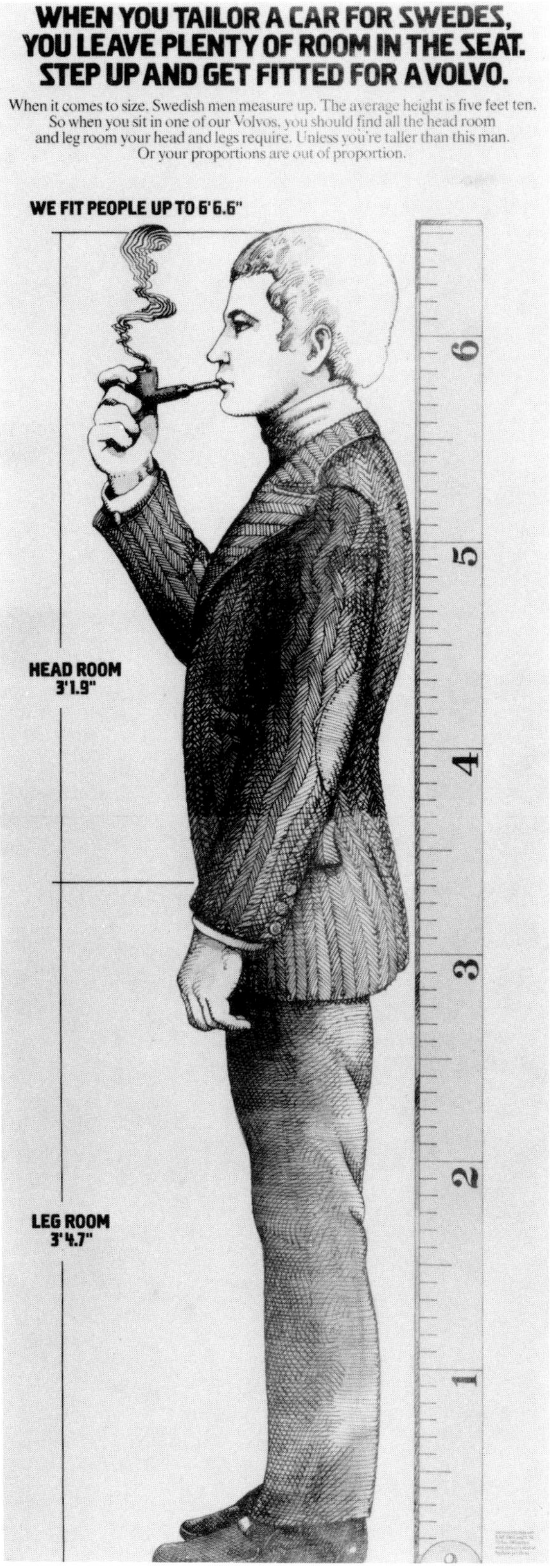
WHEN YOU TAILOR A CAR FOR SWEDES, YOU LEAVE PLENTY OF ROOM IN THE SEAT. STEP UP AND GET FITTED FOR A VOLVO.
When it comes to size, Swedish men measure up. The average height is five feet ten. So when you sit in one of our Volvos, you should find all the head room and leg room your head and legs require. Unless you're taller than this man. Or your proportions are out of proportion.
WE FIT PEOPLE UP TO 6'6.6"
HEAD ROOM 3'1.9"
LEG ROOM 3'4.7"
6
5
4
3
2
1

IT'S RUMORED THAT IN SCANDINAVIA VOLVOS LAST LONGER THAN FJORDS.

193

194

Made in Japan.
Every year, Americans salute more and more American flags that weren't made in America. Flags that bear the stars and stripes and little tags reading Made in Japan or Taiwan or Hong Kong.
Those flags aren't the only things with such labels. As low-wage, foreign goods flood the market, American industries shut down. As industries shut down, people lose jobs.
When people lose their jobs, they can't buy the things you make. Chances are if Betsy Ross (the Philadelphia seamstress who made the first American flag for George Washington) were alive today, she'd be standing in line for her unemployment check.
So help yourself and help us by looking for the union label in everything you buy. You can find our label in women's and children's garments.
This label stands for the creativity of American design, the skill of American workmanship, the importance of American jobs.
ILGWU
Made in U.S.A.
Union Label Department, International Ladies' Garment Workers' Union, 22 W. 38th Street, New York, N.Y. 10018

195

Baseball.
The Great Un-American Game.
Exhibit A
IMPORTED
Most of the baseballs and baseball gloves we use aren't made in America any more.
They're made in foreign countries at starvation wages. Such imports are destroying the jobs of American workers.
When Americans don't buy what other Americans make, Americans lose their jobs. To keep America at work, look for this label when you buy women's and children's clothes.
The job you save may be your own.
STOP IMPORTING UNEMPLOYMENT
ILGWU
Made in U.S.A.

196

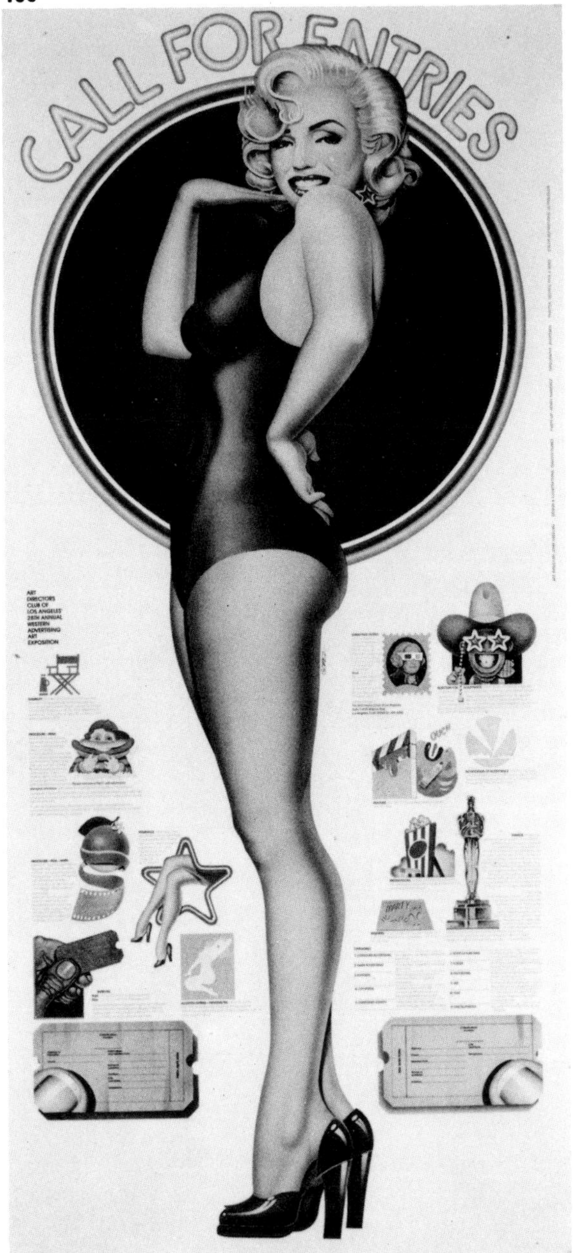
CALL FOR ENTRIES
ART DIRECTORS CLUB OF LOS ANGELES' 28TH ANNUAL WESTERN ADVERTISING ART EXPOSITION

197

Made in America
Closed factories, lofts, stores. More and more unemployment. Who did it? Many of us.
Because when Americans don't buy the goods that Americans make—that puts Americans out of work.
So save American jobs by looking for the union label when you buy women's and children's apparel.
The job you save may be your own.
STOP IMPORTING UNEMPLOYMENT
INT. LADIES GARMENT WORKERS UNION
UNION MADE
ILGWU
AFL-CIO
Made in U.S.A.

195
Art Director: Jim Raniere
Copywriter: Peter Nord
Designer: Jim Raniere
Photographer: Buddy Endress
Agency: Solow-Wexton, Inc.
Client: ILGWU

196
Art Director: John Anselmo
Copywriter: A.D.L.A.
Designer: Ignacio Gomez
Artist: Ignacio Gomez
Client: Art Directors Club of Los Angeles

197
Art Director: Jim Raniere
Copywriters: Peter Nord
Martin Solow
Designer: Jim Raniere
Photographer: Charles Wiesehahn
Agency: Solow-Wexton, Inc.
Client: ILGWU

199
Art Director: Bob Tabor
Copywriter: Elliot Firestone
Photographer: Michael Pateman
Agency: Richard K. Manoff Inc.
Client: New York City Off-Track
Betting Corporation

199

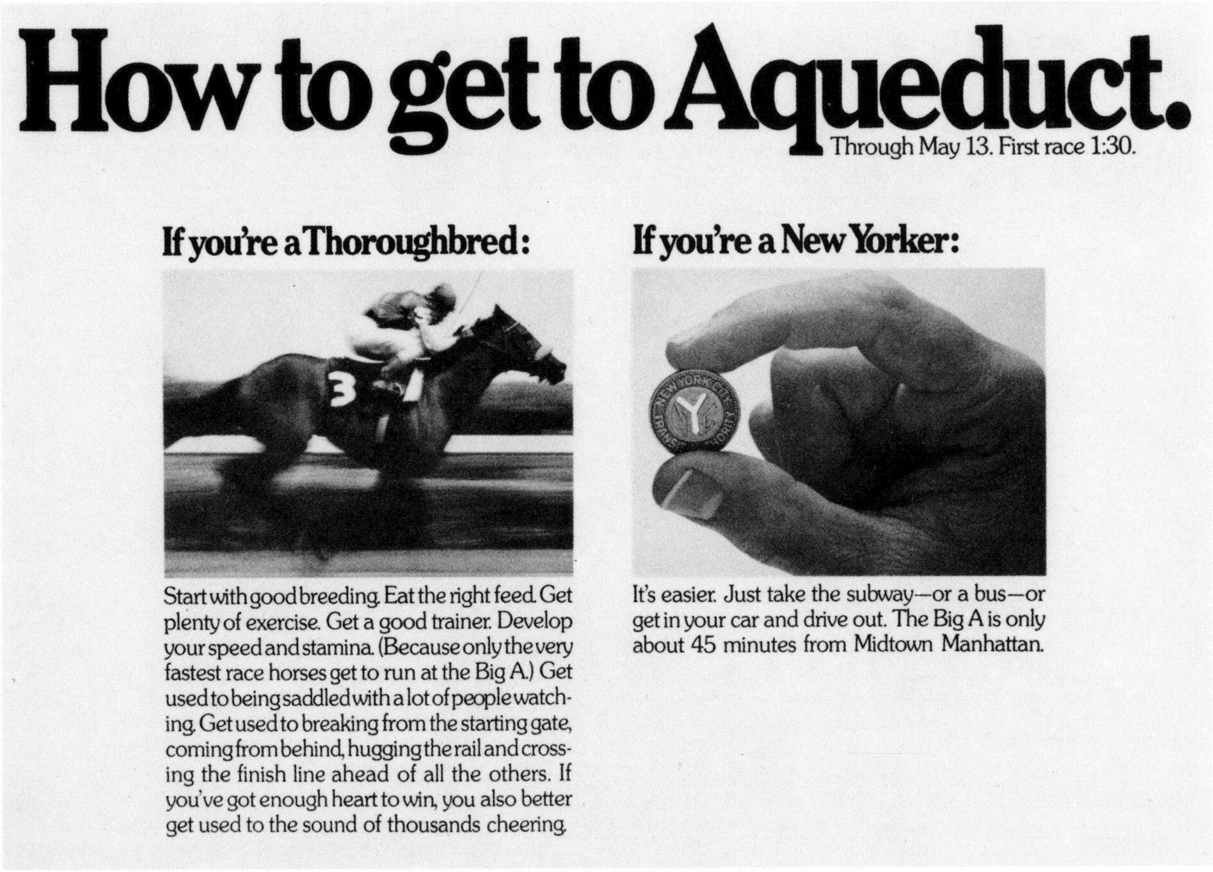
How to get to Aqueduct.
Through May 13. First race 1:30.
If you're a Thoroughbred:
3
Start with good breeding. Eat the right feed. Get plenty of exercise. Get a good trainer. Develop your speed and stamina. (Because only the very fastest race horses get to run at the Big A.) Get used to being saddled with a lot of people watching. Get used to breaking from the starting gate, coming from behind, hugging the rail and crossing the finish line ahead of all the others. If you've got enough heart to win, you also better get used to the sound of thousands cheering.
If you're a New Yorker:
NEW YORK CITY
Y
It's easier. Just take the subway—or a bus—or get in your car and drive out. The Big A is only about 45 minutes from Midtown Manhattan.

200

201

50¢
NEW YORK STATE
Lottery
Commissioner of Taxation and Finance
SERIES
ACCOUNTING NUMBER
DRAWING DATE
TICKET NUMBER
247809
Play it again, Sam.

Posters/Single

200
Art Director: Harvey Gabor
Copywriter: Pacy Markman
Designer: Harvey Gabor
Photographers: Jack Elness
Tony Garcia
Agency: McCann-Erickson, Inc.
Client: New York Racing Association

201
Art Director: Ron Carmel
Copywriter: Dan Berolzheimer
Designer: Ron Carmel
Agency: Fuller & Smith & Ross Inc.
Client: New York State Lottery

202
Art Director: William J. Conlon
Copywriter: Tom Mabley
Designer: William J. Conlon
Photographer: Burk Uzzle
Agency: J. Walter Thompson Company
Client: United States Marine Corps

203
Art Director: George Lois
Copywriter: Ron Holland
Designer: Kurt Weihs
Photographer: Tasso Vendikos
Agency: Lois Holland Callaway, Inc.
Clients: Cutty Sark
Buckingham Corporation

204
Art Director: Allan Beaver
Copywriter: Larry Plapler
Designer: Allan Beaver
Photographer: Mike Cuesta
Agency: Levine, Huntley, Schmidt
Client: E. F. Timme & Son, Inc.

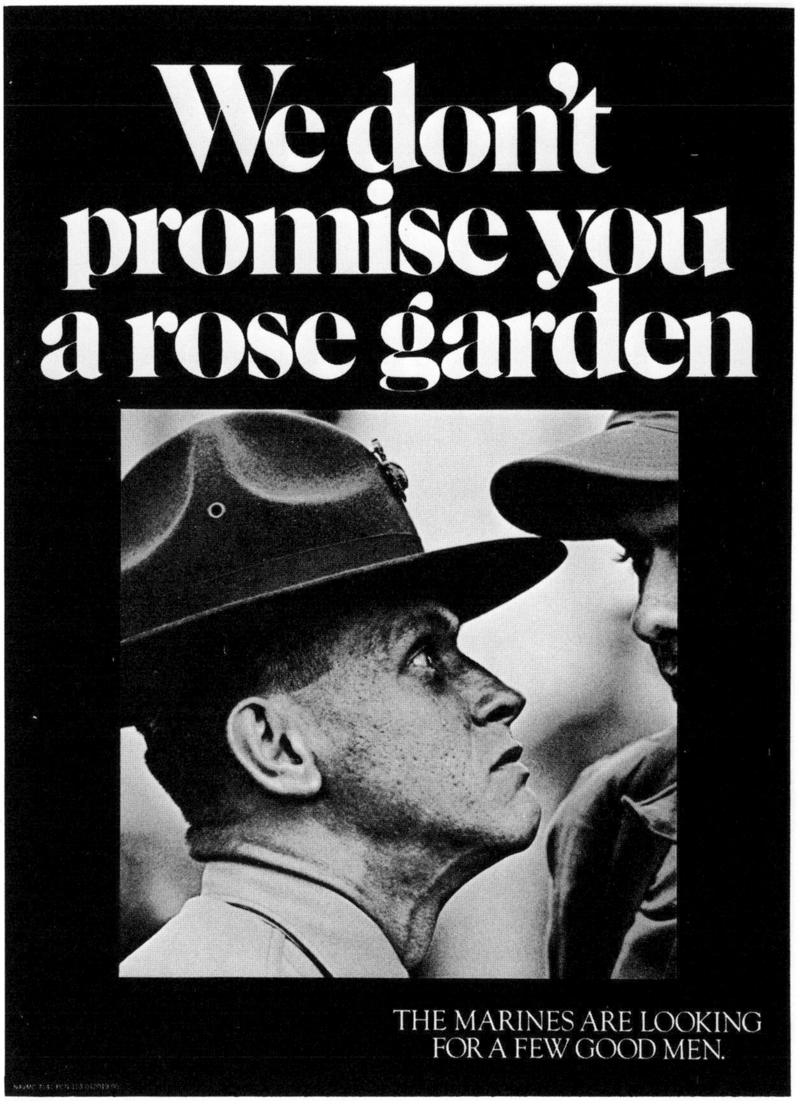
We don't promise you a rose garden
THE MARINES ARE LOOKING FOR A FEW GOOD MEN.

202

203

When you've had it up to here with graffiti...
Distilled and Bottled in Scotland under British Government Supervision
CUTTY SARK
BLENDED
"Don't give up the ship!"

204

With a Timme fake, you can have a beautiful tiger skin. And he can keep his.
Timme fabrics for home sewers.

205

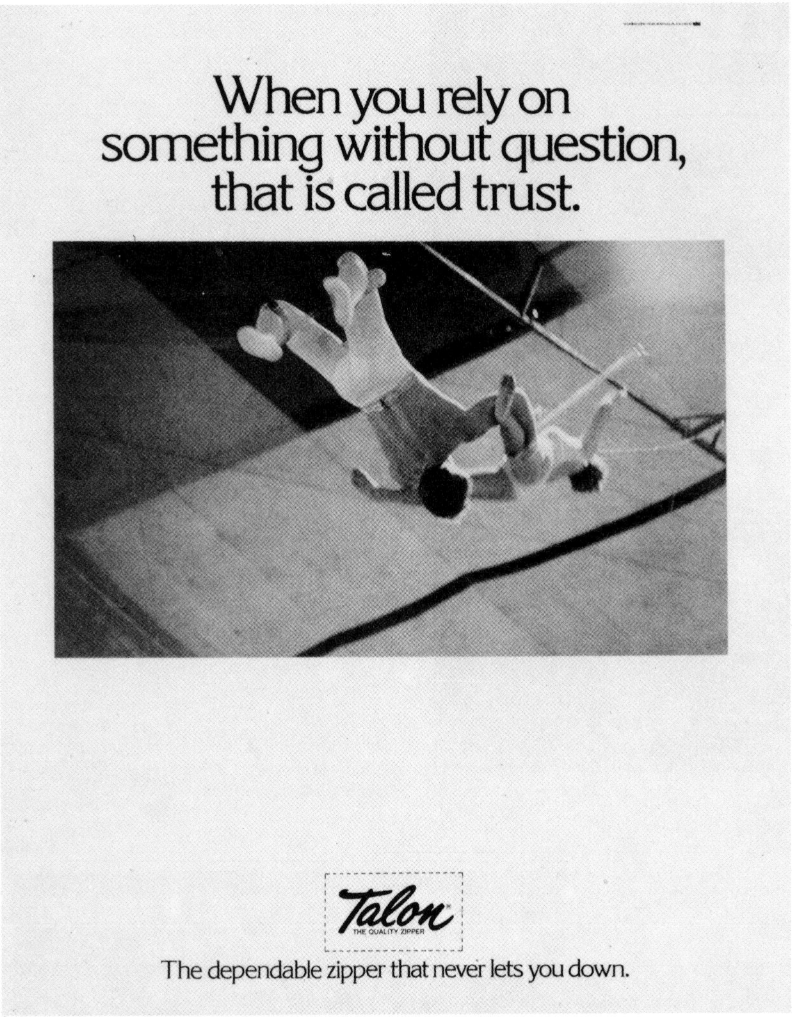
When you rely on
something without question,
that is called trust.
Talon
THE QUALITY ZIPPER
The dependable zipper that never lets you down.

When you are careful not
to hurt anything or anybody,
that is called gentleness.
Talon
The soft nylon zipper that doesn't pinch.

When you can endure all the
burdens and pressures of life,
that is called strength.
Talon
The rugged zipper that never gives up.

205
Art Director: Mike Withers
Copywriter: Joy Golden
Designer: Mike Withers
Photographers: Ernst Haas
David McCabe
Benno Friedman
Agency: DKG Inc.
Client: Talon

206
Art Director: Ivan Chermayeff
Designers: Ivan Chermayeff
William Sontag
Photographers: Dennis Stock
Bert Glynn
Phillip Jones
Anthony Edgeworth
Agency: Chermayeff & Geismar Associates
Client: Pan American Airways

Argentina
Pan Am's World

New Zealand
Pan Am's World

Pan Am's World
Africa

Panama
Pan Am's World

A CURE FOR URBAN LEPROSY.
Dresden, Germany 1945.
East New York, 1972.
Give a damn.
New York Urban Coalition

207

100,000 KIDS ARE GOING BLIND FROM A DISEASE YOU NEVER HEARD OF.
How do you tell a child who likes movies and ballet and Louisa May Alcott and 'All in the Family' and bike riding that even though she can see perfectly well right now, she will almost certainly be blind before she is 20? Maybe before she is fifteen.
That she has a disease called Retinitis Pigmentosa which she can't even pronounce, let alone spell. And that you never even heard of it yourself until you found out that your daughter had it.
That it is a hereditary disease, but you didn't even know it was in your family or even which side. That there has been virtually no research done and there's absolutely no cure. That you love her more than anything in the world and would give her your own eyes if you could. But there is nothing you can do about it.
How do you say that to your own child?
We can't. We are the parents of children who have Retinitis Pigmentosa and we refuse to give up.
We have just started the National Retinitis Pigmentosa Foundation to establish a laboratory in the Massachusetts Eye and Ear Infirmary in Boston. It will be staffed with biochemists, anatomists, electrophysiologists, and geneticists, who will devote themselves entirely to this disease. Nobody has ever even tried to do that before. (If you think one of your children, or anyone in your family could have Retinitis Pigmentosa, please write to us. We will do everything we can to help.)
All that we need now is half a million dollars to make it come true.
We know you get asked for money for very worthy causes every day and we don't like to add to your burden. But we have no choice.
If it were your child, what would you do?
RETINITIS PIGMENTOSA
BOX 29
SYOSSET, NY. 11791
I would like to help and am enclosing_____dollars.
My name is_____
Address_____
City_____State_____Zip_____
RETINITIS PIGMENTOSA
All contributions are fully tax exempt.

208

209

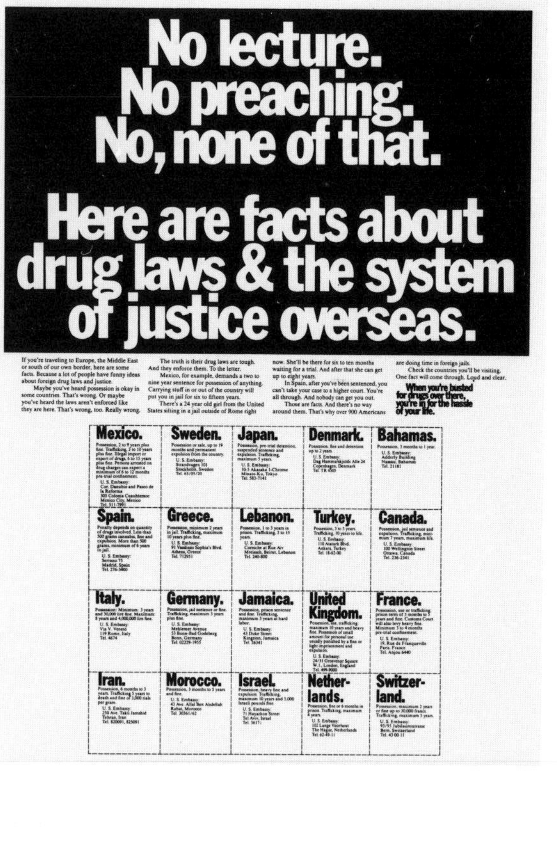

No lecture.
No preaching.
No, none of that.
Here are facts about drug laws & the system of justice overseas.
If you're traveling to Europe, the Middle East or south of our own border, here are some facts. Because a lot of people have funny ideas about foreign drug laws and justice.
Maybe you've heard possession is okay in some countries. That's wrong. Or maybe you've heard the laws aren't enforced like they are here. That's wrong, too. Really wrong.
The truth is their drug laws are tough. And they enforce them. To the letter.
Mexico, for example, demands a two to nine year sentence for possession of anything. Carrying stuff in or out of the country will put you in jail for six to fifteen years.
There's a 24 year old girl from the United States sitting in a jail outside of Rome right now. She'll be there for six to ten months waiting for a trial. And after that she can get up to eight years.
In Spain, after you've been sentenced, you can't take your case to a higher court. You're all through. And nobody can get you out.
Those are facts. And there's no way around them. That's why over 900 Americans are doing time in foreign jails.
Check the countries you'll be visiting. One fact will come through. Loud and clear.
When you're busted for drugs over there, you're in for the hassle of your life.
Mexico.
Possession, 2 to 9 years plus fine. Trafficking, 3 to 10 years plus fine. Illegal import or export of drugs, 6 to 15 years plus fine. Persons arrested on drug charges can expect a minimum of 6 to 12 months pre-trial confinement.
U. S. Embassy: Cor. Danubio and Paseo de la Reforma 305 Colonia Cuauhtemoc Mexico City, Mexico Tel. 511-7991
Sweden.
Possession or sale, up to 19 months and permanent expulsion from the country.
U. S. Embassy: Strandvagen 101 Stockholm, Sweden Tel. 63/05/20
Japan.
Possession, pre-trial detention, suspended sentence and expulsion. Trafficking, maximum 5 years.
U. S. Embassy: 10-5 Akasaka 1-Chrome Minato-Ku, Tokyo Tel. 583-7141
Denmark.
Possession, fine and detention up to 2 years.
U. S. Embassy: Dag Hammarskjolds Alle 24 Copenhagen, Denmark Tel. TR 4505
Bahamas.
Possession, 3 months to 1 year.
U. S. Embassy: Adderly Building Nassau, Bahamas Tel. 21181
Spain.
Penalty depends on quantity of drugs involved. Less than 500 grams cannabis, fine and expulsion. More than 500 grams, minimum of 6 years in jail.
U. S. Embassy: Serrano 75 Madrid, Spain Tel. 276-3400
Greece.
Possession, minimum 2 years in jail. Trafficking, maximum 10 years plus fine.
U. S. Embassy: 91 Vassilissis Sophia's Blvd. Athens, Greece Tel. 712951
Lebanon.
Possession, 1 to 3 years in prison. Trafficking, 3 to 15 years.
U. S. Embassy: Corniche at Rue Aiv Mreisseh, Beirut, Lebanon Tel. 240-800
Turkey.
Possession, 3 to 5 years. Trafficking, 10 years to life.
U. S. Embassy: 110 Ataturk Blvd. Ankara, Turkey Tel. 18-62-00
Canada.
Possession, jail sentence and expulsion. Trafficking, minimum 7 years, maximum life.
U. S. Embassy: 100 Wellington Street Ottawa, Canada Tel. 236-2341
Italy.
Possession: Minimum: 3 years and 30,000 lire fine. Maximum: 8 years and 4,000,000 lire fine.
U. S. Embassy: Via V. Veneto 119 Rome, Italy Tel. 4674
Germany.
Possession, jail sentence or fine. Trafficking, maximum 3 years plus fine.
U. S. Embassy: Mehlemer Avenue 53 Bonn-Bad Godeberg Bonn, Germany Tel. 02229-1955
Jamaica.
Possession, prison sentence and fine. Trafficking, maximum 3 years at hard labor.
U. S. Embassy: 43 Duke Street Kingston, Jamaica Tel. 26341
United Kingdom.
Possession, use, trafficking: maximum 10 years and heavy fine. Possession of small amount for personal use usually punished by a fine or light imprisonment and expulsion.
U. S. Embassy: 24/31 Grosvenor Square W.1., London, England Tel. 499-9000
France.
Possession, use or trafficking: prison term of 3 months to 5 years and fine. Customs Court will also levy heavy fine. Minimum 3 to 4 months pre-trial confinement.
U. S. Embassy: 19, Rue de Franqueville Paris, France Tel. Anjou 6440
Iran.
Possession, 6 months to 3 years. Trafficking 5 years to death and fine of 3,000 rials per gram.
U. S. Embassy: 250 Ave. Takti Jamshid Tehran, Iran Tel. 820091, 825091
Morocco.
Possession, 3 months to 5 years and fine.
U. S. Embassy: 43 Ave. Allal Ben Abdellah Rabat, Morocco Tel. 30361/62
Israel.
Possession, heavy fine and expulsion. Trafficking, maximum 10 years and 5,000 Israeli pounds fine.
U. S. Embassy: 71 Hayarkon Street Tel Aviv, Israel Tel. 56171
Netherlands.
Possession, fine or 6 months in prison. Trafficking, maximum 4 years.
U. S. Embassy: 102 Lange Voorhout The Hague, Netherlands Tel. 62-49-11
Switzerland.
Possession, maximum 2 years or fine up to 30,000 francs. Trafficking, maximum 5 years.
U. S. Embassy: 93/95 Jubilaumsstrasse Bern, Switzerland Tel. 43 00 11

210

This space contributed by the publisher as a public service.
Lick cancer.
Cancer c/o Postmaster Your Town, State, Zip
Send a contribution. We want to wipe out cancer in your lifetime. American Cancer Society.

Print/Public Service/Single

I WAS IN LOVE WITH A GIRL NAMED CATHY.
I KILLED HER.
"It was last summer, and I was 18. Cathy was 18 too. It was the happiest summer of my life. I had never been that happy before. I haven't been that happy since. And I know I'll never be that happy again. It was warm and beautiful and so we bought a few bottles of wine and drove to the country to celebrate the night. We drank the wine and looked at the stars and held each other and laughed. It must have been the stars and the wine and the warm wind. Nobody else was on the road. The top was down, and we were singing and my hair was blowing all over my face and I didn't even see the tree until I hit it."
Every year 8,000 American people between the ages of 15 and 25 are killed in alcohol related crashes. That's more than Viet Nam. More than drugs. More than suicide. More than cancer.
The people on this page are not real. But what happened to them is very real.
The automobile crash is the number one cause of death of people your age. And the ironic thing is that the drunk drivers responsible for killing young people are most often other young people.
DRUNK DRIVER, DEPT. Y
BOX 1969
WASHINGTON, D. C. 20013
I don't want to get killed and I don't want to kill anyone. Tell me how I can help.
My name is
Address
City State Zip
STOP DRIVING DRUNK.
STOP KILLING EACH OTHER.
U.S. DEPARTMENT OF TRANSPORTATION • NATIONAL HIGHWAY TRAFFIC SAFETY ADMINISTRATION

211

207
Art Director: Dick Calderhead
Copywriter: Dick Jackson
Designer: Barbara Schubeck
Photographer: Harold Krieger
Agency: Calderhead, Jackson Inc.
Client: The New York Urban Coalition

208
Art Director: Alan Kupchick
Copywriter: Enid Futterman
Designer: Alan Kupchick
Photographer: Phoebe Dunn
Agency: Service Art Studio
Client: National Retinitis Pigmentosa Foundation

209
Art Director: Al Shapiro
Copywriter: Tom Hemphill
Artist: Howard Brady
Agency: Vansant Dugdale
Client: White House Special Action Office for Drug Abuse Prevention

210
Art Director: Ivan Liberman
Copywriter: Al Hampel
Photographer: Geoffrey Forest
Agency: Benton & Bowles, Inc.
Client: American Cancer Society

211
Art Director: Alan Kupchick
Copywriter: Enid Futterman
Designer: Alan Kupchick
Photographer: Joe Toto
Agency: Grey Advertising, Inc.
Client: National Highway Traffic Safety Administration

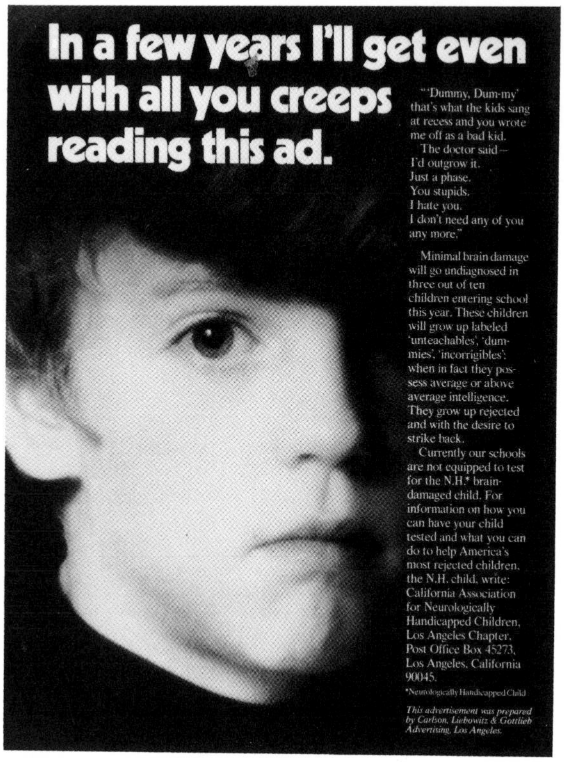

In a few years I'll get even with all you creeps reading this ad.
"'Dummy, Dum-my' that's what the kids sang at recess and you wrote me off as a bad kid.
The doctor said—
I'd outgrow it.
Just a phase.
You stupids.
I hate you.
I don't need any of you any more."
Minimal brain damage will go undiagnosed in three out of ten children entering school this year. These children will grow up labeled 'unteachables', 'dummies', 'incorrigibles': when in fact they possess average or above average intelligence. They grow up rejected and with the desire to strike back.
Currently our schools are not equipped to test for the N.H.* brain-damaged child. For information on how you can have your child tested and what you can do to help America's most rejected children, the N.H. child, write: California Association for Neurologically Handicapped Children, Los Angeles Chapter, Post Office Box 45273, Los Angeles, California 90045.
*Neurologically Handicapped Child
This advertisement was prepared by Carlson, Liebowitz & Gottlieb Advertising, Los Angeles.

212

BY THE TIME YOU FINISH THIS NEWSPAPER, A DRUNK DRIVER WILL HAVE KILLED SOMEONE.

It happens every 20 minutes.

Every 20 minutes of an average day, there's a fatal car accident caused by a drunk driver.

Sometimes he kills a man. Sometimes a woman. Sometimes a child. And sometimes he kills himself.

He doesn't mean to. But he can't help it. And it keeps happening.

Every 20 minutes.

It's probably not the first time he was drunk and driving. And he's probably very drunk. Something like eight shots of bourbon in a couple of hours. In fact, the chances are two out of three that he's a heavy, serious problem drinker.

The problem drinker is the problem. And we have to get him off the road because he can't get himself off.

There are many things that can be done to help him and to help us. Stricter drunk driving laws, stricter law enforcement, scientific breath tests, and court supervised treatment among them. There's a huge national highway safety project just beginning that needs you to understand and to help.

Help.

DRUNK DRIVER
BOX 1969
WASHINGTON, D.C. 20013

I want to help. Please tell me how.

My name is__________
Address__________
City______ State_____ Zip_____

GET THE PROBLEM DRINKER OFF THE ROAD. FOR HIS SAKE. AND YOURS.

213

214

When was the last time you had your period?

If you're two weeks overdue, don't wait. Consult your doctor. And if you *are* pregnant and you want an abortion, consult us.

We can help you get a legal, safe, inexpensive abortion. By an M.D. in a clinic or hospital.

If you have the abortion during the first 10 weeks of pregnancy, it will cost only about $150. And no matter when you have it, there's no charge for our service.

Even if you got your period yesterday, we're a good number to remember: (212) 489-7794 Monday through Friday, between 10 a.m. and 5 p.m. New York time.

Free Abortion Referral Service from ZPG-New York

212
Art Director: Israel Liebowitz
Copywriter: Janet Carlson
Designer: Israel Liebowitz
Photographer: Tom Bartone
Agency: Carlson, Liebowitz & Gottlieb
Client: California Association for Neurologicall
Handicapped Children

213
Art Director: Alan Kupchick
Copywriter: Enid Futterman
Designer: Alan Kupchick
Agency: Grey Advertising, Inc.
Client: National Highway Traffic
Safety Administration

214
Art Director: Don Slater
Copywriter: Jim Parry
Agency: Parry Associates
Client: Zero Population Growth

Print/Public Service/Single

215
Art Director: Jerry Torchia
Copywriter: Michael Gaffney
Designer: Jerry Torchia
Photographer: John Whitehead
Agency: Cargill, Wilson & Acree, Inc.
Client: Richmond Red Cross

216
Art Director: Don Slater
Copywriter: Jim Parry
Agency: Parry Associates
Client: Zero Population Growth

217
Art Director: Alan Kupchick
Copywriter: Enid Futterman
Designer: Alan Kupchick
Agency: Grey Advertising, Inc.
Client: National Highway Traffic Safety Administration

When your husband and kids are out of the house, you'll have time to get involved with a stranger.

215

216

The main difference between a $150 abortion and a $1000 abortion is the doctor makes an extra $850.
Expensive abortions are a hangover from when abortions were illegal. But today we can help you get a legal, safe—and inexpensive—abortion. By an M.D. in a clinic or hospital.
If you have the abortion during the first 10 weeks of pregnancy, it will cost only about $150. And no matter when you have it, there's no charge for our service.
We know some doctors who care more about people than money.
Call us at (212) 489-7794 Monday through Friday, between 10 a.m. and 5 p.m. New York time.
Free Abortion Referral Service from ZPG-New York

217

DRUNK DRIVER
BOX 1969
WASHINGTON, D.C. 20013
I want to help stop the killing on the highways.
My name is
Address
City State Zip
THIS COUPON COULD SAVE YOUR LIFE.
Every day 150 people die on our streets and highways. And drunk drivers are responsible for one-third of those deaths.
A drunk driver doesn't kill on purpose. He can't help it. But it keeps happening.
It's probably not the first time he's drunk and driving. And he's probably very drunk. Something like eight drinks in a couple of hours. In fact, the chances are two out of three that he's a heavy, serious problem drinker.
The problem drinker is the problem. And we have to get him off the road because he can't get himself off.
There are many things that can be done to help him and to help us. Stricter drunk driving laws, stricter law enforcement, scientific breath tests, and court supervised treatment among them. We can't tell you everything you should know here. But if you send us the coupon, we'll send you a booklet that can. There's a huge national highway safety project just beginning that needs you to understand and to help.
Help.
GET THE PROBLEM DRINKER OFF THE ROAD. FOR HIS SAKE. AND YOURS.
U.S. DEPARTMENT OF TRANSPORTATION • NATIONAL HIGHWAY TRAFFIC SAFETY ADMINISTRATION

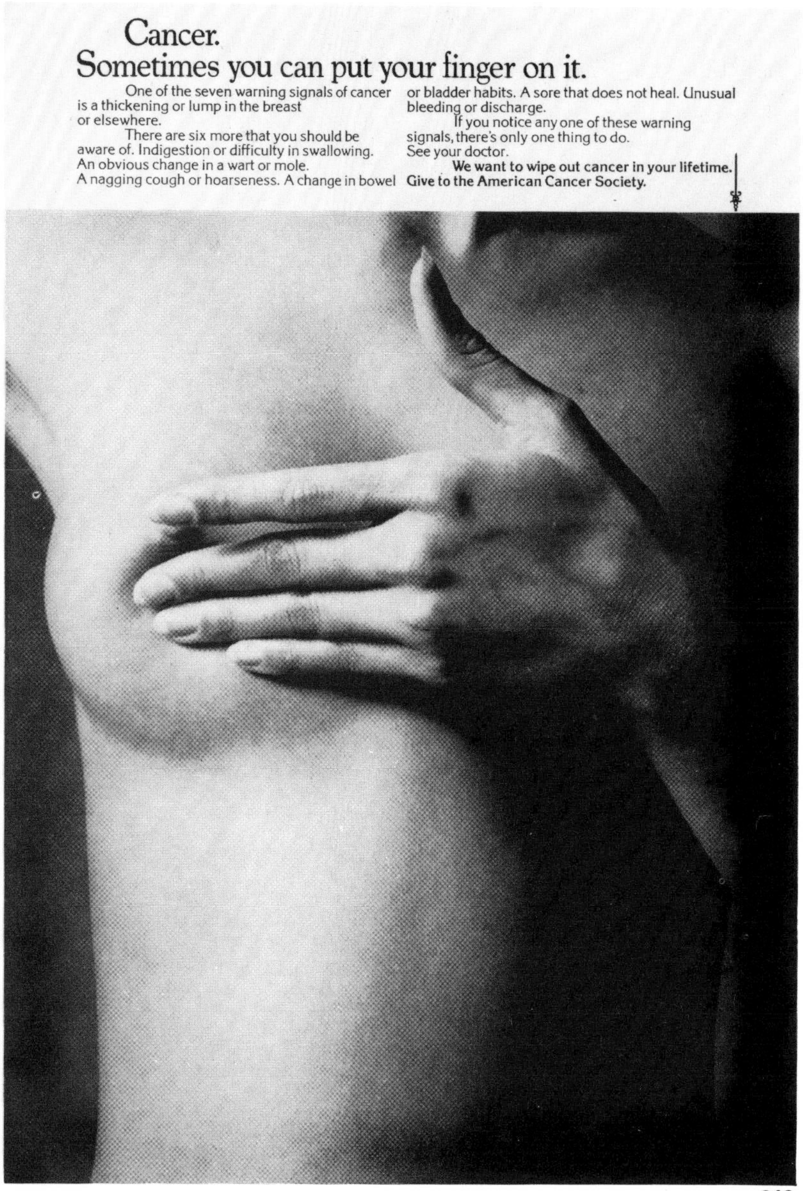
Cancer.
Sometimes you can put your finger on it.
One of the seven warning signals of cancer is a thickening or lump in the breast or elsewhere.
There are six more that you should be aware of. Indigestion or difficulty in swallowing. An obvious change in a wart or mole. A nagging cough or hoarseness. A change in bowel or bladder habits. A sore that does not heal. Unusual bleeding or discharge.
If you notice any one of these warning signals, there's only one thing to do. See your doctor.
We want to wipe out cancer in your lifetime. Give to the American Cancer Society.

218

218
Art Director: Ivan Liberman
Copywriter: Suellen Gelman
Photographer: Richard Avedon
Agency: Benton & Bowles, Inc.
Client: American Cancer Society

219
Art Director: Hal Goluboff
Copywriter: Gloria Remen
Photographer: Menken/Seltzer
Agency: Richard K. Manoff Inc.
Client: Planned Parenthood World Population

220
Art Director: Arthur Gelb
Copywriter: Mike Silverman
Designers: Arthur Gelb, Kenneth Ferretti
Photographer: Rupert Callender
Agency: Art Gelb Advertising, Inc.
Client: The Development Council

221
Art Director: Stan Block
Copywriter: Deanna Cohen
Designer: Stan Block
Photographers: Arnold Newman, Manny Gonzales
Agency: Doyle Dane Bernbach Inc.
Client: The Brooklyn Institute of Arts and Sciences

222
Art Director: Joe Gregorace
Copywriter: Martin Solow
Designer: Joe Gregorace
Artists: Vietnamese Children
Agency: Solow-Wexton, Inc.
Client: Campaign to End the War

Photo by Menken/Seltzer
Your girlfriends can get you pregnant faster than your husband.
Sometimes it looks like there's a conspiracy to get you to have children.
You're married and it's great being alone with your husband, discovering each other and feeling free to do whatever you want.
But already your girlfriends are telling you how wonderful children are and how selfish it is to wait and anything else they can think of to make you feel guilty.
Actually the girls are only part of it.
Let us not forget the future grandparents, bless their impatient hearts.
There's an awful lot of pressure on you.
It becomes hard to resist.
But if you want to, you have to know the facts of birth planning. (Lots of people who think they know, don't. Research statistics show that more than half the pregnancies each year are accidental.)
As for the pressure from relatives and friends, just remember that if you're going to have a baby it should be because you really want one.
Not because you were talked into it.
Planned Parenthood
Children by choice. Not chance.
For further information, write Planned Parenthood, Box 431, Radio City Station, New York, N.Y. 10019.
Planned Parenthood is a national, non-profit organization dedicated to providing information and effective means of family planning to all who want and need it.
advertising contributed for the public good

219

220

221

222

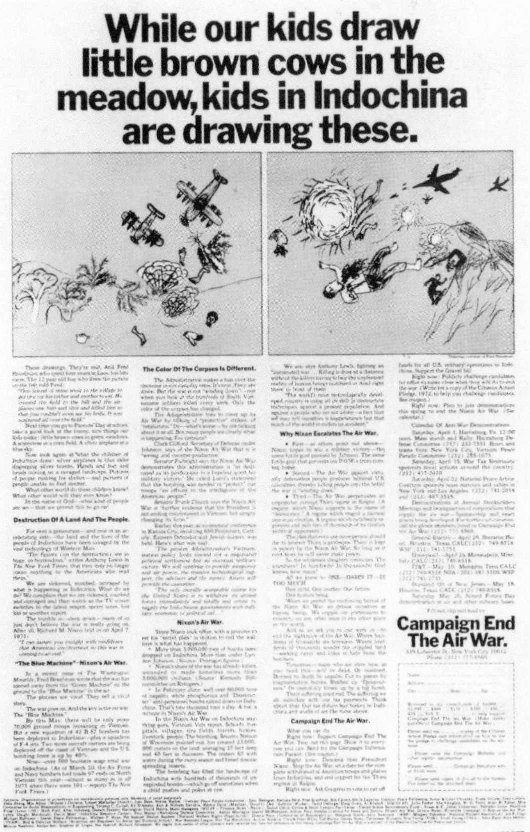

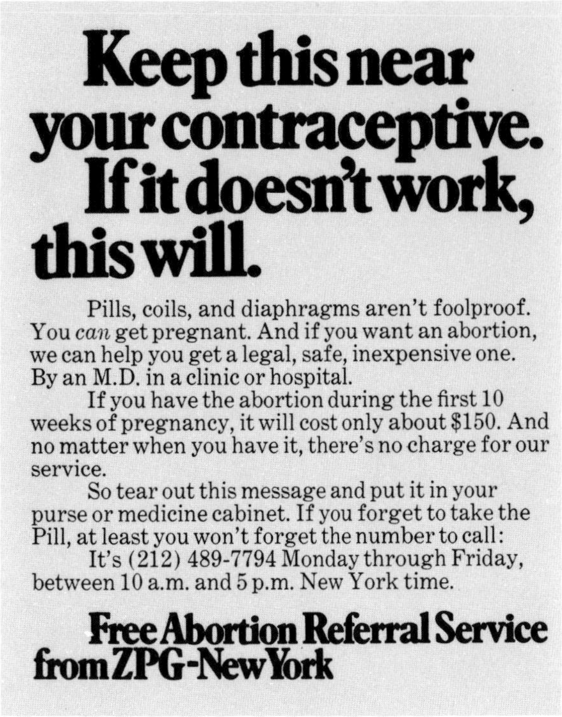
Keep this near your contraceptive. If it doesn't work, this will.
Pills, coils, and diaphragms aren't foolproof. You *can* get pregnant. And if you want an abortion, we can help you get a legal, safe, inexpensive one. By an M.D. in a clinic or hospital.
If you have the abortion during the first 10 weeks of pregnancy, it will cost only about $150. And no matter when you have it, there's no charge for our service.
So tear out this message and put it in your purse or medicine cabinet. If you forget to take the Pill, at least you won't forget the number to call:
It's (212) 489-7794 Monday through Friday, between 10 a.m. and 5 p.m. New York time.
Free Abortion Referral Service from ZPG-New York

223

Print/Public Service/Single

223
Art Director: Don Slater
Copywriter: Jim Parry
Agency: Parry Associates
Client: Zero Population Growth

224
Art Director: Tom Clemente
Copywriters: Jim Dunaway
Hank Simons
Designer: John McInnes
Photographer: John McInnes
Agency: Newspaper Advertising Bureau
Client: Anti-Shoplifting Campaign of U.S. and Canada

225
Art Directors: Dick Calderhead
Norm Siegel
Copywriter: Wally Weis
Designer: Barbara Schubeck
Artist: Stan Mack
Agency: Calderhead, Jackson Inc.
Client: Committee for No-Fault Insurance

224

This is where shoplifting stops being "fun."
If you've ever thought about doing a little shoplifting, think again.
Think how easy it is to get caught.
Think how it must *feel* to get caught.
Think how you'd answer the question that's on every job application, "Have you ever been arrested? If so, explain."
Think how—to the people you know, and the people you love, and yes, even to yourself—you can never be the same person again.
Think about it.
Presented as a public service by: NEWSPAPER LOGO OR LIST OF SPONSORING MERCHANTS HERE

225

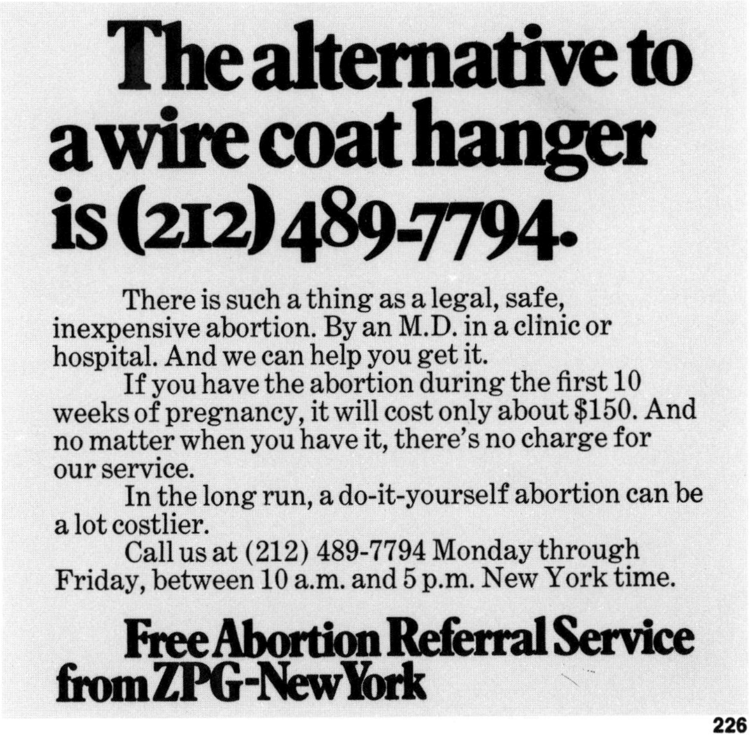
The alternative to a wire coat hanger is (212) 489-7794.
There is such a thing as a legal, safe, inexpensive abortion. By an M.D. in a clinic or hospital. And we can help you get it.
If you have the abortion during the first 10 weeks of pregnancy, it will cost only about $150. And no matter when you have it, there's no charge for our service.
In the long run, a do-it-yourself abortion can be a lot costlier.
Call us at (212) 489-7794 Monday through Friday, between 10 a.m. and 5 p.m. New York time.
Free Abortion Referral Service from ZPG-New York

226

226
Art Director: Don Slater
Copywriter: Jim Parry
Agency: Parry Associates
Client: Zero Population Growth

227 Silver Award
Art Director: Michael Uris
Copywriter: Frada Wallach
Photographers: Bob Gomez
Carl Fischer
Agency: Doyle Dane Bernbach Inc.
Client: Federation of Jewish Philanthropies of New York

227

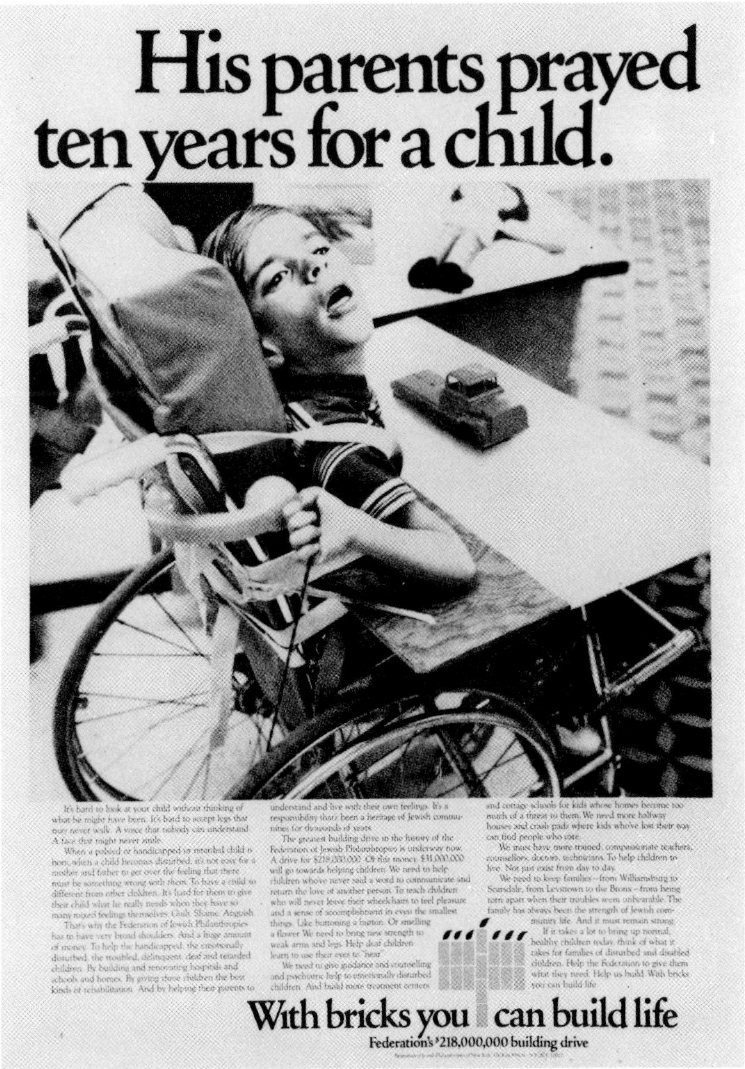
His parents prayed ten years for a child.
It's hard to look at your child without thinking of what he might have been. It's hard to accept legs that may never walk. A voice that nobody can understand. A face that might never smile.
When a palsied or handicapped or retarded child is born, when a child becomes disturbed, it's not easy for a mother and father to get over the feeling that there must be something wrong with them. To have a child so different from other children. It's hard for them to give their child what he really needs when they have so many mixed feelings themselves. Guilt. Shame. Anguish.
That's why the Federation of Jewish Philanthropies has to have very broad shoulders. And a huge amount of money. To help the handicapped, the emotionally disturbed, the troubled, delinquent, deaf and retarded children. By building and renovating hospitals and schools and homes. By giving these children the best kinds of rehabilitation. And by helping their parents to understand and live with their own feelings. It's a responsibility that's been a heritage of Jewish communities for thousands of years.
The greatest building drive in the history of the Federation of Jewish Philanthropies is underway now. A drive for $218,000,000. Of this money, $31,000,000 will go towards helping children. We need to help children who've never said a word to communicate and return the love of another person. To teach children who will never leave their wheelchairs to feel pleasure and a sense of accomplishment in even the smallest things. Like buttoning a button. Or smelling a flower. We need to bring new strength to weak arms and legs. Help deaf children learn to use their eyes to "hear."
We need to give guidance and counselling and psychiatric help to emotionally disturbed children. And build more treatment centers and cottage schools for kids whose homes become too much of a threat to them. We need more halfway houses and crash pads where kids who've lost their way can find people who care.
We must have more trained, compassionate teachers, counsellors, doctors, technicians. To help children to live. Not just exist from day to day.
We need to keep families—from Williamsburg to Scarsdale, from Levittown to the Bronx—from being torn apart when their troubles seem unbearable. The family has always been the strength of Jewish community life. And it must remain strong.
If it takes a lot to bring up normal, healthy children today, think of what it takes for families of disturbed and disabled children. Help the Federation to give them what they need. Help us build. With bricks you can build life.
With bricks you can build life
Federation's $218,000,000 building drive

You can get tan. And you can get cancer.

Maybe you think you look better tan.
Tan looks healthy.

But under that healthy glow you could be
giving skin cancer a head start.

So if you spend a lot of time in the sun, or
if you work outdoors and you have a sore that doesn't
seem to heal, see your doctor. Almost all skin

cancers can be cured if diagnosed early.
If you have fair skin, cover up.
And if you've been lucky so far, plan on a little
less sun this year. You'll be better off for it
in the long run.

We want to wipe out cancer in your lifetime.
Give to the American Cancer Society.

A kid with leukemia can die from a cold.

Leukemia is a disease of the blood-forming
tissues. It keeps the body from producing the
necessary amounts of normal white blood cells to
fight infection.

An infection that means a day in bed for a
normal child is a threat to the life of a child
with leukemia.

Today research has made enormous progress.
A few time, leukemia victims lived only a few
months. Now, in some cases, we can prolong their

lives a few years. That's good. But not good enough.
Then though we're closer to a cure,
leukemia is still the major cause of disease and death
in kids between the ages of 3 and 14.

We want to save the life of every
leukemia victim.

We can't do it without a healthy contribution
from you.

We want to wipe out cancer in your lifetime.
Give to the American Cancer Society.

Cancer.
Sometimes you can put your finger on it.

One of the seven warning signals of cancer
is a thickening or lump in the breast
or elsewhere.

There are six more that you should be
aware of. Indigestion or difficulty in swallowing.
An obvious change in a wart or mole.
A nagging cough or hoarseness. A change in bowel

or bladder habits. A sore that does not heal. Unusual
bleeding or discharge.
If you notice any one of these warning
signals, there's only one thing to do.
See your doctor.

We want to wipe out cancer in your lifetime.
Give to the American Cancer Society.

Print/Public Service/Campaign

228
Art Director: Ivan Liberman
Copywriters: Al Hampel
 Suellen Gelman
 Creative Team
Photographers: Richard Avedon
 Horn/Griner
 Tony Petrucelli
Agency: Benton & Bowles, Inc.
Client: American Cancer Society

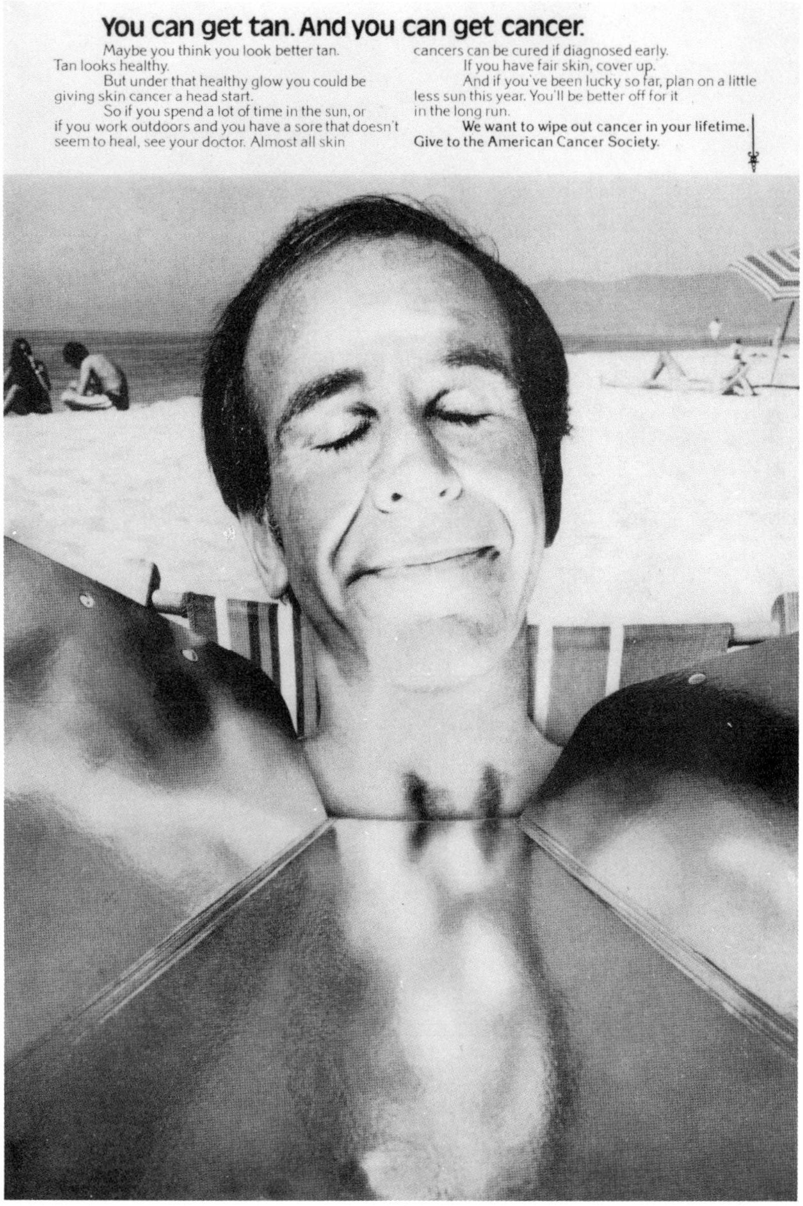

228

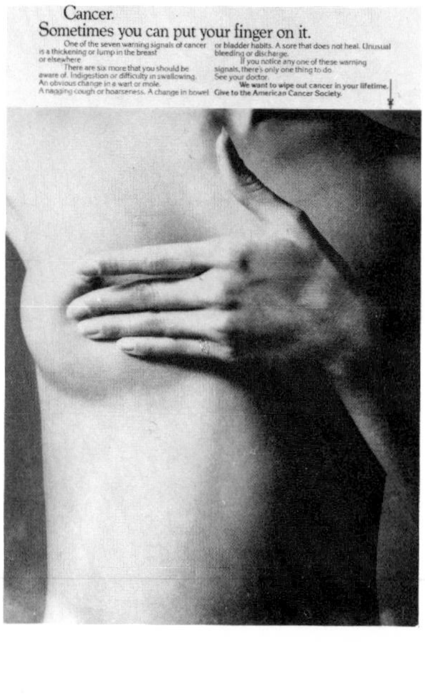

229 Silver Award
Art Director: Don Slater
Copywriter: Jim Parry
Agency: Parry Associates
Client: Zero Population Growth

229

When was the last time you had your period?

If you're two weeks overdue, don't wait. Consult your doctor. And if you *are* pregnant and you want an abortion, consult us.

We can help you get a legal, safe, inexpensive abortion. By an M.D. in a clinic or hospital.

If you have the abortion during the first 10 weeks of pregnancy, it will cost only about $150. And no matter when you have it, there's no charge for our service.

Even if you got your period yesterday, we're a good number to remember: (212) 489-7794 Monday through Friday, between 10 a.m. and 5 p.m. New York time.

Free Abortion Referral Service from ZPG-New York

The alternative to a wire coat hanger is (212) 489-7794.

There is such a thing as a legal, safe, inexpensive abortion. By an M.D. in a clinic or hospital. And we can help you get it.

If you have the abortion during the first 10 weeks of pregnancy, it will cost only about $150. And no matter when you have it, there's no charge for our service.

In the long run, a do-it-yourself abortion can be a lot costlier.

Call us at (212) 489-7794 Monday through Friday, between 10 a.m. and 5 p.m. New York time.

Free Abortion Referral Service from ZPG-New York

The main difference between a $150 abortion and a $1000 abortion is the doctor makes an extra $850.

Expensive abortions are a hangover from when abortions were illegal. But today we can help you get a legal, safe—and inexpensive—abortion. By an M.D. in a clinic or hospital.

If you have the abortion during the first 10 weeks of pregnancy, it will cost only about $150. And no matter when you have it, there's no charge for our service.

We know some doctors who care more about people than money.

Call us at (212) 489-7794 Monday through Friday, between 10 a.m. and 5 p.m. New York time.

Free Abortion Referral Service from ZPG-New York

230 Gold Award
Art Director: Bob Kwait
Copywriter: Aaron Buchman
Designer: Bob Kwait
Photographer: Anonymous
Agency: Aaron Buchman
Client: United Jewish Appeal

SOME PEOPLE COME TO ISRAEL TO DIE.
The first law passed in 1948 by Israel's first parliament guarantees that any Jew, anywhere in the world, will always be welcome in Israel.
So they still come, by the thousands.
Only thousands are old. And helpless. Like her.
Like her, they want to live out their days as free people. In a land where they feel they belong.
But caring for them takes millions of dollars. And Israel simply doesn't have them to spare.
She won't as long as she needs almost every penny to keep the peace from one day to the next.
As long as she does, it's up to us—the United Jewish Appeal, you—to provide for the living who can't provide for themselves.
So the Law can survive.
Keep the promise.
The United Jewish Appeal.

230

SO FAR, THEY'VE ONLY BEEN SCARED TO DEATH.
Keep the promise.
The United Jewish Appeal.

SOME JEWS GIVE MORE THAN OTHERS.
Keep the promise.

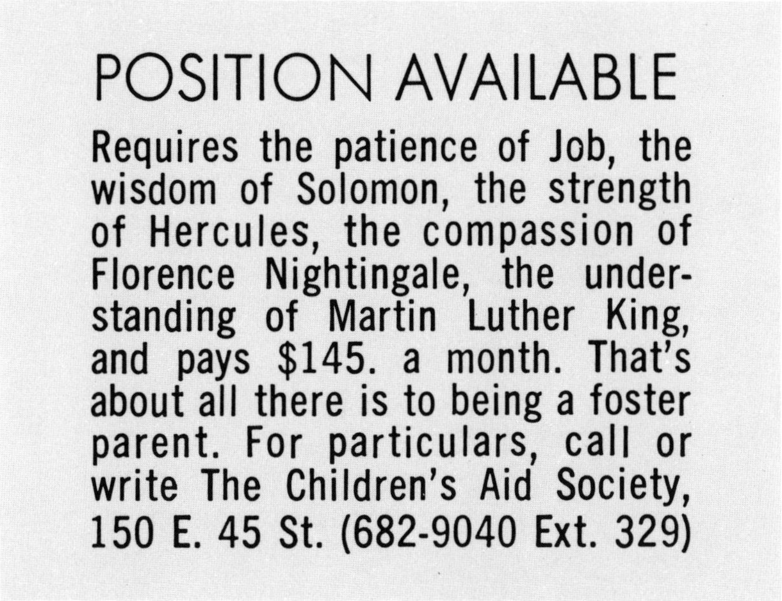
POSITION AVAILABLE
Requires the patience of Job, the wisdom of Solomon, the strength of Hercules, the compassion of Florence Nightingale, the understanding of Martin Luther King, and pays $145. a month. That's about all there is to being a foster parent. For particulars, call or write The Children's Aid Society, 150 E. 45 St. (682-9040 Ext. 329)

231

232

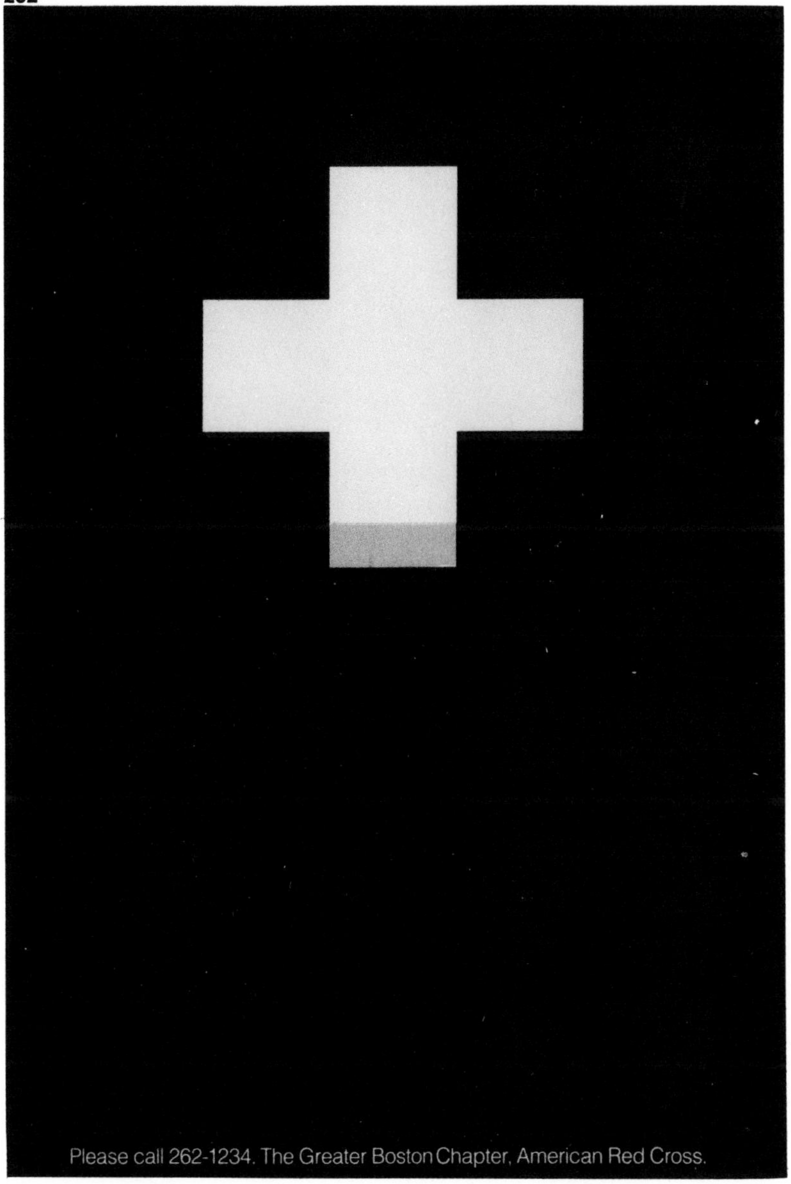
Please call 262-1234. The Greater Boston Chapter, American Red Cross.

231 Gold Award
Art Director: Rene Vidmer
Copywriter: Lew Petterson
Designer: Rene Vidmer
Agency, Hecht, Vidmer, Inc.
Client: Children's Aid Society

232
Art Director: Robert F. Baker
Copywriter: Robert F. Baker
Designers: Russ Veduccio
Robert F. Baker
Artist: Russ Veduccio
Agency: Harold Cabot, Inc.
Client: Boston Red Cross Blood Donor Program

GIVE $5. TO ODYSSEY HOUSE.
IT MIGHT SAVE YOU $500.
In 1972, in New York City, 75 percent of all crimes against property were committed by addicts.
Odyssey House helps rehabilitate addicts. Your contribution, any amount, will help.
Odyssey House, 309 East 6th Street, New York, N.Y. 10003

233

234

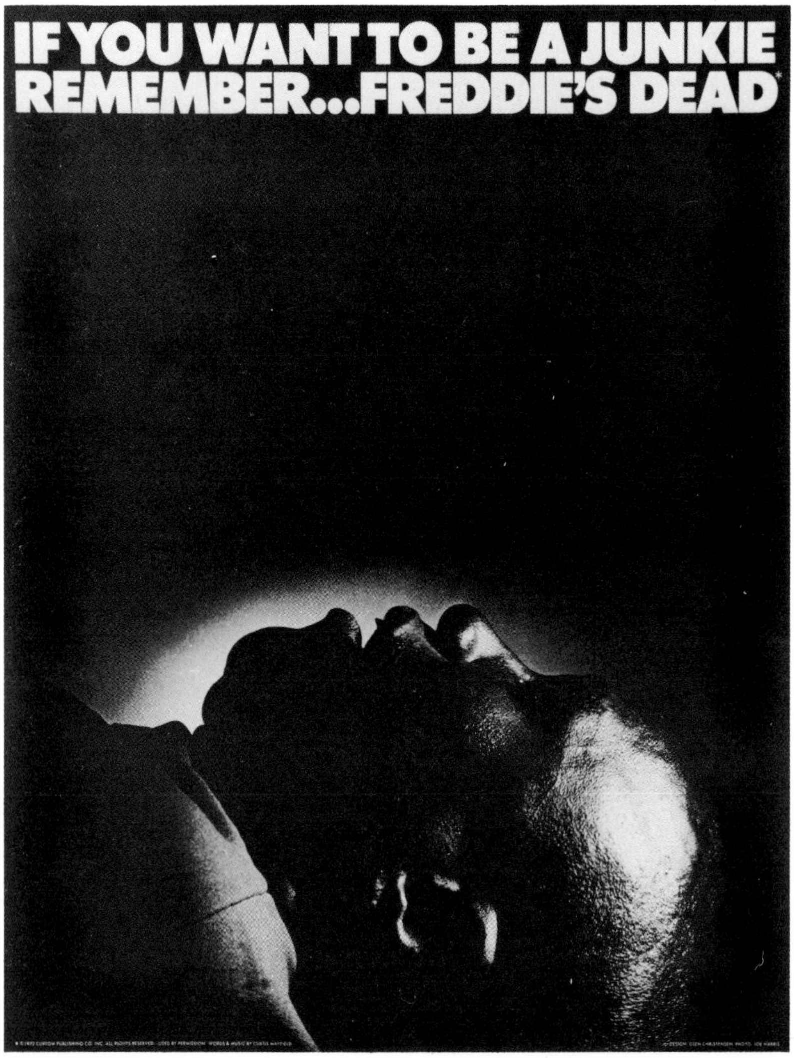
IF YOU WANT TO BE A JUNKIE
REMEMBER...FREDDIE'S DEAD*

233
Art Directors: Phyllis Kaye
Richard Wilde
Copywriters: Phyllis Kaye
Frank Young
Designers: Richard Wilde
Frank Young
Photographer: Ken Ambrose
Agency: School of Visual Arts
Public Advertising System
Client: Odyssey House

234
Art Director: Glen Christensen
Copywriter: Curtis Mayfield
Designers: Glen Christensen
Dominic Sicilia
Photographer: Joe Harris
Agency: The Buddah Group
Client: Curtom Records

235
Art Directors: Dean Koutsky
Gary Maag
Copywriters: Jim Stein
F. F. Gootee
Agency: Campbell-Mithun, Inc.
Client: Minnesota VD Awareness Committee

236
Art Director: Bernard Roer
Copywriter: Lee Cirillo
Photographer: Frank Poli
Agency: N. W. Ayer & Son, Inc., Chicago
Client: Girl Scouts of Chicago

Clap.

IN MINNESOTA, IT'S NOT APPLAUSE. DIAL OUT VD. (612) 339-7033.

A message from the Minnesota VD Awareness Committee.

235

236

One buck never did so much good.
Buy Girl Scout Cookies.
COOKIES
688
231

238

238
Art Director: Ed Thrasher
Copywriter: Ed Thrasher
Designers: John Van Hamersveld
Ed Thrasher
Photographer: Ed Thrasher
Client: Ed Thrasher

239
Art Director: Jill Richards
Copywriter: Helen Nolan
Designer: Jill Richards
Photographer: Joe Toto
Agency: Young & Rubicam International, Inc.
Client: Mayor's Narcotics Control Council

240
Art Director: Jill Richards
Copywriter: Helen Nolan
Designer: Jill Richards
Photographer: Joe Toto
Agency: Young & Rubicam International, Inc.
Client: Mayor's Narcotics Control Council

241
Art Director: Jill Richards
Copywriter: Helen Nolan
Designer: Jill Richards
Photographer: Joe Toto
Agency: Young & Rubicam International, Inc.
Client: Mayor's Narcotics Control Council

242
Art Director: Jill Richards
Copywriter: Helen Nolan
Designer: Jill Richards
Photographer: Joe Toto
Agency: Young & Rubicam International, Inc.
Client: Mayor's Narcotics Control Council

WITH FRIENDS LIKE THIS,
YOU DON'T NEED ENEMIES.
DON'T JOIN THE LIVING DEAD.

239

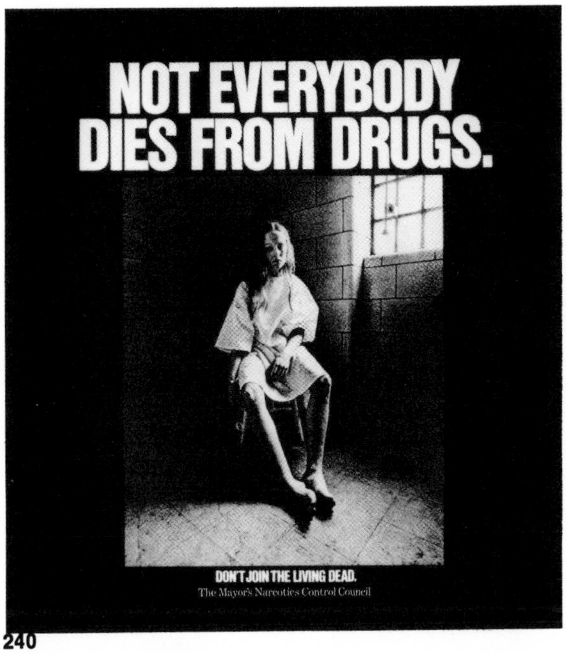
NOT EVERYBODY
DIES FROM DRUGS.
DON'T JOIN THE LIVING DEAD.
The Mayor's Narcotics Control Council

240

241

THIS IS A DRUG ADDICT
BEING COOL.
DON'T JOIN THE LIVING DEAD.
The Mayor's Narcotics Control Council

242

DON'T JOIN
THE LIVING DEAD.
If you think reality is tough for you, take a look at what it's like for kids on drugs.
Drugs don't make anything better. Only your head can do that.
The Mayor's Narcotics Control Council

243
Art Director: Ed Cain
Copywriters: Ed Cain
Frank Young
Designers: Gary Shapiro
Richard Wilde
Photographer: Frank Young
Agency: School of Visual Arts
Public Advertising System
Client: Education in Sickle Cell Disease

243

YOUR HEALTHY LOOKING CHILD MAY HAVE SICKLE CELL DISEASE.
You can be fooled.
Your child may look healthy but have a mild form of the disease called Sickle Cell Trait.
Some symptoms are blood in the urine and stomach pain.
The severe form of the disease is called Sickle Cell Anemia.
Some symptoms are easy fatigue, bed wetting, pain in legs and stomach.
The only sure way to know whether your child has the disease is to get a test.
WHERE TO GET TESTED:
Jamaica Hospital:
89th Avenue & Van Wyck Expressway, Jamaica, N.Y.
St. Luke's Hospital Center:
421 West 113th Street, New York, N.Y.
Sydenham Hospital:
Manhattan Avenue at 123rd Street, New York, N.Y.
Morrisania Hospital:
Out-Patient Clinic—Adults and Children
Walton Avenue & 168th Street, Bronx, N.Y.
Kings County Hospital:
Out-Patient Clinic—Adults-Pediatric
Pediatric Clinic—Children,
451 Clark Avenue, Brooklyn, N.Y.
For further information write:
Foundation for Research and Education in Sickle Cell Disease
423-431 West 120th Street,
New York, N.Y. 10027. Telephone: (212) 222-8500.
PAS
PUBLIC ADVERTISING SYSTEM
A DIVISION OF THE SCHOOL OF VISUAL ARTS SCHOLARSHIP FUND
PRINTED AT THE SCHOOL OF VISUAL ARTS BY THE VISUAL ARTS PRESS

244
Art Director: Gary Goldstein
Copywriter: Stevie Pierson
Designer: Gary Goldstein
Photographer: Tom Bolington
Agency: Doyle Dane Bernbach Inc.
Client: Youth Citizenship Fund

FIGHT
CITY
HALL.
Now, you and 39 million others under 30 have the power to change America. Register and vote.
Where ______ when ______

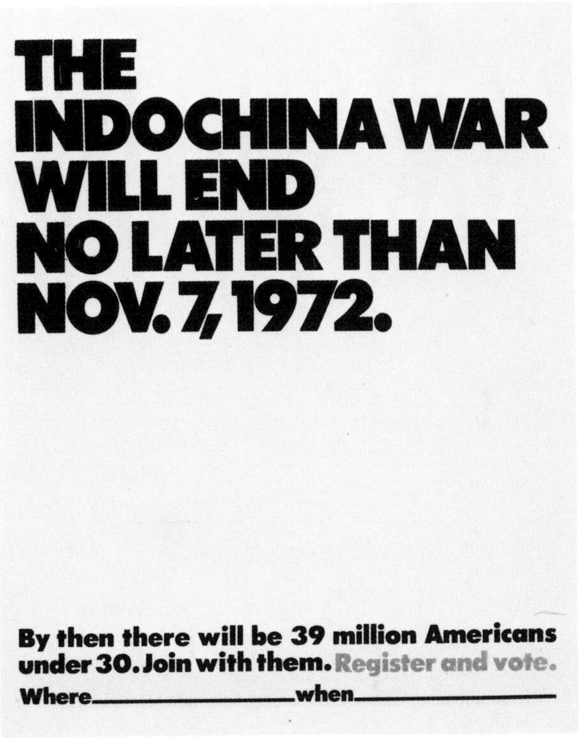
THE
INDOCHINA WAR
WILL END
NO LATER THAN
NOV. 7, 1972.
By then there will be 39 million Americans under 30. Join with them. Register and vote.
Where ______ when ______

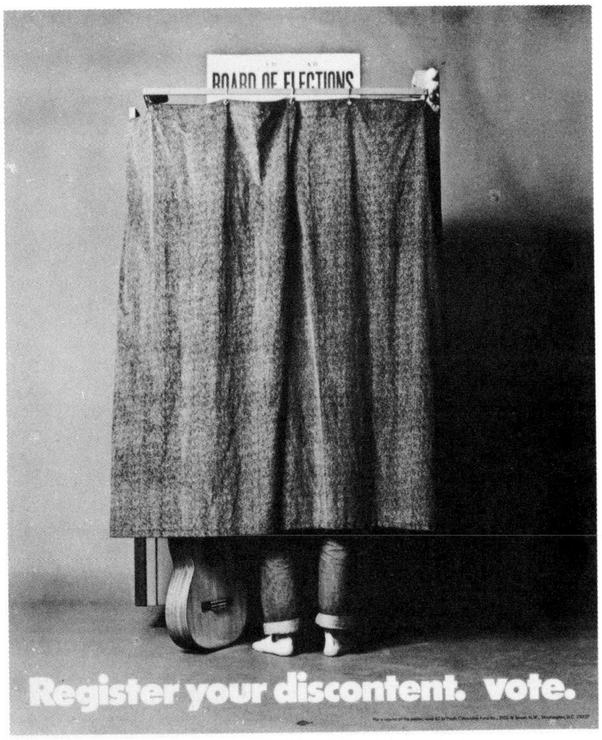
Register your discontent. vote.

244

"I had syphilis."

When I first thought I had syphilis, I was frightened, ashamed and horribly alone.

The symptoms were all there, a constant burning and itching sensation.

But I still couldn't accept it. Even with all the symptoms, I really couldn't believe it. The only way I could have gotten it was from my boyfriend, because I always keep myself as clean as possible.

Much to my relief, the symptoms slowly disappeared. I was really happy. I honestly thought I had conquered it by hoping and wishing it away.

But about a month later the symptoms returned, and much worse. I knew I had to be treated, but again I felt that awful stigma attached to the disease and I was embarrassed to call my doctor.

So I went to another neighborhood, to a clinic. I thought it would be less personal than a private doctor, and save me some humiliation. I even gave a false name.

But you know something, I learned a lot that day at the clinic. When I left I didn't feel like a freak or a deviate. I wasn't alone. There were many other people at the clinic waiting to be tested, Black, Spanish, White, all ages, men and women.

The test was simple and there was no judgment involved. And I felt so much better—so much better that I am not ashamed to tell about it.

Take my advice. If you have the slightest reason to believe you have V.D., don't hesitate to be treated. The test is painless and only takes a few minutes. The treatment is just as easy. They gave me penicillin, and I took antibiotics orally for a week.

If you don't want to be treated by your own doctor, go to a clinic. Almost all clinics are free and treatment is always confidential, even if you're under 18.

Ignoring it, or pretending it doesn't exist when symptoms are present can only seriously hurt you. V.D. can cripple, mentally retard, even kill you.

Looking back now I see how silly all my fears had been. When I think about it I am more ashamed about the foolish way I procrastinated, than about getting infected.

Listen, anyone can get V.D.... don't be ashamed.

New York City Health Department V.D. Clinics
Manhattan—Riverside, 160 West 100th Street—UN 6-8785
Central Harlem, 140 West 125th Street—749-0162
Washington Heights, 600 West 168th Street—WA 7-6300
Lower West Side, 303 Ninth Avenue—LA 4-8846
East Harlem, 158 East 115th Street—TR 6-0300 or TR 6-3811
Bronx—Morrisania, 1309 Fulton Avenue—WY 2-4200 or 992-7575
Brooklyn—Bedford, 485 Throop Avenue—574-5300
Brownsville, 259 Bristol Street—HY 8-6742
Fort Green, 295 Flatbush Avenue Ext.—TR 5-8020 or TR 5-8126
Queens—Corona, 34-33 Junction Boulevard—HI 6-3570
Jamaica, 90-37 Parsons Boulevard—758-7910
Far Rockaway, 67-10 Rockaway Beach Boulevard—NE 4-7700
Richmond Health Center—51 Stuyvesant Place, St. George, S.I.—SA 7-6000

PAS
PUBLIC ADVERTISING SYSTEM

"I had syphilis."

Yes, you're reading right. I had it, I was cured, and I'm fine.

You know, we have a very uptight attitude about venereal diseases. I'd heard about syphilis but I always thought that you had to be a prostitute or dirty to get it.

Well you can imagine my reaction, one morning as I was showering, when I noticed a sore right on the side of my vagina. Zap!

I thought that maybe it would go away if I took some aspirin or better yet, some penicillin pills.

But a week or so later that damned sore was still there. I knew I had to be treated. The infection wasn't going to pick up and leave all by itself. I also knew that the longer I put it off, the worse it would get, but I was very uptight about it.

I thought of my family doctor, but how can you sit down and tell your own doctor—a staunch believer in virginity-till-marriage—who's known you all of your life....

So I called the Health Department and asked for a V.D. treatment center near me, and I went.

I thought it would be a drag, but it wasn't. Nobody hassled me, or pressed me for information.

And they didn't notify my parents, or anything.

I got a couple of shots of penicillin. It was really cool and it was free.

So if you have even the smallest suspicion that you have V.D., please, don't sit around thinking "what if" or "suppose they" or "it couldn't be me." Stop jiving! Anybody can get V.D.

New York City Health Department V.D. Clinics
Manhattan—Riverside, 160 West 100th Street—UN 6-8785
Central Harlem, 140 West 125th Street—749-0162
Washington Heights, 600 West 168th Street—WA 7-6300
Lower West Side, 303 Ninth Avenue—LA 4-8846
East Harlem, 158 East 115th Street—TR 6-0300 or TR 6-3811
Bronx—Morrisania, 1309 Fulton Avenue—WY 2-4200 or 992-7575
Brooklyn—Bedford, 485 Throop Avenue—574-5300
Brownsville, 259 Bristol Street—HY 8-6742
Fort Green, 295 Flatbush Avenue Ext.—TR 5-8020 or TR 5-8126
Queens—Corona, 34-33 Junction Boulevard—HI 6-3570
Jamaica, 90-37 Parsons Boulevard—758-7910
Far Rockaway, 67-10 Rockaway Beach Boulevard—NE 4-7700
Richmond Health Center—51 Stuyvesant Place, St. George, S.I.—SA 7-6000

PAS
PUBLIC ADVERTISING SYSTEM

"Yo tuve syphilis."

Sí, Ud. lo esta leyendo correctamente. La Tuve y me cure, y ahora me siento perfectamente bien.

Siempre crei que solamente una prostituta ó una persona, sucia podia tener tal infección, pero no es tal cosa.

Una vez mientras me bañaba pude notar, algo cerca de la area vaginal que me intranquilizo, y me puse a pensar que diria el Dr. de la familia si lo consultase, y mas confusa me puse.

Por ultimo mé decidí consultar los doctores del Dept. De Salud y cuan grande fué mí sorpresa, cuando ellos me examinaron y me empezaron el tratamiento basado meramente en varias inyecciones de Penicilina, no fuí interrogada, y ni tan siquiera notificaron mis padres.

Asi pués, si Ud. tiene la mera idea de que Ud. pueda ser victima de esta infección proceda rapidamente a tratarse....

Cualquier persona puede contraer tal infección:—Los siguientes son oficinas del Dept. De Salud:—

New York City Health Department V.D. Clinics
Manhattan—Riverside, 160 West 100th Street—UN 6-8785
Central Harlem, 140 West 125th Street—749-0162
Washington Heights, 600 West 168th Street—WA 7-6300
Lower West Side, 303 Ninth Avenue—LA 4-8846
East Harlem, 158 East 115th Street—TR 6-0300 or TR 6-3811
Bronx—Morrisania, 1309 Fulton Avenue—WY 2-4200 or 992-7575
Brooklyn—Bedford, 485 Throop Avenue—574-5300
Brownsville, 259 Bristol Street—HY 8-6742
Fort Green, 295 Flatbush Avenue Ext.—TR 5-8020 or TR 5-8126
Queens—Corona, 34-33 Junction Boulevard—HI 6-3570
Jamaica, 90-37 Parsons Boulevard—758-7910
Far Rockaway, 67-10 Rockaway Beach Boulevard—NE 4-7700
Richmond Health Center—51 Stuyvesant Place, St. George, S.I.—SA 7-6000

PAS

"I had gonorrhea"

The first few days my urine was burning I didn't take it very seriously. I passed it off—a slight irritation or something I drank. About a week went by and the burning got a lot worse. It hurt like hell.

Well, I never thought that I would get it. It's like a lot of things, you never think it's going to happen to you. But there it was, no question about it. I had the clap. I was worried. I didn't want to admit it to myself, but I was a little ashamed.

I had to find a doctor. My family doctor was out of the question. I knew too many people there, and I didn't want a lecture. Maybe one of the guys at school or at work would know someone to go to. I was worried they would laugh their heads off. I finally found a clinic. Well what's really terrific is how it all worked out. They were great. Nobody stared at me, no one questioned me, and I didn't have to give him any personal information.

The cure was simple and painless. Just a couple shots of penicillin. It was easy.

So, if you think you have it don't kid yourself or wait around. Get treated. Don't be ashamed. Anyone can get V.D.

New York City Health Department V.D. Clinics
Manhattan—Riverside, 160 West 100th Street—UN 6-8785
Central Harlem, 140 West 125th Street—749-0162
Washington Heights, 600 West 168th Street—WA 7-6300
Lower West Side, 303 Ninth Avenue—LA 4-8846
East Harlem, 158 East 115th Street—TR 6-0300 or TR 6-3811
Bronx—Morrisania, 1309 Fulton Avenue—WY 2-4200 or 992-7575
Brooklyn—Bedford, 485 Throop Avenue—574-5300
Brownsville, 259 Bristol Street—HY 8-6742
Fort Green, 295 Flatbush Avenue Ext.—TR 5-8020 or TR 5-8126
Queens—Corona, 34-33 Junction Boulevard—HI 6-3570
Jamaica, 90-37 Parsons Boulevard—758-7910
Far Rockaway, 67-10 Rockaway Beach Boulevard—NE 4-7700
Richmond Health Center—51 Stuyvesant Place, St. George, S.I.—SA 7-6000

PAS
PUBLIC ADVERTISING SYSTEM

245
Art Directors: Gary Shapiro
Ava Sanders
Cynthia Nathan
Chris Argyros
Copywriters: Ava Sanders
Cynthia Nathan
Chris Argyros
Frank Young
Designers: Gary Shapiro
Frank Young
Richard Wilde
Photographer: Frank Young
Agency: School of Visual Arts
Public Advertising System
Client: NYC Dept. of Health, VD Information

246
Art Director: Kurt Haiman
Copywriters: Ruth Scott
Andrea Grill
Designer: Kurt Haiman
Photographer: Leonard Nones
Agency: Grey Advertising, Inc.
Client: Department of Justice

246

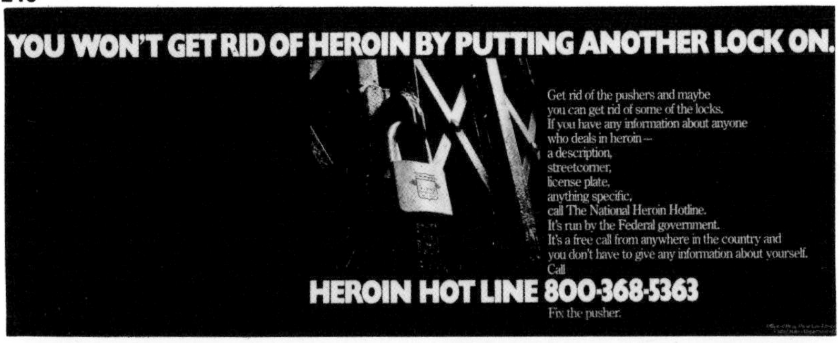
YOU WON'T GET RID OF HEROIN BY PUTTING ANOTHER LOCK ON.
Get rid of the pushers and maybe
you can get rid of some of the locks.
If you have any information about anyone
who deals in heroin—
a description,
streetcorner,
license plate,
anything specific,
call The National Heroin Hotline.
It's run by the Federal government.
It's a free call from anywhere in the country and
you don't have to give any information about yourself.
Call
HEROIN HOT LINE 800-368-5363
Fix the pusher.

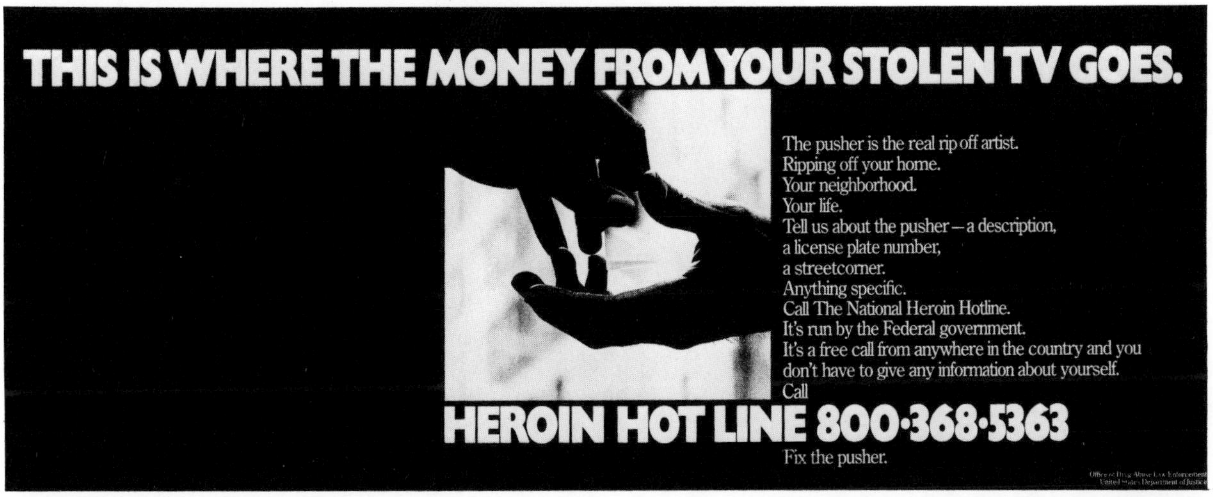
THIS IS WHERE THE MONEY FROM YOUR STOLEN TV GOES.
The pusher is the real rip off artist.
Ripping off your home.
Your neighborhood.
Your life.
Tell us about the pusher—a description,
a license plate number,
a streetcorner.
Anything specific.
Call The National Heroin Hotline.
It's run by the Federal government.
It's a free call from anywhere in the country and you
don't have to give any information about yourself.
Call
HEROIN HOT LINE 800·368·5363
Fix the pusher.

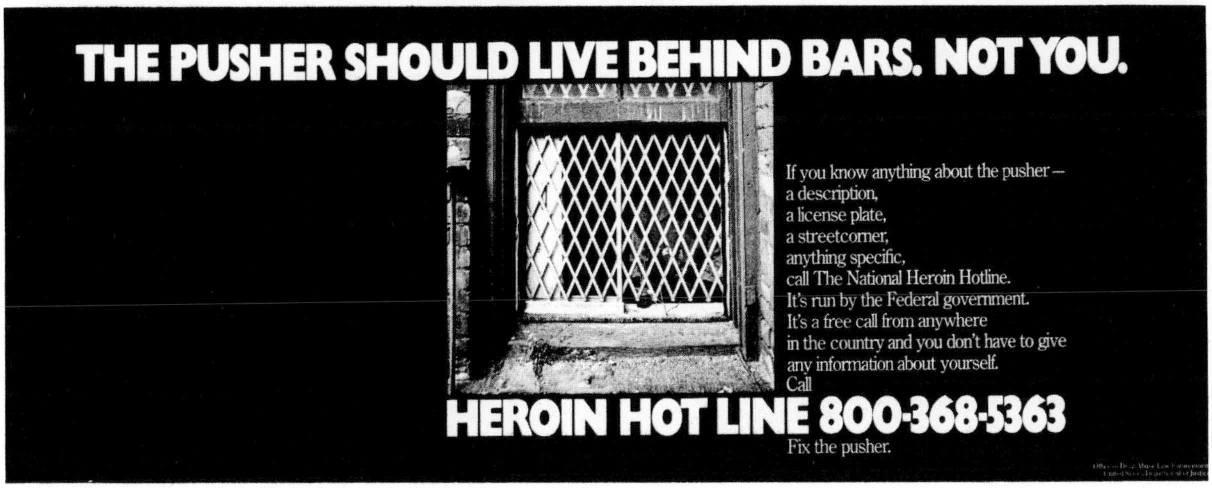
THE PUSHER SHOULD LIVE BEHIND BARS. NOT YOU.
If you know anything about the pusher—
a description,
a license plate,
a streetcorner,
anything specific,
call The National Heroin Hotline.
It's run by the Federal government.
It's a free call from anywhere
in the country and you don't have to give
any information about yourself.
Call
HEROIN HOT LINE 800-368-5363
Fix the pusher.

247

Julia Child is
a dirty street fighter.
How about you? Help the Mayor keep the streets clean.

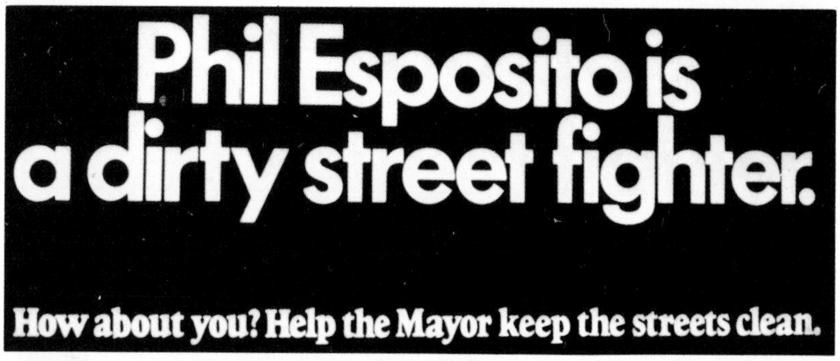
Phil Esposito is
a dirty street fighter.
How about you? Help the Mayor keep the streets clean.

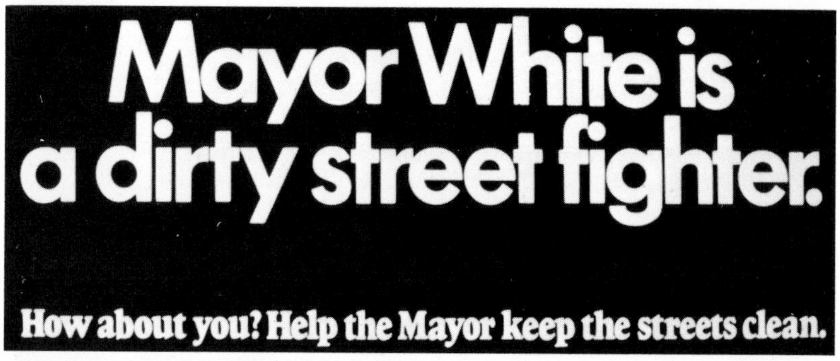
Mayor White is
a dirty street fighter.
How about you? Help the Mayor keep the streets clean.

Boston loves a
dirty street fighter.
Be one. Help the Mayor keep the streets clean.

247
Art Directors: Stavros Cosmopulos
Dick Pantano
Copywriter: Stavros Cosmopulos
Designer: Stavros Cosmopulos
Agency: Hill, Holliday, Connors, Cosmopulos, Inc.
Client: City of Boston

248
Art Director: Jill Richards
Copywriter: Helen Nolan
Designer: Jill Richards
Photographer: Joe Toto
Agency: Young & Rubicam International, Inc.
Client: Mayor's Narcotics Control Council

DON'T JOIN
THE LIVING DEAD.
If you think reality is tough for you, take a look at what it's like for kids on drugs.
Drugs don't make anything better. Only your head can do that.
The Mayor's Narcotics Control Council

WITH FRIENDS LIKE THIS,
YOU DON'T NEED ENEMIES.
DON'T JOIN THE LIVING DEAD.
The Mayor's Narcotics Control Council

NOT EVERYBODY
DIES FROM DRUGS.
DON'T JOIN THE LIVING DEAD.
The Mayor's Narcotics Control Council

THIS IS A DRUG ADDICT
BEING COOL.
DON'T JOIN THE LIVING DEAD.
The Mayor's Narcotics Control Council

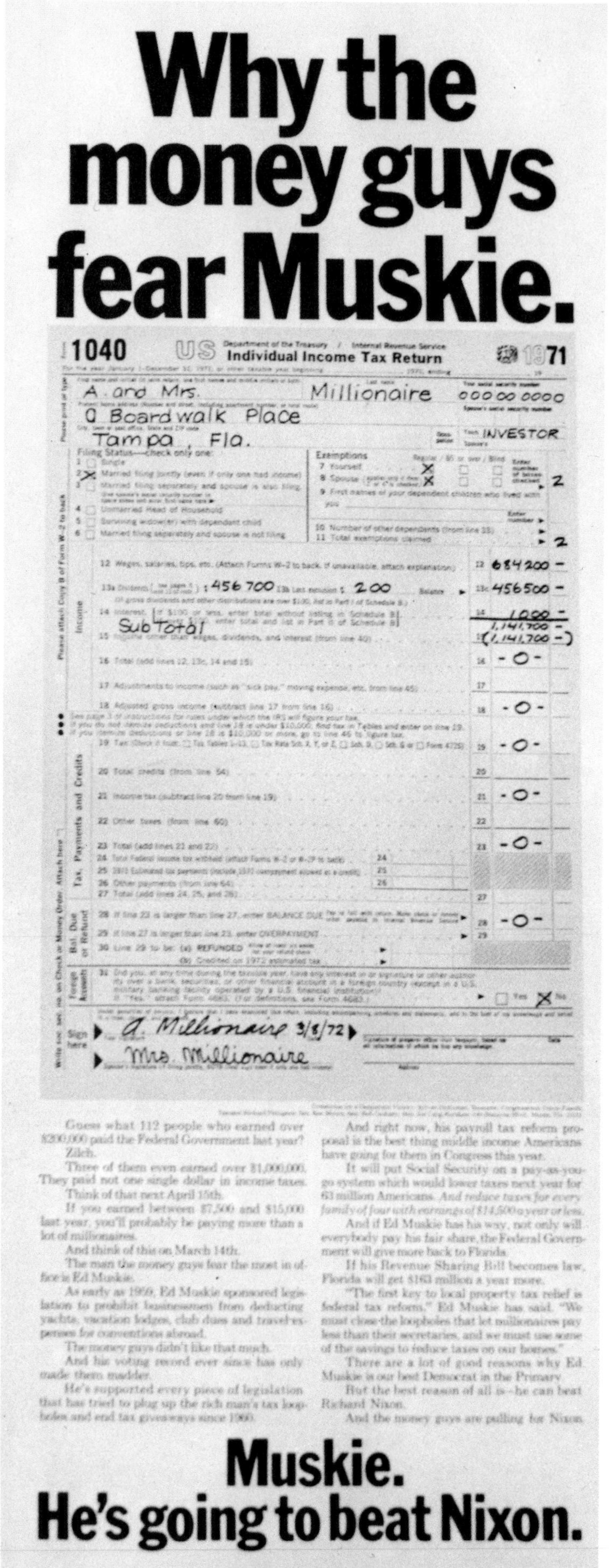

Print/Political

249
Art Director: R. Wall
Copywriters: T. Isidore
R. Fairchild
Agency: Lois Holland Callaway Inc.
Client: Floridians for Muskie

250 Gold Award
Art Directors: Seymour Chwast
Herb Lubalin
Editor: Bill Maloney
Designers: Herb Lubalin
Seymour Chwast
Artist: Ellen Shapiro
Agency: Lubalin, Smith, Carnase, Inc.
Push Pin Studio
Client: Citizens Committee for
McGovern/Shriver

251
Art Director: R. Wall
Copywriters: T. Isidore
R. Fairchild
Agency: Lois Holland Callaway Inc.
Client: Floridians for Muskie

250

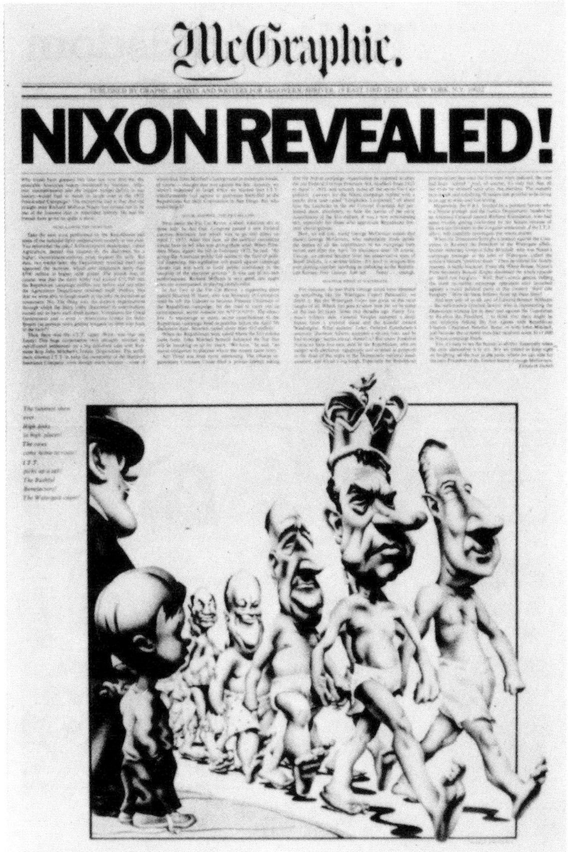
The McGraphic.
NIXON REVEALED!

251

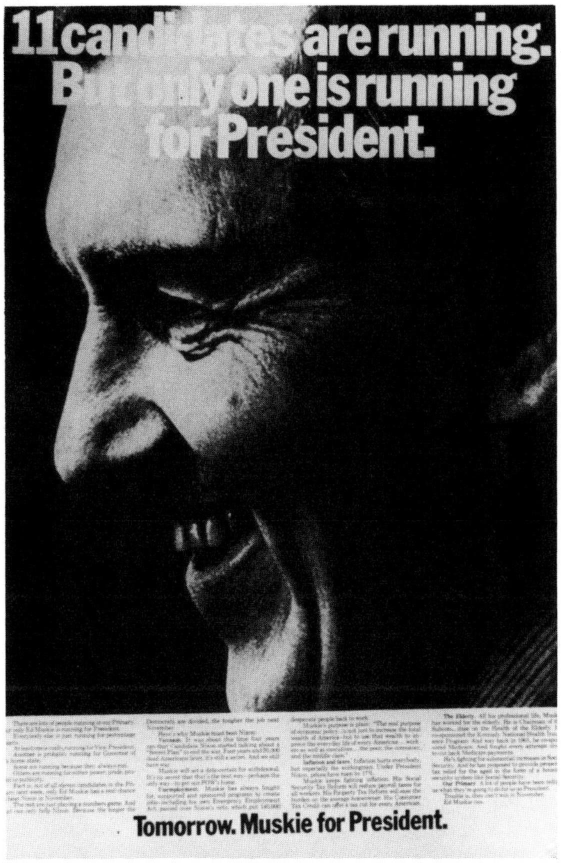
11 candidates are running.
But only one is running
for President.
Tomorrow. Muskie for President.

252
Art Director: R. Wall
Copywriters: T. Isidore
R. Fairchild
Agency: Lois Holland Callaway Inc.
Client: Floridians for Muskie

253
Art Director: Mary Moore
Copywriter: Scott Miller
Designer: Mike Solazzo
Agency: Marttila and Associates
Client: The Committee To Re-Elect
Congressman Drinan

252

253

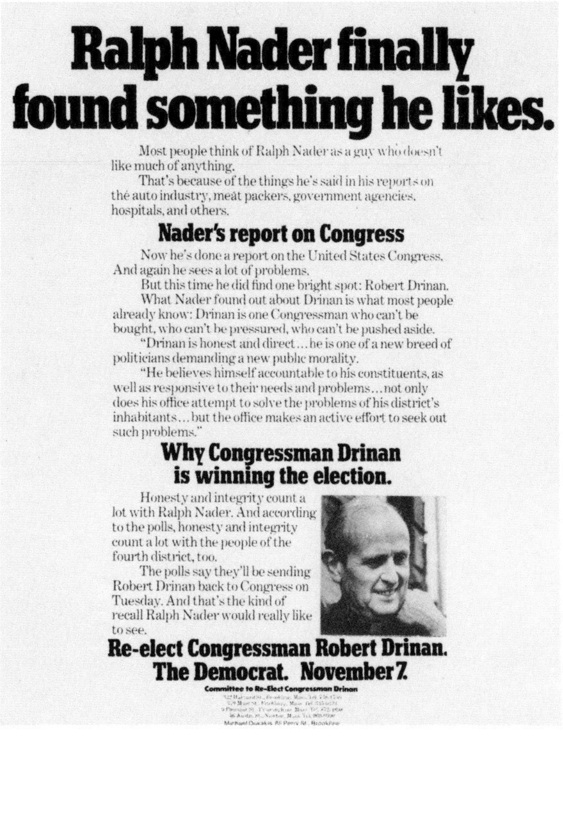
Ralph Nader finally found something he likes.
Most people think of Ralph Nader as a guy who doesn't like much of anything.
That's because of the things he's said in his reports on the auto industry, meat packers, government agencies, hospitals, and others.
Nader's report on Congress
Now he's done a report on the United States Congress. And again he sees a lot of problems.
But this time he did find one bright spot: Robert Drinan.
What Nader found out about Drinan is what most people already know: Drinan is one Congressman who can't be bought, who can't be pressured, who can't be pushed aside.
"Drinan is honest and direct ... he is one of a new breed of politicians demanding a new public morality.
"He believes himself accountable to his constituents, as well as responsive to their needs and problems ... not only does his office attempt to solve the problems of his district's inhabitants ... but the office makes an active effort to seek out such problems."
Why Congressman Drinan is winning the election.
Honesty and integrity count a lot with Ralph Nader. And according to the polls, honesty and integrity count a lot with the people of the fourth district, too.
The polls say they'll be sending Robert Drinan back to Congress on Tuesday. And that's the kind of recall Ralph Nader would really like to see.
Re-elect Congressman Robert Drinan.
The Democrat. November 7.
Committee to Re-Elect Congressman Drinan

254
Art Director: David Falcon
Copywriter: Paul Solovay
Designer: David Falcon
Artist: David Falcon
Agency: Miller, Addison, Steele, Inc.
Client: Political Consultants of America
for Leonard M. Simon

254

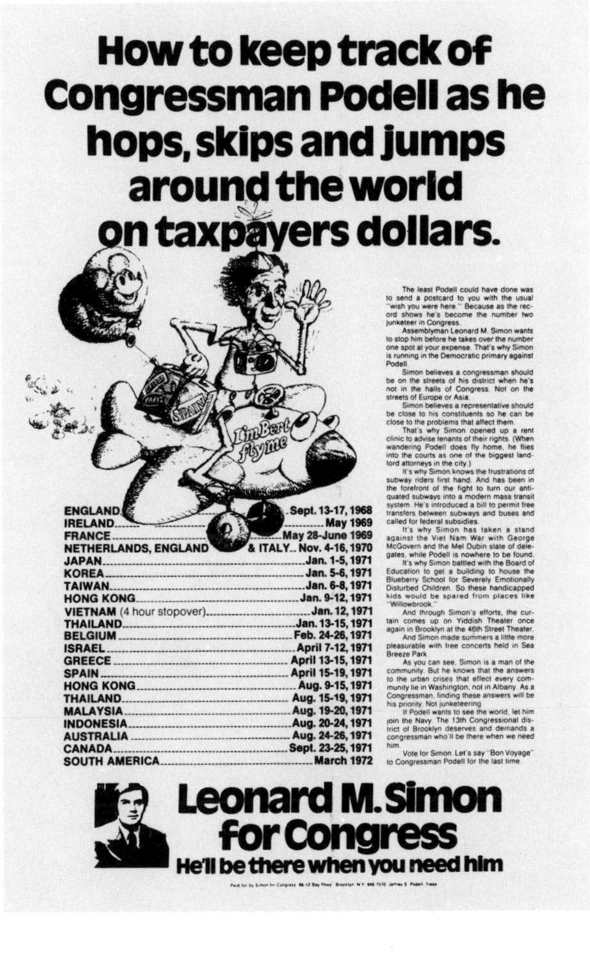

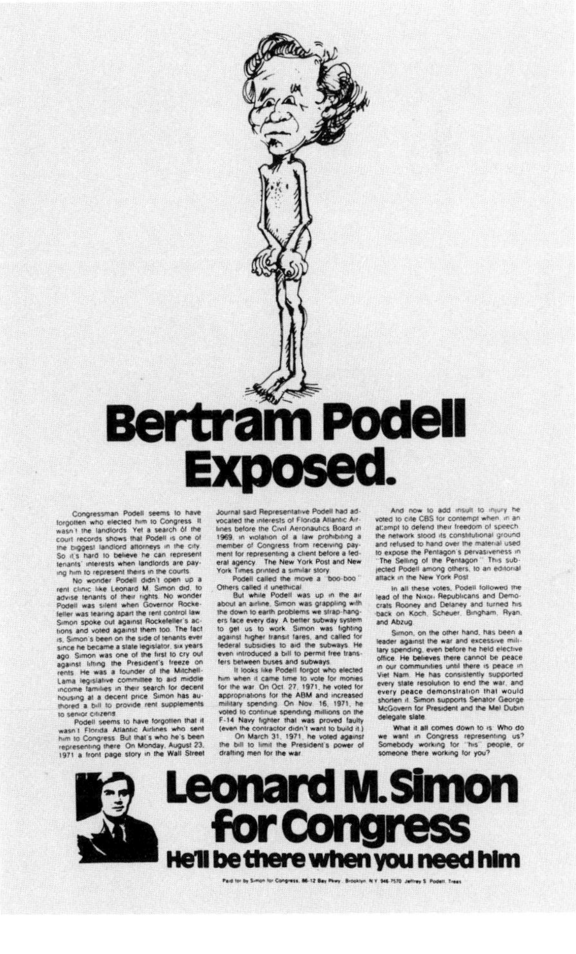

255
Art Director: R. Wall
Copywriters: T. Isidore
R. Fairchild
Agency: Lois Holland Callaway Inc.
Client: Floridians for Muskie

"I'm going to beat Nixon."
Richard Nixon has done some things wrong and some things right.
I think it's a mistake to forget either.
The things he did right, he did because he had to. And I thank God he had the good sense to do them.
But it's what he did wrong that makes me want to beat him next November.
When he went to China, that was right.
But he said yes to Anti-Ballistic Missiles, too. And that was wrong.
He established wage and price controls. A little late. But right.
But he said no to the hundreds of thousands of jobs that would have been created by either my Emergency Employment Act or the Accelerated Public Works Bill.
And he was all wrong. Because today we have an unemployment rate of 6.2%—our highest in 9 years.
He said no to desperately needed funds for vital educational and health needs. And that was wrong.
He said yes to the SST. And that was wrong.
He turned down aid for elementary and secondary schools, handicapped children and vocational students. And that was wrong.
He didn't turn down aid for a mismanaged corporation facing bankruptcy. And he was wrong again.
In fact, for three years now, Richard Nixon has been saying no to a lot of things I would have said yes to. And yes to a lot of things I would have said no to.
So I've got lots of reasons for wanting to beat him in November.
And I'm going to do it.
Somebody has to.
Tomorrow. Muskie for President.

255

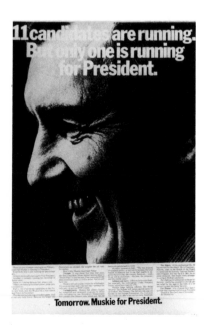

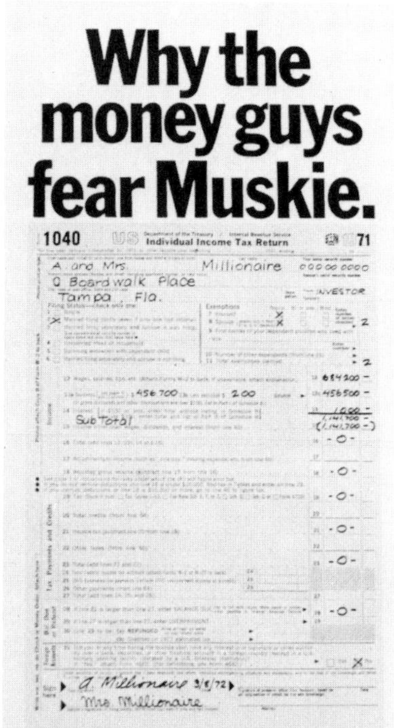
Why the money guys fear Muskie.
1040
Individual Income Tax Return
71
Muskie.
He's going to beat Nixon.

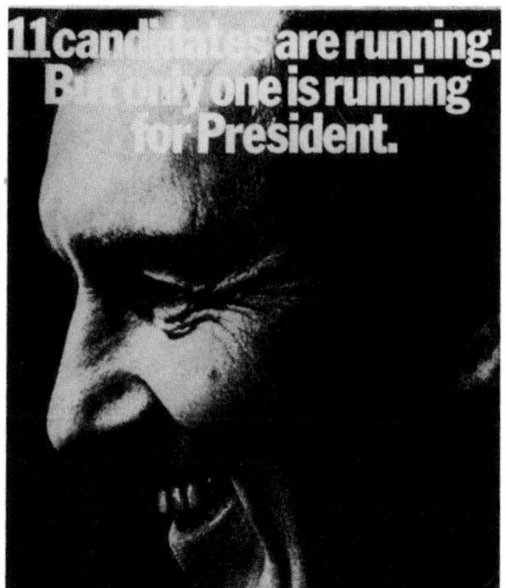
11 candidates are running. But only one is running for President.
Tomorrow. Muskie for President.

If you wouldn't give him the Presidency, don't give him our Primary.
Vote for Ed Muskie. He's going to beat Nixon.

Radio / Single

256 Gold Award
Copywriter: Ed McCabe
Producer: Ed McCabe
Production Company: The Mix Place
Agency: Scali, McCabe, Sloves, Inc.
Client: Perdue Farms, Inc.

Giblets
60-second

ANNCR.: Ladies and gentlemen, the President of Perdue Farms, Mr. Frank Perdue. . .

FRANK PERDUE: Some women have told me that when they get a chicken home, they find they've been gypped on the giblets. They bought a chicken without an interior. I wouldn't stand for that. I think when you pay for a chicken, you should get a whole chicken. Not an empty shell. I pack my tender, young Perdue chickens with all the things a chicken should be packed with. Liver, gizzard, heart, neck, and recipe. The recipe is there so that you'll know what to do with the giblets once you've got them. Instead of wasting them all on your cat.

If you're willing to settle for less in a chicken, that's your business. But I can't see it. Next thing you know someone will be trying to make the wings optional.

ANNCR.: When it comes to chicken, Frank Perdue is even tougher than you are. He *has* to be. Because every one of his chickens comes with a money-back quality guarantee.

It takes a tough man to make a tender chicken.

Perdue.

257 Silver Award
Copywriter: Ed McCabe
Producer: Ed McCabe
Production Company: The Mix Place
Agency: Scali, McCabe, Sloves, Inc.
Client: Perdue Farms, Inc.

Diet Food
60-second

ANNCR.: Ladies and gentlemen, the President of Perdue Foods, Mr. Frank Perdue. . .

FRANK PERDUE: Today, more and more people are becoming diet-conscious. What's amazing to me is how many diet-conscious people are unconscious of the fact that my Perdue chickens are one of the all-time great diet foods.

To begin with, chicken is one of the best sources of high quality protein there is. Chickens are lower in calories and have less saturated fat than equal servings of any red meat. That's why I eat chicken every day. And do I sound fat?

Aside from being good for your figure, my chickens are also cheap. They cost less per pound than any other quality meat. Do you realize that my fresh, juicy, tender young broilers even cost less per pound than hot dogs? Than hot dogs! Boy, that really galls me!

I just can't believe that in this day and age anyone would want to pay extra to be fat.

ANNCR.: Send Frank Perdue the wing-tags from two of his chickens, and he'll send you a new cookbook containing more than a hundred ways to enjoy Perdue chicken without getting fat.

It takes a tough man to make a tender chicken.

Perdue.

258
Copywriter: Ed McCabe
Producer: Ed McCabe
Production Company: The Mix Place
Agency: Scali, McCabe, Sloves, Inc.
Client: Perdue Farms, Inc.

Two Questions
60-second

ANNCR.: Ladies and gentlemen, the President of Perdue Foods, Mr. Frank Perdue. . .

FRANK PERDUE: When people ask me about my chickens, two questions invariably come up. The first is "Perdue, your chickens have such a great golden yellow color it's almost unnatural. Do you dye them?" Honestly, there's absolutely nothing artificial about the color of my chickens. If you had a chicken and fed it good yellow corn, alfalfa, corn gluten, and marigold petals, it would just naturally be yellow. You can't go around dyeing chickens. They wouldn't stand still for it.

The other question is "Perdue, your chickens are so plump and juicy, do you give them hormone injections?" This one really gets my hackles up. I do nothing of the kind. When chickens eat and live as well as mine do, you don't have to resort to artificial techniques. Why I've got a whole department that works on nothing but perfecting the dwellings my chickens live in. We've tested houses, apartments, modern, traditional, different lighting and color schemes—even soul music! And ended up with a house that's just chicken heaven. A chicken that lives right tastes right. You can't fake that.

ANNCR.: It takes a tough man to make a tender chicken.

Perdue.

259
Copywriter: David Altschiller
Producers: Maurene Kearns
David Altschiller
Production Company: Tabby Andriello
Agency: Carl Ally Inc.
Client: W.T.S. Pharmacraft-Allerest

Different Sneeze
60-second

ANNCR. (VO): Listen to the difference between a sneeze from a cold and a sneeze from an allergy.

First, the sneeze from a cold . . . (SFX)

Now the sneeze from an allergy . . . (SFX)

Now listen to the difference between a runny nose from a cold and a runny nose from an allergy.

First, the cold . . . (SFX)

Now the allergy . . . (SFX)

They sound alike, don't they. Well they look alike, too. This can be confusing, because allergies and colds are very different ailments. And a medicine that's perfect for one may not be perfect for the other.

If you have an allergy, maybe you should be taking something made specifically for allergies. Allerest.

Allerest helps relieve the runny nose, the itchy, watery eyes, and the sneezing of allergies.

Allerest comes in tablets and in time-release capsules. If you have an allergy, it's made just for what you've got.

Radio/Single

260
Copywriter: Ed McCabe
Producer: Ed McCabe
Production Company: No Soap Radio
Agency: Scali, McCabe, Sloves, Inc.
Client: Volvo, Inc.

Winter
60-second

ANNCR. (VO): In Sweden, we demand more of a car than you do. We have to. In parts of our country winter arrives in October and doesn't leave until May.

Our cars better not break down. A man could freeze to death waiting for help. If a heater doesn't function properly, it's more than an inconvenience. It could be a catastrophe.

We use raw salt on the roads. But our cars can't rust out on us. Swedish automobile inspections are so strict, badly rusted cars are ordered off the road.

In Sweden, our cars have to survive many winters. Swedes simply can't afford to buy a new car every couple of years. The cost of living in Sweden is as high as it is in the United States. But our incomes are lower.

In Sweden, the car most in demand is Volvo.

Volvo. We build them the way we build them because we have to.

261
Composers: William Backer
Billy Davis
Roger Cook
Roger Greenaway
Producer: Billy Davis
Production Company: Sherman, Kahan
Agency: McCann-Erickson, Inc.
Client: Coca-Cola, U.S.A.

Have A Good Day
60-second

(WHISTLE)

(WORDS AND MUSIC)

SONG: Hey what you say
Give 'em a song, pass it along, tell 'em
Have a good day . . . (have a good day) . . .

Rainy day blues got no chance to stay
Hey there ain't no way . . . (there ain't no way) . . .
Just tell 'em a joke, buy 'em a Coke and say
Have a good day . . . (have a good day)

They want the real thing . . . (like Coke is)
They want to have a good day (Coca-Cola)
What the world wants is

(2-BAR WHISTLE)

Yeah, the real thing

Buy 'em a Coke and tell 'em you hope
they're gonna have a good day . . .
(have a good day)
Have the real thing . . . (Coke is)
It's the real thing . . . (Coca-Cola) . . .

262
Composers: Loretta Lynn
Billy Davis
Producer: Billy Davis
Production Company: Sherman, Kahan
Agency: McCann-Erickson, Inc.
Client: Coca-Cola, U.S.A.

Sing With Me
60-second

(WORDS AND MUSIC)

SONG: I'm gonna sing my song like I never sang before
I'm gonna sing about life and the real things we need more
Well I hope you don't mind if I sip on my Coke
While I sing my song 'cause it cools my throat
And you can have one too and sing along with me

I'm gonna sing about the mountains and the valleys
And the real things in life that surround me
Things like the ocean, true love and devotion
So have a Coke and sing along with me

About the real thing . . . (Coke is)
It's the real thing . . . (Coca-Cola)
Sing along with me . . . (it's the real thing)
About the real things . . . (Coca-Cola)
Let me hear you all sing . . . (Coca-Cola)
And have a Coke with me . . . (Coca-Cola)
Everybody sing . . . (Coca-Cola)
About the real things . . . (it's the real thing)
. . . It's the real thing . . .

263
Composer: Billy Ed Wheeler
Producer: Billy Davis
Production Company: A.I.R. London
Agency: McCann-Erickson, Inc.
Client: Coca-Cola, U.S.A.

Life Is
60-second

(WORDS AND MUSIC)

SONG:Remember those days back when
We were friends
And love was just starting out
We walked and talked for hours
Asking what it's all about
We covered philosophy, having power,
Being rich and a movie star
And now that we've lived it a little bit
We know where we are

Life is remembering
Being a friend
It's an arm around you when you cry
Life is walking down a country road
Drinking Coke when you're dry

Life is a baby's laugh
It's being one half of a love that can make you whole
It's sitting and talking and drinking Coke
Planning how to reach your goal

It's the real thing . . . (like Coke is) . . .
It's laughing and remembering
It's the real thing . . . (Coca-Cola)
It's the real thing . . . (Coke is)
It's the real thing . . . (Coca-Cola) . . .

Radio/Single

264
Copywriter: George Dusenbury
Producer: George Dusenbury
Production Company: No Soap Radio
Agency: Scali, McCabe, Sloves, Inc.
Client: Volvo, Inc.

Taxes
60-second

ANNCR. (VO): In Sweden, we pay the highest taxes in the world. Perhaps it's a touch of irony that the tallest building in Sweden is the Tax Office.

We do get a lot for our tax money though. A generous retirement pension. Medical expenses. Education, through college, is free.

But that doesn't help when we buy things. Gas is 80 cents a gallon. And on a $4000 car, we pay $1000 more for tax.

So you'd think the car that would sell best in Sweden would be an inexpensive economy car. Not at all. We think buying cheap is false economy. Because our taxes are so high, the only sensible thing to do with our money is invest it in something substantial. Perhaps that explains why the largest selling car in Sweden is Volvo.

With our taxes, people can't afford to settle for less.

Volvo. We build them the way we build them because we have to.

265
Composers: William Backer
Billy Davis
Roger Cook
Roger Greenaway
Producer: Billy Davis
Production Company: Sherman, Kahan
Agency: McCann-Erickson, Inc.
Client: Coca-Cola, U.S.A.

Hello Summertime
60-second

(WORDS AND MUSIC)

Song: Birds 'n bees and all the flowers 'n trees
And fishes on the line
Girls and guys and yellow butterflies
Say hello summertime

The sun shinin' down on the back of my neck
And nothin' on my mind
And ice cold Coke on the back of the throat
Say hello summertime

Summertime in the back of your mind
Yeah summertime
Is the real thing
What you're hopin' to find
In the back of your mind
It's the real thing and . . . (Coca-Cola)
Like summertime Coca-Cola is the real thing . . . (Coke is)
Like summertime Coca-Cola is the real thing . . . (Coke is) . . .

266
Copywriter: Jim Paddock
Producer: Jim Paddock
Production Company: Kintel Studios
Agency: Burton, Campbell and Kelley
Client: Bankers Trust of South Carolina

Hold-Up
60-second

A: Ah, excuse me. Stick-em up. I'm a robber. You see my mask?

B: Yeah. Is-is this a real one?

A: Yeah, this is the real thing.

B: You know. I read about these things in the paper. And I say . . .

A: You never think it's . . .

B: It'll never happen . . .

(LAUGHS)

A: Do you have any money? Could we get on with this?

B: By the way. I've always wanted to ask one of you guys this. Does that mask, that stocking, does it hurt? Because it would seem to me, you know, that . . .

A: Well, it's not that bad. I used to have trouble talking through it.

B: Well, you do well. I can understand every word you're saying.

A: Thank you.

A: Do you have the money?

B: I don't have any. Really. I was looking for a dime just for the parking meter. Will you take Master Charge? How about that?

A: No. No, I don't take credit cards.

B: Oh, oh yeah. Well, let me see . . . Now my checking account's pretty low. I know what I'll do. I'll use my new Bankers Trust Master Checking account. Have you seen that?

A: No, I'm not familiar with that.

B: It's fantastic. I use it like a regular checking account.

A: Yeah?

B: But the checks are billed to my Master Charge. So you see . . .

A: It's like writing yourself a loan then?

B: Yeah. That's really what it is. Yes. Do you think this will cover it?

(SFX: Tearing out check)

A: This is o.k. That's fine. I'll add a zero on to this. This'll be fine.

ANNCR.: Bankers Trust Master Checking. A sneaky way to use your Master Charge.

267
Copywriters: Ed McCabe
George Dusenbury
Producers: Ed McCabe
George Dusenbury
Production Company: No Soap Radio
Agency: Scali, McCabe, Sloves, Inc.
Client: Volvo, Inc.

Engineers
60-second

ANNCR. (VO): In Sweden, precision is a national preoccupation.

The smallest unit of measurement in the world is Swedish. The Angstrom, one tenmillionth of a millimeter.

The ball bearing is a Swedish invention.

A Swedish engineer developed the block gauge. A precision instrument that allowed a famous man from Detroit to enter into mass production of cars.

Today, Sweden is often referred to as a nation of engineers. Engineering is the largest industry, employing nearly 40% of the total labor force.

At Volvo alone, there are 1,035 engineers. And only 29 stylists. We have to put a lot of emphasis on engineering. Since Volvo is the largest-selling car in Sweden, a lot of our customers are engineers too.

Volvo. We build them the way we build them because we have to.

Radio/Single

268
Copywriters: Ed McCabe
George Dusenbury
Producers: Ed McCabe
George Dusenbury
Production Company: No Soap Radio
Agency: Scali, McCabe, Sloves, Inc.
Client: Volvo, Inc.

Big
60-second

ANNCR. (VO): If you want a big station wagon, buy one that's built for big people. The Volvo station wagon is built for Swedes. And Swedish men, on an average, are two inches taller than American men. That's a big reason the Volvo 145 has leg and headroom for drivers up to six feet six and a half inches tall.

It also has a rear seat wide enough for three adults. And, with the rear seat down, room to carry a sofa 72 inches long. The 145 has all this room because Swedes need it. They travel more than anybody else in Europe.

They also own more cars per capita than anybody in Europe. Which means crowded streets, and explains why the Volvo station wagon is shorter outside and more maneuverable than most Detroit compact sedans.

The Volvo 145 station wagon is built for Sweden. Which is why it's just what you may need in America.

269
Copywriters: Ed McCabe
George Dusenbury
Producers: Ed McCabe
George Dusenbury
Production Company: No Soap Radio
Agency: Scali, McCabe, Sloves, Inc.
Client: Volvo, Inc.

Inspection
60-second

ANNCR. (VO): In Sweden, the national automobile inspections are perhaps the roughest in the world.

200 components are examined. And if your car fails, you're either served with a summons ordering you to have it fixed. Fast. Or you're forbidden to drive it at all. It has to be towed away.

So when Swedes buy a new car, how well it'll do in the inspections is one of their biggest concerns. And they can get a good idea of just how well that will be. Published reports give the results on all makes of cars sold in Sweden.

As you might imagine, these reports can really hurt an automobile manufacturer if they're bad. Or really help him if they're good. Volvo is the largest selling car in Sweden. You see, when we build a Volvo, how well it'll do in the inspections is one of our biggest concerns too.

Volvo. We build them the way we build them because we have to.

270
Art Director: George Lois
Copywriter: Ron Holland
Lyricist: Frank Gehrecke
Composer: Claiborne Richardson
Producer: Ed Murphy
Production Company: Famous Commercials
Agency: Lois Holland Callaway Inc.
Client: Restaurant Associates

Spats
60-second

(WORDS AND MUSIC)

ANNCR. (VO): Let's go to
Spats . . . For the food that ya like to eat . . .
Spats . . . Filled with folks that ya'd like to meet . . .
Spats . . . Phone your wife that you'll meet her on . . .
33rd Street.
Spats . . . It's a spot filled with lots of cheer . . .
Spats . . . Lots of fun, lots of atmosphere . . .
Spats . . . Guaranteed that you'll like it here . . .
Where? Spats.
Day time or night . . .
Spats serves you right . . .
For any mood . . .
Spats has the food.
Cocktail or two, maybe a brew . . .
Whatever you wish, Spats is your dish.
That's Spats . . . It's a nest that was built for you . . .
Spats . . . Slightly west of the Avenue . . .
Spats . . . All New Yorkers are tippin' their hats!
Why don't you tell your date . . .
There's heaven on a plate . . .
Next to the Empire State . . .
Let's go to Spats.

ANNCR. (VO): 33 West 33rd Street

Radio/Campaign

271 Gold Award
Composers: William Backer
Billy Davis
Roger Cook
Roger Greenaway
Billy Ed Wheeler
Producer: Billy Davis
Production Companies: A.I.R. London
Sherman, Kahan
Agency: McCann-Erickson, Inc.
Client: Coca-Cola, U.S.A.

Getting This World Together
60-second

(WORDS AND MUSIC)

SONG: Together—together—together —together . . .

Getting this world together
Getting this world together
Putting our dreams together
Putting our dreams together
Pull up a friendly chair
Show someone that you care . . .

(Hey) talk about what you feel now
Talk about what you feel now
Talk about what is real now
Talk about what is real now
Let's have some Coca-Cola
And talk it over now . . .

Getting this world together . . . (getting this world together)
Putting our dreams together . . . (sharing our dreams)
More people talk it over
Having a Coca-Cola
For sitting and talking it over
It's the real thing . . . (Coca-Cola) . . .

Let's have some Coke together
It's the real thing . . . (Coke is) . . . (Coca-Cola)
Coca-Cola . . . (getting this world together)
It's the real thing
Coca-Cola
Let's have some Coke together
It's the real thing
Coke is . . .

Life Is
60-second

Have a Good Day
60-second

272 Silver Award
Copywriter: Adrienne Cohen
Music: Stock
Producer: John Scott
Production Company: Audio Directors
Agency: Young & Rubicam International, Inc.
Client: Eastern Air Lines

Bahamas II
60-second

(SFX UNDER)

ORSON WELLS: A lacy fern does its perpetual dance in the undulating light below you as you float lazily in the blue sea. You take a breath, you dive to watch a yellow haze become a thousand iridescent fish moving as one current. They don't flee for now you're one of them with your snorkel and mask gliding over coral and rippled sand just a few hundred yards off Nassau shore and ten feet below it, in the Bahamas, a place for people. One of the places that makes Eastern Air Lines what it is, the airline more people fly than any other in the world, but one.

The Wings of Man.

Houston III
60-second

Cleveland I
60-second

Jamaica I
60-second

Atlanta (Fox Theater)
60-second

273
Art Director: Frank Fristachi
Copywriter: Joe Tantillo
Composer: Michael Small
Producer: Maggi Durham
Production Company: Aura Productions
Agency: DKG Inc.
Client: Getty Oil

Dollars & Cents
60-second

(GETTY MUSIC: UP AND UNDER)

ANNCR. (VO): We at Getty have been telling you that you can save money on our premium gasoline, because it's priced a few cents less per gallon than most other major premiums . . . Well now we'd like to tell you just how much money you can save with Getty premium.

(SFX: CAR DRIVING. DRIVES OVER CORD BELL. BELL RINGS TWICE)

(SFX: "Fill 'er up")

(SFX: GAS PUMP BELL STARTS TO RING AND CONTINUES TO RING UNDER)

With your first gallon of Getty premium you save about three cents. With five gallons, about fifteen cents. A twenty gallon fill up saves about sixty cents. Use Getty for a month and you save about two fifty. Use it for six months and save around fifteen dollars. And if you use Getty for a year, or around 12,000 miles of driving, you can save around thirty dollars. Thirty dollars for doing nothing more than filling up with Getty. That's enough to buy another seventy-five gallons. Which is enough gas to take you about 1,000 miles.

(SFX: CAR PULLS OUT OF STATION. CORD BELL RINGS TWICE. MUSIC UP)

At Getty, we give you more gas for your money. So you get more miles for your money.

75 Gallons
60-second

N.Y. to Florida
60-second

274
Art Director: John Caggiano
Copywriter: Michael Kahn
Music: Stock
Producer: Rosemary Barre
Production Companies: Clack Studio
Media Sound
Agency: Doyle Dane Bernbach Inc.
Client: Porsche/Audi

The Duke of Klaxon
60-second

(MUSIC THROUGHOUT WITH SOUND OF CARS BEING DRIVEN)

ANNCR. (VO): On April 8th, the Honorable George Whittingham-Raston, 4th Duke of Klaxon, suffered a financial setback. He saw fit, after much deliberation, to sell his entire stable of motor cars.

He decided to purchase a car that had just about the same headroom and legroom as his Rolls-Royce Silver Shadow. A car with front-wheel drive like his Cadillac Eldorado and the same type of steering system as his Porsche. A car that not only had an interior as stately as his Mercedes-Benz 280SE, but also promised the same expert service as his beloved, little Volkswagen.

(PAUSE)

The car he purchased was an Audi.
And owing to its rather minimal cost, the Duke felt that, indeed, it was a lot of cars for the money.

It's a Lot of Cars for the Money
60-second

Italian Count
50-second

275
Art Director: Frank Ginsberg
Copywriter: Lou Linder
Lyricists: Lou Linder
Frank Ginsberg
Composers: Mike Appel
Jim Cretecos
Producer: Cindy Woodward
Production Company: Wes Farrell Organization
Agency: The Marschalk Company
Client: Coca-Cola U.S.A.
Mr. PiBB

Folk Rock
60-second

(MUSIC THROUGHOUT)

SONG: It's nice to live in an easy way.
Without any cares from day to day.

Slow down the time, slow down the moment,
Mr. PiBB. Smooth and easy Mr. PiBB.

It's nice to have your clouds erased. So
just slow down to its easy taste.

Slow down the time. Slow down the moment.
Taste Mr. PiBB. It goes down good, Mr. PiBB.
(It goes down good.)

ANNCR. (VO): Mr. PiBB is not a cola—not a root beer. It's an easy new soft drink from the Coca-Cola Company. Taste it. It goes down good.

SONG: It goes down good.

Country Western
60-second

1950's
60-second

276
Copywriter: Ed McCabe
Producer: Ed McCabe
Production Company: The Mix Place
Agency: Scali, McCabe, Sloves, Inc.
Client: Perdue Farms, Inc.

Leg Shortage
60-second

ANNCR.: Ladies and gentlemen, the President of Perdue Farms, Mr. Frank Perdue . . .

FRANK PERDUE: I've got a problem here that you can help me with. My breasts aren't moving as fast as my legs. For some reason, people are buying a lot more of my Perdue chicken legs than Perdue chicken breasts. Of course, I really appreciate the support you're giving my legs. But we've got to get this breast problem straightened out or there'll be no end of grief. You see, a chicken only has two legs. And no matter how you slice it, you can't get more than two breasts out of one chicken. Now I'm not one to complain about having a few extra breasts on my hands. But I'm on the brink of a major leg shortage. You're just going to have to start buying more Perdue chicken breasts, or I'm going to have to start coming up with three-legged chickens.

ANNCR.: When it comes to chicken breasts, Frank Perdue is even tougher than you are. He has to be. Every one of them comes with his money-back quality guarantee.

It takes a tough man to make tender chicken breasts.

Perdue.

Giblets
60-second

Two Questions
60-second

277
Copywriters: Don Wood
Ted Kandle
Lyricists: Don Wood
Jon Silbermann
Composers: Don Wood
Jon Silbermann
Producers: Don Wood
Jon Silbermann
Production Company: MZH, Inc.
Agency: N.W. Ayer & Son, Inc., New York
Client: AT&T Long Lines

Imagine My Surprise
30-second

(MUSIC)

SONG: Imagine my surprise when I picked up the phone to find you on it . . .
I don't think I've ever been so pleased.
Your voice so gentle and understanding,
life was suddenly undemanding,
you'll never know how much those minutes mean . . .

la lalala lala lalala la lalala lala
lalala

ANNCR. (VO): It's surprising what a phone call can do for someone you love. Why not dial Long Distance and find out for yourself.

Old Time Places
60-second

Hello Sunshine
30-second

Country Blues
60-second

278
Art Director: Michael Ulick
Copywriter: Jeffrey Frey
Lyricists: Jeffrey Frey
Charles Moss
Composers: Neil Warner
Larry Levinson
Producer: Barbara Michaelson
Production Company: Warner/Levinson
Agency: Wells, Rich, Greene, Inc.
Client: Bonanza International

Eating with the Kids in the Car
60-second

(MUSIC THROUGHOUT)

SONG: Mustard on my nose
Ketchup on my clothes
Eating with the kids in the car . . .
Burgers in a sack
French fries down my back
Eating with the kids in the car . . .
These drive-ins are driving me crazy . . .
They're driving me out of my mind . . .
It's not that I'm mean or I'm lazy,
But I really wish I could find . . .
A place where a father could take his kids,
Sit down to a meal and relax . . .
And he won't have to take out a bank loan,
To pay for the tips and the tax.

ANNCR. (VO): Fathers of America, come to Bonanza and you won't have to eat in the car. Your kids can still have hamburgers but you can have a steak.

Bonanza. The family restaurant even a father could love.

The Highway Song
60-second

You've Gotta Be Rich
60-second

Radio/Campaign

279
Copywriters: Ed McCabe
George Dusenbury
Producers: Ed McCabe
George Dusenbury
Production Company: No Soap Radio
Agency: Scali, McCabe, Sloves, Inc.
Client: Volvo, Inc.

Size
60-second

ANNCR.: In many countries, the biggest-selling car is a small car. But not in Sweden. It's not that Swedes' egos are too big to stoop to a small car. It's that their bodies tend to be.

Swedish men, on an average, are two inches taller than American men. Swedish women are tall, too. That's one reason New York's biggest modeling agency goes to Sweden, more than to any other country, in search of tall, thin models.

Needless to say, this tendency for Swedes to be tall has a lot to do with the way we design cars at Volvo.

Volvos have enough leg and headroom for drivers up to six feet six and a half inches. The rear seat is wide enough for three adults. And the trunk is bigger than the trunk in big American cars.

The fact is, you just don't get to be the biggest-selling car in Sweden by building a little car.

Volvo. We build them the way we build them because we have to.

Driving
60-second

Taxes
60-second

280
Copywriter: Spencer Michlin
Lyricist: Spencer Michlin
Composer: John Hill
Production Company: Michlin & Hill, Inc.
Agency: Michlin & Hill, Inc.
Client: Pepsico, Inc.

Put a Little Ya-hoo in your Life
60-second

(MUSIC UP)

SONG: Put a little (bing, bing) in your life
Put a little (bonk, bonk) in your life
Put a little (ding, ding)
Put a little (clang, clang)
Put a little (bong, bong)
Put a little (beep, beep)
Put a little Ya-hoo in your life
Put Mountain Dew in your life
Put a little Ya-hoo in your life

(MUSIC UNDER)

ANNCR. (VO): There's a little Ya-hoo in everyone. Lemony Mountain Dew turns it loose. Mountain Dew. With the sparkly look of lemon, and the sparkly taste of lemon. Put a little in your life!

(MUSIC UP)

SONG: Put a little (bing, bing) in your life
Put a little (bonk, bonk) in your life
Put a little (ding, ding) . . .
Put a little (clang, clang)
Put a little (bong, bong)
Put a little (beep, beep)
Put a little Ya-hoo in your life
Put Mountain Dew in your life
Put a little Ya-hoo in your life
Put Mountain Dew in your life
Put a little Ya-hoo in your life
Put Mountain Dew in your life
Put a little Ya-hoo in your life.

(MUSIC UNDER)

Basic
30-second

Jug Band
30-second

Country/Mountain Dew
30-second

281
Copywriters: Sara Bragin
Mark Yustein
Producers: Sara Bragin
Mark Yustein
Production Company: National Recording Studios
Agency: Della Femina, Travisano & Partners, Inc.
Client: Blue Nun

Happy Anniversary
60-second

ANNCR.: Stiller & Meara.

(SFX: DOOR SLAMS)

STILLER: Hi, Naomi, I'm home. Happy Anniversary.

MEARA: You remembered?

STILLER: How could I forget? It was a year ago today your mother moved out and I moved back in. How about a hug?

MEARA: Ouch. Warren, watch your hands!

STILLER: That wasn't my hands. It was my claw. I mean, it was my lobster.

MEARA: What are you talking about?

STILLER: I thought I'd surprise you and bring home your favorite food for dinner. Lobster.

MEARA: But to surprise you, I made your favorite dish. Meatloaf.

STILLER: Hey, that's great. We can have both. And what's more, I brought home a little Blue Nun.

MEARA: No wonder she's blue, it's freezing out there. Bring her inside.

STILLER: No, Blue Nun wine. See.

MEARA: But that looks like white wine. How can you drink white wine with meatloaf.

STILLER: Very simple. Blue Nun is a delicious white wine that's correct with any dish—lobster or meatloaf.

MEARA: Warren, the lobster, it's attacking the meatloaf!

STILLER: Hey, Naomi, that gives me an idea.

MEARA: Warren, you devil.

ANNCR.: Blue Nun. The delicious white wine that's correct with any dish.

Another Sichel wine imported by Schieffelin & Company, New York.

MEARA: Warren, please not in front of the lobster.

Beef Wellington
60-second

Smorgasbord
60-second

282
Copywriter: Ed McCabe
Producer: Ed McCabe
Production Company: The Mix Place
Agency: Scali, McCabe, Sloves, Inc.
Client: Barney's

Just Looking
60-second

ANNCR.: If you like to shop for clothes without being bothered by salesmen, you'll appreciate Barney's unique new "just looking" button. Our hostess will give you one at the door. When you put it on, it lets our salesmen know that you want to "just look" in peace. This leaves you free to explore every nook and cranny of Barney's 21 dens, shops, and rooms without walking around repeating over and over again "just looking," "just looking."

And at Barney's, there's plenty to look at. Men's fashions in every size and style. The famous designers of Europe and the States. Most of the big name brands. You can also relax and have a cup of coffee at our espresso bar. Check out our barber shop. Or just watch the grapes grow in our glass-enclosed garden.

Come to Barney's and look around. As long as you wear the "just looking" button, we'll treat you like you're not even here. Barney's. 7th Avenue and 17th Street. We know you go out of your way to get here. We've got to pay you back.

Rainmaker Room
60-second

How to Get to Barney's
60-second

Radio/Campaign

283
Art Director: George Lois
Copywriter: Ron Holland
Lyricist: Frank Gehrecke
Composer: Claiborne Richardson
Producer: Ed Murphy
Production Company: Famous Commercials
Agency: Lois Holland Callaway Inc.
Client: Restaurant Associates

Ma Bell's
60-second

(MUSIC IS BOUNCY JAZZ) TWO VERSIONS —ONE MAN, ONE WOMAN ON PIANO

SONG: Hello—Hello—Hello—Hello—Hello —Ma Bell's restaurant! Everybody's talkin' to—everybody's walkin' to Ma Bell's—Ma Bell's the most harmoniest, telephoniest spot in town.

Everybody's night and day over Shubert Alley way, at Ma Bell's—Ma Bell's. They all love meetin' there, drinkin' and the eatin' where? At Ma Bell's. Why you can head right for a table—or the long long distance bar—there's a phone on every table—where you can call your wife and tell her where you are.
Drop around and have a ball, need a drink and make a call at Ma Bell's—Ma Bell's. The newest, brightest, light right off of Broadway. The fun and food and phones galore— Shubert Alley way—

At Ma Bell's, at Ma Bell's, at Ma Bell's—Ma Bell's—Ma Bell's—Ma Bell's . . .

ANNCR. (VO): Ma Bell's—at Shubert Alley . . . 45th Street—West of Broadway . . .

Spats/Man
60-second

Spats/Woman
60-second

284
Copywriter: Evan Stark
Producer: Christopher Hall
Production Company: Six West Recording
Agency: Doyle Dane Bernbach Inc.
Client: Mobil Oil Corporation

Dirt Sings
60-second

ANNCR.: Every car engine has an enemy. Dirt . . .

MR. DIRT: I'm dirt . . . I'm dirt . . . and it's car engines I love to hurt.

I try to make them stall and stutter and stop . . . And if I do . . . what can you do . . . ha . . .you can't even call a cop . . . you can't arrest dirt . . . And I'm dirt . . . I'm dirt . . . I'm filthy, rotten dirt . . . I'll try to make your engine whine and whimper and yelp and cry for help . . . I'm dirt . . . ha, ha . . .I'm dirt . . . ha, ha . . . I'm dirt . . .
and one more time . . .

I'm not good for your carburetor . . . cause I'll try to get it sooner or later . . . I'm no good for your engine my friend . . . Cause I don't bow and I don't bend. I'm just no good . . . on your car I'm rough . . . and if you don't like it that's just tough . . . Cause you can have trouble when I'm around . . . and when I'm around, I am around . . . I'm dirt . . . ha, ha . . . I'm dirt . . . ha, ha . . . I'm dirt.
And one more time I'm no good for your carburetor . . .
Cause . . .

(FADE OUT)

ANNCR.: But dirt has an enemy, too.
Mobil Detergent Gasoline.
Mobil fights dirt to help keep your engine clean and to help your car run smoothly . . .
Mobil Detergent Gasoline—it hates dirt.

Dirt Waxes Poetic
60-second

Driving Game
60-second

285
Copywriter: Arthur Einstein Jr.
Producer: Laurie Kahn
Production Company: Cinema Sound
Agency: Lord, Geller, Federico, Peterson Inc.
Client: The New Yorker Magazine

Kicks and Screams
60-second

MOELING: I'm John Moeling, Corporate and Financial Advertising Manager of *The New Yorker Magazine.* Most corporate advertising gets into print over the kicks and screams of the top management. Somebody gives them a bill of goods about how they have to say something warm and pleasant about their companies and they sort of go along with it, but they're not really thrilled because unfortunately advertising is considered to be a direct reduction of the bottom line. So what they'll do is write a long story about their corporation and what it does, then at the bottom they'll say write for our annual report. Then after several weeks they count up the number of requests they've gotten and rate media on a cost per inquiry basis. We lose more often than we win on this basis. The sort of portfolio that they want to interest is not the portfolio that's going to take up its pencil and write in for an annual report. It will do one of two things, it will call its broker and say send me one or it will call its broker and say, why in God's name do I have to read about this company in *The New Yorker?*

Little Shop
60-second

Interviewed in Hong Kong
60-second

TV / Single / :30 or under

286
Art Director: Henry Holtzman
Copywriter: Larry Spinner
TV Director: Melvin Sokolsky
TV Producer: Linda Mevorach
Production Company: Sokolsky Films
Agency: Young & Rubicam International, Inc.
Client: Dr. Pepper

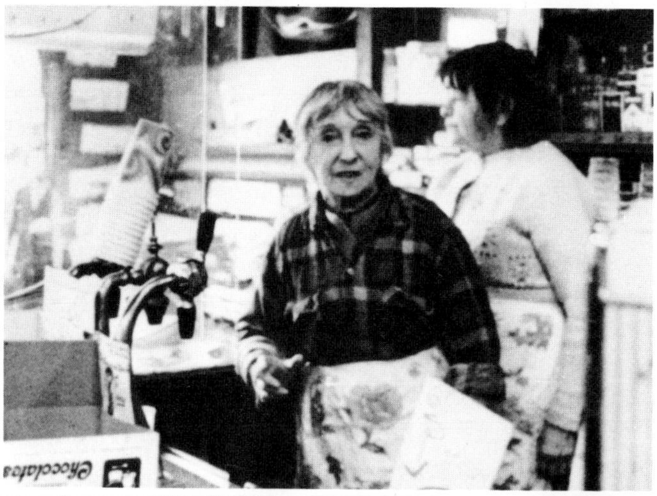

Candy Store
30-second

SCENE IS TYPICAL URBAN NEIGHBORHOOD CANDY STORE WITH ALL THE LOCAL COLOR, NOISE, ACTIVITY WITH PEOPLE COMING IN AND OUT. CITY SOUNDS ARE HEARD. CAMERA COMES IN ON CANDY STORE LADY. (SHE IS A 'RECOGNIZABLE' TYPE BECAUSE OF HER ACCENT AND HER DIRECTNESS)

CANDY STORE LADY: The first time a salesman came into my candy store to sell me Dr. Pepper, I told him to go take a walk. Then all of a sudden my customers start asking me for Dr. Pepper, Dr. Pepper. So I called the salesman and said, "Morris, bring back the Dr. Peppers." I thought it was another cola. But it's got an altogether different taste. Better, if you ask me. So now I got a big seller on my hands. Who knew?

('CANDID' TOUCH AT FINISH INCLUDES CUSTOMER WAVING INTO LENS, TRYING TO GET INTO PICTURE)

287
Art Director: Julio Dilorio
Copywriter: Gene Case
TV Director: Barry Brown
TV Producer: Barbara Fine
Production Company: Brillig Productions Inc.
Agency: Case & McGrath, Inc.
Client: The Mennen Company

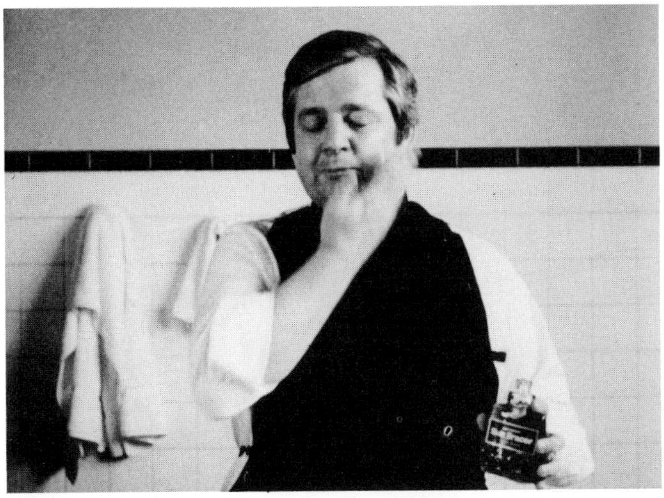

Japanese
30-second

CLERGYMAN IN BATHROOM

ANNCR. (VO): America wakes up with Skin Bracer . . .

(MUSIC)

CLERGYMAN SLAPS HIMSELF

CLERGYMAN (ON CAMERA): Thanks. I needed that.

SKIN BRACER BOTTLE

ANNCR. (VO): Skin Bracer is the morning after-shave. Its skin-tightener and chin-chillers wake you up like a cold slap in the face . . .

DISSOLVE TO JAPANESE IN BATHROOM

ANNCR. (VO): and now, the world discovers Bracer . . .

JAPANESE SLAPS HIMSELF

JAPANESE (ON CAMERA): Domo. Sorega Hitsuyodattanose.

SUBTITLE: "Thanks. I needed that."

TV/Single/:30 or under

288
Art Director: Mike Withers
Copywriter: Barry Greenspan
TV Director: Bill Alton
TV Producer: Dave De Vries
Production Company: Alton-Melsky
Agency: DKG Inc.
Client: Dollar Savings Bank

Stocks
30-second

OPEN ON MAN WALKING DOWN WALL STREET SPEAKING TO CAMERA AS HE WALKS

MAN: In 1955 I took five thousand dollars and put it into the stock market. By '59 I had myself around seven thousand bucks.

STOPS AT HOT DOG STAND

By '62 it was down to around four thousand.

But . . . by 1969 I was right back up to seven and a half.

Now? I'm just about where I started, give or take a few hundred.

Mostly take, I guess.

There's got to be a better way.

TURNS AND WALKS AWAY

ANNCR. (VO): Dollar Savings Bank. Maybe we're the better way.

SUPER: DOLLAR SAVINGS BANK
The better way.

289
Art Director: Mas Yamashita
Copywriter: Elizabeth Hayes
TV Director: Harry Hamburg
TV Producer: Mel Kane
Production Company: McGraw-Hill Pacific Productions
Agency: Doyle Dane Bernbach Inc.
Client: Hills Bros. Coffee, Inc.

On the Docks
30-second

OPEN ON BEAN BUYER ON THE SAN FRANCISCO DOCKS. BAGS OF COFFEE BEANS ARE BEING DUMPED IN SLING FROM SHIP

CU OF BEAN BUYER. BAGS ARE JUST FINISHING BEING LOWERED IN FRONT OF HIM. HE HOLDS A BAG CUTTING BEAN SCOOPER

BEAN BUYER: As the bean buyer for Hills Bros. I'm here to make sure we get what we pay for.

CUT TO SCOOPER CUTTING INTO BAG AND SCOOPING OUT BEANS. EXAMINES BEANS

The Hills family is very picky about the beans they put in their coffee. They have been for nearly 100 years.

BACK TO MEDIUM SHOT OF BEAN BUYER

Last year about a million pounds of beans didn't make it from here . . . to there.

GESTURES TOWARD HILLS BROS. PLANT BEHIND HIM

The Hills family rejected them right on the spot. I had to turn them over to a coffee broker.

BUYER MOVES AROUND BAGS AND LEANS ON THEM

And he sold them to somebody else.

MEANINGFUL LOOK TO CAMERA

ANNCR. (VO): When your own name is on the can . . . you're very picky about what goes inside.

CLOSE UP OF PRODUCT
PULL BACK TO SHOW ENTIRE CAN

TV/Single/:30 or under

290
Art Director: Kathe Mooslie
Copywriter: John Annarino
TV Director: Jack Desort
TV Producer: James Grumish
Production Company: Desort and Sam Productions, Inc.
Agency: Doyle Dane Bernbach Inc.
Client: Jack-in-the-Box

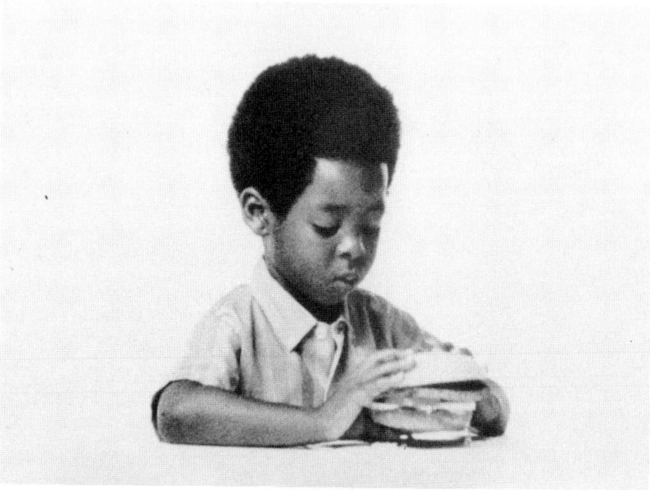

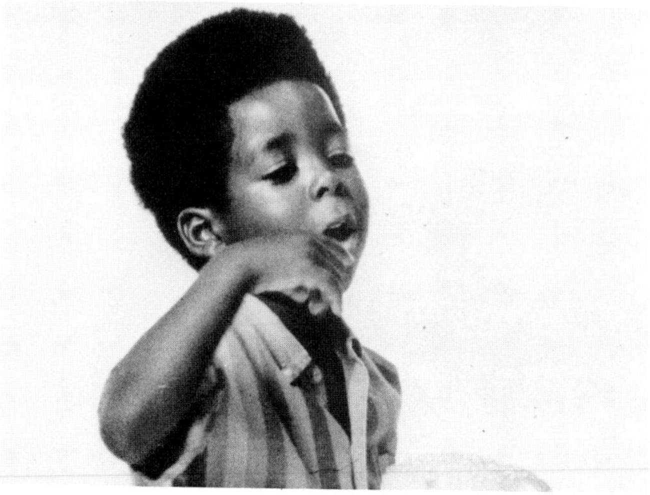

Rodney Rides Again
30-second

RODNEY SEATED WITH JUMBO JACK IN FRONT OF HIM. MAN IS OFF CAMERA

MAN: Hi, haven't I seen you on TV before?

RODNEY SPEAKS TO MAN, STILL OFF CAMERA

RODNEY: Yeah.

MAN: What's your name?

RODNEY: Rodney.

MAN: Rodney what?

RODNEY: Rodney Allen Rippy.

MAN: What's that in front of you?

RODNEY: A Jumbo Jack.

MAN: A Jumbo Jack?

RODNEY: From Jack-in-the-Box.

MAN: Did you ever get a bite out of it?

RODNEY: It too big a eat.

MAN: Think you'll be able to get a bite now? Give it a try Rodney.

RODNEY BITES INTO JUMBO JACK

Tell us how you like it.

RODNEY POINTS TO HIS MOUTH AS IF TO SAY HE CAN'T TALK WITH HIS MOUTH FULL

RODNEY: I can't, I got . . .

(SFX: LAUGHTER)

SUPER: THE JUMBO JACK AT JACK-IN-THE-BOX

291 Gold Award
Art Director: Roy Grace
Copywriter: Marcia Bell Grace
Designer: Roy Grace
TV Directors: Roy Grace
Bob Gaffney
TV Producer: Susan Calhoun
Production Company: Lofaro & Associates
Agency: Doyle Dane Bernbach Inc.
Client: American Luggage Works

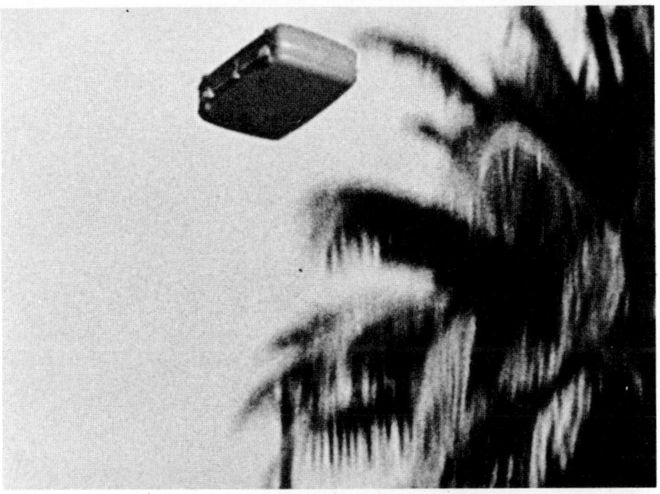

Flying
30-second

OPEN ON SUITCASE FALLING OUT OF UNSEEN HELICOPTER

SUPER: SLOW MOTION PHOTOGRAPHY

(SFX THROUGHOUT: WIND WHIRLING)

SLOW MOTION SHOTS (FROM GROUND) OF SUITCASE TUMBLING THROUGH THE SKY

MAN: What would you call a suitcase . . .

SUITCASE STILL FALLING

that could fall five hundred and fifty feet . . .

and survive twenty-two out of twenty-six times?

SUITCASE LANDS ON THE GRASS
(SFX: CRASH AS LANDS)
SUITCASE BOUNCES, THEN SETTLES

WOMAN: Fantastic!

MAN: No. American Tourister.

SUPER: AMERICAN TOURISTER FROM $20

292
Art Director: Sam Scali
Copywriter: Dan Bingham
TV Director: Franta Herman
TV Producers: Sam Scali
Dan Bingham
Production Company: Televideo Productions
Agency: Scali, McCabe, Sloves, Inc.
Client: WCBS-TV

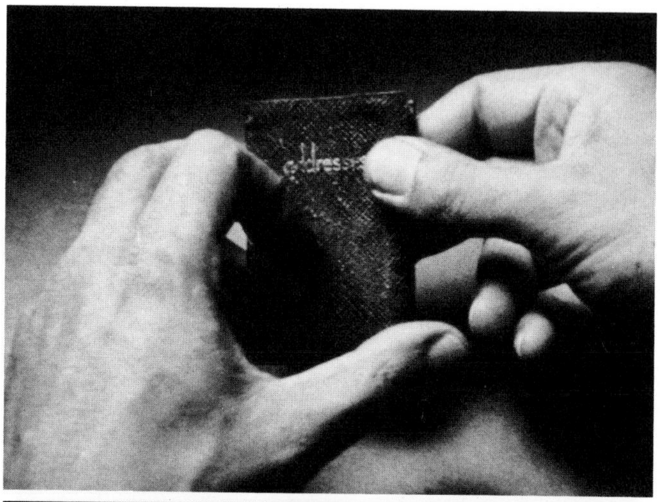

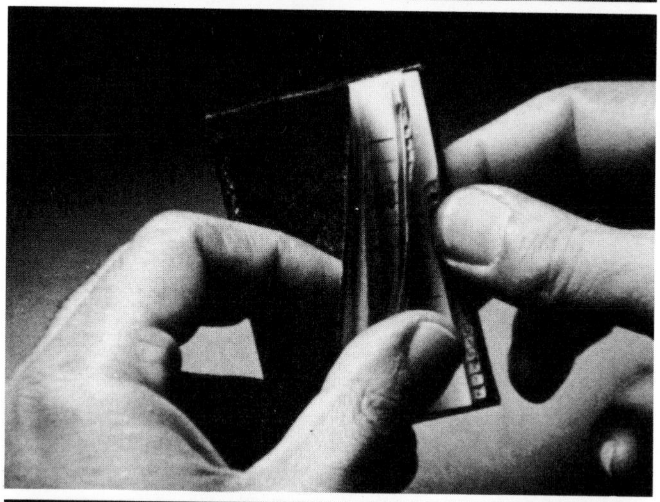

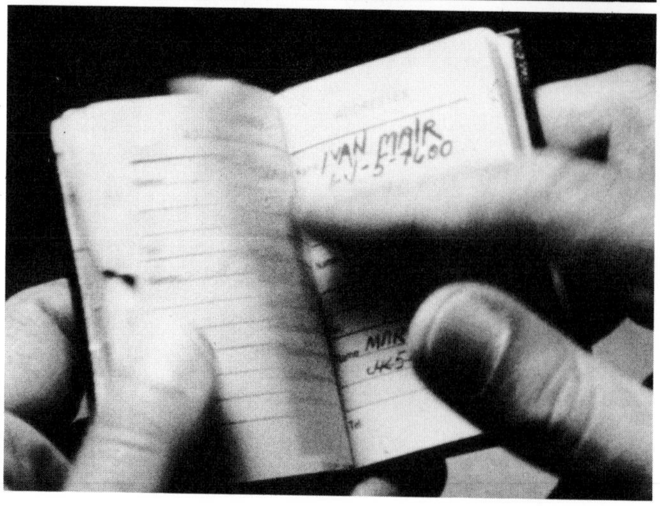

Little Black Book
30-second

SHOT OF TYPICAL, SLIGHTLY WORN, LITTLE BLACK ADDRESS BOOK

ANNCR. (VO): This little book contains the names of 24 stool pigeons . . .

CAMERA MOVES IN ON HANDS PICKING UP BOOK

12 power brokers, and innumerable informants.

HANDS BEGIN TO OPEN BOOK

All of them on a first-name basis with Chris Borgen . . .

CU OF BOOK HELD OPEN SHOWING NAMES AND PHONE NUMBERS

WCBS-TV News Crime Reporter.

CU OF FINGERS TURNING PAGES

So when Borgen wants to get all the facts behind a crime story . . .
all he has to do . . .
is let his fingers do the walking . . .

SUPER OVER BOOK: TO STAY INFORMED, YOU HAVE TO KNOW INFORMERS

through his little black book.

SUPER: THE 6 & 11 O'CLOCK REPORT ON WCBS-TV

ANNCR. (VO): See Chris Borgen weeknights on the 6 and 11 O'Clock Report.

293
Art Director: Sam Scali
Copywriter: Dan Bingham
Cameraman: Steve Horn
TV Director: Steve Horn
TV Producers: Sam Scali
Dan Bingham
Production Company: Horn/Griner Productions
Agency: Scali, McCabe, Sloves, Inc.
Client: WCBS-TV

You can't be the best
unless you do it all the time.

Day Off
30-second

DOORMAN PUSHING CART WITH NEWSPAPERS DOWN APARTMENT BUILDING HALLWAY

DOORMAN: Keane . . . Hultgren.

STOPS AT JIM JENSEN'S APARTMENT, STARTS DROPPING NEWSPAPERS BY THE DOOR

Jensen, Jensen, Jensen, Jensen . . .

ANNCR. (VO): When Jim Jensen of WCBS-TV News relaxes on his day off, he relaxes by doing what he enjoys the most. Reading about the news.

In fact, even when it is not his day off, he does what he enjoys the most. Telling you about the news.

JENSEN STEPS OUT OF HIS APARTMENT AND PICKS UP THE NEWSPAPERS

ANNCR. (VO): See Jim Jensen weeknights on the 6 and 11 O'Clock Report.

TV / Single / :30 or under

294
Art Director: Sam Scali
Copywriter: Ed McCabe
TV Director: Franta Herman
TV Producers: Sam Scali
Ed McCabe
Production Company: Televideo Productions
Agency: Scali, McCabe, Sloves, Inc.
Client: Perdue Farms, Inc.

Hot Dogs
10-second

FRANK PERDUE IN FRONT OF A BUTCHER SHOP WINDOW

FRANK PERDUE: My tasty young Perdue chickens cost less per pound, than *hot dogs*!

Than *hot dogs*!

Boy, that really galls me.

SUPER: IT TAKES A TOUGH MAN TO MAKE A TENDER CHICKEN

295
Art Director: Sam Scali
Copywriter: Ed McCabe
TV Director: Franta Herman
TV Producers: Sam Scali
Ed McCabe
Production Company: Televideo Productions
Agency: Scali, McCabe, Sloves, Inc.
Client: Perdue Farms, Inc.

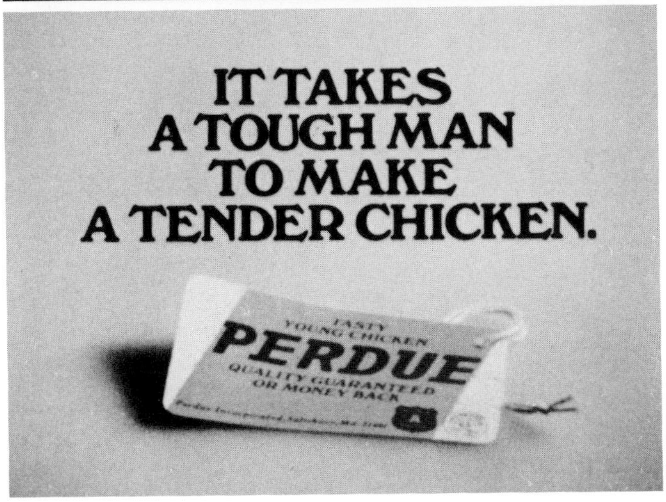

Shape Up Folks
30-second

OPEN: FRANK PERDUE IN BUTCHER SHOP

FRANK PERDUE: My fresh young chickens are one of the best sources of protein there is.

(SFX)

SHOW CHICKENS IN BIN

PERDUE: And they have fewer calories . . .

CUT TO WAIST-HIGH SHOT OF HEFTY WOMAN SHOPPER

and less saturated fat than any red meat.

VOICE IN STORE: Give me a bunch of those.

CUT TO HOT DOGS, THEN BACK TO PERDUE AT COUNTER WITH SHOPPERS

PERDUE: It's pretty obvious to me that a lot of people aren't aware of that.

C'mon folks, shape up! Start eating more of my chickens.

(SFX)

SUPER: IT TAKES A TOUGH MAN TO MAKE A TENDER CHICKEN

TV/Single/:30 or under

296
Art Director: Joe Gregorace
Copywriter: Edward Smith
Designer: Charles Piccirillo
TV Director: Andy Jenkins
TV Producer: Jerry Gold
Production Company: Jenkins-Covington
Agency: Doyle Dane Bernbach Inc.
Client: Volkswagen of America

Vote
30-second

IT'S A STREET SCENE. THERE IS A HIGH SCHOOL MARCHING BAND . . . PEOPLE JAM THE SIDEWALKS ON BOTH SIDES. A BANNER HANGS ACROSS THE STREET. IT'S A TOWN ELECTION

(SFX: CROWDS CHEERING, NOISE-MAKING, MARCHING BAND MUSIC)

MARCHING BAND COMES DOWN STREET FOLLOWED BY FANCY CONVERTIBLE. INSIDE SITS MAN WHO LOOKS LIKE 'INCUMBENT' (WAVING)

ANNCR. (VO): This is a very fancy limousine convertible. The most expensive you can buy.

(SFX: MUSIC, CROWD NOISES UNDER)

SAME VIEW OF STREET WITH TOWNSPEOPLE REVEALS ONE-MAN MARCHING BAND WALKING. HE IS DRUMMING, PLAYING GUITAR, KAZOO

(SFX: SAME MUSIC AND NOISES UNDER)

VOLKSWAGEN COMES INTO VIEW

ANNCR. (VO): This is a Volkswagen Convertible. The least expensive four-passenger convertible you can buy. . . . Now . . . which man would you vote for?

(SFX: BIG CROWD NOISES UNDER)

297
Art Director: Reinhold Schwenk
Copywriter: Lore Parker
Designer: Reinhold Schwenk
Cameraman: Lou Addams
TV Director: Tony Lover
TV Producer: Barbara Cowan
Production Company: D.S.I.
Agency: Doyle Dane Bernbach Inc.
Client: Sony Corporation

Actual TV broadcast.
SONY® Ask anyone.

18,000 Hours
30-second

(SFX OF TELEVISION PROGRAM)

YOUNG MAN INTENTLY WATCHING TV. ALL SEEN FROM TV'S-EYE-VIEW

CAMERA SLOWLY BEGINS A 180 DEGREE TURN AROUND THE MAN

ANNCR. (VO): Jim Rogers, Transmitter Supervisor. . . .

NOW WE SEE MAN IN PROFILE

. . . . for Channel 40 in Sacramento, California

CONTINUE TURN. NOW WE SEE THE SONY TRINITRON HE IS WATCHING

. . . . has played this Sony Trinitron for 18,000 hours.

NOW WE LOOK OVER HIS SHOULDER SQUARELY AT THE SET

That's the same as if *you* in your home, played it four hours a day for 12 years.

MOVE IN OVER HIS SHOULDER FOR CLOSER LOOK AT SET

18,000 hours—and still going strong!

EXTREME CLOSE-UP

Sony. Ask Jim Rogers.

SUPER: SONY. ASK ANYONE

Ask anyone.

TV/Single/:30 or under

298 Silver Award
Art Director: Bernie Vangrin
Copywriter: Ray Werner
Cameraman: Andy Jenkins
TV Director: Andy Jenkins
TV Producers: Bernie Vangrin
Ray Werner
Production Company: Jenkins/Covington
Agency: Ketchum, MacLeod & Grove, Pittsburgh
Client: C&P Telephone

Margie Schumaker
30-second

OPEN ON TWO GUYS IN TELEPHONE BOOTHS WHICH ARE STANDING SIDE-BY-SIDE. FRED FUMBLES WITH A BIT OF CRUMPLED PAPER

DIALOGUE SLIGHTLY OVERLAPS BETWEEN CONVERSATIONS

FRED: Hello Operator, I'm looking for the number of a Margie Shumaker.

AT THE SAME TIME, BOB IS LEAFING THROUGH THE DIRECTORY, RUNNING HIS FINGER DOWN A PAGE . . . PUTS A DIME IN THE PHONE, DIALS THE NUMBER

BOB: Shumaker, Shumaker, Margie Shumaker.

FRED: Well, could be a U or an O.

BOB: Jefferson Street.

FRED: On Jackson Street. Oh, I'm sorry that's Jefferson Street. What, what was that . . . 555-26. . . . Thank you very much.

FRED WRITES DOWN NUMBER

(SFX: DIALING SOUND)

FRED DIALS THE NUMBER AS BOB BEGINS TALKING TO HER

BOB: Hello Margie. Big Bob here. Uh, the fellow from the party in the brown sweater. (LAUGH) Yeh, how could you forget. Hey listen, ah, how you doin'?

(SFX: FRED GETS BUSY SIGNAL)

SUPER: Look it up yourself. It's faster.

299
Art Director: Ron Barrett
Copywriter: David Altschiller
TV Director: Jacques Lemoine
TV Producers: Paul Wollman
David Altschiller
Client: Fiat
Agency: Carl Ally Inc.

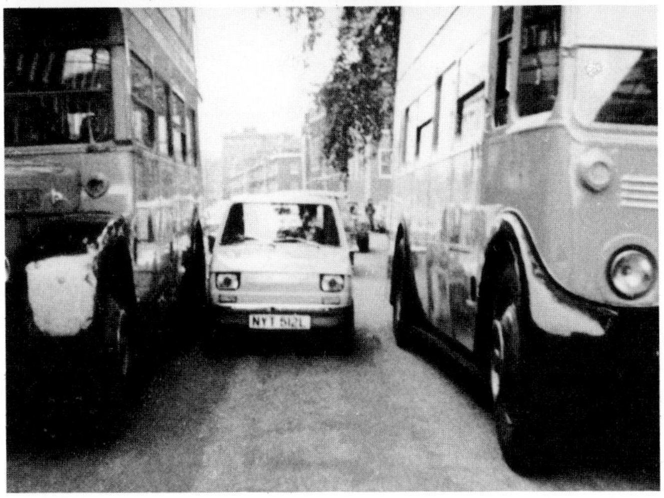

Fiat 126
30-second

(MUSIC THROUGHOUT)

OPEN SHOT OF ARCH IN EUROPEAN CITY

SHOW DIFFERENT CITIES AND TRAFFIC CRUNCH IN EACH THROUGHOUT

ANNCR. (VO): We took a good hard look at what city driving is really like and we made the new Fiat 126.

ONE SHOT SHOWS STOPPED TRAFFIC

MORE JAMMED TRAFFIC (COP TRYING TO MAKE IT WORK)

(SFX: HONKING HORNS, VOICES, TEMPERS FLARING)

MORE SCENES OF INTERSECTIONS HOPELESSLY TIED UP

ORANGE FIAT SMOOTHLY ENTERS

WENDS WAY THROUGH CARS

It's smaller outside than almost any other car for handling

FIAT DRIVING IN BETWEEN TWO BUSES

But it's very large inside for handling people

FIAT PULLS UP TO CURB AND FOUR BUSINESS MEN GET OUT OF THE SMALL CAR

If you live in the city should you drive the city car? The Fiat 126.

SUPER: Fiat 126
The City Car

TV / Single / :30 or under

300
Art Director: Roy Grace
Copywriter: Evan Stark
Designer: Roy Grace
TV Director: Howard Zieff
TV Producer: Susan Calhoun
Production Company: Zieff Films
Agency: Doyle Dane Bernbach Inc.
Client: Mobil Oil Corporation

Mr. Dirt's Bag of Tricks
30-second

DIRT IN DARK GARAGE (SMIRKING)

ANNCR. (VO): Every car engine has an enemy—dirt.

DIRT MOVES TO CAR

DIRT: If I have my way, this engine could stall.

DIRT GOES TO WORK INSIDE MOTOR

DIRT: I won't give it a little, I'll give it my all.

REALLY AT IT NOW

DIRT: I'll glob it and gook it with sludge and with grime.

STORM OF DIRT RISES FROM ENGINE

DIRT: What I'll do to this engine's worse than a crime!

ADDS BAG OF MORE DIRT

Yes, engines are what I love to hurt . . . that's why they call me Mr. Dirt.

SHOT DISSOLVES INTO GASOLINE WHIRLING AROUND IN WASHING MACHINE EFFECT

ANNCR. (VO): But dirt has an enemy. Mobil Detergent Gasoline.

PULL AWAY. CIRCLE TURNS INTO RED "O" OF MOBIL

Mobil hates dirt.

301
Art Director: Guy Noerr
Copywriter: Richard De Pascal
TV Director: Dom Rossetti
TV Producer: Dom Rossetti
Production Company: Z Productions
Agency: Young & Rubicam International, Inc.
Client: Dr. Pepper

Lifeboat
30-second

EIGHT SHIPWRECKED PEOPLE IN A LIFEBOAT, EXHAUSTED AND THIRSTY

COWARD: It's been nine days since the ship went down.

YOUNG HUSBAND: Excuse me . . . is there anything left.

LEADER: Some salted peanuts . . . and one bottle of Dr. Pepper.

COWARD: (PANICS, GETS HYSTERICAL) *One* bottle. . . . is that all there's left to drink!! It's not going to be enough!!

OTHERS HAVE TO RESTRAIN HIM.

LEADER: *Look!* . . . look at the size of this bottle . . tadah . . .

HOLDS UP DR. PEPPER 48-OZ. BOTTLE. LEADER POURS AS DEPRESSED CREW TURNS INTO PARTY MOOD

(MUSIC) THEY START DANCING

ANNCR. (VO): Dr. Pepper's new 48-oz Party-Size Bottle. It's economical, resealable and just one bottle takes care of everybody.

SUPER: DR. PEPPER PARTY-SIZE BOTTLE

TV/Single/:30 or under

302
Art Director: Alan Chalfin
Copywriter: Dick Tarlow
TV Director: Jeff Metzner
TV Producer: Ray Lofaro
Production Company: Lofaro & Associates
Agency: Sacks, Tarlow, Rosen, Inc.
Client: Cricketeer

Doubleknit Flannel Suit
30-second

OPEN ON MAN IN GRAY FLANNEL SUIT SITTING IN LOTUS POSITION

ANNCR. (VO): Cricketeer brings you peace of body.

MAN CHANGES TO A DIFFERENT YOGA POSITION. HE CONTINUES TO TAKE DIFFERENT INTRICATE POSITIONS THROUGHOUT (EXPRESSIVE OF A 'CRICKET')

A Cricketeer suit is so flexible, you can do anything in it you can do out of it. Without it losing its shape or even wrinkling. Because we believe a man should feel relaxed even in a suit, we'll give you a guidebook to yoga. The book will give you peace of mind.

CU OF MAN WITH HEAD BOWED AND HANDS IN PRAYER POSITION

Our suit will give you peace of body.

SUPER: CRICKETEER
(NAME OF STORE)

303
Art Director: Julio Dilorio
Copywriter: Gene Case
TV Director: Barry Brown
TV Producer: Barbara Fine
Production Company: Brillig Productions
Agency: Case & McGrath, Inc.
Client: The Mennen Company

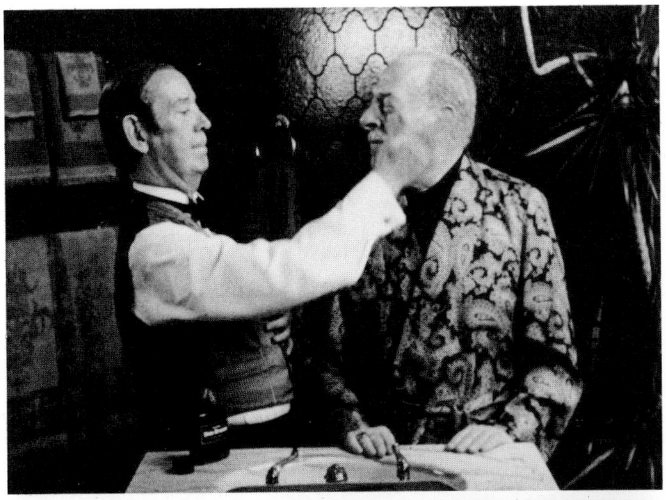

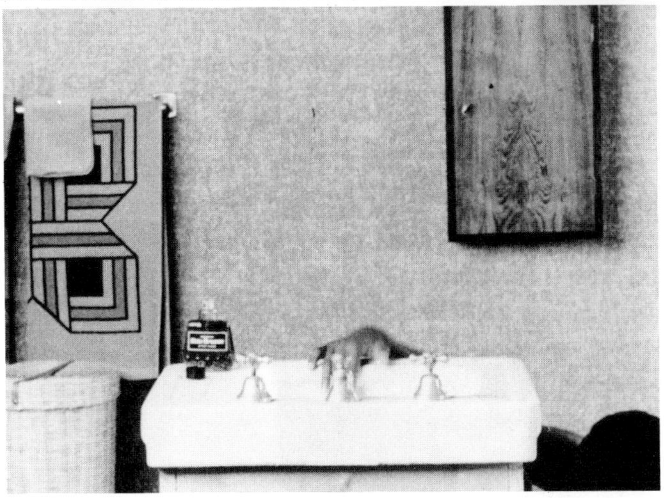

Joe Frazier
30-second

VALET AND MILLIONAIRE IN LUXURIOUS BATH

ANNCR. (VO): America wakes up with Skin Bracer . . .

(MUSIC)

(SFX: SLAP! SLAP!) VALET SLAPS MILLIONAIRE.

MILLIONAIRE (ON CAMERA): Thanks. I needed that.

DISSOLVE TO SKIN BRACER BOTTLE

ANNCR. (VO): If *you* need waking up, slap on some Bracer. Its skin-tightener and chin-chillers . . . can help you . . . come out smokin' . . .

JOE FRAZIER AT SINK. SLAPS HIMSELF OUT OF PICTURE ENTIRELY

(SFX: SLAP! THUMP!)

FRAZIER'S HAND GROPES FOR EDGE OF SINK

FRAZIER (OFF-CAMERA): Thanks. I needed that.

TV / Single / :30 or under

304
Art Director: Joe Genova
Copywriter: Jim Symon
TV Director: Barry Brown
TV Producer: John Fengler
Production Company: Brillig Productions
Agency: Kurtz & Symon, Inc.
Client: Fram Corporation

Cash Register
30-second

(SFX: RING CASH REGISTER)

CUSTOMER LEAVES GARAGE OFFICE. GARAGE OWNER SEATED BEHIND DESK GESTURES AT CUSTOMER OUTSIDE. YOU CAN SEE CUSTOMER THROUGH GLASS AS HE WALKS DEJECTED

GARAGE OWNER: That poor guy's just paid me $200.00 for a ring job. $200.00.

HE SWIVELS IN CHAIR, TAKES FRAM OIL FILTER FROM DISPLAY

This is a Fram oil filter. About $4.00.

OUTSIDE CUSTOMER HAS OPENED HOOD AND SLAMMED IT

OWNER: If he'd paid me $4.00 when he had his oil changed, chances are he wouldn't be paying me 200 bucks now.

PUTS FRAM OIL FILTER CAN NEXT TO CHECK. BY NOW CUSTOMER HAS GOTTEN INTO CAR

The choice is yours. You can pay me now. Or . . .

(CASH REGISTER BELL RINGS AGAIN AS HE PUTS CHECK IN)

pay me later.

CUSTOMER IS SEEN DRIVING OFF

SUPER: FRAM OIL FILTERS

305
Art Director: Roy Grace
Copywriter: Evan Stark
Designer: Roy Grace
Cameramen: Ed Rosson
Chuck Roscher
TV Director: Howard Zieff
TV Producer: Susan Calhoun
Production Company: Zieff Films
Agency: Doyle Dane Bernbach Inc.
Client: Mobil Oil Corporation

Mr. Dirt's Underground Garage
30-second

OPENS ON STAIRCASE

(SFX)

DOOR OPENS AND SMILING MR. DIRT DANCES DOWN STAIRS

ANNCR. (VO): Every car engine has an enemy—dirt.

DIRT PRANCES AROUND CARS DURING ENTIRE SEQUENCE, BANGING ON TOP OF HOODS, GENERALLY WHOPPING IT UP

DIRT: I'm dirt! I'm dirt! And it's car engines I love to hurt.

(SFX)

I try to make them stall and stutter and stop, and if I do, what can you do? Ha! You can't even call a cop.

HE APPEARS COMING OUT FROM ENGINE AS HOOD LIFTS

I try to make your engine whine and whimper and yelp and cry for help.

WALKS TOWARD ROWS OF CARS

I'm dirt! Ha-Ha! I'm dirt!

SHOT DISSOLVES INTO GASOLINE WHIRLING AROUND IN WASHING MACHINE EFFECT

ANNCR. (VO): But dirt has an enemy, Mobil Detergent Gasoline.

PULL AWAY. CIRCLE TURNS INTO RED "O" OF MOBIL

Mobil hates dirt!

TV/Single/:30 or under

306
Art Director: Mark Ross
Copywriter: Brendan Kelly
Cinematographer: Glen Kirkpatrick
TV Director: Rick Levine
TV Producer: Mark Ross
Production Company: Wylde Films
Agency: Ogilvy & Mather Inc.
Client: American Express Travelers Checks

Purse Snatcher
30-second

SCENE IS A CROWDED STREET. NOTHING UNUSUAL

ANNCR. (VO): You are about to witness a crime.

CLOSE UP

Two women on vacation . . . and carrying a lot of money.

SLOW MOTION: SUDDENLY A MAN MOVES IN FAST, TAKES PURSE

WOMAN: Oh, stop that man . . .

SCENE OF MAN RUNNING AMIDST CONFUSED CROWD

WOMAN: Hey, somebody stop him.

HE IS LOST AND GONE (CAMERA GOES BACK TO NORMAL SPEED)

ANNCR. (VO): Protect your vacation. Instead of cash carry American Express Travelers Checks.

BACK TO CROWD ON STREET

If they're ever stolen or lost, you can get them replaced—usually on the same day.

CU CHECKS

SUPER: American Express Travelers Checks. Because it could happen to you.

307
Art Director: Roy Grace
Copywriter: Evan Stark
Designer: Roy Grace
Cameramen: Ed Rosson
Chuck Roscher
TV Directors: Howard Zieff
Dick Lowe
TV Producer: Susan Calhoun
Production Companies: Zieff Films
Gomes Lowe, Inc.
Agency: Doyle Dane Bernbach Inc.
Client: Mobil Oil Corporation

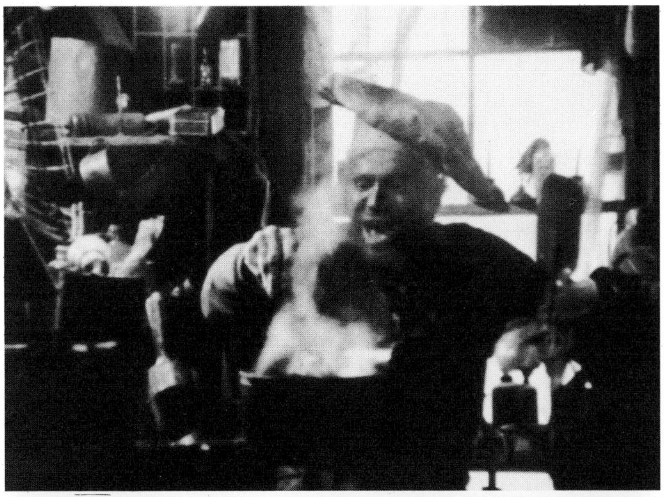

Mr. Dirt's Bag of Tricks
30-second

DIRT IN DARK GARAGE (SMIRKING)

ANNCR. (VO): Every car engine has an enemy—dirt.

DIRT MOVES TO CAR

DIRT: If I have my way, this engine could stall.

DIRT GOES TO WORK INSIDE MOTOR

DIRT: I won't give it a little, I'll give it my all.

REALLY AT IT NOW

DIRT: I'll glob it and gook it with sludge and with grime.

STORM OF DIRT RISES FROM ENGINE

DIRT: What I'll do to this engine's worse than a crime!

ADDS BAG OF MORE DIRT

Yes, engines are what I love to hurt . . . that's why they call me Mr. Dirt.

SHOT DISSOLVES INTO GASOLINE WHIRLING AROUND IN WASHING MACHINE EFFECT

ANNCR. (VO): But dirt has an enemy. Mobil Detergent Gasoline.

PULL AWAY. CIRCLE TURNS INTO RED "O" OF MOBIL

Mobil hates dirt.

Mr. Dirt's Bi-plane
30-second

Mr. Dirt's Underground Garage
30-second

TV/Campaign/:30 or under

308
Art Director: Sam Scali
Copywriter: Dan Bingham
TV Directors: Joe DeVoto
Franta Herman
TV Producers: Sam Scali
Dan Bingham
Production Companies: Richards & Myers Films
Televideo Productions
Horn/Griner Productions
Agency: Scali, McCabe, Sloves, Inc.
Client: WCBS-TV

Boys in the Back Room
30-second

OPEN: FLURRY OF REPORTERS AT CITY HALL IN REAL 'POLITICAL' BACK ROOM SET-UP

MAN: I have a statement. Gentlemen, I have a statement. If you'll please let me through, I have a statement to make.

ANNCR. (VO): When WCBS-TV News sends someone to cover a political story, we send an ex-politician.

SHOT OF JEROME WILSON TAKING IT ALL DOWN

Watch former state Senator Jerome Wilson report what actually goes on in the smoke-filled rooms.

See Jerome Wilson weeknights on the 6 and 11 O'Clock Report.

Little Black Book
30-second

Gary Essex
30-second

309

Art Director: Tom Heck
Copywriters: Bob Hildt
Dick Williams
Designer: Tom Heck
TV Directors: Jerry Shore
Ted Devlet
Micky Trenner

TV Producer: Telpac
Production Companies: Jerry Shore
D.V.I.
E.U.E.
Agency: F. William Free & Company
Client: National Airlines

Peggy, Cindy, Diane
30-second

(MUSIC UNDER)

CU OF PEGGY IN GARDEN

PEGGY (SINGING IN NATURAL AMATEUR VOICE): Come on and fly me, in the big blue sky . . .

CUT TO CU OF CINDY IN PLANE

CINDY (SINGING): Come on and fly me, together we'll fly high . . .

CUT TO DIANE IN TERMINAL

DIANE (SINGING): I'm National, fly me.

CUT TO CU OF CINDY IN PLANE

CINDY: I'm Cindy. I've got the only direct service to both Los Angeles and San Francisco. Fly me.

CUT TO TITLE: I'M NATIONAL. FLY ME. CALL YOUR TRAVEL AGENT.

GIRL (VO): I'm National, fly me.

Eileen Salyer
30-second

Mrs. Goldblum
30-second

TV/Campaign/:30 or under

310
Art Director: George Lois
Copywriter: Bob Elgort
TV Director: Joe Coffey
TV Producer: Edward Murphy
Production Company: Famous Commercials
Agency: Lois Holland Callaway Inc.
Client: Ovaltine Food Products

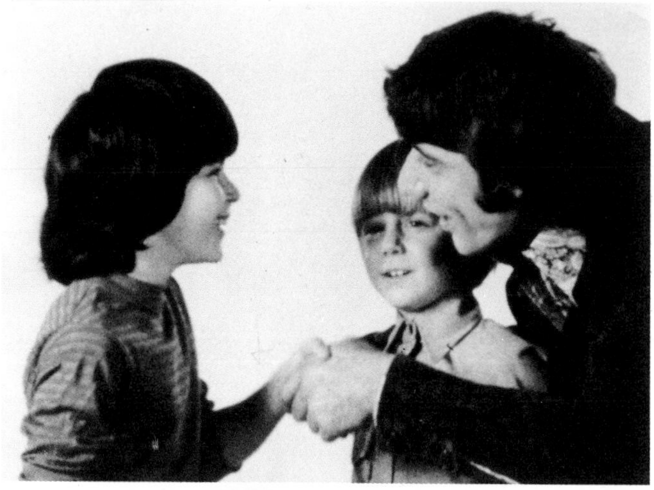

Joe Meets Kids
30-second

TITLE CARD: JOE NAMATH MEETS THE OVALTINE GANG

CU OF JOE NAMATH AND TWO YOUNG BOYS. JOE HAS ARM AROUND ONE BOY

BOY WITH JOE: Meet Jo-Jo Rizzo.

NAMATH AND JO-JO SHAKE HANDS

NAMATH: My o-o-old pal Jo-Jo Rizzo.

CUT TO A SECOND BOY

BOY WITH JOE: Mitch Goldman.

NAMATH AND MITCH SHAKE HANDS

NAMATH: My o-o-old pal Mitch Goldman.

CUT TO THIRD BOY

BOY WITH NAMATH: Eddie Alvarez.

NAMATH AND EDDIE SHAKE HANDS

NAMATH: My o-o-old pal Eddie Alvarez.

MS OF NAMATH AND BOY HOLDING GLASS OF OVALTINE

BOY WITH NAMATH: Put it there, pal. Shake hands with a glass of Ovaltine.

NAMATH: My o-o-old pal Ovaltine.

PRODUCT SHOT

ANNCR. (VO): The chocolate sensation that tastes great in milk. Ovaltine gives you more of the vitamins you need all day than any other milk flavoring.

MS OF NAMATH AND ALL THE BOYS

EVERYONE (IN UNISON): My o-o-old pal Ovaltine.

Kid Meets Joe's Friends
30-second

Joe Talks to Parents
30-second

311 Gold Award
Art Director: Sam Scali
Copywriter: Ed McCabe
TV Director: Franta Herman
TV Producers: Sam Scali
Ed McCabe
Production Company: Televideo Productions
Agency: Scali, McCabe, Sloves, Inc.
Client: Perdue Farms, Inc.

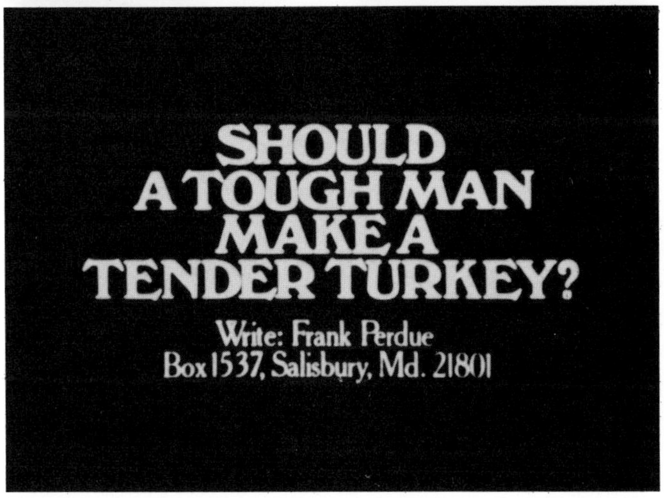

Turkey
30-second

FRANK PERDUE ALONE IN HIS DEN READING A BOOK ON "CARE AND FEEDING OF TURKEYS"

(SILENT)

PERDUE (FACE FRONT): Recently, a lady told me she had a great Perdue turkey. That's odd. I never raised a turkey.

I'm strictly a chicken man . . . But it's not a bad idea.

PERDUE SERIOUS (FORWARD)

A turkey as good as a Perdue chicken. It would require a lot of work. And I'm not going to waste my time if you're happy with the turkeys you're getting now.

Let me know what you think.

(PERDUE GOES BACK TO READING "THE CARE AND FEEDING OF TURKEYS")

SUPER: SHOULD A TOUGH MAN MAKE A TENDER TURKEY? Write: Frank Perdue

Parts Inspection
30-second

Parts
30-second

312
Art Director: Henry Holtzman
Copywriter: Larry Spinner
TV Directors: Mike Cuesta
Melvin Sokolsky
Jeffrey Metzner
TV Producer: Linda Mevorach
Production Companies: Stan Lang Productions
Sokolsky Films
Lofaro & Associates
Agency: Young & Rubicam International, Inc.
Client: Dr. Pepper

YOU'VE GOT TO BE GOOD TO MAKE IT IN NEW YORK.
Dr Pepper

Kid
30-second

SCENE IS BUSY CITY NEIGHBORHOOD. KID IN STREET. FRIENDS CROWD AROUND HIM

KID: I was thirsty one day, you know. Hey, man, cut it out.

FRIEND IN BACKGROUND THROWS SNOWBALL AT KID

So my mother gives me this Dr. Pepper. I say, "I'm no fool, man, that's a medicine." She says, "No, it's a new soda." It looks like all them other sodas to me. But I taste it, you know? Man, it's fantastic. Now all the kids drink it. Watch this.

(TO ONE OF THE KIDS)

Hey, Frankie, you want some Dr. Pepper?

FRANKIE: Yeah.

Candy Store
30-second

Cab Driver
30-second

313
Art Director: Julio Dilorio
Copywriter: Gene Case
TV Director: Barry Brown
TV Producer: Barbara Fine
Production Company: Brillig Productions Inc.
Agency: Case & McGrath Inc.
Client: The Mennen Company

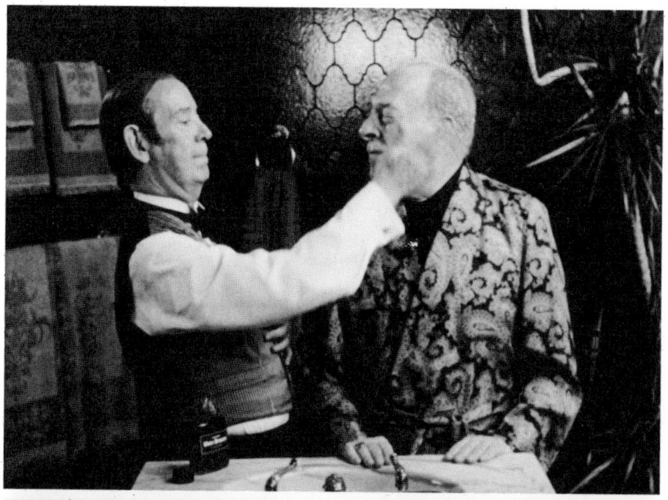

Joe Frazier
30-second

VALET AND MILLIONAIRE IN LUXURIOUS BATH

ANNCR. (VO): America wakes up with Skin Bracer . . .

(MUSIC)

(SFX): SLAP! SLAP! VALET SLAPS MILLIONAIRE

MILLIONAIRE (ON CAMERA): Thanks. I needed that.

DISSOLVE TO SKIN BRACER BOTTLE

ANNCR. (VO): If *you* need waking up, slap on some Bracer. Its skin-tightener and chin-chillers . . . can help you . . . come out smokin' . . .

JOE FRAZIER AT SINK. SLAPS HIMSELF OUT OF PICTURE ENTIRELY

(SFX: SLAP! THUMP!)

FRAZIER'S HAND GROPES FOR EDGE OF SINK

FRAZIER (OFF-CAMERA): Thanks. I needed that.

Japanese
30-second

Handcuffs
30-second

TV/Campaign/:30 or under

314 Silver Award
Art Directors: Jim Handloser
Mark Yustein
Copywriter: Frank DiGiacomo
Designers: Jim Handloser
Mark Yustein
TV Director: Bob Giraldi
TV Producer: Joan Scoccimarro
Production Company: Jerry Shore Productions
Agency: Della Femina, Travisano & Partners, Inc.
Client: WABC-TV Eyewitness News

Wedding
30-second

CU OF TEAM COMING UP STAIRS LED BY HERALDO. SHOW WEDDING, DANCING

DANCING STOPS. CUT TO HERALDO INTRODUCING TEAM

HERALDO: Come on, I'll guarantee everybody a good time. Amigos, por favor—Silencio—My good friends, I'd like you to meet my good friends, Melba, Roger, Tex, Frank and Jim.

CUT TO TEAM. CU WEDDING MOTHER WHO RECOGNIZES ROGER. SHE HAS HIM ON DANCE FLOOR AND CROWD ADVANCES

MOTHER: Ahhh, Hello Roger Grimsby, Come on, come on . . .

(MUSIC)

MOTHER AND ROGER DANCING. GIRL GOES TO HERALDO. JIM AND FRANK GET INTO SCENE. MELBA DANCES. SHOT OF PRIEST, OTHERS IN CROWD. BOUTON IN BACKGROUND

ANNCR. (VO): The Eyewitness News Team. The reason people like them so much is because they like people so much.

TITLE: EYEWITNESS NEWS (7)

CUT TO ROGER AND MOTHER DANCING AND PEOPLE ABOUT

Football
30-second

Toast
30-second

TV/Single/:60

315
Art Director: Michael Ulick
Copywriter: Jeff Frey
TV Director: Howard Zieff
TV Producer: Barbara Michelson
Production Company: Zieff Films
Agency: Wells, Rich, Greene, Inc.
Client: Midas International, Inc.

Midas
We install mufflers for a living.
We have to do a better job.

Waiting Inventory
60-second

MECHANIC IN GARAGE OFFICE.

BERT: I'll have that muffler on in no time.

BERT (ON PHONE): Phil, can you send me a muffler right away?

PHIL: Hold on Bert.

CU PHILS AUTO, TABS INVENTORY

ANNCR. (VO): Most places that install mufflers as a sideline don't carry a large inventory, so you might have to wait.

CUSTOMER EYES BERT ON PHONE

PHIL: It's on its way Bert.

BERT: Thanks . . . ah darling . . . The little lady . . . You married?

CUSTOMER: Say, you're sure you got that muffler?

BERT: My twins. Wendy and Wendell!

TAKES OUT PICTURE IN WALLET

CUSTOMER: Look, I'm in sort of a hurry.

BERT: Ha-have you seen the shop?

BERT SHOWS OFF SHOP

ANNCR. (VO): At Midas we carry a large inventory so you'll get the muffler you need instead of an excuse.

CUSTOMER: It's very interesting but . . .

BERT: . . . but you're in a hurry. Why don't you pull your car on the rack?

CUTS TO PHONE

BERT: Phil, where is it? I don't know how much longer I can hold him.

(SFX: CAR HORN)

BERT WAVES AT CUSTOMER IN HIS CAR UP ON LIFT

CUSTOMER: Hey, what's going on? Hey, you put me down. Put me down.

BERT CONCEALS HIMSELF BEHIND THE OFFICE DOOR

SUPER: MIDAS. WE INSTALL MUFFLERS FOR A LIVING. WE HAVE TO DO A BETTER JOB.

TV/Single/:60 or over

316
Art Director: Don Tortoriello
Songwriters: Dottie West
Billy Davis
Cameraman: Steve Horn
TV Director: Steve Horn
TV Producer: Ann Curry
Production Company: Horn/Griner Productions
Agency: McCann-Erickson, Inc.
Client: Coca-Cola, USA

Country Sunshine
60-second

CAB ON COUNTRY ROAD: GIRL INSIDE

SONG: I was raised on country sunshine . . .

ALL COUNTRY SCENES—SWINGING, FISHING, FATHER ON TRACTOR, MOTHER ON PORCH, HAY LOFT . . .

Green grass beneath my feet . . .
runnin' thru fields of daisies
wadin' thru the cheek . . .
You love me and it's invitin' . . .
to go where life is . . .
more excitin' . . .
But I was raised . . .

CUS OF FAMILY REACTING TO CAB

on country sunshine . . .
I was raised . . .
on country sunshine. I'm a happy . . .
with the simple things . . . a Saturday night dance . . .

CAB ARRIVING AT HOUSE

a bottle of Coke . . .
the joy that the bluebird brings.
I love you, please believe me . . .
and don't you ever leave me . . .
cause I was raised on country sunshine.

GREETINGS

It's the real thing . . .
like Coke is . . .

KIDS DRINKING COKE

that you're hoping to find . . .

GUY GETTING OUT OF TRUCK, EMBRACES GIRL

like country sunshine, it's the real thing . . .
Coca-Cola

SUPER: IT'S THE REAL THING

317
Art Director: William Moore
Songwriter: Sandy Mason Theoret
Cameraman: Steve Horn
TV Director: Steve Horn
TV Producer: John Jenkins
Production Company: Horn/Griner Productions
Agency: McCann-Erickson, Inc.
Client: Coca-Cola, USA

Playground Counselor
60-second

COUNSELOR WALKS DOWN STEPS OF ROW HOUSE

SONG: Hey, look at you lookin' at the sunrise . . .
There's such a brighter . . .
look in your eyes . . .

THEY CROSS THE STREET. NOW COUNSELOR AND THREE KIDS WALK DOWN SIDEWALK

Now that I know you've felt the wind . . .
that's blowing, reaching out . . .
and wanting life's good things.
Now that you're seeing . . .

PLAYGROUND GATE OPENS AND KIDS RUSH IN.

all things grow.

(MUSIC UP)

CU PASSING BALL TO BOY.
COUNSELOR JOGS TO BOY BEHIND FENCE.
CU TOGETHER CU BOY

There is more love in . . .
you than anyone . . .

TV/Single/:60 or over

318
Art Director: John Danza
Copywriter: Ed McCabe
TV Director: Bo Widerberg
TV Producers: John Danza
Ed McCabe
Production Company: James Garrett & Partners
Agency: Scali, McCabe, Sloves, Inc.
Client: Volvo, Inc.

Cost of Living
60-second

SCENE: YOUNG SWEDISH FAMILY IN THEIR HOME. MAN IS WORKING ON BOOKS. THROUGHOUT QUIET TALK BETWEEN THEM. LITTLE GIRL IS DRAWING

ANNCR. (VO):The cost of living in Sweden is as high as it is in the United States. But the average income is lower.

So when it comes to buying things, the Swedes are inclined to be exceedingly practical. Especially when it comes to something as expensive as a car. A 40% down payment is required. A car *has* to be economical. Gasoline is 80¢ a gallon.

This family could buy an inexpensive import. But their car has to hold up through many long, cold, Swedish winters.

FAMILY HAS TAKEN OUT CAR BROCHURES, EXAMINED THEM CLOSELY. WIFE AND HUSBAND RELATE

They can't afford to buy a new car every couple of years. So like most Swedes, they'll spend a little more and get the car that will live up to these demands.

THEY LOOK AT PICTURE OF VOLVO. THAT'S THE ONE THEY'LL BUY

Volvo. We build them the way we build them, because we have to.

SUPER: VOLVO

319
Art Director: Ralph Ammirati
Copywriter: Marty Puris
TV Director: Howard Zieff
TV Producer: Janine Marjollet
Production Company: Zieff Films
Agency: Carl Ally Inc.
Client: Fiat

Ferrari's New Car
60-second

MAN STANDING IN DRIVEWAY

MAN: Ladies and gentlemen of America, what you are about to see is Enzo Ferrari's new car.

In performance, it is what you would expect. It has front wheel drive. It has a transverse-mounted, overhead cam engine. It has rack and pinion steering.

In front, it has self-adjusting disk brakes . . . and it has four wheel independent suspension.

In comfort, it is fantastic.

The car has more room on the inside than American cars four feet longer.

HE GESTURES TO GARAGE

(SFX)

Of course, this is not the car Ferrari builds. This is the car Ferrari drives. The Fiat 128.

Just think, for the price of a Fiat you can drive around like Ferrari.

ANNCR. (VO): The P.O.E. price of the Fiat 128 is $1,992 which includes everything but delivery charges, dealer preparation and taxes.

TV/Single/:60 or over

320
Art Director: Sam Scali
Copywriter: Dan Bingham
Cameraman: Steve Horn
TV Director: Steve Horn
TV Producers: Sam Scali
Dan Bingham
Production Company: Horn/Griner Productions
Agency: Scali, McCabe, Sloves, Inc.
Client: WCBS-TV

Boyhood Heroes
60-second

(STILLS FROM OLD PICTURES RUN THROUGH THREE-QUARTERS OF SPOT)

STILL OF BABE RUTH AT BAT

ANNCR. (VO): Every red-blooded American boy has had a boyhood hero.

STILL OF 'THE SHADOW' FROM THE COMICS

RADIO ANNCR. (UNDER): 'The Babe' . . . The 'Shadow' . . .

CU 'THE SHADOW' . . . STILL OF JOE E. LOUIS FROM *THE RING*

ANNCR. (VO): The 'Brown Bomber'. . .

STILL OF YOUNG BOY BY RADIO

ANNCR. (VO): When Jim Jensen was a boy, he also had his boyhood heroes . . . H. V. Kaltenborn . . . Gabriel Heatter . . . Edward R. Murrow . . .

(SFX: MURROW'S VOICE)

In fact, while most kids ran home to the thrilling adventures of Jack Armstrong, Jim Jensen ran home to the thrilling adventures of Edward R. Murrow as he covered the London Blitz.

CU OF YOUNG JENSEN BY HIS RADIO

And when the 'News Bug' bites a kid at that age, you've got yourself a reporter.

JIM JENSEN ON CAMERA

JENSEN: Good evening, everyone. I'm Jim Jensen. Tonight's top story centers on the . . .

SUPER OVER JENSEN: You can't be the best unless you do it all the time.

ANNCR. (VO): See Jim Jensen week nights on the 6 and 11 O'clock Reports.

SUPER: The 6 & 11 O'clock Report. On WCBS-TV

321
Art Director: John Danza
Copywriter: Ed McCabe
TV Director: Bo Widerberg
TV Producers: John Danza
Ed McCabe
Production Company: James Garrett & Partners
Agency: Scali, McCabe, Sloves, Inc.
Client: Volvo, Inc.

Swedish Winter
60-second

OPEN ON MS OF SNOW-COVERED FOREST SCENE (SFX THROUGHOUT)

A CAR CAN BE SEEN IN DISTANCE. CAMERA PULLS BACK TO SHOW CAR EMERGING FROM WOODS

ANNCR. (VO): In Sweden, we demand as much of a car as you do.

CAR CONTINUES TO COME TOWARDS CAMERA ON SNOW COVERED ROAD, WOODS IN BACKGROUND

We have to. In parts of our country, winter arrives in October . . .

CUT TO CAR INTERIOR TO SHOW BACK OF PASSENGERS AND WINDSHIELD

(SFX: PEOPLE TALKING)

and doesn't leave till May . . . Our cars better not break down.

CUT TO CAR STILL COMING DOWN FOREST ROAD TOWARDS CAMERA

A man could freeze to death waiting for help . . . If a heater doesn't function properly, it's more than an inconvenience. It could be a catastrophe.

CUT TO CAR INTERIOR

We use raw salt on the roads.

CUT TO MS OF REAR OF CAR, STILL GOING DOWN ROAD, BUT NOW APPROACHING TOWN

And our cars better not rust out on us. Swedish automobile inspections are so strict, badly rusted cars are ordered off the road.

CAR PULLS INTO PARKING LOT

In Sweden, the car most in demand is a Volvo.
Volvo. We build them the way we build them because we have to.

SUPER: VOLVO

TV/Single/:60 or over

322
Art Director: John Danza
Copywriter: Ed McCabe
TV Director: Bo Widerberg
TV Producers: John Danza
Ed McCabe
Production Company: James Garrett & Partners
Agency: Scali, McCabe, Sloves, Inc.
Client: Volvo, Inc.

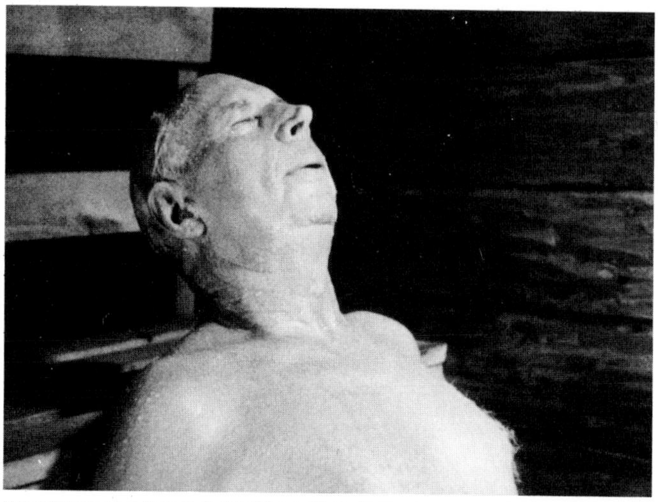

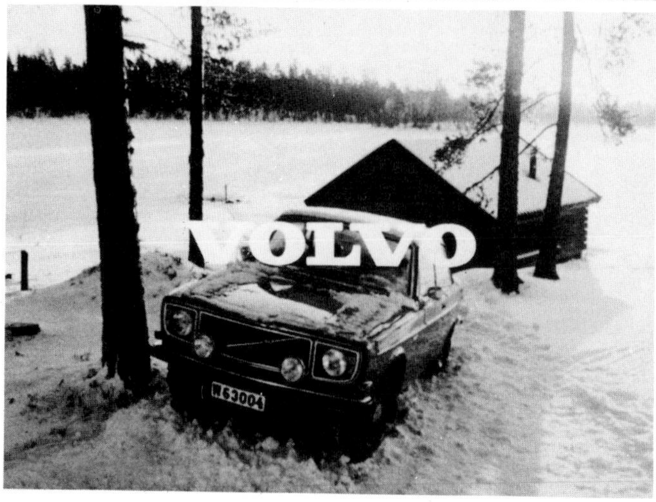

Sauna
60-second

OPEN ON CU OF STOVE IN SAUNA ROOM

SFX THROUGHOUT

VIGOROUS OLD MAN ENTERS, SITS DOWN, RELAXES

ANNCR. (VO): The life expectancy in Sweden . . . is 77 years . . .the longest on earth.

SHOTS OF MAN ENJOYING SAUNA. HE POURS WATER ON STOVE TO INCREASE STEAM

The Swedes have a passion for fitness . . . thinking, perhaps, the more they can endure, the longer they will last.

MAN COMES RUNNING OUT OF CABIN INTO SNOW. CUT TO LS OF SNOW COVERED CABIN WITH CAR PARKED OUTSIDE

The Swedish people expect of their cars exactly what they expect of themselves.

MAN RUNS TO HOLE IN ICE AND JUMPS IN WATER

So it's not surprising that the largest selling car in Sweden . . .

SWIMS AROUND IN ICE WATER

is the Volvo.

In Sweden, Volvos have a life expectancy of 14 years.

CUT TO CABIN AND VOLVO

Volvo. We build them the way we build them because we have to.

SUPER: VOLVO

323
Art Director: William J. Conlon
Copywriter: Tom Mabley
Designer: Wilson Seibert
Film Editor: Doug Johnston
TV Producer: Nicholas DeMarco
Production Company: Pelco
Agency: J. Walter Thompson Company
Client: United States Marine Corps

Rose Garden
60-second

BUS SHOTS, MILITARY RECRUITS ARRIVING

SONG: I beg your pardon . . .
I never promised you a rose garden . . .

Along with the sunshine . . .

TRAINING SHOTS

There's gotta be a little rain sometimes . . .

(MUSIC UNDER)

YOUNG CIVILIAN ON STREET

ANNCR. (VO): We don't promise you a rose garden. So if you just want to be one of the boys, stick with the boys. The Marines are looking for a few good men.

MILITARY STILLS

For almost two hundred years, we've kept our standards high, and our ranks small. Today, we're still a tough club to join . . . a tough team to make . . . and that's exactly the way we're going to keep it.

TRAINING STILLS

So we're looking for quality, not quantity.

STILLS OF TWO BLACK MARINES

We're looking for a few good men who can stand with the United States Marines.

LIVE ACTION: PARRIS ISLAND RECRUIT GRADUATION

No compromises. No shortcuts. No promises . . . except one.
You'll be a Marine. One of the few . . . and one of the finest.

SUPER: THE MARINES

The Marines are looking for a few good men.

TV/Single/:60 or over

324 Gold Award
Art Director: Jeff Cohen
Copywriter: Lester Colodny
TV Producers: Syd Rangell
Allen Kay
Lois Korey
Production Company: Richards & Myers Films
Agency: Needham, Harper & Steers
Client: Xerox Corporation

Football
90-second

THE DAY OF THE "BIG GAME"

LESS THAN TWO MINUTES TO GO: COACH IS TEARING HIS HAIR OUT

COACH (EXCITEDLY): Allright now. Pressure's on. Two minutes to go. No. No. No. Kramer, you idiot. Whatever happened to the game play we talked about? Come on. Come on. Never mind the tarp. Make that block stick. No. No. No.

COACH LOOKS DOWN THE BENCH FOR A SUB. SPOTS THE LEAST LIKELY

Colodny . . . Colodny . . . Colodny. Quick, Colodny, this is critical. All right. This is R 78, power reverse. I've got to get this into the ballgame as soon as I can.

This is . . . Colodny, pay attention. This is as important as anything you're going to do for this club. Way to go, Colodny. . . .

COLODNY DASHES UP TO XEROX IN LOCKER ROOM

ANNCR. (VO): Xerox is . . . applying its technology to all phases of communication, whether it be . . . in business, government, education. . . .

. . . medicine, . . . or even landing men on the moon . . .

. . . at Xerox, we're working to find new ways of getting information . . .
. . . to people who need it.

COACH: Here it is. Everyone gets one. Okay, here we go.

ANNCR. (VO): And most important . . . When they need it.

QUARTERBACK FLIPS TOWEL ON CENTER'S BACKSIDE, TUCKS IN XEROX PLAYERS PEER AT PLAYS ON GROUND, IN HAND, OFF TO THE SIDE, ETC.

QUARTERBACK: . . . 385, . . . 384 . . .

BALL SNAPS BACK TO QUARTERBACK . . . WHO HANDS IT TO BACK CARRYING HIS COPY, HANDS BALL TO END
PAST GOAL LINE, END READS PLAY. MEANWHILE, OPPONENTS TACKLE WRONG PLAYERS. LONG PASS THROWN TO END, LOOKS UP FROM PLAY JUST IN TIME TO CATCH GAME WINNING PASS

SUPER: XEROX

325
Art Director: Allen Kay
Copywriter: Lester Colodny
TV Director: Larry Elikan
TV Producers: Allen Kay
Lois Korey
Syd Rangell
Production Company: Plus Two Productions
Agency: Needham, Harper & Steers, Inc.
Client: Xerox Corporation

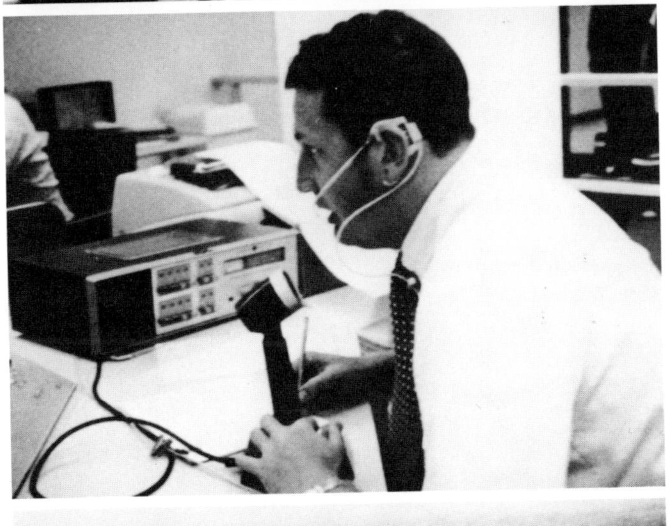

Traffic Control
90-second

MAN ON FREEWAY PEERS UNDER STALLED CAR HOOD

(SFX: TRAFFIC SLOWING—SQUEALING TIRES, HORNS)

ANNCR. (VO): 5:36 P.M. The Santa Monica Freeway. Vehicle stalled in the fast lane.

CARS SLOW AROUND STALLED CAR . . . GO OVER ELECTRONIC SENSORS

ANNCR. (VO): Sensing wires in the road-bed, linked to a Xerox computer, detect a problem.

CU: XEROX COMPUTERS

(SFX: INTERIOR SOUNDS OF HQ POST. VOICES)

ANNCR. (VO): At Division of Highways control center, the computer blinks red danger lights on an electronic map pinpointing the hazard. 5:37 P.M. Helicopters are dispatched to send back "live" pictures of the incident.

HQ: ACCIDENT SCENE TRANSMITTED "LIVE" FROM THE HELICOPTER TO MONITOR

ANNCR. (VO): The computer flashes warnings on message signs to approaching motorists . . . 5:39 P.M. Police cars and other safety equipment arrive at scene . . .

PATROLMEN MOVE TRAFFIC. TOW PICKS UP CAR

Within minutes after the first computer print-out, stalled vehicle is removed . . . 5:43 P.M. Traffic is back to normal.

INSIDE CONTROL ROOM

ANNCR. (VO): The California Business and Transportation Agency is using computers to keep traffic moving and to keep minor incidents from becoming major accidents . . .

For some motorists these Xerox computers mean they'll get home on time . . . For others, it means they'll get home. Whether you're in education, medicine, science, industry or traffic . . . Xerox computers are in the business of making your business run smoother.

SUPER: XEROX

TV/Single/:60 or over

326
Art Director: Dom Rossetti
Copywriter: Tom Attea
TV Director: Dom Rossetti
TV Producer: Dom Rossetti
Production Company: Z Productions
Agency: Young & Rubicam International, Inc.
Client: Dr. Pepper

DR PEPPER
Once you try it,
you'll love the difference.

Bride and Groom
60-second

SCENE: INTERIOR OF AN ELEGANT HOTEL ROOM. GROOM (AGITATED) IS KNOCKING ON THE BATHROOM DOOR

GROOM: Honey, I know you're in there. Can't we at least talk about it? Come on now, please. Susan! There are better ways to begin a marriage. This is crazy! And for such a simple thing. Sweetheart, it's our wedding night . . . I'm not asking for the world. Please. You know I love you.

(MUSIC UNDER)

BRIDE: All right. If it will make you happy.

BRIDE GINGERLY OPENS THE DOOR THE TINIEST BIT. GROOM HANDS HER A DR. PEPPER

FULL CHORUS: Dr. Pepper . . . so misunderstood.

BRIDE TAKES A DRINK OF DR. PEPPER . . .

BRIDE: Oh, I love it . . .

SHE CLOSES THE DOOR. GROOM IS STILL LEFT OUTSIDE

(SFX: LAUGHTER)

ANNCR. (VO): Dr. Pepper, it looks like a cola, but it tastes different. And millions of people who've tried it, love the difference.

GROOM: Oh, honey. Ohh . . .

ANNCR. (VO): Once you try it, you'll love the difference.

(SHE STILL WON'T LET HIM IN.)

GROOM: Susan . . .

CUT TO PRODUCT SHOT

SUPER: DR. PEPPER

327
Art Director: Woody Litwhiler
Copywriter: Don Marowski
TV Director: Marshall Stone
TV Producers: Ian Shand
Mike Shapiro
Production Company: M.P.O. Videotronics
Agency: Young & Rubicam International, Inc.
Client: General Cigar Co.

Get'cha Somac
60-second

(SILENT)

OPEN ON MAN SITTING IN LIVING ROOM

MAN: Sooner or later, you're gonna try a White Owl. And when you do, we got'cha.

(MUSIC)

Maybe we'll get'cha with that White Owl mildness. Maybe we'll get'cha with that White Owl flavor.

(MUSIC)

Or maybe we'll get'cha with one of those great White Owl shapes.

(MUSIC)

CU OF MAN: But we're gonna get'cha.

(MAN LAUGHS)

You know we're gonna get'cha. You don't stand a chance.

(MUSIC)

We're gonna get 'em.

(MAN LAUGHS)

(MUSIC)

(CHORUS SINGS)

TV/Single/:60 or over

328
Art Director: Nick LaMicela
Copywriter: Doon Arbus
Designer: Nick LaMicela
Cameraman: Jack Horton
TV Director: Richard Avedon
TV Producer: Paul Rosen
Production Company: Independent Artists
Agency: Norman, Craig & Kummel, Inc.
Client: Chanel No. 5

Chanel No. 5
60-second

CATHERINE DENEUVE. CAMERA EXPLORES HER BEAUTY IN ONE SLOW CONTINUOUS SHOT

DENEUVE: It's not important that I'm Catherine Deneuve. I know he loves me for what I am deeply. I know because he cares about the little things. He brings my coffee always in a small cup because it is precious to me. He gives me Chanel No. 5 because I love to put it in a special place behind my knee. When I send him flowers he understands what I mean. He takes me by the waist because he knows it touches me very much. He understands I cannot speak about feelings. He lets me show him in other ways.

CU OF SPRAY PERFUME AND COLOGNE SET: "$12.00"

DENEUVE (V.O.): Chanel No. 5 Spray Perfume and Spray Cologne.

CU OF SPRAY COLOGNE AND BATH POWDER SET: "$12.00"

Spray Cologne and Bath Powder.

CUT TO EAU DE COLOGNE: "FROM $4.00 TO $20.00"

HOLD ON DENEUVE WHO HOLDS UP CLASSIC BOTTLE

You don't have to ask for it. He knows what you want. Chanel.

329 Silver Award
Art Director: John Lindner
Copywriter: Robert Minicus
Cinematographer: Glen Kirkpatrick
TV Director: Rick Levine
TV Producer: Aram Bohjalion
Production Company: Wylde Films
Agency: Kracht, Ryder, Minicus
Client: Saab

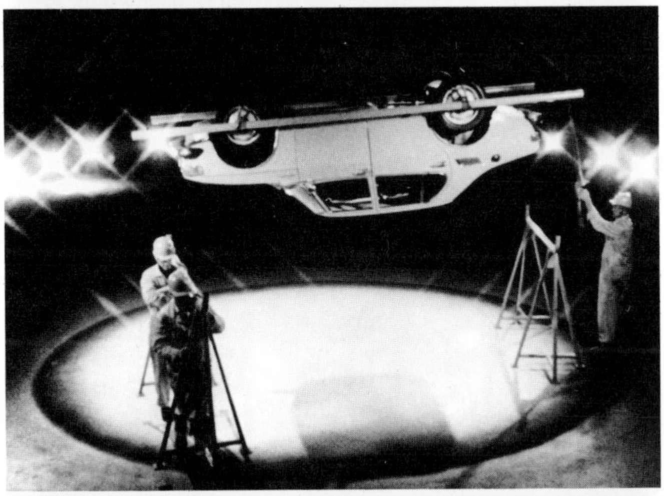

Roll Cage Drop
60-second

OPEN TWO GARAGE DOORS

SAAB IS BEING PUSHED OUT DURING INTRICATE MANEUVER WORKED WITH TECHNICIANS

ANNCR. (VO): From Trollhagen, Sweden, the front wheel drive five passenger SAAB 99E.

OVERHEAD SHOT OF SAAB

(SFX: FACTORY EMPLOYEES SPEAKING IN SWEDISH WITHIN GLASS ENCLOSED ROOM)

CONTINUE INTRICATE MANEUVER, CAR UPSIDE DOWN TO BE PUT ON BARS ACCURATELY

Some day there may be a law that all cars must have roll cage construction surrounding the passenger compartment. Because a simple roll-over can crush a car. The SAAB people agree—they wouldn't build this car without it. They tested it by dropping the car six and one-half feet onto concrete.

(SFX: ENGINEERING ACTIVITY . . . VERBAL COUNTDOWN . . . OTHER DETAILS)

(SFX: FACTORY EMPLOYEES AGAIN IN ROOM SPEAKING; CRASH SOUND OF CAR WHEN DROPPED)

DROPPED IN SLOW MOTION

The passenger compartment remains intact. We challenge any other car to try this. It's about time a car was built like this.

ENGINEERS GO AROUND TO LOOK AT CAR

SUPER: SAAB 99E

TV/Single/:60 or over

330
Art Director: Mark Ross
Copywriters: Terry Stern
Brendan Kelly
Cinematographer: Glen Kirkpatrick
TV Director: Rick Levine
TV Producer: Mark Ross
Production Company: Wylde Films
Agency: Ogilvy & Mather Inc.
Client: American Express Travelers Checks

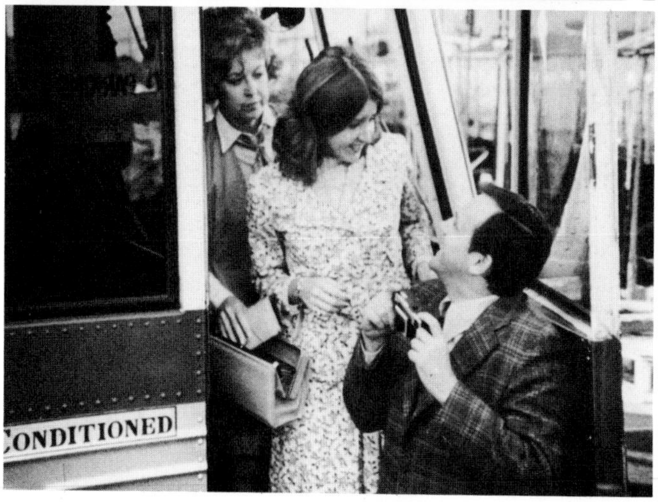

Tour Bus
60-second

CROWDED SIGHT-SEEING BUS. DRIVER CONDUCTS TOUR

ANNCR. (VO): You are about to witness a crime.

(SLOW MOTION) WOMAN OPENS PURSE. MAN AND WOMAN PICK-POCKET TEAM GIVE EACH OTHER GO-AHEAD

An open hand bag, an expert eye, a nod. Teams like this are one way a million travelers will lose their money this year. This is the squeeze play.

GROUP DESCENDS FROM BUS . . . MAN STOPS ABRUPTLY, JOLTING WOMAN BEHIND INTO FEMALE TEAM MEMBER. APOLOGIES ARE MADE—AS PICK-POCKET LIFTS WOMAN'S WALLET

MAN: Ah . . . sorry . . .

ANNCR. (VO): Did you see what happened? Watch again?

STOP ACTION AND FULL RE-PLAY

Pick-pockets are so expert, many people don't even realize they've been robbed. Protect your money. Don't carry cash. Carry American Express Travelers Checks. If they're ever stolen or lost, you can get them replaced, usually on the same day.

GROUP WALKS ON—WOMAN PICK-POCKET DROPS WALLET INTO ANOTHER TEAM MEMBER'S BAG

NOTHING IS NOTICED

American Express Travelers Checks. Because it could happen to you.

SUPER: AMERICAN EXPRESS TRAVELERS CHECKS.

TV/Campaign/:60 or over

331
Art Director: Michael Ulick
Copywriter: Jeff Frey
TV Director: Howard Zieff
TV Producer: Barbara Michelson
Production Company: Zieff Films
Agency: Wells, Rich, Greene, Inc.
Client: Midas International, Inc.

Midas presents how not to install a muffler.

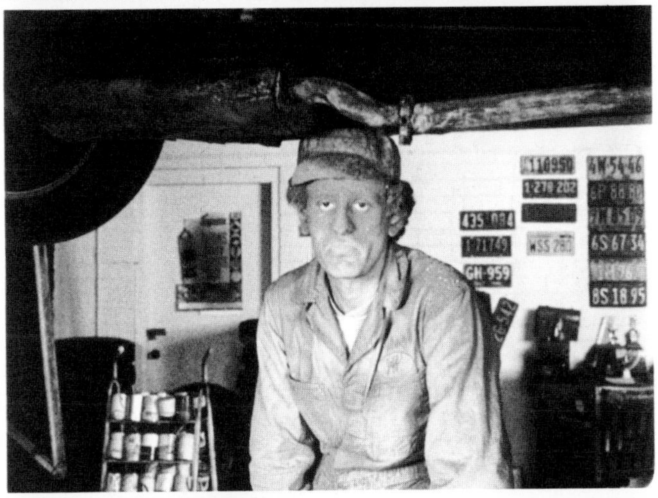

Midas
We install mufflers for a living.
We have to do a better job.

Expert
60-second

SCENE: A GARAGE. A CAR IS ON THE LIFT. AN OLD LADY WITH WHITE GLOVES AND POODLE IS LEAVING IT BE FIXED. THE "EXPERT" MECHANIC GREETS HER

SUPER: MIDAS PRESENTS HOW *NOT* TO INSTALL A MUFFLER

ANNCR. (VO): Midas presents how *not* to install a muffler.

(SFX: MUSIC THROUGHOUT)

MECHANIC SHAKES LADY'S HAND —WIPES DIRT OFF HER GLOVES WITH A CLOTH. LADY WALKS OUT

HE BEGINS TO WORK, HITS HEAD ON CAR, GOES UNDER CAR, TAPS OLD MUFFLER WITH HAMMER. HE'S COVERED WITH DUST. HE PULLS ON MUFFLER, COMES OUT FROM UNDER CAR. MUFFLER FALLS OFF. HE GOES TO RACK, FINDS NEW MUFFLER, CARRIES IT TOWARD CAR KNOCKING DOWN EQUIPMENT ON BARRELS, STEPS ON DOLLY AND ROLLS AWAY FROM CAR AND OUT OF FRAME. COMES BACK, GOES UNDER CAR TO INSTALL IT, MOVES LEVER TO LOWER CAR TO FLOOR

ANNCR. (VO): As muffler experts, Midas will be happy to install a muffler correctly anytime you like.

LADY WALKS BACK INTO FRAME. MECHANIC ACKNOWLEDGES THAT EVERYTHING IS O.K. HE HITS ROOF OF CAR. CAR FALLS APART. MECHANIC JUMPS INTO FRONT SEAT OF CAR TO GET AWAY FROM LADY. SHE CHASES HIM

ANNCR. (VO): At Midas we install mufflers for a living. We have to do a better job.

SUPER: MIDAS. WE INSTALL MUFFLERS FOR A LIVING. WE HAVE TO DO A BETTER JOB.

Waiting
60-second

Menace
60-second

TV/Campaign/:60 or over

332
Art Director: George Jacoma
Copywriters: Hanno Fuchs
Michael Shalette
TV Directors: Norman Griner
Joe Pytka
David Nagata
TV Producers: Vinnie Infantino
Manning Rubin
Ray Rivas

Production Companies: Horn/Griner Productions
Sandler Films
M.P.O. Videotronics
Agency: Grey Advertising, Inc.
Client: Ford Motor Company

When you get back to basics,
you get back to Ford.

Split Screen
60-second

(MUSIC THROUGHOUT)

MAN PUTS APPLES IN CAR TRUNK, DRIVES OFF. LADY AND FARM IN BACKGROUND

ANNCR. (VO): From the first day we built Pinto, we've measured it in our minds against the toughest competitor in the world. Ourselves.

SPLIT SCREEN: MODEL A (BOTTOM) SEPIA. '72 PINTO (TOP) REGULAR COLOR. RUNNING SIDE SHOT SPLIT SCREEN FRONT SHOT. CARS MOVE TOWARD CAMERA

We decided to invent the basic little economy car all over again.

SPLIT SCREEN SIDE SHOTS

The car that would run and run and run.

CARS PASS GAS STATIONS

And get lots of miles to the gallon. And hardly ever see a repair shop. A car that would cost very little . . . and would feel good on the road. The Ford Pinto was built 40 years after the Ford Model A. But we think it's got the same kind of toughness . . . dependability . . . and value.

SIDE AND BACK RUNNING SHOTS. CARS PASS THRU TOWN. OLD AND NEW MILK TRUCK, BIKE

Because, deep down . . . it's the same basic idea.
And when you get back to basics, you get back to Ford . . .

CU, OLD AND NEW DRIVERS THROUGH WINDSHIELD . . . '72 PINTO, RUNNING SHOT. PASSES MODEL A. DISSOLVE TO CAR PARKED WITH TRUNK OPEN

Pinto . . . 2-door sedan or 3-door runabout . . . at your Ford-Dealer's.

SUPER: WHEN YOU GET BACK TO BASICS YOU GET BACK TO FORD.

Basic Black
60-second

Family Tree
60-second

Woodie
60-second

333 Gold Award
Art Director: John Danza
Copywriter: Ed McCabe
TV Director: Bo Widerberg
TV Producers: John Danza
Ed McCabe
Production Company: James Garrett & Partners
Agency: Scali, McCabe, Sloves, Inc.
Client: Volvo, Inc.

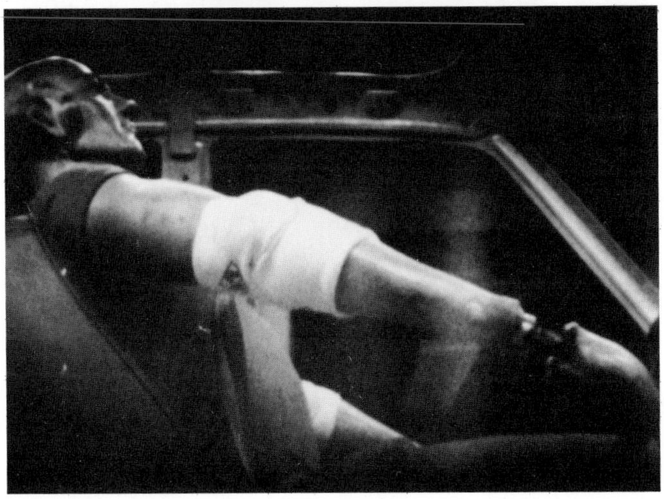

Engineering
60-second

SCENE TAKES PLACE IN A VOLVO FACTORY IN SWEDEN

OPEN ON CU OF PRECISION WORK BEING DONE BEFORE BLUEPRINT AND DIALS

MAN (VO): In Sweden precision is a national preoccupation.

CAMERA MOVES TO CORRIDOR WHERE ENGINEERS ARE ALL AT WORK

Ours is a nation of engineers. Engineering is the largest industry, employing nearly 40 percent of the total labor force.

CAMERA ROAMS FACTORY WITH VIEWS OF ENGINEERS AT THEIR WORK

MOVE TO CAR ON LIFT

(SFX: UNDER)

Thirty-five engineers to every styling. Which shows where we put the emphasis.

We have to. Since Volvo is the largest selling car in Sweden a lot of our customers are engineers too.

CU MAN WORKING ON CAR

LONG VIEW OF CAR ON RACK

MAN AT CONTROL PANEL

VIEW OF VOLVO

VIEW INSIDE OF MECHANICAL MAN GIVING CAR A WORKOUT

(SFX)

Volvo. We build them the way we build them because we have to.

SUPER: VOLVO over tracks.

Sauna
60-second

Swedish Winter
60-second

TV/Campaign/:60 or over

334
Art Director: Mark Ross
Copywriters: Terry Stern
Brendan Kelly
Cinematographer: Glen Kirkpatrick
TV Director: Rick Levine
TV Producer: Mark Ross
Production Company: Wylde Films
Agency: Olgivy & Mather Inc.
Client: American Express Travelers Checks

Tour Bus
60-second

CROWDED SIGHT-SEEING BUS. DRIVER CONDUCTS TOUR

ANNCR. (VO): You are about to witness a crime.

(SLOW MOTION) WOMAN OPENS PURSE. MAN AND WOMAN PICK-POCKET TEAM GIVE EACH OTHER GO-AHEAD

An open hand bag, an expert eye, a nod. Teams like this are one way a million travelers will lose their money this year. This is the squeeze play.

GROUP DESCENDS FROM BUS . . . MAN STOPS ABRUPTLY, JOLTING WOMAN BEHIND INTO FEMALE TEAM MEMBER. APOLOGIES ARE MADE—AS PICK-POCKET LIFTS WOMAN'S WALLET

MAN: Ah . . . sorry . . .

ANNCR. (VO): Did you see what happened? Watch again?

STOP ACTION AND FULL RE-PLAY

Pick-pockets are so expert, many people don't even realize they've been robbed. Protect your money. Don't carry cash. Carry American Express Travelers Checks. If they're ever stolen or lost, you can get them replaced, usually on the same day.

GROUP WALKS ON—WOMAN PICK-POCKET DROPS WALLET INTO ANOTHER TEAM MEMBER'S BAG. NOTHING IS NOTICED

American Express Travelers Checks. Because it could happen to you.

SUPER: AMERICAN EXPRESS TRAVELERS CHECKS.

Elevator
30-second

Purse Snatcher
30-second

335
Art Director: Robert Gage
Copywriters: Phyllis Robinson
John Noble
Designer: Robert Gage
TV Director: Robert Gage
TV Producer: Cliff Fagin
Production Company: D.S.I.
Agency: Doyle Dane Bernbach Inc.
Client: Polaroid Corporation

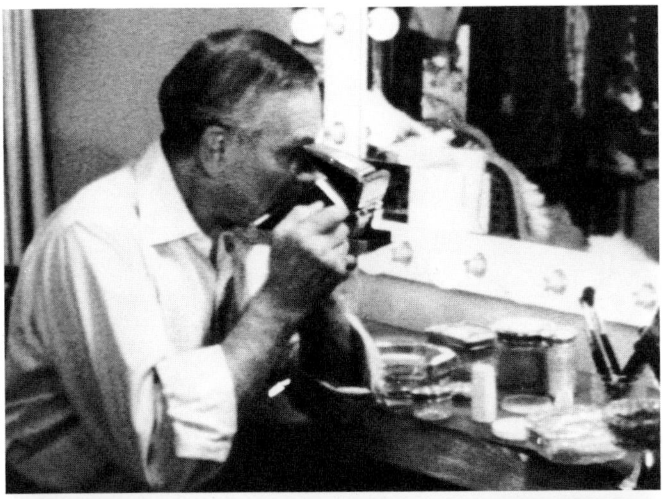

Dressing Room
60-second

LAURENCE OLIVIER SITTING AT MAKE-UP TABLE IN DRESSING ROOM

OLIVIER: You're about to see a magnificent performance. The cast of characters? A simple bowl of fruit . . . and Polaroid's new SX-70.

HE HOLDS UP CAMERA

(SFX: CAMERA BEING ADJUSTED)

Just touch the button . . .

(SFX)

and it hands you the picture.

(MUSIC)

CUT TO PRINT HE HAS TAKEN OUT OF CAMERA

There's nothing to peel,

CAMERA MOVES IN ON SLIDE

nothing even to throw away, nothing to time.

AN IMAGE BEGINS TO APPEAR ON SLIDE

In minutes, you will have a finished photograph of such dazzling beauty, that you will feel you're looking at the world for the first time.

CU OF NOW FULLY-DEVELOPED PICTURE

BACK TO OLIVIER

The new SX-70 Land Camera. From Polaroid.

Olivier on Stage
60-second

Stop Motion
60-second

TV/Campaign/:60 or over

336

Art Directors: Allan Kay
Jeff Cohen
Copywriters: Lois Korey
Lester Colodny
TV Directors: Chuck Braverman
Syd Myers
Larry Elikan
TV Producers: Lois Korey
Allen Kay
Syd Rangell

Production Companies: Braverman Productions
Richards & Myers Films
Plus Two Productions
Agency: Needham, Harper & Steers, Inc.
Client: Xerox Corporation

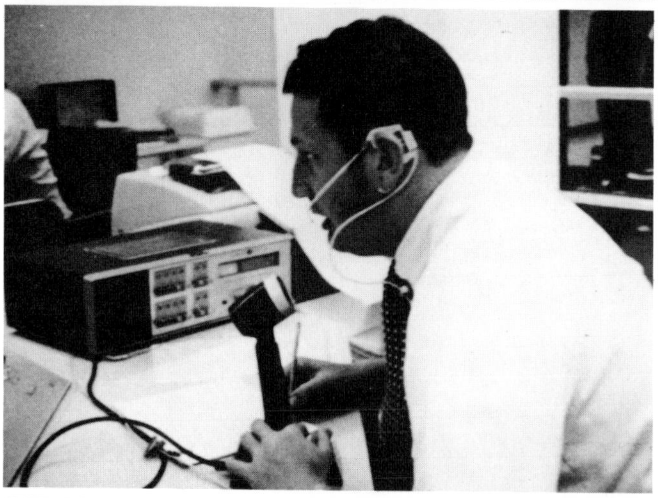

Traffic Control
90-second

MAN ON FREEWAY PEERS UNDER STALLED CAR HOOD

(SFX: TRAFFIC SLOWING—HORNS)

ANNCR. (VO): 5:36 P.M. The Santa Monica Freeway. Vehicle stalled in the fast lane.

CARS SLOW AROUND STALLED CAR . . . GO OVER ELECTRONIC SENSORS

ANNCR. (VO): Sensing wires in the road-bed, linked to a Xerox computer, detect a problem.

(SFX: INTERIOR SOUNDS OF HQ POST. VOICES)

ANNCR. (VO): At Division of Highways control center, the computer blinks red danger lights on an electronic map pinpointing the hazard. 5:37 P.M. Helicopters are dispatched to send back "live" pictures of the incident.

HQ: ACCIDENT SCENE TRANSMITTED "LIVE" FROM THE HELICOPTER TO MONITOR

ANNCR. (VO): The computer flashes warnings on message signs to approaching motorists . . . 5:39 P.M. Police cars and other safety equipment arrive at scene . . .

PATROLMEN MOVE TRAFFIC. TOW CAR

Within minutes after the first computer print-out, stalled vehicle is removed . . . 5:43 P.M. Traffic is back to normal.

INSIDE CONTROL ROOM

ANNCR. (VO): The California Business and Transportation Agency is using computers to keep traffic moving and to keep minor incidents from becoming major accidents . . .
For some motorists these Xerox computers mean they'll get home on time . . . For others, it means they'll get home. Whether you're in education, medicine, science, industry or traffic . . . Xerox computers are in the business of making your business run smoother.

SUPER: XEROX

Football
90-second

Black History
90-second

337

Art Directors: Nick Striga
Marc Surrey
Steve Versandi
Angelo Gallo
Copywriters: Stan Schulman
John Zukowski
Mort Scharfman
Charles Harding
Don Adams
TV Directors: Don Adams
Gus Jekel
Joe Pytka
TV Producers: Manning Rubin
Vinnie Infantino
Ray Rivas
Production Companies: Entertainment Concepts
Film Fair
Agency: Grey Advertising, Inc.
Client: Aurora

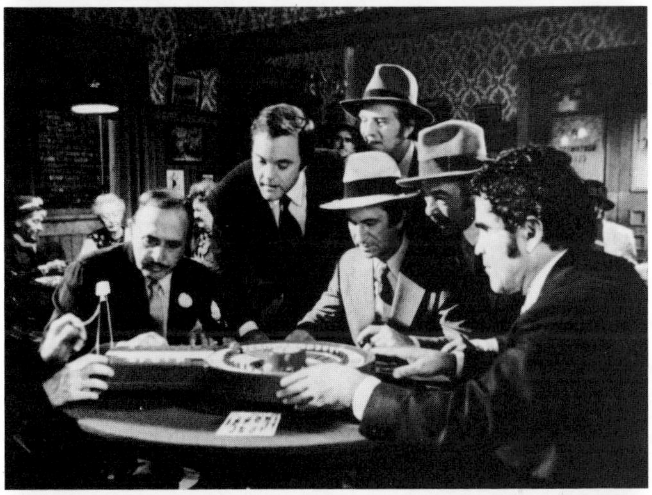

The Don of Dons
60-second

CAR PULLS UP, MAFIA-TYPE GANG GETS OUT. THE ACTION IS TAKE-OFF ON TOUGH-GUY DON ADAMS STYLE. DIALOGUE EXCERPTS

DON: Alright, tell me about this new competition on the near-north-west-south side.

FLUNKIE: It's a numbers game.

SEE SIGN "BINGO" TONIGHT

2ND THUG: With letters too!

DON: What is this? Some kind of a joke? You guys brought me to a Bingo game?

THEY GO INSIDE

FLUNKIE: This is different, boss. Skittle Bingo. You gotta shoot for numbers.

2ND THUG: You shoot, boss. Get it?

CALLER: You gentlemen come to play?

2ND THUG: Move it.

FLUNKIE: You see, boss. You shoot the small ball for the letters and the big ball for the numbers.

CALLER: G-8.

DON: Hey, I got it!

CALLER: 1-5 . . . 1-4

DON: That's it. Bingi!

CALLER: The name of the game is Bingo.

DON: Change it!

CALLER: Skuttle Bingo by Aurora.

DON: You changed the wrong word.

CALLER: Skapple Bingo by Bango.

2ND THUG: It's Skittle Skuttle by Bango.

DON: Who asked ya?

CALLER: Skapple Bingo by Bango

FLUNKIE: Skittle Skattle Bingo.

FLUNKIE: What about Bangi Bingi?

DON: I like it. I like it.

CALLER: Who asked ya?

ANNCR. (VO): It's Skittle Bingo by Aurora.

TV/Campaign/:60 or over

338 Silver Award
Art Directors: William Moore
Al Scully
Don Tortoriello
Songwriters: William Backer
Billy Davis
Roger Cook
Roger Greenaway
Dottie West
Sandy Mason Theoret
Cameraman: Steve Horn
TV Directors: Steve Horn
Peter Israelson
TV Producers: John Jenkins
Phil Messina
Ann Curry
Production Companies: Horn/Griner
E.U.E.
Agency: McCann-Erickson, Inc.
Client: Coca-Cola, USA

It's the real thing. Coke.
Trade-mark®
Coke

Raft
60-second

BIRDS, BOY, GIRL ON RAFT

SONG: Birds and bees
and all the flowers and trees . . .
and fishes on the line . . .

THROUGHOUT SCENES OF BEING TOGETHER, DANCING, SWINGING, WITH CALF . . .

Girls and guys
and yellow butterflies
say hello summertime.
The sun shining down . . .
on the back of my neck
nothing on my mind . . .

DRINKING COKE

An ice cold Coke
on the back of my throat
saying hello summertime . . .
Summertime
in the back of your mind
Yes, summertime . . .
it's the real thing.
What you're hoping to find . . .

BOY AND GIRL ON PICNIC

in the back of your mind
it's the real thing.
That's Coca-Cola

BOY AND GIRL ON RAFT SINGING

like summertime.
Coca-Cola
it's the real thing.

SUNSET, BOY EMBRACES GIRL. GIRL HOLDS COKE

Coke is . . .
Like summertime.

COKE BOTTLES ON KEY TITLED "IT'S THE REAL THING" "COKE"

Coca-Cola
Is the real thing.

Raft
60-second

Playground Counselor
60-second

Country Sunshine
60-second

339

Art Directors: Tony Angotti
Alan Kupchick
Copywriters: Enid Futterman
Joan Small
Angela Amoroso
TV Directors: Horn/Griner
Judd Maze

TV Producers: Maura Dausey
Patty Wineapple
Steve Novick
Production Companies: Horn/Griner
Flickers
Agency: Grey Advertising, Inc.
Client: Marine Midland Bank

Lovey Dovey
30-second

THEATER MARQUEE READS "LOVE CONQUERS ALL." MOVIE IS ENDING AND COUPLES PILE OUT OF THEATER. GIRL WAS DEEPLY TOUCHED AS WAS BOY

FRED: Diane.

DIANE: Fred.

Fred: That was beautiful. I love a happy ending.

Diane: I love a happy ending too. Let's get married tonight.

Fred: Tonight????????

(THE PROBLEM—HOW CAN THEY—NO MONEY)

ANNCR: (VO): If you need cash and the banks are closed, come to Moneymatic, Marine Midland's new twenty-four-hour money machine. You can get a cash advance or draw on your checking account, anytime of the day or night, seven days a week.

All you need is a special Moneymatic Master Charge card. Press a few buttons, and the money is yours.

CUS OF MONEYMATIC MACHINE

Moneymatic can do almost anything a bank can do. You can deposit money, transfer money between accounts, even make payments on loans.

Marine Midland feels when a person has to go to the bank, there should be a bank for him to go to.

BACK TO COUPLE WHO HAIL TAXI—IN A BIG HURRY

FRED: Niagara Falls.

DIANE: And step on it.

MONEYMATIC

ANNCR. (VO): Moneymatic from Marine Midland. To us people are worth more than money.

Teller
60-second

Ralph Bounces Back
30-second

TV/Campaign/:60 or over

340
Art Director: Woody Litwhiler
Copywriter: Don Marowski
TV Director: Marshall Stone
TV Producers: Ian Shand
Mike Schapiro
Production Company: M.P.O. Videotronics
Agency: Young & Rubicam International, Inc.
Client: General Cigar Co.

Get'cha Irving
60-second

MAN ALONE ON CAMERA

MAN: Sooner or later you're gonna try a White Owl, and when you do . . . we got'cha.

(MUSIC)

MAN: Maybe we'll get'cha with ah, the White Owl mildness . . . or maybe we'll get'cha with the White Owl flavor . . . or maybe, maybe we'll get'cha with a—one of our great White Owl shapes. But ah, we're gonna get'cha . . . um hu, um, oh, yeh, would I lie.

(MUSIC)

(CHORUS SINGING)

(FADING)

(FADE OUT)

Get'cha Somac
60-second

Get'cha Doyle
60-second

341
Copywriters: James Lawson
John Crawford
Music: Public Domain
Producer: Christopher Hall
Production Company: Six West Recording
Agency: Doyle Dane Bernbach Inc.
Client: National Clearing House for Drug Abuse Information

Ten Little Indians
60-second

SONG: Ten little indians up there flyin'
One stayed up then there were nine . . .
Nine little indians feelin' great
One O.D. 'ed, then there were eight
Eight little indians in cocaine heaven . . .
Convulsions took one, then there were seven
Seven little indians gettin' a fix
One got hepatitis, then there were six . . .
Six little indians pushin' to stay alive
One got busted then there were five . . .
Five little indians trying to score
One got a bad bag then there were four . . .
Four little indians droppin' LSD
One freaked out then there were three . . .
Three little indians sniffin' glue
Brain damaged one, then there were two . . .
Two little indians on a run
One of 'em crashed left just one . . .
One little indian poppin' "Reds"
Popped too many then he was dead . . .
Acids, Bennies, Needles, Pills
If one don't get you, the other one will . . .

342
Copywriter: Ken Swope
Producer: Ken Swope
Production Company: Fleetwood Recording
Agency: Effenson, Nusbaum & Richard Advertising, Inc.
Client: Massachusetts Teacher's Association

Drinking And Driving
30-second

FEMALE VOICE: If you've been drinking . . . and now you're driving . . . listen.

Pain, screams, blood, and even death may be waiting for you around the next curve.

But worse . . . maybe you'll live . . . and a station wagon full of children won't.

It's for these children that the people of the Massachusetts Teacher's Association are begging you, right now, to let someone else drive, someone sober. And if there is no one else, get food. Go for coffee. Anything.

Just get the hell off the road before something happens that will haunt your conscience for the rest of your life.

Radio/Public Service/Campaign

343
Art Director: Bob Wall
Copywriter: Bob Wall
Producer: Bob Wall
Production Company: Tabby Andriello
Agency: Lois Holland Callaway Inc.
Client: New York Voter Registration

Speech
60-second

ANNCR. (VO): Naturally I talk to my kids about the good old days. Except we couldn't vote until we were 21. Now my two kids, 18 and 20, could vote this year. And can you believe it, they didn't realize they had to register first.

(SFX: STREET DEMONSTRATION CHANT; 1968 DEMOCRATIC CONVENTION, CHICAGO)

The whole world is watching.

Same thing with your kids. Here's your chance to give them a lesson. Make them register. And if they're away at college, rush them a registration ballot.

N.Y. State Teen-age registration days are September 30th through October 2nd.

Three days that can shake the world.

(SFX: STREET DEMONSTRATION CHANT; 1968 DEMOCRATIC CONVENTION, CHICAGO)

The whole world is watching.

Truman vs. Dewey
30-second

Stevenson vs. Ike
60-second

344 Gold Award
Art Director: Manny Perez
Copywriter: Helen Nolan
Cameraman: Steve Horn
TV Director: Steve Horn
TV Producer: Manny Perez
Production Company: Horn/Griner Productions
Agency: Young & Rubicam International, Inc.
Client: New York City Drug Addiction Agency

Karen
60-second

INTERIOR. KAREN ENTERS KITCHEN. HER FATHER IS BUSY MAKING HIMSELF SOME DINNER

FATHER: Karen, are you going to have something to eat?

KAREN (AGITATED): I can't. I'm going out.

FATHER: O.K.

KAREN: Daddy, I need $20.00.

FATHER: What for? Hey, hey, what's the matter?

KAREN: Daddy, I'm sick . . . I did it again.

CAMERA THROUGHOUT CLOSE ON FATHER AND KAREN

FATHER: You mean, you're back on drugs? Are you back on drugs, Karen?

KAREN: Yes, yes, yes, yes.

FATHER: But you promised. . . .

KAREN: I'm sorry. I'm sorry, it's the last time, Daddy. I promise, it's the last time. I'll go to the hospital, I'll get help, it's the last time, Daddy. Daddy, you've got to give me $20.00.

FATHER: No.

KAREN: I need the money, I need it now, Daddy, please, help me, help me . . .

FATHER: All right, baby. All right. Here, here, that's all I've got.

KAREN EXITS APARTMENT. CUT TO EXTERIOR HALLWAY. KAREN IS VERY COOLY COUNTING THE MONEY. SHE SMILES . . . WALKS AWAY DOWN THE CORRIDOR

ANNCR. (VO): The only thing worse than what drug addicts do to the people they love, is what they do to themselves.

FADE TO BLACK

SUPER: DON'T JOIN THE LIVING DEAD

TV/Public Service/Single

345 Silver Award
Art Director: William Taubin
Copywriter: Frada Wallach
TV Director: Tony Lover
TV Producer: Herb Strauss
Production Company: Liberty Studio
Agency: Doyle Dane Bernbach Inc.
Client: Federation of Jewish Philanthropies

Joy Ride
60-second

KIDS IN A GANG HAVING A WILD TIME, RUN OUT ON THE STREET

(SFX: YELLING, SCREAMING, PUSHING)

MOMENTUM BUILDS ("C'MON, GET IN . . .")

THEY FIND A CAR, STEAL IT AND TAKE OFF. RANDOMNESS AND MOMENTUM BUILD DURING WILD RIDE

ANNCR. (VO): Kids can do some pretty wild things out of boredom, frustration and anger.

CONFUSION OF KIDS RACING, REVVING UP MOTOR

(SCREECHING: A BIG CRASH)

Don't let them.

LIGHTING OF MENORAH MADE OF BRICKS

The greatest building drive in our history is underway now.
With bricks you can build life.

SUPER OVER BRICKS: UNITED JEWISH APPEAL

346
Art Director: Bob McDonald
Copywriter: Helen Nolan
Cameraman: Steve Horn
TV Director: Steve Horn
TV Producer: Manny Perez
Production Company: Horn/Griner Productions
Agency: Young & Rubicam International, Inc.
Client: New York City Drug Addiction Agency

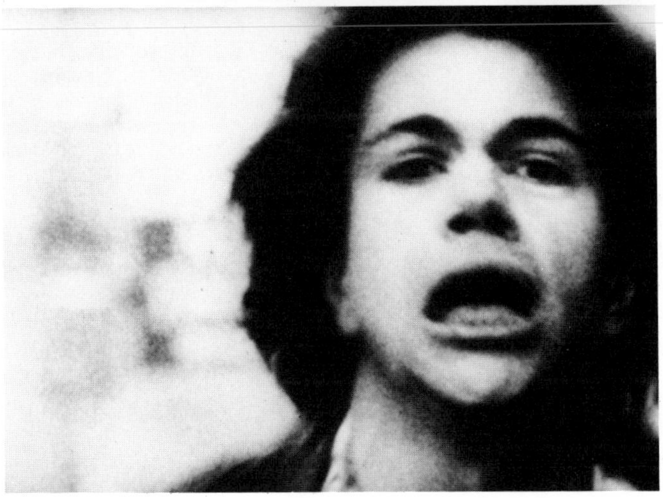

The Animal
60-second

INTERIOR, AUTOMAT
PUSHER IS SITTING AT A TABLE EATING SOUP. ENTER JOEY

JOEY: Hey man, what's happenin'? I'm sick. I need a bag.

PUSHER: Ten dollars, Joey.

JOEY: I only got five.

PUSHER: Ten dollars.

JOEY: Hey come on, you know I'm good for it.

PUSHER: Joey, the stuff is dynamite. Ten dollars or nothing.

JOEY: Please, please man . . .

PUSHER: Joey, get the money.

MOVE TO SERIES OF STRAIGHT CUTS: JOEY STEALING MONEY FROM HIS MOTHER'S POCKETBOOK; TRYING TO FORCE HIS KID BROTHER TO GIVE HIM SOME MONEY; VOMITING ON THE SIDEWALK; MUGGING A WOMAN AND STEALING HER POCKETBOOK; TURNING ON IN AN ABANDONED BUILDING

ANNCR. (VO): This is a drug addict. Unlike a man, he has no sense of right and wrong. No use for reason. He only feels. And what he feels most of the time is fear. He runs away from reality, because reality is what scares him most of all. He lives off human beings . . . because he's afraid to live like a human being. He's alive . . . but you couldn't call this really living.

FADE TO BLACK. SUPER: DON'T JOIN THE LIVING DEAD

347
Art Director: Stan Paulus
Copywriter: Tom Hemphill
Cameraman: Joe Mangine
TV Directors: Arnie Blum
Mike Johnson
TV Producers: Arnie Blum
Mike Johnson
Production Company: Family of Man Films
Agency: Vansant Dugdale
Client: White House Special Action Office
for Drug Abuse Prevention

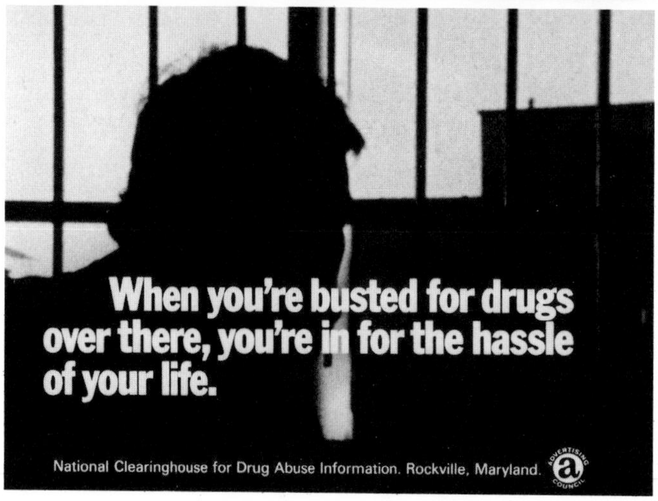
When you're busted for drugs over there, you're in for the hassle of your life.
National Clearinghouse for Drug Abuse Information. Rockville, Maryland.

Inside Outside
60-second

INTERVIEW ON STREET
SUPER: TEHERAN, IRAN

GUY ON STREET: That's what people tell me. I have no desire to . . . to try to score any kind of dope here. I didn't . . . most places in Europe the penalties are just too strict and there's nothing you can do once you get busted.

PROFILE: GUY IN PRISON CELL

GUY NO. 1 IN PRISON: Well, if I understood the laws a little more I would have definitely copped out because I realize it's just too heavy . . .

STREET SCENE

GUY ON STREET: There's no one that can help you.

BACK TO CELL

GUY NO. 1: And everybody says like it's not worth it . . . and it's true.

STREET SCENE

GUY ON STREET: The laws are very strict and they enforce them, and if you smoke and you get caught then you have to be willing to pay the dues.

PROFILE: GUY NO. 2

GUY NO. 2 IN PRISON: Well I still have 5½ years left so it's quite a long time before I am free of this. I can't even see the end of it.

STREET SCENE

GUY ON STREET: You just say goodbye to it for awhile.

ANNCR. (VO): There are over 900 United States citizens doing time on drug charges in foreign jails. They didn't know . . . or they didn't care. When you're busted for drugs over there, you're in for the hassle of your life.

GUY NO. 1: SILHOUETTE

GUY NO. 1: It's been a lot of pain to a lot of people I know.

SUPER: WHEN YOU'RE BUSTED FOR DRUGS OVER THERE YOU'RE IN FOR THE HASSLE OF YOUR LIFE.

348
Art Director: Allen Kay
Copywriters: Lois Korey
Lester Colodny
TV Director: David Langley
TV Producers: Allen Kay
Lois Korey
Syd Rangell
Production Company: David Langley Photography
Agency: Needham, Harper & Steers, Inc.
Client: League of Women Voters

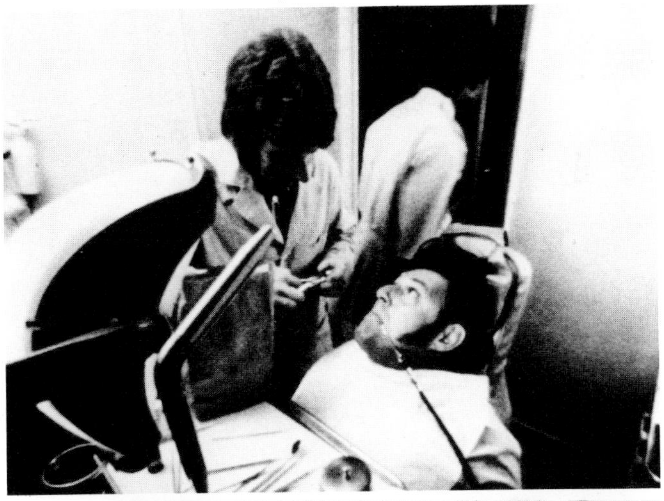

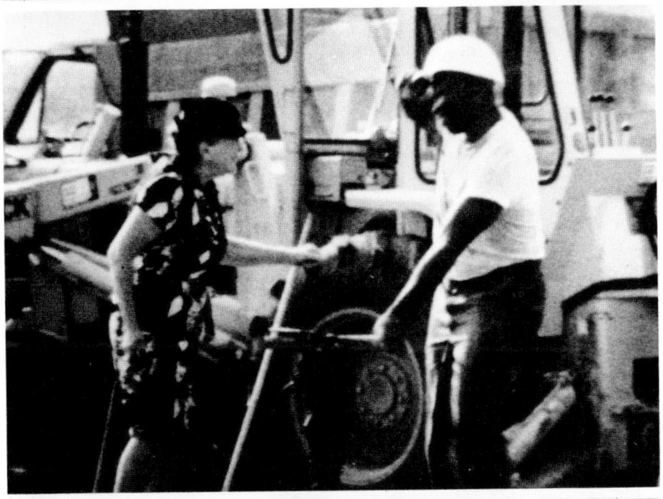

Help Someone Vote
60-second

(MUSIC)

OLD LADY RELIEVES LABORER AT JACK HAMMER

ANNCR. (VO): On November 7th get out and . . . help someone vote.

YOUNG GIRL RELIEVES POLICEMAN DIRECTING TRAFFIC

CLEANING LADY RELIEVES CHAIRMAN AT BOARD MEETING

DELIVERY BOY RELIEVES DENTIST ABOUT TO TREAT A PATIENT . . .

ANNCR. (VO): On November 7th get out and . . . help someone vote.

STAGE MANAGER TAKES THE PLACE OF ONE OF THE ROCKETTES IN A ROUTINE

ANNCR. (VO): On November 7th get out . . . and help someone vote.

LIVE RECREATION OF GRANT WOOD'S "AMERICAN GOTHIC." HIPPIE COMES ALONG. TAKES THE PLACE OF THE FARMER'S WIFE

SUPER: LEAGUE OF WOMEN VOTERS AD COUNCIL LOGO

349
Art Director: Hal Goluboff
Copywriter: Gloria Remen
TV Director: Rick Levine
TV Producer: Wayne Lachman
Production Company: Wylde Films
Agency: Richard K. Manoff Inc.
Client: Planned Parenthood/World Population

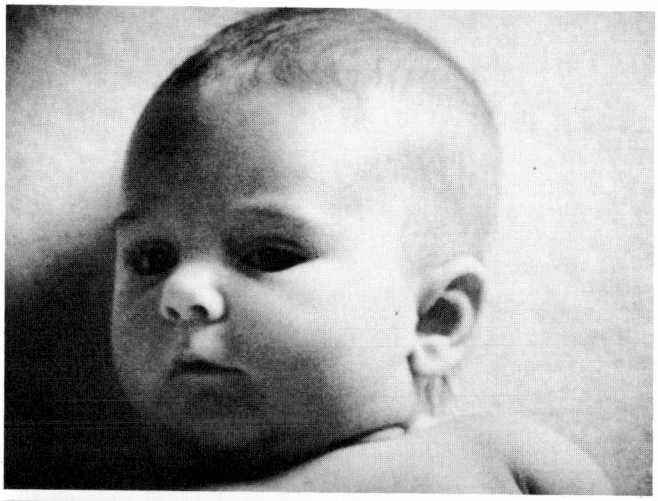

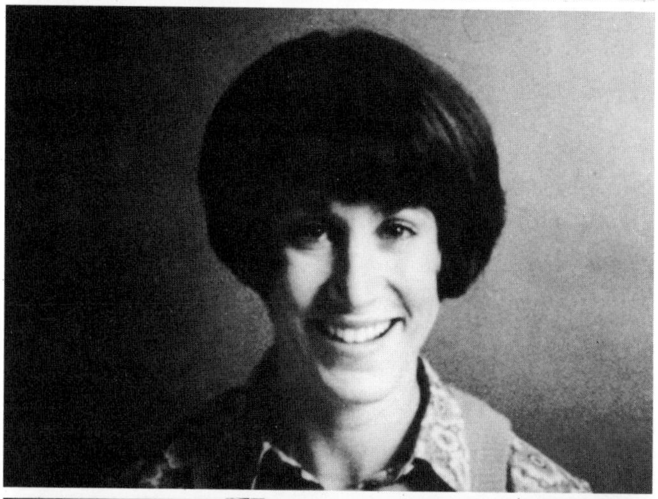

Wrong Reasons
60-second

OPEN ON BABY

ANNCR. (VO): A lot of people have children for the wrong reasons.

CUS OF VARIOUS PEOPLE THROUGHOUT COMMERCIAL

GRANDMOTHER: You've been married a year now. When are we going to see some grandchildren?

YOUNG MAN: You want to have a baby, Evelyn? All right, we'll have a baby! Maybe that'll patch things up!

YOUNG WIFE: We only want two children. But if one of them isn't a boy—we'll keep trying.

WOMAN: Why knock myself out working when I can have a baby.

MAN: Heh-heh, hey Harry. What are you and Marge waiting for—huh?

YOUNG GIRL: Sure I want another baby. What else is a woman for?

ANNCR. (VO): As we said, there are a lot of wrong reasons to have a child —but only one right reason: because you really want one. And that takes planning.

For more information, write Planned Parenthood.

SUPER: PLANNED PARENTHOOD
Children by choice.
Not chance.

350
Art Director: Bob Kuperman
Copywriter: Peter Murphy
Designer: Bob Kuperman
TV Director: Howard Zeiff
TV Producer: James Dubaris
Production Company: Zieff Films
Agency: A Little Help Inc.
Client: National Council on Alcoholism

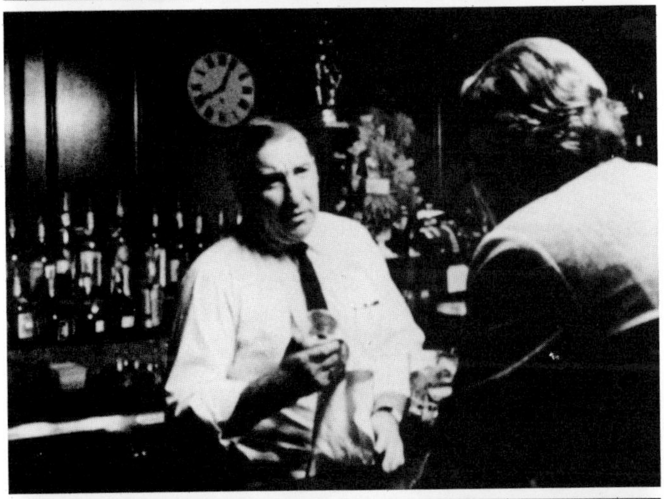

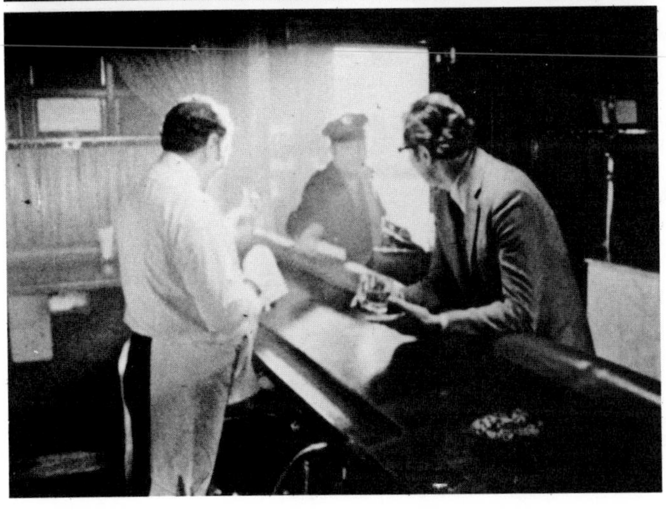

Man in Bar
30-second

IDLE CHATTER BETWEEN THE BARTENDER AND CUSTOMER IN VERY DIMLY LIT BAR

ANNCR. (VO): It's nice to relax and have a drink or two.

SHOT OF BARTENDER BEHIND THE BAR . . . CLOCK READS 8:05

But would you give up one of those drinks—just one, and send us the money so we can help the nine million alcoholics in this country before it's too late.

DOOR OPENS—SUNLIGHT FLOODS INTO THE BAR—MAILMAN POPS IN AND TOSSES MAIL ON BAR

BARTENDER: Morning Bob.

MAILMAN: Morning Lou.

DOOR CLOSES

BARTENDER: Freshen that for you?

CUSTOMER: Yeah!

ANNCR. (VO): What we're really asking is can you spare the price of a drink?

TV/Public Service/Single

351
Art Director: William Taubin
Copywriter: James Lawson
TV Director: Tony Lover
TV Producer: Sylvan Markmann
Production Company: Liberty Studio
Agency: Doyle Dane Bernbach Inc.
Client: National Clearing House for Drug Abuse Information

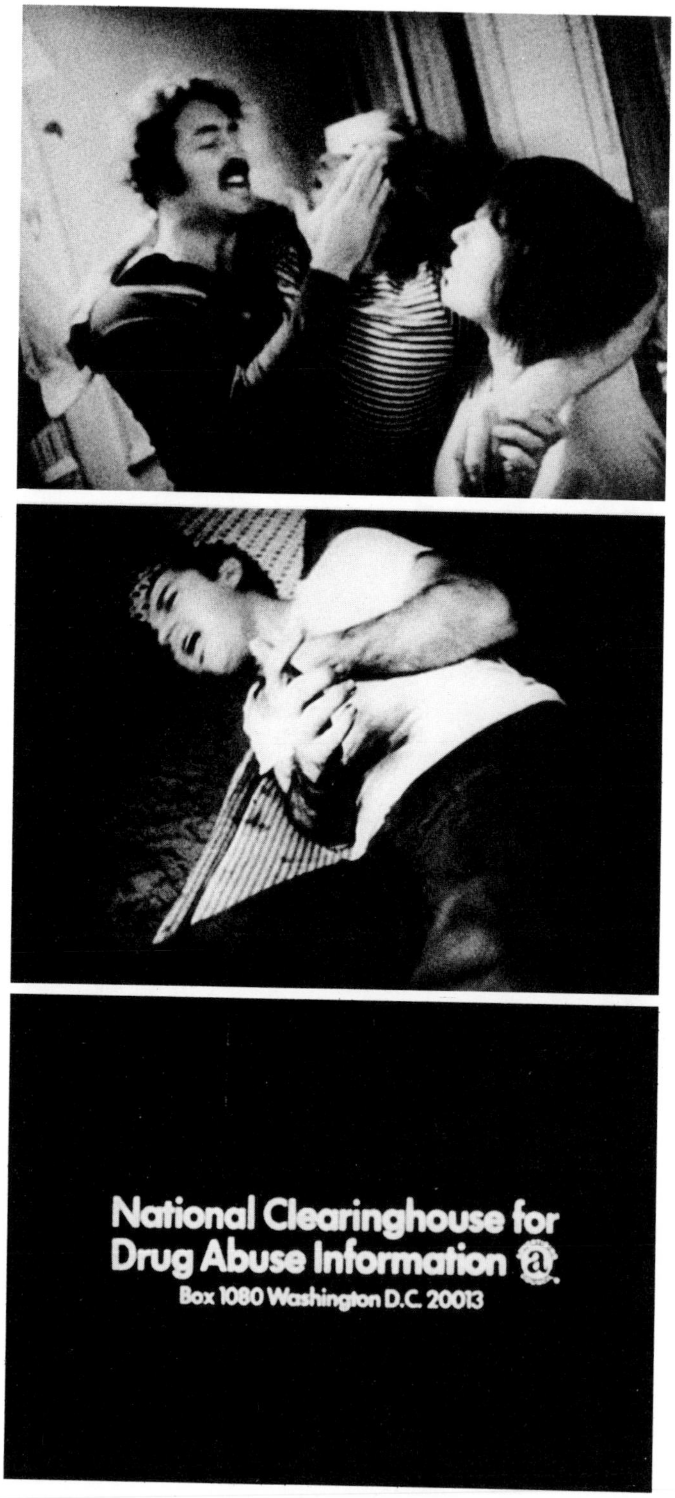

Ten Little Indians
60-second

THROUGHOUT SHOTS OF THE KIDS —INCREASINGLY STRIDENT VIEWS AS THEIR NUMBERS DECREASE

(SUNG TO ACCOMPANIMENT OF HAND CLAPPING BY A GROUP OF YOUNG BLACK KIDS)

SONG: Ten little indians, up there flyin',
One stayed up, then there were nine.

Nine little indians, feelin' great,
One O.D.'d, then there were eight.

Eight little indians, in cocaine heaven,
Convulsions took one, then there were seven.

Seven little indians, gettin'a fix,
One got hepatitis, then there were six.

Six little indians, pushin' to stay alive,
One got busted, then there were five.

Five little indians, tryin' to score,
One got a bad bag, then there were four,

Four little indians, droppin' L.S.D.
One freaked out, then there were three.

Three little indians, a sniffin' glue,
Brain damaged one, then there were two.

Two little indians, on a run,
One of them crashed, left just one.

One little indian, poppin' reds,
Popped too many, then he was dead.

Acid, bennies, needles, pills,
If one don't get you, the other one will.

352
Art Director: Alan Kupchick
Copywriter: Enid Futterman
Cameraman: Steve Horn
TV Director: Norman Griner
TV Producer: Steve Novick
Production Company: Horn/Griner Productions
Agency: Grey Advertising, Inc.
Client: National Highway Traffic Safety Administration

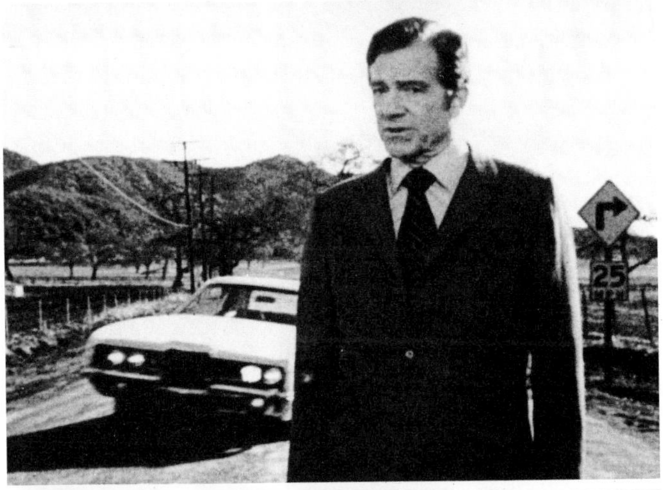
25

GET THE
PROBLEM DRINKER
OFF THE ROAD.
NATIONAL HIGHWAY TRAFFIC SAFETY ADMINISTRATION

Dana Andrews Highway
60-second

OPEN: DANA ANDREWS STANDING ON EMPTY TWO LANE HIGHWAY TALKING TO CAMERA

ANDREWS: I'm Dana Andrews and I'm an alcoholic. I don't drink anymore, but I used to. All the time. When I was drunk I was about as good a driver as my two-year-old grandson.

CUT TO WEAVING CAR HEADING TOWARD CAMERA

I had accidents but I never did kill anybody. If it had gone on, I'm sure I would have. Because the people who were responsible for 19,000 traffic deaths last year, are people just like I was. Drunk.

BACK TO DANA ANDREWS AS CAR APPROACHES AND NARROWLY MISSES HIM

I'm talking about heavy, serious problem drinkers. They're sick. And we have to help them, because they can't always help themselves. But they're killing people. And we have to stop them because they can't stop themselves.

FREEZE FRAME OF CAR AND TITLE

Get the problem drinker off the road. For his sake. And yours.

ANNCR. (VO): Write to Drunk Driver, Box 1969, Washington, D.C. We'll tell you how you can help.

TV/Public Service/Single

353
Art Director: Alan Kupchick
Copywriter: Enid Futterman
TV Directors: Cal Bernstein
Haskell Wexler
TV Producer: Maura Dausey
Production Company: Dove Films
Agency: Grey Advertising, Inc.
Client: National Highway Traffic Safety Administration

Backyard
60-second

OPEN ON MOTHER (JANIE) IN HAMMOCK HOLDING BABY

SONG (JANIE):
I want to watch the sun come
up another fifty years
I want to write a novel that
will bring the world to tears . . .
And I want to see Venice . . .

DISSOLVE TO SHOT OF MOTHER AND FATHER LAUGHING WITH BABY

I want to see my kids have kids;
I want to see them free . . .
I want to live my only life; I want the most of me . . .
I want to dance . . .
I want to love
I want to breathe . . .

FREEZE FRAME OF MOTHER AND SLEEPING BABY

ANNCR. (VO): Janie died
on an endless road in America
because a lonely man was
driving drunk out of his mind.
Problem drinkers who drive are responsible for more than 40 deaths every day.
Get the problem drinker off the road.

FRAME CHANGES TO BLACK AND WHITE AS PULL OUT TO REVEAL FREEZE FRAME HAS BECOME A PHOTOGRAPH ON THE WALL IN COUPLE'S EMPTY BEDROOM

I want to know what's out there
beyond the furthest star . . .
I even want to go there if
we ever get that far
And I want to see Venice . . .

ANNCR. (VO): Help do something about the problem drinker. For his sake. And yours.

354
Art Director: Jon Fisher
Copywriter: Sandi Butchkiss
Designer: Jon Fisher
TV Producer: Joanne Ruesing
Production Company: Audio Productions
Agency: Benton & Bowles Inc.
Client: American Cancer Society

Men Who Flirt with Death
60-second

HEADLINE ON SCREEN:
MEN WHO FLIRT WITH DEATH

ANNCR. (VO): Men who flirt with death.

MEN ON MOTORCYCLES RIDING THROUGH A WALL OF FLAME

The daredevil Novellises who risk their lives daily as they speed through hoops of flame.

MAN ON TIGHTROPE WALKING ACROSS WATER HIGH ABOVE

Lawrence Jessy who puts his life on the line as he tip-toes across treacherous churning waters.

LONG SHOT OF MEN BEING SHOT OUT OF A CANNON

The Zuchinis who flirt with death as they become human cannon balls hurtling through space.

MAN ATOP WING OF AN AIRPLANE

Johnny Fisher who daringly hangs upside down thousands of feet above the ground.

MAN WITH "HOME-MADE" WINGS ON HIS BACK, LEAPS INTO SPACE AND LANDS IN THE WATER

Sir James Terwilliger who tempts the fates as he flaps his wings in futile flight.

MAN IN A SWINGING HAMMOCK READING A BOOK

And Jerry Ross who lies there taking his life in his hands, because he hasn't had a medical check-up in over ten years.

ANNCR. (VO): Don't live dangerously. We want to wipe out cancer in your lifetime.

SUPER: AMERICAN CANCER SOCIETY

355
Art Director: George Lois
Copywriter: Ron Holland
TV Director: George Silano
TV Producer: Edward Murphy
Production Company: Famous Commercials
Agency: Lois Holland Callaway Inc.
Client: Mayor's Office

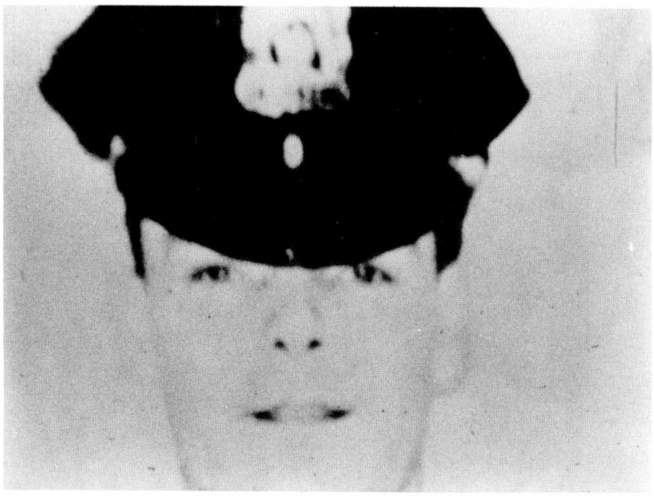

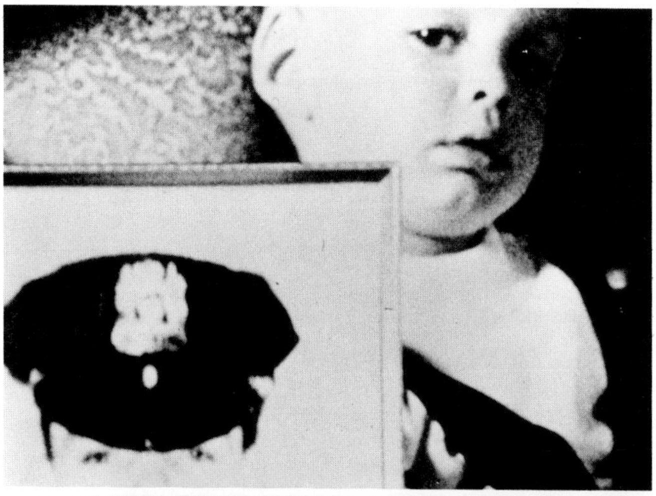

Widow
30-second

OPEN ON CU OF PHOTOGRAPH OF YOUNG POLICE OFFICER

ANNCR. (VO): In the middle of a routine day, John Joseph Darcy, Patrolman, . . .

CAMERA PULLS BACK ON PHOTOGRAPH

was suddenly, senselessly, needlessly struck down.

PULL BACK TO SHOW YOUNG CHILD SITTING BEHIND PHOTOGRAPH

He leaves behind his young son, . . .

PULL BACK TO SHOW BEGINNING OF FAMILY SHOT

his young daughter, . . .

PULL BACK TO SHOW MS OF WOMAN AND TWO CHILDREN

his young widow.

SUPER: BE FAIR TO COPS COMMITTEE

Be fair to cops. You never know when you might need one.

356
Art Director: Chuck Bua
Copywriters: Paula Green
Peggy Courtney
Designer: Peggy Courtney
TV Director: Mike Glynn
TV Producer: Paula Green
Production Company: Gordon Glynn
Agency: Green Dolmatch Inc.
Client: United States Public Health

If at first
you don't succeed
quit, quit again.

Write for
free Quitter's Aid
Rockville, Md. 20852
U.S. Department of Health, Education, and Welfare

Three People
60-second

CAMERA CUTS TO EACH FOR FACE FRONT TESTIMONIALS

BOB: I smoked for 18 years. Everytime I tried to stop, I felt anger, petulance.

GERALDINE: I was an addict. I used to smoke 60 cigarettes a day.

KEVIN: I quit smoking a lot of times, a lot of times.

BOB: Four years ago, I did a play.

GERALDINE: Then my husband got ill, and he was told he could never smoke again and I realized I would have to give it up.

KEVIN: It got to the point where I had to do something, cigarettes were just killing me.

BOB: I was going to have no chance at all of cutting it in this play unless I quit smoking.

GERALDINE: I spent as much time as I could in places where I never smoked. Like in bed or in the bathtub.

KEVIN: I took the damn things. I destroyed them. I would buy fresh packages and stamp on them.

GERALDINE: And finally I lived through the places where I used to smoke the most.

BOB: I quit. No withdrawal.

KEVIN: I beat the habit. And it worked. And I feel good.

TV/Public Service/Single

357
Art Director: Stan Paulus
Copywriter: Tom Hemphill
Cameraman: Joe Mangine
TV Directors: Arnie Blum
Mike Johnson
TV Producers: Arnie Blum
Mike Johnson
Production Company: Family of Man Films
Agency: Vansant Dugdale
Client: White House Special Action Office for Drug Abuse Prevention

NA 70
9512

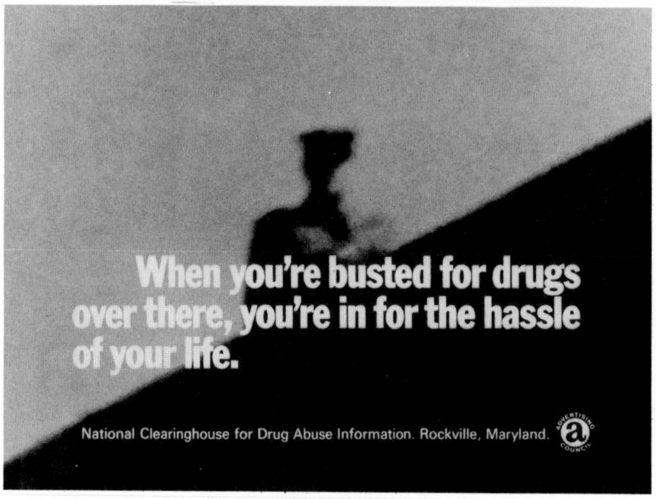
When you're busted for drugs over there, you're in for the hassle of your life.
National Clearinghouse for Drug Abuse Information. Rockville, Maryland.
ADVERTISING COUNCIL

Wall
60-second

EXTERIOR SHOT OF PRISON GUARDS STANDING ABOUT

ANNCR. (VO): Okay, America. Here it is.

SHOT OF TOWER AT CORNER OF WALL

Sixty seconds of truth in words and pictures. And the picture doesn't get any better.

CAMERA PANS WALL

Because you're looking at the outside of a prison wall in Europe. There are a lot more like this one. And locked behind them are over 900 United States citizens, busted on drug charges. Like the girl in Rome, who'll wait six to ten months for her trial. With no bail. Not even a chance for it. And the guy in Spain. He's in a foreign jail cell for six years and a day.

CAMERA MOVES IN TOWARDS GUARD ON ROOF

The drug laws overseas are tough. And they're enforced to the letter. And if somebody tells you they're not, that's a bunch of baloney. So before you leave, check the laws of the countries you plan to visit. One fact will come through. Loud and clear.

When you're busted for drugs over there, you're in for the hassle of your life.

358
Art Director: Robert J. O'Dell
Copywriter: Richard A. Feleppa
Designer: Robert J. O'Dell
Cameraman: Frank Maresca
TV Director: Robert J. O'Dell
TV Producer: KFO, Inc.
Production Company: M.P.O. Videotronics
Agency: KFO, Inc.
Client: Hamilton-Madison House

Wellington Chou
60-second

SPOT IS CHOREOGRAPHED WITH STILLS (CITY FACES)

ANNCR. (VO): They fill Mr. Wellington Chou's older years with companionship.

ELDERLY CHINESE IN CLUBHOUSE

They helped Rosa care for her mother when she got out of the hospital.

ROSA AND MOTHER

They provide care and education for Mrs. John's children because she has to work.

CHILDREN

They gave Mr. Miller somebody to talk to when he needed to talk out his problems.

MR. MILLER AND CONFIDANT

They replaced the missing father in Susie's life.

SUSIE AND FRIEND

They helped Carlos and John stay off drugs.

TWO NEIGHBORHOOD BOYS

They help Ernesta get into the right college.

GIRL WITH HER BOOKS

They helped Mr. Kovaks buy food that he can afford at the co-op.

MR. KOVAKS IN THE CO-OP

They translated a sewing pattern into Chinese for Mrs. Wong so that she can sew for her family.

SEWING SCENE

They give Mrs. Chinchosi's child a head start before she goes to public school.

CHILD

They helped keep the Leonard family together.

FAMILY

Who is they? Hamilton-Madison House. Serving the lower East side of New York.

Send what you can please.
They need it.

359
Art Director: Ed Nussbaum
Copywriter: Stanley Schulman
Designer: Ed Nussbaum
Cameraman: Norman Griner
TV Director: Norman Griner
TV Producer: Philip Peyton
Production Company: Horn/Griner Productions
Agency: Grey Advertising, Inc.
Client: National Alliance of Businessmen

Homecoming
60-second

(MUSIC THROUGHOUT: JOHNNY DESMOND SINGING "LONG AGO AND FAR AWAY" WITH THE GLENN MILLER AIR FORCE BAND)

1945. G.I. EXITS CAB IN FRONT OF FRAME HOUSE

INTERIOR. G.I. ENTERS
FAMILY AND FRIENDS EMOTIONALLY WELCOME HIM HOME

CU OF GIRLFRIEND
SOLDIER AND GIRL EMBRACE

ANNCR. (VO): 1945. Remember? People made quite a fuss about returning servicemen.

SOLDIER ENTHUSIASTICALLY FILLING UP HIS PLATE FROM BUFFET

There were block parties, parades, The 5220 Club, but most of all, there were jobs.

SOLDIER AND SAILOR FRIEND COMPARING SERVICE STORIES

Today's Vietnam veteran wants to settle down and go to work too.

SOLDIER AND GIRL ALONE IN KITCHEN WHILE PARTY CONTINUES

But for many, the jobs just aren't there. You can help do something about it.

FADE TO BLACK AND SUPER: NATIONAL ALLIANCE OF BUSINESSMEN

Call us, we're The National Alliance of Businessmen.

FADE TO SEPIA SNAPSHOT OF SOLDIER, GIRL AND ENTIRE FAMILY IN FRONT OF HOUSE. ZOOM IN ON GIRL'S FACE

Today's veteran needs his chance.

360 Gold Award
Art Directors: Bob McDonald
Manny Perez
Copywriter: Helen Nolan
Cameraman: Steve Horn
TV Director: Steve Horn
TV Producer: Manny Perez
Production Company: Horn/Griner Productions
Agency: Young & Rubicam International, Inc.
Client: New York City Drug Addiction Agency

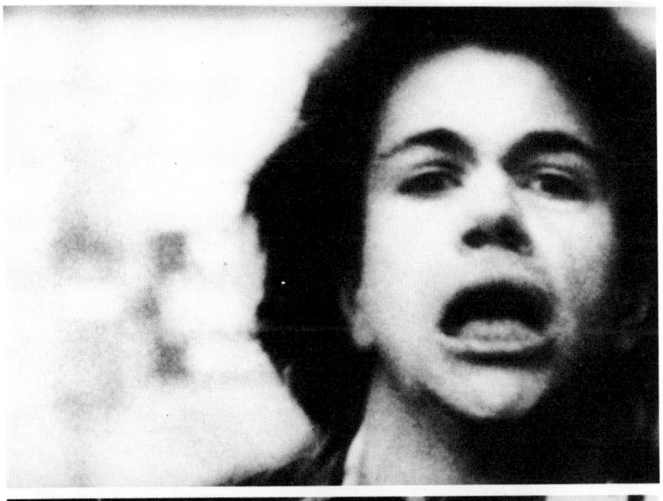

The Animal
60-second

INTERIOR, AUTOMAT. PUSHER IS SITTING AT A TABLE EATING SOUP. ENTER JOEY

JOEY: Hey man, what's happenin'? I'm sick. I need a bag.

PUSHER: Ten dollars, Joey.

JOEY: I only got five.

PUSHER: Ten dollars.

JOEY: Hey come on, you know I'm good for it.

PUSHER: Joey, the stuff is dynamite. Ten dollars or nothing.

JOEY: Please, please man . . .

PUSHER: Joey, get the money.

MOVE TO SERIES OF STRAIGHT CUTS: JOEY STEALING MONEY FROM HIS MOTHER'S POCKETBOOK; TRYING TO FORCE HIS KID BROTHER TO GIVE HIM SOME MONEY; VOMITING ON THE SIDEWALK; MUGGING A WOMAN AND STEALING HER POCKETBOOK; TURNING ON IN AN ABANDONED BUILDING

ANNCR. (VO): This is a drug addict. Unlike a man, he has no sense of right and wrong. No use for reason. He only feels. And what he feels most of the time is fear. He runs away from reality, because reality is what scares him most of all. He lives off human beings . . . because he's afraid to live like a human being. He's alive . . . but you couldn't call this really living.

FADE TO BLACK. SUPER: DON'T JOIN THE LIVING DEAD

Peer Group
60-second

Karen
60-second

TV/Public Service/Campaign

361 Silver Award
Art Director: Michael Ulick
Copywriter: Paul Margulies
Cameraman: Steve Horn
TV Director: Steve Horn
TV Producer: Philip Peyton
Production Company: Horn/Griner Productions
Agency: Wells, Rich, Greene, Inc.
Client: National Kidney Foundation

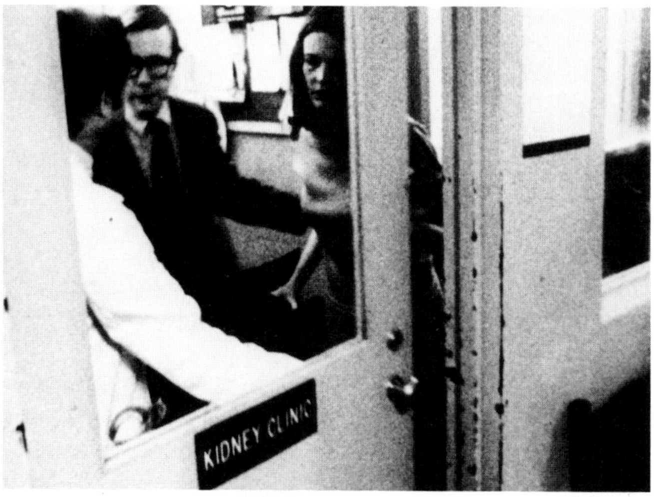
KIDNEY CLINIC

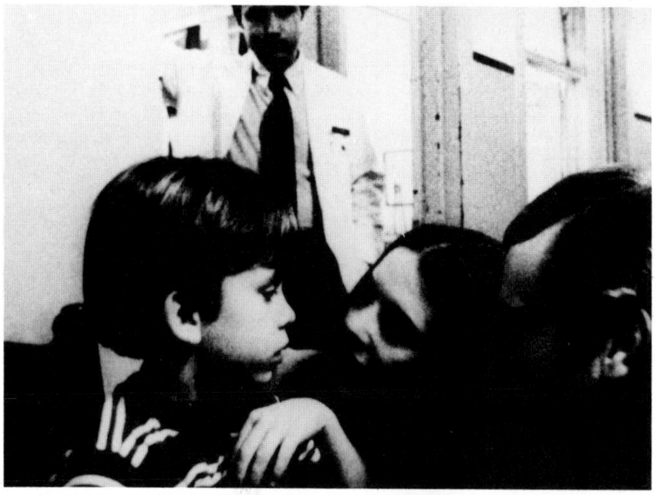

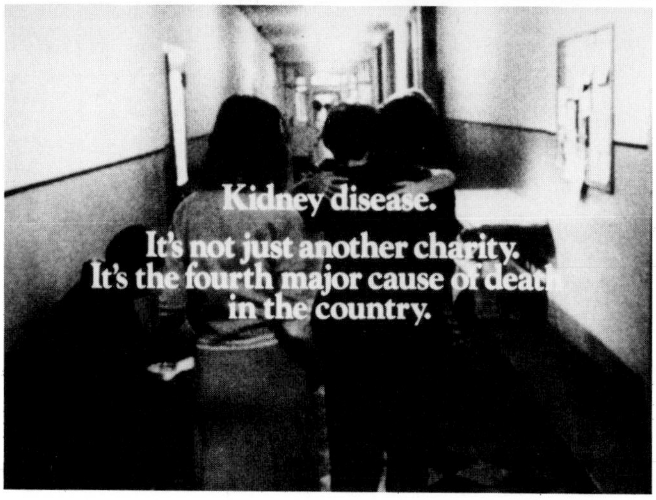
Kidney disease.
It's not just another charity.
It's the fourth major cause of death
in the country.

Kidney Machine/Kid
60-second

DOCTOR'S OFFICE. PHYSICIAN TALKING TO YOUNG COUPLE

DOCTOR: I'm sorry I can't be more definite. Yes, with a kidney machine, Jack will live. The problem is this machine costs a fortune to run and there's just not enough money in the kidney program.

Look . . . there are eight million people in this country with kidney disease and no one will take it seriously. It's not only Jack, we could save thousands of lives. I know it sounds stupid . . . now a solution to a disease and not enough money to use it.

You know I'll do everything I can. At least Jack has age in his favor.

PARENTS EXIT OFFICE TO CORRIDOR, WHERE JACK, AGE SIX, IS SITTING WITH NURSE

PARENTS: Thank you, doctor.

NURSE: See Jack! I told you Mommy and Daddy would be right out.

MOTHER: Daddy and I have decided to go out to dinner tonight. You can have anything you want. You can even have two desserts . . .

THE THREE WALK AWAY DOWN CORRIDOR

FADE TO BLACK. SUPER: SUPPORT THE NATIONAL KIDNEY FOUNDATION BOX 353, NEW YORK, NEW YORK 10016

ANNCR. (VO): It just doesn't make sense . . . to have answers to a disease and not enough money to use them.

SUPER: KIDNEY DISEASE. IT'S NOT JUST ANOTHER CHARITY, IT'S THE FOURTH MAJOR CAUSE OF DEATH IN THE COUNTRY

Funeral
60-second

Empty Chair
60-second

362
Art Director: Grey Advertising Creative Team
Writer: Grey Advertising Creative Team
TV Producer: Grey Advertising Creative Team
Production Company: James Garrett & Partners
Agency: Grey-North Advertising Inc.
Client: The National Institute on Alcohol Abuse and Alcoholism

THE NATIONAL DRINKING GAME.

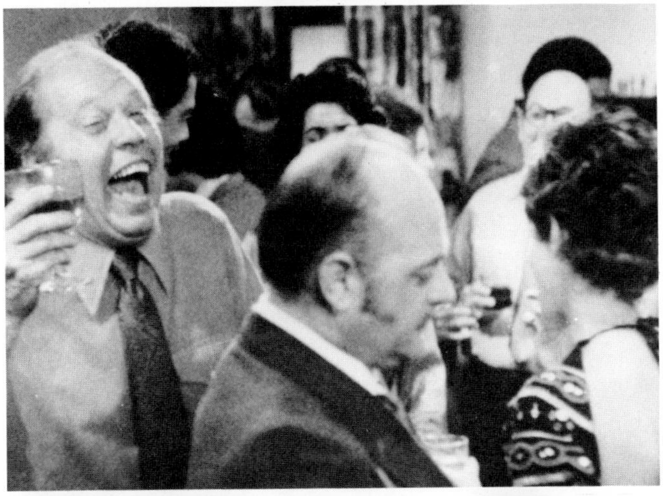

National Drinking Game
60-second

PARTY CROWD WHOOPING IT UP

ANNCR. (VO): Because so many Americans think getting drunk is fun, we thought you might like to join us in the National Drinking Game.

TITLE CARD: THE NATIONAL DRINKING GAME

(SFX: "WHOOPEE, A GAME. GET YOUR PENCIL, ETC. . .")

Just answer yes or no to the following 10 questions.

One: Do you talk a lot about drinking?

(SFX: "ONLY WHEN I'M AWAKE")

Two: Do you drink more than you used to?

(SFX: "I TRY TO . . .")

Three: Do you gulp your drinks?

Four: Do you often take a drink to feel better?

("YEAH, MUCH BETTER.")

Five: Do you drink alone?

Six: Do you ever forget what you did while you were drinking?

("NOT UNTIL THE NEXT DAY.")

Seven: Do you keep a bottle hidden somewhere for quick pick-me-ups?

("HOW DOES *HE* KNOW?")

Eight: Do you sometimes start drinking without really thinking about it?

Nine: Do you need a drink to have fun?

(SFX: THROAT CLEARING)

Ten: Do you ever take a drink in the morning to relieve a hangover? Congratulations. If you had four or more "yes" answers, then you may be one of over nine million Americans with a drinking problem.

ANNCR.: If you won—you lose.

SUPER: NATIONAL INSTITUTE ON ALCOHOL ABUSE AND ALCOHOLISM

Bill and Helen
60-second

Good Old Harry
60-second

363
Art Director: William Taubin
Copywriter: Frada Wallach
TV Director: Tony Lover
TV Producer: Herb Strauss
Production Company: Liberty Studio
Agency: Doyle Dane Bernbach Inc.
Client: Federation of Jewish Philanthropies

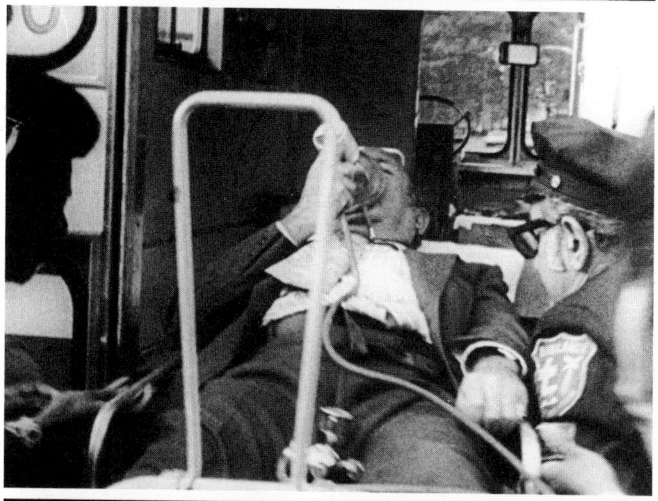

Heart Attack
30-second

SCENE OPENS ON A MAN COMING DOWN THE STEPS OF A BUILDING. SUDDENLY HE BEGINS TO GASP FOR BREATH AND FALL

HE DROPS AS PEOPLE COME RUSHING UP, TRYING TO HELP

(SFX: VOICES IN CROWD, CONSTERNATION)

ANNCR. (VO): Where will they take him?

AMBULANCE PULLS UP

To a hospital that can't afford cardio-pacs, cardio-emergency rooms or temporary pace makers?

DRIVES AWAY

It's like playing Russian Roulette, if you're trying to save a life. The hospitals of the Federation of Jewish Philanthropies must have the most modern equipment there is.
We can't afford to gamble.

MENORAH SHOWING BRICKS BEING LIT

Help us build.
With bricks you can build life.

SUPER: FEDERATION OF JEWISH PHILANTHROPIES

Joy Ride
30-second

Menorah
60-second

Aged
30-second

364
Art Director: Edward Lukas
Copywriters: Evan Stark
Indiana Sweda
Cameraman: Fred Sweda
TV Director: Fred Sweda
TV Producer: Sonya Hoover
Production Company: Sweda Enterprises Ltd., Inc.
Agency: Sweda Enterprises Ltd., Inc.
Client: N.Y.C. Environmental Protection Administration

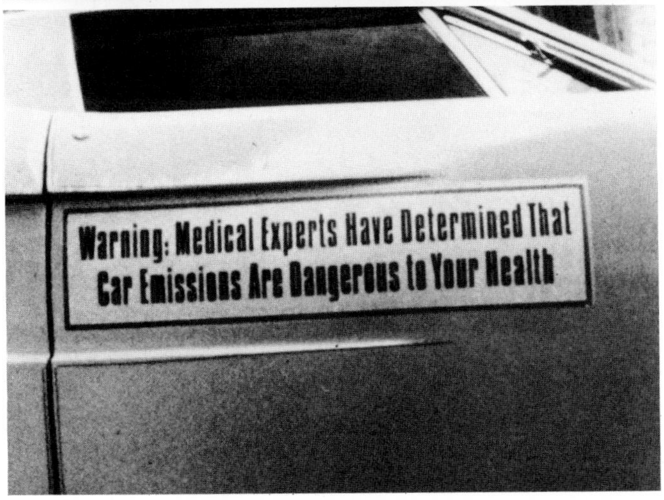
Warning: Medical Experts Have Determined That
Car Emissions Are Dangerous to Your Health

New Car
60-second

RUNNING SHOT OF NEW CAR (CUSTOM MODEL)

ANNCR. (VO): America, here it is! The sleek, sensuous lines you've dreamed of, this year's new car . . . A power engine you'll love to accelerate. Fully automatic transmission. Four barrel carburetor, front and rear disc brakes. The luxurious comfort you thought you couldn't afford.

CU OF SIGN ON DOOR THAT READS: "WARNING: MEDICAL EXPERTS HAVE DETERMINED THAT CAR EMISSIONS ARE DANGEROUS TO YOUR HEALTH"

ANNCR. (VO): Maybe we can't afford it!

Talkin' Big City
60-second

Driving to Work
60-second

EDITORIAL

Consumer Pages and Sections
Trade Pages and Sections
Complete Issues

Classroom Debate

Should the President's War-Making Powers Be Curbed?

NO

By EUGENE V. ROSTOW

NEW HAVEN, Conn. The Javits war-powers bill confirms Oliver Wendell Holmes' quip that "great cases like hard cases make bad law" more vividly than any proposal since that of the Bricker Amendment. Responding to Vietnam, the Javits bill would radically change the constitutional relationship between Congress and the Presidency in making foreign policy. Ignoring their own repeated votes for Vietnam, the sponsors contend that the cause of the Vietnam tragedy is a modern usurpation of the war power by the President. As Senator Cooper points out, this claim rewrites history.

The Javits bill would annul the military provisions of all outstanding treaties and Congressional resolutions authorizing the use of force by the President, including NATO and the Middle East Resolution, as well as all Presidential commitments.

The bill is full of paradox. While it purports to assure the nation that a pacific Congress will keep jingoistic Presidents from engaging in limited wars like Korea or Vietnam, the bill would not have prevented Vietnam, which was authorized by Congress through the very procedures proposed in the bill as constitutionally proper. In Korea, the Javits bill would have required President Truman to obtain a Congressional resolution within thirty days—which would surely have been voted at the time, although Truman and the Congressional leaders thought it unwise to do so under the circumstances.

But if the Javits bill had been on the books, it would have prevented President Kennedy from handling the Cuban missile crisis as he did. There was no claim on that occasion that we were acting to forestall an imminent threat of armed attack. Under the Javits bill, Mr. Johnson could not have moved the fleet to keep the Soviet Union out of the Six-Day War in 1967. Mr. Nixon could not have used the same method to avert general war in the Middle East in 1970, or to confine the India-Pakistan War of 1971. Nor could earlier Presidents have used force or the threat of force to induce France to leave Mexico in 1865-66, to avoid war with Britain and Spain over Florida, or to send Commodore Perry to Japan.

The Javits bill would deprive the Presidency of powers which were used by George Washington and by nearly every President since—the powers of credible deterrent diplomacy the nation needs most if there is to be any hope of avoiding nuclear war.

With admirable candor, Senator Javits has said that the purpose of his bill is to reduce the elective Presidency, which the Founding Fathers were at pains to establish as an equal branch of the tripartite government, to the humble posture of George Washington during the Revolution, when he functioned as Commander in Chief, appointed by the Congress, and its creature in every respect.

Congress has made no bid for supremacy so bold, and so foreign to the Constitution, since the impeachment of Andrew Johnson. The legal theory of the bill would permit a plenipotentiary Congress to dominate the Presidency (and the courts) more completely than the House of Commons governs in Great Britain.

I do not favor increased Presidential power. But I do defend the constitutional pattern of enforced cooperation between Congress and President we have inherited. Its corollary, however, is democratic responsibility. It is unseemly for astute and worldly men who spoke and voted for SEATO, the Tonkin Gulf Resolution, and other legislative steps into the Vietnam War now to claim that they were brainwashed, and therefore that we — and the world — should treat public acts of the United States as if they never happened.

Korea and Vietnam did not come about because the Presidency arrogated Congress' powers over foreign policy. The Congress fully supported those efforts when they were undertaken. The country is in a foreign policy crisis, however—not a constitutional crisis, but an intellectual and emotional crisis caused by growing tension between what we do and what we think. The ideas which guided our response to Korea and Vietnam have suddenly lost their power to command. Those who now believe Korea and Vietnam were errors should recall the prudent wisdom of an earlier time, when the powers of the Supreme Court were left untouched even after the catastrophic error of Dred Scott. We have never needed the strong Presidency we have developed in nearly 200 years of intense experience more than we need it today. The Javits bill would turn the clock back to the Articles of Confederation, and emasculate the independent Presidency it was one of the chief aims of the men of Annapolis and Philadelphia to create.

Eugene V. Rostow, professor of law at Yale, is author of the forthcoming book, "Peace in the Balance: The Future of American Foreign Policy."

YES

By RICHARD B. MORRIS

Prof. Eugene Rostow's recent analysis of the Javits-Stennis war-powers bill constitutes so serious a distortion of American constitutional history and so warped an interpretation of the bill's provisions and likely effects that it should not go unanswered. Nothing in the bill justifies his condemnation of it as a "bold" bid for constitutional supremacy unrivalled "since the impeachment of Andrew Johnson" nor his contention that it is based upon a legal theory which would permit "a plenipotentiary Congress to dominate the Presidency (and the courts) more completely than the House of Commons governs in Great Britain."

This is nonsense. If any branch of the Government has usurped the war-making powers of the Constitution it has been the executive arm and not Congress, with consequences that have proven detrimental to the national interest.

The Constitution is clear on its allocation of the war powers. That document clearly distinguished between declaring war and supporting it on the one hand, and conducting its operations on the other. Article I, section 8 vests in Congress the right to declare war and raise and support armies, but limits to a maximum of two years the appropriation of money to their use. On the other hand, Article II, section 2 describes the President as Commander in Chief.

Throughout the debates on the drafting of the Constitution and its ratification one finds a deep concern about executive usurpation matched by an equal concern (and remarkable prescience) that the war powers remain lodged in the legislative branch of the Government, wherein they had been previously vested from the start of the American Revolution. At the same time the Founding Fathers made certain that the executive arm which they were in the throes of fashioning was given emergency powers for military defense.

To allay widespread fears that the war-making powers under the Constitution would subvert republican institutions, the authors of The Federalist papers made a point of construing the President's role rather narrowly. The early Presidents used their military powers with caution. Even Washington's authority to issue a proclamation of neutrality seemed moot, James Madison contending that neutrality was merely the negative side of a declaration of war and required Congressional approval.

It is the undeclared war now being waged in Indochina, not the prospect of passage of the Javits-Stennis bill, which is damaging our prestige and credibility abroad, tragically dividing the American people, and diverting resources from the most urgent tasks of domestic reconstruction. In my considered judgment, that bill sets the constitutional balance true. It provides urgently needed clarification of the war-making powers in the spirit of the drafters and ratifiers of the Constitution without hampering the President in his capacity as Commander in Chief.

Professor Rostow and others protest that the Javits-Stennis bill would have inhibited the President in the Cuban missile confrontation. They scrupulously avoid mentioning the misconceived Bay of Pigs invasion or the dubious intervention in Santo Domingo. What the bill seeks to eliminate are brinkmanship and tiltmanship, the bankruptcy of the latter strategy all too evident in our recent posture during the India-Pakistan war.

The fact of the matter is that our disastrous involvement in Indochina did not come as a flashing meteor in the skies but resulted from a state of political erosion in that area going back a quarter of a century. Indubitably during that considerable period of time there must have been some moment when the issue of war or peace could have been put to Congress on a basis more candid and substantial than the Gulf of Tonkin Resolution.

Instead of candid communication between the executive and Congress we have had unparalleled doubletalk, evasion and concealment. We have seen a phantom undeclared war, which was supposed to contract, continue to escalate, one which was supposed to shorten spitefully drag on, one which still rages on land and expands in the skies.

Richard B. Morris is Gouverneur Morris Professor of History at Columbia.

365

366

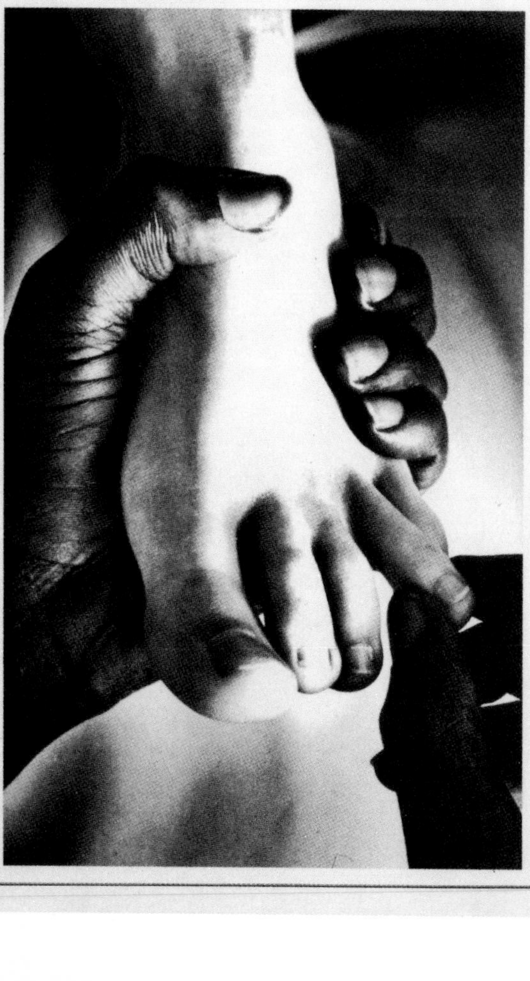

the art of sensual MASSAGE

by Gordon Inkeles & Murray Todris with photographs by Robert Foothorap

There is but one temple in the Universe, says the devout novalis, and that is the human body. Nothing is holier than that high form. We touch heaven when we lay our hand on the human body.
—Thomas Carlyle, 'The Hero As Divinity'

There are no special tricks to massage. With a warm quiet place and a bottle of scented oil you can spread pleasure over every inch of your partner's body. You don't need a lot of money or a room full of special equipment to do this. And you don't need an intensive course in anatomy to lay your hands on another human being. The art of sensual massage is much older than any labels moderns have invented for the body.

Throughout history massage has been used to relieve suffering. The most ancient medical records speak of it routinely as though it were one of the physician's most valuable tools. We will discuss therapeutic applications of various movements occasionally. But when you work with these strokes you'll discover their healing power for yourself.

Pleasure and therapy. Depends on what you want to do.

PREPARATION FOR MASSAGE

Massage aims to relax all the senses. Your preparation should center on this side.

Light: Nobody's eyes stay open through a massage. Make it easy for your partner to drift away from visual distractions. Lighting should be soft and indirect.

Quiet: If you're indoors listen to the room. Every room has its own sounds and they become very apparent while you're stroking. If the two of you like the message you may want to let it go on. Otherwise music is a wonderful way to fill a massage room. Something easy and smooth. Flutes, classical guitar, slow blues, a raga or chant. If you're outdoors, it's all there waiting for you.

Warm: 70 to 80 degrees. Motion generates heat. Your partner barely moves while you're stroking. And be sure your hands are warm.

Taste: You know what your partner likes.

The Body: Some people like a hot bath before massage. A sauna is fine, too, if you have one. Whatever you decide on, be sure both of you are clean. Trim your fingernails.

Your partner needs to rest on a fairly even level surface. It's easy to create one on a warm beach or a grassy field. Indoors, look for a thick rug or a few large flat pillows. Or for a few dollars you can cover your pillows with velvet, linen, silk and satin cloths the way we did. You may want to give extra support with pillows under the small of the back, below the ankles, and behind the neck.

Incense: Sure – the long burning kind.

Massage, like music, is rhythmic. Strokes blend into each other slowly and evenly. Put everything where you want it before you begin so you can avoid short jerky motions and interruptions.

Repeat movements three times (unless otherwise noted). When your partner gets excited about something you're doing, keep it up for awhile. But if anything you do causes pain, stop and go on to another part of the massage. *Never hurt your partner.* Use pressures that feel good to him.

Be silent.

Oils and Essences: The Biblical word "anoint" very often meant to massage with oil. The ancient Jews used olive and vegetable oils to warm the skin of those they wished to bless. In the past 5000 years no better massage oils have been discovered.

Any vegetable oil, with the exception of peanut oil, makes a fine base. Coconut oil is exceptionally clean and easy to use. When it is heated it liquifies into a smooth almost odorless medium. Keep your oil in a bottle or metal bowl that isn't likely to tip over while you're working. Use a coffee warmer or candle to heat the bowl so that you have warm oil throughout the massage. Cold oil on warm skin will shock your partner and break the mood.

Once your oil is warm, scent it with an essence extract, a perfume, or a few drops of fresh lemon juice. Odor determines mood as surely as lighting, music, and touch. So pick your scent carefully. It's a good idea to have a few bottles on hand for your partner to choose from.

Oil each part of the body before you begin massaging it. Oiling is a delicious feeling – let your partner relish it. Spread the oil slowly with even circular strokes. You need just enough oil so that your hands will move smoothly. Too much oil will leave your partner dripping. Hairy parts of the body take a bit more oil than smooth skin. Go easy on the head and hands.

Oil comes off with a soft towel. Wipe it off gently before your partner turns over, after you finish the feet, and once again after completing the massage. Rubbing down the skin with alcohol is an even more effective way of removing oil. Alcohol has to be used cold, though, and cold alcohol is a jolt. But some people love it and won't do without an alcohol rubdown during a massage.

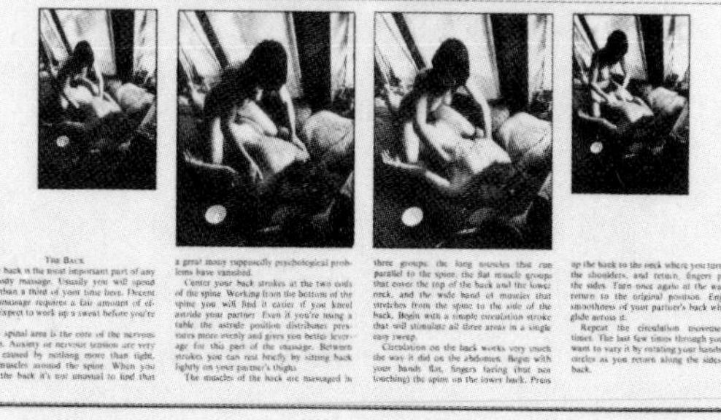

THE BACK

The back is the most important part of any full body massage. Usually you will spend more than a third of your time here. Decent back massage requires a fair amount of effort. Expect to work up a sweat before you're done.

The spinal area is the core of the nervous system. Anxiety or nervous tension are very often caused by nothing more than tight, sore muscles around the spine. When you relax the back it's not unusual to find that a great many supposedly psychological problems have vanished.

Center your back strokes at the two ends of the spine. Working from the bottom of the spine you will find it easier if you kneel astride your partner. Even if you're using a table the astride position distributes pressures more evenly and gives you better leverage for this part of the massage. Between strokes you can rest briefly by sitting back lightly on your partner's thighs.

The muscles of the back are massaged in three groups: the long muscles that run parallel to the spine, the flat muscle groups that cover the top of the back and the lower neck, and the wide band of muscles that stretches from the spine to the side of the back. Begin with a simple circulation stroke that will stimulate all three areas in a single easy sweep.

Circulation on the back works very much the way it did on the abdomen. Begin with your hands flat, fingers facing (but not touching) the spine on the lower back. Press up the back to the neck where you turn, circle the shoulders, and return, fingers pressing the sides. Turn once again at the waist and return to the original position. Enjoy the smoothness of your partner's back while you glide across it.

Repeat the circulation movement ten times. The last few times through you might want to vary it by rotating your hands in tiny circles as you return along the sides of the back.

Consumer/Pages, Spreads/B/W

365
Art Director: Joseph J. Sinclair
Editor: Terrence Dewhurst
Designer: Joseph J. Sinclair
Artist: Michael Gross
Publisher: The New York Times
School Weekly

366 Silver Award
Art Director: Robert Kingsbury
Writers: Gordon Inkeles
Murray Todris
Designer: Robert Kingsbury
Photographer: Robert Foothorap
Publisher: Straight Arrow Publishers, Inc.
Rolling Stone

367
Art Director: Robert Kingsbury
Writer: Elmo Rooney
Designer: Robert Kingsbury
Photographer: Annie Leibovitz
Publisher: Straight Arrow Publishers
Rolling Stone

367

ROLLING STONE/DECEMBER 21, 1972 PAGE 59

An Interview with
the Four-Year-Old Perfect Guru
Mahamarjoe
By Elmo Rooney

A great man once said, "In my Father's house there are many mansions." He might have added that in His world there are many saints. In the following interview we shall meet one of them—and a very special one, for he is among the fastest-rising youngsters on the spiritual horizon today: the famous four-year-old Perfect Guru Mahamarjoe.

The Universal Mind works in wondrous ways, Its miracles to perform. We never planned to interview Mahamarjoe: On the contrary, on that particular day we were under the impression we were going to speak with quite another guru, the reknowned Swami Quentin F. Chowdery. But when we arrived at the appointed time and place, lo! there was Mahamarjoe, with his parents, Mahamama and Mahababa, and a host of his followers, who providentially were equipped with tape recorders and cameras which they graciously put at our disposal.

But Mahamarjoe's life has been attended with miracles from the very first. His was not, for instance, merely a case of virgin birth: He was actually found under a lotus leaf in his parents' back yard. The fourth Perfect Guru in his family—and the youngest—he received his calling but one and a half eventful years ago. By his own count he has already, at his tender age, officiated at some 850 Nirvanas, 1100 Perfect Enlightenments and about the same number of weddings. He might as well be listed in the Yellow Pages under "Transports of Bliss"!

The interview was conducted in a casually comfortable, pillow-lined office in the Perfect Guru Mahamarjoe Universal Salvation Centre in the newly incorporated town of Growthburg, Nevada, while we waited for Swami Chowdery to appear (in vain, as it turned out; and we should like to know why he sent us that last-minute note changing the place where we should meet him—it's quite a drive to Growthburg, you know). During the interview the Perfect Guru consumed a large dish consisting of fruits, nuts and iced milk and grinned from ear to ear.—E.R.

Your tiny reverence, you have said that you are on a crusade to bring a message to the world. Just to start out, would you tell us, if I may make so bold, what your message is?

Certainly. It is this: We are all one.

That's it?

O yes.

That's the message!

O yes. Is it not a nice one?

Certainly certainly, it's just that . . . well, here you are, traveling all around the world, and your message—I think I've already gotten that particular message. I mean, I've heard it before.

Really? My goodness!

Don't you have some kind of, say, new message that I've never heard?

You've heard that one! My goodness me!

Yes, I have, I'm afraid.

O but wait. There's another part, and it is this: I am the One Who Is.

Ah. Well, that raises a very fascinating question. You have been called a "Maharishi." What exactly does this title signify?

There are Maharishis and Paramahansas and Satgurus and Avataras. But only one of each speciality can exist in one age.

What are the differences between them?

"It is such a terribly immense problem in our age, this business of the pre-school girls."

"Everything that I am today I owe to Shri Mahamama, my mother the saint."

"I see a bright golden time, with peace and charity for all and sensible clothing."

Approximately the same. However, I am all four. Four in one.

But your reverence . . .

Large economy size [laughter]. Big bargains. Shop no further, I am your boy! One stop, no fuss.

But your reverence, there are so many claimants to each of these titles. What of the others?

O they are phonies, coocoo. Bees in the bonnet. Spooks in the noggin. However, I allow them to exist. Indeed, we are rather close friends and every so often we get together and have a merry time.

As the One Who Is, what modes of activity do you pursue?

I am acting constantly at all levels to bring about spiritual growth of all individuals. Believe me when I say it. Often I am all tuckered out by bedtime. For instance, I give *darshana*, which is to say, I let people visit me and give gifts, then I bless them. This alone is very tuckering, and Mahamama will not allow me to do it every day.

Another mode of activity I pursue is the starting up of foundations. Currently I am working with pre-teens who are alcoholics and narcotics and prostitutes and venereal diseases and the rest. It is a very immense problem in our age, and I feel I am uniquely equipped to save these many souls. For instance, being four years old I am, I feel, uniquely equipped to relate, if I may use that term, to the pre-teen vibe. If any of you out there would like to help me in my great labor to save our younger brothers and sisters, then let him send in money to my Perfect Guru Mahamarjoe Pre-Teen Rehabilitation Centre. It will be used, I fully assure you, for my great labor and not for any silly purposes.

It is such a terribly immense problem in our age, this business of the preschool girls going about with the short skirts and no bra and the young boys going to loose women and diddling their mamas and so forth. Pardon me to say it, but you Americans talk about that last one all the time, but why does no one do anything? And do you know how many pregnancies are affecting the pre-school girls? The shame to their parents! But the fault is to the parents, because they allow their little ones to wear the short skirts and no bra and pink underthings which only excite the lusts, man and boy. They should only wear nice black lace panties, and we have only the black panties at my Centre, I fully assure you.

And the drinking and cursing and going steady and violent movies and pollution all over the world. I am so concerned about many things. Mankind is truly in a terrible pickle, and we must learn to place our faith and submission in the Great Mother.

Speaking of that, I'd wanted to ask you about your family. I've noticed your mother is along on your current world tour.

O my. Everything that I am today I owe to Shri Mahamama, my mother the saint. She is the glorious All-Mother and an exemplary for all motherkind.

Besides having found you under a lotus leaf, in what way, your reverence, is she exemplary?

She raised me in a wholly exemplary manner. For instance, when I was little, sometimes she had to discipline me to keep me at my studies. But observe, she always used the correct disciplines: The Discipline of Smothering with the Pillow and the Discipline of Immersing the Head in Water. It is forbidden to use upon a Perfect Guru any Disciplines that would bruise or mar his lotus flesh.

Are there any special spiritual practices that you teach?

It is my mission here on this plane to teach the supreme topknot of all meditations. This is my Universal Salvation Mission.

Would you explain what is meant by Universal Salvation?

Certainly. One arranges an altar laden with sweet succulent fruits and sweet-smelling scents of herbs and spices. Then one assumes a worshipful position. Let it arise at the root of the tongue and gather until it overflows your lips. Flow with it, flowingly, as it leaves your mouth and rolls down your chin. Salivate freely and feel it flowing down from the highest Chakra, or spot, down your neck, down your chest—always flowing with it, flowing with it—down your tum-tum, until it reaches the Bib of Universal Salvation. As it merges into the Bib you will be freed and the most delicious of sensations will overwhelm you. These Bibs, which will absorb up to a cup and a half of Salvation and keep your floors very neat, may be obtained from the Perfect Guru Mahamarjoe Salvation Centre for a thank-offering of $5 or more.

Another part of my mission is the yogic practice which I alone teach, known as Negative Breathing. By this practice one obtains all his earthly desires. It is very simple and is done on this wise: Take a deep breath and hold it down as deep as you can, pressing it past the Lotus Chakra and the rest, deeper and deeper to the root-bottom of the Dandelion Chakra. For every minute you keep that breath your karmic force is increased tenfold. Try this one on your parents!

There are other practices that I teach, but they are secret and only for initiated devotees.

Now that you have visited the United States, do you have any observations? Any predictions?

O yes. Now that I have seen your great land, which contains six percent of the world's souls, I am saddened but encouraged, for I have sensed a great spiritual hunger among this nation's youth. Did you know that your preteen pop-singing group, the Almond Brothers, have accepted me as their Perfect Guru?

Pardon me, but I must say, I see terrible times for your country in the future. I see increasing social and spiritual decay, more degradation and misery and smoking and suffering; it is inevitable. On the other hand, I see also a great spiritual rebirth: So many people are trying things for world peace—this thing, that thing, hopping around from carrying a sign to building a bomb to shaving off one's hair and climbing in bed for a week on television. But none of it works for very long, eh what? The beat goes on. But when they get into Universal Salvation, I see a bright golden time, with peace and charity for all and sensible clothing for tiny tots and all kinds of goodies.

I must mention that my current tour of youth campuses is under the sponsorship of the Tiptop Toy Company, manufacturers of the Perfect Guru Mahamarjoe Image. This pure devotional image walks, talks, salivates for all mankind and performs the Yoga of Negative Breath in three degrees of color change. Also available from them is the Perfect Guru Mahamarjoe's Book of Beloved Mandalas, which is printed in a clear black-and-white outline form so that the devotee may fill in the spaces with appropriate colors, whether by watercolor, crayon or any other means. For those who wish to become my special devotees there are many other things to be had, among them a line of delicious pure foods, Spiritual Growth-Chain Letters and good sound bargains in Nevada real estate.

So many of your devotees speak highly of your 'darshana,' or blessing plan, that I wonder if you would give me a sample?

O yes. I offer perfect freedom, perfect love, perfect chat with God. Look into my eyes.

All right.

Look deeply, deeply into my eyes . . . deeper . . . you are becoming calm . . . calm . . . peace . . . peace . . . serenity . . . serenity . . . chastity . . . no more the drugs and prostitutionhoods and alcoholics and the rest. . . .

. . . .

Mr. Rooney? Are you still on the Spiritual Jumbo Plane?

Uh, yes!

Was it not neato?

Gee, that was far out. What happened?

Never you mind. Do you have some little giftie for me?

That's really funny. I do have the strangest desire to give you . . . twenty dozen pair of underwear, black. . .

Whatever you feel like. Thank you for sharing my vibrations, and come again soon.

THE NEW YORK TIMES, SATURDAY, SEPTEMBER 30, 1972

Is Paris Happening?

ABROAD AT HOME

Aleksandr I. Solzhenitsyn

Art—for Man's Sake: I

368

THE NEW YORK TIMES, FRIDAY, AUGUST 18, 1972

Nixon's Campaign Strategy

WASHINGTON

The Sakharov Memorandum

Andrei D. Sakharov

First Nixon, Then Shriver

FOREIGN AFFAIRS

369

370

The New York Times Book Review

Edward Weston.

Collected Poems 1951-1971

By A. R. Ammons.
396 pp. New York:
W. W. Norton & Co. $12.50.

By GEOFFREY H. HARTMAN

WITH these "Collected Poems" a lag in reputation is overcome. A. R. Ammons's 400 pages of poetry, written over the space of a generation, manifest an energy, wit and an amazing compounding of mind with nature that cannot be overlooked. Even with the ommission of Ammons's longest continuous work, "Tape for the Turn of the Year" (1965), this is a remarkable book, enriched by three long poems (together almost 80 pages) that must have been composed since "Uplands" (1970) and "Briefings" (1971). Indeed, with "Hibernaculum," 112 stanzas in length, a high point of the poet's delayed career is reached. His first book, "Ommateum" ("Compound Eye"), caused no stir when it appeared in 1955; and even the mid-sixties' explosion of "Expressions at Sea Level" (1964), "Corson's Inlet" (1965) and "Northfield Poems" (1966) did not make of him an inescapable presence. Ammons snared some academic admirers, but many remained suspicious of this prolific nature bard who kept turning it out like prose. His distinction as a major American poet will now be evident.

There is a problem of bulk. Ammons is a poetic Leviathan, "Created hugest that swim the Ocean stream." The intrepid mass and inner paradoxes of his verse delight and alarm at the same time. Perception is enough, Ammons seems to say, or too much. Nature-news flashes all around us, "bends and blends of sight," "the news to my left over the dunes. . . ." The ticker-tape effect is especially remarkable in such poems as "Saliences" or the microcosmic "Corson's Inlet." It bespeaks, however, no simple vitalism, for nature's plenty makes us feel poor.

Ammons yields to every solicitation from nature only to find he has no identity left, or no firm power of naming. "So I said I am Ezra," he begins his first poem, conjoining saying and naming. But, he continues, "the wind whipped my throat/gaming for the sounds of my voice." Ammons's best poems about this loss of self and voice to nature are "Gravelly Run" and the late and very beautiful "Plunder." In the latter, reality accuses the mind of "stealing" from it to create language, and the punishment for this strange new Prometheanism is, clearly enough, that the poet cannot collect himself, even in these "Collected Poems."

A man, says Emerson, "cannot be a naturalist until he satisfies all the demands of the spirit. Love is as much its demand as perception." This clarifies, perhaps, the difficulty of all nature-poetry, but especially that of Ammons. For he subdues himself totally to love of perception, refusing all higher adventure. "No arranged terror: no forcing of image, plan, /or thought: /no propaganda, no humbling of reality to precept: /terror pervades but is not arranged, all possibilities /of escape open: no route shut, except in /the sudden loss of all routes" ("Corson's Inlet"). Nature herself, as in Wordsworth, must lead to a loss of the way.

This means, however, that Ammons can only extend the Wordsworthian revolution: emptying lyric poetry of false plots, then keeping the emptiness open for a confluence (always gracious or chancy) of event and significance. Hence his "eddies of meaning" or "swervings of action /like the inlet's cutting edge," which produce an essayistic type of poem of variable length and tenuous meter; hence also those fine, organic minglings of mind and nature, or interfacings of figure and ground. But what is often given up is the formal, graduated perfection we still feel in many poems like "Gravelly Run," "Laser," "The City Limits" and "Periphery."

Undeceived poets like Ammons are aware that nature cannot suffice even when they claim that "somehow it seems sufficient / to see and hear whatever coming and going is." Their nature poetry is an almost religious kind of discipline: it acknowledges the mind's defeat, chastens self-concern, and tempers the philosophical quest for meanings. At some point, then, the "Overall" or "sum of events" must be reckoned with. This is what happens preeminently in "Essay on Poetics," "Hibernaculum" and "Extremes and Moderations," which revive modern poetry's quest for the long poem.

In these extravagant and beautiful poems — verse essays really—Ammons maintains a virtuoso current of phrasing that embraces all types of vocabulary, all motions of thought, and leads us back now to Whitman and now to the accumulative (if hopefully cumulative) strain of Pound's "Cantos" or Williams's "Paterson." Building on a non-narrative base, that is, on a will-to-words almost sexual in persistence, he changes all "fleshbody" to "wordbody" and dazzles us with what he calls "interpenetration" — a massively playful nature-thinking, a poetic incarnation of smallest as well as largest thoughts.

Let me quote two sequences from "Hibernaculum" to show the difficult integrity of these longer poems. Here is Ammons at his worst:

I see
Aggregates of definition, plausible
emergences, I see
reticulations of ambience . . .
what do I see: I see a world made,
unmade, and made again
and near crying either way: I look
to the ground for the
lost, the ground's lost. I see grime,
just grime, grain
grist, grist.

Continued on Page 40

Geoffrey H. Hartman is author of "Beyond Formalism," "Wordsworth's Poetry" and other books, and teaches comparative literature at Yale.

November 19, 1972

39

368
Art Director: J. C. Suares
Editor: Harrison Salisbury
Designer: J. C. Suares
Artist: Randall L. Deihl
Publisher: The New York Times Op-ed page

369
Art Director: J. C. Suares
Editor: Harrison Salisbury
Designer: J. C. Suares
Artist: Murray Tinkelman
Publisher: The New York Times Op-ed page

370
Art Director: J. C. Suares
Editor: John Leonard
Designer: J. C. Suares
Artist: Edward Weston
Publisher: The New York Times Book Review

Consumer/Sections/B/W

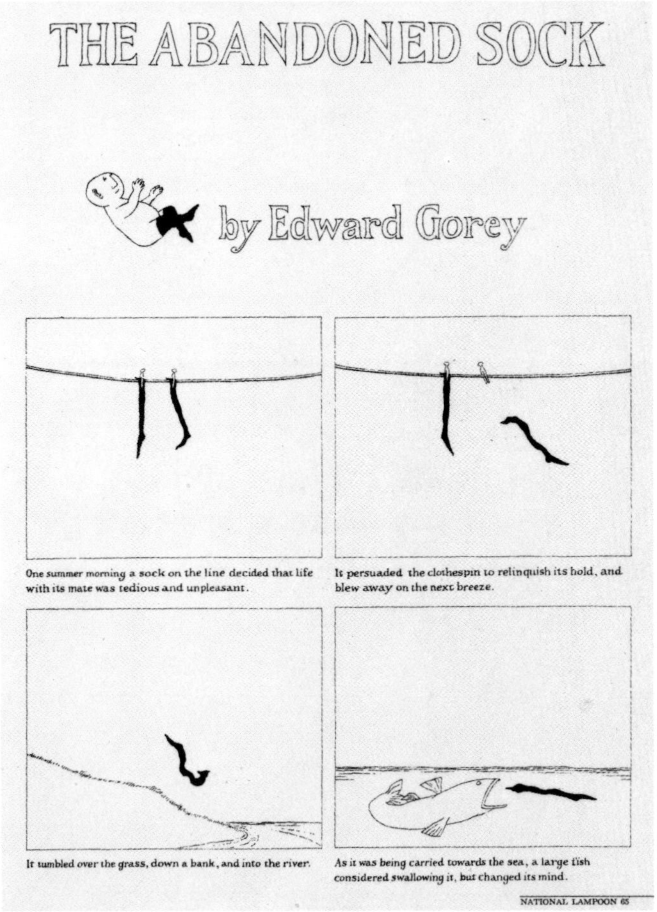
THE ABANDONED SOCK
by Edward Gorey
One summer morning a sock on the line decided that life with its mate was tedious and unpleasant.
It persuaded the clothespin to relinquish its hold, and blew away on the next breeze.
It tumbled over the grass, down a bank, and into the river.
As it was being carried towards the sea, a large fish considered swallowing it, but changed its mind.
NATIONAL LAMPOON 65

371

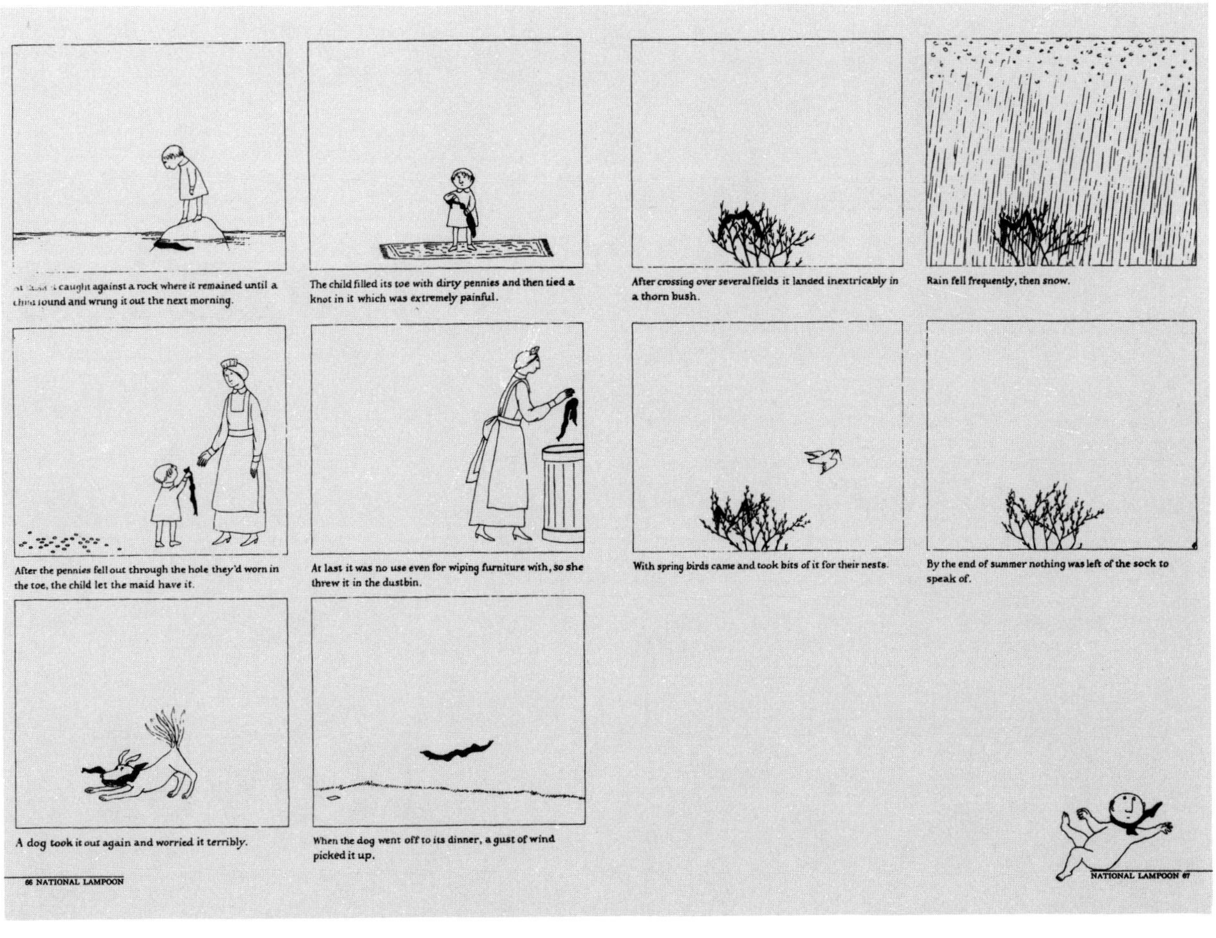
caught against a rock where it remained until a
found and wrung it out the next morning.
The child filled its toe with dirty pennies and then tied a knot in it which was extremely painful.
After the pennies fell out through the hole they'd worn in the toe, the child let the maid have it.
At last it was no use even for wiping furniture with, so she threw it in the dustbin.
A dog took it out again and worried it terribly.
When the dog went off to its dinner, a gust of wind picked it up.
66 NATIONAL LAMPOON
After crossing over several fields it landed inextricably in a thorn bush.
Rain fell frequently, then snow.
With spring birds came and took bits of it for their nests.
By the end of summer nothing was left of the sock to speak of.
NATIONAL LAMPOON 67

371
Art Director: Michael Gross
Writer: Edward Gorey
Designer: Michael Gross
Artist: Edward Gorey
Publisher: Twenty-First Century Communications National Lampoon

Consumer/Sections/B/W

372
Art Director: J. C. Suares
Editor: John Leonard
Designer: J. C. Suares
Artist: J. C. Suares
Publisher: The New York Times Book Review

372

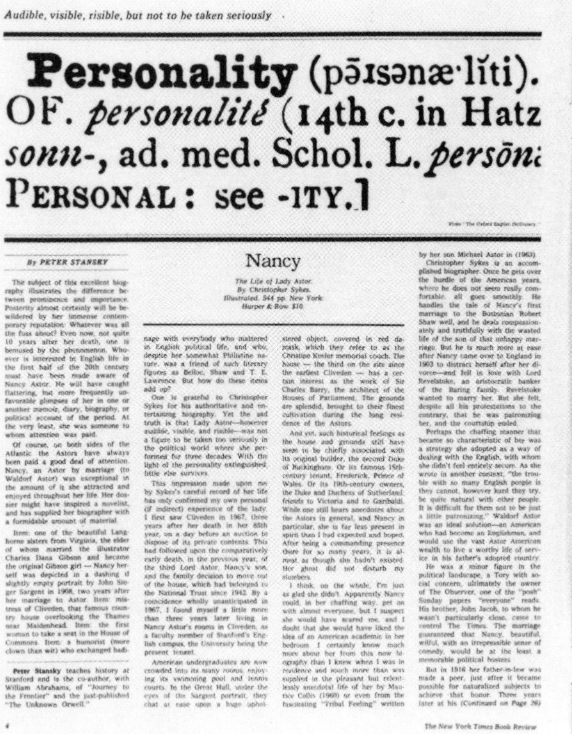

Audible, visible, risible, but not to be taken seriously

Personality (pǝɪsǝnæ·lɪti). OF. *personalité* (14th c. in Hatz *sonn-*, ad. med. Schol. L. *persōni* PERSONAL: see -ITY.]

From "The Oxford English Dictionary."

By PETER STANSKY

Nancy

The Life of Lady Astor.
By Christopher Sykes.
Illustrated. 544 pp. New York: Harper & Row. $10.

Peter Stansky teaches history at Stanford and is the co-author, with William Abrahams, of "Journey to the Frontier" and the just-published "The Unknown Orwell."

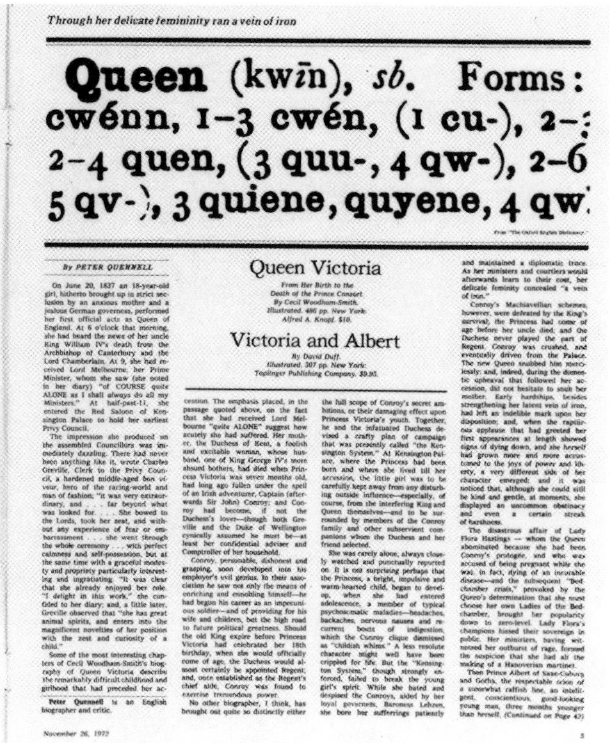

Through her delicate femininity ran a vein of iron

Queen (kwīn), *sb.* Forms: cwénn, 1–3 cwén, (1 cu-), 2– 2–4 quen, (3 quu-, 4 qw-), 2–6 5 qv-), 3 quiene, quyene, 4 qw

From "The Oxford English Dictionary."

By PETER QUENNELL

Queen Victoria

From Her Birth to the Death of the Prince Consort.
By Cecil Woodham-Smith.
Illustrated. 486 pp. New York: Alfred A. Knopf. $10.

Victoria and Albert

By David Duff.
Illustrated. 307 pp. New York: Taplinger Publishing Company. $9.95.

Peter Quennell is an English biographer and critic.

November 26, 1972

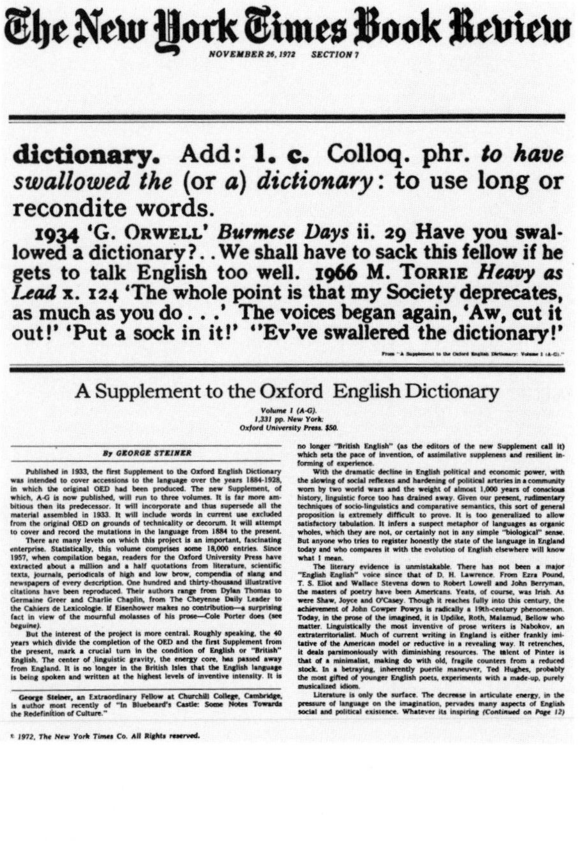

The New York Times Book Review

NOVEMBER 26, 1972 SECTION 7

dictionary. Add: **1. c.** Colloq. phr. *to have swallowed the* (or *a*) *dictionary*: to use long or recondite words.

1934 'G. ORWELL' *Burmese Days* ii. 29 Have you swallowed a dictionary?.. We shall have to sack this fellow if he gets to talk English too well. **1966** M. TORRIE *Heavy as Lead* x. 124 'The whole point is that my Society deprecates, as much as you do...' The voices began again, 'Aw, cut it out!' 'Put a sock in it!' ''Ev've swallered the dictionary!'

From "A Supplement to the Oxford English Dictionary: Volume 1 (A-G)."

A Supplement to the Oxford English Dictionary

Volume 1 (A-G).
1,331 pp. New York: Oxford University Press. $50.

By GEORGE STEINER

George Steiner, an Extraordinary Fellow at Churchill College, Cambridge, is author most recently of "In Bluebeard's Castle: Some Notes Towards the Redefinition of Culture."

© 1972, The New York Times Co. All Rights reserved.

A funny horror story about falling in love with the wrong people

futurism

62: A Model Kit

By Julio Cortázar.
Translated by Gregory Rabassa.
281 pp. New York: Pantheon Books. $6.95.

By LEO BERSANI

Novel

373
Art Director: Robert Kingsbury
Writer: Hunter S. Thompson
Designer: Robert Kingsbury
Artist: Ralph Steadman
Publisher: Straight Arrow Publishers
Rolling Stone

373

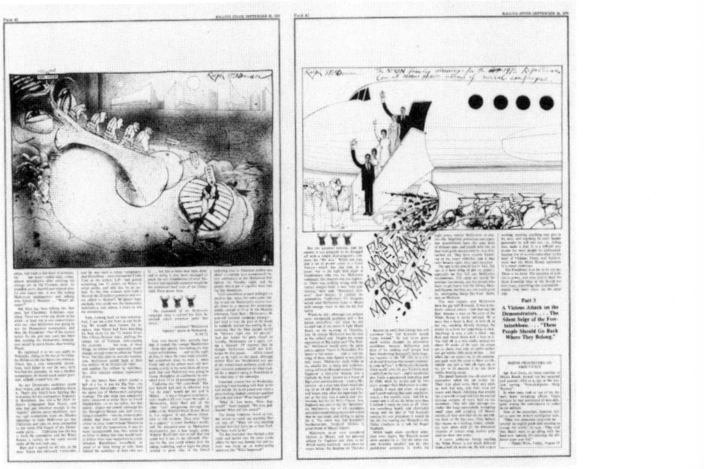

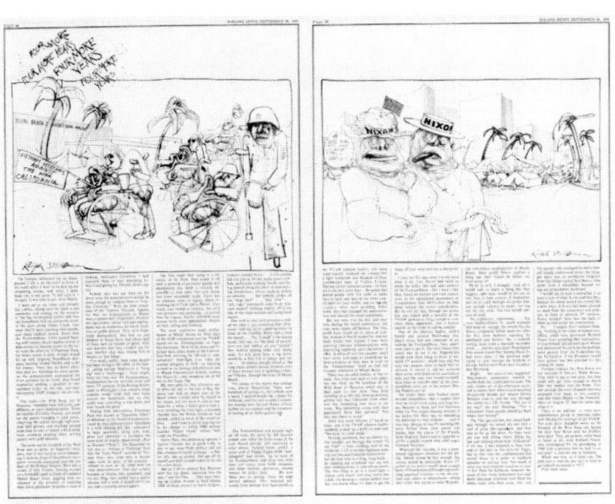

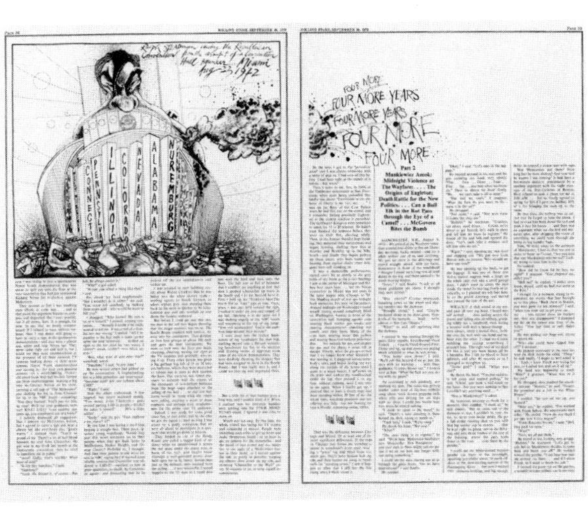

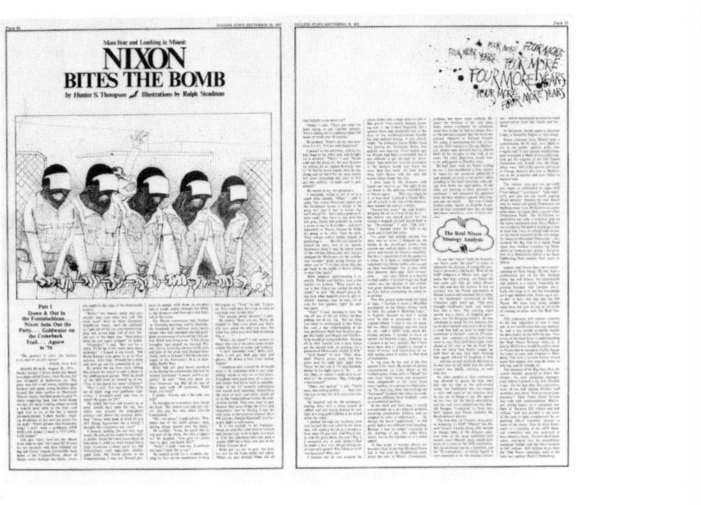

374 Gold Award
Art Director: Lawrence Miller
Writers: Modecai Siegal
Matthew Margolis
Lawrence Miller
Designers: Lawrence Miller
Vance Jonson
Artist: Reynold Ruffins
Publisher: N.Y.C. Environmental Protection Administration
Agency: Marketing Design Alliance
Client: N.Y.C. Environmental Protection Administration

374

First, read this newspaper. Then give it to your dog.
The purpose of this newspaper is to help you train your dog to go to the bathroom indoors, on newspaper, all the time.
By JEROME KRETCHMER
ENVIRONMENTAL PROTECTION ADMINISTRATOR
CITY OF NEW YORK
Traditionally, dog-owners have been allowed to let their pets relieve themselves in city streets and parks. It is a custom that dates from an era of many open spaces, little congestion and a small population.
There are already more than half a million dogs in New York City, and the number is rising.
Many concerned citizens, dog-owners and non-dog-owners alike, have come to believe that the right to own a dog should be balanced against the public's right to streets and parks free of dog litter.
For many dog-owners, "pooper-scoopers" provide a workable alternative. More and more of these devices are coming on the market. Another alternative—which the purpose of this brochure is to explore—is training dogs to go on paper indoors as a permanent form of behavior. Dog-trainers who believe that paper-training holds great promise still disagree on many details. And results can vary according to the size, sex, breed and temperament of one's pet.
The Environmental Protection Administration believes paper-training is a significant option for dog-owners, and one that should be better known.
The text that follows is excerpted and adapted from
"GOOD DOG, BAD DOG."
By Mordecai Siegal and Matthew Margolis. Copyright © 1973 by Mordecai Siegal and Matthew Margolis. Granted with the permission of Holt Rinehart & Winston, Inc., publishers.

NOW TURN TO THE CENTER.

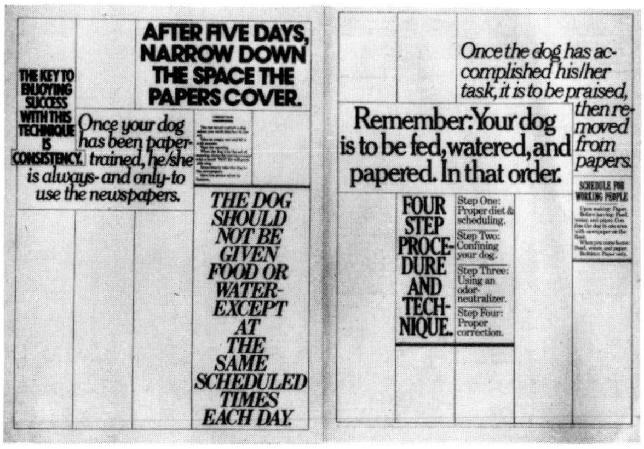
AFTER FIVE DAYS, NARROW DOWN THE SPACE THE PAPERS COVER.
THE KEY TO ENJOYING SUCCESS WITH THIS TECHNIQUE IS CONSISTENCY.
Once your dog has been paper-trained, he/she is always- and only-to use the newspapers.
THE DOG SHOULD NOT BE GIVEN FOOD OR WATER-EXCEPT AT THE SAME SCHEDULED TIMES EACH DAY.
Once the dog has accomplished his/her task, it is to be praised, then removed from papers.
Remember: Your dog is to be fed, watered, and papered. In that order.
FOUR STEP PROCEDURE AND TECHNIQUE.
Step One: Proper diet & scheduling.
Step Two: Confining your dog.
Step Three: Using an odor-neutralizer.
Step Four: Proper correction.
SCHEDULE FOR WORKING PEOPLE

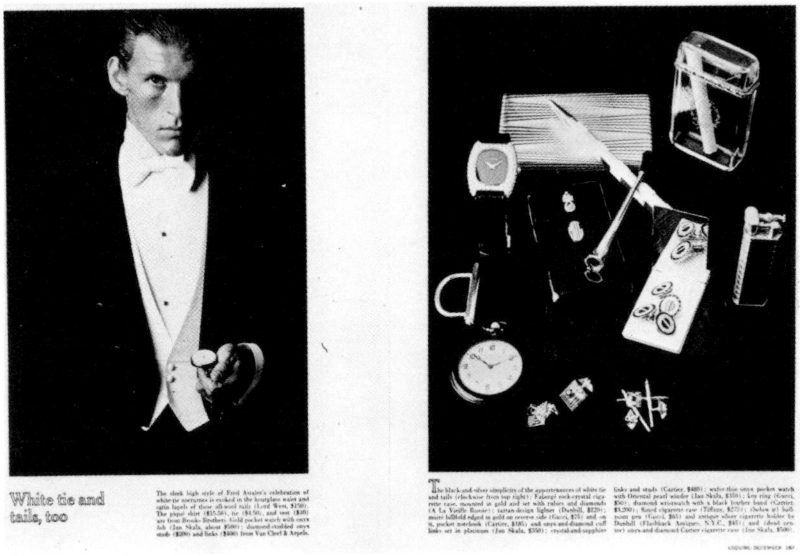
White tie and
tails, too

375

Very Special Vegetables
Frozen vegetables, always in season, are always available and ready to prepare when you need them. But they are more than convenient—they can be spectacular if you know how to combine them and how to enhance them with herbs, seasonings and savory sauces. Redbook has discovered many exciting, quick ways to dress up frozen vegetables, including our own magic Seasoned Butter Cubes to make in advance and freeze for instant use later. A collection of these easy recipes begins on page

376

377

With the holidays soon upon us, the time to take note of your looks is now. On these pages, the basics of head-to-toe maintenance, plus some quick beauty tricks for this busy season
HAIR GOES NATURAL
The signals are coming through loud and clear: The now and future direction of hair is natural. This doesn't mean messy or uncontrolled. You can "go natural" and still look as if you had just stepped out of an expensive salon. It starts with the cut, and the trick here is to have your hair cut the way it wants to go. If it's straight, choose a flattering straight style—the sleek, chin-length cut at right is a good example. If it's curly, don't fight it. Invest in a good, basic, layered cut that works with your hair, not against it. Maintenance is quick and easy. With the available profusion of gentling shampoos and new conditioners, plus the help of a blower-dryer, even the woman with / turn to page 132
YOUR
HOLIDAY
BEAUTY
BOOK

Consumer/Pages, Spreads/Color

375
Art Director: Richard Weigand
Writer: George Frazier
Designer: Henry Wolf
Photographer: Henry Wolf
Publication: Esquire Magazine

376
Art Director: William Cadge
Editor: Sey Chassler
Designer: Cal Holder
Photographer: Ben Rose
Publisher: McCall's Corporation
Redbook

377
Art Director: Alvin Grossman
Writer: Marilyn Mercer
Designer: Carveth Kramer
Photographer: Henry Wolf
Publisher: McCall Publishing Company
McCall's Magazine

Consumer/Pages, Spreads/Color

378
Art Director: William Cadge
Editor: Sey Chassler
Designer: Verdun Cook
Photographer: Pete Turner
Publisher: McCall's Corporation
Redbook

379
Art Director: Alvin Grossman
Writer: Marilyn Mercer
Designer: Alvin Grossman
Photographers: Bill Binzen
Roger Prigent
Publisher: McCall Publishing Company
McCall's Magazine

380
Art Director: Alvin Grossman
Editor: Anna Fisher Rush
Designer: Alvin Grossman
Photographer: Otto Storch
Publisher: McCall Publishing Company
McCall's Magazine

381
Art Director: Alvin Grossman
Writer: Marilyn Mercer
Designer: Carveth Kramer
Photographer: Henry Wolf
Publisher: McCall Publishing Company
McCall's Magazine

382
Art Director: Margaret Howlett
Writer: Margaret Howlett
Designer: Margaret Howlett
Artist: Margaret Howlett
Publisher: Scholastic Publications
Art and Man

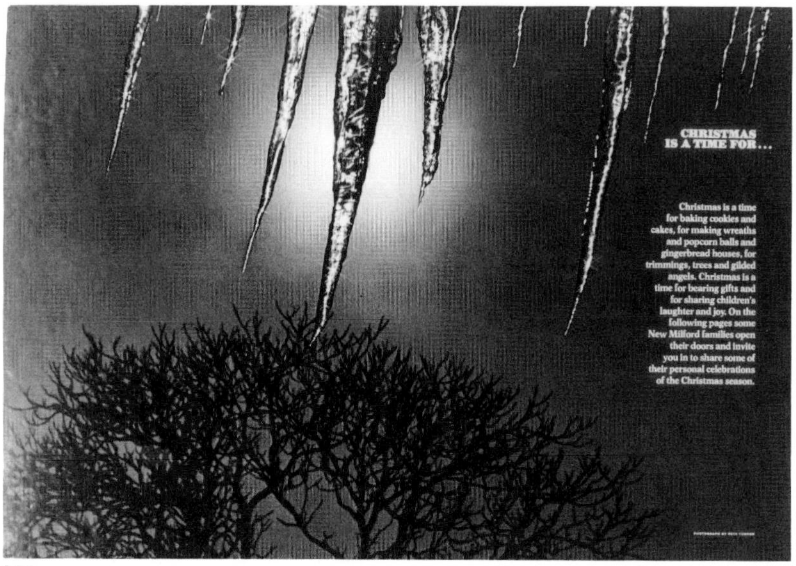
CHRISTMAS IS A TIME FOR...
Christmas is a time for baking cookies and cakes, for making wreaths and popcorn balls and gingerbread houses, for trimmings, trees and gilded angels. Christmas is a time for bearing gifts and for sharing children's laughter and joy. On the following pages some New Milford families open their doors and invite you in to share some of their personal celebrations of the Christmas season.

378

379

A SUMMER BEAUTY PLAN TO DISPLAY YOU AT YOUR BEST
BINZEN and PRIGENT

380

THIS MAN CAN BE STOPPED!
A COMPLETE GUIDE TO THE LATEST IN HOME-PROTECTION EQUIPMENT

THE LIGHT BRIGHT LOOK

In makeup, light and lively is the look to aim for. The honey-and-apricot face here, with eyes subtly emphasized and brilliant color on the lips, is a good example. The basic techniques behind the finished product, both day-to-day skin care and application of makeup, are a matter of minutes. For the particulars, see page 132

HAIRSTYLES BY KENNETH
MAKEUP BY DAMON OF KENNETH SALON

381

382

LAW AND DISORDER

Dick Tracy. Reproduced through the courtesy of the Chicago Tribune-New York News.

Still from *Little Caesar*. Warner Brothers, 1931. Photograph Culver Pictures.

The shrill blast of a police whistle, the sound of marching feet, the hoarse cough of a tommy gun, an announcer's urgent voice exclaiming, "And now—*Gangbusters*." This was the introduction to one of the most popular programs on radio, attracting millions of listeners each week. Not only did they hear "authentic police case histories," but they also received a terse description of some "public enemy" on the lam. Why, they might even have the thrill-of-a-lifetime chance to spot the miscreant and turn him in!

For this wasn't just entertainment, it was part of a crusade. One symptom of deep social unrest in the thirties was an enormous increase in crime—not only the racketeering that had started during Prohibition, but also the far more alarming street crimes of robbery, assault, and murder. People were justifiably worried and frightened by this "crime wave," and longed for a return to "law and order."

Some might take a cynical view, like that shown in the painting at right, with a police chief, a politician, and a gangster in sly cahoots. But most people looked for simpler answers. Criminals, though they might seem rather romantic in the tabloid newspapers and in movies like *Little Caesar* (above right), were simply guys who "went wrong." They richly deserved to be "sent up" or "filled full of lead." The real heroes, on the other hand, were cops like Dick Tracy (left), who got his start, guns blazing, in 1931.

Today, things don't seem so easy. There doesn't appear to be such a clear line between the law-abiding "us" and the lawbreaking "them." "Law and order" seems only part of the answer. But in a world of complex, ambiguous values it is not surprising that the old simplicities still exert a strong and nostalgic appeal.

Jack Levine (b. 1915). *The Feast of Pure Reason*, 1937. Museum of Modern Art, on extended loan from WPA Arts Program.

6

Consumer/Pages, Spreads/Color

383
Art Director: Alvin Grossman
Writer: Marilyn Mercer
Designer: Carveth Kramer
Photographer: Henry Wolf
Publisher: McCall Publishing Company
McCall's Magazine

384
Art Director: Thaddeus A. Miksinski, Jr.
Writer: Peggy Thomson
Designer: Thaddeus A. Miksinski, Jr.
Photographers: Domsea Farms
Steven C. Wilson
Publisher: United States Press and Publicati
Topic Magazine
Agency: United States Information Agency

385
Art Director: William Cadge
Editor: Sey Chassler
Designer: Bob Ciano
Artist: Gilbert Stone
Publisher: McCall's Corporation
Redbook

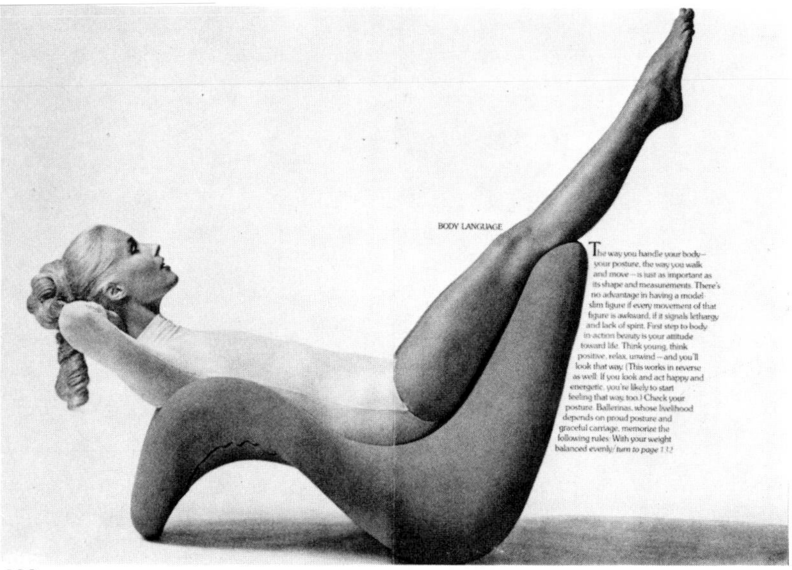
BODY LANGUAGE
The way you handle your body—your posture, the way you walk and move—is just as important as its shape and measurements. There's no advantage in having a model slim figure if every movement of that figure is awkward, if it signals lethargy and lack of spirit. First step to body in-action beauty is your attitude toward life. Think young, think positive, relax, unwind—and you'll look that way. (This works in reverse as well. If you look and act happy and energetic, you're likely to start feeling that way, too.) Check your posture. Ballerinas, whose livelihood depends on proud posture and graceful carriage, memorize the following rules: With your weight balanced evenly/ turn to page 112

383

384

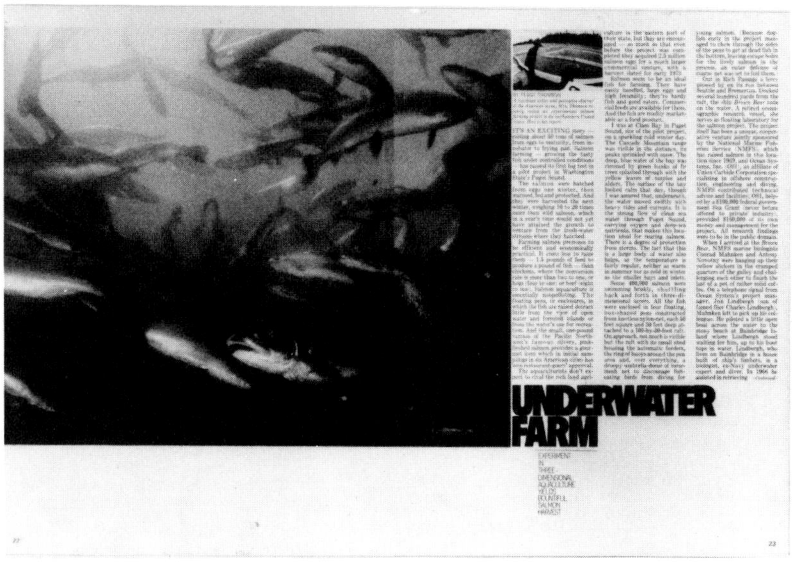
UNDERWATER FARM

385

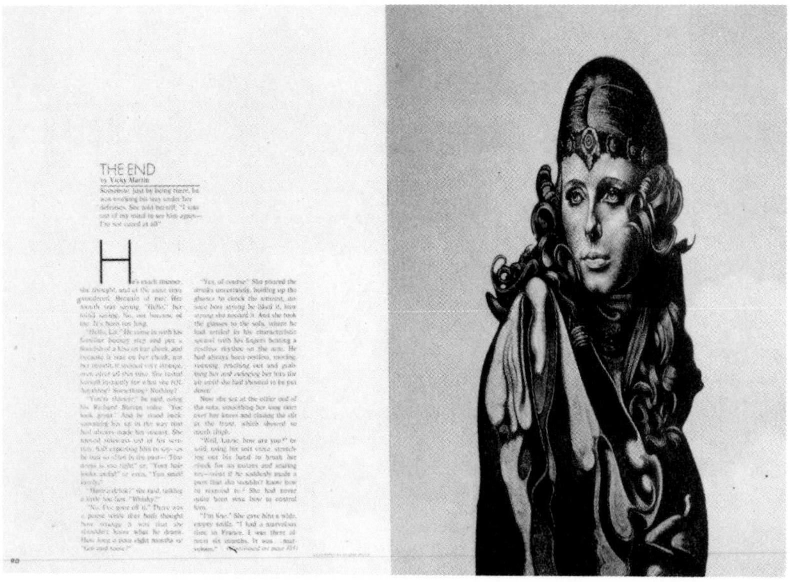
THE END
by Vicky Martin

THE PRIDE OF PASTRY CHEFS—PUFF PASTE
Puff Paste is a delicate, feather-light pastry made of sweet butter and simple dough rolled and folded into hundreds of tissue-thin, flaky layers. If you think it is far beyond your cooking prowess, you are wrong. Dare a little. All it takes is tender loving care—plus time for the dough to rest, relax and chill between its many rolling and folding sequences. After the final basic step you can keep the dough in the refrigerator or freezer, ready to shape and bake into a variety of delectable pastry concoctions you can use in many impressive ways. Some are shown here. From left to right, a Cream Horn, Napoleon, Jelly-filled Tartlet and a Palm Leaf. Recipes for these and more, together with illustrated step-by-step techniques for making them, begin on page 000.

386

387

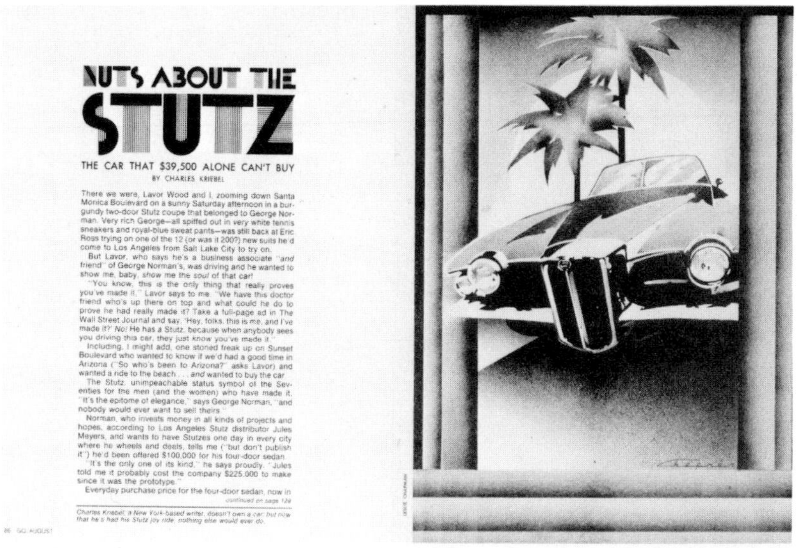

NUTS ABOUT THE STUTZ
THE CAR THAT $39,500 ALONE CAN'T BUY
BY CHARLES KRIEBEL
There we were, Lavor Wood and I, zooming down Santa Monica Boulevard on a sunny Saturday afternoon in a burgundy two-door Stutz coupe that belonged to George Norman. Very rich George—all spiffed out in very white tennis sneakers and royal-blue sweat pants—was still back at Eric Ross trying on one of the 12 (or was it 200?) new suits he'd come to Los Angeles from Salt Lake City to try on.
But Lavor, who says he's a business associate "and friend" of George Norman's, was driving and he wanted to show me, baby, show me the soul of that car!
"You know, this is the only thing that really proves you've made it," Lavor says to me. "We have this doctor friend who's up there on top and what could he do to prove he had really made it? Take a full-page ad in The Wall Street Journal and say, 'Hey, folks, this is me, and I've made it?' No! He has a Stutz, because when anybody sees you driving this car, they just know you've made it."
Including, I might add, one stoned freak up on Sunset Boulevard who wanted to know if we'd had a good time in Arizona ("So who's been to Arizona?" asks Lavor) and wanted a ride to the beach . . . and wanted to buy the car.
The Stutz, unimpeachable status symbol of the Seventies for the men (and the women) who have made it. "It's the epitome of elegance," says George Norman, "and nobody would ever want to sell theirs."
Norman, who invests money in all kinds of projects and hopes, according to Los Angeles Stutz distributor Jules Meyers, and wants to have Stutzes one day in every city where he wheels and deals, tells me ("but don't publish it") he'd been offered $100,000 for his four-door sedan.
"It's the only one of its kind," he says proudly. "Jules told me it probably cost the company $225,000 to make since it was the prototype."
Everyday purchase price for the four-door sedan, now in
continued on page 128
Charles Kriebel, a New York-based writer, doesn't own a car, but now that he's had his Stutz joy ride, nothing else would ever do.

388

THE MAN WHO WANTED SOMETHING
by Patience Wales
79

386
Art Director: William Cadge
Editor: Sey Chassler
Designer: Bob Ciano
Photographer: Carmine Macedonia
Publisher: McCall's Corporation
Redbook

387
Art Director: Harry Coulianos
Writer: Charles Kriebel
Designer: Harry Coulianos
Artist: Leslie Chapman
Publisher: Gentlemen's Quarterly

388
Art Director: William Cadge
Editor: Sey Chassler
Designer: Pat Stetson
Artist: Carol Anthony
Photographer: Alen MacWeeney
Publisher: McCall's Corporation
Redbook

Consumer/Pages, Spreads/Color

389

390

391

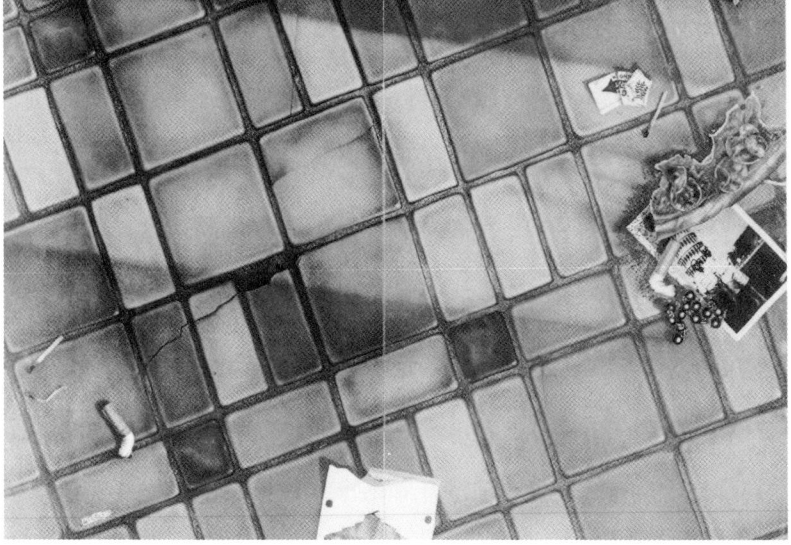

389
Art Director: William Cadge
Editor: Sey Chassler
Designer: Cal Holder
Photographer: Jerry Sarapochiello
Publisher: McCall's Corporation
Redbook

390
Art Directors: Bert Greene
Joanne Robertson
Editors: Esquire's Wear & Care Guide
Designer: Holly Dale Shapiro
Photographer: Peter Levy
Client: Esquire

391
Art Directors: Kenny Kneitel
Michael Gross
Writer: Michael O'Donoghue
Designer: Kenny Kneitel
Artist: Charles White III
Publisher: Twenty-First Century
Communications
National Lampoon

392

393

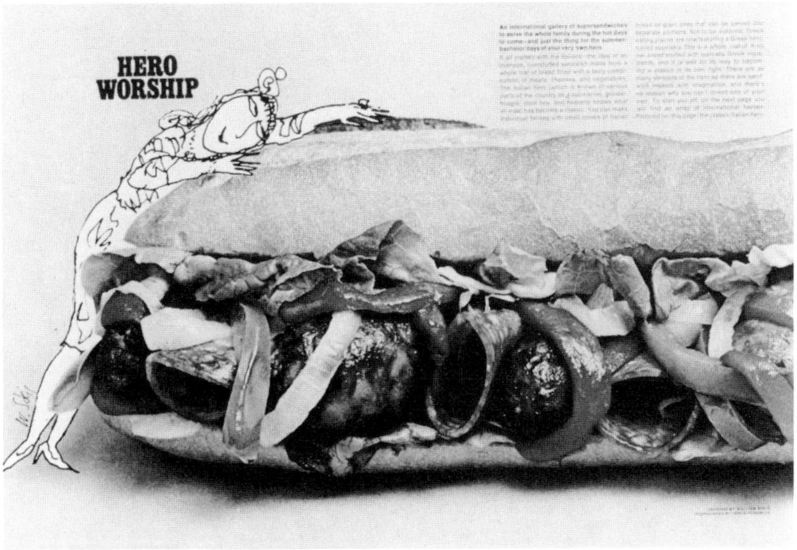

394

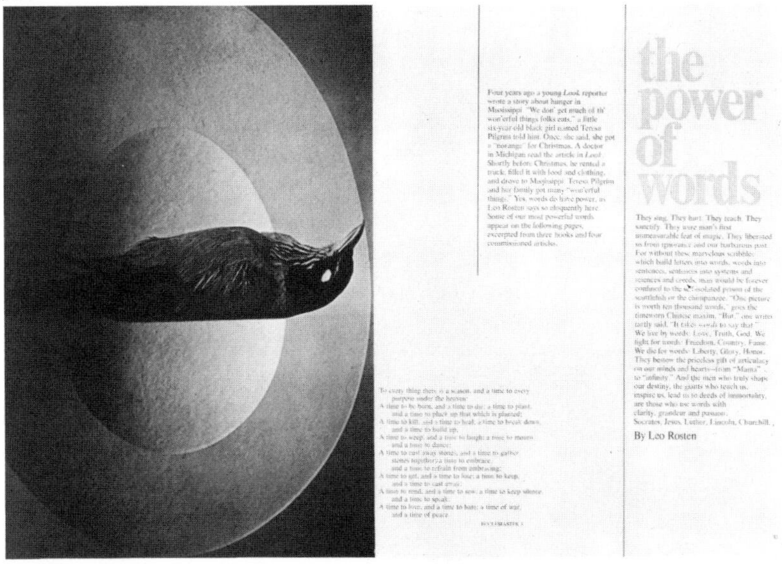

392
Art Director: Alvin Grossman
Editor: Gloria Plaut
Designer: Alvin Grossman
Photographer: James Houghton
Publisher: McCall Publishing Company
McCall's Magazine

393 Gold Award
Art Director: Alvin Grossman
Writer: Alvin Grossman
Designer: Alvin Grossman
Artist: William Steig
Photographer: Irwin Horowitz
Publisher: McCall Publishing Company
McCall's Magazine

394
Art Director: Allen F. Hurlburt
Writer: Leo Rosten
Designer: Allen F. Hurlburt
Photographer: Art Kane
Publisher: Cowles Communications, Inc.
The Look Years

HUSBANDS
IN
CRISIS

395

395
Art Director: Alvin Grossman
Editor: Don McKinney
Designer: Alvin Grossman
Photographer: Bill Binzen
Publisher: McCall Publishing Company
McCall's Magazine

396
Art Director: Harry Coulianos
Writer: Robert J. Misch
Designer: Brian Burdine
Artist: Wilson McLean
Publisher: Gentlemen's Quarterly

396

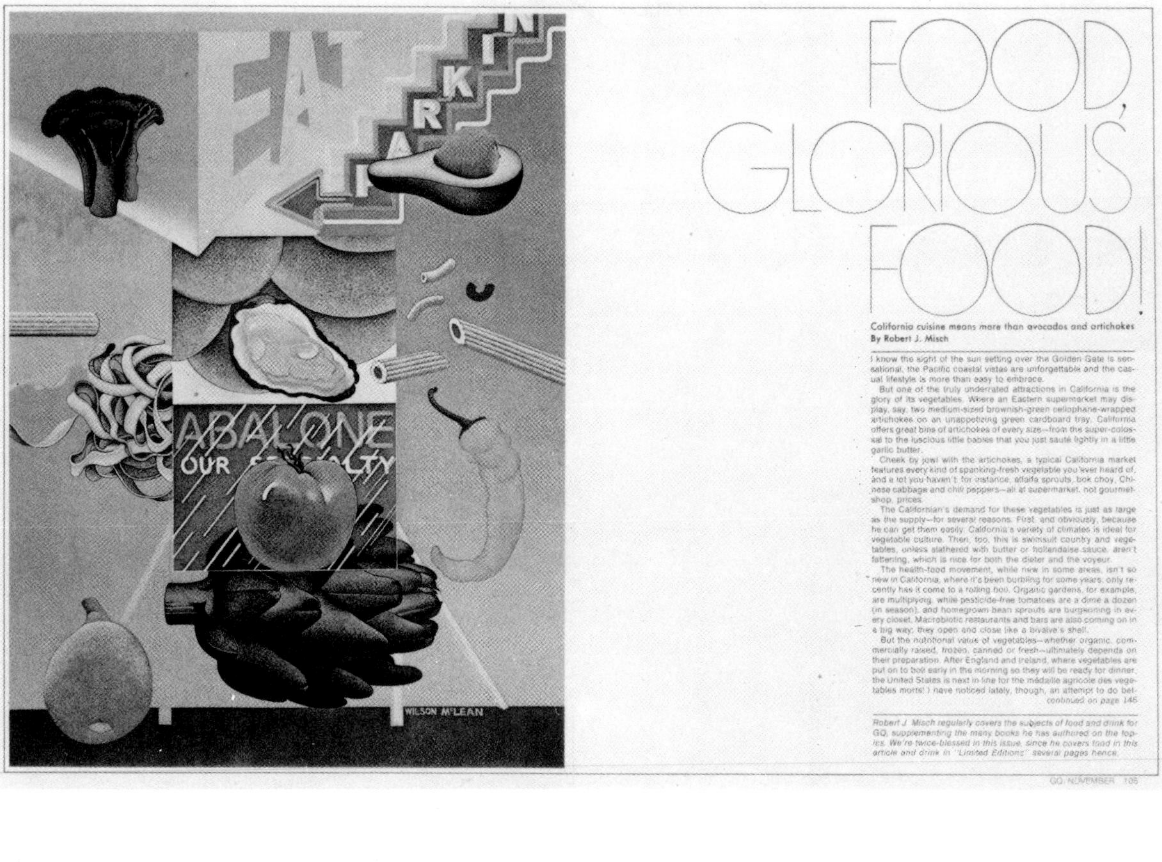
EAT
KIN
KRA
ABALONE
OUR SPECIALTY
WILSON McLEAN
FOOD, GLORIOUS FOOD!
California cuisine means more than avocados and artichokes
By Robert J. Misch
I know the sight of the sun setting over the Golden Gate is sensational, the Pacific coastal vistas are unforgettable and the casual lifestyle is more than easy to embrace.
But one of the truly underrated attractions in California is the glory of its vegetables. Where an Eastern supermarket may display, say, two medium-sized brownish-green cellophane-wrapped artichokes on an unappetizing green cardboard tray, California offers great bins of artichokes of every size—from the super-colossal to the luscious little babies that you just sauté lightly in a little garlic butter.
Cheek by jowl with the artichokes, a typical California market features every kind of spanking-fresh vegetable you've ever heard of, and a lot you haven't: for instance, alfalfa sprouts, bok choy, Chinese cabbage and chili peppers—all at supermarket, not gourmet-shop, prices.
The Californian's demand for these vegetables is just as large as the supply—for several reasons. First, and obviously, because he can get them easily. California's variety of climates is ideal for vegetable culture. Then, too, this is swimsuit country and vegetables, unless slathered with butter or hollandaise sauce, aren't fattening, which is nice for both the dieter and the voyeur.
The health-food movement, while new in some areas, isn't so new in California, where it's been burbling for some years; only recently has it come to a rolling boil. Organic gardens, for example, are multiplying, while pesticide-free tomatoes are a dime a dozen (in season), and homegrown bean sprouts are burgeoning in every closet. Macrobiotic restaurants and bars are also coming on in a big way; they open and close like a bivalve's shell.
But the nutritional value of vegetables—whether organic, commercially raised, frozen, canned or fresh—ultimately depends on their preparation. After England and Ireland, where vegetables are put on to boil early in the morning so they will be ready for dinner, the United States is next in line for the médaille agricole des vegetables morts! I have noticed lately, though, an attempt to do bet-
continued on page 146
Robert J. Misch regularly covers the subjects of food and drink for GQ, supplementing the many books he has authored on the topics. We're twice-blessed in this issue, since he covers food in this article and drink in "Limited Editions" several pages hence.
GQ NOVEMBER 105

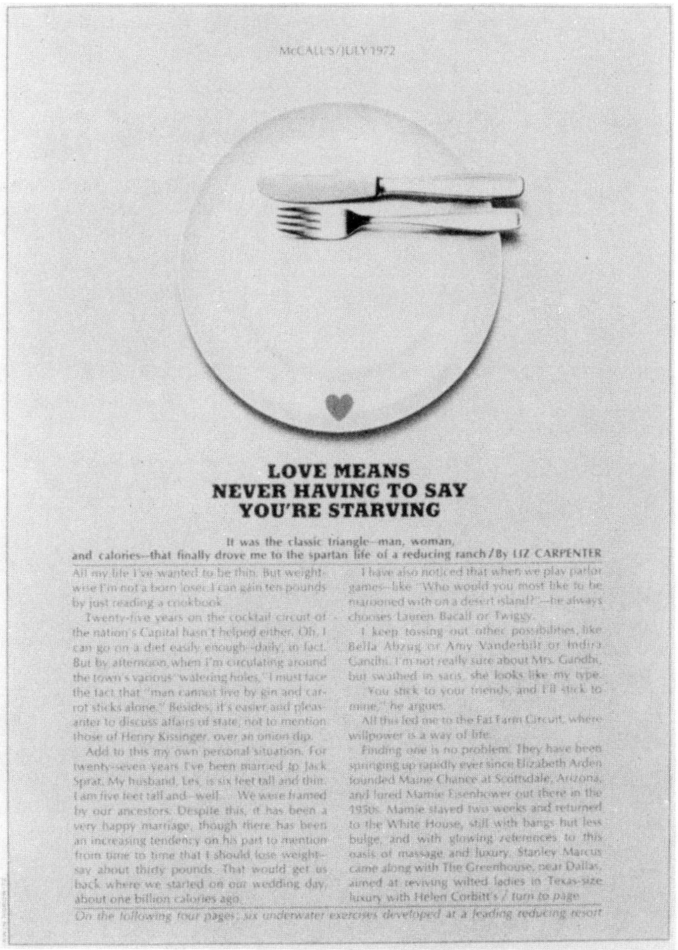

McCALL'S/JULY 1972

LOVE MEANS NEVER HAVING TO SAY YOU'RE STARVING

It was the classic triangle—man, woman, and calories—that finally drove me to the spartan life of a reducing ranch/By LIZ CARPENTER

All my life I've wanted to be thin. But weight-wise I'm not a born loser. I can gain ten pounds by just reading a cookbook.

Twenty-five years on the cocktail circuit of the nation's Capital hasn't helped either. Oh, I can go on a diet easily enough—daily, in fact. But by afternoon, when I'm circulating around the town's various "watering holes," I must face the fact that "man cannot live by gin and carrot sticks alone." Besides, it's easier and pleasanter to discuss affairs of state, not to mention those of Henry Kissinger, over an onion dip.

Add to this my own personal situation. For twenty-seven years I've been married to Jack Sprat. My husband, Les, is six feet tall and thin. I am five feet tall and—well . . . We were framed by our ancestors. Despite this, it has been a very happy marriage, though there has been an increasing tendency on his part to mention from time to time that I should lose weight—say about thirty pounds. That would get us back where we started on our wedding day, about one billion calories ago.

I have also noticed that when we play parlor games—like "Who would you most like to be marooned with on a desert island?"—he always chooses Lauren Bacall or Twiggy.

I keep tossing out other possibilities, like Bella Abzug or Amy Vanderbilt or Indira Gandhi. I'm not really sure about Mrs. Gandhi, but swathed in saris, she looks like my type.

"You stick to your friends, and I'll stick to mine," he argues.

All this led me to the Fat Farm Circuit, where willpower is a way of life.

Finding one is no problem. They have been springing up rapidly ever since Elizabeth Arden founded Maine Chance at Scottsdale, Arizona, and lured Mamie Eisenhower out there in the 1950s. Mamie stayed two weeks and returned to the White House, still with bangs but less bulge, and with glowing references to this oasis of massage and luxury. Stanley Marcus came along with The Greenhouse, near Dallas, aimed at reviving wilted ladies in Texas-size luxury with Helen Corbitt's / *turn to page*

On the following four pages: six underwater exercises developed at a leading reducing resort

397

397
Art Director: Alvin Grossman
Designer: Abelardo Menendez
Photographer: Irwin Horowitz
Publisher: McCall Publishing Company
McCall's Magazine

398
Art Directors: Louis Silverstein
Stan Mack
Editor: Mary Ann Crenshaw
Designer: Stan Mack
Artist: Ray Cruz
Publisher: The New York Times
Children's Fashion Magazine

398

S is for smocks translated from the French, just like a grown-up's schoolgirl dress.

1
A French schoolgirl's smock is translated into "tiny." Here, in a cartoon print on cotton. R.A.R. Moppets. 4 to 6x, $11. Fourth floor, Macy's. LeRoi tights. Sandler shoes.

2
A red calico smock is meant to be worn, as here, over pants. By Emma Zaiman for Sunny Lee. 4 to 6x, $13; 7 to 14, $14. Second floor, Saks Fifth Avenue.

3
A giant blue, red and yellow plaid is printed onto a pinafore smock of Avril and cotton. R.A.R. Moppets. 4 to 6x, $8; 7 to 14, $9. Second floor, Bloomingdale's. The socks by Absorba are really French.

4
Raggedy Ann flops up and down on a cotton smock dress. By Howard Jacobson for Youngland. 4 to 6x, $9; 7 to 14, $10. On the second floor, B. Altman & Co.

1 2 3 4

48 CHILDREN'S FASHIONS

K is for knits, carefree and colorful, in sweaters, skirts, pants and just-larking-about clothes.

1
Blocks of brilliance mark off the front of a navy blue acrylic knit sweater (far left.) May Knitting. 7 to 14, $9. Third floor, Franklin Simon. Navy knitted Orlon skirt by Piccolino Sport. 4 to 6x, $9; 7 to 14, $11. Sixth floor, Bergdorf's. The bright tights here are by Trimfit.

2
A hip guy wears a color-blocked black sweater over a knitted shirt with a gingham collar. Both by Wonderknit. 8 to 20. Shirt, $6.50. Acrylic sweater, $8.50. Both, Barney's Boystown.

3
A multi-colored, multi-patterned sweater of Orlon looks great over a shirt. By Justin Charles. 7 to 14, $7. Seventh floor, Lord & Taylor.

4
That ubiquitous smock turns up as a sweater—here in red Orlon blocked with color. Justin Charles. 7 to 14, $9. Fourth floor at Macy's.

1 2 3 4

THE NEW YORK TIMES MAGAZINE / AUGUST 13, 1972 49

399

New World
of Design
FOR DETAILS ON THIS
FOLDABLE, STACKABLE,
SEE-THROUGH CHAIR,
PLUS NEWS OF OTHER
EXCITING FURNITURE,
TURN THE PAGE

399
Art Director: William Cadge
Editor: Sey Chassler
Designer: Bob Ciano
Photographer: William Cadge
Publisher: McCall's Corporation
Redbook

400
Art Director: Alvin Grossman
Writer: Marilyn Mercer
Designer: Modesto Torre
Photographer: Guy Fery
Publisher: McCall Publishing Company
McCall's Magazine

401
Art Director: Alvin Grossman
Editor: Gloria Plaut
Designer: Verdun Cook
Photographer: Otto Storch
Publisher: McCall Publishing Company
McCall's Magazine

400

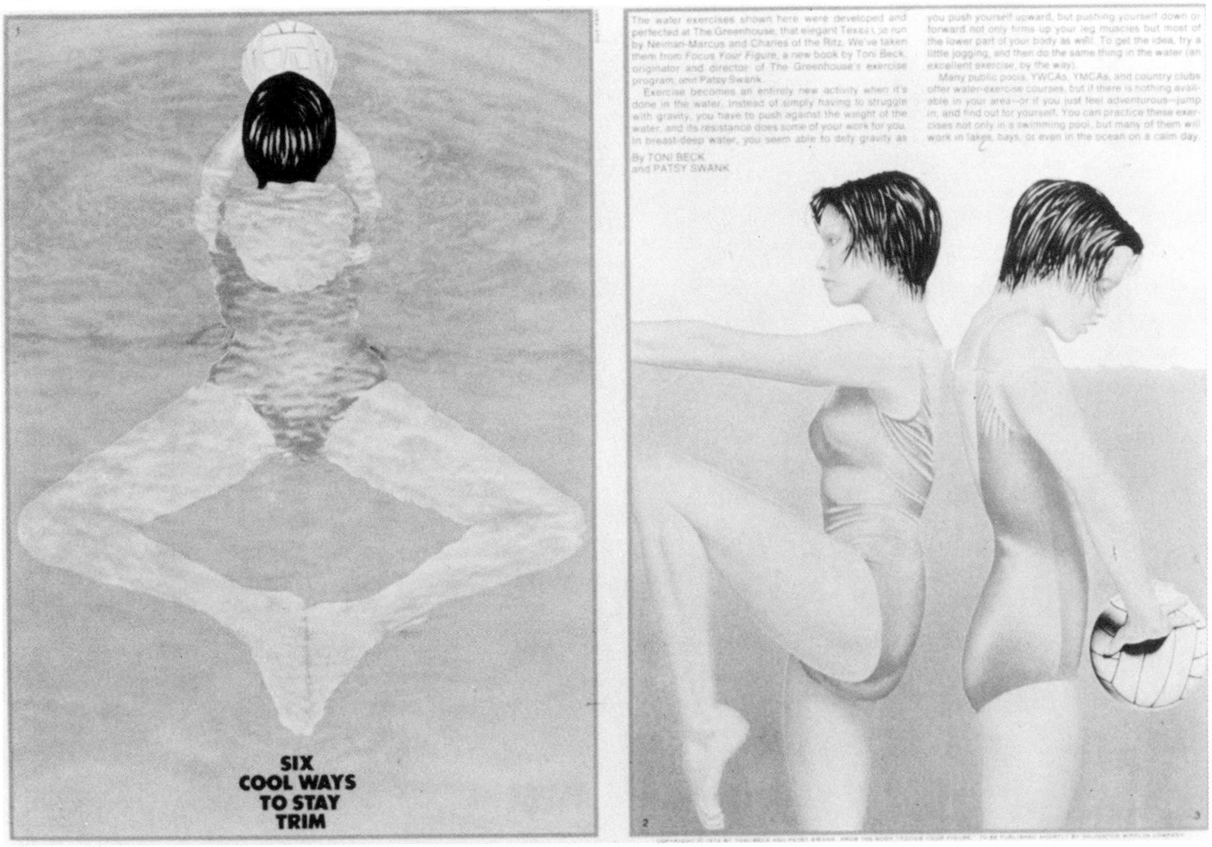
The water exercises shown here were developed and perfected at The Greenhouse, that elegant Texas spa run by Neiman-Marcus and Charles of the Ritz. We've taken them from *Focus Your Figure*, a new book by Toni Beck, originator and director of The Greenhouse's exercise program, and Patsy Swank.
Exercise becomes an entirely new activity when it's done in the water. Instead of simply having to struggle with gravity, you have to push against the weight of the water, and its resistance does some of your work for you. In breast-deep water, you seem able to defy gravity as you push yourself upward, but pushing yourself down or forward not only firms up your leg muscles but most of the lower part of your body as well. To get the idea, try a little jogging, and then do the same thing in the water (an excellent exercise, by the way).
Many public pools, YWCAs, YMCAs, and country clubs offer water-exercise courses, but if there is nothing available in your area—or if you just feel adventurous—jump in, and find out for yourself. You can practice these exercises not only in a swimming pool, but many of them will work in lakes, bays, or even in the ocean on a calm day.
By TONI BECK
and PATSY SWANK
SIX
COOL WAYS
TO STAY
TRIM

401

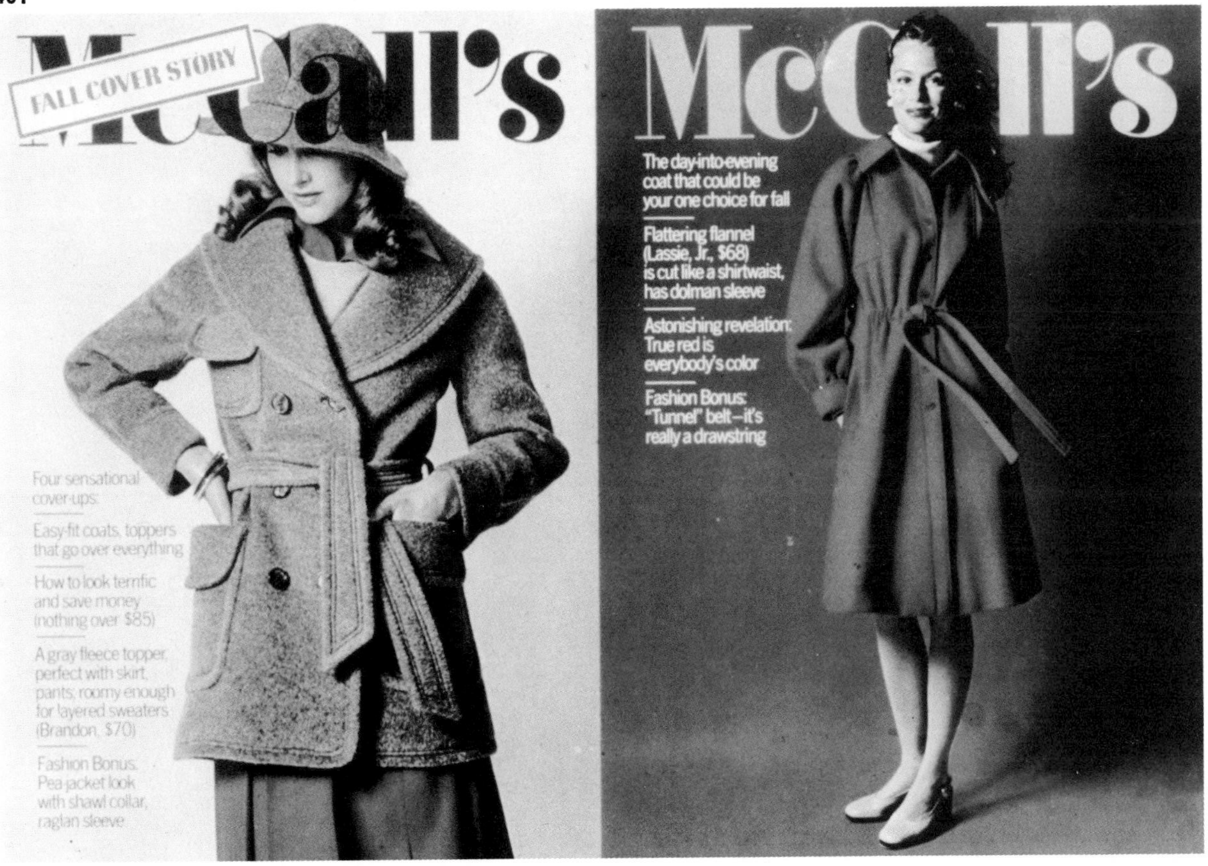
McCall's
FALL COVER STORY
Four sensational cover-ups:
Easy-fit coats, toppers that go over everything
How to look terrific and save money (nothing over $85)
A gray fleece topper, perfect with skirt, pants; roomy enough for layered sweaters (Brandon, $70)
Fashion Bonus: Pea-jacket look with shawl collar, raglan sleeve
McCall's
The day-into-evening coat that could be your one choice for fall
Flattering flannel (Lassie, Jr., $68) is cut like a shirtwaist, has dolman sleeve
Astonishing revelation: True red is everybody's color
Fashion Bonus: "Tunnel" belt—it's really a drawstring

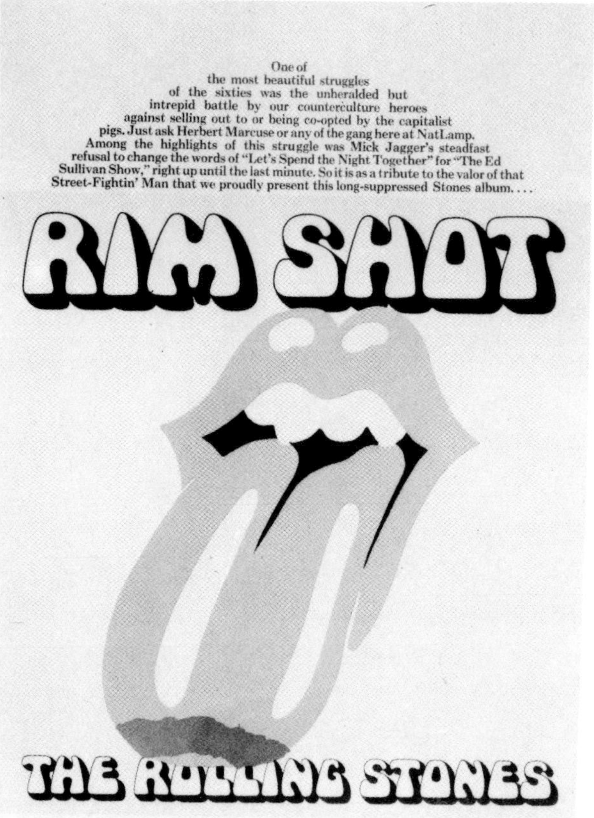
One of the most beautiful struggles of the sixties was the unheralded but intrepid battle by our counterculture heroes against selling out to or being co-opted by the capitalist pigs. Just ask Herbert Marcuse or any of the gang here at NatLamp. Among the highlights of this struggle was Mick Jagger's steadfast refusal to change the words of "Let's Spend the Night Together" for "The Ed Sullivan Show," right up until the last minute. So it is as a tribute to the valor of that Street-Fightin' Man that we proudly present this long-suppressed Stones album. . . .
RIM SHOT
THE ROLLING STONES

ark Meat
know you Negros
know you're fine
know you jigaboos
it in the daytime!
ark meat!
ur body really rates.
ark meat!
bet you'll kiss on first date.
ome on colored girl,
ll make you an upstairs made,
d while mother's playing bridge below,
ll be trumping spades!
ark meat!
bet you do it great.
ark meat!
et's integrate.
ill you do it for a dollar?
ill you do it for two?
ill you do it the way the animals
o it in the zoo?!
ark meat!
our rhythm's really crude.
ark meat!
o you do it in the nude?
ill you do those things,
hat white girls never do?
ike let me step in your stomach,
ith a high-heeled shoe?
ark meat!
ou'll do anything I please.
ark meat!
lthough you'll give me some disease.
've taken a shine to you.
respect your entire race.
've taken a shine to you.
Sit on my face!
Dark meat!!!!
That's How Bad I Am
I'm bad news, baby,
I drive with my lights off in the fog.
I'm bad news, sister,
I don't curb my dog.
I don't brush my teeth.
When my aunt died
I didn't send a wreath.
I voted for Heath.
That's how bad I am!
Ahhhhhhhhhh!! . . .
Rape and carnage!!
Ahhhhhhhhhh!! . . .
I won't take out the garbage!!
I'm a shoplifter, baby,
I use my hand to blow my nose.
I'm a mean shoplifter, baby,
I got mud on my school clothes.
I drop litter on the ground.
I use the girls' rest room
When no one's around.
I make rude sounds.
That's how bad I am!
(refrain)
I'm a bad boy, honey,
I walk on the red.
I'm a bad, bad boy, honey,
I wet my bed.
I sass my mom.
I play with my thingy
And call it "Tom."
Got a hairy palm.
That's how bad I am!
(refrain)
Exile on Forty-second Street
We're little girls!
Isn't that droll?
We're all little girls,
And we're nine years old.
We take candy from strangers,
Take rides in strange cars,
And we might just go all the way,
If you're going all that far.
We go down for pennies.
We wear patent-leather shoes
So you can peek up our tunics
And see the good news.
We're a bunch of little girls!
Isn't that the rage?
And whenever it is that we grow up
We'd love to go onstage.
Standing at the intersection
In our sailor suits and pleats,
At thirty-five can you imagine
Looking half so sweet?
Would you like to take us boating?
Would you like to buy us treats?
Would you like to sniff our knickers
Or our tricycle seats?
We're a bunch of little girls!
It's the very latest flash!
We're a gaggle of Lolitas
For the right amount of cash.
New in town, big fellow?
By all means let's be frank
Me and the boys in the band here
Mince all the way to the bank!
Don't you ever get a yen to wear
Your girl-friend's Chanel suit?
And all five of us are married
We just do this to be cute.
Madonna Vomit
(sotto voce a capello)
(con brio)
Away in a manger,
No crib for a bed,
His Mother blew her lunch
All over Baby Jesus' head!
Madonna Vomit!
Uuuuuuulllllllgggh!
Madonna Vomit!
Uuuuuuulllllllgggh!
Madonna Vomit!
Uuuuuuulllllllgggh!
Jesus came from heaven
To save the human race,
But even Virgin Mary
Shot her cookies in his face!
Madonna Vomit!
Uuuuuuulllllllgggh!
etc.
The seraphim are gathered
And the whole angelic squad
To see the Blessed Virgin
Flash the hash all over God!
Madonna Vomit!
Uuuuuuulllllllgggh!
etc.
A tender little tableau
The star shines down upon:
The Virgin treating Jesus
To a Technicolor yawn!
Madonna Vomit!
Uuuuuuulllllllgggh!
etc.
(sotto voce a capello)
The Boss
On the cross
Died,
Clyde.
Under My Heel
(Bianca's Song)
Under my heel
The rat who
Thinks he's such big stuff
Under my heel
The brat who
Likes to take it rough
He's under me, oh yeah
There's a difference in the clothes he wear
Under me
I make him kneel
Under my heel
Under my heel
The bum who's
Just a little twit
Under my heel
The scum who
Takes it where he sits
He's under me, oh yeah
He begs for British discipline
Under me
His last appeal
Under my heel
Under my heel, he's
So weak
He's putty in my hands
Under my heel, there's
No cheek
He bows to my commands
He's under me, oh yeah
His petticoat is disarranged
Under me
You should hear him squeal
Under my heel
He's under me, oh yeah
He begs for mercy, but he stays
Under me
I'm his evening meal, he's
Under my heel
Under my heel, with
Buns bared
He does just what I want
Under my heel, He's
More scared
Than he was at Altamont
He's under me, his spic chick
Watch him cringe when I crack the whip
Under me
It's his great ordeal
Under my heel

RIM SHOT
Front Side:
Dark Meat (P. J. O'Rourke)
Gay Rat (Rick Ballen)
Chocolate Speedway Boogie (Sean Kelly)
Under My Heel (Dean Latimer)
Back Side:
Exile on Forty-second Street (P. J. O'Rourke)
I Got the Reds (Rick Ballen)
Madonna Vomit (O'Donoghue-Kelly)
Flatulent Girl (Rick Ballen)
That's How Bad I Am (P. J. O'Rourke)
Produced by Sean Kelly
Album design: David Kaestle
Front cover illustration: Michael Gross
Photography: Steve Myers
A and R: Tony Hendra
GIMME SKELTER
Flatulent Girl
Waitin' for a girl who's got boogers in her nose
Waitin' for a girl who's got spiders on her clothes
Crotch beginnin' to decompose
Waitin' for a flatulent girl
Waitin' for a girl and she licks my dirty feet
Waitin' for a girl who's got hair on her teeth
She eats dog shit off the street
Waitin' for a flatulent girl
Waitin' for a girl who goes "poot" everywhere
Waitin' for a girl who's got insects in her hair
She's a model on Times Square
Waitin' for a flatulent girl
Gay Rat
I hear the lisping of your lips in my ear
I know you're a well-hung honey
I'm no mincing fairy
My legs are quite hairy
I can see that you are going to persist
No, I don't like your new purse
You know I ball twenty girls every day
I'm no mincing fairy
My legs are quite hairy
Oh yeah, you're a gay rat
Oh no, don't do that
Oh yeah, you're a gay rat
Listen man, please don't do that
Not there! Down farther . . .
Chocolate Speedway Boogie
Gonna sneak up from behind you
Gotta underhanded plan
Gonna turn your head around
Cause I'm a backdoor man
Like a doggie in a manger
Like a piggie at the trough
I know you hate it baby
That's what gets me off!
I Got the Reds
Every time . . . etc.

402
Art Director: David Kaestle
Writers: Sean Kelly
P. J. O'Rourke
Michael O'Donoghue
Rick Ballen
Designer: David Kaestle
Artist: Michael Gross
Photographer: Steve Myers
Publisher: Twenty-First Century Communications
National Lampoon

403
Art Directors: Walter Bernard
Milton Glaser
Writer: Susan Strauss
Designer: Tom Bentkowski
Artist: Chas. B. Slackman
Publisher: New York Magazine

403

JUNE, 1972 VOL. 2, NO. 3

NEW YORK

HANDBOOK

A PARENTS' GUIDE TO SCHOOLS AND CLINICS IN NEW YORK

How to Get Special Care for Special Children

By Susan Strauss

"The children are everywhere . . . it would probably not be inaccurate to state that one or more such children could be found in the majority of elementary classrooms. . . ." (Syracuse University Research Institute.)

Learning disabilities in children vary widely. Labels include: brain-injured, mentally retarded, emotionally disturbed, autistic, hyper-kinetic, perceptually impaired, neurologically handicapped—or perhaps simply unmanageable. In many cases intelligence is inherently normal. These labels are rarely helpful—most children present symptoms in more than one category—except in acknowledging that a problem does exist. The real and devastating difficulty for such a child and his parents is that he does not constructively fit into regular school, camp and childhood activities.

In deciding whether to seek help for a child, the criterion seems to be: trust yourself as a parent. If aspects of a child's development genuinely concern you—perhaps not talking at an appropriate age or showing an unwillingness to play with other children—chances are that it's worth looking into. Beware of a too-prolonged "he'll outgrow it" syndrome. The least you will get from a professional evaluation is reassurance; at most, a problem may be diagnosed early, when treatment is likely to have a better chance of success. Parents living in New York are fortunate because they have a wide range of facilities to turn to. This Handbook's aim is to present a selective list and description of some of these facilities.

Particularly with a very young child, centralized services—i.e., clinics—make sense for these reasons: tests and consultations take place at one location; there is often the possibility of treatment within the clinic, or a wide range of referrals. Medical services at clinics are generally excellent, and usually cost less than private care.

If, after professional diagnosis, it is felt that a child needs special teaching, the first recourse of parents should be the public schools. In cases where no suitable facilities are available for a particular child, $2,000 in tuition will be paid by the State of New York directly to a private or voluntary school. (See box, page 43.) Many of these schools are excellent. The League School has pioneered education for deeply disturbed children; students of special education from all over the world visit Gateway School; Shield Institute emphasizes teaching retarded children from the earliest months of life.

The following schools and diagnostic centers for special children are only a selection of those available in New York. Every one that I mention I have visited.

IN THIS ISSUE:
Evaluation Clinics
Schools for Special Children
Public School Facilities

Additional copies of this Handbook can be obtained for 25 cents from New York Magazine, Department H, 207 East 32nd Street, N.Y., N.Y. 10016.

Illustrated by chas b slackman

NEW YORK 37

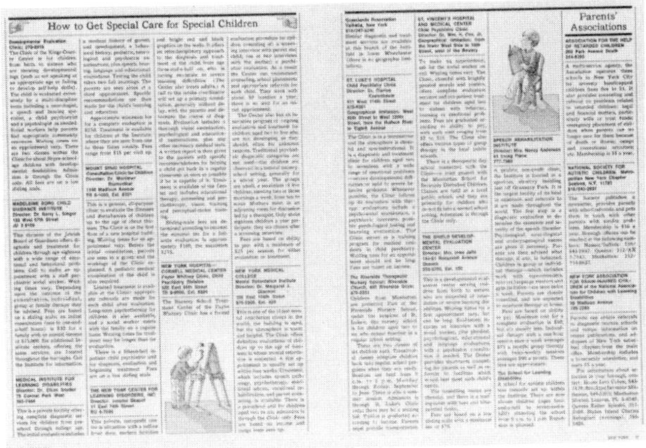

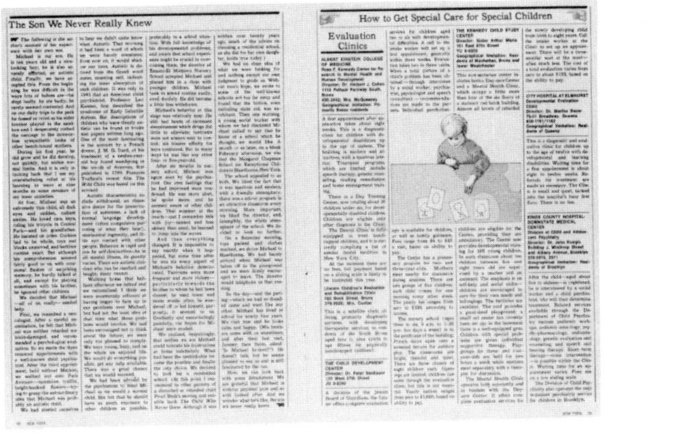

404
Art Directors: Milton Glaser
Walter Bernard
Writer: Nicholas Gage
Designers: Walter Bernard
Rochelle Udell
Artists: Paul Davis
Mark English
Burt Silverman
Harvey Dinnerstein
Richard Hess
James McMullan
Alex Guidziejko
Publisher: New York Magazine

404

THE SHOOTING OF FRANK COSTELLO: *The successor to Lucky Luciano was walking through the lobby of his apartment building on May 2, 1957, when he heard someone say, "This is for you, Frank." The speaker was a henchman of Vito Genovese, who wanted Costello's job as Mafia boss. Costello was only wounded, but he got the message and took an early retirement.*

Painting by Paul Davis

THE KILLING OF JOEY GALLO

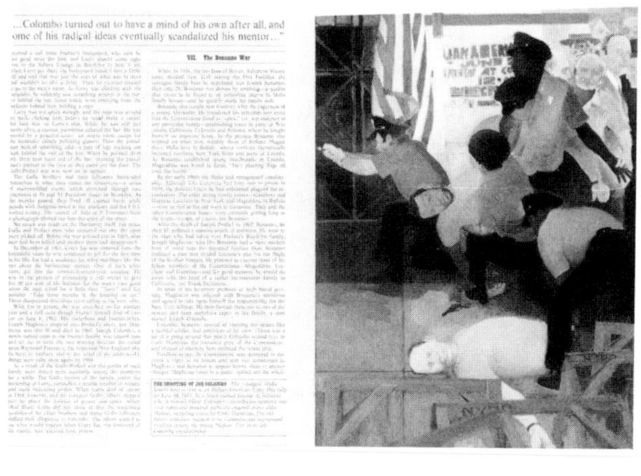

...Colombo turned out to have a mind of his own after all, and ome of his radical ideas eventually scandalized his mentor..."

VII. The Bonanno War

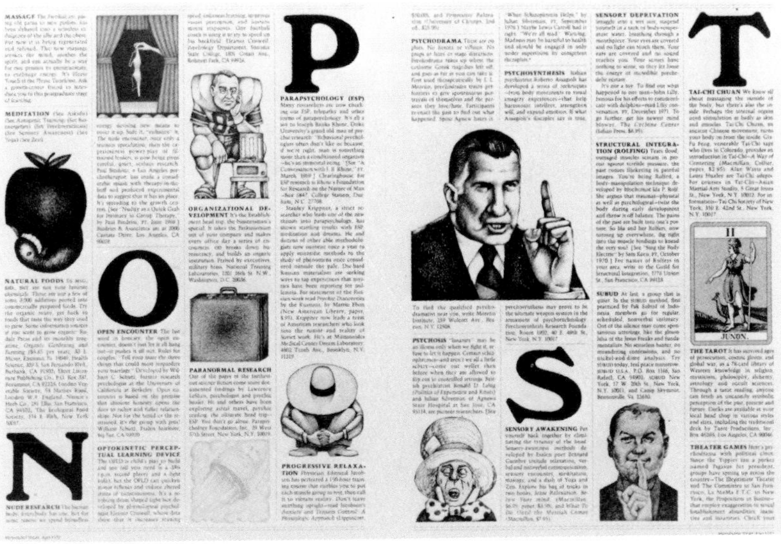

405 Silver Award
Art Director: Tom Gould
Writers: Eleanor Criswell
Severin Petersen
Designer: Mabey Trousdell
Artist: Mabey Trousdell
Publisher: C.R.M. Publishing
Psychology Today

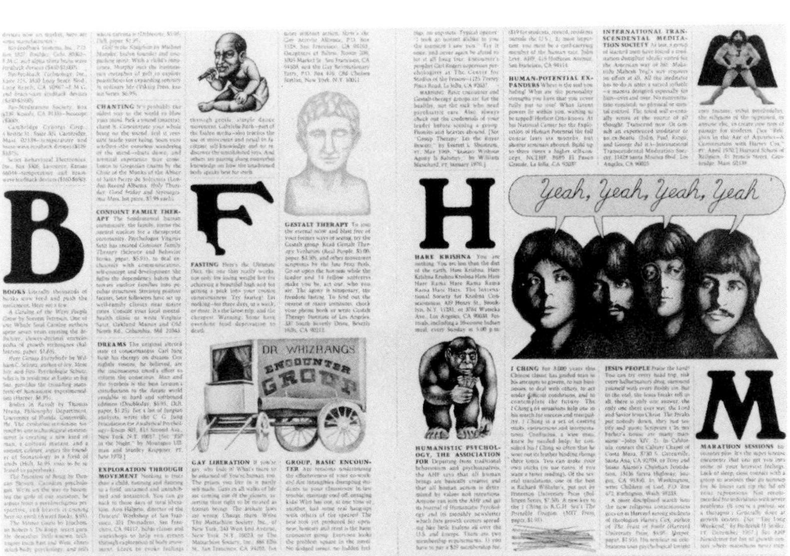
Yeah, Yeah, Yeah, Yeah

405

Higher Grumbles of the Soma—
A Partial Compendium of Humanistic Psychology and Its Technology of Personal Growth
by Eleanor Criswell & Severin Peterson
The Whole Soul Catalog

406
Art Director: Kenneth Munowitz
Writer: Roy Bongartz
Designer: Kenneth Munowitz
Artist: Claes Oldenburg
Publisher: American Heritage Publishing
Horizon Magazine

406

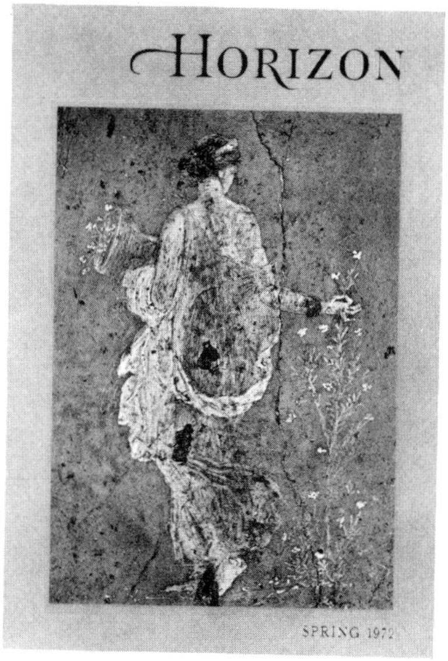

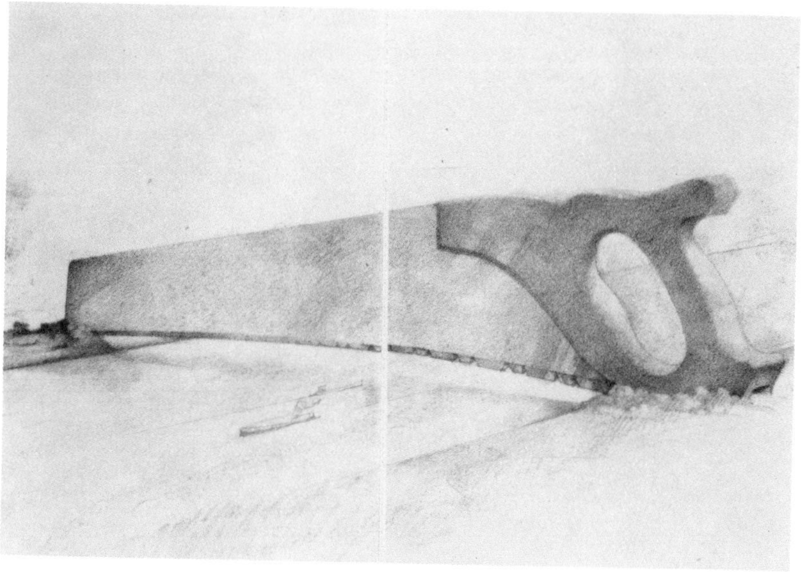

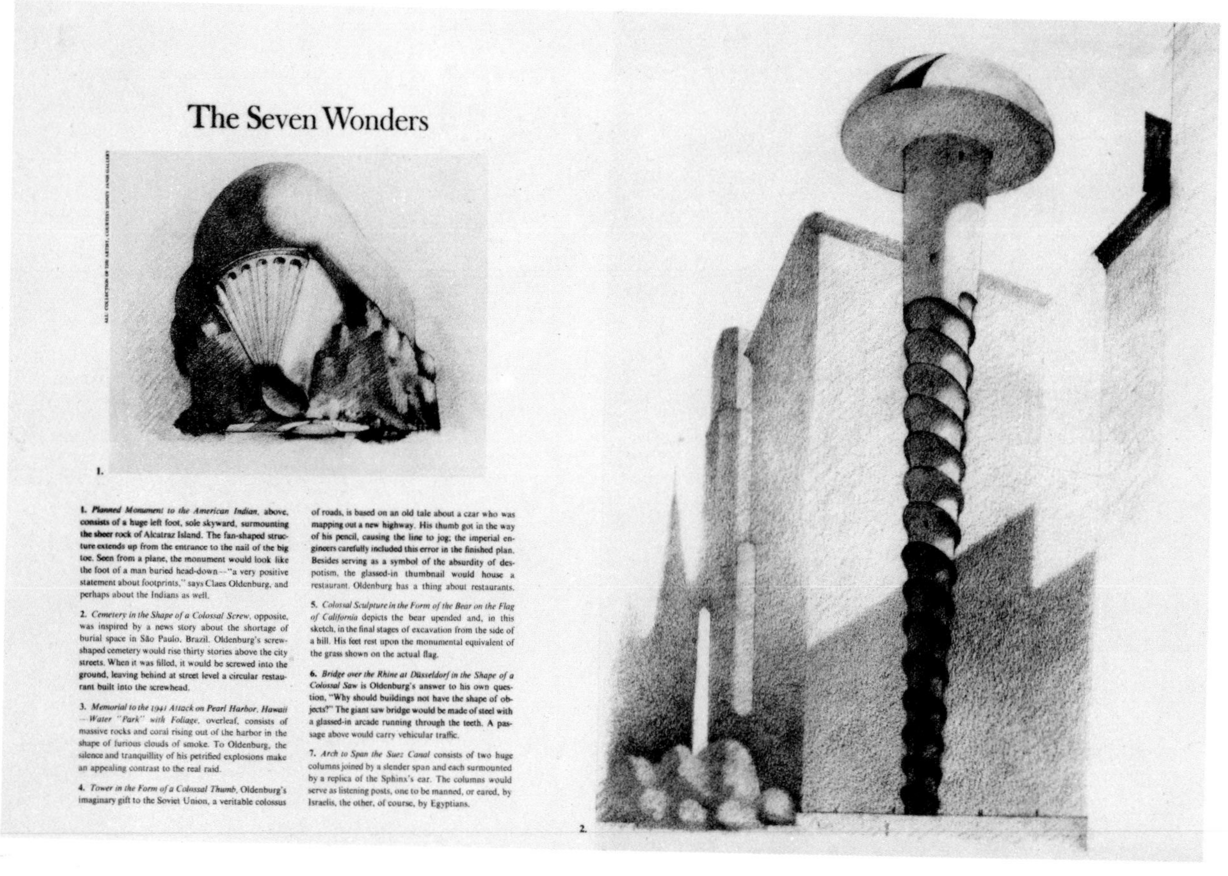

The Seven Wonders

1.

1. ***Planned Monument to the American Indian*, above, consists of a huge left foot, sole skyward, surmounting the sheer rock of Alcatraz Island. The fan-shaped structure extends up from the entrance to the nail of the big toe. Seen from a plane, the monument would look like** the foot of a man buried head-down—"a very positive statement about footprints," says Claes Oldenburg, and perhaps about the Indians as well.

2. *Cemetery in the Shape of a Colossal Screw*, opposite, was inspired by a news story about the shortage of burial space in São Paulo, Brazil. Oldenburg's screw-shaped cemetery would rise thirty stories above the city streets. When it was filled, it would be screwed into the ground, leaving behind at street level a circular restaurant built into the screwhead.

3. *Memorial to the 1941 Attack on Pearl Harbor, Hawaii —Water "Park" with Foliage*, overleaf, consists of massive rocks and coral rising out of the harbor in the shape of furious clouds of smoke. To Oldenburg, the silence and tranquillity of his petrified explosions make an appealing contrast to the real raid.

4. *Tower in the Form of a Colossal Thumb*, Oldenburg's imaginary gift to the Soviet Union, a veritable colossus of roads, is based on an old tale about a czar who was mapping out a new highway. His thumb got in the way of his pencil, causing the line to jog; the imperial engineers carefully included this error in the finished plan. Besides serving as a symbol of the absurdity of despotism, the glassed-in thumbnail would house a restaurant. Oldenburg has a thing about restaurants.

5. *Colossal Sculpture in the Form of the Bear on the Flag of California* depicts the bear upended and, in this sketch, in the final stages of excavation from the side of a hill. His feet rest upon the monumental equivalent of the grass shown on the actual flag.

6. ***Bridge over the Rhine at Düsseldorf in the Shape of a Colossal Saw* is Oldenburg's answer to his own question, "Why should buildings not have the shape of objects?" The giant saw bridge would be made of steel with a glassed-in arcade running through the teeth. A passage above would carry vehicular traffic.**

7. *Arch to Span the Suez Canal* consists of two huge columns joined by a slender span and each surmounted by a replica of the Sphinx's ear. The columns would serve as listening posts, one to be manned, or eared, by Israelis, the other, of course, by Egyptians.

2.

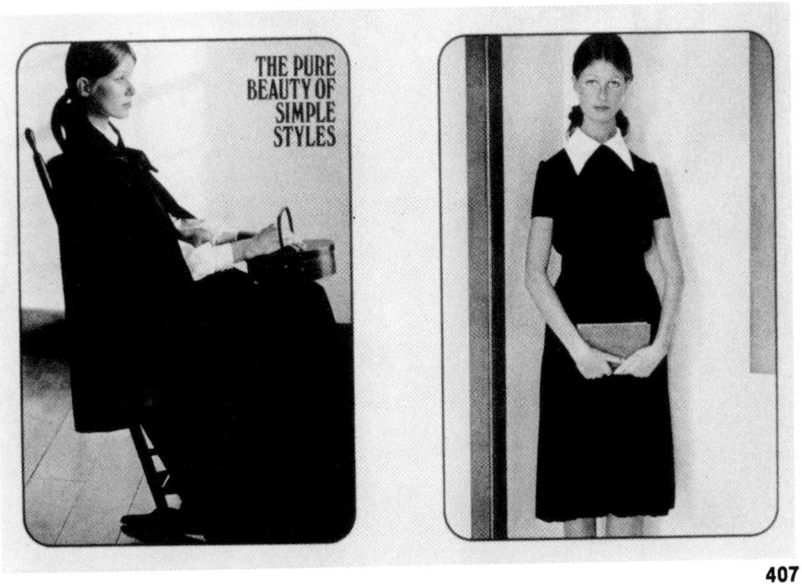
THE PURE
BEAUTY OF
SIMPLE
STYLES

407

407
Art Director: Alvin Grossman
Editor: Gloria Plaut
Designer: Alvin Grossman
Photographer: Jack Ward
Publisher: McCall Publishing Company
McCall's Magazine

408
Art Director: William Cadge
Editor: Sey Chassler
Designer: Rostislav Eismont
Photographer: Gordon E. Smith
Publisher: McCall's Corporation
Redbook

408

409
Art Directors: Milton Glaser
Walter Bernard
Writer: Phyllis Harris
Designer: Rochelle Udell
Artist: Phillipe Weisbecker
Publisher: New York Magazine

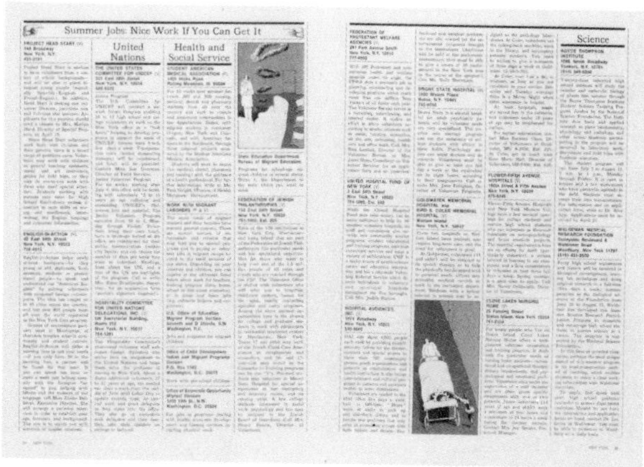
Summer Jobs: Nice Work If You Can Get It
United Nations
Health and Social Service
Science

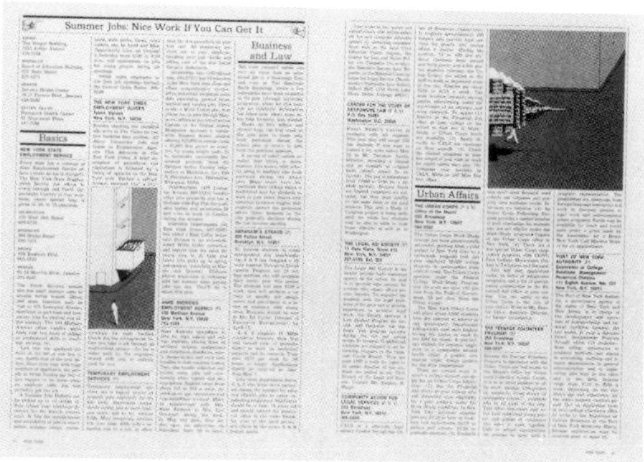
Summer Jobs: Nice Work If You Can Get It
Basics
Business and Law
Urban Affairs

409

MARCH, 1972 VOL. 2, NO. 2

NEW YORK
HANDBOOK
A STUDENT'S GUIDE TO SUMMER EMPLOYMENT

Nice Work If You Can Get It

By Phyllis Harris

Summer may seem light-years away, but for students interested in working during summer vacation, the season began around Christmas, when, armed with résumés, Social Security cards and working papers, they began scouring the city trying to interest local employers in their talents.

The student job market has always been tight, and this year there are even fewer jobs to go around. This Handbook has been compiled to offer a wide range of job possibilities and to suggest further avenues of exploration. (Job listings are keyed "P" or "V" to indicate whether they are paid or volunteer.) It's a good idea to supplement your job hunt by checking with your high school guidance counselor or with your college's financial aid and placement offices. At the library, take a look through the *College Placement Annual* for the names and addresses of corporations and government agencies which recruit college seniors and graduate students for permanent employment and offer summer jobs to undergraduates. The capsule descriptions in the *Encyclopedia of Associations* and the *Information Bulletins* of the Vocational Foundation, Inc. may also give you ideas.

And, if you can afford to *give*, not sell, your time, by all means consider volunteer work—there are countless agencies, hospitals and, of course, campaign headquarters, that desperately need young people to help them out during summer months.

You will have to be more resourceful in the pursuit of this summer's job than ever before. But the essential ingredients couldn't be simpler: a handful of tokens for getting to interviews, stamps and stationery for letters of inquiry, patience and determination. Get going.

WORKING PAPERS

If you are under 18, working papers are necessary for certain jobs—not babysitting, caddying or cutting lawns, but just about any other kind of work. Check the by-laws describing the work proscribed for certain age groups (factory work is illegal for those 15 and under, driving trucks for those 17 and under).

Getting the papers is not complicated. Your school guidance office should have the necessary forms; or go to the offices listed below (open Monday-Friday, 8:15 a.m. to 3:30 p.m.), where you can also get a doctor's certificate showing that you are physically able to do the job—or bring a letter from your family doctor. Your parent or guardian has to sign the application form; a pledge of employment is filled out by the employer; your birth certificate will prove your age.

Borough Locations for Working Papers

MANHATTAN
The Commercial Building
350 Avenue of the Americas
(near West Fourth Street)
477-3980

Illustrated by Phillippe Weisbecker

NEW YORK 39

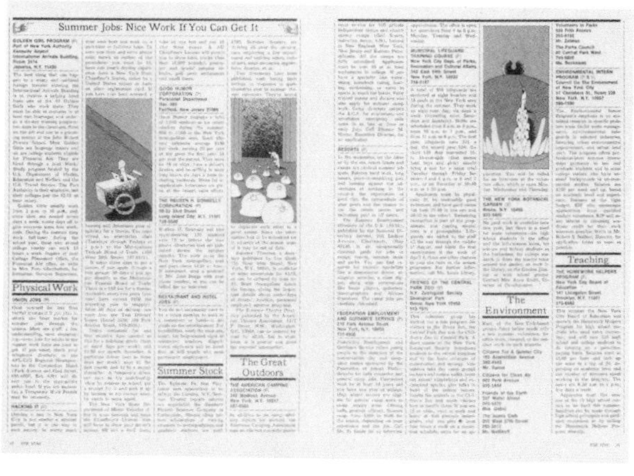
Summer Jobs: Nice Work If You Can Get It
Physical Work
Summer Stock
The Great Outdoors
The Environment
Teaching

410
Art Director: Alvin Grossman
Writer: Archibald MacLeish
Designer: Alvin Grossman
Photographer: Lord Snowdon
Publisher: McCall Publishing Company
McCall's Magazine

410

"The Amish spotted the idea of progress for what it is long before the rest of us"

When you ask their children why the Amish don't live in the city, they say, "Where would we keep our horses?"

Consumer/Sections/Color

MAGIC
Tricks and the Trade

411
Art Directors: Milton Glaser
Seymour Chwast
Vincent Ceci
Writer: Frank Bergon
Designers: Milton Glaser
Seymour Chwast
Vincent Ceci
Artist: Christian Piper
Publisher: Hill Publishing
A Handbook of Magic

411

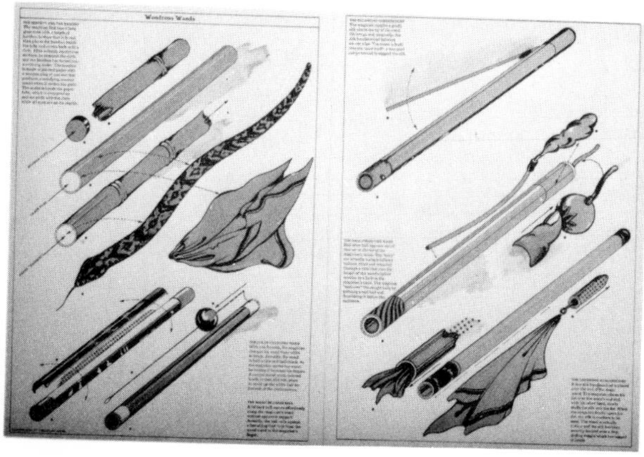
Wondrous Wands

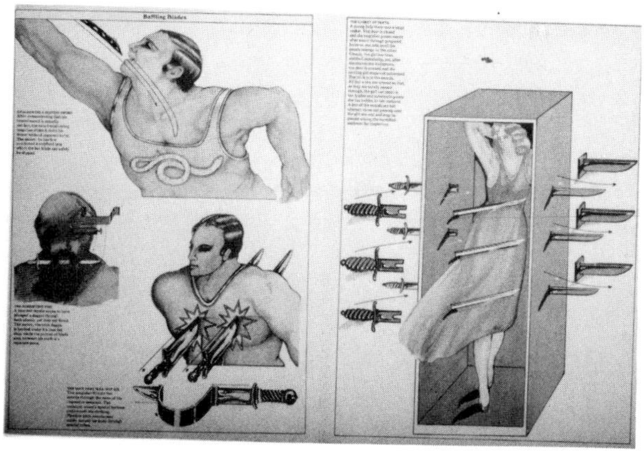
Baffling Blades

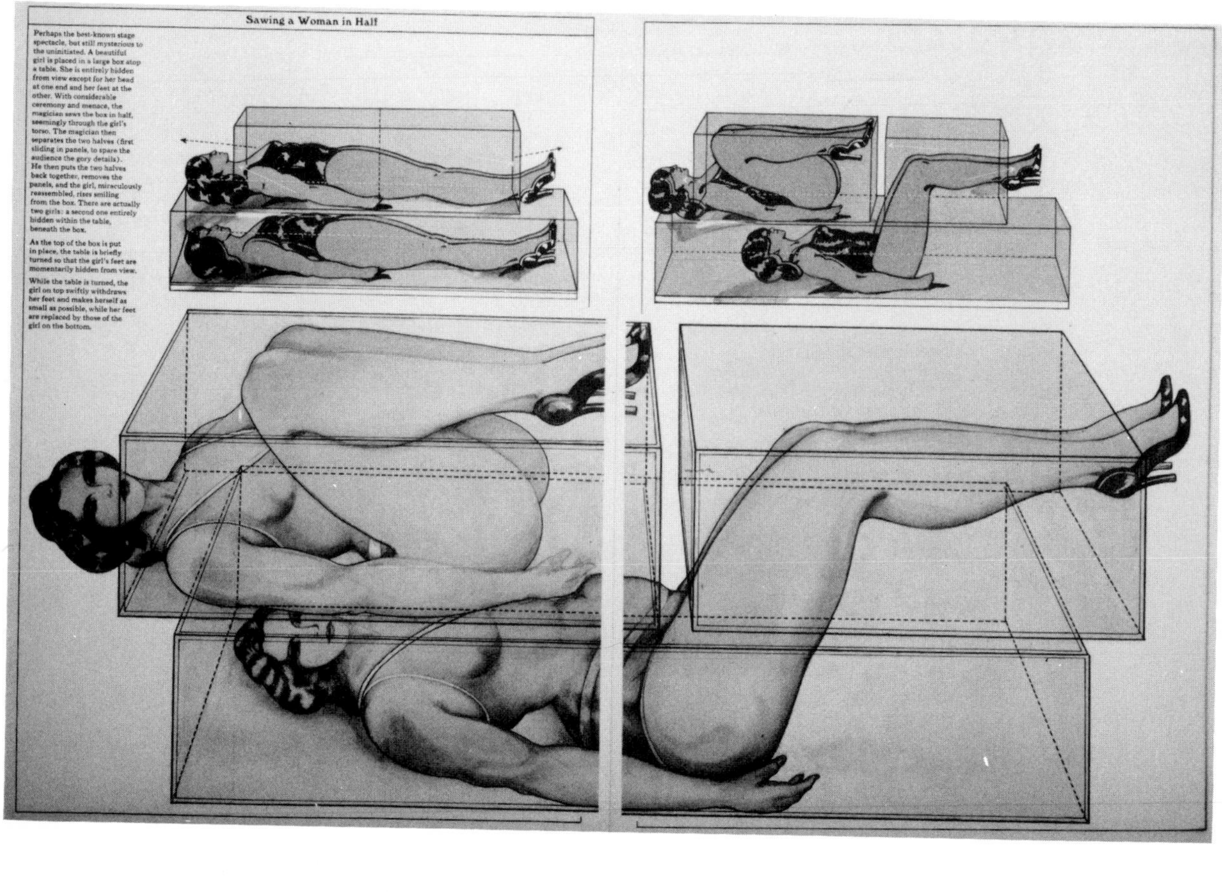
Sawing a Woman in Half
Perhaps the best-known stage spectacle, but still mysterious to the uninitiated. A beautiful girl is placed in a large box atop a table. She is entirely hidden from view except for her head at one end and her feet at the other. With considerable ceremony and menace, the magician saws the box in half, seemingly through the girl's torso. The magician then separates the two halves (first sliding in panels, to spare the audience the gory details). He then puts the two halves back together, removes the panels, and the girl, miraculously reassembled, rises smiling from the box. There are actually two girls: a second one entirely hidden within the table, beneath the box.
As the top of the box is put in place, the table is briefly turned so that the girl's feet are momentarily hidden from view.
While the table is turned, the girl on top swiftly withdraws her feet and makes herself as small as possible, while her feet are replaced by those of the girl on the bottom.

412
Art Director: Joe Sapinsky
Copywriter: Alfred Gescheidt
Photographer: Alfred Gescheidt
Publisher: ASMP
Infinity

purpose of photography for me. And that is my point-of-view, which keeps me in a rage of enthusiasm. But what has really always puzzled me, is the army of technicians—technician-photographers—who couldn't care less what their skills are geared up to. (Most of advertising.) Of course the money's there. But it is not that this army of skilled workers are concerned by the dilemma. on the contrary they seem to relish it. "You tell me what you want and I'll do it."

This is not my road: and I don't have the easy acceptance of so many who have reduced themselves to photographic hands.

I have been very fortunate to have kept working in photography for the past 24 years. I have no idea what the future holds. I do know that sketches, ideas, photographs that I now submit—pictures which were previously considered preposterous and without market value—have found startling acceptance! The world has changed, and so has photography. We're reaching out. But even here, "new trends" are equated with new gadgets, or only with scientific instruments. Rarely is that most intangible and personal horizon considered: Human imagination.

I know that I have more ideas and projects in my head, and on paper, than ever before. I hope to do them all. My hope is to keep working, as I happily ride, run, walk, or even crawl—doing it—into the sunset. □

Alfred Gescheidt's photographs have been widely published. He says: "The only market I haven't cracked is postage stamps."

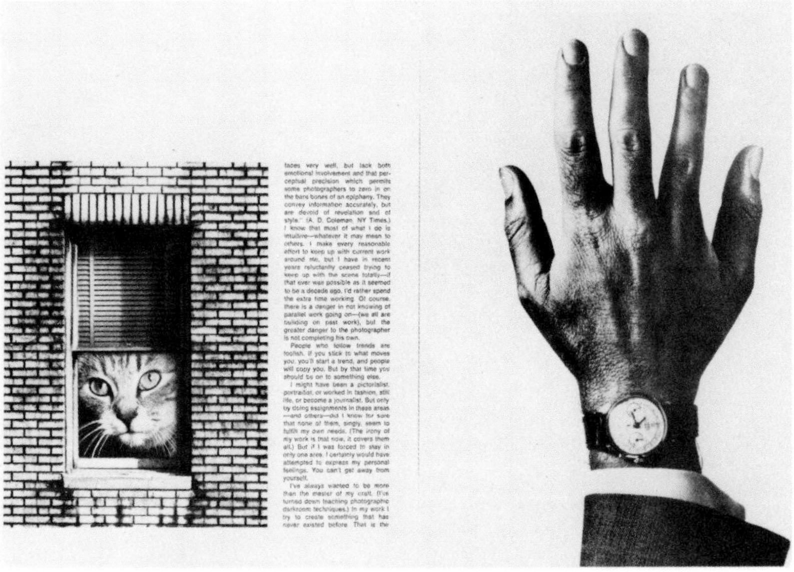

faces very well, but lack both emotional involvement and that perceptual precision which permits some photographers to zero in on the bare bones of an epiphany. They convey information accurately, but are devoid of revelation and of style." (A. D. Coleman, NY Times.) I know that most of what I do is intuitive—whatever it may mean to others. I make every reasonable effort to keep up with current work around me, but I have in recent years reluctantly ceased trying to keep up with the scene totally—if that ever was possible as it seemed to be a decade ago. I'd rather spend the extra time working. Of course, there is a danger in not knowing of parallel work going on—(we all are building on past work), but the greater danger to the photographer is not completing his own.

People who follow trends are foolish. If you stick to what moves you, you'll start a trend, and people will copy you. But by that time you should be on to something else.

I might have been a pictorialist, portraitist, or worked in fashion, still life, or become a journalist. But only by doing assignments in these areas —and others—did I know for sure that none of them, singly, seem to fulfill my own needs. (The irony of my work is that now, it covers them all.) But if I was forced to stay in only one area, I certainly would have attempted to express my personal feelings. You can't get away from yourself.

I've always wanted to be more than the master of my craft. (I've turned down teaching photographic darkroom techniques.) In my work I try to create something that has never existed before. That is the

412

Humor and Beyond
By ALFRED GESCHEIDT

■ I've never gotten over my feelings of awe and amazement upon seeing my first photographic image appear in the developer tray. The picture, as I remember, was an old, textured barn door, shot late in the afternoon. The year was 1948, and I was a student at the University of New Mexico, where I had taken an "elective course in photography. Prior to that time I had never held a camera in my hand.

Well, the thrill hasn't left me; and today, I still marvel at the process of photography—the craft and the art. For me, much of it remains as mysterious and exciting as when I first watched men walking on the moon.

My photographic philosophy is a very personal one: I admire all those who look beyond the camera as a tool, who have something to say, and feel passionate about saying it. The individual is the medium. (I'm even peeved by those strange words: AP photo; Black Star photo; LIFE photo; Miami Chamber of Commerce photo, etc., because no organization or corporate structure creates pictures. Individual photographers do and we shouldn't forget it).

We live in a world of categories. We want to file people for easy reference and recall. Much of my work is not funny. It is dead serious. Or it is neither. (But, I'm told, "Don't complain. You're lucky, these days, to be remembered for anything!")

I don't think a photographer-artist can even be objective about his own work, and I'm constantly amazed and beguiled by the word precision and descriptive power of our critics, ". . . (so-and-so's) . . . . images are excellent reportage but generally short on insight, they record sur-

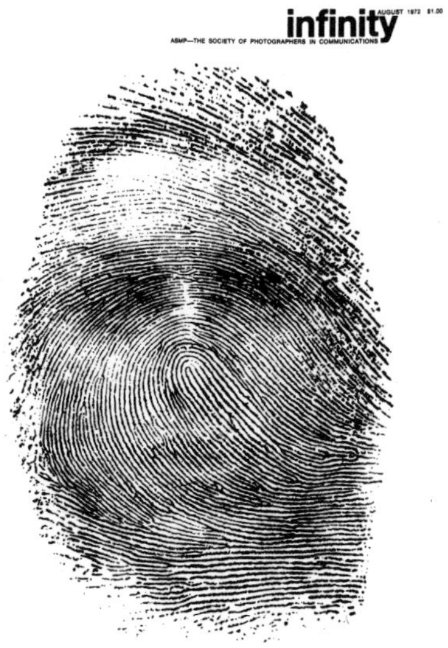

413

Learning disabilities

The Wooster approach

Every child in first grade really wants to learn, but by the time a youngster reaches third or fourth grade, that's not always true. If for any reason a child isn't doing well in first or second grade you have to find out why. If you don't, the prospects for salvaging that child grow dimmer with each year.

Thus pediatrician Morris Dixon of the Wooster Clinic believes that finding and helping children who have real or potential learning disabilities is an important, though time-consuming element of well child care. "But too few physicians and too few pediatricians have much skill or interest in working with such children." Dr. Dixon's experience in Wooster, a 16-member multispecialty group located in this north-central Ohio community of 18,000, and that of fellow pediatrician Roger Moyer show what can be done when a handful of interested and determined professionals take the time and make the effort to solve a problem that affects so many school-age children.

"Some learning disabled (LD) children are difficult for the physician to miss," says Dr. Dixon. "The one with a neurologic problem such as seizures or palsy is relatively easy to detect. But other LD children aren't, unless you make a point of hearing what you're listening to and seeing what you're looking at. For example, when a mother casually mentions that Johnny is absent-minded and says, 'Whenever I send him to the basement to bring up six items, he comes back with only one, or none,' pay attention. She's angry and considers Johnny a behavior problem and it's easy to agree unless you stop to consider the existence of some perceptual problem. Any time we hear complaints that a child is 'lazy' or 'isn't learning' we suspect some form of learning disability and rule it in or out."

Dr. Moyer says, "It's essential that such children be identified early." Some authorities have found that if behavioral and attitudinal change isn't encouraged in an LD child by the time he reaches fourth grade, his learning problems will haunt him (and others) throughout his lifetime. Then the objective becomes not remediation but the development of self-awareness by building on his strengths and ignoring his weaknesses.

"Our hope is that within the next 10 to 15 years we'll eliminate from junior and senior high school classrooms the incorrigible kids who've turned everything off—youngsters who today are monumental behavior problems are either dropped from school or allowed to sit drugged in semi-consciousness."

Both physicians agree that learning disabilities aren't exclusively problems for the pediatrician to handle. "They're educational problems as well, and we feel the best place to deal with them is in the classroom," says Dr. Dixon. "But in our area, and I suspect in most others, teachers with formal training in identifying and working with LD children are difficult to find. We're making progress in Wooster and surrounding Wayne County. It's not rapid and certainly not solely by our own efforts, but we are moving forward."

The pediatricians credit a number of factors for their success. The community is largely agricultural but has a broad industrial base and includes four colleges. Not surprisingly, the faculty members tend to have a heightened appreciation of the problems and aims of modern education. Since many of them have children enrolled in the local schools, it's been a little easier to master the kind of parent and community support that help to achieve success.

Also of vital importance have been the efforts of Ken Black, director of pupil personnel for Wayne County public schools, and George

continued

GROUP PRACTICE / JUNE 1973 27

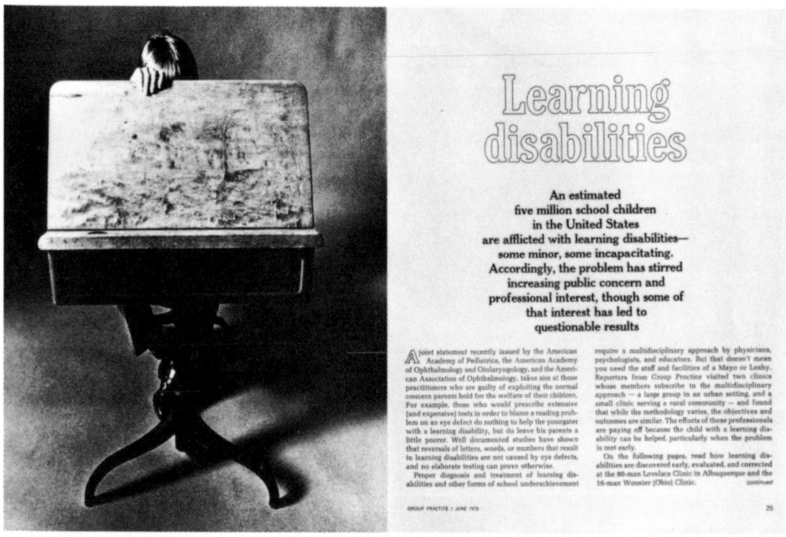

Learning disabilities

An estimated five million school children in the United States are afflicted with learning disabilities—some minor, some incapacitating. Accordingly, the problem has stirred increasing public concern and professional interest, though some of that interest has led to questionable results

A joint statement recently issued by the American Academy of Pediatrics, the American Academy of Ophthalmology and Otolaryngology, and the American Association of Ophthalmology, takes aim at those practitioners who are guilty of exploiting the normal concern parents hold for the welfare of their children. For example, those who would prescribe extensive (and expensive) tests in order to blame a reading problem on an eye defect do nothing to help the youngster with a learning disability, but do leave his parents a little poorer. Well documented studies have shown that reversals of letters, words, or numbers that result in learning disabilities are not caused by eye defects, and no elaborate testing can prove otherwise.

Proper diagnosis and treatment of learning disabilities and other forms of school underachievement require a multidisciplinary approach by physicians, psychologists, and educators. But that doesn't mean you need the staff and facilities of a Mayo or Leahy. Reporters from *Group Practice* visited two clinics whose members subscribe to the multidisciplinary approach — a large group in an urban setting, and a small clinic serving a rural community — and found that while the methodology varies, the objectives and outcomes are similar. The efforts of these professionals are paying off because the child with a learning disability can be helped, particularly when the problem is met early.

On the following pages, read how learning disabilities are discovered early, evaluated, and corrected at the 80-man Lovelace Clinic in Albuquerque and the 16-man Wooster (Ohio) Clinic.

continued

GROUP PRACTICE / JUNE 1973 25

Learning disabilities

The Albuquerque approach

Pediatrician George Brown of the Lovelace Clinic is busy year 'round. But come the start of the school term each fall things get a little hectic for him, and they stay that way long after the traditionally traumatic first day back. Problems that may have been submerged all summer suddenly surface and become magnified when a child is confronted, perhaps for the first time, with demands to behave, read, spell, and write as his peers do.

However, seldom does an isolated or acute event prompt parents and teachers to seek Dr. Brown's help; rather an accumulation of events spanning a period of years builds up. He recalls such a case:

"Billy's mother told us of his five difficult years in the same public school. She suspected something was wrong as early as first grade, but blamed his reading difficulties on the fact that the class was taught all year by substitutes because the regular teacher was ill. When his problems worsened in second grade, she blamed them on those of the first grade. The third grade teacher said Billy lived in his own world, and neither mother nor Billy liked that teacher. His fourth grade teacher gave him special attention and he improved. Now in the fifth grade, trying hard, and seeming more confident, he has a teacher who is 'sarcastic' about his abilities. Finally, someone at the school advised the mother to bring Billy to me."

Teachers and counselors in the Albuquerque school system initiate about half of the referrals Dr. Brown receives for learning disability evaluations. That's how Billy came to him. Another 40% of the referrals come from parents themselves. The remaining 10% come from physicians and other professionals. "These evaluations," says Dr. Brown, "comprise only about 10% of the patients seen, but they occupy nearly one-third of my time."

"It is not enough," says Dr. Brown, "for someone to tell us that Billy can't read. We must learn his style—what he can do and how he does it. How does he sleep, run, draw? How does he face the challenge of new people, places, things, tasks? How does he handle frustration or anger? How does he see, hear, speak, learn, think? Is he more capable of dealing with direct experience than he is with words? What are his expectations and views of himself? Our job here is to understand what makes Billy tick and to learn why he seems out of phase with his world. When we know the answers to these questions, and only then, can we begin to suggest a course of action to Billy's parents and his school instructors."

Accumulating all the information required for such a thorough evaluation of a child with behavioral or learning difficulties cannot be done by any one specialist, says Dr. Brown. An interdiscipline approach is essential, and at Lovelace any of the clinic's professional staff can be consulted.

When a mother first calls the clinic, Dr. Brown speaks with her briefly and asks her to have the child's school and the family physician forward reports to him in time for the first appointment. Dr. Brown obtains a detailed history from the mother at the first interview while the child is in another room. He pays special attention to details of her pregnancy and delivery, and the child's early development and medical history. Here the emphasis is on a history of high fevers, coma, trauma, seizures, poisonings or other possible central nervous system injuries, and CNS abnormalities in the parents or in their families.

This interview serves many purposes. "Of course, we get data about the child's health. But it is our first and best opportunity to see the problem as the parent sees it and to see the child as the parent sees him." Dr. Brown says. "I try to make it clear that, for the time being, what

continued

GROUP PRACTICE / JUNE 1973 31

413
Art Director: Mel Abfier
Editor: Irving J. Cohen
Designer: Mel Abfier
Photographer: Gordon E. Smith
Publisher: Fischer-Murray Group Practice

This is the March-April 1972 issue of Dealer News with Marketing Letter for the Photofinisher.
KODAK PUTS IT ALL IN YOUR POCKET

414

415

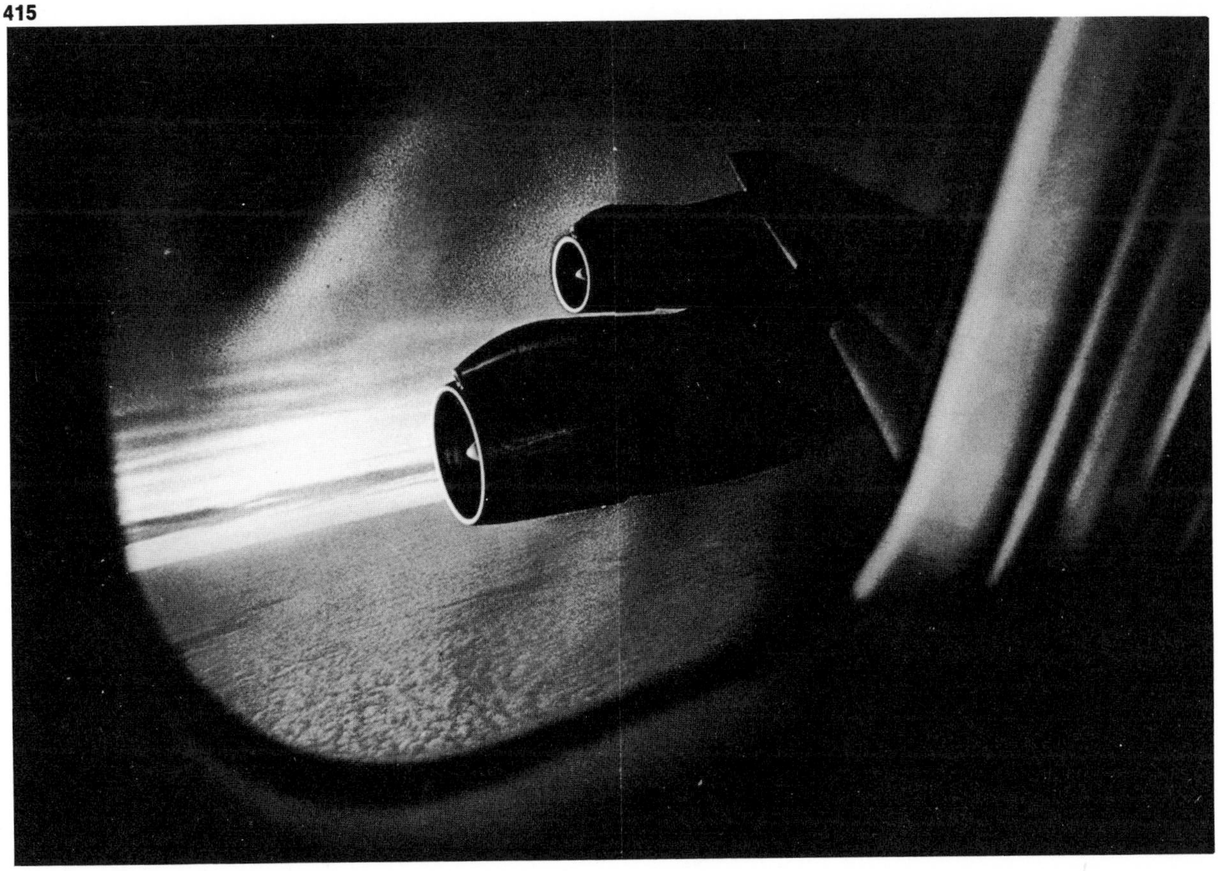

414
Art Director: Anatol Timov
Copywriter: Kenn Jacobs
Designer: Anatol Timov
Photographer: Neil Montanus
Agency: Rumrill-Hoyt, Inc.
Client: Eastman Kodak Company

415
Art Director: Stanley Spellar
Photographer: Pete Turner
Publisher: Filipacchi Photo

416

417

416
Art Director: Stanley Spellar
Photographer: Pete Turner
Publisher: Filipacchi Photo

417
Art Director: Pete Turner
Editor: Allen Porter
Designer: Pete Turner
Photographer: Pete Turner
Publisher: Camera Magazine
Agency: Pete Turner
Client: Pete Turner

Consumer / Complete Issue

418
Art Director: Kenneth Munowitz
Editor: Charles L. Mee, Jr.
Designer: Kenneth Munowitz
Publisher: American Heritage Publishing
Horizon

418

THE RITES OF SPRING
APRIL IN CHINA
(A.D. 1120)
When fair weather finally broke winter's hold
on the Yellow River valley,
a whole great civilization went on holiday.
And a Sung dynasty
painter lovingly recorded every detail
By WALTER KARP

HORIZON
SPRING 197

THE RITES OF SPRING

Twenty-five hundred years ago this spring, Greek maidens were dancing wildly on Mount Parnassus to honor the great god Dionysus. Four thousand years ago this spring, Babylonians were taking part in mock battles and stripping their king of his official regalia. These were the magical rites of spring, carried out to ensure the renewal of the earth's fertility, the celebrations of ancient people steeped in superstition. Or so, at any rate, it once seemed. When Sir James Frazer published *The Golden Bough* in 1890, his Victorian readers confidently concluded that modern man in his marvelous progress had laid aside such childish toys. Today we are not so certain that ancient festivals were quite so childlike or that the need for seasonal rituals was merely the province of myth-ridden barbarians. Despite the vast changes wrought by history, the seasons themselves have not changed, and modern man still shares with his ancient forebears the same environment of the calendar: the annual waxing and waning of daylight; the longest day, about June 22; the longest night, about December 22; the breakup of winter's frigid routines; the lifting of summertime torpor. In our response to the unchanging seasons lies a common bond between us and our ancestors and the common bond among ourselves.

The psychology of the seasons is still an obscure subject, but common experience indicates its salient principle: at certain junctures of the year there arises among men a general fever of the blood, a sort of common malaise, a complex yearning for something outside the ordinary round of life. Men can give it public form and expression or, if they choose, can ignore it. The calendrical malaise, however, is inextinguishable; it returns each year with the moment that excites it.

The cruelest month? The rites of spring resemble Sadie Hawkins Day in James Thurber's cover for The New Yorker *of April 27, 1940. Above, Picasso's flowery gift celebrates the season in gentler fashion.*

Take, for example, the juncture known as the winter solstice, the moment when the shrinking day has shrunk to its smallest and will begin once again to roll back the night. It is at one and the same time the mark of winter's onset and the distant harbinger of summer light. Pagan Rome gave expression to the complex emotions it arouses in a holiday known as the Saturnalia, a week of general license in which schools were closed, declarations of war forbidden, and distinctions of rank momentarily discarded. Roman paganism died out, but the winter solstice did not; the early Christians located the celebration of Christ's nativity at the same place in the year. The religious change involved was, of course, enormous, but the underlying passion of the solstice has remained. Indeed, it appears to be a "Saturnalian" one, as Christian moralists have had cause to complain throughout the Christian Era. We see its force today in the annual frenzy of Christmas shopping, a sort of Saturnalian release appropriate to a society of consumers. We see its expression in the annual office Christmas party, which, like the pagan Saturnalia, is an occasion for ignoring distinctions of rank. One way or another the urge of a season finds its outlet.

But it is spring that arouses in us the strongest, most insistent, and most complex of all seasonal emotions. On the following pages we have tried to exhibit something of its singular force and variety—in the Dionysian rites of ancient Greece, in the twisted career of a single spring holiday, May Day; as a phenomenon of biology, as an event in the history of modern music, as the subject for one of the most remarkable of paintings. The essay on *The Golden Bough* shows how the central theme of spring—the annual renewal of life—runs like a bright thread through an enormous tapestry of ancient rites and enduring myths. Mankind has never failed to respond to that annual renewal of life. It arises within us as the fever in the blood known as spring.

W.K.

5

Consumer/Complete Issue

419 Gold Award
Art Director: Kenneth Munowitz
Editor: Charles L. Mee, Jr.
Designer: Kenneth Munowitz
Publisher: American Heritage Publishing
Horizon

419

"Shockingly Mad, Madder Than Ever, Quite Mad!"

So said Horace Walpole about a painting by Henry Fuseli. But the young Romantic Age had a penchant for madness; hence all the mad scenes that marked its artists' revolt against reason

The art of the preceding epoch had celebrated the Great and the Beautiful; it was an age of equestrian statues and of paintings of gentlewomen being serenaded in pleasure gardens. But then, almost as though the French Revolution had given the starting signal for this kind of terror as well, the rococo dream dissolves into the romantic nightmare, and the arts proceed to disgorge all the suppressed fears and ferocities of the human imagination. Now it is not field marshals on horseback but demons of lust who ride wildcats and broomsticks in Goya's *Caprichos*, the only beautiful women are the ones being sold by hideous whoremongers, and the myth of a polite, perfectible society is transformed into repulsive images.

Here, a century before Freud, Goya provides the illustrations for a jungle book of the psychopathic subconscious. In the *capricho* entitled *The Sleep of Reason Produces Monsters* (right) he even shows us how it was done: a portrait of the artist as a young dreamer, haunted by the phantoms that have sprung from his own overheated brain. We know that Goya had firsthand knowledge of the sleep of reason, for he went to the madhouse of Saragossa to study scenes of demonic possession among the violently insane. The result is a typically ambiguous painting known as *The Madhouse* (page 81), in which the half-naked lunatics perform their antics before black-robed visitors who seem, on closer inspection, to be rather more sinister than the inmates.

Goya is a very Spanish painter, but these were not merely local lunacies, escaped from an asylum where the Inquisition still held sway and madness was regarded as a kind of *lèse-majesté* against God. Throughout Europe there were young romantics who were as fascinated by the irrational as their fathers had been by the promise that reason would solve everything. The French Revolution, originally advertised as the culmination of the age of reason, had served to destroy both the old order and the belief that intellect could be elevated to take its place. Now it was the emotions' turn to be consulted

The Sleep of Reason Produces Monsters *is Goya's title for this engraving, one of the famous* Caprichos *series, published in 1799.* Mad Kate *(opposite), the melodramatic study of a demented woman, is the work of Henry Fuseli, the Swiss painter who transplanted himself to London in the 1760's and became part of the English romantic movement. Kate is an illustration for a poem by William Cowper (himself intermittently mad), which features her as the village lunatic, driven out of her wits by the death of her lover. Fuseli shows her crouching on a rock, hair and dress aswirl—an apt symbol of the mad underworld of European romanticism.*

By FREDERIC V. GRUNFELD

75

Our Crumbling Institutions

The institutions of civilized life—essentially unchanged since the agricultural revolution of ten thousand years ago—are showing signs of strain, if not collapse. Here, and on the following pages, HORIZON documents Professor Plumb's thesis.

The Family

HORIZON

SUMMER 1972

Trade/Complete Issue

420
Art Director: Dick Hess
Editor: Steve Abel
Designer: Dick Hess
Artist: Seymour Chwast
Publisher: Babcock & Wilcox
Interface

420

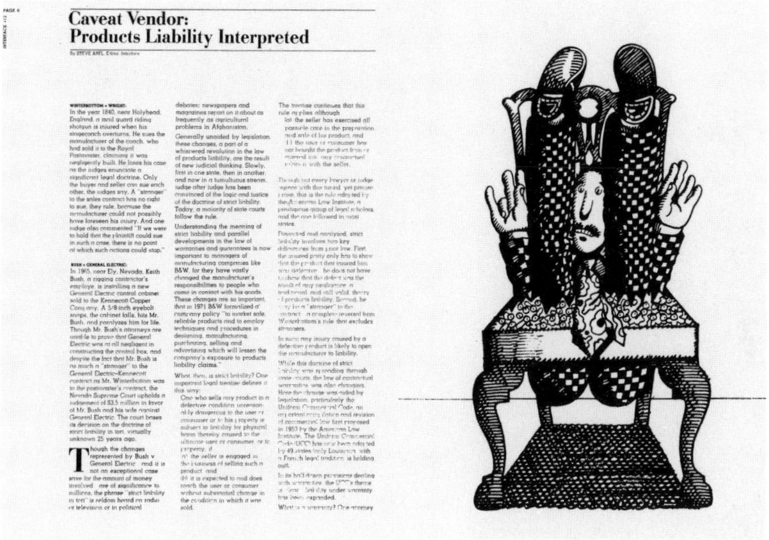

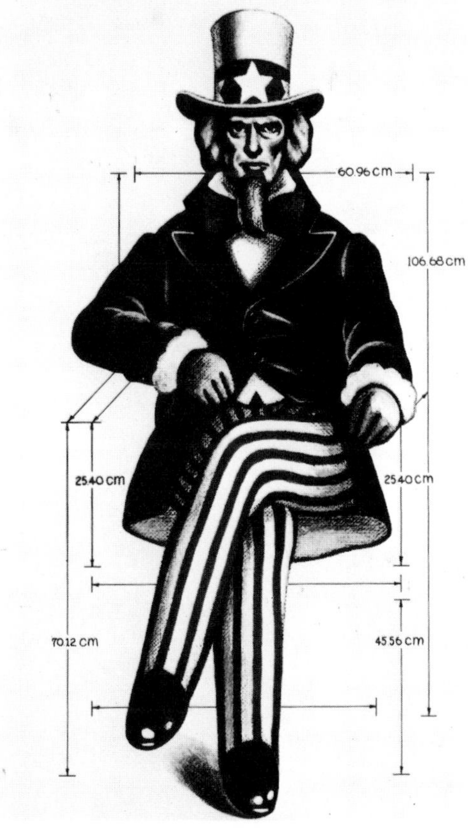

Blocking the smooth conversion of a manufacturing operation from the customary to the metric system of measurement, are many imponderables which make it difficult for an individual coordinator or task force to foresee every detail in the procedure or to anticipate every bottleneck.

To simplify planning, the U. S. Metric Study developed some reasonable assumptions which have been followed in the preparation of this guide. These assumptions may not be valid in every instance but they provide a background that allows a company to develop conversion plans that have a reasonable chance of being compatible with national programs.

That the United States will move toward complete metrication under a nationally coordinated program during a ten-year period is the first assumption. It is further assumed that the program will specify that American schools begin teaching the metric system as the primary means of measure, and that comparable parts, materials, and other out-of-plant production items and services will be available at reasonable cost.

The U. S. Metric Study also assumed that replacement of manufacturing equipment with its metric equivalent will follow normal obsolescence programs. When a machine can be easily converted, however, such as by changing dials, verniers and indicators, it is expected that conversion kits will be available at reasonable cost.

Finally, *and perhaps most important*, it is assumed that, in general, only new or redesigned products will be designed and manufactured to metric measurement. Unless there are distinct economic or performance advantages to be accrued from conversion, existing U.S. products will remain unchanged until the normal life cycle of the product is complete and a new metric product replaces it. Old product lines with sufficient sales volume to justify continued production would not be converted until near the end of the transition period. Meanwhile, soft conversion of drawings, specifications and instruction manuals would be used for foreign customers.

Because metrication cuts across department lines, the conversion process must start with the appointment of a metric coordinator. To be successful, he must be thoroughly familiar with all product lines, as well as the applicable engineering and manufacturing procedures. He should report to the chief operating executive because at times he'll need real clout to get the job done.

His first assignment will be to develop a basic plan for metric conversion. From there, he will move on to a working plan, involving almost every element of the company.

The basic plan must originate from the engineering side of the organization (product design, manufacturing engineering and internal standards) because metric conversion, briefly defined, means to adapt or develop products that will be functionally acceptable in a metric world. Hopefully, the metric conversion program will be an addition to an existing long-range new product development and marketing program.

Working within a long-term product-marketing plan, the first step in developing the basic plan is to classify products into groups and to assign priorities for the metric conversion of each product group. Where, for instance, a product becomes noncompetitive because of changes in technology or markets, a decision to redesign will, at the same time, establish a high priority for metric conversion.

H. H. Gorrie, retired senior vice president and director of B&W's Bailey Meter Co. subsidiary, became interested in the metric system because of Bailey's involvement in world markets. Shortly before retiring in 1970, Mr. Gorrie headed Bailey's metric conversion cost analysis in cooperation with the U.S. Metric Study. In addition, he chaired committees of the Scientific Apparatus Manufacturers Association that studied metrication and international standards activities.
A graduate of Rensselaer Polytechnic Institute, Mr. Gorrie joined Bailey Meter in 1927 as an engineer. He was promoted to chief engineer in 1953 and elected a vice president in 1955.
The author of several technical papers, Mr. Gorrie also holds 37 patents.

Conversely, a product acceptable to the metric market because of its technical superiority should be given a low metric conversion priority.

Priorities for mature products with low sales or high retooling costs or both are more difficult to determine. In some cases, the low-cost approach will be to phase out the product; in other cases it will be advisable to convert to metric dimensions with a minimum of redesign and tooling. In any event, at some stage in the conversion program, products using the old measurements will become a nuisance and management must decide whether to convert or discontinue the product.

With custom built or special product lines, metrication will be determined by acceptability in the market place or by company progress in the conversion program. In either case, conversion will be decided on an individual product basis.

In operations such as those of the Power Generation Group where products are very highly engineered, it is important to consider the availability of relevant metric standards.
As the basic criteria for a specific product line redesign, they can accelerate or retard the redesign priority. In some cases, a lack of metric standards will establish the priority for an interim metric interface redesign, in which only parts connecting to metric parts are redesigned.

A second major factor in all of these decisions is a company's marketing strategy. Industries that look to world markets will want to make their products acceptable in a metric environment as fast as economically possible. Other industries that do not currently have international marketing ambitions will tend to delay action until metric conversion in the United States has progressed to a point where their profitability declines unless they convert.

Internal considerations that will come into play in establishing metric conversion priorities include projected growth in total product sales and the availability of manpower to develop acceptable company metric standards, specifications and procedures. External factors include the

The In-Basket Syndrome

By JOHN E. LEE

In the manager's world, that not always trustworthy vehicle known as the "In" basket on the edge of the desk can be a useful communications tool or an imprisoning trap which can diminish administrative efficiency.

When I was given my first managerial assignment some years ago, my office desk often seemed to be an island completely surrounded by a sea of paper, channeled through the "In" basket and eventually overflowing whatever makeshift floodgates I'd been able to invent by way of drawer space, shelves, cabinets or circular file. I could have developed a profitable recycling business out of the deluge of paper that descended on me daily. There were memos and publications and edifying corporate speeches of impressive bulk, financial reports of companies having nothing to do with mine, news clippings, direct-mail ads from book publishers, invoices and purchase orders and elaborately done up proposals for additional assignments my already overburdened crew should be able to accomplish in the interests of improved productivity.

With a staff of four reporting to me, I in turn reported to a unit manager with a staff of 25. So I had to become something of a master of cryptography to find my way through the scribbled notes requiring or requesting me to *do* something or, at the very least, react. I sometimes felt I'd unwittingly fallen in with a crowd of Speedwriting graduates who had flunked speed-reading, else they'd have been more discerning and considerate in the choice of reading matter they passed on to me.

Was it the intention of the staff, in a one-upsmanship game, to impress me with the range of their interests? Were they clearing their own desks? Or did they simply lack the skill to cull?

Yet I developed an almost paranoiac fear of rechanneling anything through the "Out" basket until or unless I had time to evaluate it. After all, there was always the chance that something of intrinsic value lay hidden somewhere within the mess.

One afternoon, my department manager buzzed me on the intercom and said, "I just had lunch with Jim Fox. He told me he doesn't know anything about the meeting you're setting up in Cleveland next week. Hunt up that memo I sent you and make sure his name was on it."

What memo?

What meeting?

Recovering from momentary paralysis, I quizzed my secretary. She vaguely remembered the context of the request. She was certain she had put the paper in my "In" basket about two weeks before. Together, we turned over just about everything in sight, hot on the trail of the missing memo. After an hour's search, we found the gem clinging as if magnetized to the back cover of a magazine that, after a lingering stay in my "In" basket, had been moved to semioblivion on a book shelf.

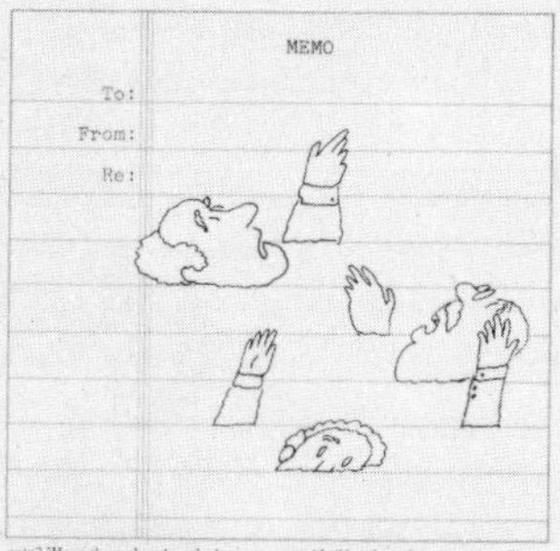

Fortunately, there still was time to make the meeting arrangements asked for.

But the experience taught me two things.

1—Never underestimate the power of a memo—to do you in.

2—In a managerial position requiring the handling of a relatively large volume of incoming paper there is a very real need for a systematic method of screening it, if necessary acting on it and then moving it on.

The system installed will, of course,

Continued on page 20

Mr. Lee is assistant manager, corporate public relations, in charge of organizational communications.

Pollution Control: Unclouding the Future

By FRED VIGEANT

In a recent speech for a United Nations committee, anthropologist Margaret Mead noted the tendency of conservationists as well as the general public to blame industry for most environmental problems. A U.S. spokesman at the first United Nations Conference on World Environment, Dr. Mead said agriculture and individual consumers actually produce more pollution than industry. In addition, she noted that public demand for more goods and services is the prime reason for industrial pollution.

Whether or not the blame is well-directed, industry is the target of new laws being enacted to specifically limit its emissions. The Federal Clean Air Act of 1970, the keystone of much new legislation, has put industry under the shadow of further limits on the matter it can release to the atmosphere. And because electricity is sought by other industries as a form of clean power in their own clean-up campaigns—the electric utility industry faces the prospect of producing more power and less dirt.

Oregon's Willamette River, for instance, was considered environmentally 'dead' less than five years ago. Today, just one paper mill on the Willamette spends $20,000 a month for electricity to operate a new waste recovery system. The cleaner Willamette, however, means that an electric utility is probably burning more fuel and that more wastes from the fuel's combustion are reaching the atmosphere.

Another example comes from California's Pacific Gas and Electric Co. In a series of ads, the utility points out that the electric-powered trains on San Francisco's new Bay Area Rapid Transit produce less pollution than the cars people would use otherwise. But to do it, PG&E has to supply the trains with as much electricity as a city of 70,000 people.

But if electric power production itself is causing pollution, it can't very well solve environmental problems. The White House Council on Environmental Quality has estimated that the power industry must invest over $10 billion during the next five years, twice as much capital as the petroleum, paper, concrete and metals industries combined, if it is to bring its air and water pollution under control.

While objection is often raised to the carbon monoxide and dioxide that flow freely out of utility stacks, these compounds are probably the least hazardous combustion products. And, trees and people produce far greater volumes of carbon dioxide than all industrial sources combined. To order utilities to emit less carbon oxides would make as much sense as asking everyone to hold their breath.

Other matter generated in utility boilers, however—particulates, nitrogen oxides and sulfur oxides—are considered dangerous. Utilities contribute about 20 million tons of particulate, 10 million tons of nitrogen oxides and 20 million tons of sulfur oxides to the atmosphere annually. This accounts for over 50 percent of all of America's sulfur oxide emissions, about 25 percent of all industrial particulates, and 25 percent of all nitrogen oxides.

These pollutants are now subject to legal control. New plants brought on line since last year, for instance, must emit several times less nitrogen oxides than the average emissions of their abundant ancestors. Sulfur and particulate emission limits on new plants are equally stri t.

For example, a modern gas-fired boiler, that if uncontrolled could emit as much as 1,000 parts per million of nitrogen oxides, must now be designed to emit less than 165 parts per million, under regulations of the U.S. Environmental Protection Agency. In some areas, such as Los Angeles and New York City, even stricter regulations must be met.

Electric utilities, however, have at least a slight edge over most other companies because they operate within defined territories and are not subjected to the competition that other businesses are. Thus, the public that demands more and cleaner power generation will ultimately pay for both. Few utilities will go out of business because expenditures on pollution control equipment force them to raise electricity prices, though getting government approval of higher rates is often a problem. Thus, the burden of providing the means to control these emissions traditionally has been on companies, such as B&W, that design and manufacture utility equipment.

Technical background and experimental pollution control advances from the Research & Development division have given the Power Generation Group the ability to design both long- and short-term solutions to utility pollution problems. And 1972 has been an important year in terms of legislation and start-ups of B&W's methods of meeting new emission limits. This article examines some air-pollution control problems and what is being done to solve them.

422

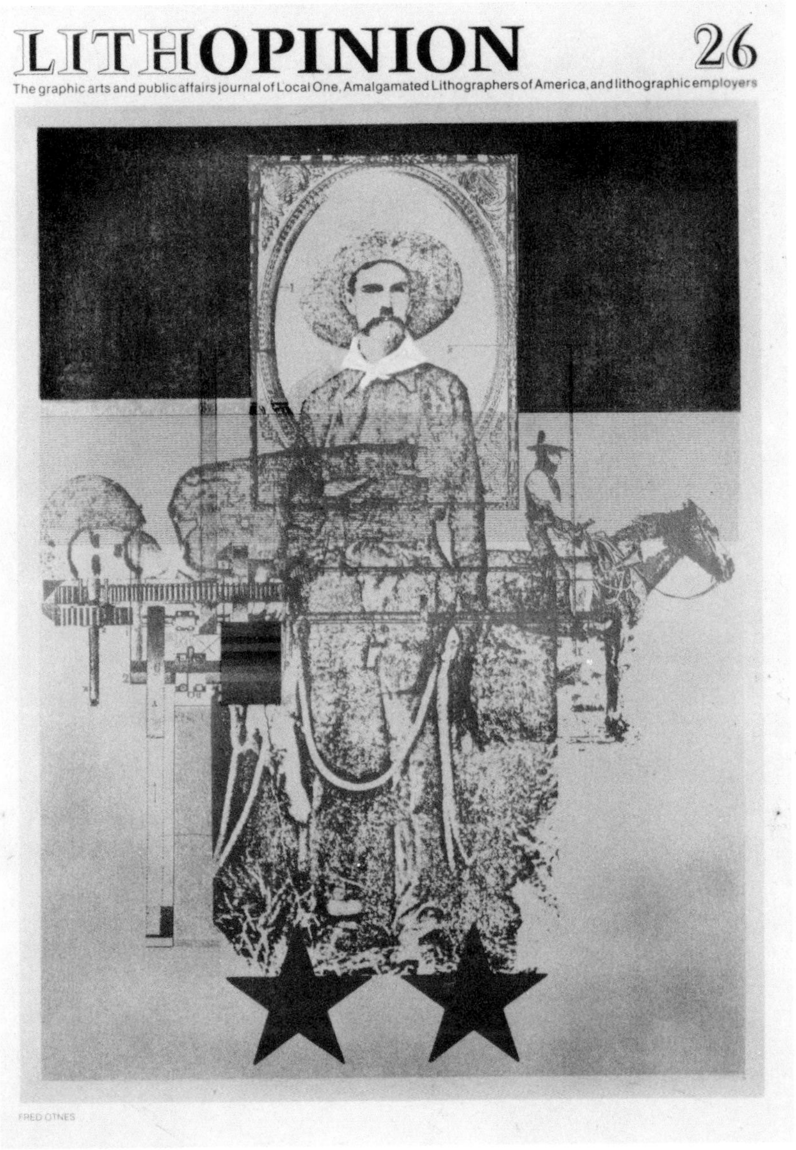
LITHOPINION 26
The graphic arts and public affairs journal of Local One, Amalgamated Lithographers of America, and lithographic employers
FRED OTNES

421
Art Director: Dick Hess
Editor: Al Farnsworth
Designer: Dick Hess
Artist: Folon
Publisher: Babcock & Wilcox
Interface
Agency: Richard Hess Inc.
Client: Babcock & Wilcox

422
Art Director: Robert Hallock
Editor: Edward Swayduck
Designer: Robert Hallock
Artists: Fred Otnes
Alan E. Cober
Murray Tinkelman
Publisher: Local One, Amalgamated
Lithographers of America
Lithopinion

423

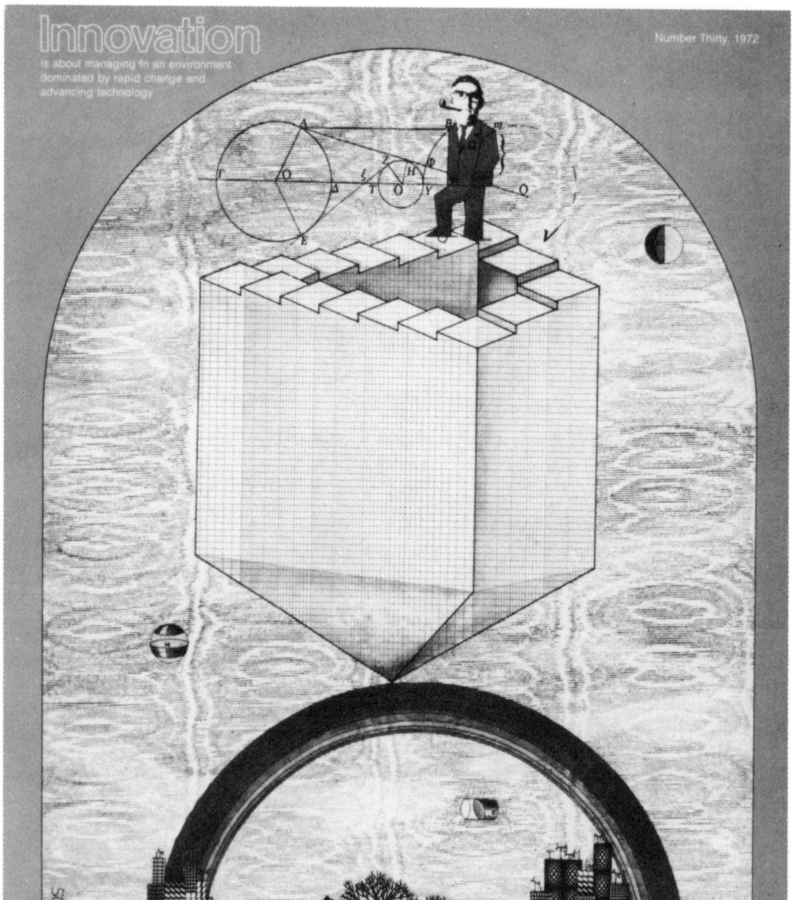
Innovation
is about managing in an environment dominated by rapid change and advancing technology
Number Thirty, 1972

423 Silver Award
Art Director: Eric Gluckman
Editor: Michael F. Wolff
Designers: Eric Gluckman
Rachel Katzen
Artists: Francois Colos
Murray Tinkelman
Publisher: Technology Communication, Inc
Innovation

WORK
new styles, new environments, new attitudes

AN INTERVIEW
What Bothers Young People About Business?
THE DECEPTION!

424 Gold Award
Art Director: Joseph R. Morgan
Editor: Leonard Reed
Designers: Judith Mays
David Moore
Joseph Morgan
Robert Banks
Thurman French
Picture Editor: Lee Battaglia
Publisher: U.S. Information Agency
America Illustrated

Америка
Этот номер посвящен Калифорнии

424

КАЛИФОРНИЯ СТОИТ НА ПЕРВОМ МЕСТЕ ПО ПРОИЗВОДСТВУ АБРИКОСОВ, АВОКАДО, ВИНОГРАДА, ПЕРСИКОВ, СЛИВ, ЛИМОНОВ, МАСЛИН, ФИНИКОВ, МИНДАЛЯ И САХАРНОЙ СВЕКЛЫ

КАЛИФОРНИЯ
МИФ ИЛИ ДЕЙСТВИТЕЛЬНОСТЬ

ALITALIA
PORTLAND
OREGON
NORTH

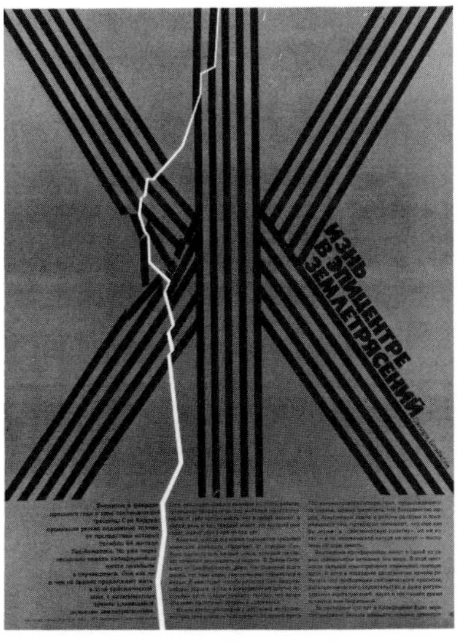
ЖИЗНЬ В ЭПИЦЕНТРЕ ЗЕМЛЕТРЯСЕНИЙ

COVERS

Magazines
Book Jackets
Record Albums

425
Art Directors: Milton Glaser
Walter Bernard
Editor: Clay Felker
Designer: Milton Glaser
Artist: King Features
Publisher: New York Magazine

426 Silver Award
Art Director: Michael Gross
Writer: Michael Choquette
Designer: Michael Gross
Photographer: Leonard Soned
Publisher: Twenty-First Century Communications
National Lampoon

427
Art Director: Stan Mack
Editor: Lewis Bergman
Designer: Stan Mack
Photographer: Michael Raab
Publisher: The New York Times Sunday Magazine

428
Art Director: Michael Gross
Writer: Tony Hendra
Designer: Michael Gross
Artist: Dick Hess
Publisher: Twenty-First Century Communications
National Lampoon

429
Art Directors: Milton Glaser
Walter Bernard
Designers: Milton Glaser
Walter Bernard
Artist: Milton Glaser
Photographer: Walter Bernard
Publisher: New York Magazine

Split to the Coast Drink Like a Fish Travel Through Time
Do Yourself In But Don't Forget to Write
NATIONAL LAMPOON
MARCH 1972
MAGAZINE 75 CENTS

426

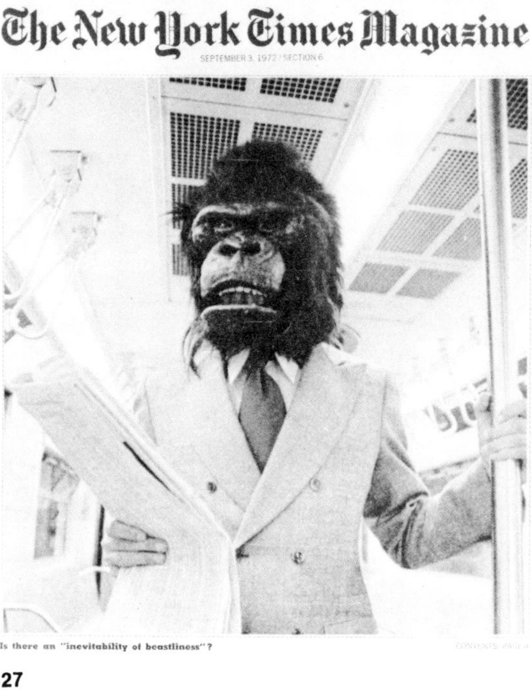
The New York Times Magazine
SEPTEMBER 3, 1972 / SECTION 6
Is there an "inevitability of beastliness"?

427

428

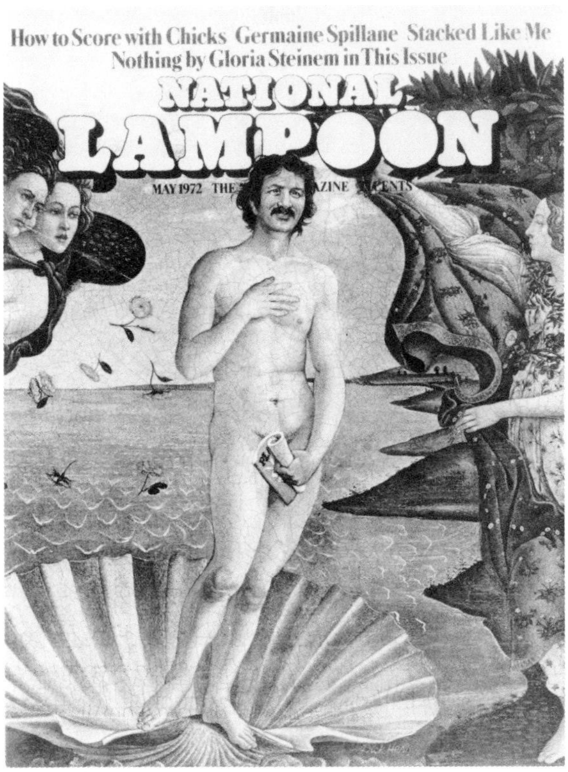
How to Score with Chicks Germaine Spillane Stacked Like Me
Nothing by Gloria Steinem in This Issue
NATIONAL LAMPOON
MAY 1972

429

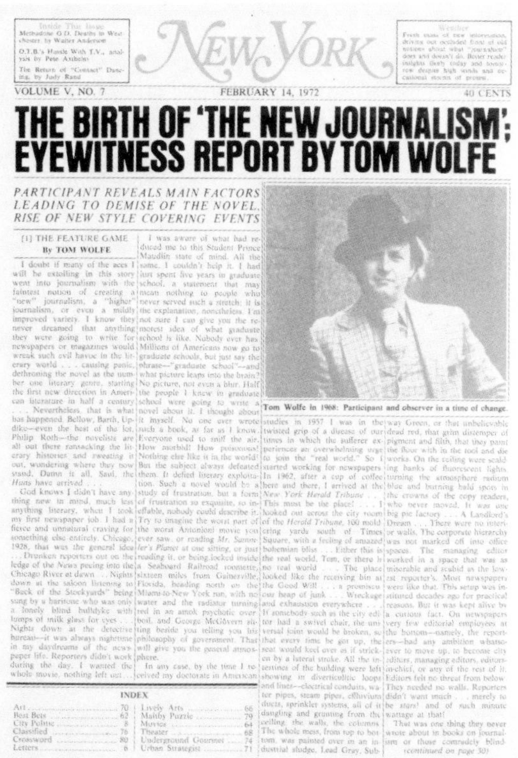

Inside This Issue
Methadone O.D. Deaths in Westchester, by Walter Anderson
O.T.B.'s Hassle With T.V., analysis by Pete Axthelm
The Return of "Contact" Dancing, by Judy Rand

NEW YORK

Weather
Fresh mass of new information, driving out occluded front of old notions about what "journalism" does and doesn't do. Better reader insights likely today and tomorrow despite high winds and occasional storms of protest.

VOLUME V, NO. 7 FEBRUARY 14, 1972 40 CENTS

THE BIRTH OF 'THE NEW JOURNALISM'; EYEWITNESS REPORT BY TOM WOLFE

PARTICIPANT REVEALS MAIN FACTORS LEADING TO DEMISE OF THE NOVEL, RISE OF NEW STYLE COVERING EVENTS

[1] THE FEATURE GAME
By TOM WOLFE

I doubt if many of the aces I will be extolling in this story went into journalism with the faintest notion of creating a "new" journalism, a "higher" journalism, or even a mildly improved variety. I know they never dreamed that anything they were going to write for newspapers or magazines would wreak such evil havoc in the literary world . . . causing panic, dethroning the novel as the number one literary genre, starting the first new direction in American literature in half a century . . . Nevertheless, that is what has happened. Bellow, Barth, Updike—even the best of the lot, Philip Roth—the novelists are all out there ransacking the literary histories and sweating it out, wondering where they now stand. Damn it all, Saul, the *Huns have arrived* . . .

God knows I didn't have anything new in mind, much less anything literary, when I took my first newspaper job. I had a fierce and unnatural craving for something else entirely. Chicago, 1928, that was the general idea . . . Drunken reporters out on the ledge of the *News* peeing into the Chicago River at dawn . . . Nights down at the saloon listening to "Back of the Stockyards" being sung by a baritone who was only a lonely blind bulldyke with lumps of milk glass for eyes . . . Nights down at the detective bureau—it was always nighttime in my daydreams of the newspaper life. Reporters didn't work during the day. I wanted the whole movie, nothing left out . . .

I was aware of what had reduced me to this Student Prince Maudlin state of mind. All the same, I couldn't help it. I had just spent five years in graduate school, a statement that may mean nothing to people who never served such a stretch; it is the explanation, nonetheless. I'm not sure I can give you the remotest idea of what graduate school is like. Nobody ever has. Millions of Americans now go to graduate schools, but just say the phrase—"graduate school"—and what picture leaps into the brain? No picture, not even a blur. Half the people I knew in graduate school were going to write a novel about it. I thought about it myself. No one ever wrote such a book, as far as I know. Everyone used to sniff the air. How morbid! How poisonous! Nothing else like it in the world! But the subject always defeated them. It defied literary exploitation. Such a novel would be a study of frustration, but a form of frustration so exquisite, so ineffable, nobody could describe it. Try to imagine the worst part of the worst Antonioni movie you ever saw, or reading *Mr. Sammler's Planet* at one sitting, or just reading it, or being locked inside a Seaboard Railroad roomette, sixteen miles from Gainesville, Florida, heading north on the Miami-to-New York run, with no water and the radiator turning red in an amok psychotic overboil, and George McGovern sitting beside you telling you his philosophy of government. That will give you the general atmosphere.

In any case, by the time I received my doctorate in American studies in 1957 I was in the twisted grip of a disease of our times in which the sufferer experiences an overwhelming urge to join the "real world." So I started working for newspapers. In 1962, after a cup of coffee here and there, I arrived at the *New York Herald Tribune* . . . This must be the place! . . . I looked out across the city room of the *Herald Tribune*, 100 moldering yards south of Times Square, with a feeling of amazed bohemian bliss . . . Either this is the real world, Tom, or there is no real world . . . The place looked like the receiving bin at the Good Will . . . a promiscuous heap of junk . . . Wreckage and exhaustion everywhere . . . If somebody such as the city editor had a swivel chair, the universal joint would be broken, so that every time he got up, the seat would keel over as if stricken by a lateral stroke. All the intestines of the building were left showing in diverticulitic loops and lines—electrical conduits, water pipes, steam pipes, effluvium ducts, sprinkler systems, all of it dangling and grunting from the ceiling, the walls, the columns. The whole mess, from top to bottom, was painted over in an industrial sludge, Lead Gray, Subway Green, or that unbelievable dead red, that grim distemper of pigment and filth, that they paint the floor with in the tool and die works. On the ceiling were scalding banks of fluorescent lights, turning the atmosphere radium blue and burning bald spots in the crowns of the copy readers, who never moved. It was one big pie factory . . . A Landlord's Dream . . . There were no interior walls. The corporate hierarchy was not marked off into office spaces. The managing editor worked in a space that was as miserable and scabid as the lowest reporter's. Most newspapers were like that. This setup was instituted decades ago for practical reasons. But it was kept alive by a curious fact. On newspapers very few editorial employees at the bottom—namely, the reporters—had any ambition whatsoever to move up, to become city editors, managing editors, editors-in-chief, or any of the rest of it. Editors felt no threat from below. They needed no walls. Reporters didn't want much . . . merely to be *stars*! and of such minute wattage at that!

That was one thing they never wrote about in books on journalism or those comradely blind-

(continued on page 30)

Tom Wolfe in 1968: Participant and observer in a time of change.

INDEX

430

431

432

433

Magazine Covers

Money
JANUARY 1973 $1.50
Adding a room, a roof or a rosebush is an investment in good living, but the **payoff on home improvements** varies widely when you sell. Knowing which projects come closest to paying their way can help you avoid the financial mistakes proliferating here. ¶Elsewhere in this issue, we suggest **what to do if you're fired**—sensible advice designed to keep a temporary setback from becoming a cascading personal disaster. ¶Ingots, medallions, plates of precious metal: **instant collectors' items** bring out the Goldfinger in us all. Too often, all that glitters is a few dollars' worth of silver.
FOR SALE
BUMSTEAD, YOU'RE FIRED!

434

435

The Miracle of Democracy
Wallace Horror Comic Equal Time Coronation of King Dick
NATIONAL LAMPOON
This issue is brought to you by the Republican Party—a leisure service of ITT.

430
Art Director: Mike Salisbury
Designer: Mike Salisbury
Artist: David Willardson
Publisher: Los Angeles Times
West Magazine

431
Art Director: Don Owens
Copywriter: Coast Magazine Staff
Designer: Kenny Kneitel
Photographer: Charles White III
Publisher: Coast Magazine

432
Art Director: Dick Hess
Designers: Dick Hess
Marleen Adlerblum
Artist: Folon
Publisher: United Nations Assoc.
Vista
Agency: Richard Hess Inc.

433
Art Director: Frank Zachary
Designer: Norman S. Hotz
Artist: Robert Kipniss
Publisher: American Express Publishing
Travel & Leisure

434
Art Director: Peter Rauch
Writer: William Simon Rukeyser
Designer: Bob Daniels
Artist: Chic Young
Photographer: Carl Fischer
Publisher: Time Inc.
Money Magazine

435
Art Director: Michael Gross
Writer: Tony Hendra
Designer: Michael Gross
Artist: Robert Grossman
Publisher: Twenty-First Century
Communications
National Lampoon

436

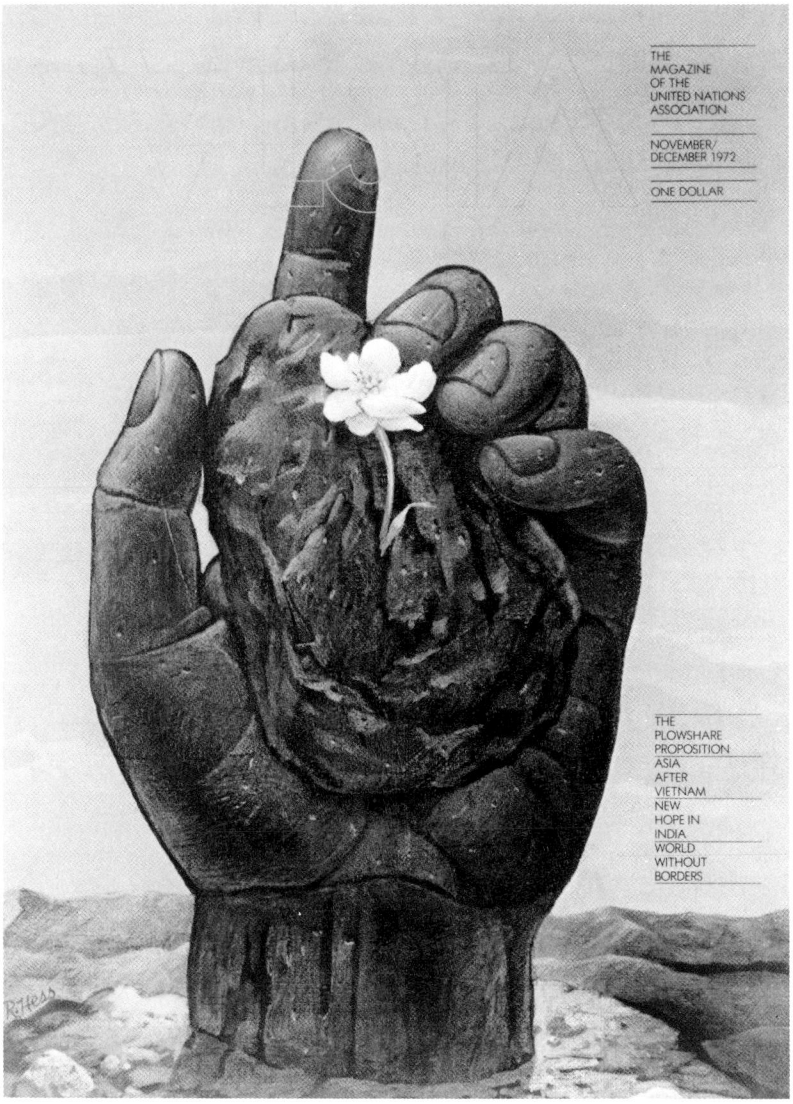
THE
MAGAZINE
OF THE
UNITED NATIONS
ASSOCIATION
NOVEMBER/
DECEMBER 1972
ONE DOLLAR
THE
PLOWSHARE
PROPOSITION
ASIA
AFTER
VIETNAM
NEW
HOPE IN
INDIA
WORLD
WITHOUT
BORDERS

436
Art Director: Dick Hess
Designers: Dick Hess
Marleen Adlerblum
Artist: Dick Hess
Publisher: United Nations Assoc.
Vista
Agency: Richard Hess Inc.

437
Art Director: Harry O. Diamond
Designer: Harry O. Diamond
Artist: Alan E. Cober
Publisher: Exxon Corporation
The Lamp Magazine

438
Art Director: Myles Ludwig
Artist: Guy Fery
Photographer: Guy Fery
Publisher: Advertising Trade Publications
Art Direction

439
Art Director: Dick Hess
Designers: Dick Hess
Marleen Adlerblum
Artist: Ronald Searle
Publisher: United Nations Assoc.
Vista
Agency: Richard Hess Inc.

440
Art Director: Michael Gross
Writer: George W. S. Trow
Designer: Michael Doret
Artists: Charles White III
Michael Doret
Publisher: Twenty-First Century
Communications
National Lampoon

The Lamp
SPRING 1972

437

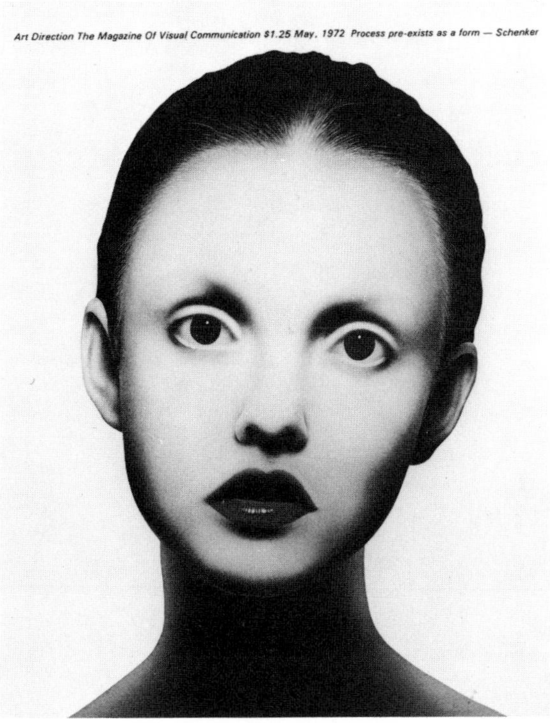
Art Direction The Magazine Of Visual Communication $1.25 May, 1972 Process pre-exists as a form — Schenker

438

439

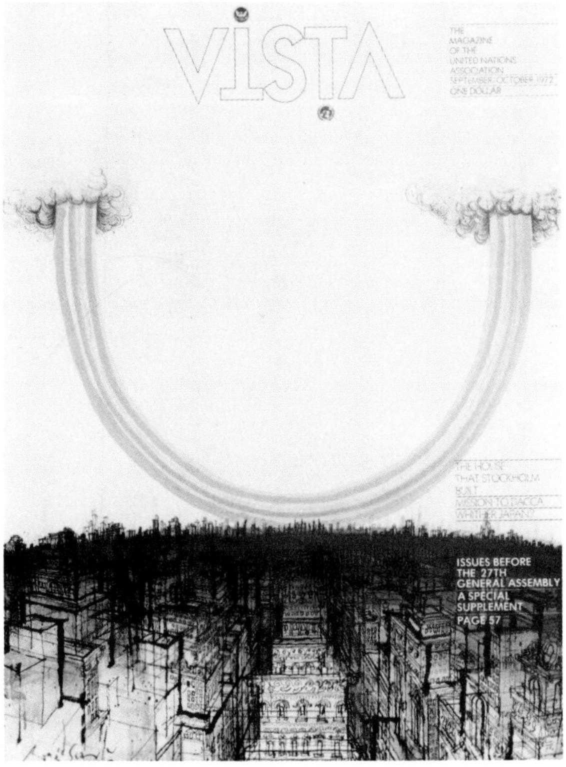
VISTA
THE MAGAZINE OF THE UNITED NATIONS ASSOCIATION SEPTEMBER/OCTOBER 1972 ONE DOLLAR
THE HOUSE THAT STOCKHOLM BUILT
MISSION TO DACCA
WHITHER JAPAN?
ISSUES BEFORE THE 27TH GENERAL ASSEMBLY
A SPECIAL SUPPLEMENT PAGE 57

440

The Wide World of Meat National Geographic Parody
George Sanders Memorial Boredom Awards
NATIONAL LAMPOON
SEPT. 1972 THE HUMOR MAGAZINE 75 CENTS
Bonnie Boredom Says: Save Boredom Stamps— You're On The Way To Stupid Gifts
ONE BORE
I'M BORED

Magazine Covers

All About Eve's Women, by Joseph Mankiewicz
McGovern and the Professors—Why the Defections?
'I Ate Everything In Bloomingdale's Food Dept.'
Mimi Sheraton's Guide to 1,900 Delicacies
50 CENTS
OCTOBER 16, 1972
NEW YORK
THE 10 WORST JUDGES IN NEW YORK

441

442

APRIL 1972
PRICE $1
Esquire
THE MAGAZINE FOR MEN
Dubious Achievements EXTRA!
Esquire's version of the Howard Hughes Affair. (If we waited till next January, we wouldn't believe it.)
"My pictures sure as hell compare favorably... I have noticed that on television... I'm pretty pleased about the way mine have stood up."
"Now, regarding Mr. Nixon, I have tried not to bother him since he has been in office..."
"How in hell could I write my name if I had 8-inch fingernails?"
"I was about to have some photographs made and released to the press... I am going to make them and look at them before I ship them out."
"It just seems to me, for the protection of the public, somebody ought to know what I look like."
"Is Bobby Jones dead? Isn't that a shame."

441
Art Directors: Milton Glaser
Walter Bernard
Designer: Milton Glaser
Artist: Milton Glaser
Publisher: New York Magazine

442
Art Director: George Lois
Designer: George Lois
Photographer: Carl Fischer
Agency: Lois Holland Callaway Inc.
Client: Esquire Magazine

443
Art Directors: Milton Glaser
Walter Bernard
Editor: Clay Felker
Designers: Walter Bernard
Milton Glaser
Photographer: Carl Fischer
Publisher: New York Magazine

444
Art Directors: Milton Glaser
Walter Bernard
Designer: Milton Glaser
Photographer: Henry Wolf
Writer: Milton Glaser
Publisher: New York Magazine

445
Art Director: Michael Gross
Writer: Ed Bluestone
Designer: Michael Gross
Photographer: Ronald G. Harris
Publisher: Twenty-First Century
Communications
National Lampoon

446
Art Director: Neil Shakery
Designer: Michael Doret
Artist: Michael Doret
Publisher: Saturday Review Company
Saturday Review Of The Arts

Buying Without Fear at New York's Auction Houses
Tubal Ligation: Why and Why Not
50 CENTS
SEPTEMBER 25, 1972
New York
The Kitchen As Erogenous Zone By Gael Greene
Apartment Living Is Easy If You Know How
Custom-Designed, Hold-Everything Closets
The Best Handymen in Town
Un-Cute Children's Furniture
What Department Store Decorators Can Do For You
25 Objects You Shouldn't Do Without

443

The Man Who Shot Rap Brown, by Robert Daley
Why the Power Vacuum Goes On and On at Time Inc.
Psyching Out McGovern's Mission, by Garry Wills
New York
Special Section
THE WHOLE GRAPE CATALOGUE
Wine Buys and Wine Intelligence for The Passionate Sipper

444

445

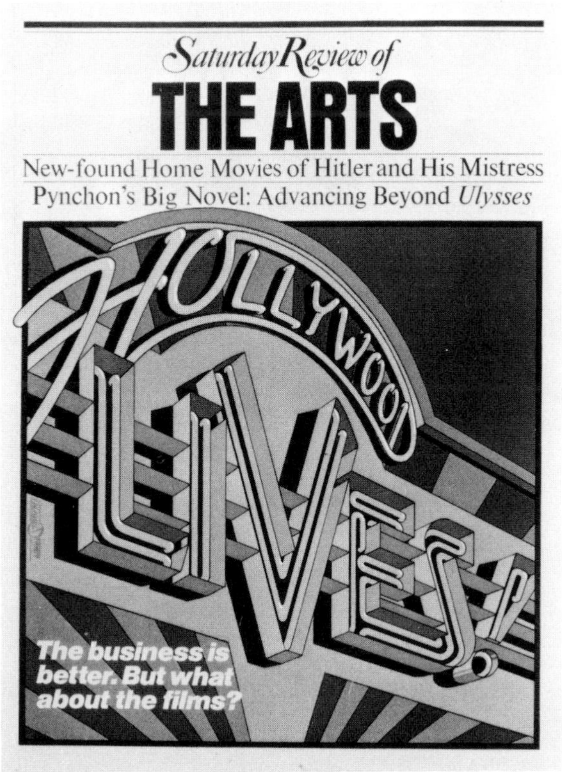

Saturday Review of
THE ARTS
New-found Home Movies of Hitler and His Mistress
Pynchon's Big Novel: Advancing Beyond *Ulysses*
Hollywood Lives!
The business is better. But what about the films?

446

Death
The Adventures of Deadman Playdead Magazine
Last-Aid Kit Suicide Letters to Santa
NATIONAL LAMPOON
JAN. 1973, THE HUMOR MAGAZINE 75 CENTS
If You Don't Buy This Magazine, We'll Kill This Dog

447

447 Gold Award
Art Directors: Milton Charles
Alan Peckolick
Designer: Alan Peckolick
Photographer: Frank Moscati
Publisher: World Publishing
Agency: Alan Peckolick Graphic Design

448

449

448 Silver Award
Art Director: Tina Rossner
Designers: Michael Doret
Kenneth Kneitel
Photographer: Charles White III
Agency: Fluid Drive Studio
Client: ABKCO Records

449
Art Director: Frank Daniel
Designer: Frank Daniel
Photographer: Frank Daniel
Client: Pickwick International, Inc.

THIS is Maurice CHEVALIER
RCA VICTOR
VPM-6055 THIS IS MAURICE CHEVALIER
Internationally famous, respected for his professionalism and loved for his charm, Maurice Chevalier was more than just an entertainer: the jaunty straw hat, the extended lower lip, the cavalier walk, the accent—combined into a kind of "esprit de coeur" that made the name Maurice Chevalier synonymous with the French spirit. A collection of songs identified with this fabulous performer has to include Mimi, Louise, Valentine; we have them again and we know... This Is Maurice Chevalier.
Amsel

450

451

PURE PRAIRIE LEAGUE
VICTOR STEREO
RCA LSP-4650
Norman Rockwell
Woman—Tears—Country Song—It's All on Me—Harmony Song—You're Between Me—Take It Before You Go—Doc's Tune

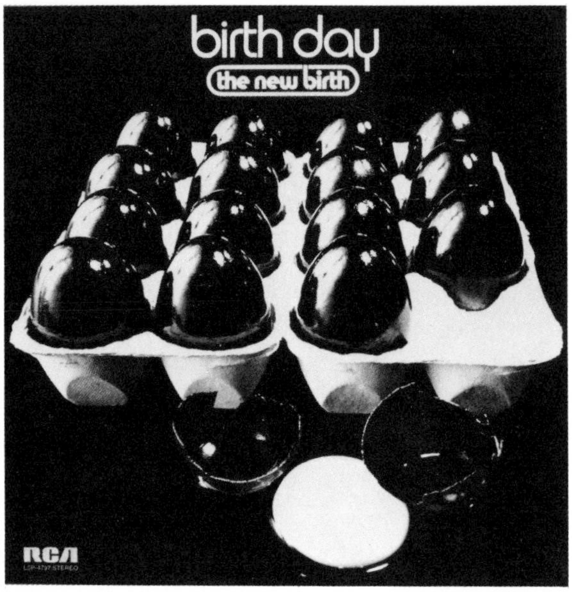
birth day
the new birth
RCA
LSP-4797 STEREO

452

453

RCA
VPM-6076
2 RECORD SET
VICTOR
THE ORIGINAL RECORDINGS
This is Helen O'Connell
VPM-6076 THIS IS HELEN O'CONNELL
AMSEL

454

455

Record Album Covers

450
Art Director: Acy Lehman
Designer: Joe Stelmach
Artist: Richard Amsel
Client: RCA Records

451
Art Director: Acy Lehman
Designer: Acy Lehman
Artist: Norman Rockwell
Client: RCA Records

452 Gold Award
Art Director: Acy Lehman
Designer: Acy Lehman
Photographer: Nick Sangiamo
Client: RCA Records

453
Art Director: Acy Lehman
Designer: Acy Lehman
Artist: Richard Amsel
Client: RCA Records

454
Art Director: Acy Lehman
Designer: Acy Lehman
Artist: Don Punchatz
Client: RCA Records

455
Art Director: David E. Krieger
Designer: David E. Krieger
Photographer: Joel Brodsky
Agency: Davis Fried Krieger Inc.
Client: The Stax Organization

Record Album Covers

457
Art Directors: Chris Whorf
Ed Thrasher
Designers: John Casado
Barbara Casado
Artist: John Casado
Photographer: Ed Thrasher
Agency: John & Barbara Casado Design
Client: Warner Bros. Records

458
Art Director: Bob Ciano
Designer: Bob Ciano
Artist: Roger Hane
Client: CTI Records

457

458

459
Art Director: Bill Levy
Designer: Fred Marcellino
Client: Paramount Records

460
Art Director: Tony Lane
Designer: Tony Lane
Photographer: Tony Lane
Client: Fantasy Records

459

460

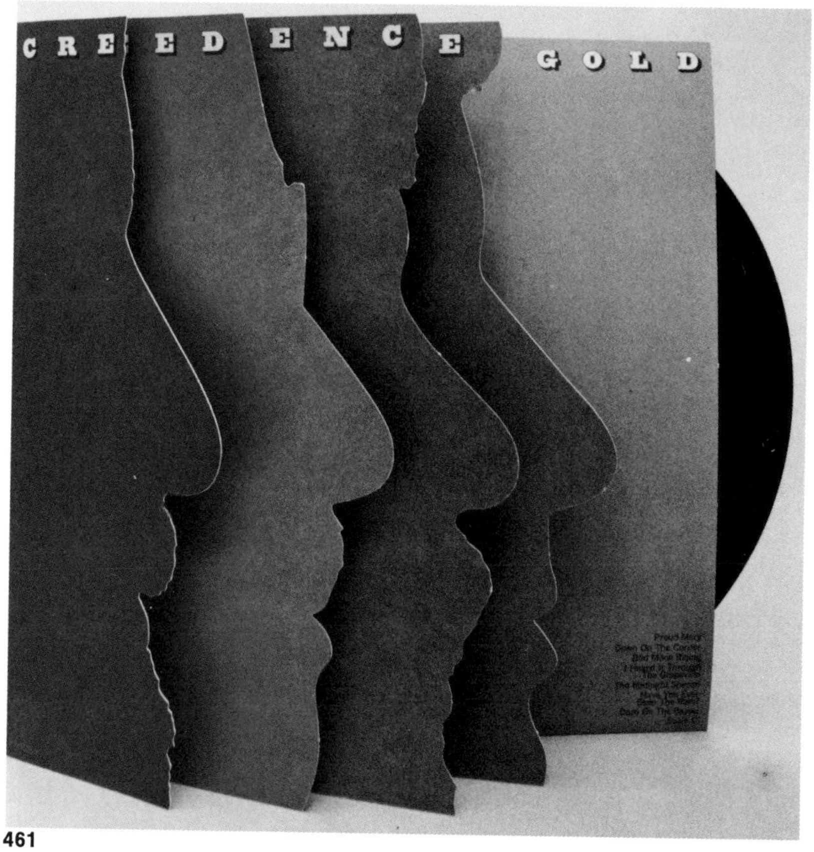
C R E E D E N C E
G O L D

461

462

CAPTAIN BEEFHEART
AND THE MAGIC BAND
REPRISE RECORDS
CLEAR SPOT
CAPTAIN BEEFHEART AND THE MAGIC BAND
STEREO

461
Art Director: Tony Lane
Designer: Tony Lane
Client: Fantasy Records

462
Art Director: Ed Thrasher
Designers: John Casado
Barbara Casado
Photographer: Jim McCrary
Client: Warner/Reprise Records

463
Art Directors: John Berg
Ed Lee
Designer: Teresa Alfieri
Artist: Roy Carruthers
Agency: Columbia Records
Client: Columbia Records

465
Art Director: Ron Coro
Designer: Ron Coro
Photographer: David Gahr
Agency: Columbia Records
Client: Columbia Records

463

465

466

467

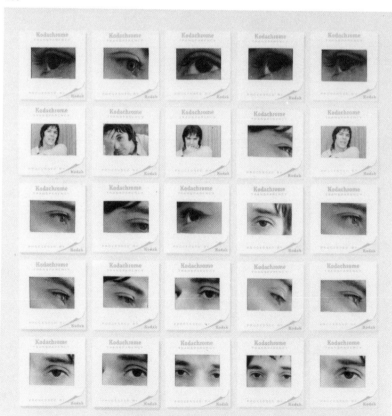

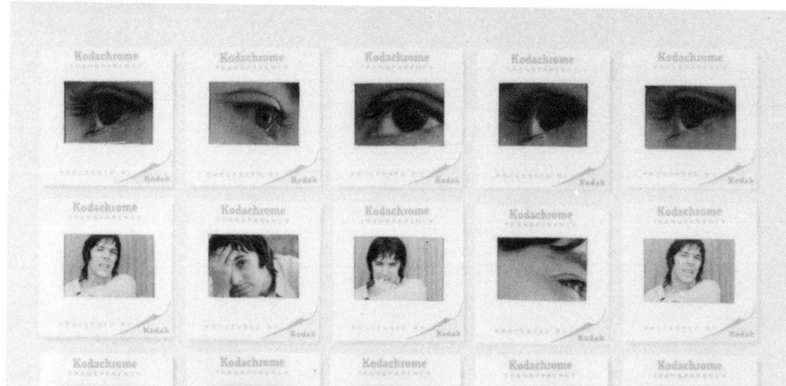

466
Art Director: Tina Rossner
Designer: Kenneth Kneitel
Photographer: Charles White III
Agency: Fluid Drive Studio
Client: ABKCO Records

467
Art Director: Ed Thrasher
Designer: Andy Warhol
Photographer: Ed Thrasher
Client: Warner/Reprise Records

SALES PROMOTION AND GRAPHIC DESIGN

Books, Booklets, Brochures
Packaging
Point-of-Sale
Annual Reports
Sales Presentations
Calendars
Direct Mail
Letterheads
Trademarks and Logotypes
Corporate Identity Programs

468
Art Director: George Lois
Copywriter: Rudy Fiala
Designer: Dennis Mazzella
Photographer: Carl Fischer
Agency: Lois Holland Callaway Inc.
Client: Olivetti Corporation of America

469
Art Director: Roland Young
Writer: Chuck Casell
Designer: Mike Salisbury
Photographer: Jim McCrary
Agency: Mike Salisbury Inc.
Client: A&M Records

468

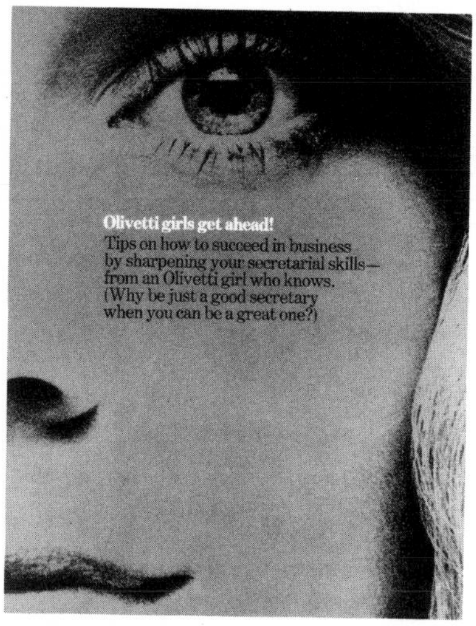
Olivetti girls get ahead!
Tips on how to succeed in business by sharpening your secretarial skills—from an Olivetti girl who knows. (Why be just a good secretary when you can be a great one?)

Don't be a clock-watcher.
If you have a job that interests you, at which you work hard, you'll be surprised how fast the time flies. If you don't, you'd better find another job.
Don't join a company that keeps you down!
Unfortunately, some companies are still pretty stuffy about women. So if you want to grow, pick an outfit you can grow in. Even if it means less salary. (Don't underestimate what the right job can mean to you in finding out who you are and what you can do.)
Know the basic tools of your trade.
It almost goes without saying, to get ahead you've got to be a whiz at typing and shorthand (not to mention spelling). So work hard at it. Of course, being an Olivetti girl gives you a head start in the typing department. You've got the typewriter with the brain inside that makes the four most common typing mistakes absolutely impossible!

469

1969
MIDDLE-OF-THE-ROCK
Joe Cocker

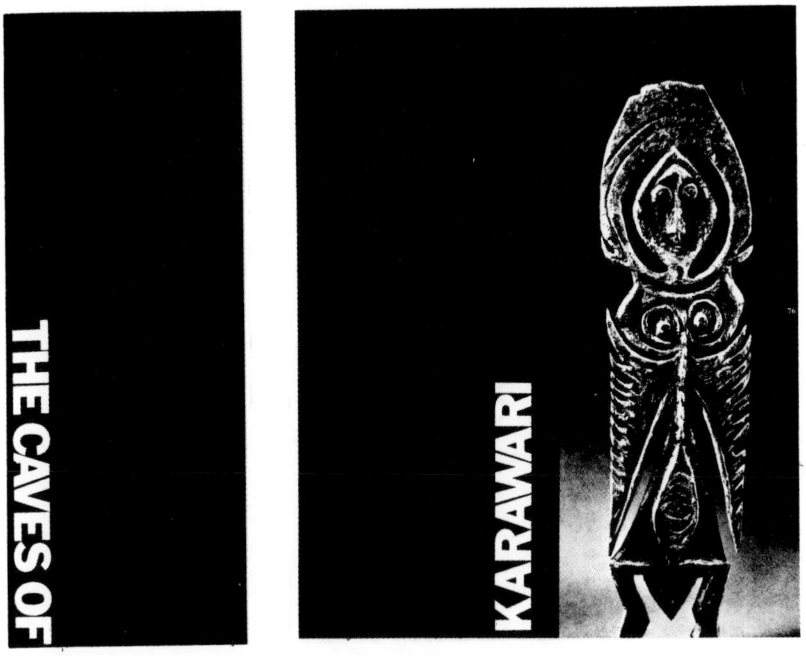

470
Art Director: George Lois
Designers: Kurt Weihs
Dennis Mazzella
Artist: Bill Viola
Agency: Lois Holland Callaway Inc.
Client: D'arcy Gallery

471
Art Director: Dick Lemmon
Copywriter: George Mead
Designer: Dick Lemmon
Artist: Donald Wilson
Agency: N. W. Ayer & Son, Inc., Chicago
Client: State of Illinois Tourism

470

20 SCENIC MOTOR TOURS
TO TAKE IN ILLINOIS.
STOCKTON
FREEPORT
MT CARROLL
OREGON
FULTON
CLINTON
DIXON
ROCK FALLS
2.
Here is a 206-mile trip for a perfect outing in the country. Visit Illinois' most glorious parks, the scene of the Lincoln-Douglas debate and the site of the Black Hawk Treaty.
0 Mi. Start at State and N. Main Streets in Rockford. Drive west on State Street to U.S. 20.
30 Mi. Freeport. A large boulder marks the site of the Lincoln-Douglas debate of 1858. According to historians, it helped make Lincoln president and hastened the start of the Civil War. Take time to observe the old stone home which houses the Stephenson County Historical Society, at 1440 S. Carroll Ave. The trees surrounding the home were brought west by covered wagon. Follow U.S. 20.
51 Mi. Stockton. Turn south here on Route 78 to Mt. Carroll, then proceed west on U.S. 52.
80 Mi. Savanna. This is a thriving rail center for the truck-farming crops destined for Chicago. It is also a turn-off point north, via Route 84.
82 Mi. Mississippi Palisades State Park. The 1300 acres of this park are dominated by a series of rugged cliffs rising above the river. The terrain is heavily wooded, and has a number of deep canyons to explore. Unusual rock formations include the Indian Head, Twin Sisters, and Bob Upton's Cave. Foot and bridle paths are clearly marked. This is a perfect spot for a snack. Now return to Savanna via Route 84 and continue south to U.S. 30. Turn west and go through Fulton to U.S. 67 in Iowa.
105 Mi. Clinton. This town was once one of the more important lumbering towns in the region. When prime timber gave out, the village managed to convert to agriculture, and is today a center of rich farming country. Turn east here on to U.S. 30 to Route 2.
133 Mi. Sterling. This town, together with adjacent Rock Falls, offers a splendid view of the Rock River. Now continue east on Route 2.
146 Mi. Dixon. The Lincoln Memorial marks the site of the Dixon Blockhouse, an important negotiating site during the Black Hawk War. Jefferson Davis, Zachary Taylor and Abraham Lincoln met here in 1832. An unusual statue of Lincoln as a youthful frontier soldier, is worth a picture for your album. Drive north on Route 2 to the south edge of Oregon and turn west on a well-marked country road.
169 Mi. White Pines Forest State Park. Just when you think you have seen all the matchless views possible in a one-day trip, you enter this land of moss-covered cliffs and the only remaining stand of virgin white pine forest in Illinois. There are children's playgrounds and a lodge which invites a rest or a bit of refreshment. Be sure to have film for your stop here, for these great trees are fast disappearing from the mid-western scene. Now return to Oregon. Cross the Rock River on Route 64 and take a county road north.
178 Mi. Lowden Memorial State Park. Dominating the landscape in this exceptionally attractive park is the 48-foot concrete statue of Black Hawk, which towers more than 250 feet above Rock River. The children will enjoy the tame deer in the park reservation. This might be a perfect spot for bringing out that picnic basket again.
Retrace your route to Oregon and continue north on Route 2. The last leg of your trip is always close to the Rock River, and passes through interesting farm country.
206 Mi. Rockford.

471

472
Art Director: Ivan Chermayeff
Copywriter: Ivan Chermayeff
Designer: Ivan Chermayeff
Photographer: Elliott Erwitt
Publisher: The Viking Press, Inc.
Studio Books

473
Art Director: Craig Braun
Designer: Tom Wilkes
Photographers: Phil Marco
Ethan Russell
Agency: Wilkes & Braun, Inc.
Client: Ode Records Inc.

472

Observations on American Architecture by Ivan Chermayeff with photographs by Elliot Erwitt

473

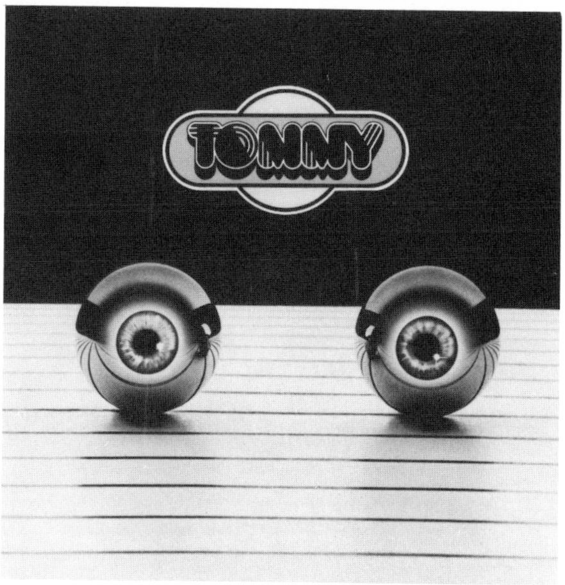
TOMMY

474
Art Director: Bob Salpeter
Designer: Bob Salpeter
Agency: Lopez Salpeter Inc.
Client: IBM

475
Art Directors: Bob Loth
Bill Bonnell III
Copywriter: Anthony Marcin
Designer: Bill Bonnell III
Photographers: Steve Deutsch
Tony Kelly
Stan Jorstad
Nick Costanza
Agency: Container Corporation of America
Client: Container Corporation of America

474

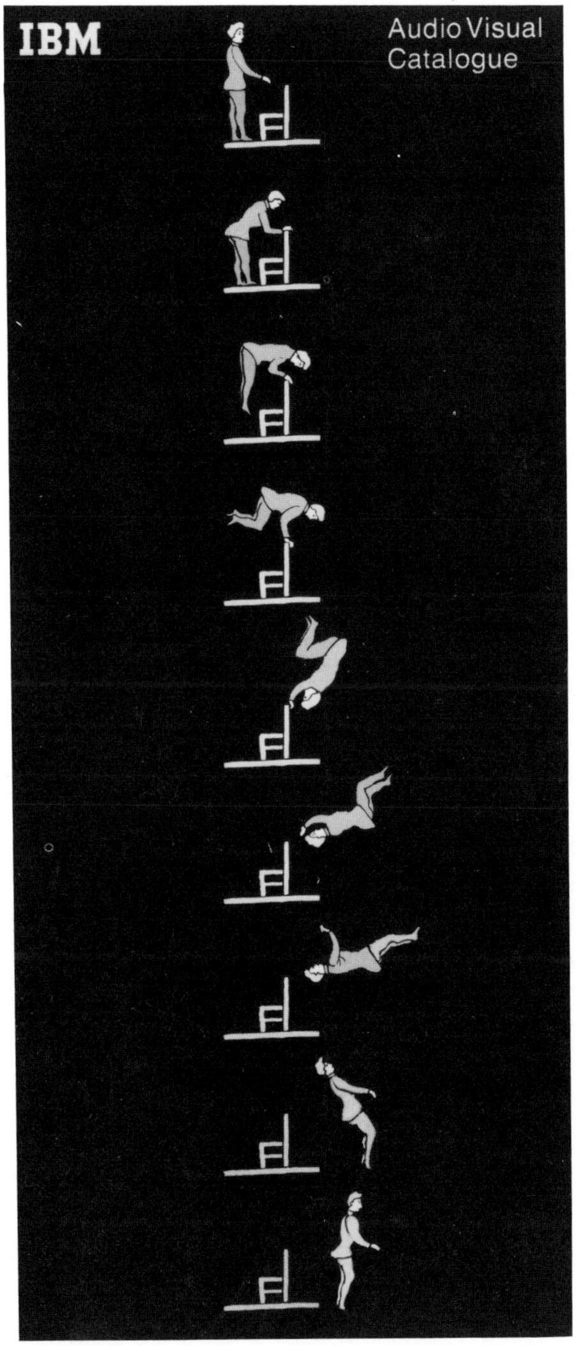

475

First, read this newspaper. Then give it to your dog.

The purpose of this newspaper is to help you train your dog to go to the bathroom indoors, on newspaper, all the time.

The text that follows is excerpted and adapted from "GOOD DOG, BAD DOG."

By Mordecai Siegal and Matthew Margolis. Copyright © 1978 by Mordecai Siegal and Matthew Margolis. Granted with the permission of Holt Rinehart & Winston, Inc., publishers.

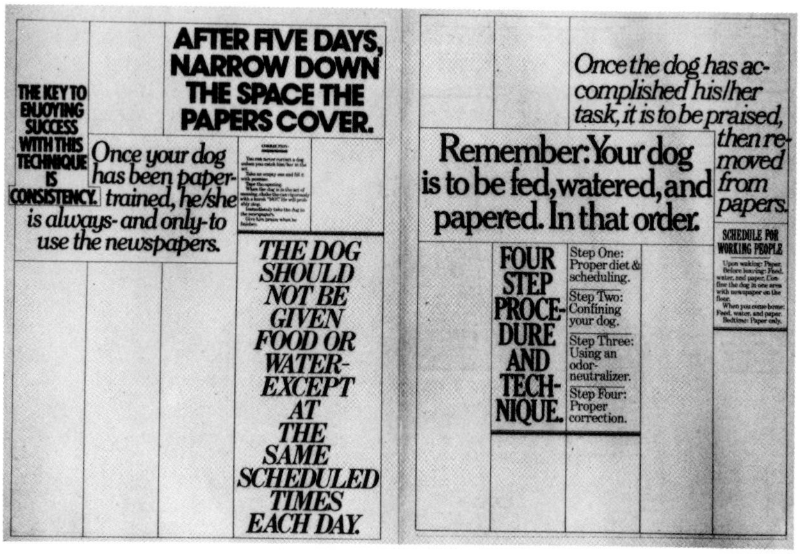

THE KEY TO ENJOYING SUCCESS WITH THIS TECHNIQUE IS CONSISTENCY.
AFTER FIVE DAYS, NARROW DOWN THE SPACE THE PAPERS COVER.
Once your dog has been paper-trained, he/she is always- and only-to use the newspapers.
THE DOG SHOULD NOT BE GIVEN FOOD OR WATER-EXCEPT AT THE SAME SCHEDULED TIMES EACH DAY.
Once the dog has accomplished his/her task, it is to be praised, then removed from papers.
Remember: Your dog is to be fed, watered, and papered. In that order.
FOUR STEP PROCEDURE AND TECHNIQUE.
Step One: Proper diet & scheduling.
Step Two: Confining your dog.
Step Three: Using an odor-neutralizer.
Step Four: Proper correction.
SCHEDULE FOR WORKING PEOPLE
Upon waking: Paper. Before leaving: Food, water, and paper. Confine the dog in one area with newspaper on the floor.
When you come home: Food, water, and paper.
Bedtime: Paper only.

476

477

THINK

CAT

After they learn to spell C-A-T
Who's going to teach them to T-H-I-N-K?

ON SATURDAY HE MIGHT SHOW THEM WHAT THE SUN DID TO ICARUS. ON SUNDAY, WHY AND HOW.

Gene London runs a delightful doubleheader of children's programs with two completely different formats. But the ends are the same: education through entertainment.

One day, he's the lovable, if bumbling, star of CARTOON CORNERS GENERAL STORE where, as a part-time reporter for a local newspaper, he digs out big stories and lets his audience know what he's learning as he's learning it. One assignment, for example, had him covering the story behind the first manned flight, and the intrepid reporter went all the way back to the tale of Icarus and Daedalus for background information.

Another day, in a somewhat more relaxed, more informal atmosphere, London tells stories, draws to music, takes youngsters on filmed tours, gives instructions on the care of pets and plants, and demonstrates simple scientific experiments that the kids can repeat at home.

Learning without tears isn't exactly a new concept for children's television. But we don't know when it has ever been in more expert hands.

And if you still can't recall the whole story of Daedalus and the problem his son had with the sun, it may be because you weren't fortunate enough to have London as a teacher.

THE GENE LONDON SHOW/
CARTOON CORNERS GENERAL STORE

HERE COMES THE MOD GOOD HUMOR MAN WITH THIS WEEK'S PACKAGE OF MUSIC, NEWS AND MYSTERY INGREDIENTS.

His name is Don Boevingloh and he mixes his special blend of entertainment and education on THE RAINBOW PALACE.

Boevingloh, a former teacher and stage director, is ideally equipped to handle the eclectic, often zany, always fast-paced format of this unique show.

It's a place where youngsters might learn how to make ice cream or what's happening to the Mississippi; and it might show them anything from young musical groups to news about kids that they can't get anywhere else.

Continuing features include a studio audience segment; a look at the handicrafts, art and creativity of other youngsters; special interviews by the kids themselves with prominent sports, political and scientific figures; and an ecology segment with the master gardener Jerry Baker.

Incidentally, it's called THE RAINBOW PALACE because the whole show takes place in a mad and mod ice cream parlor that's alive with the colors, the designs and the atmosphere that have captured the younger generation's fancy.

More important, it's alive with the excitement that captures their imagination. And if it all sounds like an entertaining way for kids to learn a whole lot about a whole lot of things, that's because it is.

THE RAINBOW PALACE

478

Introducing The Auto-Train.™
For only $190, it'll take you, your car
and 3 other people to or from Florida.
Luxuriously.

476 Gold Award
Art Director: Lawrence Miller
Writers: Mordecai Siegal
Matthew Margolis
Lawrence Miller
Designers: Lawrence Miller
Vance Jonson
Artist: Reynold Ruffins
Publisher: N.Y.C. Environmental Protection Administration
Agency: Marketing Design Alliance
Client: N.Y.C. Environmental Protection Administration

477
Art Director: Lou Dorfsman
Copywriters: Lou Dorfsman
Peter Nord
Designers: Lou Dorfsman
Ira Teichberg
Artist: John Alcorn
Agency: CBS/Broadcast Group
Client: CBS Television Stations Division

478
Art Director: Ken Berris
Copywriter: Richard Raboy
Designer: Ken Berris
Artist: Sims Tabark
Agency: Della Femina, Travisano & Partners, Inc.
Client: Autotrain

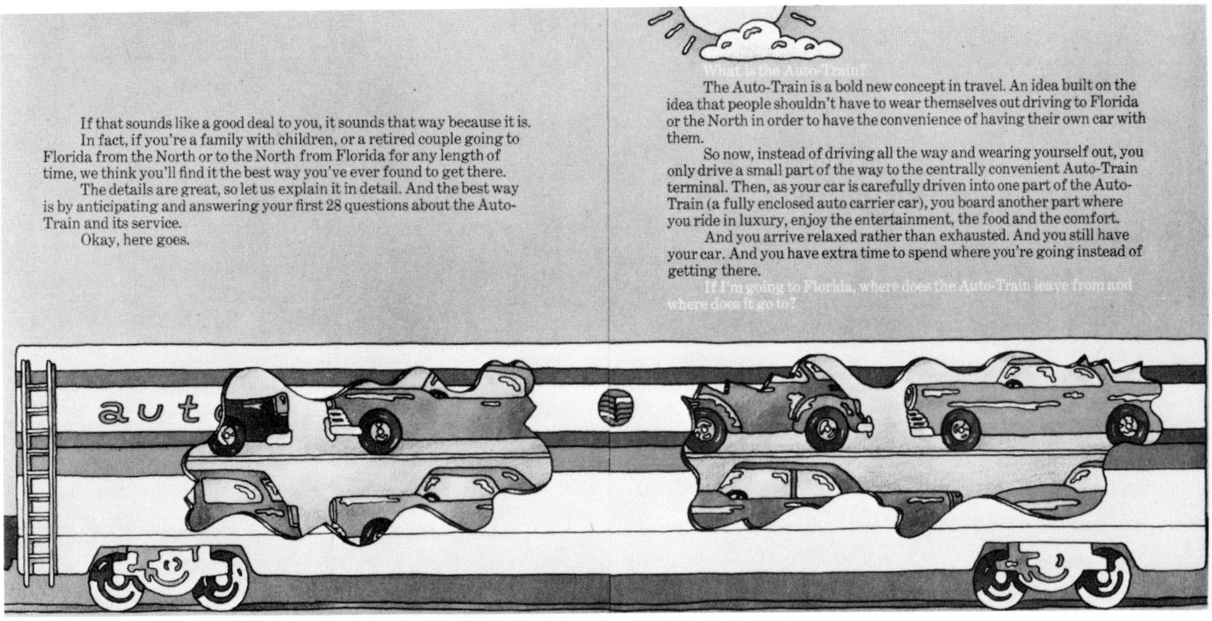
If that sounds like a good deal to you, it sounds that way because it is.
In fact, if you're a family with children, or a retired couple going to Florida from the North or to the North from Florida for any length of time, we think you'll find it the best way you've ever found to get there.
The details are great, so let us explain it in detail. And the best way is by anticipating and answering your first 28 questions about the Auto-Train and its service.
Okay, here goes.
What is the Auto-Train?
The Auto-Train is a bold new concept in travel. An idea built on the idea that people shouldn't have to wear themselves out driving to Florida or the North in order to have the convenience of having their own car with them.
So now, instead of driving all the way and wearing yourself out, you only drive a small part of the way to the centrally convenient Auto-Train terminal. Then, as your car is carefully driven into one part of the Auto-Train (a fully enclosed auto carrier car), you board another part where you ride in luxury, enjoy the entertainment, the food and the comfort.
And you arrive relaxed rather than exhausted. And you still have your car. And you have extra time to spend where you're going instead of getting there.
If I'm going to Florida, where does the Auto-Train leave from and where does it go to?
aut

479

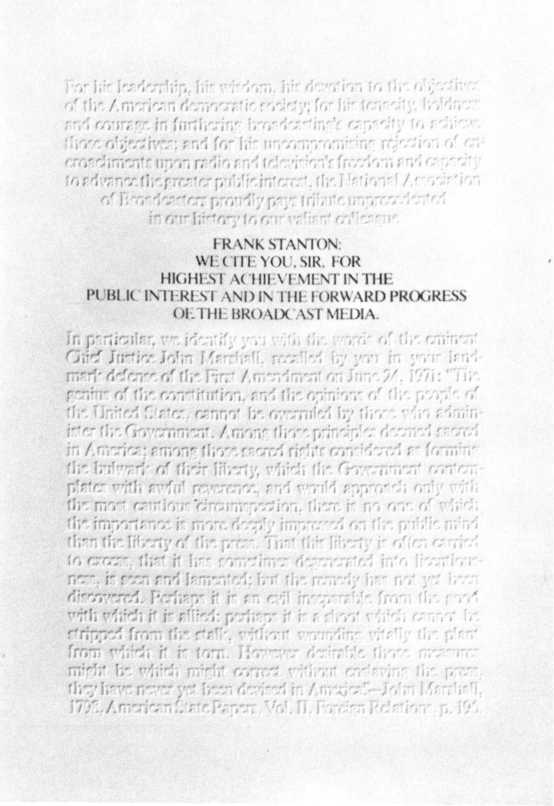

For his leadership, his wisdom, his devotion to the objectives of the American democratic society; for his tenacity, boldness and courage in furthering broadcasting's capacity to achieve those objectives; and for his uncompromising rejection of encroachments upon radio and television's freedom and capacity to advance the greater public interest, the National Association of Broadcasters proudly pays tribute unprecedented in our history to our valiant colleague

FRANK STANTON:
WE CITE YOU, SIR, FOR
HIGHEST ACHIEVEMENT IN THE
PUBLIC INTEREST AND IN THE FORWARD PROGRESS
OF THE BROADCAST MEDIA.

In particular, we identify you with the words of the eminent Chief Justice John Marshall, recalled by you in your landmark defense of the First Amendment on June 24, 1971: "The genius of the constitution, and the opinions of the people of the United States, cannot be overruled by those who administer the Government. Among those principles deemed sacred in America; among those sacred rights considered as forming the bulwark of their liberty, which the Government contemplates with awful reverence, and would approach only with the most cautious circumspection, there is no one of which the importance is more deeply impressed on the public mind than the liberty of the press. That this liberty is often carried to excess, that it has sometimes degenerated into licentiousness, is seen and lamented; but the remedy has not yet been discovered. Perhaps it is an evil inseparable from the good with which it is allied; perhaps it is a shoot which cannot be stripped from the stalk, without wounding vitally the plant from which it is torn. However desirable those measures might be which might correct without enslaving the press, they have never yet been devised in America."—John Marshall, 1798, American State Papers, Vol. II, Foreign Relations, p. 196.

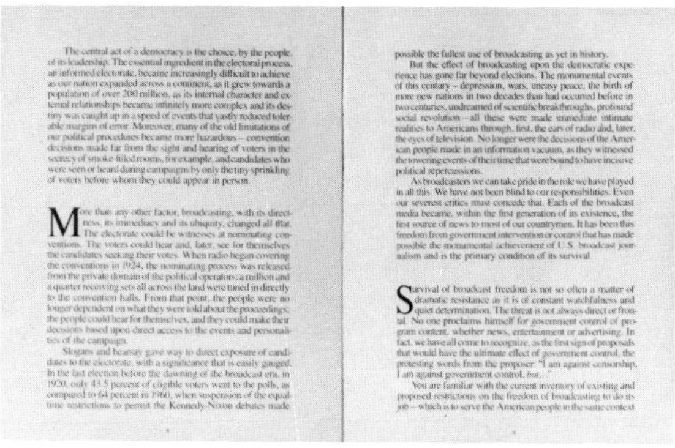

The central act of a democracy is the choice, by the people, of its leadership. The essential ingredient in the electoral process, an informed electorate, became increasingly difficult to achieve as our nation expanded across a continent, as it grew towards a population of over 200 million, as its internal character and external relationships became infinitely more complex and its destiny was caught up in a speed of events that vastly reduced tolerable margins of error. Moreover, many of the old limitations of our political procedures became more hazardous – convention decisions made far from the sight and hearing of voters in the secrecy of smoke-filled rooms, for example, and candidates who were seen or heard during campaigns by only the tiny sprinkling of voters before whom they could appear in person.

More than any other factor, broadcasting, with its directness, its immediacy and its ubiquity, changed all that. The electorate could be witnesses at nominating conventions. The voters could hear and, later, see for themselves the candidates seeking their votes. When radio began covering the conventions in 1924, the nominating process was released from the private domain of the political operators; a million and a quarter receiving sets all across the land were tuned in directly to the convention halls. From that point, the people were no longer dependent on what they were told about the proceedings; the people could hear for themselves, and they could make their decisions based upon direct access to the events and personalities of the campaign.

Slogans and hearsay gave way to direct exposure of candidates to the electorate, with a significance that is easily gauged. In the last election before the dawning of the broadcast era, in 1920, only 43.5 percent of eligible voters went to the polls, as compared to 64 percent in 1960, when suspension of the equal-time restrictions to permit the Kennedy-Nixon debates made possible the fullest use of broadcasting as yet in history.

But the effect of broadcasting upon the democratic experience has gone far beyond elections. The monumental events of this century – depression, wars, uneasy peace, the birth of more new nations in two decades than had occurred before in two centuries, undreamed of scientific breakthroughs, profound social revolution – all these were made immediate intimate realities to Americans through, first, the ears of radio and, later, the eyes of television. No longer were the decisions of the American people made in an information vacuum, as they witnessed the towering events of their time that were bound to have incisive political repercussions.

As broadcasters we can take pride in the role we have played in all this. We have not been blind to our responsibilities. Even our severest critics must concede that. Each of the broadcast media became, within the first generation of its existence, the first source of news to most of our countrymen. It has been this freedom from government intervention or control that has made possible the monumental achievement of U.S. broadcast journalism and is the primary condition of its survival.

Survival of broadcast freedom is not so often a matter of dramatic resistance as it is of constant watchfulness and quiet determination. The threat is not always direct or frontal. No one proclaims himself for government control of program content, whether news, entertainment or advertising. In fact, we have all come to recognize, as the first sign of proposals that would have the ultimate effect of government control, the protesting words from the proposer: "I am against censorship, I am against government control, *but*..."

You are familiar with the current inventory of existing and proposed restrictions on the freedom of broadcasting to do its job – which is to serve the American people in the same context

480

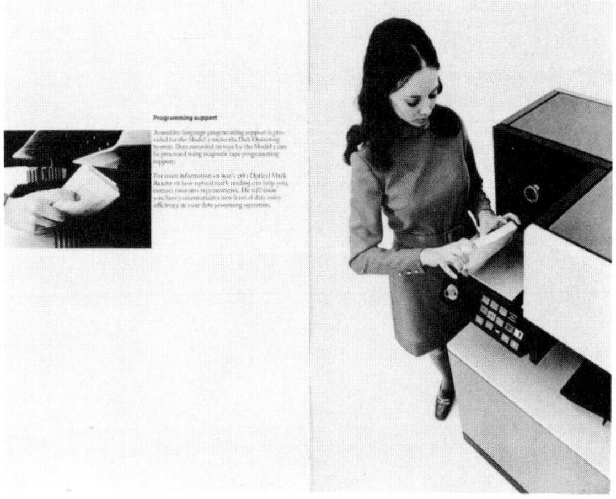

479
Art Director: Lou Dorfsman
Designers: Lou Dorfsman
Ted Andresakes
Agency: CBS/Broadcast Group
Client: Columbia Broadcasting System, Inc.

480
Art Director: John Milligan
Designer: John Milligan
Photographer: Jim Broderick
Client: IBM

481

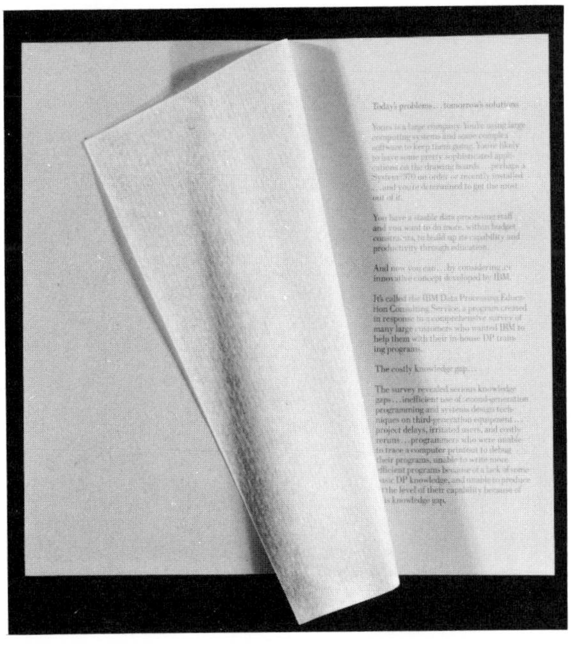

482

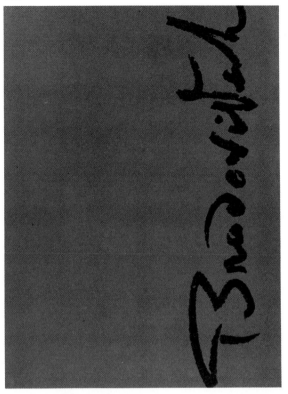

481
Art Director: Bob Paganucci
Designer: Bob Paganucci
Artist: Bob Paganucci
Client: IBM

482
Art Director: Richard Hood
Writer: George Bunker
Designer: Richard Hood
Photographers: Alexey Brodovitch
Richard Avedon
Irving Penn
Henri Cartier-Bresson, etal.
Publisher: Philadelphia College of Art
Smithsonian Institution
Client: Philadelphia College of Art

MARINE AIR

22
Huey UH-1. This multi-use machine is called the workhorse of the Marine "chopper" fleet. Because it is fast, has a low silhouette, and the ability to land and take-off from unprepared clearings, the Huey can sweep in to drop off Marine ground troops or supplies. In this role it can carry a Marine reconnaissance team, or 2,000 lbs. of cargo. When fully armed, the Huey becomes an effective gunship for landing-zone protection and troop support. Depending upon the mission, a crew of two usually operates the Huey—pilot and co-pilot, who sit side by side in the cockpit. The co-pilot's job also includes that of observer and gunner. The Huey is a lightweight helicopter that cruises at 100 mph, and has a maximum speed of 120 mph. It is jet powered, with two engines in the latest model. Besides troop transport, the craft is also used for medical evacuation, airborne command and control, escort of larger helicopters, liaison and courier, and search and rescue missions.

483
Art Director: William J. Conlon
Copywriter: Thomas Mabley III
Designer: William J. Conlon
Photographer: Jim Berberian
Agency: J. Walter Thompson Company
Client: United States Marine Corps

484
Art Director: John Noneman
Copywriter: Corinne A. Forti
Designer: Patricia Noneman
Photographer: John T. Hill
Agency: Noneman and Noneman, Inc.
Client: Grace Institute

485
Art Director: Robert Leydenfrost
Designer: John Haines
Publisher: Port Authority of New York and New Jersey
Client: Port Authority of New York and New Jersey

483

Grace Institute 75 Years of Excellence

484

TheNewYork-
NewJersey
Metropolitan
Area
Industrial
Development
Guide
The Port
of New York
Authority

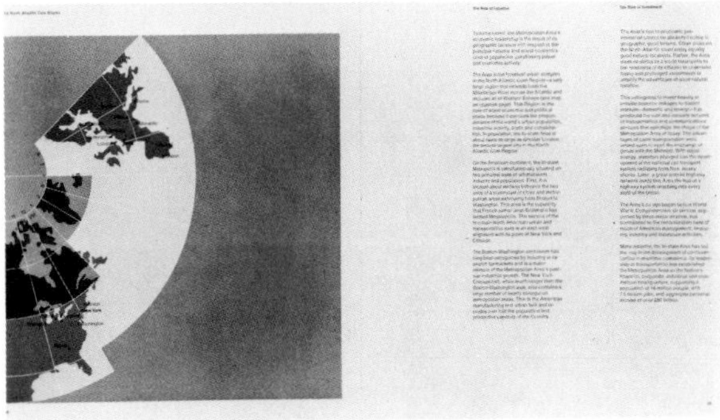

485

486

CNR
PROSPECTUS
'72,'74

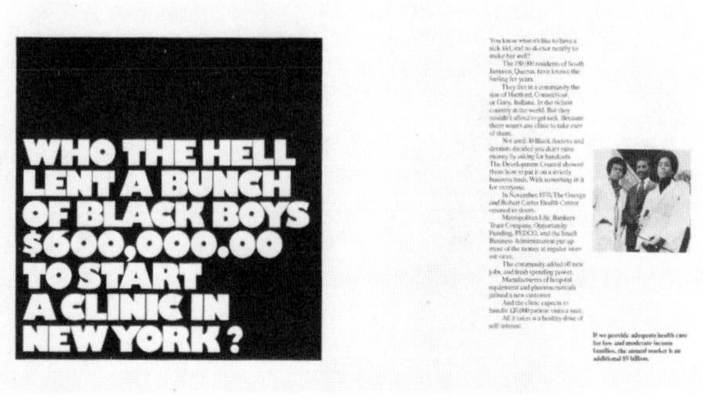
WHO THE HELL
LENT A BUNCH
OF BLACK BOYS
$600,000.00
TO START
A CLINIC IN
NEW YORK ?

487

SELF-INTEREST
PAYS OFF.
FOR EVERYONE.

488

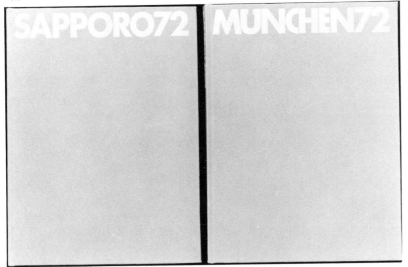

486
Art Director: Ginny Aromando
Writers: Ginny Aromando
Meg Schimpf
Designer: Ginny Aromando
Artist: Ginny Aromando
Agency: Ginny Aromando
Client: College of New Rochelle

487
Art Director: Arthur Gelb
Writer: Mike Silverman
Designers: Arthur Gelb
Kenneth Ferretti
Photographers: Ann Schwartz
Rupert Callender
Agency: Art Gelb Advertising, Inc.
Client: The Development Council

488
Art Director: Willy Fleckhaus
Writer: Walter Umminger
Designer: Willy Fleckhaus
Photographer: Erwin Fieger
Publisher: Olympische Sport Bibliothek Munchen
Client: Deutsche Sporthilfe

489
Art Director: Kevin Miller
Copywriter: Fred Murphy
Designer: Kevin Miller
Photographers: Phil Marco
Dick Faust
Agency: Rumrill-Hoyt, Inc.
Client: Eastman Kodak Company

490
Art Director: Ivan Chermayeff
Designers: Ivan Chermayeff
Sandra Erickson
Photographers: Ivan Chermayeff
various others
Agency: Chermayeff & Geismar Associates
Client: Metropolitan Museum of Art

491
Art Director: Fred J. Korge
Designer: Tom Ballenger
Artist: Tom Ballenger
Agency: Baxter & Korge, Inc.
Client: Southwestern Bell Telephone Company

492 Silver Award
Art Director: Carl Stewart
Copywriter: Michael Schiffrin
Photographer: Henry Sandbank Studios
Agency: Gaynor & Ducas, Inc.
Client: Birmingham Small Arms

489

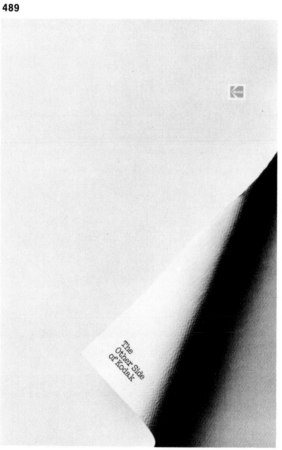

490

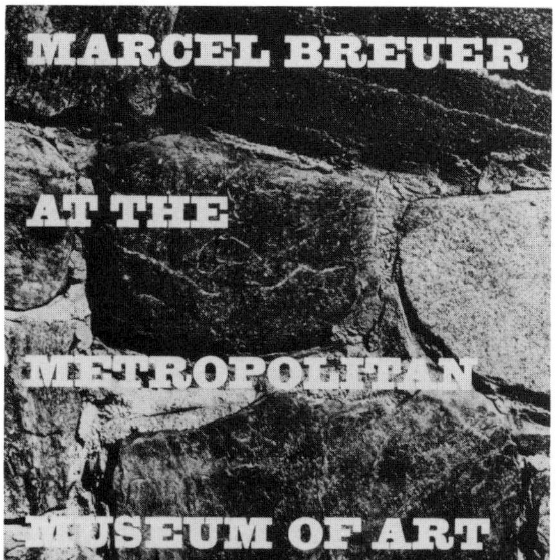

MY
TELEPHONE
BOOK

8
THIS IS A TELEPHONE REPAIRMAN.
9
THIS IS A TELEPHONE TRUCK.

491

492

The 1973
Tiger 750 (TR7RV)
TRIUMPH

Books, Booklets, Brochures

493
Art Directors: Ed Gold
David Crowder
Writers: Jim Gollin
Bob Kristan
Jan Krukowski
Designer: David Crowder
Photographer: Al Giese
Agency: Barton-Gillet Company
Client: New York University

493

Where can you get an education like no other in theater, film, television or dance?
NYU

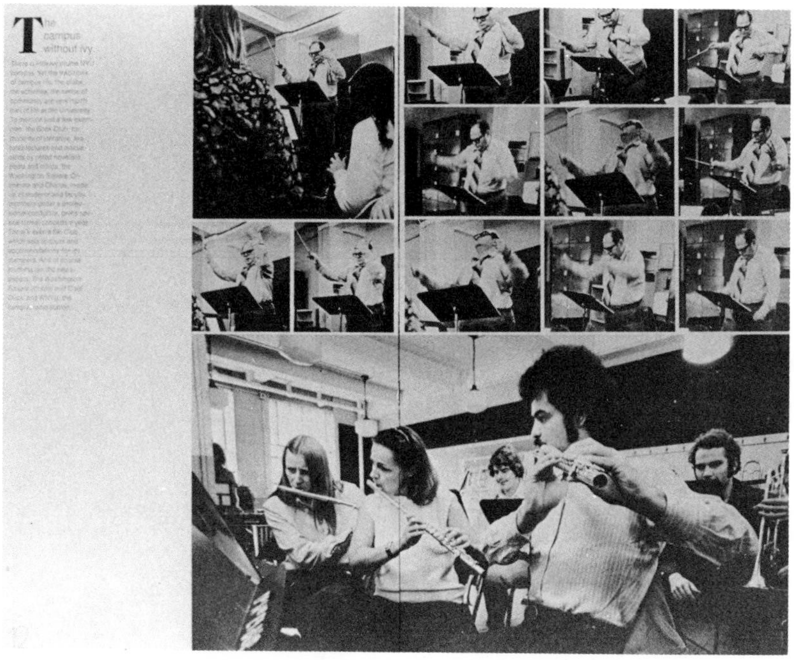
The campus without ivy.

An important part of your education in education will be the greatest classroom in the world.
NYU

It's time to debunk the prevailing myth of the organization man.
NYU

If you want to study the best of man and his works, there is a place for you that is like no other.
NYU

494
Art Director: Lou Musachio
Copywriter: Mike Racz
Designer: Lou Musachio
Photographer: Charles Wiesehahn
Agency: Acme Communications
Client: Acme Communications

495
Art Director: Jim Benedict
Copywriter: Jim Benedict
Designer: Jim Benedict
Artist: Push Pin Studios
Agency: Hurvis, Binzer & Churchill
Client: Collins, Miller & Hutchings

Acme may have already worked for you . . .

494

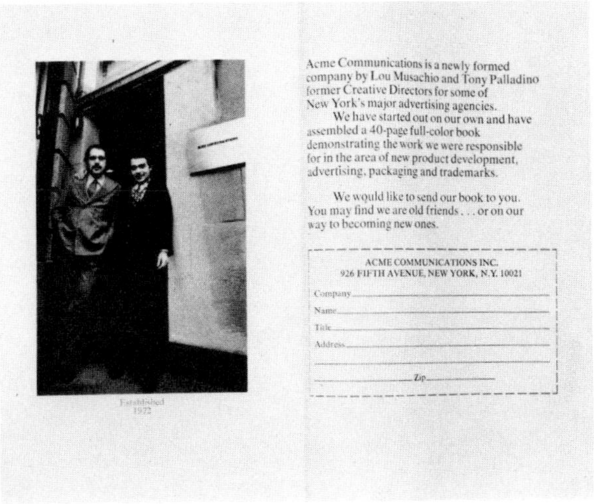

495

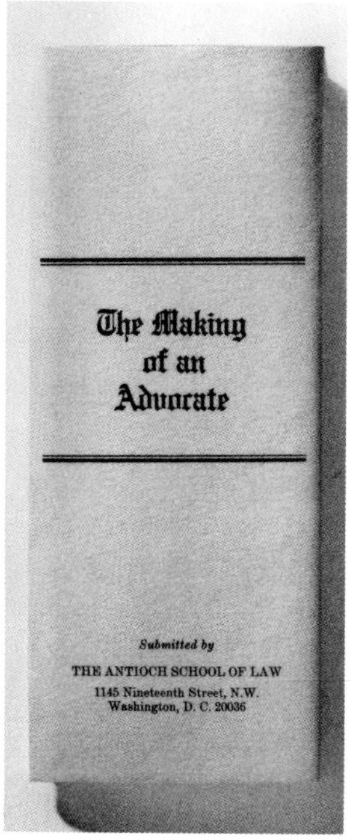
The Making of an Advocate
Submitted by
THE ANTIOCH SCHOOL OF LAW
1145 Nineteenth Street, N.W.
Washington, D. C. 20036

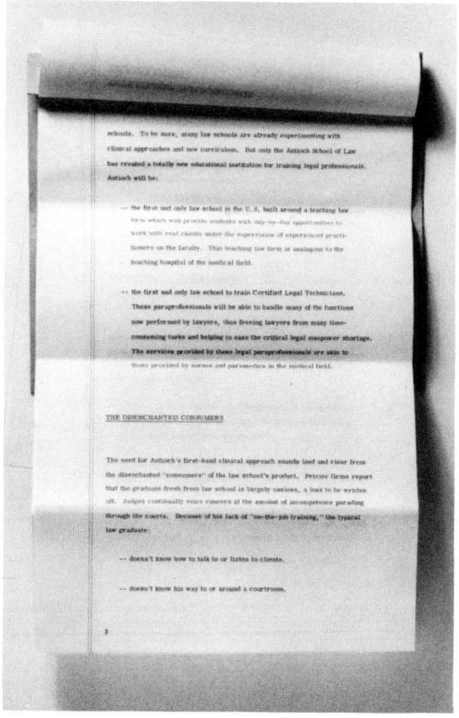
schools. To be sure, many law schools are already experimenting with clinical approaches and new curriculum. But only the Antioch School of Law has created a totally new educational institution for training legal professionals. Antioch will be:
-- the first and only law school in the U.S. built around a teaching law firm which will provide students with day-by-day opportunities to work with real clients under the supervision of experienced practitioners on the faculty. This teaching law firm is analagous to the teaching hospital of the medical field.
-- the first and only law school to train Certified Legal Technicians. These paraprofessionals will be able to handle many of the functions now performed by lawyers, thus freeing lawyers from many time-consuming tasks and helping to ease the critical legal manpower shortage. The services provided by these legal paraprofessionals are akin to those provided by nurses and paramedics in the medical field.
THE DISENCHANTED CONSUMERS
The need for Antioch's first-hand clinical approach sounds loud and clear from the disenchanted "consumers" of the law school's product. Private firms report that the graduate fresh from law school is largely useless, a loss to be written off. Judges continually voice concern at the amount of incompetence parading through the courts. Because of his lack of "on-the-job training," the typical law graduate:
-- doesn't know how to talk to or listen to clients.
-- doesn't know his way to or around a courtroom.
3

496

497

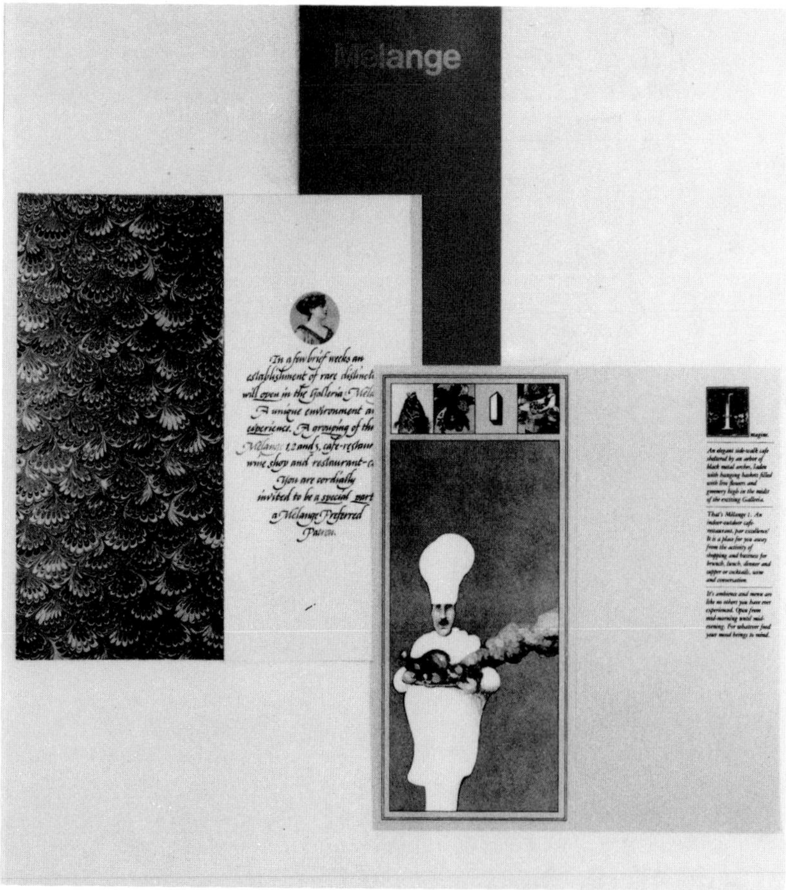
Melange

496
Art Director: Jack Odette
Writer: Jerrold Weitzman
Designers: Valerie Lieberman
Jack Odette
Agency: Sid Green Associates
Client: Antoich School of Law

497
Art Director: Jerry Herring
Copywriter: Jack Douglas
Designer: Jerry Herring
Artist: Jerry Jeanmard
Agency: Kelvin Group Partnership
Client: Melange

498
Art Director: Ted Schmitt
Copywriters: Ted Bell
Patti Mullen
Designer: Ted Schmitt
Photographer: Elliott Irwin
Agency: Tinker Dodge & Delano
Client: Australian Tourist Commission

499
Art Director: Jack Odette
Writer: Barrett J. Riordan
Designer: Jack Odette
Photographers: James Karales
Jeff Gould
Peter Gould
Burk Uzzle
Christa Armstrong
Joel Baldwin
Arthur Tress
Tim Kantor
Fred Lyon
Bruce Roberts
Joan Sudlow
Agency: Odette Associates, Inc.
Client: First National City Bank of New York

AUSTRALIA

Where the good old days are now.

"We'd rather cart you off for a beer than give you a glass of water.

We've got to save the water to keep the blasted geraniums alive."

"I'm Don Smyth, licensee of The Hero of Waterloo pub in Sydney. Because Australia has no aristocracy, I get wharfies, politicians, businessmen, students and roustabouts all talking together here. Especially at night, when two old fellas play the squeezebox and bush bass for singalongs. If you don't know the words to Waltzing Matilda, you'll learn them soon.

"Although we have some of the best beer in the world, pub-hopping's not the only thing we like to do. Here in Sydney alone, we have over 2,000 restaurants, 22 beaches, golf courses, tennis courts, horse racing, cricket and football arenas.

"When the sun goes down, head for King's Cross, Sydney's Montmartre. You'll hear every tongue on earth in the bohemian coffee houses, not to mention world famous jazz artists. If symphony and ballet are more to your liking, you'll find them first rate, too.

"Of course you can't miss our new Opera House. The architecture's so out of the ordinary, it's been practically unbuildable.

"Down in Melbourne there's a saying that they have all the ideas and we Sydneysiders just carry them out. That's nonsense of course, but I have to admit it's a right elegant city with its tree-lined, house-proud streets, financial center, fashionable shops, and Victorian Arts Centre. Me, I like to go down there for horse racing. Those Melburnians are so sports-minded that they made a public holiday out of a horse race, the Melbourne Cup.

"At night, there's dinner and dancing at hotels and restaurants, plus night clubs around St. Kilda. With many legitimate theatres, Melbourne's Australia's theatre center. During the spring and summer, there are concerts, ballet, opera and plays presented at Sidney Myer Music Bowl, a striking open-air amphitheatre.

"Back in 1912, we had an international contest to see who would plan our capital city, Canberra. One of your Frank Lloyd Wright's boys, Walter Burley Griffin, won. Even though it isn't finished yet, it's already one of the country's most exciting cities.

Blasted geraniums overlooking Sydney's Harbor.

"Try your luck at the opal fields around Lightning Ridge. Anyone can stake a claim for $1, but be careful you don't get opalitis. It's easy to get hooked. Of course, if you're not lucky you can buy opal on the fields or in Digger's Rest Pub. There's dances out back every night and wild celebrations when someone strikes. And since they don't get many Yanks there, they love to tell you stories of blokes like Jimmy the Murderer, who killed his pet monkey in a rage and never forgave himself.

"Or take a trip to a sheep station like Oxford and join in the roundup and droving. Then come back to the homestead for a barbecue.

"Just across the Bass Strait is Tasmania, so different from the rest of Australia that it seems more like England. Hobart, the capital of

498

499

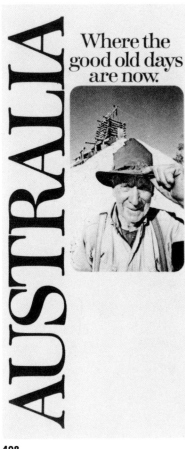

Waste Disposal and Pollution

Pollution is nothing new. Nearly every human activity produces residue of some sort. Cutting a piece of wood leaves sawdust, washing one's hands creates dirty water, and simply breathing produces carbon dioxide. Nature has an enormous capacity to assimilate and neutralize waste material. But in recent decades, as cities and their surrounding areas have become more densely populated, as industrial processes have grown increasingly complex, and as the nation's living standards have reached ever higher levels, disposing of the inevitable residue has become a major problem.

In Western countries, the discharge of untreated human and industrial sewage into the waterways and the discharge of gaseous waste into the air now seriously disturb the public, whose mood has changed drastically in just a few years. Only a short time ago, from Pennsylvania to Northern Italy, people in mining towns and factory cities accepted dirt and stench without question or complaint. Today, even the Japanese seem to have reached their limit, though they still often live amid conditions of pollution that most Americans would not tolerate.

The problem has become acute because the normal economic forces that actively help determine social behavior have not been brought to bear on waste disposal decisions. The rivers, seas and air have been readily available free of charge for use as public dumping grounds. Since the producer of waste tries to rid himself of it as cheaply as possible, these seemingly costless facilities have been employed as a matter of course. The best way to correct the consequent abuses, as will be seen, is to harness the powerful forces of the marketplace that, until now, have been absent.

The Economics of Pollution

Pollution is an injustice because, while people have no direct vote in the waste disposal decision, they may be directly affected by the result. Whenever an individual imposes an undesired burden upon others, the total, or social, costs of his actions exceed the costs he must bear privately. Ending this divergence between social and private costs is the key to pollution control.

A familiar example of cost divergence is the factory which dumps its wastes into a river at no cost to itself and contaminates the drinking water of communities downstream. There are many other, more ordinary examples of individual actions that produce detrimental side effects: the person who smokes a cheap cigar in a crowded room, the suburbanite who, to the dismay of his neighbors, raises chickens on his front yard. Costs such as these are common to our everyday world; the point at which they become a problem depends upon the amount of harm and the number affected.

Pollution is a major problem today, not because of some moral failure of our society, but because our economy does not compel polluters to assume the costs they inflict upon others. In our economic

500
Art Director: Einar Vinje
Writers: Jonathan Thompson
Karl Ludvigsen
Designer: Einar Vinje
Photographer: Jesse Alexander
Publisher: Bond/Parkhurst Publications
Client: Bond/Parkhurst Publications

501
Art Director: Willy Fleckhaus
Writer: Willy Fleckhaus
Designer: Willy Fleckhaus
Photographers: Tassilo Trost
David Hamilton
Publisher: Ciba-Geigy, Basel
Client: Ilford Fotochemie

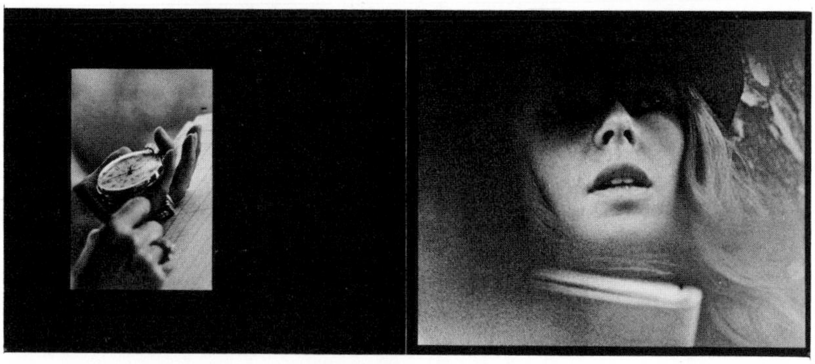

500

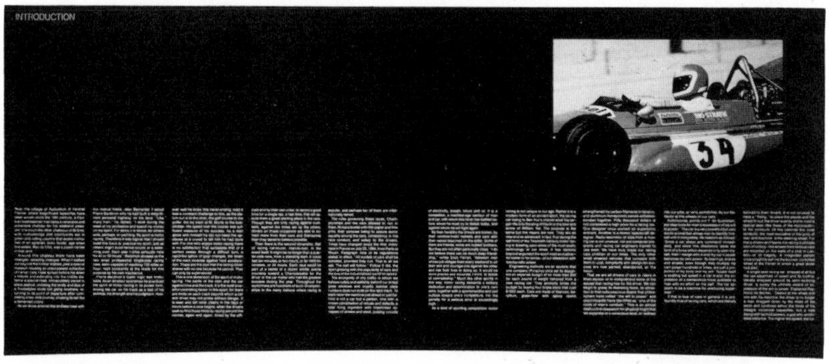

501

In the Summertime.
A classical Hamilton photo
from his book "Dreams of a
Young Girl". Details, details,
flowers, skin, curls, bonnets,
light, warmth of a summer
day, remembered.
Ideal specimens for a
pleasant book.

Unis.
Un Hamilton classique,
cette photo tirée de son
livre célèbre de jeunes filles...
Une abondance de détails,
où le dessin de la peau,
le dessin du contrôle
flou des reflex.
que l'ombre négligemment
estompés.
Souvenirs d'un jour d'été,
charme, comme une
image d'un ouvrage d'art
sur la photographie.

In Sommer.
Ein klassisches
Hamilton-Photo aus
seinem Buch
«Mädchenträumes.
Viele Details:
Haus, Blonden, Haar.
Erinnerungen
an den Sommer
Licht, Wärme.
Ein Photo als Vorlage
für ein Prachtsbuch.

D'estate.
Una classica foto di
Hamilton e il suo libro
«Sogni di una ragazzina».
Molti dettagli: l'Pelle, fiori,
capelli.
Ricordo sull'estate, luce,
calore.
Una foto d'introduzione
ad un libro di fotografia.

Verano.
Una clásica foto Hamilton
tomada de su libro «Sueños
de muchacha».
Abundancia de detalles:
piel, flores, cabello. Recuerdos de un verano, luz, calor.
Foto para una obra de arte
fotográfica.

På sommaren.
Ett klassiskt Hamiltonbild
ur hans bok «Drömmar om
en Ung Flicka».
Mängd detaljer: hud,
blommor, hår.
Minnen av sommaren,
ljus, värme.
Ett foto som inpress till
en fotobok.

ILFOMAR A1

TEAGUE TRIST
KRISTO
ILFOBROM

DAVID HAMILTON
SORA
ILFOMAR

ILFOBROM A H2

Each photographer shown
here at their his her work.

Un album Ilford à l'affiche
de deux photographes de
réputation internationale:
David Hamilton et
Teague Trist.

Dieses Ilford-Album
präsentiert zwei inter-
national Photographen:
David Hamilton und
Teague Trist.

Questo Album Ilford
presenta due fotografi
internazionali:
David Hamilton e
Teague Trist.

Este album Ilford presenta
a dos fotógrafos
internacionales:
David Hamilton y
Teague Trist.

Det här fotoalbumet
presenterar två
internationella fotografer:
David Hamilton och
Teague Trist.

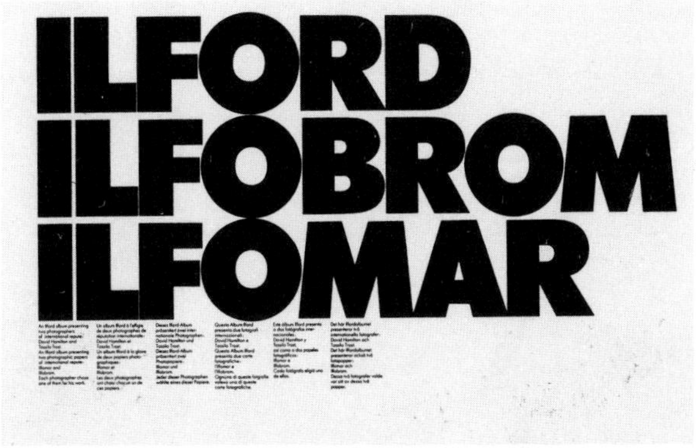

ILFORD
ILFOBROM
ILFOMAR

502
Art Director: Mickey Tender
Copywriter: Pat Cuningham
Designer: Mabey Trousdell
Artists: Jim Smith
George Parrish
Paul Blakey
Photographer: Cailor/Resnick
Agency: N. W. Ayer & Son, Inc.
Client: United States Army

503
Art Director: Richard Danne
Writer: J. Alexander McGhie
Designer: Richard Danne
Photographer: Robert Pastner
Agency: McGhie Associates, Inc.
Client: William Blanchard Co.

502

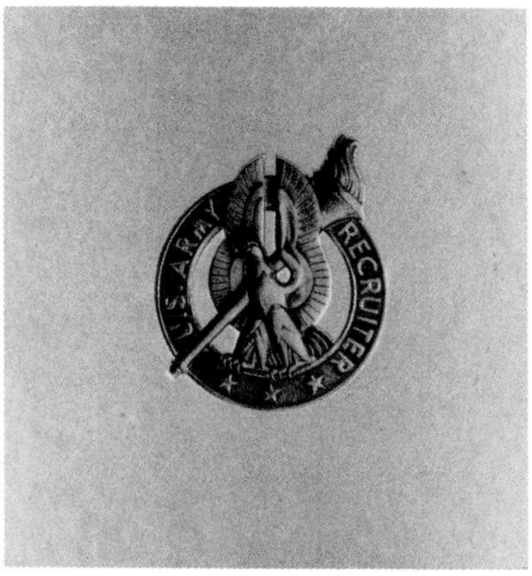

This is what your prospects will be reading the next few months.

503

Blanchard

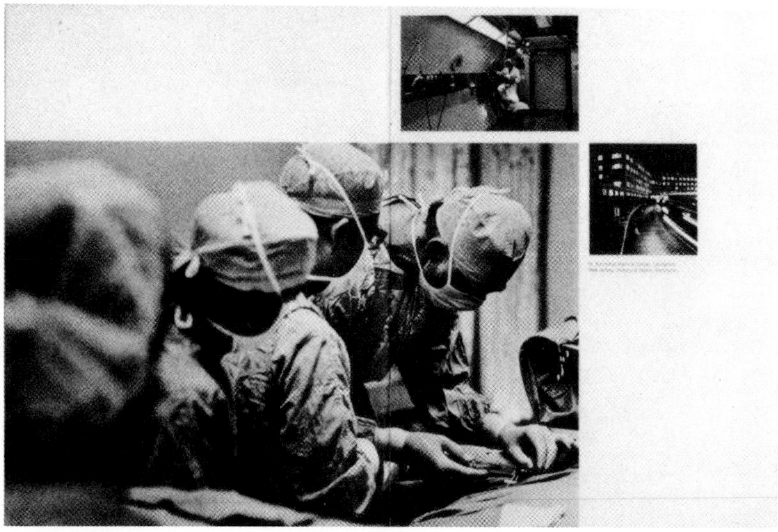

Packaging

504
Art Director: Eugene J. Grossman
Designer: Willi Kunz
Agency: Anspach Grossman Portugal Inc.
Client: The Meadville Corporation

505
Art Directors: Hal Frazier
Paul Hauge
Designers: Hal Frazier
Paul Hauge
Artists: Hal Frazier
Paul Hauge
Copywriter: Newmarket Design Associates Staff
Agency: Neumarket Design Associates
Client: Karzen Corporation

504

505

Packaging

506
Art Director: Jerome Gould
Designer: Jerome Gould
Artist: Jerome Gould
Copywriter: Robert Marona
Agency: Gould & Associates
Client: Morton Salt Company

507
Art Directors: Michael Peters
Ian Butcher
Designers: Michael Peters
Ian Butcher
Geoffrey Hockey
Artists: Tony Meuwissen
Hargreave Hands
George Hardie
Bob Laurie
John Gorham
Alan Manham
Philip Castle
Barry Craddock
Arthur Robins
Camden Play Centre
Keishn H. Careieu
Agency: Michael Peters & Partners
Client: Winsor & Newton, Limited

506

507

508
Art Director: Glen Christensen
Designer: Glen Christensen
Artist: Glen Christensen
Agency: The Buddah Group
Client: Curtom Records

509
Art Directors: Art Goodman
Saul Bass & Associates
Designers: Mamoru Shimokochi
Saul Bass & Associates
Artists: Mamoru Shimokochi
Saul Bass & Associates
Agency: Saul Bass & Associates
Client: Quaker Oats Co., Inc.

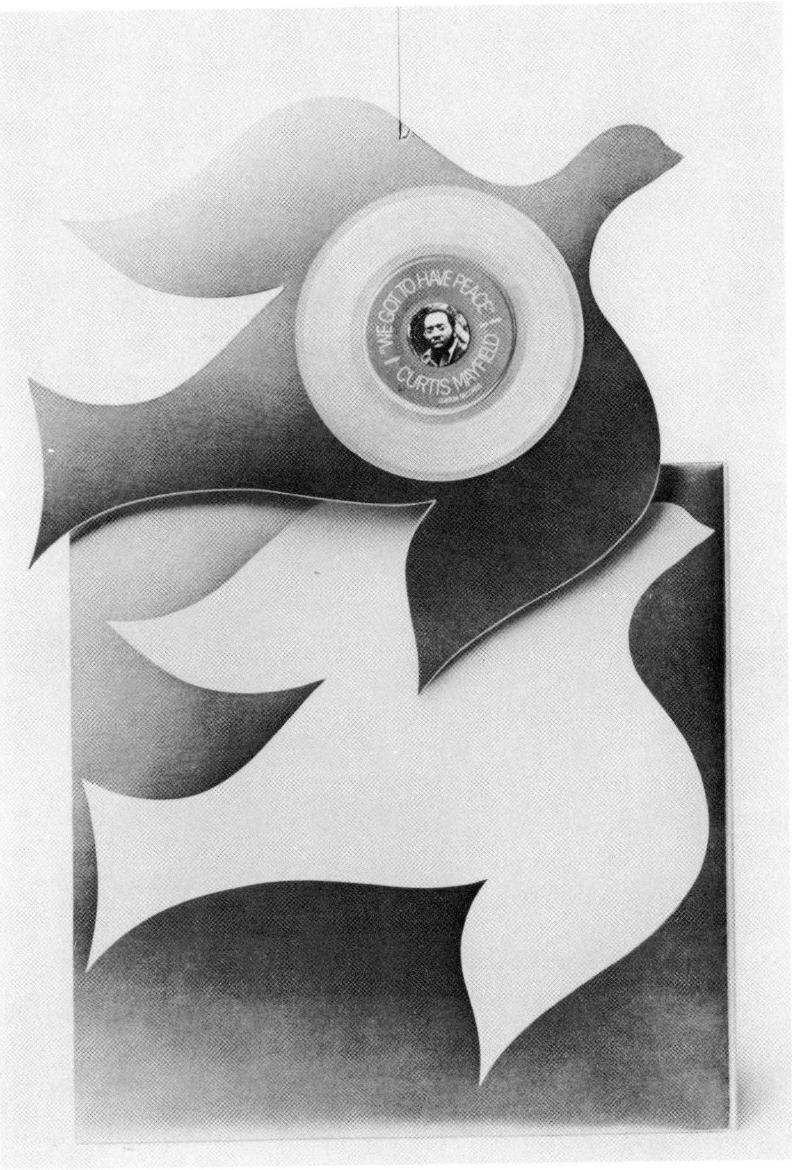

508

509

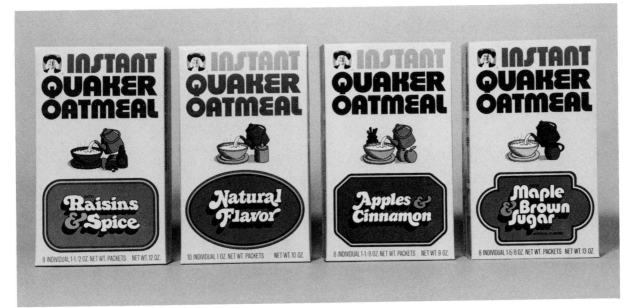

510

511

512

513

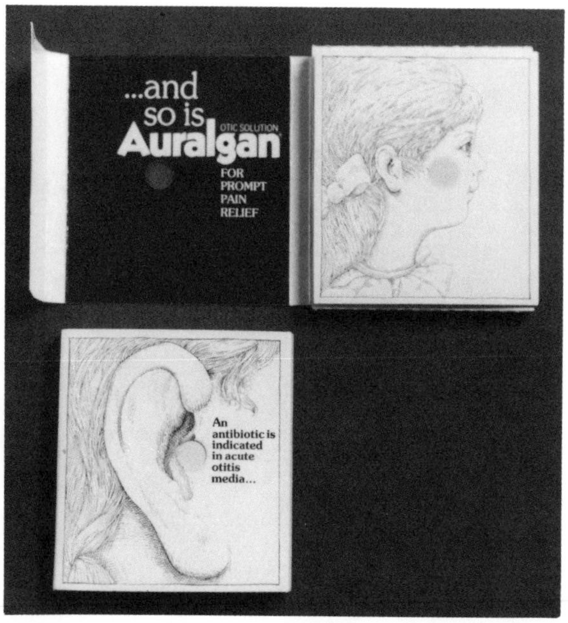

Packaging

510
Art Director: Lou Dorfsman
Designers: David November
Akihiko Seki
Artist: Akihiko Seki
Agency: CBS/Broadcast Group
Client: CBS News

511
Art Director: William R. Tobias
Designer: William R. Tobias
Photographer: Leonard Soned
Client: Birthday Book

512
Art Director: Alfonso Marino
Photographer: Charles Kirk
Copywriter: Martin Friedman
Agency: Herbert Arthur Morris Advertising
Client: Exquisite Form Industries

513
Art Director: Jim McFarland
Designer: Jim McFarland
Artist: Tom di Grazia
Copywriter: Mike Norton
Agency: Sudler & Hennessey, Inc.
Client: Ayerst Labs.

514 Gold Award
Art Director: Meg Crane
Designers: Ira Sturtevant
Meg Crane
Photographer: Ivor Parry
Copywriter: Ira Sturtevant
Agency: Ponzi & Weill
Client: The Flavorbank Company, Inc.

515
Art Director: Irv Koons
Designers: Irv Koons
Frank Weitzman
Artist: Frank Weitzman
Client: American Sound & Tape Corporation

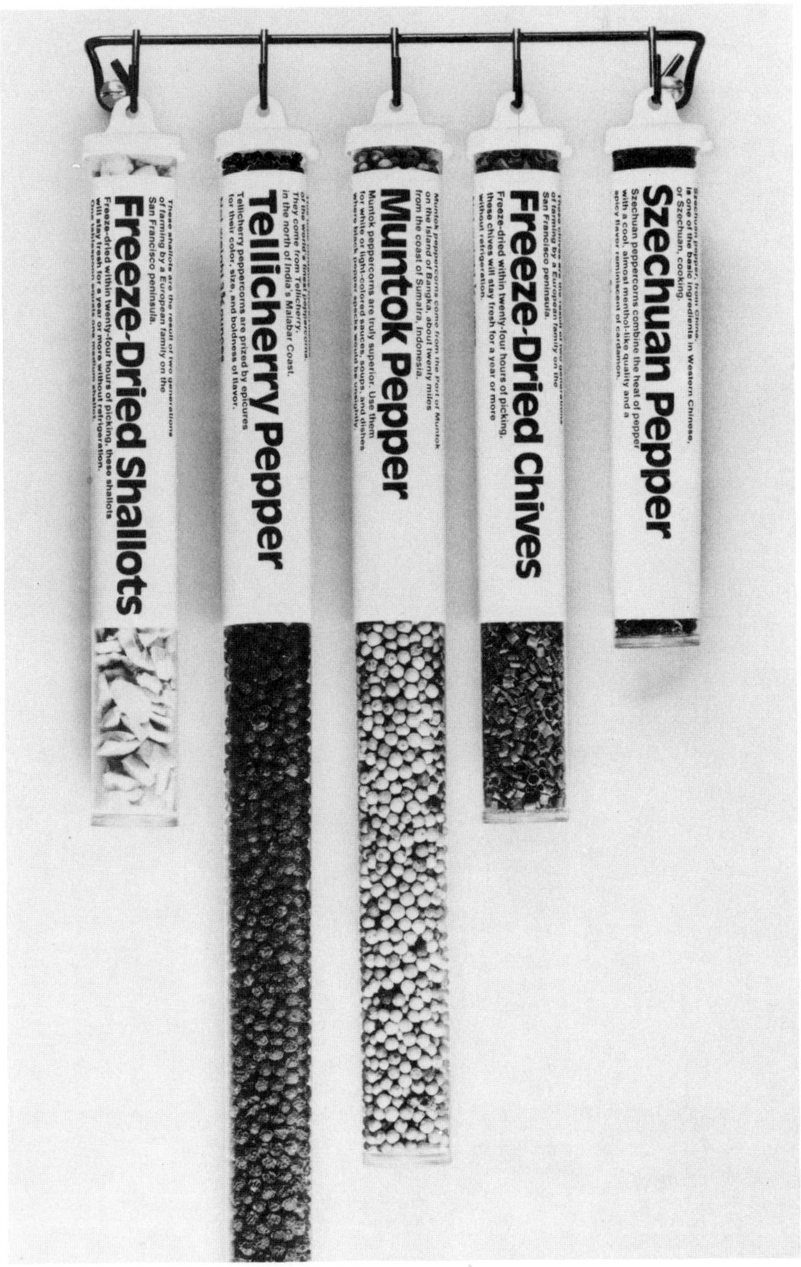

514

515

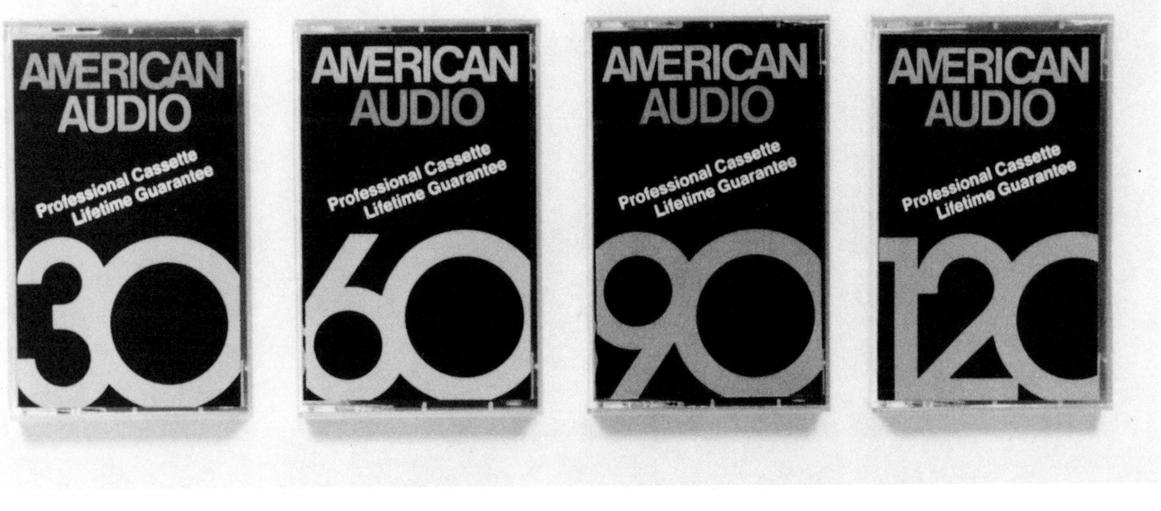

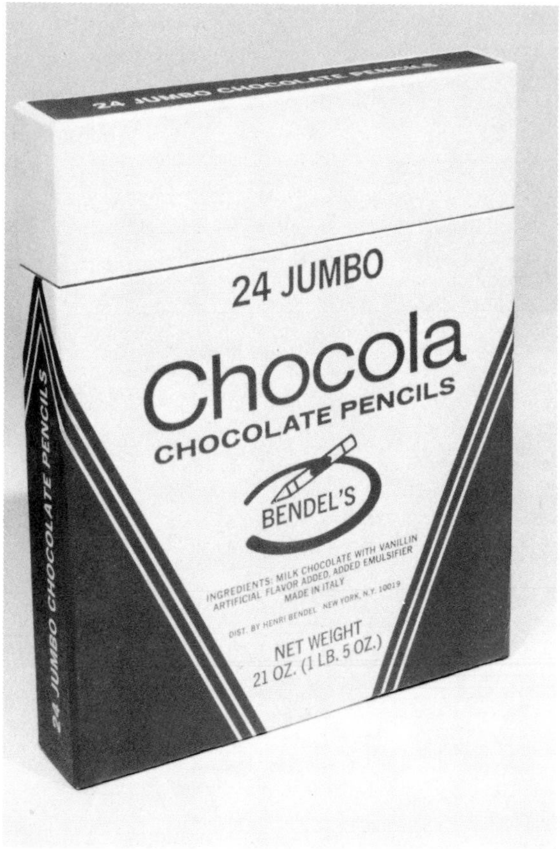
24 JUMBO CHOCOLATE PENCILS
24 JUMBO
Chocola
CHOCOLATE PENCILS
BENDEL'S
INGREDIENTS: MILK CHOCOLATE WITH VANILLIN
ARTIFICIAL FLAVOR ADDED, ADDED EMULSIFIER
MADE IN ITALY
DIST. BY HENRI BENDEL · NEW YORK, N.Y. 10019
NET WEIGHT
21 OZ. (1 LB. 5 OZ.)
24 JUMBO CHOCOLATE PENCILS

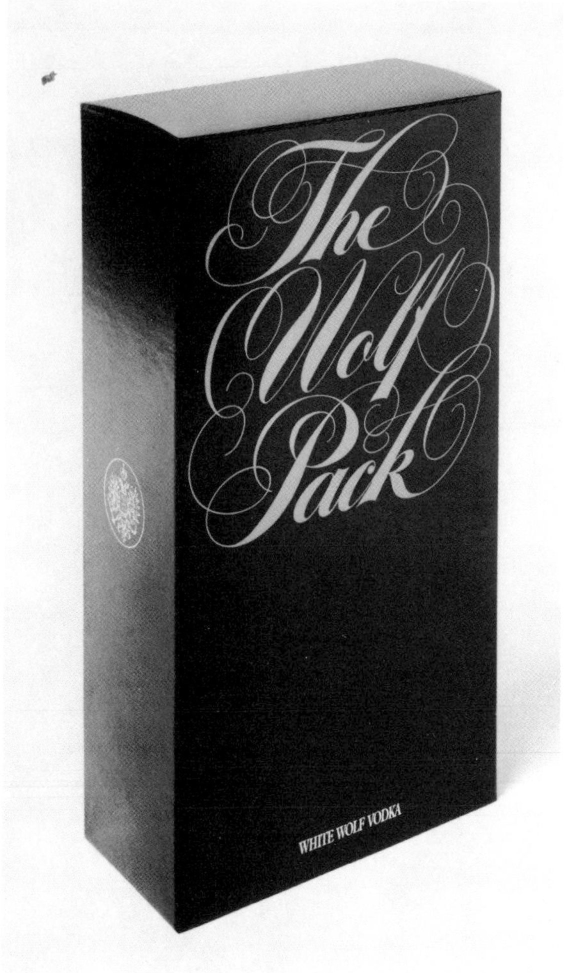
The Wolf Pack
WHITE WOLF VODKA

516 517

518

WHEAT
GERM
BREAD
SOYA
BEAN
BREAD
NATURAL FOODS
OROWEAT BAKING CO.
SAN FRANCISCO, CALIF. 94080 U.S.A.
net weight 16 ounces (1 pound)
SPROUTED
WHEAT
BREAD
STONE GROUND

Packaging

516 Silver Award
Art Director: Stanley Church
Designers: George Gropper
Pat Slade
Copywriter: George Gropper
Agency: Stanley Church Inc.
Client: Food For Thought

517
Art Directors: Jerry Berman
Gene Icardi
Designers: Jerry Berman
Gene Icardi
Artist: Richard Leech
Copywriter: Len Alaria
Agency: Berman, Icardi Inc.
Client: House of Sobel

518
Art Director: Richard C. Runyon
Designers: Richard C. Runyon
Julie Morris
Artist: Julie Morris
Client: Oroweat Baking Company

519

520

521

519
Art Director: J. Michael Essex
Designer: J. Michael Essex
Photographer: John Bilecky
Copywriter: J. Michael Essex
Agency: WQED Design Centre
Client: Earth Rise Designs Inc.

520
Designers: Frank Ginsberg
Eric Small
H. L. Vander Berg
Copywriter: Lou Linder
Agency: The Marschalk Company
Client: Coca-Cola, U.S.A.

521
Art Director: John DiGianni
Designer: Gianninoto Associates, Inc.
Agency: Gianninoto Associates, Inc.
Client: Beatrice Foods Company

522
Designer: Helmut Krone
Agency: Case & McGrath Inc.
Client: The Mennen Company

523
Art Director: Raymond Lee
Designer: Raymond Lee
Retoucher: Ron Hills
Agency: Raymond Lee & Associates Ltd.
Client: Mead Johnson, Canada

524
Art Director: Herb Lubalin
Designer: Herb Lubalin
Agency: Martin Landey, Arlow Advertising, Inc.
Client: Mennen Company

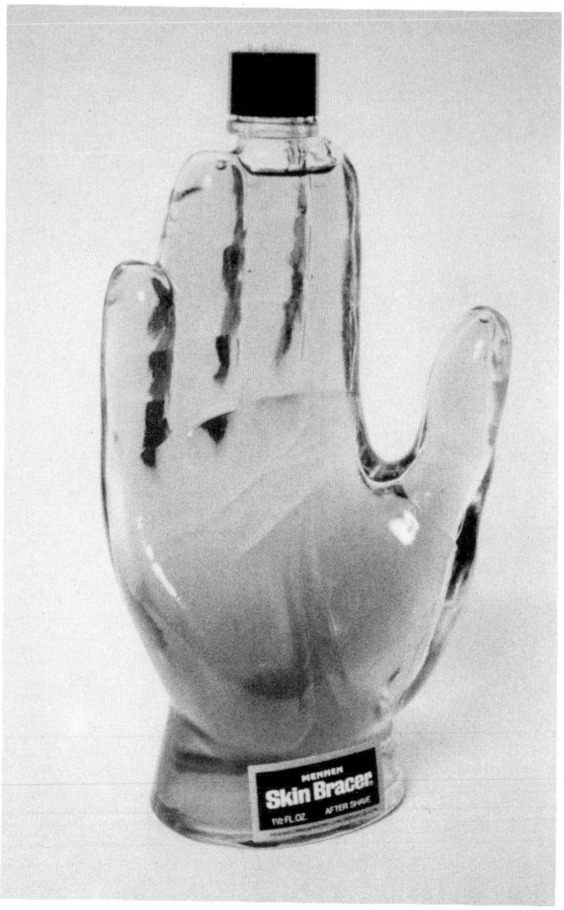

522

523

524

525

525
Art Director: Annegret Beier
Designer: Annegret Beier
Artist: Peter Weiss
Agency: Lubalin, Delpire et Cie.
Client: Corolle

526
Art Directors: Don Weller
Dennis Juett
Designer: Don Weller
Artists: Don Weller
Jim Van Noy
Agency: Weller & Juett Inc.
Client: McCulloch Corporation

527
Art Director: Annegret Beier
Designer: Annegret Beier
Artist: John Alcorn
Agency: Delpire Advico
Client: Corolle

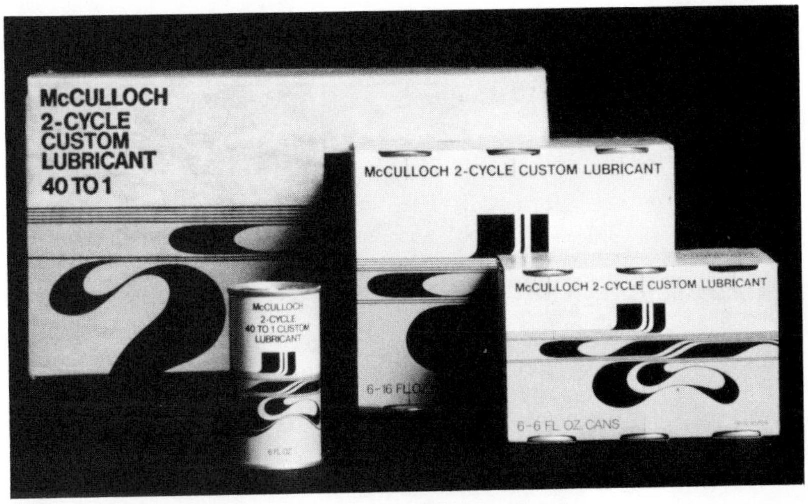

526

527

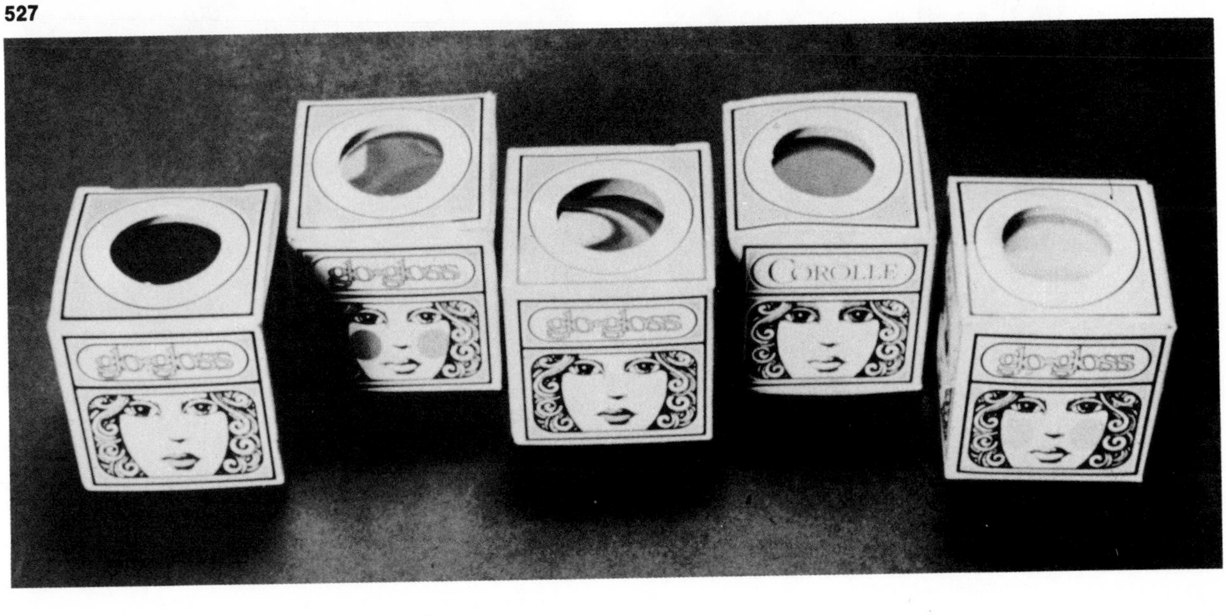

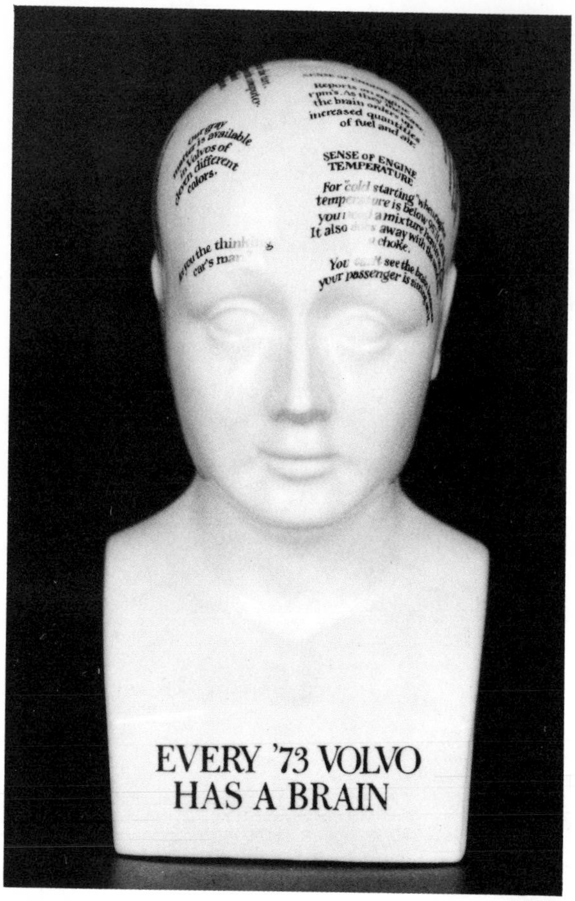

528

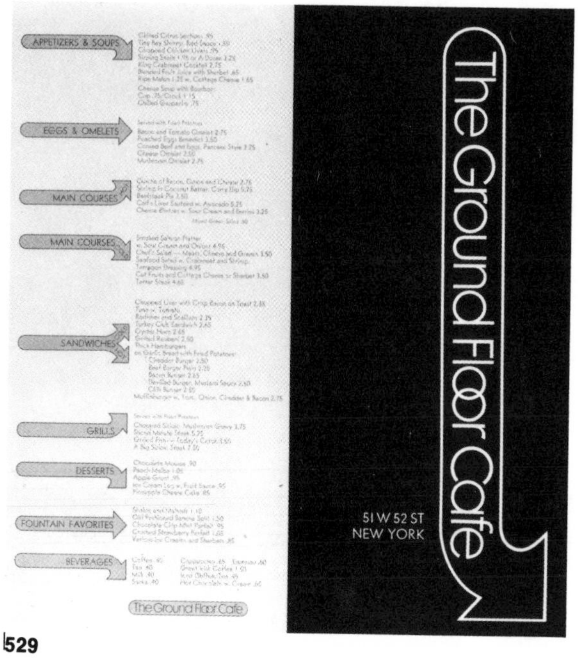

529

530

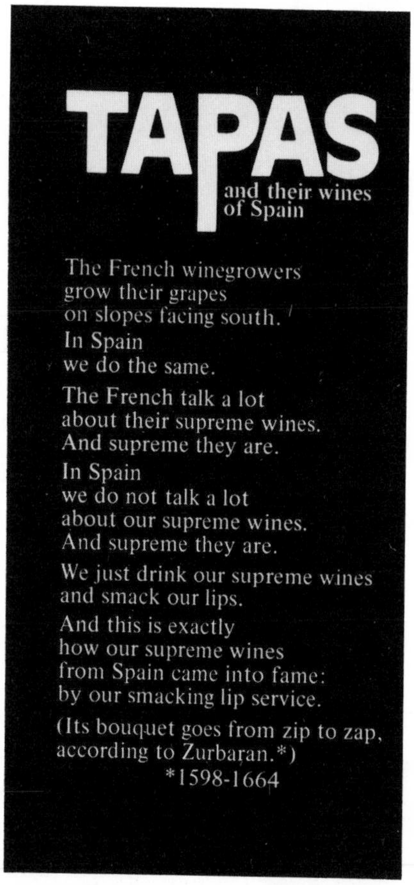
TAPAS
and their wines
of Spain
The French winegrowers
grow their grapes
on slopes facing south.
In Spain
we do the same.
The French talk a lot
about their supreme wines.
And supreme they are.
In Spain
we do not talk a lot
about our supreme wines.
And supreme they are.
We just drink our supreme wines
and smack our lips.
And this is exactly
how our supreme wines
from Spain came into fame:
by our smacking lip service.
(Its bouquet goes from zip to zap,
according to Zurbaran.*)
*1598-1664

531

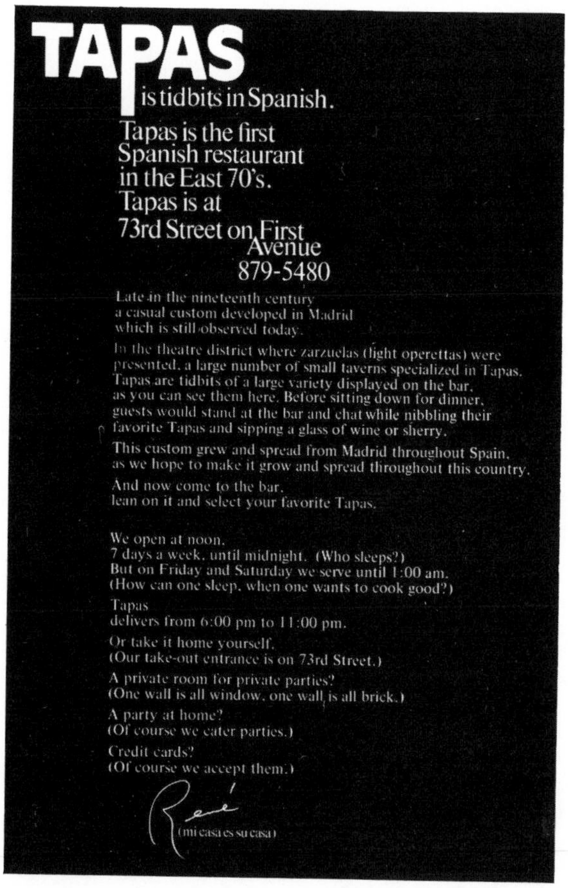
TAPAS
is tidbits in Spanish.
Tapas is the first
Spanish restaurant
in the East 70's.
Tapas is at
73rd Street on First
Avenue
879-5480
Late in the nineteenth century
a casual custom developed in Madrid
which is still observed today.
In the theatre district where zarzuelas (light operettas) were
presented, a large number of small taverns specialized in Tapas.
Tapas are tidbits of a large variety displayed on the bar,
as you can see them here. Before sitting down for dinner,
guests would stand at the bar and chat while nibbling their
favorite Tapas and sipping a glass of wine or sherry.
This custom grew and spread from Madrid throughout Spain,
as we hope to make it grow and spread throughout this country.
And now come to the bar,
lean on it and select your favorite Tapas.
We open at noon,
7 days a week, until midnight. (Who sleeps?)
But on Friday and Saturday we serve until 1:00 am.
(How can one sleep, when one wants to cook good?)
Tapas
delivers from 6:00 pm to 11:00 pm.
Or take it home yourself.
(Our take-out entrance is on 73rd Street.)
A private room for private parties?
(One wall is all window, one wall is all brick.)
A party at home?
(Of course we cater parties.)
Credit cards?
(Of course we accept them.)
René
(mi casa es su casa)

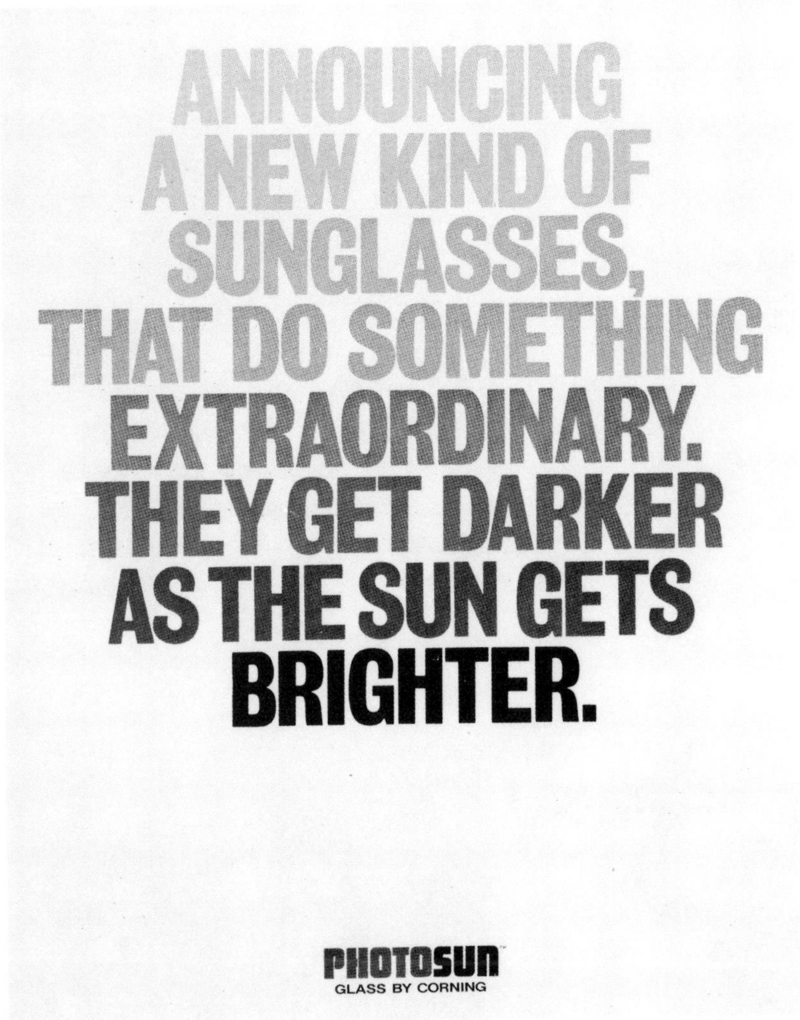
ANNOUNCING
A NEW KIND OF
SUNGLASSES,
THAT DO SOMETHING
EXTRAORDINARY.
THEY GET DARKER
AS THE SUN GETS
BRIGHTER.
PHOTOSUN
GLASS BY CORNING

532

533

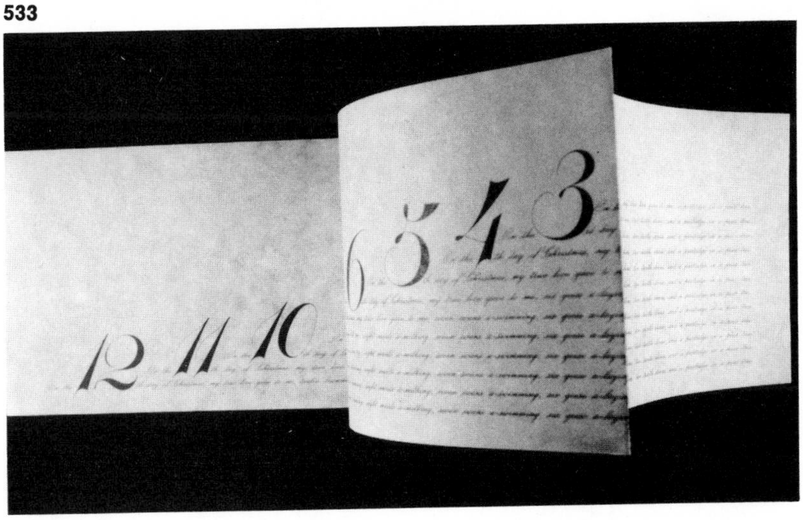

528
Art Director: Joe Schindelman
Copywriter: Ray Myers
Designer: Joe Schindelman
Agency: Scali, McCabe, Sloves, Inc.
Client: Volvo, Inc.

529
Art Director: Kurt Weihs
Designer: Kurt Weihs
Artist: Kurt Weihs
Agency: Lois Holland Callaway Inc.
Client: Restaurant Associates

530
Art Director: Dennis Mazzella
Copywriters: Barbara Brenner
Kurt Weihs
Designer: Kurt Weihs
Agency: Brenner, Mazzella, Weihs
Client: Tapas Restaurant

531
Art Director: Kurt Weihs
Copywriters: Barbara Brenner
Kurt Weihs
Designer: Dennis Mazzella
Agency: Brenner, Mazzella, Weihs
Client: Tapas Restaurant

532
Art Director: Rod Capawana
Copywriter: Rod Capawana
Designer: Rod Capawana
Agency: Warner, Bicking & Fenwick, Inc.
Client: Corning Optical

533 Silver Award
Art Director: Herb Lubalin
Designer: Herb Lubalin
Artist: Tom Carnase
Agency: Lubalin, Smith, Carnase Inc.
Client: Georg Jensen

'72
IT'S A GREAT YEAR
ANY WAY YOU LOOK AT IT

534

Cafe America!

535

536

Suppertime!
Meet Old-fashioned
Mr. Jennings
(the ice-cream parlor man)
Always be polite to Mr. Jennings.
He'll keep us young forever.
He doesn't care for war,
he doesn't care for jewels,
he doesn't care for architecture.
Mr. Jennings knows what counts.
Sodas.
And heavenly sweets.
Ethereal creams.
Blasphemous blendings of
delectable fruits.
(And it's a wondrous place
to spend lunchtime, dinnertime–
even suppertime.)
No matter how many years you live,
everything in Mr. Jennings' place
tastes as good as treats did
when you were a kid.
Guaranteed.
Le Sandwich
1) Mr. Jennings' Club 3.25
2) Sliced Turkey (white meat) 2.45
3) Mr. Jennings' Junior Club 2.65
4) Imported Danish Ham & Swiss Cheese 2.45
5) Tunafish, Sliced Egg with Tomato 2.65
6) Steakburger
served with cabbage slaw 2.25
7) Cheeseburger
served with cabbage slaw 2.55
8) Chicken Salad, Tomato & Lettuce 2.25
9) Grilled Cheese, Bacon & Tomato
center dish cabbage slaw 2.45
Les Salads
A) Mr. Jennings' Fresh Fruit Bowl
with cottage cheese 3.25
B) Chicken Salad
served with fresh fruit, lettuce & tomato 3.25
C) Salmon Platter
individual can salmon, egg, tomato
& cabbage slaw 3.35
D) Tunafish Salad
served with sliced egg, lettuce & tomato
& cabbage slaw 3.25
(all our salads served with melba toast)
Mr. Jennings' Scream Delights
Scream Surprise 3.35
Scream Banana Split 4.25
Scream Fresh Fruit Sundae 3.35
Scream Fudge, Butterscotch 3.35
Scream Flaming Josephine 3.25
Scream Tricolour 3.25
(open evenings til midnight)

Point-of-Sale

534
Art Director: Herb Lubalin
Designer: Herb Lubalin
Artist: Tom Carnase
Agency: Lubalin, Smith, Carnase, Inc.
Client: Georg Jensen

535
Art Director: Kurt Weihs
Designer: Kurt Weihs
Artist: Pat Valenti
Agency: Lois/Chajet Design Group
Client: Restaurant Associates

536
Art Director: George Lois
Designer: Tom Courtos
Artists: George Lois
Tom Courtos
Agency: Lois/Chajet Design Group
Client: Old-fashioned Mr. Jennings

537
Art Director: Kurt Weihs
Copywriter: Ron Holland
Designer: Kurt Weihs
Artist: Kurt Weihs
Agency: Lois/Chajet Design Group
Client: Marriott

538
Art Director: Dennis Mazzella
Copywriter: Ron Holland
Designer: Dennis Mazzella
Agency: Lois/Chajet Design Group
Client: Marriott

539
Art Director: Sam Scali
Copywriter: Ed McCabe
Designer: Sam Scali
Agency: Scali, McCabe, Sloves, Inc.
Client: Barney's

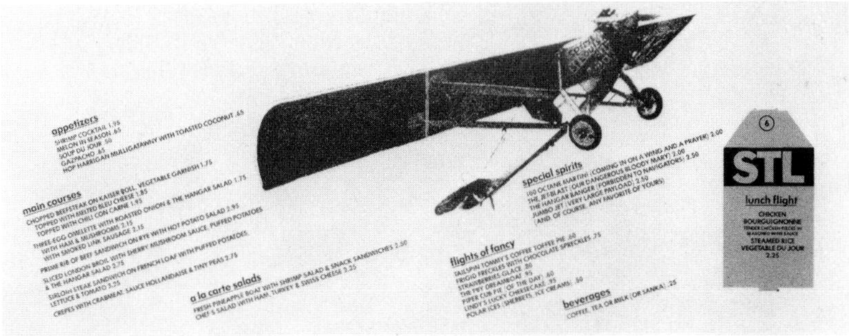

537

538

539

540

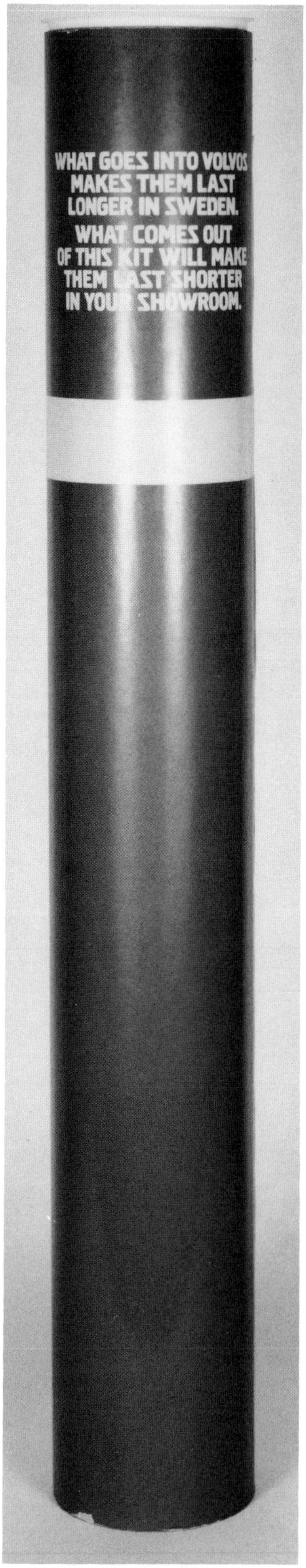

541

Point-of-Sale

540
Art Director: Joe Schindelman
Copywriter: Ray Myers
Designer: Joe Schindelman
Agency: Scali, McCabe, Sloves, Inc.
Client: Volvo, Inc.

541 Gold Award
Art Director: Bill Berenter
Copywriter: Tom Nathan
Designer: Bill Berenter
Agency: Scali, McCabe, Sloves, Inc.
Client: Volvo, Inc.

542
Art Director: Howard C. Grant
Copywriter: Charles R. Tyson, Jr.
Designers: Howard C. Grant
Dante E. Evangelista
Artist: Dante E. Evangelista
Agency: N. W. Ayer & Son, Inc.
Ayer Design
Client: First Pennsylvania Bank

543
Art Director: Mike Gaines
Copywriter: John Weibusch
Designer: Peter Palombi
Artist: Peter Palombi
Agency: National Football League
Properties Inc.
Client: National Football League

544
Art Director: George Lois
Designer: Kurt Weihs
Photographer: Kurt Weihs
Agency: Lois/Chajet Design Group
Client: Noxell

Target Saving:
A unique system designed to organize, remind and reward you into saving.
Target Saving starts here. Take a free starter kit today.
Your target might be:
Home
Emergency
Wedding
Travel
Retirement
Vacation
Moving
Home Remodeling
A New Kitchen
Education
Second Home
Car
Anniversaries
Anything
TARGET SAVING
TARGET SAVING

542

SUPER BOWL VI
AFC VS. NFC FOR THE NFL CHAMPIONSHIP
AND THE VINCE LOMBARDI TROPHY
Miami vs. Dallas
Sunday, January 16, 1972 • 1:30 P.M. Tulane Stadium, New Orleans

543

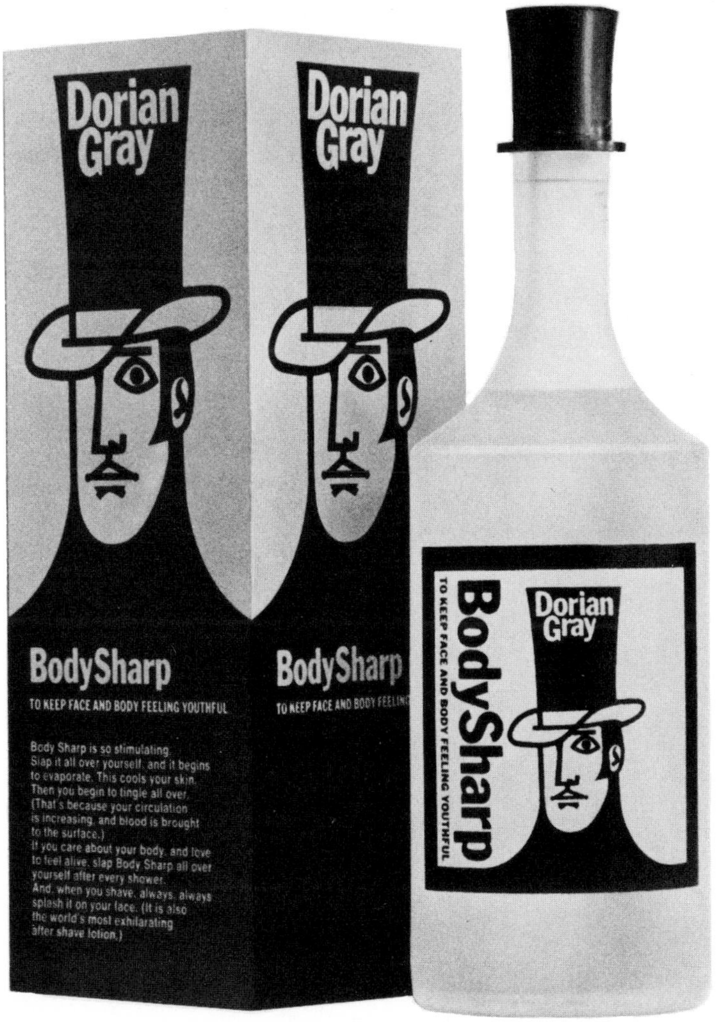
Dorian Gray
Dorian Gray
BodySharp
TO KEEP FACE AND BODY FEELING YOUTHFUL
Body Sharp is so stimulating.
Slap it all over yourself, and it begins
to evaporate. This cools your skin.
Then you begin to tingle all over.
(That's because your circulation
is increasing, and blood is brought
to the surface.)
If you care about your body, and love
to feel alive, slap Body Sharp all over
yourself after every shower.
And, when you shave, always, always
splash it on your face. (It is also
the world's most exhilarating
after shave lotion.)
BodySharp
Dorian Gray
BodySharp
TO KEEP FACE AND BODY FEELING YOUTHFUL

544

545
Art Director: Bill Telford
Copywriter: Joan McDonald
Designer: Fluid Drive Studio
Photographer: Charles White III
Agency: Telford Assts.
Client: Questor Corporation

546
Designer: Peter Harrison
Copywriter: SCM Public Relations Dept.
Photographer: Wolf von dem Bussche
Client: SCM Corporation

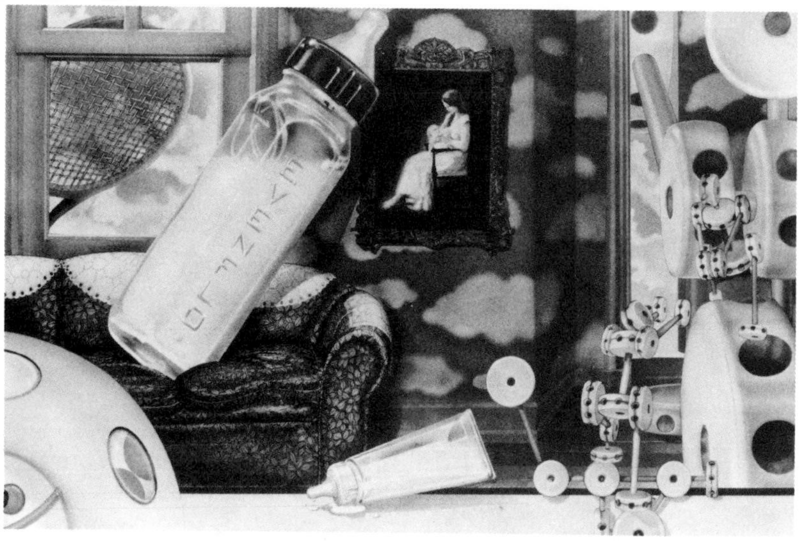

545

546

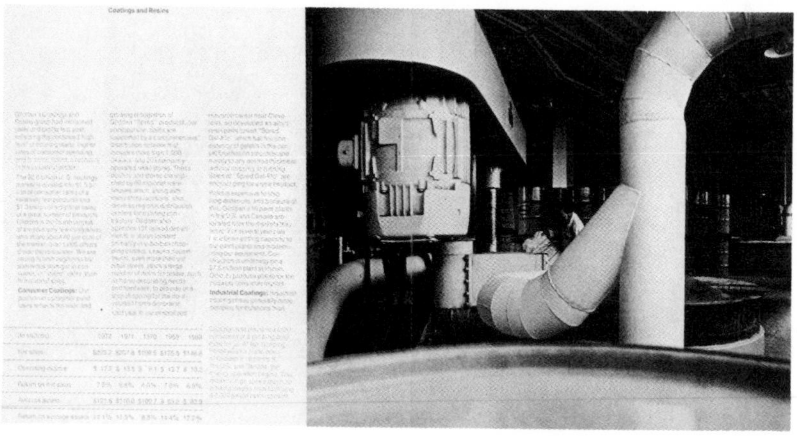

How Cybermatics Inc. avoided
the 6 fatal mistakes that
caught up with
computer companies in 1971.

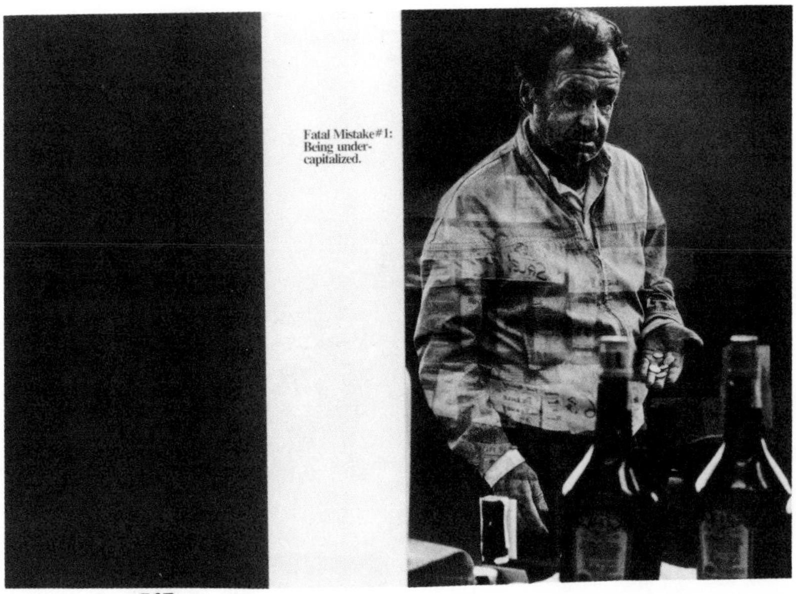
Fatal Mistake #1:
Being under-
capitalized.

547

548

The Flying Tiger Corporation · 1971 Annual Report
COMMON
SEE REVERSE FOR
CERTAIN DEFINITIONS
COUNTERSIGNED:
BY
AUTHORIZED SIG

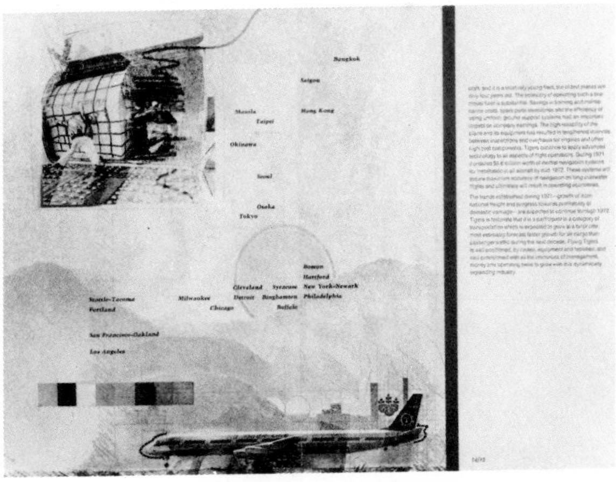

547 Silver Award
Art Director: Harry Webber
Copywriter: Bob Taft
Photographer: Manny Gonzalez
Agency: Case & McGrath Inc.
Client: Cybermatics Inc.

548
Art Director: Robert Miles Runyan
Copywriter: Ed Rees
Designer: Rusty Kay
Artist: Marty Gunsaullus
Photographer: Steve Kahn
Agency: Robert Miles Runyan & Associates
Client: The Flying Tiger Corporation

Annual Reports

549
Art Director: William R. Tobias
Copywriter: Crosby-Kelly, Ltd. Staff
Designer: William R. Tobias Design
Artist: Mike Menoogian
Photographer: Wolf Von Dem Busche
Client: Esterline Corporation

550
Art Director: Robert Miles Runyan
Copywriter: Lynda Olsen
Designer: Scott Reid
Photographer: Robert Stevens
Agency: Robert Miles Runyan & Associates
Client: Environmental Systems International

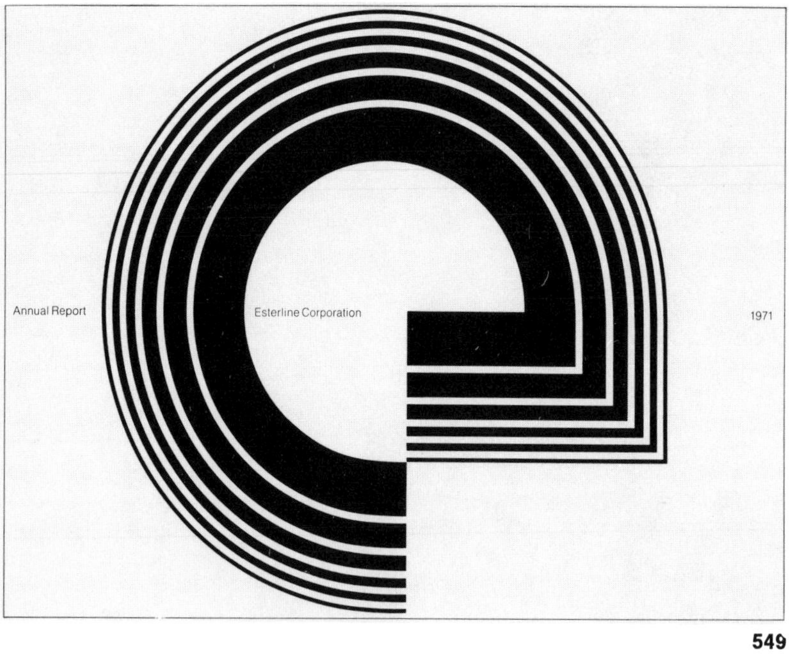

549

550

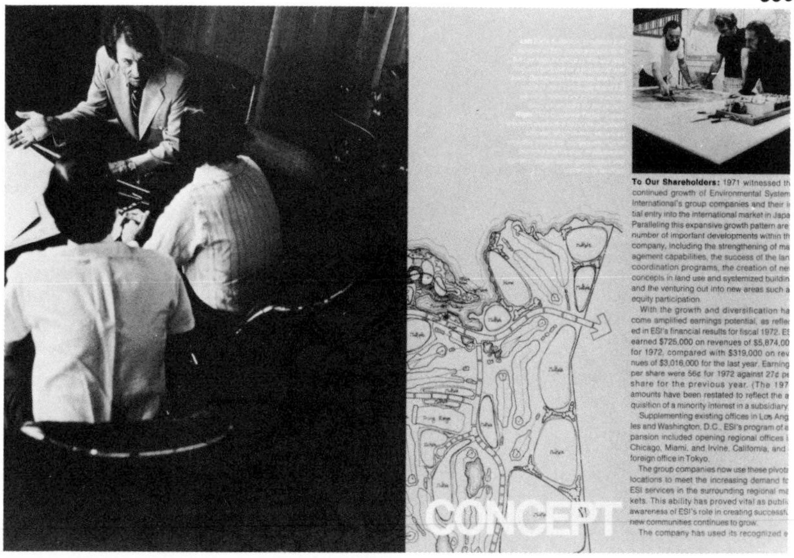

551
Art Directors: Woody Pirtle
Stan Richards
Copywriter: Dave Crellin
Designer: Woody Pirtle
Photographer: Greg Booth
Agency: The Richards Group
Glenn Public Relations
Client: Centex Corporation

552
Art Director: Robert Miles Runyan
Copywriter: Ruder & Finn
Designer: Gary Hinsche
Artist: Dick Ellescas
Photographer: Bob Stevens
Agency: Robert Miles Runyan & Associates
Client: Mattel, Inc.

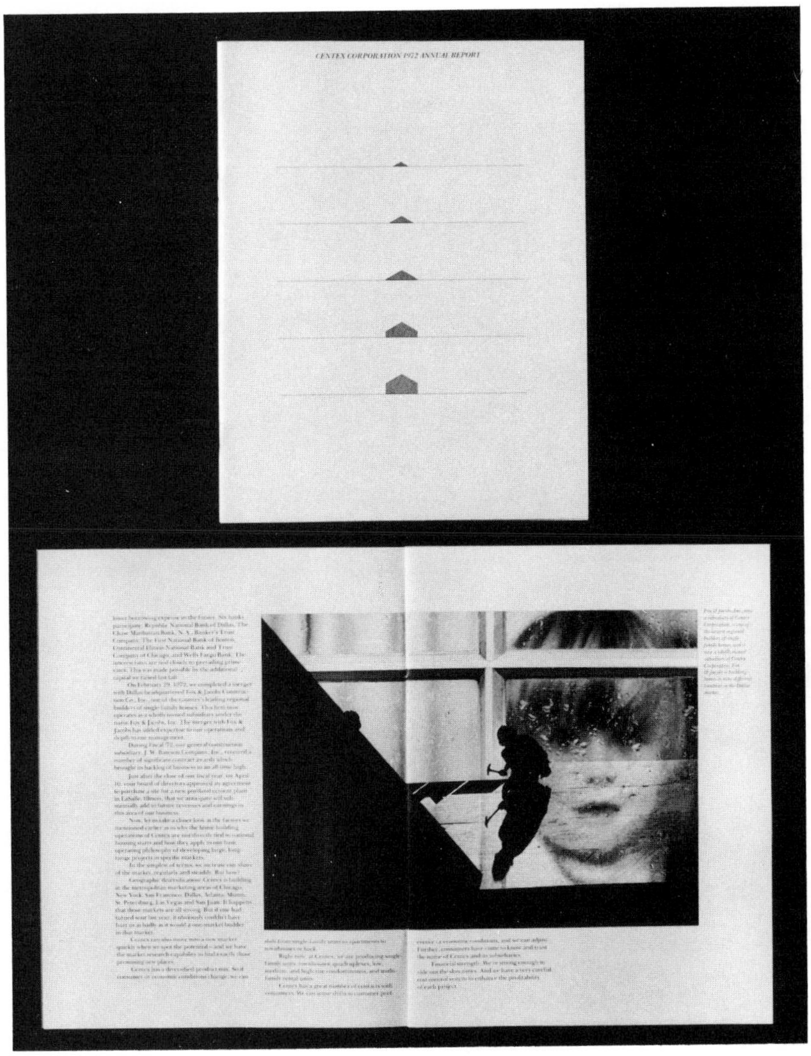

551

552

553
Art Director: George Tscherny
Copywriter: Rubenstein, Wolfson & Co. Staff
Designer: George Tscherny
Photographers: Morton Shapiro
George Tscherny
Burk Uzzle
Agency: Rubenstein, Wolfson & Co., Inc.
Client: Colonial Penn Group, Inc.

554
Art Director: Advertising Designers, Inc.
Copywriter: Paul Warda
Designer: Carl Seltzer
Photographers: Bob Schaar
Kurt Lenk
Agency: Advertising Designers, Inc.
Client: National Medical Enterprises

553

554

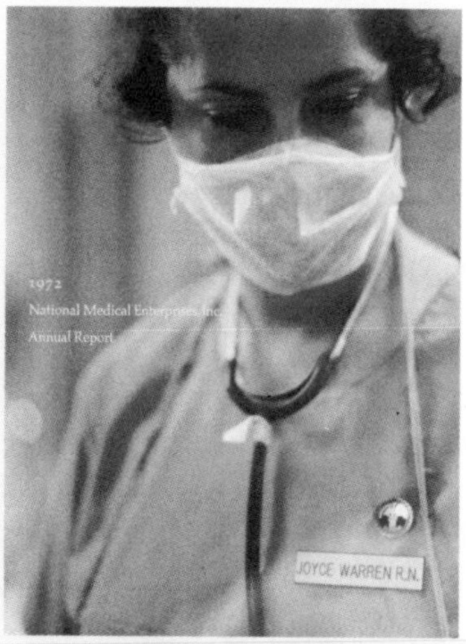

555
Art Director: John Morning
Copywriter: Bedford-Stuyvesant Restoration Corp.
Designer: John Morning
Photographers: Ace Creative Photos
LeRoy W. Henderson
Buford Smith
Pope Studio
Agency: Bedford-Stuyvesant Restoration Corp.
Client: Bedford-Stuyvesant Restoration Corp.

556
Art Director: Michael Reid
Copywriter: Archibald McKinlay Jr.
Designer: Michael Reid
Photographer: Michael Reid
Agency: Michael Reid Design
Client: Rush-Presbyterian-St. Luke's Medical Center

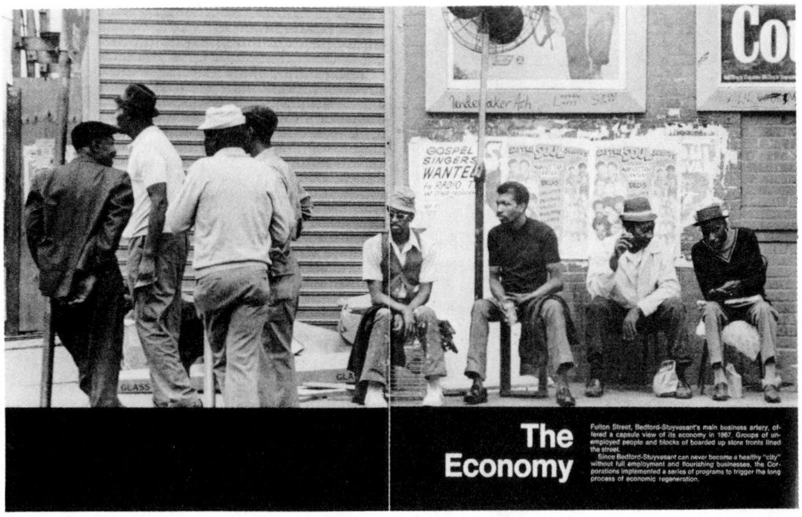
GOSPEL SINGERS WANTED
The Economy
Fulton Street, Bedford-Stuyvesant's main business artery, offered a capsule view of its economy in 1967. Groups of unemployed people and blocks of boarded up store fronts lined the street.
Since Bedford-Stuyvesant can never become a healthy "city" without full employment and flourishing businesses, the Corporations implemented a series of programs to trigger the long process of economic regeneration.

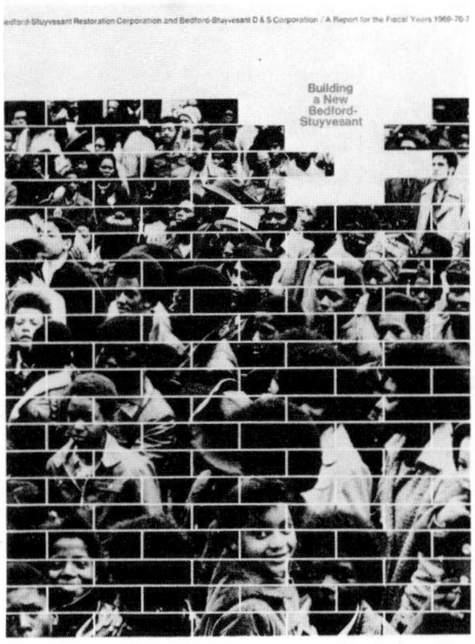
Stuyvesant Restoration Corporation and Bedford-Stuyvesant D & S Corporation / A Report for the Fiscal Years
Building a New Bedford-Stuyvesant

555

556

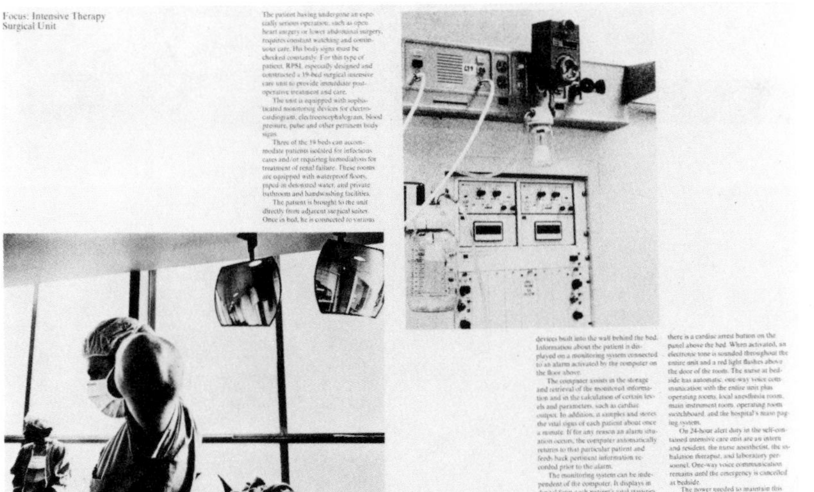
Focus: Intensive Therapy
Surgical Unit

Rush-Presbyterian-St. Luke's Medical Center Annual Report
7172
"You, and all of us involved in RPSL, are creating–not just talking about–a comprehensive and balanced health care system. We are closing the loop between delivering quality health care and producing the manpower to do the job . . . Truly, Rush-Presbyterian-St. Luke's is having an impact on health care in America that will be felt for many years to come."

557
Art Director: Mel Abert
Copywriter: Mel Newhoff
Designer: Mel Abert
Photographers: Lamb and Hall
Hank Hinton
Agency: Abert, Newhoff & Burr
Client: Alison Mortgage Investment Trust

557

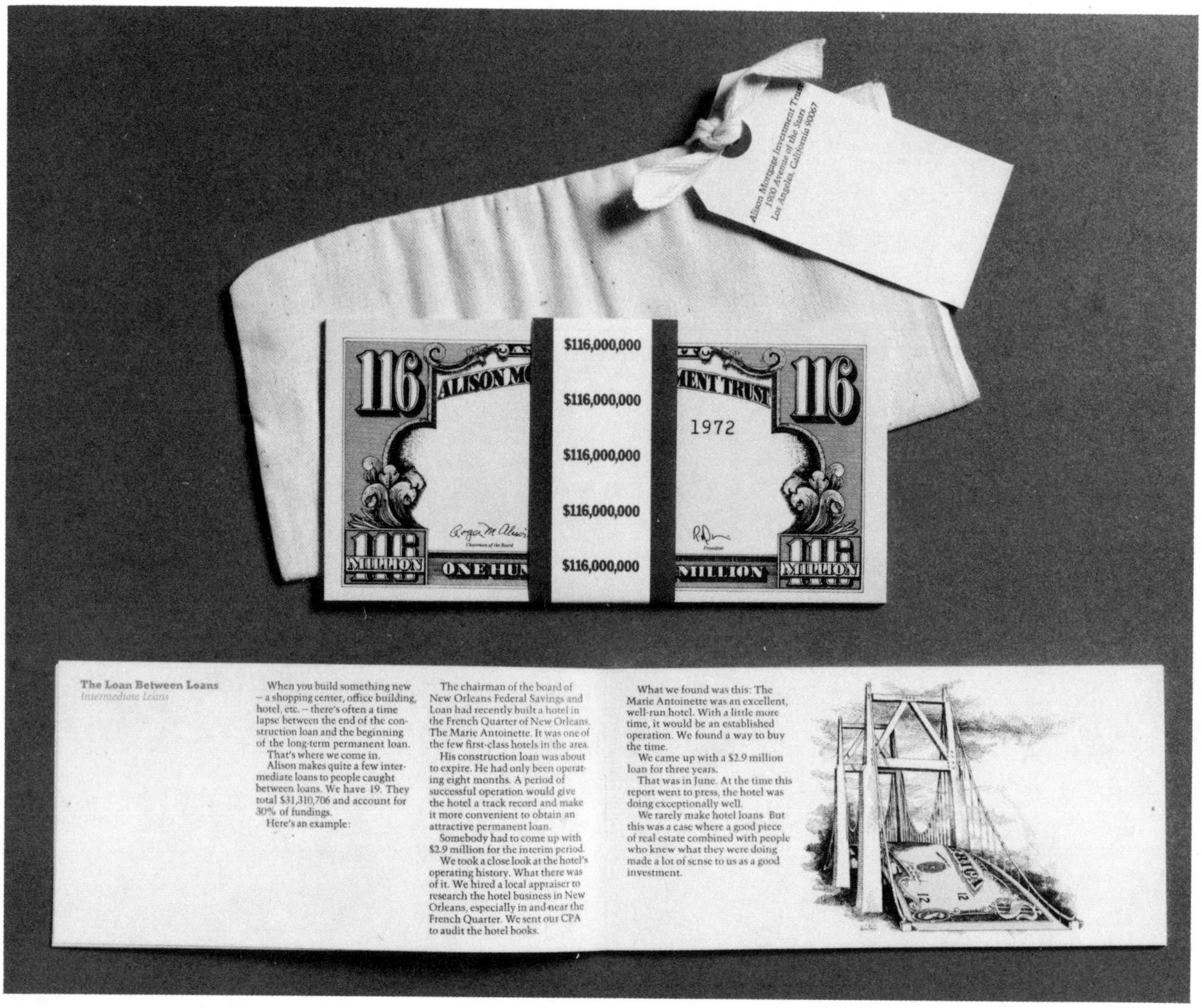
Alison Mortgage Investment Trust
1900 Avenue of the Stars
Los Angeles, California 90067
$116,000,000
$116,000,000
$116,000,000
$116,000,000
$116,000,000
116
ALISON MO
MENT TRUST
1972
MILLION
The Loan Between Loans
Intermediate Loans
When you build something new – a shopping center, office building, hotel, etc. – there's often a time lapse between the end of the construction loan and the beginning of the long-term permanent loan.
That's where we come in.
Alison makes quite a few intermediate loans to people caught between loans. We have 19. They total $31,310,706 and account for 30% of fundings.
Here's an example:
The chairman of the board of New Orleans Federal Savings and Loan had recently built a hotel in the French Quarter of New Orleans. The Marie Antoinette. It was one of the few first-class hotels in the area.
His construction loan was about to expire. He had only been operating eight months. A period of successful operation would give the hotel a track record and make it more convenient to obtain an attractive permanent loan.
Somebody had to come up with $2.9 million for the interim period.
We took a close look at the hotel's operating history. What there was of it. We hired a local appraiser to research the hotel business in New Orleans, especially in and near the French Quarter. We sent our CPA to audit the hotel books.
What we found was this: The Marie Antoinette was an excellent, well-run hotel. With a little more time, it would be an established operation. We found a way to buy the time.
We came up with a $2.9 million loan for three years.
That was in June. At the time this report went to press, the hotel was doing exceptionally well.
We rarely make hotel loans. But this was a case where a good piece of real estate combined with people who knew what they were doing made a lot of sense to us as a good investment.

558

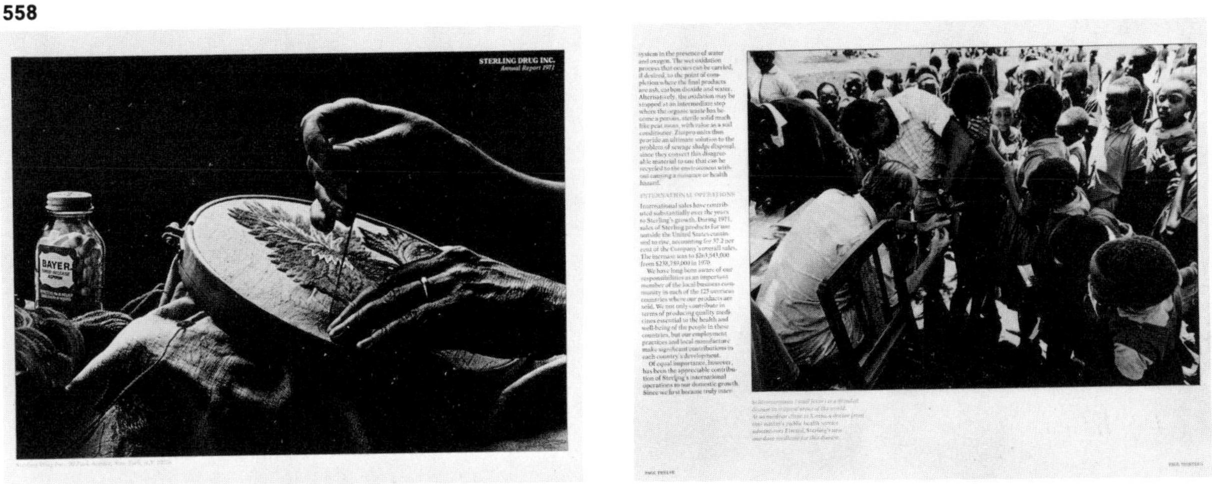

559

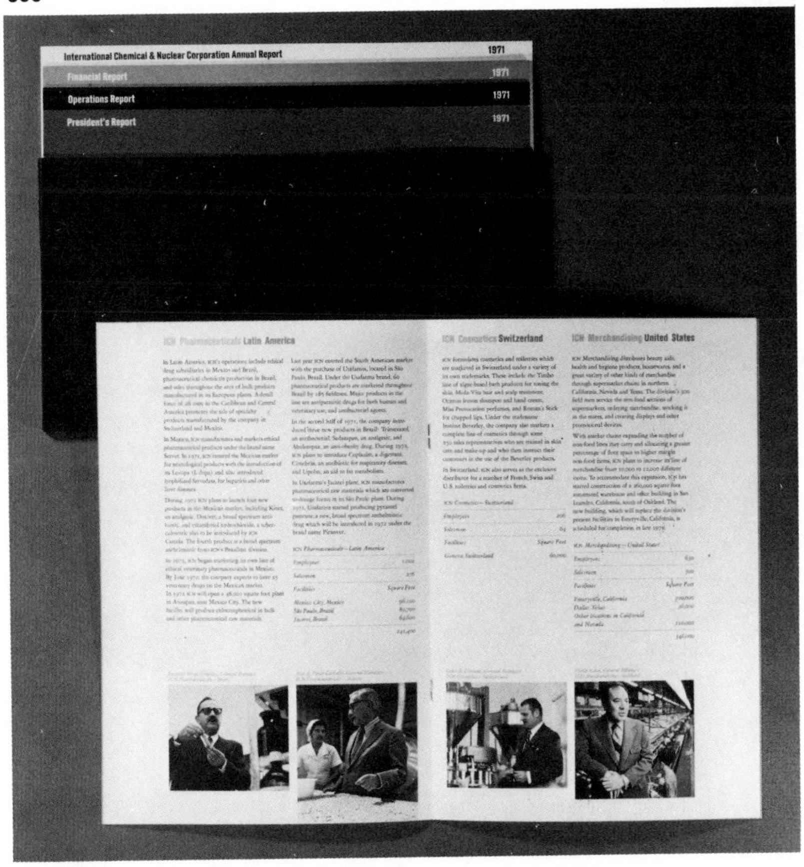

558
Art Director: Len Fury
Copywriter: Richard Blodgett
Designer: Len Fury
Photographers: Phil Marco
Marvin Koner
Gerry Cranham
Lance Nelson
Bob Gomel
Richard Saunders
Carl Roodman
Leonard Soned
Agency: Corporate Annual Reports Inc.
Client: Sterling Drug Inc.

559
Art Director: James Cross
Copywriter: Ray Winship
Designers: James Cross
Kenton Lotz
Photographer: William Claxton
Agency: James Cross Design Office, Inc.
Client: ICN Pharmaceuticals, Inc.

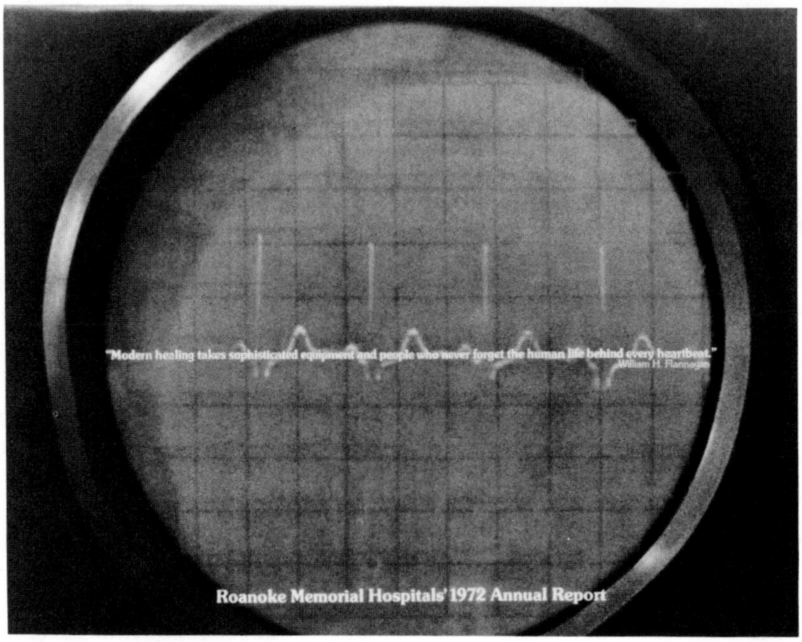
"Modern healing takes sophisticated equipment and people who never forget the human life behind every heartbeat."
William H. Flannagan
Roanoke Memorial Hospitals' 1972 Annual Report

1 2 3 4 5 6 7
Independence Day
8 9 10 11 12 13 14
15 16 17 18 19 20 21
22 23 24 25 26 27 28
29 30 31
July 1973
The microscope was the invention of the famous Italian scientist Galileo. It was developed in 1609 as a by product of his famous telescope. Galileo's microscope failed to give a clear picture for complicated optical reasons. Due to the high degree of magnification the images were blurred and distorted. Two 17th century scientists made Galileo's invention more precise and effective. More than 300 years passed before there was any improvement.

560 Gold Award
Art Directors: John Chepelsky
Kent Puckett
Copywriter: Doris Sanders
Designer: John Chepelsky
Photographer: The Workshop, Inc.
Agency: Brand Edmonds Packett
Client: Roanoke Memorial Hospitals

561
Art Director: Jim Laird
Copywriter: John Ott
Designer: Jim Laird
Photographer: Bob Stahman
Agency: Laird-Penczak Design, Inc.
Client: International Basic Economy Corpo

562
Art Director: Michael Reid
Copywriter: Eileen Ganz
Designer: Michael Reid
Photographer: David Windsor
Agency: Michael Reid Design
Client: Saint Joseph Hospital

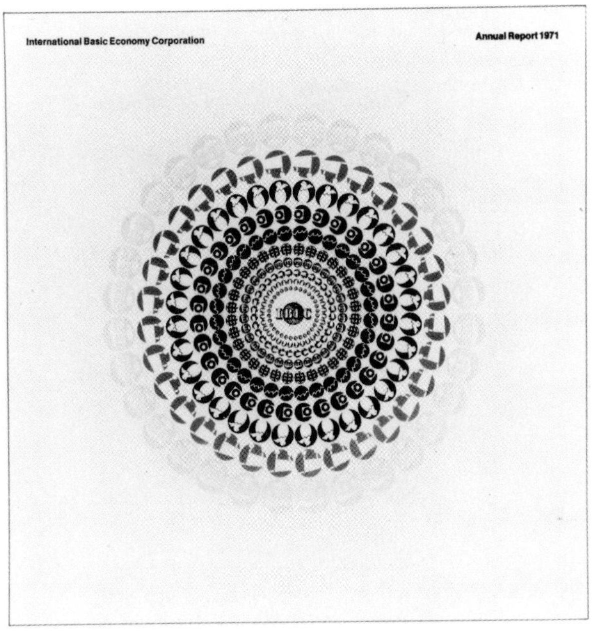
International Basic Economy Corporation
Annual Report 1971

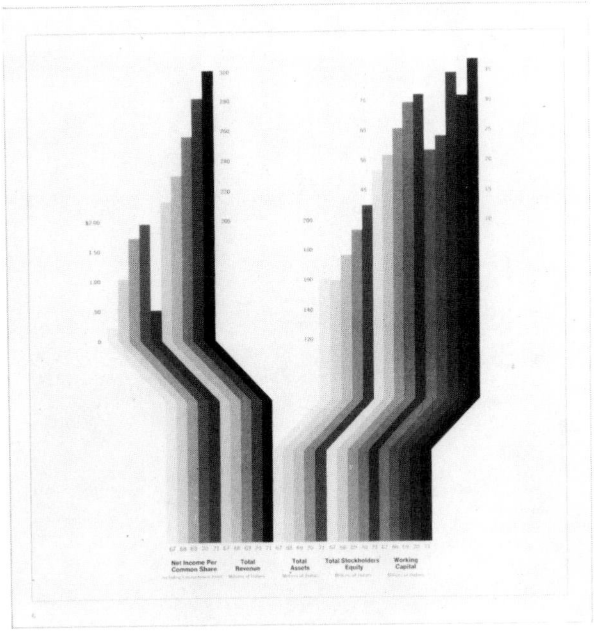
Net Income Per Common Share
Total Revenue
Total Assets
Total Stockholders Equity
Working Capital

561

562

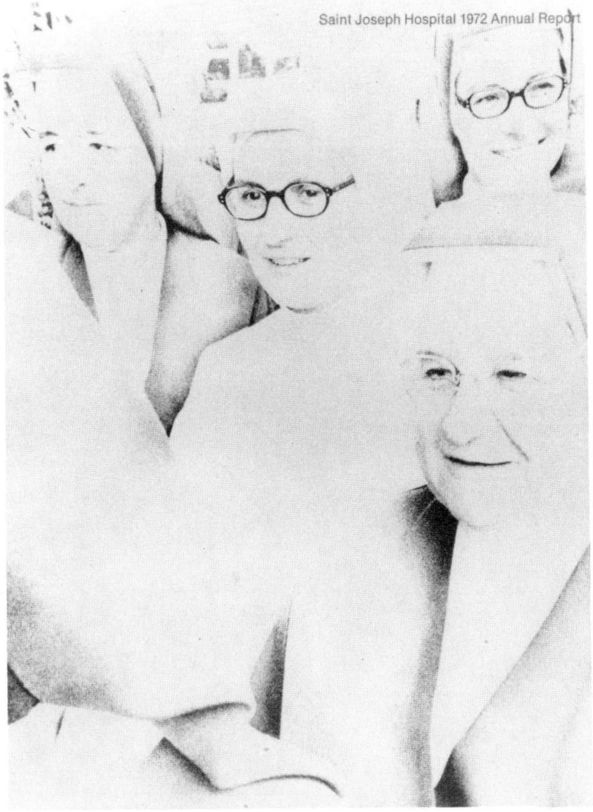
Saint Joseph Hospital 1972 Annual Report

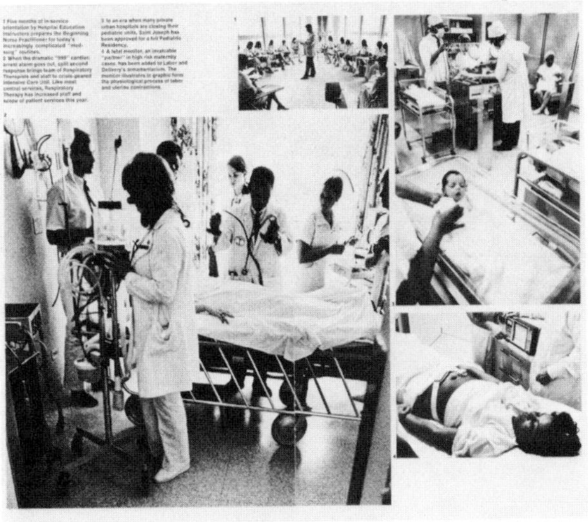

Annual Reports

563
Art Director: Michael Reid
Copywriter: Blossom Porte
Designer: Michael Reid
Artist: Mary Nolan
Photographer: Archie Lieberman
Agency: Michael Reid Design
Client: Children's Memorial Hospital

564
Art Director: Alicia Landon
Copywriter: Lowell Farley
Designer: Alicia Landon
Photographers: Doug Corry
Robert Oei
Wolf von dem Bussche
Margot Granitsas
Agency: Corporate Annual Reports, Inc.
Client: International Paper Company

563

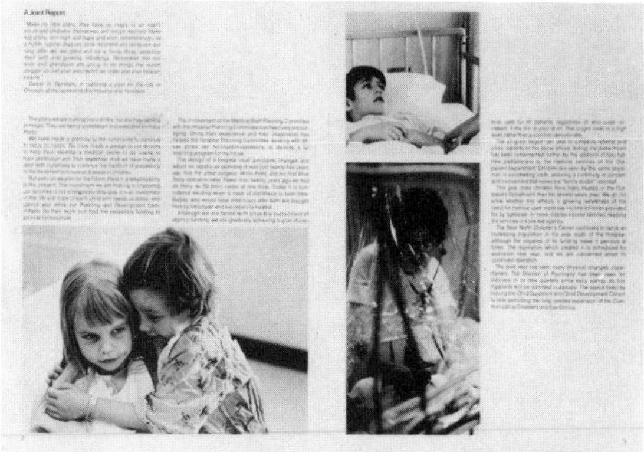

564

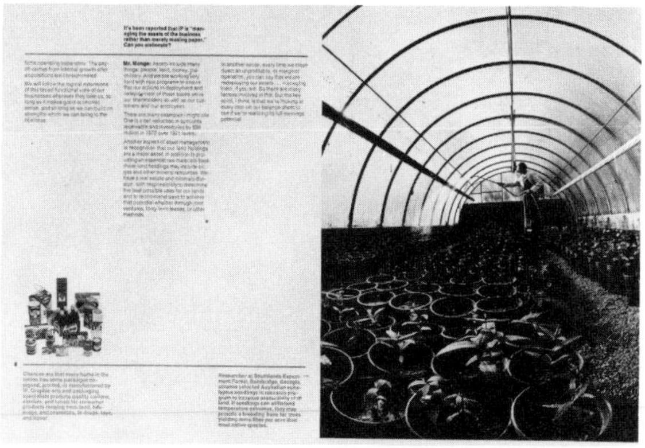

565
Art Director: Kit Hinrichs
Copywriters: Harshe-Rotman & Druck Staff
Designers: Kit Hinrichs
Leo Choplin
Gene Daniels
Photographers: Ted Rozumalski
John Rees
John Messina
Black Star
Agency: Hinrichs Design Associates
Client: Foster Grant Co., Inc.

566
Art Directors: Peter J. Blank
Don Menell
Copywriter: William Kemsley
Designers: Peter J. Blank
Don Menell
Photographers: James Karales
Stu Smith
Agency: WKA Corporate Graphics
Client: The Washington Post Company

565

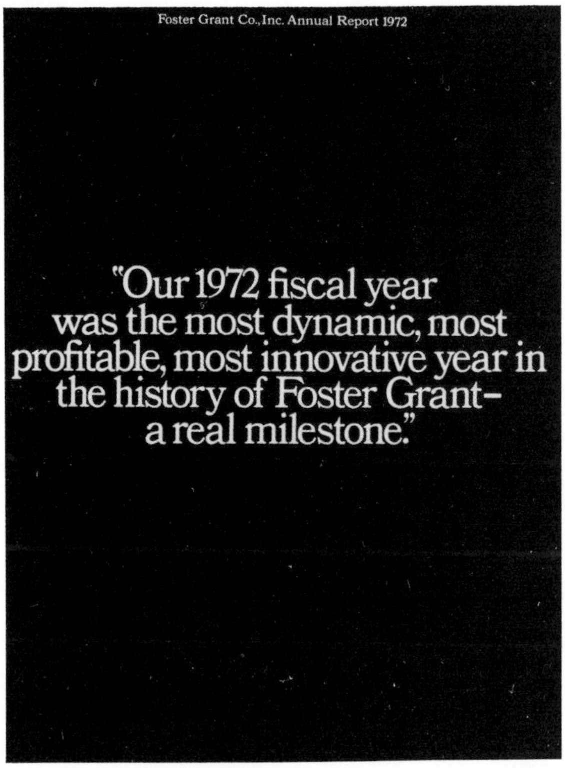
Foster Grant Co., Inc. Annual Report 1972
"Our 1972 fiscal year was the most dynamic, most profitable, most innovative year in the history of Foster Grant– a real milestone."

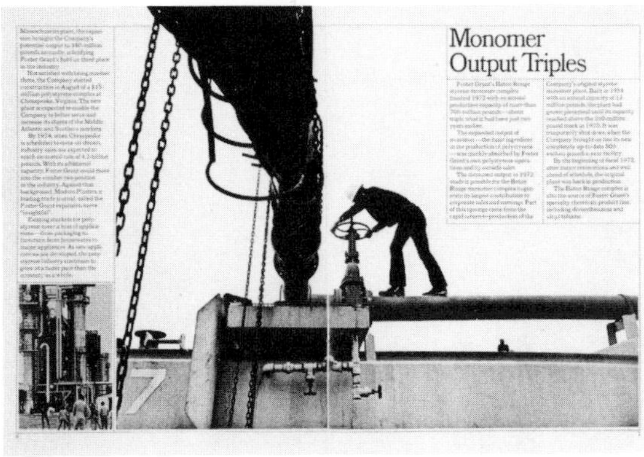
Monomer Output Triples

566

ANNUAL REPORT...1971
The Washington Post Company
The Washington Post Company is a growing communications enterprise that has expanded from newspaper publishing to include magazines, broadcasting and books; its operations extend around the world. The Company, which made its first public offering in 1971, is traded on the American Stock Exchange.
The Washington Post itself, the Company's original base, is one of America's major dailies—the only morning newspaper in the nation's capital and one of its two Sunday newspapers.
The Company publishes Newsweek, which appears simultaneously each week in 179 countries. It also publishes books, which are sold primarily by direct mail, and Art News magazine, America's oldest fine arts monthly.
The broadcast operation consists of three VHF television stations and two AM radio stations. The television stations, each affiliated with a national network, are WTOP-TV in Washington, D.C., WPLG in Miami and WJXT in Jacksonville, Florida. The radio stations are WTOP in Washington and WCKY in Cincinnati.
The Company also owns 83 per cent of Robinson Terminal Warehouse Corporation in Alexandria, Virginia and 49 per cent of Bowaters Mersey Paper Company Limited, a newsprint company in Liverpool, Nova Scotia. The Company is a partner in a joint venture that publishes the International Herald Tribune in Paris and another joint venture that operates the Los Angeles Times-Washington Post News Service.

THE WASHINGTON POST

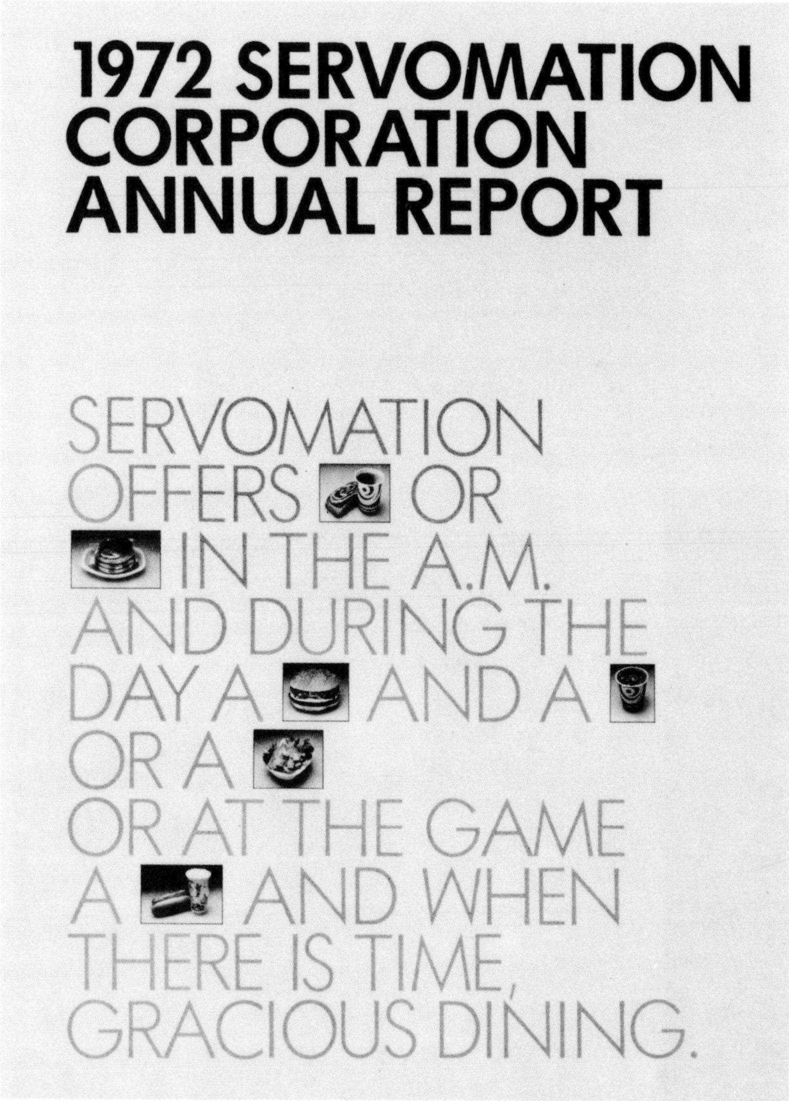
1972 SERVOMATION
CORPORATION
ANNUAL REPORT
SERVOMATION
OFFERS OR
IN THE A.M.
AND DURING THE
DAY A AND A
OR A
OR AT THE GAME
A AND WHEN
THERE IS TIME,
GRACIOUS DINING.

COFFEE & PASTRY. THE BREAKFAST AND MID-MORNING SNACK PREFERRED MOST BY PEOPLE ON THE MOVE. SERVOMATION SERVES MORE THAN 1,800,000 CUPS OF COFFEE AND 550,000 PASTRIES EACH WORKING DAY.
SERVOMATION

567
Art Directors: Peter J. Blank
Don Menell
Copywriter: William Kemsley
Designers: Peter J. Blank
Don Menell
Photographers: Charles Gold
Stu Smith
Agency: WKA Corporate Graphics
Client: Servomation Corporation

568
Art Director: Ronald Rampley
Copywriter: Richard E. Cruikshank
Designer: Ronald Rampley
Photographer: Don Shapero
Agency: Logan Carey & Rehag
Client: Dean Witter & Co., Inc.

569
Art Director: Ivan Chermayeff
Copywriter: Rufus Stillman
Designers: Ivan Chermayeff
Angela Reeves
Photographer: Ivan Hill
Agency: Chermayeff & Geismar Associates
Client: Torin Corporation

568

569

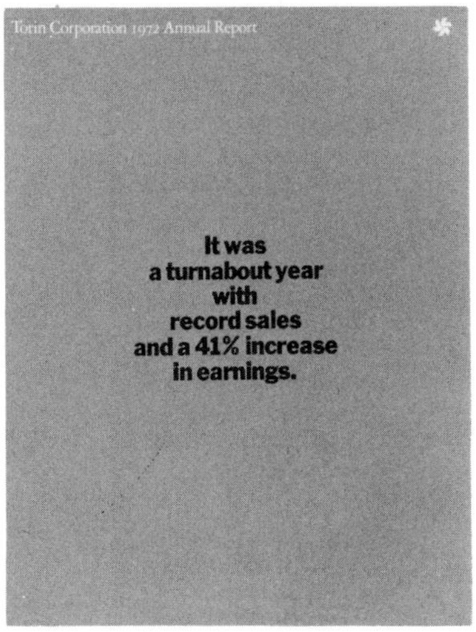

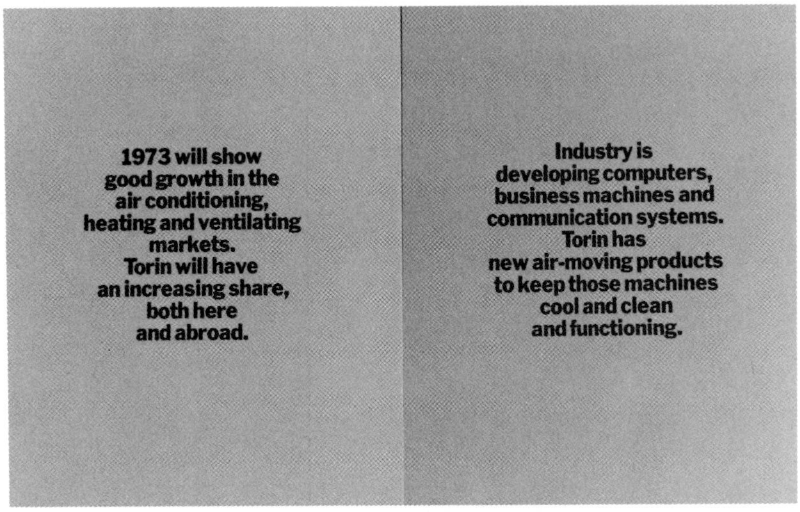

Sales Presentations

570

571

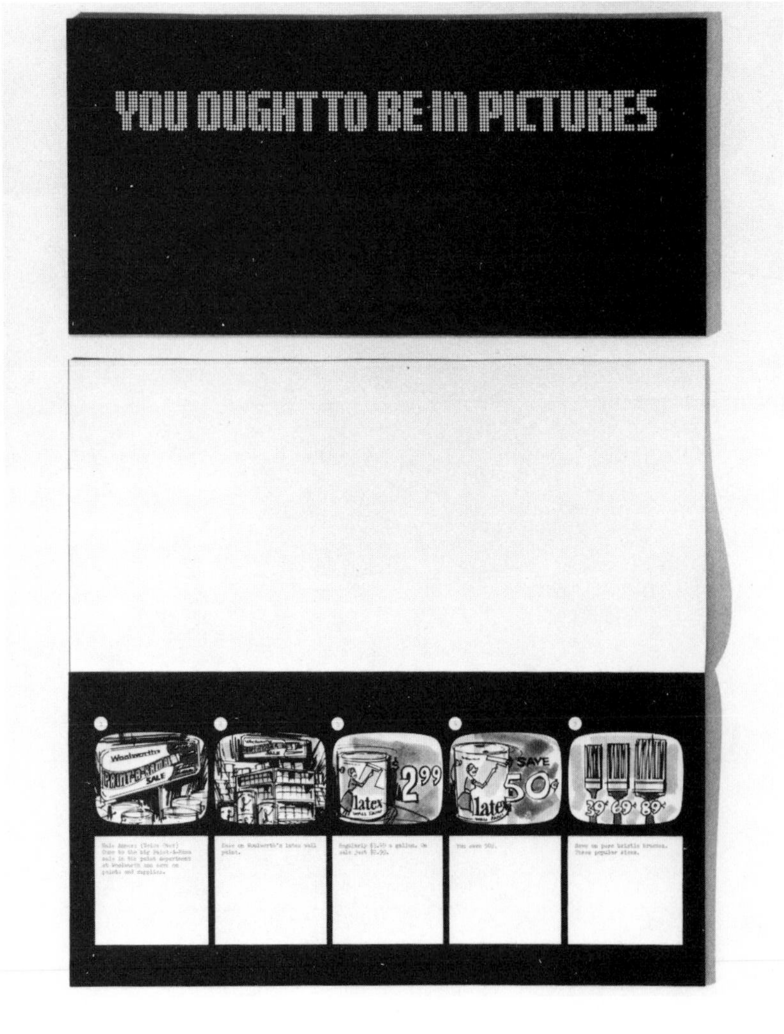

570
Art Director: Ted Andresakes
Designers: Ted Andresakes
Ira Teichberg
Photographer: CBS Photo
Agency: CBS/Broadcast Group
Client: CBS Television Network

571
Art Director: Lou Dorfsman
Copywriters: Lou Dorfsman
Steve Sohmer
Designers: Lou Dorfsman
Ted Andresakes
Artist: Peter Tomlinson
Agency: CBS/Broadcast Group
Client: CBS Television Stations

572
Art Directors: Tom Clark
Lee Elliot
Copywriter: Lee Elliot
Designer: S. Schlatner
Artist: Stan Moldof
Agency: The Infinity Group, Inc.
Client: Certain-Teed Products Corp.

573
Art Director: J. Michael Essex
Copywriters: J. Michael Essex
Walt Duka
Margie Moeller
Designer: J. Michael Essex
Artist: Ed Zelinsky
Agency: WQED/Design Centre
Client: National Assoc. of Educational Broadcasters
The Corporation for Public Broadcasting

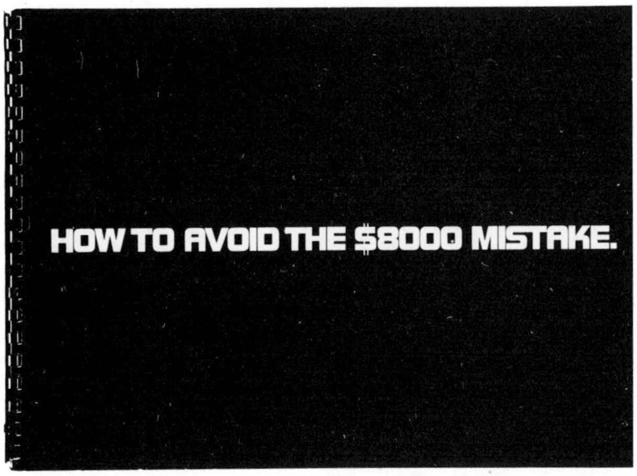
HOW TO AVOID THE $8000 MISTAKE.

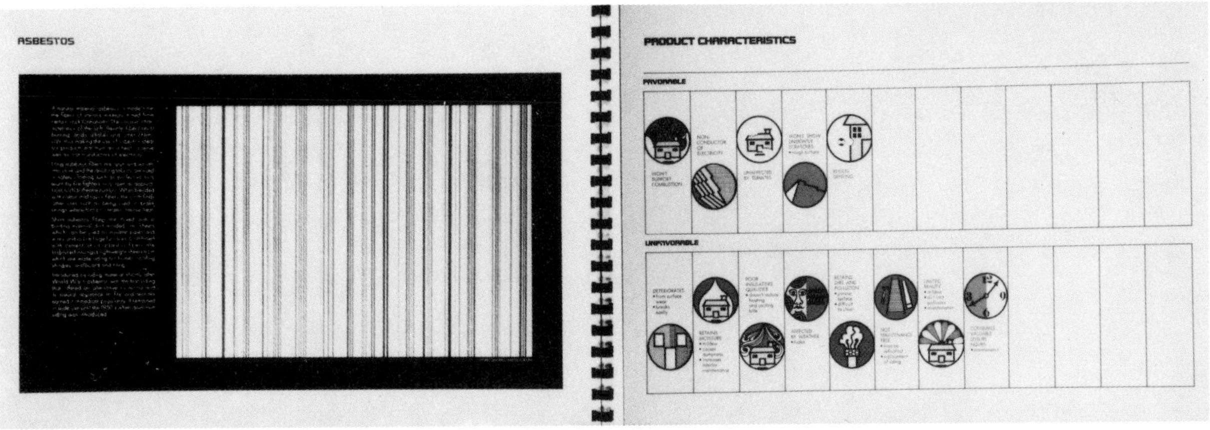
ASBESTOS
PRODUCT CHARACTERISTICS
FAVORABLE
UNFAVORABLE

572

573

AGENDA
Get Yourself Together
Get Yourself Together.
Call for Entries
Get Yourself Together
Get Yourself Together
Get Yourself Together
Get Yourself Together
The 1972 National Conference on Public Relations in Public Television

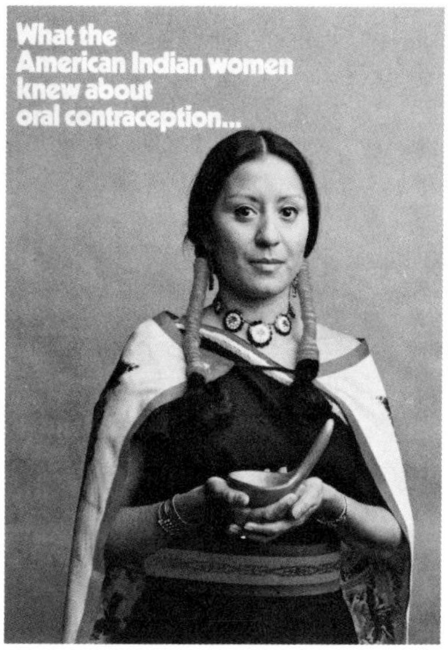

What the American Indian women knew about oral contraception...

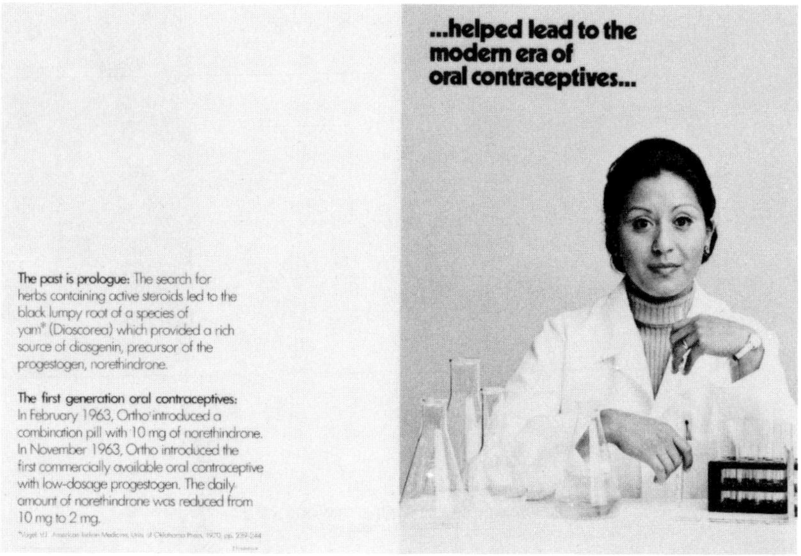

...helped lead to the modern era of oral contraceptives...

The past is prologue: The search for herbs containing active steroids led to the black lumpy root of a species of yam* (Dioscorea) which provided a rich source of diosgenin, precursor of the progestogen, norethindrone.

The first generation oral contraceptives: In February 1963, Ortho introduced a combination pill with 10 mg of norethindrone. In November 1963, Ortho introduced the first commercially available oral contraceptive with low-dosage progestogen. The daily amount of norethindrone was reduced from 10 mg to 2 mg.

*Vogel, V.J. American Indian Medicine, Univ. of Oklahoma Press, 1970, pp. 239-244

...which led Ortho to Ortho-Novum 1/50-21 for the woman of today's world.

The past is prologue: The search for herbs containing active steroids led to the black lumpy root of a species of yam* (Dioscorea) which provided a rich source of diosgenin, precursor of the progestogen, norethindrone.

The first generation oral contraceptives: In February 1963, Ortho introduced a combination pill with 10 mg of norethindrone. In November 1963, Ortho introduced the first commercially available oral contraceptive with low-dosage progestogen. The daily amount of norethindrone was reduced from 10 mg to 2 mg.

*Vogel, V.J. American Indian Medicine, Univ. of Oklahoma Press, 1970, pp. 239-244

Ortho-Novum 1/50 21

Each tablet contains 1 mg norethindrone and 0.05 mg mestranol

Ortho-Novum 1/50 21 offers:

...high effectiveness, when taken as directed;

...a usually well-tolerated combination, easy on your patient and easy for her to stay with;
(Please see detailed information on contraindications, warnings, precautions and adverse reactions)

...easy regimen, 3 weeks on...1 week off, a simple regimen to remember;

...low dosage, 1 mg norethindrone and 0.05 mg mestranol;

...and the unique Dialpak Tablet Dispenser

574

575

ATC One of the Significant Developments in Incandescent Bulbs Since Edison

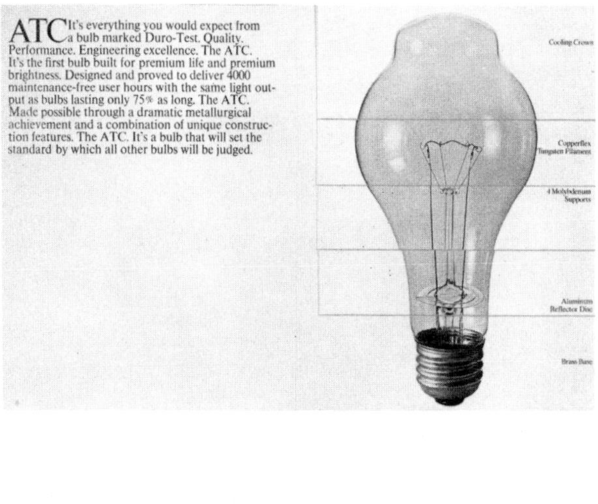

ATC It's everything you would expect from a bulb marked Duro-Test. Quality. Performance. Engineering excellence. The ATC. It's the first bulb built for premium life and premium brightness. Designed and proved to deliver 4000 maintenance-free user hours with the same light output as bulbs lasting only 75% as long. The ATC. Made possible through a dramatic metallurgical achievement and a combination of unique construction features. The ATC. It's a bulb that will set the standard by which all other bulbs will be judged.

574
Art Director: Alfred Zalon
Copywriter: Al Gerstein
Designer: Alfred Zalon
Photographer: Carl Fischer
Agency: Kallir Philips Ross
Client: Ortho Pharmaceutical Corporation

575
Art Directors: Kit Hinrichs
Jack C. Wright
Copywriter: Mike Rudner
Designer: Kit Hinrichs
Photographers: Richard Jeffery
Leonard Soned
Agency: Hinrichs Design Associates
Client: Duro-Test Corporation

576
Art Director: Walter Kaprielian
Copywriter: Richard Seideman
Designers: Harold Florian
Joel Benay
Walter Kaprielian
Artist: Push Pin Studios
Agency: Ketchum, MacLeod & Grove, Inc.
Client: General Foods

JELL-O
BRAND GELATIN
The Dessert America Grew Up With Serves You An Exciting New Opportunity.

576

IMPROVED
JELL-O
NEW FORTIFIED JELL-O GELATIN
Your Opportunity To Serve More Nutrition In Your Meals.
The latest National Nutrition Survey* indicates a deficiency of Vitamins A and C and Iron in the diets of numerous American children. While a balanced diet can eliminate these deficiencies, it is frequently difficult to get children to eat properly. As an aid to better nutrition, Jell-O® Gelatin has now been fortified with Vitamin A, Vitamin C and Iron. Jell-O® Gelatin has always been a food that children eat readily. New fortified Jell-O® Gelatin will provide your children with added nutrition at no extra cost. It will provide a source of more nutrition throughout your weekly menus at less than 2¢ per serving. In addition, fortified Jell-O® Gelatin offers even more flavor appeal because it tastes more fruit-like. A nationwide survey of dietitians and food service managers shows an enthusiastic reaction to fortified Jell-O® Gelatin. We believe you, too, will have the same favorable attitude.
*Department of Health, Education and Welfare, Ten State Nutrition Survey 1968-70.
NUTRITIOUS
VITAMINS A AND C+IRON
NEW FORTIFIED JELL-O GELATIN
Gives You Two More Good Reasons To Serve More Of America's Favorite Gelatin.
New Fruitier Taste
Fortified Jell-O® Gelatin is more flavorful because it tastes more fruit-like. It's made with a new formulation that achieves a more natural-tasting fruit flavor while providing the economy Jell-O® Gelatin has always offered.
New Nutritional Bonus
Fortified Jell-O® Gelatin has been formulated to provide a nutritional bonus of Vitamin A, Vitamin C and Iron—some of the important nutrients found in many of the fruits served in the school lunch program.
FRUITIER
Taste
NEW FORTIFIED JELL-O GELATIN
Fortified With Vitamin A, Vitamin C And Iron
One 4 oz. (1/2 cup) serving of fortified Jell-O® Gelatin delivers 160% of the Vitamin A...40% of the Vitamin C...125% of the Iron of the composite average of 1/2 cup servings of the fruits listed below:
Apples Bananas Blackberries Blueberries Grapes Peaches Pears Raspberries Strawberries Cherries
A 4 oz. (1/2 cup) serving of fortified Jell-O® Gelatin supplies these percentages of Minimum Daily Requirements:
Vitamin A Child 14% Adult 10%
Vitamin C Child 30% Adult 20%
Iron Child 10% Adult 7%
Or these percentages of the Recommended Daily Dietary Allowances for children 10 to 12 years of age.
Vitamin A 9%
Vitamin C 15%
Iron 4%

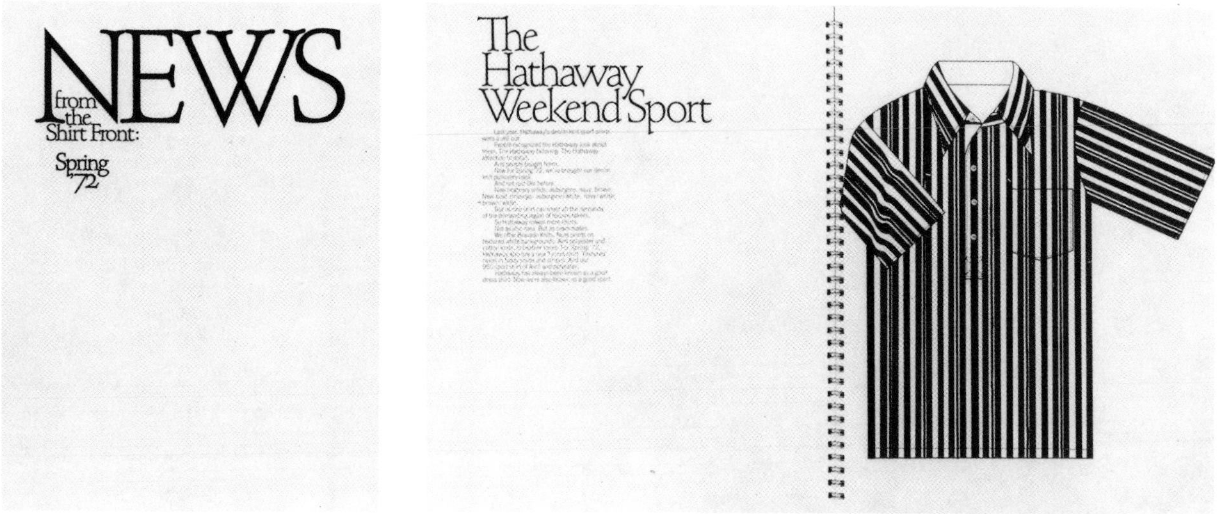
NEWS
from the Shirt Front:
Spring '72
The Hathaway Weekend Sport

577

578

DRAMA SPECIALS FOR YOUTH
WORLD CULTURES
A Proposal From
WQED
Metropolitan Pittsburgh
Public Broadcasting
4802 Fifth Avenue
Pittsburgh, Pennsylvania 15213
NANCY AND FRIENDS
American
Revolution
GEORGE WASHINGTON, ESQUIRE
DOCUDRAMA

577
Art Directors: Andy Romano
Chuck Bua
Designer: Andy Romano
Artist: Marilyn Hoffner
Photographer: Leonard Nomes
Copywriters: Peggy Courtney
Paula Green
Agency: Green Dolmatch Inc.
Client: Hathaway Shirts

578
Art Director: Ed Zelinsky
Designer: Ed Zelinsky
Agency: WQED Design Centre
Client: Metropolitan Pittsburgh Public Broadcasting

579
Art Director: George McCathern
Copywriter: Morris Shriftman
Designer: George McCathern
Artist: Century Expanded
Photographer: Alan Breslau
Agency: Century Expanded
Client: American Dietaids Company

579

Dear Friend:
During the past twenty-five years, American Dietaids has assisted hundreds of health food retailers in starting and then successfully building their businesses.
We offer an effective approach to health food marketing through a well planned program of advertising and store promotion of our fine products as well as other nationally known brands.
This kit contains everything you need to conduct a sustained program of newspaper advertising designed to stimulate interest in your existing business, attract new customers to your store and to enhance your reputation as an active and responsible member of the business community. Most importantly, it will make a meaningful contribution to your increased sales and profits.
After all, at American Dietaids we're in business for your health and the health of your business.
Cordially,
Milton Okin
President
American Dietaids Company

580

581

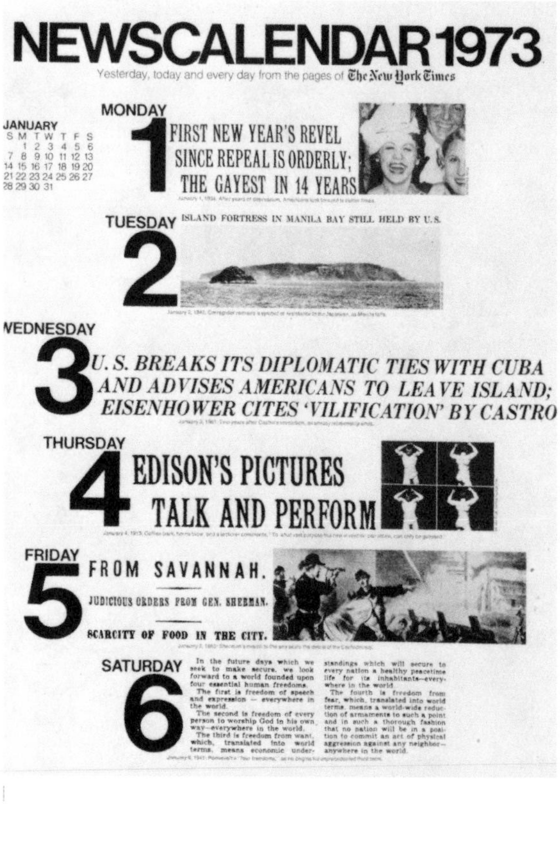
NEWSCALENDAR 1973
Yesterday, today and every day from the pages of The New York Times

JANUARY

S	M	T	W	T	F	S
		1	2	3	4	5	6
7	8	9	10	11	12	13
14	15	16	17	18	19	20
21	22	23	24	25	26	27
28	29	30	31			

MONDAY 1
FIRST NEW YEAR'S REVEL SINCE REPEAL IS ORDERLY; THE GAYEST IN 14 YEARS

TUESDAY 2
ISLAND FORTRESS IN MANILA BAY STILL HELD BY U.S.

WEDNESDAY 3
U. S. BREAKS ITS DIPLOMATIC TIES WITH CUBA AND ADVISES AMERICANS TO LEAVE ISLAND; EISENHOWER CITES 'VILIFICATION' BY CASTRO

THURSDAY 4
EDISON'S PICTURES TALK AND PERFORM

FRIDAY 5
FROM SAVANNAH.
JUDICIOUS ORDERS FROM GEN. SHERMAN.
SCARCITY OF FOOD IN THE CITY.

SATURDAY 6
In the future days which we seek to make secure, we look forward to a world founded upon four essential human freedoms.
The first is freedom of speech and expression — everywhere in the world.
The second is freedom of every person to worship God in his own way—everywhere in the world.
The third is freedom from want, which, translated into world terms, means economic understandings which will secure to every nation a healthy peacetime life for its inhabitants—everywhere in the world.
The fourth is freedom from fear, which, translated into world terms, means a world-wide reduction of armaments to such a point and in such a thorough fashion that no nation will be in a position to commit an act of physical aggression against any neighbor—anywhere in the world.

582

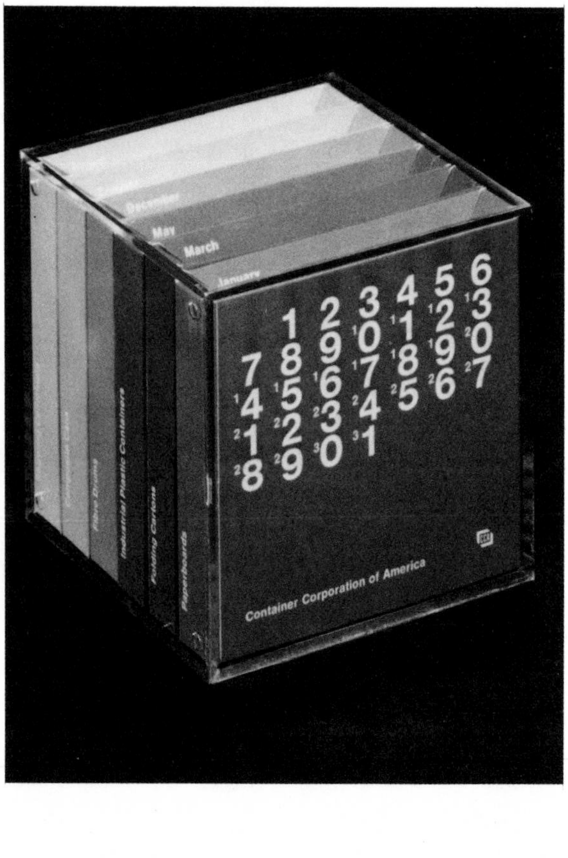

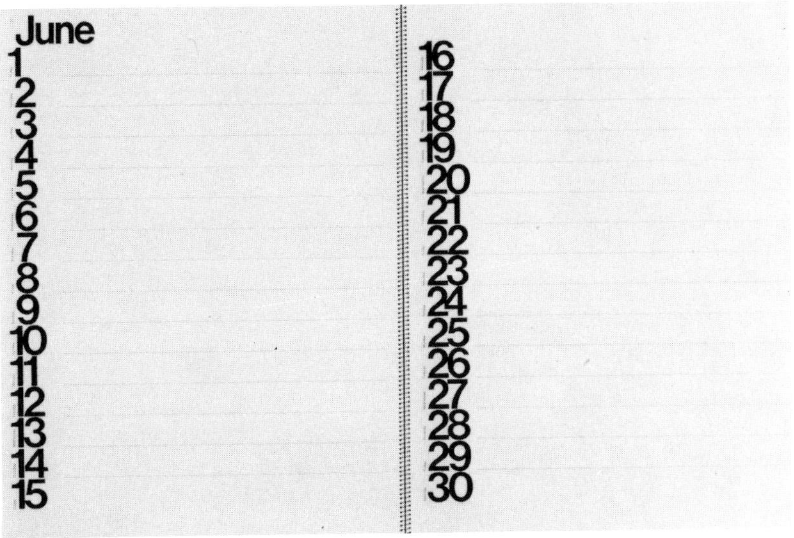

583

584

GASOLINE COSTS 80¢ A GALLON IN SWEDEN. AND SWEDES GAS UP MORE VOLVOS THAN ANY OTHER CAR.
FRIDAY/MAY
5
VOLVO: AS ADVERTISED IN SPORTS ILLUSTRATED TODAY. AS SOLD IN OUR SHOWROOM NOW.
THURSDAY/MAY
4
IF YOU WANT TO SEE A VOLVO'S PAINT JOB REALLY SHINE, DRIVE ONE THROUGH MUD, ROCKS, TAR, DIRT AND ROAD SALT.
3

580 Silver Award
Art Director: James Cross
Designers: James Cross
Kenton Lotz
Photographers: George Meinzinger
Dave Holt
Stan Caplan
Nick Rozsa
Gary Krueger
Roger Marshutz
Allan Walker
Ken Biggs
Lamb/Hall
Ken Marcus
Tom Engler
Dan deWolfe
Agency: James Cross Design Office, Inc.
Client: Ingram Paper Company

581
Art Directors: Louis Silverstein
Helen Silverstein
Designers: Louis Silverstein
Helen Silverstein
Photographer: News Photographers
Copywriter: Helen Silverstein
Client: The New York Times

582 Gold Award
Designer: Bill Bonnell III
Agency: Container Corporation of America
Client: Container Corporation of America

583
Art Directors: Richard Danne
Robert Sloan
Designer: Richard Danne
Client: Richard Danne

584
Art Director: Bill Berenter
Designer: Bill Berenter
Copywriter: Tom Nathan
Agency: Scali, McCabe, Sloves, Inc.
Client: Volvo, Inc.

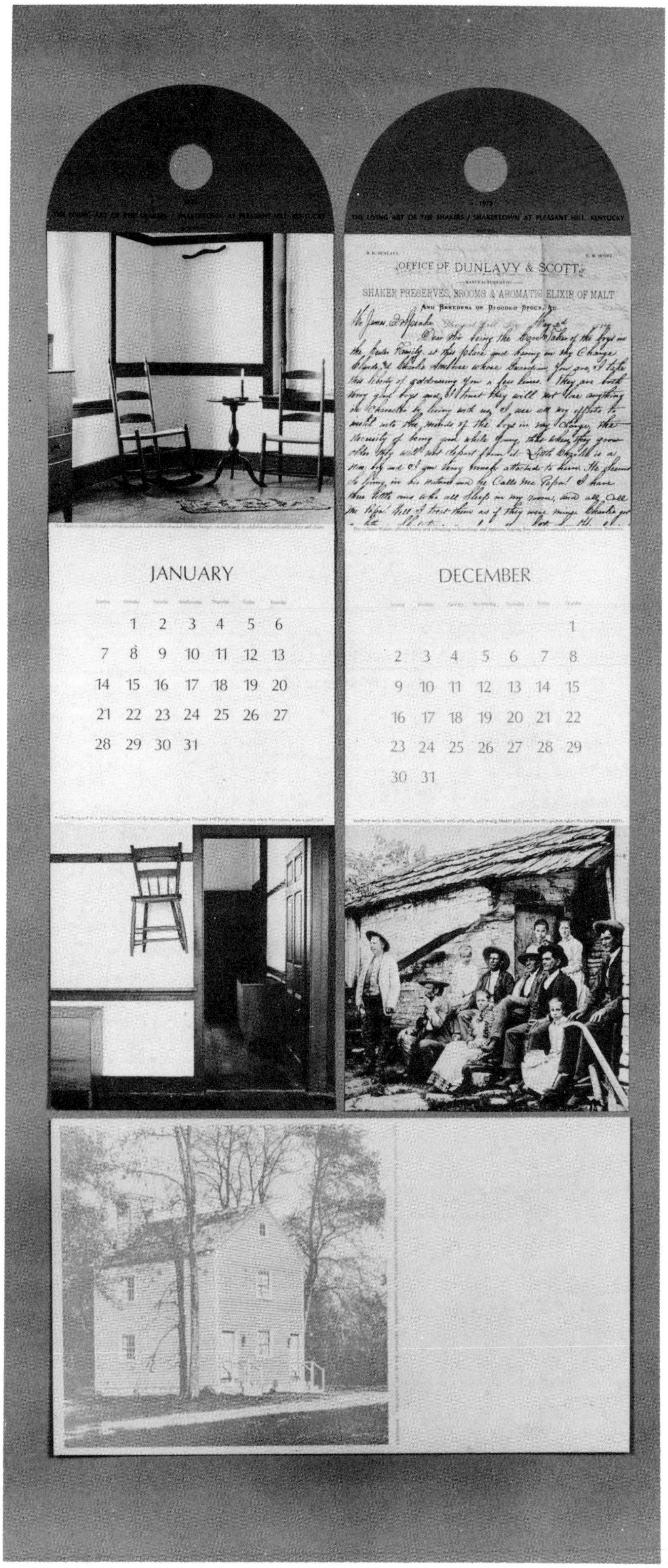

585
Art Director: Susan Jackson Keig
Designer: Susan Jackson Keig
Photographer: James L. Ballard
Copywriter: Susan Jackson Keig
Client: Shakertown at Pleasant Hill, Ky.

586
Art Director: Joseph Smith
Copywriter: Joseph Smith
Designer: Joseph Smith
Artist: Joseph Smith
Agency: Ruben, Montgomery & Associates
Client: Art Director's Club of Indiana

587
Art Director: Allan Wash
Copywriter: Allan Wash
Designer: Allan Wash
Artist: Allan Wash
Client: Allan Wash, Copywriter

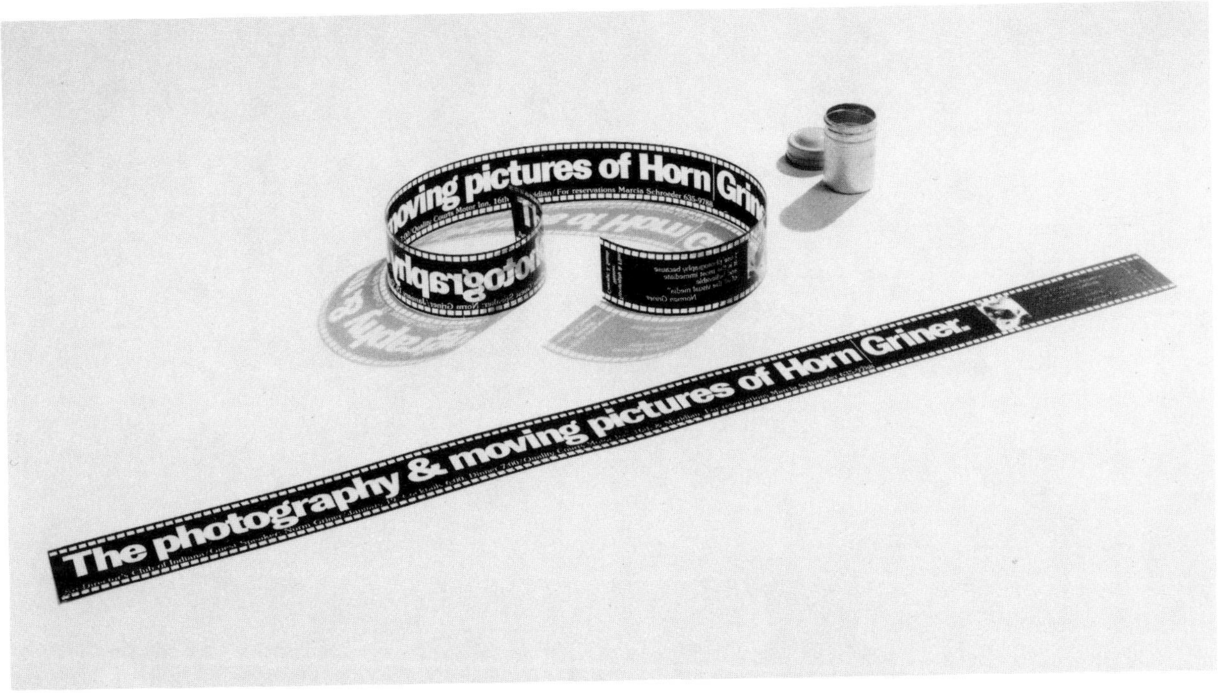

586

587

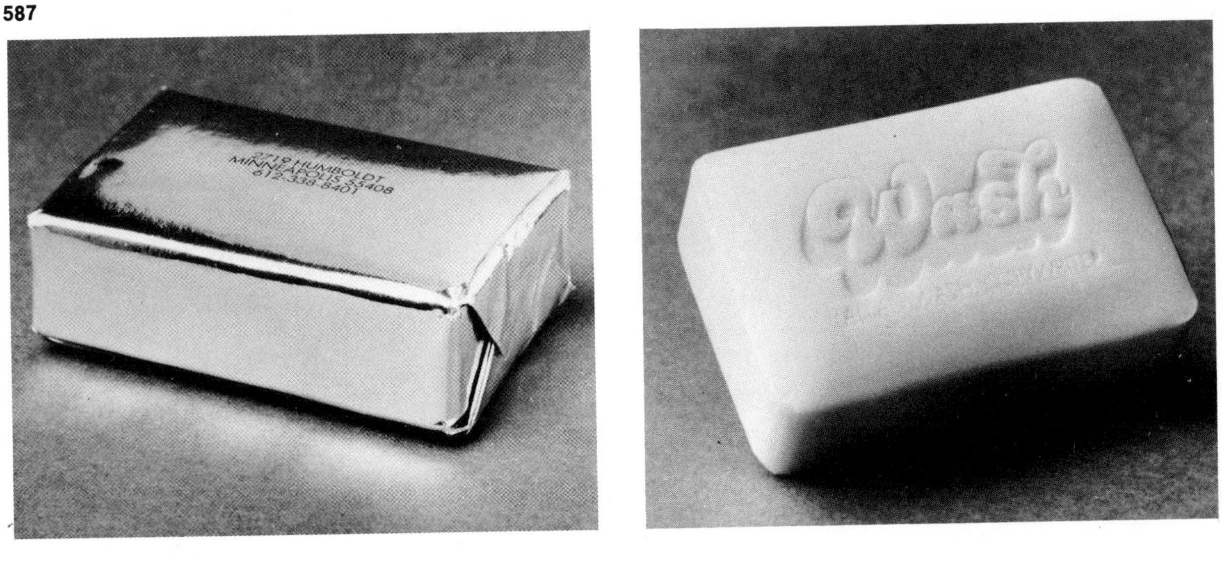

588

589

588
Art Director: Aves Advertising Creative Staff
Copywriter: Aves Advertising Creative Staff
Designer: Aves Advertising Creative Staff
Agency: Aves Advertising, Inc.
Client: Evans Products Company

589
Art Directors: Jerry Herring
Tom Poth
Ken Harshfield
Copywriter: Jerry Herring
Designers: Jerry Herring
Tom Poth
Ken Harshfield
Artists: Jerry Herring
Tom Poth
Ken Harshfield
Maurice Lewis
Agency: Baxter & Korge, Inc.
Client: Kimberly-Clark Corporation

Our Policy:
For 3¢ more, Airmail insures you the most reliable letter service going.
Airmail is more reliable because it gets priority over all regular mail. Unlike many first-class letters, that fly standby when space is available, Airmail always catches the first plane out.
Airmail insures that cities in the Continental U.S. are only two days away.
Airmail hardly ever takes more than two days to arrive—often only one. (Just make sure your letters get to an Airmail box by our last pickup of the day.)
This helps you know when to follow up on correspondence. It also insures you of important time to plan ahead.
Airmail insures that your letters will be processed first and fastest.
Airmail letters always get handled and processed first, before other mail. In fact, when you use Airmail you save up to half a day in handling alone.
Airmail insures your letters will be treated with respect on their arrival.
Airmail commands attention because it looks important.
It says that you're concerned enough to mail your letters the fastest, most reliable way.
What it all adds up to is this: Airmail gets on the plane first, gets handled first, and gets where it's going first. Airmail. An inexpensive insurance policy that's good business.
AIRMAIL
Your Postal Service

590

591

590
Art Director: Sandy Carlson
Copywriters: Bruce Goldman
Steve Herz
Designer: Sandy Carlson
Artist: Isador Seltzer
Agency: Needham, Harper & Steers
Client: U. S. Postal Service

591
Art Director: Ted Andresakes
Designer: Kathy Palladini
Artist: Jerry Darvin
Agency: CBS/Broadcast Group
Client: CBS Television Stations

Direct Mail

592
Art Director: James Miho
Copywriter: David Brown
Designer: James Miho
Artist: James Miho
Client: Champion Papers

592

To the traveler through Brazil's colonial towns, buildings faced with tiles are an exciting display of color and craftsmanship. Blue and white predominate, but you can find yellow, green, and brown if you search carefully.
Today, some of Brazil's leading artists create new designs for this old form... and artisans preserve the tilemaker's art with reproductions of the very old ones. They're beautifully made, still inexpensive, and durable.

593

594

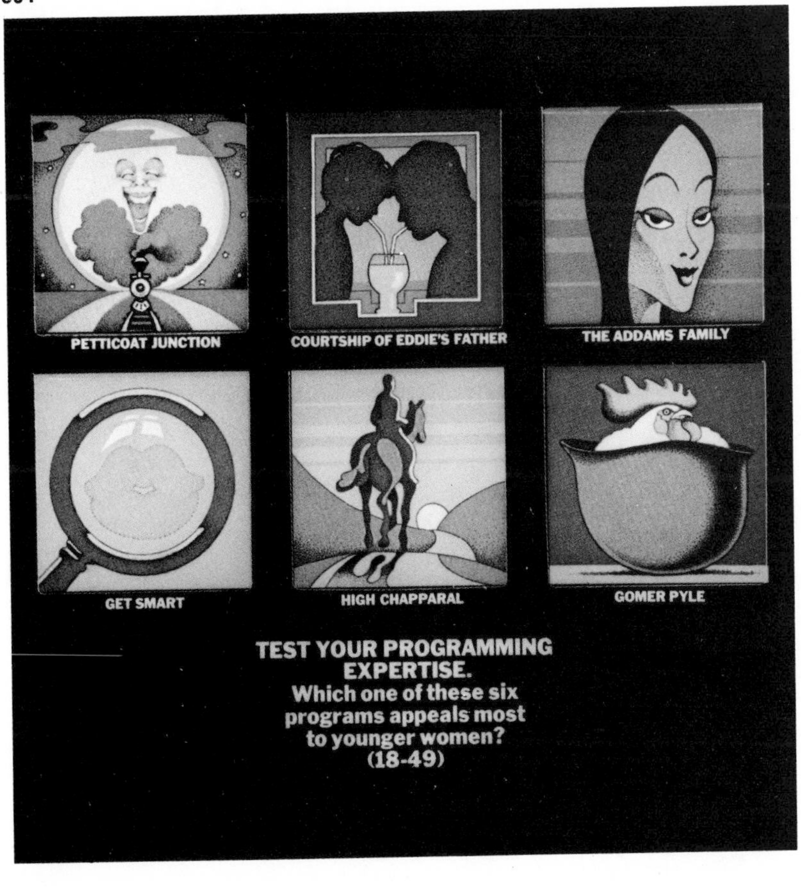
PETTICOAT JUNCTION
COURTSHIP OF EDDIE'S FATHER
THE ADDAMS FAMILY
GET SMART
HIGH CHAPPARAL
GOMER PYLE
TEST YOUR PROGRAMMING EXPERTISE.
Which one of these six programs appeals most to younger women? (18-49)

593 Gold Award
Art Director: Frank Rogers
Copywriter: Jack O'Brien
Designer: Mabey Trousdell
Artist: Mabey Trousdell
Agency: Kincaid Advertising
Client: First National City Bank

594
Art Director: Rene Vidmer
Copywriter: Lew Petterson
Designers: Rene Vidmer
Alan Mitelman
Artist: Sean Harrison
Agency: Hecht, Vidmer, Inc.
Client: MGM

"DON'T
WORRY, DEAR.
ALL THAT HARD WORK'S
FINALLY GOING TO PAY OFF."
MEANWHILE, UP ON THE AWARDS STAGE...

"FOR THE
CATEGORY:
BEST CREATIVE
BANK MARKETING SERVICES...
THE
AWARD
WINNER IS...
NBC

595

596

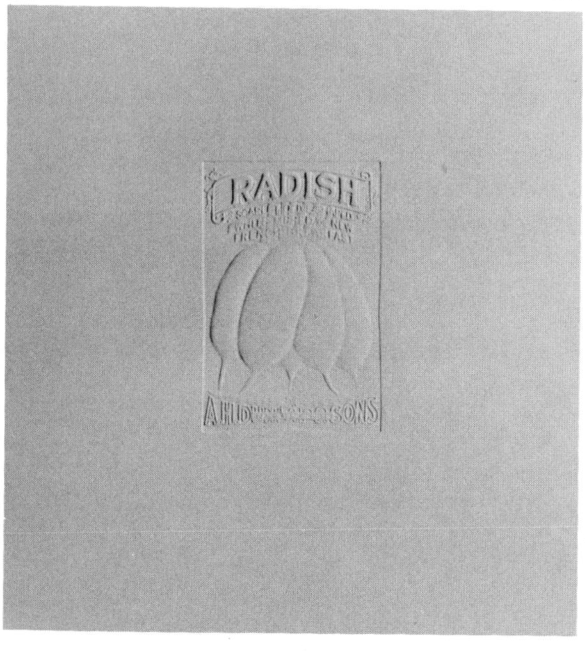
RADISH

The ABC's of NFL Football
A Primer

595
Art Director: Tom Lewis
Copywriter: Bruce Levitt
Designers: Tom Lewis
 Bruce Levitt
Photographer: Culver Pictures
Agency: John H. Harland Company
Client: John H. Harland Company

596
Art Directors: Ralph Moxcey
 Jim Witham
Copywriter: Nelson Lofstedt
Designers: Ralph Moxcey
 Jim Witham
Artists: Jim Baldwin
 Gahan Wilson
 John Martucci
 Joe Veno
 Gail Cooper
 John Carlson
 Jerry Pinkney
 Carol Anthony
 Gregory Fossella
 Tom Norton
 Alain Lenoir
Photographers: Bill Bruin
 Jerry Freedman
 Phil Marco
 Frank Foster
Agency: Humphrey, Browning, MacDougall
Client: S. D. Warren Paper Company

597
Art Director: Mike Gaines
Designer: Mabey Trousdell
Artist: Mabey Trousdell
Agency: Mabey Trousdell Inc.
Client: N.F.L. Properties

597

E **is for ENDS.** For the past decade and a half or so, most pro teams have used three ends or receivers. The flanker actually is the fourth member of the backfield and, as such, must remain one yard behind the line of scrimmage. Like the flanker, the wide receiver also is split out, but he lines up on the line of scrimmage with the rest of the offensive line. The tight end, usually a big, strong man, lines up next to a tackle.

F **is for FIELD.** A football field is 100 yards long and 53-1/3 yards wide. It is bisected by lines five yards apart, beginning from each goal line. The 50-yard line is the midpoint and the other yardlines graduate out on either side of it. The tiny lines that are slightly more than 23 yards from each sideline are called hashmarks. They are one yard apart and each series of plays with the football begins either within them or directly on them. On each end of the field is the end zone, which is 10 yards deep.

G **is for GOAL POST.** The goal post is the part of the football field that is, essentially, just for kicks. It is 18 ft., 6" wide, 10 ft. high at the crossbar and 20 ft. high at the endposts. All conversions (the point after a touchdown) and field goals must pass over the crossbar between the endposts to be good.

H **is for HALL OF FAME.** The legends of the past are a part of the Hall of Fame in Canton, Ohio. Seventy-four men have been honored and a selection committee makes yearly additions. The impressive building also holds memorabilia from pro football's most notable games, featuring some of the sport's great teams.

Direct Mail

598

598
Art Director: Rene Vidmer
Copywriter: Rene Vidmer
Designers: Rene Vidmer
Alan Mitelman
Photographer: Anonymous
Agency: Hecht, Vidmer, Inc.
Client: MGM

599 Silver Award
Art Directors: John Casado
Barbara Casado
Copywriter: Barbara Casado
Designers: John Casado
Barbara Casado
Artists: Barbara Casado
Art Krebs
Agency: John & Barbara Casado Design
Client: John & Barbara Casado

600
Art Director: Pete Coutroulis
Copywriters: Howard Krakow
Jim Weller
Designers: Pete Coutroulis
Tom Conrad
Agency: Jim Weller & Partners
Client: United Performing Arts Fund

599

600

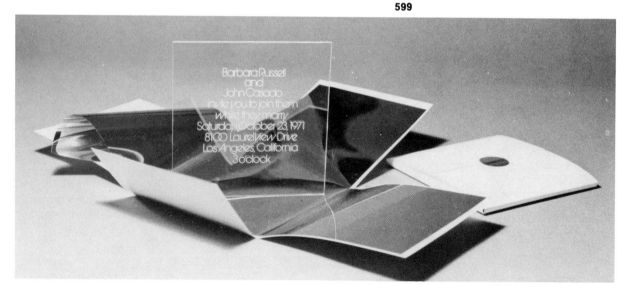

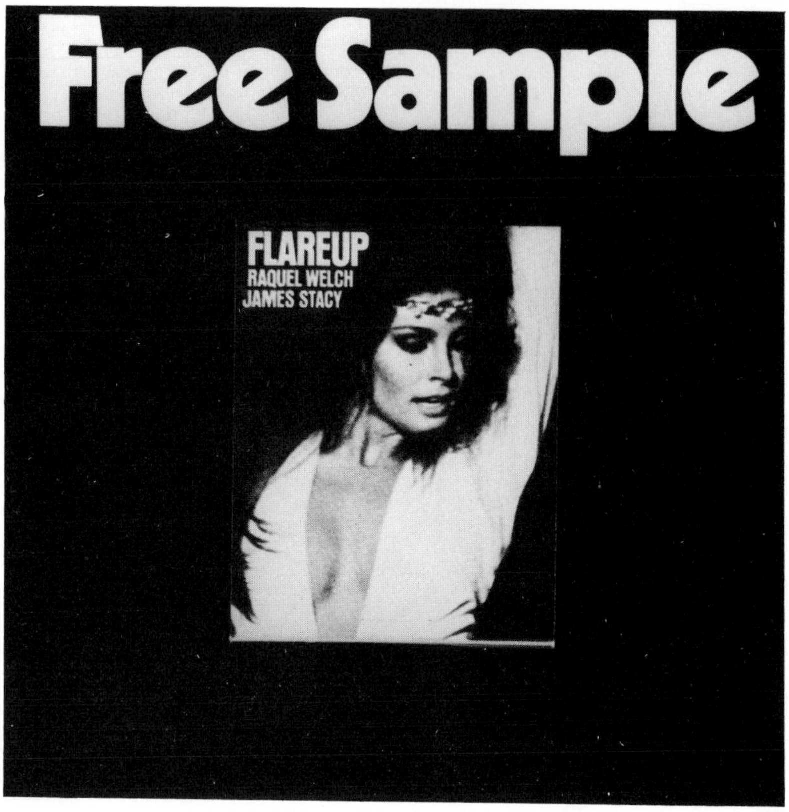

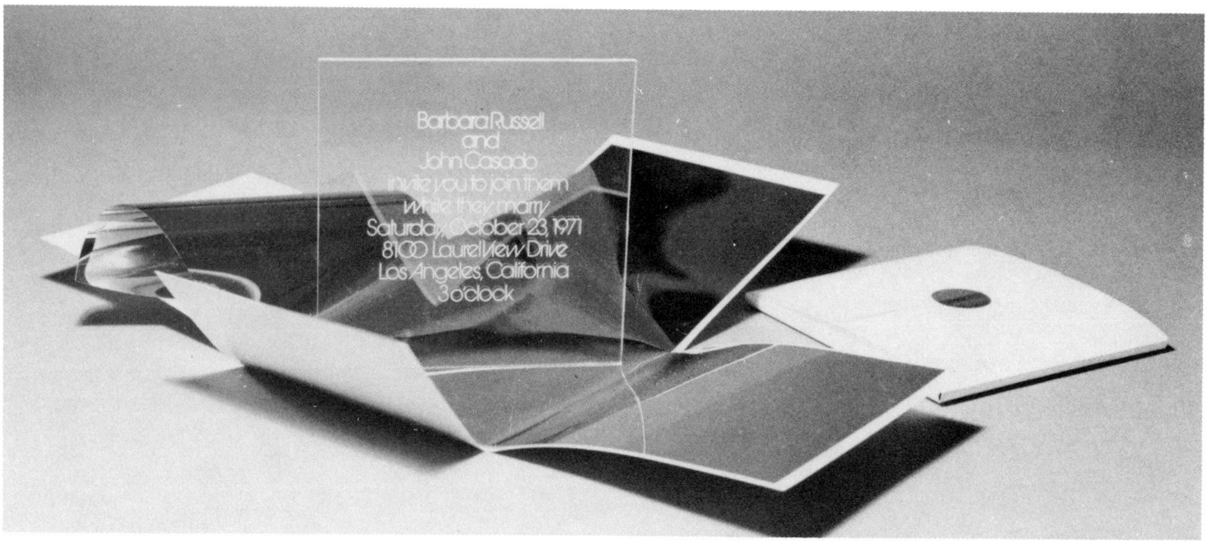

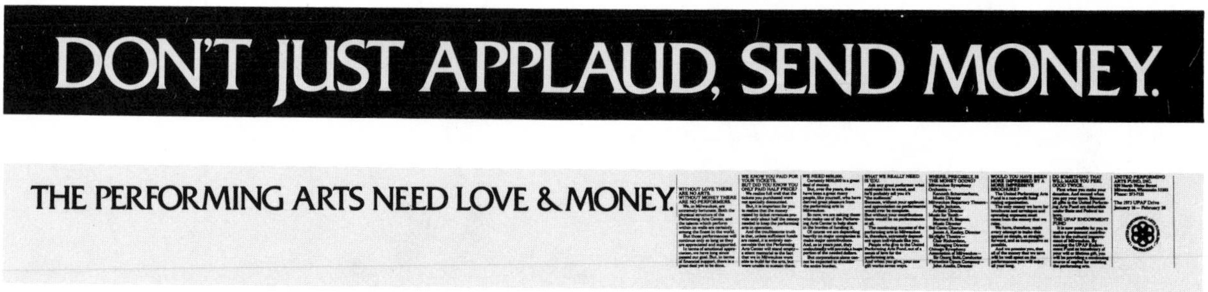

601
Art Director: Dave Haggerty
Copywriter: Bob Meury
Designer: Dave Haggerty
Photographer: Dave Haggerty
Client: Joe Calabrese

601

JOE CALABRESE.
THE HANDS OF A SURGEON.

BOARDMAN
509 LORIMER STREET · BROOKLYN, NEW YORK 11211 · 212·387·4059

Direct Mail

602
Art Director: Richard Nava
Copywriter: Jean Zerries
Designer: Richard Nava
Photographer: Peter Papadopolous
Agency: Image Communications Inc.
Client: Talon

603
Art Director: Mabey Trousdell
Copywriter: Mabey Trousdell
Designer: Mabey Trousdell
Artist: Mabey Trousdell
Client: Mabey Trousdell

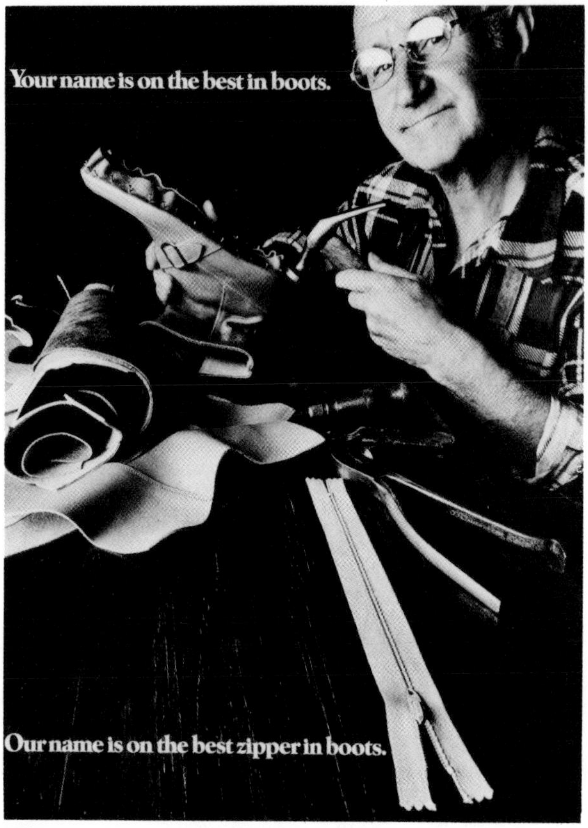
Your name is on the best in boots.
Our name is on the best zipper in boots.

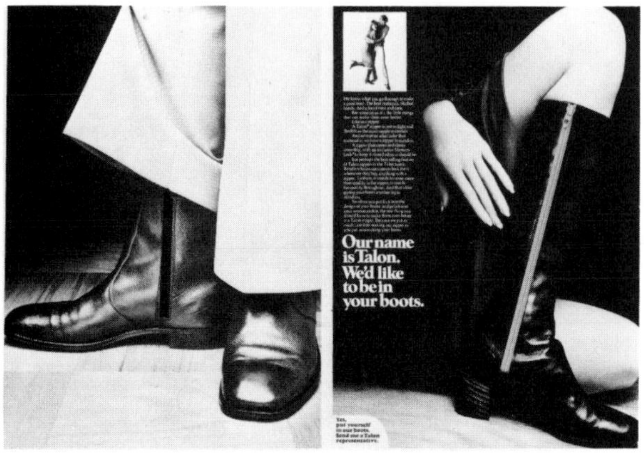
Our name is Talon. We'd like to be in your boots.

602

603

"SHOULD AULD ACQUAINTANCE BE FORGOT"
1973 JANUARY 1973

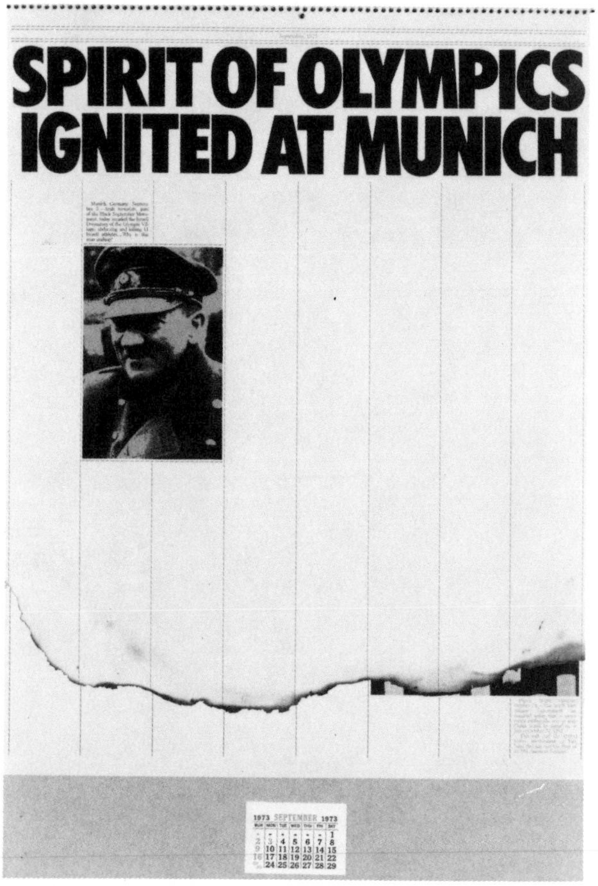
SPIRIT OF OLYMPICS IGNITED AT MUNICH
1973 SEPTEMBER 1973

Letterheads

604
Art Director: Larry Phillips
Designer: Mabey Trousdell
Artist: Mabey Trousdell
Agency: Garner Lyon
Client: WAPE Radio

605
Art Director: Robert Fiore
Designer: Robert Fiore
Agency: Gaynor & Ducas, Inc.
Client: Birmingham Small Arms

604

605

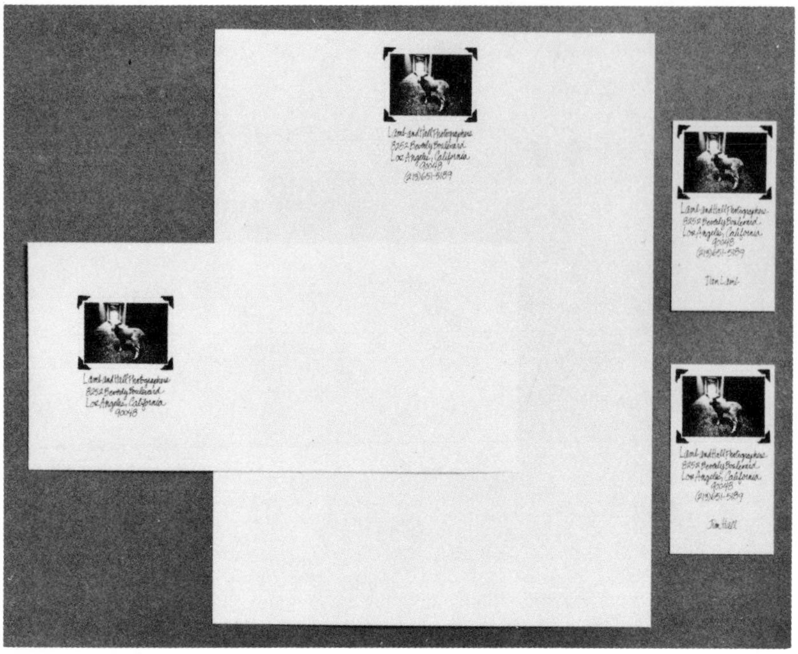

606

607

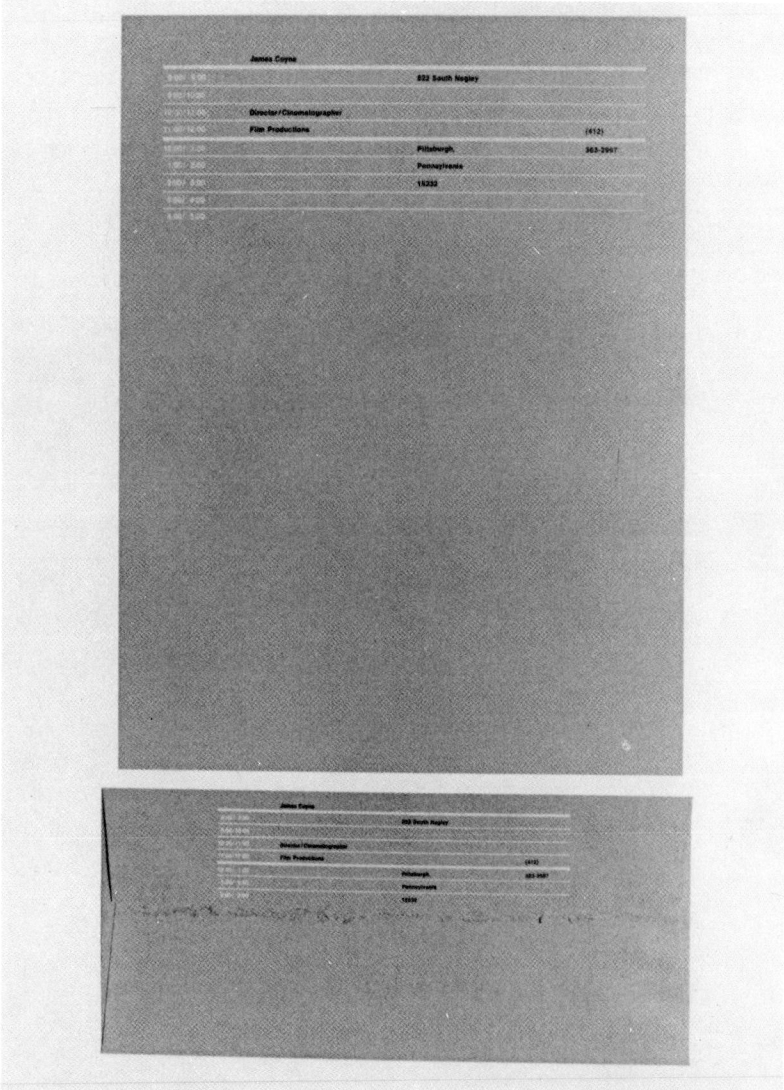

Letterheads

606
Art Director: Mel Abert
Designer: Mel Abert
Photographer: Lamb & Hall
Retoucher: Alan Williams
Agency: Abert, Newhoff & Burr
Client: Lamb & Hall Photographers

607
Art Director: J. Michael Essex
Designer: J. Michael Essex
Agency: WQED Design Centre
Client: James Coyne

608
Art Director: Craig Braun
Designer: Tom Wilkes
Agency: Wilkes & Braun Inc.
Client: Terry Knight Ent. Ltd.

609
Designer: Richard Moore
Agency: Richard Moore Associates
Client: Richard Moore Associates

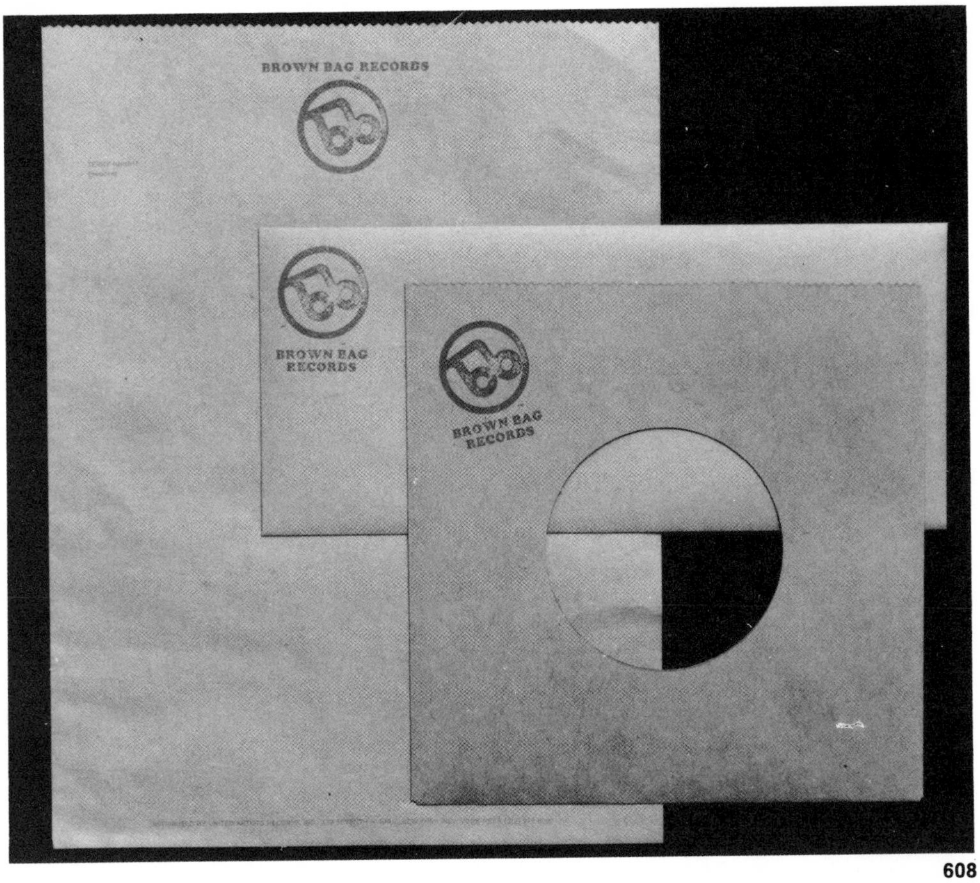

BROWN BAG RECORDS
BROWN BAG
RECORDS
BROWN BAG
RECORDS

608

609

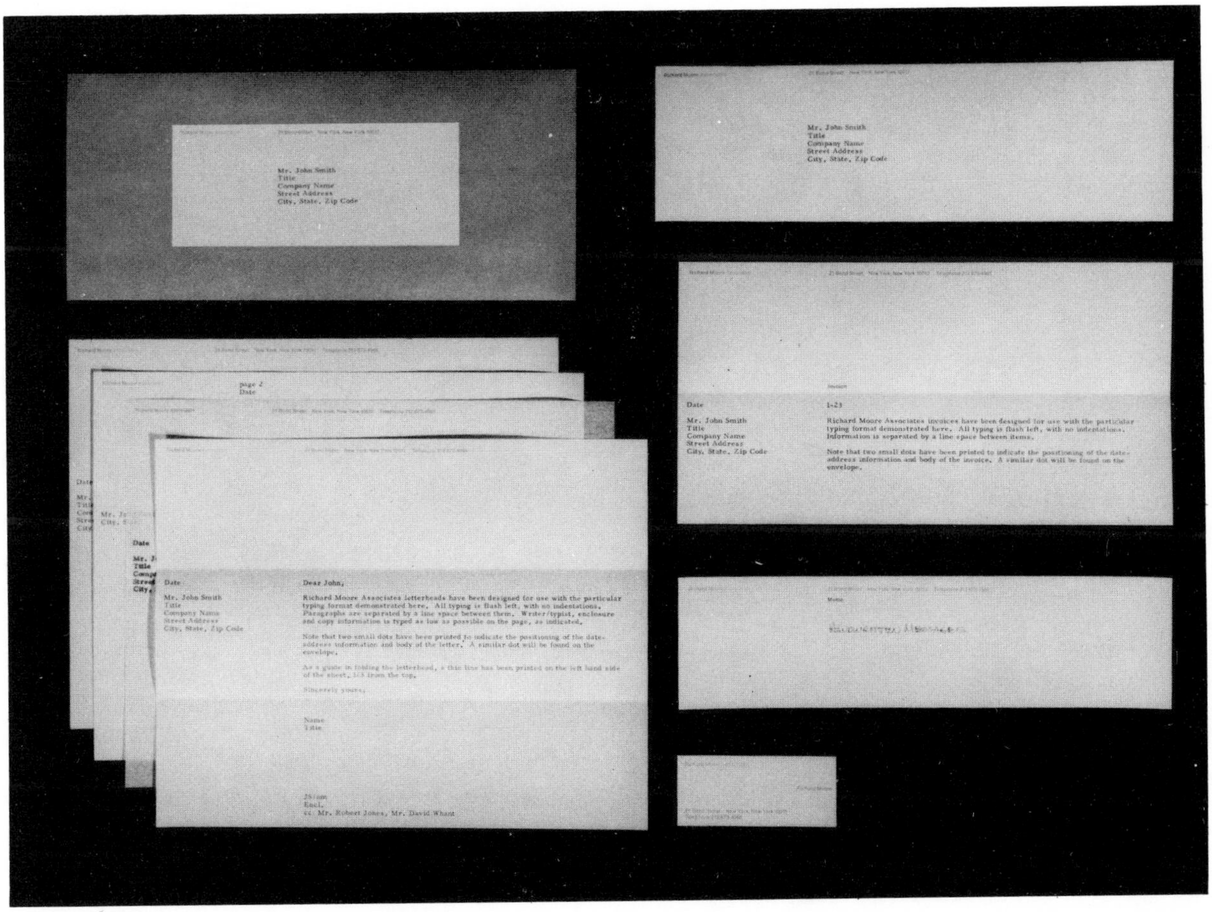

Mr. John Smith
Title
Company Name
Street Address
City, State, Zip Code
Mr. John Smith
Title
Company Name
Street Address
City, State, Zip Code
page 2
Date
Date
Mr. John Smith
Title
Company Name
Street Address
City, State, Zip Code
Dear John,
Richard Moore Associates letterheads have been designed for use with the particular typing format demonstrated here. All typing is flush left, with no indentations. Paragraphs are separated by a line space between them. Writer/typist, enclosure and copy information is typed as low as possible on the page, as indicated.
Note that two small dots have been printed to indicate the positioning of the date-address information and body of the letter. A similar dot will be found on the envelope.
Name
Title
Encl.
cc. Mr. Robert Jones, Mr. David Whant
Date
1-23
Mr. John Smith
Title
Company Name
Street Address
City, State, Zip Code
Richard Moore Associates invoices have been designed for use with the particular typing format demonstrated here. All typing is flush left, with no indentations. Information is separated by a line space between items.
Note that two small dots have been printed to indicate the positioning of the date-address information and body of the invoice. A similar dot will be found on the envelope.

610

611

612

613

Letterheads

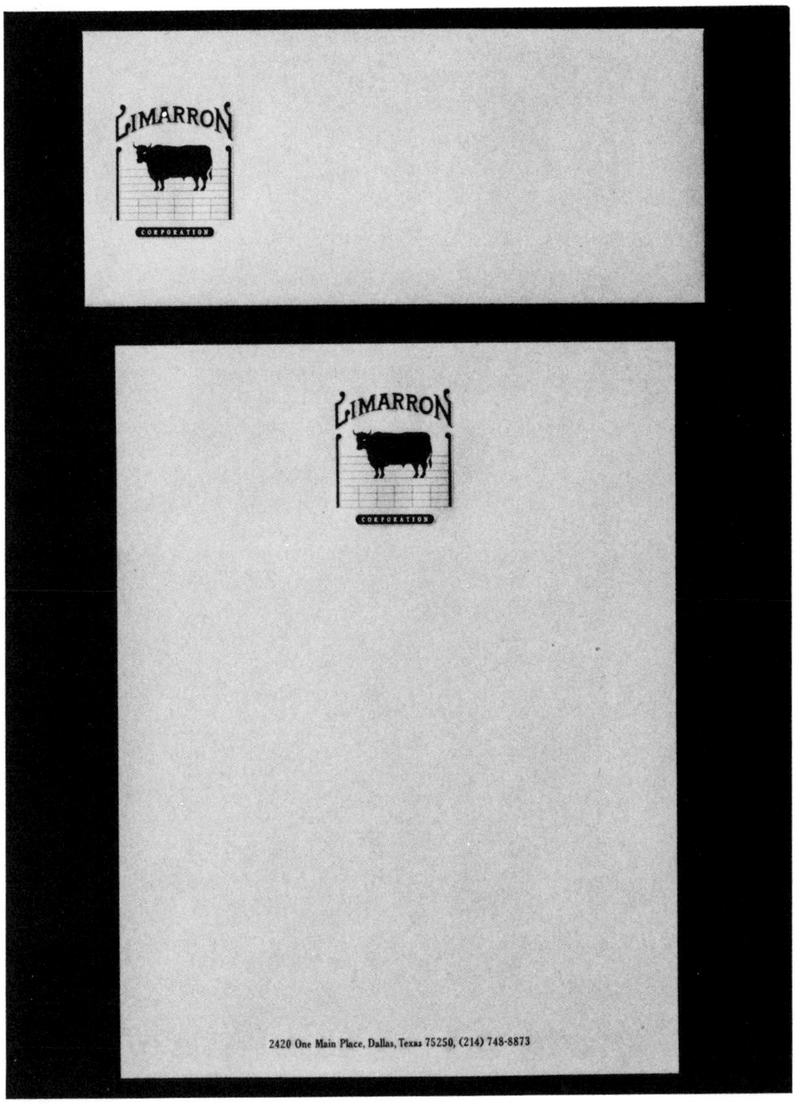

614

615

610
Art Director: Steve Frankfurt
Designer: Tony Palladino
Artist: Bob Geissman
Agency: Acme Communications
Client: Frankfurt Communications

611
Art Director: Tony Palladino
Designer: Tony Palladino
Artist: David Wilcox
Agency: Acme Communications
Client: Acme Communications

612
Art Director: Herb Lubalin
Designer: Herb Lubalin
Artist: Tom Carnase
Agency: Lubalin, Smith, Carnase, Inc.
Client: Ampersand Productions

613
Art Director: John Casado
Designers: John Casado
Barbara Casado
Artist: John Casado
Copywriter: Adrienne Lowe
Agency: John & Barbara Casado Design
Client: Set The Date Campaign

614
Art Director: Woody Pirtle
Designer: Woody Pirtle
Artist: Woody Pirtle
Agency: The Richards Group
Client: Cimarron Corporation

615 Silver Award
Art Director: Michael Doret
Designer: Michael Doret
Artist: Michael Doret
Client: Whitmore Movie Works

Letterheads

616
Art Director: J. Michael Essex
Designer: J. Michael Essex
Artist: Ed Zelinsky
Agency: WQED Design Centre
Client: Wallis & Marshall Katz

617
Art Director: Woody Pirtle
Designer: Woody Pirtle
Artist: Woody Pirtle
Agency: The Richards Group
Client: Linda Pirtle

616

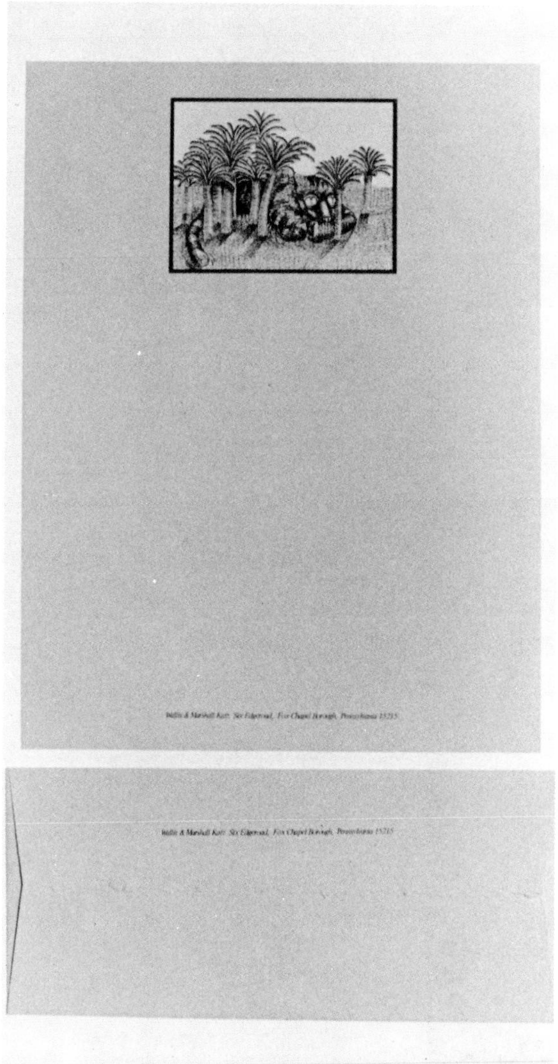

617

Lithographix, Inc.
811 North Highland
Los Angeles, Calif. 90038
213:462-7236

618

619

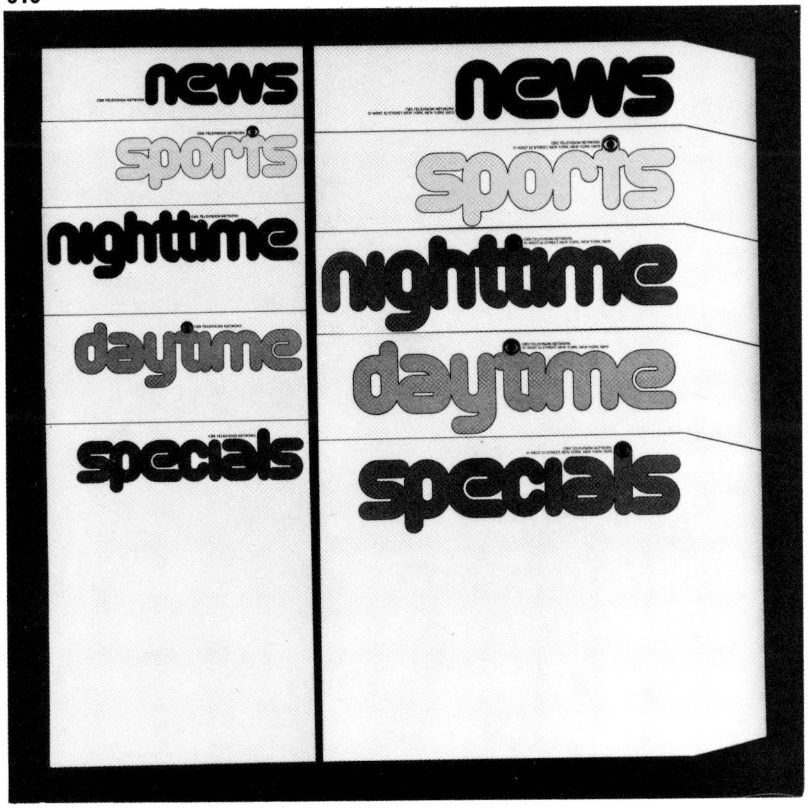

618
Art Directors: Don Weller
Dennis Juett
Designer: Dan Hanrahan
Artist: Dan Hanrahan
Agency: Weller & Juett Inc.
Client: Lithographix, Inc.

619
Art Director: David November
Designers: David November
Akihiko Seki
Artist: Akihiko Seki
Agency: CBS/Broadcast Group
Client: CBS Television Network

620 Gold Award
Art Directors: Dennis Juett
Don Weller
Designers: Dennis Juett
Don Weller
Jack Hermsen
Artist: Bob Maile
Photographer: Don Weller
Agency: Weller & Juett Inc.
Client: Quality Real Estate Investments

621
Art Directors: Dennis Juett
Don Weller
Designer: Don Weller
Agency: Weller & Juett Inc.
Client: Pierce, Lacey/Cannell & Chaffin

622
Art Director: Lawrence Miller
Designer: Lawrence Miller
Artist: Lawrence Miller
Copywriter: Lawrence Miller
Agency: Marketing Design Alliance
Client: Lawrence Miller and Associates

620

621

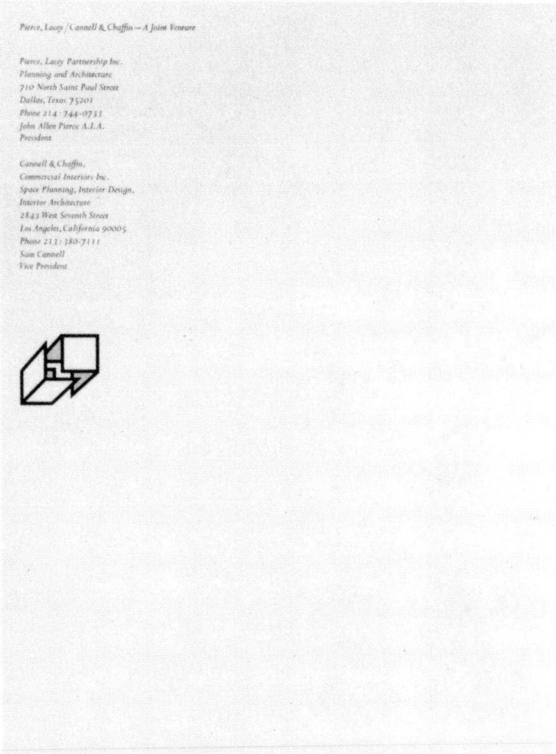

622

623

624

625

623
Art Director: Roger Ferriter
Designer: Roger Ferriter
Artist: Tom Carnase
Agency: Lubalin, Smith, Carnase Inc.
Client: Bayhead Yacht Corporation

624 Silver Award
Art Director: Michael Salisbury
Designer: Michael Doret
Artist: Michael Doret
Publisher: Los Angeles Times
West Magazine

625
Art Director: Herb Lubalin
Designer: Herb Lubalin
Artist: Tom Carnase
Agency: Lubalin, Smith, Carnase Inc.
Client: Typographic Communications

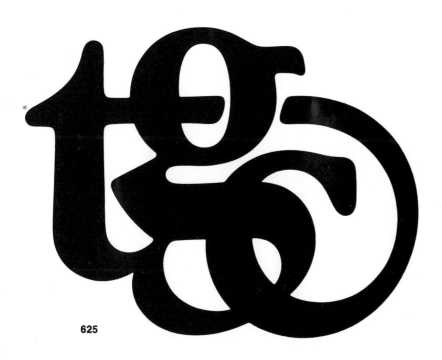

Trademarks, Logotypes

626
Art Director: Annegret Beier
Designer: Annegret Beier
Artist: Kohei Miura
Agency: Delpire Advico
Client: Meridien Hotel

627
Art Director: Herb Lubalin
Designer: Herb Lubalin
Artist: Kohei Miura
Agency: Delpire Advico
Client: Meridien Hotel

628
Art Director: Annegret Beier
Designer: Annegret Beier
Artist: Kohei Miura
Agency: Delpire Advico
Client: Meridien Hotel

626

627

628

629
Art Director: Alan Peckolick
Designer: Alan Peckolick
Artist: Mike Dorat
Agency: Alan Peckolick Graphic Design
Client: Loft's Candy Company

630
Art Director: Ellen Shapiro
Designer: Tony Dispigna
Artist: Tony Dispigna
Agency: Artissimo, Inc.
Client: Ellen Shapiro

629

630

631

632

633

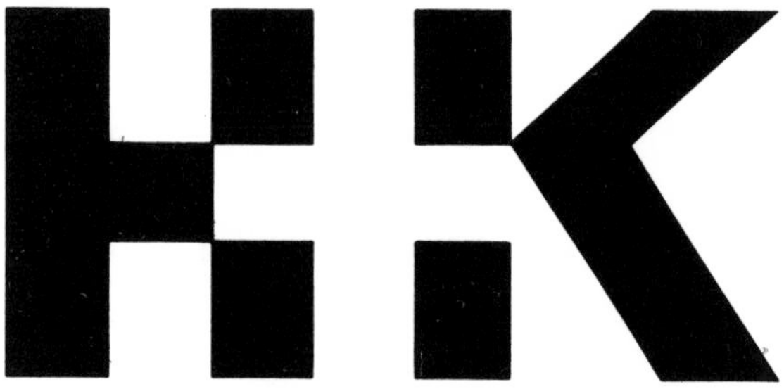

634

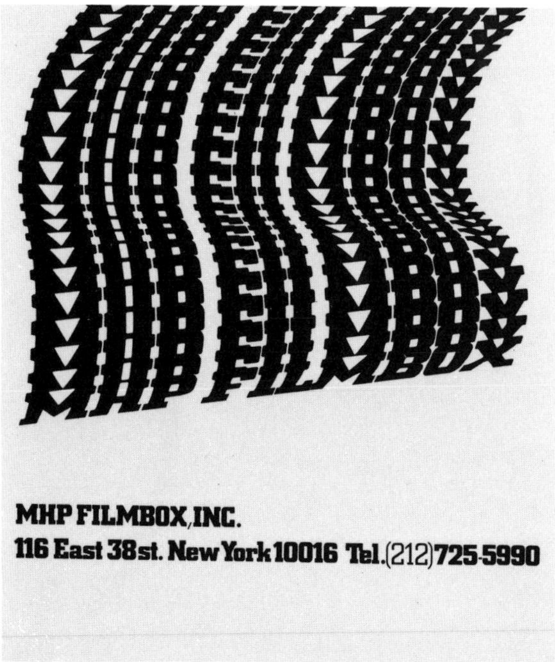

631
Art Director: Dennis Mazzella
Designer: Kurt Weihs
Copywriters: Barbara Brenner
Kurt Weihs
Agency: Brenner, Mazzella, Weihs
Client: Leasemobile

632
Art Director: Kurt Weihs
Designer: Dennis Mazzella
Photographer: Kurt Weihs
Agency: Brenner, Mazzella, Weihs
Client: Suburban Pontiac Inc.

633
Art Director: Hill and Knowlton Graphics
Designer: Hill and Knowlton Graphics
Artist: Hill and Knowlton Graphics
Agency: Hill and Knowlton, Inc.

634
Art Director: Gene Sercander
Designer: Gene Sercander
Artists: Gene Sercander
Benny Rivera
Agency: Design 35
Client MHP Filmbox

635

636

637

635
Art Directors: Don Weller
Dennis Juett
Designer: Dan Hanrahan
Artist: Dan Hanrahan
Photographer: Roger Marchutz
Agency: Weller & Juett Inc.
Client: Lithographix, Inc.

636
Art Director: Annegret Beier
Designer: Annegret Beier
Artist: Fumiko Higuchi
Client: Sheila Hicks

637
Art Director: Kurt Weihs
Designer: Kurt Weihs
Photographer: Kurt Weihs
Copywriter: Ron Holland
Agency: Lois/Chajet Design Group
Client: Marriott

638

639

Trademarks, Logotypes

638
Art Director: Tom Courtos
Designer: Tom Courtos
Artist: Tom Courtos
Agency: Lois/Chajet Design Group
Client: Restaurant Associates

639
Art Director: George Lois
Designer: Dennis Mazzella
Artist: John Pistelli
Copywriter: Ron Holland
Agency: Lois/Chajet Design Group
Client: Restaurant Associates

640
Art Director: Dennis Mazzella
Designer: Kurt Weihs
Agency: Brenner, Mazzella, Weihs
Client: Myrtle Motors Corp.

641
Art Director: Kurt Weihs
Designer: Kurt Weihs
Artist: Kurt Weihs
Agency: Lois/Chajet Design Group
Client: Restaurant Associates

642
Art Director: Kurt Weihs
Designer: Kurt Weihs
Agency: Lois/Chajet Design Group
Client: Tonsil Records

Myrtle
Motors
Pontiac
Mm
Myrtle Motors Corp.
61-20 Fresh Pond Rd.
Maspeth, Queens
366-5050

640

641

The Ground Floor Cafe
751-5152

642

Tonsil Records

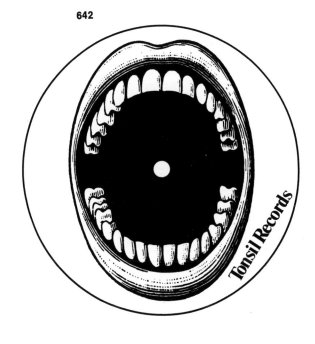

644

643

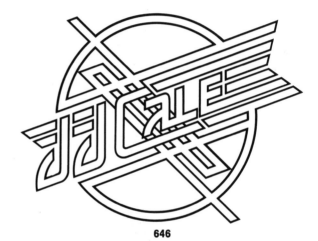

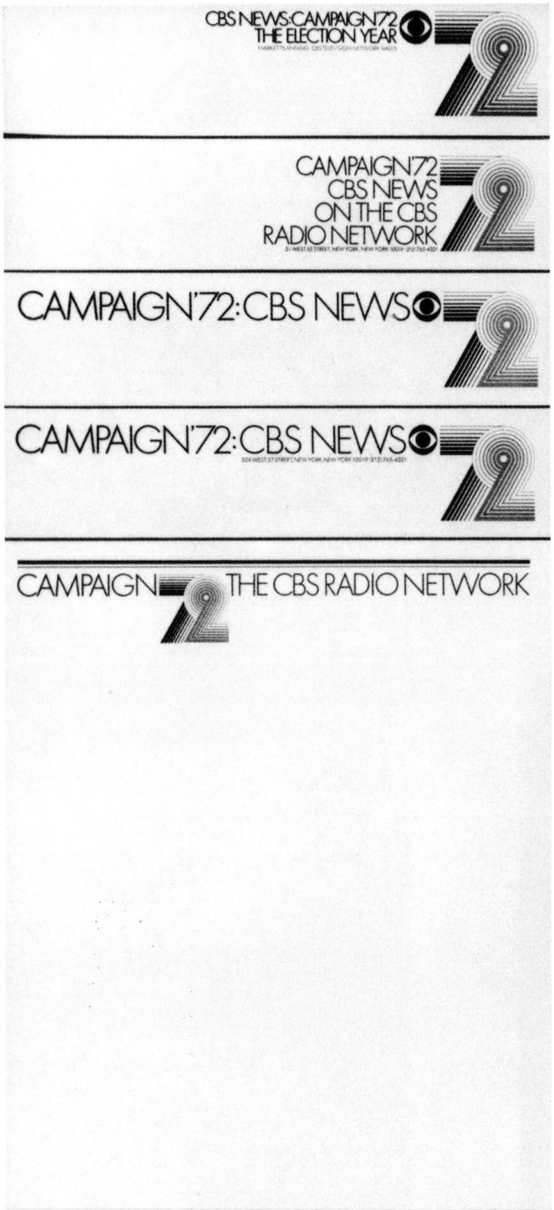

646

647

648

649

643
Art Director: Lou Dorfsman
Designer: Akihiko Seki
Artist: Akihiko Seki
Agency: CBS/Broadcast Group
Client: CBS News

644
Art Director: Bob Ciano
Designer: Bob Ciano
Artist: Roger Hane
Client: CTI Records

646
Art Directors: Gene Brownell
John C. LePrevost
Designer: John C. LePrevost
Artist: Severine Nelson
Agency: Gene Brownell Studio
Client: Shelter Records

647
Art Director: Arie J. Geurts
Designer: Arie J. Geurts
Artist: Arie J. Geurts
Client: Charolais Breeders

648
Art Director: Steve Frankfurt
Designer: Tony Palladino
Artist: Bob Geissman
Agency: Acme Communications
Client: Frankfurt Communications

649
Art Director: Don Kano
Designer: Don Kano
Artist: Don Kano
Agency: Will Martin Design Associates
Client: Senate of Priests
Archdiocese of Los Angeles

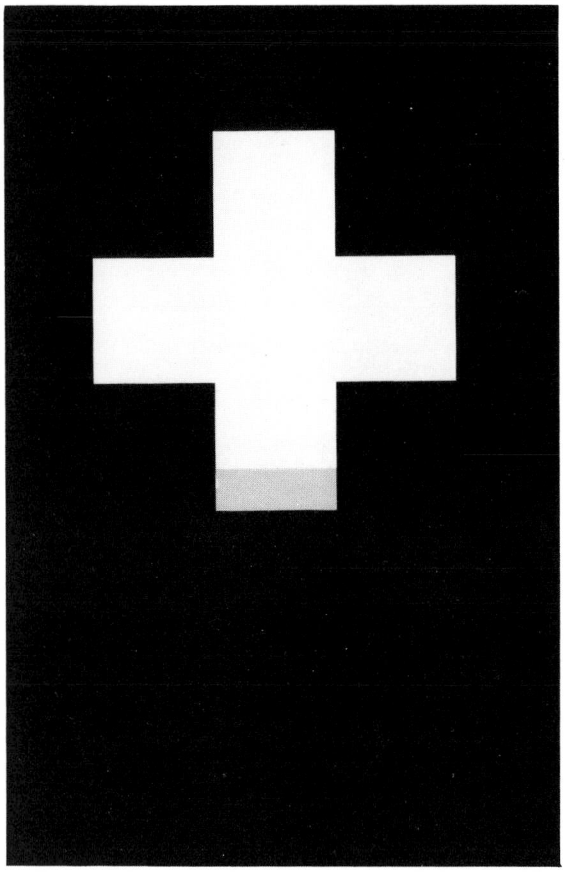

650

651

652

653

654

655

650
Art Director: Robert F. Baker
Designers: Russ Veduccio
Robert F. Baker
Artist: Russ Veduccio
Copywriter: Robert F. Baker
Agency: Harold Cabot, Inc.
Client: Boston Red Cross
Blood Donor Program

651
Art Directors: John Casado
Cheri Ramey
Designers: John Casado
Barbara Casado
Artists: John Casado
Barbara Casado
Agency: John & Barbara Casado Design
Client: The Potting Shed

652
Designer: Kenneth Walker
Agency: Kenneth Walker Design Group
Client: Kenneth Walker Design Group

653
Art Directors: Robin Rickabaugh
Heidi Rickabaugh
Designers: Robin Rickabaugh
Heidi Rickabaugh
Artist: Robin Rickabaugh
Client: Electrical Appliance Service Inc.

654
Art Director: Thomas A. Rigsby
Designer: Thomas A. Rigsby
Artist: Richard Vartian
Agency: TriArts Inc.
Client: Uniforms Unlimited, Inc.

655
Art Directors: Robin Rickabaugh
Heidi Rickabaugh
Designers: Robin Rickabaugh
Heidi Rickabaugh
Artist: Robin Rickabaugh
Client: Edgefield Lodge

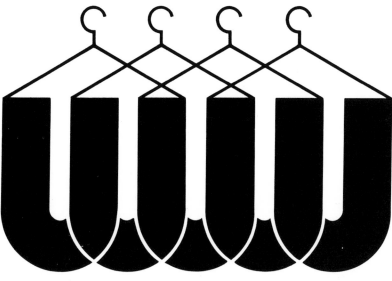

656
Art Director: John Casado
Designer: John Casado
Artists: John Casado
Bette Duke
Agency: Dancer, Fitzgerald & Sample
Client: The Bubble Machine

657 Gold Award
Art Director: Michael Reid
Designer: Michael Reid
Artist: Halina Logay
Agency: Michael Reid Design
Client: Rush-Presbyterian-St. Luke's
Medical Center

658
Art Director: Raymond Lee
Designer: Raymond Lee
Agency: Raymond Lee & Associates Ltd.
Client: Durastone Ltd.

656

657

658

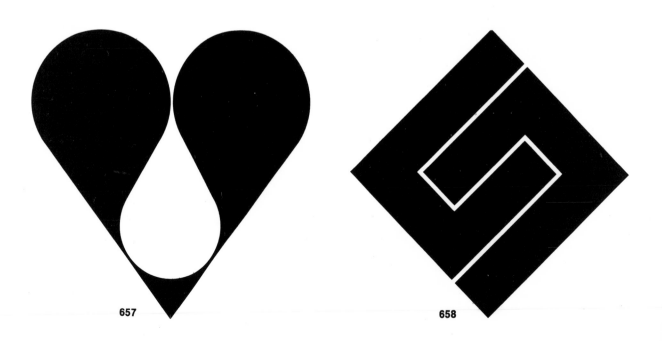

659
Art Director: Mel Abert
Designer: Mel Abert
Photographer: Lamb & Hall
Retoucher: Alan Williams
Agency: Abert, Newhoff & Burr
Client: Lamb & Hall Photographers

660
Art Director: Glen Christensen
Designer: Glen Christensen
Artists: Sir John Tenniel
Glen Christensen
Agency: The Buddah Group
Client: The Famous Charisma Label

661
Art Director: Glen Christensen
Designers: Glen Christensen
Mona Mark
Artist: Mona Mark
Agency: The Buddah Group
Client: Kama Sutra Records

659

660

661

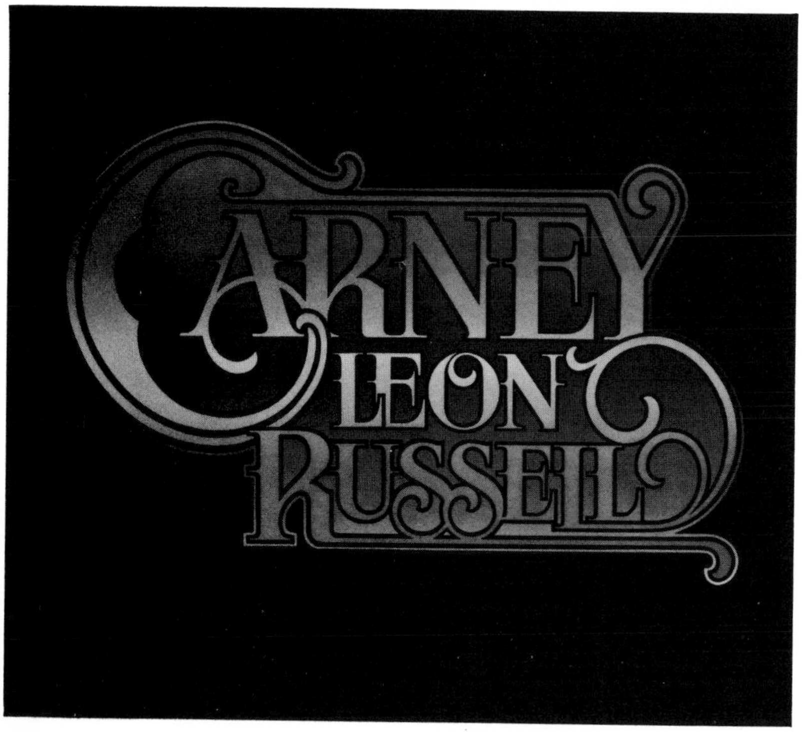

662

662
Art Directors: Gene Brownell
John C. LePrevost
Designer: John C. LePrevost
Artist: John C. LePrevost
Agency: Gene Brownell Studio
Client: Shelter Records

663
Art Director: Kurt Weihs
Designer: Kurt Weihs
Artist: Kurt Weihs
Agency: Lois/Chajet Design Group
Client: Marriott

664
Art Director: George Lois
Designer: Tom Courtos
Artist: George Lois
Agency: Lois/Chajet Design Group
Client: Old-fashioned Mr. Jennings

663

664

665
Art Director: Mel Abert
Designer: Mel Abert
Photographer: Lamb & Hall
Retoucher: Alan Williams
Agency: Abert, Newhoff & Burr
Client: Lamb & Hall Photographers

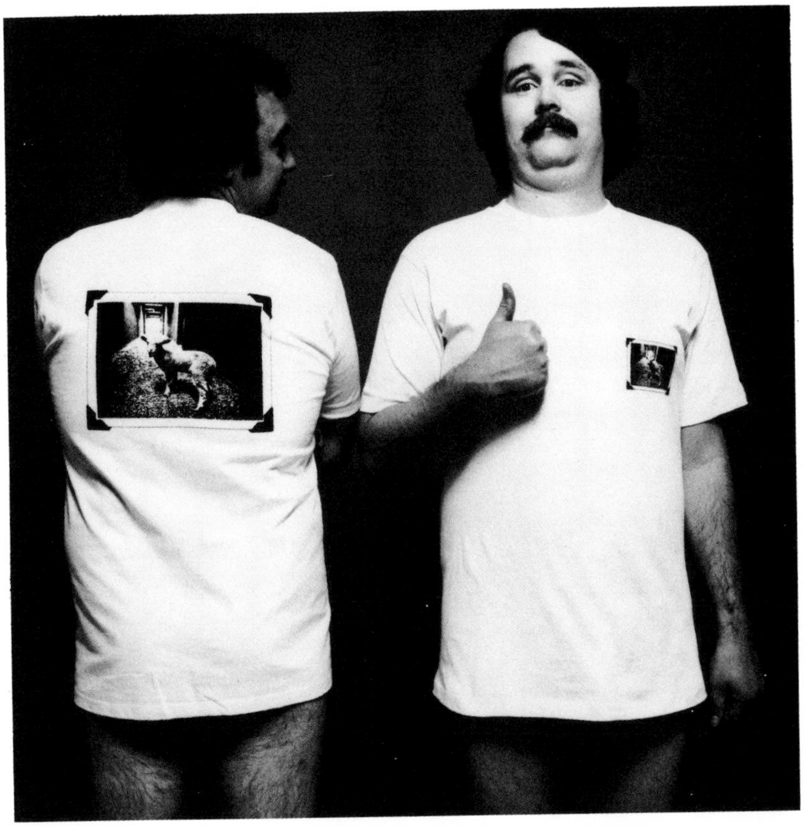

665

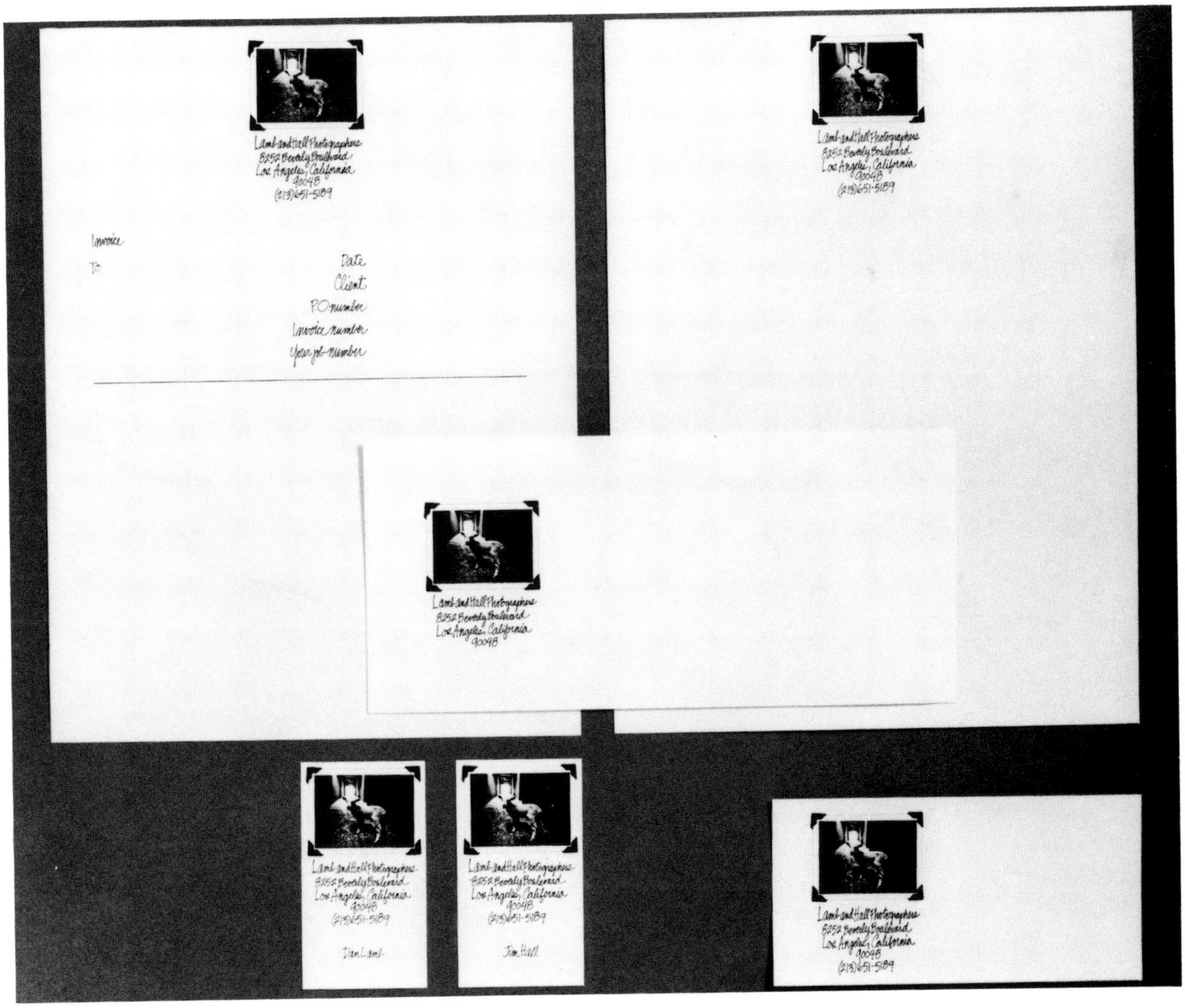

BirthdayBook
BirthdayBook
740 Madison Avenue, NewYork 10021
Telephone 212-249-2408
PhelpsK.Manning
Invoice
Purchase Order

666

667

Office Memorandum
Invoice

666
Art Director: William R. Tobias
Designers: William R. Tobias
Upendra Shah
Artist: James Orlandi
Client: Birthday Book

667
Designers: Richard Moore
Rei Yoshimura
Agency: Byron Osterweil Associates
Client: Marshall & Ilsley Corporation

668
Art Director: Walter Halucha
Designer: Walter Halucha
Artist: Ted Lodigensky
Copywriter: Jane Talcott
Agency: Doyle Dane Bernbach Inc.
Client: Snark Products Inc.

668

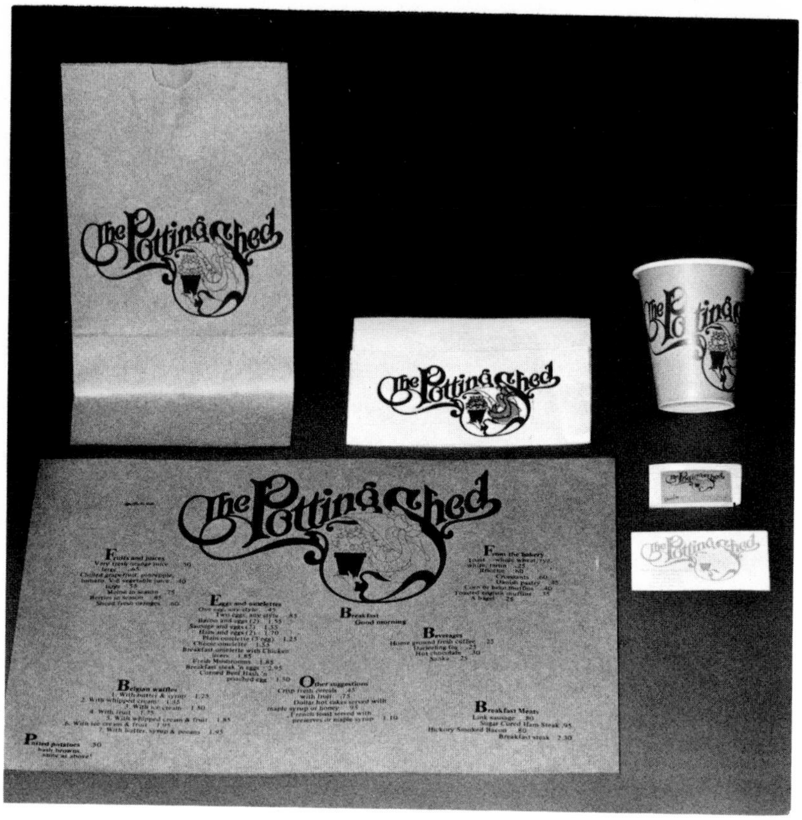

669

670

669
Art Director: Cheri Ramey
Designers: Cheri Ramey
John Casado
Artist: John Casado
Copywriter: Adrienne Lowe
Agency: Lynda Resnick Agency
Client: Spectrum Foods
The Potting Shed

670
Art Director: Cheri Ramey
Designer: Cheri Ramey
Artist: Michael Stern
Copywriter: Adrienne Lowe
Agency: Lynda Resnick Agency
Client: Spectrum Foods
The Greenhouse

ART AND PHOTOGRAPHY

Editorial Photography
Advertising and Promotion Photography
Editorial Art
Advertising and Design Art

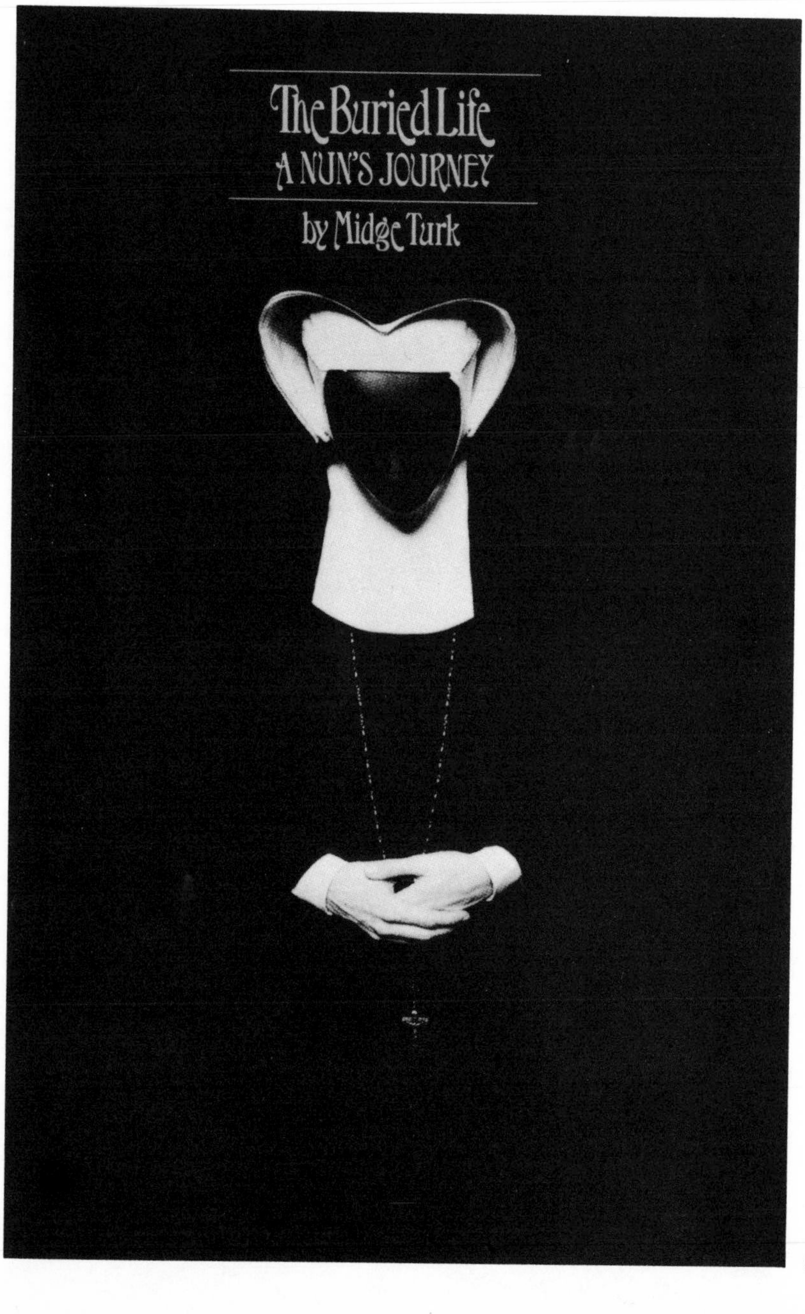

671
Art Director: Alan Peckolick
Designer: Alan Peckolick
Photographer: Frank Moscati
Publisher: World Publishing
Agency: Alan Peckolick Graphic Design

671

672
Art Director: Harry Redler
Designer: Harry Redler
Photographer: Philippe Cornut
Copywriter: Arthur Goldsmith
Publication: Famous Photographers School

The initials TAM are those of a French publication rarely seen by most Gallics, but often reviewed by editors and others interested in photography. The initials stand for "Land, Air, Sea," and TAM is the magazine of the French Army.

Among TAM's brightest contributors is FPS student Philippe Cornut, a young newspaper photographer who was assigned to the magazine in order to enable him to continue his profession while serving his tour of military duty. Only his assignments differ. Instead of shooting local subject matter, he's covering (mostly in color) subjects of special interest to soldiers—new sports cars, major athletic events, Alpine scenes and maneuvers, pop recording musicians, and the like.

Philippe began his professional career two and a half years ago. Now 21, he has been an FPS student for two years. An article in the French magazine *Photo-Cinéma* recently featured a cross-section of his photographs, some of which are shown on these pages. As you can see, his work ranges from straight documentary through human interest to esoteric mood shots. In *Photo-Cinéma*, author J. de Coutter describes Philippe as "a likable, calm young man beginning a photographic career with confidence, intelligence, and a total lack of pretension." He adds further: "Cornut's ambition is to 'write life with a 35 mm camera the way others do with a ball-point pen.'"

We particularly like the closing lines of M. de Coutter's article, which could apply to the work and photographic aspirations of many FPS students: "The prints are displayed before me like playing cards. I am trying to read in them the destiny of Philippe Cornut. Doubtless he has read my thoughts for he concluded himself, 'The future is each day. It is the offspring of the young and the reality of what one sees in the newspapers. Photography must help lead the way for those who are looking.'"

Portfolio: Philippe Cornut, France

Ballet dancers, twin-lens reflex, Tri-X, 1/60 second at f/3.5

672

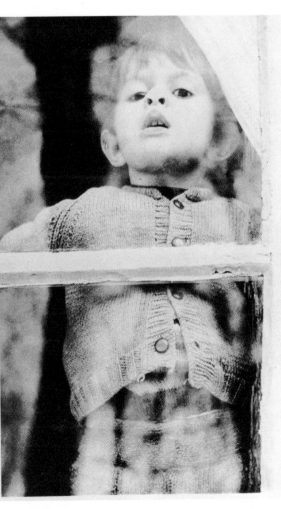

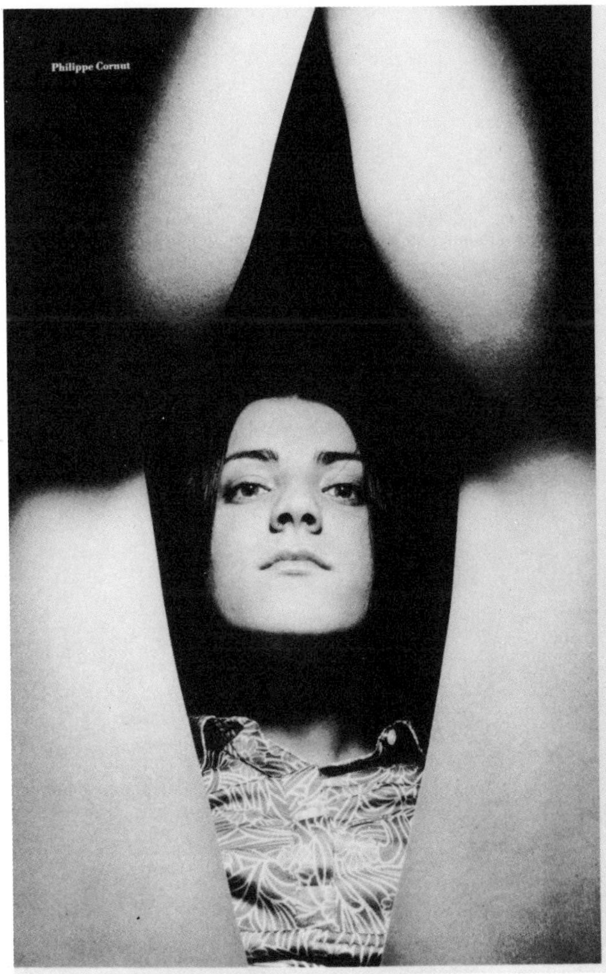

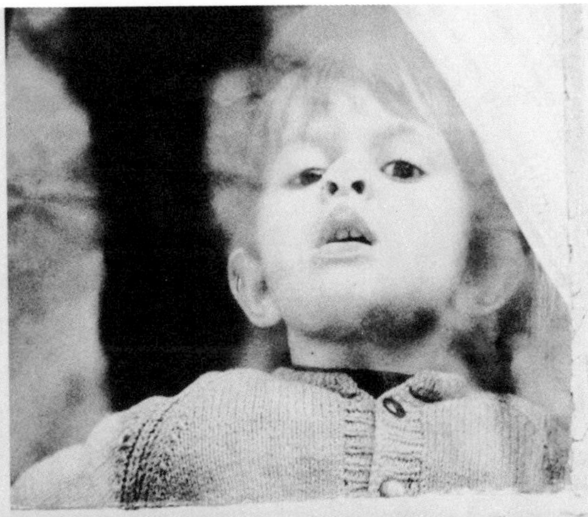

Rainer Kiedrowski

Burro, Southern Spain

Any way you consider him, Rainer Kiedrowski of Düsseldorf, West Germany, is quite a remarkable young man. Up until last summer, when he became a student of FPS, Rainer's knowledge of photography was totally self-taught. He had never worked in a studio or with a professional photographer, had never taken a course in photography. Yet within the three years prior to joining FPS, he had set up a studio and processing lab, been saluted on a television program, and honored in three professional photographic exhibits, including the recent Photokina in Cologne. In addition, he has traveled on photographic assignments throughout Europe, Africa, and Asia, and was a top prizewinner in the second Asahi Pentax World Contest.

Rainer credits his FPS Course as being an important factor in his most recent successes. "The FPS studies," he writes, "have served to refine my knowledge in the technical and figurative aspects of photography--especially through the stimuli and specific problem confrontations that are so important a part of formal training."

Rainer describes himself at present as having two "crucial interests" insofar as his career is concerned.
[1] He wants to further develop his experimental work, which has already resulted in assignments to produce posters, book jackets, and editorial material for magazines.
[2] He has a strong urge to continue to travel and produce "photographic observations of people and life under critical social stresses." Intermingled with his experimental and documentary interpretations, Rainer isn't overlooking the practical bread-and-butter necessity of taking the kinds of pictures in ready demand --feature picture stories, travel-tourism material for carrier lines, and a backlog of genre photographs to be distributed by stock-photo agencies.

What about specialization? Now 24 years old, Rainer is understandably in no hurry to specialize in subject matter. "I am clearly an all-around photographer at this point," he writes. "I want to continue for an indefinite period to feel free and unbound in my work. I am still learning, still building new interests and new skills as I go along."

West German boy

Experimental portrait

25

673
Art Director: Harry Redler
Designer: Harry Redler
Photographer: Rainer Kiedrowski
Copywriter: Arthur Goldsmith
Publication: Famous Photographers School

674
Art Director: Ernest Scarfone
Designer: Ernest Scarfone
Photographer: Laurence Sackman
Publisher: Ferdinand Brothers
Nikon World

675
Art Director: J. C. Suares
Designer: J. C. Suares
Photographer: Jerry Uelsmann
Editor: Harrison Salisbury
Publisher: The New York Times
Op-ed page

674

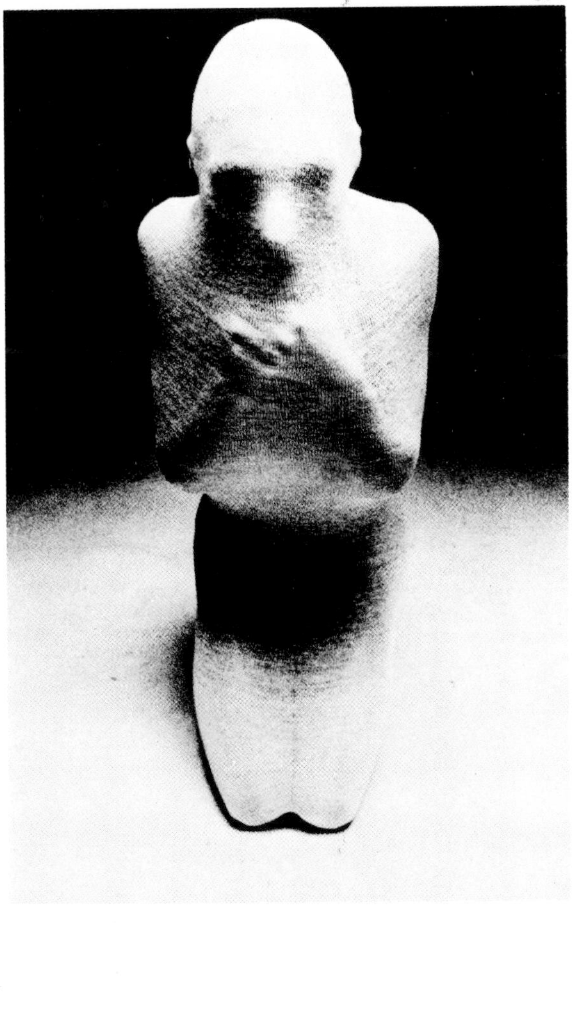

675

Hope Against Hope

AT HOME ABROAD

Obituary: Motherhood

'Welfare Is Not an Evil Word'

"We have for centuries segregated certain groups from the mainstream of life."

All You Have to Do Is Dream

". . . so that even the most bizarre dream could be understood."

'To Whom Should I Write a Letter?'

"One feels like a child throwing paper planes against a blank wall."

676

676 A

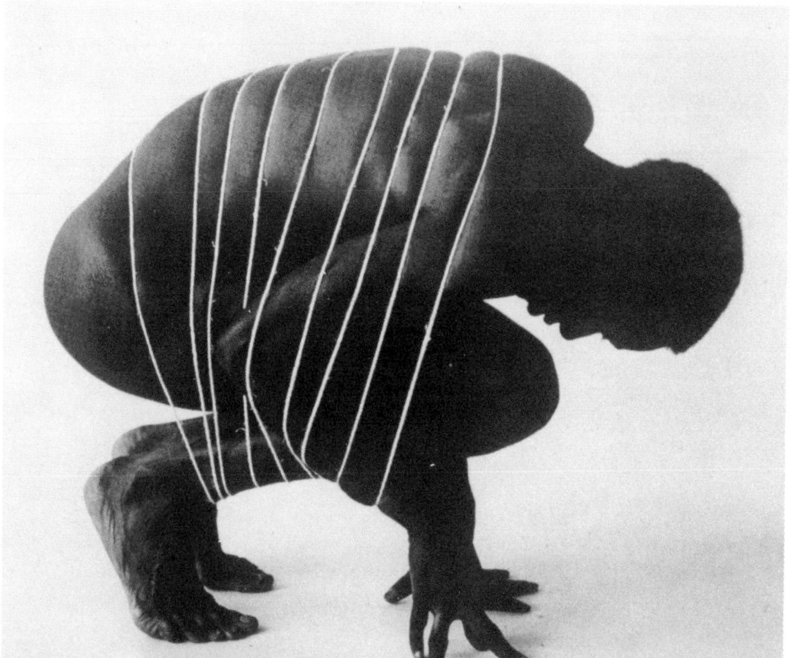

677

... Schmerzen für den Gott

Stärke und Selbstdisziplin. Narben, Ringe, Farben sind mit Stolz getragene Embleme seines sozialen Status, der männlichen Reife, der Stammeszugehörigkeit, und der Rolle, die er in der Gemeinschaft spielt. In anderen Fällen ergreift ein göttlicher bzw. dämonischer Geist Besitz von dem Lebenden, und seine Gegenwart wird durch Farbzeichen offenbar. Übrigens bemalten sich auch die Heerführer der alten Römer bei Siegesfeiern das Gesicht mit roter Farbe, um so dem Gott Jupiter ähnlich zu werden.

Bei der Geburt bleibt der junge Massai zunächst namenlos, um den Dämon des Todes zu täuschen. Erst nach ca. 6 Jahren erhält er in einer feierlichen Zeremonie einen Namen. Dabei durchsticht ihm die Mutter beide Ohrläppchen, was bedeutet, daß er nun in den Clan aufgenommen ist. Fortan gilt seine Sorge dem Ohrenschmuck. Von Zeit zu Zeit wird die Wunde wieder geöffnet, Holzstäbchen und Steine hindurchgeschoben, um eine möglichst große Öffnung zu schaffen. Mit der Beschneidung des geschlechtsreifen Knaben, wird dieser in den Rang des Kriegers erhoben und darf zum ersten Mal sein Ohr verzieren. Dabei wählt er meist rote und blaue Perlenringe, Zeichen seiner Ergebenheit für den Gott enkAi, dessen Güte (blau) und Zorn (rot) dadurch symbolisiert wird. Im Verlauf seines Lebens wechselt die Ohrzierden entsprechend den Stationen seiner Erfahrung und Reife. Die Bedeutung des Ohrläppchens ist für den Massai der seiner Genitalien vergleichbar, sein Verlust eine soziale Katastrophe. Nur der Frau ist es erlaubt, ihn dort zu berühren, der Versuch jedes anderen bedeutet eine Aufforderung zum Kampf.

Bei der Bedeutung, die der Massai diesem Körperteil beimißt, fragt man sich, was ihn veranlassen kann, sich mit einer Konservendose, Abfallprodukt der Zivilisation, auszustaffieren? Der Grund ist simpel. Blechdosen sind leichter und bequemer als Steine, um das Loch im Ohrläppchen zu dehnen.

676
Art Director: Ernest Scarfone
Designer: Ernest Scarfone
Photographer: Don Carstens
Publisher: Ferdinand Brothers
Nikon World

676A
Art Director: Dick Hess
Designer: Marleen Adlerblum
Photographer: Art Kane
Publisher: United Nations Assoc.
Vista
Agency: Richard Hess Inc.

677
Art Director: Klaus Von Seggern
Designer: George Guther
Photographer: Pete Turner
Publication: Er

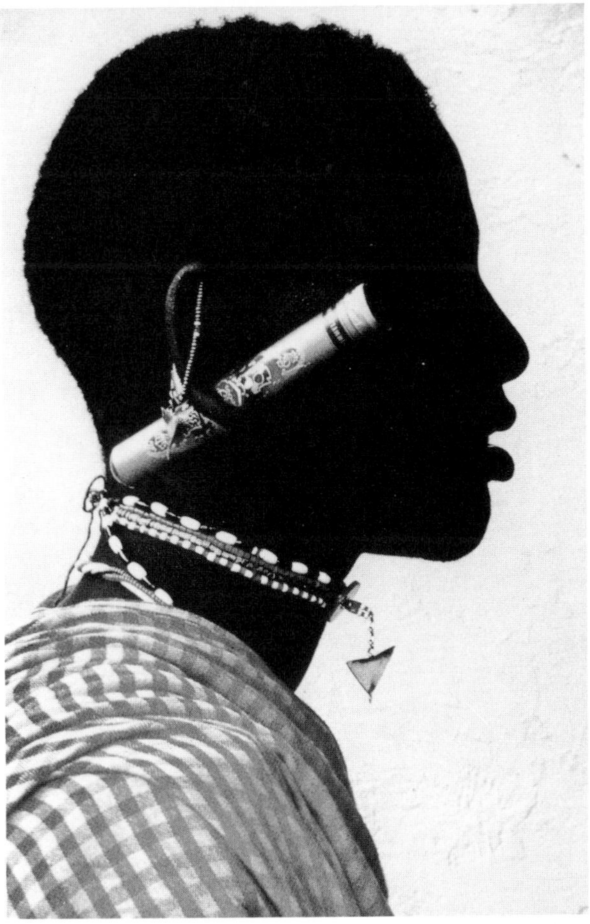

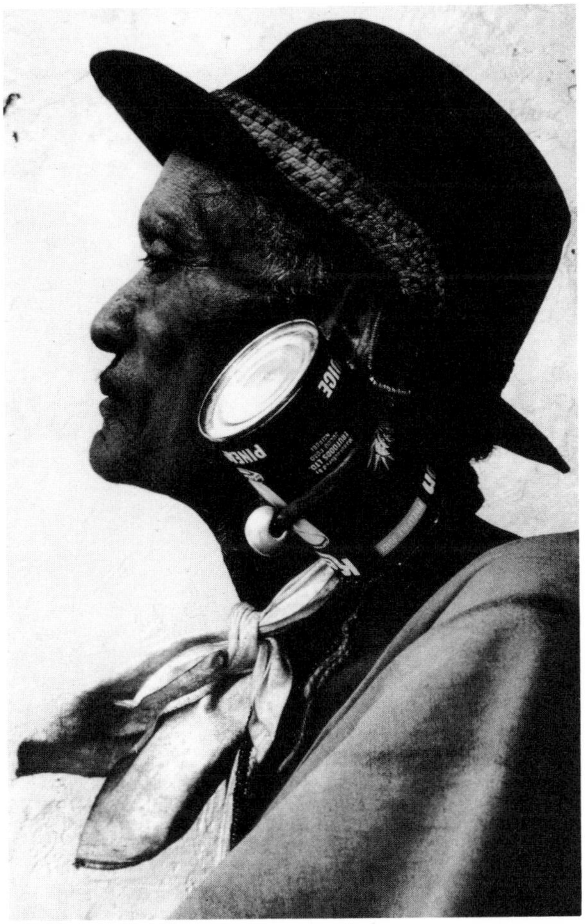

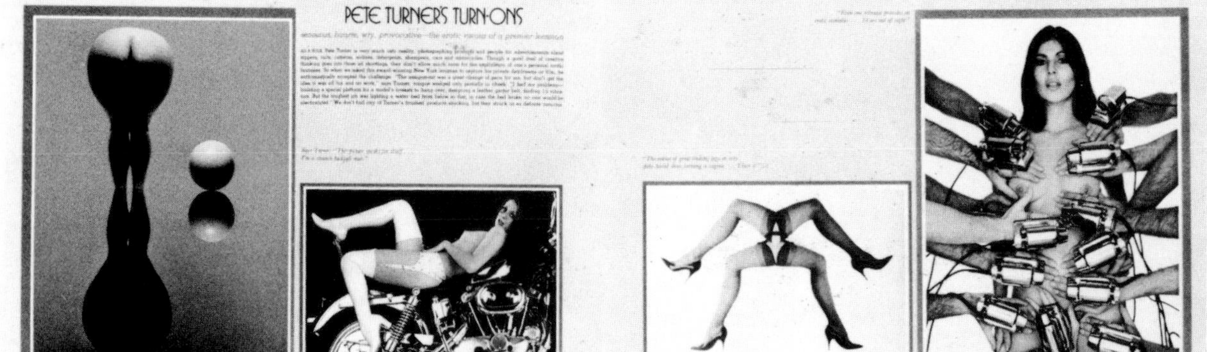
PETE TURNER'S TURN-ONS

678
Art Director: Art Paul
Photographer: Pete Turner
Publisher: Playboy Publications
Playboy

679
Art Director: William Cadge
Designer: Cal Holder
Photographer: Ben Rose
Editor: Sey Chassler
Publisher: McCall's Corporation
Redbook

680
Art Director: David Hillmann
Designer: David Hillmann
Photographer: Christa Peters
Publisher: Nova Magazine

Very Special Vegetables
Frozen vegetables, always in season, are always available and ready to prepare when you need them. But they are more than convenient—they can be spectacular if you know how to combine them and how to enhance them with herbs, seasonings and savory sauces. Redbook has discovered many exciting, quick ways to dress up frozen vegetables, including our own magic Seasoned Butter Cubes to make in advance and freeze for instant use later. A collection of these easy recipes begins on page

679

680

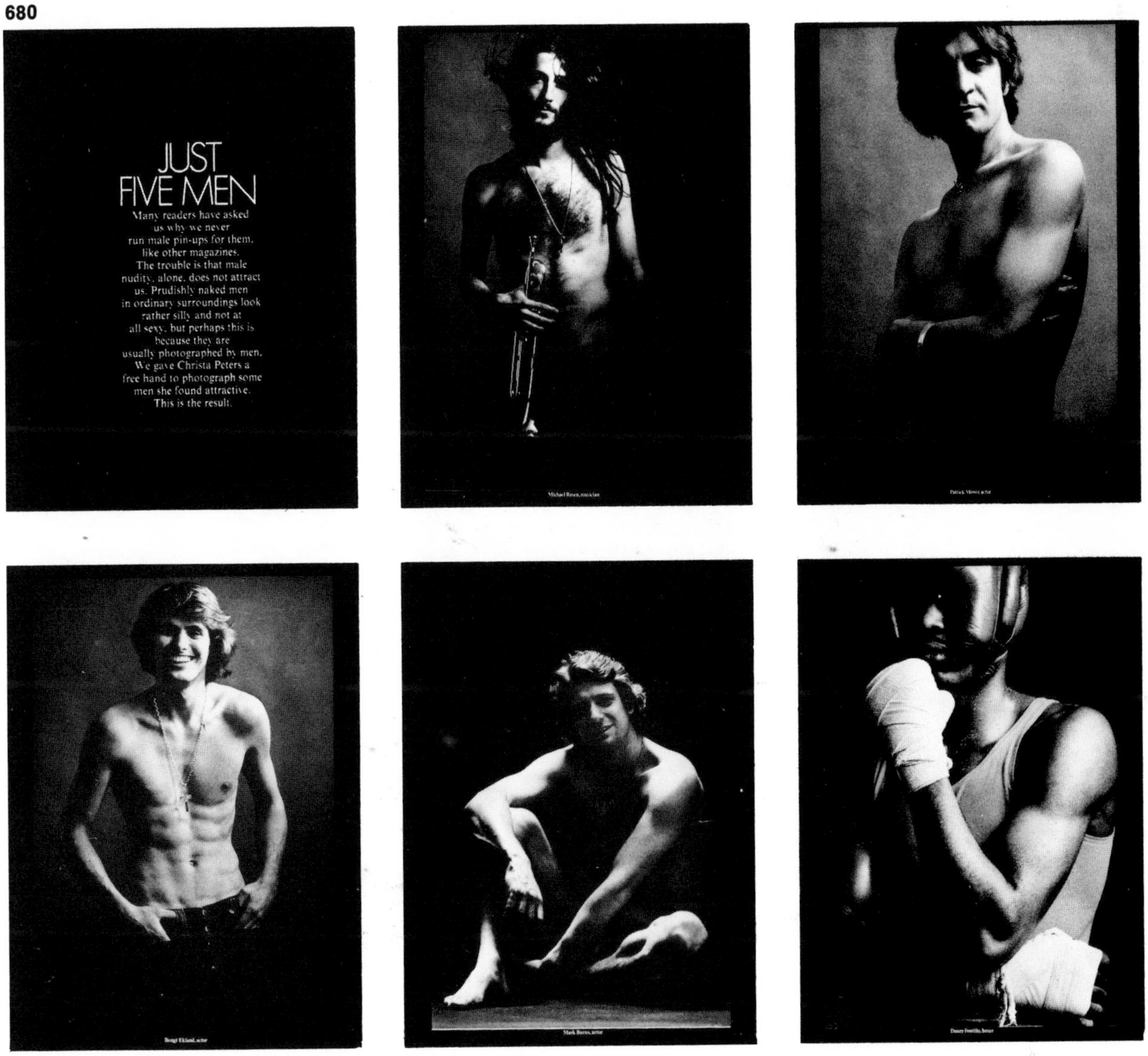
JUST FIVE MEN
Many readers have asked us why we never run male pin-ups for them, like other magazines. The trouble is that male nudity, alone, does not attract us. Prudishly naked men in ordinary surroundings look rather silly and not at all sexy, but perhaps this is because they are usually photographed by men. We gave Christa Peters a free hand to photograph some men she found attractive. This is the result.

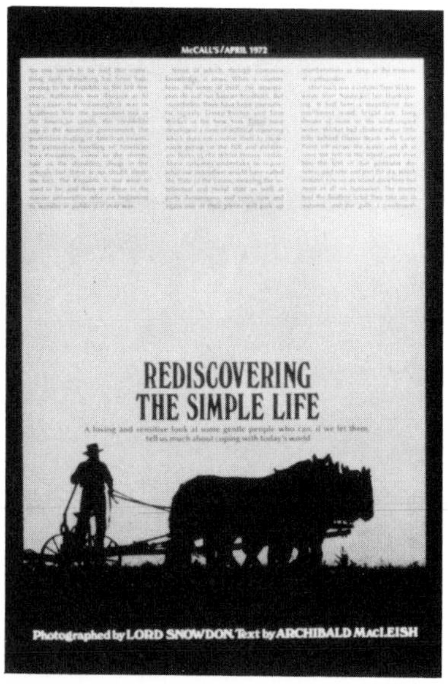
McCALL'S/APRIL 1972
REDISCOVERING THE SIMPLE LIFE
A loving and sensitive look at some gentle people who can, if we let them, tell us much about coping with today's world
Photographed by LORD SNOWDON. Text by ARCHIBALD MacLEISH

"When you ask their children why the Amish don't live in the city, they say, 'Where would we keep our horses?'"

681

"The Amish spotted the idea of progress for what it is long before the rest of us"

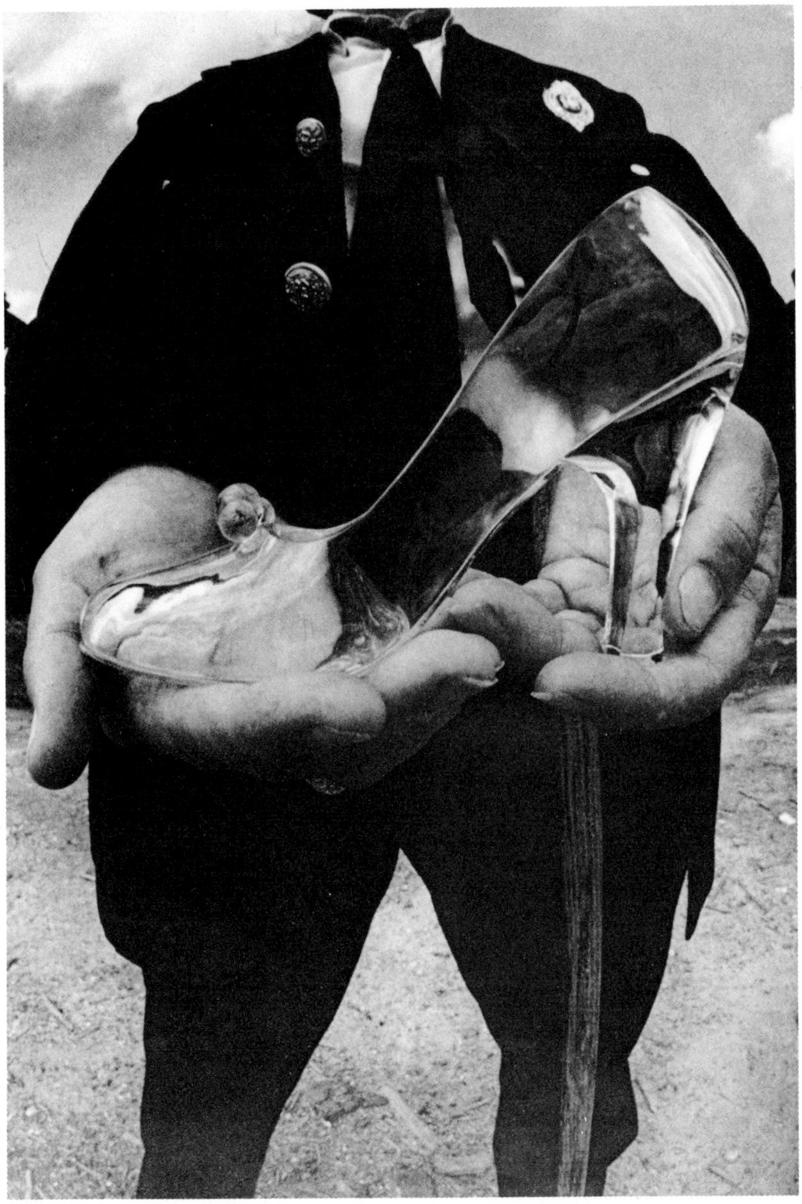

681
Art Director: Alvin Grossman
Designer: Alvin Grossman
Photographer: Lord Snowdon
Publisher: McCall Publishing Company
McCall's Magazine

682 Gold Award
Art Director: Richard Weigand
Photographer: Art Kane
Writer: Bob Dylan
Publication: Esquire Magazine

682

BOB DYLAN: The Metaphor at the End of the Funnel

But is it art? . . .

Milton! Thou shouldst be living at this hour! But thou ain't, Milton; instead, we have Bob Dylan (Doctor of Music, Princeton University), whom Jack Newfield called "the Walt Whitman of the jukebox, the Brecht of the electric guitar." Of course we also have Norman Mailer, who said, "If Dylan's a poet, I'm a basketball player." Well, we believe that Mailer is a basketball player, Jack Newfield is the Dizzy Dean of the catachresis, and Bob Dylan is right on and groovy; and anybody who doubts that view of Dylan must confront the general and constant opinion of mankind for lo these five or six years at least. We, of course, are but one voice; other voices are those of Frank Kermode, one of the foremost English language critics; Stephen Spender, poet and former editor of Encounter*; and photographer Art Kane. Professor Kermode, indeed, takes Dylan seriously enough to have planned a book on him (defeated by copyright technicalities); Mr. Spender, as you shall see, doesn't take him seriously at all; Mr. Kane responded to the images in six Dylan songs with the pictures on the following seven pages. Finally, we called up Dylan, after months of fruitless trying, and asked the Wordsworth of the microgroove himself.*

"Well, how do you see me?" he responded.

"Well, as a kind of human metaphor at the end of a corporate funnel," we answered.

"Well, that ain't bad," he said, and hung up.

Photographed by Art Kane

683

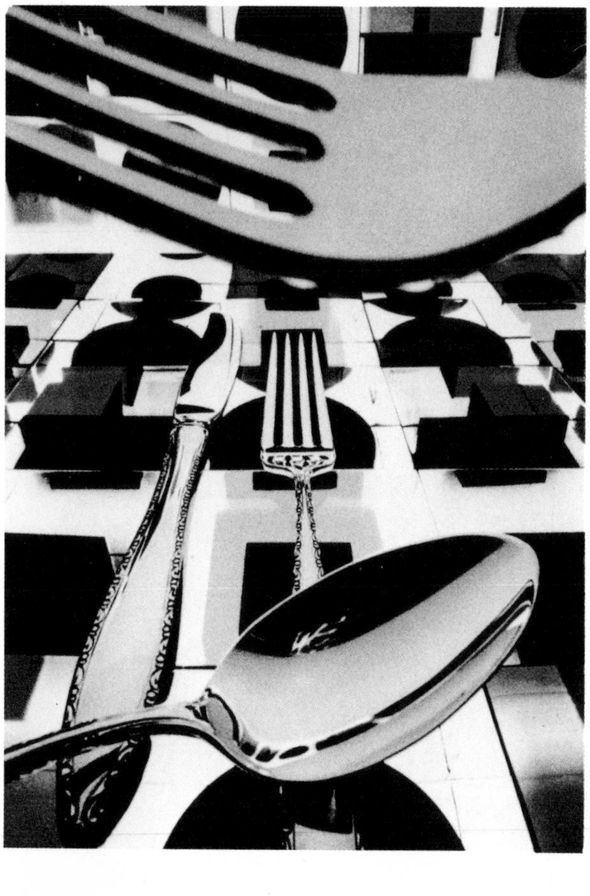

684

Couverts d'argent. Recherche personnelle de Turner, dans son studio de Carnegie Hall, à New York, en 1968. Objectif f : 3,5 de 20 mm. Flash électronique. Kodachrome II. F : 22 au 1/60 s.

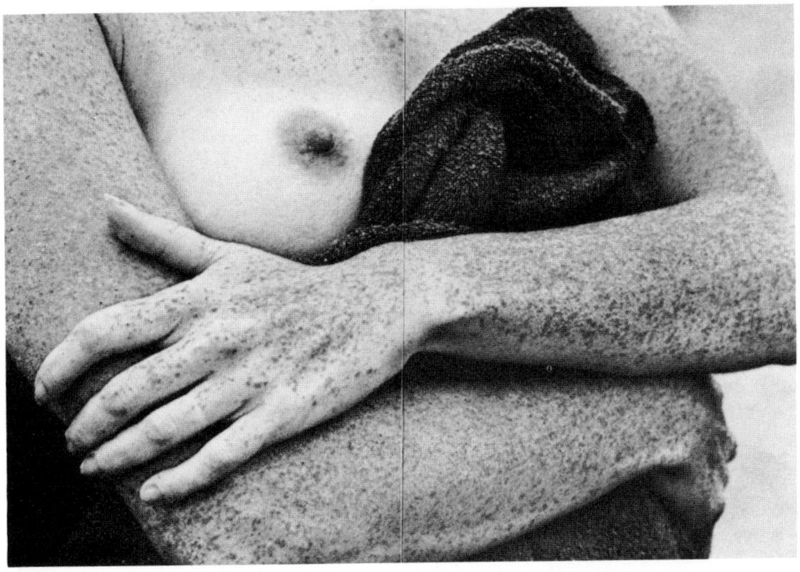

689

690

article
MY FIRST ORGY
BY DAN GREENBURG
the craven coward in me said no, but the journalist in me said yes, yes, yes!

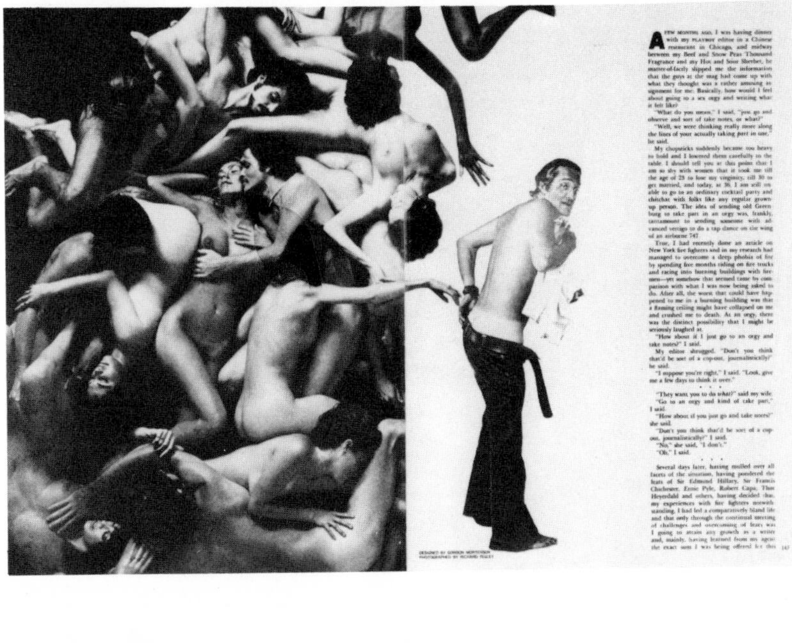

A FEW MONTHS AGO, I was having dinner with my PLAYBOY editor in a Chinese restaurant in Chicago, and midway between my Beef and Snow Peas Thousand Fragrance and my Hot and Sour Sherbet, he matter-of-factly slipped me the information that the guys at the mag had come up with what they thought was a rather amusing assignment for me. Basically, how would I feel about going to a sex orgy and writing what it felt like?

"What do you mean," I said, "just go and observe and sort of take notes, or what?"

"Well, we were thinking really more along the lines of your actually taking *part* in one," he said.

My chopsticks suddenly became too heavy to hold and I lowered them carefully to the table. I should tell you at this point that I am so shy with women that it took me till the age of 23 to lose my virginity, till 30 to get married, and today, at 36, I am still unable to go to an ordinary cocktail party and chitchat with folks like any regular grown-up person. The idea of sending old Greenburg to take part in an orgy was, frankly, tantamount to sending someone with advanced vertigo to do a tap dance on the wing of an airborne 747.

True, I had recently done an article on New York fire fighters and in my research had managed to overcome a deep phobia of fire by spending five months riding on fire trucks and racing into burning buildings with firemen—yet somehow that seemed tame by comparison with what I was now being asked to do. After all, the worst that could have happened to me in a burning building was that a flaming ceiling might have collapsed on me and crushed me to death. At an orgy, there was the distinct possibility that I might be seriously laughed at.

"How about if I just go to an orgy and take notes?" I said.

My editor shrugged. "Don't you think that'd be sort of a cop-out, journalistically?" he said.

"I suppose you're right," I said. "Look, give me a few days to think it over."

* * *

"They want you to do *what?*" said my wife.

"Go to an orgy and kind of take part," I said.

"How about if you just go and take notes?" she said.

"Don't you think that'd be sort of a cop-out, journalistically?" I said.

"No," she said, "I don't."

"Oh," I said.

* * *

Several days later, having mulled over all facets of the situation, having pondered the feats of Sir Edmund Hillary, Sir Francis Chichester, *Ernie Pyle*, Robert Capa, Thor Heyerdahl and others, having decided that, my experiences with fire fighters notwithstanding, I had led a comparatively bland life and that only through the continual meeting of challenges and overcoming of fears was I going to attain any growth as a writer and, mainly, having learned from my agent the exact sum I was being offered for this

687
Art Director: Hans Albers
Photographer: Tom Bartone
Copywriter: Jeanne Voltz
Publisher: Los Angeles Times
Home Magazine

688
Art Director: Ernest Scarfone
Photographer: Alan Ira Kaplan
Publisher: Billboard Publications
Modern Photography Annual

689
Art Director: Ernest Scarfone
Designer: Ernest Scarfone
Photographer: Jerome Ducrot
Publisher: Ferdinand Brothers
Nikon World

690
Art Director: Arthur Paul
Designers: Arthur Paul
Gordon Mortensen
Photographer: Richard Fegley
Publisher: Playboy Enterprises
Playboy Magazine

Sophia Loren
The Last of the Love Goddesses

691
Art Director: Tom Ridinger
Designer: Mesney's Third Bardo
Photographer: Douglas Mesney
Publisher: H & R Publications
Show Magazine

691

Advertising, Promotion Photography

692
Art Director: Morton Goldsholl
Designer: Morton Goldsholl
Photographer: Tom Freese
Client: Goldsholl Associates

693
Art Director: Tom Conrad
Designer: Tom Conrad
Photographer: Victor Skrebneski
Copywriters: Jim Weller
Roger Myers
Agency: Jim Weller & Partners
Client: Rosemary Bischoff

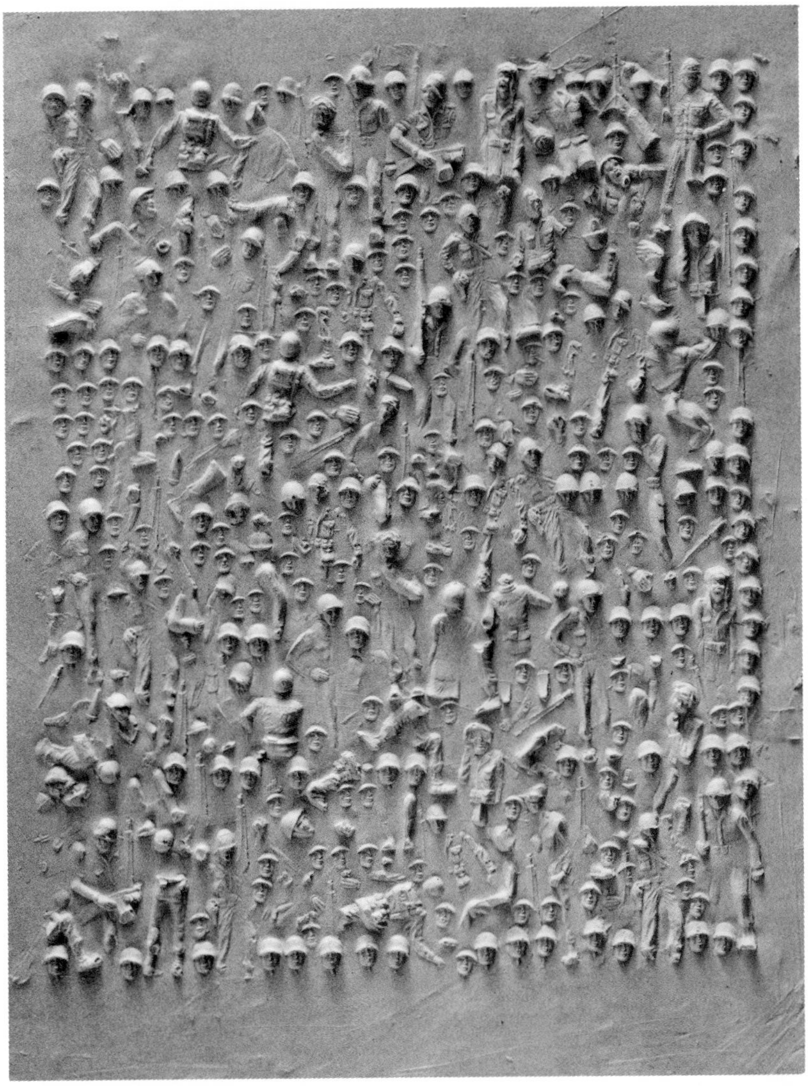

692

693

694
Art Director: Pete Coutroulis
Photographer: Victor Skrebneski
Copywriter: Howard Krakow
Agency: Jim Weller & Partners
Client: Florence Eiseman

695
Art Director: Pete Coutroulis
Designer: Pete Coutroulis
Photographer: Victor Skrebneski
Copywriter: Howard Krakow
Agency: Jim Weller & Partners
Client: Florence Eiseman

694

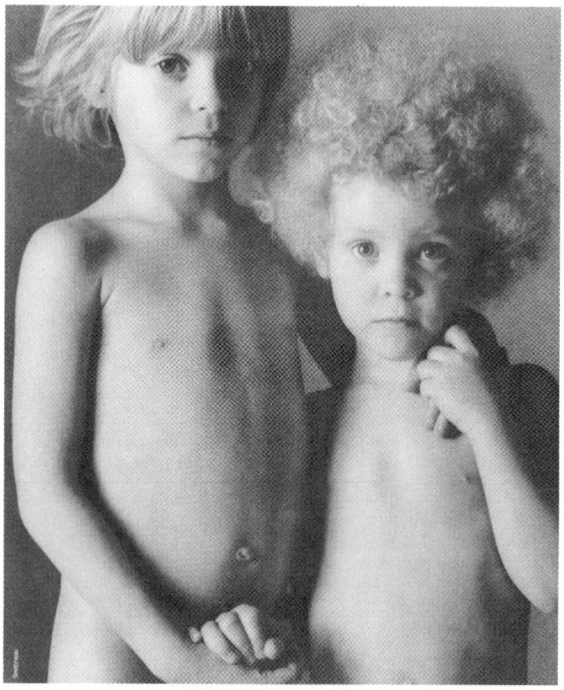

695

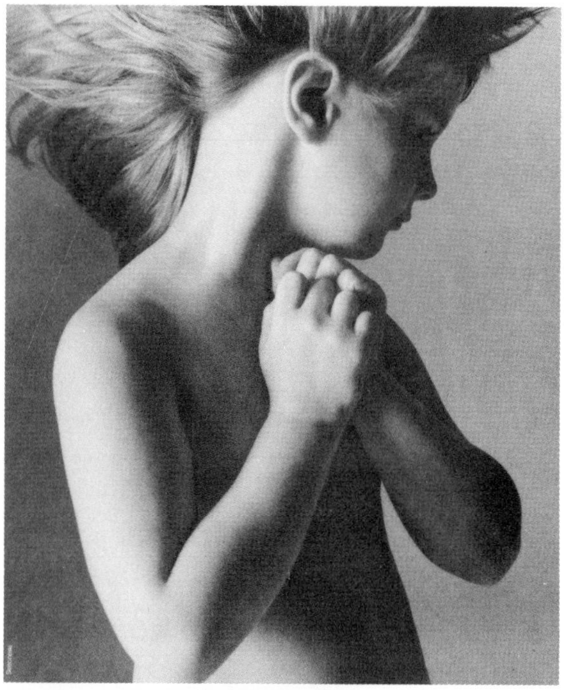

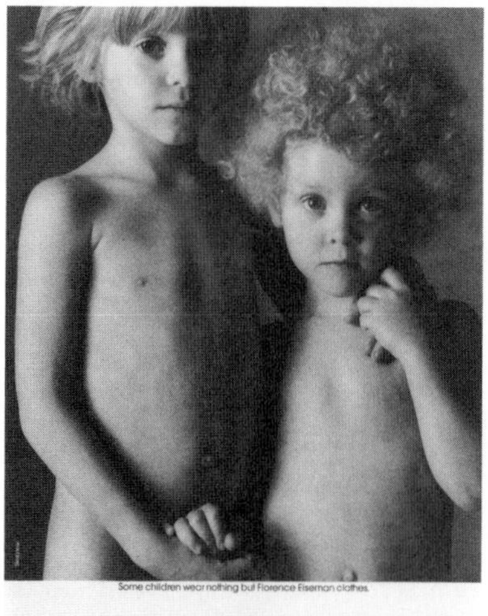
Some children wear nothing but Florence Eiseman clothes.

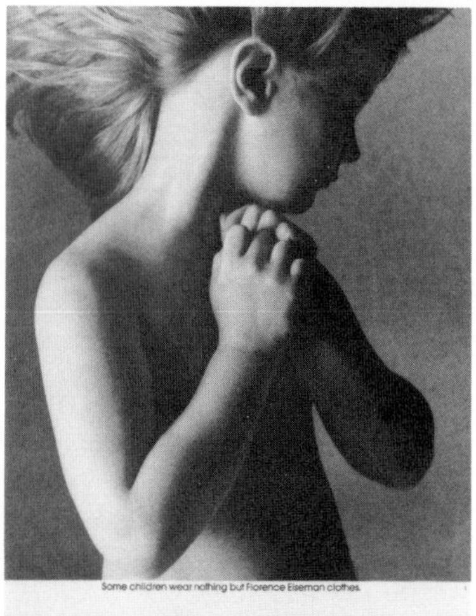
Some children wear nothing but Florence Eiseman clothes.

After raising 43 children over the last 30 years, Clara Hale has started a new family.
New York City: It's still a hell of a town.
New York Telephone

696

697

EASTERN'S PERSON-TO-PERSON WEEKENDS.
EASTERN THE WINGS OF MAN

696
Art Director: Bob Steigelman
Designer: Bob Steigelman
Photographer: Bruce Davidson
Copywriter: Ray Demsey
Agency: Young & Rubicam International, Inc.
Client: New York Telephone

697
Art Director: Jim Swan
Designer: Jim Swan
Photographer: Art Kane
Copywriter: Phil Peppis
Agency: Young & Rubicam International, Inc.
Client: Eastern Airlines

698
Art Director: Michael Uris
Designer: Michael Uris
Photographer: Jack Wallach
Copywriter: Frada Wallach
Agency: Doyle Dane Bernbach Inc.
Client: Federation of Jewish Philanthropies

699 Silver Award
Art Directors: William Taubin
Michael Uris
Designers: Wiliam Taubin
Michael Uris
Photographer: Jack Wallach
Copywriter: Frada Wallach
Agency: Doyle Dane Bernbach Inc.
Client: Federation of Jewish Philanthropies

698

699

What if she dies first?
With bricks you can build life

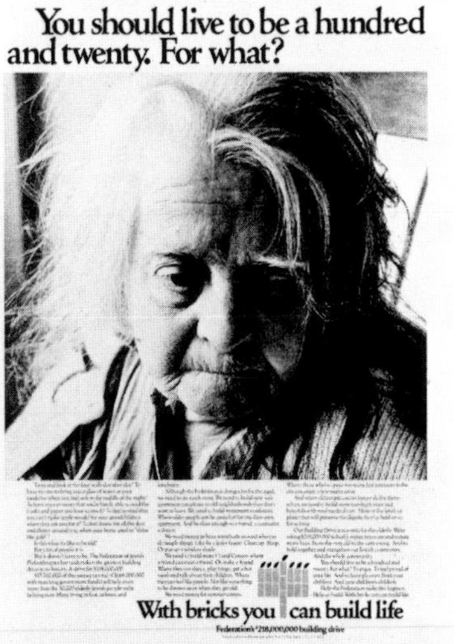
You should live to be a hundred and twenty. For what?
With bricks you can build life

700
Art Director: Jim Swan
Designer: Jim Swan
Photographer: Art Kane
Copywriter: Phil Peppis
Agency: Young & Rubicam International, Inc.
Client: Eastern Airlines

701
Art Director: Jim Swan
Designer: Jim Swan
Photographer: Art Kane
Copywriter: Phil Peppis
Agency: Young & Rubicam International, Inc.
Client: Eastern Airlines

700

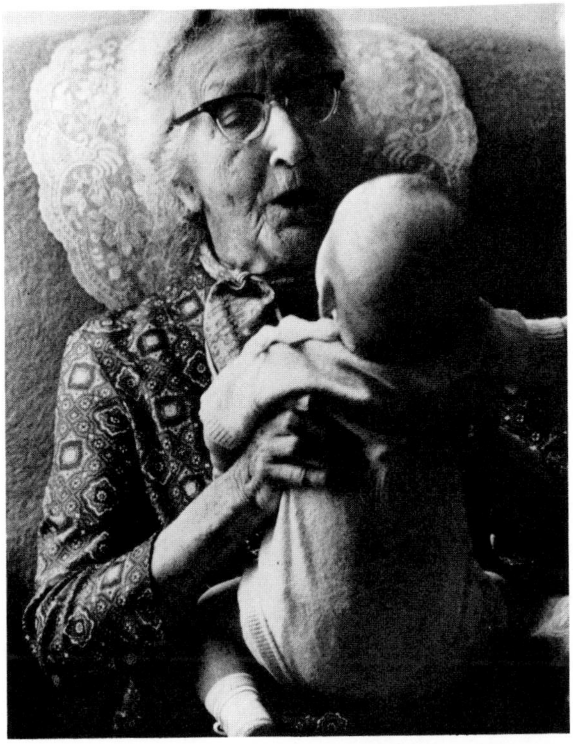

701

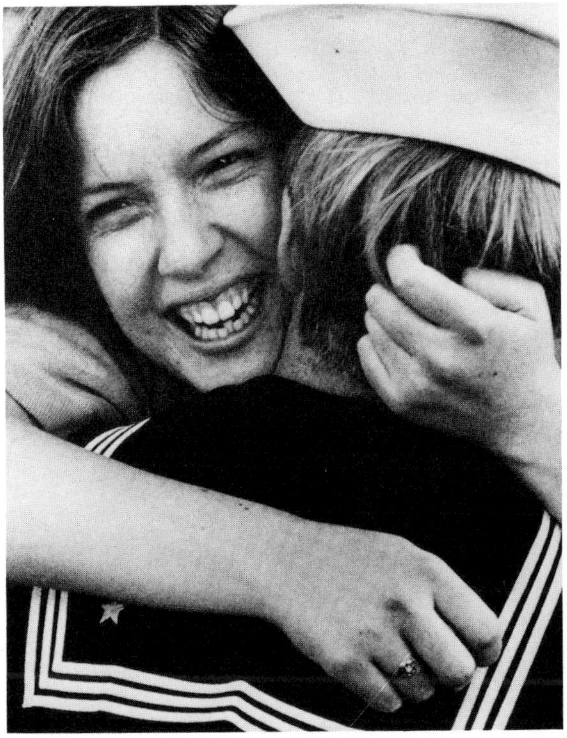

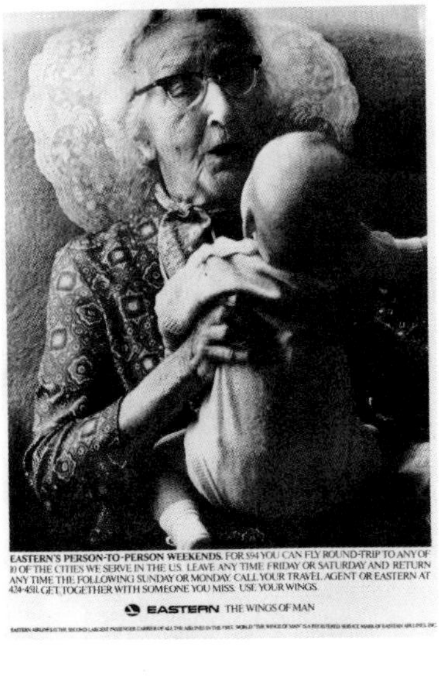

702
Art Director: Jim Swan
Designer: Jim Swan
Photographer: Art Kane
Copywriter: Phil Peppis
Agency: Young & Rubicam International, Inc.
Client: Eastern Airlines

703
Art Director: Dan Piel
Designer: Dan Piel
Photographer: Ed Jaffe
Copywriter: Bill Zeitung
Agency: Marsteller Inc.
Client: Marine Office, Appleton & Cox

704
Art Director: Rod Capawana
Designer: Simon Lo
Photographer: Tasso Vendikos
Copywriter: Charles Sawyer
Agency: Warner, Bicking & Fenwick, Inc.
Client: Ilford Inc.

EASTERN'S PERSON-TO-PERSON WEEKENDS. FOR $94 YOU CAN FLY ROUND-TRIP TO BOSTON OR PHILADELPHIA. LEAVE ANY TIME FRIDAY OR SATURDAY AND RETURN ANY TIME THE FOLLOWING SUNDAY OR MONDAY. CALL YOUR TRAVEL AGENT OR EASTERN AT 355-7392. GET TOGETHER WITH SOMEONE YOU MISS. USE YOUR WINGS.
EASTERN THE WINGS OF MAN

702

703

One reason we're so big in commercial inland marine insurance is our local loss handler who can get to the scene before the smoke settles down.
MOAC Marine insurance is our only business

We couldn't perfect black and white
without perfecting the gray scale.
While America was perfecting color.
Ilford was perfecting black and white.
© ILFORD INC.

While America was perfec
color, Ilford was perfecting
black and white.

Here it is in black and white.
While America was perfecting color, Ilford was perfecting black and white.

705

705
Art Director: Tom Conrad
Designer: Tom Conrad
Photographer: Victor Skrebneski
Copywriters: Jim Weller
Roger Myers
Agency: Jim Weller & Partners
Client: Rosemary Bischoff

706 Gold Award
Art Director: Stan Jones
Photographer: Dick Richards
Copywriter: John Annarino
Agency: Twentieth Century Fox
Client: Twentieth Century Fox

708
Art Director: George Lois
Designers: Dennis Mazzella
Tom Courtos
Photographer: Carl Fischer
Copywriter: Rudy Fiala
Agency: Lois Holland Callaway Inc.
Client: Olivetti Corporation of America

706

708

709
Art Directors: Ralph Moxcey
Jim Witham
Designers: Ralph Moxcey
Jim Witham
Photographer: Bill Bruin
Copywriter: Nelson Lofstedt
Agency: Humphrey, Browning, MacDougall
Client: S. D. Warren Paper Company

710
Art Directors: Barry Kaufman
Richard Lomonaco
Designers: Barry Kaufman
Richard Lomonaco
Photo Graphics: Communications Quorum, Inc.
Photographer: Romain Vishniac
Agency: Communications Quorum, Inc.
Client: United Jewish Appeal

709

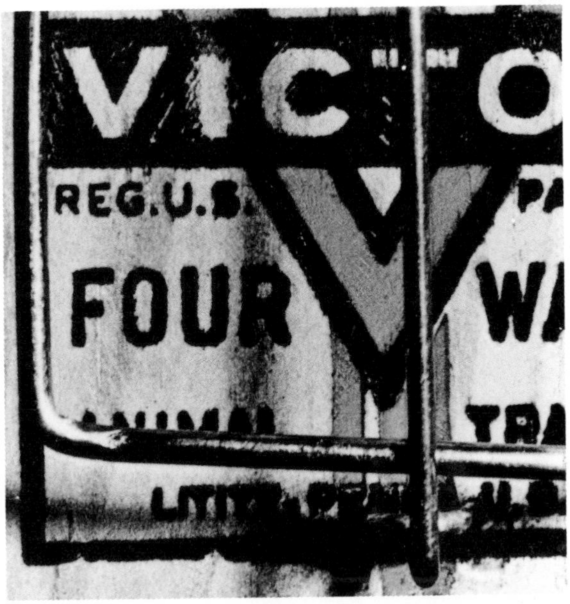

...never bet against the mouse.

710

711
Art Director: Herb Lubalin
Designer: Herb Lubalin
Photographer: Pete Turner
Copywriter: Lois Wyse
Agency: Lubalin, Smith, Carnese, Inc.
Client: Garret Press

712
Art Directors: Sal Lodico
Ed Bianchi
Designer: Sal Lodico
Ed Bianchi
Photographer: Maureen Lambray
Copywriters: Roz Levenstein
Bill Waites
Agency: Young & Rubicam International, Inc.
Client: Puerto Rican Rums

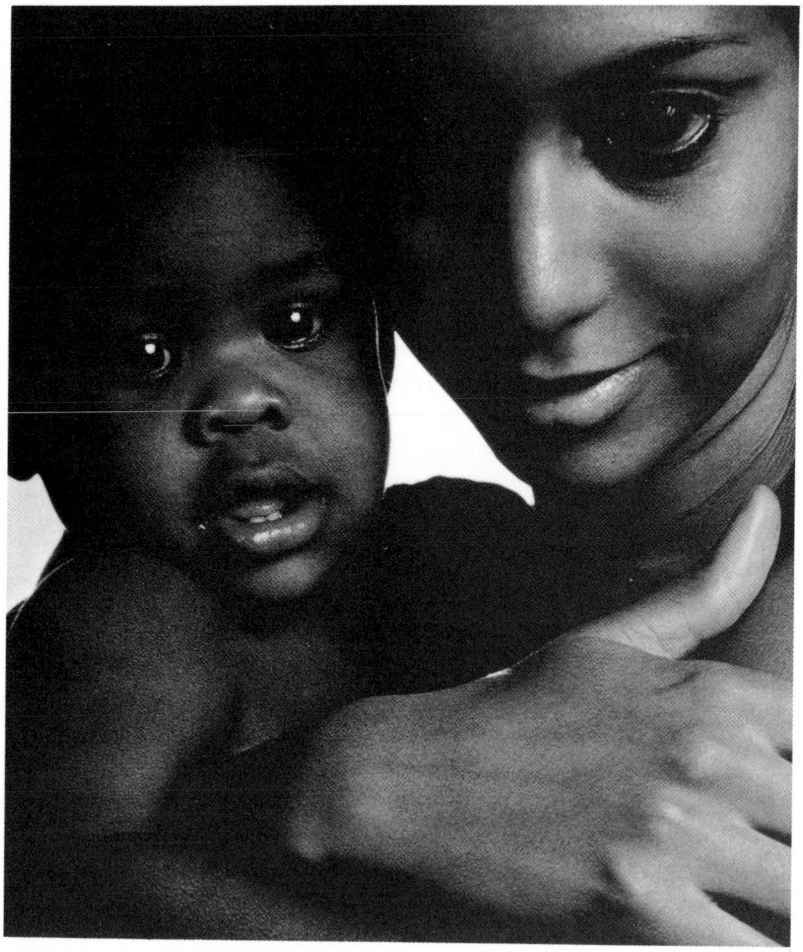

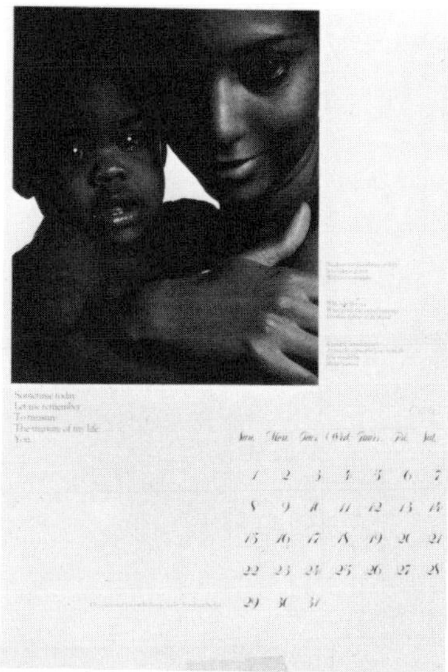

711

712

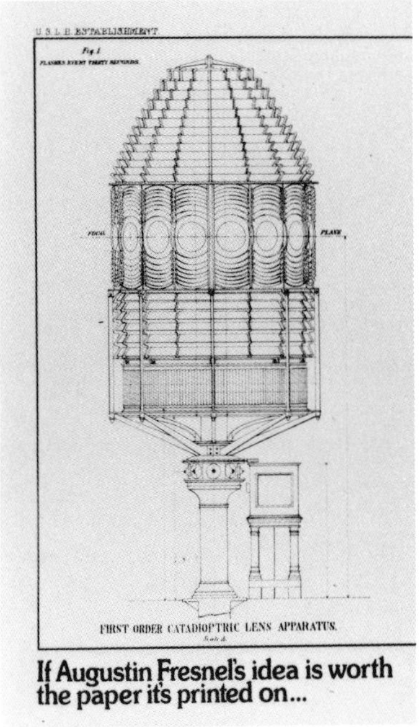
FIRST ORDER CATADIOPTRIC LENS APPARATUS.
If Augustin Fresnel's idea is worth the paper it's printed on...

713

714

BEAUTYREST. THE ULTIMATE OVERNIGHT VACATION.

713
Art Directors: Ralph Moxcey
Jim Witham
Designers: Ralph Moxcey
Jim Witham
Artist: Terry Walker
Photographer: Frank Foster
Copywriter: Nelson Lofstedt
Agency: Humphrey, Browning, MacDougall
Client: S. D. Warren Paper Company

714
Art Directors: Matt Basile
Jerry Sandler
Designers: Matt Basile
Jerry Sandler
Photographer: Howard Krieger
Copywriter: Greta Basile
Agency: Young & Rubicam International, Inc.
Client: Simmons

When you can endure all the burdens and pressures of life, that is called strength.
Talon
The rugged zipper that never gives up

715

716

The idea of Reverence for Life
offers itself as the realistic answer
to the realistic question of how
man and the world are related . . .
Albert Schweitzer
Joel Carl Freid
Photographer
301-474-0585
Greenbelt, Maryland 20770

717

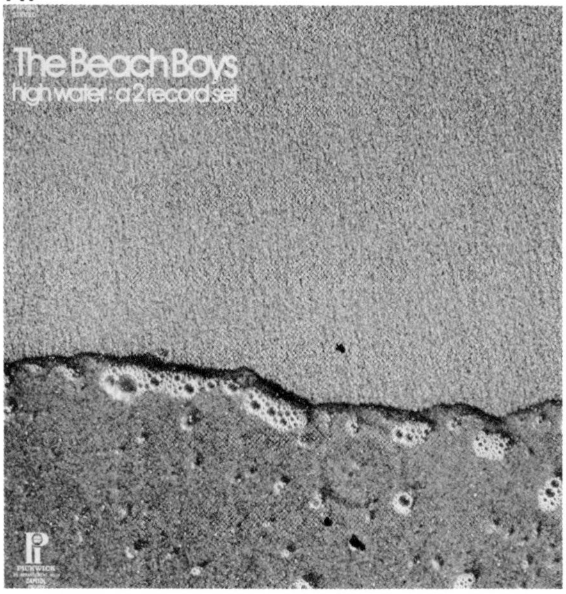
The Beach Boys
high water : a 2 record set

718

719

720

715
Art Director: Mike Withers
Designer: Mike Withers
Photographer: Ernst Haas
Copywriter: Joy Golden
Agency: DKG Inc.
Client: Talon

716
Art Director: Robert Rytter
Designer: Robert Rytter
Photographer: Joel Carl Freid
Writer: Albert Schweitzer
Client: Joel Carl Freid

717
Art Director: David Lartaud
Designer: David Lartaud
Photographer: David Lartaud
Client: Pickwick International, Inc.

718
Art Director: Bob Ciano
Designer: Bob Ciano
Photographer: Pete Turner
Client: CTI Records

719
Art Director: Bob Ciano
Designer: Bob Ciano
Photographer: Pete Turner
Client: CTI Records

720
Art Director: Bob Ciano
Designer: Bob Ciano
Photographer: Pete Turner
Client: CTI Records

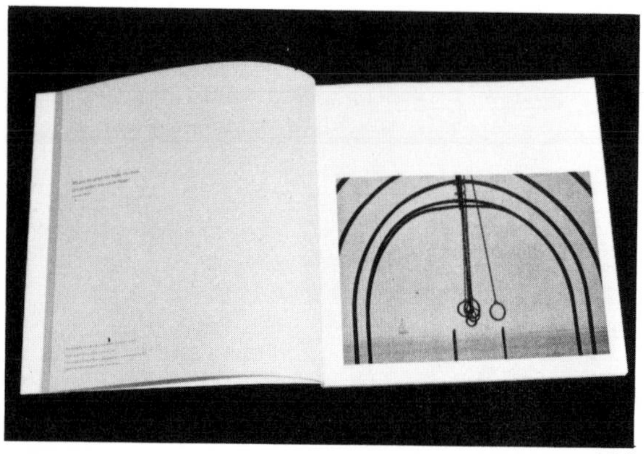

721

722

723

721
Art Directors: Don Weller
Dennis Juett
Designers: Don Weller
Dennis Juett
Photographers: Don Weller
Dennis Juett
Copywriter: Edmund Waller
Agency: Weller & Juett Inc.
Client: Koltun Brothers

722
Designer: David Hedrich
Photographer: David Hedrich
Client: David Hedrich Photography

723
Art Director: Guglielmo Nardelli
Designer: Guglielmo Nardelli
Photographer: Guglielmo Nardelli
Client: Nardelli Photography

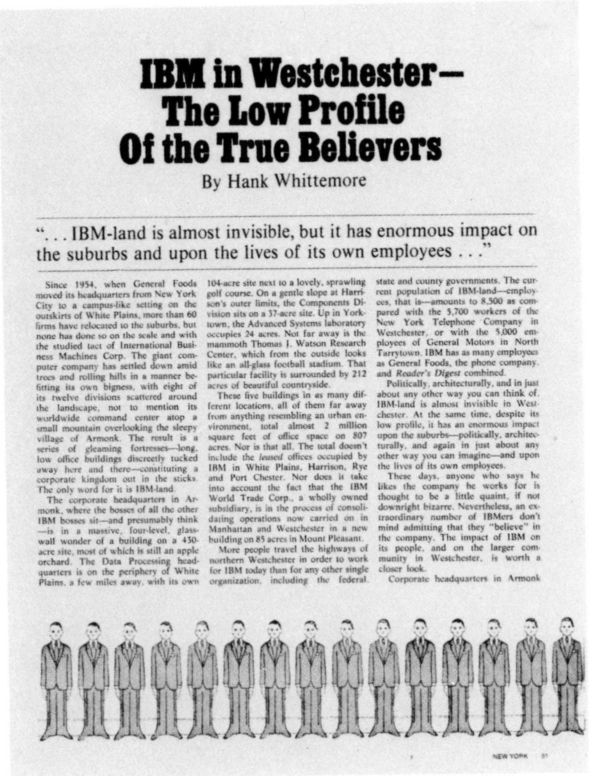

IBM in Westchester— The Low Profile Of the True Believers

By Hank Whittemore

"... IBM-land is almost invisible, but it has enormous impact on the suburbs and upon the lives of its own employees ..."

Since 1954, when General Foods moved its headquarters from New York City to a campus-like setting on the outskirts of White Plains, more than 60 firms have relocated to the suburbs, but none has done so on the scale and with the studied tact of International Business Machines Corp. The giant computer company has settled down amid trees and rolling hills in a manner befitting its own bigness, with eight of its twelve divisions scattered around the landscape, not to mention its worldwide command center atop a small mountain overlooking the sleepy village of Armonk. The result is a series of gleaming fortresses—long, low office buildings discreetly tucked away here and there—constituting a corporate kingdom out in the sticks. The only word for it is IBM-land.

The corporate headquarters in Armonk, where the bosses of all the other IBM bosses sit—and presumably think—is in a massive, four-level, glass-wall wonder of a building on a 430-acre site, most of which is still an apple orchard. The Data Processing headquarters is on the periphery of White Plains, a few miles away, with its own 104-acre site next to a lovely, sprawling golf course. On a gentle slope at Harrison's outer limits, the Components Division sits on a 37-acre site. Up in Yorktown, the Advanced Systems laboratory occupies 24 acres. Not far away is the mammoth Thomas J. Watson Research Center, which from the outside looks like an all-glass football stadium. That particular facility is surrounded by 212 acres of beautiful countryside.

These five buildings in as many different locations, all of them far away from anything resembling an urban environment, total almost 2 million square feet of office space on 807 acres. Nor is that all. The total doesn't include the *leased* offices occupied by IBM in White Plains, Harrison, Rye and Port Chester. Nor does it take into account the fact that the IBM World Trade Corp., a wholly owned subsidiary, is in the process of consolidating operations now carried on in Manhattan and Westchester in a new building on 85 acres in Mount Pleasant.

More people travel the highways of northern Westchester in order to work for IBM today than for any other single organization, including the federal, state and county governments. The current population of IBM-land—employees, that is—amounts to 8,500 as compared with the 5,700 workers of the New York Telephone Company in Westchester, or with the 5,000 employees of General Motors in North Tarrytown. IBM has as many employees as General Foods, the phone company, and *Reader's Digest* combined.

Politically, architecturally, and in just about any other way you can think of, IBM-land is almost invisible in Westchester. At the same time, despite its low profile, it has an enormous impact upon the suburbs—politically, architecturally, and again in just about any other way you can imagine—and upon the lives of its own employees.

These days, anyone who says he likes the company he works for is thought to be a little quaint, if not downright bizarre. Nevertheless, an extraordinary number of IBMers don't mind admitting that they "believe" in the company. The impact of IBM on its people, and on the larger community in Westchester, is worth a closer look.

Corporate headquarters in Armonk

NEW YORK 51

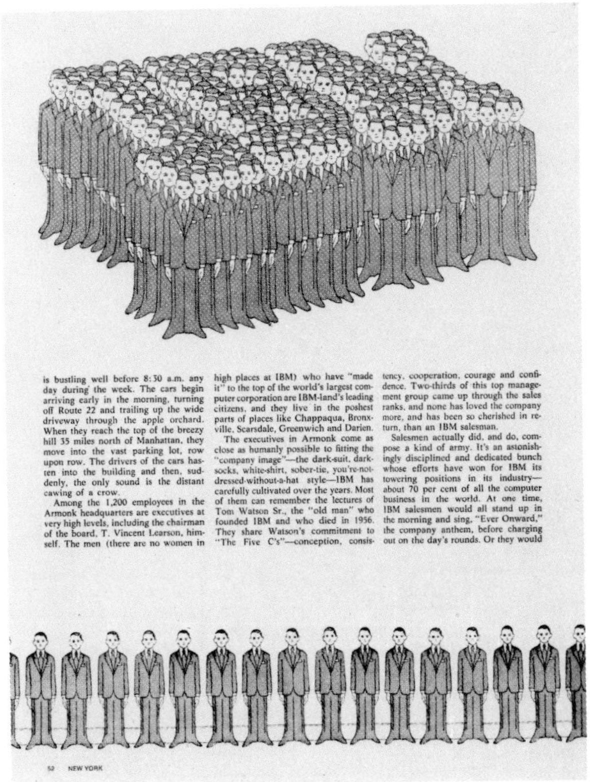

is bustling well before 8:30 a.m. any day during the week. The cars begin arriving early in the morning, turning off Route 22 and trailing up the wide driveway through the apple orchard. When they reach the top of the breezy hill 35 miles north of Manhattan, they move into the vast parking lot, row upon row. The drivers of the cars hasten into the building and then, suddenly, the only sound is the distant cawing of a crow.

Among the 1,200 employees in the Armonk headquarters are executives at very high levels, including the chairman of the board, T. Vincent Learson, himself. The men (there are no women in high places at IBM) who have "made it" to the top of the world's largest computer corporation are IBM-land's leading citizens, and they live in the poshest parts of places like Chappaqua, Bronxville, Scarsdale, Greenwich and Darien.

The executives in Armonk come as close as humanly possible to fitting the "company image"—the dark-suit, dark-socks, white-shirt, sober-tie, you're-not-dressed-without-a-hat style—IBM has carefully cultivated over the years. Most of them can remember the lectures of Tom Watson Sr., the "old man" who founded IBM and who died in 1956. They share Watson's commitment to "The Five C's"—conception, consistency, cooperation, courage and confidence. Two-thirds of this top management group came up through the sales ranks, and none has loved the company more, and has been so cherished in return, than an IBM salesman.

Salesmen actually did, and do, compose a kind of army. It's an astonishingly disciplined and dedicated bunch whose efforts have won for IBM its towering positions in its industry—about 70 per cent of all the computer business in the world. At one time, IBM salesmen would all stand up in the morning and sing, "Ever Onward," the company anthem, before charging out on the day's rounds. Or they would

52 NEW YORK

724

725

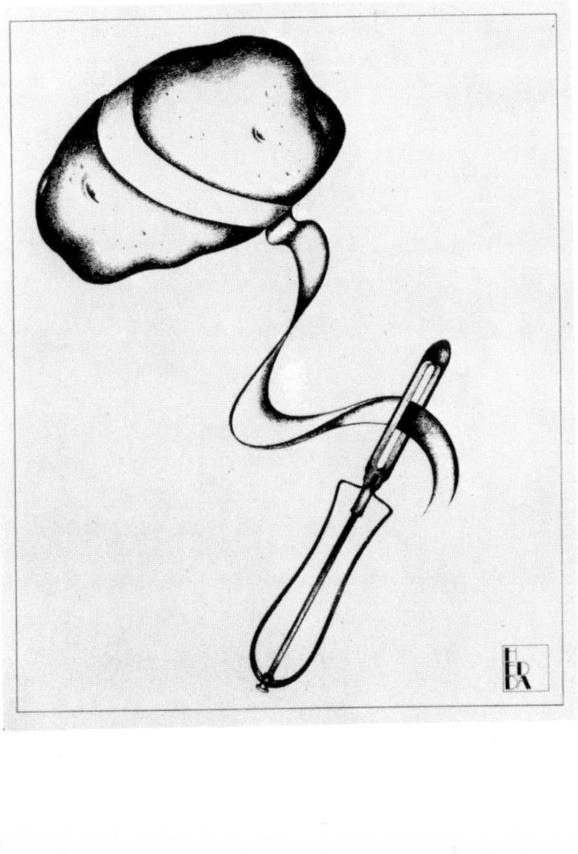

724
Art Directors: Milton Glaser
Walter Bernard
Designers: Milton Glaser
Walter Bernard
Artist: Chas. B. Slackman
Publisher: New York Magazine

725
Art Director: Myrna Davis
Designer: Paul Davis
Publisher: The Hampton Day School Press

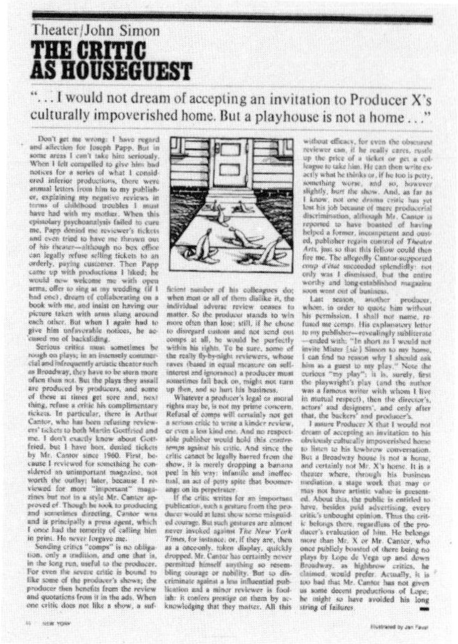

Theater/John Simon

THE CRITIC AS HOUSEGUEST

"... I would not dream of accepting an invitation to Producer X's culturally impoverished home. But a playhouse is not a home ..."

Don't get me wrong: I have regard and affection for Joseph Papp. But in some areas I can't take him seriously. When I felt compelled to give him bad notices for a series of what I considered inferior productions, there were annual letters from him to my publisher, explaining my negative reviews in terms of childhood troubles I must have had with my mother. When this epistolary psychoanalysis failed to cure me, Papp denied me reviewer's tickets and even tried to have me thrown out of his theater—although no box office can legally refuse selling tickets to an orderly, paying customer. Then Papp came up with productions I liked; he would now welcome me with open arms, offer to sing at my wedding (if I had one), dream of collaborating on a book with me, and insist on having our picture taken with arms slung around each other. But when I again had to give him unfavorable notices, he accused me of backsliding.

Serious critics must sometimes be rough on plays; in an intensely commercial and infrequently artistic theater such as Broadway, they have to be stern more often than not. But the plays they assail are produced by producers, and some of these at times get sore and, next thing, refuse a critic his complimentary tickets. In particular, there is Arthur Cantor, who has been refusing reviewers' tickets to both Martin Gottfried and me. I don't exactly know about Gottfried, but I have been denied tickets by Mr. Cantor since 1960. First, because I reviewed for something he considered an unimportant magazine, not worth the outlay; later, because I reviewed for more "important" magazines but not in a style Mr. Cantor approved of. Though he took to producing and sometimes directing, Cantor was and is principally a press agent, which I once had the temerity of calling him in print. He never forgave me.

Sending critics "comps" is no obligation, only a tradition, and one that is, in the long run, useful to the producer. For even the severe critic is bound to like some of the producer's shows; the producer then benefits from the review and quotations from it in the ads. When one critic does not like a show, a sufficient number of his colleagues do; when most or all of them dislike it, the individual adverse review ceases to matter. So the producer stands to win more often than lose; still, if he chose to disregard custom and not send out comps at all, he would be perfectly within his rights. To be sure, some of the really fly-by-night reviewers, whose raves (based in equal measure on self-interest and ignorance) a producer must sometimes fall back on, might not turn up then, and so hurt his business.

Whatever a producer's legal or moral rights may be, is not my prime concern. Refusal of comps will certainly not get a serious critic to write a kinder review, or even a less kind one. And no respectable publisher would hold this *contretemps* against his critic. And since the critic cannot be legally barred from the show, it is merely dropping a banana peel in his way: infantile and ineffectual, an act of petty spite that boomerangs on its perpetrator.

If the critic writes for an important publication, such a gesture from the producer would at least show some misguided courage. But such gestures are almost never invoked against *The New York Times*, for instance, or, if they are, then as a once-only, token display, quickly dropped. Mr. Cantor has certainly never permitted himself anything so resembling courage or nobility. But to discriminate against a less influential publication and a minor reviewer is foolish: it confers prestige on them by acknowledging that they matter. All this without efficacy, for even the obscurest reviewer can, if he really cares, rustle up the price of a ticket or get a colleague to take him. He can then write exactly what he thinks or, if he too is petty, something worse, and so, however slightly, hurt the show. And, as far as I know, not one drama critic has yet lost his job because of mere producerial discrimination, although Mr. Cantor is reported to have boasted of having helped a former, incompetent and ousted, publisher regain control of *Theatre Arts*, just so that this fellow could then fire me. The allegedly Cantor-supported *coup d'état* succeeded splendidly: not only was I dismissed, but the entire worthy and long-established magazine soon went out of business.

Last season, another producer, whom, in order to quote him without his permission, I shall not name, refused me comps. His explanatory letter to my publisher—revealingly subliterate—ended with: "In short as I would not invite Mister [*sic*] Simon to my home, I can find no reason why I should ask him as a guest to my play." Note the curious "my play": it is, surely, first the playwright's play (and the author was a famous writer with whom I live in mutual respect), then the director's, actors' and designers', and only after that, the backers' and producer's.

I assure Producer X that I would not dream of accepting an invitation to his obviously culturally impoverished home to listen to his lowbrow conversation. But a Broadway house is not a home, and certainly not Mr. X's home. It is a theater where, through his business mediation, a stage work that may or may not have artistic value is presented. About this, the public is entitled to have, besides paid advertising, every critic's unbought opinion. Thus the critic belongs there, regardless of the producer's evaluation of him. He belongs more than Mr. X or Mr. Cantor, who once publicly boasted of there being no plays by Lope de Vega up and down Broadway, as highbrow critics, he claimed, would prefer. Actually, it is too bad that Mr. Cantor has not given us some decent productions of Lope; he might so have avoided his long string of failures. ■

44 NEW YORK

Illustrated by Jan Faust

726
Art Directors: Milton Glaser
Walter Bernard
Designers: Milton Glaser
Walter Bernard
Artist: Jan Faust
Writer: John Simon
Publisher: New York Magazine

727
Art Director: John Quinan
Artist: John Quinan
Publisher: The Evening Star

728
Art Director: Walter Bernard
Designer: Tom Bentkowski
Artist: Marvin Mattelson
Publisher: New York Magazine

726

727

728

The Insatiable Critic/Gael Greene

RECIPE FOR A POLITICAL RESTAURANT

"... Frosted-glass partitions and green-shaded lights give the room a classy intimacy. Will Jimmy's mellow into an institution?..."

Listen, all you bums and poets. This is New York ... where politics and chopped chicken liver are born bedfellows. If you don't want to be a judge or run for Mayor and you haven't saved up enough cash to emigrate to Brazil, what else can you do if you're a politician's politician and a Mayor's muscle-plus-fount-of-patronage? You open a restaurant.

The party is over at City Hall. Big John is beautiful but he isn't going to be President. You grew up riding herd on youth gangs in the great gung-ho days of the Lindsay adolescence. You cut your teeth riding in a big fat limousine with red power beams flashing ... and a private phone to check in with your broker. You thrive on pressure and deadlines and the soulful seduction of men's minds at 4 a.m. Eight hours' straight sleep makes you a nervous wreck.

So you open a restaurant. Who is to say ex-Deputy Mayor Richard Aurelio and former Administrative Assistant Sid Davidoff were not destined to move into the wounded space that once housed Toots Shor's to run a saloon-of-sorts called Jimmy's?

If Paris is the perfect
setting for romance,
New York is the perfect city
in which to get over one,
to get over anything.
Cyril Connolly*

Politics, Dick Schaap assures me, teaches you to lie and cheat and connive. Certainly these skills are not superfluous in the restaurant business. Contacts, contracts, high-wire acts, symbiotic bonhomie—what's good for the city is good for the saloon. A good campaign needs compelling graphics: what graphics designer Phil George did for the Lindsay Presidential printware, he's done for Jimmy's innards and menus. And there's a winning slogan: "The restaurant for people who love New York."

"I'd rather be a lamppost
in New York
Than a millionaire in any
other city."
Michael Burke*

*Quote hanging on the wall at Jimmy's.

For energy, guts and a mastery of hyperbole, who can rival the political advance man? Surely serving a decidedly lightweight—it looked less than two and a half pounds to me—lobster when the menu promises three and a half pounds at $16.75, as Jimmy's did one autumn evening, is only as bold as eyeing a crowd of 15,000 and judging it as 35,000.

Actually, Sid Davidoff and Richard Aurelio *do* have certain undeniable qualifications for running a restaurant. They both eat out a lot. Sid's folks owned a candy store in Brooklyn, and later one in Queens. "I started working behind the counter when I was only five," he confided to Leonard Lyons. "I was the Marjoe of the short-order cooks." He also worked his way through school booking bands in local clubs, waiting tables in the Catskills, selling DDT to tenement dwellers in Chelsea. He came to Lindsay as chauffeur-bodyguard-troubleshooter in 1966, proud of his biceps and his image as a health nut, modest about ranking seventh in his law school class at N.Y.U.

Now that Aurelio stalks his nighttime fief at 33 West 52nd Street (days are dedicated to his public-relations business), old friends of his *Newsday* night-editor days recall intimations of a gastronomic destiny. Remember that night in Bay Shore when Sunny Aurelio ordered lobster and ate only the lobster's liver? Is the tale apocryphal? *Newsday* chums remember it well. Freelance writer Harvey Aronson remembers Dick Aurelio as The Sheik of *Newsday*. "We were all little kids at *Newsday*, fresh out of college. He was kind of suave. He wore sweaters. At night we used to send out across the street to this diner for sandwiches and he would invent these gourmet combinations. Instead of just plain tuna, he would order tuna, bacon and a slice of tomato on rye with mayo.

"Dick was always crazy about New York," Aronson recalls. "Whenever we went into Manhattan, we'd ask him where to eat, what shows to see. Once he took us to this French restaurant. Everybody knew him. The waiter brought out the food still in the cooking pots for us to smell. I was so impressed. Fourteen years ago we had a housewarming, bring-your-own-bottle. Dick could have brought Scotch or rye, even gin. We would have found that sophisticated. You know what he brought? Tequila. And he went out to the kitchen for lemons. You're supposed to suck the lemon and drink the tequila. Wait. I think the bottle is still here. Yes, it is. Do you think I should throw it out?"

So you see, all you bums and poets! Dick and Sid bring solid experience, taste and sophistication to West 52nd Street. They also, by incredible coincidence, lucked into an experienced partner of estimable assets: the Irving half of the extraordinary Riese Brothers. The Murray half surrendered his stock in Jimmy's to Dick and Sid. The Riese Brothers are not interested in food. That has not kept them from becoming

729
Art Director: J. C. Suares
Designer: J. C. Suares
Artist: Paul Giovanopoulos
Editor: Harrison Salisbury
Publisher: The New York Times

730
Art Director: Eric Seidman
Designer: Eric Seidman
Artist: Paul Bruner
Editor: Robert Clugman
Publisher: The New York Times Week in Review

731
Art Director: J. C. Suares
Designer: J. C. Suares
Artist: Anita Siegel
Editor: Harrison Salisbury
Publisher: The New York Times

THE NEW YORK TIMES, SATURDAY, FEBRUARY 19, 1972

Nixon in China—A Political Pilgrim

By VINCENT P. MICELI

Some incurable optimists would have us see Mr. Nixon in Peking as an American Moses confronting Mao, the Chinese Pharaoh, with a divine mandate to convert at once and return to the "family of nations." Needless to say, this religious analogy, projected and enhanced with moralistic rhetoric, is an impious fraud. There has been no missionary mandate from God, Church or Country to "Go Down Nixon." Neither has there been any appeal from godless self-god Mao to "Come, let us reason together." The plain truth is that the President of the United States is a mendicant pilgrim to Peking. And perhaps the most depressing aspect of this truth is that he is a mere political pilgrim.

We get the uneasy feeling that we have been down this road before. History is an implacable witness, teaching us, in the wise saying of Santayana, that "those who cannot remember the past are condemned to repeat it." In the era of Nazism, Neville Chamberlain visited Munich for the purpose of inviting Hitler's Germany back into the "family of nations." In order to satisfy Hitler's voracious appetite, Mr. Chamberlain, with the connivance of the Western world, fed Austria and other small European nations to the Nazi beast. Umbrella in hand and smile on his face he returned to London proclaiming to the world "peace in our time."

While Nazism was digesting its new victims and London's ambassador to peace was celebrating his taming of the German monster, Mr. Churchill shrewdly applied the following analogy to the reality of the situation: Mr. Chamberlain thinks that if he feeds the crocodile often enough, this beast will eventually be satisfied; in reality the crocodile's appetite will become so voracious from these frequent feedings that it will never be sated short of devouring Mr. Chamberlain and the whole of Europe.

It might be well for Mr. Nixon to recall the tragic fate of Mr. Chamberlain and the Europe, not to mention the world, of the nineteen-forties as he begins to feed the Dragon of China with small nations of Asia.

Now the bargaining with Red China over the destiny of Free China and the Far East contradict the professed policy of the United States for the last 25 years. America has sacrificed thousands of American lives and vast treasure in Korea and Vietnam to guarantee the freedom of the Far East. It helped create SEATO for that specific purpose. Communist China remains today as great an aggressor as she was when branded such by the United Nations on the occasions of her invasions of Tibet and India and her perpetration of genocide in the conquered territories.

What new evidence has presented itself to explain the President's sudden respect for the Chinese Communist State? It is evident to the whole world that Red China has undergone no perceptible moral conversion. Indeed, a recent Senate subcommittee document reports that Mao's regime murdered between 34 and 64 million persons, primarily political dissidents and minority ethnic groups. The mere passage of time cannot make a hardened aggressor-nation fit to enter the community of nations as a trustworthy member. Is it possible America no longer has any stomach for the ugly truth that Mao's China remains a criminal state dedicated to the conquest of its free and peaceful neighbors?

We are driven to seek the explanation for the President's pilgrimage to Peking in the mind of the President himself. Some cynics explain that Mr. Nixon, realizing he is in political trouble, is visiting Peking for the sole purpose of guaranteeing his re-election. If he can monopolize the peace issue by this visit, his enemies will be left naked before the electorate on the matters of both war and peace.

As a moral philosopher I would propose a deeper motive for the President's new China policy. It flatters the pride of all men, but especially of men in high position and power, to think that they are above the radical metaphysical conflict raging eternally between the forces of good and evil. Instead of aligning themselves with the good against the evil, they fall into the magnificent delusion of thinking themselves capable of harmonizing these irreconcilable enemies. Vain and presumptuous enterprise! The moral philosopher knows that God himself cannot stand above the conflict between good and evil. Indeed, being the essence of moral goodness, God is necessarily the eternal punisher of men and societies addicted to criminal activity. Thus, what God himself necessarily keeps asunder, Mr. Nixon is trying to join together — a world dedicated to criminal aggression and a world dedicated to civil liberty. Consequently, the President's new China policy is foredoomed to failure as a peace move, though it may succeed in getting him re-elected as a political ploy. But the transcendent moral reality that must be confronted by all Americans is this truth: When politicians become gods, citizens and nations become pawns in the ruthless struggle for power.

The Rev. Vincent P. Miceli, Visiting Professor of Philosophy at the Gregorian University in Rome, is author of "The Gods of Atheism."

729

730

731

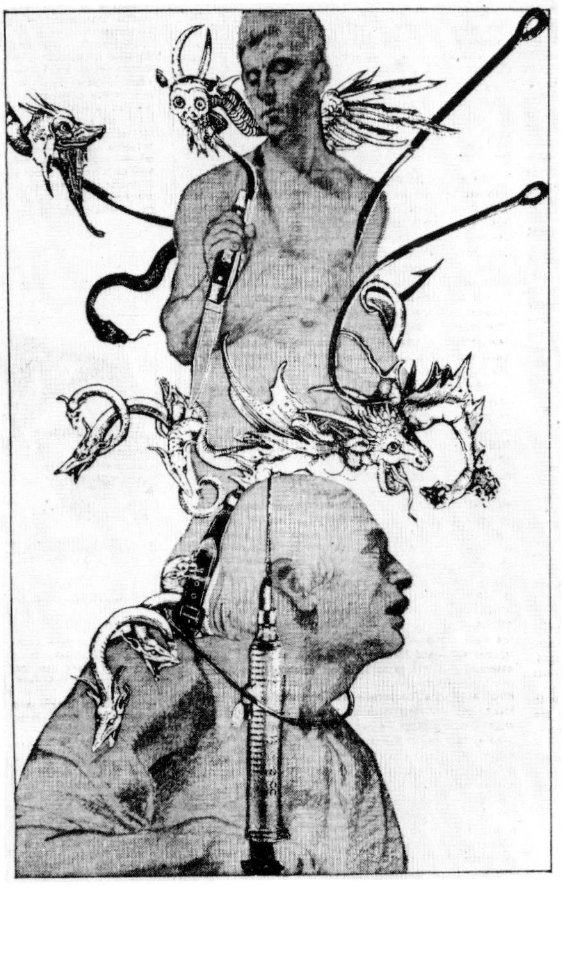

Editorial Art/B/W

732
Art Director: William Cadge
Designer: Bob Ciano
Artist: Bob Zoell
Editor: Sey Chassler
Publisher: McCall's Corporation
Redbook

733
Art Directors: Milton Glaser
Walter Bernard
Designers: Milton Glaser
Walter Bernard
Artist: Robert Grossman
Copywriter: Nicholas Pileggi
Publisher: New York Magazine

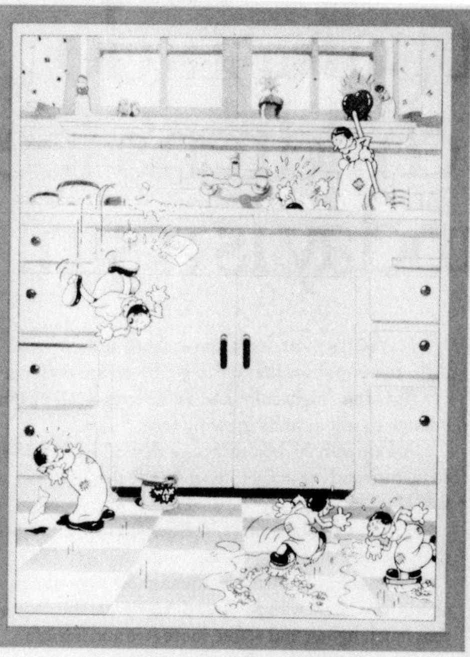

HOW TO RUN A KITCHEN

Third of a series on the kitchen: How to make it work, how to work in it—and how to get out of it in a hurry when you want to. This article will help you face the challenge of keeping a kitchen clean

A shining-clean, shipshape kitchen is the only suitable setting for food preparation. But keeping this action-packed room clean every day presents some special challenges. As part of a continuing series on how to run a kitchen—without its entirely running you—Redbook has prepared a guide to the most efficient and painless ways to keep kitchens clean. Our clean-up guide covers a range of the materials, surfaces and equipment found in most kitchens: the kind of care they need, daily and periodically, to keep them at their peak of good looks and efficiency.

The sink. For porcelain-enameled sinks, use the mildest, least-abrasive cleaning method that works. Harsh cleansers eat away the surface gradually, leaving pits and scars in the surface that in turn must be treated with a harsh cleanser to keep them presentable. To clean a porcelain sink in good condition, apply a liquid light-duty dishwashing detergent and rub with a soft cloth or sponge. Scrub stubborn stains with a mild cleanser. For a sink already rough or stained, use the mildest cleanser that will work to remove stains and make the sink look clean.

Stainless-steel sinks need no cleansers. Wash them with a sudsy soft cloth or sponge and then rinse well with clear water. To prevent water-spotting, particularly in hard-water areas, wipe the sink dry with a cloth or paper towel. Use this same method of washing, rinsing and drying on all chromium trim.

Countertops. Plastic laminates used on tables, cabinets and countertops are heat- and stain-resistant but are not indestructible. The care you give them is as important as the cleaning. You should not set a hot pot on them, use them for a cutting board or scrub with harsh cleansers. Any of these practices will mar the surface and make it more susceptible to staining. To protect this kind of surface and make it a snap to wipe clean, apply one of the self-cleaning waxes designed for kitchen use. Or use a spray cleaner made for cleaning laminated surfaces. If a slight stain remains, it often will disappear after a few days. If a stain persists, treat it in one of the following ways: (1) Pour a small amount of liquid chlorine bleach onto the stain and let it stand for a few seconds and then wipe it off. Rinse the spot with a detergent-and-water solution and wipe it dry. (2) Pour a small amount of rubbing alcohol (isopropyl) onto the stain and let it stand for one minute to "lift" the stain free from the surface. Then pour a small amount of liquid chlorine bleach on this area to remove the color of the stain. Let the bleach stand for a few seconds or more, until the stain disappears (but never let it stand more than five minutes); then wipe up the liquid with a sponge or cloth. Rinse with detergent and water and wipe dry. Rewax the treated area.

Linoleum counters, like linoleum floors, look better and are easier to keep clean if they are protected with a wax. Between periodic waxings, a linoleum surface needs only daily wiping with a damp or sudsy cloth.

Ceramic-tile or stainless-steel counters are easy to maintain. Wipe them with a damp or sudsy cloth, then a dry one. Special glass-ceramic counters or inserts, which are rugged enough to withstand knife blades, hard knocks and bubbling-hot pots, can be cleaned with a damp cloth, or when necessary for a stubbornly sticky spot, cleansing powder.

Wooden work surfaces such as a counter insert, dishwasher top, cutting board and butcher-block table should be wiped clean with a damp cloth and then wiped dry. Neither soak them with water nor let liquid spills remain for any length of time or you will damage the wood. Remove stains by rubbing them with liquid detergent and very fine steel wool. Then wipe with a damp cloth, followed by a dry one. Lubricate the wood occasionally by rubbing it with a little mineral oil.

Cabinets. Wash metal and plastic-laminate cabinets with a solution of all-purpose cleaner and water. Use a heavy-duty spray cleaner if the surface has *(Continued on page 58)*

56

ILLUSTRATED BY BOB ZOELL

732

733

734
Art Director: Peter Rauch
Designer: Bob Daniels
Photographer: Carl Fischer
Copywriter: Jeremy Main
Publisher: Time Inc.
Money Magazine

735
Art Directors: Milton Glaser
Walter Bernard
Designer: Walter Bernard
Artist: Julio Fernandez
Writer: Julie Baumgold
Publisher: New York Magazine

What to Do If You're Fired

Losing a job is a brutal shock, but if you keep your head at the crucial moment you can probably minimize the damage. *by Jeremy Main*

734

735

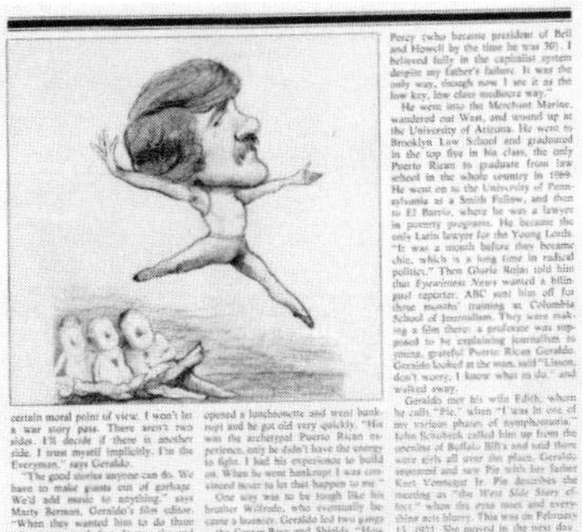

736

737

Editorial Art/Color

736
Art Director: Herb Bleiweiss
Designer: Bruce Danbrot
Artist: Mark English
Writer: Colette
Publisher: Downe Communications
Ladies Home Journal

737
Art Director: Herb Bleiweiss
Designer: Bruce Danbrot
Artist: Mark English
Writer: Dale Funson
Publisher: Downe Communications
Ladies Home Journal

738
Art Director: William Cadge
Designer: Bob Ciano
Artist: Gilbert Stone
Editor: Sey Chassler
Publisher: McCall's Corporation
Redbook

739 Silver Award
Art Director: Arthur Paul
Designers: Arthur Paul
Roy Moody
Photographer: Mike Medow
Publisher: Playboy Enterprises
Playboy Magazine

738

739

MAN'S HIDDEN ENVIRONMENT

article By DAVID DEMPSEY *saint or misanthrope, success or failure—what you are can be shaped by where you are*

EVER SINCE ADAM AND EVE were banished from the Garden of Eden, man has known that his surroundings influence his behavior. The houses we live in, our offices, the space around us, the sounds that intrude on our daily lives, smells, colors, even the arrangement of furniture, determine many of our actions. (A well-known contemporary architect, for example, claimed that he could design a house that would guarantee a divorce for any couple who lived in it a month.)

Man obviously has evolved along with his environment, modifying it to suit his needs. But somewhere along the line, the process got out of hand: the technical side of modern civilization assumed a life of its own that no longer reflected the true needs of its users. Technology, in conquering nature, has surrounded us with a unique man-made environment, but for most of us, our physical comforts have made us ill at ease psychologically. And our psychological landscape has a profound effect on how we behave. For example:

The decor of a room can influence the speed at which we work. In an experiment at Brandeis University, lab assistants were assigned three rooms—"ugly," "beautiful" and "average"—for the purpose of giving tests. Examiners in the ugly room almost always finished their testing faster than those in the two other rooms. Moral: Beauty in the environment may not be a virtue if there is work to be done.

A change in the color of our surroundings changes the pattern of human

740

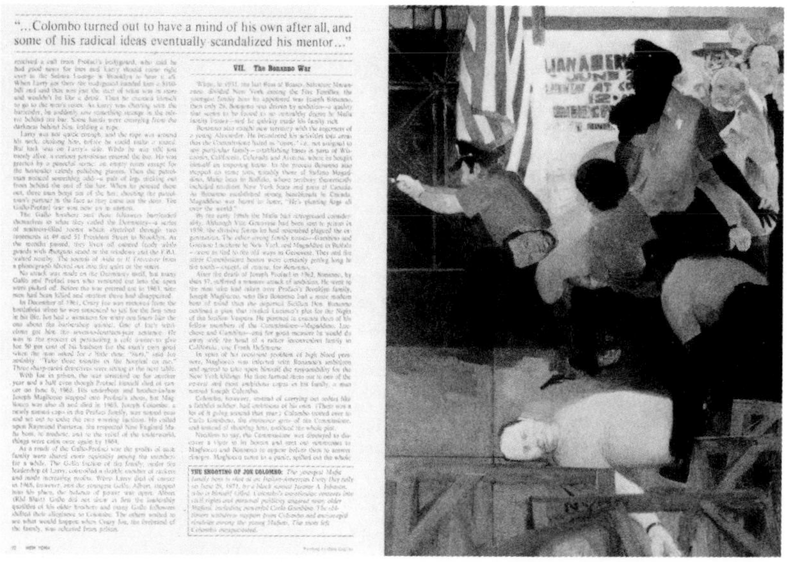
"...Colombo turned out to have a mind of his own after all, and some of his radical ideas eventually scandalized his mentor..."

VII. The Bonanno War

THE SHOOTING OF JOE COLOMBO:

THE SHOOTING OF FRANK COSTELLO: The successor to Lucky Luciano was walking through the lobby of his apartment building on May 2, 1957, when he heard someone say, "This is for you, Frank." The speaker was a henchman of Vito Genovese, who wanted Costello's job as Mafia boss. Costello was only wounded, but he got the message and took an early retirement.
NEW YORK

THE KILLING OF JOEY GALLO: Blamed for planning the shooting of Joe Colombo, Gallo is shot to death and his bodyguard wounded at 5:30 a.m. on April 7, 1972, in Umberto's Clam House in Little Italy. Gallo was celebrating his 43rd birthday with people close to him, including his bride and her young daughter. A Colombo associate named Joseph Luparelli later turned himself in to the F.B.I. saying that he waited outside in a getaway car while four Colombo men took part in the Gallo killing.
NEW YORK

740 Gold Award
Art Directors: Milton Glaser
Walter Bernard
Designers: Walter Bernard
Rochelle Udell
Artists: Paul Davis
Mark English
Burt Silverman
Publisher: New York Magazine

741
Art Director: Neil Shakery
Designer: Neil Shakery
Artist: Roger Hane
Publisher: Saturday Review
Saturday Review of the Arts

742
Art Director: John B. Mastrianni
Designer: John B. Mastrianni
Photographer: James Smith
Copywriter: Marilyn Van Saun
Agency: Aetna Life & Casualty
Client: Driver Education Services
Magazine

741

742

743

IN THIS SET OF APOCALYPTIC ETCHINGS, ARTIST CHARLES BRAGG PRESENTS HIS VISION OF MAN AS HE HAS BEEN AND AS HE MIGHT BE
THE GNOME OF DEATH presides, it's true. We watch from a corner (overinformed and underknowledged) while our generals hump the planet and our priests bless them on their way (call it the way of the cross), while lizard kings do a death-grip waltz on the bones of the same dance done before and the tribal legions raise their banners one against the other, while the garbage and the bones collect waist-deep around the men who proclaim each absurd war holy.
And informed sources said today that God is on our side. Although the Lord was not around to comment, Death had this to say: "Kiss my rumpled ass and sing power. There are no fair fights and only I can save you from love gone wrong." It is stylish to despair.
The FORCES of DEATH and the FORCES of LIFE

"Kiss your own dead ass and be damned, Death... No one needs saving from love."
Still, imagination holds out—for what isn't, and never was, but might, some say, come to be. It's a fool's vision, perhaps, but they have found it in caves, on ruined walls and in the notebooks of young dead poets. Dumb dreams of the artist depicting a planet in love with itself, where the Gnome is silly for a time. Where men can tweak his beard and dare to be naked and vulnerable, loving and inefficient, and without the borrowed power of Death over one another.
It's true the Gnome has his way over man in the end; the game isn't fair, it just is. Still, there's no reason to serve the dark bastard, to run his errands for him, to extend a soulless kingdom while we have the light. For if death is his threat, life is our only revenge. Sing: "Kiss your own dead ass and be damned. There are no real fights among men, and no one needs saving from love."

743
Art Director: Arthur Paul
Designers: Arthur Paul
Tom Staebler
Artist: Charles Bragg
Publisher: Playboy Enterprises, Inc.
Playboy Magazine

744
Art Director: Dick Hess
Designer: Marleen Adlerblum
Artist: Edward Sorel
Publisher: United Nations Assoc.
Vista
Agency: Richard Hess Inc.

745
Art Director: Arthur Paul
Designers: Arthur Paul
Fred Nelson
Artist: Roy Carruthers
Publisher: Playboy Enterprises, Inc.
Playboy Magazine

746
Art Director: Alvin Grossman
Designer: Modesto Torre
Artist: Roger Hane
Publisher: McCall Publishing Company
McCall's Magazine

The Disarmers: A Look at the ACDA

744

BLACK MAGIC
an all-season offshoot of the blazer

attire **By ROBERT L. GREEN** No, that's not Dirk Butkus; it's artist Roy Carruthers' fanciful rendering of a rather substantial fellow in a black brushed-cotton single-breasted two-button jacket with notched lapels and patch pockets, $125, that's worn with a multicolor striped silk shirt with long-pointed collar and two-button cuffs, $65, both by Jackie Rogers; and a pair of natural-color brushed-cotton jeans with Western pockets and straight legs, by New Man for Jackie Rogers, $25. Real tough!

745

746

She had lost her heart to another woman's child—a little girl who was "different." Now she was determined to sacrifice anything, or anyone, to keep her

THE INNOCENTS
By MARGERY SHARP

Editorial Art/Color

747
Art Directors: Dick Hess
Marleen Adlerblum
Designer: Marleen Adlerblum
Artist: Dick Hess
Publisher: United Nations Assoc. Vista
Agency: Richard Hess Inc.

748
Art Director: Dick Hess
Designers: Dick Hess
Marleen Adlerblum
Artist: Dick Hess
Publisher: United Nations Assoc. Vista
Agency: Richard Hess Inc.

747

748

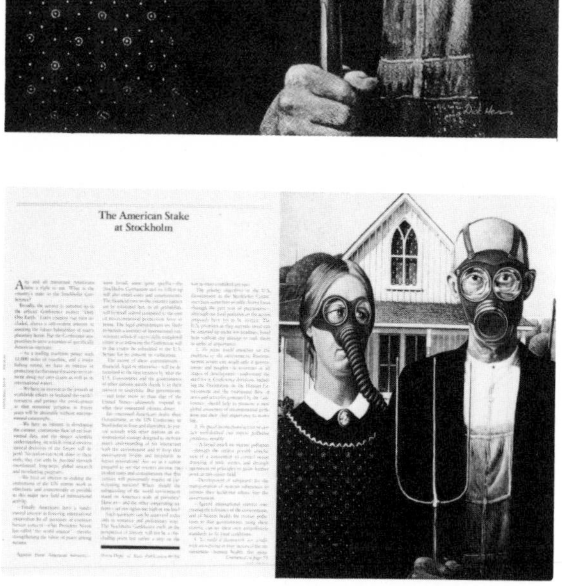

The American Stake at Stockholm

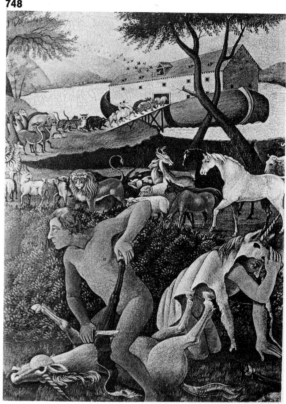

SOME WHYS AND WHEREFORES OF THE UN CONFERENCE ON THE HUMAN ENVIRONMENT

Where Did The Dodo Go?

749
Art Director: Dick Hess
Designer: Marleen Adlerblum
Artist: Rene Magritte
Publisher: United Nations Assoc.
Vista
Agency: Richard Hess Inc.

750
Art Director: Arthur Paul
Designers: Arthur Paul
Kerig Pope
Artist: George Roth
Publisher: Playboy Enterprises, Inc.
Playboy Magazine

Where Will They Live?
Who Speaks For Mankind?

749

750

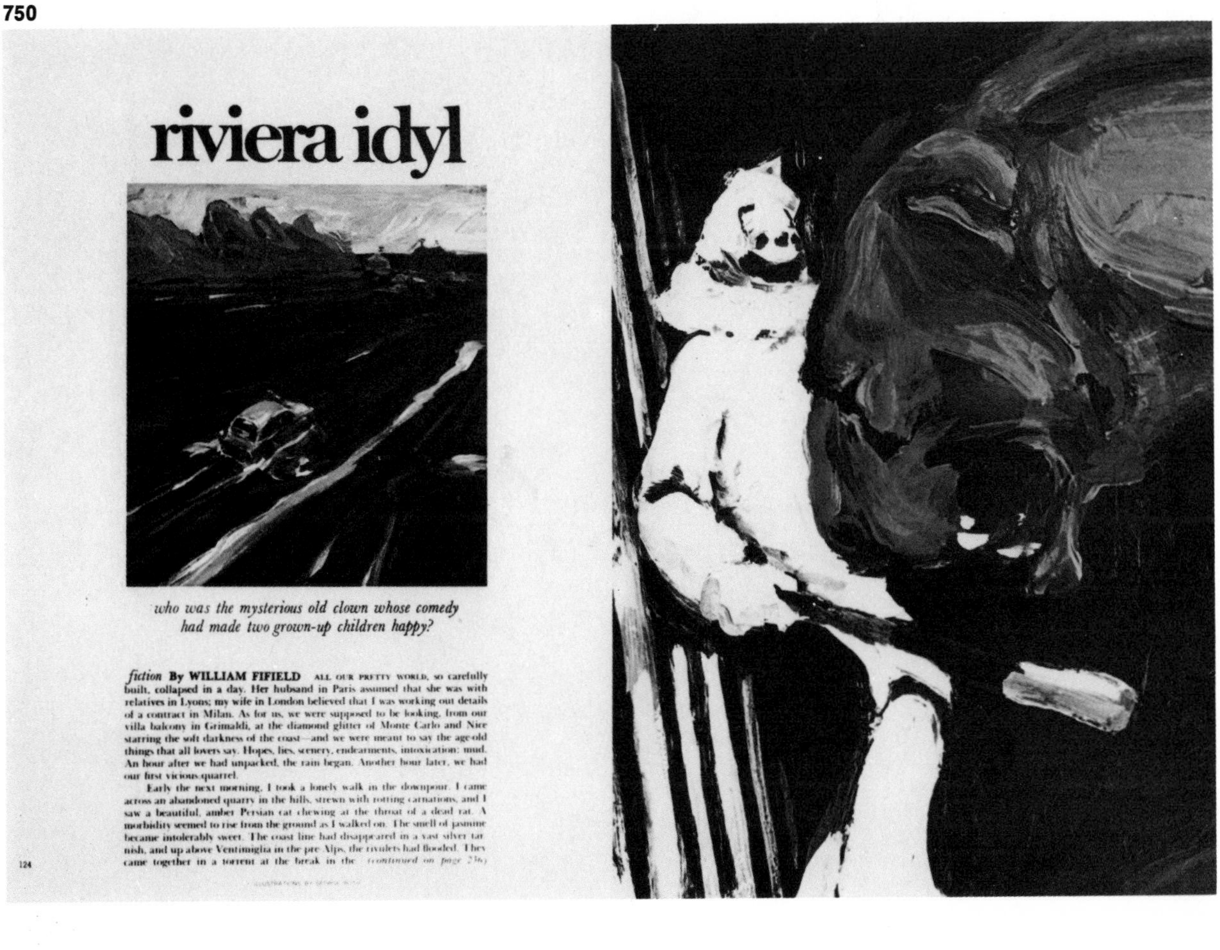

riviera idyl

who was the mysterious old clown whose comedy had made two grown-up children happy?

fiction **By WILLIAM FIFIELD** ALL OUR PRETTY WORLD, so carefully built, collapsed in a day. Her hubsand in Paris assumed that she was with relatives in Lyons; my wife in London believed that I was working out details of a contract in Milan. As for us, we were supposed to be looking, from our villa balcony in Grimaldi, at the diamond glitter of Monte Carlo and Nice starring the soft darkness of the coast—and we were meant to say the age-old things that all lovers say. Hopes, lies, scenery, endearments, intoxication: mud. An hour after we had unpacked, the rain began. Another hour later, we had our first vicious quarrel.

Early the next morning, I took a lonely walk in the downpour. I came across an abandoned quarry in the hills, strewn with rotting carnations, and I saw a beautiful, amber Persian cat chewing at the throat of a dead rat. A morbidity seemed to rise from the ground as I walked on. The smell of jasmine became intolerably sweet. The coast line had disappeared in a vast silver tarnish, and up above Ventimiglia in the pre-Alps, the rivulets had flooded. They came together in a torrent at the break in the *(continued on page [illegible])*

124

751

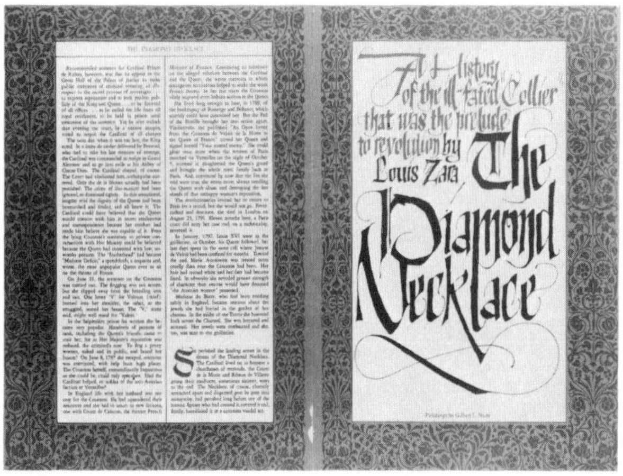
A History of the ill-fated "Collier" that was the prelude to revolution by Louis Zara
The Diamond Necklace

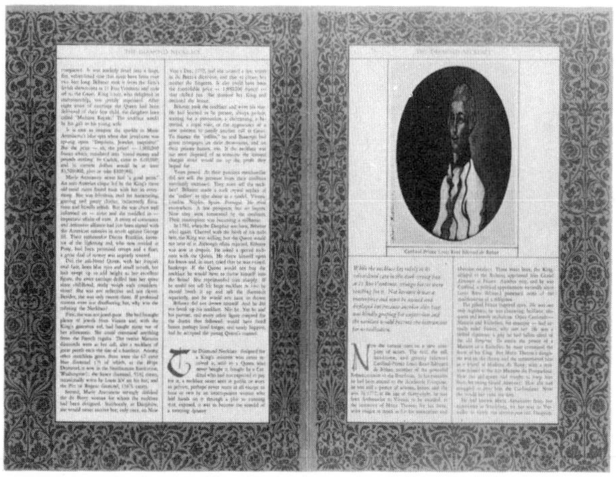

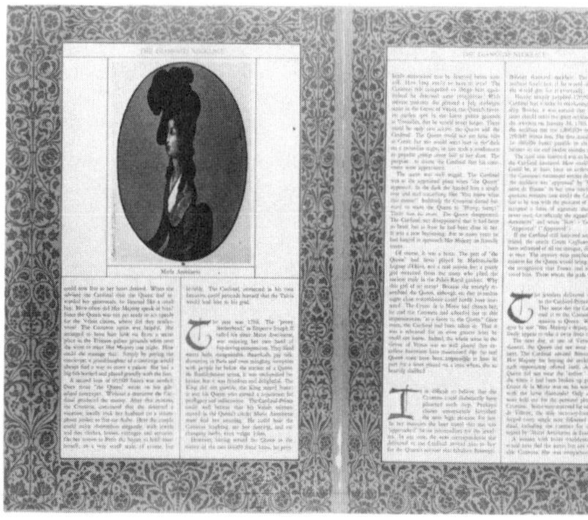

Editorial Art/Color

751
Art Director: Robert Sadler
Designer: Robert Sadler
Artist: Gilbert L. Stone
Copywriter: Louis Zara
Publication: Mineral Digest

751 A Silver Award
Art Directors: Milton Glazer
Walter Bernard
Designer: Tom Bentkowski
Artist: James McMullan
Publisher: New York Magazine

752
Art Director: Arthur Paul
Designers: Arthur Paul
Bob Post
Artist: Etienne Delessert
Publisher: Playboy Enterprises, Inc.
Playboy Magazine

A Robert B. Radnitz / Martin Ritt Film
SOUNDER
Released by 20th Century-Fox
50/4 David Lee (KEVIN HOOKS) and his coon hound Sounder set off on a long journey in search of the boy's father.

751 A

752

article By DONN PEARCE HARVARD. Brick sidewalks. Old cemeteries. Black picket fences. Traffic jams. Granite. Money. Umbrellas. Two Halloween pumpkins on a Victorian porch. John Kenneth Galbraith reading the paper while getting a shoe shine at the valeteria. Paul Revere. Longfellow. Freaks with beards in country overalls. Professors with ties and raincoats, hair short and gray. Political posters. Student centers. Memorial plaques. Bicyclists wearing safety vests of Day-Glo orange. A lighted window. A face bent over a book.

My feet are slow and stealthy as I limp along those dark and rainy streets. I am cold. I am worried. I have been sent to do a guy named B. F. Skinner. Mister *1984*. The Brainwasher. The Pigeon Man. The guy who wants to do away with our freedom and our dignity. Professor of psychology, author of ten books, inventor of the air crib, designer of the teaching machine, architect of communes, recipient of 15 honorary degrees, visiting lecturer, high on the best-seller list, darling of the talk shows, winner of a hatful of awards, grants and fellowships. He has already been attacked by the church, by *Time*, by the Freudians, humanists and existentialists, by Spiro Agnew and the *New York Times Book Review*. Now it's my turn.

• • •

Psychology. The great pseudo science. A few phenomena explained, a few theories advanced. But no predictions. Because nobody really knows. The tool has not yet been invented that enables scientists to peer into the mind, the personality, the brain, the soul or whatever it is that makes us tick. Until the microscope was invented, man could only speculate about the nature of disease. Until the telescope, we knew nothing of the universe. And until their fantastic gadget does come along, psychologists will remain, in effect, witch doctors.

We have had Freud, whose frame of reference was the past; Adler, who dealt with the present; Jung, who looked to the mystic future. The psychoanthropologists believe man is the product of his evolutionary instincts. Piaget thinks it is all a matter of development. As for therapy, there has been psychoanalysis, electric shock, surgery, drugs, ice packs, hypnosis, sexual tutoring, psychodrama, group confession, electrodes implanted in the brain, dream interpretation, massage, touch exercises and marathon encounters. Carl Rogers says the only thing that counts is the self. Rollo May says a cause-and-effect science cannot be applied to human psychology. R. D. Laing says we should all go crazy in order to become sane. Thomas Szasz says there's no such thing as crazy.

And then there is B. F. Skinner. He denies the very existence of the mind. Since it cannot be measured, it cannot scientifically exist. Only behavior itself can be observed and measured, only behavior can be modified. Skinner is a determinist. He is an empiricist. He is an atheist. To him, all meaningful behavior is a unique, personal set of responses that are contingent upon the individual's environment. The rest is pretension and vanity. The idea of an autonomous inner man with a free, responsible soul is merely old superstition. Skinner assumes that human behavior is orderly. To control human behavior by controlling man's environment is what Skinnerism is all about.

And this would be the key to *(continued on page 86)*

GOD IS A VARIABLE INTERVAL

this distinguished, gentle man has a vision—today pigeons, tomorrow the world

Advertising, Design Art/B/W

753
Art Director: Ed Bianchi
Designer: Ed Bianchi
Artist: Ted Lodigensky
Copywriter: Chet Lane
Agency: Young & Rubicam International, Inc
Client: Eastern Airlines

754
Art Director: Ford, Bryne & Brenan Staff
Designer: Ford, Bryne & Brenan Staff
Artist: Wally Neibart
Agency: Ford, Bryne & Brenan
Client: Insurance Company of North America

755
Art Director: Dolores Gudzin
Designer: Dolores Gudzin
Artist: Gilbert Stone
Agency: National Broadcasting Company
Client: National Broadcasting Company

756
Art Director: Jim Uhlir
Designer: Mabey Trousdell
Artist: Mabey Trousdell
Copywriter: Mabey Trousdell
Agency: Foote Cone & Belding, Inc.
Client: International Harvester

757
Art Director: Lou Dorfsman
Designers: Lou Dorfsman
Ira Teichberg
Artist: John Alcorn
Copywriters: Lou Dorfsman
Peter Nord
Agency: CBS/Broadcast Group
Client: CBS Television Stations Division

758
Art Director: Frank Biancalana
Designer: Frank Biancalana
Photographer: Tim Lewis
Copywriter: Ethan Revsin
Agency: Lee King & Partners
Client: GATX

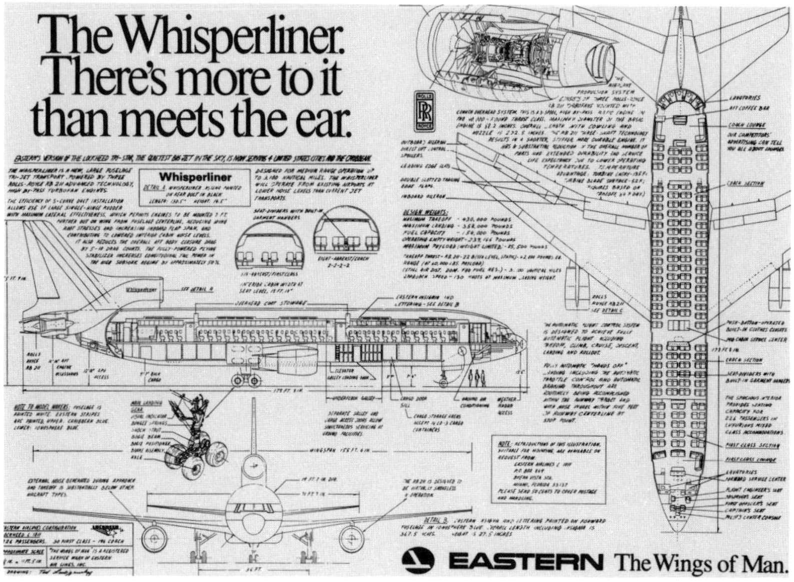

The Whisperliner.
There's more to it
than meets the ear.
Whisperliner
EASTERN The Wings of Man.

753

754

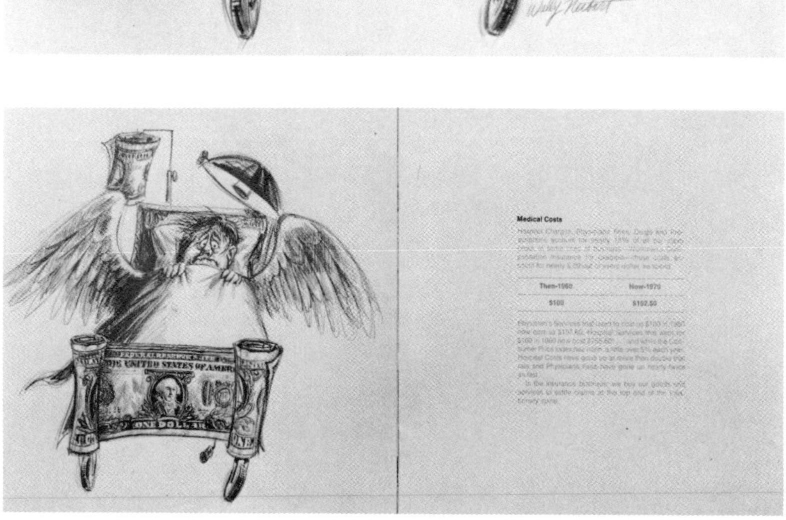

Medical Costs

ESCAPE
A JACK WEBB PRODUCTION • SUNDAY AT 10 PM ON NBC

755

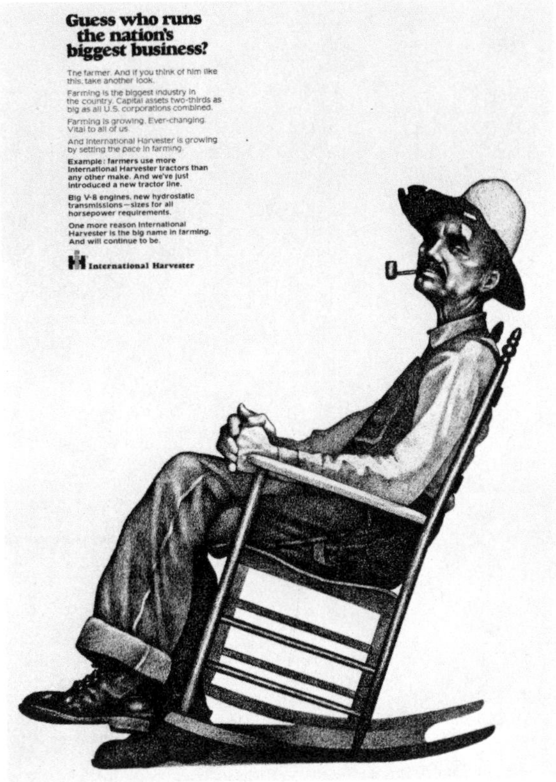

756

757

After they learn to spell C-A-T
CAT
Who's going to teach them to T-H-I-N-K?
THINK

758

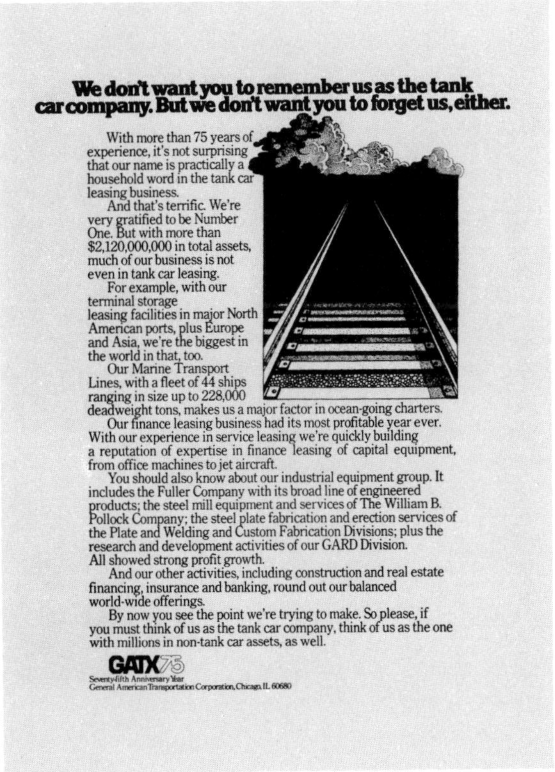

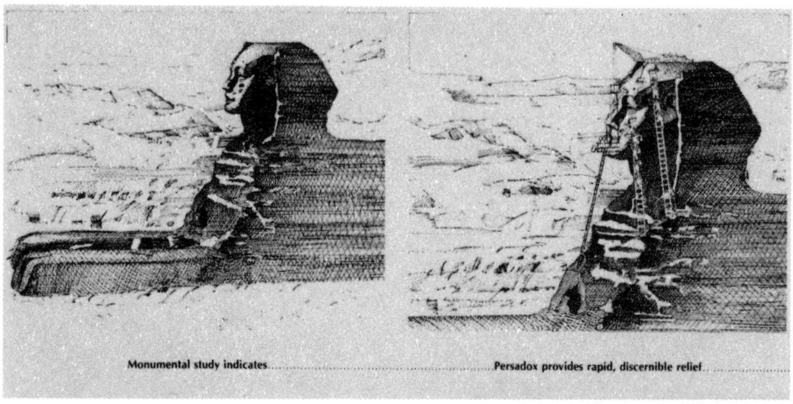
Monumental study indicates...
...Persadox provides rapid, discernible relief...

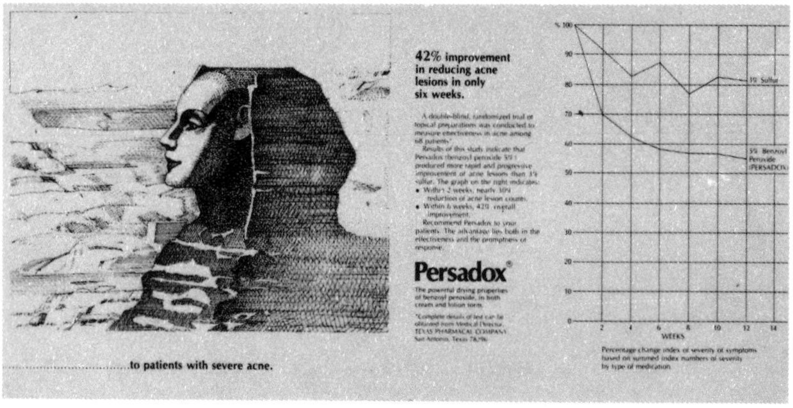
...to patients with severe acne.
42% improvement in reducing acne lesions in only six weeks.
Persadox®
% 100
90
80
70
60
50
40
30
20
10
0
2
4
6
8
10
12
14
WEEKS
5% Sulfur
5% Benzoyl Peroxide (PERSADOX)
Percentage change index of severity of symptoms based on summed index numbers of severity by type of medication.

759

760

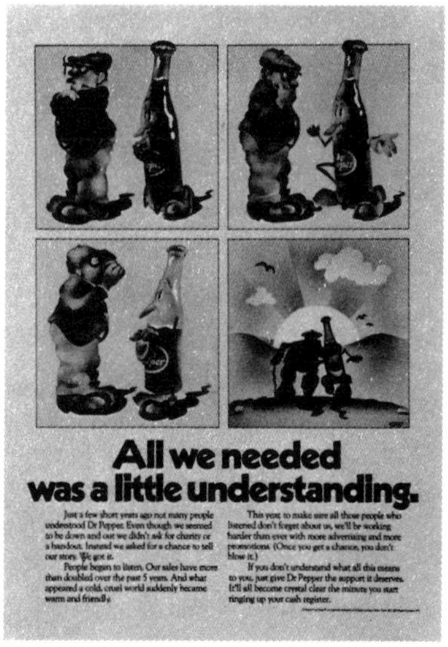
All we needed was a little understanding.
Just a few short years ago not many people understood Dr Pepper. Even though we seemed to be down and out we didn't ask for charity or a handout. Instead we asked for a chance to tell our story. We got it.
People began to listen. Our sales have more than doubled over the past 5 years. And what appeared a cold, cruel world suddenly became warm and friendly.
This year, to make sure all those people who listened don't forget about us, we'll be working harder than ever with more advertising and more promotions. (Once you get a chance, you don't blow it.)
If you don't understand what all this means to you, just give Dr Pepper the support it deserves. It'll all become crystal clear the minute you start ringing up your cash register.

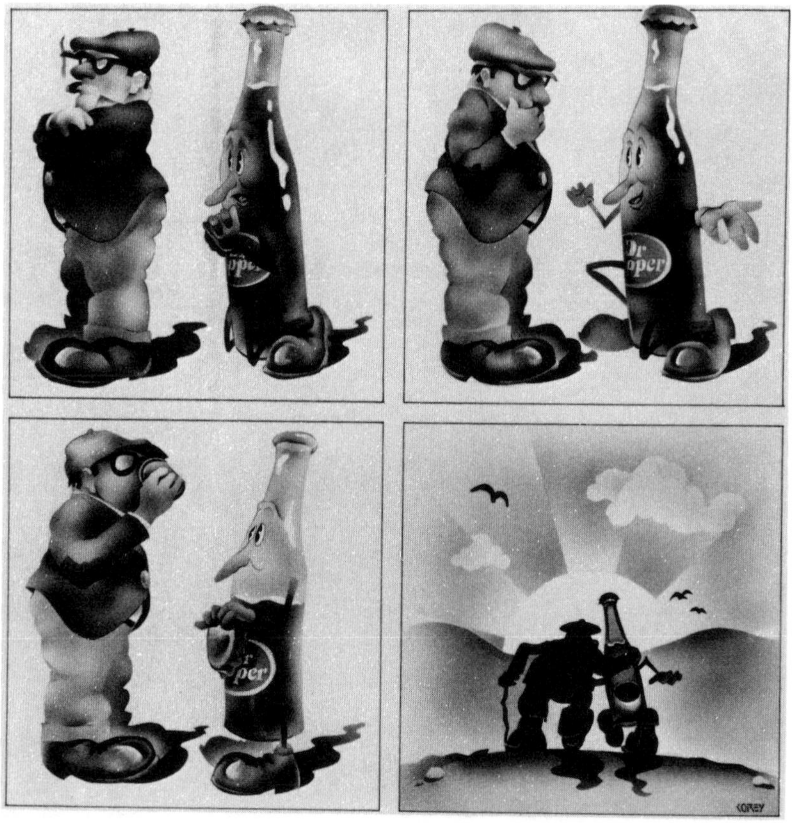
COREY

Behind every great furniture design
is a great furniture designer,
or reasonable facsimile thereof.

761

762

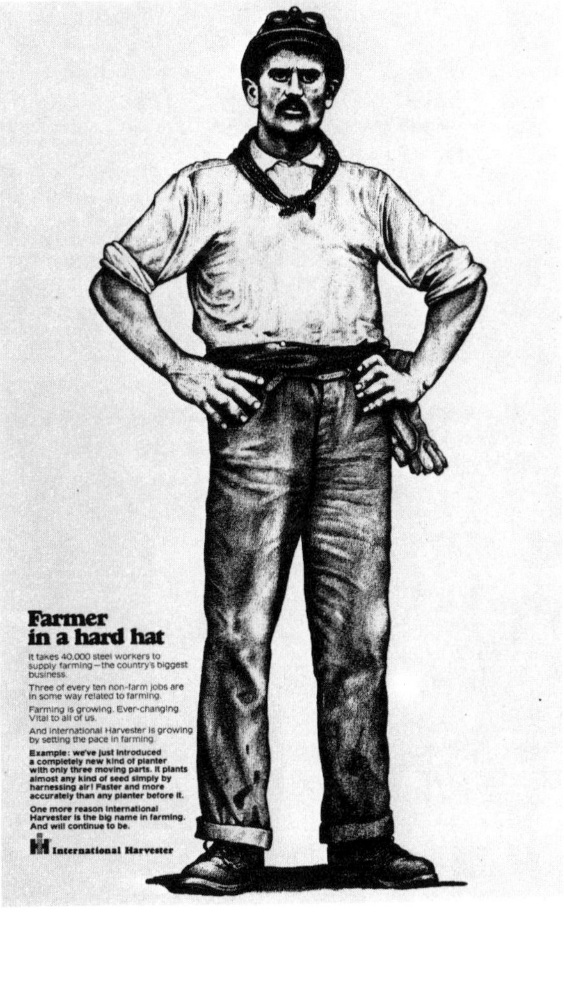
Farmer
in a hard hat
It takes 40,000 steel workers to supply farming—the country's biggest business.
Three of every ten non-farm jobs are in some way related to farming.
Farming is growing. Ever-changing. Vital to all of us.
And International Harvester is growing by setting the pace in farming.
Example: we've just introduced a completely new kind of planter with only three moving parts. It plants almost any kind of seed simply by harnessing air! Faster and more accurately than any planter before it.
One more reason International Harvester is the big name in farming. And will continue to be.
International Harvester

759
Art Director: Tom Knott
Designer: Tom Knott
Artist: John Cook
Copywriter: Dick Baker
Agency: The Bloom Agency
Client: Texas Pharmacal Company

760
Art Director: Guy Noerr
Designer: Guy Noerr
Artist: Chris Corey
Copywriter: Allen Salisbury
Agency: Young & Rubicam International, Inc.
Client: Dr. Pepper

761
Art Director: Pete Coutroulis
Designer: Pete Coutroulis
Artist: Joe Saffold
Copywriter: Howard Krakow
Agency: Jim Weller & Partners
Client: Fisher Office Furniture, Inc.

762
Art Director: Jim Uhlir
Designer: Mabey Trousdell
Artist: Mabey Trousdell
Copywriter: Mabey Trousdell
Agency: Foote Cone & Belding, Inc.
Client: International Harvester

His mother needed an air force.
All you need is Birds Eye Combinations.
They should have given her a medal as big as the Empire State Building.
At Birds Eye, we never forget the little boy who lives inside every man.
We're just for tasty vegetables.
5¢ off the vegetables mother never had. 5¢
Green Peas and Pearl Onions
5¢
5¢

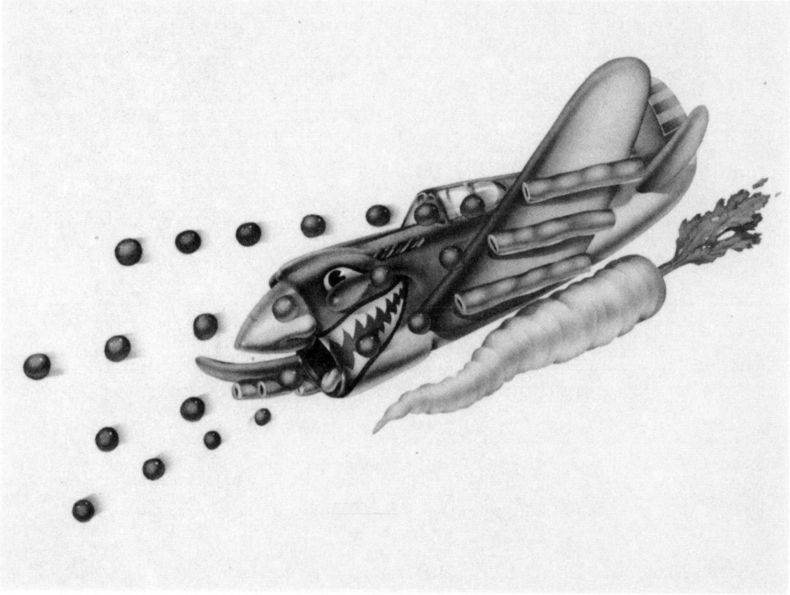

764

765

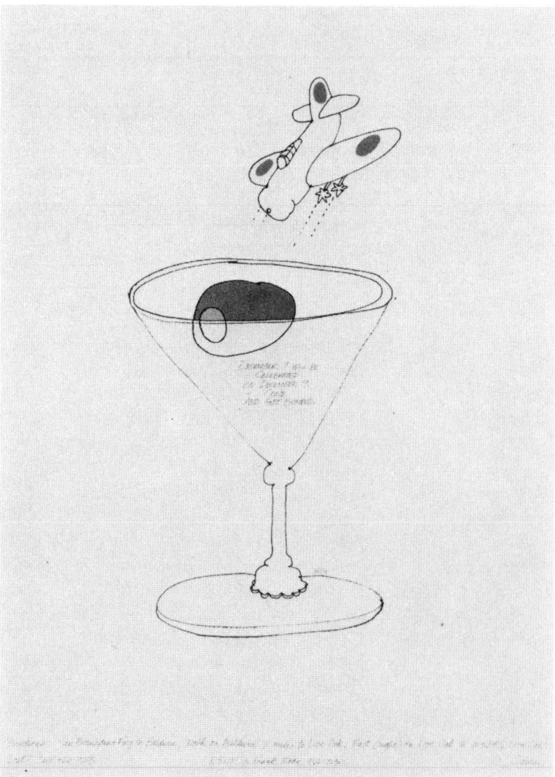

766

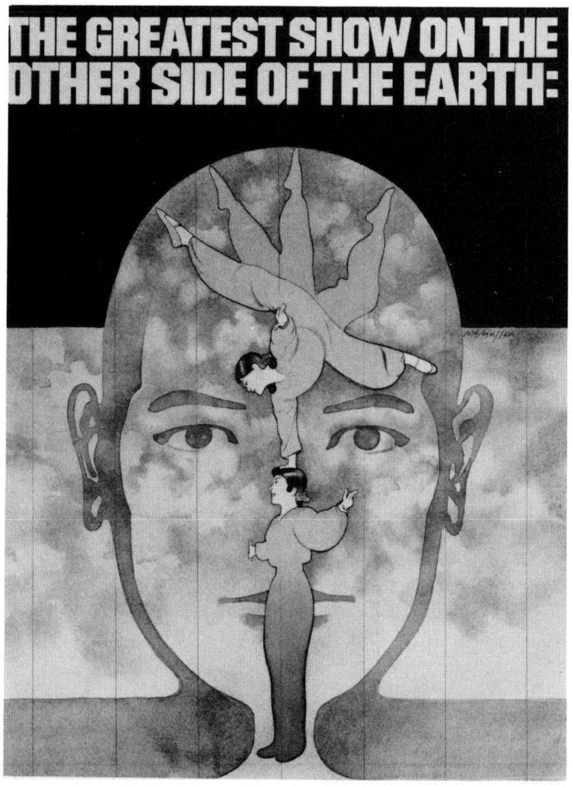
THE GREATEST SHOW ON THE
OTHER SIDE OF THE EARTH:

Riders of the Purple Sage Unite! Throw off your wing-tipped shackles and join the masters of the fine art of poking cows, grunting homilies and collecting network residuals! Come to Texas! Come to the wildest of the wild, wild wests! Slap your chaps into the lopin'-along saddle and ride off into the John Ford Sunset, smilin' under sweatin' Stetson. Here's what cowboy'n's all about:
SO YOU WANNA BE A COWBOY?
You had to have a bandana. It covered your nose and mouth in a dusty stampede. Good for hiding behind when robbing a stage coach, it made an adequate tourniquet. In case you were unlucky.
The singing cowboy really existed. he sang on the range at night to calm down the restless herd, and believe it or not one of his favorite's was Home On The Range. In real life the cowboy was usually a southerner and 26% were black.
How to Roll a Cigarette
The cowboy rolled his own cigarette. Some guys could go through the entire exercise with one hand. Isn't that impressive?
The Lone Ranger's silver bullets were probably made out of tin foil. Because everyone else's were made out of paper. Hard to re-load.
The ten-gallon hat. So called because cowboys used it for watering their horses. It also kept them out of the rain and was unmatched for those dramatic sunset ride offs and a hearty "High O Silver".
The tenderfoot. Wore celluloid collars and drank sarsaparilla—a sort of root beer. Could drink anyone under the table, which is where he usually was when the six-guns came out.
You don't really need these. The horse needs them even less. Send them to the SPCA.
The Longhorn. The cowboy spent all summer fattening him up for the fall roundup. Then he drove him to market and by the time he got there he was skinny again. You figure it out.

764
Art Director: Woody Litwhiler
Designer: Woody Litwhiler
Artist: Charles White
Photographer: Joe Toto
Copywriter: Don Marowski
Agency: Young & Rubicam International, Inc.
Client: General Foods

765
Art Director: Don Weller
Designer: Don Weller
Artist: Don Weller
Copywriter: Frank Noda
Agency: Weller & Juett Inc.
Client: Mary Catone
Frank Noda

766
Art Director: Richard Nava
Designer: Richard Nava
Artist: James McMullan
Agency: Image Communications, Inc.
Client: Norton Simon Communications

767
Art Director: Frank Rogers
Designer: Mabey Trousdell
Artist: Mabey Trousdell
Agency: Cargill, Wilson & Acree
Client: First Union National Bank

767

768

The
ABC
of NFL Football
A Primer
A
G
is for GOALPOST.
M
is for MOTIVATION.
T
is for TOUCHDOWN.
B
is for BALL.
N
is for NFL.
U
C
is for COACH.
H
is for HALL OF FAME.
O
is for OFFENSIVE LINEMEN.
V
is for VICTORY.
D
is for DEFENSE.
I
is for INTERMISSION.
J
is for JOGGING.
P
is for PLAYS.
W
is for WHISTLE.
E
is for ENDS.
K
is for KICKING GAME.
Q
is for QUARTERBACK.
X
R
is for RUNNING BACKS.
Y
is for YARDS.
F
L
S
is for SUPER BOWL.
Z
is for ZONE.
NO PASSING ZONE

769

orioles
colts

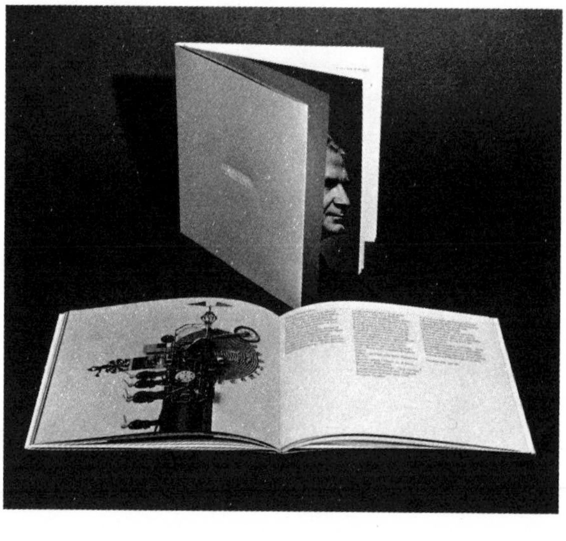

771

"If you will it, it is no dream."
—Theodore Herzl

768
Art Director: Mike Gaines
Designer: Mabey Trousdell
Artist: Mabey Trousdell
Agency: Mabey Trousdell Inc.
Client: N.F.L. Properties

769
Art Director: Henry Epstein
Designer: William Duevell
Artist: Fred Otnes
Copywriter: Joel Cohen
Agency: ABC Art Department
Client: ABC News

771
Art Directors: Barry Kaufman
Richard Lomonaco
Designers: Barry Kaufman
Richard Lomonaco
Artist: Fred Otnes
Photographer: Morecraft/Oliwa
Agency: Communications Quorum, Inc.
Client: United Jewish Appeal

772
Art Director: Mike Gaines
Designer: Mabey Trousdell
Artist: Mabey Trousdell
Agency: Mabey Trousdell Inc.
Client: N.F.L. Properties

773
Art Directors: Barry Tucker
Ernie James
Designer: Ernie James
Artists: Barry Tucker
Ernie James
Ray Condon
Editor: George Doszla
Agency: Tucker & James
Client: Sandoz Australia Pty. Ltd.

774
Art Director: David Krieger
Designer: David Krieger
Artist: Tim Lewis
Agency: Davis Fried Krieger Inc.
Client: Chess/Janus Records

775
Art Directors: Frank Perry
Art Christy
Designers: Frank Perry
Art Christy
Artist: Gordon Kibbee
Copywriters: Frank Perry
Mitch De Groot
Clem Bittner
Art Christy
Agency: Fuller & Smith & Ross Inc.
Client: Mobil Oil Corporation

776
Art Directors: Frank Perry
Art Christy
Designers: Frank Perry
Art Christy
Artist: Ettienne Delessert
Copywriters: Frank Perry
Mitch De Groot
Clem Bittner
Art Christy
Agency: Fuller & Smith & Ross Inc.
Client: Mobil Oil Corporation

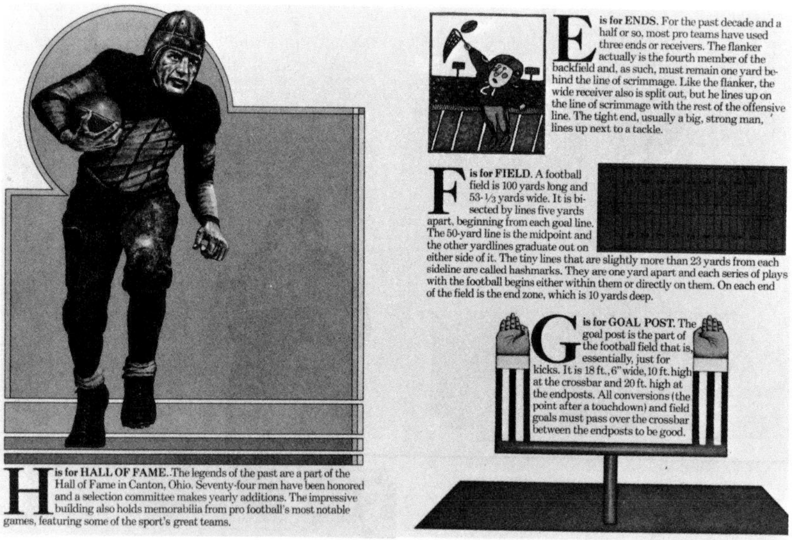
E is for ENDS. For the past decade and a half or so, most pro teams have used three ends or receivers. The flanker actually is the fourth member of the backfield and, as such, must remain one yard behind the line of scrimmage. Like the flanker, the wide receiver also is split out, but he lines up on the line of scrimmage with the rest of the offensive line. The tight end, usually a big, strong man, lines up next to a tackle.
F is for FIELD. A football field is 100 yards long and 53-1/3 yards wide. It is bisected by lines five yards apart, beginning from each goal line. The 50-yard line is the midpoint and the other yardlines graduate out on either side of it. The tiny lines that are slightly more than 23 yards from each sideline are called hashmarks. They are one yard apart and each series of plays with the football begins either within them or directly on them. On each end of the field is the end zone, which is 10 yards deep.
G is for GOAL POST. The goal post is the part of the football field that is, essentially, just for kicks. It is 18 ft., 6" wide, 10 ft. high at the crossbar and 20 ft. high at the endposts. All conversions (the point after a touchdown) and field goals must pass over the crossbar between the endposts to be good.
H is for HALL OF FAME. The legends of the past are a part of the Hall of Fame in Canton, Ohio. Seventy-four men have been honored and a selection committee makes yearly additions. The impressive building also holds memorabilia from pro football's most notable games, featuring some of the sport's great teams.

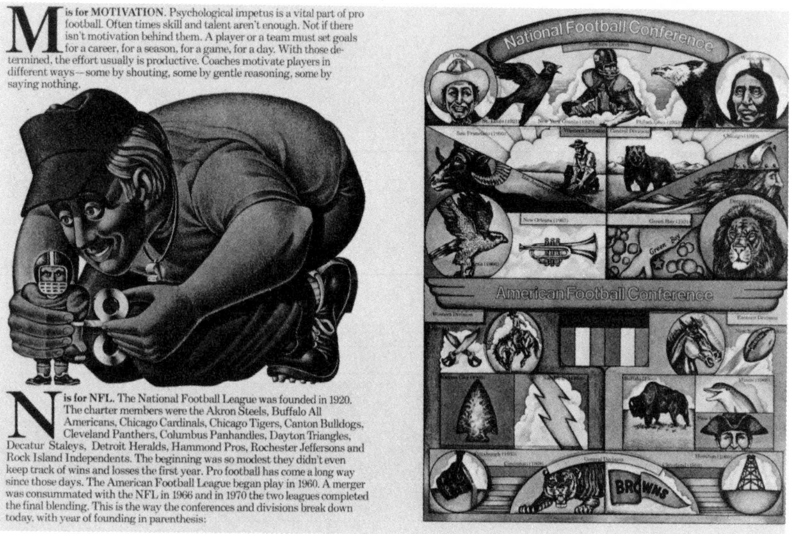
M is for MOTIVATION. Psychological impetus is a vital part of pro football. Often times skill and talent aren't enough. Not if there isn't motivation behind them. A player or a team must set goals for a career, for a season, for a game, for a day. With those determined, the effort usually is productive. Coaches motivate players in different ways—some by shouting, some by gentle reasoning, some by saying nothing.
N is for NFL. The National Football League was founded in 1920. The charter members were the Akron Steels, Buffalo All Americans, Chicago Cardinals, Chicago Tigers, Canton Bulldogs, Cleveland Panthers, Columbus Panhandles, Dayton Triangles, Decatur Staleys, Detroit Heralds, Hammond Pros, Rochester Jeffersons and Rock Island Independents. The beginning was so modest they didn't even keep track of wins and losses the first year. Pro football has come a long way since those days. The American Football League began play in 1960. A merger was consummated with the NFL in 1966 and in 1970 the two leagues completed the final blending. This is the way the conferences and divisions break down today, with year of founding in parenthesis:
National Football Conference
American Football Conference
BROWNS

772

773

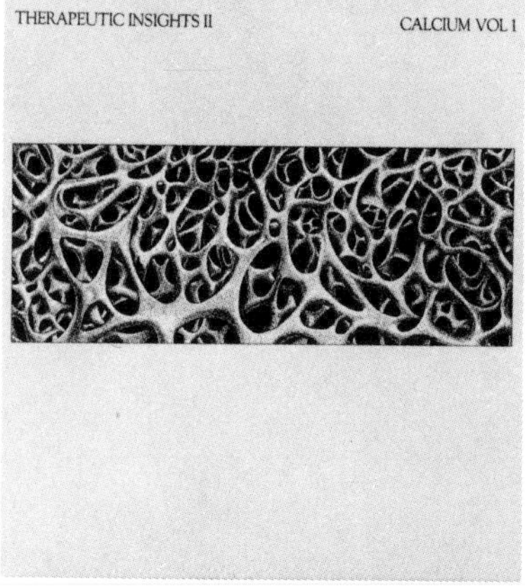
THERAPEUTIC INSIGHTS II
CALCIUM VOL 1

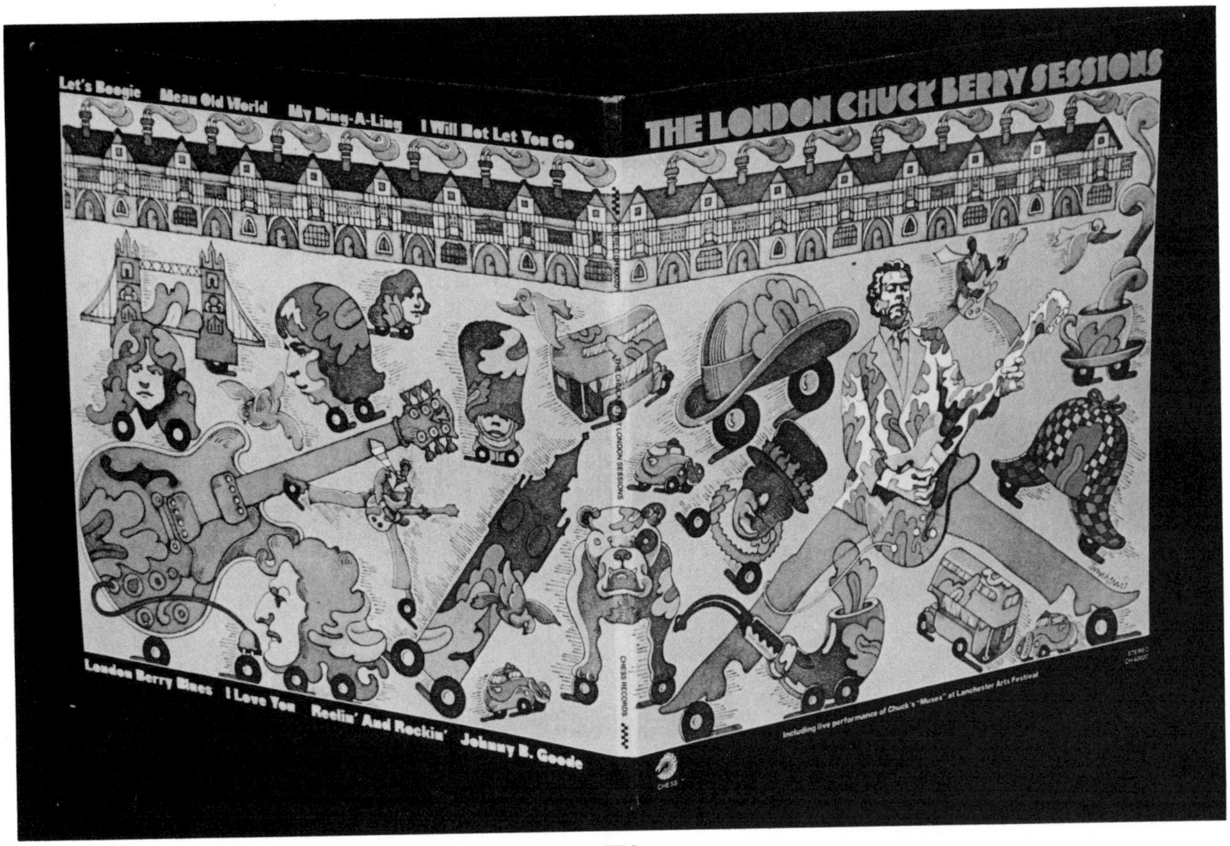
Let's Boogie
Mean Old World
My Ding-A-Ling
I Will Not Let You Go
THE LONDON CHUCK BERRY SESSIONS
London Berry Blues
I Love You
Reelin' And Rockin'
Johnny B. Goode
Including live performance of Chuck's "Muses" at Lanchester Arts Festival

774

775

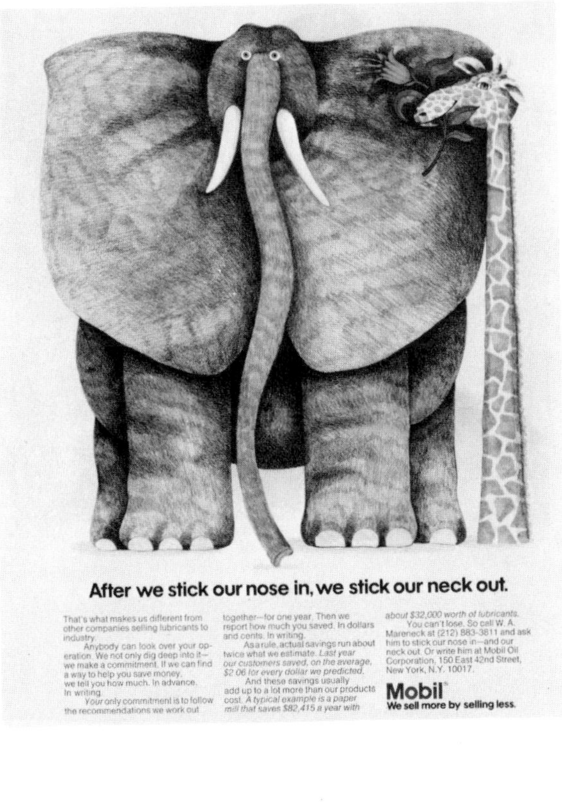
After we stick our nose in, we stick our neck out.
That's what makes us different from other companies selling lubricants to industry.
Anybody can look over your operation. We not only dig deep into it—we make a commitment. If we can find a way to help you save money, we tell you how much. In advance. In writing.
Your only commitment is to follow the recommendations we work out together—for one year. Then we report how much you saved. In dollars and cents. In writing.
As a rule, actual savings run about twice what we estimate. *Last year our customers saved, on the average, $2.06 for every dollar we predicted.*
And these savings usually add up to a lot more than our products cost. *A typical example is a paper mill that saves $82,415 a year with about $32,000 worth of lubricants.*
You can't lose. So call W. A. Mareneck at (212) 883-3811 and ask him to stick our nose in—and our neck out. Or write him at Mobil Oil Corporation, 150 East 42nd Street, New York, N.Y. 10017.
Mobil
We sell more by selling less.

776

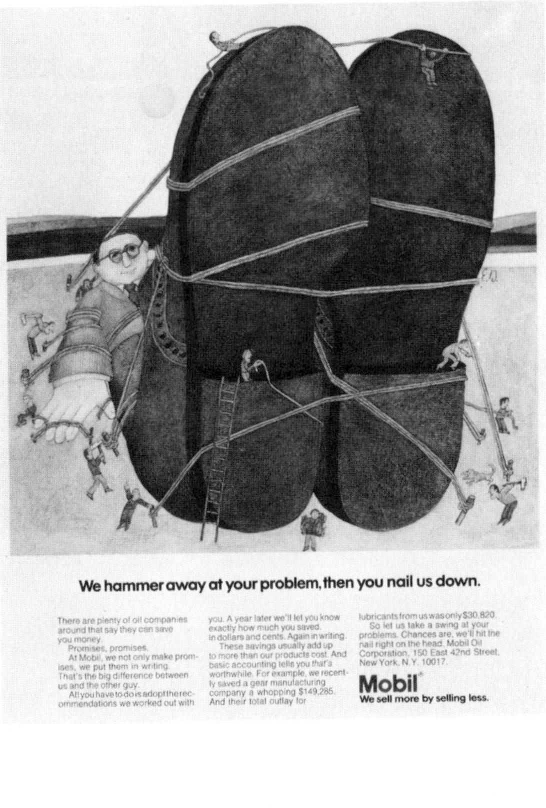
We hammer away at your problem, then you nail us down.
There are plenty of oil companies around that say they can save you money.
Promises, promises.
At Mobil, we not only make promises, we put them in writing. That's the big difference between us and the other guy.
All you have to do is adopt the recommendations we worked out with you. A year later we'll let you know exactly how much you saved. In dollars and cents. Again in writing.
These savings usually add up to more than our products cost. And basic accounting tells you *that's* worthwhile. For example, we recently saved a gear manufacturing company a whopping $149,285. And their total outlay for lubricants from us was only $30,820.
So let us take a swing at your problems. Chances are, we'll hit the nail right on the head. Mobil Oil Corporation, 150 East 42nd Street, New York, N.Y. 10017.
Mobil
We sell more by selling less.

IMPROVED
JELL-O
NUTRITIOUS
VITAMINS A AND C+IRON
FRUITIER
Taste
NEW FORTIFIED JELL-O GELATIN
Your Opportunity To Serve More Nutrition In Your Meals.
NEW FORTIFIED JELL-O GELATIN
Gives You Two More Good Reasons To Serve More Of America's Favorite Gelatin.
New Fruitier Taste
New Nutritional Bonus
NEW FORTIFIED JELL-O GELATIN
Fortified With Vitamin A, Vitamin C And Iron
Apples
Bananas
Blackberries
Blueberries
Grapes
Peaches
Pears
Raspberries
Strawberries
Cherries
Vitamin A
Vitamin C
Iron
Child
Adult

JELL-O
BRAND GELATIN
The Dessert America Grew Up With Serves You An Exciting New Opportunity.

777

778

Once we get to the root of your problem, we go out on a limb.
That's the difference between us and the other oil companies. They say their recommendations will save you money. But we tell you exactly how much. In advance. Before you commit yourself to anything.
If you decide to go ahead, all you have to do is follow the recommendations we work out together. And a year later we'll get together again, figure out the actual savings and give you a report. In writing.
These savings usually add up to more than our products cost. For example, we recently saved a Northwest truck fleet $57,410—yet the lube costs were only $800.
Can you use savings like these?
Call W. A. Mareneck at (212) 883-3811 and get all the details. Or write him at Mobil Oil Corporation, 150 East 42nd Street, New York, New York, 10017.
Mobil
We sell more by selling less.

779

Advertising, Design Art/Color

777
Art Director: Walter Kaprielian
Designers: Harold Florian
Joel Benay
Walter Kaprielian
Artist: Push Pin Studios
Copywriter: Richard Seideman
Agency: Ketchum, MacLeod & Grove, Inc.
Client: General Foods

778
Art Directors: Frank Perry
Art Christy
Designers: Frank Perry
Art Christy
Artist: Don Ivan Punchatz
Copywriters: Frank Perry
Mitch De Groot
Clem Bittner
Art Christy
Agency: Fuller & Smith & Ross Inc.
Client: Mobil Oil Corporation

779
Art Director: Ed Thrasher
Designers: Chris Whorf
John Casado
Barbara Casado
Artist: Don Ivan Punchatz
Client: Warner/Reprise Records

780
Art Director: Frank Biancalana
Designer: Frank Biancalana
Artist: Charles White III
Copywriter: Ethan Revsin
Agency: Lee King & Partners
Client: GATX

781
Art Director: Frank Biancalana
Designer: Frank Biancalana
Artist: David Wilcox
Copywriter: Ethan Revsin
Agency: Lee King & Partners
Client: GATX

782
Art Director: Frank Biancalana
Designer: Frank Biancalana
Artist: Paul Davis
Copywriter: Ethan Revsin
Agency: Lee King & Partners
Client: GATX

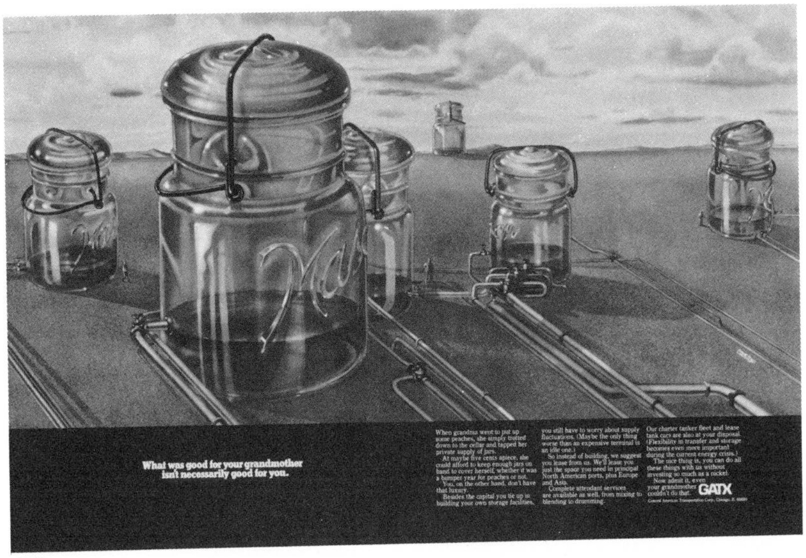
What was good for your grandmother isn't necessarily good for you.
GATX

780

Old tank cars don't die, they just slowly depreciate.
GATX

781

782

Your ships can't cross the water the way ours can.
GATX

Paul Davis

Ex-New Yorker
returns to town.
For years, the snowy egret had been migrating to Jamaica Bay in the springtime.
Then suddenly, it disappeared. Mainly because something else had disappeared from Jamaica Bay. Clean water and the plant and fish life necessary to support bird life.
Then in 1968, Herbert Johnson was appointed to the Jamaica Bay Wildlife Refuge by the city's Parks Administration.
Immediately, he and his fellow workers set out to restore the ecological balance.
They planted bayberry and chokeberry. And pine. Even wheat, oats and rye.
Herb Johnson also fought for clean water. And spoke to Audubon societies, school children and politicians about the dangers of destroying our wildlife and waterways.
Today, over 300 species of birds may be seen in Jamaica Bay – including a flourishing colony of lovely, graceful snowy egrets.
Only a few years ago, Herb Johnson probably felt like a lonely voice crying in a rapidly disappearing wilderness.
Today, he has lots of company in his crusade to save the 600 miles of woodlands and waterways of our great town.
It's the story of a great comeback. But then New Yorkers have always been known for their great comebacks.
New York City:
It's still a hell of a town.
New York Telephone

783

You can't tell a tiger
by his stripes.
INDUSTRY WEEK

784

785

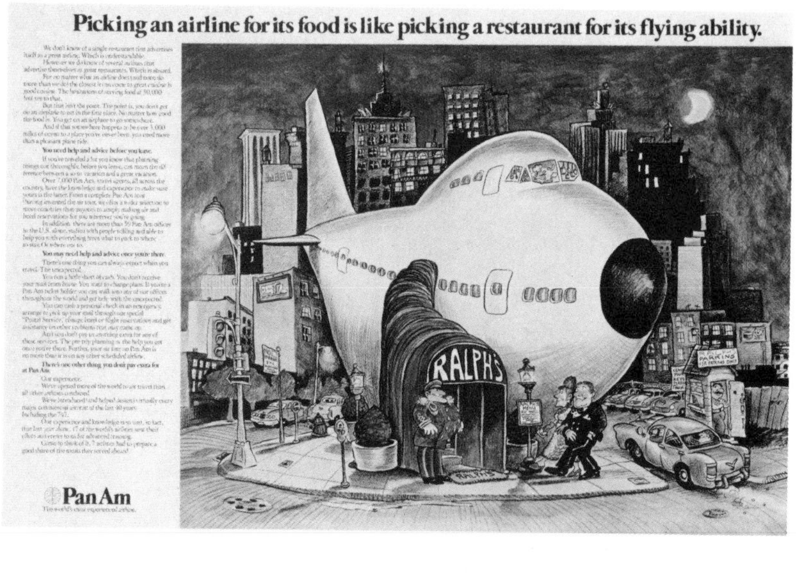
Picking an airline for its food is like picking a restaurant for its flying ability.
RALPHS
Pan Am

783
Art Director: Bob Steigelman
Designer: Bob Steigelman
Artist: Paul Davis
Copywriter: Ray Dempsey
Agency: Young & Rubicam International, Inc.
Client: New York Telephone

784
Art Director: Tom Gilday
Designer: Tom Gilday
Artist: Arnold Varga
Copywriter: Joyce Spetrino
Agency: Griswold-Eshleman Co.
Client: Penton Publishing Co.

785
Art Director: Amil Gargano
Artist: Rick Meyrowitz
Copywriters: Jim Durfee
Bob Kaplan
Agency: Carl Ally Inc.
Client: Pan American Airways

786
Art Directors: Howard C. Grant
Richard P. Ritter
Designers: Howard C. Grant
Richard P. Ritter
Photographer: Ryszard Horowitz
Copywriter: Diamond Information Center
Agency: N. W. Ayer & Son, Inc.
Ayer Design
Client: De Beers Consolidated Mines, Ltd.

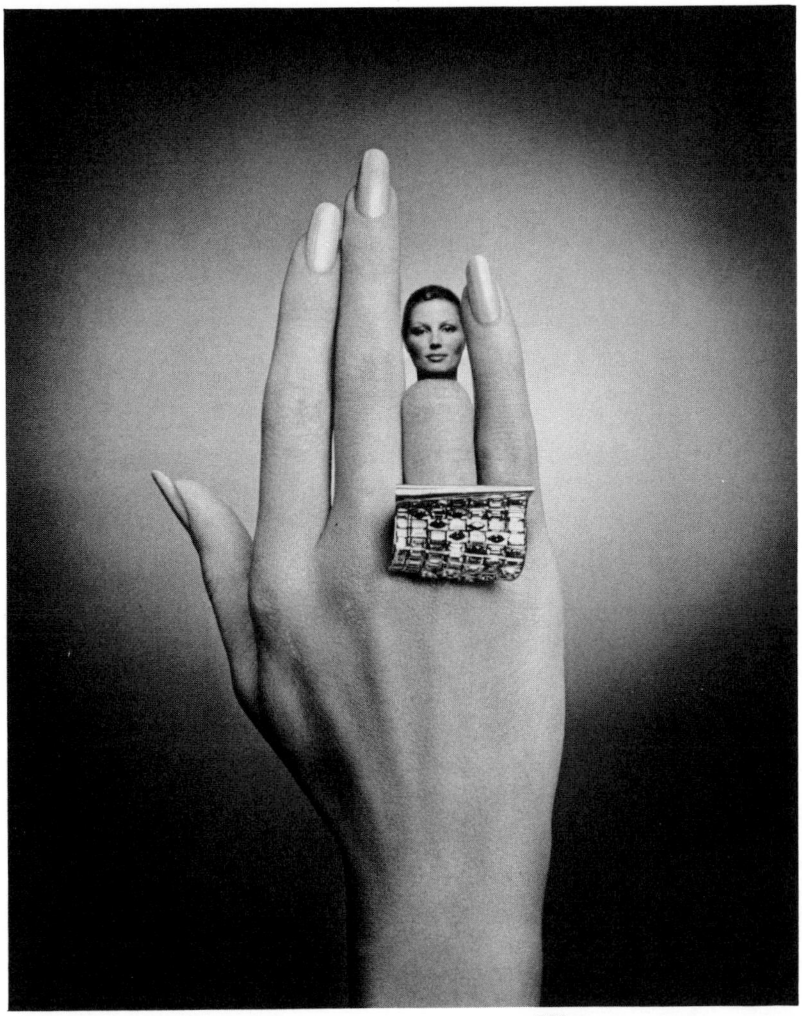

786

787
Art Directors: Gene Brownell
John C. LePrevost
Designer: John C. LePrevost
Artist: Marilyn LePrevost
Photographer: Gene Brownell
Agency: Gene Brownell Studio
Client: Shelter Records

788 Gold Award
Art Directors: Howard C. Grant
Richard P. Ritter
Designers: Howard C. Grant
Richard P. Ritter
Photographer: Ryszard Horowitz
Copywriter: Diamond Information Center
Agency: N. W. Ayer & Son, Inc.
Ayer Design
Client: De Beers Consolidated Mines, Ltd.

787

788

789
Art Director: Harvey Gabor
Designer: Harvey Gabor
Artist: David Leffel
Copywriter: Pacy Markman
Agency: McCann-Erickson, Inc.
Client: New York Racing Association

790
Art Director: Walter Kaprielian
Artist: J. McCaffery
Designers: Walter Kaprielian
Peter Welsch
Harold Florian
Katsuji Asada
Arton Associates, Inc.
Copywriter: Arthur X. Tuohy
Agency: Ketchum, MacLeod & Grove, Inc.
Client: Newark District Ford Dealers

You're a Thoroughbred and
today you're going to race in New York.
All that breeding, all that training helped make you
fast enough to run at Beautiful Belmont Park.
And those people relaxing in the stands
are here to watch you run.
Good luck.
DAVID A. LEFFEL

789

790

FILMS AND TELEVISION

Station I.D.'s
Station or Network Promotions
Program Promotions

Station IDs

791
Art Director: Lou Dorfsman
Designer: George McGinnis
TV Directors: Lou Dorfsman
George McGinnis
TV Producer: George McGinnis
Production Company: Edstan Studio
Agency: CBS/Broadcast Group
Client: CBS Television Network

CBS 'Eye' Logo
5-second

MUSIC ACCOMPANIES THE ART

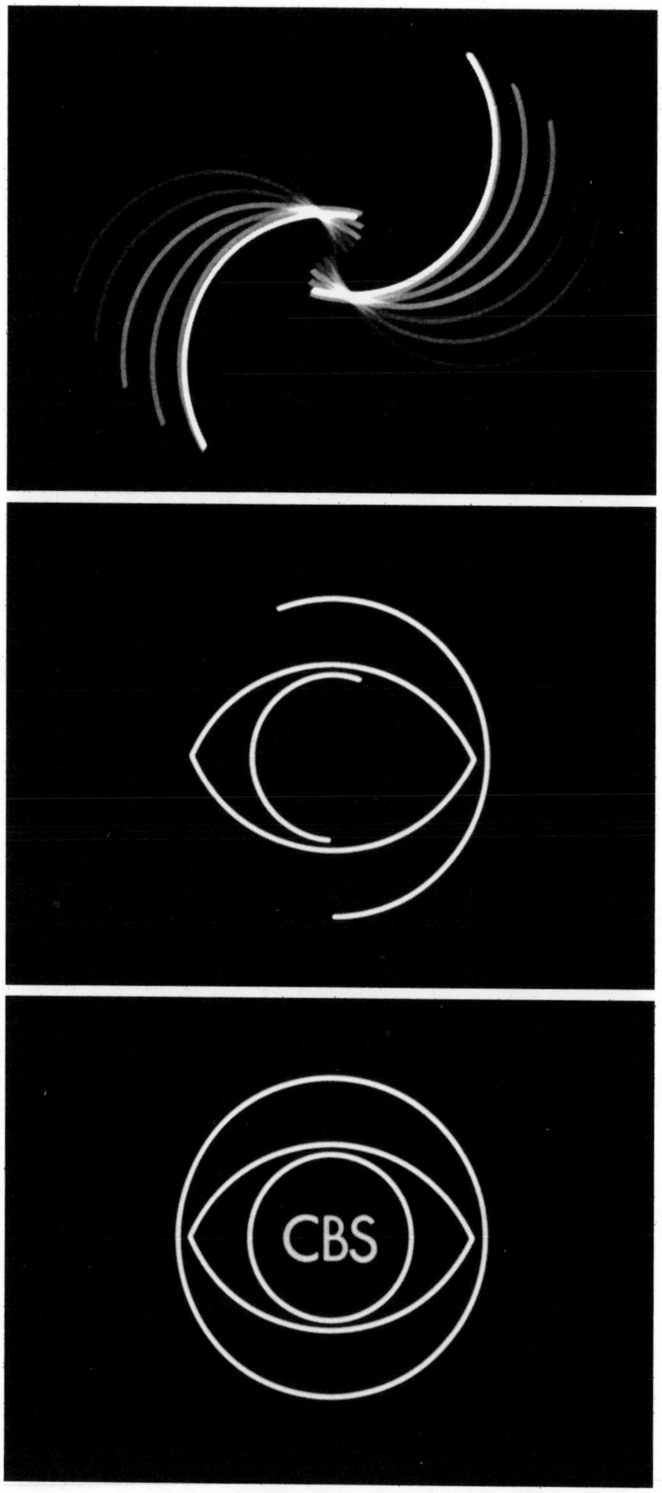

792 Silver Award

Art Directors: Ernie Smith
Herb Lubalin
Annegret Beier
Copywriters: Ron Aigen
Gil Perlman
Designers: Ernie Smith
Herb Lubalin
Annegret Beier
Artists: Marie Michal
Tony DiSpigna

TV Directors: Herb Lubalin
Gil Perlman
TV Producers: Lawrence K. Grossman Inc.
Production Companies: Sel Animation
July Studio
Merlin Studio
Agency: Lawrence K. Grossman Inc.
Client: Public Broadcasting Service,
Washington D.C. and WHA-TV

The Freeloader Analyzed
60-second

PSYCHIATRIST'S OFFICE, PATIENT LYING ON COUCH

DOCTOR: This guilt . . . you feel it only in the evening?

PATIENT: I think so.

DOCTOR: How do you spend your evenings?

PATIENT: Watching TV, mostly . . .uh, Masterpiece Theatre . . . Hollywood Television Theatre . . . William F. Buckley . . .

DOCTOR: Very interesting.

PATIENT: Why?

DOCTOR: They're all *public* television programs?

PATIENT: Well, sure. That's my favorite station.

DOCTOR: May I ask you a very *personal* question?

PATIENT: How personal?

DOCTOR: Have you sent a check to your public TV channel?

PATIENT: Well, no. Most of my extra money is spent on this couch.

DOCTOR: Yes, I know. But it's quite possible that your guilt stems from watching public TV programs and not helping to *pay* for them . . . Face it: You're a free-loader!

(SFX: "BOING!")

ZOOM IN ON PATIENT'S FACE . . . THE "BELL" HAS RUNG IN HIS HEAD

PATIENT: Am I cured?

SUPER: SEND US A CHECK.
OR A NOTE FROM YOUR DOCTOR.

Keep Television Beautiful
60-second

May Is Bustin' Out All Over
60-second

Station, Network Promos

793
Art Director: Ted Andresakes
Designer: Ted Andresakes
Artist: Ted Andresakes
TV Director: Karl Fischer
Production Company: Pumpernickel Inc.
Agency: CBS/Broadcast Group
Client: CBS Television Network

CBS Christmas Deer
20-second

MUSIC ACCOMPANIES THE ART

794 Gold Award
Art Director: Barry Vetere
Copywriter: Jan Zechman
TV Director: Joe Sedelmaier
TV Producers: Jan Zechman
Barry Vetere
Production Company: Sedelmaier Film Productions, Inc.
Agency: Zechman Lyke Vetere, Inc.
Client: KMOX-TV

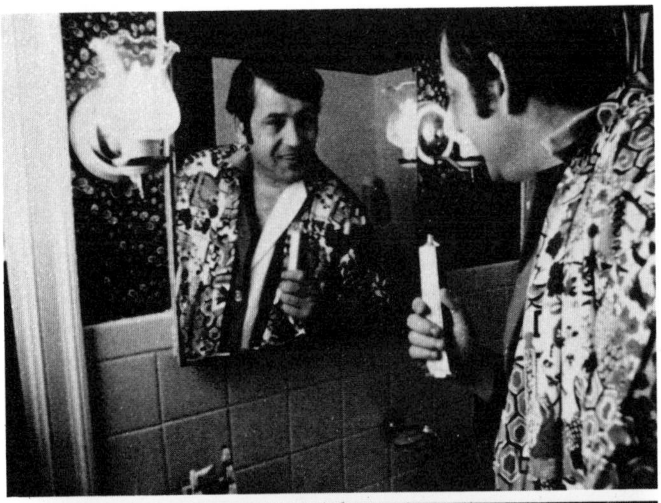

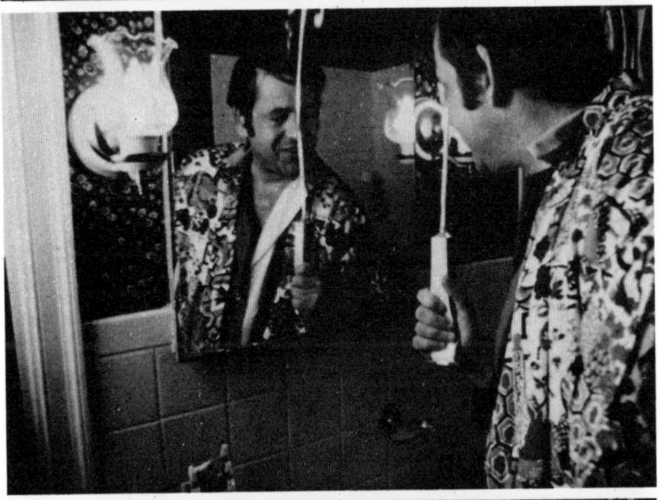

Bob Buck
10-second

OPEN ON BATHROOM. BOB BUCK ENTERS. WALKS JAUNTILY TO SINK, UP TO MIRROR

ANNCR. (VO): We've always insisted on 24 hour-a-day sportscasters.

BUCK PICKS UP TOOTHPASTE TUBE AND HOLDS IT LIKE HAND MIKE

BUCK: (A LITTLE LIKE HOWARD COSELL) Hello sports fans!

IN HIS ENTHUSIASM, BUCK SQUEEZES THE TOOTHPASTE ALL OVER HIS HAND AND PAJAMA TOP

ANNCR. (VO): What have we done?

SUPER: NEWS SERVICE
6 & 10 P.M.

Jim Bolen
10-second

Max Roby
10-second

Tom Jones
10-second

795
Art Director: Morton Goldsholl
Copywriter: Jerry Chodera
Designer: Morton Goldsholl
Cameraman: Tom Freese
TV Director: Morton Goldsholl
TV Producer: Jerry Chodera
Production Company: Goldsholl Associates
Agency: Campbell-Mithun, Inc.
Client: Accent International

The Honeymooners
5-minute

SCENE I: INTERIOR AL AND GERT'S SMALL APARTMENT, 1890 CONVERTED BROWNSTONE, SEEDY. MID MORNING. CU CHUBBY HAND AND NEWSPAPER. HAND GROPES FOR CAN OF BEER. AL DRINKS

SCENE 2: GERT, NEWLY-WED, AL'S MATE, CHUBBY, LOVABLE. ENTERS LIVING ROOM FROM KITCHEN IN ROBE AND CURLERS. THEY LOOK AT ONE ANOTHER, BORED

SCENE 3: MONTAGE CUTS: AL AND GERT AROUND APARTMENT, AIMLESSLY LOOKING OUT OF WINDOW AT BRICK WALL

SCENE 4: GERT TURNS ON RADIO. IT WON'T PLAY. A WHACK

(SFX: NEWS PROGRAM COMES ON)

(SFX: AL BELCHING FROM BEER)

SHE SIPS COFFEE

(SFX: RADIO PLAYS ACCENT JINGLE)

GERT LOOKS AT AL. (EYES GET SOFTER)

SCENE 5: FANTASY MONTAGE: LS, SLOW MOTION SKY, AL RUNNING, ARMS OUTSTRETCHED TO SCREEN

CUT TO APARTMENT. AL GETTING INTERESTED IN GERT

MONTAGE: GERT RUNNING TOWARD CAMERA, ARMS OUTSTRETCHED, HAPPY. BACK IN APARTMENT AGAIN, THEY COME CLOSE TOGETHER

SCENE 6: MORE FANTASY MONTAGE

MORE SCENES IN APARTMENT WHERE THEY NUZZLE, PLAY HANDS, GETTING CLOSER

MANY INTER-CUTS UNTIL IN APARTMENT THEY AT LAST ARE SO CLOSE BELLIES COLLIDE. THEY BOUNCE BACK, EMBRACE MADLY

SCENE 7: (SFX: FIREWORKS)

BOLD COLOR FIREWORKS FINISH

796
Art Director: Lou Dorfsman
Designers: Lou Dorfsman
George McGinnis
TV Directors: Lou Dorfsman
George McGinnis
TV Producer: George McGinnis
Production Company: Edstan Studio
Agency: CBS/Broadcast Group
Client: CBS Television Network

Thursday Night Movie
30-second

MUSIC ACCOMPANIES THE ART

Program Promos

797
Art Director: Lou Dorfsman
Designers: Lou Dorfsman
George McGinnis
TV Directors: Lou Dorfsman
George McGinnis
TV Producer: George McGinnis
Production Company: Edstan Studio
Agency: CBS/Broadcast Group
Client: CBS Television Network

Late Movie Opening
38-second

MUSIC ACCOMPANIES THE ART

798
Art Director: Lou Dorfsman
Designers: Lou Dorfsman
George McGinnis
TV Directors: Lou Dorfsman
George McGinnis
TV Producer: George McGinnis
Production Company: Edstan Studio
Agency: CBS/Broadcast Group
Client: CBS Television Network

Sunday Movie
38-second

MUSIC ACCOMPANIES THE ART

Program Promos

799
Art Director: Elinor Bunin
Designer: Elinor Bunin
Cameraman: Jim Walker
TV Directors: Elinor Bunin
Robert Young
TV Producers: Elinor Bunin
Chiz Schultz
Production Company: Elinor Bunin Productions
Client: Chiz Schultz, Inc.

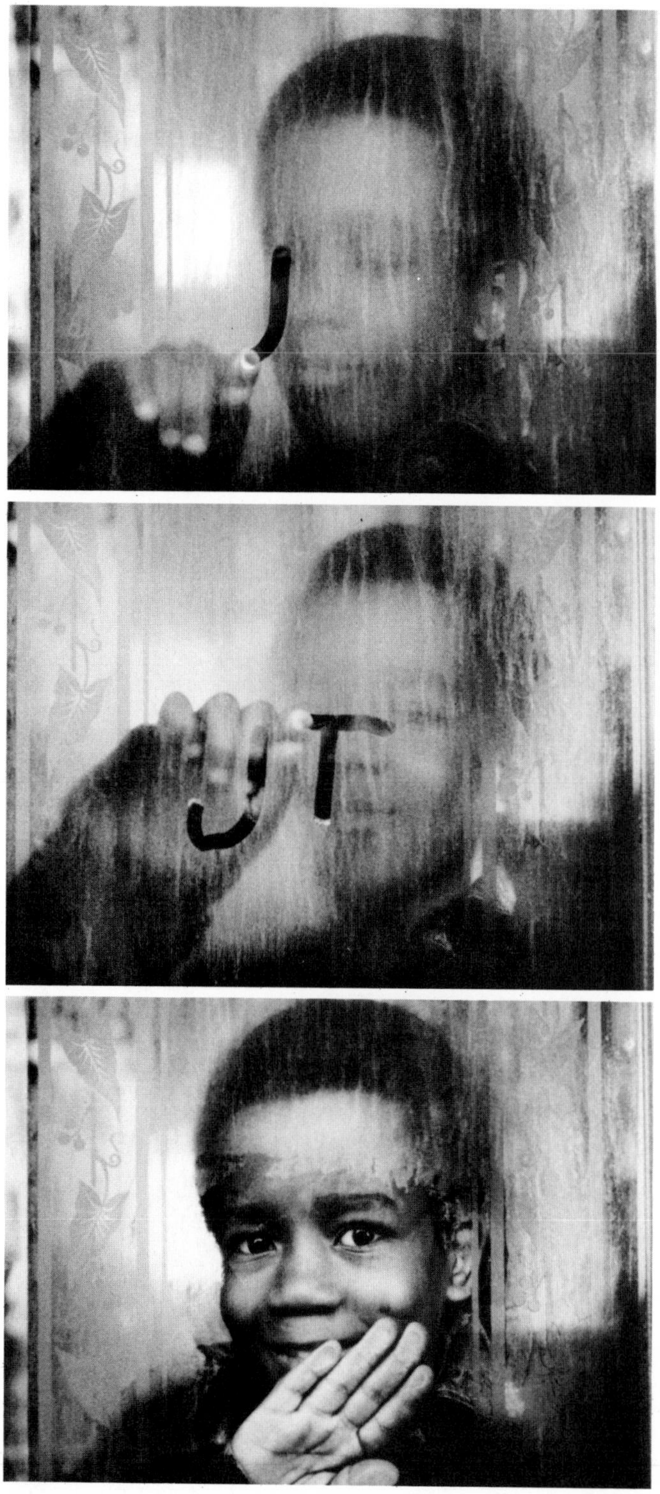

J.T.
24-second

IN THIS TITLE SEQUENCE FOR A SERIES, THE CAMERA FOCUSES THROUGHOUT ON A SOLE SMALL BOY IN HARLEM. HE IS PREOCCUPIED DRAWING HIS INITIALS, J.T., ON A CLOUDY, WINTRY WINDOW

WOMAN'S VOICE (CALLING EXCITEDLY): J.T. . .J.T. . .

J.T. QUICKLY RUBS THE WINDOW CLEAR, REVEALING AN ENDEARING, EXPECTANT FACE

FINISH CLOSE

THE ART DIRECTORS CLUB

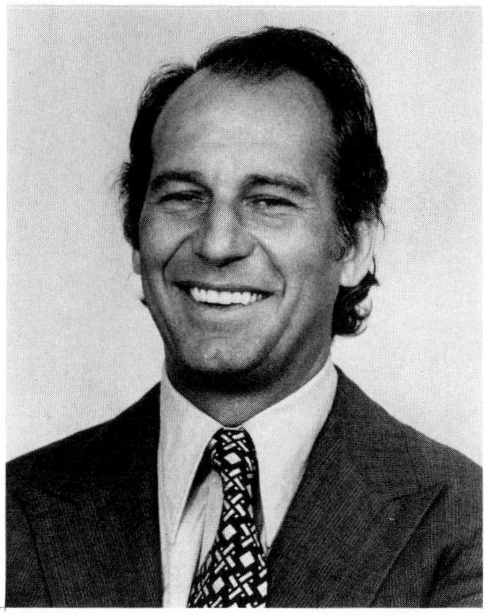

1971–1973
George Lois
Dave Davidian
Dave Epstein
Gene Federico
George Krikorian
Bill McCaffery
Gene Milbauer
Bob Reed
Arnold Roston
Ernie Scarfone
Bob Wall
William Cadge

Words between the outgoing

With the creative partnership of the Art and Copy Clubs in a new Show this year, a new significance has been brought to The Art Directors Club's awards system that records the good and great work done over the past 52 years. The history of the creative forces involved in our business is contained in our 51 awards show annuals and has helped inspire the people in our business to produce work of which we all can be proud.

The inception last year of The Art Directors Hall of Fame has awakened in us the need to understand the past and to study and know the great pioneers of our crafts. The history of design in our country has generally been neglected and, with the continuing research into people deserving of our Hall of Fame, our Club can teach and give incentive to the new talent continuously coming into our business. The better an art director searches and understands the past, the better an art director he or she can become.

Along with that search, from 1971 to 1973, The Art Directors Club has been involved in making important changes in direction. One of the Club's most important functions was and will remain our awards show, but the understanding that our membership can influence and cause progressive change in our business and in our educational system sets us on a path that can make The Art Directors Club take its rightful place as the most meaningful professional club in the world.

The vast majority of the membership (now happily with the beginning of an influx of women) wants our club to *be* more than a meeting place with a bar, to *do* more than give an occasional scholarship. Last year's "Making New York Understandable" show, lauded by Ada Louise Huxtable for its foresight, was an initial way of "getting our feet wet" in trying to help solve the problems of our city. With the aid and partnership of The Copy Club, we can even do more to help make our business one that does credit not only to ourselves, but brings honor to those who want to work in our business and lead useful, creative lives.

Our new President is Herb Lubalin—one of the great pioneers in the graphic arts and a man who knows how to get things done. He and a gung-ho executive committee, along with the Club's advisory board, want and need the involvement of every member to keep the Club going in the right direction.

Nothing much nicer could happen to The Art Directors Club than to have Herb Lubalin and his new board at the helm. Give em' hell, Herb!

George Lois

and the incoming presidents.

Them's kind words, and it has always been my feeling that the membership has never realized, or understood, its potential as a force for the social good.

This membership comprises more talent and more creativity, more ability to influence people and make them react than any other creative group I know of.

If all this affluence of ability could be harnessed for the betterment of social conditions in such areas as communications, education, living conditions, environmental conditions, philanthropic activities and—even in making each other better people by closer personal relationship—all of us would be the happier for it.
I'm glad to say that, during the past two years, the gap between promises and delivery has narrowed and the dynamism of this club has accelerated under the direction of George Lois and an admirable executive board. Because of an attempt to change the attitude of the club from that of a professional social organization to one that can play a more significant role in our society, a certain amount of controversy has come about, which is always inherent when new, untried ideas are explored. I am fully in support of these programs and will try my best, as the incoming President of the New York Art Directors Club to implement that which has already been started. It's my hope to add a few ideas of my own and those of the incoming board, a selection of talent I feel honored to be working with.

Additionally, I plan to call on the full membership to become participants rather than spectators. If every member contributed just a few hours of his time during the course of a year, the synergistic result could be overwhelming.

In brief, try to stop thinking of us as an organization that concentrates its total activity towards an exhibition—however good—a conference and an annual book extolling our glory—however unpretentious—as individuals in the fields of advertising and editorial art and design, and start thinking of us as an organization with the obligation to try to influence properly, people in the matters of government, education, business—our own profession. And, also, all those so-called "little people" out there who find it difficult to talk to one another.

If you're in sympathy with the direction we're taking, let us know about it. We want to hear from you. We can sure use all the help we can get. If you disagree, let us know that, too. We'll get together and talk about it. A fair exchange is never any robbery.

Herb Lubalin

1973–1974
Herb Lubalin
Jerry Andreozzi
Dave Davidian
Dave Deutsch
Lou Dorfsman
Gene Federico
Marilyn Hoffner
George Krikorian
George Lois
Gene Milbauer
Bill Taubin
Henry Wolf

The One Show

At the One Show judgings.

At the One Show awards dinner.

THE NEW YORK
ART DIRECTORS CLUB

THE ONE SHOW
THE ART DIRECTORS CLUB INC.
THE COPY CLUB OF NEW YORK

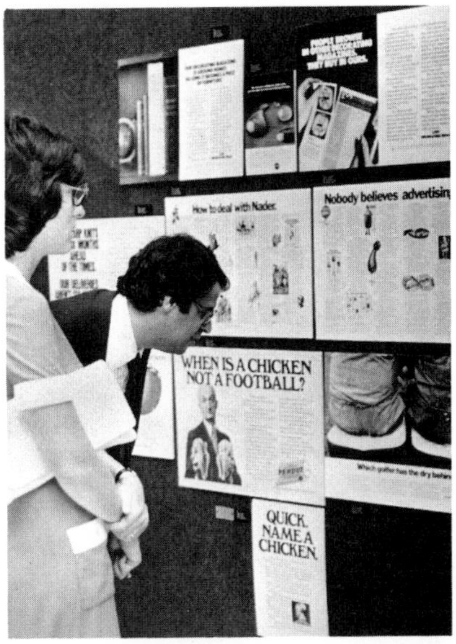
How to deal with Nader.
Nobody believes advertising
WHEN IS A CHICKEN NOT A FOOTBALL?
QUICK. NAME A CHICKEN.

At the One Show exhibition. Olivetti Building, New York City.

The One Show Credits

Staff Assistants: Melissa Merkling, Wendy Smith, Glenda Spencer, Jackie Weir
The One Show Call Pencil Concept: Alan Peckolick, Peter Nord
The One Show Medal: Kurt Weihs, George Lois
The One Show Certificates: Kurt Weihs
Olivetti Building Exhibition: Kenneth Walker Design Group
Dorothy Schuster, Project Director
Hanging Committee: Kurt Weihs, Chairman
George Lois, Charlie Rosner, Dorothy Schuster
TV Editor: Robert Smith
Radio Editor: The Mix Place
Data Processing: AMIC
TV Judgings Location: CBS, MPO Videotronics
Radio Judgings Location: Horn/Griner Productions
Awards Ceremonies: Shep Kurnit, Chairman
Photos: Jim Demetropoulos, Joe Corto

THE NEW YORK
ART DIRECTORS CLUB

A first event in the City. The proclaiming of "Communications Week." At the signing (from l.): councilman-at-large Kenneth Haber: in-coming ADC president Herb Lubalin; "Inside New York" conference chairman David Enock; out-going ADC president George Lois; One Show Awards Dinner chairman Shep Kurnit; Copy Club president Ed McCabe; *Advertising Age* Creative Workshop director Bob Heady. Front and center: New York City Mayor John V. Lindsay.

Editor's note: This report covers activities from 1971 through 1973—with projection into 1974 activities.

THE NEW YORK
ART DIRECTORS CLUB

A few of 100 hosts.

Carl Fischer

Tony Schwartz

"Inside New York" credits
Art Director: Ralph Tuzzo
Secretary: Glenda Spencer
Assistant: Judy Schloss

Bill Cadge

Allan Hurlburt

Stan Eisenman David Enock

Peter Hirsch

Henry Wolf

"INSIDE NEW YORK"

This year's conference was designed to continue an idea that was started last year, bringing together people from all over the country and the world to visit over 100 of New York's most influential communicators. Groups of 6 to 15 visitors traveled around New York from office to office and spent an hour to an hour and a half with each host.

For the first time, *Advertising Age* held its Creative Workship in New York City and for the first time, The New York Art Directors Club and *Advertising Age* joined together for a full week of communications programs. The *Ad Age* workshops ran from Monday to Thursday morning. The Wednesday workshops were coordinated with The Art Directors Club. Thursday and Friday were the visits to New York's offices.

The best way that one can assess the real value of this conference is to have been a visitor or a host. Being chairman this year gave me the opportunity to witness unanimous enthusiasm (visitors' and hosts').

Unfortunately, this enthusiasm does not always last beyond the actual experience. For this reason I feel we should continue to meet, exchange ideas, find out why we do things the way we do, explore problems of morality in advertising, budget problems, the attitude of the consumer, how to improve our profession and what part communication plays in our lives (for communication is "the essence of being human").

In fact, the "Inside New York" visits concept is so valuable I think New Yorkers should do this several times a year—among themselves.

The participation of the hosts helps to reinforce my belief in the validity of conferences which provide such personalized meetings.

David Enock
Art Directors 18th Communications
Conference Chairman

THE NEW YORK
ART DIRECTORS CLUB

Making New York Understandable
September 6 thru September 27. New York Cultural Center. 2 Columbus Circle.
11 am–6 pm. Tuesday thru Sunday. Thursday to 9 pm. The Art Director's Club, Inc.

HOW TO GET DOWNTOWN FASTER THAN AN ANT

If the bus I get on gives me more Peter Max than destination or route information or just plain service, then I've really got a problem.

If the front pages of our dailies tell us about 000,000 of this and 000,000 of that and 000,000 of deaths and 000,000,000 of dollars and we can't comprehend the 000,000,000s, then we've all got a problem.

If you can't find a bathroom in Central Park or you don't know where to get (simply) a drink of water in New York on a hot day, then we're lost in more ways than one.

The more we learn, the more complex our society becomes. The more we develop our tools of communication, the harder it gets to make things clear. The decay of the city increases as it becomes less understandable to its citizens. Even that half-compliment, "It's a nice place to visit, but—" may no longer apply to New York.

Those of us who live and work in this growing confusion of a city can't sit back and expect a mayor or a governor or more policemen to solve our problems; particularly if we are art directors and designers and writers and photographers and filmmakers—i.e., communicators. We're the ones who must face up to the responsibility of relating our work to the lives we live and the life we observe around us. We must apply our skills and tools to the job of giving form and order and meaning to urban processes. By making the city even a bit more understandable, we make it a bit more livable.

Efforts in this direction were presented in a major exhibition—"Making New York Understandable" at the New York Cultural Center. These ideas and solutions comprised part of our 17th annual communications conference.

Going to Paris won't make you a better artist, chatting in pubs won't make you a better novelist, and going to communications conferences won't make you a better communicator. What may is doing your thing where you live. So that's what we decided to do in New York. We thought we and everybody else in the city would benefit if we could come up with just a few good ideas that would help make New York understandable.

There was much enthusiasm for the project and lots of excited talk about it. Over a period of months I talked with a couple of hundred art directors and designers, and quite a bit of literature was issued on the subject of the kinds of contributions the communicator could make to clarify public information, etc. After all, that's supposed to be what it's all about. Except that when the show date drew near, only a few ideas had been completed by Club members.

Believing the overall concept to be important and viable, we went out looking for solutions beyond the membership and found that many already existed or were in the works, often in unexpected places. So, welcoming ideas from everyone, we put together a sort of starter set. In any event, it was the first show where communicators applied their skills in this area.

We hope the ideas interest you. More importantly, we hope they spur you to some kind of action on your own toward making your own home town understandable, whether it's New York or anywhere else.

You know, if life is the real issue, it could be that the real hope for all our lives is in making use of the powers we already have.

William McCaffrey
Art Directors 17th Communications
Conference Chairman

P. S. Since these events took place it has become increasingly clear that the lack of information being made public can affect all of our lives gravely. This was only a beginning.

THE NEW YORK
ART DIRECTORS CLUB

Information graphics were displayed.
Reprinted by permission of
The New York Times, Sunday, September 24, 1972

DOING THE HARD THINGS FIRST

There is a very well intentioned and quite amiable little show at the New York Cultural Center called "Making New York Understandable," a theme close to this writer's heart. It is a timeless and open-ended subject, and the questions it raises will last long after the closing date of Oct. 11.

For nine years this fall, we have been struggling to make New York understandable, knowing that it is an impossible task. New York will never be understandable in anything except detail or microcosm; both its spirit and its physical facts are contradictory and evasive, full of the paradoxes of the too large, too tragic, too rich, and too real.

Reality, as New York puts it together, consists of nirvana and the lower depths with every gradation in between. It offers punishments and rewards of the body and soul that defy even the most sophisticated analysis.

The simplistic mind that demands reason and order and proper hues of black and white reduces New York falsely to its own level of inadequacy. Define humanity under pressure. Or civilization at its most brutal and complex. Or survival, primary and profound. At best one only senses New York, given revelatory glimpses of its scale, processes and meanings, beauties and enormities. Equally, understand the workings of the universe.

Madison Avenue Mall model.

Vestpocket park ideas.

Nevertheless, the kind of understanding that the exhibition at the Cultural Center seeks is both laudable and logical. It takes the form of a sampling of the devices used to give information about the city to city dwellers—to clarify their surroundings, to aid them in their daily lives, to reveal the city's services and form. It proceeds from basic graphics—in posters, street and subway signs, publications and films—to the necessities and amenities of public transportation and vest pocket parks, right up to the Olympian manipulations of the environment by planners in new-towns-in-town such as Welfare Island and Battery Park City.

The range is from the direct guide, as maps, to methods of making the city more livable and workable, as in the currently stalemated proposal for a Madison Avenue mall. There are models, photographs, films and books, and even a copy of New York's Master Plan.

Re-vamped subway signage.

The exhibition was conceived and assembled by the Art Directors' Club, in connection with its 17th annual communications conference, held in New York from Sept. 6 to 8. The idea came from William McCaffery, program chairman of the conference. Material included is the work of Art Directors' Club members and other designers, writers, filmmakers, architects, and planners, all with a stake in making the city visible, comprehensible, or better in some way.

"The decay of the city increases as it becomes less understandable to its citizens," Mr. McCaffery says. The entrance wall label calls for the city's "communicators" in visual and verbal fields to address themselves to the problem of communication between the citizen and his habitat.

The show, necessarily spotty because of its scope, is cheerful, even optimistic. But something else emerges from the casual assemblage of plans and projects. It goes beyond the pleasant, rational novelty of the model of the Prattaxi developed by Pratt students, or the Ginkelvan by Van Ginkel Associates for the city's Office of Midtown Planning and Development, or the promise of subway sense and style emerging from MTA chaos by MTA consultants Unimark International, or the eloquent plea for the care and handling of city trees by landscape architect Robert Zion.

Assembled in the most offhand way is the most solidly impressive evidence of the planners' work in New York on a very large and sophisticated scale, almost all in construction now.

The Bedford-Stuyvesant superblock, by landscape architect M. Paul Friedberg and Associates and architect I. M. Pei and Partners, is a completed and successful experiment in bringing urban amenity to the ghetto slums.

The Harlem River Bronx State Park, a 65-acre project of recreational open space with housing, schools, shops, pools, gyms, athletic fields, amphitheater, and marina, by Friedberg and Davis, Brody Associates, is currently rising on a desolate industrial riverfront site. The client is the State Park Commission for the City of New York.

*

Battery Park City, a 91-acre new community for 55,000 residents, designed by the team of Philip Johnson and John Burgee, Harrison and Abramovitz, and Conklin and Rossant, with active handholding by the city's planners, is going ahead now, under the auspices of the Battery Park City Authority.

Welfare Island, master-planned by Johnson and Burgee, with all of its well-aired troubles, has still managed to break ground for housing. With Ed Logue, a man of steely commitment and impressive achievement heading the State Urban Development Corporation, its construction is no real gamble.

In one of the most curious understanding gaps of all, New Yorkers fail to grasp that these massive schemes are going ahead; that these things are actually happening. Brought up on paper plans and no action, the people and the media maintain habits of easy cynicism.

A new idea for inner-city transportation.

New hospital signage promotes understanding.

Useful sidewalk solutions for residents and visitors.

The exception is the young. Raised on science fiction and the moon, in a world where anything can, and does, happen, their reality is broader. They carry the badge of New York cynicism like a cheerful flag, but they accept what their elders reject.

*

The day we visited the show, a high-school class on a cultural outing suddenly brought the galleries to sharp life, their reactions instinctive, totally New York. The girls, to a Ms, teetered on four-inch platform soles, with fingernails of black, silver and dried blood. The boys vied in rainbow sneakers. They didn't bother with wall labels. They wrote their own script.

"Welfare Island?" (Granny glasses, wide cuffed pants.)

"Is that what they're making now?" (Broad-brimmed black hat and glasses, six-inch cork platform soles.)

"You mean just for welfare recipients?" (Jean Harlow hairdo and blouse, rhinestone pin, wedgies.)

"Don't be crazy; it's the city of the future." (White stocking cap, jeans, red-white-and-green sneakers.)

"It's going to be our city?" (Purple body shirt, red-white-and-blue sneakers.)

"Sure. But don't worry about it. You'll be dead." (Hair and Aquarius deshabille.)

Laughter. (All.)

All they really underestimated was the time it would take, but then, time is notoriously long for the young. We give it 10 years, and we expect to be around. The big dreams are the most real thing about this unreal city these days. They have the substance of money, law and steel. If there is another lesson in the show, it may be that it is easier to build immense, planned developments than to get a rational taxi or a clear street sign. We do the hard things first.

In New York, in fact, we only do the impossible. Understand a city like that?

Ada Louise Huxtable

"Making New York Understandable" credits
Exhibition: David Enock Photos: Ernie Costa

THE NEW YORK
ART DIRECTORS CLUB

PUTTING YOUR MONEY WHERE YOUR MOUTH IS

If we are to influence and improve the quality of work, it really begins with what we do for the kids. Kids are disturbed about corruption in high places, disillusioned about our commercial society in general. Sixty percent of the people in a Harris poll believed that this corruption was a fact of life. Yet old people have been bellyaching about the kids. Everybody promises. Nobody seems to be telling it straight.

The point is—we can put our money where our mouth is. For this reason, the ADC in very recent years has increased its Scholarship Fund activities, finding money to give to talented and needy kids so that they can enter the field. The emphasis has been on the underprivileged. The record includes some innovations.

The Fund as an independent corporation was so organized due largely to the prescience of Arnold Roston a decade ago (he is still its active president). Traditionally, the ADC had given to young people over the years, but the Fund put it under one umbrella. Fund directors this year, who add their names to a prestigious list, are Dave Epstein, Marilyn Hoffner, George Lois, Herb Lubalin, and Arnold Roston.

Scholarship winners at ceremonies with Arnold Roston, George Lois, Joseph Papp.

For the directors it's engrossing but time-consuming work to select scholarship applicants. It means going to student exhibitions, corresponding with art and regular high schools, and then later reviewing portfolios.

This is from recent Annual Scholarship reports:

☐ The ADC Fund was among the first to come to the aid of the New York Public Library—to fight against its curtailment of services. (The Government had pledged monies if professional organizations would assist.) The ADC donated over $3,000 to abate this library crisis. It was an important contribution for the Club because of the belief in our role as (simply) a 'citizen' of the City.

☐ Money was given to promising young people to attend Cooper Union, Pratt, Cornell, Parsons, SVA, and other schools. Of the 14 scholarship recipients, nine happily were women (thus the Club could do its small bit to even the sex ratio among a.d.s!). The recipients: Julie Baron, Donna Chapin, Doris Chin, Ruth Fanelli, Diana Farrell, Talita Long, Jussara Luz Padillia, Joseph McDermott, Nancy Rapoport, Alex Rosenberg, Gale Saddy, Percy Scott, Stewart Suskind, Peter Voorhies.

Now how is all this money raised? Mostly through hounding companies, magazines, etc. Contributions don't, of course, always come with groans—agencies, art and type studios, and individual members have given generously out of their hearts. And, when there's money in the till, the Club donates separately to the Fund. Also, the Club sponsors special fund-raising events. This year, the Club raised close to $600 at its wild and wonderful communications industry preview of "Slither," the first feature made by award-winning commercial director Howard Ziéff.

To continue the report—

☐ Close to $700 went to the Children's Art Workshop in the Public Theater Building (Joseph Papp's on Lafayette Street). This project, a cooperative venture with Cooper Union, has taken 40 young kids 'off the streets' and put them into graphics. (Not only did the kids buy and renovate a printing press, they're now into filmmaking.)

☐ The ADC answered a call for help from member George Halpern, who is Chairman, Commercial Art Department, N.Y.C. Community College. The problem: poor urban kids just can't afford art materials so they can't do their homework. The Club gave toward their purchase.

☐ The Club helped innovate a new program — giving the seed money for a new Art Therapy Program established by the Philadelphia College of Art in association with Philadelphia hospitals. Its goal: the training of therapists in one of the country's pioneer art therapy degree programs.

For some time we have known art can heal. This program—using art to aid the increasing numbers of mentally ill Americans—will combine medicine, education, and art. Today, there only are 235 practicing art therapists. Tomorrow, who knows?

Dave Epstein and Pratt class, ADC.

THE NEW YORK
ART DIRECTORS CLUB

MATCHING WORDS WITH ACTION

Education chairman Dave Epstein puts it this way: "What we have been doing is to break with the past to some extent . . . to stimulate more of our own members to 'give a damn' . . . to reassert a proper claim of leadership as far as the schools are concerned . . . it has taken an incredible number of man hours."

Working with him: Eileen Hedy Schultz, Bob Farber, Bill Brockmeier, Hoyt Howard, Lee Epstein, Steve Weinstein, Bill Bossert, Sandford Silverberg, Mike Perez, Charles Rosner, Stan Bloom, John Okladek.

This—from the education report:

□ A new course in art direction—taught by individual members or teams of members—is being devised for this school year at the request of Parsons School of Design. The course should have long-ranging, solid ramifications. (Notwithstanding an excellent education to be gotten in art schools generally beyond the freshman year, Epstein finds a gaping omission in the introduction and history of American advertising and visual communication for first-year students.)

□ The committee, at the request of some schools and in close liaison with all the schools, is working on formulating core curriculum for students entering the field. Teachers and professionals will give closer consideration to what it is about now—today. Not what it was we got out of school. And, by defining the basic requirements for professionalism, perhaps we can better profile the professional visual communicator for ourselves to contemplate.

□ A potpourri of activities—hosts at Art Career Day Expositions—pow-wows run by N.Y.'s School Art League. Art Directors, illustrators, architects rap with students, offering counseling and general direction . . . host to on-hand classes from Pratt and N.Y. Institute of Technology . . . host to graduates at special Portfolio Review sessions . . . aid to schools like Haaron High in re-vamping its publication . . . A sell-out program was an 'Encounter-Dialogue' so successful it will be run yearly. Panels of star talent were challenged by faculty and students. Some of what happened is here.

"The Magazine Malaise" encounter.

"Graphics Man (or Woman)—a cultural necessity?"—a dialogue to examine the role of the communicator in a society under stress. The panelists did much purging themselves, asking—are we needed, said Epstein . . .

What is the cultural commitment for the young person entering graphic arts, asked George Sandek, Cooper Union, and David Levy, Parsons.

"Conscience and Standards." George Lois reported the ADC had circulated the Council on Economic Priorities study on corporate ads. CEP's Alice Tepper Marlin said the public's need for truthful information is growing . . . "People in advertising have enormous power—to move clients. They can provide needed facts." . . .

TV commercials encounter.

ALL ABOUT WOMEN ART DIRECTORS . . . AND OTHER NOTES OF IMPORT ON MEMBERSHIP

If we aren't to be constantly renewed with new and emerging talents—who join because of what we've been up to—then all of this is so much sound and fury.

Happily—we report positive support. In three years, membership has grown close to 600—a mix of a small group of junior members (art directors for a minimum of a year), associates (from related creative areas), and non-residents.

The most important, timely news is about women members. The ADC began an active push for women two years ago (with a "Boy A.D. Meets Girl A.D." bash). A steady push has brought results: women members are up—over 30.

This from Marilyn Hoffner, who is secretary and was one of the earlier women members of the ADC, is a personal perspective on where women stand—for women in the Club and women readers in general: Marilyn remembers it was "big news when Cipe Pineles (now Burtin) became the first female member in the nearly-500 male group in the 50's . . . and feeling daring as the first woman to propose her husband for membership . . .

"Now we cover every field of design—in key positions at agencies, in publishing, throughout industry. No longer do we handle only feminine accounts, but the fight really isn't over. Our salaries aren't all equal and we still have account execs telling us that the lightline gothic caps and milano roman we plan to use isn't 'masculine' enough while the a.d. in the next office calmly uses the same types . . . but this too shall pass. And our female membership will grow to reflect our true numbers in the art world."

Membership chairman were (two men) Peter Adler and Eric Gluckman. They and their committees worked hard.

It's been a very good few years.

TOURING SHOWS

Under the auspices of the United States Information Agency, the ADC's Annual Shows of Advertising, Editorial and Television Art and Design have been seen by world citizens of every race and tongue. Yearly, shows are mounted in small museums and galleries, embassies, stores—goodwill ambassadors for that special folk art-science-business known as American advertising and communications. It is interesting to wonder at the high popularity of the touring exhibits. The AD Club of Tokyo ran a double feature—their show and our own last year, attended by over 3,000 in one week. People in Bogota, Budapest, Caracas, Prague, Paris, Paramaribo, Teheran have seen the shows in recent years. The One Show will continue the global tours (in its first two days at the Olivetti Building in New York, no less than six cities asked to have it!).

AD Club of New York shows with AD Club of Tokyo.

HALL OF FAME SPECIAL

Following its exhibit at New York's Cultural Center last September, the first Hall of Fame Exhibition was requested for showing by Syracuse University's College of Visual and Performing Arts—shown at their Lubin House Gallery, New York. This is from their publication honoring Dr. Agha, Lester Beall, Alexey Brodovitch, A. M. Cassandre, Rene Clarke, Bob Gage, William Golden, Paul Rand: "We have often acknowledged the genius of the media man, the art director, for his special cleverness. Today, the art director's success as creative artist, thinker, inventor concerns us." (Cynics of advertising please note.) "*They* have bridged the gap between art and commerce." . . . Helping the art-going public and educators to bridge the gap, Syracuse plans one-man retrospectives a season on each ADC famer.

SPEAKER, SPEAKER

What do Judith Crist, *New York* movie critic, Chico Hamilton, drummer, Immie Fiorentino, lighting impressario, Aaron Burns, type impressario, Jacqueline T. Robertson, Madison Avenue Mall (a project which the ADC supported), Frank Braynard, New York's South Street Seaport, Pat Caufield, photographer-naturalist, Jim Henson, "Sesame Street's" muppets creator, Robert Clive, *Life* a.d. Gershon Kingsley, Moog fame, have in common? All were guests at Wednesday Speakers Programs—a partial listing at that. The varied programs were arranged by Bert Littmann and Meg Crane. Specials also included incisive panels—

The lunch crowd.

one on "Opening Your Own Business," another on "How Magazine Economies are Affecting Creativity." The new events were part of the Club's expanded concept of exploring all of the disciplines that touch our lives. Evenings there were joint sessions of the American Society of Magazine Photographers and the ADC (sample discourses—"New Communication Between Art Director and Photographer" and "The New Pornography") . . . Tuesday noons Dick Ross' Dixieland Band played and Tuesday evenings the Modern Jazz Quartet . . . And more: "Free Movies" series included a preview of Bob Levinson's feature "Hail to the Chief," non-commercial and public service films by commercial-makers, student films . . . And: Felix Kent, one of the world's legal experts on advertising, ran, for the ADC, the industry's first 'course' on "Creating in the New Climate of Legalism."

MORE FOR SHOW

Bob Ciano, head of Clubhouse Exhibitions, and committee members Len Fury, Harvey Gabor, Carveth Kramer say this activity is ripe for expansion since the ADC space is ideal and not used to maximum. These shows, however, were heavily-trafficked—Arnold Varga (illustrations), Kiyoshi Kanai (type), corporate advertising, posters, selected photographers' works. Upcoming for 1974: Members Painting Show, set for Lever House, and "Freetime Photography Show," (members photos), Nikon House.

Judith Crist.

Chico Hamilton plays at the Club.

Members List

Adamec, Donald
Adams, Gaylord
Adams, George C.
Adler, Jane
Adler, Peter
Adorney, Charles S.
Agha, M. F.
Aguirre, Lawrence
Albrektson, Evald J.
Aldoretta, Warren P.
Allen, Lorraine
Allner, Walter H.
Alston, Robert
Ammirati, Carlo
Andreozzi, Gennaro R.
Andresakes, Ted
Ansel, Ruth
Anthony, Al
Anthony, Robert
Arlow, Arnold
Asano, Tadashi
Aster, Jeanne
Aufricht, Gabor M.
Aymar, Gordon C.

Bach, Robert O.
Baker, Frank
Ballarino, Carmine J.
Barbini, Edward
Barkoff, Ira A.
Barron, Don
Bartel, Clyde W.
Basile, Matthew
Bastian, Rufus A.
Batlin, Leon
Beckerman, Alvin
Beckerman, Jay
Bee, Noah
Belliveau, Peter
Belsky, Murray
Bennett, Edward J.
Benson, Laurence Key
Berenter, William
Berg, John
Berkovitz, Edward
Berkowitz, Seymour
Berliner, Saul
Berry, Park
Bertulis, Frank
Bethune, Lloyd
Biondi, Aldo
Biondo, Frank
Birbower, Stewart
Blank, Peter
Blattner, Robert H.
Blend, Robert
Block, David S.
Blod, Francis
Blomquist, Arthur T.
Bloom, Stan
Bode, Robert W.
Boden, James J.
Bohman, Robert J.
Boothroyd, John Milne
Boroff, Sanford
Bossert, William T.
Bostrom, Thor F.
Boudreau, James
Bourges, Jean
Bowman, Harold A.
Boyd, Douglas
Braguin, Simeon
Brattinga, Pieter
Brauer, Fred J.
Brockmeier, William P.
Brody, Marc
Brody, Ruth
Brooke, John
Brugnatelli, Bruno E.
Brussel-Smith, Bernard
Brzoza, Walter C.
Bua, Charles
Buckley, William H.
Buksbaum, Hal
Burns, Aaron
Burns, Herman F.
Burtin, Cipe Pineles

Cadge, William
Calluori, Michael E.
Campanelli, Rocco E.
Campbell, Stuart
Capone, Anthony
Cappiello, Tony
Carlu, Jean
Cavallo, Joseph
Cerullo, C. Edward
Charney, David H.
Cherry, John V.
Chessman, William O.
Chiesa, Alfred F.
Chin, Kay
Church, Stanley
Chwast, Seymour
Ciano, Robert
Ciofalo, John
Civale, Frank, Sr.
Clark, Herbert
Clemente, Thomas F.
Cline, Mahlon A.
Clive, Robert
Coiner, Charles T.
Collins, Benjamin
Confalonieri, Giulio
Conrad, Ernest
Cook, John
Cook, Verdun P.
Costa, Ernest
Cotler, Sheldon
Cottingham, Edward M.
Counihan, Thomas J.
Craddock, Thomas J.
Craig, James Edward
Crane, Meg
Cranner, Brian
Craw, Freeman
Crozier, John Robert
Crump, Frank
Cummings, Richard
Cupani, Joseph
Cutler, Charles

Dadum, Royal
Dahlmann, William
Daidone, Benedetto
D'Amato, Joseph
Danar, Nat
Dane, Norman R.
DaRold, Thierry L. H.
Davi, Dick
Davidian, David
Davis, Hal
Davis, Herman A.
Davis, Philip
Davis, Sy
Dederick, Jay G., Jr.
Del Sorbo, Joseph R.
Delvecchio, Pat
Demner, Marius
Demoney, Jerry C.
Deppe, Florian R.
Deutsch, David S.
Dickens, Madlyn
Dickinson, Charles R.
Diehl, Edward P.
Dignam, John F.
Divet, Andre J.
Dixon, Kenwood
Doe, Gerald
Dolobowsky, Robert
Donald, Peter
Donatiello, Michael
Dorfsman, Louis
Dorian, Marc
Doyle, J. Wesley
Dubin, Morton
Duffy, Donald H.
Duffy, William R.
Dunning, Robert
Dusek, Rudolph

Eberman, Edwin
Eckstein, Bernard
Edgar, Peter
Eidel, Zeneth
Eisenman, Stanley
Elton, Wallace
Emery, Rod A.
Engler, Elliot
Enock, David
Epstein, David
Epstein, Henry
Epstein, Lee
Erikson, Rolf
Ermoyan, Suren
Essman, Robert N.

Farber, Bob
Farrar, Louis
Farrell, Abe
Federico, Gene
Fenga, Michael
Fernandez, George R.
Ferrara, Aniello
Fertik, Samuel A.
Finegold, Rupert J.
Fiorenza, Blanche
Firpo, Gonzalo
Fischer, Carl
Fitzgerald, John E.
Flack, Richard
Fliesler, Alan
Flock, Donald
Flynn, J. Walter
Fortune, William
Foster, Robert
Fraioli, Jon M.
Francis, Robert D.
Frankel, Ted
Frankfurt, Stephen O.
Franznick, Philip E.
Free, William
Freedman, Mel
Freyer, Fred
Friedman, Martin
Frohlich, L. W.
Frost, Oren S.
Fujita, S. Neil
Fury, Leonard W.

Gabor, Harvey
Gage, Robert

Garlanda, Gene
Gatti, David
Gauss, Joseph T.
Gavasci, Alberto P.
Geoghegan, Walter B.
Georgi, Carl H.
Gering, Joseph
Germakian, Michael
Gertner, Richard
Giammalvo, Nick
Giglio, Salvatore
Gillis, Richard B.
Giuliani, Wendy Swensen
Giusti, George
Glaser, Milton
Glessmann, Louis R.
Gluckman, Eric
Glusker, Irwin
Goff, Seymour R.
Gold, William
Goldberg, Irwin
Goldgell, Hazel
Goldman, Edward
Golub, William
Grace, Roy
Graham, Edward
Graham, John
Greenberg, Albert
Greenberg, Nancy
Greenwell, Robert
Griffin, John J.
Griner, Norman
Groody, Geraldine
Grossberg, Manuel
Grossman, Alvin
Grotz, Walter
Gruen, Chuck
Gruppo, Nelson
Guild, Lurelle V. A.
Guild, S. Rollins
Gunn, William

Haber, Norbert
Hack, Robert H.
Haiman, Kurt
Hainline, Wallace F.
Halpern, George
Halpert, A.
Halvorsen, Everett
Hanke, Lou
Hanson, Thurland
Hartelius, Paul V., Jr.
Hautau, Janet
Havemeyer, Mitch
Hawkins, Arthur
Heff, Saul
Heiffel, Eugene
Hemmick, Bud
Heyman, Wesley F.
Hill, John J., Jr.
Hipwell, Grant I.
Hirsch, Peter M.
Hodes, Ronald
Hoffner, Marilyn
Holeywell, Arnold C.
Holtane, George
Hopkins, William P.
Horton, John
Horton, Robert J.
Hovanec, Joe
Howard, Hoyt
Hungerford, Robert
Hurlburt, Allen F.

Imhoff, Howard C.
Irrera, Paul
Irwin, William A.

Jaccoma, Edward G.
Jacobs, Harry M.
Jaggi, Moritz S.
Jamison, John
Joiner, James
Jones, Bob
Jones, Dick
Joslyn, Roger
Jossel, Leonard
Julia, Christian

Kambanis, Aristedes
Kanai, Kiyoshi
Kaprielian, Walter
Karsakov, Leonard
Katzen, Rachel
Kaufmann, M. R.
Keil, Tom S.
Kelly, Kenneth Roy
Kent, Seymour
Kenzer, Myron W.
Kittel, Frederick H.
Kleckner, Valerie
Klein, Gerald
Kner, Andrew
Knoepfler, Henry O.
Komai, Ray
Kosarin, Norman
Krauss, Oscar
Krikorian, George
Kurnit, Shep

LaGrone, Roy E.
Laird, James E.
Lamarque, Abril
Lampert, Harry
Larkin, John J.
LaRotonda, Anthony
LaSala, Anthony C.
Lawler, Paul G.
Lazzarotti, Sal
Lenoff, Jerome H.
Leonard, Jack A. D.
Leslie, Dr. Robert
Leu, Olaf
Levine, David T.
Levinson, Julian P.
Leydenfrost, Robert
Liberman, Alexander
Limeburner, Reeve
Lipsitt, Martin
LiPuma, Sal
Littmann, Bert W.
Lockwood, Richard
Lois, George
Longo, Vincent R.
Longyear, William L.
Lord, Richard
Lotito, Rocco
Louise, John
Lowry, Alfred
Lubalin, Herbert
Lucci, John
Ludekens, Fred
Luden, Richard B.
Luria, Richard
Lyon, Robert W., Jr.

MacDonald, John
MacFarlane, Richard
Macri, Frank
Madia, Anthony
Madris, Ira B.
Magdoff, Samuel
Magnani, Louis A.
Malone, Martin J.
Mancino, Anthony
Manzo, Richard
Marinelli, Jack
Marshall, Al F.
Marshall, Daniel
Martin, Raymond M.
Martinott, Robert T.
Massey, John
Matyas, Theodore S.
Maximov, George
Mayhew, Marce
Mayshark, C. B.
Mazzella, Dennis
McCaffery, William A.
McCallum, Robert
McFadden, Keith
McOstrich, Priscilla
Medler, James V.
Menell, Don
Menna, Louis
Merlicek, Franz
Messina, Joseph
Messina, Vincent N.
Metzdorf, Lyle
Milbauer, Eugene
Minko, William
Mohtares, Alexander
Morang, Kenneth E.
Morgan, Burton A.
Morgan, Wendy Jo
Moriber, Jeffrey M.
Morrison, William R.
Morton, Thomas Throck
Moskof, Martin Stephen
Moss, Tobias
Munch, Jacob A.
Murray, John R., Jr.
Mutter, Ralph

Nappi, Nick
Negron, William
Nelson, Andrew K.
Newby, Ben
Nichols, Mary Ann
Nield, Walter K.
Nissen, Joseph
Noda, Ko
Noll, Verne
Norris, Edgar S.
Nussbaum, Edward

O'Dell, Robert
O'Hehir, Joseph
Okladek, John
Olden, Georg
Olivo, Gary
Orr, Garrett P.
Osborn, Irene Charles
Otter, Robert David
Ottino, Larry
Owett, Bernard S.

Paccione, Onofrio
Paces, Zlata
Palladino, Tony
Palmer, Edward A.
Parker, Paul E., Jr.
Pearl, Leonard
Peckolick, Alan
Peltola, John J.

Pento, Paul
Peter, John
Petrocelli, Robert H.
Pfeffer, Elmer
Philiba, Allan
Philips, Gerald M.
Philpotts, Randy
Piera, Ricardo
Pioppo, Ernest
Pittmann, Stuart
Platt, Melvin
Pliskin, Robert
Podeszwa, Raymond
Popcorn, Faith
Portuesi, Louis
Posnick, Paul
Post, Anthony
Price, Gordon
Pride, Benjamin
Prueitt, Gerald
Prusmack, A. John
Pulise, Santo

Quell, Henry

Rada, George A.
Radtke, Gary
Rafalaf, Jeffrey S.
Raffel, Samuel
Rand, Paul
Redler, Harry
Reed, Robert C.
Reed, Samuel
Reed, Sheldon
Reeves, Patrick A.
Reinke, Fred
Reinke, Herbert O.
Rich, King
Ricotta, Edwin C.
Rienecke, William
Rizzo, Dominic G.
Robbins, Morris
Roberts, Kenneth
Robertson, Raymond
Robinson, Clark L.
Rocchio, Robert
Rocker, Harry
Rockwell, Harlow
Romagna, Leonard A.
Rondell, Lester
Rose, Jacqueline
Rosenblum, Morris L.
Rosenthal, Herbert
Rosner, Charles
Ross, Andrew
Ross, Dick
Ross, James Francis
Roston, Arnold
Rothman, Jack
Rothstein, Arthur
Rubenstein, Mort
Russell, Henry N.
Russo, Vincent, Jr.
Rustom, Mel
Ruther, Donald
Ruzicka, Thomas
Ryan, William Lawrence

St. Louis, Leonard A.
Saks, Robert
Salpeter, Robert
Santandrea, James, Jr.
Sattler, Ernest
Sauer, Hans
Savage, W. Lee
Savitsky, Joseph
Scali, Sam
Scarfone, Ernest G.
Scheck, Henry
Scherr, Alfred J., Jr.
Scheuer, Gustavo
Schleider, Irene
Schmalenberger, Robert F.
Schneider, Richard M.
Schneider, William H.
Schreiber, Martin
Schultz, Eileen Hedy
Schwietzer, Alvin
Segal, Leslie
Seide, Allan
Seide, Ray
Seidler, Sheldon
Sellers, John L.
Settle, Raoul
Shakery, Neil
Sheldon, William
Shipenberg, Myron
Shutak, Sandra
Shure, G. Don
Siano, Jerry J.
Sieber, Richard E.
Simkin, Blanche
Silverberg, Sanford
Silverstein, Louis
Simpson, Milton
Skolnik, Jack
Sloves, Matt
Smith, David
Smith, Paul
Smith, Robert Sherrick
Smith, Rollin
Smith, Sidney
Smokler, Jerold
Smollin, Michael J.
Sneider, Kenneth P.
Solomon, Martin
Sosnow, Harold
Spiegel, Ben
Stabin, Mel
Stahlberg, David
Stapelfeldt, Karsten
Stauf, Alexander
Stech, David H.
Steinbrenner, Karl H.
Stenzel, Alfred B.
Sternglass, Lila
Stevens, Martin
Stone, Bernard
Stone, Loren B.
Storch, Otto
Streisand, Sheldon Jay
Strosahl, William
Stuart, Kenneth
Suares, Jean-Claude
Sunshine, Norman
Sutnar, Ladislav
Sweret, Michael
Sykes, Philip

Taibbi, Salvatore J.
Tanaka, Soji
Tarallo, Joseph
Tashian, Melcon
Taubin, William
Temple, Herman B.
Tesoro, Ciro
Thompson, Bradbury
Thorner, Lynne
Tillotson, Roy W.
Tinker, John Hepburn
Todaro, John
Toland, Truman
Tollin, Helaine Sharon
Tortoriello, Don
Tompkins, Gilbert
Toth, Peter
Townsend, William P. T.
Trasoff, Victor
Travisano, Ronald
Treidler, Adolph
Troop, Roger J.
Trumbauer, J. Robert
Tsao, Alex
Tuzzo, Ralph

Urbain, John A.

Vaccari, Anthony
Velez, Miguel
Venti, Tony
Versandi, Robert
Vitale, Frank A.

Wade, Edward R.
Wagener, Walter A.
Wagman, John
Wagner, Bernard
Waivada, Ernest
Wall, Robert
Wallace, Joseph O.
Wallace, Robert G.
Wallis, Hal
Walsh, Michael
Wasserman, Rose
Watt, James C.
Watts, Ron
Weber, Jessica Margot
Weihs, Kurt
Weil, Tycho R.
Weinstein, Stephen
Weisbord, Abbot A.
Weithas, Art
Wells, Sidney A.
Welti, Theo
Wetzel, Ronald
West, Jack
Weyant, Constance B.
Wheaton, Ned
White, Peter A.
Wilbur, Gordon M.
Wilde, Richard
Wilson, Ronald L.
Wilvers, Robert
Witalis, Rupert
Wolf, Henry
Wohl, Jack
Wollman, Michael

Yablonka, Hy
Yonkovig, Zen
Yuranyi, Steve

Zalon, Alfred
Zeidman, Robert
Zeigler, John
Zlotnick, Bernard
Zules, Anthony

INDEX

Art Directors

Copywriters, Writers

Designers

Artists, Photographers

Agencies

Clients

Publishers, Publications

TV and Radio Directors

TV and Radio Producers

Composers, Lyricists

Production Companies

ADVERTISING

The Japanese Print—One of a series
Color separations and reproduction by Pioneer-Moss Reproductions Corp.
Lithographed on Curtis Rag 70 lb. offset

浮世絵

Ukiyo-e was originally a Buddhist expression translated as "The every day world of sorrows and troubles" emphasizing the transitory nature of human life as opposed to blissful eternal life. As time passed the meaning of the expression changed and its religious and solemn overtones were replaced with a new emphasis on the pursuit of a pleasurable and lighthearted life and an interest in "now." The word ukiyo-e contains three characters. "uki" which means "floating" or transitory" —"yo" signifying "world" and "e" meaning pictures". Translated, ukiyo-e becomes "pictures of the floating world." Today this term is generally applied to the prints and paintings of the latter part of the 17th century through the 19th century that were produced in the area of Edo (today called Tokyo). In its period ukiyo-e also applied to the other popular and stylish fads of the day, and was used as a prefix for activities devoted to daily amusements, whims and pleasures without any concern for tomorrow.

The ukiyo-e artist was the illustrator of his day. He chose his subjects from the theatre, the "pleasure districts" and other everyday scenes. Morunobu (1618-1695) was the first artist to make use of woodcuts as an inexpensive means of reproducing drawings of the contemporary life of the people. The production of color prints flourished in the late 18th century after full range color printing was developed about 1765 and it was no longer necessary to hand color black and white block prints.

The beautiful results obtained by the outstanding ukiyo-e artists such as Harunobu, Shunsho, Kiyonaga, Sharaku, Utamaro, Hokusai, Toyokuni, Hiroshige, Eisen, Kuniyoshi, Kunisada and the last of their era, Kyosai and Yoshitoshi, are all the more wonderous when the methods of producing these prints are known. The artist's drawing was made with India ink and brushed on very thin rice paper. This was laid face down on a cherrywood block by the engraver. He then proceeded to cut the reversed design in relief on the block. Proofs were pulled from this block and the artist would specify the colors and positions on the proof. The engraver then cut a block for each color required. In order to register the blocks, the engraver cut a small line at the lower right hand side, and a corner cut in the top left hand side in the same position of each block. When the blocks were completed to the artist's satisfaction they were turned over to the printer. He inked each block with the proper color and pressed a sheet of paper that had been dampened slightly to the block, using a bamboo fiber mat as his press. He used the corner lines on the block as a guide, feeding the edges of the paper to these two register marks. The prints were produced and printed under the direction of the publisher. To a great extent the taste of the publisher and his marketing ability determined both the quality and commercial success of the final print. A combination of talents by the artist, engraver and printer was required to obtain a worthwhile print. Both the artist and publisher were extremely zealous in choosing engravers and printers who would interpret and produce the print to their satisfaction. Many poor prints were made by inferior craftsmen and also by running too

many impressions from worn blocks. Very often poor quality duplicate blocks were produced that bore little relationship to the original blocks.

Since the prints were used as illustrations for books in many cases, they inevitably assumed a political character. Important officials of the day were represented in various and unflattering ways. In 1789 the prints became subject to censorship. In 1842 the censor's personal seal appeared on all prints. In 1847 the censors worked in pairs with two seals appearing on the prints and in 1852 a combination date and censor's seal appeared. These seals did more to help collectors date the prints than restrict the subject matter, since artists and publishers found many ways to circumvent the censorship.

Prior to the works of Hokusai and Hiroshige most prints dealt with heroic subjects, the theatre and beautiful women. Hokusai perfected the color print as a medium for landscapes and Hiroshige within a few years rivaled Hokusai in this field only with less seriousness and with somewhat of a self-taught western influence and perspective. In 1849 the great Hokusai died, leaving Hiroshige the undisputed master in the landscape field. Hiroshige traveled extensively in search of material and turned out a large number of print series including the famous work on the To-kaido (eastern seaboard highway extending from Edo to Kyoto). He died in 1858 at the age of 62 during a cholera epidemic that raged through Japan and killed 28,000 in Edo alone. His farewell poem reads: "Leaving my brush on the Azuma (To-kaido) road, I depart to enjoy the wondrous sights of paradise."

In 1861, Kuniyoshi died, followed by Kunisada in 1864. This left Kyosai and Yoshitoshi (pupils of Kuniyoshi) as the only first rate artists among the mediocre artists of the Imperial Restoration period that began in 1868. This era marked the end of the ukiyo-e period. Chemical colors, over-refined engraving and printing methods and European drawing techniques eliminated the simple beauty of the ukiyo-e print. Among the impressions left on western painters by the Japanese print were Whistler's "Nocturnes" and the terrible copies in oil by Van Gogh of Hiroshige's "Ohashi Bridge" and "Plumblossom Garden". In 1861 Captain Sherard Osborn, an English naval officer published a book reproducing Hiroshige prints. In describing one of his prints he writes ". . . our embryo Turner has striven hard to reproduce the combined effects of water, mountain, cloud, and sprays touched by the bright beams of a rising sun". Turner of course was acclaimed by the following generation of western art lovers as one of the greatest landscape artists of all time. Hiroshige undoubtedly belongs in this category as well.

Hiroshige 1797-1858. Mt. Fuji viewed from Mt. Rokuso-Zan across the lake. No. 35 of "The 36 Views of Mt. Fuji" 8⅝ x 13¼ signed Hiroshige Ga Published by Tsuta-ya 1858

冨士三十六景
上総鹿埜山
廣重画

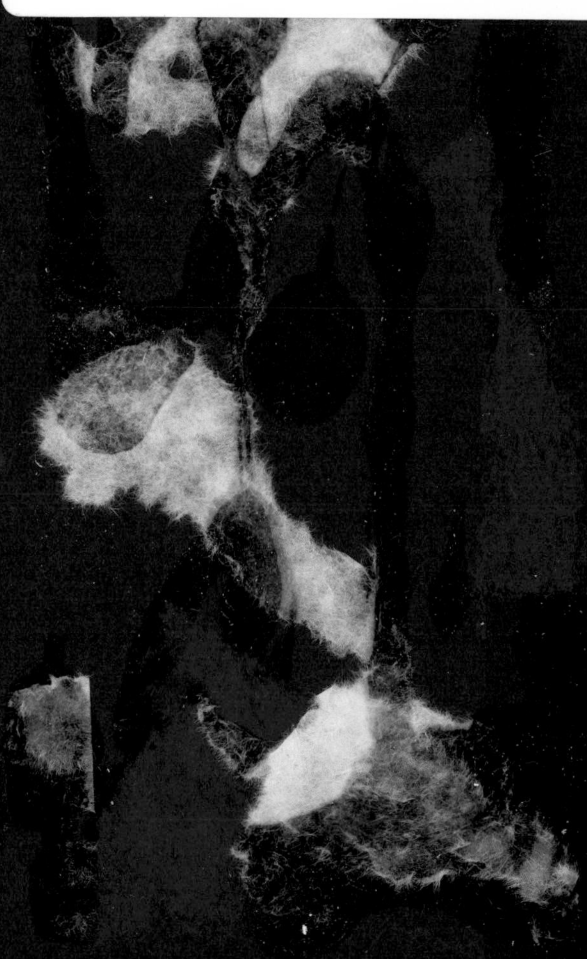